Intellectual Property Law and Taxation

Eighth Edition

Intellectual Property Law and Taxation

Eighth Edition

Nigel A. Eastaway, OBE, FCA, FCCA, CTA (Fellow),
CPA, FTIHK, MRICS, FCMA, CGMA, FCIS, FOI, TEP,
AIIT, MAE, MEWI, SBV, FRSA
MHA MacIntyre Hudson

Richard J. Gallafent, BSc, CPA, EPA, RTMA,
ETMA, MITMA, CPhys, MInstP
Gallafents LLP, Chartered Patent Attorneys and European Patent Attorneys

Victor A.F. Dauppe, BSc FCA CTA AIIT TEP
Arram Berlyn Gardner

Jacquelyn Kimber, BA (Hons), CTA
Moore Stephens LLP

SWEET & MAXWELL

THOMSON REUTERS

Eighth Edition   2013

Published in 2013 by Sweet & Maxwell, 100 Avenue Road, London NW3 3PF part of Thomson Reuters (Professional) UK Limited (Registered in England & Wales, Company No 1679046.
Registered Office and address for service: Aldgate House, 33 Aldgate High Street, London EC3N 1DL)

For further information on our products and services, visit *www.sweetandmaxwell.co.uk*

Typeset by Letterpart Limited, Caterham on the Hill, Surrey CR3 5XL

Printed and bound by CPI Group (UK) Ltd, Croydon CR0 4YY.

No natural forests were destroyed to make this product; only farmed timber was used and re-planted.

A CIP catalogue record of this book is available for the British Library.

ISBN: 978-0-414-02885-2

Thomson Reuters and the Thomson Reuters logo are trademarks of Thomson Reuters.

Sweet & Maxwell ® is a registered trademark of Thomson Reuters (Professional) UK Limited.

Crown copyright material is reproduced with the permission of the Controller of HMSO and the Queen's Printer for Scotland.

All rights reserved. No part of this publication may be reproduced or transmitted in any form or by any means, or stored in any retrieval system of any nature, without prior written permission, except for permitted fair dealing under the Copyright, Designs and Patents Act 1988, or in accordance with the terms of a licence issued by the Copyright Licensing Agency in respect of photocopying and/or reprographic reproduction. Application for permission for other use of copyright material, including permission to reproduce extracts in other published works, shall be made to the publishers. Full acknowledgement of author, publisher and source must be given.

© 2013 Sweet & Maxwell

Preface

In the first edition of this book in 1981, I wrote:

"Intellectual property law and taxation have been the subject of very considerable development over the past few years and the authors expect this development to continue. Against this background it is convenient to consider intellectual property primarily in the individual areas of patents, designs, trade marks, copyright and the various rights which are given common law protection (i.e. passing-off, unfair competition, know-how and show-how and endorsement). However, these various areas interact and overlap and many real life situations contain components from more than one of them. It is in these messy situations that the possibilities for proper or incompetent planning are to be found and it is hoped that this book will assist in inclining practitioners and beneficiaries to the former rather than allowing a gradual slide to the latter.

This book is addressed to those who wish to use intellectual property law and taxation for legitimate ends. The intricate nature of these subjects provides a fascinating set of ground rules which may be used by the skilled operator to his advantage. Those who wish to take advantage of those rules must first know them, in general if not in detail, and Part One of this work therefore deals with the main areas of intellectual property law. Each area is discussed within a single chapter but, for ease of comparison with the other areas, all the chapters in Part One follow the same format: an introduction explains the basic concepts behind the particular branch of intellectual property law concerned, followed by more detailed sections on the method of obtaining protection, the form of protection, exploitation, international systems and comparisons with other countries' laws on the subject." This edition, although now more than twice as long, attempts to continue this ideal.

In Part Two of the book, various tax matters relating to intellectual property are dealt with and in Part Three each type of intellectual property is again discussed within a single chapter, but from the tax point of view. Part Four is concerned with tax planning generally and applies to all types of intellectual property, while Part Five deals with specific taxation applications.

Part Six gives practical examples, cautionary tales and what we hope is a clear illustration of how intellectual property law and taxation interact in the form of nine case studies which follow the progress of an author, an inventor, a rock group, a bricklayer, and various entrepreneurs from the inception of their ideas to the resolution of their tax planning problems.

I would like to thank, in addition to my co-authors, my partners in BDO LLP and MHA MacIntyre Hudson for their encouragement and in particular Richard Jones at BDO, who helped to check my input and correct my errors and

PREFACE

omissions, and my secretary Julie Bell.

Nigel Eastaway OBE
MHA MacIntyre Hudson
New Bridge Street House
30–34 New Bridge Street
London
EC4V 6BJ
October 2013

Abbreviations

CA 1956	Copyright Act 1956
CA 2006	Companies Act 2006
CAA 1990	Capital Allowances Act 1990
CCR	County Court Rules
CDPA 1988	Copyright, Designs and Patents Act 1988
CFC	controlled foreign company
CTA	Corporation Tax Act 2010
CTMO	Community Trade Marks Office
DSS	Department of Social Security
FA	Finance Act
IHTA 1984	Inheritance Tax Act 1984
IM	Inland Revenue Manual
IRS	Internal Revenue Service (US)
ITEPA 2003	Income Tax (Earnings and Pensions) Act 2003
ITTOIA 2005	Income Tax (Trading and Other Income) Act 2005
ITA 2007	Income Tax Act 2007
NIC	National Insurance contributions
PA 1977	Patents Act 1977
RDA 1949	Registered Designs Act 1949
SA 1891	Stamp Act 1891
SERPS	State Earnings Related Pension Scheme
SI	Statutory Instrument

ABBREVIATIONS

SP	Statement of Practice
TA 1988	Income and Corporation Taxes Act 1988
TCGA 1992	Taxation of Chargeable Gains Act 1992
TIOPA	Taxation (International and Other Provisions) Act 2010
TMA 1938	Trade Marks Act 1938
TMA 1994	Trade Marks Act 1994
TMA 1970	Taxes Management Act 1970
VAT	value added tax
VATA 1994	Value Added Tax Act 1994

TABLE OF CONTENTS

	PAGE
Preface	v
Abbreviations	vii
Table of Cases	xxvii
Table of Statutes	xliii
Table of Statutory Instruments	lxi
Table of Treaties and Conventions	lxiii
Table of European Provisions	lxv

PARA

Part 1
LAW

1. Introduction 1–001

2. Patents
   Introduction 2–001
   Obtaining protection 2–005
      Patentable inventions 2–006
      Novelty 2–008
      The application 2–009
      Search 2–010
      Examination 2–011
      Patent agents/attorneys 2–012
   Form of protection 2–013
   Exploitation 2–018
      Assignment 2–019
      Licensing 2–020
      Exhaustion 2–024
   International systems 2–025
      The international convention 2–026
      The Patent Co-operation Treaty and the European Patent
         Office 2–028
      The European Patent Office 2–030
   The Community Patent 2–031
      The United States 2–032
   Petty patents 2–034
   Conclusion 2–036

CONTENTS

3. Designs
Introduction 3–001
Obtaining protection 3–002
Form of protection 3–006
Exploitation 3–008
International systems 3–009
Conclusion 3–012

4. Trade marks
Introduction 4–001
Obtaining protection 4–004
Registrable marks 4–005
The application 4–006
Form of protection 4–009
    Infringement 4–010
Exploitation 4–011
    Licensing and permitted use arrangements 4–012
    Assignment 4–013
    Franchising 4–014
International systems
    The basic framework 4–015
    The EU system of registration 4–016
    The Madrid Agreement and Protocol 4–019
    The rest of the world 4–020
Conclusion 4–021

5. Copyright and design right
Introduction 5–001
Obtaining protection 5–002
Form of protection 5–004
Design right 5–006
Exploitation 5–012
International aspects 5–014
Conclusion 5–017

6. Common law protection
Introduction 6–001
Passing off and unfair competition law 6–002
Know-how and show-how 6–008
Endorsement 6–009

7. Commercial exploitation of intellectual property
Introduction 7–001
Policy 7–002

8. Specific applications
Introduction 8–001
Biotechnology 8–002

CONTENTS

Computers 8–007
Broadcasting..8–010
Film 8–012
Franchising...8–013
Conclusion..8–014

Part 2
PRINCIPLES OF TAXATION

9. Individuals and Partnerships
General principles 9–001
    Personal allowances...9–003
        Rate of tax 9–004
Self-assessment 9–005
    Tax returns 9–006
    Disclosure of tax avoidance schemes 9–008
    Enquiries into returns by HMRC 9–009
    Payment 9–010
    Estimates and amendments..9–011
    Penalties 9–012
    Internet services...9–013
    Partnerships..9–014
    Accounts and computations...9–015
    Post-transaction rulings 9–016
    Repayment claiming 9–017
Residence 9–018
    Residence and ordinary residence prior to April 6, 2013..........9–019
    Residence after April 6, 2013..9–022
        Ordinary residence 9–026
        Dual residence 9–027
Domicile..9–028
    Remittance basis..9–031
    Gifts overseas 9–037
Business Investment Relief...9–038
Employees...9–039
    Benefits in kind 9–040
    P11Ds...9–041
    Allowances...9–042
    PAYE..9–043
    Emoluments 9–044
Self-employed 9–045
    Current year basis..9–046
    Adjusted accounts..9–048
    Cash basis 9–049
        Capital allowances 9–051
Loss Relief..9–053
Cap on unlimited tax reliefs 9–055

CONTENTS

Annual payments 9–056
   Failure to deduct tax 9–058
   Pure income profits 9–059
Income from UK land 9–061
   Enveloped Dwellings 9–064
Income from investments
   Interest and discounts 9–065
   Taxed investment income 9–066
Foreign securities and possessions 9–067
Casual profits 9–069
National insurance 9–070
Capital gains tax 9–071
   Chargeable gains and losses 9–072
   Entrepreneurs' relief 9–073
   Losses 9–076
   Transfers between husband and wife 9–077
   Re-structuring of companies 9–078
   Roll-over relief 9–079
   Other provisions 9–080
Partnerships
   Self-assessment by partners 9–081
   Non-resident partner 9–083
   Partnership carried on outside the United Kingdom 9–084
   Corporate partner 9–085
Limited partnerships 9–086
Limited liability partnerships 9–087
   Proposed changes 9–088
Inheritance tax 9–090
   Taxpayer's estate 9–091
   Conditionally exempt transfers 9–092
   Trusts 9–093
   Close companies 9–094
   Reliefs 9–095
   Gifts with reservation of benefit 9–096
   Pre-owned asset charge 9–097
   Other provisions 9–098

10. Companies and trusts
Companies and corporation tax
   Background 10–001
   Structure of corporation tax 10–002
   Rate of tax 10–003
   Losses 10–004
   Charges on income 10–005
   Trading companies 10–006
   Groups of companies 10–007
   Substantial shareholding exemption 10–008
   Deduction of tax at source 10–009

CONTENTS

Dividend receipts 10–010
Corporation tax payments and accounting periods 10–011
Disclosure of tax avoidance schemes 10–013
Trusts 10–014
Income tax 10–015
Other trusts (life interest trusts) 10–017
Discretionary and accumulation trusts: particular features ... 10–018
Tax return 10–019
Capital gains tax 10–020
Foreign trusts 10–021
Inheritance tax 10–022

11. Value added tax
Introduction 11–001
Place of supply of goods 11–003
Exports out of or into the European Union and intra-EU
  movements 11–004
Place of supply of services 11–005
Time of supply 11–007
Rate of VAT 11–008
Recovery of VAT in general 11–009
VATable persons 11–010
Collection of VAT 11–011
Treatment of intellectual property 11–012

12. Valuation
Intellectual property 12–001
Market value 12–002
Special purchasers 12–004
Real sales 12–005
Optimum lotting 12–006
Hindsight 12–007
Willing parties 12–008
Discounted cash flows—net present value of incremental cash
  flows 12–009
Weighted average cost of capital 12–010
Industry price multiple—capitalisation of earnings 12–012
Royalty comparisons—relief from royalty methods 12–013
Hybrid valuations—cost based valuations 12–014
Excess profits—notional maximum royalties payable 12–015
External factors—comparable market transactions 12–016
Goodwill—premium sales price—gross profit differential 12–017
Brands 12–019
Real options methods 12–020
Binomial model 12–021
Monte Carlo simulation 12–022
Location of assets 12–023
International Financial Reporting Standard 3 (IFRS 3) 12–024

CONTENTS

Case law 12–026
Further case law 12–027
    Issue *a*: conclusion
HMRC's Corporate Intangible Research and Development Manual
    deals with valuation issues at CIRD10240 12–028
CIRD30515 sets out notes on accounting practice for intangible
    assets under FRS11 and IAS36 12–029
IAS36 12–030
CIRD30520 covers FRS7/IFRS3 12–031
Scope 12–032
Meaning of Fair Value 12–033
Impaired Assets—Effect on Fair Value 12–034
CIRD30525—Intangible assets: notes on accounting practice: FRS
    for Smaller Entities (FRSSE) 12–035
    Other intangible assets and goodwill 12–036
CIRD30535 deals with goodwill 12–037
Negative Goodwill 12–038

13. Transfer pricing

Introduction 13–001
    The main provisions 13–002
        Interest 13–007
        Documentation and penalties 13–008
Foreign legislation 13–012
Arbitration Convention 13–013
Theory of international transfer pricing 13–014
The OECD Transfer Pricing Guidelines for multinational enterprises
    and tax administrations (Report of July 22, 2010) 13–017
    Transfer pricing methods to arrive at the arm's-length
        price 13–018
    Transaction-based methods 13–019
        Comparable uncontrolled price method (CUP) 13–020
        Re-sale price method 13–021
        The cost-plus method 13–022
    Transactional profit methods 13–023
        The transactional profit-split method 13–024
        Transactional net margin method 13–026
        Global methods 13–027
Arm's-length range 13–028
Intangibles 13–029
US royalties 13–031
Customs valuations 13–034
Double taxation treaties 13–035
Future developments 13–037

14. Controlled foreign companies

Introduction 14–001
Definition of CFC 14–002

CONTENTS

Residence 14–003
Control 14–004
The gateways 14–006
Profits attributable to UK activities 14–007
Non-trading finance profits 14–008
Trading finance profits 14–009
Captive insurance 14–010
Solo consolidation 14–011
Finance company exemption 14–012
Entity-level exemptions 14–013
The temporary period of exemption 14–014
The excluded territories exemption 14–015
The low profits exemption 14–016
The low profits margin exemption 14–017
The tax exemption 14–018
Clearances 14–019
Apportionment of CFC chargeable profits 14–020
Chargeable profits 14–021
Creditable tax 14–024
Cell companies 14–025
Double charges 14–026
Foreign systems 14–027

15. Research and Development

Introduction 15–001
Frascati 15–003
SSAP 13 and Guidelines 15–004
Accounting treatment of R&D expenditure 15–007
Taxation treatment 15–010
Capital expenditure on R&D, R&D allowances 15–011
Trading deduction for R&D costs 15–013
R&D relief for small and medium-sized companies—"super deduction" 15–014
Cap on relief 15–015
Qualifying R&D expenditure 15–016
Staffing costs 15–017
Software or consumable items 15–018
Other conditions 15–019
Irrevocable election for connected persons treatment 15–020
Pre-trading expenses 15–021
SME R&D tax credits 15–022
Appeals, etc. 15–024
Tax relief on R&D expenditure for large companies 15–025
Qualifying R&D expenditure 15–026
The relief 15–027
Definitions 15–028
Vaccine research relief 15–029
Cap on relief 15–030

CONTENTS

Qualifying expenditure 15–031
R&D expenditure credits under the large company scheme..................15–032
    SME's expenditure on sub-contracted R&D—ss.104C–104E..................15–034
    SME's expenditure on subsidised qualifying expenditure—ss.104F–104H......15–035
    Capped R&D expenditure—s.104I..................................15–036
Amount and payment of credit..15–037
Insurance companies and groups..15–039
Anti-avoidance and interpretation.....................................15–040
Tax relief for television production and video games developments.....15–041

Part 3
INTELLECTUAL PROPERTY TAXATION

16. Patents

Introduction..16–001
Annual payments—post-April 5, 2007—pre-December 5, 2011—individuals....16–002
Patent royalties—post-December 5, 2012................................16–005
    Form R185..16–007
    Excess charges...16–008
Companies—deduction of tax at treaty rate.............................16–009
Companies paying gross under Directive................................16–010
    Foreign patents..16–013
    Non-residents..16–014
Patent income...16–015
    Trading income...16–017
    Investment income..16–018
    Lump sum receipts treated as capital...........................16–020
    Keep out covenants...16–023
    Lump sum receipts treated as income............................16–025
Taxation of capital receipts as income................................16–028
    Non-residents: capital sums....................................16–030
    Costs of acquisition...16–032
    Effect of winding up...16–033
    Lump sum for previous use......................................16–034
    Conclusion...16–035
Expenses..16–036
Capital allowances
    Licensee's capital payment.....................................16–037
    Post-March 31, 1986 expenditure................................16–038
Employee awards...16–039
Enterprise Investment Scheme: roll-over relief on reinvestment and venture capital trusts..16–043
Capital gains tax...16–044

CONTENTS

Inheritance tax 16–045
Stamp duty 16–046
VAT
    Treatment of patents 16–047

17. Trade and Service Marks and Designs
Introduction 17–001
Income 17–002
    Averaging 17–003
Investment income 17–006
Expenses 17–007
Royalties 17–008
Lump sums 17–009
Relief to purchaser 17–010
Royalties paid 17–011
Dealing and investment 17–012
Stamp duty 17–013
VAT 17–014

18. Copyright
Introduction 18–001
Professional income 18–002
Acquired copyright royalties 18–004
Post-cessation receipts 18–005
Post-cessation expenses 18–006
Assignment of copyright 18–007
    Future copyright 18–008
    Income of assignee 18–009
    Capital receipts 18–010
    Film rights and outright sales 18–011
    Publishing and casual receipts 18–014
Casual authors 18–016
Averaging provisions 18–017
Deduction of tax at source 18–018
    Non-residents 18–019
    Non-resident authors 18–023
Realisation of investments 18–026
Prizes and grants 18–027
    Arts Council awards and bursaries 18–029
    Public lending right 18–032
Leasing 18–033
Expenses 18–034
Purchase of copyright
    Capital allowances 18–035
    Deferred revenue expenditure 18–036
BIM4220 Deductions: timing: deferred revenue expenditure: reaching consistency of treatment.
    Background 18–039

CONTENTS

The cut off 18–040
Detail 18–041
Cases where the return is closed 18–042
Claims from taxpayers that the cut off date is retrospective 18–043
Particular situations 18–044
Cases where a non-depreciation policy has been adopted 18–045
Double deductions 18–046
Combined capital and deferred revenue expenditure
   depreciated 18–047
Appeals 18–048
Film and Audio products 18–049
   Expenditure treated as revenue expense the F(No2) A 1992
      rules 18–050
   Allocation of expenditure income matching method 18–051
   Allocation of expenditure cost recovery method 18–052
   Miscellaneous provisions 18–053
   Qualifying films 18–054
   100 per cent write off the F(No2)A 1997 rules 18–055
   Three-year spread 18–057
   Preliminary expenses 18–058
   Capital allowances 18–059
   Video tapes for rental 18–060
Film related trading losses
   The FA 2004 rules
      Trade profits: Films and sound recordings 18–061
   Film related trading losses, the ITA 2007 rules 18–062
   The ITTOIA 2005 rules 18–063
   Anti-avoidance measures—The FA 2005 rules 18–064
Settlement opportunity 18–066
HMRC settlement opportunity—UK GAAP partnerships and
   sideways loss relief 18–067
UK GAAP Partnerships 18–068
Terms of Settlement 18–069
What to do now 18–070
Film and sound recordings
   The FA 2006 schemes 18–071
   Entitlement to film tax reliefs 18–072
   Corporation tax treatment of sound recordings 18–075
Capital taxes 18–076
Stamp duty 18–077
VAT 18–078

19. Know-how and Show-how
Introduction 19–001
   Definitions 19–002
Income 19–003
Lump sums
   Case law 19–004

CONTENTS

    Statutory provisions 19–008
    Common control 19–009
    Disposal of know-how and goodwill 19–010
    Non-trading know-how 19–011
    Restrictive covenants 19–012
Planning aspects 19–013
Allowance to purchaser 19–014
Commercial know-how 19–015
    Divers 19–016
Stamp duty 19–017
VAT 19–018
Double taxation 19–019

20. Merchandising and endorsement
Introduction 20–001
Merchandising 20–002
Income 20–003
Endorsement fees 20–007
Stamp duty 20–009
VAT 20–010

21. Corporate Intangible fixed assets
Introduction 21–001
Scope 21–002
Basis 21–003
Application 21–005
Excluded assets 21–006
Definition 21–009
Accounting issues—UK GAAP 21–010
Smaller entities 21–012
Impairment review 21–013
Commencement and transitional provisions 21–014
Royalties 21–016
Date of acquisition 21–017
Allowable costs (debits) 21–018
Amortisation 21–020
Fixed rate allowance 21–022
Amortisation following part realisation 21–023
Taxable receipts (credits) 21–024
Revaluations 21–025
Negative goodwill 21–026
Reversal of previous accounting loss 21–027
Change of accounting policy 21–028
Realisation of intangible fixed assets 21–029
Anti-avoidance 21–032
How credits and debits are given effect 21–033
    Corporate partners 21–036

Rollover relief on reinvestment 21–037
    Rollover relief on reinvestment: groups 21–041
    Rollover relief on acquisition of shares 21–042
Degrouping 21–043
    Group definition 21–046
    Degrouping charge 21–049
    Relieving provisions 21–050
    Demergers 21–051
    Bona fide commercial merger 21–052
Transfer of business or trade 21–053
Transfer of trade between EU companies 21–054
Formation of a Societas Europaea by merger 21–055
Incorporation of an overseas permanent establishment 21–056
Clearance 21–057
Life assurance businesses and building societies 21–058
Finance leasing 21–059
Controlled foreign companies 21–060
    Consequential amendments 21–061
Double taxation relief 21–062
Value shifting 21–063

22. The Patent Box

Introduction and background 22–001
Outline 22–002
Elections 22–004
Companies qualifying for the patent box 22–005
Qualifying intellectual property 22–006
The development condition 22–008
The active ownership condition 22–011
Election 22–012
Calculation of relevant intellectual property profits of a
    trade 22–013
Total gross income of trade (TI) 22–014
Relevant intellectual property income (RIPI) 22–015
Particular cases: software 22–018
Particular cases: medical treatments 22–020
Notional royalty 22–021
Calculating profits of trade
    CTA 2010 s.357CG 22–022
Routine return 22–025
Marketing assets return figure 22–026
Profits arising before grant of right 22–030
Streaming 22–031
Mechanics of relief 22–033
Losses 22–034
Anti-avoidance 22–037
Cost-sharing arrangements 22–039

23. General Principles and Non-corporates

Introduction 23–001
Trading and professional income 23–008
    Current year basis 23–009
    Investment income 23–010
Losses 23–012
    Trading losses 23–013
    Non-trading losses 23–015
Post-cessation receipts 23–016
Income not otherwise charged to tax 23–018
Capital gains 23–019
ITEPA 2003 23–020
    Arising basis 23–021
    "Golden handshakes" 23–022
    Inducement payments 23–023
Pension schemes 23–024
    Unfunded pensions 23–027
Keyman insurance 23–028
Trusts 23–029
    Income tax on trusts 23–030
    Capital taxes on trusts 23–031

Part 4
TAX PLANNING

24. International tax planning

Introduction 24–001
    Non-residents 24–002
Overseas rights 24–003
Foreign partnerships 24–004
    Control and management 24–007
    Assessment of Foreign Income 24–008
Remittance basis 24–009
    Gifts overseas 24–012
Withholding taxes 24–014
Double taxation relief 24–015
Royalty structures 24–018
Film distribution agreements 24–022
Authors 24–023
Dividend routing 24–024
Loan routing 24–025
Tax havens 24–026
    Switzerland 24–027
    Liechtenstein 24–028
    Luxembourg 24–029
    Isle of Man and Channel Islands 24–030
    Republic of Ireland 24–031

CONTENTS

    Other havens 24–032
  Transfers of assets abroad 24–033
    Liability of non-transferors 24–036
    Power to obtain information 24–041
  Changes in the transfer of assets abroad rules—FA 2013 24–042
  Gains of non-resident settlements 24–043
    Supplementary charge 24–045
    Payments by and to companies 24–046
    Trustees ceasing to be resident in United Kingdom 24–048
  Capital gains tax charge on settlor 24–052
  Limbo trusts 24–056
  General anti-avoidance provisions 24–057

25. Stamp duty
  Introduction 25–001
  Intellectual property 25–002

26. Package deals
  Introduction 26–001
  Manufacturing agreements 26–002
    Licensor's position 26–003
    Licensee's position 26–005
    Common control 26–006
  Publishing deals 26–007
  Ethical drugs 26–008
  Broadcasting 26–010
  Recording agreements 26–011

Part 5
SPECIFIC TAXATION APPLICATIONS

27. Entertainers and sportsmen
  Introduction 27–001
  Employed or self-employed 27–002
    HMRC guidance 27–013
    Theatrical non-performing workers 27–015
    Musicians 27–016
    Film and television workers 27–017
    Agency workers 27–018
    Sportsmen 27–019
    Benefit years 27–020
    Athletes 27–021
  National Insurance 27–022
  Personal service companies (IR35) 27–023
  Restrictive covenants 27–026
  Date royalties taxable 27–027
  Simpler accounts for small businesses 27–031

CONTENTS

Advance royalties 27–032
Investment income 27–033
Angels 27–034
Compensation 27–035
Inducement payments 27–036
Capital receipts 27–037
Expenses 27–038
Returns 27–039
Employment companies 27–040
Company partnerships 27–042
Alternative assessments 27–043
Anti-constellation provisions 27–044
    Exemptions 27–046
Non-resident entertainers and sportsmen 27–047
    Reduced withholding agreements 27–049
    Double taxation agreements 27–050
    Benefits and apportionment 27–051
Image Rights 27–053
VAT 27–054

28. Franchising
Advantage to franchisor 28–001
Advantage to franchisee 28–002
Disadvantage to franchisor 28–003
Disadvantage to franchisee 28–004
Agreements 28–005
Code of conduct 28–006
The franchisor's tax position
    Analysis of agreement 28–008
    Initial lump sums 28–009
    Amortisation 28–010
    Restrictive covenants 28–011
    Know-how 28–012
    Show-how 28–013
    Advertising pools 28–014
        Royalties 28–015
    Turn-key operations 28–018
The franchisee's tax position 28–019
    Initial payment 28–020
    Deferred revenue expenditure 28–025
    Advertising contributions 28–027
    Pre-trading expenditure 28–028
VAT 28–029
International considerations 28–030

29. Computer software, the internet and the Cloud

Introduction 29–001
Software 29–002
   New media 29–003
The internet 29–004
The Cloud 29–005
Acquisition for distribution 29–006
Exploitation for own use 29–007
Capital allowances 29–008
Revenue expenditure 29–009
Royalties 29–010
Withholding tax 29–011
"Treaty shopping" 29–012
Development expenditure 29–013
Transfer pricing 29–014
VAT 29–015

Part 6
CASE STUDIES

Case Study 1: Peter Roberts, author
Introduction CS1–001
The product CS1–002
Initial income CS1–003
The companies CS1–005
The discretionary trust CS1–007
Strompy takes off CS1–008
Selling out CS1–011
The beneficiaries' income CS1–013
The trading trust CS1–014
The future CS1–015

Case Study 2: Andrew Rankin, inventor
Introduction CS2–001
The product CS2–002
The company CS2–003
The children's trust CS2–004
First year's growth CS2–005
Overseas trading income CS2–006
Selling out CS2–007
The Safteemyle partnership CS2–009
Safteemyle Ltd CS2–011
Andrew Rankin: trading structure

CONTENTS

Case Study 3: Brighton Rock, entertainers
Introduction CS3–001
The product CS3–002
The partnership's income CS3–005
The companies CS3–006
The pension funds CS3–009
The children's trusts CS3–010
The small companies' rate CS3–011
Another record CS3–012
The overseas companies CS3–013
Double taxation CS3–014
The film CS3–016
Gift of future copyright to trust CS3–017

Case Study 4: Albert Potcher, bricklayer extraordinare
Introduction CS4–001
The product CS4–002
Protecting the idea CS4–003
Beginning commercial exploitation CS4–004
The company CS4–006
Taking the idea abroad CS4–008
Another trade mark CS4–009
The competitors CS4–010
The outcome CS4–011

Case Study 5: Tanaday, the pill or potion to help you love the sun
The product CS5–001
Loot Pharmaceuticals Plc CS5–002
The joint development agreement CS5–003
Licences and sub-licences CSS–004
Further development of the discovery CS5–005

Case Study 6: Gribs by Night
The product CS6–001
Terms of the merchandising licence agreement CS6–002
Exploitation of the licence CS6–004
Manufacture of licensed articles CS6–005
The tax position CS6–006

Case Study 7: Nuttabun, fast food for the third millennium
The product CS7–001
The companies CS7–003
Franchise outlets CS7–004
Other licenses and agreements CS7–006
The future CS7–008

CONTENTS

Case Study 8: Transporterplane, economic transport for the 21st century
- The product CS8–001
- Applications for patents CS8–002
- The consortium company CS8–003
- The outcome CS8–004

Case Study 9: Yuri Rakovsky, conductor/composer
- Introduction CS9–001
- Nationality CS9–003
- Domicile CS9–004
- Residence CS9–005
- Sources of income CS9–007
- World tour CS9–009
- VAT on the tour CS9–012
- The video CS9–013
- Jacko Records CS9–014
- Girlfriend CS9–015
- Uli CS9–016

PAGE

Appendices
- Appendix 1: Copyright, Designs and Patents Act 1988 617
- Appendix 2: Patents Act 1977 621
- Appendix 3: Treaty on the Functioning of the European Union ... 627
- Appendix 4: Countries with Double Taxation Agreements with the UK—rates of withholding tax for the year ended April 5, 2012 629
- Appendix 5: HMRC FEU50, A Guide to Paying Foreign Entertainers 639
- Appendix 6: Guidelines on the Special NIC rules for Entertainers 653
- Appendix 7: Film, Television and Production Industry Guidance Notes 2003 edition 663
- Appendix 8: Guidelines on the Meaning of R&D for Tax purposes 681

PAGE

Index 693

TABLE OF CASES

Addison v London Philharmonic Orchestra [1981] I.C.R. 261, EAT 27–002

Agassi v Robinson (Inspector of Taxes); Sub Nom: Agassi v Robertson (Inspector of Taxes); Set v Robinson (Inspector of Taxes) [2006] UKHL 23; [2006] 1 W.L.R. 1380; [2006] 3 All E.R. 97; [2006] S.T.C. 1056; 77 T.C. 686; [2006] B.T.C. 372; 8 I.T.L. Rep. 1106; [2006] S.T.I. 1542; (2006) 103(22) L.S.G. 27; (2006) 156 N.L.J. 880; (2006) 150 S.J.L.B. 671, HL 20–006, 27–048, 27–053

Airfix Footwear Ltd v Cope [1978] I.C.R. 1210; [1978] I.R.L.R. 396; (1978) 13 I.T.R. 513, EAT 27–003

Alchemist (Devil's Gate) Film Partnership v Revenue and Customs Commissioners TC/2012/0618 18–066

Alianza Co Ltd v Bell (Surveyor of Taxes) (1906) 5 T.C. 172 17–010

Alloway v Phillips (Inspector of Taxes) [1980] 1 W.L.R. 888; [1980] 3 All E.R. 138; [1980] S.T.C. 490; [1980] T.R. 111; (1980) 124 S.J. 346, CA (Civ. Div.); affirming [1979] 1 W.L.R. 564; [1979] S.T.C. 452; 53 T.C. 372; [1979] T.R. 35; (1979) 123 S.J. 338, Ch D.. 18–015, ... 23–018

Alternative Book Co Ltd v Revenue and Customs Commissioners (2008) S.T.C. (SCD) 830 27–002

Andrews v King (Inspector of Taxes) [1991] S.T.C. 481; [1991] I.C.R. 846; 64 T.C. 332; [1991] S.T.I. 654; (1991) 88(31) L.S.G. 39; (1991) 135 S.J.L.B. 84, Ch D. 27–002

Ansell (Inspector of Taxes) v Brown [2001] S.T.C. 1166; 73 T.C. 338; [2001] B.T.C. 381; [2001] S.T.I. 847; (2001) 98(31) L.S.G. 37, Ch D. 27–021

Archer Shee v Baker (1927) 11 T.C. 749 16–017, ... 23–030

Argent v Minister of Social Security [1968] 1 W.L.R. 1749; [1968] 3 All E.R. 208; 5 K.I.R. 344; (1968) 112 S.J. 801, QBD 27–002

Aschrott, Re; Sub Nom: Clifton v Strauss [1927] 1 Ch. 313, Ch D 12–005

Asher v London Film Productions Ltd [1944] K.B. 133, CA 27–034

Associated Portland Cement Manufacturers Ltd v Inland Revenue Commissioners (1945) 27 T.C. 103 19–014

Association of British Travel Agents Ltd v Inland Revenue Commissioners; Sub Nom: ABTA v Inland Revenue Commissioners [2003] S.T.C. (S.C.D.) 194; [2003] S.T.I. 275, Sp Comm 13–013

Atherton v British Insulated and Helsby Cables (1925) 10 T.C. 77 . 9–048, 17–010, 18–036, 21–009, 28–020, 28–026

Attorney General v Jameson [1904] 2 I.R. 644 12–005

Attorney–General v Pottinger (1861) 6 H&N 733 9–028

Attorney General of Ceylon v Mackie [1952] 2 All E.R. 775; 45 R. & I.T. 793; (1952) 31 A.T.C. 435; [1952] T.R. 431, PC (Cey) 12–006, ... 12–016

Australia Mutual Provident Society v Chaplin (1978) 18 A.L.R. 385 27–013

Australian Mutual Provident Society v Inland Revenue Commissioners (1947) 28 T.C. 388 9–027

Aykroyd v Inland Revenue Commissioners (1942) 24 T.C. 515 24–034

BE Studios Ltd v Smith & Williamson Ltd [2005] EWHC 1506 (Ch); [2006] S.T.C. 358; [2005] B.T.C. 361; [2005] S.T.I. 1260, Ch D 15–004

BSC Footwear Ltd v Ridgway [1972] A.C. 544; [1971] 2 W.L.R. 1313; [1971] 2 All E.R. 534; 47 T.C. 495; (1971) 50 A.T.C. 153; [1971] T.R. 121; (1971) 115 S.J. 408, HL 27–029

Ball v Johnson (1971) 47 T.C. 155 18–027

Balloon Promotions Ltd v Wilson (Inspector of Taxes); Vela–Castro v Rodin (Inspector of Taxes) [2006] S.T.C. (S.C.D.) 167; [2006] S.T.I. 623, Sp Comm 12–017, ... 28–024

Bambridge v Inland Revenue Commissioners [1955] 1 W.L.R. 1329; [1955] 3 All E.R. 812; 48 R. & I.T. 814; 36 T.C. 313; (1955) 34 A.T.C. 181; [1955] T.R. 295; (1955) 99 S.J. 910, HL 24–034

Barclays Mercantile Business Finance Ltd v Mawson (Inspector of Taxes); Sub Nom: ABC Ltd v M (Inspector of Taxes) [2004] UKHL 51; [2005] 1 A.C. 684; [2004] 3 W.L.R. 1383; [2005] 1 All E.R. 97; [2005] S.T.C. 1; 76 T.C. 446; [2004] B.T.C. 414; 7 I.T.L. Rep. 383; [2004] S.T.I. 2435; (2004) 154 N.L.J. 1830; (2004) 148 S.J.L.B. 1403, HL 12–025, 23–003

Barnett v Brabyn (Inspector of Taxes) [1996] S.T.C. 716; 69 T.C. 133, Ch D. 27–002, 27–003

Barrett v Revenue and Customs Commissioners [2008] S.T.C. (S.C.D.) 268; [2007] S.T.I. 2416, Sp Comm 9–019, 9–020

Bartlett v Barclays Bank Trust Co Ltd (No.1) [1980] 2 W.L.R. 430; [1980] 1 All E.R. 139; (1980) 124 S.J. 85, Ch D. 24–035

TABLE OF CASES

Bartlett v Barclays Bank Trust Co Ltd (No.2) [1980] Ch. 515; [1980] 2 W.L.R. 430; [1980] 2 All E.R. 92; (1980) 124 S.J. 221, Ch D. 27–035

Battle v Inland Revenue Commissioners [1980] S.T.C. 86;.[1979].T.R..483, Ch D. . . 12–008

Bayliss v Gregory [1988] S.T.C. 476 . . . . 23–003, 23–006

Beare (Inspector of Taxes) v Carter (1940) 23 T.C. 353 . . . . 18–010, 18–011, 18–012

Beatty v Inland Revenue Commissioners (1940) 23 T.C. 574 24–034

Beauchamp (Inspector of Taxes) v FW Woolworth Plc [1990] 1 A.C. 478; [1989] 3 W.L.R. 1; [1989] S.T.C. 510; 62 T.C. 542; (1989) 133 S.J. 850, HL 28–020

Bentleys Stokes & Lewless v Beeson (Inspector of Taxes) [1952] 2 All E.R. 82; [1952] 1 T.L.R. 1529; 45 R. & I.T. 461; 33 T.C. 491; (1952) 31 A.T.C. 229; [1952] T.R. 239; [1952] W.N. 280; (1952) 96 S.J. 345, CA 27–038

Bhadra v Ellam (Inspector of Taxes) [1988] S.T.C. 239; 60 T.C. 466; (1988) 85(2) L.S.G. 37, Ch D. 27–002

Bheekhun v Williams; Bheekhun v Stafford [1999] 2 F.L.R. 229; [1999] Fam. Law 379, CA (Civ. Div.) 9–030

Billam v Griffith 23 T.C. 757 . 18–011, 18–013

Birmingham and District Cattle By–Products Co. Ltd v Inland Revenue Commissioners (1919) 12 T.C. 92 28–028

Bishop (Inspector of Taxes) v Finsbury Securities Ltd; Sub Nom: Finsbury Securities Ltd v Inland Revenue Commissioners; Finsbury Securities Ltd v Bishop (Inspector of Taxes) [1966] 1 W.L.R. 1402; [1966] 3 All E.R. 105; 43 T.C. 591; (1966) 45 A.T.C. 333; [1966] T.R. 275; (1966) 110 S.J. 636, HL 12–015

Black Nominees Ltd v Nicol (Inspector of Taxes); Sub Nom: Nicol (Inspector of Taxes) v Black Nominees Ltd [1975] S.T.C. 372; 50 T.C. 229; [1975] T.R. 93; (1975) 119 S.J. 613, Ch D. 27–040

Borland's Trustee v Steel Bros & Co Ltd [1901] 1 Ch. 279, Ch D. 12–001

Bowden (Inspector of Taxes) v Russell and Russell [1965] 1 W.L.R. 711; [1965] 2 All E.R. 258; 42 T.C. 301; (1965) 44 A.T.C. 74; [1965] T.R. 89; (1965) 109 S.J. 254, Ch D. 27–038

Bradberry, Re; National Provincial Ltd v Bradberry; Fry, Re; Tasker v Gulliford [1943] Ch. 35, Ch D. 12–007

Bradbury v Arnold (1957) 37 TC 665 18–015

Brandwood v Banker (1928) 14 T.C. 44 16–027

Bray (Inspector of Taxes) v Best [1989] 1 W.L.R. 167; [1989] 1 All E.R. 969; [1989] S.T.C. 159; 62 T.C. 705; (1989) 86(17) L.S.G. 43; (1989) 139 N.L.J. 753; (1989) 133 S.J. 323, HL 23–021

Bricom Holdings Ltd v Inland Revenue Commissioners [1997] S.T.C. 1179; 70 T.C. 272; [1997] B.T.C. 471, CA (Civ. Div.) 13–015, ... 14–020

Brigg Neumann & Co v Inland Revenue Commissioners 12 T.C. 1191, DC 12–002

Bristol Myers Co's Application [1968] F.S.R. 407; [1969] R.P.C. 146, QBD 2–008

British Dyestuffs Corp. (Blackley) Ltd v Inland Revenue Commissioners (1924) 12 T.C. 586 . . . . 19–006, 28–009

British Sugar Manufacturers Ltd v Harris (Inspector of Taxes) 21 T.C. 528 26–005

British Sugar Plc v James Robertson & Sons Ltd [1997] E.T.M.R. 118; [1996] R.P.C. 281; (1996) 19(3) I.P.D. 19023, Ch D. 4–010

British Transport Commission v Gourley [1956] A.C. 185; [1956] 2 W.L.R. 41; [1955] 3 All E.R. 796; [1955] 2 Lloyd's Rep. 475; 49 R. & I.T. 11; (1955) 34 A.T.C. 305; [1955] T.R. 303; (1956) 100 S.J. 12, HL 27–035

Brodies Will Trustees v Inland Revenue Commissioners (1933) 17 T.C. 432 9–056

Brooke v Inland Revenue Commissioners (1917) 7 T.C. 261 9–021

Brown v Burt (1911) 5 T.C. 667 . . . 9–019

Buckingham v Francis, Douglas & Thompson; Sub Nom: Buckingham v Francis [1986] 2 All E.R. 738; (1986) 2 B.C.C. 98984; [1986] P.C.C. 347, QBD (Comm) 12–007

Buswell v Inland Revenue Commissioners [1974] 1 W.L.R. 1631; [1974] 2 All E.R. 520; [1974] S.T.C. 266; 49 T.C. 334; [1974] T.R. 97; (1974) 118 S.J. 864, CA (Civ. Div.) 9–030

Cadbury Schweppes Plc v Inland Revenue Commissioners (C–196/04) [2007] Ch. 30; [2006] 3 W.L.R. 890; [2007] All E.R. (EC) 153; [2006] S.T.C. 1908; [2006] E.C.R. I–7995; [2007] 1 C.M.L.R. 2; [2006] C.E.C. 1026; [2008] B.T.C. 52; 9 I.T.L. Rep. 89; [2006] S.T.I. 2201, ECJ (Grand Chamber) 13–020, 14–001

Cadbury Schweppes Plc v Williams (Inspector of Taxes) [2006] EWCA Civ 657; [2007] S.T.C. 106; [2006] B.T.C. 440; [2006] S.T.I. 1572, CA (Civ. Div.) 23–003

Caillebotte v Quinn [1975] 1 W.L.R. 731; [1975] 2 All E.R. 412; [1975] S.T.C. 265; 50 T.C. 222; [1975] T.R. 55; (1975) 119 S.J. 356, Ch D. 27–038

TABLE OF CASES

Cairns v MacDiarmid (Inspector of Taxes) [1983] S.T.C. 178; 56 T.C. 556; [1983] B.T.C. 188; (1983) 127 S.J. 89, CA (Civ. Div.) 23–003

Campbell (Trustees of Davies Education Trust) v Inland Revenue Commissioners; Sub Nom: Davies Educational Trust (Campbell) v Inland Revenue Commissioners; [1970] A.C. 77; [1968] 3 W.L.R. 1025; [1968] 3 All E.R. 588; 45 T.C. 427; [1968] T.R. 327; (1968) 112 S.J. 864, HL . . . 9–056, 9–059, 9–060

Carmichael v National Power Plc [1999] 1 W.L.R. 2042; [1999] 4 All E.R. 897; [1999] I.C.R. 1226; [2000] I.R.L.R. 43; (1999) 96(46) L.S.G. 38; (1999) 143 S.J.L.B. 281, HL 27–003

Carson (Inspector of Taxes) v Peter Cheyney's Executor [1959] A.C. 412; [1958] 3 W.L.R. 740; [1958] 3 All E.R. 573; 51 R. & I.T. 824; 38 T.C. 240; (1958) 37 A.T.C. 347; [1958] T.R. 349; (1958) 102 S.J. 955, HL 18–002, 18–003, 18–023, 18–033

Carter (Inspector of Taxes) v Sharon [1936] 1 All E.R. 720; 20 T.C. 229, KBD 9–037, 24–012

Castle Construction Chesterfield) Ltd v Revenue and Customs Commissioners (2009) S.T.C. (SCD) 27–002, 27–011

Catnic Components Ltd v Hill & Smith Ltd (No.1); Sub Nom: Catnic Components Ltd v Hills & Rutter [1981] F.S.R. 60; [1982] R.P.C. 183, HL 2–014

Chancery Lane Safe Deposit & Offices Co Ltd v Inland Revenue Commissioners [1966] A.C. 85; [1966] 2 W.L.R. 251; [1966] 1 All E.R. 1; 43 T.C. 83; (1965) 44 A.T.C. 450; [1965] T.R. 433; (1966) 110 S.J. 35, HL 15–010

Chen Hsong Machinery Co. Ltd v Inland Revenue Commissioners (Hong Kong) (D52/96) 12–015

Cicutti v Suffolk CC [1981] 1 W.L.R. 558; [1980] 3 All E.R. 689; [1980] E.C.C. 424; 79 L.G.R. 231; (1981) 125 S.J. 134, Ch D. 9–026

Clark v Green [1995] S.T.C. (SCD) 99 12–008

Clark v Inland Revenue Commissioners [1979] 1 W.L.R. 416; [1979] 1 All E.R. 385; [1978] S.T.C. 614; 52 T.C. 482; [1978] T.R. 335; (1979) 123 S.J. 252, Ch D.. . . . . . 24–038, 27–045

Clark v Oxfordshire Health Authority [1998] I.R.L.R. 125 27–004

Clark (Inspector of Taxes) v Oceanic Contractors Inc [1983] 2 A.C. 130; [1983] 2 W.L.R. 94; [1983] 1 All E.R. 133; [1983] S.T.C. 35; 56 T.C. 183; (1982) 13 A.T.R. 901; (1983) 133 N.L.J. 62; (1983) 127 S.J. 54, HL 27–011

Clayton v Newcastle–under–Lyme Corp. (1888) 2 T.C. 416 28–014

Clinch v Inland Revenue Commissioners [1974] Q.B. 76; [1973] 2 W.L.R. 862; [1973] 1 All E.R. 977; [1973] S.T.C. 155; 49 T.C. 52; [1973] T.R. 157; (1973) 117 S.J. 342, QBD 24–041

Coalite & Chemical Products v Treeby 48 T.C. 171; [1971] T.R. 425 . . . . 19–005, 28–009

Colquhoun v Brooks (1889) L.R. 14 App. Cas. 493; 2 T.C. 490, HL 9–067, 24–005

Commissioner of Taxes v Nchanga Consolidated Copper Mines [1964] A.C. 948; [1964] 2 W.L.R. 339; [1964] 1 All E.R. 208; (1964) 43 A.T.C. 20; [1964] T.R. 25; (1964) 108 S.J. 73, PC (Rho) 28–022

Congreve v Inland Revenue Commissioners [1948] 1 All E.R. 948; (1948) 41 R. & I.T. 319; 30 T.C. 163; [1948] W.N. 197; [1948] L.J.R. 1229; (1948) 92 S.J. 407, HL 24–034

Constantinesco v R. (1927) 43 T.L.R. 727; 11 T.C. 730 16–025

Cooke (Inspector of Taxes) v Blacklaws [1985] S.T.C. 1; 58 T.C. 255; (1984) 81 L.S.G. 3259, Ch D. 27–002

Cooper v Blakiston (1908) 5 T.C. 347 . . . . 18–027, 27–020

Copeman (Inspector of Taxes) v William Flood & Sons (1941) 24 T.C. 53 9–048

Corbett v Duff (Inspector of Taxes) (1941) 23 T.C. 763 . . . . 18–027, 27–020

Corbett's Executrices v Inland Revenue Commissioners (1943) 25 T.C. 305 24–034

Cottingham's Executors v Inland Revenue Commissioners (1938) 22 T.C. 344 24–034

Couch (Inspector of Taxes) v Administrators of the Estate of Caton; Sub Nom: Administrators of the Estate of Caton v Couch (Inspector of Taxes); Caton's Administrators v Couch (Inspector of Taxes) [1997] S.T.C. 970; 70 T.C. 10; [1997] B.T.C. 360; (1997) 94(30) L.S.G. 29, CA (Civ. Div.); affirming [1996] S.T.C. 201, Ch D.; reversing [1995] S.T.C. (S.C.D.) 34, Sp Comm 12–008

Courthope (dec'd), Re (1928) 7 A.T.C. 538 12–009

Crabtree v Hinchcliffe (Inspector of Taxes); Sub Nom: Hinchcliffe (Inspector of Taxes) v Crabtree [1972] A.C. 707; [1971] 3 W.L.R. 821; [1971] 3 All E.R. 967; 47 T.C. 419; [1971] T.R. 321; (1971) 115 S.J. 891, HL 12–008

Cramer v Cramer [1987] 1 F.L.R. 116; [1986] Fam. Law 333; (1986) 83 L.S.G. 1996, CA (Civ. Div.) 9–027

TABLE OF CASES

Craven (Inspector of Taxes) v White; Inland Revenue Commissioners v Bowater Property Developments Ltd; Craven (Inspector of Taxes) v White; Baylis (Inspector of Taxes) v Gregory [1989] A.C. 398; [1988] 3 W.L.R. 423; [1988] 3 All E.R. 495; [1988] S.T.C. 476; (1988) 85 (34) L.S.G. 49; (1988) 138 N.L.J. Rep. 219; (1988) 132 S.J. 1120, HL . 22–001, 23–003, 23–006
Crossland (Inspector of Taxes) v Hawkins [1961] Ch. 537; [1961] 3 W.L.R. 202; [1961] 2 All E.R. 812; 39 T.C. 493; (1961) 40 A.T.C. 126; [1961] T.R. 113; (1961) 105 S.J. 424, CA 24–023, 24–033, 27–040, CS1–012
Crossman, Re (1936) 15 A.T.C. 94 . . . . 12–001, 12–005
Cunard's Trustees v Inland Revenue Commissioners (1945) 27 T.C. 122 20–004
Curtis v Jarvis (1929) 14 T.C. 744 18–019
Daphne v Shaw (1926) 43 T.L.R. 45; 11 T.C. 256 18–035
Davies v Braithwaite (1933) 18 T.C. 198 . . . . 23–008, 24–005, 24–009, 27–001, 27–002, 27–008
Davis v Harrison (1927) 11 T.C. 561 . . . . 18–027, 27–020
De Lasteyrie du Saillant v Ministere de l'Economie des Finances et de l'Industrie (2004) SWTI 890 24–048
Dealler v Bruce (1934) 19 T.C. 9 9–056
Degorce (Patrick) v Revenue and Customs Commissioners (2013) UKFT 178 (TC). 18–066
Delage v Nugget Polish Co. Ltd (1905) 21 T.L.R. 454 . . . . 17–011, 19–003
Denekamp v Pearce (Inspector of Taxes) [1998] S.T.C. 1120; 71 T.C. 213; [1998] B.T.C. 413, Ch D. 12–008
Desoutter Bros v Hanger & Co; Artificial Limb Makers Ltd (1936) 15 A.T.C. 49 . . . . 16–017, 16–021
Deuce and Ball v Robinson [2003] S.T.C. (SCD) 382 27–047
Down v Compton (1937) 21 T.C. 60b 18–028
Dragonfly Consultancy Ltd v Revenue & Customs Commissioners (2008) S.T.C. 3030. 27–002
Drummond v Collins (Surveyor of Taxes) (1915) 6 T.C. 525 9–056
Duff v Williamson [1973] S.T.C. 434; 49 T.C. 1; [1973] T.R. 171 18–027

Duke of Buccleuch v Inland Revenue Commissioners; Sub Nom: Duke Devonshire's Trustees v Inland Revenue Commissioners [1967] 1 A.C. 506; [1967] 2 W.L.R. 207; [1967] 1 All E.R. 129; [1967] R.V.R. 25; [1967] R.V.R. 42; (1966) 45 A.T.C. 472; [1966] T.R. 393; (1967) 111 S.J. 18, HL 12–003, 12–005, 12–006, 12–008
ECC Quarries Ltd v Watkis (Inspector of Taxes) [1975] S.T.C. 175 28–025
Earl Fitzwilliam v Inland Revenue Commissioners; Sub Nom: Inland Revenue Commissioners v Earl Fitzwilliam [1914] A.C. 753, HL; affirming [1913] 2 K.B. 593, CA; 28–024
Earl Haig Trustees v Inland Revenue Commissioners (1939) 22 T.C. 725 18–015
Earl Howe v Inland Revenue Commissioners (1919) 7 T.C. 289 . . . . 9–059, 9–060
Earl Iveagh v Inland Revenue Commissioners [1930] I.R. 431 9–030
Earl of Ellesmere v Inland Revenue Commissioners [1918] 2 K.B. 735, KBD 12–006
Eastern National Omnibus Co Ltd v Inland Revenue Commissioners [1939] 1 K.B. 161, KBD 25–002
Eclipse Film Partners No 35 LLP v Revenue & Customs Commissioners 2012 SFTD 823 18–066
Edward Collins & Sons v Inland Revenue Commissioners (1924) 12 T.C. 773 28–014
Edwards (Inspector of Taxes) v Bairstow; Edwards (Inspector of Taxes) v Harrison [1956] A.C. 14; [1955] 3 W.L.R. 410; [1955] 3 All E.R. 48; 48 R. & I.T. 534; 36 T.C. 207; (1955) 34 A.T.C. 198; [1955] T.R. 209; (1955) 99 S.J. 558, HL 27–007
Edwards (Inspector of Taxes) v Clinch [1982] A.C. 845; [1981] 3 W.L.R. 707; [1981] 3 All E.R. 543; [1981] S.T.C. 617; 56 T.C. 367; [1981] T.R. 393; (1981) 125 S.J. 762, HL; affirming [1981] Ch. 1; [1980] 3 W.L.R. 521; [1980] 3 All E.R. 278; [1980] S.T.C. 438; [1980] T.R. 189; (1980) 124 S.J. 397, CA (Civ. Div.) 27–002
Edwards (Inspector of Taxes) v Warmsley Henshall & Co [1968] 1 All E.R. 1089; 44 T.C. 431; (1967) 46 A.T.C. 431; [1967] T.R. 409, Ch D. 27–038
Eilbeck (Inspector of Taxes) v Rawling [1981] S.T.C. 174 23–003
Ellis v Lucas [1967] Ch. 858; [1966] 3 W.L.R. 382; [1966] 2 All E.R. 935; 43 T.C. 276; [1966] T.R. 87; (1966) 110 S.J. 605, Ch D. 18–027
Elmhirst v Inland Revenue Commissioners (1937) 21 T.C. 381 9–026

TABLE OF CASES

English Electric Co v Musker; Sub Nom: Inland Revenue Commissioners v English Electric Co 41 T.C. 556; (1964) 43 A.T.C. 119; [1964] T.R. 129, HL 19–004, 28–009

Ensign Tankers (Leasing) Ltd v Stokes (Inspector of Taxes) [1992] 1 A.C. 655; [1992] 2 W.L.R. 469; [1992] 2 All E.R. 275; [1992] S.T.C. 226; 64 T.C. 617; [1992] S.T.I. 364; (1992) 89(17) L.S.G. 49; (1992) 136 S.J.L.B. 89, HL 12–025, 18–066, 23–003, 23–005

Erichsen v Last (1881) 1 T.C. 351 24–006

Erven Warnink BV v J Townend & Sons (Hull) Ltd (No.1) [1979] A.C. 731; [1979] 3 W.L.R. 68; [1979] 2 All E.R. 927; [1979] F.S.R. 397; [1980] R.P.C. 31; (1979) 123 S.J. 47, HL 6–004, 6–005

Express & Echo Publications Ltd v Tanton [1999] I.C.R. 693; [1999] I.R.L.R. 367; (1999) 96(14) L.S.G. 31, CA (Civ. Div.). 27–005

Exxon Corporation and Others v Exxon Insurance Consultants International Ltd. [1982] R.P.C. 69 5–013

Fall (Inspector of Taxes) v Hitchen [1973] 1 W.L.R. 286; [1973] 1 All E.R. 368; [1973] S.T.C. 66; 49 T.C. 433; [1972] T.R. 285; (1972) 117 S.J. 73, Ch D. . 27–001, 27–002, 27–008, 27–014

Faye v Inland Revenue Commissioners (1961) 40 T.C. 103 9–029

Ferguson v John Dawson & Partners (Contractors) Ltd [1976] 1 W.L.R. 1213; [1976] 3 All E.R. 817; [1976] 2 Lloyd's Rep. 669; 8 B.L.R. 38; [1976] I.R.L.R. 346; (1976) 120 S.J. 603, CA (Civ. Div.) 27–003, 27–010

Ferguson (Harry) (Motors) v Inland Revenue Commissioners [1951] N.I. 115; 33 T.C. 15; (1954) 33 A.T.C. 422 16–026

Fetherstonaugh (formerly Finch) v Inland Revenue Commissioners; Sub Nom: Finch v Inland Revenue Commissioners [1985] Ch. 1; [1984] 3 W.L.R. 212; [1984] S.T.C. 261; (1984) 81 L.S.G. 1443; (1984) 128 S.J. 302, CA (Civ. Div.); reversing [1983] 1 W.L.R. 405; [1983] S.T.C. 157; (1982) 126 S.J. 838, Ch D. 9–095

Fielden v Inland Revenue Commissioners (1965) 42 T.C. 501 9–030

Findlay's Trustees v Inland Revenue Commissioners (1938) 22 A.T.C. 437 . . . . 12–008, 12–016, 12–017

First World Software Ltd v Revenue and Customs Commissioners (2008) S.T.C. (SCD) 389 27–002

Floor v Davis (Inspector of Taxes) [1980] A.C. 695; [1979] 2 W.L.R. 830; [1979] 2 All E.R. 677; [1979] S.T.C. 379; (1979) 123 S.J. 374, HL; affirming [1978] Ch. 295; [1978] 3 W.L.R. 360; [1978] 2 All E.R. 1079; [1978] S.T.C. 436; [1978] T.R. 71; (1978) 122 S.J. 437, CA (Civ. Div.) 23–003

Force One Training Ltd (LON/95/1594A October 1995 (13619)) 28–029

Fragmap Developments v Cooper 44 T.C. 366; [1967] T.R. 169 12–015

Franchise Development Services Ltd (LON/95/2530A July 1996 (14295)) 28–029

Fry (Inspector of Taxes) v Burma Corp Ltd [1930] A.C. 321; 15 T.C. 113, HL 9–021

Fry, Tasker v Gulliford, Re [1943] Ch.35 12–007

Fuge v McClelland 49 R. & I.T. 546; 36 T.C. 571; (1956) 35 A.T.C. 274; [1956] T.R. 245 27–002

Furniss (Inspector of Taxes) v Dawson [1984] A.C. 474; [1984] 2 W.L.R. 226; [1984] 1 All E.R. 530; [1984] S.T.C. 153; 55 T.C. 324; (1984) 15 A.T.R. 255; (1984) 81 L.S.G. 739; (1985) 82 L.S.G. 2782; (1984) 134 N.L.J. 341; (1984) 128 S.J. 132, HL 23–003, 23–005, 23–006, 23–007

Furse (Deceased), Re; Sub Nom: Furse v Inland Revenue Commissioners [1980] 3 All E.R. 838; [1980] S.T.C. 596; [1980] T.R. 275, Ch D. 9–030

Fynn v Inland Revenue Commissioners [1958] 1 W.L.R. 585; [1958] 1 All E.R. 270; 51 R. & I.T. 142; 37 T.C. 629; (1957) 36 A.T.C. 313; [1957] T.R. 323; (1958) 102 S.J. 381, Ch D. 24–034

Gaines–Cooper v Revenue and Customs Commissioners [2007] EWHC 2617 (Ch); [2008] S.T.C. 1665; [2007] B.T.C. 704; 10 I.T.L. Rep. 255; [2008] W.T.L.R. 209; [2007] S.T.I. 2651, Ch D. . . . 9–019, 9–020, 9–030

Gajapatiraju v Revenue Divisional Officer Vizagaptam; Sub Nom: Gajapatiraju v Vizagapatam (Revenue Divisional Officer) [1939] A.C. 302; [1939] 2 All E.R. 317, PC (Ind) 12–004

Gardner Mountain & d'Ambrumenil Ltd v Inland Revenue Commissioners; Sub Nom: Inland Revenue Commissioners v Gardner Mountain & d'Ambrumenil Ltd [1947] 1 All E.R. 650; (1947) 80 Ll. L. Rep. 297; 29 T.C. 69; 177 L.T. 16, HL . . 27–027, 27–030

Garforth (Inspector of Taxes) v Tankard Carpets Ltd [1980] S.T.C. 251; 53 T.C. 342; [1980] T.R. 29, Ch D. 28–020

Gaspet Ltd (formerly Saga Petroleum (UK)) v Elliss (Inspector of Taxes) [1987] 1 W.L.R. 769; [1987] S.T.C. 362; (1987) 84 L.S.G. 1241, CA (Civ. Div.); 15–011

TABLE OF CASES

Gerritse v Finanzamt Neukolln–Nord (C234/01) [2004] S.T.C. 1307; [2003] E.C.R. I–5933; [2004] 3 C.M.L.R. 22; 5 I.T.L. Rep. 978; [2003] S.T.I. 1145, ECJ (5th Chamber) 27–050

Glamorgan Quarter Sessions v Wilson [1910] T.C. 537 9–058

Glantre Engineering Ltd v Goodhand (Inspector of Taxes) [1983] 1 All E.R. 542; [1983] S.T.C. 1; 55 T.C. 165; [1982] B.T.C. 396; (1983) 14 A.T.R. 126; (1982) 126 S.J. 838, DC 23–023, 27–036

Glass v Inland Revenue Commissioners 1915 S.C. 449; (1915) 1 S.L.T. 297, VAC 12–002, ... 12–004

Glasson v Rougier 26 T.C. 86 18–011

Glenrothes Development Corp v Inland Revenue Commissioners [1994] S.T.C. 74, SP 11/91 25–003

Global Plant Ltd v Secretary of State for Health and Social Security; Sub Nom: Global Plant Ltd v Secretary of State for Social Services [1972] 1 Q.B. 139; [1971] 3 W.L.R. 269; [1971] 3 All E.R. 385; (1971) 11 K.I.R. 284; (1971) 115 S.J. 506, QBD 27–002

Gold Coast Selection Trust Ltd v Humphrey (Inspector of Taxes) [1948] A.C. 459; [1948] 2 All E.R. 379; 64 T.L.R. 457; 41 R. & I.T. 469; 30 T.C. 209; [1948] L.J.R. 1507; (1948) 92 S.J. 527, HL ... 12–002, 27–021

Grainger (Inspector of Taxes) v Maxwell (1925) 10 T.C. 139 23–010

Gray v Inland Revenue Commissioners; Sub Nom: Executors of Lady Fox v Inland Revenue Commissioners; Lady Fox's Executors v Inland Revenue Commissioners [1994] S.T.C. 360; [1994] 38 E.G. 156; [1994] R.V.R. 129; [1994] S.T.I. 208; [1994] E.G. 32 (C.S.); [1994] N.P.C. 15, CA (Civ. Div.) 12–005

Greater London Council v Minister of Social Security [1971] 1 W.L.R. 641; [1971] 2 All E.R. 285; 69 L.G.R. 251, QBD 27–022

Green v Brace (1960) 53 R. & I.T. 757; 39 T.C. 281; (1960) 39 A.T.C. 296; [1960] T.R. 281 16–029

Greenbank Holidays Ltd v Revenue and Customs Commissioners (2010) SFTD 1101 16–001

Gresham Life Assurance Society v Styles (Surveyor of Taxes) (1892) 3 T.C. 185, HL 16–002, 17–011, 23–015

Greycon Ltd v Klaentschi (Inspector of Taxes) [2003] S.T.C. (S.C.D.) 370; [2003] S.T.I. 1598, Sp Comm 23–028

Griffin (Inspector of Taxes) v Citibank Investments Ltd; Sub Nom: Citibank Investments Ltd v Griffin (Inspector of Taxes) [2000] S.T.C. 1010; 73 T.C. 352; [2000] B.T.C. 324; [2000] S.T.I. 1546; (2000) 97(45) L.S.G. 42; (2000) 144 S.J.L.B. 266, Ch D 23–003

Grimm v Newman [2002] EWCA Civ 1621; [2003] 1 All E.R. 67; [2002] S.T.C. 1388; [2002] B.T.C. 502; [2002] S.T.I. 1507; (2002) 146 S.J.L.B. 261, CA (Civ. Div.); reversing [2002] S.T.C. 84; [2002] B.T.C. 135; [2001] S.T.I. 1406; [2001] N.P.C. 155, Ch D. 9–037, 24–012

Gripple Ltd v Revenue and Customs Commissioners (2010) S.T.C. 2283, (2010) EWHC 1609 (Ch) 15–004, 15–017

Grosvenor Place Estates v Roberts [1961] Ch. 148; [1961] 2 W.L.R. 83; [1961] 1 All E.R. 341; 39 T.C. 433; (1960) 39 A.T.C. 442; [1960] T.R. 391; (1961) 105 S.J. 87, CA 9–058, 23–010

Grove, Re; Sub Nom: Vaucher v Treasury Solicitor (1889) L.R. 40 Ch. D. 216, CA 9–028

Halifax Plc and others v Customs & Excise Commissioners (2006) S.T.C. 919 24–057

Hall (Inspector of Taxes) v Lorimer [1994] 1 W.L.R. 209; [1994] 1 All E.R. 250; [1994] S.T.C. 23; [1994] I.C.R. 218; [1994] I.R.L.R. 171; 66 T.C. 349; [1993] S.T.I. 1382; (1993) 90(45) L.S.G. 45; (1993) 137 S.J.L.B. 256, CA (Civ. Div.); affirming [1992] 1 W.L.R. 939; [1992] S.T.C. 599; [1992] I.C.R. 739; (1992) 136 S.J.L.B. 175, Ch D. .. 27–002, 27–003, 27–006, 27–007, 27–013

Hallstroms Pty v Federal Commissioner of Taxation [1946] H.C.A. 34 16–022

Hancock (Surveyor of Taxes) v General Reversionary and Investment Co Ltd (1918) 7 T.C. 358 23–027

Handley Page v Butterworth 19 T.C. 328 .... 17–009, 25–002, CS8–002

Harmel v Wright (Inspector of Taxes) [1974] 1 W.L.R. 325; [1974] 1 All E.R. 945; [1974] S.T.C. 88; 49 T.C. 149; [1973] T.R. 275; (1973) 118 S.J. 170, Ch D.. . 9–034, 24–009

Harrods (Buenos Aires) v Taylor Gooby 41 T.C. 450; (1964) 43 A.T.C. 6; [1964] T.R. 9; (1964) 108 S.J. 117, CA 24–016

Hart (Inspector of Taxes) v Sangster; Sub Nom: Sangster v Hart (Inspector of Taxes) [1957] Ch. 329; [1957] 2 W.L.R. 812; [1957] 2 All E.R. 208; 50 R. & I.T. 349; 37 T.C. 231; (1957) 36 A.T.C. 63; [1957] T.R. 73; (1957) 101 S.J. 356, CA; 9–064

Hartland v Diggines (Inspector of Taxes) (1926) 10 T.C. 247 9–043

TABLE OF CASES

Hasloch v Inland Revenue Commissioners 47 T.C. 50; (1971) 50 A.T.C. 65; [1971] T.R. 45 27–045

Hawkings–Byass v Sassen (Inspector of Taxes) [1996] S.T.C. (S.C.D.) 319, Sp Comm 12–004

Heather (Inspector of taxes) v PE Consulting Group Ltd [1973] Ch. 189; [1972] 3 W.L.R. 833; [1973] 1 All E.R. 8; 48 T.C. 293; [1972] T.R. 237; (1972) 116 S.J. 824, CA (Civ. Div.) 9–048

Heaton (Inspector of Taxes) v Bell (1969) 46 T.C. 211 23–021

Helvering v Gregory (1931) 69 F2d 809 23–005

Henriksen (Inspector of Taxes) v Grafton Hotel Ltd (1942) 24 T.C. 453 ... 28–021, 28–022

Herbert Smith (A Firm) v Honour (Inspector of Taxes) [1999] S.T.C. 173; 72 T.C. 130; [1999] B.T.C. 44; [1999] E.G. 23 (C.S.); (1999) 96(11) L.S.G. 70; (1999) 149 N.L.J. 250; (1999) 143 S.J.L.B. 72; [1999] N.P.C. 24, Ch D 15–010, 18–038, 18–043

Higgs (Inspector of Taxes) v Olivier [1952] Ch. 311; [1952] 1 T.L.R. 441; 45 R. & I.T. 142; 33 T.C. 136; (1952) 31 A.T.C. 8; [1952] T.R. 57; (1952) 96 S.J. 90, CA 27–026, 28–011

Hitch v Stone (Inspector of Taxes); Sub Nom: Stone (Inspector of Taxes) v Hitch [2001] EWCA Civ 63; [2001] S.T.C. 214; 73 T.C. 600; [2001] B.T.C. 78; [2001] S.T.I. 104; [2001] N.P.C. 19, CA (Civ. Div.) 23–003

Hobbs v Hussey (Inspector of Taxes) (1942) 24 T.C. 153 .... 18–014, 18–015

Hochstrasser (Inspector of Taxes) v Mayes; Jennings v Kinder (Inspector of Taxes) [1960] A.C. 376; [1960] 2 W.L.R. 63; [1959] 3 All E.R. 817; 53 R. & I.T. 12; 38 T.C. 673; (1959) 38 A.T.C. 360; [1959] T.R. 355, HL 9–044

Holt, Re (1953) 32 A.T.C. 402 . 9–043, 12–005, 12–007, 12–008, 12–016

Horner v Hasted (Inspector of Taxes) [1995] S.T.C. 766; 67 T.C. 439, Ch D. 27–002

Horton v Young (Inspector of Taxes) [1972] Ch. 157; [1971] 3 W.L.R. 348; [1971] 3 All E.R. 412; 47 T.C. 60; [1971] T.R. 181; (1971) 115 S.J. 388, CA (Civ. Div.) 9–061

Housden (Inspector of Taxes) v Marshall [1959] 1 W.L.R. 1; [1958] 3 All E.R. 639; 52 R. & I.T. 60; 38 T.C. 233; (1958) 37 A.T.C. 337; [1958] T.R. 337; (1959) 103 S.J. 16, Ch D. 18–014

Household v Grimshaw; Sub Nom: Household v Grimshaw (Inspector of taxes) [1953] 1 W.L.R. 710; [1953] 2 All E.R. 12; 46 R. & I.T. 347; 34 T.C. 366; (1953) 32 A.T.C. 133; [1953] T.R. 147; (1953) 97 S.J. 372, Ch D. 18–012

Howson (Inspector of Taxes) v Monsell [1950] 2 All E.R. 1239 (Note); 66 T.L.R. (Pt. 2) 916; 31 T.C. 529; [1950] T.R. 333; [1950] W.N. 544; (1950) 94 S.J. 742, Ch D. 18–012

Huhtala v Her Majesty's Revenue and Customs (2010) UKFTT 429 (TC) 18–015

Humberstone v Northern Timber Mills (1949) 79 C.L.R. 389 27–009

Hume v Asquith; Sub Nom: Asquith v Hume [1969] 2 Ch. 58; [1969] 2 W.L.R. 225; [1969] 1 All E.R. 868; 45 T.C. 251; [1968] T.R. 369, Ch D ... 16–014, 18–004, 18–009, 18–023, CS1–014

ITV Services Ltd v Revenue and Customs Commissioners FTT [2010] UKFTT 586 (TC) 27–014

Icebreaker 1 LLP v Revenue and Customs Commissioners (2011) S.T.C. 1078 18–066

Iliffe News and Media Ltd & Others v Revenue & Customs Commissioners (2012) UKFFT 696 (TC) 12–026

India v Taylor; Sub Nom: Delhi Electric Supply & Traction Co Ltd, Re [1955] A.C. 491; [1955] 2 W.L.R. 303; [1955] 1 All E.R. 292; 48 R. & I.T. 98; (1955) 34 A.T.C. 10; [1955] T.R. 9; (1955) 99 S.J. 94, HL 16–014

Indofood International Finance Ltd v JP Morgan Chase Bank NA London Branch [2006] EWCA Civ 158; [2006] S.T.C. 1195; [2006] B.T.C. 8003; 8 I.T.L. Rep. 653; [2006] S.T.I. 582, CA (Civ. Div.) 24–019

Ingram v Inland Revenue Commissioners [1986] Ch. 585; [1986] 2 W.L.R. 598; [1985] S.T.C. 835; (1986) 83 L.S.G. 45; (1985) 239 S.J. 813, Ch D 23–003

Ingram v Inland Revenue Commissioners [2000] 1 A.C. 293; [1999] 2 W.L.R. 90; [1999] 1 All E.R. 297; [1999] S.T.C. 37; [1999] L. & T.R. 85; [1998] B.T.C. 8047; [1998] E.G. 181 (C.S.); (1999) 96(3) L.S.G. 33; (1999) 143 S.J.L.B. 52; [1998] N.P.C. 160, HL 9–096

Inland Revenue Commissioners v Anglo American Asphalt Co. Ltd (1941) 29 T.C. 7 16–017

Inland Revenue Commissioners v Bowater Property Developments Ltd (1986) 130 S.J. 15 23–006

TABLE OF CASES

Inland Revenue Commissioners v Brebner [1967] 2 A.C. 18; [1967] 2 W.L.R. 1001; [1967] 1 All E.R. 779; 1967 S.C. (H.L.) 31; 1967 S.L.T. 113; 43 T.C. 705; (1967) 46 A.T.C. 17; [1967] T.R. 21; (1967) 111 S.J. 216, HL 21–032, 27–045
Inland Revenue Commissioners v British Salmson Aero Engines Ltd (1938) 22 T.C. 29 ......9–056, 16–015, 16–020, 28–011
Inland Revenue Commissioners v Brown (1926) 11 T.C. 292 9–019
Inland Revenue Commissioners v Buchanan [1914] 3 K.B. 466 12–002, 12–004, ...12–008
Inland Revenue Commissioners v Bullock [1976] 1 W.L.R. 1178; [1976] 3 All E.R. 353; [1976] S.T.C. 409; 51 T.C. 522; [1975] T.R. 179; (1976) 120 S.J. 591, CA (Civ. Div.) 9–030
Inland Revenue Commissioners v Burmah Oil Co Ltd [1982] S.T.C. 30; 1982 S.C. (H.L.) 114; 1982 S.L.T. 348; 54 T.C. 200; [1980] T.R. 397; [1982] T.R. 535, HL 22–001, 23–003, 23–005, 23–006, 23–007
Inland Revenue Commissioners v Church Commissioners for England [1977] A.C. 329; [1971] 1 W.L.R. 1761; [1976] 3 W.L.R. 214; [1976] 2 All E.R. 1037; [1976] S.T.C. 339; 50 T.C. 516; [1976] T.R. 187; (1976) 120 S.J. 505, HL 9–056
Inland Revenue Commissioners v City of London (as Epping Forest Conservators); Sub Nom: London Corp (as Conservators of Epping Forest) v Inland Revenue Commissioners [1953] 1 W.L.R. 652; [1953] 1 All E.R. 1075; (1953) 117 J.P. 280; 46 R. & I.T. 315; 34 T.C. 293; (1953) 32 A.T.C. 111; [1953] T.R. 123; (1953) 97 S.J. 315, HL 9–056
Inland Revenue Commissioners v Clay; Inland Revenue Commissioners v Buchanan [1914] 3 K.B. 466, CA ..12–002, 12–004, 12–008
Inland Revenue Commissioners v Cohen (1937) 21 T.C. 301 9–030
Inland Revenue Commissioners v Coia (t/a Achilles Motor Co) 1959 S.C. 89; 1959 S.L.T. 122; 52 R. & I.T. 519; 38 T.C. 334; (1959) 38 A.T.C. 12; [1959] T.R. 15, IH (1 Div) 28–023
Inland Revenue Commissioners v Combe (1932) 17 T.C. 405 9–019
Inland Revenue Commissioners v Desoutter Bros Ltd (1945) 29 T.C. 155 16–016
Inland Revenue Commissioners v Dowdall O'Mahoney & Co [1952] A.C. 401; [1952] 1 All E.R. 531; [1952] 1 T.L.R. 560; 45 R. & I.T. 204; 33 T.C. 259; [1952] 31 A.T.C. 126; [1952] T.R. 85; (1952) 96 S.J. 148, HL.....................24–016
Inland Revenue Commissioners v Duchess of Portland [1982] S.T.C. 149 9–029

Inland Revenue Commissioners v Duke of Westminster [1936] A.C. 1; 19 T.C. 490, HL....................23–005
Inland Revenue Commissioners v Europa Oil (NZ); Sub Nom: New Zealand Inland Revenue Commissioners v Europa Oil (NZ) [1971] A.C. 760; [1971] 2 W.L.R. 55; (1970) 49 A.T.C. 282; [1970] T.R. 261; (1970) 114 S.J. 909, PC (NZ) 13–015
Inland Revenue Commissioners v Eversden; Sub Nom: Inland Revenue Commissioners v Greenstock's Executors; Essex (Somerset's Executors) v Inland Revenue Commissioners [2003] EWCA Civ 668; [2003] S.T.C. 822; 75 T.C. 340; [2003] B.T.C. 8028; [2003] W.T.L.R. 893; [2003] S.T.I. 989; (2003) 100(27) L.S.G. 38; (2003) 147 S.J.L.B. 594, CA (Civ. Div.) 9–096
Inland Revenue Commissioners v Falkirk Ice Rink Ltd [1975] S.T.C. 434; 1975 S.L.T. 245; 51 T.C. 42; [1975] T.R. 223, IH (1 Div) 18–027
Inland Revenue Commissioners v Goodwin; Inland Revenue Commissioners v Baggley [1976] 1 W.L.R. 191; [1976] 1 All E.R. 481; [1976] S.T.C. 28; 50 T.C. 583; [1976] T.R. 1; (1976) 120 S.J. 99, HL 27–045
Inland Revenue Commissioners v Kleinwort Benson [1969] 2 Ch. 221; [1969] 2 W.L.R. 696; [1969] 2 All E.R. 737; [1969] 1 Lloyd's Rep. 152; 45 T.C. 369; [1968] T.R. 455; (1969) 113 S.J. 286, Ch D.................24–038, 27–045
Inland Revenue Commissioners v Lithgows Ltd 1960 S.C. 405; 1961 S.L.T. 160; 39 T.C. 270; (1960) 39 A.T.C. 430; [1960] T.R. 363, IH (1 Div) ....12—004
Inland Revenue Commissioners v Lo & Lo (A Firm) [1984] 1 W.L.R. 986; [1984] S.T.C. 366; (1984) 128 S.J. 516, PC (HK) 28–014
Inland Revenue Commissioners v Longmans Green & Co. Ltd (1932) 17 T.C. 272 ....18–021, 18–024, 18–025
Inland Revenue Commissioners v Lysaght; Sub Nom: Lysaght v Inland Revenue Commissioners [1928] A.C. 234; [1928] All E.R. Rep. 575; 13 T.C. 511, HL................9–019, 9–026
Inland Revenue Commissioners v McGuckian; McGuckian v Inland Revenue Commissioners [1997] 1 W.L.R. 991; [1997] 3 All E.R. 817; [1997] S.T.C. 908; [1997] N.I. 157; 69 T.C. 1; [1997] B.T.C. 346; (1997) 94(27) L.S.G. 23; (1997) 141 S.J.L.B. 153, HL (NI).........23–003
Inland Revenue Commissioners v Marr's Trustees (1906) 44 S.L.R. 647 12–005
Inland Revenue Commissioners v Maxse (1919) 21 T.C. 41 18–014

TABLE OF CASES

Inland Revenue Commissioners v Mills; Sub Nom: Mills v Inland Revenue Commissioners [1975] A.C. 38; [1974] 2 W.L.R. 325; [1974] 1 All E.R. 722; [1974] S.T.C. 130; 49 T.C. 367; [1974] T.R. 39; (1974) 118 S.J. 205, HL .. 16–025, 27–040, 11–012

Inland Revenue Commissioners v Morris (1967) 44 T.C. 685 18–027

Inland Revenue Commissioners v National Book League [1957] Ch. 488; [1957] 3 W.L.R. 222; [1957] 2 All E.R. 644; 50 R. & I.T. 603; 37 T.C. 455; (1957) 36 A.T.C. 130; [1957] T.R. 141; (1957) 101 S.J. 553, CA 9–059

Inland Revenue Commissioners v Olive Mill, Ltd; Sub Nom: Inland Revenue Commissioners v Olive Mill Spinners, Ltd (in liquidation) [1963] 1 W.L.R. 712; [1963] 2 All E.R. 130; 41 T.C. 77; (1963) 42 A.T.C. 74; [1963] T.R. 59; (1963) 107 S.J. 476, Ch D.. 23–007

Inland Revenue Commissioners v Plummer [1980] A.C. 896; [1979] 3 W.L.R. 689; [1979] 3 All E.R. 775; [1979] S.T.C. 793; 54 T.C. 1; [1979] T.R. 339; (1979) 123 S.J. 769, HL 9–029

Inland Revenue Commissioners v Pratt [1982] S.T.C. 756; 57 T.C. 1; (1982) 79 L.S.G. 1444.................... 24–033

Inland Revenue Commissioners v Regent Trust Co Ltd [1980] 1 W.L.R. 688; [1980] S.T.C. 140; 53 T.C. 54; [1979] T.R. 401; (1980) 124 S.J. 49, Ch D............ 16–017

Inland Revenue Commissioners v Rolls Royce Ltd (No.2) (1944) 29 T.C. 137 16–017

Inland Revenue Commissioners v Sangster (1919) 12 T.C. 208 18–002

Inland Revenue Commissioners v Schroder [1983] S.T.C. 480; 57 T.C. 94; [1983] B.T.C. 288, Ch D. 24–034

Inland Revenue Commissioners v Scottish Provident Institution [2005] S.T.C. 15 23–003

Inland Revenue Commissioners v Titaghur Jute Factory Co Ltd [1978] S.T.C. 166; 1978 S.C. 96; 1978 S.L.T. 133; 53 T.C. 675; [1977] T.R. 341, IH (1 Div)...... 28–014

Inland Revenue Commissioners v Willoughby [1997] 1 W.L.R. 1071; [1997] 4 All E.R. 65; [1997] S.T.C. 995; 70 T.C. 57; [1997] B.T.C. 393; (1997) 94(29) L.S.G. 28; (1997) 147 N.L.J. 1062; (1997) 141 S.J.L.B. 176, HL; affirming [1995] S.T.C. 143; (1995) 92(10) L.S.G. 39; (1995) 139 S.J.L.B. 44, CA (Civ. Div.) 24–033

Inland Revenue Commissioners v Zorah (1926) 11 T.C. 289 9–019

Innocent (Inspector of Taxes) v Whaddon Estates [1982] S.T.C. 115; 55 T.C. 476; [1981] T.R. 379, ... 23–012

International Combustion Ltd v Inland Revenue Commissioners (1932) 16 T.C. 532 16–017

Irving (Inspector of Taxes) v Tesco Stores (Holdings) [1982] S.T.C. 881; 58 T.C. 1; [1982] B.T.C. 305, Ch D. 12–004

JP Hall & Co Ltd v Inland Revenue Commissioners [1921] 3 K.B. 152, CA; reversing [1921] 1 K.B. 213; 12 T.C. 382, KBD 27–027, ... 27–030

Jarrold v Boustead; Sub Nom: Large v McInnes; Simms v McInnes; McInnes v Large; McInnes v Simms [1964] 1 W.L.R. 1357; [1964]3 All E.R. 76;41 T.C. 701; (1964) 43 A.T.C. 209; [1964] T.R. 217; (1964) 108 S.J. 500, CA 27–036

Jarvis v Curtis Brown Ltd (1929) 14 T.C. 744 18–002

Jenners Princes St Edinburgh v Inland Revenue Commissioners (1998) S.T.C. (SCD).................... 18–039

Joffe v Thain 48 R. & I.T. 565; 36 T.C. 199; (1955) 34 A.T.C. 212; [1955] T.R. 205 24–008

John v James [1986] S.T.C. 352, Ch D. 27–035

John & E Sturge Ltd v Hessel (Inspector of Taxes) [1975] S.T.C. 573; 51 T.C. 183; [1975] T.R. 205, CA (Civ. Div.) 19–005, 28–009

John Mills Productions Ltd (In Liquidation) v Mathias (Inspector of Taxes) (No.3) 44 T.C. 441; [1967] T.R. 181; 117 N.L.J. 756 27–035

Johnston (Inspector of Taxes) v Britannia Airways [1994] S.T.C. 763; 67 T.C. 99, Ch D. 9–047, 15–010, 28–014, 28–025

Jones v Garnett (Inspector of Taxes) [2007] UKHL 35; [2007] 1 W.L.R. 2030; [2008] Bus. L.R. 425; [2007] 4 All E.R. 857; [2007] S.T.C. 1536; [2007] I.C.R. 1259; [2007] 3 F.C.R. 487; 78 T.C. 597; [2007] B.T.C. 476; [2007] W.T.L.R. 1229; [2007] S.T.I. 1899; (2007) 157 N.L.J. 1118; (2007) 151 S.J.L.B. 1024, HL 27–023

Jones v Inland Revenue Commissioners (1919) 7 T.C. 310 16–021

Jones v Inland Revenue Commissioners; Sweetmeat Automatic Delivery Co v Inland Revenue Commissioners [1895] 1 Q.B. 484, QBD 25–003

Kelly (J. D.) v GE Healthcare Ltd (2009) EWHC 181(Pat) 16–041

Kinloch v Inland Revenue Commissioners (1929) 14 T.C. 736 9–026

Kirby (Inspector of Taxes) v Thorn EMI Plc [1988] 1 W.L.R. 445; [1988] 2 All E.R. 947; [1987] S.T.C. 621; [1987] 2 F.T.L.R. 403; 60 T.C. 519; (1987) 84 L.S.G. 2693; (1987) 131 S.J. 1456, CA (Civ. Div.) 16–024, 28–011, 28–012

TABLE OF CASES

Kirke v Good 48 R. & I.T. 793; 36 T.C. 309; (1955) 34 A.T.C. 262; [1955] T.R. 275 16–016 16–016
Kirke v Inland Revenue Commissioners (1944) 26 T.C. 208 16–016
Kleinwort Benson Ltd v Lincoln City Council; Kleinwort Benson Ltd v Birmingham City Council; Kleinwort Benson Ltd v Southwark LBC; Kleinwort Benson Ltd v Kensington and Chelsea RLBC [1999] 2 A.C. 349; [1998] 3 W.L.R. 1095; [1998] 4 All E.R. 513; [1998] Lloyd's Rep. Bank. 387; [1999] C.L.C. 332; (1999) 1 L.G.L.R. 148; (1999) 11 Admin. L.R. 130; [1998] R.V.R. 315; (1998) 148 N.L.J. 1674; (1998) 142 S.J.L.B. 279; [1998] N.P.C. 145, HL 9–058, 23–011
Kneen (Inspector of Taxes) v Martin (1934) 19 T.C. 33 .... 9–034, 24–0009
Kronospan Mielec sp z oo v Dyrektor Izby Skarbowej w Rzeszowie (2011) S.T.C. 80 15–004
Lane v Shire Roofing Co (Oxford) Ltd [1995] T.L.R. 104 27–003
Lankhorst–Hohorst GmbH v Finanzamt Steinfurt (C–324/00) [2003] S.T.C. 607; [2002] E.C.R. I–11779; [2003] 2 C.M.L.R. 22; [2003] B.T.C. 254; 5 I.T.L. Rep. 467; [2002] S.T.I. 1807, ECJ (5th Chamber) 12–002
Latilla v Inland Revenue Commissioners [1943] A.C. 377; 25 T.C. 107, HL 24–034
Lawrence v Inland Revenue Commissioners (1940) 23 T.C. 333 18–015
Lawson (Inspector of Taxes) v Johnson Matthey [1992] 2 A.C. 324; [1992] 2 W.L.R. 826; [1992] 2 All E.R. 947; [1992] S.T.C. 466; 65 T.C. 39; [1992] S.T.I. 529; (1992) 136 S.J.L.B. 164, HL 28–020
Lawton, Re (1958) 37 A.T.C. 216; [1958] T.R. 249 9–029
Leather Cloth Co v American Leather Cloth Co 11 E.R. 1435; (1865) 11 H.L. Cas. 523, HL 25–002
Lee v Inland Revenue Commissioners (1941) 24 T.C. 574 24–034
Lee Ting Sang v Chung Chi–Keung [1990] 2 A.C. 374; [1990] 2 W.L.R. 1173; [1990] I.C.R. 409; [1990] I.R.L.R. 236; (1990) 87(13) L.S.G. 43; (1990) 134 S.J. 909, PC (HK) 27–003, 27–009
Leeming v Jones (1930) 15 T.C. 333 18–016
Levene v Inland Revenue Commissioners [1928] A.C. 217; [1928] All E.R. Rep. 746; 13 T.C. 486, HL 9–019, 9–023
Lincolnshire Sugar Co Ltd v Smart (Inspector of Taxes) [1937] A.C. 697; 20 T.C. 643, HL 18–027, 27–032
Littlewood v Revenue and Customs Commissioners (2009) S.T.C. 243 27–002

Loewenstein v De Salis (1926) 10 T.C. 424 9–019
London Bank of Mexico and South America Ltd v Apthorpe (1891) 3 T.C. 143 .... 23–008, 24–005
Lord Chetwode v Inland Revenue Commissioners [1977] 1 W.L.R. 248; [1977] 1 All E.R. 638; [1977] S.T.C. 64; 51 T.C. 647; [1977] T.R. 11; (1977) 121 S.J. 172, HL 24–034
Lord Howard de Walden v Inland Revenue Commissioners (1941) 25 T.C. 121 24–034
Lord Inchiquin v Inland Revenue Commissioners 41 R. & I.T. 570; 31 T.C. 125; [1948] T.R. 343, CA 9–019
Lord Vestey's Executors v Inland Revenue Commissioners; Lord Vestey's Executors v Colquhoun (Inspector of Taxes) [1949] 1 All E.R. 1108; (1949) 42 R. & I.T. 314; (1949) 42 R. & I.T. 325; 31 T.C. 1; [1949] T.R. 149; [1949] W.N. 233, HL 24–036
Loss v Inland Revenue Commissioners [1945] 2 All E.R. 683 27–001
Lunt v Wellesley (1945) 27 T.C. 78 27–034
Lupton (Inspector of Taxes) v FA & AB Ltd; Sub Nom: FA & AB Ltd v Lupton (Inspector of Taxes) [1972] A.C. 634; [1971] 3 W.L.R. 670; [1971] 3 All E.R. 948; 47 T.C. 580; [1971] T.R. 284; (1971) 115 S.J. 849, HL 12–015
Lynall v Inland Revenue Commissioners; Sub Nom: Lynall (Deceased), Re [1972] A.C. 680; [1971] 3 W.L.R. 759; [1971] 3 All E.R. 914; 47 T.C. 375; [1971] T.R. 309; (1971) 115 S.J. 872, HL .12–003, 12–004, 12–005, 12–007, 12–008
MKM Computing Ltd v Revenue and Customs Commissioners (2008) S.T.C. (SCD) 403 27–002
MacFarlane and Skivington v Glasgow City Council EAT/1277/99 27–005
McGowan (Inspector of Taxes) v Brown & Cousins (t/a Stuart Edwards) [1977] 1 W.L.R. 1403; [1977] 3 All E.R. 844; [1977] S.T.C. 342; (1977) 244 E.G. 133; 52 T.C. 8; [1977] T.R. 183; (1977) 121 S.J. 645, Ch D. 18–027, 27–013
Mackenzie v Arnold (Inspector of Taxes) 45 R. & I.T. 556; 33 T.C. 363; (1952) 31 A.T.C. 369; [1952] T.R. 337, CA 18–012
McManus v Griffiths (Inspector of Taxes) [1997] S.T.C. 1089; 70 T.C. 218; [1997] B.T.C. 412; (1997) 94(33) L.S.G. 27, Ch D. 27–002
McMeechan v Secretary of State for Employment [1997] I.C.R. 549; [1997] I.R.L.R. 353, CA (Civ. Div.) 27–004
McNamee v Inland Revenue Commissioners (1954) I.R. 214 12–005

TABLE OF CASES

MacNiven (Inspector of Taxes) v Westmoreland Investments Ltd; Sub Nom: Westmoreland Investments Ltd v MacNiven (Inspector of Taxes) [2001] UKHL 6; [2003] 1 A.C. 3ll; [2001] 2 W.L.R. 377; [2001] 1 All E.R. 865; [2001] S.T.C. 237; 73 T.C. 1; [2001] B.T.C. 44; 3 I.T.L. Rep. 342; [2001] S.T.I. 168; (2001) 98(11) L.S.G. 44; (2001) 151 N.L.J. 223; (2001) 145 S.J.L.B. 55, HL 23–003, 23–004, 23–005
McVeigh v Arthur Sanderson & Sons Ltd (1968) 45 T.C. 273 18–035
Magnavox Electronics Co (In Liquidation) v Hall (Inspector of Taxes) [1986] S.T.C. 561; 59 T.C. 610, CA (Civ. Div.) 23–003
Mairs (Inspector of Taxes) v Haughey [1994] 1 A.C. 303; [1993] 3 W.L.R. 393; [1993] 3 All E.R. 801; [1993] S.T.C. 569; [1993] I.R.L.R. 551; 66 T.C. 273; [1993] B.T.C. 339, HL (NI) 9–044
Mallalieu v Drummond (Inspector of Taxes) [1983] 2 A.C. 861; [1983] 3 W.L.R. 409; [1983] 2 All E.R. 1095; [1983] S.T.C. 665; (1983) 80 L.S.G. 2368; (1983) 133 N.L.J. 869; (1983) 127 S.J. 538, HL 9–048, 27–021
Mankowitz, Ex p.; Sub Nom: Mankowitz v Special Commissioners of Income Tax 46 T.C. 707; [1971] T.R. 53 24–041
Margerison v Tyresoles Ltd (1942) 25 T.C. 59 . . . . 16–024, 28–011
Market Investigations Ltd v Minister of Social Security [1969] 2 Q.B. 173; [1969] 2 W.L.R. 1; [1968] 3 All E.R. 732; (1968) 112 S.J. 905, QBD . . . 27–002, 27–003, 27–008, 27–010, 27–013
Marks & Spencer Plc v Halsey (Inspector of Taxes) (C–446/03) [2006] Ch. 184; [2006] 2 W.L.R. 250; [2006] All E.R. (EC) 255; [2006] S.T.C. 237; [2005] E.C.R. I–10837; [2006] 1 C.M.L.R. 18; [2006] C.E.C. 299; [2006] B.T.C. 318; 8 I.T.L. Rep. 358; [2006] S.T.I. 41, ECJ 10–004
Marren v Swinton and Pendleberry Borough Council [1965] 1 W.L.R. 576 27–004
Marren (Inspector of Taxes) v Ingles [1980] 1 W.L.R. 983; [1980] 3 All E.R. 95; [1980] S.T.C. 500; 54 T.C. 76; [1980] T.R. 335; (1980) 124 S.J. 562, HL 9–076
Marshall (Inspector of Taxes) v Kerr [1995] 1 A.C. 148; [1994] 3 W.L.R. 299; [1994] 3 All E.R. 106; [1994] S.T.C. 638; 67 T.C. 81; (1994) 91(30) L.S.G. 32; (1994) 138 S.J.L.B. 155, HL 12–005
Mason (Inspector of Taxes) v Innes [1967] Ch. 1079; [1967] 3 W.L.R. 816; [1967] 2 All E.R. 926; 44 T.C. 326; [1967] T.R. 143; (1967) 111 S.J. 376, CA (Civ. Div.) . . . 12–015, 13–016, 18–007, 18–008, 18–009, 23–019, CS1–014

Massey v Crown Life Insurance Co [1978] 1 W.L.R. 676; [1978] 2 All E.R. 576; [1978] I.C.R. 590; [1978] I.R.L.R. 31; (1978) 13 I.T.R. 5; (1978) 122 S.J. 791, CA (Civ. Div.) 27–003, 27–013
Merchant (Peter) v Stedford 42 R. & I.T. 28; 30 T.C. 496; [1948] T.R. 359; (1949) 93 S.J. 40, CA 28–014
Midland Sinfonia Concert Society v Secretary of State for Social Services [1981] I.C.R. 454, QBD 27–002
Miesegaes v Inland Revenue Commissioners (1957) 37 T.C. 493 9–026
Mills v Jones (1929) 14 T.C. 769 16–025
Mitchell v Rosay; Sub Nom: Rosay v Mitchell (1954) 47 R. & I.T. 508; 35 T.C. 496; (1954) 33 A.T.C. 299; [1954] T.R. 289, CA 27–033, 27–034
Mitchell (Inspector of Taxes) v Ross; Mitchell (Inspector of Taxes) v Hirtenstein; Mitchell (Inspector of Taxes) v Marshall; Taylor–Gooby (Inspector of Taxes) v Tarnesby; Taylor–Gooby (Inspector of Taxes) v Drew [1962] A.C. 813; [1961] 3 W.L.R. 411; [1961] 3 All E.R. 49; 40 T.C. 11; (1961) 40 A.T.C. 199; [1961] T.R. 191; (1961) 105 S.J. 608, HL . . 27–002, 27–005, 27–009
Moore v Griffiths (Inspector of Taxes); Sub Nom: Hurst v Griffiths; Griffiths (Inspector of Taxes) v Moore [1972] 1 W.L.R. 1024; [1972] 3 All E.R. 399; 48 T.C. 338; [1972] T.R. 61; (1972) 116 S.J. 276, Ch D. 18–027, 27–020
Moorhouse (Inspector of Taxes) v Dooland [1955] Ch. 284; [1955] 2 W.L.R. 96; [1955] 1 All E.R. 93; 48 R. & I.T. 29; 36 T.C. 1; (1954) 33 A.T.C. 410; [1954] T.R. 393; (1955) 99 S.J. 60, CA 18–027, 27–020
Moriarty (Inspector of Taxes) v Evans Medical Supplies Ltd; Sub Nom: Evans Medical Supplies Ltd v Moriarty (Inspector of Taxes) [1958] 1 W.L.R. 66; [1951] 3 All E.R. 718; 51 R. & I.T. 49; 37 T.C. 540; (1957) 36 A.T.C. 277; [1951] T.R. 297; (1958) 102 S.J. 67, HL . . . 19–004, 19–005, 19–007, 28–009
Moss Empires Ltd v Inland Revenue Commissioners (1937) 21 T.C. 264 9–056
Munby v Furlong (Inspector of Taxes) [1971] Ch. 359; [1971] 3 W.L.R. 270; [1971] 2 All E.R. 953; [1971] S.T.C. 232; 50 T.C. 491; (1977) 121 S.J. 87, CA (Civ. Div.) 18–035
Murgatroyd (inspector of Taxes) v Evans–Jackson [1961] 1 W.L.R. 423; [1961] 1 All E.R. 881; 43 T.C. 581; (1966) 45 A.T.C. 419; [1966] T.R. 341; (1966) 110 S.J. 926, Ch D. 27–038
Murray v Imperial Chemical Industries Ltd (1967) 44 T.C. 175 16–023, ... 28–011

xxxvii

TABLE OF CASES

Musgrave, Re; Sub Nom: Machen v Parry [1916] 2 Ch. 417, Ch D. 9–058
Narich Pty v Commissioner of Payroll Tax [1984] I.C.R. 286, EAT 27–003
Neely v Rourke (Inspector of Taxes) [1988] S.T.C. 216, CA (Civ. Div.) 12–008
Nethermere (St Neots) Ltd v Gardiner; Sub Nom: Nethermere (St Neots) Ltd v Taverna [1984] I.C.R. 612; [1984] I.R.L.R. 240; (1984) 81 L.S.G. 2147; (1984) 134 N.L.J. 544, CA (Civ. Div.) 27–013
New Zealand Commissioner of Inland Revenue v Challenge Corp. Ltd [1986] S.T.C. 548 23–005
News International v Shephard [1989] S.T.C. 617 23–003
Newstead (Inspector of Taxes) v Frost [1980] 1 W.L.R. 135; [1980] 1 All E.R. 363; [1980] S.T.C. 123; [1980] T.R. 1; (1980) 124 S.J. 116, HL 24–007, 27–042
Noddy Subsidiary Rights Co v Inland Revenue Commissioners [1967] 1 W.L.R. 1; [1966]3 All E.R. 459; 43 T.C. 458; (1966) 45 A.T.C. 263; [1966] T.R. 237; (1966) 110 S.J. 764, Ch D. 20–005
Norman v Golder (Inspector of Taxes) [1945] 1 All E.R. 352; 26 T.C. 293, CA 27–021, 27–038
O2 Holdings Ltd v Hutchison 3G UK Ltd (Preliminary Ruling); Sub Nom: O2 (UK) Ltd v Hutchinson 3G UK Ltd [2005] EWHC 344 (Ch); [2005] Eu. L.R. 745; [2005] E.T.M.R. 62; (2005) 28(6) I.P.D. 28045, Ch D. 6–006
Odeon Associated Theatres Ltd v Jones; Sub Nom: Odeon Associated Cinemas v Jones [1973] Ch. 288; [1972] 2 W.L.R. 331; [1972] 1 All E.R. 681; 48 T.C. 257; [1971] T.R. 373: (1971) 115 S.J. 850, CA (Civ. Div.) 9–048, 15–010, 27–029, 28–014
Ogilvie v Kitton (1908) 5 T.C. 338 . . . . 9–067, 23–008, 24–005
O'Kelly v Trusthouse Forte Plc [1984] Q.B. 90; [1983] 3 W.L.R. 605; [1983]3 All E.R. 456; [1983] I.C.R. 728; [1983] I.R.L.R. 369, CA (Civ. Div.) 27–002, 27–008
Orchard Wine & Supply Co v Loynes; Sub Nom: Orchard Wine & Spirit Co v Loynes 33 T.C. 97; (1952) 31 A.T.C. 46; [1952] T.R. 33 . . . . 17–002, 17–009
Ostime v Duple Motor Bodies; Duple Motor Bodies v Inland Revenue Commissioners [1961] 1 W.L.R. 739; [1961] 2 All E.R. 167; 39 T.C. 537; (1961)40 A.T.C. 21; [1961] T.R. 29; (1961) 105 S.J. 346, HL 27–029
Ostime (Inspector of Taxes) v Australian Mutual Provident Society (1959) 38 T.C. 492 . . . . 24–005, 24–015

Overseas Containers (Finance) Ltd v Stoker (Inspector of Taxes) [1989] 1 W.L.R. 606; [1989] S.T.C. 364; 62 T.C. 473, CA (Civ. Div.) 24–025
Owen v Southern Railway of Peru Ltd (1956) 36 T.C. 602 28–014
Padmore v Inland Revenue Commissioners [1989] S.T.C. 493; 62 T.C. 352; [1989] B.T.C. 221, CA (Civ. Div.) 24–006
Padmore v IRC (No.2) [2001] S.T.C. 280 24–006
Pardoe (Inspector of Taxes) v Energy Property Development Corporation; Sub Nom: Energy Property Development Corporation v Pardoe (Inspector of Taxes) [2000] S.T.C. 286; 72 T.C. 617; [2000] B.T.C. 87; [2000] S.T.I. 216; (2000) 97(10) L.S.G. 37, Ch D. 27–046
Paterson Engineering Co. Ltd v Duff (1943) 25 T.C. 43 . . . . 16–013, 26–004, 28–008
Pattison (Inspector of Taxes) v Marine Midland Ltd [1984] A.C. 362; [1984] 2 W.L.R. 11; [1984] S.T.C. 10; 57 T.C. 219, HL 28–020
Paulin, Re (1936) 15 A.T.C. 94 12–005
Peel v Inland Revenue Commissioners (1927) 13 T.C. 443 9–026
Petrotim Securities Ltd v Ayres (Inspector of Taxes) (No.1) [1964] 1 W.L.R. 190; [1964] 1 All E.R. 269; 41 T.C. 389; (1963)42 A.T.C. 421; [1963] T.R. 397; (1963) 107 S.J. 908, CA . . . . 12–016 , 18–007, 26–006
Philippi v Inland Revenue Commissioners [1971] 1 W.L.R. 1272; [1971] 3 All E.R. 61; 47 T.C. 75; (1971) 50 A.T.C. 16; [1971] T.R. 167; (1971) 115 S.J. 427, CA (Civ. Div.) 24–034
Pommery & Greno v Apthorpe (1886) 2 T.C. 182 24–006
Prevost Car Inc v R. 2008 TCC 231; 10 I.T.L. Rep. 736, Tax Ct (Can) 24–019
Prince v Mapp (Inspector of Taxes) [1970] 1 W.L.R. 260; [1970] 1 All E.R. 519; 46 T.C. 169; [1969] T.R. 443; (1969) 119 N.L.J. 1116; (1969) 114 S.J. 110, Ch D. 27–021, 27–038
Pritchard (Inspector of Taxes) v Arundale [1972] Ch. 229; [1971] 3 W.L.R. 877; [1971] 3 All E.R. 1011; 47 T.C. 680; [1971] T.R. 277; (1971) 115 S.J. 658, Ch D. 9–044, 23–023, 27–036
R. v Barnet LBC Ex p. Shah, *The Times*, July 21, 1980 9–026
R. v Charlton [1966] S.T.C. 1418 12–015
R. v Inland Revenue Commissioners Ex p. Fulford–Dobson [1987] Q.B. 978; [1987] 3 W.L.R. 277; [1987] S.T.C. 344; 60 T.C. 168, QBD 9–020
RTZ Oil and Gas Ltd v Elliss (Inspector of Taxes) [1987] 1 W.L.R. 1442; [1987] S.T.C. 512; 61 T.C. 132; (1987) 131 S.J. 1188, Ch D. 17–010

TABLE OF CASES

Rahman v Chase Bank (CI) Trust Co Ltd, February 12, 1990, Royal Ct. Jersey 24–035, 24–056
Ramsay v Inland Revenue Commissioners (1935) 20 T.C. 79 9–056
Ramsay v Liverpool Royal Infirmary; Sub Nom: Liverpool Royal Infirmary v Ramsay [1930] A.C. 588; 1930 S.C. (H.L.) 83, HL 9–030
Ramsay (WT) Ltd v Inland Revenue Commissioners; Eilbeck (Inspector of Taxes) v Rawling [1982] A.C. 300; [1981] 2 W.L.R. 449; [1981] 1 All E.R. 865; [1981] S.T.C. 174; 54 T.C. 101; [1982] T.R. 123; (1981) 11 A.T.R. 752; (1981) 125 S.J. 220, HL 22–001, 23–003, 23–004, 23–005, 23–006, 23–007
Ramsden v Inland Revenue Commissioners 50 R. & I.T. 662; 37 T.C. 619; (1957) 36 A.T.C. 325; [1957] T.R. 247 24–034
Ready Mixed Concrete (South East) Ltd v Minister of Pensions and National Insurance; Minister for Social Security v Greenham Ready Mixed Concrete Ltd; Minister for Social Security v Ready Mixed Concrete (South East) Ltd [1968] 2 Q.B. 497; [1968] 2 W.L.R. 775; [1968] 1 All E.R. 433; 4 K.I.R. 132; (1967) 112 S.J. 14, QBD 27–009, 27–010, 27–013
Reed (Inspector of Taxes) v Clark [1986] Ch. 1; [1985] 3 W.L.R. 142; (1985) S.T.C. 323; 58 T.C. 528; (1985) 82 L.S.G. 2016; (1985) 129 S.J. 469, Ch D............ 9–021
Reed (Inspector of Taxes) v Seymour (1927) 11 T.C. 625 .... 18–027, 27–020
Rees Roturbo Development Syndicate Ltd v Inland Revenue Commissioners (1928) 13 T.C. 366 16–027
Regal (Hastings) Ltd v Gulliver (1944) 24 A.T.C. 297 9–058
Regent Oil Co Ltd v Strick (Inspector of Taxes); Sub Nom: Strick (Inspector of Taxes) v Regent Oil Co Ltd; Inland Revenue Commissioners v Regent Oil Co Ltd; Regent Oil Co Ltd v Inland Revenue Commissioners [1966] A.C. 295; [1965] 3 W.L.R. 636; [1965] 3 All E.R. 174; 43 T.C. 1; (1965) 44 A.T.C. 264; [1965] T.R. 277; (1965) 109 S.J. 633, HL .. 16–022, 28–020, 28–025
Reid v Inland Revenue Commissioners (1926) 10 T.C. 673 9–026
Revenue and Customs Commissioners v Halycon Films LLP (2010) S.T.C. 1125 18–066
Revenue and Customs Commissioners v Micro Fusion 2004–1 LLP (2010) S.T.C. 1541 18–066
Revenue and Customs Commissioners v Phillips Electronics UK Ltd (Case C–18/11) 10–084
Revenue and Customs Commissioners v Tower MCashback LLP 1(2011) UKSC 19 .... 12–025, 18–066
Revenue and Customs Commissioners v Wright [2007] S.T.C. 1684 27–011
Ridge Securities Ltd v Inland Revenue Commissioners [1964] 1 W.L.R. 479; [1964] 1 All E.R. 275; 44 T.C. 373; (1963) 42 A.T.C. 487; [1963] T.R. 449; (1964) 108 S.J. 377, Ch D............ 12–016
Riley v Coglan [1967] 1 W.L.R. 1300; [1968] 1 All E.R. 314; 44 T.C. 481; [1967] T.R. 155; (1967) 111 S.J. 606, Ch D........ 27–036
Robert Addie & Sons Collieries Ltd v Inland Revenue Commissioners (1924) 8 T.C. 671 28–022
Robinson Bros (Brewers) Ltd v Durham Assessment Committee; Sub Nom: Robinson Bros (Brewers) Ltd v Houghton and Chester–le–Street Assessment Committee [1938] A.C. 321, HL..................... 12–004
Robson v Dixon [1972] 1 W.L.R. 1493; [1972] 3 All E.R. 671; 48 T.C. 527; (1972) 116 S.J. 863, Ch D. 9–021
Rolls Royce Ltd v Jeffrey (Inspector of Taxes); Sub Nom: Inland Revenue Commissioners v Rolls Royce Ltd [1962] 1 W.L.R. 425; [1962] 1 All E.R. 801; 40 T.C. 443; (1962) 41 A.T.C. 17; [1962] T.R. 9; (1962) 106 S.J. 261, HL 19–004, 19–004, 28–009
Royal Bank of Canada v Inland Revenue Commissioners [1972] Ch. 665; [1972] 2 W.L.R. 106; [1972] 1 All E.R. 225; 47 T.C. 565; (1971) 115 S.J. 968, Ch D..................... 24–041
Rustproof Metal Window Co v Inland Revenue Commissioners [1947] 2 All E.R. 454; 29 T.C. 243; [1947] L.J.R. 1479; 177 L.T. 657, CA..................... 16–026
Rye and Eyre v Inland Revenue Commissioners (1935) 19 T.C. 164 18–023
S Ltd v O'Sullivan (1972) TL(I) 108 .... 28–025, 28–026
St. John's College School Cambridge v Secretary of State for Social Security, unreported, June 12, 2000 27–002
Salomon v Customs and Excise Commissioners; Sub Nom: Solomon v Customs and Excise Commissioners [1967] 2 Q.B. 116; [1966] 3 W.L.R. 1223; [1966] 3 All E.R. 871; [1966] 2 Lloyd's Rep. 460; (1966) 110 S.J. 833, CA..................... 12–002
Salt v Buckley (Inspector of Taxes) [2001] S.T.C. (S.C.D.) 262; [2001] S.T.I. 1526, Sp Comm 18–034
Salt v Golding (Inspector of Taxes) [1996] S.T.C. (S.C.D.) 269, Sp Comm 15–011, 18–034
Samarkand Film Partnership No 3 v Revenue and Customs Commissioners (2012) SFTD 1 18–066

TABLE OF CASES

Sassoon v Inland Revenue Commissioners (1943) 25 T.C. 154 24–034
Scott v Ricketts; Sub Nom: Ricketts v Scott [1967]1 W.L.R. 828; [1967] 2 All E.R. 1009; 44 T.C. 303; (1967) 46 A.T.C. 133; [1967] T.R. 123; (1967) 111 S.J. 297, CA (Civ. Div.) 27–019, 27–021
Sebright, Re (1944) 23 A.T.C. 190 9–058
Sharkey (Inspector of Taxes) v Wernher; Sub Nom: Wernher v Sharkey (Inspector of Taxes) [1956] A.C. 58; [1955] 3 W.L.R. 671; [1955] 3 All E.R. 493; 48 R. & I.T. 739; 36 T.C. 275; (1955) 34 A.T.C. 263; [1955] T.R. 277; (1955) 99 S.J. 793, HL 13–016, 18–007
Shepherd v Revenue and Customs Commissioners; Sub Nom: Shepherd v Inland Revenue Commissioners [2006] EWHC 1512 (Ch); [2006] S.T.C. 1821; 78 T.C. 389; [2007] B.T.C. 426; [2006] S.T.I. 1518, Ch D. 9–019, 9–020
Sherburn Aero Club Ltd v Revenue and Customs Commissioners (2009) S.T.C. (SCD) 27–002
Shilton v Wilmshurst (Inspector of Taxes) [1991] 1 A.C. 684; [1991] 2 W.L.R. 530; [1991] 3 All E.R. 148; [1991] S.T.C. 88; 64 T.C. 78; (1991) 135 S.J. 250, HL 9–044, 23–023, 27–020, 27–036
Shine, Re [1892] 1 Q.B. 522, CA 27–022
Shiner v Lindblom; Lindblom v Shiner [1961] 1 W.L.R. 248; [1960] 3 All E.R. 832; 39 T.C. 367; (1960) 39 A.T.C. 291; [1960] T.R. 277; (1961) 105 S.J. 128, Ch D. 18–026, 27–037
Short v Treasury Commissioners [1948] A.C. 534; [1948] 2 All E.R. 509; 64 T.L.R. 400; [1949] L.J.R. 143; (1948) 92 S.J. 573, HL; affirming [1948] 1 K.B. 116; [1947] 2 All E.R. 298; 63 T.L.R. 472; [1947] L.J.R. 1463; 177 L.T. 338; (1947) 91 S.J. 482, CA 12–001
Sidey v Phillips (Inspector of Taxes) [1987] S.T.C. 87; 59 T.C. 458; (1987) 84 L.S.G. 342; (1987) 131 S.J. 76, Ch D. 27–002, 27–009
Simpson v John Reynolds & Co (Insurances) Ltd [1975] 1 W.L.R. 617; [1975] 2 All E.R. 88; [1975] 1 Lloyd's Rep. 512; [1975] S.T.C. 271; 49 T.C. 693; [1975] T.R. 33; (1975) 119 S.J. 287, CA (Civ. Div.) 18–027
Skinner v Berry Headlands [1970] 1 W.L.R. 1441; [1971]1 All E.R. 222; 46 T.C. 377; (1970) 49 A.T.C. 237; [1970] T.R. 219; (1970) 114 S.J. 808, Ch D. 12–016
Smyth v Inland Revenue Commissioners (1941) I.R. 643 12–006

Southern Railway of Peru Ltd v Owen (Inspector of Taxes); Sub Nom: Owen (Inspector of Taxes) v Southern Railway of Peru Ltd; Peru v Owen (Inspector of Taxes) [1957] A.C. 334; [1956] 3 W.L.R. 389; [1956] 2 All E.R. 728; 49 R. & I.T. 468; 36 T.C. 634; (1953) 32 A.T.C. 147; [1956] T.R. 197; (1956) 100 S.J. 527, HL 28–014
Spearmint Rhino Ventures Ltd v Revenue and Customs Commissioners (2007) EWHC 613 (Ch) 27–002
Spelling Goldberg Productions Inc v BPC Publishing Ltd (Application for Intervention) [1981] R.P.C. 280, CA (Civ. Div.) 5–013
Spiers v Mackinnon (1929) 14 T.C. 386 24–005
Sports Club v Inspector of Taxes [2000] S.T.C. (S.C.D.) 443; [2000] S.T.I. 1364, Sp Comm 27–020
Stagecraft Ltd v Minister of National Insurance 1952 S.C. 288; 1952 S.L.T. 309, IH (2 Div) 27–002
Stainer's Executors v Purchase (Inspector of Taxes); Sub Nom: Purchase (Inspector of Taxes) v Gospel (Stainer's Executors); Gospel v Purchase (Inspector of Taxes) [1952] A.C. 280; [1951] 2 All E.R. 1071; [1951] 2 T.L.R. 1112; 45 R. & I.T. 14; 32 T.C. 367; (1951) 30 A.T.C. 291; [1951] T.R. 353; (1951) 95 S.J. 801, HL 18–002, 23–016, 27–033, 27–034
Stanley v Gramophone & Typewriter Ltd (1908) 5 T.C. 358 24–003
Stanyforth v Inland Revenue Commissioners [1930] A.C. 339, HL 12–003
Steiner v Inland Revenue Commissioners [1973] S.T.C. 547; 49 T.C. 13; [1973] T.R. 177, CA (Civ. Div.) 9–030
Stokes v Bennett [1953] Ch. 566; [1953] 3 W.L.R. 170; [1953] 2 All E.R. 313; 46 R. & I.T. 436; 34 T.C. 337; (1953) 32 A.T.C. 256; [1953] T.R. 255; (1953) 97 S.J. 438, Ch D. 16–014
Street v Mountford [1985] A.C. 809; [1985] 2 W.L.R. 877; [1985] 2 All E.R. 289; (1985) 17 H.L.R. 402; (1985) 50 P. & C.R. 258; [1985] 1 E.G.L.R. 128; (1985) 274 E.G. 821; [2008] B.T.C. 7094; (1985) 82 L.S.G. 2087; (1985) 135 N.L.J. 460; (1985) 129 S.J. 348, HL 25–003
Stringfellow Restaurant Ltd v Nadine Quashie (2012) EWCA Civ 1735 27–002
Sun Newspapers v Federal Commissioner of Taxation 61 C.L.R. 337 28–020
Tavener Rutledge Ltd v Trexapalm Ltd [1975] F.S.R. 479; [1977] R.P.C. 275; (1975) 119 S.J. 792, Ch D. 5–013
Taylor v Caldwell (1863) 3 B. & S. 826 25–003

TABLE OF CASES

Taylor v Dawson (1938) 22 T.C. 189 27–032

Temperley v Smith [1956] 1 W.L.R. 931; [1956] 3 All E.R. 92; 49 R. & I.T. 650; 37 T.C. 18; (1956) 35 A.T.C. 291; [1956] T.R. 275; 10 S.J. 550, Ch D. . . 18–027, 20–008, 27–021

Tennant v Smith (Surveyor of Taxes) (1892) 3 T.C. 158 23–021

Test Claimants in the Thin Cap Group Litigation v Inland Revenue Commissioners (C–524/04) [2007] S.T.C. 906; [2007] 2 C.M.L.R. 31; [2008] B.T.C. 348; 9 I.T.L. Rep. 877; [2007] S.T.I. 538, ECJ (Grand Chamber) 12–004

Thiele v Thiele (1920) 150 L.T.J. 387 9–028

Thomson v Minister of National Revenue [1946] 1 D.L.R. 689, Sup Ct (Can) 9–019

Thomson (Inspector of Taxes) v Gumeville Securities Ltd; Gumeville Securities Ltd v Thomson (Inspector of Taxes) [1972] A.C. 661; [1971] 3 W.L.R. 692; [1971] 3 All E.R. 1071; 47 T.C. 633; [1971] T.R. 299; (1971) 115 S.J. 851, HL 12–015

Thomson (Inspector of Taxes) v Moyse [1961] A.C. 967; [1960] 3 W.L.R. 929; [1960] 3 All E.R. 684; 39 T.C. 291; (1960) 39 A.T.C. 322; [1960] T.R. 309; (1960) 104 S.J. 1032, HL 9–034, 24–009

Thomsons (Carron) Ltd v Inland Revenue Commissioners [1976] S.T.C. 317; 51 T.C. 506; [1976] T.R. 145, CS . . 19–007, 28–009

Threlfall v Jones (Inspector of Taxes); Gallagher v Jones (Inspector of Taxes) [1994] Ch. 107; [1994] 2 W.L.R. 160; [1993] S.T.C. 537; 66 T.C. 77; (1993) 90(32) L.S.G. 40; (1993) 137 S.J.L.B. 174, CA (Civ. Div.) . . . 9–048, 15–010, 18–038, 18–039, 18–043, 28–014

Tod (Inspector of Taxes) v South Essex Motors (Basildon) Ltd [1988] S.T.C. 392; 60 T.C. 598, Ch D. 9–076

Tootal Broadhurst Lee Co v Inland Revenue Commissioners [1949] 1 All E.R. 261; 42 R. & I.T. 74; 29 T.C. 352; [1949] T.R. 37; [1949] W.N. 43; (1949) 93 S.J. 132, HL 16–017

Tower Mcashback LLP v Revenue and Customs Commissioners [2007] S.P.C. 619 .... 23–003, 26–019

Trustees of Ferguson (dec'd) v Donovan [1929] I.R. 489 24–003

Trustees of Johan Thomas Salvesen v Inland Revenue Commissioners (1930) 9 A.T.C. 43 ..... 12–006, 12–007, 12–008, 12–016

Tucker v Granada Motorway Services Ltd [1979] 1 W.L.R. 683; [1979] 2 All E.R. 801; [1979] S.T.C. 393; (1979) 123 S.J. 390, HL; affirming [1979] 1 W.L.R. 87; [1979] 1 All E.R. 23; [1978] S.T.C. 587; [1978] T.R. 167; (1978) 122 S.J. 730, CA (Civ. Div.); affirming [1977] 1 W.L.R. 1411; [1977] 3 All E.R. 865; [1977] S.T.C. 353; [1977] T.R. 167; (1977) 121 S.J. 664, Ch D. 28–023

Turvey v Dentons (1923) Ltd [1953] 1 Q.B. 218; [1952] 2 All E.R. 1025; [1952] 2 T.L.R. 996; 45 R. & I.T. 772; (1952) 31 A.T.C. 470; [1952] T.R. 471; (1952) 96 S.J. 852, QBD 9–058, 23–011

Udny v Udny (1866–69) L.R. 1 Sc. 441; (1869) 7 M. (H.L.) 89, HL 9–028

United States of America v Silk (1946) 331 U.S. 704 27–008

Universal City Studios Inc v Mukhtar & Sons [1976] 1 W.L.R. 568; [1976] 2 All E.R. 330; [1976] F.S.R. 252; (1976) 120 S.J. 385, Ch D. 5–013

Usher's Wiltshire Brewery Ltd v Bruce (1915) 6 T.C. 399 28–021

Vallambrosa Rubber Co Ltd v Farmer (Surveyor of Taxes) (1910) 5 T.C. 529 28–020

Vaughan–Neil v Inland Revenue Commissioners [1979] 1 W.L.R. 1283; [1979] 3 All E.R. 481; [1979] S.T.C. 644; 54 T.C. 223; [1979] T.R. 257; (1980) 130 N.L.J. 865; (1979) 123 S.J. 506, Ch D. 23–023, 27–036

Vestey v Inland Revenue Commissioners [1962] Ch. 861; [1962] 2 W.L.R. 221; [1961] 3 All E.R. 978; 40 T.C. 112; (1961) 40 A.T.C. 325; [1961] T.R. 289, ChD 9–056

Vestey v Inland Revenue Commissioners (No.1); Baddeley v Inland Revenue Commissioners; Payne v Inland Revenue Commissioners (No.1) [1980] A.C. 1148; [1979] 3 W.L.R. 915; [1979] 3 All E.R. 976; [1980] S.T.C. 10; 54 T.C. 503; [1979] T.R. 381; (1979) 123 S.J. 826, HL 24–034, 24–036

Vodafone Cellular Ltd v Shaw (Inspector of Taxes) [1997] S.T.C. 734; 69 T.C. 376; [1997] B.T.C. 247; (1997) 141 S.J.L.B. 93, CA (Civ. Div.) 28–020

Waddington v Waddington (1920) 36 T.L.R. 359 9–028

Wain v Cameron (Inspector of Taxes) [1995] S.T.C. 555; 67 T.C. 324; [1995] S.T.I. 732; (1995) 92(20) L.S.G. 40; (1995) 139 S.J.L.B. 118, Ch D. 18–013

Walker (Inspector of Taxes) v Carnaby, Harrower, Barham & Pykett [1970] 1 W.L.R. 276; [1970] 1 All E.R. 502; 46 T.C. 561; [1969] T.R. 435; (1969) 114 S.J. 35, Ch D. 18–027

TABLE OF CASES

Wallach (Deceased), Re; Sub Nom: Weinschenk v Treasury Solicitor [1950] 1 All E.R. 199; 66 T.L.R. (Pt. 1) 132; [1950] W.N. 40; (1950) 94 S.J. 132, PDAD 9–028
Walls v Sinnett (Inspector of Taxes) [1987] S.T.C. 236; 60 T.C. 150, DC 27–002, 27–009
Walsh v Randall (1940) 23 T.C. 55 .... 9–034, 24–0009
Walton v Inland Revenue Commissioners [1996] S.T.C. 68; [1996] 1 E.G.L.R. 159; [1996] 21 E.G. 144; [1996] R.V.R. 55; [1995] E.G. 191 (C.S.), CA (Civ. Div.)................... 12–005
Watson Bros v Hornby (Inspector of Taxes) [1942] 2 All E.R. 506, KBD 12–016
Werle & Co v Colquhoun (1888) 2 T.C. 402 24–006
West (Inspector of Taxes) v Trennery; Sub Nom: Tee v Inspector of Taxes; Trennery v West (Inspector of Taxes) [2005] UKHL 5; [2005] 1 All E.R. 827; [2005] S.T.C. 214; 76 T.C. 713; [2005] B.T.C. 69; [2005] W.T.L.R. 205; [2005] S.T.I. 157; (2005) 149 S.J.L.B. 147; [2005] N.P.C. 10, HL.................... 23–003
Weston's Settlement, Re (1968) 47 A.T.C. 324 24–048
Whimster & Co v Inland Revenue Commissioners; Sub Nom: Whimster & Co v Inspector of Taxes (1925) 23 Ll. L. Rep. 79; 1926 S.C. 20; 1925 S.L.T. 623; 12 T.C. 813, IH (1 Div)............. 27–029
Whitworth Park Coal Co v Inland Revenue Commissioners; Sub Nom: Inland Revenue Commissioners v Whitworth Park Coal Co; Ramshaw Coal Co v Inland Revenue Commissioners; Brancepath Coal Co v Inland Revenue Commissioners [1961] A.C. 31; [1959] 3 W.L.R. 842; [1959] 3 All E.R. 703; 52 R. & I.T. 789; 38 T.C. 531; (1959) 38 A.T.C. 295; [1959] T.R. 293; (1959) 103 S.J. 938, HL 9–056
Wild v Ionides (1925) 9 T.C. 392 16–027
Wilkie v Inland Revenue Commissioners [1952] Ch. 153; [1952] 1 All E.R. 92; [1952] 1 T.L.R. 22; 45 R. & I.T. 29; 32 T.C. 495; (1952) 31 A.T.C. 442; [1951] T.R. 371; (1951) 95 S.J. 817, Ch D.......... 9–025
Wilkins v Rogerson [1961] Ch. 133; [1961] 2 W.L.R. 102; [1961] 1 All E.R. 358; 39 T.C. 344; (1960) 39 A.T.C. 425; [1960] T.R. 379; (1961) 105 S.J. 62, CA 23–021
Williams v Singer (1920) 7 T.C. 387................ 16–017, 23–030
Willingale (Inspector of Taxes) v International Commercial Bank Ltd [1978] A.C. 834; [1978] 2 W.L.R. 452; [1978] 1 All E.R. 754; [1978] S.T.C. 75; 52 T.C. 242; [1978] T.R. 5; (1978) 122 S.J. 129, HL 27–029
Winans v Attorney General (No.1) [1904] A.C 287, HL 9–030
Winans v Attorney General (No.2); Sub Nom: Winans v King, The [1910] A.C. 27, HL 9–091
Winter v Inland Revenue Commissioners; Sub Nom: Sutherland's Estate, Re; Sutherland (Deceased), Re [1963] A.C. 235; [1961] 3 W.L.R. 1062; [1961] 3 All E.R. 855; (1961) 40 A.T.C. 361; [1961] T.R. 349; (1961) 105 S.J. 929, HL 12–008, 12–013
Winter Garden Theatre (London) Ltd v Millennium Productions Ltd; Sub Nom: Millennium Productions Ltd v Winter Garden Theatre (London) Ltd [1948] A.C. 173; [1941] 2 All E.R. 331; 63 T.L.R. 529; [1941] L.J.R. 1422; 177 L.T. 349; (1947) 91 S.J. 504, HL................. 25–003
Withers v Wynyard (1938) 21 T.C. 724 9–019
Withers (Inspector of Taxes) v Nethersole [1948] 1 All E.R. 400; 64 T.L.R. 157; 41 R. & I.T. 159; 28 T.C. 501; [1948] T.R. 31; [1948] W.N. 105; [1948] L.J.R. 805; (1948) 92 S.J. 193, HL............... 18–011
Wolf Electric Tools Ltd v Wilson (Inspector of Taxes) [1969] 2 All E.R. 724; 45 T.C. 326; [1968] T.R. 391, Ch D. ... 19–007, 28–009
Wombles Ltd v Wombles Skips Ltd [1975] F.S.R. 488; [1971] R.P.C. 99, Ch D....................... 5–013
Wright v Revenue and Customs Commissioners (2009) SFTD 84 27–011
Yarmouth v France (1887) L.R. 19 Q.B.D. 647, QBD 18–035
Yates (Inspector of Taxes) v GCA International; Sub Nom: GCA International v Yates (Inspector of Taxes) [1991] S.T.C. 157; 64 T.C. 37; [1991] B.T.C. 107, Ch D............ 9–068, 24–016, 28–017
Young and Young v Phillips (Inspector of Taxes) [1984] S.T.C. 520; 58 T.C. 232; (1984) 81 L.S.G. 2776, DC 23–003

TABLE OF STATUTES

1890	Partnership Act (53 & 54 Vict. c.39) 9–068

1890 Partnership Act (53 & 54 Vict.
  c.39) 9–068
  s.4(2) 24–004
1891 Stamp Act (54 & 55 Vict. c.39)
  s.59 . . . . 16–046, 25–002
  s.62 . . . . 16–046, 25–002
  s.122(1) 25–001
1907 Limited Partnerships Act (7 Edw.7
  c.24) 9–086, 24–004
1927 Finance Act (17 & 18 Geo.5 c.10)
  s.26 18–023
1949 Registered Designs Act (12, 13 & 14
  Geo.6 c.88) . . . 3–002, 5–005, 5–007,
              5–009, 5–010,
              17–003
  s.1 3–007
  (2) 3–002
  (3) 3–002
  (b) 3–002
  s.7(1) 3–006
  s.19(5) 3–008
  s.24B(1) 3–007
  (3) 3–007
1956 Copyright Act (4 & 5 Eliz.2
  c.74) 5–006, 5–007, 5–010
1968 Design Copyright Act 5–006
1970 Taxes Management Act (c.9)
  s.7 9–005
  s.8 9–006
  s.8B 9–007
  s.9(4)(b) 9–007
  s.16 . . . . 18–032, 27–039
  s.29 9–011
  s.59A 9–066
  s.59B 9–066
  (1)(b) 17–005
  s.59D 10–011
  Sch.1A 21–039
  Sch.1B 17–005
1973 Domicile and Matrimonial Proceedings
  Act (c.45) 9–029
1976 Restrictive Trade Practices Act
  (c.34) 28–008
1977 Patents Act (c.37) . 2–002, 2–005, 2–009,
              23–006
  s.1(1)(b) 2–007
  (c) 2–007
  (2) 2–006
  s.2 2–008
  s.4 2–007
  s.7(2) 2–009
  ss.8–12 2–009
  s.15(1) 2–009
  s.16 2–010
  s.17 2–010
  s.18 2–011
  ss.30–36 2–019

  s.30 2–018
  s.33 2–019
  s.40(1) 16–041
  s.61(3) 2–017
  s.71 2–017
  s.96 2–011
  s.97(3) 2–011
  s.98 2–015
  s.130 2–015
1979 Public Lending Right Act
  (c.10) 18–078
1984 Inheritance Tax Act (c.51)
  ss.1–2 9–090
  ss.1–4 9–002
  s.3 . . . . 9–090, 16–045
  s.3A 9–080, 16–045
  s.4 9–090
  s.5 9–091
  s.6 . . . . 9–002, 9–091
  s.7 9–090
  ss.10–17 9–091
  s.10 16–045
  s.18 9–091
  s.19 9–091
  s.20 9–091
  s.21 9–091
  s.22 9–091
  ss.23–29A 9–091
  ss.30–35 9–092
  s.30 18–076
  s.31 18–076
  ss.32–33 18–076
  ss.36–42 9–092
  s.48 9–091
  ss.49–57A 9–093
  ss.58–70 . . . . 9–091, 9–093
  ss.58–85 10–023
  s.6 9–093
  s.65 9–093
  s.66 9–093
  s.71 . . . . 9–093, 10–022
  ss.71A–71D 10–022
  ss.94–102 9–094
  s.98 . . . . CS2–011
  ss.103–105 9–095
  ss.103–114 16–045
  s.105(1)(a) 9–095
  ss.106–112 9–095
  s.113 9–095
  s.113A 9–095
  s.113B 9–095
  s.114 9–095
  ss.114–124B 9–095
  s.125 9–095
  s.130 9–095
  s.141 9–095
  ss.142–147 9–095

TABLE OF STATUTES

s.150	9–095
ss.151–153	9–090
s.158	9–095
s.159	9–095
s.160	9–095, 12–002, 12–024, 16–045
s.161	9–095
s.168	9–095
s.170	9–095
s.171	9–095
ss.172–176	9–095
ss.178–189	9–095
ss.190–198	9–095
ss.199–214	9–098
ss.214–261	9–098
ss.227–229	9–098
s.234	9–098
ss.262–266	9–098
s.267	9–002, 9–030, 9–032, 9–037, 9–091, 9–098, 24–012
s.268	9–098
Sch.1	9–090
Films Act (c.21)	
Sch.1	18–055, 18–063, 18–071, 18–072

1986 Finance Act (c.41)
s.102	9–091, 9–096, 9–097
(5)	9–096
ss.102A–102C	9–096
Sch.20	9–091

1988 Income and Corporation Taxes Act (c.1)
s.4(2)	9–058
s.7(2)	13–019
s.8	22–061
(1)(a)	12–014, 15–012
(m)	9–056, 12–014
s.105	18–006
s.109	18–005
ss.118ZE–118ZO	18–067
s.119	22–061
s.188	9–040
s.209	
(2)(da)	12–007
ss.249–251	9–078
s.297(4)	18–059
s.298(5)	18–059
s.337	21–061
s.337A	21–061
s.338	21–061
s.338A	21–061
s.338B	21–061
(1)	21–061
(2)	21–061
(3)	21–061
(4)	21–061
s.339	21–061, 21–061
s.348	9–057, 9–058, 16–003
(2)(a)	16–002
s.349	9–058, 16–003
(1)	16–015
(b)	16–002

s.350	9–058
s.353	15–012
s.362	15–012
s.380	18–061
s.381	18–061
(4)	15–012
s.387	16–011
s.393(9)	10–006
s.401	28–028
s.403(1)	14–023, 14–033, 14–034
s.416	24–054
s.438(1)	15–012
s.439(1)(a)	15–012
s.527(1)	16–034
s.531	26–005
s.587B(2)(a)(ii)	21–061
s.681(4)	27–040
s.686	16–017
s.703(1)	27–045
s.739	24–036
s.741	24–038
s.775	CS1–014
s.788	9–027
(3)	9–027
s.790	9–027
s.795(4)	21–062
s.797A	21–062
s.797B	21–062
(4)	21–062
(5)	21–062
s.799	13–008
s.808A	12–016
s.811	21–062
s.821	18–032
(3)(a)	18–032
s.826	14–023, 14–034, 15–022
(3A)	15–024
(8BA)	15–024
s.837A	15–001, 14–003, 14–011, 14–014
s.837B	15–001
s.908(4)	28–025
Sch.16	21–061
Sch.18	10–012
Sch.28AA	12–007, 12–008, 12–010, 12–013, 12–017, 12–018, 13–001
Sch.28B, para.4(5)	18–059
para.5(1)	18–059
Finance Act (c.39)	
s.338B(5)	21–061
s.797B(1)–(3)	21–061
Copyright, Designs and Patents Act (c.48)	5–002, 5–005, 5–010, 24–002
Pt.II	27–001
Pt.III	18–001
s.3(1)	5–003
s.4	5–002
(1)(b)	5–002
(2)	5–002
s.9	5–003
s.11	5–003

TABLE OF STATUTES

s.16	5–004
(2)	5–004
ss.17–21	5–004
s.17(3)	5–006
s.51	5–005
s.52	5–005
s.91	18–008, 23–019
s.97(2)	5–011
s.153	5–003
s.154	5–003
s.155	5–003
s.213	5–007
s.215(2)	5–009
s.216	5–008
s.226(2)	5–008
(3)	5–008
s.276	2–012

1989 Finance Act (c.26)
- s.43 18–037

1990 Capital Allowances Act (c.1)
- s.68 .... 18–035, 18–050
- (9) 18–054
- ss.136–139 15–002

1991 Finance Act (c.31)
- s.46 9–019
- s.72 18–061

1992 Taxation of Chargeable Gains Act (c.12) 10–002

s.2	9–001
(1)	9–071
s.3	9–071, 10–020
s.4	9–071
s.5	9–075
s.8	10–002
s.10	9–001, 24–048
(1)	9–071
s.10A	9–001
s.12	9–001, 9–071
(1)	9–036, 24–011
s.13	9–071, 24–047
(4)	24–047
(10)	24–047
s.16	9–076
(2A)	9–076
s.16A	9–076
s.17	9–075, 10–002, 12–016, 18–007
s.18	9–075, 10–002, 12–016
(1)	12–013
(3)	9–076
s.19	9–075, 12–016
s.20	9–075, 13–016
ss.21–28	9–075
s.21	16–024, 17–009, 19–010, 23–019, 27–043, 28–009, 28–011, 28–012
(1)	28–024
s.22	16–024, 28–011
s.28	21–017, 21–038
ss.29–34	9–071, 12–016
s.29	CS2–011
s.33A	21–063

s.35	9–072, 23–019
(5)	23–019
s.37	9–072, 18–007
(1)	9–072, 23–019
s.38	9–072, 12–005, 23–019
ss.39–41	9–072
s.42	9–075, 23–019
s.43	9–075
s.44	9–075, 18–076
s.45	9–075
s.46	9–075
s.47	9–075
s.48	9–076
s.49	9–076
s.51(2)	16–042
s.53	23–019
s.57	9–075
s.58	9–077
s.59	9–077
s.62	9–077, 9–079, 23–016
s.71(1)	24–047
s.76	24–047
s.77	24–053
s.78	24–051
s.80	24–048, 24–051
s.81	24–048
s.82	24–049
s.83	24–049, 24–051
s.84	24–050
s.85	24–051
s.86	10–021, 24–043, 24–051, 24–052, 24–053, 24–057
s.87	10–021, 24–038, 24–043, 24–044, 24–047, 24–051
s.88	24–044
s.89	24–043, 24–044
s.90	24–044
s.91	24–043, 24–045
s.96	24–046, 24–047
s.97(1)	24–046
s.98	24–047, 24–057
s.98A	24–057
ss.104–114	9–077
ss.114–ll7B	9–077
ss.126–140B	9–078
s.130(1)(5)	21–015
s.135	9–076
s.136	21–053
(1)	21–053
s.138	21–053, 21–057
ss.139–140B	21–053
s.139	21–014
s.140	21–056
s.140A	21–014, 21–054
s.140B	21–054
s.140E	21–014
s.142	9–078
ss.143–149A	9–078
ss.150–151B	9–078
s.150A	16–043

TABLE OF STATUTES

s.150C 16–043
ss.152–159 21–003
ss.152–160 9–079
s.152 . . . . . 21–015, 24–048, 24–050
s.153A 21–039
s.155 . . . . . 9–079, 16–044, 21–015,
 21–037, 21–044,
 28–009, 28–024
s.162 . . . . CS2–003, CS2–011
s.164I(5) 18–059
s.164N(1) 18–059
s.165 . . . . . 9–079, 16–044, 18–007,
 21–020, 23–019,
 24–049, 24–050,
 CS2–011
ss.166–169 9–079
s.169B 24–050
s.169C 24–050
ss.169H–169S 9–073
s.170 21–046
 (12)–(14) 21–047
ss.171–191 21–003
s.171 . . . . . 10–007, 19–013, 21–048,
 21–056, 21–063
s.171A 10–007, 21–048
s.175 21–041
s.178 19–013
ss.179–181 21–049
s.179 . . . . . 19–013, 21–015, 21–044,
 21–063
 (2) 21–015
 (4) 21–015
 (6) 21–015
 (8) 21–015
ss.184A–184I 10–002
s.184G 24–057
s.187 21–031
s.190 21–044
s.215 21–058
s.216 21–058
ss.222–226 9–080
s.256 9–080
s.257 9–080
s.258 . . . . 9–080, 18–076
 (3) 18–076
 (5) 18–076
ss.260–261 9–080
s.260 . . . . . 10–020, 16–044, 24–049
s.262 . . . . 9–080, 18–076
s.263 9–080
ss.272–291 9–080
ss.271F–835J 18–020
s.272 . . . . . 12–002, 12–016, 12–024
s.273 12–016
s.275 9–071
 (1)(g) 9–071, 12–022
 (h) 9–071
 (k) 12–022
s.286 12–016
Sch.1 10–020
Sch.2, para.16 23–019
para.17 23–019

Sch.5 . . . . 24–043, 24–051, 24–052
 para.9(1A) 24–055
 (10C–11) 24–055
 para.10A 24–055
 para.10B 24–055
Sch.5A 24–057
Sch.5AA 21–053
Sch.5B 16–043
Sch.7A 10–002
Sch.7AB 21–044
Sch.7AC 10–008, 19–013
Sch.8 9–075
Finance (No.2) Act (c.48) 26–017
 ss.40A–40B 18–050
 ss.40A–40C 18–061
 ss.40A–43 18–63
 ss.40A–43 18–055
 s.40A 18–050
 (1) 18–050
 (2) 18–050
 (3) 18–050
 (4)(b) 18–050
 (5) 18–050
 s.40B 18–057
 (1)–(3) 18–051
 (4) 18–051
 (c) 18–051
 (5)–(7) 18–052
 s.40C(2) 18–051
 s.40D 18–050, 18–059, 18–065
 ss.41–43 . . . . 18–054, 18–063
 s.41 . . . . 18–058, 18–059
 s.42 . . . . . 18–055, 18–059, 18–063,
 18–064
 (1) 18–057
 (b) 18–057
 (2), (5) 18–057
 (6) 18–057
 (7) 18–057
 (8) 18–057
 s.42D 18–057
 s.43(1) 18–056
 (2) 18–056
 (3) 18–056
Friendly Societies Act
 (c.40) 21–046
Trade Marks Act (c.26) . . 4–004, 4–006,
 4–010, 17–007
 s.2(2) 6–004
 s.3 4–006
 (1) 4–007
 (3) 4–007
 (4) 4–007
 s.10 4–009
 (3) 4–010
 s.11 4–009
 ss.28–31 4–012
 s.46 4–008
 s.50 4–002
 s.56 4–015
 s.60 4–015
 s.63 4–004

	Sch.2 4–002		s.129 . . . . . 18–077, 20–009, 25–001
	Value Added Tax Act		Sch.12 27–023
	(c.23) 29–029		Sch.19 15–001
	s.5(2)(b) 11–012, 16–047		para.2(b) 14–023
	s.6 11–007		Sch.20 15–001
	s.8 11–005		Sch.21 15–001
	(1) 27–056	2001	Capital Allowances Act
	s.9 16–048		(c.2) 16–028, 21–008, 21–017,
	s.39 27–057		29–002
	s.48(1) 27–055		Pt.2 14–023
	Sch.1, para.1(1) 27–054		Pt.6 22–025
	Sch.3B 29–017		Pt.8 . . . . 16–016, 22–025
	Sch.4A11–005. 29–017		s.2(1) 9–051
	para.1 27–056		s.5 . . . . 18–055, 18–063, 21–017
	para.9 27–055		s.6(4) 9–051
	Sch.8 11–008		ss.11–270 9–051
	Sch.9 11–008		s.25 9–051
1995	Finance Act (c.4)		s.28 9–051
	Sch.6, para.19(2)–(3) 9–063		ss.29–33 9–051
1996	Finance Act (c.8). 21–086		s.49 9–051
	Ch.2, Pt.4 21–061		ss.71–73 21–008
1997	Finance (No.2) Act (c.58)		s.71 . . . . 9–051, 29–008
	s.48 . . . . . 18–055, 18–056, 18–057,		s.72 21–008
	18–061, 18–063,		ss.83–88 29–008
	18–064		s.161 9–051
	(1) 18–055		s.264 9–051
	(2)(a) 18–055		ss.271–360 9–051
	(b) 18–055		ss.361–393 9–051
	(3) 18–055		ss.394–436 9–051
	(4),(6) 18–055		ss.437–451 . 9–051, 16–002, CS2–004
	(6A) 18–055		s.437 15–011
	(7) 18–055		s.438(1) 15–011
	(8) 18–055		(2) 15–011
	(9) 18–055, 18–063		(3)–(6) 15–011
	(10) 18–055		(3) 15–011
	Plant Varieties Act (c.66)		s.439 15–011
	s.7 21–005		(1) 15–012
1998	Finance Act (c.36)		(2)–(4) 15–011
	s.36 21–045		(5) 15–011
	s.37 21–045		s.440 15–011
	Sch.18		s.441 . . . . 15–011, 15–012
	para.10(2) 15–023		(1) 15–011
	para.15 . . . . 15–038, 22–004		(3) 15–011
	para.52 14–034		s.442(1) 15–012
	(2)(ba) 15–024		(2) 15–012
	(5)(ab) 15–024		(3) 15–012
	paras 54–65 21–039		(4) 15–012
	para.55 21–039		(5) 15–012
	para.57 21–039		s.443(1) 15–012
	para.83A 15–023		(3) 15–012
	para.83B 15–023		(4) 15–012
	para.83C 15–023		(5) 15–012
	para.83D 15–023		(6) 15–012
	para.83E 15–023		s.444(1)–(3) 15–012
	para.83F 15–023		(4) 15–012
	paras 83M–83R 14–034		s.445(1)–(3) 15–012
2000	Limited Liability Partnerships Act		(4) 15–012
	(c.12) 9–087, 24–004		(5) 15–012
	Finance Act (c.17). 15–001		(6) 15–012
	s.60 27–023		s.446 15–012
	s.68 15–001		s.447(1) 15–012
	s.69 . . . . . . 15–001, 15–014, 14–015		(2) 15–012

TABLE OF STATUTES

(3) 15–012	(6) 16–038
s.448(1) 15–012	s.482 16–028
(2) 15–012	s.483 16–016
(3) 15–012	s.531 9–051
(4) 15–012	ss.537–543 16–031
(5) 15–012	s.547–549 15–012
s.449 15–012	s.563(6) 16–031
s.450 15–012	s.567–570 . . . . 16–028, 19–014
s.451 15–012	s.567(1) 16–028
ss.452–463 19–014	s.572(1)–(3) 16–028
s.452 . . . . . 19–002, 19–014, 28–026	Sch.2 9–051
s.453 . . . . 19–017, 28–026	para.68 12–008
s.454 19–014	para.82 9–051
s.455(1) 19–014	Sch.3, para.100 16–028
(2) 19–014	2002 Finance Act (c.23). 9–048, 19–001,
(3) 19–014	21–001, 21–061
s.456 19–014	s.1 21–061
s.457 19–014	ss.2–4 21–061
s.458(1)–(4) 19–014	s.3(1) 21–034
(5) 19–014	s.5 21–062
(6) 19–014	s.5(2) 21–062
s.459 19–014	s.5(4) 21–062
s.460 19–014	s.30(5) 21–062
s.461 19–014	s.52 14–031
s.462 . . . . . 19–008, 19–014, 28–012	s.53 . . . . 15–001, 15–025
(2) 19–014	s.54 15–001
s.463 19–014	s.56 15–001
ss.464–477 16–038	s.84 . . . . 15–001, 21–001
ss.464–483 16–016	s.90(2)(16) 13–002
s.466 16–037	ss.99–101 18–063
ss.467–468 16–038	s.99 . . . . . . 18–055, 18–063, 18–065
s.467 16–038	(1)–(3) 18–056
s.468(3) 16–038	(4)(16) 18–056
s.469 16–038	(6) 18–056
s.470 16–038	s.100 . . . . 18–055, 18–065
s.471 16–038	s.101 . . . . 18–055, 18–063
(3) 16–038	s.116 . . . . 19–017, 25–001
(4) 16–038	s.129 26–003
(5) 16–038	Sch.12 . . . . 15–001, 15–025
(6) 16–038	Sch.13 15–001
s.472(1)–(3) 16–038	Sch.14 15–001
(4) 16–038	Sch.29 . . . . . 12–026, 15–001, 21–001,
(5) 16–028, 16–038	21–062
(6) 16–038	Sch.30 . . . . 21–001, 21–034, 21–061
s.473 16–038	Sch.34 26–003
s.474 16–038	2003 Income Tax (Earnings and Pensions) Act
s.475 16–038	(c.1) . 9–001, 9–044, 23–020, 23–023,
s.476 16–038	23–027,
s.477(1) 16–038	24–009, 24–020,
(2) 16–038	CS3–007
(3) 16–038	Pt.2 . . 9–039, 9–040, 9–044, 23–021,
s.478 16–038	27–025
s.479 16–038	Pt.3 . . . . 9–040, 21–020, 23–021
(4) 16–038	Pt.4 9–040
s.480 16–038	Pt.5 . . . . 9–040, 9–041, 23–021
(4) 16–038	Pt.6 9–040
s.481 16–038	Pt.7 9–040
(1) 16–038	Pt.9 9–55
(2) 16–028, 16–038	Pt.10 9–040
(3) 16–038	Pt.11 9–043
(4) 16–038	Pt.12 9–042
(5) 16–038	s.6 9–033

TABLE OF STATUTES

s.7 . . . . 9–033, 23–023, 23–027	s.175 9–040
s.10 . . . . 9–033, 23–027	s.180 9–040
(2) 9–040, 23–020, 23–020, 23–021	s.205 9–040
s.15 9–001	s.212 9–040
(1) 23–020	s.215 9–040
(2) 9–043	s.221 9–040
s.17(1)–(3) . . . 9–034, 9–039, 24–009	s.222 9–040
(2) 9–043	s.223 9–040
(3) 9–043, 24–009	s.225 . . . . 23–023, 27–026
s.18 . . . . 9–043, 23–021	s.226 23–023
s.19 23–021	s.237(2) 9–042
ss.20–27 9–001	s.240 9–042
ss.20–41 9–033	ss.250–254 9–042
s.21(1) 23–020	s.261 9–042
ss.22–24 24–009	ss.271–289 9–41
s.22 . . . . 9–031, 9–032, 9–042	s.288 9–042
(1) 23–020	s.315 9–040
(2) 9–043, 23–020	s.318 9–040
s.23 9–042	s.327 23–021
s.25(1) 23–020	s.341 9–042
s.26 . . . . 9–031, 9–032	s.343 9–042
(1) 23–020	s.346 9–042
s.27(1) 23–020	s.352 . . . . 9–042, 27–014
s.30(1)–(3) 9–034	s.356(1) 9–042
s.30(1) 24–009	s.370 9–042
s.30(3) 24–009	s.372 9–040
s.31 23–021	s.373 9–042
s.32 23–021	s.386 23–023
s.41 27–023	s.388 23–027
ss.44–47 27–025	ss.401–416 18–027
s.47(2)(a) 27–018	s.401 23–023
ss.48–61 . . . . 27–002, 27–025	s.403 23–023
s.49(1)(c) 27–023	s.617 9–042
s.50 27–023	s.637 9–042
s.51 27–023	s.684 . . . . 23–021, 27–011
s.52 27–023	s.686 23–021
s.53 27–023	s.688A 27–025
s.54 27–023	Finance Act (c.14)
s.55 27–024	s.23 29–017
s.56 27–024	s.185 9–096
s.57 27–024	Sch.2 29–017
s.58 27–024	Sch.22 9–040
ss.59–61 27–024	2004 Finance Act (c.12) 12–010, 13–060
s.61A–61J 27–025	ss.119–123 . 18–061, 18–062, 18–063
s.61B 27–025	s.119 18–061
s.61C 27–025	s.120 18–061
s.61D 27–025	s.121 18–061
s.61E 27–025	s.122 18–061
s.61F 27–025	s.122A 18–062
s.61G 27–025	s.123 18–061
s.61H 27–025	s.124 18–065
s.61I 27–025	s.125 18–065
s.6J 27–025	ss.149–284 23–024
s.62(2) 9–040, 23–021	s.246(2) 21–018
(b) 18–027	ss.306–319 24–057
s.65 9–041	s.306 9–008
s.70 9–040	Sch.15 9–097
s.105 . . . . 9–040, 23–021	para.3 9–097
s.106 . . . . 9–040, 23–021	para.6 9–097
s.150 9–040	para.7 9–097
ss.167–168 9–040	para.8 9–097
	para.9 9–097

TABLE OF STATUTES

	para.10(1)(a) 9–097	(7) 18–018
	(2)(a) 9–097	s.87 15–013
	para.11 9–097	(2) 15–013
	para.12 9–097	(3) 15–013
	para.13 9–097	(4) 15–013
	Patents Act (c.16) 2–009	s.88 15–013
2005	Income Tax (Trading and Other Income)	(3) 15–013
	Act (c.5) 9–001, 13–015	(5) 15–013
	Ch. 3A 9–049	(6) 15–013
	Pts 2–5 . . . . 9–034, 9–036	(7) 15–013
	Pt.2 . . . 9–033, 9–044, 9–045, 9–048,	s.89 . . . . 9–048, 15–013, 16–036
	9–049,	s.90 . . . . 15–013, 17–007
	9–056, 9–061, 9–067,	ss.92–94 9–048
	13–015, 15–016,	s.130 18–063
	15–026, 18–063,	s.131 18–063
	20–003, 24–003,	s.133 18–063
	24–005, 24–006,	s.134 18–063
	24–007, 24–008,	s.135 18–063
	24–009	ss.136–138A 18–063
	Pt.3 . . . 9–061, 9–062, 9–065, 9–067,	s.137 18–063
	9–082	s.138 18–064
	Pt.4 . . . 9–056, 9–065, 9–066, 9–067,	s.138A 18–063, 18–064
	9–082,	ss.139–144 18–063
	24–003	s.139 18–063
	Pt.5 . . 9–056, 9–051, 9–069, 24–002,	s.140 18–063
	24–033,	s.140A 18–063
	24–037	s.141 18–063
	Pt.7 9–063	s.142 18–063
	Pt.8 . . . . 9–033, 9–067	ss.142A–142E 18–064
	Pt.9 24–009	s.143 . . . . 18–063, 18–065
	ss.5–8 . . . . 17–003, 18–002, 18–003,	s.144 18–065
	18–005, 18–007,	s.145A 18–064
	18–009, 18–010,	ss.148A–148FD 18–065
	18–016, 20–007,	s.163 27–023
	27–019	s.164 27–023
	s.6 . . . . 9–001, 24–004	s.172B 13–016
	(1) 24–009	ss.192–195 28–012
	(2) 24–004	s.192 19–002
	(3) 24–009	s.192(1) . . . 19–002, 19–015, 28–001,
	s.13 27–047	28–012, 28–025,
	(2)(4) 27–048	28–026
	(4)(b) 27–052	(3) 19–012, 28–012
	(5) 27–048	(4) 28–012
	(7) 27–052	s.193 19–009
	s.14 . . . . 27–047, 27–052	(1) 19–008, 28–012
	s.15(2) 19–016	(2) 19–008
	s.21 9–063	s.194 . . . . 19–014, 28–012
	s.25 . . . . . 15–010, 17–011, 18–036,	(2) 19–010
	27–027	(4) 19–010
	ss.32–94 18–034	(5) 19–010
	s.33 . . . . 9–048, 17–007, 17–010	s.195 . . . . 19–009, 19–014
	s.34 . . . . . . 9–048, 12–015, 20–003,	s.197 9–046
	26–008, 27–021,	s.198 9–046
	27–038, 28–016,	s.199 9–046
	28–019, 29–004	s.200 9–046
	s.45 . . . . 9–048, 12–015, 27–038	(2) 9–046
	s.46 27–038	(3) 9–046
	s.51 . . . . 9–048, 9–056, 12–014	(4) 9–046
	s.55 12–015	s.201 9–046
	s.57 . . . . 9–048, 17–002, 28–028	s.202 9–046
	s.58 9–048	s.205 9–047
	s.66(1) 18–018	s.206 . . . . 9–047, 9–054

1

TABLE OF STATUTES

s.214	9–046
s.216	9–046
s.217	9–046
s.218	9–046
s.219	9–046
s.220	9–047
(3)	9–047
ss.221–225	17–003, 17–012, 18–017, 18–032, CS1–003
s.221(1)	17–003
(2)	17–003
(3)	17–003
(4)	17–003
s.222	17–004
(4)	17–004
(5)	17–004
(6)	17–004
s.223(1)	17–003
(4)	17–004
s.224(1)	17–004
(3)	17–003
(4)	17–005
(5)	17–005
s.225(4)	17–005
ss.226–240	27–028
ss.227–240	9–048
ss.241–257	23–016
ss.241–259	18–002, 18–005
s.243	23–017
(3)	23–016
(4)	18–005
(5)	24–008
s.246	23–017
(1)	18–005
(3)–(4)	23–016
s.247(1)	18–005
s.250	18–006
s.251	23–017
s.252	23–016
s.253	23–016
(1)	18–005
ss.254–255	18–006, 23–017
s.254	18–005
(1)(a)	18–032
s.255	23–017
s.256	23–017, 23–018
(1)(b)	18–005
s.257	18–005, 23–017
s.260	9–001
s.269	9–068
s.272	9–061
ss.308A–308C	9–062
s.368	9–001
s.397	9–066, 10–010
s.397A	9–067
s.397AA	9–067
s.397B	9–067
s.509(3)	16–030
s.525	18–032, 18–034
s.577	9–001
s.577(2)	18–015
ss.578–581	17–012
ss.578–582	18–001, 18–002, 18–004, 18–009, 18–015, 18–016, 20–003
s.578	16–018
s.579	9–056, 16–002, 16–013, 17–002, 17–006, 17–008, 18–018, 20–003, 24–003, 27–043
s.580	23–010
s.581	18–009
s.582	17–012, 18–016, 18–034
ss.583–586	26–005, 28–012
s.583	19–011
(1)	28–012
(2)	28–012
(4)	28–001, 28–012, 28–025, 28–026
(5)	28–001, 28–012, 28–025, 28–026
s.585(2)	19–011
ss.587–599	16–018, 16–028
s.587	16–006, 16–016, 16–030, 16–038, 24–002
s.588	16–018, 16–030
s.589	16–018
ss.590–592	16–019
s.590	16–018, 16–030
(3)	16–018
s.591	16–019
(3)	16–019
(4)	16–019
(5)	16–019
s.592	16–019
(3)	16–019
(4)	16–019
(5)	16–019
s.593	16–016
(1)	16–019
(2)	16–019
(4)	16–019
s.594	16–016, 16–033
s.596	16–019
s.597	16–031
s.598	16–031
s.599	16–031
s.600	16–036
s.601	16–036
s.602	16–031
s.603	16–031
s.604	16–031
s.605	16–031
s.606	16–031
s.608	16–031
s.619	CS1–006, CS1–014
s.620	27–040
s.624	9–097
ss.629–632	23–030
s.629	27–040
ss.683–686	20–004
s.683	20–004, 27–034, 27–043
(3)	20–004

TABLE OF STATUTES

s.684(1)	20–004
s.687	18–014, 18–015, 18–028, 18–034, 19–011, 20–007, 23–018, 27–019, 27–021, 27–034, 27–043
s.688	23–018
s.727	16–005
ss.757–767	16–010, 17–011, 20–004
s.757	16–011
s.758	16–010, 16–011, 16–012
s.759	16–011
s.760	16–011
s.761	16–011
s.763	16–010, 16–012
s.764	16–012
s.765	16–012
s.766	16–012
s.767	16–012
s.776	18–028
ss.809B–809C	9–084
s.830	9–031, 9–032, 24–011
s.831	9–031, 9–032
ss.832–832B	24–037
s.832	9–001, 9–068, 24–008
s.832A	9–033
s.833	9–034, 24–009
s.848	9–081
s.849	9–081
(3)	9–083
s.850	9–081
ss.849–856	24–006
ss.851–856	9–082
s.853	9–082
s.857	9–033, 9–067, 9–084, 24–006, 24–009, 27–042, 27–043
(3)	24–003
s.882	8–005
Sch.1, para.381	17–005
Sch.2, paras 31–38	18–063
Finance Act (c.7)	
s.58	18–055
s.59	18–054
ss.60–65	18–054
s.65(1)	18–056
ss.72–79	18–057
s.101	22–027
Sch.3	18–054
para.3(1)	18–054
para.6(1)	18–055
Sch.10	22–027
Finance (No.2) Act (c.22)	21–061
2006 Finance Act (c.25)	9–075, 9–090, 10–004, 10–022, 10–028, 18–071, 21–007, 21–008
s.46	18–058
s.47	18–063
ss.65–68	27–053
ss.158–161	23–024
Sch.5, paras 15–23	18–072
Companies Act (c.46)	21–067
s.1	21–046
ss.381–384	21–012
2007 Income Tax Act (c.3)	9–001, 15–001, 16–002, 16–004, 17–011
Pt.5	9–055
Pt.5A	9–055
s.2	16–005
s.3	24–039
s.8	23–030
s.12	10–016, 10–017
s.19	24–003
ss.23–24	23–015
ss.23–25	23–014
s.23	9–057, 9–066, 16–003
s.24	16–005
s.24A	9–055, 9–082, 9–087
s.27A	18–065
s.35	9–003
s.36	9–003
s.37	9–003
s.38	9–003
s.46	9–003, 21–005
ss.61–63	23–014
s.61(2)	23–013
s.62	23–014
s.62(2)	23–013
s.63	23–014
s.64	9–053, 9–055
s.65	23–013
(2)	9–054
s.67	9–054
s.68	9–054
s.71	9–076
s.72	9–054, 9–055, 23–013
s.74A	9–053
s.74B	9–053
s.74C	9–053
s.74D	9–053
ss76–79	9–053
ss.83–85	23–014
s.83	9–054
s.88	23–015
ss.89–93	23–014
s.89	9–054
s.90	9–054
s.95	23–015
ss.102–116	18–065
ss.103–114	9–045
s.103C	9–082, 9–086
(6)	9–082
ss.104–105	9–086
ss.107–114	9–087
s.107	23–008
ss.117–124	9–061
ss.120–124	9–063
s.120	9–055
s.129	23–013
ss.131–135	23–014
ss.131–151	9–054, 9–055

TABLE OF STATUTES

ss.152–155 23–015
s.195 16–043
s.213 23–013
s.214 23–013
s.306 16–043
ss.447–452 16–002
s.448 . 9–056, 9–057, 13–015, 16–001
   (2) 16–003
   (4) 16–003
s.449 . . . . . 11–012, 16–001, 16–003
s.450 16–003
s.452 16–003
s.461 16–034
s.479 . . . . 10–015, 23–030
s.484 10–018
s.486 10–017
s.491 . . . . 10–015, 10–018
s.492 10–015
s.493 16–017
s.499 16–001
ss.714–735 . 24–038, 24–039, 24–041
ss.714–751 . 14–020, 24–013, 24–033,
                                    CS3–015
s.714(4) 24–038
ss.715–735 24–040
s.715 24–034
ss.716–750 . . . . CS3–012
s.716 24–033
s.718 24–039
s.719 . . . . . 24–033, 24–036, 24–038
ss.720–735 9–037
s.720 . . . . . 24–036, 24–038, 24–040,
                        CS1–011, CS3–012
s.721(5) 24–033
ss.722–723 24–038
s.722 24–033
s.724 24–039
s.725 . . . . 13–015, 24–033
s.726 24–040
s.727 24–040
s.728(3) 24–033
s.729 24–040
s.730 24–040
ss.731–735 . 21–032, 24–036, 24–037,
                                    25–038
s.733(1) 24–036
s.734 24–038
ss.735–742 24–034
ss.736–742 . . . . CS1–011
s.738 24–034
s.743 24–040
s.745 24–039
s.747 24–038
ss.748–750 . . . . . . 24–041, 24–048
s.748 24–041
s.749 24–041
s.750 24–041
s.751 24–040
ss.773–785 . . . . . 27–040, CS1–011,
                       CS1–012, CS1–013,
                       CS1–014,
                       CS2–008, CS3–007,
                       CS3–012
ss.773–789 . . . . . . 23–008, 27–044,
                       CS3–015
s.773(2)(a) 27–045
   (b) 27–045
s.774(a) 27–045
   (b) 27–045
ss.776–779 27–044
s.777 27–045
   (7) 18–009, 27–045
s.778 27–045
   (2) 18–009
   (3) 18–009
s.779 27–045
   (3) 18–009
s.781 27–045
s.784 . . . 27–044, 27–046, CS1–011,
                       CS1–012, CS2–008
s.785 27–046
s.786 27–046
s.788 27–046
ss.796–803 18–062
s.796 18–062
s.797 18–062
s.798 18–062
s.799 18–062
s.800 18–062
s.801 18–062
s.802 18–062
s.803 18–062
ss.809A–809Z 9–001, 9–068,
                       24–009, 24–012
s.809B 9–031, 9–032, 9–067,
                       24–006, 24–043
s.809C . 9–031, 9–032, 9–032, 9–067,
                       24–011,
                       24–043
s.809D . 9–003, 9–031, 9–032, 24–043
s.809E 9–031, 9–032
s.809H 9–032, 9–034
s.809I 9–032
ss.809K–809Z 9–034
ss.809L–809U 9–037
s.809L 24–009
s.809M 9–034
ss.809P–809R 9–034, 24–010
s.809V–Z6 9–034
s.809V 9–032
ss.809X–809Z 24–010
s.809Z 9–031, 9–032, 9–071
s.811 . . . . . . 9–001, 10–021, 16–017
   (4)(a) 16–014
s.812 16–017
s.813 16–017
s.826 16–017
ss.829–833 9–019
s.829 9–021
s.830 . . . . 9–020, 9–021
s.831 . . . . 9–019, 9–020, 9–025
s.832 . . . . 9–019, 9–020, 9–025

TABLE OF STATUTES

s.835C 18–020
ss.835T–835X 18–020
ss.847–849 16–013
s.848 . . . . 16–001, 23–010
ss.898–902 . 17–008, 18–004, 20–003
ss.898–905 . 16–003, 16–013, 28–016
ss.898–910 16–009
s.898 . . . . . 9–056, 17–001, 17–011,
18–001
  (1) 16–002
  (a) 18–018
  (b) 18–018
ss.899–905 16–017
ss.899–902 . . . . 18–001, 20–004
s.899 . . . . . 16–002, 16–006, 16–013,
16–017, 17–001,
17–011, 18–018,
20–003, 27–034
  (2) 16–010, 16–013
  (3)(a)(ii) 16–002
  (4)(a) 16–002
ss.900–902 17–011
ss.900–903 17–008
s.900 . . . . . 13–015, 17–001, 18–018,
20–003
  (1) 16–003
  (c) 16–003
  (2) 16–003
  (3) 16–003, 17–001
s.901 . . . . . 11–012, 16–003, 17–001
  (2) 18–020
s.902 . . . . . 16–003, 17–001, 20–003
s.903 . . . . . 9–066, 13–015, 16–003,
16–005, 16–006,
16–010, 16–020,
16–046, 18–001
  (5) 16–006
  (6) 16–006
s.904 16–005
s.905 16–006
ss.906–909 . . 17–008, 17–0ll, 20–004
ss.906–910 18–001
s.906 . . . . . 16–010, 17–001, 17–008,
17–011, 18–019,
18–022, 18–023,
18–024, 18–032,
18–033, 24–002,
28–016, 29–010
  (2) 14–023
  (4) 18–020, 18–022
  (5) 18–019
s.907 17–001
  (1)(a) 18–022
  (1)(c) 18–032
  (2) 18–022
s.908 18–020
  (1) 17–0008
  (2) 17–008
s.909 . . . . 17–001, 18–019
  (1) 18–021
  (2) 18–019, 18–021

s.910 . . . . . 16–028, 16–029, 16–030,
16–034
ss.911–917 . . . . 16–006, 17–011
s.911 . . . . . 11–012, 16–009, 28–016
  (1)(c) 16–009
  (2) 16–009
s.912 . . . . 16–009, 28–016
s.913 16–009
  (2) 16–009
s.914 16–010
  (2) 16–010
  (3) 16–010
s.915 16–010
s.917 16–010
s.933 . . . . 10–009, 11–012
s.944 . . . . 27–044, 27–046
ss.945–955 10–009
ss.945–962 . 16–009, 17–001, 18–022
s.946 11–012
s.946(5) 18–022
s.951 9–058
s.963 . . . . . 9–057, 16–009, 16–014,
17–001, 18–022
s.964 . . . . . 17–001, 18–022, 27–034
s.966 . . . . 18–072, 27–024
s.975 . . . . 16–007, 16–034
s.989 21–005
s.993 . . . . . 12–013, 15–026, 16–038
s.994 16–038
s.997 18–036
  (1), (3) 21–005
s.1003 . . . . 15–001, 15–003
s. 1006 . . . 15–001, 15–003, 15–011,
15–013, 21–008
  (2) 15–003
  (3) 15–003
  (4) 15–003
  (5) 15–003
s.1015(3) 27–044
s.1025 . . . . 16–003, 16–006
s.1026 16–003
Sch.1, para.299 27–046
para.300 27–046
Finance Act (c.11)
  s.25 27–025
  s.27 9–076
  ss.68–70 23–024
  Sch.3 27–025
  Sch.14 13–011
Legal Services Act (c.29) 2–012
2008 Finance Act (c.9)
  s.60 18–065
  ss.90–92 23–024
  Sch.10 15–015, ...15–030
2009 Corporation Tax Act (c.4). 16–001,
23–010
  Pt.2 23–010
  Pt.3 15–016
  Pt 8 . . . . . 16–001, 17–001, 18–001,
19–001, 21–001,
21–008, 21–009,
21–018, 21–020,

TABLE OF STATUTES

	21–036, 21–037, 21–059, 21–061, 21–062, 26–004, 26–005, 26–008
Pt.9	16–001, 23–010, 24–002, 24–003
Pt.9A	10–010
Pt.12	22–025
Pt.13	14–040
Pt.15	21–002, 21–007
Pt.17	21–036
s.2	10–001
s.5	10–001, 16–017
s.8	21–061
s.9	9–10, 10–011
s.10	14–023
s.14	14–003
s.18	10–001, 14–003
s.19	10–001, 10–003, 16–017
ss.24–25	10–001
ss.35–45	15–026
s.43	21–050
s.46	15–010, 27–030
s.52	21–046
s.54	13–015, 20–007, 28–017, 28–019, 29–005
s.56	21–018
(2)(c), (d)	21–041
(3)	21–041
s.57(2)	23–008
s.59	13–015
s.61	15–021, 23–008
s.87	15–013
(2)	15–013
(3)	15–013
(4)	15–013
s.88	15–013
(1)(a)	15–024
(3)	15–013
(5)	15–013
(6)	15–013
ss.89–90	15–013
s.104A	15–033, 15–040
ss.104M–104N	15–037
ss.104P–104Q	15–037
ss.104R–104T	15–038
ss.104U–104W	15–039
ss.104X–104Y	15–040
s.109	21–041
s.117	21–001
s.118	21–017
s.150	18–075
s.151	18–075
(4)	18–075
s.152	18–075
s.157	13–016
ss.176–179	16–023
s.176	28–011
(1)	19–002
(3), (4)	19–012, 28–012
s.177	28–012
(1), (2)	19–008, 28–012
s.178	19–009, 28–012
(1)	19–014, 19–010
(2)	19–014, 19–010
(3)	19–014, 19–010
(4)	19–010
(5)	19–010
(6)	19–010
s.179(1)	19–013, 19–014
(2)	19–013, 19–014
(3)	19–014
s.180	18–036
s.201(2)	16–018
s.330	15–021
s.371	21–015
s.388(7)	15–013
ss.449–451	21–050
s.486B	22–014
s.499	21–046
s.577A	21–018
s.637(1), (2), (4)	21–038
ss.711–879	16–001, 19–001
ss.711–906	13–017, 17–001, 18–001
ss.711–931	16–044
s.712(3)	22–031
s.714	21–015, 21–016
s.716	21–015
s.719	21–015, 21–040
s.721	21–015, 21–058
ss.726–732	21–043
s.727	21–015
s.728(2), (3)	21–016
s.729	CS7–005
ss.733–741	21–056, 21–059
s.735	21–040
s.736	21–040
s.741	21–015, 21–047, 21–049, 21–054, 21–055, 21–056, 21–058
(1)	21–038
(3)	21–058
(4)	21–038, 21–058
ss.747–749	21–049, 21–050
ss.751–753	21–049
ss.754–763	21–037, 21–043
s.754	14–022, 21–037
s.755	21–043
s.756	21–037, 21–039, 21–059
(1)	21–038
(b)	21–039
(2)	21–038
(3)	21–038
(4)	21–038
s.757	21–039, 21–041
s.758(1)	21–015, 21–039
(2)	21–039, 21–042
(3)	21–039
(4)	21–039
(5)	21–039
(a)	21–039
(6)	21–039
s.759(1), (2), (3)	21–040
s.761	21–039

TABLE OF STATUTES

(2)–(7) 21–039
s.762 21–038
s.763 21–038
   (2) 21–038
ss.764–773 . . . . 21–041, 21–056
s.764 21–046
s.765 21–046
s.766(1) 21–046
s.767 21–047
s.768 21–047
s.769(1)–(3) 21–047
s.770(1)–(2) 21–047
s.772 21–047
s.773 21–047
   (3) 21–041
ss.774–799 21–041
ss.775–802 21–047
s.775 . . . . . 21–020, 21–049, 21–063
   (1) 21–043, 21–047
   (4) 21–043, 21–047
s.776 . . . . . 21–015, 21–020, 21–054,
                    21–058
   (1)–(5) 21–048
ss.777–779 . . . . 21–048, 21–052
s.778(1)–(4) 21–042
s.779(1)–(5) 21–042
   (7) 21–042
ss.780–799 21–043
ss.780–785 21–063
s.780 . . . . 21–043, 21–058
   (1)(a)–(c) 21–049
   (2) 21–049
   (3) 21–049
   (5) 21–050
s.781(5) 21–049
s.783(1) 21–050
s.784 21–050
s.785 . . . . . 21–043, 21–050, 21–058
   (1)–(3) 21–050
   (4) 21–049
   (6) 21–050
s.786 21–050
s.787 21–051
s.788(1)–(3) 21–052
ss.789–790 21–052
s.789(1) 21–052
s.791 21–038
   (1)–(5) 21–043
ss.792–796 21–044
s.792(1) 21–52
   (1)–(4) 21–043
s.793(1)–(5) 21–043
s.794 21–038
   (1) 21–043
   (5) 21–044
   (6) 21–044
ss.795–897 21–045
s.795 21–044
   (1) 21–044
   (2) 21–045
   (3)(b) 21–044
   (4) 21–044
s.796 21–044
s.797(3)–(5) 21–045
s.798(1) 21–045
   (4)–(6) 21–045
s.799 21–052
ss.808–813 21–059
ss.810–813 21–016
ss.817–833 . . . . 21–049, 21–053
s.818 21–055
   (1)–(6) 21–053
s.819 21–054
   (3), (4) 21–054
ss.820–832 21–055
s.820(2) 21–054, 21–055
ss.821–822 21–055
s.826 21–058
s.828 21–056
s.829(1), (3)–(5) 21–056
s.830 21–056
s.831 . . . . . 21–054, 21–055, 21–056
s.832 . . . . . 21–054, 21–056, 21–057
   (1)–(3), (5) 21–057
s.833 21–057
   (2)–(4) 21–057
s.839 16–038
s.839 16–038
ss.845–846 21–049
ss.846–849 21–049
s.846(1) 21–047
s.850(1)–(2) 21–038, 21–045
s.851 . . . . 21–018, 21–053
s.852(2)–(4) 21–058
ss.854–855 21–059
   (1) 21–059
s.854 21–059
s.855 21–059
   (6), (7) 21–059
s.868 21–018
s.869 21–018
ss.880–900 . 16–001, 17–001, 18–001
ss.881–889 21–047
ss.881–905 21–038
s.881 19–001
s.882 21–038
   (1) 21–020, 21–038
s.883 21–017
   (3), (5), (7) 21–017
s.884 21–017
s.885(1), (7) 21–017
s.886 18–074
s.887(1), (2) 21–017
s.888 21–017
s.889 21–017
s.896 . . . . 16–008, 17–011
   (1), (2) 21–016
s.897 21–038
   (3) 21–038
ss.898–900 21–038
s.898(2)(c), (d) 21–038
   (4) 21–038
ss.899–900 . . . . 21–038, 21–045
s.899(7) 21–038, 21–045

TABLE OF STATUTES

ss.901–906 . . . . 16–001, 19–001
s.904 21–058
s.905 21–038
   (6), (7) 21–038
s.906(1), (2) 21–005
ss.907–931 16–001
s.908(1) 19–011, 19–012
   (4) 19–002, 19–015, 28–011,
                          28–012, 28–026
s.909(2)–(4) 19–011
   (5), (6) 19–013
s.910 16–036
   (1) 19–011
ss.912–915 . 16–018, 16–028, 16–038
ss.912–917 16–033
ss.912–920 16–034
s.912 . . . . . 16–006, 16–016, 16–028,
                    16–030, 22–014,
                    24–002, 24–003
   (2) 16–030, 24–003
   (3) 16–001
s.913 16–032
ss.914–918 16–018
s.914 . . . . 16–029, 16–030
   (4) 16–030
s.915 16–029
s.916 16–030
s.917 16–030
s.918 . . . . . 16–016, 16–028, 16–033
s.919 . . . . . 16–031, 16–032, 16–033
s.920 16–033
s.921 16–028
   (3), (4) 20–010
s.922 16–028
s.923 16–028
s.924 . . . . 16–036, 16–038
s.925 16–036
s.925(4) 16–028
ss.926–931 16–028
s.927 16–036
ss.931A–931Q 24–003
s.977 . . . . 20–004, 20–007
s.1015 15–016
ss.1039–1084 15–019
ss.1039–1142 . . . . . 15–001, 15–040
ss.1040A–1040Y 15–025
s.1042 . . . . 15–016, 15–028
s.1042 15–016
ss.1043–1073 . . . . . 15–010, 15–014
s.1044 . . . . 15–014, 15–016, 15–022
s.1045 15–021
s.1046 15–019
s.1047 15–021
s.1048(1)–(5) 15–023
s.1049 15–023
s.1050 . . . . 15–014, 15–016, 15–019
   (7) 15–019
s.1052 . . . . 15–016, 15–019
s.1053 . . . . 15–016, 15–019
ss.1054–1057 15–022
s.1054 15–022
s.1056(2) 15–022

s.1058(2) 15–022
s.1060(4)–(7) 15–022
s.1061 16–022
ss.1063–1067 15–016
s.1063 5–019
s.1065 . . . . 15–016, 15–019
s.1066 . . . . 15–016, 15–019
s.1067 . . . . 15–016, 15–019
ss.1071–1072 15–019
ss.1074–1084 . . . . . 15–010, 15–019,
                    15–025, 15–029
s.1074 . . . . 15–026, 15–027
s.1075 15–025
s.1076 15–026
s.1077 15–026
s.1078 15–026
s.1079 15–026
s.1080–1082 15–027
s.1082(2)–(3) 15–027
ss1083–1084 15–027
s.1084(1)–(3) 16–023
s.1085–1142 15–019
s.1086 . . . . 15–023, 15–029, 15–031
s.1087 15–031
s.1091 15–029
   (3)–(4) 15–029
s.1098–1102 15–031
s.1101 15–030
ss.1101–1102 15–031
ss.1113–1118 . . . . . 15–015, 15–030
ss.1113–1142 15–014
ss.1119–1121 15–025
ss.1119–1122 15–014
s.1122 . . . . 15–025, 15–026
ss.1123–1127 15–031
ss.1123–1128 15–028
s.1123 . . . . 15–017, 15–020
s.1124 . . . . 15–017, 15–020, 21–018
   (2) 15–017
   (4) 15–017
s.1125 15–018
   (2) 15–018
s.1126 15–018
ss.1127–1132 16–017
s.1130 15–020
s.1132 15–031
s.1133 . . . . 15–019, 15–020
   (5) 15–020
   (6) 15–020
s.1134 15–020
s.1135 15–020
s.1136 15–019
s.1138 . . . . 15–019, 15–019, 15–031
   (4) 15–019
s.1140 . . . . 15–016, 15–031
s.1142 . . . . 15–025, 15–028
s.1172 15–029
s.1181 18–071
s.1182 18–071
s.1183 18–071
s.1184 18–071
s.1185 18–071

TABLE OF STATUTES

s.1186 18–071	(3)(a) 15–022
s.1188 . . . . 18–073, 18–074	(3)(b) 15–022
s.1189 18–073	s.45 . . . . . . 10–004, 15–022, 16–008
s.1190 18–073	ss.99–104 15–022
s.1191 18–073	s.99 . . . . 10–004, 21–034
s.1192 18–073	s.102 21–034
s.1193 18–073	s.103 21–034
s.1194 18–073	s.104 21–034
ss.1195–1216 18–072	s.105 21–034
ss.1195–1198 18–072	s.113 10–004
s.1195 18–071	s.137 16–022
s.1196 18–071	s.152 15–027
s.1197 18–071	s.189 10–005
s.1198 18–071	ss.265–268 21–033
s.1199 . . . . 18–072, 18–073	s.357B 22–005
s.1200 . . . . 18–072, 18–073	(4) 22–010
s.1201 18–072	s.357BB 22–006, 22–007
s.1202 18–072	s.357BD 22–008
s.1203 18–072	s.357C 22–013
s.1205 18–072	s.357CA 22–014, 22–022
s.1206 18–072	s.357CB 22–014
s.1207 18–072	s.357CC 22–015, 22–018
s.1208 18–073	(2) 22–020
s.1209 18–073	s.357CF 22–016
s.1210 18–073	s.357CG 22–022
s.1211 . . . . 18–073, 18–074	s.357CH 22–022
s.1212–1216 18–072	s.357CI 22–025
s.1218 10–006	s.357CJ 22–025
s.1219 10–006	s.357CN 22–027
ss.1256–1272 9–085	s.357CO 22–027
s.1271 16–033	s.357CP 22–029
s.1272 16–028	s.357CQ 22–013, 22–030
s.1273 16–028	s.357D 22–021, 22–031
s.1275 14–023	s.357DB 22–032
s.1285 10–010	s.357DC 22–032
s.1289 21–018	(2) 22–032
s.1298 . . . . 13–015, 21–018	s.357EA 22–034
s.1301 13–015	s.357EB 22–034, 22–036
s.1304 . . . . 13–015, 21–018	s.357EC 22–034
s.1316 15–026	s.357EE 22–036
(2) 19–013	s.357F 22–037
Sch.1 21–015	s.357FA 22–038
Sch.2, paras 113–114 15–028	s.357FB 22–038
para.115 15–029	s.357G 22–004
para.128 . . . . 18–072, 18–073	s.357GB 22–004
para.130 18–074	(2) 22–032
para.132 18–073	(6) 22–011
Finance Act (c.10)	s.357GC 22–039
Sch.6 9–053	s.357GD 22–036
2010 Corporation Tax Act (c.4)	s.360 18–065
Pt.5 . . . . . . 10–004, 18–073, 21–047	s.439 10–003
Pt.8A 22–001	ss.450–451 24–046
Pt.11 21–034	s.491 15–024
Pt.23 21–020	ss.711–906 12–017
s.9A 14–022	s.882(2) 14–005
ss.19–32 . . . . CS3–015	s.967(1)–(3) 14–024
ss.24–25 10–003	s.1020 13–011
ss.25–30 22–026	s.1021 13–011
s.25(3)(a) 10–003	ss.1075–1077 21–051
s.26 10–003	s.1088 21–051
s.34 10–003	s.1101 15–031
s.37 . . . . 10–004, 18–073	

TABLE OF STATUTES

s.1122 . . . . 12–013, 14–005, 15–020,
15–026, 16–038,
21–019
s.1123 . . . . 15–020, 21–019
s.1124 13–004
s.1127 . . . . 15–010, 18–036
s.1134 15–003
s.1138 . . . . 15–003, 15–011, 15–013,
15–022
(2) 15–003
(3) 15–003
(4) 15–003
(5) 15–003
ss.1141–1143 29–011
s.1154(2) 21–046
Taxation (International and Other
Provisions) Act (c8)
Pt.4 . . . . . 13–007, 13–010, 13–011,
13–015, 21–016,
21–018, 21–020,
21–024, 21–048,
26–006, 29–014
Pt.9A 14–001, 14–021, 21–060
ss.2–7 24–015
s.2 28–016
s.6(1) 24–058
ss.8–17 . . . . 24–016, 28–017
ss.8–56 24–016
s.9 24–016
ss.18–35 24–016
ss.36–39 24–016
s.38 24–017
s.40 24–016
s.41 24–016
ss.42–56 24–016
s.47 24–017
s.63 24–005
ss.112–115 24–016
s.112 28–017
s.124 13–012
s.127 13–013
s.131 . . . . 13–016, 16–012
s.132 16–012
ss.146–217 . 12–015, 13–001, 24–008,
CS5–004
s.152 13–008
s.159 13–004
ss.161–162 13–007
s.163 13–004
s.164 13–017
s.165 13–003
ss.166–173 13–003
ss.174–180 13–002
s.174 13–011
ss.213–214 13–011
s.371BC 14–020
s.371BD 14–020
s.371DG 14–007
s.371DH 14–007
s.371DI 14–007
s.371DJ 14–007
s.371DK 14–007

ss.371EB–371EE 14–008
s.371PA 14–024
s.371QC–QF 14–024
s.371RC 14–005
s.371RD(3)(c)(d) 14–004
(5) 14–004
(7) 14–005
s.371RE 14–005
s.371SD 14–021
s.371SE 14–021
s.371SF 14–022
ss.371TA–371TC 14–003
s 371VB 14–023
(6) 14–023
Sch.6 . . . . 16–017, 18–020
Finance Act (c.13). 9–064
s.63 27–053
Sch.3 9–053
2012 Finance Act (c.14) 10–083, 14–001
s.13 27–053
s.54 18–036
Sch.3, para 1 15–016
Sch.3, para 2 15–014
Sch.3, para 3 15–016
Sch.3, para 6 . . . . . . 15–016, 15–025
Image Rights (Bailiwick of Guernsey)
Ordinance (Ordinance No. XLVII of
2012) 27–053 . . . . . . 15–016, 15–025
2013 Finance Act (c.29) 9–002, 9–091,
18–022, 24–057
s.8 27–053
s.9 27–053
s.15 . . . . 16–001, 16–005
s.17 . . . . 9–049, 27–028
s.18 27–028
s.34 15–025
s.48 23–025
s.61 24–047
s.174 9–091
s.177 9–002
ss.206–215 . . . . . . 24–057, CS3–015
s.205 24–058
s.207 24–057
s.208 24–058
ss.210–211 24–058
s.210 24–058
s.211 24–058
s.212 24–058
s.213 24–058
s.214 24–058
s.215 24–058
ss.214–216 9–022
s.215 24–012
s.216 24–012
s.218 9–022
s.219 9–022
Sch.3 9–055
Sch.4 9–049
Sch.10 . . . . 24–039, 24–042
Sch.14 . . . . 15–025, 15–040
Schs 15–16 15–041
Sch.34 9–091

TABLE OF STATUTES

Sch.41 . . . . 24–057, CS3–015
Sch.43 . . . . 24–012, 24–058
Sch.44 24–012
Sch.45 9–022
Sch.46 9–022
2014 Finance Act. 9–089

TABLE OF STATUTORY INSTRUMENTS

1970 Double Taxation Relief (Taxes on Income) (General) Regulations SI 1970/488 16–014
Double Taxation Relief (Taxes on Income) (Austria) Order SI 1970/1947 Art.12 24–019
1973 Double Taxation Relief (Taxes on Income) (Jamaica) Order SI 1973/1329 19–019
1978 Double Taxation Relief (Taxes on Income) (Hungary) Order SI 1978/1056 . . . . CS7–005
Social Security (Categorisation of Earners) Regulations SI 1978/1689 . . . . 27–002, 27–022
1986 Companies (Northern Ireland) Order SI 1986/1032 21–046
1987 Income Tax (Entertainers and Sportsmen) Regulations SI 1987/530 27–047
reg.2 27–047
reg.3 27–047
(2) 20–006, 20–008
reg.4 . . . . 27–047, 27–048
reg.5 27–049
reg.6 27–047
reg.7 27–048
reg.10 27–048
reg.12 27–048
reg.16 27–051
reg.17 27–051
1992 Value Added Tax (Place of Supply of Services) Order SI 1992/3121
art.13 27–056
art.15(a) 27–054
(c) 27–056
1993 Income Tax (Employments) Regulations SI 1993/744 9–041
1995 Value Added Tax Regulations SI 1995/2518 18–078
regs 173–197 27–055
1996 Deregulation (Restrictive Trade Practices Act 1976) (Amendment) (Variation of Exempt Agreements) Order SI 1996/346 28–008
1998 Civil Procedure Rules SI 1998/3132
Pt.63 2–017
Pt.63PD 2–017
Corporation Tax (Instalment Payments) Regulations SI 1998/3175 10–012
2000 Films (Modification of the Definition of "British Film") Order SI 2000/756 18–071
Research and Development (Prescribed Activities) Regulations SI 2000/2081 15–001

2002 Corporation Tax (Finance Leasing of Intangible Assets) Regulations SI 2002/1967 21–059
Double Taxation Relief (Taxes on Income) (The United States of America) Order SI 2002/2848
art.4(6) 9–028
art.12 24–015
art.16 . . . . CS3–013
2003 Finance Act 2002, Schedule 13 (Appointed Day) Order SI 2003/1472 15–029
Income Tax (Pay As You Earn) Regulations SI 2003/2682 27–011
2004 Research and Development (Prescribed Activities) Regulations SI 2004/712 . . . . 15–001, 15–003
Tax Avoidance Schemes (Information) Regulations SI 2004/1864 9–008
2005 Recovery of Taxes etc Due in Other Member States (Amendment of Section 134 of the Finance Act 2002) Regulations SI 2005/1479 16–014
2006 Definition of "British Film" Order SI 2006/643 18–071
Tax Avoidance Schemes (Prescribed Descriptions of Arrangements) Regulations SI 2006/1543 . . . . 9–008, 10–013
Registered Designs Rules SI 2006/1975
r.31 3–005
Films and Sound Recordings (Appointed Day) Order SI 2006/3399 18–074
2007 Corporation Tax (Surrender of Terminal Losses on Films and Claims Relief) Regulations SI 2007/678 18–074
Corporation Tax (Taxation of Films) Transitional Provisions Regulations SI 2007/1050 18–074
Patents Rules SI 2007/3291 . . . . 2–002, 2–009
Recovery of Foreign Taxes Regulations SI 2007/3507 16–014
Recovery of Duties and Taxes Etc. Due in Other Member States (Corresponding UK Claims, Procedure and Supplementary) (Amendment) Regulations 2007 SI 2007/3508 16–014
2008 Trade Marks Rules SI 2008/1797 4–005

TABLE OF STATUTORY INSTRUMENTS

2009 Double Taxation Relief and International Tax Enforcement (Taxes on Income and Capital) (Netherlands) Order SI 2009/227 24–019

2012 Tax Avoidance Schemes (Information) Regulations SI 2012/1836 9–008

Controlled Foreign Companies (Excluded Territories) Regulations SI 2012/3024 14–015

TABLE OF TREATIES AND CONVENTIONS

1883 International Union for the Protection of Industrial Property (Paris Union) (International Convention) . . 2–026, 2–027, 3–009, 4–015, 4–020, 5–011

1886 Berne Copyright Convention 5–003, 5–015
Art.4 5–015

1891 Madrid Agreement Concerning the International Registration of Marks 4–019

1925 Hague Agreement Concerning the International Registration of Industrial Designs (Hague Agreement) 3–010

1952 Universal Copyright Convention 5–003, 5–015
Art.III 5–016

1957 Treaty of Rome
Art.85 . . . . 1–004, 6–003
Art.86 . . . . 1–004, 6–003

1961 International Convention for the Protection of New Varieties of Plants (UPOV) 1961 8–004
International Convention for the Protection of Performers, Producers of Phonograms and Broadcasting Organisations (Rome Convention) 5–016, 8–011

1969 UK/Austria Double Taxation Treaty (SI 1970/1947) CS6–006

1970 Patent Co–operation Treaty. 2–026, 2–028, 2–029, 2–030

1973 Convention on the Grant of European Patents (European Patent Convention) 2007 . . . . . . 2–030, 16–013, 16–030, 22–006, 22–020

1975 UK/Cyprus Double Taxation Treaty (SI 1975/425) 24–019

1976 UK/Ireland Double Taxation Treaty (SI 1976/2151) 24–023, CS5–003
UK/Spain Double Taxation Agreement (SI 1976/1919)
Art.4(2)(c) 24–005

1980 Hungary/Japan Double Taxation Treaty 24–020
United Nations Model Double Taxation Convention 13–036

1989 Agreement Relating to Community Patents (Community Patent Convention) 2–028, 2–031
Madrid Protocol to the 1891 Madrid Agreement Concerning the International Registration of Marks and the Protocol Relating to that Agreement 4–019

1990 Convention 90/436/EEC on the Elimination of Double Taxation in Connection with the Adjustment of Transfers of Profits between Associated Undertakings (EE90/436) . 13–013, 13–014, 13–037
Art.2, para.4 13–014

1992 OECD Model Tax Convention on Income and Capital . 13–001, 13–036, 27–050, 29–001, 29–011
Art.5 . . . . 29–004, 29–011
Art.7 13–036
Art.9 . . . . . 13–001, 13–014, 13–037, 22–021, 22–029, 24–008
Art.11(6) 13–037
Art.12 13–036
(4) 13–036
Art.25 13–037
United States/Netherlands Income Tax Treaty 24–019

1993 Treaty of the European Community
Art.43 14–001
Art.49 14–001
Art.56 14–001

1994 Trade Related Aspects of Intellectual Property Rights (TRIPs) Agreement 1–004, 2–024
Trademark Law Treaty. 4–020

2002 UK/US Double Taxation Treaty (SI 2002/2848) 24–015, 24–019, CS3–013, CS6–005
Art.4(6) 9–029

2006 United States Model Income Tax Convention 13–036

2007 OECD Convention on Mutual Assistance in Tax Matters 16–014

2009 Treaty on the Functioning of the European Union 2–020, 2–028
Art.101 . . . 2–020, 6–003, CS4–010, 2–023
Art.102 6–003
UK/Netherlands Double Taxation Treaty (SI 2009/227) CS6–006

2011 UK/Hungarian Double Taxation Treaty (SI 2011/2726)
Art.12 . . . . CS7–005

lxiii

TABLE OF EUROPEAN PROVISIONS

1988 First Council Directive 89/104/EEC of 21 December 1988 to approximate the laws of the Member States relating to trade marks (European Design Harmonisation Directive) [1989] OJ L40/1 . . 3–002, 3–011, 4–016, 5–007, 5–010

1990 European Union Arbitration Convention (Convention 90/436/EEC) [1990] OJ L225/10 . . . . 13–013, 13–037
Art.4(2) 13–014
Council Directive 90/434/EEC of 23 July 1990 on the common system of taxation applicable to mergers, divisions, transfers of assets and exchanges of shares concerning companies of different Member States (Mergers Directive) [1990] OJ L 225/1 . . . . 21–054, 21–081
Council Directive 90/435/EEC of 23 July 1990 on the common system of taxation applicable in the case of parent companies and subsidiaries of different Member States (Parent/Subsidiary Directive) [1990] OJ L 225/6 24–024

1993 Council Regulation (EC) No 40/941 of 20 December 1993 on the Community trade mark [1994] OJ L 11/1 4–016

1998 Directive 98/71/EC of the European Parliament and of the Council of 13 October 1998 on the legal protection of designs [1998] OJ L 289/28 . . . . . . 3–011, 5–008, 5–010

2001 Council Directive 2001/44/EC of 15 June 2001 amending Directive 76/308/EEC on mutual assistance for the recovery of claims resulting from operations forming part of the system of financing the European Agricultural Guidance and Guarantee Fund, and of agricultural levies and customs duties and in respect of value added tax and certain excise duties [2001] OJ L 175/17 16–014
Council Regulation (EC) No 2157/2001 of 8 October 2001 on the Statute for a European company (SE) [2001] OJ L 294/1 21–055

Council Regulation (EC) No 6/2002 of 12 December 2001 on Community designs [2002] OJ L 3/1) 3–011, 5–009

2003 Commission Recommendation of 6 May 2003 concerning the definition of micro, small and medium–sized enterprises 2003/361/EC [2003] OJ L 124/36 . . . . 10–010, 15–014
Council Directive 2003/49/EC of 3 June 2003 on a common system of taxation applicable to interest and royalty payments made between associated companies of different Member States (Interest and Royalties Directive) [2003] OJ L 157/4 (Interest and Royalties Directive) . 13–015, 13–016, 16–006, 16–010, 16–012, 16–016, 24–001, 24–019
Council Regulation (EC) No 1782/2003of 29 September 2003 establishing common rules for direct support schemes under the common agricultural policy and establishing certain support schemes for farmers and amending Regulations (EEC) No 2019/93, (EC) No 1452/2001, (EC) No 1453/2001, (EC) No 1454/2001, (EC) 1868/94, (EC) No 1251/1999, (EC) No 1254/1999, (EC) No 1673/2000, (EEC) No 2358/71 and (EC) No 2529/2001 [2003] OJ L 270/1 21–015

2006 Council Directive 2006/112/EC of 28 November 2006 on the common system of value added tax [2006] OJ L 347/1 16–014
Directive 2006/114/EC of the European Parliament and of the Council of 12 December 2006 concerning misleading and comparative advertising [2006] OJ L 376/ 21 6–005

PART 1

LAW

CHAPTER 1

Introduction

Broadly speaking, intellectual property is about copying, and the temptation to do so is an ever present human condition. The emergence of legal protection and legal remedies reflects this, and sets limits, trying to define boundaries between what may legitimately be done and what is illegitimate, between the areas of new development which are, for longer or shorter periods, fenced off and what then passes into (or always is in) that pool of common knowledge from which all may freely take.   1–001

Being able to stop copying is a desire of many businesses, for the straightforward reason that it impels customers to come to the originator for the product or service in question. Accordingly, intellectual property law has a major impact on the actual conduct of business across a very wide range of human endeavour.

This impact has increased in recent years, in the face of a general move against monopolies or trade restrictions of any type. The impact, however, continues to be dissipated: there is no overall "unfair copying" statute, only the well-established patent, trade mark and copyright laws and the relatively more recent additions such as the protection of registered designs. All of these areas of law were subject to major revisions in the last half of the twentieth century in order to match and adapt intellectual property law to meet the desire by innovators for the protection of their new ideas in all the multifarious areas of modern technology and newly developed marketing methods, particularly the rise in sales of goods and provision of services ordered via the internet, and rendered possible by the invention of the World Wide Web.

However, while technological change occurs rapidly, legislative change does not, and this has given rise to a host of problems as producers of goods and suppliers of services seek to restrain rapid adoption by copying of what they have taken time and effort to develop. This impact differs from one area to another; the high speed development in communications and the "information business", for example, initially left the practical application of copyright law and protection in disarray, while franchising and endorsement have led to a general questioning of the functions of the trade mark rights which they exploit. Genetic engineering has raised a whole new issue of ethical dimensions: should new plants and animals be patented? The rapid technological advances have the effect that the pace of change in the area of intellectual property law is increasing, while at the same time the boundaries between it and other areas of commercial, property and consumer law become ever less definite. Accordingly the term "intellectual property law" becomes less and less exact as time goes on.   1–002

INTRODUCTION

The general caveat notwithstanding, however, one can still discern not only various branches of the subject but also some common themes which various branches share, and it is the purpose of this brief introduction to bring these elements together. Once this has been done, certain aspects of the law discussed in the following chapters should appear, if not more logical, at least more comprehensible.

The principal characteristic of all forms of intellectual property is the so-called "incorporeal" nature of that property. It is an abstraction, intangible, and as such more difficult to protect than other less nebulous forms of property. The distinction between the two types of property can be seen by considering what is before your eyes, this book, and the respective rights of its owner and its authors. The owner has absolute control over it as an object and is at perfect liberty to do what he will with it. The reader may benefit from the ideas contained in it but—and here the authors' rights take over—you cannot treat the authors' presentation of them as your own: you cannot re-publish this book in any form yourself and neither can you make an adaptation or translation of it for publication. The authors still retain a legal interest in this book by virtue of our work in preparing its contents, no matter how great or how meagre the intellectual effort which that involved. Not only can the authors prevent the unauthorised copying of this work but we can also control its transformation into some other form, whether by translation, dramatisation, animated cartoon or any other means. An inventor or designer may have similar rights: if, for example, he designs a new gearbox or a new way of making a button, he can prevent others from copying the basic design or process involved.

1–003 The second characteristic of intellectual property law, however, is that its application is not solely intellectual. To be eligible for legal protection the author's or inventor's work must have been rendered into some tangible or perceptible form, be it a book, a gearbox, a dramatic performance, or whatever. There is no copyright in mere ideas. Legal protection would have been available for the creators of *La Grande Jatte* or the *Communist Manifesto* but Seurat could not have claimed any rights over the idea of pointillism, nor Marx and Engels over that of Communism. Whatever example of intellectual property, properly so-called, is discussed it will be seen that something embodying it already exists in a tangible form and is therefore capable of being copied: were it not, there would be no need, according to the theories and public policy considerations which have been responsible for shaping this branch of the law, for legal protection.

A third characteristic of intellectual property law is its general economic exclusionary approach. The grant of an intellectual property right, whether automatic or following some form of application and registration process, does not give the owner of the right any necessary ability to exploit their creation. That ability is determined by the intellectual property rights of others. Thus, the naming of a newly-introduced product, even if rights by way of registration have been obtained in respect of the name of that product, may attract the exercise of an earlier intellectual property right, in particular a trade mark right, by others where the new mark chosen is simply too close to one giving rise to an existing earlier right. Likewise, in the case of a patent, the ability to exploit a particular invention may be prevented by third parties holding an earlier patent right which

INTRODUCTION

would be infringed by such exploitation. Intellectual property rights are accordingly primarily a right to stop other people doing things: in some cases for a relatively short period of time, such as in the case of unregistered design rights, for a longer term as in the case of patents or registered designs, for a considerable period of time as in the case of literary, artistic and musical copyrights, or, indeed, essentially in perpetuity for trade marks.

In practice, therefore, the term "intellectual property" denotes the rights relating to producing tangible or perceptible objects or providing actual services which copy in some way an original object or service made or supplied by a person whose mental efforts created that original. To a very large extent, this has dictated the form of the rights granted to that person: ideas are not protected but copying the outcome of the application of those ideas is proscribed. Obviously, only something which is likely to be copied needs protection but, if it is genuinely useful, that protection should be granted in such a way that it does not prevent or discourage the dissemination of knowledge about it. The law does not make a value judgment as to whether or not the property it is desired to protect really is useful, but instead provides enough sticks and carrots to ensure that anything which could be exploited by copying is protected and, at the same time, to encourage the owner of the property to exploit it himself. Thus an author or inventor may be given the right to prevent unauthorised copying (a right which he can exploit commercially by making copies himself or by selling subsidiary rights), but this right is usually limited in time (which encourages the owner to make use of his monopoly while he still has it). In the case of inventions, this system is usually backed up by a state agency (once usually called a Patent Office, but increasingly called an Intellectual Property Office) whose function is to assist the inventor in protecting his intellectual property rights while also ensuring, through the public deposit of details of the inventor's work, that the benefits of that work are not lost to the community at large.

Ideas and copying know no national boundaries, so intellectual property law systems in different countries need to interact. Many countries are party to various international agreements which have been formulated as mutual protection societies to ensure that rights in one country are not rendered worthless by an absence of such rights in another country. There are international organisations to develop and monitor international progress, most notably a United Nations agency, the World Intellectual Property Organisation, whose headquarters are in Geneva and which administers most of the multilateral intellectual property treaties. A number of multilateral interest groups have emerged, particularly in the patent area, for example the "trilateral" of the European/US/Japanese Patent Offices. These groups seek to co-operate in important practical areas, such as work-sharing, as well as playing an important role in assisting the orderly development of policy, particularly but not exclusively in the field of patents, and concentrating at an international level. Intellectual property systems have also been the subject of attention in multilateral trade talks; the Uruguay Round of GATT negotiations identified trade-related aspects of intellectual property systems as a specific subject for study and reflection and this resulted, at the end of that round of negotiations, in the Trade-Related Aspects of Intellectual Property Rights (TRIPs) Treaty by

1–004

INTRODUCTION

which an increasing number of states are bound. The Doha round made further progress in the area of availability of patented medicines.

All international work in this area is slow, not only because of the inter-governmental negotiating process but also because of the difficulty of producing a centrally accepted approach which will suit all parties and which can be implemented uniformly despite the differing bases of the legal systems of the various countries concerned: Roman-Dutch law, the Napoleonic code and Anglo-Saxon common law. Some progress towards an "international patent" has already been made, and certain regional patent, design and trade mark offices are already in operation for some years. However, there is still much "global harmonisation" which is desired by business but which has yet to be achieved.

It can be seen from this brief analysis that although what the law of intellectual property is really concerned with is the protection of original intellectual effort, it is commerce, rather than intellect, which is the principal factor in the development of this area of law. Intellectual property rights are marketable commodities and it is therefore not surprising to find that on occasions they are subject to the general rules of commercial, particularly competition, law. As mentioned earlier, intellectual property rights allow their owners to limit the activities of others. If those others are competitors, the question arises at once as to whether or not that restraint is too anti-competitive: if it is, it may be illegal. Over the past 50 years, intellectual property law has received a great impact from competition law, particularly in the developing field of so-called "EU anti-trust" law, based originally on arts 85 and 86 of the Treaty of Rome and is still surviving in the TPEU (see App.3). The concepts of the exhaustion of rights and their possession (as opposed to their exercise) have been the subject of detailed government and professional scrutiny and the law in this area is still developing. Yet with the general governmental view that competition should be stimulated, other ways of preventing competitors doing what they wish are becoming less available and less effective, thus placing an ever greater burden on the intellectual property systems to hold a fair balance between preventing copying in order to provide a legitimate reward to originators and allowing copying so that all may freely use new developments which are believed to be "good" for national and regional economies. Much recent development in the legislative area may be seen as altering this balance, sometimes consciously.

Various recent developments are discussed at various stages in the remainder of Pt I but the point to be emphasised again here is that intellectual property of all forms is subject to a diverse body of laws which offers great scope, when approached from the right angle, for commercial exploitation. The following chapters examine those laws predominantly from this viewpoint.

CHAPTER 2

Patents

INTRODUCTION

These used to be called *letters patent* and many years ago (in countries which were still monarchies) were issued under the seal of the sovereign. Letters patent for inventions were but one of the variety of letters patent which the sovereign granted and, indeed, letters patent for UK life peers, for example, are still granted by the sovereign. All the somewhat archaic phrase means is royal or state document which is open to inspection by anybody, which might well be headed by the time-honoured phrase "To whom it may concern". Letters patent for inventions were awarded to inventors as part of a bargaining system between the state or Crown on the one hand and the inventor on the other. Nowadays, in the operation of a modern patent system, those participants are conventionally replaced by the state on the one hand, acting through the Intellectual Property Office, and the company which employs the inventor on the other. Patents continue, of course, to be granted to individual inventors, some of whom still exist and even thrive.

2–001

In order to understand the basis of the patent system it is still convenient (though changes in the law have rendered this technically somewhat unsound) to take the metaphor of a bargaining system between the state and the inventor. The impetus to set up the bargaining system arises from a view held by certain states that the progress of technology can be advanced by encouraging people to publish their new discoveries, techniques and the like. They therefore bargain with the inventor on the following basis: if the inventor comes to the state with an invention and reveals that invention to the state, then in return the state will reveal the invention to everyone else but, for a limited period of time, will restrict the use of the invention only to the person who brought the invention to the state, or those whom he permits to use it. Early patent laws more explicitly reflect this bargaining approach as the underlying basis of patent law than more recent attempts at statutory codification.

This simple approach to the state/inventor bargain requires more detailed consideration of two aspects before it can be fully appreciated. The first of these is the nature of "invention" itself, and the second is the way in which the state restricts the use of the invention to the "patentee", the person to whom the patent is granted.

Turning first to the question of the nature of an "invention", it should first of all be appreciated that the patent system is not designed to protect every new idea against copying by others. Essentially patent protection is available for inventions which are directly to do with manufacture, either because the invention resides in

2–002

a new manufactured article, or because it is a new manufacturing process. In contrast, certain things which can undoubtedly be described as inventive do not have the same directness of application to manufacture. For example, mathematical theories, medical treatment methods, ways of playing games and doing business, and computer programs have traditionally been excluded from the possibility of being protected by patents, although certain aspects of them may be the subject of copyright protection (see Ch.5), but these exclusions are being eroded, as will appear below.

Secondly, the way in which the state restricts the use of the invention to the patentee is by forbidding others to use the invention rather than giving the patentee positive clearance to use it. Thus a patentee's manufacturing or processing activities may be circumscribed by the patents of others but are generally in no way affected by his ownership of his own patents. It is, of course, to be hoped that the possession of a patent, by keeping competitors off, will enable the inventor or his company to exploit an invention exclusively without the competition copying that exploitation, at least for the number of years that the patent can be kept effective.

The fundamental bargaining approach between the state and inventor is nowadays very difficult to discern, since it is overlaid by the practical considerations of running the bargaining system. As soon as the industrial revolution started there was an immediate and enormous increase in the number of people inventing things and wanting state protection to enable them to develop their inventions, i.e. wanting patents. The system accordingly developed from a system of contacting various court officials and securing a royal grant to a highly systematised operation run by a special government office set up for the purpose and acting under the authority of a statute (currently the Patents Act 1977) and rules made under the statute (the Patents Rules 2007). Some aspects of this growth in the mechanics of the system deserve detailed consideration.

2–003 First of all, it soon became necessary for the inventor not merely to allege that an invention had been made connected with, for example, ploughs or leather, at the same time undertaking to make the information concerning the invention available to third parties, but to explain in detail, in writing, precisely what the invention was and how it could be employed. This grew into a statutory requirement for filing a description of the invention with the government office concerned, and for obvious reasons, principally that others need to be able to carry out the invention after the statutory period of protection has come to an end, the description has to be adequate, i.e. written in adequate detail to enable others in the field (conveniently thought of as competitors) to put the invention into effect in their own manufacturing processes or new products.

In addition to the requirement to provide a full description of the invention, the practice arose of asking the inventor to supply a definition of his invention as well. This definition had to be designed to do two things: first, it had to act to distinguish the invention in question from what had been done before, i.e. from the so-called "state of the art". Secondly, it was used to delimit the monopoly claimed, i.e. to define that area out of which, by virtue of the grant of a patent, other people were meant to keep. These definitions, which have come to be known in jargon as "claims", are little more than an attempt in wording accurately to identify an invention in terms which will enable someone assessing the patent to judge whether a given process, article or the like does or does not embody the invention, or does or does not fall within the scope of the claims, to put it in more formal language.

Much time is taken up in patent matters with the consideration of whether an invention is obvious or not, or whether it involves an inventive step or not, compared with what people were doing before. It is a matter for skilled value judgment and much time and effort has been expended over the years in the courts in arguing obviousness or lack of it in respect of inventions on which patents have been granted. While several lines of approach and, indeed, certain principles have emerged from all that litigation, every case on obviousness or lack of inventive step is peculiar to its own facts, and what is obvious to one judge at one stage in time does not affect what another judge or judges consider as obvious in some other field of technology at some other time. Much can be written about obviousness and, indeed, much has been written about it, both in the court reports and elsewhere, but it is beyond the compass of this volume to do more than indicate the problem area. It is sufficient for present purposes to say that obviousness usually represents the chief attack on a patent made by someone who wishes to destroy that patent.

Most industrialised countries now have individual Intellectual Property Offices which operate to grant several tens of thousands of patents per year, extending over the entire field of subject matter and what they protect varies from very simple to very complex inventions. International/supranational Patent Offices have also been founded to operate central patent application processing systems covering several (or more) countries. Of course, the system for granting patents as operated by government or even international Patent Offices does little more than provide a preliminary sieving and evaluation process. Detailed consideration of whether an invention is new and unobvious, against a background of expert evidence in the particular field and very thorough searching of the prior literature, is simply impractical for the vast majority of patents. However, the system is self-adjusting to this extent: if an invention is of little commercial value, then it does not merit having that sort of money spent on it. The originator may put it into practice, but it is perhaps unlikely that it will be widely copied, certainly not on a sufficient scale to make it worthwhile bothering to take any proceedings for patent infringement. If, on the other hand, an invention is important, sufficiently important to make it worthwhile for parties other than the patentee to consider whether or not to put the invention into practice, then an attempt may be made to destroy the patent or to limit its effects by the interested third party. Such an attempt is not very often made as a mere academic exercise; rather the approach often adopted is that of commencing to use the invention and considering the position if the patentee decides to take action. 2–004

OBTAINING PROTECTION

Patent protection is obtained by asking the government for it and paying the fees. Grant is not automatic in most countries. 2–005

PATENTS

In the United Kingdom, the grant of patents for inventions is now subject to the provisions of the Patents Act 1977, and it is useful to consider what is necessary to secure a patent under that Act.

Patentable inventions

2–006 First, the Act defines (albeit somewhat unsatisfactorily by way of exclusion) the categories of invention for which a patent may be obtained. Thus, PA 1977 s.1(2) states that the following (amongst other things) are not patentable inventions:
Anything which consists of:

(a) a discovery, scientific theory or mathematical method;
(b) a literary, dramatic, musical or artistic work or any other aesthetic creation whatsoever;
(c) a scheme, rule or method for performing a mental act, playing a game or doing business, or a program for a computer; and
(d) the presentation of information.

However, these exclusions are stated to apply "only to the extent that a patent or application for a patent relates to that thing as such", a phrase which might be thought to fail to assist in providing clear guidance. In the field of "software" or "computer-implemented inventions", it has received much judicial attention resulting in an unsurprising outcome: some are patentable and some not depending on the particular case concerned and how "applied" the inventive step was.

It should be noted, however, that, in practice, the same approach can give rise to different results in Europe and, more broadly, the United States has a much more straightforward approach, enabling inventive business methods and computer programs to be patented.

2–007 A further time-honoured category of invention which has often been stated to be unpatentable, though, in some such cases, on no very clear statutory basis, is a process for treating the human body for the prevention or cure of disease. However, this approach is subject to erosion; it was criticised heavily in a decision in the High Court of New Zealand ([1980] R.P.C. 305). In some countries, notably the United States, it has been possible to obtain patents for the medical treatment of human beings for some time.

In this area, the boundary between the "patentable" and the "excluded from patentability" categories is coming under increasing pressure because of developments in the fields of genetic engineering and biotechnology broadly. Following widespread debate extending over years as to whether an individual "gene sequence" is patentable, the unsurprising consensus is emerging that a modified gene sequence **can** be patented, while a natural one may be categorised as a mere discovery. An analogous area for dispute is how, if at all, to protect stem cell preparations for use in the prevention or cure of genetic disease.

Still under the heading of what constitutes an invention, it is necessary to have something which is new and inventive or, in the wording of PA 1977 s.1(1)(b) "involves an inventive step". In addition, PA 1977 sets out the additional requirement that an invention must be "capable of industrial application" (s.1(1)(c)) and this last requirement is the current basis on which the British Patent Office would undoubtedly reject a claim directed to a method of medical treatment (for the definition of industrial application, see PA 1977 s.4).

Novelty

As noted above, an invention, to be patentable, must be "new". The justification for this, in a patent system reflecting the bargaining approach described above, is that there is no virtue in the state granting a patent in return for a disclosure of something which was already known, in the legal phrase, something "in the public domain". There is now a statutory definition of the word "new" in this connection: PA 1977 s.2, states that an invention is new if it does not form part of "the state of the art"; and that splendid phrase covers everything which has been made available to the public in any way at all, e.g. by printed publication, oral disclosure or use. From a consideration of this, it follows that for an invention to be new at a given date, no one else but the inventor must know about it unless those people that the inventor has told are duty bound not to reveal it any further. In the classic words of Lord Parker in *Re Bristol Myers Co's Application* [1968] R.P.C. 146: "if the information has been communicated to a single member of the public without inhibiting fetter, that is enough to amount to a making available to the public" and a valid patent cannot subsequently be obtained. Thus, in order to obtain a patent, i.e. in order to come to a bargain with the state, the inventor must tell the state about the invention first, before he reveals the invention to the public in any other way.

2–008

The stress on timing reflects the fact that the consideration of novelty must be related to a given point in time—what was new last week is not new now. In patent law, the all-important point in time is the date on which the invention was first communicated, by way of an application for a patent, to a government patent office. This date is usually known as the "priority date", as the first filing creates a right of priority which can be invoked later in a second application for a patent for the same invention filed within a year of the first one.

As noted above, in addition to the requirement of novelty at the priority date, in order to be patentable an invention must involve "an inventive step". This is another way of saying that the invention must not be obvious. There are all sorts of ways of making obvious modifications to articles and processes which will render the modified article or process new, but there may be nothing inventive about doing so. For example, the motor car having a door held on to the chassis by five separate hinges may be totally novel, but could hardly be described as embodying an inventive step. As with assessing novelty, the question of whether an invention was obvious is also related to the priority date; it is obviousness at the priority date which should be considered.

The application

Against this background, it is useful to see how these general ideas are reflected in practice in the working of the current UK Patents Act and the associated Patents Rules 2007 made thereunder.

2–009

PATENTS

The general structure of the system is as follows: the inventor (or someone else entitled to apply for a patent on his/her invention such as the employer) writes down a description of the invention and takes or sends it to the Intellectual Property Office and requests, on an official form, that he be granted a patent (the use of forms reflects the traditional paper-based application processing, but most applications for patents are now filed electronically). The Intellectual Property Office examines what it receives to see if it is in good order formally and then to see if the invention is patentable and, while this is going on, it publishes the details of the invention, essentially of the application as filed, in order to disseminate the information. If, after examination, the Office thinks a patent ought to be granted, then the patent is granted. The examination process is split into two main parts, in the first of which—the search stage—the materials submitted are checked for formal requirements and a search among literature, mostly patent literature, is made in order to establish the technical background against which the invention as described and "claimed", i.e. as defined by the applicant, is to be judged. In the second stage detailed scrutiny is effected to ensure that the materials filed in support of the application are clear and internally consistent and the question of whether the invention as set out is really an invention, having regard to the prior art known to the Examiner (i.e. usually what has been revealed by the search), is then carefully considered.

Broken down into fine detail, the normal procedure is as follows: first of all, it is necessary for the inventor to write down a description of his invention and take or send it to the Intellectual Property Office, "filing", before the invention has become public knowledge. This clearly needs to be done early, usually in order that the inventor, by their own efforts, does not make the invention part of "the state of the art" (see para.2-008, above), whereafter it cannot be validly patented. The filing date, i.e. the day on which the Office receives the application becomes the priority date for the patent application in question. Normally the inventor applies or, if he is employed, his employer applies. The application is usually, though not always, made in the name of the person to whom it is intended that the patent should be granted (see PA 1977 s.7(2)). Questions of entitlement to the grant of a patent may be dealt with by the Intellectual Property Office in the case of disputes (see PA 1977 ss.8–12). In order to secure a filing date, the requirements are fairly minimal (PA 1977 s.15(1)), namely, that a patent is requested, the applicant is named and there is a description of the invention. No fee is payable just for filing—though fees do need to be paid to the Office sooner or later. These three things constitute the minimum requirement for securing a date but they do not, of course, enable the Office to deal fully with the application. All that the Office does do, if an application is filed with the minimum requirements, is set up a file, award an "application number" and "filing date" and then simply wait for the remaining requirements to be fulfilled. If the requirements are not fulfilled, then the application lapses. The remaining requirements for the search stage are to file claims (brief definitions of the invention), an abstract (a brief description of what the invention is and, usually, what it is useful for—to aid those who look at the published application papers later), and a request for preliminary examination and search and to pay the respective application and search fees. If these are not all done within a year of the filing date, the application is deemed withdrawn.

Search

Once the request for preliminary examination and search has been filed and the fees paid, the Office examines the case from two points of view, first, that of compliance with the miscellaneous formalities concerning typing, pagination, drawings and the like and, secondly, a patent examiner makes a search to see what material should be cited in the search report as the appropriate technical background against which the invention is going to be judged. This search is carried out, usually expeditiously, under PA 1977 s.17. It has to be carried out fairly fast if the request for preliminary examination and search is not filed until the last possible day (one year after the priority date), since there is a requirement (PA 1977 s.16) that as soon as practicable after 18 months from the priority date, the Office must publish the application papers as filed and a practice that, unless the papers as filed are inadequate to enable a sensible search to be effected, the search report is published at the same time. Thus, the Office is geared to carry out both the formalities examination and the search within the space of a few months and to communicate the results of such examination and search to the applicant.

2–010

At this stage the applicant can consider whether or not to proceed further with the application. If the search has turned up material which quite clearly discloses the invention, or something so close as to make the invention really rather obvious, then the applicant can simply abandon the matter at that stage. Indeed, if the applicant acts sufficiently fast, as soon as the results of the search emerge, the application can be withdrawn before preparations for its publication are complete and, in those circumstances, the description of the invention in the application is never published. This is not adverse to the public interest since the invention is effectively already known. The applicant does not have to react in any way to the search report, though he may do so if he wishes, e.g. by submitting amended claims. In contrast, if the preliminary examination has revealed deficiencies in the formalities—usually inadequately drawn drawings or the lack of a statement of how the applicant (if not the inventor) is entitled to apply for the patent, and giving the inventor's name(s)—then those deficiencies must be remedied. If this is not done, the Office will simply deem the application withdrawn. Usually there is no possibility of reinstatement if that happens and if, by then, the invention has become known (e.g. by virtue of commercial use having started) the ability to secure a patent is wholly lost. It is thus very important to react to problems raised by the formalities examination at this stage.

If the applicant does not withdraw the case, and provided any requirements identified in the preliminary examination report are met, the Office, a little while after the 18-month period has elapsed, publishes the application papers as a printed patent specification. These are numbered in a series starting at 2,000,000 and the number is followed by a suffix letter A to indicate that this is the publication of the specification as originally filed, and *not* of the specification of a granted patent. Publication does two things: first, it disseminates technical information, thought to be for the common good. Secondly, it enables third parties, who may be aware of material much more relevant when considering patentability than whatever is listed in the search report, to draw the existence of such material to the attention of the Office (which in turn alerts the applicant with the details), so enabling more constructive substantive examination of patentability to take place.

At publication, the full details of the application, including copies of most of the documents on file, become available online via the internet. This includes correspondence between the applicant (or his attorney) and the Office, and can be viewed on the Office's Ipsum database. As processing continues, the further documents arising during the examination process are added, so it is possible for interested parties to keep a watch on pending applications made by others. They may also file documents to assist the Office, for example, details of relevant prior art which has not been cited in the search report.

Examination

2–011   Within six months of that publication, if the applicant wants to proceed with his application, a request for substantive examination must be filed. This once done, the examiner then, under the provisions of PA 1977 s.18, investigates, to the extent that he considers necessary in view of the results of the search previously carried out, whether the application complies with the requirements of the Act and the Rules. The principal areas considered by the examiner are whether the invention, as described and particularly as claimed, is new and possesses an inventive step relative to "the state of the art" and whether the documents are internally self-consistent. To do this the examiner looks at the claims which have been submitted and holds them up as a yardstick against what has been described or done before the application was filed. If he finds, for example, that the claims, looked at as definitions, contain within their scope matter which forms part of the state of the art, then he will point out this fact to the applicant, who then has a chance to amend the definitions (claims) in order to exclude from them the earlier known subject matter. Quite clearly, the definitions cannot be any good as definitions of an invention if they include within their scope something that is not new, or something which is effectively obvious. Another example is if the examiner decides that the claims cover more than one invention. This can happen if there is more than one ingenious idea underlying a new mechanism or process. In such a case, the application may be split up into two or more applications (called a parent application and one or more "divisionals"), each capable of becoming a separate patent.

The examiner may carry out this substantive examination process several times, each time giving the applicant a further chance to amend the papers in order to overcome the objections which he has raised, but finally the examiner has to make a decision either to pass the application to grant or to refuse it. In the former case, the Office grants a patent to the applicant and sends him a "Certificate of Grant" to prove it. From the date of grant onward the applicant, now the patentee, can in theory stop other people using his invention. If the examiner, despite the pleas of the applicant, is not convinced of the patentability of the invention and issues a decision refusing the application the applicant may appeal to the Patents Court, a special court established by PA 1977 s.96 and forming part of the Chancery Division of the High Court. If the applicant still fails to convince the Patents Court that a potential invention is present, then, provided that the Patents Court itself gives leave, a further appeal may be made, under PA 1977 s.97(3), to the Court of Appeal, or, even in appropriate cases, to the Supreme Court.

It can be seen from the above observations that securing a patent usually takes considerable time, e.g. three or more years from when the inventor first applies. This can be very disadvantageous in certain industrial and commercial circumstances. However, if the Office receives requests for search and examination (and the respective fees) simultaneously, it combines search and examination, thus shortening the procedure, and time to grant can be further shortened by asking the Office to publish the application before the 18 months from the priority date have elapsed. The Office will not usually move a case through to grant before three months after publication, so that anyone who wants to make observations on patentability has time to do so. If commercial considerations arise, for example an early infringement by a competitor, the Office will accelerate the processing of a specific case even more.

Patent agents/attorneys

As can be seen, the system under the current Patents Act, as in previous systems before it, is fairly complex and since the nineteenth century a separate profession has evolved to act on behalf of people seeking patents. In the United Kingdom they are called patent attorneys (though the old title of patent agent is still used by a few) and the use of these titles is statutorily controlled. Under CDPA 1988 s.276, no one may describe themselves as a patent agent or patent attorney unless they are duly entered on the Register of Patent Agents kept for the purpose by a Registrar acting under the authority of the Intellectual Property Office. To qualify for entry on that Register it is necessary to pass qualifying examinations which are jointly administered by the relevant UK professional bodies, the Chartered Institute of Patent Attorneys and the Institute of Trade Mark Attorneys (as there is a separate Register for Trade Mark Agents, and the two Institutes, which have many members in common, administer the examinations for both via a "Joint Examination Board"). The patent and trade mark professions are regulated professions under the auspices of the Legal Services Act 2007 and the regulation is carried out by IPReg, the Intellectual Property Regulation Board; more details are available from its website (*http://www.ipreg.org.uk*). 2–012

The background to this legislation is the feeling that the public should be entitled to distinguish between qualified practitioners and unqualified practitioners whose competence it would be beyond the power of the applicant to determine. Quite clearly, an inventor who made a very good invention could be wholly denied his just rewards if his patent matters were not handled properly. Of course, the right of a person to file and prosecute his own patent application is still available to individuals and, indeed, is still made use of by some. It is not, however, a course that can be unreservedly recommended, particularly since the inventor himself is not always best able to take a detached or objective view of what he has invented, certainly not one sufficiently detached or objective to enable him or her properly to assess what has actually been invented. The skill of patent attorneys, however, is not merely the intellectual one of assessing wherein an invention may lie, but the practical ones of being able to reflect the invention in clear and adequately broad wording, and of knowing the extensive rules and formalities in the system of applying for patents at the UK Intellectual Property Office (and elsewhere,(see below). Since failure to observe the rules can lead to the application being deemed withdrawn (however meritorious or brilliant the invention) and since (because of the novelty requirement) it is often not possible to "go round again", the benefits of using only qualified patent attorneys are clear. Mention should be made of the fact that, in addition to the profession of patent attorneys qualified by examination, solicitors are able to act before the Intellectual Property Office in all matters as agent for an inventor or applicant. Most solicitors, however, prefer to see such work done by a patent attorney, particularly if the matter in question is of a highly technical nature. Only a small proportion of solicitors is qualified technically, while almost all patent attorneys have university degrees in science or engineering.

It is, of course, necessary in making and pursuing an application for a patent to pay certain government fees and if an attorney is used his professional fees will also need to be paid.

FORM OF PROTECTION

2–013   Turning now to consider that other aspect of the bargain noted above, namely, the way in which the state restricts the use of an invention to patentees or those whom they permit to use the invention, it is important to note carefully how the so-called patent monopoly works. The act of trying to secure a patent publishes details of the invention so that all may know about it, but the grant of the patent to the successful applicant restricts people other than the patentee from using the invention. It is important to remember that the restriction is placed on the people who are not the patentee, rather than any positive permission to operate the invention being granted to the patentee. A brief consideration of the results, were the latter course to be followed, will show why this is so.

Consider the first man to invent safety glass, i.e. two sheets of glass stuck either side of a sheet of transparent plastics. Assume that he invents it against a background "state of the art" consisting only of single sheets of glass which tend to shatter and do damage. Safety glass is clearly an invention, judged against that background, and he secures a patent, which can last up to 20 years. Consider now the man who, 10 years after the first man invented safety glass, invents a much improved safety glass, by the use of a particular material for the plastics interlayer. This, let us assume, is also inventive, so he obtains a patent too.

Now, if the grant of a patent were an entitlement to work the invention, the grant of the second patent for the improved safety glass clearly diminishes the "monopoly" held up to that time by the first patentee, the man who actually invented safety glass in the first place. The grant of permission to the second man to operate would clearly detract from the previous 20-year "monopoly" held by the first man.

2–014   In contrast, the system works the other way, and the grant of the patent simply gives the patentee a right to stop third parties. Thus, in the example given in para.2-013, the first patentee is in a position to stop anybody else making safety glass. This position continues to exist even when the second man comes along and secures his patent, which enables him in turn to stop anybody producing the improved safety glass, and this includes an ability to stop the original patentee of safety glass doing so. In this simple illustration neither party can produce the improved safety glass without the permission of the other. Of course, two reasonable men wishing to operate their inventions in the best possible fashion would each agree to let the other do so, but it might pay the second man to wait until the first man's patent runs out and then hope to take away his entire business by selling a better product which the first man could not produce.

The term of a patent, i.e. the time period for which the state allows the patentee to prohibit third parties from using an invention is currently 20 years in the United Kingdom and much the same sort of period outside it. The practice in the United Kingdom and most other countries is to pay for the operation of the patent system by means of fees collected from applicants and patentees. Since running a patent system in an Intellectual Property Office is rather an expensive business, particularly in view of the necessity to employ technically competent searching and examining staff, costs would be very high to the applicant if he had to pay a cost equating to the cost of providing those services as he used them. This would act as a deterrent to patenting, clearly not seen as good public policy, so for many years many countries have adopted an alternative approach by keeping the initial application processing fees low and then charging patentees "renewal fees" which must be paid annually if the patent is to be kept in force. These start at a modest level, but increase as the years pass and the patent ages. The theory is that if, after 15 or more years, the patent is still doing useful work for a company or inventor in excluding others from a certain field, then it is worth his while to pay for it.

As noted, the patent gives the right to the patentee to stop other people using the invention, i.e. to stop other people infringing. Infringement is a very straightforward concept and while in detail, in practice, it is sometimes a little difficult to apply, the principles can be very simply stated: the claims at the end of the specification of the granted patent are definitions, usually of articles or processes, which, it is alleged, embody the invention which has been made. In order to determine whether infringement has occurred, it is only necessary to take the yardstick of the wording of the claim and hold it up, mentally, adjacent to the possibly infringing process or product and see if it fits. The sort of question which is simply posed is: does the product or process under consideration fall within the category of all products or processes embraced by the defmition constituting (usually) claim 1 of the patent in question? If it does, then there is infringement and if not, not. This sort of question is sometimes difficult to answer, especially if it is difficult to see just what the allegedly infringing process or product does or is. It also depends on the construction of the wording of the claims (definitions), and that can be difficult sometimes. In addition even words with straightforward meanings should, at least on occasion, be given a "purposive" construction (*see* Lord Diplock's remarks in *Catnic* [1982] R.P.C. 183, at 244).

If a patentee decides that his patent is being infringed by a third party, his usual course of action is to ask the third party to stop, pointing out that he has a patent monopoly. This may or may not immediately have the desired effect and, 2–015 indeed, in practice usually does not, though it may bring the parties together for discussions to settle the matter on an amicable basis. This is discussed more fully below in terms of licensing.

If, on the other hand, there is no question of settlement on an amicable basis, and the infringement continues, then the patentee either simply gives up (e.g. because he cannot afford to litigate, or the infringement is, commercially, tolerable) or he asks the government to stand by its side of the bargain and stop the infringer infringing. The patentee does this by commencing an action before the relevant court, in England and Wales, the Intellectual Property Enterprise Court (the re-named Patents County Court) or the Chancery Division of the High Court. Cases may be brought in Scotland or Northern Ireland if desired in the appropriate court (see PA 1977 ss.98 and 130). The major object of the action is usually to seek an injunction stopping the infringer from continuing with his infringement or from infringing the patent in any other way.

The normal response given by an infringer to being sued falls into two parts. First of all, there is usually a denial that infringement is actually taking place. That denial may be more or less substantial in different cases. More fundamentally, however, in most cases there is an attack on the validity of the patent which has been granted to the patentee. In other words, what the infringer will say is that even if what he is doing falls within the scope of the claims, the patent cannot be used against him because it is a bad bargain made between the inventor and the state. The bargain can be bad for one of two types of reasons. It may be intrinsically bad, for example, because the invention is not one for which a patent may properly be granted or because the description of the invention provided by the applicant is insufficient. Alternatively, it may be bad because unbeknownst to the Patent Office and the inventor, what they thought was an invention, i.e. what they thought was new and unobvious, is not really so at all, but rather something that has been done before or something so close to what has been done before that there is no inventive step in doing what the applicant, now patentee, described.

2–016 Technically, the defendant in such a case raises a defence that the patent is invalid and, normally, counterclaims against the complainant patentee for the revocation of the patent. The matter proceeds as a civil action brought between two civil litigants, but there are special rules and practices designed to provide speedy and expeditious resolution of the dispute. Trial takes place before a single judge, usually, though not invariably, one of the specialist judges with patents experience, and judgment is usually reserved. After judgment is delivered there is an automatic right to appeal to the Court of Appeal. The judge will normally issue an order, if he finds in favour of the patentee, restraining the defendants from continuing to infringe. The order may also compel delivery up of infringing material and may direct an inquiry as to damages which have been suffered by the patentee as a result of the unauthorised infringement.

If an appeal is filed and subsequently lost there is a further right of appeal to the Supreme Court, but only, in accordance with the usual rules, on a point of law and with leave of the Supreme Court.

Many cases which are brought in the United Kingdom do not even reach trial, the parties preferring to settle their differences in some amicable fashion rather than face the time and expense of a legal patent action. It is not unusual for patent actions to require the assistance of expensive expert witnesses, the performance of experiments, attendance on demonstrations and possibly weeks in court, though this is now rare save in cases of major importance to two substantial litigants.

Even if the parties do not wish to be amicable, the court will often seek, at an early stage, to see if some form of alternative dispute resolution (ADR) can be effective. If it seems appropriate, courts will encourage parties to attempt to resolve their differences by mediation, and, in recent years, both the UK-IPO and the World Intellectual Property Organisation (WIPO) have set up mediation services to assist with patent case resolution.

2–017

Separately, and without any binding effect, the UK-IPO will issue an "opinion" on any question of patent infringement or validity in informal proceedings which usually take less than 10 weeks from start to finish. Asking the UK-IPO for such an opinion is valuable, as others can be involved, apart from whoever asks for their opinion, and the process can clarify issues fast and in a very cost-effective way; money spent on such an opinion may well substantially reduce, or even avoid entirely, the cost of subsequent litigation.

Although the provisions have never been used, it is also possible to bring infringement actions before the Intellectual Property Office, rather than before the court, but only if both parties agree (PA 1977 s.61(3)). Also, if there is a question of whether a particular process or product is or is not an infringement, the person who wants clearance can, if the patentee refuses to give it, apply to the Intellectual Property Office or the Intellectual Property Enterprise Court for a ruling (PA 1977 s.71).

The Intellectual Property Enterprise Court, which started operations in 1990, is now the preferred forum for settling patent infringement disputes. It has the same rules of procedure (CPR Pt 63, supplemented by a practice direction, PD63) and the ability to deal with any patent or design matter which previously would have had to be litigated in the High Court. A major difference in practice is that the High Court "standard legal team" of barrister, solicitor and patent attorney can be dispensed with—all three may conduct the litigation and may appear before the Intellectual Property Enterprise Court to plead the case, individually or in any combination. In both Intellectual Property Enterprise Court and High Court patent cases, written pleadings are now extensive and they, and case conferences, are intended to serve rapidly to clarify what is in issue between the parties and move the genuine issues to expeditious resolution. Most cases take less than a year from start to judgment.

EXPLOITATION

Turning now to the commercial rather than the technical aspects of patents, it is as well to reiterate that the patent does not give the patentee any right to use the process or in any way enhance directly the patentee's ability to manufacture or sell the product in question. His rights are determined by the patents of others, but his own patent is like an agreement with the state, whereby the state grants him a right to stop others using the invention.

2–018

This right, once technically known merely as a "chose in action" but now simply as a patent, is regarded, in the United Kingdom at least, as personal property, which can, however, be licensed and can be assigned (see PA 1977 s.30).

Assignment

2–019   Assignment is the easier concept. In exactly the same way as fishing rights along a river bank can be sold, patent rights can be sold by the patentee to anyone who is willing to buy them. It is customary (and necessary if the subsequent proprietor of the patent wants to take any legal action) to register the change in ownership at the Intellectual Property Office. In the United Kingdom this is governed by PA 1977 ss.30–36 and it is worth observing in passing that the effect of these sections is to render the registration of an assignment very desirable. If an assignment from A to B is not registered by B, B will certainly lose out on the possibility of collecting damages from an infringer C until B's name is entered on the UK-IPO database as the proprietor of the patent. Possibly more importantly, if A then purports to sell to C, and C registers his assignment before B has registered his, then, by virtue of PA 1977 s.33, the assignment to B is void. It accordingly behoves assignees to record at the UK Intellectual Property Office the fact that they are the new proprietors.

Licensing

2–020   Licensing is a very broad field in which a wide variety of arrangements is possible. The easiest way of thinking of licences is to think of a contractual arrangement between the patentee, who is the licensor, and someone who wishes to do something which, if done in the absence of a licence, would render him liable to a suit for infringement of the patent. Such a position should be at the heart of any licensing arrangement, but straightforward "no strings" arrangements between a patentee and a user, although the simplest cases to analyse, are not particularly common. Quite often, parties come to arrangements which cover more than one patent or more than one product type or more than one market. Different patents may apply to different products and patent licences may contain agreement clauses between the parties which deal with collateral matters such as exchange of technical information, purchase of special materials, communication of improvements and the like. However, patent licence matters can often be broken down into a number of component parts each of which is relatively straightforward to understand.

The licence granted by a patent licence to a licensee is a permission to do that which, in the absence of the licence, would be restrainable. Accordingly, patent licences should make it quite clear just what patent or patents are being licensed and what, if any, restrictions are placed on the licensee in terms of the availability of the whole of the patented field. Thus, if the consideration for the licence is a royalty payment on products sold, it is quite clear that in most cases that royalty should be payable only on products the manufacture of which, if carried out by an unlicensed party, would be an infringement of the patent. This is, however, a purist approach which is not always observed, sometimes for sound practical reasons and sometimes for no apparent reason at all. Patent licences have been known where the patents have been recited but royalty has been payable on royalty bearing products which have been defined in a way not coextensive with the protection afforded by the broadest claims of the patent. Such arrangements need to be looked at very carefully in practice, though they rarely give rise to very much difficulty as between a willing licensor and a willing licensee. Care should, however, be taken not to attempt to hang too much on too slender a patent licence peg, since if that attempt is made difficulties may arise, for example, in terms of the fundamental propriety of the licence or its effect, particularly its effects in relation to competition and anti-trust law. In this connection, it is noteworthy that one area of very substantial activity in the closing decades of the twentieth century by the European Commission has been an attempt to regulate patent licensing, particularly to prevent abuse of patents (and for that matter other industrial property rights) by their being used to cloak with apparent propriety an agreement between undertakings which was contrary to what is now art.101 of the Treaty on the Functioning of the European Union (see App.3).

Most licence arrangements take the form of a licence being granted from the licensor to the licensee with a payment by the licensee to the licensor as a result. However, the way in which licence payments are made varies very widely and, as will be seen subsequently, this can have a quite substantial effect on the ultimate return to the patentee.

2–021 The classical approach is to pay a licence royalty either as a percentage of net sales price or in terms of some fixed sum per article processed or manufactured. Percentage royalty arrangements have the advantage of being self-adjusting when the sales price rises. Fixed price royalties, however, need to be looked at rather more carefully and consideration should always be given in any licence agreement to including some form of escalation clause, either at a predetermined rate or, for example, tied to the general rate of inflation using some appropriate index. Additionally, or alternatively, royalty rates may vary in accordance with the amount of material produced or processed and in this respect, depending upon circumstances, it may be entirely appropriate and agreeable to the parties that the royalty rate rises or falls with increasing manufacture under licence.

In some cases, in contrast, the parties will agree for the purchase of a licence for a fixed sum, either by way of an immediate total payment or by way of appropriate deferred payment terms. Such arrangements are relatively unusual, however, not least because they saddle the patentee with a licensee from whom he may not be able to detach himself. This can be embarrassing if the licensee does not in fact operate the patent and some other party wants to take a licence. While the first licence is still in existence, the second party may be disinclined to do so.

To avoid this sort of problem, minimum payments are often specified in licence arrangements, partly to ensure return to the patentee and partly also to act as an incentive to the licensee to commence operating under the license. Care invariably needs to be taken to ensure that the intentions of the parties concerning any minimum royalties are clearly expressed. In particular, attention needs to be given to the question of whether the licensee can keep a licence in force merely by paying the stipulated minimum royalties, even if no operations under licence have taken place.

2–022   In addition to the obligations normally placed on the licensee in a patent licence to work the invention and pay appropriate monies, obligations are sometimes placed on the licensor. For example, it is not unusual for a licence arrangement to require the patentee to keep patents in force and neither is it unusual to find provision made in the agreement for the situation where an unlicensed third party starts to infringe. In those circumstances, a wide variety of options is open to licensor and licensee, ranging from no obligations on the licensor at all through to a positive obligation to sue. This last could be an extremely expensive obligation and more than erode any profit from the licence. It is accordingly one which should be adopted only with adequate safeguards.

A particularly important area of licensing practice is the question of termination. While, quite obviously, the parties are always capable of agreeing mutually to terminate, many circumstances arise where it is in the patentee's interest to terminate, for example, if production by the licensee is inadequate or fails to meet standards of quality or if the licensee goes into liquidation or is taken over by some third party whom the licensor feels is undesirable as a licensee. Very varied clauses may be set out in licence agreements to meet the varying circumstances of varying parties and various types of licensed product or process.

No discussion of patent licensing is complete without reference to the terms "sole" and "exclusive". The patentee who has (unless circumscribed by the patent rights of others) the ability to work his invention may wish to extend that ability to not more than one licensee. If so, then the patentee simply grants a sole licence and the effect of that is simply to leave the patentee and the sole licensee as the only two parties able properly to exploit the invention. This may be advantageous from the commercial point of view but of course it excludes the possibility of granting a third licence to an infringer who appears and leaves open, should third party infringement commence, only the possibilities of ignoring it or commencing suit to stop it. The first may not be very satisfactory and certainly cannot be expected to improve the relationship between the licensor and the sole licensee; the second can be very expensive.

2–023   In contrast, in the case of an exclusive licence, the licensee becomes the only person entitled to work under the patent, i.e. the patentee himself is excluded. Exclusive licences have been entered into on many occasions in the past and they can be very attractive to the patentee from a financial point of view. They suffer, however, from problems with regulatory agencies, notably the European Commission, which has expressed the view that in appropriate circumstances the existence of an exclusive licence can itself give rise to a contravention of art.101(1) of the Treaty on the Functioning of the European Union. The argument is that an exclusive licence is an agreement between two parties which has as its object or effect the prevention or restriction or distortion of competition since the patentee himself is no longer able to compete with the licensee. One way of avoiding this problem, though it needs to be deployed with care, is to sell the patent to the would-be exclusive licensee against a deferred consideration which is dependent on the amount of use made of the patent. A reversion provision, triggered in appropriate circumstances, may be very advisable.

In substitution for one or more separate licences with individual payments, royalties and the like, it is possible to come to package deal arrangements either from a patent holder to a non-patent holder or as between patent holders who may "cross-license" relevant patents or bundles of patents which they wish mutually to exploit. In some such arrangements, there may be no need for money to pass from one party to another, but consideration always needs to be given when such complex arrangements are being contemplated as to whether it is desirable for each party to have no net receipts and no net outgoings. Additionally, anything with a hint of a "patent pool" or "cartel" about it tends to interest regulatory authorities, either transnational ones like the European Commission, or national ones (e.g. UK Office of Fair Trading, German Bundeskartellamt, US Federal Trade Commission).

In recent times, a major stimulus to the development of patent pools has been the rise of modern communications technology, particularly in the "mobile telephone" area, where a single viable communications unit may need to use large numbers of patented technologies. Such pools are justified if they consist of patents which need to be used to meet international standards. In such cases, these are unobjectionable, in competition law terms, provided licenses are available to new entrants to the market on a so-called "FRAND" basis (Fair, Reasonable and Non-Discriminatory).

Finally, consideration always needs to be given when considering patent licences to questions of the ability to sub-license or sub-contract manufacture or processing on the part of the licensee and questions of so-called "exhaustion" in respect of the goods where patented goods are in question. It does need to be made quite clear to the licensee whether or not he is entitled to extend a sub-licence under his main licence and, if so, whether any restrictions are placed on such sub-licensing. Likewise, if the subject matter is a patented product, consideration should always be given as to whether a licence to manufacture and sell the product includes the possibility of the licensee sub-contracting the manufacture rather than doing it himself.

Exhaustion

"Exhaustion" is a term which has received much consideration in recent years in connection with alleged attempts by patentees to partition markets, most notably in the European Union, by the use of patents and restrictive licences. The approach which has been adopted is to say that once a patented article has been placed on the market with the consent of the patentee, or indeed by his direct actions. then the rights in such patents as the patentee may hold are effectively exhausted, as far as that article is concerned, in such a fashion that neither the patent in the country where the article is first placed on sale nor any corresponding patents in other countries can subsequently be used as a barrier to the free movement of those goods. The current position in the European Union is that intra-community exhaustion applies—i.e. goods placed legitimately on the EU market in any EU state by the patentee can be sold anywhere else in the European Union. However, "International Exhaustion" is not recognised, so grey market imports into the European Union can be restrained. The TRIPs agreement explicitly avoided the subject. Generally speaking, what is important to remember is that a potential licensee needs to take great care to ensure that the licence he receives from the licensor gives him all the freedom necessary to do

2–024

what he wants to and, in addition, that his customers are likewise free to use the goods (or occasionally the process) in the way contemplated.

INTERNATIONAL SYSTEMS

2–025   Until now only the basic structure of the patent system and the way it is put into effect in the United Kingdom have been considered. Patents however, are considered by almost all countries to be a Good Thing and were even obtainable behind the former Iron Curtain. In all cases the general approach is the same, save with the important but now rapidly becoming historical, exception of the United States in connection with the approach to novelty and filing. Most countries require application to be made *before* the invention is disclosed publicly (see paras 2-004 to 2-005, above), to a government office, and the office subsequently grants patents which have much the same effect in the country concerned as UK patents do in the United Kingdom. However, in the United States and a small number of the countries outside Europe, an application made after public disclosure, though only within certain limits, (usually six months or a year from disclosure) can result in a valid patent in the country concerned. In the United States, following the changes brought in by the America Invents Act which came into force in 2013, the rule is that the patent should be awarded to the first inventor to file for protection (as opposed to the old "first to invent" rule).

The international convention

2–026   Most countries' patent systems require the applicant to apply before the invention is disclosed **anywhere**—the so-called absolute novelty requirement. At the date on which the first application is made, the "state of the art" noted above is all that was known or used before that date. Accordingly, inventors who want protection in a lot of countries would obviously be faced with a very major problem of expenditure if they had to apply in all of them before the invention was disclosed anywhere, and thus, generally, before the inventor has any idea whether the invention is "commercial". This problem was solved in the nineteenth century by means of an international treaty which is formally known as the *International Union for the Protection of Industrial Property*. Informally, it is known as the *Paris Union* (referring to the diplomatic conference in Paris in 1883 which settled the basic form of the treaty) or the *International Convention.*

While this convention deals with a wide variety of matters affecting industrial property law, it is of particular note as it sets up a mutual arrangement between the Member States that avoid the aforementioned problem. A provision in the treaty ensures that the signatory states enact in their national industrial property laws a provision enabling a so-called claim of priority to be made by an applicant for an industrial property right (the treaty covers designs and trade marks as well as patents). Applied to patents, the system is quite straightforward: when an applicant makes a first application for a patent at a patent office in any member country (called a "regular national filing") making the application generates a "right of priority", which is why the application date is often simply referred to as the "priority date". Within one year of making that original application in the original country, he may make applications in other patent offices in the other member countries claiming the priority right so that the patent offices in each of the other countries will consider the application as though it had been filed on the same day as the original application in the original country. The original application is normally, for reasons of convenience and sometimes necessarily for reasons of domestic law and internal security, in the home country of the applicant.

About 140 countries are now members of the treaty and these include all the principal European countries and the majority of the developed world. Certain states have bilateral arrangements with other countries which work on much the same basis: however, there is nowadays a major incentive to join the Paris Union as membership is a prerequisite to membership of the Patent Cooperation Treaty (see below), and compliance with its major provisions is required by the TRIPs agreement.

Using the provisions of the Paris Union Treaty, therefore, an inventor or company can make a single application in their home country relatively inexpensively and then proceed to try to exploit the invention. The disclosure inevitably associated with such attempts does not adversely affect their ability, within one year of the original filing, to file patents for the invention in the other countries. If the invention is a failure and there is no commercial need to continue, the expenditure has been relatively small and the initial application may be allowed to lapse or pursued just in the applicant's home country. If, on the other hand, the invention is by that time shown to have potential or, even better, has actually started to make a profit for the applicant, then at that stage he can make a reasoned decision as to how much to spend and where he wants to secure foreign patents. The priority date system thus enables the inventor to protect himself widely but at a low initial cost.

2–027

Even the International Convention arrangements do not render the cost of filing foreign patents trivial, nor of protecting an invention in a number of countries something which is lightly undertaken. In the last third of the twentieth century, international agreements were reached which both made life easier for applicants by reducing unnecessary duplication of search and examination effort for the granting authorities in a number of countries, while maintaining the desirable effect of patents granted after a thorough search and examination commanding respect as they are assumed to be validly granted.

The Patent Co-operation Treaty and the European Patent Office

International co-operation in the patent field led in 1973 to three international treaties, two of which came into force in 1978. These two might be described conveniently as central systems intended to avoid the duplication of effort but which nevertheless grant national patents as the end result. The third treaty proposed the grant of a single patent having effect in all countries of the European Union; it was never able to command the necessary support, however, and has now been replaced by action under the provisions of the TFEU.

2–028

Signature of the Patent Co-operation Treaty in Washington concluded negotiations for a treaty which has, as one of its principal objects the avoidance of the duplication of search and examination in various different countries. It is administered by the so-called "International Bureau" of the World Intellectual Property Organisation in Geneva and works on the following basis: if an inventor wishes to secure patents in some of the member countries, he files an application at the Patent Co-operation Treaty Office (in fact, physically, usually with his own national patent office) which then remits the papers to the International Bureau which in turn sends them to a patent office with good search facilities, known as an International Searching Authority. The examiner there carries out a search and finds any literature which he thinks relevant to the consideration of patentability, and communicates this to the applicant by way of an "International Search Report" which lists out the material he found relevant and an "Opinion of the International Searching Authority" which says why the examiner considers it relevant. If the applicant wishes, the claims may be amended at this time (within two months of the date of issue of the search report), in order more clearly to distinguish the invention from the "prior art". The applicant may also, following issuance of the search report and the Opinion of the International Searching Authority, choose to move the discussion of patentability forward by asking for "International Preliminary Examination", optionally submitting amended claims with such a request. Following exchanges with the International Preliminary Examining Authority (usually the same patent office as did the search), a patentability report (called the "International Preliminary Examination Report") is issued, which sets out the examiner's considered view as to whether the invention is patentable in view of the material he has found in the search. If the international preliminary examination route is not chosen by the applicant, then, around 30 months from the priority date, the International Bureau issues the written opinion of the International Searching Authority as an "International Preliminary Report on Patentability".

As with the national systems of many of the PCT member countries, the application is published (including publication of the search report) by the International Bureau shortly after 18 months have elapsed from the priority date. Since most PCT applications are "second filings", i.e. they are in respect of inventions for which a first regular national "priority" filing has already been made. This is usually a little after six months from the filing date of the PCT application.

2–029 Search and optional preliminary examination are the so-called international phase of processing an application under the Patent Co-operation Treaty. Following these international stages, the papers are sent by the International Bureau to each of the national Patent Offices in the various countries of the system designated and to the several regional patent offices, so that if the applicant wishes, usually by 30 months after the priority date, though in some cases the term can be a little longer, the patent application can then be processed in accordance with the relevant national law. This may range from the national or regional office continuing the examination proceedings and making the applicant argue his case if he wants to get a patent, at one end of the scale, to simply granting a patent without any guarantee of its validity at the other. However, it is at this stage that the applicant must decide whether to proceed at all, and if so for which countries. If it is desired to proceed, action needs to be taken in those countries, usually including paying fees to the local office, appointing local attorneys and, very often, filing a translation of the specification into the local language of the respective chosen countries.

The Patent Co-operation Treaty system is useful when it is desired to delay the cost of patenting, particularly as it enables the cost of making translations into foreign languages of the specification to be delayed. The usefulness of the system is slightly compromised by the fact that some important industrialised countries (most notably Taiwan) are not members of the Treaty, but membership reached 148 countries in 2013. The system has become very popular with applicants: the number of applications made via the Patent Cooperation Treaty rises each year—in 2012 the number was 194,400.

The European Patent Office

The other major treaty currently operative is the European Patent Convention, which led to the setting up of the European Patent Office. This organisation, which has its headquarters in Munich but branches elsewhere, operates in a fashion very similar to a national patent office. The application is searched and if the applicant, following a review of the search report, wishes to proceed, then examination by the European Patent Office examiner then takes place. If the examiner is convinced that patentable subject matter is present, once the papers are brought into order and the claims directed to that subject matter, the European Patent Office grants not a single European patent but rather a bundle of patents in each of the countries which were members of the system at the date of application. These patents then rank equally with patents granted by the national patent office of each country. If they are to be kept in force then payment of annual renewal fees is essential. In some countries, certain formalities must be observed if a patent granted by the European Patent Office is to be effective there, most notably (and expensively) the filing of a translation (sometimes only of the claims) into the local language. The way in which the European Patent Office operates necessitated very substantial harmonisation of patent laws throughout the member countries and the substantive conditions set out in the national statutes of each individual country for patentability, the nature of patentable invention and the like, are now common to all member countries. As at July 1, 2013, the European Patent Convention covers 39 countries including all of the 28 European Union countries, most of the EEA countries and some others, including so-called extension states, certain countries previously parts of the Soviet Union or Yugoslavia, which have agreed to provide a local patent corresponding to the granted European Patent so long as certain formalities are observed, including stating that protection is desired in that country when the European application is filed.

2–030

The European Patent Office is, in the language of the Patent Cooperation Treaty, a "Regional Office". There are three other such "Regional Offices", the Eurasian Patent Office which covers most of the FSU in similar fashion to the way the EPO covers Western Europe, and two regional African Offices covering respectively most of the sub-Saharan Anglophone or Francophone countries (though South Africa maintains a separate system).

THE COMMUNITY PATENT

2–031   The third treaty signed in 1973 aimed to provide a unitary "community patent" using the European Patent Office organisation to grant a single patent effective throughout the countries of the European Union. Implementation of the Community Patent Convention (CPC) ran into numerous problems which resulted, more than 30 years after signature, in the European Union Member States deciding to introduce a "Community Patent" by regulation, rather than by multilateral treaty. A regulation was agreed in 2012 and, at the time of writing, work is under way on the necessary implementing regulations. The fees levels have not yet been set, and there are extant European law challenges with respect to some provisions and constitutionality. Collaterally to the agreement on granting "EU"-wide patents is an agreement on a European Patent Court, so that both securing a patent and enforcing it after grant could be done on an EU-wide basis. This agreement is also facing certain challenges, and it is unlikely that either system will actually come into operation before 2015 or possibly later. What is wholly unclear is how users of the patent system will react, especially if fee levels are set high. The ability to choose a subset of EU countries for grant by the European Patent Office will also eventually disappear, which may lead to certain users of the system electing to revert to nationally granted patents in the countries of interest, especially if that is still available even if, using the PCT system, the EPO has carried out the search and issued the opinion on patentability.

The international systems keep down costs by reducing the duplication of efforts by national patent offices, both at the search stage and, later, during examination, where there are now a number of agreements in place formally recognising the right of an applicant and national patent office to take into account the results of earlier interaction between the applicant and a different national patent office. So-called "Patent Prosecution Highway" arrangements are increasing, as well as the tendency of Examiners to watch, via the internet, the progress of applications in other countries corresponding to the one they are in the process of examining. This leads to increased consistency of approach. The systems also reduce duplication of work by patent attorneys throughout the world. Most UK patent attorneys are also European Patent Attorneys, the restricted class of people who are allowed to act for others before the European Patent Office. In PCT matters, for many countries, local patent attorneys do not need to become involved until around 30 months from the priority date, i.e. after the initial application has been made, the search carried out, the papers published and any preliminary examination report sought also settled.

For UK, the UK Patent Attorney can thus find him or herself acting first before the UK-IPO for the initial application, then before the International Bureau of the World Intellectual Property Organisation, for the PCT application, then before the European Patent Office when the case passes into the European Regional Phase and, finally, as the agent for the European Patent (UK) when the EPO has granted the patent and it ranks equally with United Kingdom patents granted via the national processing route.

If, by this time, the original UK application has also turned into a UK patent, one or other will be surrendered.

The United States

2–032
In the United States following the enactment of the America Invents Act in 2012, the principal differences between US practice and practice elsewhere, revolve around the stress placed on the role of the inventor, and the one-year "grace period" preventing the inventor's own disclosures from disentitling him to receive a patent.

The first springs from the Constitution of the USA, which reserves to **inventors** the fruits of their labours. For this reason in the United States until recently the inventor's employer, who may be entirely entitled to ownership of the invention, could not apply for the patent initially. Instead, the inventor had to apply. Nowadays, the company which owns the rights may apply, though the application must be accompanied by, or rapidly followed up with, proof of assignment from the inventor, who must in any case be named, and who must still authorise the filing by the company.

In the United States, the emphasis on the inventor was further reflected in the concept of granting the patent, not to the first man to come to the Patent Office with the invention, but to the first to invent. Thus in the past if two inventors made the same invention at different times and the later inventor files an application at the US Patent Office before the earlier inventor does, that did not stop the patent for the invention being awarded to the earlier inventor, even though he applied later. Nowadays, the patent is awarded to the "first inventor to file", and the later inventor, if the first to file, secures the patent.

2–033
For the same reasons the novelty requirements are different in the United States from those in other countries. The invention has to be new and inventive, but the relevant date at which the "prior art" ends, for most categories, is not the date of filing but one year earlier. Note, however, that the detailed rules applicable are not as simple as this: see 35 USC s.102. Thus in the United States it is possible to invent, reduce to practice and come out on the market and find that the invention is commercially worthwhile before applying for a patent. In addition, if the invention is made in the United States, the application to patent it must be made in the United States before any corresponding patent is applied for elsewhere (unless a permit for foreign filing is obtained first), and, in the case of a non-US originating invention, the application must be filed in the USA before the invention is actually patented, i.e. a patent is granted covering it, anywhere.

In practice, these differences of approach in the United States do not lead to very great difficulties or incompatibilities between the patent system there and those elsewhere in the world. There is, however, one caveat which should be carefully noted: it has long been the practice in the United States because of the one-year "grace period" to "wait and see" before filing. As noted above, this does not jeopardise the validity of the US patents which might subsequently issue on the invention but, of course, public use or disclosure in the United States before filing there, and accordingly before setting up a priority date, may well make it quite impossible for the inventor to secure any valid patent protection outside of the United States. Unless, therefore, interest is going to be limited only to the United States, it is wise for the US inventor or his company to file an application at the US Patent Office before the invention is released to the public. There is some pressure for an extension of the grace period approach to other countries, but while there is some consensus that it could assist in some cases, there is concern that any adoption by other countries of a "grace period" rule in order to enable discounting of disclosures made by the inventor before filing from counting as part of the "state of the art" which would need primary legislation in lots of countries to effect such a proposal would need to occur substantially simultaneously and everywhere. This may make it impossible to introduce such a system in practice.

PETTY PATENTS

2–034 Not all inventions make the same technical contribution to progress in their particular field. They may nevertheless be useful, and many legislatures, particularly those requiring a high standard of inventiveness for patentability, have felt in the past that some sort of protection was needed for "minor inventions". A variety of systems have grown up in individual jurisdictions and there is no uniformity of identifying name. The term "petty patent" may be applied to the concept generally for English-speaking countries, though the normal English language term for the Japanese type is "utility model". The French and Italians have "certificates of utility", while the German variety is almost invariably known by its German term "Gebrauchsmuster".

Protection by way of petty patent is generally characterised by being:

(1) of shorter term than protection by patent, and
(2) being obtained with no or relatively little formality.

Thus, for example, a German Gebrauchsmuster may be secured by filing an application to receive one accompanied by a specification and claims drafted exactly as they would be drafted for a patent application. However, there is no examination or search and grant occurs immediately and automatically.

2–035 In some countries, petty patent protection is restricted to mechanical subject matter, or at least to subject matter which can be illustrated in a drawing. However, in other countries the system can, for example protect chemical inventions as well.

Because of the rapidity of obtaining them and the relative lack of formality, petty patents can be a useful form of protection, particularly where a product with a likely relatively short market life is concerned, and where there might be doubts as to whether the item had sufficient inventiveness to support a normal patent. Manufacturing industry in countries which have petty patent systems tends to use such systems and in recent years several countries which did not previously provide such protection have chosen to enact petty patent laws to provide it. There is no immediate prospect of such being enacted in the United Kingdom, though there has in the past been pressure by way of a projected European Union directive. This was proposed on the basis that the current differences in availability of this sort of protection within the European Union could distort inter-state trade and hamper the completion of the internal market. The evidence for this proposition is thin. Generally, EU "small industry" enthusiastically supports the introduction of petty patent protection throughout the European

Union as it is perceived as a cheaper route to protection than the patent system. Large industry is generally opposed, mindful of the extra burden on industry *as a whole* of the existence of a large number of unexamined rights which materially would increase the difficulty of being able to be sure that one could proceed with any particular product or process without fear of infringement. No rapid change seems likely.

In terms of exploitation, petty patents may be considered as equivalent to patents for most practical purposes, though in view of their shorter term, licence arrangements tend to be shorter term also. If exploitation needs to be offensive, by way of an infringement suit, a prerequisite to bringing such suit may be to have a novelty search carried out by the national patent office of the country concerned so that the court and defendant may both have a chance of assessing the likelihood of validity immediately an action is started. Such a requirement acts as a deterrent to the owner of the petty patent right bringing actions for infringement casually and possibly oppressively, e.g. against smaller companies or individuals, but large industry fears it might be "held to ransom" if use of the petty patent systems (and the systems themselves) become more international.

CONCLUSION

Patents are useful, and can act at least for a short time to keep others away from encroaching on new technology, once the exploitation of a new invention occurs. They can be built up into a portfolio to secure a technological lead in a field and ensure that any competitor is kept at bay.

2–036

However, there is a need to have ideas which are new, and not obvious, and to use the complex technical legal systems to secure protection. Once protected, the invention can be exploited by licence or by the patentee's own manufacture, or both.

Patents are useful pegs on which to hang know-how and licensing deals and can assist in transferring funds. The printed specifications also constitute an enormous body of literature on technology (rather than science) which is generally available and can be usefully studied because it is all classified by subject matter, and is available in computer database form enabling relevant technical material to be located with ease and precision. In particular, all patents now in force in all the major industrialised countries which are members of the Paris Union can now be found by computer searching, making infringement clearance searches materially easier, though not easy.

CHAPTER 3

Designs

INTRODUCTION

"Design" is not only the least well-defined of the standard types of intellectual property, but the most subject to variation globally. Metaphorically, design law has long been the Cinderella of registered intellectual property rights, being largely disregarded compared to its two uglier elder sisters, patents and trade marks. The term "uglier" is only used by way of comparison, since aspects of form and beauty and elegance rarely figure in patent matters and only occasionally (there is some overlap as will appear below) in connection with trade marks, particularly their presentation as logotypes.

3–001

Originally, design protection was devised to provide encouragement to designers of manufactured articles who, particularly when those articles were for "consumer" use, took the trouble to make the items look good. The advent of mass production during the industrial revolution opened up and started to sensitise large consumer markets, and it became rapidly apparent that a well-designed article—from a pair of Staffordshire china dogs though to an elegant barouche—sold better. The design of consumer articles accordingly started to assume substantial importance and systems started to be put in place whereby protection could be achieved for a particular design provided that it was new or original, a copy of the design was deposited and the usual formal procedures associated with securing a registered intellectual property right were followed.

A major advantage of registering a design was that it provided the owner of the design with a clear right to stop others producing usually the same type of article that looked the same, whether as a result of copying or as pure coincidence. Traditionally, design law protects a particular design applied to a particular item, be it bicycle, cloth or perfume bottle. However, in the European Union at least, following a directive, the focus has shifted to protecting new and original designs as such—and irrespective of the "article" to which the designer applied the design. Infringement became broader, but, at the same time, in order to be validly registered, a design had to be new in the broad sense—nothing looking like it had to be known already.

Design registration, however, still provides a quick, relatively inexpensive way of securing protection for the look of an article and can be invoked irrespective of whether the look of the infringing article is as a result of intentional copying or unintentional near-identity. Not having to prove copying makes enforcement of registered design rights considerably simpler.

OBTAINING PROTECTION

3–002 In the United Kingdom, the registration of designs is governed by the Registered Designs Act (RDA) 1949 which is nowadays a heavily amended version of the original Act. The amendment took place in 2001, when UK design law was substantially amended to harmonise with design law elsewhere in Europe, in order to meet the obligations under the European Design Harmonisation Directive of a few years earlier. Under the amended s.1(2) of the 1949 Act, "design":

"means the appearance of the whole or a part of a product resulting from the features of, in particular, the lines, contours, colours, shape, texture or materials of, the product, or its ornamentation".

This is very broad, broadness underlined by the definition of product which appears in s.1(3) of the Act which covers any industrial or handicraft item (though it specifically excludes computer programs) and which is stated in particular to cover "packaging, get-up, graphic symbols, typographic typefaces, and parts intended to be assembled into a complex product".

This means that a design can, for example, be embodied in a logo on a T-shirt, a pattern on fabric, or the particular shaping or configuration of a vehicle tailfin. As is so often the case, there are some statutory exclusions stating that certain types of design are not protectable. These are designs which are solely dictated by their technical function and designs contrary to public policy or accepted principles of morality. Apart from that, any design is registrable if it has the two necessary properties of being new and of having "individual character". Individual character was a relatively new concept when the law changed and is defined as possessed by a design:

"if the overall impression it produces on the informed user differs from the overall impression produced on such a user by any design which has been made available to the public before the relevant date." (s.1(3)(b))

3–003 However, a design applied to or incorporated in a product which constitutes a component part of a "complex product", e.g. a car, is only considered to have novelty and individual character if, when it is in the complex product, it is visible during normal use. Just what this means has yet to emerge.

It is noteworthy that the definition of individual character is not tied down to any particular article or product to which the design might be applied. Thus, a design of a perfume bottle in the shape of the Eiffel Tower would not have individual character, even if no-one had ever thought of producing an Eiffel Tower-shaped bottle before.

In parallel to this, novelty means that no identical design or design whose features differ only in immaterial details has been made available to the public earlier on. Note that it does not matter whether the design was applied to something completely different earlier on. If the design (irrespective of what it was applied to) is old, valid design protection by registration is not available. Note also that disclosure of the design by its originator within the preceding 12 months also does not count; there is a so-called "grace period" enabling a manufacturer to see, e.g. which of a range of designs is selling before deciding which to register.

OBTAINING PROTECTION

3–004
The approach to securing a registered design is straightforward: an application is made to the Designs Registry in the Intellectual Property Office and the relevant application fee is paid. The application must include so-called "representations" showing the design, and even though registration is of the design itself, i.e. essentially detached from any "article", the representations usually show the design as it might be applied to a particular article and one of the formalities necessary is to identify, in the application, an article to which the design might be applied. This is straightforward for many three-dimensional items (car, soft toy, lampshade), but can be trickier where surface pattern or ornament is involved.

A single application can be made covering a plurality of designs, whether those designs have anything in common or not. Representations of the design, and an indication of a possible use for it, are needed in each case.

The Designs Registry, which is part of the UK Intellectual Property Office, checks that applications meet the formal grounds and, if that check reveals no problems, a designs registration certificate then issues, usually a few weeks after the application has been filed. The certificate is attached to a set of the representations of the design, usually photographs or drawings. In cases where the designer wants protection early, but does not want disclosure of the designs to occur until they are launched—e.g. the fashion industry—it is possible (on payment of an extra fee) to defer publication of the design for up to 12 months from the date of application.

The proprietor of the design, i.e. the person who can apply to register it, will normally be the actual designer, but not in the case where the designer is employed and the design is created in the course of that employment (where the employer owns the design), nor (at present—there is a proposal to align the position with copyright) in the case of any commissioned work where the commissioner owns the design. If a design was created by computer where there really was no human author, the person who made the arrangements necessary for the creation of the design is deemed to be the author and thus the proprietor of the design.

3–005
Even though the design is identified as being registered in respect of a particular article, the basic reason for that requirement is to enable designs to be classified in a fairly rough and ready way. There is a so-called "Locarno" classification for designs which curiously categorises articles into 31 different classes ranging from foodstuffs through musical instruments to machines and appliances for preparing food or drink not elsewhere specified, and a final class (engagingly called Class 99) which is headed "miscellaneous" and which is presumably used by classifiers to put items in, which simply do not appear to fit in any of the other classes. Classification in this way starts to make "subject matter" searching of designs a possibility, though this will remain for some considerable time a somewhat inexact exercise. However, the introduction of the Designview database (to be found on *http://www.tmdn.org*) is assisting in enabling searches at least to see if a design is registered in one or more of the major European jurisdictions.

The Intellectual Property Office maintains a database of design applications and registrations, and the data is available via the internet for all registered designs in force. Copies of the representations filed in respect of any design registration may easily be found and viewed if the registration number is known, and searching on the Locarno Classification is also possible. However, it is not yet possible—because there is no classification for the designs themselves (only for the articles to which they may be applied) to search for similar designs.

However, a manufacturer who wants to check whether a proposed item would infringe any registered design in force can ask the Registry to carry out a check (Designs Form 21, Registered Design Rules, r.3l). Two specimens of the design proposed or two representations showing the design (e.g. photographs or drawings) have to be supplied and a fee paid. The Registrar's view expressed as a result of such a search is not conclusive, but it is a prudent step to take if it is proposed to launch a new item in a field where design protection is often taken out.

FORM OF PROTECTION

3–006   When a registration certificate is issued (usually within a few months of applying), the proprietor of that registration then acquires the exclusive right in the United Kingdom and the Isle of Man to use the design and any design which does not produce on the informed user a different overall impression (RDA 1949 s.7(1)). Such right includes the making, offering, putting on the market, importing, exporting or using of a product in which the design is incorporated or to which it is applied and it includes stocking such a product for any of those purposes.

As with patents, the right given is a right to stop other people, and it includes a right to prevent both manufacture and importation of products incorporating or bearing the registered design or a design not producing on the informed user a different overall impression. The nature of the informed user will depend on the particular type of design in question, and seems curiously to depend also on the field of use, but it is probably rarely going to be a normal end user. However, infringement will be established, even if the article in question is not of the type identified in the registration and, particularly noteworthy, irrespective of whether the infringement was derived by copying from the original, or just by chance has come to give the informed user the same "overall impression".

In the United Kingdom, registration lasts initially for five years, counted from the original date of application. It may be extended four times, each time for a further five years, on payment of a fee.

3–007   It is of very great importance to remember that infringement of a registered design can take place without any ill intent or bad faith and without any copying taking place. If two parties independently conceive the same, or substantially the same, new teapot shape, one registers and the other produces, then since the shapes are substantially the same, the teapot as produced will infringe the registered design. In such a case, the so-called "innocent infringer" does get let off damages (RDA 1949 s.24B(1)), but can still be enjoined from further manufacture (RDA 1949 s.24B(3)).

There is provision (RDA 1949 s.1) for declaring a registered design invalid by any person interested on the basis of any ground on which the Registrar could have refused to register. Such actions are rarely brought before the Registrar, registered designs usually being attacked only by defendants in infringement proceedings brought in the Intellectual Property Enterprise Court or the High Court.

EXPLOITATION

As noted above, once the proprietor has his design registration, he can stop other people producing or offering for sale items which infringe it. The procedure parallels that for patent infringement (see paras 2-018 to 2-023, above). Equally, the proprietor can permit such activity to take place in return for a licence fee, either a lump sum, or a royalty, or a combination of the two, or, in certain cases, some other form of consideration. Licences and other documents affecting the registered design may be registered on the register kept for that purpose. Registration is valuable if court proceedings are contemplated as, by RDA 1949 s.19(5), documents in respect of which no entry has been made in the Register of Designs shall not be admitted in any court as evidence of the title of any person to a registered design or share or interest in a registered design unless the court otherwise directs. Quite clearly, the court will always take registration of a licence, or an assignment, in the register as prima facie evidence of entitlement. 3–008

As just noted, an assignment can be registered, and, indeed, should be, in order to claim entitlement if the registration is sold or otherwise transmitted.

INTERNATIONAL SYSTEMS

Many countries protect so-called "industrial designs" and this is usually effected by means of a registration system which varies quite widely from country to country. There is not that uniformity often encountered in patent and trade mark law, although design laws are covered by the provisions of the International Convention. 3–009

In a manner analogous to the one-year priority period for patents, there is a six-month priority period for designs, i.e. if an application to register the design is made in, for example, the United Kingdom, then, within six months, an application can be made to register in other countries claiming the UK priority date and the applications in those other countries will be considered as though they had been filed on the same date as the UK application. The British Registry will provide a certificate for use abroad, if so requested.

Although in many overseas countries design registration is virtually automatic and little searching is carried out, there is one notable exception and that is the United States. In that country, the Patent Office carefully examines applications for "design patents" and the procedure is very similar to the normal patent prosecution procedure there. The American Examiner will quite often issue an official action on a design patent application, citing earlier designs which bear some resemblance to the design applied for and asserting that the differences are insubstantial. Prosecuting design applications in the United States is accordingly generally much more costly than prosecuting design applications elsewhere, and "unobviousness" is a requirement for design patent validity. There is no direct parallel in the United States to the "Industrial Design" registration systems of other countries.

3–010 There are two major multinational systems for protecting designs, an "International Design" deposit system run by the World Intellectual Property Organisation, which provides protection in up to 69 countries via a single deposit (the relevant treaty is called the Hague Agreement) and the European Community designs system.

The United Kingdom is not a member of the Hague Agreement (though there is a proposal to join), but the European Union is, and accordingly any UK resident individual or company can use it, even though the United Kingdom is not a direct signatory. The system is administered by WIPO in Geneva. It operates by granting an international registration covering those countries chosen by the applicant. The International Bureau in Geneva tells the local national designs offices in the designated countries that a design has been registered, and the local designs office can, if it has concerns, raise them with the design owner However, such objections are very rare.

The Community Designs Office (the designs part of the properly named Office for Harmonisation in the Internal Market (Trade Marks & Designs)) located in Alicante, Spain, commenced operations on April 1, 2003 and it provides throughout the European Union design protection of identical scope to that provided under British law.

3–011 The fee structure and the ease of filing—which can be done simply and effectively electronically—is such that it is expected to become the design registration office of choice for many UK applicants and if protection is needed in three or four major EU countries, it is cheaper than going for individual national registrations. It is also very fast—there is no searching for earlier similar designs, and if all the formalities are in order on electronic filing, registration occurs a few days later. The system which operates the Community Designs Office is set out in the Council Regulation on Community Designs, Council Regulation 6/2002. The detailed operation is governed by implementing regulations made under that Regulation, and the Regulation is specifically designed to be wholly compatible with the earlier European Community Harmonisation Directive on designs. One point to note is that if a design is possibly invalid (due to being too close to an earlier published design), then an application to cancel the design registration can be filed before the office, i.e. one does not have to apply to the court. If one fears being accused of design infringement, then applying to the Office to invalidate the design may be a good tactical move, especially as if the design owner then sues, the court seized of the matter may well decide to suspend the proceedings until the Community Office has made a decision.

The success of what must be considered for almost all Community member countries a new designs regime will not be easily measured for several years, but it is to be hoped that major benefits will flow from the harmonisation and centralisation now achieved in Europe. Whether the focus on design as such, rather than on the article which embodies it, will lead to an increased investment in design, or will make suing non-competitors, e.g. the toymaker who produces a replica car, easier remains to be seen.

CONCLUSION

In summary, the simple major rules about industrial designs are: 3–012

(1) Designs intended for application to industrially produced articles, or which may be used by others to make such articles can be protected by registration, so long as the design is new and has individual character.
(2) Once the design is registered, the protection extends to any type of article so long as the design on the potentially infringing article gives the informed user the same overall impression.
(3) It is much easier to prosecute a copyist under a clear design registration than under copyright or unfair competition law, even if either of the latter can be made to apply, which is not always the case.
(4) Design registration is probably the quickest and cheapest form of protection available for a manufactured product. It is restricted in its scope, but it may serve as a rapidly usable weapon to keep down competition from competitors who copy your products.

CHAPTER 4

Trade marks

INTRODUCTION

For many centuries craftsmen and traders have sought to leave their marks on goods as a means of identifying those goods. The motives for doing so may be mixed, but at least one central component has always been to attempt to identify the product in order to promote repeat business. In some technical areas, for example, the manufacture of precious metal wares and ceramics, very extensive marking systems have been in operation for centuries and these serve as an invaluable guide to the historian or even to the archaeologist. However, their original purpose was simply to identify the trade source, whether that was a manufacturer in post-industrial revolution times or a craftsman. Additionally, particularly after the industrial revolution, trade sources included an increasing number of people who were not manufacturers but merely traders who placed identifying marks on goods which passed through their hands with a view to spreading their own reputation and thus promoting repeat business. At the same time, service industries started to develop, and there too individual operators needed to distinguish from one another, though often this was merely by way of the names of the founders, as is the case with many banks.

4–001

With the use of marks to identify goods or services with their provider arose the use of counterfeit marks, i.e. marks used improperly by those who wished to trade on the reputation of the original genuine provider. The object of doing so was to enhance the commercial prospects of the improper user at the expense of the legitimate user. It has long been held that attempts of this nature to secure a "free ride" or improper commercial advantage are wrong. Originally such attempts generally involved an element of dishonesty on the part of the perpetrator but nowadays, particularly with very substantial international trade, dishonesty is not a necessary component. What is, however, almost invariably present is an ability, if not an intention, to cause deception or confusion among those who encounter the marked goods or services, usually simply thought of as the relevant purchasing public. This has for many years been regarded as unacceptable and strong trade mark laws are one of the weapons in the state armoury against public deception, sometimes denoted "consumer protection", which many administrations regard as a Good Thing.

Not all markings associated with goods or services are "trade marks". For example, markings may indicate other attributes, such as date of manufacture, geographical source, compliance with standards or safety warnings, and their use may be controlled by other areas of law. Generally, a clear line is drawn legislatively between such markings and "trade marks", so that the former cannot be "registered" as the latter. However, an area of overlap developed in connection with certain very well-known symbols which, while protected by international treaty, are not protected by such treaty as much as desired by their "owners", the International Olympic Committee. The development of restrictive rights in connection with the 1912 Summer Olympics illustrated that there was a potential "association right" which those who market goods needed to take into account.

4–002 Other than the mention in this paragraph, this chapter does not concern itself with two particular categories of trade mark which might be thought of as "other markings" but which are, nevertheless, protected by trade mark law. There are certification marks and collective (or guarantee) marks. Both of these types of mark are open to use by a number of traders and so do not serve as an unambiguous indicator of origin. Use of a collective mark may be restricted to members of a given trade association or some other grouping, while use of a certification mark may be restricted only to those whose goods meet some set of independent criteria. Typical examples of this last sort of mark are the British Standards Institution "Kitemark" and the Woolmark. The use of certification marks is generally controlled independently of any particular trade or manufacturing source (for a statutory basis in the United Kingdom see TMA 1994 s.50 and Sch.2). The rules permitting use of a certification mark have to be open to public view, and this is achieved by requiring the rules to be approved before registration can be achieved.

Thus, in what follows, the term "trade mark" is used to denote exclusively marks used by an individual trader, or sometimes a consortium of traders or more than one trader by agreement, to denote origin or identify source, either on or in connection with goods or in connection with services.

The use of trade marks expanded enormously with the coming of the industrial revolution and the colossal expansion in trade in manufactured goods, and accordingly in the legislative history of many countries there appears during the nineteenth century a realisation of the necessity to set down quite clearly the law relating to trade marks and to unify practices which may have differed as between different areas of trade. This unification generally adopted as its central element the creation of so-called trade mark registers, i.e. lists of trade marks together with their respective goods or services and proprietors, which were maintained by the governments concerned. It had long been the practice in certain industries to control trade marks by the creation of a central register, often operated by the regulating body of the industry itself, and in some cases these systems were simply taken over by the states which set up a central state-controlled register. In almost all the then industrialised countries by 1900 there was some sort of codified trade mark law and a register of trade marks.

4–003 The system of registering trade marks on an independently maintained, statutory register still left the individual tradesman, craftsman or manufacturer free to adopt and use any trade mark which he pleased (provided, of course, that such use was not misleading or confusing) and there has never been any necessity, at least as far as most countries are concerned, to secure trade mark registration before a mark could be used and trade commenced. Instead, what the registration system provides is a register covering all classes of goods and services on which traders may enter notice of their rights, both as a warning to others of their existence and to form a statutory right on the basis of which action can be taken.

Trade mark registers are open to inspection by any member of the public in order that they may be searched with a view to ascertaining the freedom or otherwise to use a particular mark. Of course, such a search cannot be exhaustive in the sense of giving a positive clearance, since not all marks in use are necessarily on the register, but it does provide a valuable starting point and nowadays a check at the trade mark registries of several industrialised countries is a sine qua non prior to the application of a new trade mark to a new line of goods which is to be manufactured and sold in substantial quantities or to the adoption of a new mark for a service business. The risks of running into a problem if such a check is not carried out, and the consequent possible expense of renaming and remarking products, or reprinting stationery, are generally unacceptable. Indeed, now that business is, because of the internet, effectively global rather than local, broad geographical searching to "clear" the use of a new mark is a wise investment, even though the cost of such clearance searches can be substantial, especially if one's first (and second, etc.) choice of mark proves identical to or too close to avoid confusion with marks already registered by others.

OBTAINING PROTECTION

In the United Kingdom, the registration of trade marks is governed by TMA 1994 under which is maintained the Register of Trade Marks (TMA 1994 s.63) on which details of all registrations are entered, and which continues the statutory office of the Registrar. This office is common with that of the Comptroller General of Patents, and the Trade Marks Registry forms a branch of the United Kingdom Intellectual Property Office (still legally the Patent Office) and operates from the same premises.

4–004

REGISTRABLE MARKS

Any sign capable of being represented graphically and which is capable of distinguishing goods or services of one undertaking from those of other undertakings can be registered. Thus, both word marks and so-called device marks or symbols can be registered as trade marks, but they must be capable of being distinctive of goods or services rather than merely being descriptive. Thus a picture showing the type of goods in question or a word describing the nature or quality of the goods or services in question will not be registrable unless (usually due to very unusual circumstances) it has in fact become distinctive. A word with no direct reference to the quality or character of the goods or services, or a picture of some different good may well be registrable: for example, a picture of a swallow is registrable in respect of ballpoint pens, or of a penguin in respect of dry cleaning services. The most distinctive sort of mark which has the merit of memorability is, of course, the invented word. The most famous invented word

4–005

mark is probably the word "Kodak". Care must always be taken when inventing words in one language to ensure that they do not have some specific meaning, particularly a pejorative or improper meaning, in another.

When applying to register a trade mark, it is necessary to specify the goods or services in respect of which registration is desired (Trade Marks Rules 2008 r.8). An application to register can be made in respect of goods or services in one class only, or for both goods and services, and for any number of classes.

The goods or services for which registration is sought are generally expressed in general terms but for convenience of classifying them it is also necessary to state the class in which they fall. Most countries now use the so-called International Classification of Goods and Services. The 34 classes of goods and 11 classes of services covered by this classification appear as a Schedule to the Trade Marks Rules.

THE APPLICATION

4–006　Under TMA 1994, in order to secure registration of a trade mark application must be made on the prescribed form and the prescribed fee paid. Both of these conditions may be fulfilled by online filing using the internet. The application needs to state the name of the proprietor, and his address, include a representation of the mark, and state the goods or services in respect of which registration is desired. The Trade Marks Registry then conducts an examination of the application to see whether the mark intrinsically qualifies for registration, i.e. whether the mark is of a type which can be registered as a trade mark as falling within TMA 1994 s.3.

A mark cannot be registered if it cannot be "represented graphically", so there may be problems with "non-standard" marks like smells or noises.

Subject to the condition that if one can prove by evidence that a mark is distinctive in fact, it can be registered, the following types of mark cannot, prima facie, be registered:

(1) marks devoid of any distinctive character;
(2) marks consisting exclusively of signs or indications which may serve in trade to designate characteristics of the goods or services in question, e.g. their type, quality, geographical origin, purpose or value; and
(3) marks consisting exclusively of signs or indications customary in current language or in bona fide and established practices in the trade in question.

4–007　In such cases, evidence of acquired distinctiveness must be supplied if the objection is to be overcome (TMA 1994 s.3(1)).

The registry can also object to registering marks the use of which would not be entitled to protection in the courts for any reason, or the use of which would be contrary to public policy or morality, or is deceptive (TMA 1994 s.3(3) and (4)).

In addition to this evaluation of the mark's intrinsic qualities, the Registrar also conducts a search of other marks on the register or the subject of earlier filed applications to see if there are any identical or similar marks already registered or applied for in respect of identical or similar goods or services. This includes, on a somewhat ad hoc basis, looking at marks applied for or registered in respect of services where those services are intimately connected with the goods applied for or vice versa. The search extends to all applications or registrations effective in the UK, including marks registered or applied for at the Community Trade Mark Office, and marks registered in the international register where the United Kingdom is a designated state. If the Registrar finds what s/he considers to be one or more relevant marks when this search is effected, the applicant is provided with the details of the earlier marks, but this is essentially advisory, though the applicant can object that some or all of the marks "cited" should *not* have been, and is given an opportunity (rarely taken but always offered) to amend the statement of goods or services with a view to avoiding one or more particular citations.

Once the Registrar is satisfied as to intrinsic registrability and a short time for objections to the list of relevant marks found by the search has expired, the Office "accepts" the application and causes the details of it to be electronically published in the weekly *Trade Marks Journal*. At the same time the Office notifies the owners of any earlier UK national registrations or international registrations effective in the UK by virtue of a national UK designation in it (see para.4–019, below) which were cited. Within two months from publication, an opposition may be filed by any interested third party on the basis of any intrinsic grounds on which the application might be refused, or on the basis of any earlier mark owned or used by them, even if that mark is not registered. If no one opposes, or if an opposition is resolved in favour of the applicant, then the mark is registered with effect from the date on which application was made. This is subject to a small caveat: if someone, on seeing an application advertised, does not wish to oppose, but does feel that for some reason the mark should not be registered, he or she can file "observations" at the Trade Marks Registry. These are communicated by the Registry to the applicant. If the Registrar thinks the observations reveal problems, then these must be resolved before the mark is registered.

4–008

In the United Kingdom, it usually takes (for an unopposed application) between four and eight months to obtain registration. However, if evidence of distinctiveness needs to be collected, or if a third party opposes registration, the time from application to registration (if achieved) can be several years.

Once registration has been secured it can be retained forever, provided that the registration is kept in force by paying renewal fees every 10 years and is kept in use. This gives a very substantial term to arrangements involving trade marks but this term perforce reflects the long term over which genuine trading reputations can extend. Of course, if a mark ceases to be used, then that reputation starts to evaporate and after a given time (five years in the United Kingdom (TMA 1994 s.46)) the mark can be removed from the register ("revoked") for non-use.

FORM OF PROTECTION

Entry of a mark on the register gives the proprietor the ability to say effectively: "My trade mark is on the register. It is therefore up to anyone who trades, and who can of course see that my mark is registered, to keep away from using, on

4–009

goods like mine or in respect of services of the same kind as I provide, any mark which is the same or confusingly similar. If despite this someone does use such a mark, then the fact that I have registered my mark gives me a *prima facie* right to stop them using their confusingly similar mark and, if they will not stop when asked politely, I will take action in the courts to compel them to stop."

This conversion of what might be described as a common law right (see Ch.6 for discussion of passing off) to a so-called prescriptive right is of very substantial importance. Not only does it create a position in which the original trade mark adopter and user can take legal action on the basis of a specific statutorily registered right, but it relieves him of the initial responsibility of demonstrating that the right in question is one which he ought to enjoy. In the contrasting case where a trader has had his mark appropriated by a third party improperly but the mark is not registered, the first trader always had to demonstrate, as a prerequisite for any success in court, that he had used his mark and thereby acquired a reputation or "goodwill" arising out of its use. This pre-requisite is still necessary in passing-off cases, but the burden of proof is difficult, and indeed often very expensive, to discharge. Providing that proof might also have adverse consequences such as the necessity of revealing the trading pattern of the original trader, including figures for trading, how the trade is carried on and the provision of examples and evidence from people in the trade. The provision of the statutory register and trade mark statute law avoids the trouble and expense of proving reputation and use, at least as a necessary step to stopping improper use. The ability to rely on such a prescriptive right, to say "this is my territory and you infringe on it at your peril", vastly simplifies disputes concerning marking.

Registration gives the proprietor of the mark the exclusive right to use it in respect of the goods or services, save for two notable exceptions (see TMA 1994 ss.10 and 11). The first of these allows the use of a trade mark in connection with goods adapted for use in connection with particular trade marked goods, for example, as accessories or spare parts. The second exempts from infringement of a registration of mark "A" the use of mark "B", where the marks are identical or nearly resemble each other and have both been registered, if mark "B" is used only on goods or services in respect of which it has been registered. These exceptions operate only if the use in question is in accordance with honest business practice.

Infringement

4–010 Basically, the right to proceed against others is limited to cases where the use is of the same or a confusingly similar mark on goods or services which are the same or similar to the goods or services in respect of which the mark is registered. Thus, if someone had registered a mark for "silverware", use of the same or of a similar mark on "goldware" by an unauthorised third party would be an infringement, Likewise, a registration in respect of "insurance services" could well be infringed by the use of the same mark by a third party for banking services, but that would be the case only if consumers saw the services as similar or likely to be related. Much will depend on the particular circumstances of each case. Thus, in the celebrated *British Sugar* case ([1996] R.P.C. 281) a "toffee spread" for putting on, e.g. toast was found to be not too similar to a dessert topping syrup.

Additionally, the 1994 Trade Marks Act introduced a new form of infringement where the mark registered has a reputation, and the use by a third party is on non-similar goods or services. If the use would cause detriment to the registered mark, it will infringe. Section 10(3) is thought to have analogous effects to the "anti-dilution" sections in some foreign trade mark laws (notably those in the United States), but there is no reported case which explores this section in any detail. The introduction of this form of infringement rendered "defensive registration" unnecessary.

If someone infringes, and refuses to stop after the infringement has been drawn to their attention, action can be taken in the Intellectual Property Enterprise Court (the re-named Patents County Court) or in the High Court to restrain infringement. The relief sought is usually an injunction and an inquiry as to damages, the former being by far the more important. The defences to infringement are usually simply that the respective marks are not confusingly similar, or that the goods or services in respect of which the alleged infringement is taking place are not covered by the registration or sufficiently similar or related thereto to cause confusion.

Validity of the registration is rarely called into question; however, a counter-attack is sometimes mounted if the owner of the registration has allowed his mark to become generic, so that it has ceased to function as a trade mark, so enabling the defendant, if successful, to have the mark removed from the register.

EXPLOITATION

Positive exploitation of registered trade mark rights (other than relying on them merely as a defensive measure) is a relatively modern phenomenon.   **4–011**

Originally, a very harsh approach was taken to the question of use of a registered trade mark by anyone other than its originator and original user, even if the trade mark proprietor was prepared to agree, it being felt that use by anyone other than the registered proprietor of the mark was effectively deceptive. With the liberalisation of trade and the growth of extensive trade practices inconsistent with this idealist approach, this is no longer the case and the practice has grown up of enabling marks to be properly used either by their original proprietor or by somebody who is licensed or permitted to use the mark.

Licensing and permitted use arrangements

Nowadays, the use of a particular trade mark on particular goods or services may be genuine in one of two different sets of circumstances: the first is, of course, the case where the goods are produced or the services rendered by the actual owner of the trade mark, who is usually the proprietor of the trade mark registration. The second is that the goods are produced or services rendered by some third party which may or may not have any other commercial connection with the proprietor, but which has an arrangement with the proprietor whereby the goods or services   **4–012** are in some way sanctioned or franked with the proprietor's approval. The usual approach is to say that the mark may be used by the third party under licence provided that the goods or services in question meet standards of quality laid down from time to time by the registered proprietor. Thus, to the member of the public who sees the goods or an advertisement for the services, the trade mark now indicates either that the goods or services emanate from the original proprietor of the trade mark, or that they are offered in the market with his approval. It is usually assumed that the proprietors of trade marks will jealously guard the reputation of their own manufacture, their own goods or their own services by ensuring that all products or services placed on the market under licence meet the high quality standards of their own product or service and, indeed, it is clearly commercially desirable in many cases to ensure that they do so. However, it should be remembered that there is nothing to stop a trade mark proprietor allowing a third party to manufacture under licence products of a markedly inferior nature with the proprietor's mark still stamped on them and with the manufacturers of the inferior goods securing an advantage for which they are prepared to pay the proprietor by virtue of the enhanced sales which the use of the mark is presumed to confer. Whether it does and whether it will continue to do so in the case of goods that are not of adequate quality is, of course, a very interesting question; generally speaking, proprietors effectively reserve to themselves the right to vary the quality of the goods they sell in response to market demand, availability of materials and so on, but they rarely allow such latitude to their licensees. Similar considerations apply in respect of services.

In the United Kingdom (and some other countries) it is possible (though not mandatory) to register permitted use arrangements, registration generally conferring the benefit that use by a licensee is deemed to be made by the proprietor and can be relied upon in any attack on the mark by virtue of alleged non-use. In the United Kingdom the provisions of TMA 1994 ss.28–31, govern the position of licensees.

Trade mark licence arrangements can be made as such or they may form part of overall arrangements between trade mark owners and users of the mark in a wide variety of circumstances. Trade marks can be particularly useful in identifying new products, particularly when the products are incapable of being protected from exploitation by others by patents.

Assignment

4–013   It should be observed that in addition to being licensed a trade mark registration is something which can be assigned. Generally speaking, trade marks are assigned with the business in respect of which the marks are used, but this need not always be the case. Sometimes assignments are effected of marks "without goodwill", either because there is effectively no subsisting goodwill or because of certain other difficulties which can arise. For example, where a registration is used on goods both for home consumption and for export, the proprietor may wish to sell the overseas business, and if so he may wish to assign the marks in the exporting countries and additionally to assign the registration of the mark in the country of manufacture only in respect of exports. Part assignment of a registration in this way is permitted, as is assignment in respect of part only of the goods or services in respect of which the mark was registered. The registration then effectively splits into two (or more) registrations, each of which must be separately maintained if the overall original extent of protection is to continue.

Franchising

One particularly important area, particularly in recent years, of exploiting trade mark rights, especially in the service industries, is the use of so-called franchise arrangements in which the proprietor of a business pays a fixed fee or royalty for the right to use a licensor's name and trade mark. A classic example of this kind is the trade mark "Wimpy" in respect of the provision of fast food services, both in terms of the sale of items such as hamburgers and in respect of the provision of restaurant services. The franchisor takes care of product and market development and national advertising, which of course enures to the benefit of all the franchise holders, or franchisees as they are called. Franchisees in turn secure the benefit of the reputation and, they believe, do better business than they otherwise would. Franchise agreements often include a number of other contractual terms; in particular, they often require the franchisee to obtain his supplies of raw materials from the franchisor or from an approved source. The subject of franchising agreements is, however, one of substantial complexity and capable of great development. Reference should be made to specialist works on the subject for detailed forms and precedents.

4–014

INTERNATIONAL SYSTEMS

The basic framework

The International Convention (see para.2–026) covers trade marks as well as patents (though coverage of trade marks used on services is not as effective as that for goods marks). There is a priority claim system with a priority period of six months, *not* one year as for patents, but it is little used since there is no requirement (in contrast to the position applying to inventions where application must be made before knowledge of the invention comes into the public domain) to apply to register before use has commenced. In some countries (e.g. the United States and Canada), although application can be made prior to use, registration will not be effected prior to use commencing. The Convention also provides that member countries will legislate to give special protection to "famous marks"—in the United Kingdom this is reflected in TMA 1994 s.56—and to enable the retrieval of a principal's mark for which the agent has, without authorisation, secured registration (TMA 1994 s.60).

4–015

The intricacies of trade mark law and registration are substantial and there is much variation in detail throughout the world. Accordingly, as with patents, a profession has grown up to deal with the matter. Most patent attorneys or patent attorney firms handle trade mark work, and in many countries, of which the United Kingdom is one, there is in addition a substantial professional body which deals solely with trade marks.

Most countries nowadays use the International Classification of Goods and Services to categorise applications and registrations (though Canada does not use a classification system at all). Countries which for many years did not use the International Classification but adopted it later usually applied a "reclassification" to existing registrations, usually on renewal.

Two slightly different approaches are adopted in various countries to the question of how specifically goods and services have to be described. Some countries, particularly the United States, make the registrant specify very precisely the goods or services on which he is using or proposing to use the mark and will, in practice, allow registration only in respect of a relatively narrow specification. However, in those countries it is general that infringement will be committed by a trader who uses the same or a confusingly similar mark on those goods or services or on goods or services of a like kind. In many other countries, a very broad description of goods—e.g. "foodstuffs"—or services—e.g. "financial services", is acceptable.

The EU system of registration

4–016   The European Community, as part of its work towards facilitating a true "common market", provided two initiatives in the trade marks area. The first was a Directive on harmonisation of national trade mark laws. This Directive was collateral to the 1992 completion of the internal market and compelled all EU countries to adopt certain basic common elements in their trade mark law. It also laid the ground for the second, namely the Community Trade Mark Regulation. The latter sets up a system of trade mark registration which is operated by the Office for Harmonisation in the Internal Market (Trade Marks and Designs), usually simply referred to (even though the EU design system is now operating from the same offices) as the Community Trade Marks Office ("CTMO"). It opened for business (in Alicante, Spain) on April 1, 1996, and grants trade mark and design registrations which are unitary throughout the European Union.

The working languages of the CTMO are English, French, German, Spanish and Italian, though applications can be filed in any one of the other official languages of the European Union (though in such a case a second language, which must be one of the five specified, must also be chosen, in which communications with the CTMO are carried out).

The CTMO examines applications for intrinsic registrability, and, if the applicant has, when applying, asked for a search to be carried out in national registers, advises those national trade mark offices which have agreed to carry out such searches details of the applications it has received. The national offices search their own registers for possibly conflicting marks, report in a rather superficial and standardised way any they find to the CTMO, and the CTMO forwards the report(s) to the applicant, but the CTMO does not, at that stage, make any assessment of any possible conflict with existing registrations or earlier applications. The CTMO carries out its own search in earlier Community applications and registrations to see if there are any possibly conflicting marks, and it draws the attention of the applicant to their existence.

If the CTMO is satisfied that a mark is intrinsically registrable, it advertises the details in the *Community Trade Mark Bulletin*, and tells the owners of any earlier potentially conflicting Community registrations or applications that it is doing so.

4-017

Advertisement starts a three-month term for oppositions by third parties which have to be based on rights which those parties hold, e.g. a national registration in an EU country, or an earlier Community trade mark registration. In opposition proceedings, the CTMO adjudicates whether bearing in mind the similarity or identity of the goods or services, a later mark is too similar to an earlier one to allow registration, and can refuse registration wholly or partially.

If no opposition is filed, or one is resolved in favour of the applicant, then the mark is registered. The registration is renewable every 10 years. A Community registration ranks equally in all countries of the European Union with its national registrations, and, to the extent that a proprietor may have overlapping national registration of the same mark, the effects of the national registration(s) are suppressed while the Community registration remains in force.

If an opposition succeeds, it may be on the basis of a conflict which is only effective in one or a few Member States of the European Union. In such a case, there are arrangements for converting the Community trade mark application (for countries where such conflicts do not apply) into one or more national applications (the applicant can choose how many), each of which is then processed by the respective national office in the usual way, each retaining the original filing date of the Community trade mark application.

4-018

As the European Union expands, the reach of community trade mark registrations likewise expands, albeit with protection against expropriation of local interests if there is a direct clash between an existing national mark and the newly effective community registration.

The Madrid Agreement and Protocol

A different approach to providing an international trade mark system has existed for several decades. It is called the "Madrid Agreement". The original agreement still does not apply in the United Kingdom since the United Kingdom has never signed up to it. Basically, the Madrid Agreement provides a system where, having secured registration in your original home country, you file a single international application with the central authority (the World Intellectual Property Organisation in Geneva) designating as many Member States of the system as you want to have your registration effective in, and paying the appropriate fees. The international organisation then publishes details of the mark (and of the original home registration) and tells the national trade mark offices in the designated Member States that registration has been sought in that state. The local office can then examine the mark and, if it is a country where there is the possibility of objecting by way of opposition proceedings, the local office may advertise the mark to see if anyone wishes to oppose. If someone opposes, or if the local office itself raises objections, the matter is then sorted out at a local level, though this may involve needing to appoint local attorneys to deal with the matter. The language of the Madrid Agreement international registration system is French.

4-019

This system worked well for several decades, but had certain technical drawbacks which prevented some countries joining. These were addressed at an inter-governmental level, and this resulted in the creation of a slightly modified arrangement (known as the Madrid Protocol) which came into operation on April 1, 1996, originally with a relatively small number of adherent member countries, but with one of them being the United Kingdom. It now has over 90 members, rather more than the original agreement now has (56). The member countries form the "Madrid Union".

All the individual EU countries are members of the Madrid Protocol, and candidate states are expected to ratify it on or prior to accession. There is also a "link" between the Madrid Protocol system and the Community trade mark system insofar as the European Union is a region which can be designated in an application made via the Madrid Protocol. The Madrid Protocol continues to attract new Member States, and these now include the USA, Japan, China, Korea, Australia, and India. When new states join, it is possible to add them into existing registrations by way of a "subsequent designation" procedure.

A major advantage of the international registration system is that even though it covers many countries, only a single renewal fee is paid to renew the registration (every 10 years) and if it changes hands, a single assignment can be recorded centrally rather than having to record the new owner in the office of each jurisdiction.

The rest of the world

4–020   Most countries have trade mark registration systems, though in a few third world countries no such laws yet exist and the only protection available is at common law and effected by publishing "cautionary notices". In many smaller countries, particularly ex-British Colonies, registration is granted to proprietors only on the basis of a first registration in a "major" country, e.g. the UK.

Most countries are signatories to the 1883 International Convention, which sets out some very basic requirements for the trade mark laws of individual countries to comply with, and which sets up the "priority term" scheme. However, that Convention allows very wide variations between national laws to co-exist. In an effort to make life easier for trade mark owners (and trade mark offices) a more recent treaty (the Trademark Law Treaty or "TLT") was agreed in 1994, which harmonises the laws and practices of the member countries much more. So far, it is in force in only 42 countries, but this number is slowly growing as those who have signed but not yet ratified, possibly because they have not yet brought their domestic laws into conformity with its provisions. A further 28 countries plus the European Union are in this situation.

CONCLUSION

4–021   Possession of a trade mark registration gives rise to an ability by its proprietor to do two things: first, by using his trade mark and by defending its integrity, for example by proceeding against anyone who uses the trade mark or one deceptively similar without authorisation, he can attempt to maintain a captive

CONCLUSION

market. He can create a reputation by selling high quality goods in a particular brand and the hope is always that the use of a trade mark will ensure that his brand is purchased rather than that of a rival manufacturer. Nowadays, no one goes into a tobacconist's and asks for a packet of cigarettes; rather, they ask for a particular brand of cigarettes and the trade marks applied to such brands (which survives the increasing mandatory "plain packaging" requirements) are of course invariably registered, if at all possible, and those registrations are jealously guarded. The registration offers a proprietary right, saving the proprietor very substantial sums of money in any litigation against a third party who unfairly uses the mark or a similar one on the right sort of goods or services and thereby injures the proprietor's trade or reputation.

Secondly, the reputation that has been built up may be traded on not only by the proprietor himself, but by licensing, with appropriate conditions to ensure that the reputation is not tarnished. Such licences can provide a very valuable source of income. The intention to license is sufficient justification for owning a registration, so, for example, a performance group may well confine its activities to stage performances, while licensing its (registered trade marked) name to third parties who produce, e.g. recordings, posters, clothing or memorabilia bearing the group's name. Income from such exploitation by licence may be more than the group (or, e.g. a famous sportsman) earns from pursuing their profession.

CHAPTER 5

Copyright and design right

INTRODUCTION

Copyright law was originally designed to protect creators from exploitation of their works by others without permission. Certain categories of creation easily lent themselves to reproduction and it was not felt right that the creator should be denied the profits from that reproduction. Thus, originally literary works, and subsequently musical, dramatic and artistic works, came to be recognised as worthy of copyright protection and gradually the area was widened and the protection codified to give the various complex systems in operation today.

5–001

One thing common to all aspects of copyright law is the concept of a copyright "work" and this stresses, rightly, the creative aspect just noted. The term "work" in this sense includes a very wide variety of things such as books, pictures, music, sculpture and photographs, but one feature common to them all is that they have a tangible or otherwise perceptible specific form. A work is conveniently to be contrasted with an idea. Thus the idea of composing music based on bird song is not something over which copyright law has any control, but a piece of music by Oliver Messiaen based on that approach is a work in which copyright can and does subsist; pointillism is an idea, but each painting by Seurat or any member of his school gave rise to a further "copyright" owned by the artist who painted it; the idea of a reusable space shuttle contrasts with the actual design of one.

It follows from this approach that copyright is a right associated with and based on a particular perceptible expression usually, though not always, the conscious product of an original mind. Both skill and labour are normally employed in the production of a copyright work and the copyright comes into being when the work itself comes into being.

Copyright in three-dimensional works outside the fine arts and architectural areas should logically operate in parallel with its operation in them. However, this can give rise to practical problems, and a new right, so-called "design right", was invented in the late 1980s to complement copyright and regulate the position in the three-dimensional design field.

OBTAINING PROTECTION

Patent and trade mark law are fairly easy to grasp and voluntary for an inventor or trader: inventors have a choice of whether or not to use the patent system, and registration under a trade mark registration system is also voluntary. The number of people inventing things and choosing to avail themselves of the patent system

5–002

each year is relatively small, as is the number of persons who choose to use trade mark registration systems. In marked contrast, copyright law in many countries, and in particular in the United Kingdom, is not in the nature of a voluntary system but is a mandatory system which gives protection automatically on creation and reduction to a permanent form. Thus, every painting done by each member of a school class, every essay done for the English master, every technical drawing of each part that goes up to make a modem jet engine and every letter, report or memorandum may be the subject of copyright protection. Copyright law thus tends to embrace or touch upon very varied fields of activity and it has developed in somewhat haphazard fashion in many countries, with the inevitable result that, in detail, copyright law is often anomalous, piecemeal and almost invariably difficult to understand.

British copyright law was thoroughly revised in 1987 in order then to provide a modern, up-to-date framework which attempts to cover the whole field of literary, artistic and musical endeavour, the areas of computer programs, sound recordings, cinematograph films, television broadcasts and sound broadcasts and published editions of works. The Act (Copyright, Designs and Patents Act 1988) aims to give a homogeneous treatment to works which are the classical products of original creation by authors, artists and others such as books, plays, music, sculptures, drawings and engravings, and more recent types of work such as holograms, video recordings and computer programs. The Act also gave statutory birth to the design right, a sort of industrial copyright applicable where the work created is a tangible, physical, three-dimensional, useful article.

The nature of the protection available under copyright or design right depends centrally on the nature of the "work" created. Copyright law tends to try to categorise works under several headings, but the terms used are not always very clear. Indeed, in some cases, such terms are defined very broadly, such as the definition of an artistic work in CDPA 1988 s.4, but this definition itself requires careful study to decide what it means and even then the boundaries are not clear. Consider a climbing frame built in the garden from old plumbing fittings and piping and set in the ground in some concrete. This is unquestionably a structure in the normal dictionary meaning of the term and "building" is stated to include "any fixed structure" in CDPA 1988 s.4(2). Artistic work in CDPA 1988 s.4(1)(b) is defined as including a work of architecture, being a building or a model for a building. Is the climbing frame a "work of architecture" or will its creator have to rely on his design right to prevent copyists?

5–003 The term "musical work" is defined in CDPA 1988 s.3(1), as meaning a "work consisting of music". If, working on some mathematical formula, a composer produces a spiked drum which, when inserted into a musical box movement and rotated, causes the box to produce "music", is the spiked drum a musical work?

Protection, if obtainable, i.e. if the work is of a kind susceptible of protection, is usually obtained merely by making the work (when it is, of course, initially "unpublished") provided that the maker was a "qualified person" (CDPA 1988 ss.153 and 154) or that first publication occurred in the United Kingdom (CDPA 1988 s.155). "Qualified person" includes all British subjects and all persons (of any nationality) resident or domiciled in the United Kingdom. The application of these provisions is extended by the relevant statutory order to citizens of, or publication in, all of the member countries of the Berne and Universal Copyright Conventions.

Copyright ownership usually belongs in the first instance to the creator of the original work, called for convenience the author of the work, a reflection perhaps of the original roots of copyright law in literary copyright (CDPA 1988 ss.9 and 11). Generally speaking, the author of the work is entitled to the copyright in it, but that copyright may be transmitted in the usual way by the author who can sell it to a third party for an appropriate consideration or it can be given away or passed by testamentary disposition. There are some cases, however, where copyright initially vests with someone other than the author by operation of law, and of course two parties can always agree that one will carry out original work and the copyright in that work shall belong to the other. Thus CDPA 1988 s.11 provides for automatic ownership of the copyright in the literary, dramatic, musical or artistic works of an employee by his employer unless there is agreement to the contrary. It should be remembered, however, that if any works such as drawings, photographs, paintings, engravings or portraits are commissioned, the commissioner does not automatically own the copyright in the work unless the parties have agreed so, explicitly.

FORM OF PROTECTION

Copyright and design right protect against unauthorised *copying*. The fundamental principle is that if someone has taken the time and trouble to produce a work in respect of which copyright or design right subsists, then others should not, at least not without appropriate permission, and/or payment, make a "copy" of that work, i.e. reproduce it in some way involving an act of copying. The number of ways in which a work can be reproduced is large and, of course, dependent upon the nature of the work itself. Current UK legislation (CDPA 1988 s.16) tries to cover the various infringing acts, enumerating copying the work, issuing copies of the work to the public, performing, showing or playing the work in public, broadcasting the work, including it in a cable programme service, or making an adaptation of the work, or doing any of the proscribed acts in relation to such an adaptation. Definitions of these various categories of action are contained in CDPA 1988 ss.17–21. The copyright owner is given the exclusive right to carry out these various acts, and by virtue of CDPA 1988 s.16(2), it is an infringement of copyright to do, without the licence of the owner, any of these exclusive acts and it is also an infringement to authorise another person to do so.

5–004

All of these exclusive acts or acts which constitute infringement can broadly be described as "copying". In some way, the copyist/infringer reproduces the actual physical detailed perceptible form of the original work, possibly transmuted into an almost unrecognisable form compared with the original, but nevertheless a copy.

Certain minor corollaries follow from this approach to copyright law. The first is that a copy of a copy is a copy of the original. Thus if a novel is written by A and illegally copied by B, C who copies B's illegal copy can still have proceedings brought against him by A and can be restrained from copying without licence.

5–005 Secondly, the other side of the coin is that independent conception is always a complete answer to a charge of copying. Even if the final works are effectively identical, as is perforce the case with certain works such as mathematical tables, copyright can still subsist in the works but is not infringed by the later independent producer of the same work.

Returning to the point raised earlier concerning ideas, it should be stressed that copyright in a particular work is not infringed by somebody who takes the idea behind the work and then produces their own reworking of that idea. Thus a line is to be drawn between making an adaptation of a work and making an analogous work starting from the same first principles.

The term of copyright, during which "copying" is restricted, is usually substantial, being in most cases (not, e.g. typographical arrangements of a published edition) from the work's coming into existence until the expiry of 70 years from the end of the year in which the death of the author occurred. In the case of sound recordings, films and broadcasts, the term of protection dates from the year of their manufacture or release. Complex provisions apply to works where the author died more than 50 years before 1996 but less than 70 years before that date.

It should be pointed out, however, that the term of any protection under the CDPA 1988 in respect of ornamental surface designs registrable under the Registered Designs Act 1949 is limited by CDPA 1988 s.52, to a period of 25 years from the date of first marketing the item. The copyright protection in a drawing may continue to subsist and, for example, making a copy *drawing* will infringe after the 25-year period. Likewise, if a design right is exploited by making reproductions of an article created first as a drawing of that article, any protection under the copyright in the drawing cannot be used to stop the article being made or copied (CDPA 1988 s.51).

DESIGN RIGHT

5–006 As explained above, copyright law evolved from the desirability of protecting the result of labour and skill in the fine arts, whether they were literary, artistic or musical. In contrast, registered design law was designed to provide protection for the applied arts, and specifically to ornamentation, shape and configuration as applied to industrially manufactured articles. In many countries these two sorts of protection exist, but separately and with little interaction. However, in the United Kingdom, there has been much interaction between the two.

The chief cause of the interaction was the ability to sue, for copyright infringement, the manufacturer of a three-dimensional article which was preceded by a drawing. The drawing attracted copyright (as drawings do, irrespective of artistic quality) and UK law has for many years (CDPA 1988 s.17(3)) deemed the making of a copy in three dimensions of a two-dimensional work an infringement of the copyright in that artistic work. Until 1968 there was, however, a specific exclusion separating protection by way of copyright and protection by way of registered design: if something was registered as a design, or could have been so registered, then no action was possible under the Copyright Act.

This had the effect that those who did not choose to register their designs but did exploit them commercially lost all protection. By an amendment to CA 1956, which became known as the Design Copyright Act 1968, the previous exclusion of suit under the Copyright Act was removed. This gave rise to substantial litigation by manufacturers of industrially produced articles, who sued the copiers of those articles for infringement of the copyright in the original design drawings.

This approach led to anomalies, particularly that if the drawings were of such a nature that the article in question was not susceptible of registration as a design under RDA 1949. The period of protection effectively given to such industrial designs under the Copyright Act was very substantial. If the design was not protectable under RDA 1949 for lack of sufficient originality, the anomaly arose that good innovative design was effectively protected for only 15 years, while trivial design was effectively protected for much longer. 5–007

After much debate, a new form of protection was devised, known as "design right" protection. This new attempt to protect design endeavour in respect of industrially produced articles worked sufficiently well (or appealed philosophically sufficiently) for it to be reflected in the European Design Harmonisation Directive, so parallel approaches now apply in EU Member states, indeed being somewhat more broadly applicable where the Designs Directive has been directly implemented into local law.

Design right, e.g. the term as statutorily defined in the United Kingdom, applies narrowly, only to features of the shape and configuration of articles (or parts of them) and only when they are original—the "commonplace" is excluded (CDPA 1988 s.213).

Design right arises once the relevant design is done, whether by drawing, sculpting, model making or otherwise, but only if the designer or commissioner of the design is an EU national (personal or corporate) or if that does not apply, if whoever markets the articles first is exclusively authorised to do so in the United Kingdom and first marketing takes place in the European Union. The nationality and location requirements may be extended outside the EU countries in due course. 5–008

The extent of protection is the right to sue others who copy the design so as to produce articles exactly or substantially to that design (CDPA 1988 s.226(2), (3)).

Like copyright, design right arises automatically, but it lasts far less long, a maximum of 15 years from the end of the calendar year in which the design right arose, but as little as 10 years from the end of the calendar year in which articles made to the design are first made available for sale or hire (CDPA 1988 s.216). For the last five years of the period of protection, a licence to copy the design is available as of right, the terms of such licence to be settled by the Comptroller General of Patents, Designs and Trade Marks in the absence of agreement between the parties.

In contrast to the position concerning copyright, the owner of design right, where the design is commissioned, is the commissioner, not the person who created the design (CDPA 1988 s.215(2)). This matches the position of commissioned designs. This is likely to change, to bring the position into line 5–009 with other EU countries but it will be possible, by agreement, for the commissioner to own the design right if both parties so wish; this is expected to become the norm for those using freelance, i.e. not employed, designers.

Design right may be assigned or licensed in the same way as other intellectual property rights and it may co-exist with registration under RDA 1949. Ownership of any registered design protection and of the design right in respect of the same article will normally be the same, but need not be so.

The relatively long protection given by the UK's design right (compare the short protection against copying provided in the European Design Regulation in which covers both the copying of an unregistered right and the infringement (copying not needed though often present) of a registered one) arose from an attempt to hold the legislative balance between the creators of original designs who should enjoy, it is felt, a certain amount of protection, and the interests of industry in being able to use designs, and indeed copy industrially produced designs, after a reasonable period of time. One area where such copying is particularly vigorous is the so-called spare parts industry, where a conflict arises between the desires of the spare parts industry to exist—and indeed prosper—and the hard commercial fact that, for many motor manufacturers, the profit on "genuine" spare parts may make the difference between commercial survival and failure.

5–010 In the United Kingdom some time ago, an action was brought under the Copyright Act in connection with the design of exhaust pipes, where the replacement exhaust pipe industry is vigorous. The House of Lords ruled that the owner of the original vehicle was entitled to have it repaired, and accordingly was entitled to have someone manufacture a copy exhaust pipe for that purpose, and by extension that manufacturers were legitimately entitled to manufacture copy exhaust pipes not to the specific order of someone who needed one but in the expectation that those who in due course would need to repair their vehicles would need to purchase one. The law concerning spare parts will no doubt develop further. The lack of clarity in this area led to an "opt-out" in the European Design Harmonisation Directive, leaving the (still) unharmonised variations in national laws and practices essentially untouched. Even design protection reflects the lack of clarity on spare parts: many of them are untouched as they are excluded from registered design protection by the "complex product" exception (see p.34).

It should be stressed that all of the above observations concerning design right, and indeed the majority of those concerning the protection of industrially applied design by the use of copyright, are applicable centrally only in the United Kingdom, and have been followed in general terms in only a relatively few countries outside of the European Union. In many countries, copyright law does not provide any remedy for the copying of industrially produced articles, and in the case of that occurring, the originator of that article may have to fall back on unfair competition law or slavish imitation law as developed in those jurisdictions in order to try to secure any relief. In some countries, copying of industrial design for which no protection has been sought under the registered design law of that country is effectively legitimate.

The interactions between copyright, design right and registered design protection should be remembered, recalling that for many articles, these types of protection are not mutually exclusive, and two or all three types may tend to be complementary. Despite the broad copyright and/or design right protection given by the CDPA 1988, it is still useful to register a design for an article which may be protected under both headings for a number of reasons. The major reason is that registration gives a clearly defined monopoly which is infringed by somebody who produces an article looking the same, whether or not copying has taken place. Thus in any action against a copyist, if action is brought under the RDA 1949, there is no need to *prove* copying. Sometimes copying is very difficult to prove, particularly if it takes place outside the jurisdiction. Secondly, the simple affixing of a copyright or design right notice to an article does not allow the competition to see in just what copyright or the design right subsists, so since the right may be in only a part of the item, but the third party can only guess as to which, copying any part (even if other parts are *not* copied) may give rise to a design right infringement—even if the overall article looks different. If a design is registered then articles produced to that design may bear the registered design number and anyone can then discover precisely what the registered design covers and, if they are so minded, take care not to infringe. Naturally, if they move away from infringement of the registered design, they are most likely (though not inevitably) to move sufficiently far to avoid copyright or design right infringement also.

This discussion has shown how very strong copyright law can be in certain areas. It should not, however, be taken as too strong since, by appropriately conducting themselves, manufacturers can still compete legitimately without copying, as follows: if a manufacturer A brings out a new range of products and manufacturer B wants to copy them, clearly manufacturer B cannot simply proceed to do so without risk. However, if there is some underlying new design idea or the like which, stripped of its particular physical embodiments, can be appropriately expressed, then manufacturer B is entitled to go to a designer (or indeed use his own) and ask to have a range of designs produced embodying that concept. Since each of those designs would be original and not copied, no copyright or design right infringement can take place even if the ultimately produced designs bear an uncanny resemblance to the original designs of manufacturer A. Independent origination is a total defence to an allegation of copying. Care should, of course, be taken in embarking on any such course of action to make quite certain that the subsequently made designs are truly independently done. The temptation must also be avoided, if manufacturer B is not quite happy with the designs produced by his designer, for manufacturer B to review and alter the new designs to render them more marketable while at the same time making them resemble manufacturer A's designs more. Such changes may convert an original work into a copy. 5–011

Actions for copyright and design infringement can be taken in the Intellectual Property Enterprise Court or in the High Court, Chancery Division, the usual remedies of an injunction against further copying, delivery up of infringing copies and an inquiry as to damages or an account of profits being normally available. In any particularly flagrant case of copyright infringement the court can award additional damages (CDPA 1988 s.97(2)), which could clearly be substantial.

EXPLOITATION

5–012 Copyrights are generally exploited by manufacture of the copyright work normally by some form of printed publication or recording or by licensing others to do so. Licences need to specify carefully what acts are permitted. The payments may be by way of lump sum or royalty. Licences to perform are often administered by societies set up for the purpose; in the United Kingdom the Performing Right Society grants such licences.

However, exploitation by total reproduction, performance, or the like is not the only way in which a return for investment of skill and labour to produce the copyright work can be secured. One related area which relies on copyright law for regulating the conduct of parties operating in it is that of character merchandising.

In recent years it has become widespread practice to attempt to sell goods on the back of usually fictional characters. In most cases (though by no means all) the origin of the character is literary and in many cases of major impact the original literary work is made into a film. If the film is widely promoted, and has particular characters or images associated with it, then it is to be expected that a wide range of articles will have their sales potentially increased by being made in the form of, or ornamented with, representations of, the characters in question. In particular, clothing is of increased appeal to certain sections of the purchasing public if it bears a representation of a well-known character.

5–013 Traditionally underlying character merchandising programmes is copyright law. It is simply not open to would-be riders on the bandwagon of success of any particular film or comic strip to avail themselves of the copyright manifestations of the particular character. Their representation cannot be used with impunity and action can often be brought very quickly to stop misuse (see, e.g. the *Jaws T-shirt* case, *Universal Studios v Mukhtar & Sons Ltd* [1976] F.S.R. 252, and the *Kojakpops* case, *Tavener Rutledge v Trexapalm* [1977] R.P.C. 275). In another case, the proprietor of a film was able to stop the sale of posters corresponding to frames in the film (*Spelling Goldberg Productions Inc v BPC Publishing* [1981] R.P.C. 280, CA). However, there are limits to the application of copyright: the refuse contractor who had the bright idea of riding on the popularity of certain furry creatures who allegedly live near and keep clean Wimbledon Common was, at least at the interlocutory level, not felt by the British courts to be reprehensible when the plaintiff, as assignee of the copyright in certain characters, sued the unlicensed user of the characters' name, for passing off (*Wombles v Wombles Skips* [1977] R.P.C. 99). Exxon were unsuccessful in their plea that copyright would enable them to stop a third party setting up as "Exxon Insurance Consultants International Ltd" though they did succeed on a passing-off basis ([1982] R.P.C. 69).

The use of copyright in character merchandising is now supplemented by the ability to register logotypes, or, e.g. representations of cartoon characters, as designs, thus enabling the originators to secure a registered right which is infringed without copying needing to be proved, even though in many cases copying will in fact have occurred.

Performance, character merchandising and other collateral activity are becoming considerably more important as a way of securing a return on the investment in developing and promoting an artist in the world of musical recording, or in the television and film industry. This follows the rise in availability of copying devices in the mass marketplace which the music and film industries assert is depriving them of revenue.

Finally, copyright is used by many "content producers" to seek to curtail, or at least to secure a return from, reproduction of that content via the internet. In recent years, many cases have been brought before the courts seeking to restrain the effectively uncontrollable dissemination of material via the internet, and many in the content industry are unhappy at the present state of copyright law and its application in the "information" age.

INTERNATIONAL ASPECTS

It cannot be stressed too much that copyright law, in contrast to patent and trade mark law, tends to vary widely from country to country, both in respect of its detailed provisions and in respect of the degree of formality necessary to secure protection. Accordingly great care needs to be taken in any matter where there is a substantial copyright element in order to secure good local advice in all the relevant countries. This is particularly important where the exploitation of the copyright is otherwise than by classical means, such as the publication of books or the printing of pictorial reproductions, e.g. by way of dissemination via the internet. 5–014

Just which works are protected and which works are not is an interesting area and there is wide variation from country to country and indeed from time to time. However, the often quoted maxim of copyright law that "what is worth copying is worth protecting" implies that, at least in the Anglo-Saxon law countries, the law will be interpreted broadly in this respect where possible.

In some countries in order to secure adequate copyright protection certain registration formalities may be necessary. The United Kingdom is not one of those, but it is worth noting that the United States is; in the United States, registration of works with the US Copyright Office is simple and relatively inexpensive (see *http//:www.copyright.gov* [Accessed September 10, 2013] for details).

As in the case of other intellectual property law, it early became desirable for countries to come to multilateral agreements concerning copyright and there are two major copyright conventions known colloquially as the Berne Convention and the Universal Copyright Convention. The first of these is an attempt to preserve some uniformity of law between the various member countries and fundamentally it is a mutual agreement between its members that, as expressed in art.4: 5–015

> "authors, the nationals of any of the [member countries] shall enjoy in countries other than the country of origin of the work for their works, whether unpublished or first published in a [member country], the rights which the respective laws do now or may hereafter grant to natives".

One of the fundamental planks of the Berne Convention is that such protection must be granted without any formalities. Formalities may be necessary in certain countries if copyright proceedings are to be taken against an infringer, but the protection is effectively automatic.

The Universal Copyright Convention is a younger convention but one which is, by virtue of its wider membership, perhaps the more important.

5–016 Under the provisions of the Universal Copyright Convention, each member agrees to give the nationals of all the other member countries the same protection for their unpublished works as it gives to the unpublished works of its own nationals. It also undertakes to give the nationals of other contracting states in respect of published works and to the nationals of any country if the work is first published in one of the member states, the same rights as it gives to works first published in its own territory. Also, if published works first published outside the territory of the contracting state in question are not the work of a national author, then the protection is to be enjoyed without formality of any sort, provided only that all published copies bear the so-called Universal Copyright Convention marking, which consists of the well-known © device, followed by the year of first publication and the name of the copyright owner (see UCC art.III). The Universal Copyright Convention does not, however, stop the member countries from requiring formalities to be observed if copyright is to be enjoyed in its territory either in respect of works first published in its territory or in respect of work of its nationals wherever first published. In addition, the member countries may require compliance with formalities if action is to be brought in the courts of that country.

As noted above, copyright affects not only dealing in physical items embodying the copyright (books, prints, tapes, magnetic discs) but also broadcasting works or performances. In the international sphere, the Rome Convention on Satellite Broadcasting seeks to provide some international regulation and acts as a harmonising influence on domestic law in this area and a series of Copyright Directories seek to provide some harmonisation of approach in the European Union.

In contrast, the internet continues to act as a powerful destabilising influence due to its rise being accompanied by the easier (and cheaper) availability of equipment for copying, and the inherent factor in the copying of digitised material that the copy is an exact copy of the original with no loss of any data, and accordingly indistinguishable from the original. This has led to the development of anti-copying techniques and to the vigorous development of weapons to disable such techniques and allow copying to occur even of "protected" material. Technology is well ahead of legal developments in the area, particularly as legal progress is retarded when lawmakers are unwilling to enact laws, even locally, which will be widely ignored and difficult, or unpopular, to enforce. To arrive at internationally acceptable solutions is a challenge currently facing governments in the copyright area, and one which is unlikely to be satisfactorily answered soon, if ever. Copyright owners or licensee exploiters, so-called content producers, seek to be able to monetise their investment while the users of content—the public—want ever more availability, and they want it without cost.

CONCLUSION

Copyright laws cover all dealings with copyright works, and specifically with reproducing those works, often in a form different from their original. Copyright adheres to the creator or part creator of the work and a work may accordingly have more than one copyright owner associated with it.

Copyrights can be exploited by making copies and selling them, by performing a "performable" work, or by licensing others to do either of these. They last for a long time and, at least in the central fields of literary, dramatic and musical works, are of wide geographical application.

What is worth copying is worth protecting, morally if not caught by statute. Independent conception is a total defence to an allegation of copying.

5–017

CHAPTER 6

Common law protection

INTRODUCTION

To a greater or lesser extent, each of the various forms of intellectual property discussed in the previous chapters stands on its own as a relatively clearly defined and easily distinguished subject, governed for the most part by statute law under which formal procedures have been established for the protection of the particular rights involved. There are some other forms of intellectual property, however, that are less easily defined and for which no formal protection is offered, other than that available from the courts. As a result, the legal rules governing such matters as breach of confidence, unfair competition and the protection of trade secrets are a good deal less clear than those regarding, for example, patents and copyright. Nonetheless, certain basic principles can be derived from the reported cases and their practical application is discussed in this chapter.

6–001

PASSING OFF AND UNFAIR COMPETITION LAW

The concept of unfair competition between commercial undertakings is of relatively recent origin, when compared to the patent and trade mark systems, and it has grown up very much as a result of activities by companies being felt to be in some way unsatisfactory or unfair.

6–002

Unfair competition law varies widely from country to country and interacts in many ways with intellectual property law. Cases of unfair competition often involve an intellectual property aspect and likewise intellectual property cases often involve an unfair competition aspect. Both should be remembered if action needs to be taken, both by a claimant wishing to assert his rights or by a defendant wishing to continue with an activity which has been complained of.

Often the law on this subject has developed on a very piecemeal basis, drawing from various other areas of law. In some countries there has been subsequent codification, but even codification in this field tends to be of a very general nature, leaving much to be decided by the courts.

In terms of unfair competition there is no question of taking any formal steps to obtain protection. Whoever trades in a particular country is protected automatically by the unfair competition law of that country, however undeveloped or highly developed that body of law may be. The form of protection is, however, usually relatively similar and consists in an ability to secure an injunction against a third party, forcing it to stop the act of unfair competition in which it is engaged. Sometimes, it is also possible to recover damages from such

6–003

third parties, but damages are not usually nearly so important as stopping the abuse. Occasionally, however, damages can be of importance, particularly in the United States in connection with anti-trust law where so-called "treble damages" can be awarded in appropriate cases.

The reason for including a brief discussion of unfair competition law in this book is simply that many unfair competition cases have, as one or more of their ingredients, a violation of patent, registered design, trade mark or copyright rights.

In terms of patents, the major area of interaction between patenting and unfair competition law is in the so-called anti-trust field. The anti-trust law was first developed in the United States under the Lanham and Sherman Acts and many volumes have been written on its detailed application. In the last three decades of the twentieth century, a substantial body of European anti-trust law emerged following cases brought under the provisions of what were then arts 85 and 86 of the Treaty of Rome (now arts 101 and 102 of the TFEU). The situation most commonly met with in this area is an arrangement, concerning a patent, between two parties which is felt by a third to be improper and unfair. Much can hang in these cases on whether a patent monopoly is or is not valid and on the ability or inability (or unwillingness) of the patentee to grant licences on reasonable terms.

6–004 Although, theoretically, there is no barrier to similar problems arising in respect of registered designs, very little activity in this field has taken place compared with that in the patents field.

Turning now to the question of trade marks, as well as being an infringement of a trade mark registration, the adoption by a third party of a trade mark that is the same as, or confusingly similar to, a registered trade mark of another trader is considered in many countries to be of itself an act of unfair competition. In the United Kingdom, for example, the application of the same or a confusingly similar trade mark may well be a central plank in an allegation by a complainant in proceedings that the defendant is attempting thereby to pass off the defendant's goods as those of the complainant. "Passing off" is a very well-established common law wrong in British jurisprudence and the courts have never been slow to act to restrain those who attempt to pass off their goods as those of others, i.e. those who attempt to trade unfairly on a reputation previously established by others. Thus in litigation in the United Kingdom where trade marks have been copied or almost copied, it is common practice for suit to be brought not only in respect of the infringement of a trade mark registration but also in respect of an attempt to pass off. Of course, if the trade mark is used and has a reputation but is not registered no action can be brought under the Trade Marks Act 1994 (see s.2(2)) and in such a case the only remedy available to the owner of the unregistered trade mark is to sue for passing off.

Passing off received a thorough judicial overhaul in the United Kingdom some years ago, sweeping aside some considerations more suited to domestic markets in a quieter age, and reflecting the major changes in the mercantile environment, which occurred during the twentieth century. In the *Advokaat* case ([1980] R.P.C. 31) an attempt was made to set out clearly the ingredients necessary for the plaintiff to succeed. They must include (per Lord Diplock):

> "(1) a misrepresentation; (2) made by a trader in the course of his trade; (3) to prospective customers of his or ultimate consumers of goods or services supplied by

him; (4) which is calculated to injure the business or goodwill of another trader (in the sense that it is a reasonably foreseeable consequence); and (5) which causes actual damage to a business or goodwill of the trader by whom the action is brought or (in a *quia timet* action) will probably do so."

6–005 The judgment in *Advokaat* carefully expressed the reservation (as passing off cases traditionally do) that no set of rules for determining the presence or absence of passing off was likely to cover every possibility, but it remains a good guide. However, the "classic trinity" formulation—reputation, misrepresentation and damage—may provide a simpler yardstick in most cases.

In somewhat similar fashion copyrights often figure in unfair competition cases. The range of instances vary from the use of copyright material, such as customer lists or price lists, by a defecting employee setting up in his own business, to the use of similar designs for business forms or packaging. It is of particular value to remember in respect of items that in themselves may be, for lack of substantiality, on the borderline of copyright protection that, if they are copied, the act of copying may in appropriate circumstances be an act of unfair competition, even though the material may ultimately be shown not to enjoy copyright protection. In one particular area, that of so-called slavish imitation, copying is often actionable as an act of unfair competition even though, for technical reasons, the item being copied may not enjoy copyright protection.

Overall, it must be stressed that what does and what does not constitute unfair competition can vary from time to time and particularly from country to country. For example, the laws on comparative advertising, which often incidentally uses other people's trade marks, vary widely from country to country. In the European Union, there are certain types of comparative advertising that are unquestionably legitimate. The consolidated Directive on misleading and comparative advertising, 2006/114 makes it clear that the use of others' trade marks is legitimate, despite the fact that much of it appears to constitute a trade-mark infringement at first glance. The formulation adopted to avoid infringement is to exempt use to identify goods or services of the legitimate proprietor or licensee, provided such use is in accordance with "honest practices in industrial or commercial matters" and does not without due cause take unfair advantage of, or be detrimental to the distinctive character or repute of, the trade mark.

6–006 An up-to-date assessment of comparative advertising practice, and which well illustrates its interaction with trade mark protection law, is to be found in the ECJ decision in *O2 Holdings Ltd et al v Hutchison 3G UK Limited* (C–533/06).

Another area of particular variability from country to country is the ability of manufacturers to make free offers, give away free prizes, on either a lottery or some other basis, and generally use tough marketing techniques, which in many other countries are accepted as part of the normal commercial rough and tumble.

Manufacturers, traders and their advisers, therefore, need to remember that behind the specific intellectual property laws is the body of general and common law in the various countries concerned, particularly the unfair competition law, which interacts in many peculiar and sometimes changing ways with intellectual property situations. The general background should be borne in mind when making arrangements and contracts, particularly when making restrictive contracts, while if problems arise during the exploitation of the contract as a result of buccaneers, pirates or sharp operators, the unfair competition law should

6–007 be checked to see whether it may not provide a simpler and often more rapid approach to commercial effectiveness than conventional litigation based on an alleged misuse of an alleged intellectual property right.

Of course, it is as well to remember that the whole situation can be looked at from the opposite point of view, in order to determine how far a trader may go in competing with other traders who have protected intellectual property rights.

Whenever action is contemplated under an intellectual property right it is as well to consider whether, in addition to mere technical infringement of that right, there is not also an unfair competition aspect of the case which may be prayed in aid. The practice of looking at things this way developed in the United States, based on its anti-trust laws, led to the practice, in many patent cases in the United States, of including a so-called anti-trust counterclaim where the defendants often allege, inter alia, that the patent in question was obtained by a fraud on the Patent Office and that an attempt to maintain it is accordingly an anti-trust violation entitling the defendant to treble damages. This approach, while understandable, is felt by many to be a regrettable situation, leading as it does to a very substantial increase in the costs, duration and complexity of American patent cases. On the other hand, the potential rewards to the successful patentee are substantial.

Another area of US legislation outside the strict field of patents comes into play where the allegedly infringing manufacturer or importer is outside the United States. In such a case it is now commonplace not to sue for infringement the importer or user of the pirated goods in the United States, but rather to commence an action before the US International Trade Commission seeking to exclude the goods from the United States on the basis that patent infringement is occurring and American domestic industry is threatened by the therefore illegitimate importation. This alternative approach is highly effective and relatively rapid in many cases.

KNOW-HOW AND SHOW-HOW

6–008 The ability of manufacturers and traders to carry on their businesses legally depends not only on their being free of restrictions of the types discussed under the headings of patents, designs, copyright and trade marks, but also on their having the knowledge, skills and abilities to do what they want to do. To take a very simple example, a man may wish to set up in business manufacturing electronic calculators. This may look like a good field to enter, but if the man has no knowledge and expertise he will have to acquire it. He may be able to do this by a diligent reading of the literature coupled with home experimenting but this is likely to be time-consuming and not very efficient. Clearly, he could employ people versed in those particular skills, but any employees who come to him would be expected to operate with the ordinary skills of the skilled persons in that field, and not to use particular trade secrets, proprietary techniques and the like, which their previous employers had regarded as part of that employer's "confidential information". If access to that information is required, it must be paid for, assuming that the possessors of the information are willing to sell it. Surprisingly often these days people are willing to sell confidential information, possibly due to the increasing industrial espionage that will render the sale impossible if not concluded fairly soon after the new techniques have been developed and put into practice. Indeed, the very existence of industrial espionage is but the other side of the know-how and show-how coin.

Conventionally speaking, the term "know-how" is used to denote information that can be committed fairly straightforwardly to paper or some other tangible form while "show-how" is used to cover information that really can be transmitted effectively only by in-house training. The person selling the show-how undertakes to train the purchaser's employees, for example, in how to polish and bloom lenses to obtain optical instruments of the highest quality. It goes without saying that paying know-how and show-how fees can generate much greater respect in an industry than trying to poach the competitors' skilled personnel.

Effectively, know-how and show-how can be transferred only once between the same two parties and any fee that passes is accordingly effectively the consideration for either information in tangible form, in the case of know-how, or a certain amount of demonstration or training in the case of show-how. Once the information has been passed or the demonstration given, the contract is effectively concluded, save for any continuing obligations on the parts of the originator and purchaser. In this respect, the purchaser will usually want some guarantee from the originator that the same information will not be widely disseminated, or at least not without the purchaser's consent, for a certain period of time. Likewise, the vendor will probably want the purchaser to undertake to keep the information it has imparted secret and to maintain working practices and the like confidential. Usually, such obligations cease in any case when the information comes into the public domain, but care needs to be taken when considering any such arrangement as to just what continuing obligations are placed on both parties to the transaction.

ENDORSEMENT

In recent years the practice of endorsement where a well-known person recommends this or that product in an advertisement launched to promote sales at the expense of competing products, has become very widespread. Certain categories of public figure, most notably sportsmen and women and "television personalities", can command very high fees by agreeing to support some particular manufacturer of goods, which are sometimes only remotely connected with the person's particular claim to public fame. Thus boxers may be called upon to extol the virtues of a particular male cosmetic or newscasters may report glowingly on their predilections for a particular make of car. For such services they are paid a fee. They are not, of course, paid a fee if the same predilection is simply revealed as an item of news. The fact that a leader of a punk rock group eats a packet of Krunchy Krisps daily for breakfast may do wonders for the sale of that product, but its mere appearance in a newspaper report attracts no fees. Advertisers generally take the trouble to agree an endorsement fee with a personality if they wish to use an item of information such as this in their advertising but, of course, it is sometimes difficult to draw the line between what

6–009

can and what cannot fairly be said about the person, either in advertising or non-advertising copy, having regard to the laws of libel and defamation.

In the United Kingdom the laws of libel and defamation and, to some extent, passing off govern the use by third parties of reference to particular living persons. In some countries, however, most notably the United States, legislators have directed their attention to the specific problems arising from the use of personalities' names, photographs and the like and widely varying local laws exist. As in other areas, therefore, care should always be taken when contemplating making money by endorsement to determine just what law is applicable and the extent to which the proposed activity could be restrained if it were unauthorised.

Endorsement fees, as with so many other fees that are paid in order to be able to do something legally, which could otherwise not have been done legally, may be paid by way of a lump sum, or, for example, in dependence upon the amount of use made of the particular endorsement. The endorser may also wish to place limits on the amount to which that endorsement is used, particularly limits in terms of time. Many personalities are happy to receive a fee for endorsing some particular product at one stage of their career, but a repeat run of the advertisement five years later at a very different stage of that personality's career might be embarrassing.

A recent innovation in Intellectual Property Law is a specific statutory "image rights" law introduced in Guernsey (see *http//:www.guernseylegalresources.gg* [Accessed September 10, 2013]). It will be interesting to see whether this approach is adopted elsewhere.

CHAPTER 7

Commercial exploitation of intellectual property

INTRODUCTION

The preceding chapters of this book have attempted to break down intellectual property into its classic divisions and to provide general details with regard to each area relating to obtaining rights, and to the validity and enforceability of rights. This has been done without any specific attempt being made to relate those rights to actual businesses. Clearly, the applicability of individual rights will vary very substantially from one business to another. The relative importance of individual types of right will vary depending upon the nature of the commercial undertaking owning and exploiting such rights, and the relative importance of intellectual property to an undertaking will vary from cardinal, in the case of a business whose business is the exploitation of such rights, for example a copyright licensing agency or a patent auction firm, to peripheral, for example in the case of a firm of central heating maintenance engineers, especially if they trade under a highly generic name and so have no "trade mark" identity.

7–001

Wherever a business or organisation is situated on this scale, however, it is likely to have some intellectual property rights, but even in those cases where there is a very conscious history and policy of obtaining those rights which do not arise automatically and without effort, there has been a tendency in many cases to see obtaining rights almost as an end in itself and certainly with a view to using the rights as little as possible.

Intellectual property rights can be thought of as a resource, and like many resources can be exploited more or less as the owner of that resource chooses. For many decades, even after the Industrial Revolution had occurred, intellectual property rights were regarded as a somewhat arcane area, at best ancillary to the central business of the organisation, and not regarded as a resource to be exploited.

As will be apparent in Part 2, various aspects of taxation impinge on the acquisition or transmission of intellectual property rights, but larger sums of money (and accordingly larger benefits from getting it right and larger dis-benefits from getting it wrong) are generally associated with the exploitation of rights. The most obvious example of this is the licensing of technology, be it patent or design protected, of reputation (such as in franchising, often based on trade mark protection), and in publishing or performance, based on copyright.

COMMERCIAL EXPLOITATION OF INTELLECTUAL PROPERTY

POLICY

7–002   Many organisations have scant internal consciousness of the existence and usefulness of intellectual property rights, but even in those which do not suffer in this way, there is often a reluctance to analyse the actual or prospective business and to settle down and try to construct some sort of identifiable policy for the exploitation of those rights. A pre-requisite for a clear formulation of policy is the identification of what intellectual property rights the business or other organisation actually has, and for this an important starting point is to carry out some form of intellectual property audit.

Such an audit should cover both what you have and what you do with it, so the first part of an audit must accordingly be regarded as a "stocktake". It is a source of constant surprise to many practitioners in the intellectual property field to find that the ignorance, and perhaps fear, that surround intellectual property issues translate into an inability among business people even to appreciate what they have. This unconsciousness is, for obvious reasons, most pronounced in those areas that do not require positive and conscious intervention in order to secure intellectual property rights. Thus, companies owning patents and registered designs generally know that they own them. On the other hand, it is not at all uncommon to find that companies remember that they have copyright only when something adverse happens, such as a product being copied together with its packaging or some rather more obvious (and potentially commercially damaging) copying takes place. Perhaps the most widely ignored area is that of trade and service marks. A trade mark is too often equated with a brand name, and overall marks of identity, for example the particular way a company represents its name as a logotype on letterhead, or particular identifying symbols, are not seen as being fully functional trade marks, despite the fact that their use is sometimes considerably more widespread than the use of a particular brand name would ever be. This often leads a company to rely on a (mistaken) belief that no-one else can use its name, on the basis that it is "registered" at Companies House, and to consternation when faced with the greater risk of failure, and much-increased cost, of litigating at common law to stop a third party, rather than being able simply and quickly to secure the desired result by threatening to sue on the basis of a trade mark or service mark registration.

Accordingly, when contemplating the exploitation of intellectual property, stage one in many cases is simply to sit down and try to identify what intellectual property a particular business or organisation has. Clearly, the intellectual property can be categorised into the divisions represented by Chs 2–6 and their relative impact on the company or organisation's business can be assessed.

7–003   Having identified what intellectual property is around, two immediate questions arise: the first is whether it is enough. Thus, for example, a company engaged in the manufacture of new domestic electrical appliances may well find, on carrying out an intellectual property stocktake, that it owns lots of design rights. However, it may own only a few registered designs, or indeed none at all. While, on account of the novelty rules explained in Ch.3 (see para.3–003), protection by way of registered design may no longer be available for some of the company's products already on the market, a decision may well be made that, as a matter of principle, it would be highly desirable to protect recently introduced

POLICY

items, and those to be introduced in future by way of registered design, conferring a potential monopoly for a maximum of 25 years, rather than simply relying on a right against copying, absolute for five years, qualified for the next five and then extinguished.

Analogously in respect of trade marks, but with the major difference here that there is no barrier on securing registration subsequent to adoption and use, and, indeed, at any time following adoption, the decision can be made to seek explicit and identifiable protection by way of registration rather than relying on being able to do something downstream if a problem arises on the basis of some common law passing-off or unfair competition approach.

The second question that arises is how can one make more of the intellectual property rights one finds one has? Here commercial considerations obviously come into play, particularly in manufacturing industry. There is little merit in licensing your technology to competitors who, for whatever reason, can cheerfully pay you a licence royalty but then proceed to make the same or a similar product, sell it in direct competition with yours, and thereby reduce your sales (and the profit consequent on those sales) to an extent greater than the compensation received for allowing the activity to take place. On the other hand, technologies may well have applications outside the immediate market and/or geographical area of commercial interest to their owner, and field- or territory-restricted licences can provide a valuable additional source of income.

Away from technology and purely into reputation, it may well be that a company, which acquires expertise in a particular servicing field, cannot exploit that reputation simply by expanding, and the problems of over-optimistic expansion are well documented in management textbooks. However, a company with a high reputation in a particular field but that works only in one area of a country may well find it highly profitable to share that expertise with someone who is willing to work a different area of the country. There is no essential reason why a London-based business with a strong reputation should not license others in the provinces to carry out the same business under the same banner for an appropriate fee. Such arrangements do not have to have the normal attributes of a franchising operation.

7–004

Looked at more internationally, the choice is clear in the case of an owner of copyright in a literary work, be it a novel or a book about mending your car. Copyright may be acknowledged on the back of the title page but wholly under-exploited. Both novels and car maintenance manuals are useful outside the country in which they are originally written, but too often little vigorous attempt is made to come to arrangements abroad involving translation and other possible localisation of the book in question with subsequent local publication and the return of royalty income.

Not so often appreciated is the fact that overseas consumer markets are not restricted to translations of books, but rather in general are not so dissimilar from one's home market that exploitation of rights there should be ignored. While clearly time and effort may be involved in securing someone abroad to exploit your ideas, be they market oriented as with the case of a good trade mark or a good design or technology oriented as in the case of a manufacturing process or product, nevertheless if you are able to make a success of the business in your own country, it is probably reasonable to suppose that someone else can make a like success of a like business in a similar country. An inducement when looking for someone to make money for themselves and give you a cut of it in an overseas country is, of course, that you are offering protection. Particularly in the case of patents and designs but also in the case of trade marks, the up-front cost of securing the protection in the overseas territory may well be something that can easily be recovered by a down payment from a willing licensee, even if the licensee insists that the payment has to be set off against initial royalties. Arranging with someone local to exploit markets overseas can often be much simpler and much less worrying than trying to do it yourself, whether by local manufacture and export on the one hand or by setting up a local operation in the country concerned on the other. Obviously if you are an existing multinational, that sort of thing presents no problems, but although multinational companies are large and there are many of them, they are vastly outnumbered by the small and medium-sized enterprises on which, it is now widely acknowledged, most economies' economic success actually depend in overall terms.

Once an organisation has identified its stock of intellectual property and taken a policy decision to try to exploit it, working through that policy decision will, if successful, generate new business and/or income. It may also give rise to certain extra outgoings. The taxation treatment of both income and outgoings is dealt with in the next part of this book and this is again broken down into individual subject headings since tax treatment is not uniform across the whole spectrum of intellectual property rights. Thus, the application of an overall intellectual property exploitation policy requires consideration of a myriad of details, with a view to securing a satisfactory return on the "intellectual property capital", which a person or an organisation can build up. It suffers from the problem of all intellectual property: it is undervalued because you cannot see it. What you can see, however, is that by exploitation individuals and organisations may make money. The following chapters give guidance as to how the money you make splits between those authorities who feel entitled to a share and the organisation that is left with the residue.

CHAPTER 8

Specific applications

INTRODUCTION

The aim of this chapter is to be illustrative, but not exhaustive, of the ways in which intellectual property rights interact with business activities. The various examples given have been selected as identifiable business areas, each with its own distinctive mix of intellectual property relevance. As will appear below, however, the nature of the mix and which ingredients of the recipe predominate vary widely. **8–001**

Some of the illustrations also touch briefly on the interaction between intellectual property and much wider areas, such as the ethical impact of advances in biotechnology and the globalisation of trade and commerce, particularly in cases where the products in question have no "weight"—software, musical recordings, films—or the service in question is one of information processing.

BIOTECHNOLOGY

Since advances in scientific knowledge revealed some of the details of how biological processes operate, their technological application has assumed major industrial and commercial importance. Of course, biotechnology existed before and, indeed, some areas, most notably brewing and wine making, date back for centuries, as, indeed, do techniques of selective breeding. However, the discoveries in biology and biochemistry in the twentieth century have spawned the biotechnology industry we have today, and the pace of discovery and development in this area shows no signs of slowing, not least because of the enthusiasm with which the investment community originally embraced the fledgling industry. **8–002**

By its very nature, biotechnology is breaking new ground and is being seen as a possible source of effective weaponry in the fights against hunger and disease. The potential commercial rewards are substantial and accordingly the demand for protection is acute, particularly having regard to the intrinsic reproducibility of many biotechnological materials once they have been initially "created".

The major important form of intellectual property protection used by the biotechnology industry is the patent system. This can be seen to stem traditionally from the use of the system by the old biotechnology industry, which relied on micro-organisms to operate novel and improved processes. Indeed, although clearly "living material", due to their unprepossessing nature, most microorganisms were regarded as just another material and, indeed, new strains could be patented. As the technical ability to manipulate life forms started to edge up towards the higher organisms, other considerations emerged, and nowadays there is a vigorous debate concerning the patenting of higher life forms and/or of methods or materials that can be used to generate new types of higher life form.

8–003 One case that focused thoughts in this area concerned the so-called "Harvard Oncomouse". This is a real live creature genetically predisposed to develop cancer, and which provided researchers a further weapon in their armamentarium to try to combat that disease. The case highlighted (though it is not the only case to do so) the previously rather dormant consideration, common in various patent laws for a long time, but not much referred to, which allowed, in this case, the European Patent Office to refuse protection to an invention the use of which would be contrary to morality. Although in the past, in certain jurisdictions, such provisions had been used to prevent manufacturers of contraceptive devices securing patent protection for their products, the existence and possible commercial value of the prohibition had almost been forgotten until biotech cases started to emerge.

There has been much ill-informed debate on the subject, but what is important to remember is that those who invest in biotechnological development expect a return, and expect the entity in which they have invested to take prudent steps to protect its own technology with a view to maximising its profits and thereby the return on the original investment. It is thus hardly surprising that, in this fast-developing field, substantial amounts of effort have been directed and continue to be directed, to seeing how far the patent system can be used to protect the fruits of research from being overly harvested by others.

Those active in the field have also realised that, potentially, the scope of protection given by way of a patent is substantially broader and more effective than that which could possibly be achieved by use of the nearest previous attempt at providing protection in the biotech field, namely plant variety protection.

8–004 It is worth looking briefly at plant variety protection since, although relevant to only a very small proportion of industry at large, the system does exist, there is an international treaty, and, particularly in the field of crop seed, there can be substantial economic effects.

It is easy to see that the plant variety protection system was erected, in a fashion similar to that for the patent system, in order to stimulate selective plant breeders to intensify their efforts and produce new strains of useful plants or, of course, ornamental ones. The proposition, essentially, was to set up a registration system whereby someone who developed a new variety was entitled to a limited period of protection against copying. The requirement for protection is simply to produce a new variety, but in order to be protectable under the various national laws (most of which are consistent with the international treaty in the area, known as the UPOV Treaty) the variety must be stable, uniform and distinct. Provided that these criteria are satisfied (and, e.g. the UK Plant Varieties Office does examine the point), protection can be secured for a period of time which can vary with the general type of plant, but is usually between 15 and 25 years.

The plant varieties legislation (and the underlying Convention) is, however, directed to the protection by way of an individual right applying to an individual plant variety. Thus, no protection is given, for instance, to a technique that may improve the pest resistance of a number of different varieties of, e.g. maize. Such a technique does not necessarily give rise to a new variety of maize, potatoes or whatever, but may be effective in improving the yield of many different varieties. If the technique is new and non-obvious (it is clearly "industrially applicable") it ought to be protectable by way of a patent.

Although there is, as mentioned above, an international treaty relating to plant varieties and national laws exist in the countries that have ratified that treaty, there is no parallel treaty in respect of animal varieties, something which was not of particular significance many years ago, but which is important to remember now, and the absence of which undoubtedly increased the pressure on using the patent system to protect investment in development of better animals. 8–005

The argument that has raged (and that continues to rage) in connection with the patenting of living material is whether, ethically, it is correct to give anyone, even for the limited monopoly term, control over something possessing a quality of "life". A point often missed by animal rights activists and others is that at least the patent system does provide the patentee with a certain amount of control, for a limited period of time, with respect to the exploitation of his invention. If, as has been argued, no patents should be granted in the area for ethical reasons, then the possibility of controlling development of any particular invention in the field or, indeed, the development of the field itself is diminished, and this hardly seems consistent with the views expressed by some that animals should simply not be used in certain ways for what are essentially industrial purposes. At least if there is a patent, use without the patentee's permission can be stopped, so reducing the amount of (in some people's views) deplorable activity.

When considering the biotechnology industry's use of patents, mention should also be made of the very considerable regulatory barriers that are placed in the way of commercialising many inventions in the field. These will undoubtedly give rise in the years to come to attempts to extend the life of patents in this area in a fashion similar to the supplementary protection certificate schemes, which operate for pharmaceuticals and agrochemicals, where their commercial introduction may be delayed by regulatory processes, effectively eroding the term of patent protection that the patentee could expect.

There have been suggestions that copyright protection might be available (or even design type protection) for huge, complex bioactive molecules, some of which can, for example, be expressed in typographic form or by way of their shape and configuration, but little progress has been made in enlisting either of these types of right in the cause of protecting biotech developments. Know-how and secrecy, however, may well provide an adequate period of protection, enabling a commercial lead to be built up, which it may be difficult for competitors to erode. However, the control of source material will not prolong a de facto monopoly. The grant of patents for any biotechnological invention that depends on a micro-organism requires it to have been deposited in a culture collection and for samples to be available to third parties. 8–006

As usual, major players in the field will have corporate identities and as the whole biotechnology industry develops, trade marks may become more important as enabling effectively identical materials to be identified with differing manufacturing sources. Also, adoption of a distinctive identity by a start-up

SPECIFIC APPLICATIONS

company may well pay a dividend when in due course one of the major players seeks to buy the business, not merely for its technology but also for its name.

COMPUTERS

8–007   Computer technology and its provision of computer treatment of information have led to the "information revolution". Computers and their uses are replete with intellectual property considerations, perhaps most importantly ones relating to copyright, since copying, particularly digital copying, is something that computers carry out with great speed and accuracy. Indeed, once anything is reduced to digital form, it is possible to create a physical copy far more exact than any mechanical copying method could produce. With the advent of computer programs capable of handling vast quantities of data and storage devices capable of storing it, the material with which computers deal moved from being text and number-based to being sound and graphics based. So-called "multi-media" computers are now within reach of most individuals, and this means that the means of copying "information" are now available to the population at large. But copyright law has not, at a global or national level, yet reflected this, and the focus has been on attempting to stop "individual" copying or the making available of means to enable such copying, e.g. by file-sharing network providers. These initiatives have been unpopular with the public at large and not conspicuously successful in reducing personal copying.

However, in addition to personal copying, which is almost impossible to control, there is a desire, particularly in the creative community, to copy material for incorporation into new works, which will then be disseminated, and for this, authorisation is needed. However, the practicalities of authorisation are substantial, if not nightmarish. The traditional approach to using other people's material almost invariably involved identifying some physical product, such as a print or book, which would have associated with it some clue as to the originator and therefore as to the then copyright owner. Nowadays, the ability to download graphics images from numerous websites on the internet, coupled with the ability to scan in printed images from books or other printed media, exacerbates what is already a difficult situation. It is not for nothing that an old European Union Green Paper in connection with copyright referred to "The Challenge of Technology", but so far that challenge, seen as a major impetus to copyright law development and revision, has not been successfully overcome.

A separate copyright area relating to computers concerns the copyright in computer programs themselves. Although some early decisions showed a certain wariness or disinclination on the part of the judiciary to equate writing a computer program with writing a novel, it seemed to become rapidly accepted that both activities required the application of skill and labour to produce an original work and as countries revised their copyright laws in the final decades of the twentieth century, for the avoidance of any doubt, most provided explicitly that copyright covers computer programs. Secondly, there has been a realisation that the language in which a copyright work is expressed is essentially irrelevant and thus it is of no consequence whether an original program is written in a higher or lower level language, or even in machine code. In any of these cases, copying is easy to achieve and, usually, easy to detect.

The distinction is often drawn between software (which runs a computer) and data (on which the computer carries out operations). Although the distinctions are not hard and fast, it is a useful practical distinction. However, as far as copyright law is concerned, there is no particular distinction to be drawn between a computer program and a stored computer text or image. In each case, if creating the original took skill or labour, there will be an underlying copyright that will be infringed by unauthorised copying.

8–008

Separately, if there is a compilation of data into a "database", this may itself attract protection by way of a so-called "database right". This sprang from the idea that the information revolution (and European economies) would be assisted by protecting the work that had gone into databases from encroachment by others, so stimulating investment in the area. The European Union legislated, the United States did not. It is by no means clear that investment in the creation and maintenance of databases in the European Union was assisted by the new rights, and when they eventually came to be litigated, at least in the United Kingdom, there was considerable disappointment at the result.

Any computer system requires, in addition to software and data, an actual computer, i.e. the hardware. In this respect, the three classical registered intellectual property rights are all important ways for the manufacturer or originator to try to protect their own business. Thus, the physical way in which a computer is manufactured, as well as individual components such as microcircuits, transducers and the like, is fit subject matter for patent protection, and inventions in these fields are all clearly protectable. What was originally not at all clear (though the current situation is not much improved) was the ability to protect software by way of patents. Indeed, the protection of software "as such" is still proscribed by many patent laws, but what has emerged as clearly patentable subject matter is a computer or other like complex piece of electronic equipment programmed to operate in a particular way. Put another way, the fact that something requires a computer program to make it work does not translate into a ban on patentability of that thing.

The particular design of computer equipment, e.g. monitors, keyboards, printers and scanners, is an area to which substantial attention is paid by manufacturers since design can serve to attract and distinguish, and accordingly promote sales. This is particularly so where intending purchasers may well have sufficient aesthetic sensitivity to prefer one design over another while being wholly unable, on a technical basis, to decide which of two pieces of equipment actually performs its intended task better. The value of design in this area is accordingly substantial.

8–009

Even more, the distinguishing power of a trade mark can materially enhance repeat business. In a market with product offerings that are not easy to distinguish in technical terms to the lay purchaser, the power of a strong and respected trade mark to secure the purchase can be material. It is perhaps mostly neatly summed up in the possibly apocryphal slogan "No one ever got fired for buying IBM".

The application of a highly distinctive trade mark to software products can also be of immense value since, in the same way as many people cannot distinguish one personal computer from another in terms of performance (though the distinction between prices is clear), so they will have difficulty in distinguishing one word processing or accounts software package from another. It should be said that some operators in the software industry have displayed a remarkable lack of invention in naming software products, which has undoubtedly led to confusion on the part of purchasers, but there are conspicuous examples of those who adopt highly distinctive branding and imaginative product naming.

BROADCASTING

8–010 At first sight, the only material intellectual property right which would seem to be connected with broadcasting is that of copyright. Sound and video recordings possess copyright, and broadcasting, save with permission, is an act of copyright infringement. Of course, nowadays the difficulty with broadcasting is that, at the receiving end, someone can make a copy. It is clear that in many jurisdictions, that act of copying is saved from being actionable only by virtue of the fact that it is done for private purposes, e.g. for "time shifting". The theoretical approach is clear and understandable and the practice is obviously unstoppable. Where the broadcasters and, indeed, other copyright owners become concerned is where the recording actually causes economic detriment. This problem is likely to increase in future rather than decrease, for example with the increasing popularity of "pay per view" programming. The "Holy Grail" of copy protection systems is still being sought by some crusaders, but the array of infidels dedicated to defeating such systems remains in place to maintain "balance", and their activities, as well as public irritation when foiled by "DRM"—digital rights management technology—have caused some notable *volte-face* within the content provider community.

As with radio broadcasting, concern has long been expressed by the phonographic industry that off-air recording of popular music was severely diminishing revenues. Attempts to meet this legitimate concern resulted in the past in the concepts of a "blank tape levy", and a surcharge on recording machines, but this tends to have little effect in practice, and in any event such approaches are overtaken by the use of the PC and subsequent handheld devices as a recording device.

The rise (and fall) of Napster has been extensively documented, and it opened up the "peer-to-peer" file-sharing business. The phonographic industry reacted with litigation and closed down a number of operators, but, by this time, the genie was out of the box, the necessary software widely available and the end users ultra aware of the ease with which they could now record (for replay as many times as desired—just like buying a "record") the music they wished to listen to. An informal "file sharing community" arose, which may not feel inclined to buy into the industry's response of combining an official site with downloadable recordings with a micro payment system. No-one who has followed the saga so far can predict the outcome a few years hence with any confidence, and the rise of a community which is not at all motivated by profit is a challenge to legislators and, probably more so, to enforcers. Ironically, the greater the industries' attempts at enforcement, the greater the potential alienation from what they want to regard as their core customer base.

8–011 The major problem arises from the global reach of the internet and the reduction of copyright material to mere digital data. In this respect, the internet is rapidly taking over from broadcasting as the prime deliverer of content—with greater flexibility and fidelity. Indeed, some courts have held placing viewable material on a website as equivalent to broadcasting.

Whether material is being transmitted through the ether, or placed on a website, there are no "national boundaries" left. International attempts to regulate the position, e.g. the Rome Convention on satellite broadcasting, may be obsolete by the time they were designed to be effective. There can be little doubt that the problems of securing an adequate return to programme creators and content will be with us for decades, if not forever, and copyright law is ill-adapted to promote such returns in practice, however admirable the concepts behind it, in the context of a global, 24/7 available, information ocean, exemplified by "the cloud", into which vast quantities of data may be placed and from which individuals can secure what they want, and when they want it.

A traditional attempt to match the desires of copyright holders to secure a return commensurate with the use made of their copyright works and the desire of broadcasters to be able to broadcast such works, particularly musical works, takes the form of so-called "copyright collecting societies". These are organisations which monitor broadcasting and which have agreements with broadcasters and others enabling broadcast to take place of material effectively "administered" by the society in return for payment. These have tended to emerge as national institutions and have fulfilled a very satisfactory role in providing the centralised mechanism of collecting performance royalties and paying the copyright owners. However, with increasing internationalisation of broadcasting, their task becomes more difficult, and to this must be added the problem of massive expansion of the amount of broadcasting which occurs. Where there were a handful of radio channels and a smaller number of television channels a few decades ago, there are now numerous local broadcast radio stations and a bewildering variety of television satellites and satellite channels. The advent of computer-based systems has, naturally, materially assisted the efficiency of the whole operation, but the sheer volume of broadcasting can tend to overwhelm attempts at comprehensive monitoring. No doubt, however, free market forces will continue to shape activity in this area, while technology may be expected to assist monitoring. The collecting societies can be expected to seek ways of collecting money for their members from internet streaming activity, but finding practical and equitable solutions is not easy, even if such solutions are to be found at all. Within the European Union, the Commission has indicated that it is by no means certain that the current collecting society model and arrangements are adequate, and there is momentum to move from a constellation of individual national collecting societies to a more pan-EU model.

SPECIFIC APPLICATIONS

FILM

8–012   As in broadcasting, the interaction between the film industry and intellectual property law is predominantly in the area of copyright. A cinematograph film (or its parallel, the video recording) is, of course, a work requiring application of skill and labour to produce it, and one accordingly which gives rise to copyright in the film or video recording itself. That copyright is to be seen as separate from usually a number of copyrights which underlie it, for example in the original story such as a novel, an adaptation made for the purpose of turning the novel into a script and/or screenplay, and sometimes also a translation. Film makers may thus need to secure copyright clearance from a number of sources before the film can be made and distributed.

Copyright law also covers the screening or public showing of a film and the industry has developed extensive licensing and distribution arrangements reflecting this.

Film production and distribution companies are naturally concerned to protect their image and this may be done via trade mark protection. The sequence which precedes the opening of a feature film almost invariably shows, often in animated form, the trade mark of the production or distribution company, and the graphic imagery of searchlights pointing skywards by a stylised imposing building and that of a man striking an enormous gong are no doubt as well known to readers as that of a roaring lion surrounded by a heraldic frame.

FRANCHISING

8–013   During the twentieth century, a way of doing business was developed in which an original successful "business formula" developed by an original organisation could be replicated by licensing others to operate in the same way. The originator became a "franchisor". This was a particularly effective way of growing a very large business without the central major capital investment otherwise required; franchisees provide the capital for their own individual operations.

What binds the franchisor and franchisee together into a coherent operation is the identity of the business, and this is protected by a mix of contractual arrangements, enabling strict control to be exercised as to how the franchisee operates, and trade mark protection for the central identity. The franchisee is a licensee or permitted user of the mark or marks in question. Registration of the mark or marks is important since once a particular business formula has been shown to be successful, imitators may emerge, and the strength of a franchised operation usually resides in the confidence of the customer that he will secure essentially the same service or product from any franchisee within the system.

In this connection, copyright can have a part to play as well as trade mark law, particularly if the franchise operation is one which relies on written contracts between the individual franchisee and its customers, e.g. in the fields of pawnbroking or television rental. The terms and conditions of the transaction between the customer and the franchisee will almost certainly be standardised by the franchisor and the need for a copyist to generate his own written contractual material is a barrier to entry into the field, albeit not an insuperable one.

CONCLUSION

Finally, many franchise operations require the would-be franchisee to undergo a period of training which is essentially the communication of know-how and, indeed, show-how from franchisor to franchisee. While many aspects of a franchise operation may not be difficult to copy, because they are effectively published as soon as the business starts up, there may well be areas of information which can be kept confidential, for example the ingredients, recipes and processing conditions to produce a foodstuff recognisably the same in Brisbane, Bombay, Beijing and Baltimore.

CONCLUSION

Any particular business or commercial activity will involve the use (and sometimes the creation) of a variety of intellectual property rights. Care should be taken to be aware of what rights are used, to secure a clear line of authority from the rights' owners if separate from the business, and to take such steps as may be appropriate to protect the business against copying by appropriate development of intellectual property rights, either in the capacity of an owner of those rights or in that of a licensee.

8–014

PART 2

PRINCIPLES OF TAXATION

CHAPTER 9

Individuals and Partnerships

GENERAL PRINCIPLES

Individuals, resident and domiciled in the United Kingdom are subject to income tax on the whole of their income arising worldwide, whether remitted to the United Kingdom or not (ITTOIA 2005 ss.6, 260, 368, 577; ITEPA 2003 s.15). A non-resident is normally taxable only on income arising in the United Kingdom although his liability may be limited to the tax deducted at source in respect of certain sources of income (ITA 2007 s.811). A non-UK domiciliary is normally liable to income tax on income arising in the United Kingdom and remittances of income arising overseas (ITEPA 2003 ss.15, 20–27; ITTOIA 2005 s.832; ITA 2007 ss.809A–809Z). If unremitted foreign income and gains exceed £2,000 in any tax year, a non-UK domiciliary over the age of 18 must pay an annual remittance basis charge in order to claim the remittance basis. If the non-UK domiciliary has been resident in the United Kingdom for seven out of the previous nine tax years prior to the relevant tax year the remittance basis charge is £30,000. The charge increases to £50,000 for a taxpayer who has been resident in the UK for 12 out of the previous 14 tax years prior to the relevant tax year. He will also lose personal allowances and the capital gains tax annual exemption as soon as he claims the remittance basis.

9–001

Income tax is applied under various charging provisions in ITEPA 2003 (which deals with employment income including pensions), ITTOIA 2005 (concerning trading income, interest and dividends, income from property and miscellaneous income) and ITA 2007, which contains a number of residual charging provisions, loss relief rules and provisions for the administration of income tax.

An individual, resident and (for tax years up to 2012/13) ordinarily resident in the United Kingdom, is also liable to capital gains tax on any chargeable gains (TCGA 1992 s.2). The concept of "ordinary residence" is abolished for 2013/14 and later years. A non-UK domiciliary is generally only liable to capital gains tax on disposals of assets situated in the United Kingdom, or remittances of gains from overseas assets sold at a profit (TCGA 1992 s.12), subject to the remittance basis charge rules described above which apply for 2008/09 and later years. Individuals not resident in the United Kingdom are generally not liable to capital gains tax even on assets situated in the United Kingdom, except where UK assets have been used for a trade or business carried on in the United Kingdom (TCGA 1992 s.10). However, where an individual who was previously UK resident, returns to the United Kingdom after being temporarily non-UK resident, he may be liable to capital gains tax in respect of certain assets disposed of whilst

INDIVIDUALS AND PARTNERSHIPS

9–002 temporarily non-UK resident. These provisions apply where there are fewer than five years of assessment falling between the year of departure and the year of return, and four out of the seven years of assessment immediately preceding the year of departure are also years of assessment in which he is resident and/or ordinarily resident in the United Kingdom (TCGA 1992 s.10A).

United Kingdom domiciliaries wherever resident are liable to inheritance tax on worldwide assets on death and on certain gifts (IHTA 1984 ss.1–4). A non-UK domiciliary is only liable to inheritance tax in respect of United Kingdom assets (IHTA 1984 s.6). In certain cases a non-UK domiciliary may be deemed to be domiciled in the United Kingdom for inheritance tax purposes, and from July 17, 2013, a non-UK domiciliary married to a UK domiciled spouse may elect to be treated as UK domiciled for the purposes of inheritance tax only (FA 2013 s.177). An individual who becomes deemed domiciled in the United Kingdom for inheritance tax purposes is not treated as UK domiciled for income tax or capital gains tax purposes (IHTA 1984 s.267).

An individual may also be subject to tax on certain deemed income or gains under various anti-avoidance provisions, designed to prevent the avoidance of tax through, in particular, the use of non-resident trusts and companies and the diversion of income to children.

Personal allowances

9–003 Individuals, including minor children under the age of 18, who are resident in the United Kingdom for a particular tax year, are entitled to basic personal allowances. Non-UK resident EEA nationals and Commonwealth citizens may also claim the personal allowance. The personal allowance, blind person's allowance and married couples' reliefs are not available to non-UK domiciled individuals claiming the remittance basis from 2008/09. There is no withdrawal of personal allowances where the remittance basis applies without the need for a claim (ITA 2007 s.809D), for example where unremitted income and gains are below £2,000. Personal allowances are withdrawn from individuals with income exceeding £100,000 at the rate of £1 for every £2 of income.

The rates of personal allowances for 2013/14 which are available are as follows:

	£
Personal allowance (ITA 2007 s.35)	9,440
Age allowance (ITA 2007 s.36)*	
65–74 single	10,500
75 or over single (ITA 2007 s.37)	10,660
Married** and born before April 6, 1935 (ITA 2007 s.46)	3,040
Married** and either spouse 75 or over	7,915
Blind person's (ITA 2007 s.38)	2,160

*The age-related allowances are progressively withdrawn if income exceeds £26,100.

**From December 5, 2005, couples who have entered into a civil partnership are entitled to the same allowances as married couples.

Rate of tax

Income tax is charged at the basic rate (20 per cent for 2013/14), higher rate (40 per cent for 2013/14) or additional rate (45 per cent for 2013/14, 50 per cent for 2011/12 and 2012/13) depending on the level of income. Savings income (broadly bank and building society interest) is taxed at the starting rate for savings of 10 per cent up to the starting rate limit. Dividend income is taxed at the rate of 10 per cent up to the basic rate threshold, at the dividend upper rate of 32.5 per cent to the extent dividend income falls within the higher rate band, and at 37.5 per cent (2013/14) in relation to income taxed at the additional rate.

9–004

The following thresholds apply for 2012/13 and 2013/14:

	2013/14	**(2012/13 in brackets)**
Starting rate for savings	£0–£2,790	(£2,710) at 10%* (10%)
Basic rate	£0–32,100	(£34,370) at 20% (20%)
Higher rate	£32,101–£150,000	(£34,371–£150,000) at 40% (40%)
Additional rate	over £150,000	at 45% (50%)

*Applies only to savings income, which is treated as forming top slice of total income.

SELF-ASSESSMENT

The mechanism for taxing individuals has been a system of self-assessment since 1996/97. The taxpayer will normally be sent a tax return at the beginning of the tax year, in April, but if he does not receive a tax return and has income or gains subject to tax he must, within six months of the end of the tax year, notify HM Revenue & Customs ("HMRC") of his liability to tax under TMA 1970 s.7 and HMRC will then send him the appropriate tax return for completion. It is not necessary to notify HMRC where the taxpayer's only income is remuneration or benefits already taxed under PAYE, or untaxed income has been taken into account in his PAYE coding, or has been subject to deduction of tax at source and the individual is not liable to tax at higher rates. Notification of chargeable gains is not required where the gain is below the annual exempt amount (£10,900 2013/14) and the gross proceeds do not exceed twice this amount (£21,800 2013/14).

9–005

INDIVIDUALS AND PARTNERSHIPS

Tax returns

9–006 Taxpayers who do receive a tax return will receive a core return plus supplementary pages tailored to their needs, for example if they have income from employment, self-employment, are a partner or a member of a limited liability partnership, have income from property, income from trusts, income from abroad or are non-resident, or have capital gains. The tax return has to be submitted by October 31, following the end of the tax year if filing a paper return, or January 31, following the tax year end if filing electronically. These deadlines apply unless the return has been issued late by HMRC, in which case the return must be submitted within three months of the date of issue. The taxpayer will normally be expected to calculate his tax liability but may submit the return by October 31, following the end of the tax year and request HMRC to calculate the tax for him. In cases where there are small amounts of other income or minor underpayments of up to £2,000 HMRC will code out the underpayment and collect the outstanding tax under the PAYE system during the following fiscal year, provided that the return is submitted by September 30, or December 30 if the return is submitted online. HMRC is to issue a consultation document over the summer of 2013 over proposals to increase the level of underpayments which can be collected through adjustments to the taxpayer's PAYE code. The taxpayer may choose to settle the underpayment directly rather than have it included in the following year's tax code.

There are two separate filing dates for paper returns and returns filed online. Paper returns must be submitted to HMRC by October 31 following the end of the tax year. Returns filed online must be submitted by January 31 following the end of the tax year (TMA 1970 s.8).

The standard tax return includes claims for reliefs and allowances which must normally be claimed in the tax return, although where the information is not available at the time, for example in respect of pension premiums paid on or before January 31 (or October 31, as appropriate) and treated as being paid in the preceding year of assessment, a claim outside the return may be made.

9–007 Under self-assessment HMRC may make corrections if the mistake is obvious under TMA 1970 s.9(4)(b). If the correction is not obvious the return has to be sent back to the taxpayer for re-submission and is not treated as a proper return. Once a return has been submitted and accepted and the calculation of tax due confirmed as correct, the return will be accepted unless it becomes the subject of an enquiry.

A taxpayer who has received a notice to file a self assessment tax return from HMRC is under an obligation to complete the return within the above deadlines, even where there is no income to report or the return has been issued in error. For 2012/13 and subsequent years, the taxpayer may request HMRC to withdraw the notice to file a return when it is agreed that no return is required (TMA 1970 s.8B).

Disclosure of tax avoidance schemes

With effect from March 18, 2004, taxpayers and advisers have been under an obligation to notify HMRC of certain planning arrangements entered into which enable a tax advantage to be obtained, or whose purpose (or one of the main purposes) is the obtaining of a tax advantage (FA 2004 s.306; SI 2004/1864). From August 1, 2006, all arrangements which seek to avoid income tax, capital gains tax, corporation tax and stamp duty land tax must be disclosed if the scheme contains one or more specified "hallmarks", such as confidentiality conditions, the existence of premium fee arrangements, the intention to generate tax-deductible losses or the scheme is mass-marketed (SI 2006/1543). Before January 1, 2011, arrangements on off market terms were also included. A proposal to put an arrangement in place which meets the relevant disclosure criteria must be notified to HMRC within five working days, even if the arrangement is not actually implemented and penalties can be imposed for non-compliance (SI 2012/1836). HMRC also have the ability to call for documents from a scheme "promoter" if non-compliance with the disclosure requirements is suspected, and from January 1, 2011, to obtain information from a person who is an "introducer" in relation to a notifiable arrangement. Once a scheme has been notified, HMRC will then issue a scheme number which the taxpayer must disclose on his self-assessment tax return, which inevitably increases the taxpayer's risk of the return being selected for enquiry by HMRC.

9–008

Enquiries into returns by HMRC

HMRC has 12 months from the filing date to enquire into a tax return, which may be a general enquiry to test the veracity of the information supplied by the taxpayer. The 12-months enquiry window applies to both returns filed online and in paper format. A general enquiry of this nature at district level will normally involve the production of the underlying books and records, and a meeting between HMRC and the taxpayer and his agent, if any. Most cases for enquiry will be chosen following HMRC's risk assessment of cases most likely to be incorrect, or may be chosen at random by HMRC's central computer. The majority of enquiry cases will be chosen following a risk assessment and only a small proportion of returns, something like one in 1,000, will be subject to random enquiry.

9–009

In addition to general enquiries HMRC may raise aspect enquiries where they are not seeking confirmation of the correctness of the taxpayer's records, but are querying the tax treatment of certain items or asking for additional information.

Under self-assessment the taxpayer has a statutory requirement to keep the records used to complete his tax return for a minimum period of 12 months following the filing date or until an enquiry is completed, if later; if the taxpayer is in business, the period becomes five years.

Payment

9–010 Tax not deducted at source is due for payment in two equal interim instalments, on January 31 in the tax year and July 31 following the tax year, with any balance being payable on January 31 following the end of the tax year, which is also the last date for submission of paper and online tax returns and the date of payment of the first instalment of tax for the following year.

Where 80 per cent or more of the tax due for the year is collected under PAYE or deducted at source or the prior year's liability was under £1,000, interim payments are not required. Nor are interim payments required in respect of capital gains.

The amount of the interim payments is based on the final tax liability for the preceding year, half that liability due for each of the two interim instalments. A claim may be made to reduce the interim instalment where there are good grounds for believing that it would be excessive, for example because of a downturn in business or loss claims.

There are fixed financial penalties or tax-geared penalties for failure to deliver tax returns as required and interest is payable on tax paid late. Failure to submit a return within the filing deadline triggers a £100 penalty. For 2009/10 and earlier years, the penalty was capped at the amount of tax outstanding on January 31, if lower, however, for 2010/11 and subsequent years the £100 penalty applies even where no tax is due. A daily penalty of £10 per day may be applied for a maximum of 90 days if a return is outstanding for three months or more after the filing deadline. If the failure to deliver a return continues six months after the "penalty date", i.e. the day after the filing date, a penalty of 5 per cent of the tax liability outstanding at the due date, or £300 if greater, applies. A further tax-geared penalty is due where the taxpayer has not filed a return 12 months after the penalty date. The amount of the penalty is dependent upon three factors: firstly, whether the withholding of information from HMRC is deliberate on behalf of the taxpayer; whether the withholding of information is concealed and finally the category in which the information falls. The three categories are determined by reference to whether the information relates to domestic or offshore matters, and if offshore, the extent to which the territory concerned has entered into tax information exchange agreements with the UK. The maximum penalty applicable is 200 per cent of the liability, which would have been shown on the return if it had been filed on the due date, or £300 if greater.

Estimates and amendments

9–011 Where information is not available to complete a tax return, the taxable income must be estimated to the best of the taxpayer's ability and the attention of HMRC drawn to the fact that this is a provisional estimate. This will be superseded by an amended self-assessment when the correct figure is known. A reasonably reliable estimate does not have to be drawn to HMRC's attention but a figure that is little more than a guess should be identified as such and the reason why the figure is not more accurate explained.

Once a return has been submitted and the enquiry period is over it becomes final unless HMRC can make a discovery under TMA 1970 s.29. A discovery may be made where there is a loss of tax and there is evidence that the situation arises owing to a taxpayer's deliberate or careless behaviour or where, on the basis of the information available to him, an officer of the Board could not reasonably have been expected to have recognised that tax had been underpaid. Where a self-assessment is reopened on discovery, it will be superseded by an amended self-assessment once a position has been agreed with HMRC.

In some cases the figures in the tax return will depend on subjective opinions, such as the value of unquoted shares, and in these cases the fact and basis of the valuation should be disclosed to HMRC. Valuations of property will normally be referred to the district valuer and valuation of unquoted shares and intellectual property referred to the Shares Valuation Division.

Penalties

Penalties may be imposed for the submission of an incorrect return if the taxpayer has acted carelessly in preparing the return or the inaccuracy is deliberate rather than a genuine mistake. As for the penalties applying on a failure to file a return, a distinction is drawn between domestic or offshore errors. For errors involving domestic matters, the maximum penalty is 100 per cent of the tax understated in the return as a result of the error, although the amount of the penalty will depend on whether the error is careless or deliberate, and whether the deliberate action was concealed or not. A reduction will be given to the penalty if the taxpayer offers full co-operation to HMRC in correcting his return or makes a voluntarily disclosure that an error has been made. For accuracies relating to offshore matters, the maximum penalty is 200 per cent of the tax understated as a result of the error. A penalty of up to £3,000 may also be levied if the taxpayer fails to keep proper records supporting the entries in his return. Penalties may also be imposed on third parties (such as accountants and tax advisers) where the person has deliberately provided false information with the intention of causing a taxpayer to understate their tax liability.

9–012

Internet services

Under self-assessment, agents are able to register with HMRC and submit taxpayers' returns over the internet, which has the advantage of avoiding transcription errors and enabling the agent to receive electronically a copy of the taxpayers' statements, which would normally be sent direct to the taxpayer, showing the amount of tax currently due and the future instalments so far as ascertained. HMRC's online self assessment service allows taxpayers and agents to access other information such as statements of account showing payments and repayments due. In addition, the individual's tax liability is calculated automatically when a self-assessment tax return is filed over the internet.

9–013

Partnerships

Under self-assessment partnerships (including limited liability partnerships) are not a taxable entity, but a nominated partner is responsible for submitting the partnership tax return to HMRC and preparing a partnership statement showing

9–014

the allocation of the taxable profit among the partners. Each individual partner is then responsible for returning his share of the partnership profits in accordance with the information on the partnership statement and to pay the tax on his share of the partnership profits. Clearly, this means that, if there is an HMRC enquiry into the partnership, this automatically extends to an enquiry into each individual partner, at least as an aspect enquiry, on his partnership income.

Where an individual partner disputes the amount of partnership profit or losses allocated to him/her on the partnership return, the individual may enter the amount of profits/losses considered to be correct and make a disclosure in the white space of the return.

Accounts and computations

9–015 Under self-assessment it is not necessary to submit accounts and computations or taxed income vouchers even where a repayment is due, except in the case of labour only sub-contractors, unless specifically requested in the course of an HMRC enquiry. In many cases, however, it will be appropriate to submit accounts and computations and such other information as the taxpayer considers necessary for the proper understanding of the tax return and to refer to the accompanying documents in the white space on the tax return. The reason for this is both to enable HMRC to have the information necessary to confirm the return in the first instance, rather than to have to go through the formality of opening a formal enquiry, and to ensure that once the enquiry period is over HMRC would not be able to make a discovery, as they would already have the appropriate information. The main reason why HMRC do not consider that accounts and computations are normally required is because the returns for partnerships and the self-employed contain an analysis of the accounts in a standardised format, together with a summary, computation and capital allowances adjustments. This should be sufficient to calculate the tax due and also give HMRC a basis for computerised risk assessment.

Post-transaction rulings

9–016 A post-transaction ruling from HMRC confirming the tax treatment in advance of submission of the return is usually available under CAP 1 (Clearances and Approvals). This facility is likely to be of most benefit to unrepresented taxpayers. In the case of capital gains involving the agreement of valuations it is possible, once the transaction has been completed, to submit details to HMRC on Form CG34 for submission to the Shares Valuation Division in order to commence the valuation enquiries at the earliest possible moment. In simple cases this will enable agreement to be reached prior to submission of the return or, in more complex cases, at least get the valuation discussion under way as soon as the transaction has been completed rather than waiting for HMRC to refer it to the Shares Valuation Division in the course of a formal enquiry at some later date.

Repayment claiming

Small repayment claims remain outside self-assessment and repayment claim forms, together with the appropriate vouchers to cover the tax repayment, must be submitted by taxpayers. HMRC may also make targeted review enquiries outside the self-assessment system to employees to check that the correct code number is being applied for PAYE purposes.

An overpayment of tax may be reclaimed on submission of the appropriate return or information to HMRC, together with repayment supplement from the date of payment or, in the case of tax deducted at source, the deemed date of payment, which is January 31 after the end of the tax year.

9–017

RESIDENCE

A statutory definition of residence is introduced for 2013/14 and later years, and the concept of ordinary residence is abolished. Prior to April 6, 2013, residence and ordinary residence were not defined by the Taxes Acts and determination of an individual's residence (and ordinary residence) relied upon case law and HMRC's published guidance (IR 20 and subsequently HMRC 6).

9–018

Residence and ordinary residence prior to April 6, 2013

In *Levene v IRC* (1928) 13 T.C. 486 the dictionary definition of place of usual abode was followed. Ordinary residence has been contrasted with casual or occasional residence (*Lysaght v IRC* (1928) 13 T.C. 511; *Thomson v Minister of National Revenue (Canada)* 1946 S.C.R. 209), and may be treated as meaning that in the normal course of his life the taxpayer had been resident in the United Kingdom. Actual cases relating to residence show that where there is some business or permanent tie in the United Kingdom, the taxpayer tended to be treated as resident, subject to the specific exemptions contained in ITA 2007 ss.829–833 although the purpose of the visit did not outweigh the time spent (*Lord Inchiquin v IRC* (1948) 31 T.C. 125). A house available for use in the United Kingdom, by a visitor to the United Kingdom for some temporary purpose only, may be ignored in determining residence (ITA 2007 s.831).

Staying in hotels implied non-residence (*IRC v Zorah* (1926) 11 T.C. 289 and *IRC v Brown* (1926) 11 T.C. 292). Living in a yacht anchored in the United Kingdom (*Brown v Burt* (1911) 5 T.C. 667) and use of a hunting lodge (*Loewenstein v De Salis* (1926) 10 T.C. 424) has resulted in residence. Temporary visits abroad did not cause United Kingdom residence to be lost (*IRC v Combe* (1932) 17 T.C. 405) nor did temporary visits to the United Kingdom give rise to residence (*Withers v Wynyard* (1938) 21 T.C. 724). Reference had to be made to the quality of a person's presence in the United Kingdom, not just the quantity of time spent in the United Kingdom (*Gaines Cooper v Revenue & Customs Commissioners* [2007] S.T.C. (SCD) 23; *Shepherd v Revenue & Customs Commissioners* [2006] S.T.C. 1821). There had to be evidence of a distinct break in the pattern of the taxpayer's life on moving abroad (*L. Barrett v Revenue & Customs Commissioners* [2008] S.T.C. (SCD) 268).

9–019

HMRC's practice relating to residence was principally set out in HMRC 6 (formerly booklet IR20) and SP3/81. Following the decision of the Special Commissioners in *Gaines-Cooper*, HMRC issued further guidance on their practice in relation to residence in Revenue & Customs Brief 01/07. If no place of abode was maintained in the United Kingdom the taxpayer was resident for any tax year in which visits to the United Kingdom total 183 days or if visits were habitual and substantial, i.e. on average 91 days or more a year for four years. If the visits were habitual and substantial, ordinary residence could also be claimed. Ordinary residence and residence could still be claimed where the absence abroad amounted to less than three years and the taxpayer visited the United Kingdom for 91 days or more in a tax year. The three-year period was reduced where there is a full-time occupation overseas and the taxpayer had been abroad for a complete tax year (subject to permitted visits to the United Kingdom). As to visits extended because of exceptional circumstances, see SP2/91 and FA 1991 s.46. HMRC's general practice prior to April 6, 2008 was to ignore days of arrival and departure in calculating the number of days an individual was present in the United Kingdom. From April 6, 2008, ITA 2007 s.832 specifies that for the 183-day test, an individual will be treated as present in the United Kingdom on a particular day if he is present at midnight, unless he is merely in transit in the United Kingdom. The "transit rule" requires the individual to arrive on one day and depart the next, without having undertaken activities substantially unrelated to his passage through the United Kingdom. For example, the transit rule would treat a businessman arriving in the United Kingdom from overseas on his way to another international destination as not present in the United Kingdom on the day of arrival, provided that during his time in the United Kingdom he did not carry out activities substantially unrelated to his passage through the United Kingdom, such as attending business meetings or visiting his employer's UK office. By contrast, HMRC's guidance on the operation of the transit rule indicate that if the individual merely met a work colleague by chance whilst staying at a hotel near the airport and they discussed business matters, the day of arrival in the United Kingdom would be ignored under the transit rule, as the chance meeting with a colleague was unrelated to the individual's transit through the United Kingdom.

9–020 Although ITA 2007 s.832 concerns only the 183-day test, HMRC has indicated in guidance notes accompanying the draft legislation that their practice in relation to the 91-day average test will be aligned such that days of arrival will be treated as days of UK presence, unless the individual is only in the United Kingdom as a transit passenger. Furthermore, a number of recent cases, notably *Shepherd, Gaines-Cooper* and *L. Barrett* have emphasised that it is not sufficient for an individual who has been resident and ordinarily resident in the United Kingdom for a number of years to achieve non-UK resident status merely be limiting the number of days spent in the United Kingdom to meet the 183-day and 91-day thresholds: the individual must leave the United Kingdom and there must be a distinct change in the pattern of his lifestyle in the United Kingdom.

If a place of abode was maintained in the United Kingdom (which is not to be ignored under ITA 2007 s.830 above, or under ITA 2007 s.831, as a result of a full-time employment overseas or being engaged full-time in a trade or profession outside the United Kingdom), the taxpayer who was normally resident in the United Kingdom, may be resident for any year in which he was physically present in the United Kingdom for however short a length of time and ordinarily resident if the visits were habitual and substantial.

Under Extra-Statutory Concession (ESC) A11 a taxpayer coming to the United Kingdom was treated for income tax purposes as resident in the United Kingdom in the year of arrival only from the date on which he arrived, and a taxpayer leaving the United Kingdom was treated as resident in the year of emigration only up until the date of his departure, although the concession was not applied where there is a tax avoidance motive (*R v IRC Ex p. Fulford-Dobson* [1987] S.T.C. 344).

However, a full year's personal allowances were given in each case against the income for the resident period (*Fry v Burma Corporation, Ltd* (1930) 15 T.C. 113). A non-resident may be liable to tax on UK income not taxed at source at basic and higher rates (*Brooke v IRC* (1917) 7 T.C. 261), provided that HMRC can collect the tax.

9–021

For capital gains tax purposes, revised Extra-Statutory Concession D2 did not exempt capital gains in the tax year realised before arrival where the individual had been either resident or ordinarily resident in the United Kingdom at any time during the five years of assessment immediately preceding the year of assessment in which he arrived in the United Kingdom. Similarly, an individual who left the United Kingdom, and was thereafter treated as not resident and not ordinarily resident here, was not charged to capital gains tax on gains from disposals made after the date of departure, provided that the individual was not resident and not ordinarily resident in the United Kingdom for the whole of at least four out of the seven years of assessment immediately preceding the year of assessment in which he left the United Kingdom. Gains which related to assets used by a trade, business, profession or vocation carried on by the taxpayer through a UK branch or agency are excluded from the concession.

Temporary absence from the United Kingdom did not make a Commonwealth or Irish citizen non-resident for tax purposes (ITA 2007 s.829), but see *Reed v Clark* [1985] S.T.C. 323, which held in the circumstances of the case that an absence for a complete fiscal year was not an absence for some temporary purpose.

A person with a full-time employment outside the United Kingdom had his residence for tax purposes determined without regard as to whether he maintained a place of abode in the United Kingdom for his use. Similar provisions applied if a trade, profession or vocation was carried on entirely outside the United Kingdom. Incidental duties in the United Kingdom were ignored (ITA 2007 s.830; *Robson v Dixon* (1972) 48 T.C. 527 and SP/A 10).

Residence after April 6, 2013

After a prolonged period of consultation, a statutory test of UK residence is introduced from April 6, 2013 (FA 2013 ss.218 and Sch.45. The concept of ordinary residence is withdrawn for 2013/14 and later years (FA 2013 s.219 Sch.46).

9–022

The statutory residence test comprises three parts; an automatic non-UK resident test, an automatic UK resident test and a "sufficient ties" test. If the conditions of one test are met, the other tests do not need to be considered, i.e. if an individual falls to be treated as automatically non-UK resident under the test, there is no need to consider the other tests, and in particular the sufficient ties test can be ignored.

An individual is automatically treated as non-UK resident in a tax year if he spends less than 16 days in the UK during the year (other than in the year of death), or he was not resident in any of the three preceding tax years, and spent fewer than 46 days in the UK in the tax year in question. The post 2008 day count rules have been carried over into the statutory residence test, so that an individual will be treated as present in the United Kingdom on a particular day if he is present at midnight, unless he is merely in transit in the United Kingdom. Days of presence caused by circumstances beyond the individual's control such as sudden illness are also discounted. An individual will also be regarded as automatically non-UK resident if he carries out sufficient work abroad. The remaining two automatic non-UK resident tests deal with the tax year in which the taxpayer dies, and provide firstly that a taxpayer will be not UK resident in the year of death if he was non-resident in the two preceding tax years, and the number of days spent in the UK is less than 46, and secondly, that a taxpayer will not be UK resident in the year of death if he was non-resident in the preceding year, and split year treatment applied to the tax year before that.

9–023 There are four automatic tests of UK residence. A taxpayer will be considered automatically resident in the UK for a tax year if he is present in the UK for 183 days or more in that year. Under the second test, a person is resident in the UK if he has a home in the UK for 91 consecutive days or more (where at least 30 days of that period fall within in the tax year in question), is present there for some time on at least 30 days in the tax year, and during that 91-day period either he has no home overseas, or he has one or more such homes but each of them is a home at which he is present on fewer than 30 days in the tax year. If he has more than one home in the UK each of them is looked at separately for this purpose. An individual will also be UK resident if he works full-time in the UK for a period of at least 365 days, all or part of which falls within the year, without a significant break (a break of more than 30 days, with exceptions for annual leave, sick leave and parenting leave). More than 75 per cent of the days in the year when he works for more than three hours must be days when he does so in the UK. "Full time" means an average of at least 35 hours per week.

On death, a taxpayer will be considered UK resident in the year of death if he was resident under any one of the automatic UK resident tests in each of the previous three tax years, and (assuming the taxpayer would not otherwise have been UK resident in the year of death) the preceding year was not a split year, and at the time of death, he had a home in the UK. "Home" means a building or part of a building or, for example, a vehicle, vessel or structure of any kind. There must be a sufficient degree of permanence or stability for a building etc to count as a home, echoing the concept of a "residence" for capital gains tax purposes set down in *Levene*. The draft guidance published by HMRC states that "a person's home is a place that a reasonable onlooker with knowledge of the material facts would regard as that person's home." The draft guidance states that a holiday home or temporary retreat is not a "home" for the purpose of the residence tests, but the distinction between a home that is used sometimes as a holiday home and occasionally on a less casual basis, for example as a base when working outside the UK, is not clear.

Where a taxpayer is neither resident nor non-resident under the automatic tests, residence is determined by reference to the "sufficient ties" test, which looks at a number of UK ties together with days spent in the UK. A taxpayer will have a tie to the UK if:

1. he has family resident in the UK. Family members include a spouse, civil partner, unmarried partner or minor children. Minor children are excluded if the individual sees the child in the UK on fewer than 61 days in the tax year. A child aged under 18 who is in full-time education in the UK, and who would not be UK-resident if the time spent in full-time education were disregarded, is treated as non-resident for this purpose if he spends less than 21 days in the UK outside term time. Term time is defined as including half term breaks;
2. he has accommodation in the UK that is available to be used by him for a continuous period of at least 91 days in a tax year, and the taxpayer spends at least one night there in the year. If the accommodation is the home of a close relative the "one night" test is extended to 16 nights, to avoid an individual being treated as having accommodation available where, for example, he makes limited visits to stay with his parents. This tie does not require the individual to own the accommodation. Note that "accommodation" is a wider concept than "home" in the automatic UK resident test, and would include holiday homes and more temporary lodgings. For example, if the taxpayer were to make a hotel booking for a continuous term of at least 91 days in a tax year, the hotel room would constitute accommodation for this purpose;
3. he works, continuously or intermittently in the UK for at least 40 days in the relevant tax year for at least three hours a day. In this context, "work" encompasses everything in connection with work, including training and travel time;
4. he spent more than 90 days in the UK in either of the two preceding tax years. It is not necessary for the individual to have been UK resident in those years, only to have exceeded the 90-day threshold; and
5. he has been UK resident in any of the three previous tax years and he spends more days in the UK than in any other single country in the tax year in question. This tie is relevant only to someone leaving the UK, making it more difficult to lose UK residence status than to acquire it.

The day counting rules applicable to the UK ties test include an additional anti-avoidance provision to counter the risk of abuse of the "midnight" rule. The anti-avoidance rule will apply where the individual was resident in at least one of the preceding three tax years, has three or more ties with the UK and there were more than 30 days in the tax year in which the individual was present in the UK at some point during the day, but had left the UK at midnight. Where the anti-avoidance rule applies, all days spent in the UK above the first 30 days are counted as days of UK presence.

9–024

INDIVIDUALS AND PARTNERSHIPS

Once the number of UK ties has been established for a particular tax year, the number of days spent in the UK will determine whether or not the individual is UK resident for that year. The day count element of the UK ties test has to be considered slightly differently depending on whether the taxpayer is a "leaver" or "arriver".

Arrivers

Days spent in the UK	Impact of ties on residence status
Fewer than 46 days	Always non-resident
46–90 days	Resident if four ties (otherwise not resident)
91–120 days	Resident if three or more ties (otherwise not resident)
121–182 days	Resident if two or more ties (otherwise not resident)
183 days or more	Always resident

Leavers

Days spent in the UK	Impact of ties on residence status
Fewer than 16 days	Always non-resident
16–45 days	Resident if four ties (otherwise not resident)
46–90 days	Resident if three or more ties (otherwise not resident)
91–120 days	Resident if two or more ties (otherwise not resident)
121–182 days	Resident if one or more ties (otherwise not resident

For leavers, split year treatment will enable a taxpayer to be treated as non-UK resident from the date of departure if he leaves to work full time overseas, or leaves to live abroad and ceases to own a home in the UK and also spends fewer than 16 days in the UK A person arriving in the UK will become UK resident from the date he acquires a home in the UK, or starts full time work in the UK or comes to live in the UK. Split year treatment will apply automatically, unless the taxpayer elects for it not to apply. Accompanying spouses will also be able to claim split year treatment, subject to certain conditions.

9–025   The statutory residence test applies for all tax years from 2013/14. As a person's residence position in the three preceding tax years may be relevant to the current year (for example in relation to the automatic overseas test), there is a transitional provision which enables a taxpayer to elect for the new rules to apply to the assessment of their residence status in any one or more of the three preceding years before 2013/14.

A temporary visitor to the United Kingdom is not liable to tax on foreign income on remittances, unless he has spent 183 days in the United Kingdom in any tax year (ITA 2007 s.831). The 183-day period in ITA 2007 s.831 is

RESIDENCE

calculated exactly (*Wilkie v IRC* (1951) 32 T.C. 495). Days of arrival and departure were generally ignored for periods prior to April 5, 2008. From 2008/09, the day of arrival is included as a day of presence in the United Kingdom for the purposes of the 183-day (ITA 2007 s.832) test, unless either the individual leaves the United Kingdom on the same day or the transit rule applies. HMRC adopt the same practice in relation to the non-statutory 91-day average test which applied for tax years up to 2012/13.

Ordinary residence

The concept of ordinary residence is abolished from April 6, 2013. As with residence (pre-April 6, 2013), there was no statutory definition of ordinary residence and it was held in the case of *Lysaght v IRC*, above, to be the converse of casual or occasional residence. It was therefore treated as meaning, in the normal course of events, that the taxpayer was resident for substantial periods of time in the United Kingdom. For example, in *Kinloch v IRC* (1929) 14 T.C. 736, it was held that a widow who lived mainly in hotels and had spent substantial periods in the United Kingdom to visit her son at school, was ordinarily resident. See also, *Peel v IRC* (1927) 13 T.C. 443; *Miesegaes v IRC* (1957) 37 T.C. 493; *Reid v IRC* (1926) 10 T.C. 673 and *Elmhirst v IRC* (1937) 21 T.C. 381; also *R v Barnet LBC Ex p Shah, The Times*, July 21, 1980, and *Cicutti v Suffolk CC, The Times*, July 30, 1980. For HMRC practice on ordinary residence, see SP 3/81.

9–026

Dual residence

Because the United Kingdom, in common with many other countries, will treat a taxpayer as resident in cases where he is habitually in the country for periods of less than 183 days it will be appreciated that it is perfectly possible for a taxpayer to be resident in two or more countries in the course of a single tax year, and thus become dual resident. This means that he may be liable to tax in both countries, perhaps on his worldwide income in both countries. This problem is frequently overcome under a double taxation treaty as a bilateral agreement between the two countries in question, under which the taxpayer is regarded as fiscally resident in one country but not the other. This is frequently known as a tie-breaker clause and residence under such a provision depends on the country in which the taxpayer has the permanent home, or if in both countries, where his centre of vital interests (i.e. his main social and economic interests) is; and if in both countries, in the country of which he is a national, unless he is a national of both countries or neither, in which case the tax authorities of both countries have to sort out his fiscal residence. This is one of the few cases where nationality has a bearing on UK taxation. The double taxation treaty may also provide that income is taxable only in the country in which the taxpayer is resident or in which the income arises, which is particularly common in the case of rents from immovable property. The United Kingdom does not give an exemption to income that is subject to foreign tax under a treaty or local domestic law but will give a credit for UK income tax or capital gains tax on the same income or gain under TA 1988 s.788 where there is a double taxation treaty or s.790 where there is no treaty and

9–027

INDIVIDUALS AND PARTNERSHIPS

the relief is given unilaterally. An international treaty normally overrules United Kingdom domestic legislation (*Australian Mutual Provident Society v IRC* (1947) 28 T.C. 388; TA 1988 s.788(3)).

DOMICILE

9–028 An individual's domicile determines the system of private international law by which he is governed in matters relating to marriage and divorce, the division of his estate on death and the legitimacy of his children. So far as the United Kingdom is concerned, it is possible to be domiciled in England and Wales, Scotland or Northern Ireland as there are three separate systems of law within the United Kingdom. For tax purposes, a reference to UK domicile or non-UK domicile is generally accepted to mean domicile within one of these three jurisdictions. A person is normally domiciled in the country in which he is considered to have his permanent home, although it is possible to be domiciled in a country in which he does not actually have such a home. No person can be without a domicile, and unlike residence it is only possible to have one domicile at any one time for any one purpose. An existing domicile is presumed to continue until it is proved that a new domicile has been acquired, and most importantly, the onus of proof lies with whoever seeks to allege the change of domicile.

Every individual acquires at birth a domicile of origin, which in the case of a legitimate child, where the father is alive at the date of birth, is the country in which the father was domiciled at that time. If the father has died or the child is illegitimate, the domicile of origin is the country in which his mother was domiciled at the time of his birth. In these days when a large number of couples live together and have children without getting married, it may no longer be presumed that a child is legitimate, if it ever could have been (*Udny v Udny* (1869) L.R.1. Sc. & Div. 441; *Re Grove* (1888) 40 Ch D. 216).

Any independent person can acquire a domicile of choice, which displaces the domicile of origin, by residing in a country with the intention of remaining there permanently or indefinitely (*Attorney-General v Pottinger* (1861) 6 H & N 733; *Waddington v Waddington* (1920) 36 T.L.R. 359; *Cramer v Cramer* (1987) 1 F.L.R. 116). If a domicile of choice is abandoned, either a new domicile of choice is acquired or the domicile of origin revives. To give up a domicile of choice requires both leaving the country of choice and giving up the intention of remaining there permanently or indefinitely (*Thiele v Thiele* (1920) 150 L.T.J. 387).

9–029 A domicile of choice is basically the country in which an individual intends to make his permanent home, but it is not possible to claim a domicile of choice without actually living in the country claimed (*IRC v Duchess of Portland* [1982] S.T.C. 149; *Plummer v IRC* [1987] S.T.C. 698).

The domicile of a child under 16 is a dependent one and would usually follow any change in the father's domicile. A minor may acquire an independent domicile of choice at the age of 16 or earlier marriage.

A woman already married on January 1, 1974 would have acquired her husband's domicile on marriage as a domicile of dependence, now regarded as one of choice, but under the Domicile and Matrimonial Proceedings Act 1973, a woman who marries after that date retains an independent domicile. A married woman with a dependent domicile can by her actions now establish an independent domicile of choice, but her domicile of origin does not automatically revert on divorce (*Faye v IRC* (1961) 40 T.C. 103), or on her husband's death (*Re Wallach dec'd, Weinschenk v Treasury Solicitor* (1949) 28 A.T.C. 486; *IRC v Duchess of Portland* [1982] S.T.C. 149). A wife who is an American citizen is deemed to have married after January 1, 1974 under art.4(6) of the UK–USA double taxation treaty (SI 2002/2848).

As domicile is very much a matter of fact and of intention (*Earl of Iveagh v Revenue Comrs* [1930] I.R. 431, Supreme Court), mere length of stay in the United Kingdom would not be sufficient to establish a UK domicile. In *Winans v Att.-Gen.* [1904] A.C. 287 and *Bowie (or Ramsay) v Liverpool Royal Infirmary* [1930] A.C. 588, residence for nearly 40 years did not establish a change of domicile. Similarly in the more recent cases of *Buswell v IRC* [1974] S.T.C. 266 and *IRC v Bullock* [1976] S.T.C. 409, a foreign domicile of origin was not overruled by residence in the United Kingdom for a considerable period, in the face of the taxpayer's avowed intention not to change his domicile. In *Steiner v IRC* [1973] S.T.C. 547, *Re Lawton* (1958) 37 A.T.C. 216; *Re Furse (Deceased), Furse v IRC* [1980] S.T.C. 596 and *Bheekhun v Williams* (1998/99) 1 I.T.E.L.R. however, a change of domicile was on the facts of each case upheld. It is difficult to throw off a UK domicile of origin (*IRC v Cohen* (1937) 21 T.C. 301; *Gaines Cooper v Revenue & Customs Commissioners* [2007] S.T.C. (SCD) 23) and if a foreign domicile of choice is obtained, a return to live in the United Kingdom would usually resurrect the domicile of origin (*Fielden v IRC* (1965) 42 T.C. 501).

9–030

It is provided by IHTA 1984 s.267, that for inheritance tax purposes a person is deemed to be UK-domiciled for three years following the acquisition of a foreign domicile or if resident in the United Kingdom for 17 out of the previous 20 fiscal years.

Remittance basis

For 2007/08 and earlier years, the remittance basis applies automatically to a non-UK domiciled individual's foreign employment income and chargeable gains, and a claim is only required in respect of relevant foreign income (ITTOIA 2005 s.831).

9–031

With effect from April 6, 2008, a non-UK domiciled individual over the age of 18 must claim the remittance basis (ITA 2007 s.809B) through their self-assessment tax return each year, unless unremitted foreign income and gains for the tax year are below a de minimis threshold of £2,000, in which case the remittance basis will automatically apply (ITA 2007 s.809D). The remittance basis will also apply without the need to make a claim where the non-UK domiciled individual is either under the age of 18 during the relevant tax year, or has been resident in the United Kingdom for fewer than six out of the previous nine tax years, provided the individual does not have any UK source income or gains in the year and has not made a remittance of foreign income or gains (ITA

2007 s.809E). "Foreign income and gains" comprise relevant foreign income (ITTOIA 2005 s.830), overseas earnings (ITEPA 2003 ss.22 and 26) and foreign chargeable gains (ITA 2007 s.809Z).

For 2008/09 and later years, an annual charge applies for long-term resident non-UK domiciliaries over the age of 18 who claim from the remittance basis of taxation (ITA 2007 s.809C). The remittance basis charge is £30,000 for non-UK domiciled individuals who have been resident in the United Kingdom for at least seven out of the previous nine tax years. For 2012/13 and subsequent years, the remittance basis charge increases to £50,000 for an individual who has been resident in the UK in at least 12 of the previous 14 tax years. It is the individual's decision each tax year as to whether they wish to claim the remittance basis or suffer income and capital gains tax on their worldwide income and gains, however, for individuals with annual foreign income or gains in excess of the grossed up amount of the charge (for 2013/14, £66,667 or £111,111 for the £30,000 and £50,000 charges respectively) it will generally be to their advantage to claim the remittance basis and pay the £30,000 charge. Remittances of foreign income and gains made during a tax year in which the individual chooses to be taxed on their worldwide income and gains on an arising basis will remain taxable in the year of remittance.

9–032 The remittance basis charge applies only where a claim is required for the remittance basis to apply; the charge is therefore not payable where the remittance basis applies automatically, such as where unremitted foreign income and gains is below the £2,000 de minimis threshold.

The remittance basis charge operates by treating as taxable on the arising basis sufficient unremitted foreign income or gains (net of any reliefs or deductions which may be due) to produce an additional tax liability for the year of £30,000/£50,000 (ITA 2007 ss.809C, 809H). This additional liability on "nominated" foreign income and/or gains is subject to the same payment rules as any other tax due for the year, and is intended to be recognised as a payment of tax on income or gains for the purposes of double tax relief.

Where the "nominated" foreign income or gains are subsequently remitted to the United Kingdom, no further tax will be charged on the remitted amount. However, there are detailed provisions specifying the order in which foreign income and gains are treated as remitted, so that where the taxpayer remits nominated income or gains whilst other income or gains remain unremitted, the unremitted amounts are treated as having been remitted in priority to the nominated income/gains (ITA 2007 ss.809H and 809I). For 2012/13 and later years, where the cumulative total of nominated income and gains remitted to the UK up to the current year does not exceed £10, the above rules do not apply. A remittance of foreign income and gains to pay the remittance basis charge is not treated as a taxable remittance if the payment is made directly to HMRC (ITA 2007 s.809V)

9–033 For tax years up to 2012/13, the remittance basis rules applied equally to foreign income (but not gains, which are taxed in the year they arise) of an individual who is UK resident but not ordinarily resident for a particular tax year, and was therefore eligible for the remittance basis in respect of foreign income. Ordinary residence is abolished from April 6, 2013, and only non-UK domiciliaries are able to claim the remittance basis from that date.

Where an individual who has been resident in the United Kingdom for four out of the previous seven tax years becomes non-UK resident for a period of less than five complete tax years, foreign income remitted to the United Kingdom during the period of temporary non-residence will be subject to income tax in the tax year in which the individual returns to the United Kingdom. This rule applies for 2008/09 and later years (ITTOIA 2005 s.832A).

If a sizeable proportion of work is done overseas it may well be desirable for a non-UK domiciliary to enter into a foreign partnership within ITIOIA 2005 s.857 under which the income is taxable under ITTOIA 2005 Pt 8; or to enter into a contract of employment with a non-resident company, in which case the remuneration would be dealt with as earnings. This would be particularly appropriate in the case of a non-UK domiciled individual because in respect of income taxed under ITTOIA 2005 Pt 2 Ch.2, a non-UK domiciled individual has no advantage under UK tax law compared with a person domiciled in the United Kingdom being taxed on his worldwide profits, whereas remuneration from a non-resident company or partnership for services performed wholly abroad would be taxed only on remittances to the United Kingdom and not on the income arising (ITTOIA 2005 s.857; ITEPA 2003 ss.6, 7, 10, 20–41). For 2008/09 and subsequent years, where the taxpayer has been resident in the United Kingdom for more than seven of the previous nine tax years, the advantage of taxation under the remittance basis must be balanced against the annual £30,000/£50,000 cost of claiming it.

Prior to 2008/09, remittances in a fiscal year following that in which the recipient ceased to be a partner would be tax-free in the United Kingdom as there would be no source of income to tax. There were therefore advantages in alternating periods of overseas activities through a series of partnerships and employments and remitting only during a fiscal year following that in which the source ceased. From April 6, 2008/09, the "source ceasing" rule ceases to apply and this planning is no longer feasible. It should also be noted that a UK domiciled and resident partner of a foreign partnership would be assessed to tax on the arising basis on his share of the profits of the foreign partnership. Remittances from a ceased employment are taxable under ITEPA 2003 ss.17(1)–(3), 30(1)–(3).

9–034

Assessments on a remittance basis include not only direct remittances to the United Kingdom but also constructive remittances, such as the satisfaction of a debt incurred in the United Kingdom under ITTOIA 2005 s.833 or ITA 2007 s.809H. A cheque drawn on an American bank account was held to be a constructive remittance when sold to a UK bank (*Thomson v Moyse* (1960) 39 T.C. 291), as was a loan enjoyed in the United Kingdom (*Harmel v Wright* (1973) 49 T.C. 149). Remittances of the proceeds of foreign securities could be a remittance of capital if the securities were acquired before the taxpayer became resident in the United Kingdom (*Kneen v Martin* (1934) 19 T.C. 33), but not if purchased out of foreign income while the taxpayer was resident in the United Kingdom (*Walsh v Randall* (1940) 23 T.C. 55). It was arguable that remittance of a physical asset was not a remittance of income, for the purposes of ITTOIA 2005 Pts 2–5 for tax years up to 2007/08, but the benefit from its use in the United Kingdom could be taxed as earnings. For 2008/09 and later years, there are specific provisions which treat a taxpayer as having made a remittance if money, property (such as artwork, antiques or cars) or services acquired using unremitted foreign income is brought into or otherwise used or received in the United Kingdom by or for the individual or another relevant person (ITA 2007 ss.809K–809Z6). A "relevant person" comprises the taxpayer, his spouse or civil partner, their minor children or grandchildren, a close company (including a company which would be close if it were UK resident) of which the taxpayer or another relevant person is a participator, the trustees of a settlement of which the taxpayer or another relevant person is a settlor or beneficiary, and anybody connected with such a settlement. For the purposes of this test, the terms "spouse" and "civil partner" include those living together as if they were married or in a civil partnership (ITA 2007 s.809M).

There are exemptions for assets brought into the United Kingdom for a temporary purpose, repair or for public display. Assets costing less than £1,000 and items for personal use (such as clothing, watches and jewellery) are also exempt from the new remittance rules (ITA 2007 s.V–Z6). The benefit of any exemption is lost if the asset is sold in the United Kingdom and a taxable remittance will arise at the time of sale. It should be noted that the above exemptions only apply to assets acquired out of unremitted foreign income: it does not extend to assets acquired out of unremitted foreign gains.

9–035 Transitional rules provided that assets acquired using untaxed foreign income and owned by the taxpayer or a relevant person at March 11, 2008 will not give rise to a remittance if brought into the United Kingdom at a later date, even if the asset was kept outside the United Kingdom on that date. Assets acquired using untaxed foreign income located in the United Kingdom at April 5, 2008 will also not give rise to a charge under the remittance basis for so long as the present owner retains the asset.

Specific rules are introduced from 2008/09 dealing with remittances from funds comprising a mix of income or gains and capital (ITA 2007 ss.809P–809R). It has been HMRC's practice to treat income as being remitted in priority to capital, on the basis that a person would exhaust their sources of income before utilising capital, however, from April 6, 2008, the legislation provides a detailed process for identifying taxable remittances using broadly a "just and reasonable" apportionment.

For years up to 2007/08, the remittance basis was not available to an individual resident in the United Kingdom and domiciled in the Republic of Ireland in respect of Irish income. This restriction is removed for 2008/09 and later years.

9–036 If a non-UK domiciled individual is assessable on a remittance basis, it is important to ensure that, so far as possible, remittances to the United Kingdom are out of capital. This means that a taxpayer may require several bank accounts. The account containing his capital prior to becoming resident in the United Kingdom may be freely remitted. An account containing the proceeds of disposals of overseas investments could be remitted, but any chargeable gains element would be taxable on the remittance basis under TCGA 1992 s.12(1). However, the effective rate of tax applicable to capital gains may be less, as a result of the flat rate of tax of 18 per cent applying to gains, than that applicable to income and, therefore, a remittance from such an account should normally be made in preference to a remittance of income, assessable under ITTOIA 2005 Pts 2–5.

Gifts overseas

Prior to 2008/09, a non-domiciled individual taxable on the remittance basis could make gifts overseas of funds from his foreign bank accounts to his wife, family and friends. An overseas bank account into which the gift passed thereby avoided the constructive remittance problems previously mentioned (*Carter v Sharon* (1936) 20 T.C. 229 and *Grimm v Newman* (2002) S.T.C. 84). If, for example, a wife bought an expensive coat or otherwise spent the money so that her husband received no benefit, or if the children paid for their own school fees, it was considered that these would not be constructive remittances. However, from 2008/09 a transfer of unremitted foreign income or gains to person falling within the category of "relevant persons" (noted above) will be treated as a taxable remittance by the taxpayer where cash, other property or services are brought into or provided in the United Kingdom (ITA 2007 ss.809L–809U).

9–037

Where the individual is not UK-domiciled for either income tax or inheritance tax purposes, the gifts mentioned above can still be made free of inheritance tax. However, if the person is deemed domiciled in the United Kingdom for inheritance tax purposes under IHTA 1984 s.267, he would need to take advantage of the potentially exempt transfer provisions or other inheritance tax exemptions.

If a non-domiciled partner makes a gift from his (Jersey) bank account to his United Kingdom partners by transferring funds to their own (Jersey) bank accounts, such a gift would be excluded property for inheritance tax purposes. However, it would be necessary to ensure that the UK partners had not made a transfer of assets to the foreign partnership, or otherwise ITA 2007 ss.720–735 could cause the gifts to be assessable as income.

BUSINESS INVESTMENT RELIEF

From April 6, 2012, a non-UK domiciliary is able to bring foreign income or gains to the UK to make qualifying investments without triggering a taxable remittance. Business investment relief applies where the funds are invested in certain qualifying investments within 45 days of the overseas funds being received in the UK. The taxpayer must have been taxable on the remittance basis in the tax year in which the foreign income or gains arose, but there is no such requirement for the tax year in which funds are brought in to the UK. Qualifying investments include an issue of shares or securities, or a loan. Shares need not be ordinary shares, and the loan need not be secured. The investment must be in an eligible trading company, a "stakeholder company" or a holding company. A trading company is defined as broadly an unquoted trading company which does not carry on a substantial level of non-trading activity. "Substantial" for this purpose means 20 per cent or more, normally by reference to turnover. A stakeholder company is an unquoted company which exists wholly for the

9–038

purpose of making investments in eligible trading companies, and the company actually holds one or more such investments, or is preparing to do so within the next two years. A holding company is defined broadly as a company which is a member of a trading group having one or more 51 per cent trading subsidiaries. For business investment relief purposes, a "trade" includes a property rental business (whether of commercial or residential property). There is also no requirement for the company to be UK resident, although it is perhaps difficult to see why a non-UK domiciliary would choose to bring funds to the UK if the investment was in an overseas company.

For relief to apply, neither the taxpayer nor any "relevant person" (as defined above) must obtain a benefit from the investment, either directly or indirectly. A benefit includes anything that would not have been made available to the taxpayer in the ordinary course of business, or would not have been provided on such favourable terms. The investor may draw a salary, dividends, loan interest etc without triggering a benefit provided they are in line with amounts payable to any other employee or investor.

Business investment relief is withdrawn on the occurrence of a chargeable event. Withdrawal is proportionate if the event does not affect the whole of the investment. Chargeable events include: the investee company ceasing to meet the requirements for a trading company, stakeholder company or holding company, as appropriate; a disposal or part disposal of the investment; the taxpayer extracts "value" from the investment, other than the normal commercial benefits of dividends, loan interest payments, etc. or the company becomes "non-operational". This excludes formal insolvency proceedings taken for genuine commercial reasons.

In the case of a chargeable event, no charge arises provided the taxpayer takes "appropriate mitigation steps". In the case of a disposal, the taxpayer must either apply the whole of the sale proceeds to the making of another qualifying investment, or take the money offshore (although amounts may be retained in the UK sufficient to fund any capital gains tax liability). For other chargeable events, such as the cessation of trading activities, the mitigating steps rule requires the taxpayer to disposal of the holding within a period of 90 days, starting with the day the taxpayer became aware (or ought reasonably to have become aware) of the potentially chargeable event. For a receipt of value, the 90-day period starts on the date value is received. HMRC has the discretion to extend the 90-day grace period, and regulations the Business Investment Relief Regulations 2012 (SI 2012/1898) currently permit an extension where there is a lock-in agreement associated with the company acquiring a listing on a recognised stock exchange which prevents the investor disposing of the shares, or there is a statutory barrier such as a "closed period" following the company's year end, or under the terms imposed by a court order.

EMPLOYEES

9–039 Employees, directors and other office holders are subject to tax under ITEPA 2003. Chapter 4 of Pt 2 of ITEPA 2003 applies to resident employees (and prior to 2013/14, ordinarily resident) and domiciled in the United Kingdom. Where an employee is resident in the United Kingdom he is taxable on his worldwide earnings. Chapter 5 of Pt 2 of ITEPA 2003 sets out the rules applying to employees resident or domiciled outside the United Kingdom. If the employee is non-UK domiciled and the earnings arise from overseas duties with a non-UK resident employer the income is only taxed if remitted to the United Kingdom at any time, whether during the currency of the employment or not (ITEPA 2003 ss.17(1)–(3), 30(1)–(3).

A non-resident who is employed part time in the United Kingdom is taxable on the income arising from those duties unless the income is taxed only in the country of residence under a double taxation treaty.

Benefits in kind

In addition to being liable to tax under ITEPA 2003 ss.10(2), 62(2), 372, on all salaries, fees, wages, perquisites and profits whatsoever, an employee is taxable on gains from share options under Ch.5 of Pt 7 of the ITEPA 2003 (as amended by FA 2003 Sch.22) on non-cash vouchers, on credit tokens on cash vouchers under Ch.4 of Pt 2 of the ITEPA 2003 and on tax paid on behalf of the employee by the employer not reimbursed within 90 days under ITEPA 2003 s.222. Living accommodation is taxable on the annual value of the accommodation under ITEPA 2003 s.105 with an additional charge under ITEPA 2003 s.106 where the cost of the accommodation exceeds £75,000.

9–040

Termination payments are taxable under Ch.3 of Pt 6 of ITEPA 2003 subject to an exemption for the first £30,000 and foreign-service payments under TA 1988 s.188. Sick pay under ITEPA 2003 s.221, maternity pay under Ch.3 Pt 10 of ITEPA 2003, income support and job-seekers allowances are taxable under Ch.4 of Pt 10 of ITEPA 2003.

Directors and employees paid at a rate of £8,500 per annum or more, inclusive of expenses and benefits, are subject to tax on expenses under ITEPA 2003 s.70, subject to a deduction for those expenses wholly exclusively and necessarily incurred in the performance of the duties of the employment including travelling expenses other than travel between home and the place of the employment under ITEPA 2003 Pt 5 Ch.2. Travelling expenses reimbursed by the employer, including related subsistence, is allowable.

Employees are also taxable on benefits in kind, normally on the cost to the employer under ITEPA 2003 Pt 3 Ch.10 except where the benefit is taxable in accordance with particular rules such as the benefit from the private use of a car or van, taxable under ITEPA 2003 Pt 3 Ch.6 on a percentage ranging from 5–35 depending on the published CO^2 emissions of the car. Where an employee is provided with a van for private use, there is a flat rate benefit in kind charge of £3,000 (rate for 2013/14). An additional £564 charge applies if the employer also meets the cost of fuel for the van's private use. These benefit in kind charges are subject to amendments where the car is unavailable for part of the year, or where payment is made for the use of the car. Corresponding adjustments are available for the use of a van. ITEPA 2003 Pt 4 exempts benefits taxed elsewhere and also allowable benefits such as car parking, canteen meals, etc. A crèche provided by an employer does not, within appropriate limits, give rise to a benefit in view of ITEPA 2003 s.318 and there are specific rules for benefits which consist of the use of an asset other than a car or van, which is normally 20 per cent of its market value under ITEPA 2003 s.205. Car fuel is taxed on the basis of a scale charge under ITEPA 2003 s.150 which depends on the size of the car, but pooled cars and vans are excluded from a taxable benefit under ITEPA 2003 ss.167–168. Beneficial loans are caught by ITEPA 2003 s.175 subject to de minimis exemptions for, e.g. season ticket loans of less than £5,000 increasing to £10,000 for 2014/15 and later years (ITEPA 2003 s.180). Beneficial share arrangements for employees are caught under Chs 8 and 9 of Pt 3 of ITEPA 2003, although there are approved share option schemes and an enterprise management incentive scheme with beneficial tax treatment provided for under Ch.6 (approved share incentive plans ("SIPs")), Ch.7 (approved SAYE option schemes), Ch.8 (approved company share option plans "CSOPs"), Ch.9 (enterprise management incentives ("EMI")) of Pt 7 of ITEPA 2003. Where the employee is provided with living accommodation, not only is the benefit of the accommodation taxed but also any expenses incurred by the employer under ITEPA 2003 s.315. Directors' tax paid by the employer is a benefit under ITEPA 2003 s.223 and a scholarship for the child of an employee is caught by ITEPA 2003 ss.212 and 215.

P11Ds

9–041   The way the benefit provisions work is that the employer or provider of the benefit if it is a third party, has to complete Form P11D for the director or higher paid employee, which has to be submitted to HMRC by July 6 following the end of the fiscal year to which it relates. This form gives particulars of all benefits provided for the employee and all expenses reimbursed unless these are covered by a dispensation negotiated with HMRC under the authority of ITEPA 2003 s.65. In addition to benefits excluded because of a dispensation as non-taxable, the employer can agree to pay the tax direct in respect of minor benefits under a PAYE settlement agreement under SI 1993/744 and SP5/96. Formal incentive schemes can also be covered by a taxed award scheme which is particularly useful for third-party benefits where it is not intended that the beneficiary should suffer a tax charge (see SP5/96 para.17).

A copy of Form P11D or the information returnable thereon has to be given to the employee by July 6 following the year end, which he in turn will use to return the taxable benefits and expenses less the claim for allowable expenses under ITEPA 2003 Pt 5 on the ITEPA 2003 employment supplementary pages of his tax return.

There are proposals for benefits in kind and expenses to be dealt with through the PAYE system for the purposes of both income tax and national insurance contributions, which may lead to the withdrawal of the requirement for employers to submit Form P11D each year.

Allowances

9–042   Specific allowances for earned income include lump-sum benefits on retirement from a pension fund under ITEPA 2003 s.637, removal expenses and benefits under ITEPA 2003 ss.271–289 up to various allowable limits. Employer-financed house-loss indemnity schemes are protected by ITEPA 2003 s.288 and allowances for expenses in connection with foreign emoluments as given by ITEPA 2003 ss.22 and 23. Relief for foreign travelling expenses, including fares of the employee's family and dependants, is given by ITEPA 2003 ss.341, 370 and 373, while foreign pensions qualify for a 10 per cent deduction under ITEPA 2003 s.617. The car parking exemption is given by ITEPA 2003 s.237(2) and sporting and recreational facilities by ITEPA 2003 s.261. There is a de minimis exemption for incidental overnight expenses given by ITEPA 2003 s.240; work-related training by ITEPA 2003 ss.250–254, and fees and subscriptions to professional bodies, etc. by ITEPA 2003 s.343. Directors' liability insurance is protected by ITEPA 2003 s.346 and the agency expenses of employed entertainers by ITEPA 2003 s.352 (see Ch.27). The payroll deduction scheme for donations to charity is governed by ITEPA 2003 Pt 12.

No deduction is available for business entertaining in view of ITEPA 2003 s.356(1). These are, however, normally disallowed on the employer in the corporation tax computation rather than on the employee under ITEPA 2003. The exception is where the employee is given a round sum entertaining allowance which is taxable on the employee and tax deductible to the employer.

PAYE

In addition to providing a copy of Form P11D or the information provided thereon, the employer must also provide the employee with the annual certificate of pay and tax deducted on Form P60 by May 31 following the end of a tax year under the Income Tax (Employments) Regulations 1993 (SI 1993/744) reg.39. The employee should therefore have the information required to complete the employment income supplementary pages using separate pages for each employment.

9–043

Tax under ITEPA 2003 is assessed on the amount received in the fiscal year, under ITEPA 2003 ss.15(2) and 22(2) irrespective of the period during which it was earned, unless it is received prior to the commencement of the employment in which case it is treated as having been received in the year of assessment in which the employment commences under ITEPA 2003 s.17(2) or the employment has ceased, in which case it is treated as having been received in the last year of assessment during which the employment was held (ITEPA 2003 s.17(3)). The time at which income is received is the time it is actually paid to the employee or credited to an account on which he can draw under ITEPA 2003 s.18. The PAYE system is governed by ITEPA 2003 Pt 11 inclusive and the Income Tax (Employments) Regulations 1993 (SI 1993/744). The payment by the employer of an employee's liability is a payment to the employee (*Hartland v Diggines* (1926) 10 T.C. 247).

Emoluments

Income is taxed on the emoluments of an office or employment under ITEPA 2003 Pt 2 Ch.2 which includes payments for a future employment (*Shilton v Wilmshurst* [1991] S.T.C. 88) but must relate to a reward for services past, present or future (*Hochstrasser v Mayes* (1959) 38 T.C. 673). If the payment does not relate to the employment it is not taxable as employment income (*Mairs v*

9–044

Haughey [1993] S.T.C. 569 and *Pritchard v Arundale* (1971) 47 T.C. 680). Whether income is properly taxable under ITEPA 2003 as income from an employment, or under ITTOIA 2005 Pt 2 Ch.2 as self-employed, is sometimes unclear and the point is dealt with further in Ch.27, below.

SELF-EMPLOYED

9–045 Self-employed individuals are taxable under ITTOIA 2005 Pt 2 Ch.2.

For most practical purposes there is no distinction between income from a trade and income from a profession or vocation. The distinction is relevant, however, when considering the application of the sideways loss relief restriction provisions of ITA 2007 ss.103–114. The introduction of self-assessment led to a major change in the basis of tax and profits of the self-employed.

A business is subject to taxation on the current year basis, i.e. on the adjusted profits of the accounting period ending in the fiscal year for which they are taxed.

The rules setting out the basis of assessment for income from a trade, profession or vocation are contained in ITTOIA 2005 Pt 2 Ch.15.

Current year basis

9–046 Under the current year basis of assessment, profits for the first year of assessment are assessed from the date of commencement to the following April 5, as under the old basis (ITTOIA 2005 s.199). However, profits for the second year of assessment depend on whether there is a 12-month accounting period ending in the year, in which case the assessment is on the profits for that period (ITTOIA 2005 s.200). If there is not a 12-month accounting period ending in the second fiscal year, the assessment is on the basis of the profits for the first 12 months from commencement under ITTOIA 2005 s.201. Where there is no accounting period ending in the second year of assessment but a change of accounting date in the third year, the change of accounting date is deemed to have taken place 12 months before the actual change under ITTOIA 2005 s.214, which may give a deemed accounting date in the second fiscal year. If this is less than 12 months from commencement, the assessment will still be on the profits for the 12 months from that date (ITTOIA 2005 s.200(2)). Where there is a change in accounting date less than 12 months from commencement, in the second year of assessment, the assessment will still be on the profits for the first 12 months (ITTOIA 2005 s.200(2)). If the change of accounting date is more than 12 months from commencement, the assessment for the second year is based on the profits to the new accounting date under ITTOIA 2005 s.200(3).

If there is no accounting date in either of the first or the second year, because the first set of accounts is for a long period, the assessable profits for the second fiscal year is on the default basis, i.e. the fiscal year itself (ITTOIA 2005 s.200(4)). In the third year of assessment, if there is a 12-month accounting period ending in the third year, that forms the basis of assessment under ITTOIA 2005 s.198. If it was an accounting period of at least 12 months ending in the second fiscal year, the basis period for the third fiscal year is 12 months from the end of the previous basis period (ITTOIA 2005 s.201). In the fourth and

SELF-EMPLOYED

subsequent fiscal years the basis period continues to be the period of 12 months after the end of the basis period for the preceding year of assessment, so long as accounts are made up for a 12-month period (ITTOIA 2005 s.198).

Where there is a change of accounting period, the new accounting date will normally apply for tax purposes provided that the new accounting date does not exceed a period of 18 months, notice of the change has been given to HMRC, there has been no previous accounting date change in the preceding five years of assessment, or if there has been such a change HMRC is satisfied that the change is made for bona fide commercial reasons (ITTOIA 2005 ss.217, 218). If there is an invalid change it will be ignored for the year in which the change takes place, but in a subsequent year it will normally become effective provided that the appropriate notice is given to HMRC that the change is to apply for tax purposes (ITTOIA 2005 s.219). Where a change in accounting date skips a fiscal year, for example where accounts are made up for a 13-month period from April 1 in one year to April 30 in the following year, the accounting date is deemed to have changed 12 months prior to the actual date of change (ITTOIA 2005 s.214). If the accounting period to the new accounting date or deemed accounting date is for less than 12 months, the assessment is on the profits for the 12-month period ending on the new date (ITTOIA 2005 s.216). If the accounting period is for more than 12 months to the new accounting date, the whole of the period is assessable for the fiscal year in which it ends. If there are two accounting dates ending in the same fiscal year these are amalgamated under ITTOIA 2005 s.197 and the basis period would be the extended period covering both sets of accounts under ITTOIA 2005 s.216. In the year in which the business ceases, the assessment is from the end of the basis period ending in the preceding fiscal year to the date of cessation under ITTOIA 2005 s.202.

It will be appreciated that under these rules the same profits may be taxed in more than one year of assessment. To the extent that the profits are doubly charged, they are overlap profits and the period taxed more than once becomes an overlap period. The overlap profits of an overlap period may be carried forward until relieved. They may be partially relieved on a change of accounting date, which has resulted in the assessment of profits of more than 12 months in the fiscal year, under ITTOIA 2005 s.220. The proportion of the overlap profits relieved is obtained by following the steps set out in ITTOIA 2005 s.220(3), which effectively relieves the overlap profits for the overlap period proportionately to the extent that the change of accounting date results in an accounting period of more than 12 months. 9–047

The balance of the overlap profits of an overlap period are relieved on cessation of the business under ITTOIA 2005 s.205. If a loss-making period is included in the basis period for two successive fiscal years, it is only included in the first such period and treated as nil in the second period under ITTOIA 2005 s.206. If the overlap relief against the profits for the final period results in there being a loss in that period, this is relievable in the normal way for loss relief or as a terminal loss.

Adjusted accounts

9–048 The starting point for the assessable profits under ITTOIA 2005 Pt 2 Ch.2 (the former Sch.D, Case I or II) is the accounting profit computed in accordance with generally accepted accounting principles (*Heather v P-E Consulting Group* (1973) 48 T.C. 293; *Threlfall v Jones, Gallagher v Jones* [1993] S.T.C. 537; *Odeon Associated Theatres Limited v Jones* (1971) 48 T.C. 257; *Johnston v Britannia Airways Limited* [1994] S.T.C. 763). Profits must generally be computed on a full accruals basis, although a cash basis is introduced for businesses with turnover up to the VAT registration threshold (£79,000 for 2013/14) with effect from 2013/14 and later years, see below. Under the accruals basis, statutory rules were introduced in FA 2002, and incorporated into ITTOIA 2005 in ss.227–240, to set out the adjustments that must be made for tax purposes where there is a change in the accounting basis. The accounts, however, require to be adjusted for tax purposes as certain income may have to be excluded, because it is taxed under some other provision, or expenses properly deducted for accounting purposes are not allowable for tax purposes as a result of statutory provisions or case law. The general rules as to deductions not allowable for tax purposes are contained in ITTOIA 2005 s.34 and include expenses not wholly and exclusively incurred for the purposes of the trade, profession or vocation. Other expenses are expressly disallowed such as capital payments (ITTOIA 2005 s.33) and patent royalties (ITTOIA 2005 s.51). The incidental costs of obtaining loan finance are specifically allowed under ITTOIA 2005 s.58 as are expenses in connection with foreign trades and travelling by ITTOIA 2005 ss.92–94. Patent and trade mark fees and expenses are specifically allowed under ITTOIA 2005 s.89. Relief for certain pre-trading expenditure is given by ITTOIA 2005 s.57. Business entertaining expenses are specifically excluded by ITTOIA 2005 s.45.

Expenses incurred partly for business and partly for private purposes may be wholly disallowed as not being wholly and exclusively for the purpose of the trade (*Mallalieu v Drummond* [1983] S.T.C. 665). On the other hand, it may be possible to apportion expenditure, for example the cost of heating a house partly used for business purposes, on some just and reasonable basis, and to allow the deduction of the business proportion (*Copeman v William J Flood & Sons Limited* (1941) 24 T.C. 53).

Capital expenditure is disallowed: this has been described as expenditure made not only once for all but with a view to bringing into existence an asset or advantage for the enduring benefit of a trade (*Atherton v British Insulated and Helsby Cables Limited* (1925) 10 T.C. 77).

Cash basis

9–049 Following consultation on how the tax regime may be simplified for smaller businesses and a review by the Office of Tax Simplification, Finance Act 2013 introduces a cash basis for calculating the profits of small unincorporated businesses (whether sole traders or partnerships) (FA 2013 s.17 and Sch.4, inserting ITTOIA 2005 Ch 3A). "Small" means cash receipts must not exceed £79,000 (the VAT registration threshold for 2013/14) or £158,000 if the taxpayer is also in receipt of the new universal credit. The cash basis can continue to be used even if receipts exceed the VAT registration threshold, provided receipts do not exceed twice the VAT registration limit.

Certain businesses are excluded from the cash basis, such as farming businesses which have a herd basis election in place, and businesses with a current profit averaging election. A business eligible for the cash basis calculates their taxable income by simply taking business income received in a year and deducting business expenses paid in a year, subject to a few exceptions. There is no requirement to make adjustments for debtors, creditors or stock, other than on a business leaving the cash basis, and in general no distinction will fall to be made between capital and revenue expenditure. Income and expenses are treated as inclusive of VAT even where the business is not VAT registered.

Capital allowances may not be claimed under the cash basis, other than in relation to motor vehicles where the flat-rate motoring expense adjustment is not claimed. Special rules apply to dealers in land, dealers in securities and ministers' religion claiming the cash basis.

Flat-rate expenses may be claimed rather than actual costs in relation to motoring costs (in relation to cars, motorcycles and goods vehicles), business use of the taxpayer's home, and private use of business premises. For motoring expenses, the deduction is based on HMRC authorised mileage allowance payments. The "simplified" flat rate deductions are in all cases optional. 9–050

The cash basis is optional, however, businesses that choose to use the cash basis will have to continue using it until "there is a change of circumstances ... which makes it more appropriate for [the] profits to be calculated in accordance with Generally Accepted Accounting Practice". A business using the cash basis is restricted to a maximum £500 loan interest which may be treated as a trading expense in an accounting period, although hire purchase interest paid is not restricted. Restrictions also apply to how losses are relieved, and a taxpayer whose business profits are computed on the cash basis is not able to claim sideways loss relief against other income and gains arising in the tax year of loss. Relief for the loss is given by carry forward against future trading profits.

Capital allowances

The prohibition of a deduction for capital expenditure extends to the depreciation provision for the diminution in value of capital assets, normally debited in a profit and loss account. The effect of this disallowance is partly countered by allowing capital allowances on certain defined items of capital expenditure. Capital allowances are given as a trading expense, (CAA 2001 s.2(1)). Capital allowances are available on machinery and plant, (CAA 2001 ss.11–270) including special provisions for ships, expensive motor cars, short life assets, long-life assets, leased assets and inexpensive cars and fixtures. Relief is also available for mineral extraction under CAA 2001 s.16l; partnerships using the property of a partner, under CAA 2001 s.264; building alterations connected with the installation of machinery or plant, under CAA 2001 s.25; expenditure on thermal insulation, under CAA 2001 s.28; computer software, under CAA 2001 s.71; expenditure relating to films, tapes and disks is however normally treated as a trading expense and not eligible for capital allowances under CAA 2001 Sch.2 para.82, whereas allowances for expenditure on fire safety and safety at sports 9–051 grounds and security is given by CAA 2001 ss.29–33. Relief for expenditure is given on certain research and development expenditure by CAA 2001 ss.437–451; dwelling houses let on assured tenancies are covered by CAA 2001 ss.49 531; mineral extraction allowances by CAA 2001 ss.394–436 and dredging by CAA 2001 ss.361–393.

Capital allowances were available on industrial buildings and structures, (CAA 2001 ss.271–360) and agricultural buildings, (CAA 2001 ss.361–393); however, writing down allowances was phased out over a four-year period commencing on April 6, 2008. With effect from March 21, 2007, a balancing adjustment does not arise on the disposal of an industrial or agricultural building.

Under the current year basis capital allowances are treated as an expense. The rate of capital allowances is given on the basis of a 12-month period and if the basis period is for a longer or shorter period the rate of writing-down allowance is adjusted accordingly. Where, however, there is an overlap of two periods of account the period common to both is deemed to fall in the first period of account only for capital allowance purposes under CAA 2001 s.6(4). The rate of writing-down allowance is 18 per cent per annum for general plant and machinery for 2012/13 and later years (20 per cent for 2008/09 to 2011/12). An 8 per cent rate of writing-down allowance (10 per cent prior to 2011/12) applies to certain long life assets and integral features.

9–052 An annual investment allowance ("AIA") was introduced with effect from April 6, 2008 for individuals and partnerships, and April 1, 2008 for companies. Expenditure up to the AIA limit on general plant and machinery (excluding cars), is treated as a revenue expense in the year in which it is incurred. The limit is £250,000 from January 1, 2013 to December 31, 2014, having previously been £25,000 from April 1, 2012 to December 31, 2012. Previous limits are £100,000 (between April 2010 and April 2012) and £50,000 (from April 2008 to April 2010). Complex transitional provisions apply to determine the level of expenditure qualifying for AIA where an accounting period straddles a change in rate. Qualifying expenditure on plant and machinery above the AIA threshold will be eligible for writing-down allowances at the standard rate of 18 per cent per annum on a reducing balance basis, unless the short life asset regime applies or the expenditure falls to be included in the special 8 per cent rate pool. Motor vehicles are allocated to the main plant and machinery pool (CO_2 emissions below 160g/km) or the special rate pool (CO_2 emissions below 160g/km) depending on their levels of carbon emissions.

Writing-down allowances at the rate of 100 per cent are available for expenditure on certain energy efficient items, including cars with very low carbon emissions (95g/km or below in 2013/14).

Short life asset treatment is available for expenditure on plant and machinery where the estimated useful life is less than eight years (four years prior to 2011/12). Qualifying expenditure on an asset which is subject to a short life asset election is placed in a single asset pool such that a disposal of the asset will produce a balancing charge or balancing allowance. If the asset is still retained at the end of eight year period, the asset is transferred to the main pool or special rate pool as appropriate without a balancing adjustment.

LOSS RELIEF

Whenever trading activities of a business result in a loss, and the business is carried on a commercial basis with a view to the realisation of profits, the adjustment of the figures for tax purposes is exactly the same as where there is a profit, except that disallowable items such as depreciation reduce the loss rather than increase the profits. Where claimed capital allowances increase the loss. Effectively, therefore, loss relief applies to losses as increased by capital allowances.

9–053

Under self-assessment, losses are calculated by reference to the loss in the accounting period ending in the fiscal year and may be set against the total income either of that year, i.e. set against other income, or against the total income of the preceding fiscal year, i.e. carrying the loss back one year (ITA 2007 s.64). An extended carry back period of three years applied for losses arising in 2008/09 or 2009/10 (FA 2009 Sch.6).

Relief for losses against other income in the year of loss or preceding year may be capped at £25,000 per annum where the taxpayer is not actively involved in carrying on the loss-making trade. The restriction applies for 2008/09 and later years (ITA 2007 ss.74A, 74B). An individual is treated as not carrying on a trade in an active capacity where he spends an average of less than 10 hours per week engaged in trading activities (ITA 2007 s.74C). Relief may also restricted for losses arising from capital allowances in relation to certain leasing activities (ITA 2007 ss.76–79), losses derived from expenditure on certain films (ITA 2007 ss.74A, 74C, 74D), and losses generated from tax avoidance arrangements (FA 2010 Sch.3).

A claim to set off losses must be made by January 31 following the end of the year of assessment in which the loss arises. The taxpayer may elect whether to set off the loss, or carry it back, but he cannot claim part of the loss in each year except to the extent that the loss exceeds the income available for relief in the chosen year. Loss relief for a loss arising in the current year takes precedence over a loss arising in a succeeding year carried back (ITA 2007 s.65(2)). A loss arising in the first four fiscal years of a trade may be carried back and set against the total income of the three preceding years, using up the earliest available income first under ITA 2007 s.72. Where a loss appears in a computation for a second time, for example under a change of accounting date, it is only given in the first year for which it is available and treated as nil in the second year (ITTOIA 2005 s.206).

9–054

Where losses are not set against other income they may be carried forward under ITA 2007 s.83 and set against the first available profits from the same trade. There are no restrictions on carry forward loss relief for non-active traders.

A loss arising in the last 12 months of trading may be set against total income for the final year and any surplus against total income for the preceding three years against the latest year first (ITA 2007 ss.89 and 90).

A capital loss on unquoted shares, as computed for capital gains tax purposes, may, where the shares have originally been subscribed for rather than acquired from an existing shareholder, be relieved for income tax purposes against total income under ITA 2007 ss.131–151. Farming losses may be subject to a restriction under ITA 2007 ss.67 and 68.

CAP ON UNLIMITED TAX RELIEFS

9–055 Certain so-called unlimited tax reliefs are subject to a cap for 2013/14 and subsequent tax years (FA 2013 Sch.3; ITA 2007 s.24A). The cap limits the amount of affected tax reliefs that can be claimed by an individual to the greater of 25 per cent of income or £50,000. Income for this purpose is defined as total income liable for income tax, adjusted for pension contributions and gift aid donations.

The cap applies only to those tax reliefs which reduce the amount of general income liable to tax, and are not currently capped. This includes: relief for trading losses against general income of the year of loss and/or the previous tax year under ITA 2007 s.64 (note that the offset of brought forward against trading income from the same source is not within the scope of the cap); loss relief in early years under ITA 2007 s.72; qualifying loan interest, for example in relation to a loan taken out to invest in a partnership; relief for losses on property income where the loss arises from capital allowances (ITA 2007 s.120); income tax relief for losses on unquoted shares (ITA 2007 ss.131–151), but note that relief is not restricted where the share subscription qualified for relief under the Enterprise Investment Scheme (ITA 2007 Pt 5) or Seed Enterprise Investment Scheme (ITA 2007 Pt 5A). Charitable donations through the Gift Aid scheme, payroll giving, community investment tax relief and relief for gifts of land and shares are not subject to the cap.

ANNUAL PAYMENTS

9–056 Annual payments are payments made under a legal obligation (*Drummond v Collins* (1915) 6 T.C. 525; *Dealler v Bruce* (1934) 19 T.C. 9). The payments must be recurring (*Moss Empires Ltd v IRC* (1937) 21 T.C. 264) over a period exceeding 12 months (*Whitworth Park Coal Co Ltd v IRC* (1959) 38 T.C. 531). They must be pure income profit of the recipient taxable under Sch.D, Case III on the gross amount received, with no expenses deductible against them (*IRC v London Corporation (as conservators of Epping Forest)* (1953) 34 T.C. 293). They must be income not capital receipts of the payee (*Campbell v IRC* (1970) 45 T.C. 427). In some cases it is necessary to divide a payment between its capital and income elements (*IRC v Church Commissioners for England* [1976] S.T.C. 339; *IRC v British Salmson Aero Engines Ltd* (1938) 22 T.C. 29; *Brodies Will Trustees v IRC* (1933) 17 T.C. 432; *Ramsay v IRC* (1935) 20 T.C. 79; *Vestey v IRC* (1961) 40 T.C. 112), see also Ch.20, para.20–003.

Annual payments (other than interest) payable out of the profits of a business and which represented pure income profit in the hands of the recipient were specifically excluded as a deduction in computing profits under Sch.D Case I/II for years up to 2004/05 (TA 1988 s.74(1)(m)), however, many payments fell outside this restriction on the basis that it dealt with payments "out of profits" rather than the computation of profits themselves. Annual payments do not feature in the rewritten rules for the calculation of trading profits in ITTOIA 2005 Pt 2, which apply from April 6, 2005. However, these contain specific exclusions from allowable expenditure, such as ITTOIA 2005 s.51, which excluded a deduction for any royalty or other sum paid in respect of the user of a patent. Royalties paid on or after April 1, 2002 to or by a company are not treated as annual payments by the company but are dealt with on an accruals basis, see Ch.21, para.21–016.

From April 6, 2007, the concept of a "charge on income" is abandoned for income tax purposes, and relief for a "qualifying annual payment" (under ITA 2007 s.898) which is unrelieved as a trading expense is obtained by deducting the gross amount of the payment in calculating the individual's net income (ITA 2007 s.448). Payments qualifying for relief include any royalty or other sum paid in respect of the user or patent. The payment must be made in the United Kingdom, and the recipient must be within the charge to income tax under ITTOIA 2005 s.579 Pt 4 Ch.7 Pt 5 Chs 4 and 7, or ITEPA 2003 Pt 9. Where the recipient is a company, the payment must either be chargeable to income tax under one of the provisions mentioned above, or be charged to corporation tax under Sch.D Case III. Donations to charity, interest and certain other payments are excluded from the definition of "qualifying annual payment".

The payer of a patent royalty or other qualifying annual payment is obliged to deduct income tax at the basic rate from the payment (ITA 2007 s.448). The tax deducted is taken into account on the payer's self-assessment tax return for the year in which the payment is made. It is worth noting that under the rules applying up to April 5, 2007, provided that the payment was made wholly out of income or gains chargeable to income tax (TA 1988 s.348), there was no compulsion to deduct tax at the basic rate, but the licensee was entitled to deduct, and only by making such a deduction could he obtain tax relief. It will be appreciated that if, as in the example, he paid tax on his total income without basic rate relief for the royalty paid but deducted tax from the actual royalty, he would have been in the same net position as if he had paid the gross royalty and claimed the amount as an expense for tax purposes provided, of course, that he is only liable to tax at the basic rate. Relief for higher rates was given, despite the annual payment not being a trading expense, by treating it as a deduction from the payer's total income.

9–057

The deduction from income is made in respect of the fiscal year in which the annual payment is paid, irrespective of the period to which it relates (ITA 2007 s.23). The method of relief for annual payments, etc. ensures that the payee suffers tax at least at the basic rate and HMRC therefore only has to collect by direct assessment any higher or additional rate tax on the payee. To the extent that the payer does not have a basic rate liability sufficient to cover the tax deducted from the annual payment, the payer must notify HMRC and income tax will be collected from the payer following the issue of an assessment under ITA 2007 s.963.

Failure to deduct tax

If the payer fails to deduct tax from an annual payment, HMRC can nonetheless assess the recipient (*Glamorgan Quarter Sessions v Wilson* [1910] T.C. 537; *Grosvenor Place Estates Ltd v Roberts* (1960) 39 T.C. 433).

9–058

If the licensee who is entitled to deduct tax from a royalty payment fails to do so he can recover the tax where there is an error of fact, e.g. whether the payment is a royalty payment or some other payment or money is paid under a mistake of law (*Kleinwort Benson Ltd v Lincoln CC* [1999] 2 A.C. 349). If there has been an honest mistake of fact, the tax not deducted could be deducted from future payments (*Re Musgrave, Machell v Parry* [1916] 2 Ch. 417; *Turvey v Dentons (1923) Ltd* (1952) 31 A.T.C. 470).

For 2007/08 and later years, the rate of tax to be deducted is the rate in force during the tax year in which the payment is made. This represents a change from the previous provision under TA 1988 s.4(2), which drew a distinction between the payment of a royalty or other annual payment out of profits or gains brought into charge to tax, under TA 1988 s.348, and payments not made out of profits or gains brought into charge to tax, and is therefore dealt with under TA 1988 ss.349, 350. In the former case, the rate of tax to be deducted is that for the fiscal year in which the amount becomes due for payment, irrespective of whether it is paid on time or not. In the latter case, the rate of tax to be deducted is that for the fiscal year in which the amount is finally paid, irrespective of when it was due for payment (ITA 2007 s.951) (See *Re Sebright Public Trustee v Sebright* (1944) 23 A.T.C. 190; *Regal (Hastings) Ltd v Gulliver* (1944) 24 A.T.C. 297).

Pure income profits

9–059   The definition of an annual payment usually turns on the question as to whether the payment is "pure income profit" in the hands of the recipient or whether the recipient has assumed reciprocal obligations involving him in expenditure such as would diminish his income from the payments. The relevant principles are stated in such cases as *IRC v National Book League* (1957) 37 T.C. 455; *Earl Howe v IRC* (1919) 7 T.C. 289 and *Campbell v IRC* (1968) 45 T.C. 427. If the payment is considered to be an annual payment, then the question of deduction of income tax is relevant.

In the *National Book League* case, Vaisey J. said of the covenanted subscriptions (at 468):

> "But the fact remains that these covenanted payments were not ordinary typical covenanted subscriptions to a charity. I think they were payments to the incorporated body, the League, in return for which the subscriber got some substantial advantage, so that these payments cannot be described as pure income payments when they reached the hands of the League and those who conducted its affairs."

Similarly, Lord Justice Morris stated (at 475):

> "The question arises whether the payments can be said to be pure gifts to the charity. In the terms of a phrase which has been used, can the payments be said to be pure income profit in the hand of the charity? If the payments were made in such circumstances that the League was obliged to afford to the covenantors such amenities and such benefits of membership as would at any particular time be offered to all members, and if those amenities and benefits were appreciable and not negligible, then I do not think that the payments were pure income profit in the hands of the charity."

9–060   In *Campbell v IRC*, Lord Donovan stated (at 446):

"The truth is, in my opinion, that one cannot resolve the problem whether a payment is an annual payment within Case III simply by asking the questions 'Must the payee give or do something in return?' or 'Did the payer make some counter stipulation or receive some counter-benefit?' or 'Was it pure bounty on his part?"

Such questions come more easily to the mind perhaps where, as here, payment to a charity is involved. But there is no warrant in the Income Tax Acts for applying a special test in the case of charities. The test must be applicable to all annual payments; and the problem must continue to be resolved, in my opinion, on the lines laid down by Scrutton L.J. in Earl Howe's case. One must determine, in the light of all the relevant facts, whether the payment is a taxable receipt in the bands of the recipient without any deduction for expenses or the like whether it is, in other words "pure income" or "pure profit income" in his hands, as those expressions have been used in the decided cases. If so, it will be an annual payment under Case III. If, on the other hand, it is simply gross revenue in the recipient's bands, out of which a taxable income will emerge only after his outgoings have been deducted, then the payment is not such an annual payment. This, of course, bas been said often enough before, but the judgement under review makes it necessary, I think, to say it again. The test makes it necessary to decide each case on its own facts. If goods and services are supplied in return for the payments in question, no doubt it will normally be found that this is done continuously or periodically during the time that the sums are payable, though there may be exceptions to this situation.

INCOME FROM UK LAND

Income from real property received by a person within the charge to income tax is taxable under ITIOIA 2005 Pt 3. Income from real property in both the United Kingdom and overseas is charged to tax under these provisions. Rental profits are computed as if the property business were a trade under ITTOIA 2005 Pt 2 (ITIOIA 2005 s.272), with certain modifications. Rules for taxation of income from real estate are totally different for companies, where the schedular system is retained. Although the income is calculated as if it arose from a business under ITIOIA 2005 Pt 2, which means that, for example, interest and capital allowances are allowed as trading expenses, the income does not qualify as trading income for loss relief, which is therefore ring fenced (ITA 2007 ss.117–124) and may be offset only against future rental income, nor does the rental business qualify for capital gains tax relief such as entrepreneurs' relief or roll-over relief on replacement of business assets. 9–061

Furnished holiday lettings, although taxed as income under ITTOIA 2005 Pt 3 Ch.6, are treated more like a trade in that capital gains tax reliefs available for a trade apply. Prior to 2011/12, a furnished holiday lettings business was also treated as a trade for loss relief purposes, and losses could be claimed against other income arising in the tax year of loss and/or the prior year. Because the rules for the calculation of trading income apply, income and expenses are calculated on an accruals basis, not on the cash basis, property by property, which was the position prior to 1995/96. Where property is let on a favourable rent below the full market value, there is no requirement to bring in a notional rent.

There may, however, be a disallowance of part of the expenses, to the extent that they exceed the income on property let out at an under value, on the grounds that the excess expenditure is not incurred wholly and exclusively for the purpose of the letting business. Apart from this, there is no need to deal with properties on an individual basis, and rents and expenses of a number of properties may be pooled.

The letting of overseas furnished holiday lettings was treated as an overseas property business and the more favourable treatment outlined above was not available. This position was potentially in contravention of EU law, and from 2011/12, the commercial letting of furnished holiday accommodation within the EEA is subject to the same deemed trade provisions as a UK furnished holiday lettings business. By concession, where an overseas furnished holiday letting business was operated prior to 2011/12 and the taxpayer's return is under enquiry, the taxpayer may claim this treatment for earlier years.

9–062 In relation to losses, from 2011/12, UK and overseas furnished holiday lettings businesses are treated as separate trades for loss relief purposes. Losses may be relieved only by carry forward against profits of the same business.

It is not uncommon to run into difficulties in agreeing allowable travelling expenses in connection with the supervision of property, as HMRC take a fairly strict line and need to be convinced that the travelling expenses are allowable and that the taxpayer's home is the base from which those expenses are computed, following *Horton v Young* (1971) 47 T.C. 60.

Furnished lettings are taxed under ITTOIA 2005 Pt 3 Ch.6 in the same way as for unfurnished property except that there is an allowance for wear and tear which is 10 per cent of the rent less council tax, water rates and other services normally borne by the tenants (ITTOIA 2005 ss.308A–308C, formerly Extra-Statutory Concession B47). Any amount received for the supply and use of furniture is treated in the same way as general rental receipts.

9–063 There is an exception to the rule that, except in the case of furnished holiday lettings, losses cannot be offset against total income which applies where the losses arise from excess capital allowances or agricultural expenses (ITA 2007 ss.120–124). Any property business losses brought forward under the "old" rules (applying for 1994/95 and earlier years) are treated as if they were expenses arising in 1995/96 under FA 1995 Sch.6 para.19(2) and (3). Income of a property business is taxed on a fiscal year basis, except in the case of partnership income or income from sub-letting surplus business premises brought into the computation of trading profits under ITTOIA 2005 s.21.

Joint ownership of the property does not necessarily amount to a partnership and each co-owner is assessed on his share of the rents less expenses.

Casual letting of a room in the taxpayer's home may be covered under the rent-a-room relief provisions in ITTOIA 2005 Pt 7 Ch.1.

Enveloped Dwellings

9–064 Finance Act 2013 introduces a range of measures concerning the taxation of UK residential property with a value at April 2012 in excess of £2 million. The measures relate to properties held by "non-natural persons" such as companies, partnerships with corporate members and collective investment schemes. There are three elements to the measures: firstly, a capital gains tax charge from April 6,

2013 at the rate of 28 per cent on the disposal of such properties by non-natural persons, including overseas companies; secondly, an annual residential property tax from April 1, 2013 on properties held by non-natural persons (the "annual tax on enveloped dwellings", or ATED); and finally an increased rate of stamp duty land tax on the acquisition of UK residential property by a non-natural person. The rate of SDLT is 15 per cent from March 22, 2012.

Various exemptions are available, such as were property is held for the purposes of a property rental business, where the letting is to independent third parties on a commercial basis, the property is held as part of a property trading or development business and properties held to provide housing to employees. There are also exemptions for working farmhouses and historic houses operated as a business. Where property is partly residential and partly commercial, only the residential element is subject to the FA 2013 provisions.

INCOME FROM INVESTMENTS

Interest and discounts

Interest and discounts are taxed under ITTOIA 2005 Pt 4 (formerly Sch.D Case III) on the income arising in the fiscal year.

9–065

Strictly speaking, each deposit on an interest-bearing account creates a new source of income (*Hart v Sangster* (1957) 37 T.C. 231).

As with rental income, taxed under ITTOIA 2005 Pt 3, partnerships are taxed on untaxed interest by reference to the accounting year ending in the fiscal year not by reference to the income arising in the fiscal year.

Taxed investment income

Income from Government securities, debentures, deposit interest from banks and building societies normally has tax deducted at source at the rate of 20 per cent, the basic rate for 2013/14. Previously, tax was deducted at the savings rate (referred to as the lower rate in 2006/07 and earlier years). The recipient is charged to income tax on the amount received under ITTOIA 2005 Pt 4. These provisions also charge income arising from overseas securities or possessions. Dividends from UK companies are taxable under ITTOIA 2005 Pt 4 Ch.3, and are deemed to carry a notional non-repayable tax credit equal to one-ninth of the dividend (ITTOIA 2005 s.397). Those paying tax at the basic rate suffer no further liability in respect of the dividend receipt; however, a taxpayer subject to the higher rate of tax will be liable on the total dividends received during the year and the credits relating thereto, as they form part of his total income under ITA 2007 s.23. The additional dividend rate is 37.5 per cent (2013/14, 42.5 per cent in 2011/12 and 2012/13). The upper dividend rate is 32.5 per cent, which combined with the notional tax credit of one-ninth of the dividend reduces the effective rate of tax on distributions to 25 per cent for a higher rate tax payer. Non-interest income from annual payments, such as patent royalties, are still subject to tax deducted at the basic rate of 20 per cent for 2013/14 (ITA 2007 s.903).

9–066

Under self-assessment, tax on investment income is payable in two instalments based on the preceding year's income, less the credit for the tax deducted at source, with the balance being payable on January 31 after the end of the fiscal year. The interim payments are dealt with by TMA 1970 s.59A and the final payment of income tax and capital gains tax by TMA 1970 s.59B.

FOREIGN SECURITIES AND POSSESSIONS

9–067 With the exception of rental income from foreign real estate, which is taxed under ITTOIA 2005 Pt 3, income from foreign securities and possessions is taxed under ITTOIA 2005 Pt 4, in the same way as income from UK securities, etc. The charge to tax is on the amount of income arising in the current fiscal year. The income is calculated on the amount arising and, in the case of foreign trades and professions, the income is calculated as if it arose under ITTOIA 2005 Pt 2 on the income arising in the accounting period ending in the fiscal year. Income from an overseas partnership is taxed as if the trade were conducted in the United Kingdom, subject to a claim for the remittance basis to apply to the profits of a non-UK domiciled partner (ITTOIA 2005 s.857; ITA 2007 ss.809B, 809C.).

For 2008/09 and later years, a non-repayable tax credit equal to one-ninth of the foreign distribution is introduced for shareholders with less than a 10 per cent interest in the overseas company. This aligned the treatment of United Kingdom and non-UK distributions received by both basic and higher rate taxpayers. For 2009/10 and later years, the foreign distribution tax credit regime is further expanded to shareholders with interests of more than 10 per cent in an overseas company where various conditions are met (ITTOIA 2005 ss.397A, 397AA, 397B).

Prior to the abolition of the schedular system for income tax purposes with effect from April 6, 2005, a trade controlled from the United Kingdom was charged under Sch.D, Case I (*Ogilvie v Kitton* (1908) 5 T.C. 338), but if controlled abroad, for example through a resident manager, under Sch.D, Case V (*Colquhoun v Brooks* (1889) 2 T.C. 490). The ITTOIA 2005 Pt 2 does not draw a distinction between trading income arising in the United Kingdom and that arising overseas, subject to a number of special provisions contained in ITTOIA 2005 Pt 8.

9–068 Where foreign income is received by a non-UK domiciliary, the amount taxable is the amount remitted to the United Kingdom, subject to the availability of the remittance basis to certain long-term resident non-UK domiciliaries from 2008/09. Income from property in the Republic of Ireland was taxable on an arising basis for 2007/08 and earlier years, but is within the remittance basis for 2008/09 and subsequent years. The remittance basis is given by ITTOIA 2005 s.832 and ITA 2007 ss.809A–809Z, and must be claimed for each fiscal year for which it is to apply, subject to limited exceptions. A non-UK domiciliary who has been resident in the United Kingdom for seven out of the previous nine tax years and who has unremitted foreign income and/or gains of more than £2,000 in the year, must pay an annual charge of £30,000 in order for the remittance basis to apply to his foreign income and gains, otherwise the non-UK domiciliary's worldwide income and gains will be taxed on the arising basis as if he were domiciled in the United Kingdom.

In the case of overseas-let property (other than furnished holiday lettings), income from each overseas property is pooled and there is one "overseas property business" (ITTOIA 2005 s.269). As there is now just one set of rules applying to income from property, whether located in the United Kingdom or overseas, the anti-avoidance provisions, such as those relating to premiums on leases, apply equally to properties abroad.

Profits and losses on overseas property income are pooled and any surplus loss is carried forward and offset against rental profits in future years. Notwithstanding the pooling of rental profits, it may be necessary to calculate the profit or loss for each property individually where foreign tax is payable in order to apply the correct double tax credit, following *Yates v GCA International Ltd* [1991] S.T.C. 157.

CASUAL PROFITS

The sweep-up provision taxing profits or gains not otherwise brought into charge for tax is ITTOIA 2005 Pt 5, which is computed on the income arising in the fiscal year except in the case of partnerships where it is by reference to the accounting period ending in the fiscal year.

9–069

NATIONAL INSURANCE

National insurance contributions are largely outside the scope of this book but the amounts levied can be substantial. For 2013/14, employees are subject to Class I contributions of up to 12 per cent on earnings between £149 and £797 per week. An additional 2 per cent is chargeable on earnings above £797 per week. The employer is subject to contributions of 13.8 per cent of the gross earnings without limit. A self-employed individual is taxed at a flat rate of £2.70 per week for 2013/14 once above the small exemption of £5,725 and is also liable to tax at 9 per cent of the annual profits between £7,755 and £41,450. An additional 2 per cent is payable on all profits above the threshold of £41,450. Those not in employment may pay a voluntary contribution of £13.55 per week.

9–070

CAPITAL GAINS TAX

Capital gains tax is payable on chargeable gains of taxpayers resident or ordinarily resident in the United Kingdom, in the year in which the disposal takes place (TCGA 1992 s.2(1)). Non-residents are normally taxable on chargeable gains in respect of assets in the United Kingdom used for the purposes of a trade, branch or agency carried on in the United Kingdom (TCGA 1992 s.10(1)), although from 2013/14 a charge may arise in relation to UK residential property held by non-individuals. Non-UK domiciliaries are only taxable on chargeable

9–071

INDIVIDUALS AND PARTNERSHIPS

gains remitted to the United Kingdom on non-UK assets (TCGA 1992 s.12). From April 6, 2008, where a non-UK domiciled individual has been resident in the United Kingdom for at least seven out of the previous nine tax years, the remittance basis is only available on payment of an annual charge of £30,000 or £50,000 depending on the length of residence, unless foreign income and chargeable gains (see ITA 2007 s.809Z) are below £2,000. United Kingdom resident non-UK domiciliaries who opt not to pay the annual charge are subject to capital gains tax on their worldwide chargeable gains in the tax year in which the disposal takes place. The situs of assets for capital gains tax purposes is given by TCGA 1992 s.275. For example, an interest in land is where the land is situated; shares or debentures are situated where the principal register is situated, if registered, or where the shares certificates are physically held if bearer shares (in a non-UK company). From March 16, 2005 shares or debentures in a company incorporated within the United Kingdom are situated in the United Kingdom. Goodwill is situated where the trade or business or profession is carried on. Patents, trade marks registered designs and corresponding rights are situated where they are registered, and, if registered on more than one register, where each register is situated, and rights or licenses to use a patent or trade mark or registered design are situated in the United Kingdom if those rights are exercisable in the United Kingdom (TCGA 1992 s.275(1)(h)); copyright, design right and franchises, rights or licences to use in the copyright, work or design in which the design right subsist and corresponding rights are situated in the United Kingdom if those rights are exercisable in the United Kingdom (TCGA 1992 s.275(1)G)). There is a de minimis exemption for capital gains tax of £10,900 for 2013/14 (TCGA 1992 s.3). This exemption is not available to non-UK domiciled individuals taxable on the remittance basis, unless unremitted foreign income and gains are less than £2,000. Capital gains above the annual exempt amount are taxable at a flat rate of 28 per cent, irrespective of the length of time for which the asset has been held or the type of asset concerned. Where gains are within the basic rate band (£32,010 for 2013/14) the rate is 18 per cent. There is limited relief for entrepreneurs (described below) which reduces the tax rate on the first £10 million of gains to 10 per cent where certain conditions are met. For self-assessment purposes interim payments are not required for capital gains tax and the tax is therefore due on January 31 following the end of the fiscal year in which the gain arose. For 2006/07 and earlier years, capital gains were subject to tax at the income tax rate as if the gains were the highest amounts of the taxpayer's income in the fiscal year (TCGA 1992 s.4).

There are complex anti-avoidance provisions enabling gains of non-resident companies to be apportioned to the shareholders, under TCGA 1992 s.13, and value shifting where rights of shares are amended, under TCGA 1992 ss.29–34.

Chargeable gains and losses

9–072 Chargeable gains are calculated on the excess of the consideration proceeds less disposal costs over the base cost plus acquisition costs (TCGA 1992 ss.37 and 38), unless the consideration has been taxed as income (TCGA 1992 s.37(1)), or the costs have been allowed for income tax purposes as deductible expenses or capital allowances (TCGA 1992 ss.39–41). The base value of assets held on

March 31, 1982 will be the market value at that date (TCGA 1992 s.35). From June 23, 2010, to the extent net gains exceed the annual exempt amount and any current year or brought forward capital losses, those gains are taxable at a single rate of 28 per cent unless they fall within the basic rate band, in which case the rate is 18 per cent.

Entrepreneurs' relief

Entrepreneurs' relief is introduced with effect from April 6, 2008 and is available on certain disposals of shares and securities (including interests therein) and assets used for the purposes of a business carried on by the taxpayer. The relief applies on a qualifying disposal of business assets by individuals and certain trustees, and is also available in respect of disposals associated with a material disposal (TCGA 1992 ss.169H–169S). The provisions also extend to the disposal of assets used by an individual for the purpose of a business which he carries on in entering into a partnership. A business carried on in partnership is treated as owned by the individual partners, and a disposal by a partner of his interest in the assets of a partnership is treated as a disposal of part of the partnership business.

9–073

The principal relief applies where a taxpayer makes a material disposal of the whole or part of a business, assets formerly used in the business following a cessation of shares or securities in a company. Where the disposal is of the whole or part of a business, the business must have been owned by the individual throughout the period of one year ending with the date of disposal. If a business ceases rather than being sold as a going concern, the assets must have been owned throughout the period of one year ending with the date of cessation. From that date there is a three year window from the date of cessation for entrepreneurs' relief to apply to gains realised on the disposal of assets formerly used in the business.

For a disposal of shares and/or securities to benefit from entrepreneurs' relief, the shareholder must, throughout the period of one year prior to the disposal, have held at least 5 per cent of the ordinary share capital and voting rights of the company, and have been an officer or employee of that company or another member of the same group throughout that time, although there is no requirement for the individual to have worked a particular number of hours in order to meet this condition. The company must also be either a trading company or holding company of a trading group during the one year pre-sale period. These terms are defined as for business asset taper relief, which means that the company must be carrying on trading activities, and those activities do not include to a substantial extent activities other than trading activities. "Substantial" means 20 per cent or more.

Entrepreneurs' relief is extended to shares awarded under an Enterprise Management Incentive option scheme from April 6, 2013. For disposals of shares taking place on or after April 6, 2013, the 5 per cent holding requirement is removed and the 12-month minimum shareholding period will commence on the date the option is granted, rather than the date the option is exercised. These changes apply to EMI shares acquired on or after April 6, 2012 where the disposal takes place on or after April 6, 2013.

9–074

Trustees may also qualify for entrepreneurs' relief on the disposal of shares or securities in a company or assets used (or formerly used) for the purposes of a business and which form part of the settled property of the settlement. For the relief to apply to a disposal by trustees there must be an individual beneficiary who has a life interest in the settlement (other than for a fixed term) in the whole of the trust assets or the part containing the business assets being disposed of. Relief claimed by the trustees on a disposal counts towards the beneficiary's lifetime £1 million total.

Shareholders and partners in a partnership may also claim entrepreneurs' relief on associated disposals of business assets on withdrawal from participation in a business, provided there is a material disposal and throughout the period of one year ending on the earlier of the material disposal or cessation of the business, the business assets were used in the business.

9–075 Where entrepreneurs' relief applies, gains are charged at the rate of 10 per cent. Subject to the lifetime limit for qualifying gains of £10 million, entrepreneurs' relief may be claimed on any number of disposals on or after April 6, 2008. A claim must be submitted on or before January 31 following the tax year in which the disposal is made. No claim may be made where a loss arises.

For 2006/07 and earlier years, the base cost of an asset may be increased by reference to indexation in accordance with the increase in the retail prices index between the date of acquisition of the asset or March 31, 1982 if later, and the date of disposal (TCGA 1992 ss.5–57) or April 5, 1998 if earlier. There is no indexation relief for periods beyond April 5, 1998, although taper relief may be available for disposals in 2007/08 and earlier years. Indexation allowance is withdrawn altogether for disposals on or after April 6, 2008.

Where the disposal is a transaction between connected parties or not at arm's length, the market value may be substituted for the proceeds, if any, under TCGA 1992 ss.17 and 18. There are anti-avoidance provisions to prevent the mitigation of capital gains tax by transferring assets in a series of transactions under TCGA 1992 ss.19 and 20. The disposal proceeds in particular cases where an asset is lost or destroyed are dealt with by TCGA 1992 ss.21–28 and part disposals and assets derived from other assets by TCGA 1992 ss.42 and 43.

Where the asset is a wasting asset, i.e. has a predictable useful life of less than 50 years, the base cost less any residual or scrap value is written off over the predictable life (TCGA 1992 ss.44 and 46), except where the asset has qualified for capital allowances (TCGA 1992 s.47), or is a tangible moveable wasting asset, which is exempt from capital gains tax under TCGA 1992 s.45. Cases with less than 50 years to run are depreciated on a curved line basis under TCGA 1992 Sch.8.

Losses

9–076 Losses are calculated in the same way as profits, but a loss on a non-UK asset of a non-domiciliary is not an allowable loss (TCGA 1992 s.16). Capital gains tax losses can only be set against chargeable gains in the same or subsequent years, except on death where capital losses may be carried back to the preceding tax year. However, trading losses can be set against capital gains in the same year to the extent that they exceed any taxable income, under ITA 2007 s.71. Losses on transactions between connected parties may only be offset against gains arising on disposals between the same connected persons (TCGA 1992 s.18(3)).

Losses may be carried forward indefinitely to set against future gains but, under self-assessment, TCGA 1992 s.16(2A) provides that losses for 1996/97 onwards must be claimed and relieved before any losses for earlier years, and have to be quantified. It has not been necessary, nor indeed possible (*Tod v South Essex Motors (Basildon) Limited* [1988] S.T.C. 392) to quantify capital losses of earlier periods except where necessary to compute the net chargeable gain.

A loss is not a capital loss if it arises directly or indirectly from arrangements, the main purpose or one of the main purposes of which is the securing of a tax advantage. This "targeted anti-avoidance rule" ("TAAR") applies to transactions taking place on or after December 6, 2006 (TCGA 1992 s.16A inserted by FA 2007 s.27).

In the first instance, in a capital gains tax computation, consideration due after the time of disposal is brought in at its full value and there is no deduction for any contingent liabilities. If the future consideration cannot be ascertained at the time of disposal, the right to the deferred element forms part of the consideration for the disposal and the value of that right is brought into account at its full value (*Marren v Ingles* [1980] S.T.C. 500 HL). If however, the consideration does not materialise or a contingent liability crystallises, an appropriate adjustment is made (TCGA 1992 ss.48 and 49). Where the deferred consideration takes the form of securities, the earn-out right itself is treated as a security and the share exchange provisions of TCGA 1992 s.135 automatically apply.

Transfers between husband and wife

Transfers between husband and wife or, after December 5, 2005, members of a civil partnership living together are exempt from capital gains tax (TCGA 1992 s.58). Business partnership gains are taxable proportionately on the partners personally, not on the firm (TCGA 1992 s.59). Death is not a chargeable event for capital gains tax purposes and therefore assets passing on death receive a capital gains tax-free uplift to the probate value at the date of death (TCGA 1992 s.62). There are rules for the identification of shares of the same class in the same company, and shares are pooled. For 2007/08 and earlier years, shares acquired since April 6, 1982 constituted a pool of shares and those acquired between April 6, 1965, when capital gains tax was introduced, and April 5, 1982, were treated as a separate pool (TCGA 1992 ss.104–114). Gilt-edged securities and qualifying corporate bonds are exempt from capital gains tax (TCGA 1992 ss.115–117B).

9–077

Re-structuring of companies

There are complex rules relating to the reorganisation or reconstruction of companies with the broad effect that where shares or securities are received in exchange for shares previously held, the gain will be deferred, which is usually known as "roll-over" on a paper for paper transaction, though any cash element will be immediately chargeable to capital gains tax (TCGA 1992 ss.126-l40B).

9–078

INDIVIDUALS AND PARTNERSHIPS

The appropriate amount in cash treated as income under the stock dividend provisions of TA 1988 ss.249–251 is deemed to be expenditure on the shares for capital gains tax purposes under TCGA 1992 s.142.

Options are treated as assets for capital gains tax purposes, but may be absorbed into the principal asset if exercised (TCGA 1992 ss.143–149A). Specific capital gains tax exemption is given to investments qualifying under the business expansion scheme or the enterprise investment scheme, personal equity plans and venture capital trusts, under TCGA 1992 ss.150–151B.

Roll-over relief

9–079 Certain classes of assets such as land and buildings, fixed plant and machinery, ships and aircraft, goodwill and certain agricultural quotas, as defined by TCGA 1992 s.155, qualify for roll-over relief under the rules relating to replacement of business assets in TCGA 1992 ss.152–160. Relief is only available to the extent that an amount equal to the whole of the proceeds on disposal is reinvested in qualifying assets within a window of opportunity commencing one year prior to and ending three years after the disposals. Any proceeds not reinvested remain chargeable.

It should be noted that intellectual property is not a qualifying asset for roll-over relief for business asset rules, see Ch.21, below.

Roll-over relief may be available on the transfer of a business to a company in exchange for shares under TCGA 1992 s.62 or as a gift of business assets under TCGA 1992 s.165. The gift relief is restricted if the donee is non-resident or a foreign controlled company, or dual resident trust, or if the donee ceases to be UK-resident (TCGA 1992 ss.166–169).

Other provisions

9–080 An individual's main residence is exempt from capital gains tax under TCGA 1992 ss.222–226. There are other exemptions or holdover reliefs in respect of charities (TCGA 1992 ss.256 and 257), works of art (TCGA 1992 s.258), chattels (TCGA 1992 s.262), cars (TCGA 1992 s.263), and gifts on which inheritance tax is chargeable (TCGA 1992 ss.260–261).

There are also provisions relating to the valuation of assets, double taxation relief, delayed remittances on foreign assets, etc. under TCGA 1992 ss.272–291.

PARTNERSHIPS

Self-assessment by partners

9–081 Partnerships are dealt with under the current year basis of assessment throughout. Partnerships under the Partnership Act 1890 are not a taxable entity for tax purposes and each partner is responsible for his own tax on his own share of the partnership profits (ITTOIA 2005 s.848).

The partnership is, however, treated as a notional individual for the purposes of the calculation of its profits chargeable to tax under ITTOIA 2005 s.849. The nominated partner will therefore have to lodge a partnership return containing details of the partnership income and a partnership statement allocating that income among the individual partners.

Each partner is treated as if he were carrying on a separate trade, the amounts of the profits of which were his share of the partnership profits (ITTOIA 2005 s.850). The effect of this is that commencement and cessation provisions do not apply to the partnership, but a partner joining the partnership is deemed to have commenced his notional sole trade and a partner leaving will be deemed to have ceased his notional sole trade which in turn means that the individual partners will have overlap relief on commencement and overlap relief on cessation in the same way as a sole trader carrying on an actual trade.

Partnership taxed income and chargeable gains are allocated to the partners entitled to receive such income and gains in the fiscal year, but other partnership income including rental income taxable under ITTOIA 2005 Pt 3; untaxed interest, income from foreign securities and foreign possessions taxable under ITTOIA 2005 Pt 4; or miscellaneous income taxable under ITTOIA 2005 Pt 5, are all calculated by reference to the accounting period ending in the fiscal year, as if it were income of a deemed second trade. The income has to be returned and is taxed in accordance with the rules applicable to the type of income, the deeming provisions only applying to allocate the income among the partners in the appropriate fiscal year. The deeming provisions also apply to the consequent adjustments for overlaps and overlap relief on a partner joining or leaving the partnership, but do not convert the investment income into trading income for any other purpose (ITTOIA 2005 ss.851–856). 9–082

Relief for trading losses arising to non-active partners against other income and gains of the tax year and preceding year is limited to £25,000 per annum (ITA 2007 s.103C). This rule does not apply to losses derived from certain expenditure on films (ITA 2007 s.103C(6)). Relief for trading losses for active partners is restricted for 2012/13 and later years under ITA 2007 s 24A to the greater of 25 per cent of income or £50,000.

The change of accounting date rules are applied at the partnership level by ITTOIA 2005 s.853 to avoid individual partners having different accounting dates other than in the years in which they join or leave the partnership.

Non-resident partner

Where a partnership contains a non-resident partner, ITTOIA 2005 s.849(3) provides that for the purpose of his tax liability the partnership is deemed to be a non-resident individual and therefore a separate partnership tax return would have to be prepared calculating the tax payable on this basis, i.e. by reference to the profits arising in the United Kingdom and excluding any non-UK profits and gains, for the purposes of allocation among the non-resident partners. The UK-resident partners would continue to have their allocation on the basis of the partnership's worldwide income. 9–083

Partnership carried on outside the United Kingdom

9-084 Where the partnership is carried on wholly or partly outside the United Kingdom and the control and management is situated abroad, a non-UK domiciled partner is taxable on his share of non-UK profits on the remittance basis (ITTOIA 2005 s.857). In the case of such a partnership the profits would be computed along United Kingdom lines on the worldwide income for any UK resident and domiciled partners, and a separate computation restricted to the UK profits, if any, for the non-UK domiciled partners. An appropriate partnership statement would be required allocating profit among each class of partner. Non-domiciled partners would then be taxable on their share of profits arising in the United Kingdom and on any remittances of overseas profits, subject to the availability of the remittance basis in 2008/09 and later years for non-UK domiciliaries who have been resident in the United Kingdom for at least seven of the previous nine tax years (ITA 2007 ss.809B, 809C).

Corporate partner

9-085 Where there is a corporate partner in the partnership, CTA 2009 ss.1256-1272 require the profits to be computed along corporation tax lines for the partnership for allocation through a separate partnership statement to the corporate partners.

LIMITED PARTNERSHIPS

9-086 Limited partnerships under the Limited Partnership Act 1907 are taxed in exactly the same way as ordinary partnerships except that there is a restriction on loss relief which cannot exceed £25,000 per annum (ITA 2007 s.103C). Prior to 2007/08, loss relief was restricted to the limited partner's contribution to the firm (CTA 2009 s.1273 for companies; ITA 2007 ss.104 and 105). Because in Scotland a partnership is a separate legal entity, Scottish limited partnerships are sometimes used to provide an entity with a separate legal existence which is transparent for UK tax purposes.

LIMITED LIABILITY PARTNERSHIPS

9-087 A new form of body corporate, the limited liability partnership (LLP) was introduced by the Limited Liability Partnership Act 2000 with effect from April 6, 2001. For most taxation purposes this new entity is treated as if it were a partnership. As for other partnerships, there are restrictions on loss relief which cannot exceed the LLP member's contribution to the firm (ITA 2007 ss.107-114). For 2012/13 and later years, relief for losses is restricted under ITA 2007 s.24A to the greater of 25 per cent of income or £50,000.

INHERITANCE TAX

Proposed changes

On May 20, 2013, as part of its review of avoidance arrangements involving partnerships, HMRC issued a consultation document on proposed changes to the rules for the taxation of partnerships and LLPs to counter "disguised employment relationships" and "artificial" allocations of partnership profits.

Members of limited liability partnerships are currently considered to be self-employed even if they are remunerated solely by means of a fixed salary. HMRC proposes to treat members of an LLP as employees for income tax and NIC purposes if either:

- on the assumption that the business of the LLP was carried on as a partnership by two or more of its members, they would be regarded as employees of that partnership; or
- they are exposed to no economic risk (such as loss of capital or a requirement to repay drawings) if the LLP makes a loss or is wound up, and they are not entitled to a share of either the profits or any surplus assets on a winding up.

9–088

This proposed change affects only members of LLPs, as there is no equivalent presumption of self-employment status for partners in a general partnership.

The second element to the proposed changes relates to the allocation of partnership profits. At present, profits and losses are allocated according to ratios agreed between the partners or members during an accounting period. It is proposed that that profits or losses will be re-allocated on a just and reasonable basis where profits are allocated to company partners that are liable to tax at the corporation tax rate rather than the higher income tax rates. Where losses in early years of trading are allocated to individual partners while subsequent profits are allocated to company partners, it is proposed that loss relief would be denied. These changes will apply only to "mixed membership partnerships", i.e. where at least one partner (or member in the case of an LLP) is an individual and one person is not liable to income tax (for example, a company or non-UK resident). An adjustment of profits or losses would only apply where it is reasonable to assume that the arrangement is intended to secure a tax advantage.

9–089

The consultation document also includes proposals to counter arrangements where a member accepts a reduced profit share in return for a payment by one or other members who will suffer a lower rate of tax on those profits, such as a corporate member. In this situation, the payment will taxed as income.

Legislation giving effect to these changes is expected in Finance Act 2014.

INHERITANCE TAX

Inheritance tax is charged on the value transferred by a chargeable transfer by an individual, after March 26, 1974, which is not a potentially exempt transfer (IHTA 1984 ss.1 and 2). The measure of a transfer of value is the reduction in the transferor's estate as a result of the transfer (IHTA 1984 s.3). A lifetime transfer by an individual on or after March 22, 2006 is a potentially exempt transfer under

9–090

IHTA 1984 s.3A if it is to an individual or a disabled person's trust. Substantial alterations were made to the inheritance tax rules relating to trusts by FA 2006, and transfers to most trusts on or after March 22, 2006 will give rise to an immediate charge to inheritance tax, to the extent that the value transferred exceeds the nil rate band or other available exemptions. Under the rules in place prior to March 22, 2006, an immediate charge to tax arose only on transfers to a discretionary trust. Transfers on death under IHTA 1984 s.4 are charged at the full rate of 40 per cent on the excess of the chargeable transfers, including potentially exempt transfers made within seven years prior to death, over the exemption of £325,000 (2013/14 rate) on cumulative chargeable transfers (IHTA 1984 Sch.1). Taper relief for gifts (not to be confused with the capital gains taper relief which applied for 1998/99 to 2007/08, see earlier editions of this book) is given by IHTA 1984 s.7 and lifetime transfers are charged at half the rate of tax applicable on death.

Taxpayer's estate

9–091   A taxpayer's estate for inheritance tax purposes includes not only all assets worldwide, beneficially owned by him, but also the assets of a pre-2006 trust in which he is a life tenant (IHTA 1984 s.5) and assets given away where he has retained an interest in the property (FA 1986 s.102 and Sch.20). Excluded property under IHTA 1984 s.6 includes property situated outside the United Kingdom, beneficially held by a non-UK domiciled individual who is not deemed to be UK domiciled under IHTA 1984 s.267. There are no specific situs rules for inheritance tax purposes, so the normal common law rules apply, for example bearer securities are situated in the country in which the documents are kept (*Winans v Att-Gen (No.2)* [1910] A.C. 27). Certain gilt-edged securities are excluded property in the hands of non-domiciliaries. Where the trust was created prior to March 22, 2006, the life tenant of an interest in possession trust is deemed to own the capital of the trust for inheritance tax purposes under IHTA 1984 s.5, and consequently the reversionary interest therein is excluded property under IHTA 1984 s.48. New interest in possession trusts created after March 22, 2006 are brought within the "relevant property" regime previously applying only to discretionary trusts (IHTA 1984 ss.58–70), and will be subject to 10-year periodic charge and exit charges. Where the relevant property regime applies, the life tenant is not treated as having an interest in the capital of the trust for inheritance tax purposes and trusts assets are not included in his chargeable estate on death.

There are specific exclusions from inheritance tax for dispositions not intended to confer gratuitous benefit on the recipient or for the maintenance of the taxpayer's family, for retirement benefits, for the benefit of employees, waivers of remuneration and dividend, the granting of tenancies of agricultural property and written variations affecting the disposition of a deceased's estate, under IHTA 1984 ss.10–17. Transfers between spouses and members of a civil partnership were exempt subject to a limit of £55,000 to a non-UK domiciled spouse by a UK domiciled spouse (IHTA 1984 s.18) for 2012/13 and earlier years. For transfers on or after April 6, 2013, this limit is increased to the level of the nil rate band, currently £325,000. Further, a non-UK domiciled spouse of a

UK domiciliary is able to elect to be treated as UK domiciled for inheritance tax purposes only. This change will apply from July 17, 2013 (the date FA 2013 received Royal Assent).

There is an annual exemption of up to £3,000 (IHTA 1984 s.19); relief for small gifts (IHTA 1984 s.20); normal expenditure out of income (IHTA 1984 s.21); gifts in consideration of marriage or civil partnership (IHTA 1984 s.22); gifts to charities, political parties, housing associations, for national purposes, public benefit and into employee trusts (IHTA 1984 ss.23–29A).

Liabilities of the estate are generally deducted from assets in arriving at the amount chargeable to inheritance tax. However, Finance Act 2013 proposes to exclude a deduction for a liability to the extent that it has been incurred to acquire excluded property, or property qualifying for business property relief or agricultural property relief (FA 2013 s.176 and Sch.36). For example, a taxpayer may take out a loan to finance his business, but secured the loan on his main residence. Under the current rules, the liability would reduce the value of the house rather than the business, but the value of the business would have been reduced to nil by business property relief. Under the FA 2013 proposals, the loan will be offset against the value of the business, which is already reduced to nil for inheritance tax purposes owing to business property relief. The loan will not be available to reduce the value of the property upon which it is secured, increasing the overall value of the estate.

Conditionally exempt transfers

There is a conditionally exempt transfer regime covering historic houses, works of art, etc. under IHTA 1984 ss.30–35. Allocation of exemptions is dealt with by IHTA 1984 ss.36–42.

9–092

Trusts

From March 22, 2006, the distinction in the inheritance tax treatment of interest in possession and discretionary trusts is removed, and with a few limited exceptions, all trusts are subject to the relevant property regime in IHTA 1984 ss.58–70 described below. Subject to the availability of reliefs and exemptions, an inheritance tax charge may arise on the settlor on creating the trust in the first instance and thereafter on the tenth anniversary of the creation of the trust with a pro rata charge on any additions to the trust fund. The 10-year charge is basically 30 per cent of the normal lifetime rate, which itself is 50 per cent of the standard rate of 40 per cent. The effective rate of the 10-year charge is therefore a maximum of 6 per cent of the value of the assets in the trust (IHTA 1984 ss.64 and 66). There is also a charge under IHTA 1984 s.65 on assets leaving a trust, calculated on the reduction in value of the trust assets as a result of the distribution. These "relevant property" rules do not apply to existing interest in possession trusts created prior to March 22, 2006 (unless there is a further addition of funds to the settlement after that date), trusts for vulnerable persons, an immediate interest in possession created by will or intestacy on death (an "immediate post-death interest"), or certain successive interests in possession arising on the death of the life tenant after March 22, 2006 ("transitional serial

9–093

interests"). All property held on pre-March 22, 2006 trusts is treated as if it were that of the life tenant under IHTA 1984 ss.49–57A.

Prior to March 22, 2006, accumulation and maintenance trusts had specific benefits under IHTA 1984 s.71. Not only was the transfer into an accumulation and maintenance settlement a potentially exempt transfer so far as the settlor is concerned, but there was no 10-yearly charge, nor was there a charge on distribution to a beneficiary. In order to qualify for this beneficial treatment, beneficiaries had to acquire an interest in possession at age 25 at latest, but this could be an interest only in the income of the trust not necessarily the trust capital. In order to preserve this beneficial treatment, accumulation and maintenance trusts created before March 22, 2006 must have amended their terms before October 6, 2008 such that beneficiaries become absolutely entitled to trust property at the age of 18, otherwise their favourable inheritance tax treatment will have been lost. New accumulation and maintenance settlements created after March 22, 2006 will not carry any inheritance tax privileges.

There are various relieving provisions available for charitable trusts, employee trusts, trusts for bereaved minors or young persons (aged 18–25) and maintenance funds for historic buildings.

Close companies

9–094   Transfers by close companies can be apportioned through and subject to inheritance tax as if they were transfers by the shareholders, under IHTA 1984 ss.94–102.

Reliefs

9–095   There are some important inheritance tax reliefs, including business property relief for assets used in a business which includes intellectual property used for the purposes of the trade, or licensed as part of a business. The relief is available on a disposal of the business or an interest in a business, unquoted shares, which includes those on the alternative investment market, all at 100 per cent. Listed securities giving the transferor control, land or building, plant or machinery used for the purpose of a business carried on by a partnership in which the transferor was a partner, or for a business carried on by a settlement, qualifies for a 50 per cent relief (IHTA 1984 ss.103–105). The value of the business is the net value of the business assets including goodwill, after deducting any liabilities incurred for business purposes (*Finch v IRC* [1983] S.T.C. 157). There are various restrictions on minimum periods of ownership, replacement assets and an exclusion for excepted assets that are basically investment assets not used in the business (IHTA 1984 ss.106–112). There are one or two traps to emphasise, in particular that relevant business property consists of a business or interest in a business, not business assets in isolation (IHTA 1984 s.105(1)(a)). Where there are contracts for sale such as buy/sell agreements, these are treated as an entitlement to cash not business assets, under IHTA 1984 s.113 and SP12/80. Where assets have been transferred within seven years of death, relief is only available where the donee has retained the assets or replacement assets, under IHTA 1984 ss.113A and

INHERITANCE TAX

113B. A broadly similar relief is available for agricultural property under IHTA 1984 ss.115–124B, but not both on the same asset (IHTA 1984 s.114).

There are other reliefs for such things as woodlands (IHTA 1984 ss.125 and 130); quick succession relief (IHTA 1984 s.141); alterations to the disposition of a deceased's estate (IHTA 1984 ss.142–147); voidable transfers (IHTA 1984 s.150); pension schemes, and in particular the cash entitlement under a pension scheme which may be paid direct to the beneficiaries without passing through the estate (IHTA 1984 ss.151–153). Double taxation relief is available for inheritance tax under IHTA 1984 ss.158 and 159 either by treaty or unilaterally. Property is to be valued on the basis of a disposal in the open market, at arm's length, with no deduction for flooding the market (IHTA 1984 s.160). For valuation purposes, assets of the transferor must be aggregated with those of his spouse and any property which has been settled on a charity and held by the charity within five years of the transfer. This is known as related property under IHTA 1984 s.161.

In the case of unquoted shares and securities, IHTA 1984 s.168 provides that the market value is on the basis of a sale in the open market on the assumption that there is available to any prospective purchaser all the information which a prudent, prospective purchaser might reasonably require for a purchase from a willing vendor by private treaty at arm's length (IHTA 1984 s.168). A lease for life is treated as an interest in possession and therefore the lessee is deemed to own the entire property (IHTA 1984 s.170). Changes occurring on death such as the receipt of insurance policy proceeds are included in the estate at death under IHTA 1984 s.171. There are allowances for funeral expenses, expenses incurred abroad, income tax and unpaid inheritance tax, future payments due on the transfer of assets, and sales of related property assets under IHTA 1984 ss.172–176. The sale proceeds can effectively be substituted for the probate value where shares are sold within a year of death under IHTA 1984 ss.178–189 or where land is sold within three years of death under IHTA 1984 ss.190–198. Adjustments have to be made for reinvestment.

Gifts with reservation of benefit

Property which has been the subject of a gift may still be caught as part of the donor's taxable estate as a gift with reservation of benefit if possession and enjoyment of the property is not assumed by the donee virtually to the entire exclusion of the donor (FA 1986 s.102; see *Tax Bulletin* November 1993 for HMRC's interpretation of "virtually to the entire exclusion".) These rules apply in respect of gifts made on or after March 18, 1986, and are intended to counteract arrangements (whether legally binding or not) whereby an individual sought to reduce the value of his taxable estate by making lifetime gifts of valuable assets, such as the family home whilst continuing to live in and enjoy the property. If it were not for the gift with reservation rules, the transfer would be exempt from inheritance tax on the assumption the donor survived seven years from the date of the gift. Following *IRC v Ingram* [1999] S.T.C. 37, lease carve-out schemes are not effective in circumventing the gift with reservation of benefit rules (FA 1986 ss.102A–102C). From June 20, 2003, arrangements, where an interest in property is transferred into an interest in possession trust and the life interest is subsequently terminated enabling the donor to benefit from the

9–096

property, are caught by the gift with reservation of benefit rules (*IRC v Eversden* [2003] S.T.C. 822 (FA 2003 s.185). There are exemptions for gifts between spouses and, from December 5, 2005, civil partners, gifts to charities and gifts in consideration of marriage (FA 1986 s.102(5)). HMRC do not regard a settlor's right of recovery from the trustees of certain non-UK resident settlements as a reservation of benefit (SP 5/92). There are other exemptions, such as where the donor pays a market rent for the use of the property.

Where the gift with reservation of benefit rules apply, the asset will continue to form part of the donor's estate on death, unless the reservation of benefit has ceased before that time. Furthermore, the property subject to the reservation of benefit will not benefit from an uplift to market value at the date of death for capital gains tax purposes, as it is only for inheritance tax purposes that the original gift is ignored and the asset treated as part of the donor's estate. There are provisions which prevent a double charge to tax where inheritance tax is levied both on the gift and on the donor's estate on death (SI 1987/1130).

Pre-owned asset charge

9–097   An annual income tax charge was introduced for 2005/06 and later years where an individual has made transfers of assets and continued to enjoy the benefit of them, without falling into the gift with reservation of benefit rules of FA 1986 s.102 (FA 2004 Sch.15). The charge applies where a person occupies land or buildings which he does not own, but for which he provided the funds or owned previously on or after March 17, 1986 (FA 2004 Sch.15 para.3). The income tax charge is based on the rental value of the property, using the same principles as those used for calculating a benefit in kind charge on the employer-provided accommodation. There is also a charge for the use of previously owned (or funded) chattels, such as works of art, cars, etc. (para.6), and intangible property comprised in settlements where the settlor retains an interest (para.8). The income tax charge is calculated by reference to the value of the chattel or intangible property using a notional rate of interest (paras 7, 9). In the case of the charge on intangible assets, any tax paid by the settlor under other anti-avoidance provisions such ITTOIA 2005 s.624 is deducted from the amount charged under the pre-owned asset rules. Various exemptions are available, including where the annual benefit is worth less than £5,000 (para.13); the transfer is between spouses/civil partners (para.10(2)(a)), or the transfer was for full market value (para.11). A charge does also not arise where the transfer concerned foreign property and the donor was not domiciled (or deemed domiciled) in the United Kingdom at the time of the transfer (para.12). Transactions on arm's-length terms are also excluded (para.10(1)(a)). There are provisions enabling those who entered into gift with reservation avoidance-type arrangements to unwind those structures and thus avoid payment of the pre-owned asset charge, without creating a double charge to inheritance tax (SI 2005/3441).

Other provisions

There are provisions dealing with the liability to tax by the transferor, his personal representatives, trustees of settled property, etc. under IHTA 1984 ss.199–214 and the administration and collection provisions are covered by IHTA 1984 ss.215–261. In particular, where the asset disposed of is land, shares or securities which gave the transferor control of the company or amounted to at least 20 per cent of his estate, or unlisted shares or securities where immediate payment of tax will create hardship, or represent at least 10 per cent of the nominal value of the issued share capital, or commercial woodlands, inheritance tax may all be paid by equal annual instalments over 10 years under IHTA 1984 ss.227–229. Interest is only due on overdue instalments in such circumstances under IHTA 1984 s.234. There are various anti-avoidance provisions relating to future payments, annuities purchased in conjunction with a life policy, transfers reported late, more than one chargeable transfer on one day under IHTA 1984 ss.262–266. Non-UK domiciliaries are deemed to be domiciled in the United Kingdom if they were domiciled in the United Kingdom within the three years immediately preceding the transfer, or were resident in the United Kingdom in at least 17 out of the previous 20 fiscal years under IHTA 1984 s.267. Associated operations may be aggregated under IHTA 1984 s.268 and treated as if they were a single disposal.

9–098

CHAPTER 10

Companies and trusts

COMPANIES AND CORPORATION TAX

Background

Until 1965 income tax applied to all entities whether they were individuals, trusts, unincorporated associations or incorporated bodies. Corporation tax was introduced in 1965 and applied to all bodies corporate which were resident in the United Kingdom.

10–001

"Bodies corporate" includes unincorporated bodies such as clubs and associations as well as the more familiar limited and unlimited companies. It does not include partnerships or trusts, or even a limited liability partnership which, although an incorporated body is transparent for tax purposes in most situations.

The residence qualification for corporation tax is important. Subject to the incorporation rule explained above, a body corporate that is resident outside the United Kingdom is not liable to corporation tax, unless it is carrying on a trade or profession in the United Kingdom through a permanent establishment (CTA 2009 ss.2, 5 and 19). Instead, such bodies are liable to income tax to the extent that the income is taxable at all. For example, foreign companies with rental income in the United Kingdom pay income tax and not corporation tax. The distinction is important principally because of the rate of tax, but also, in respect of the regulations, returns and general compliance which differ as between income tax and corporation tax.

Although residence is a question of fact, a company will nonetheless be deemed to be resident in the United Kingdom if it was incorporated there, unless it is also resident in a treaty country such that under the double tax treaty in question it is considered more resident in the other country. In such circumstances the company will be treated as resident in that other country (CTA 2009 s.18).

Structure of corporation tax

A company's taxable profit or Profit Chargeable to Corporation Tax is comprised of its total income (usually from various sources) after deduction of all available reliefs. The main types of taxable income are trading income, property income, interest or profits from loan relationships, non-trading gains on intangible fixed assets and overseas income. There are special rules which principally affect trading losses, retainable charges and the deduction of tax at source.

10–002

Chargeable gains are not separately chargeable to corporation tax but are added in to the total amount chargeable to corporation tax (TCGA 1992 s.8). In consequence, the amount on which corporation tax is chargeable is the sum of chargeable income and profits and chargeable gains computed in accordance with the Taxation of Chargeable Gains Act 1992.

Chargeable gains are broadly computed in the same way as for individuals with a number of important exceptions: indexation relief applies to companies; net chargeable gains after losses are added to the income and profits charged to corporation tax; there is no equivalent annual exemption for companies and net chargeable gains simply form part of the overall corporation tax assessment. The same rate of tax applies to a company's gains as to its other profits. Capital losses may be offset only against capital profits, and similar restrictions apply as for individuals in relation to the offset of losses on transactions between connected parties or otherwise not on arm's-length terms (TCGA 1992 ss.17, 18).

A "targeted anti-avoidance rule" ("TAAR") was introduced with effect for transactions taking place on or after December 5, 2005. This rule prevents a loss being an allowable loss if it accrues to a company directly or indirectly in consequence of, or in connection with, any arrangements where the main purpose or one of the main purposes is the securing of a tax advantage (TCGA 1992 ss.184A–184I). There are also specific anti-avoidance rules restricting the set-off of capital losses and gains of companies joining a new group (TCGA 1992 Sch.7A).

Rate of tax

10–003   Companies pay tax at a standard rate on the total assessable profit, traditionally referred to as the chargeable amount. The standard rate from April 1, 2013 is 23 per cent (Finance Act 2012), from April 1, 2014 will be 21 per cent and from April 1, 2015 will be 20 per cent (Finance Act 2013), bringing the main rate in line with the small companies rate of tax.

Companies with profits of not more than £300,000 are defined as small companies and pay tax at a lower rate of 20 per cent (rate applicable from April 1, 2011). Profits falling within the range of £300,000 to £1,500,000 are taxable at an overall intermediate rate, and companies with profits in excess of £1,500,000 will pay tax at the full standard rate. In cases where a company's profits fall between £300,000 and £1,500,000 an alternative way of defining this is that the first £300,000 of profits are taxable at the small companies' rate and the final tranche at 25 per cent for financial year 2012 and at 23.75 per cent for financial year 2013.

The rate for small companies is subject to an anti-abuse provision which allocates the relevant limits (e.g. £300,000 and £1,500,000) between the number of associated companies—broadly companies under common control or which are in a parent subsidiary relationship (CTA 2010 ss.24 and 25). In arriving at the number of associated companies, it is possible to ignore dormant companies which carry on no activities and which do not either pay or receive dividends from their associated companies (CTA 2010 s.25(3)(a)). Certain non-trading holding companies paying dividends equal to the amount of dividend income arising can also be ignored (CTA 2010 s.26).

COMPANIES AND CORPORATION TAX

Closely-held investment companies are not permitted to use the small company rate unless their income is predominantly rental income (CTA 2010 s.34). A company is close if it is controlled by five or fewer participators (broadly shareholders and certain loan creditors) or any number of directors (CTA 2010 s.439).

Losses

Trading losses for corporation tax can be offset against the total profits, including chargeable gains, of the year or of the preceding year (CTA 2010 s.37). Otherwise trading losses can be carried forward against future trading profits only, but without time limit (CTA 2010 s.45). Trading losses may also be grouped for relief if there is an appropriate group relationship (CTA 2010 s.99). 10–004

Relief for other income losses largely follows the income tax rules restricting relief to that particular source of income only.

Capital gains tax losses, computed in a similar way as for personal capital gains tax, can be offset only against capital gains of the same company in the same year; any unused capital losses can be carried forward indefinitely in the same company. There is no group relief in respect of capital losses, but two companies within a group can elect for an asset sold by one of them to a person outside the group to be treated as though it had been transferred to the other immediately prior to the sale.

Following the European Court of Justice ruling in the case of *Marks & Spencer Plc v Halsey* [2006] S.T.C. 237, where it was held that the United Kingdom was in breach of the principle of freedom of establishment by not permitting a parent company to obtain loss relief in respect of the losses of a foreign subsidiary, provisions were introduced by FA 2006 permitting limited relief for such losses (CTA 2010 s.113). The amended legislation, now contained in CTA 2010 Pt 5 Ch.3, enables UK companies to claim losses from group companies resident in the EEA (European Economic Area) in certain circumstances. Further, following the Court of Justice of the European Union (CJEU) ruling in *Phillips Electronics UK Ltd*, legislation in the Finance Act 2013 s.30 amends the restrictions on when companies resident in the EEA can surrender losses attributable to their UK permanent establishment. From April 1, 2013, UK permanent establishment losses will only be denied to the extent that they are actually relieved (rather than whether they could be relieved) in another country.

Charges on income

Those costs which are not specifically deductible but which constitute annual charges are deducted from the total profits liable to corporation tax including capital gains (CTA 2010 s.189). Such charges are comprised of any annuity or other annual payment not being within the loan relationship regime (e.g. interest) or intangible assets regime (e.g. royalties). 10–005

Trading companies

10–006　Charges, where not relieved against profits and gains of the year, can be carried back against the chargeable amount for the previous year or added to any unrelieved trading losses for the year and carried forward for offset against future trading profits only (CTA 2010 s.45). To the extent that the charges relate to non-trading activities, they cannot be carried either backwards or forwards.

Special rules apply to investment companies which incur costs which are not properly deductible under any of the appropriate schedules and cases and consequently would otherwise not rank for relief at all. Such costs are treated as management expenses and relieved against profits and gains of the year or carried back to the previous year, or added to the management expenses of the subsequent year for relief in the same fashion (CTA 2009 s.1219).

It is important to note that an investment company is one defined as carrying on activities wholly or partly in the making of investments (CTA 2009 s.1218). There is therefore a category of company which is neither a trading company nor an investment company and which may have a number of costs which simply do not qualify for relief as being neither management expenses on the one hand nor permitted deductions under the various schedules and cases or for capital gains tax purposes.

Groups of companies

10–007　In recognition of the close association that companies within a group have with each other, important concessions are made in respect of both income and capital gains.

For income, losses and excess charges of one company may be offset against another in the same 75 per cent group. For capital gains tax purposes, transactions between companies within the same 75 per cent group do not give rise to a capital gains tax gain or loss, and the acquiring company effectively stands in the shoes of the disposing company in respect of the original base cost of the asset (TCGA 1992 s.171). There is, however, no group relief in respect of capital gains tax and it was therefore common to transfer assets intra group to the company that has capital gains tax losses in order that gains on disposal outside the group can be crystallised in the company which has capital gains tax losses, thereby achieving relief for the losses. Companies in the same 75 per cent group are able to enter into a joint election for a gain realised in one company to be treated as arising in another company, so that capital losses in one group company can be used to shelter gains arising to another member of the group (TCGA 1992 s.171A).

Substantial shareholding exemption

10–008　Where a company disposes of a "substantial shareholding" in broad terms a holding of at least 10 per cent in a company (the investee company), the disposal is exempt provided that the shares have been held throughout a continuous period of 12 months beginning not later than two years before the disposal. Various further conditions apply, including a requirement that the vendor company be a trading company or a member of a trading group and the investee company must also be a trading company or alternatively the holding company of a trading group (TCGA 1992 Sch.7AC).

Deduction of tax at source

Unlike individuals, who may retain tax deducted at source and thus obtain basic rate relief, companies are obliged to retain tax at source and pay it over to HMRC on a quarterly basis using Form CT61 (ITA 2007 ss.945–955). Every quarter, therefore, companies return and pay over to HMRC the tax they have deducted from retainable charges, patent royalties and interest after taking credit for any tax deducted from their income by other companies. Thus, a net amount of tax is paid over. To the extent that tax suffered on income exceeds tax deducted on payments, an amount is refundable. However, any refund is made only to the extent that previous payments have been made to HMRC in the tax year. Any unclaimed excess may be deducted from net tax payable on the corporation tax assessment. Consequently, if net tax is being suffered, relief will be available only on the tax payment date, i.e. nine months after the year end. The requirement to deduct tax at source is relaxed in certain circumstances for payments between companies where the recipient is within the charge to corporation tax thereon (ITA 2007 s.933).

10–009

Dividend receipts

It has been a feature of corporation tax that companies within its scope do not pay tax on franked investment income (dividends from UK resident companies). This income is outwith the scope of tax (CTA 2009 s.1285). From July 1, 2009, most dividends received from non UK companies are also exempt from corporation tax. When deciding whether a dividend is exempt, there are different rules for small companies, as defined in the Annex to Commission Recommendation 2003/361/EC of May 6, 2003 and all other companies. The rules can be found in CTA 2009 Pt 9A. If an overseas dividend is not exempt, double tax relief via credit relief can be obtained.

10–010

Individuals, trusts and other persons who are not companies, within the scope of corporation tax, are entitled to a tax credit in respect of a dividend (ITTOIA 2005 s.397). The tax credit, which is non-refundable, amounts to 10 per cent of a "gross" dividend (i.e. the dividend plus the tax credit). For dividends within a taxpayer's basic rate band the credit discharges the recipient's liability to income tax other than a liability at the dividend higher rate.

Corporation tax payments and accounting periods

Corporation tax is payable in respect of accounting periods which have event specific commencements and terminations CTA 2009 ss.9 and 10). An accounting period begins when a company is incorporated; when a company begins to trade; immediately after the end of the previous accounting period; or 12 months after the beginning of the previous accounting period. An accounting period ends when a company ceases to trade, or 12 months after it began. In consequence, an

10–011

accounting period cannot exceed 12 months, and if accounts are made up for, say, an 18-month period, this will, for corporation tax, be treated as a 12-month period followed by a six-month period, i.e. two separate accounting periods of different lengths.

The rate of tax is determined by the tax year, which is defined as a period from April 1 to the subsequent March 31. Accounting periods (however short) that straddle March 31 will therefore fall across two financial years and may have two different tax rates requiring apportionment or allocation of profits, income and gains.

For companies other than large companies (see below) corporation tax is due nine months after the end of the accounting period (TMA 1970 s.59D). An 18-month accounting period therefore has two tax payment dates, one nine months after the expiry of the first 12-month period and one nine months after the expiry of the second six-month period.

10–012 For large companies, currently companies with profits in excess of £1,500,000 in any 12-month accounting period, a system of quarterly accounting for corporation tax applies. A company is not a large company in respect of an accounting period where its profits do not exceed £10,000,000 and it was not a large company in the 12 months prior to that accounting period. The first instalment is due six months and 13 days from the commencement of the accounting period and the final instalment is due three months and 14 days from the end of the accounting period. In the case of a 12-month accounting period ending on December 31, 2013 instalments will be due on July 14, 2013, October 14, 2013, January 14, 2014 and April 14, 2014 (SI 1998/3175).

Under corporation tax self assessment ("CTSA"), companies are required to calculate their liability to corporation tax for each accounting period (FA 1998 Sch.18 para.7). Tax is payable either by instalments or nine months after the year end whether or not accounts are submitted, but accounts must be submitted within 12 months of the end of the period of account. Consequently, with, say, an 18-month accounting period, the accounts need not be submitted until 12 months from the end of the 18 months, whereas tax payment dates are determined by the end of the strict accounting periods. The submission of accounts must be accompanied by a tax return (Form CT600) which incorporates a signed declaration by the taxpaying company or its agent.

Disclosure of tax avoidance schemes

10–013 The disclosure of tax avoidance scheme rules (DOTAS) apply to the avoidance of corporation tax, and taxpayers who are party to arrangements which seek to avoid income tax, capital gains tax, corporation tax and stamp duty land tax must disclose the arrangements to HMRC if one or more specified "hallmarks" are present, such as confidentiality conditions, the existence of premium fee arrangements, off-market arrangements are used or the scheme is mass-marketed (SI 2006/1543). A proposal to put an arrangement in place which meets the relevant disclosure criteria must be notified to HMRC within five working days, even if the arrangement is not actually implemented, and penalties can be imposed for non-compliance. HMRC also have the ability to call for documents from a scheme "promoter" if non-compliance with the disclosure requirements is

TRUSTS

suspected. Once a scheme has been notified, HMRC will then issue a scheme number which the taxpayer must disclose on his CTSA return and complete supplementary form CT600J.

TRUSTS

Trusts are recognised as separate bodies and the trustees are personally liable for income tax and capital gains tax arising on trust assets.   **10–014**

Income tax

For income tax purposes trusts pay tax at a rate dependent upon whether or not they are discretionary and accumulation trusts on the one hand or any other kind of trust (principally life interest trusts) on the other. Discretionary and accumulation trusts pay tax at the trust rate of 45 per cent or dividend trust rate of 37.5 per cent as appropriate on income above the first £1,000. The first £1,000 of taxable income is chargeable at the dividend ordinary rate or the basic rate, according to the type of income (ITA 2007, s.479). Where the settlor has made more than one settlement (whether in the United Kingdom or overseas), the £1,000 first slice of income is split across the number of settlements in existence during the tax year, but cannot be reduced below £200 per settlement (ITA 2007 ss.491, 492).   **10–015**

Discretionary or accumulation trusts for the benefit of certain vulnerable persons, such as the disabled or minor children, where at least one parent is deceased, may elect to be taxed according to the particular financial circumstances of each beneficiary rather than being subject to the trust rates of tax. This enables the trustees to obtain the benefit of each beneficiary's annual personal allowance and basic rate band.

Other trusts, such as life interest trusts, pay tax at the basic, or dividend rate of tax, as appropriate to the type of income being taxed.

Whatever the kind of tax, when the beneficiary receives an income distribution, tax will be treated as deducted from that income at 45 per cent, in the case of a discretionary or accumulation trust, and at a computed rate derived from the mix of dividend income and other income, in respect of life interest trusts.

For discretionary and accumulation trusts, broadly, the gross income of the trust is computed and the trust's administration expenses properly chargeable to revenue (such as bank charges, non-deductible interest income related charges of professional trustees, etc.) are also computed. The trust rates of tax do not apply to administration expenses incurred by the trustees, and relief is given for these by deducting the expenses first from the net savings income within ITA 2007 s.12 (income charged at the starting rate for savings) and income taxed at source (principally taxed interest and net dividends) before grossing up at 100/80 or 100/90 for dividend income and applying tax at 20 per cent. From this tax payable are deducted any tax deducted at source and tax credits. If the trustees' savings income is insufficient to absorb the expenses, they are set against non-savings income.   **10–016**

COMPANIES AND TRUSTS

Example

In the year ended April 5, 2012 the Harum Discretionary Trust had the following income and expenses:

	£
Property rents	40,000
UK dividends (including tax credits of £200)	2,000
Taxed interest (tax deducted at source £700)	3,500
	£45,500

Trust administration expenses proportion	£	
chargeable to revenue	1,350	
Overdraft interest	1,050	£2,400

The tax liability of the trust for 2011/12 is as follows:

	£	£
Rental income:		18,000
£40,000 at 45%		
Taxed interest (net)	2,800	
Net dividends	1,800	
Deduct: Expenses	(2,400)	
	£2,200	
£2,200 grossed up at 100/80 = £2,750 @25% (45% less 20%)		688
Tax payable by trustees under self assessment		18,688
Add: Tax deducted at source	700	
Tax credits	200	900
Total tax borne		£19,588

TRUSTS

Notes

(a) Expenses (including in this example the overdraft interest) are set first against income falling within ITA 2007 s.12 (savings income) and within this classification set first against dividend income. The effect is that to the extent that expenses exceed dividend income, the expenses, grossed up at 20 per cent, save tax at 20 per cent (the difference between the 20 per cent rate and the trust rate).

(b) The net revenue available for distribution to the beneficiaries at the trustees' discretion will be £23,512 (£45,500 less £19,588 less £2,400).

Any income distribution to the beneficiary is treated as having tax deducted at a flat rate of 45 per cent which is treated as his gross income, and tax credits can be recovered in line with tax deducted at source from other income.

A 19-year-old student is one of the beneficiaries to whom the trustees can pay the settlement income. The trustees make a payment of £3,000 to him on January 31, 2013. He has no other income in the year 2012/13 and is unmarried.

	£
Net income	3,000
Tax @45/55	2,455
Gross income	£5,455

He can claim a tax repayment for 2012/13 of:

	£
Total income	5,000
Deduct: Personal allowance	(5,000)
Tax	nil
Tax accounted for by trustees	2,455
Repayment due	£2,455

The mechanism for tax relief on expenses is to offset them first against net savings income within ITA 2007 s.12, and within this classification set first against dividend income, i.e. expenses to the extent they exceed dividend income are relievable against other savings income. Expenses are then set against basic rate income. This deduction, grossed up, effectively gives relief at 25 per cent the difference between the 45 per cent rate applicable to trusts and the 20 per cent basic rate.

Other trusts (life interest trusts)

10-017 Life interest trusts pay tax at the basic rate on other income. There is no relief to the trustees in respect of trust expenses chargeable to revenue which was paid out of net income, but they reduce the beneficiary's income.

Example
The Wonga settlement is a life interest settlement which has the following income and expenses in the year 2012/13.

	£	£
Property income		500
Taxed interest income (tax deducted at source £300)		1,500
Dividends	900	
Add: Tax credits	100	1,000
		£3,000
Expenses chargeable to revenue		£900

A is sole life tenant of the Wonga settlement and therefore receives all the settlement income. A's income for 2012/13 from the Wonga settlement is as follows:

	£	£
Trust dividend and interest income (gross)	2,500	
Other trust income (property income)		500
Deduct: tax at basic rate (20%)	(500)	
		(100)
	2,000	
Trust expenses (Note (b))	900	
Net income entitlement of beneficiary:		
Trust interest income £1,200 (tax deducted £300)		
Other trust income £400 (tax deducted £100)		
Grossed-up amounts: £1,200 x 100/80	£1,500	
£400 x 100/20		£500

TRUSTS

Notes

(a) This income falls to be included in A's return even if it is not actually paid to him, as he is absolutely entitled to it. He will receive a tax certificate (Form R185 (Trust Income)) from the trust agents, showing two figures for gross income (£1,500 and £500), tax deducted (£300 and £100) and net income (£1,200 and £400).

(b) The trust expenses are deducted from income falling within ITA 2007 s.12 (savings income) in priority to other income (ITA 2007, s.486). Within this category of income the expenses are first set against dividend income, in this example extinguishing that income (£900–£900 $ad nil).

(c) That part of A's trust income which is represented by savings income (£1,200 net) is treated in A's hands as if it were savings income received directly by A.

The tax assessable on the trustees will be £100 (£500 at 20 per cent). The expenses are not deductible in arriving at the tax payable by the trustees.

Discretionary and accumulation trusts: particular features

Income received by a trust which is to be accumulated, or payable at the discretion of the trustees or some other person is, , taxed at the trust rate and dividend trust rate rather than at the basic rate. The trust rate for 2013/14 is 45 per cent, and the trust dividend rate is 37.5 per cent, or such other rates as Parliament may determine. The trust rate does not apply where: **10–018**

(1) the trust is exempt as a charity;
(2) the income arises from property held for the purpose of certain retirement benefit or personal pension schemes; or
(3) the income is income of any person other than the trustees or treated as income of a settlor.

As regards (3), the position is considered before the income is distributed, so that income paid to the settlor's unmarried minor children does not fall within the exemption. The trustees may offset expenses incurred in the management of the trust against trust income for the purpose of determining income chargeable at the trust rate, although income so relieved remains subject to basic rate tax (ITA 2007 s.484). Where the trustees receive income which is not subject to income tax, (e.g. interest on certain gilt-edged securities received by non-resident trustees) expenses relating to that income are excluded from relief (ITA 2007 s.491).

Tax relief in respect of expenses is given by deduction for the whole expense from savings income in preference to other income. Expenses are deducted against dividend income in priority to other savings income. In consequence, relief will be obtained at the dividend ordinary rate in respect of dividend income, and 20 per cent in respect of other trust income. Computations must therefore be done in respect of dividend income at the 10 per cent rate, and for other income at the 20 per cent rate as appropriate to arrive at the net income entitlement which is then grossed up at 20 per cent and tax deducted.

The beneficiary is treated as having received all the net income of the trust whether or not it is actually paid to him and the certificate of tax deduction (Form R185 (Trust Income)) will show the different streams of gross income and the tax deducted from net income. The beneficiary will then be assessed on the gross income at the basic or higher rates as appropriate, with credit for the tax treated as deducted by the trustees.

Tax return

10–019 Trusts are within the scope of self-assessment, as it applies to individuals. The normal time limits for the submission of the SA900 return will apply, i.e. January 31, following the end of the year of assessment, for returns filed online and October 31 for paper returns.

Capital gains tax

10–020 The taxation of capital gains in trusts is, by comparison with the income tax treatment, relatively straightforward. Trusts pay tax on capital gains at the rate of 28 per cent. The computation of the gain itself follows ordinary capital gains tax principles in that the base cost and costs of sale are deducted from sale proceeds in order to arrive at the gain. Trusts pay capital gains tax at the same flat rate of 28 per cent as for individuals, with no deductions for indexation relief or taper relief. Trustees are, however, eligible to claim entrepreneurs' relief in respect of certain disposals where there is a qualifying beneficiary. Trusts benefit from the capital gains tax annual exemption but only to the extent of 50 per cent of the exemption available to individuals. Furthermore, this exemption has to be shared by all "connected trusts", subject to a minimum exemption of £200 (TCGA 1992 s.3 as modified by Sch.1).

Holdover relief under TCGA 1992 s.260 is applicable in respect of any transfer either into or out of a relevant property settlement as inheritance tax will be payable on the transfer, albeit that this may be only at the nil rate.

The effect of a claim is to reduce the base cost of the asset transferred in the hands of the trustees, thus increasing the amount of tax suffered by the trustees in respect of any future disposal of the asset.

Foreign trusts

10–021 This is a highly complicated area, full of anti-avoidance legislation, and should be approached with great care. The position is particularly complex following the various changes to the tax treatment of non-UK domiciliaries having effect from April 6, 2008. Nonetheless, basic principles are followed.

Foreign trustees are not UK persons and as such will bear tax only on UK income. Overseas trustees are technically liable to the trust rate of tax if they are discretionary or accumulation trusts. Non-resident trustees are outwith the scope of capital gains tax due to their non-residence, however, gains may be apportioned to a UK resident or domiciled settlor or beneficiary under TCGA 1992 ss.86 and 87. From April 6, 2008 gains may also be also apportioned to non-UK domiciled beneficiaries under TCGA 1992 s.87 where the beneficiary receives a capital payment from the trustees. United Kingdom dividends received by non-resident trusts do not give rise to a credit which can be carried through to an income beneficiary of the trust unless the offshore trust makes full returns and pays all its tax as if it were a UK trust under Extra-Statutory Concession B18. The liability of a non-UK resident trust to UK income tax may be limited to the tax deducted at source in certain circumstances, broadly, where the settlor is not able to benefit under the terms of the trust (ITA 2007 s.811). Gains on post-March 1991 offshore settlements, in which the settlor or his family can benefit, have any capital gain assessed directly on the settlor. From March 17, 1998 pre-1991 trusts are similarly treated unless certain conditions are met. The scope for non-UK domiciled individuals to use offshore trusts as an effective tax planning strategy has been significantly curtailed by changes introduced for 2008/09 and later tax years.

In respect of inheritance tax, if the overseas settlement is created by a non-domiciled settlor in respect of non-UK property, the settlement will be an excluded property settlement irrespective of any subsequent change in the settlor's domicile. In order to retain the offshore nature of the settlement assets, an offshore company should be inserted beneath the trust to hold any UK assets (other than UK residential property being occupied by a beneficiary) as this will retain the excluded property character of the settlement.

Inheritance tax

The inheritance tax regime applying to trusts was significantly altered by FA 2006, which introduced changes with effect from March 22, 2006. Prior to this date, there were effectively two separate regimes applying to life interest trusts on the one hand and accumulation and discretionary trusts on the other. The regime for discretionary trusts is unchanged by the FA 2006 provisions, except in relation to those discretionary trusts which were accumulation and maintenance trusts.

10–022

Before March 22, 2006, life interest trusts were not treated as separate persons for inheritance tax. Instead, the trust's assets were deemed to belong to the life tenant and were aggregated with his estate for all purposes. Any tax payable by virtue of transfers involving a life interest trust was payable by the trustees out of the trust assets even though the tax due was computed by reference to the life tenant's personal inheritance tax circumstances. Potentially exempt transfers could be made and there were no 10-yearly charges on the trust's assets.

Accumulation and discretionary trusts, in contrast, were and are treated as separate taxable persons and therefore have their own inheritance tax "clock". Transfers out of such settlements therefore are transfers of value subject to inheritance tax. The computational rules in respect of transfers from such trusts, both within the first 10 years and subsequently, are complicated and outwith the scope of this brief overview. However, it should be noted that accumulation and discretionary trusts cannot make potentially exempt transfers and that they are subject to an additional 10-yearly charge (effectively an internal gift on which inheritance tax is payable). This 10-yearly charge is the reference by which any distributions out of the settlement in the subsequent 10 years are computed. Before the introduction of the changes in FA 2006, most accumulation trusts were outside the scope of 10-yearly charges and there was also no charge on a beneficiary becoming absolutely entitled to trust property, usually on attaining age 18 or 25. In order to remain within the tax-favoured regime, accumulation trusts in existence at March 22, 2006 must have amended their terms such that a beneficiary becomes absolutely entitled to property aged 18, or if the trust is a will trust for minor children, existing treatment continues provided the beneficiaries become absolutely entitled to property at aged 25 (IHTA 1984 ss.71, 71A–71D).

10–023　New life interest trusts created after March 22, 2006 are treated in the same way as discretionary trusts and are subject to the "relevant property" regime of IHTA 1984 ss.58–85. The creation of the trust is a chargeable lifetime transfer rather than a potentially exempt transfer, and there is a 10-yearly charge on trust assets. Inheritance tax charges also apply on property leaving the trust, e.g. on the appointment of capital to a beneficiary. Assets within the trust are not treated as belonging to the life tenant and will not be included in his taxable estate on death.

Life interest trusts in existence at March 22, 2006 are generally unaffected by the changes until the life interest in place on the above date is terminated, e.g. on the death of the life tenant, although there are a number of exceptions to this rule such as where a new life interest is appointed to the existing life tenant's spouse.

Trusts created under will by a parent for their minor children are outside the new rules, as are Immediate Post Death Interest in possession trusts (IPDI) and trusts for the disabled and charitable trusts.

CHAPTER 11

Value added tax

INTRODUCTION

Value added tax ("VAT") is the tax on the supply or deemed supply of goods and services unless those goods and services are exempt or outside the scope of UK VAT. The tax is charged on the supplier who has an obligation to register if his turnover exceeds the registration threshold. The VAT charge (output tax) is accounted for by the supplier to HMRC, either quarterly, monthly or in some instances annually, depending on his circumstances. **11–001**

To the extent that a recipient of a VATable supply uses the supply for his business to make VATable supplies in his turn, he may recover the VAT he has incurred (input tax) by set-off against any VAT output tax he may owe in any return period, or by direct repayment if his input tax exceeds his output tax. If input tax is not attributable to the making of taxable supplies (because the supplies made are either exempt or outwith the scope of VAT), such input tax will not be recoverable.

Apart from those clearly identifiable supplies, "supply" includes anything done for a consideration. There is a specific exclusion that the supply of money itself (in return for a supply) does not itself constitute a supply. However, in any barter-type transaction there will be cross-supplies in the same way as there is for direct tax.

The distinction between supplies of goods and supplies of services is largely concerned with the time and place of supply. There are also important differences in connection with the international supply of goods and services. **11–002**

The supply of goods is defined as any transfer of property or possession in goods, the supply of power, heat, refrigeration or ventilation or the grant of a major interest (freehold or lease exceeding 21 years) in land. The supply of goods also includes transfer of own goods between EU Member States and there are a number of deemed or self-supplies which are supplies of goods. The supply of services is defined as anything which is not a supply of goods and consequently covers a huge range of supplies.

Where a business or part of a business is sold or transferred to another person there may be a transfer as a going concern which is outside the scope of VAT and, unless an "option to tax", no VAT is charged or recovered on the proceeds of sale of assets including goodwill.

VALUE ADDED TAX

PLACE OF SUPPLY OF GOODS

11–003 The place of supply of goods not involving their removal from or to the United Kingdom is the United Kingdom if the goods are there and outside the United Kingdom if they are not there. Goods supplied as part of an installation or assembly are treated as supplied where they are assembled.

Goods supplied under other circumstances are supplied in the United Kingdom if the goods enter the United Kingdom by or under the direction of the supplier or if they are acquired in the United Kingdom by an unregistered person from a supplier in another EU state. Further tiers of rules apply in increasingly uncommon circumstances.

A supply within a country not involving the goods passing over any border is a straightforward matter involving the charging of VAT by the supplier and its payment to HMRC and the recovery of the VAT input charge from HMRC by the recipient. Where goods cross the border, however, different rules apply.

EXPORTS OUT OF OR INTO THE EUROPEAN UNION AND INTRA-EU MOVEMENTS

11–004 Supplies of goods involving an export where the goods physically move across a border out of the European Union are zero-rated provided that the zero-rating conditions (principally involving the removal of the goods outside the European Union within the time limit, such that the goods are not delivered, collected or used by any UK person, including the customer in the interim) are satisfied. The importer will deal with any import duty, etc. when importing the goods into the country of destination. It is, of course, possible for the supplier to export the goods to himself in a foreign country, dealing with the importation into that country on his own account before making an onward sale to his customer in that country. This would make him liable to whatever sales, tax, etc. might be applicable in that country.

With the abolition of border controls, cross-border movements of goods within the European Union have to be dealt with on a self-assessed basis. The terminology is amended to refer to "dispatches" in substitution for "exports" and "acquisitions" in substitution for "imports". Generally, the dispatch of goods from a supplier in one EU state to a recipient in another is treated as zero-rated for the supplier and as an acquisition by the recipient. The recipient must charge himself his own country's VAT and then recover it, if it is in respect of an onward taxable supply by him. The effect, in the case of fully taxable persons, will be that the VAT by the recipient is both charged by him and recovered by him on the same VAT return, i.e. merely a set of book entries. This applies also to the movement of goods across a border without change in ownership. Consequently, a UK importer taking goods to France for his own business would make a dispatch in the United Kingdom outwith the scope of VAT and have to charge himself French TVA with appropriate recovery, quite possibly incurring a liability to register in France in respect of the transaction. It should be noted that the dispatch may be treated as zero-rated only if the supplier quotes his customer

VAT registration number on the VAT invoice, the goods physically cross an EU border, and documentary evidence of dispatch is available.

The importation by an EU trader of goods from outside the European Union and its onward supply to an EU trader in another EU state will involve the rules of import and supplies of goods followed by the rules on intra-EU supplies of goods. It is important to identify the person importing the goods into the European Union, so that if it is the person making the supply from outside the EU, he will need to register for VAT in the country of importation and be responsible for VAT on the onward supply.

Goods are acquired and become liable to VAT on acquisition when they have crossed an EU border into the acquirer's EU state. It is important to determine the person making the acquisition and this will often depend on when and where title passes. This is particularly noticeable in triangular trade where, for example, goods are supplied from supplier A to customer C in another EU state but have been invoiced to an intermediate supplier, B, in a third Member State, who reinvoices to customer C. While the goods may pass from the supplier's EU state to the end user's EU state, crossing only one border, the change in ownership from A to B and then to C gives B a potential liability to register for VAT in C's state to account for VAT on their acquisition and their subsequent onward supply to C. All EU states have agreed in these circumstances that, provided that B is not registered in C's state, the acquisition and onward supply by B is completely ignored and this supply is treated in its simplest form as a dispatch by A and an acquisition by C. This simplification procedure is at B's option and is compulsory on all parties once he so opts. Notification must be made to HMRC and the proper procedures complied with.

PLACE OF SUPPLY OF SERVICES

Services have different places of supply depending upon the type of service. Supplies in relation to land are considered to be supplied: where the land is physically situated; B2C supplies of intangible listed in VATA 1994 Sch.4A supplied to a customer who belongs outside of the EU are supplied where the customer belongs; supplies relating to cultural, artistic, sporting, scientific, education or entertainment services or relating to exhibitions, conferences and meetings are supplied where the activities take place in the case of B2C transactions; and where the event takes place in respect of admission charges (and their ancillary services) in B2B transactions. Any other supplies follow the general rule. **11–005**

The general rule is that the place of supply of services in a B2B transaction is treated as being where the customer belongs, which in turn means where he has his place of business or, if more than one, where he has the place of business most concerned with the receiptof a particular supply. If the transaction is not B2B (i.e. it is B2C), the general rule is the place of supply is where the supplier belongs.

The counterpart to import and acquisition VAT is the reverse charge on services received (VATA 1994 s.8). This, applies to all B2B general rule services

VALUE ADDED TAX

where the supplier belongs outside of the UK, unless the supply is exempt or zero-rated. The receipt of such services in the UK count toward the VAT registration limit.

11–006 The reverse charge is extended to also apply to B2B (and not B2C) particular services made in the UK where the recipient of the supply is already UK VAT registered and the supplier belongs outside of the UK. The particular services are land and property; services supplied where performed; passenger transport; hired goods; telecommunications services; radio and TV broadcasting services; and electronically supplied services. This extension does not count towards VAT registration and if received by a non-VAT registered person it has no reverse charge effect. The receipt of such services causes the recipient to charge himself UK VAT and pay it over to Customs, while at the same time allowing him to recover the VAT input tax, if appropriate, on the same VAT return. It is, therefore, in the case of a fully taxable trader, a book entry. The reverse charge of itself, if sufficiently large, can cause a trader to register where otherwise he would not have an obligation to do so except in the case of reverse charge extension.

The receipt of reverse charge services from another EU state is treated as neither a supply of goods nor a supply of services if the EU recipient would use the supply for any EU business, whether or not it is a business which makes taxable (rather than exempt) supplies. Although not obligatory, it is common and recommended practice to quote the recipient's VAT registration number on the supplier's invoice. There is no equivalent to the simplification involving triangular supplies of goods.

TIME OF SUPPLY

11–007 The time of a supply is the earlier of the date of an invoice for the supply, the completion of the supply or the receipt of cash in respect of the supply (VATA 1994 s.6). The receipt of part of the cash triggers the VAT liability only on that part of the cash received, rather than the whole of the supply.

RATE OF VAT

11–008 VAT is chargeable upon all supplies of goods and services by way of business (or, under EU law, in the pursuance of an economic activity). That specific profit-making motive is required. Those transactions which are not by way of business are outwith the scope of VAT. A business may make some supplies which are outwith the scope of VAT because they are not in pursuance of the business, or indeed any business carried on by that person.

If a supply is within the charge to VAT it is chargeable at a zero rate if within Sch.8 to the VATA 1994 or, failing this, it is an exempt supply if it is within Sch.9 to the VATA 1994 and is otherwise a standard-rated or reduced-rated supply chargeable to VAT.

RECOVERY OF VAT IN GENERAL

11–009

The recovery of VAT input tax is possible only if it relates to specific taxable supplies or is in pursuance of a taxable activity. Furthermore, there is a category of supplies which is outwith the scope of VAT but which nonetheless ranks for VAT input tax credit. If, however, a business is an exempt business, i.e. making exempt supplies only, it will not be able to recover any VAT. Most exempt businesses, however, are not wholly exempt but are partially exempt and this requires an allocation of input tax between the exempt and the non-exempt (taxable) parts. Non-recoverable VAT input tax (exempt input tax) may nevertheless be recovered if it comes within the de minimis limits (less than £625 per month, on average, and where exempt supplies are less than 50 per cent of the output of the business). Certain other exempt supplies are treated as not exempt for partial exemption purposes, including, e.g. bank interest received by a business.

VATABLE PERSONS

11–010

VAT is a tax on transactions carried out by a legal person, and not on particular supplies, so that every business carried on by a VAT-registered person must be aggregated for one VAT return. A business consultant who is also a portrait photographer would have one VAT registration in respect of both of his businesses. VAT recognises the individual, the partnership and the company and they must be separately registered. Furthermore, partnerships with a different partnership composition are treated as separate partnerships even if there is only one partner different between them. Anti-avoidance provisions exist to counteract the fragmentation of a business between VATable persons with a view to avoiding VAT registration.

There is a special relieving provision under which companies forming a group, or even those under common control, can share a VAT registration such that all transactions within the group are deemed to occur within the same VATable entity. One company is chosen as the representative member and all supplies are deemed to be made by or to the representative member. The same concept is applied, with interesting regional variations, in other EU states. Complex anti-avoidance provisions arise in respect of companies leaving or joining such a VAT group.

COLLECTION OF VAT

11–011

Only businesses which are registered for VAT have to charge VAT on taxable supplies made. Anyone who makes taxable supplies is eligible to register for VAT, however it is not obligatory for any business which has a turnover of less than £73,000 per year (from April 5, 2013).

VAT registered businesses which make only taxable supplies add VAT at either the standard rate of 20 per cent, the reduced rate of 5 per cent or 0 (zero) per cent on the provision of goods or services. Likewise, such businesses will also pay

VALUE ADDED TAX

VAT on expenses incurred. Each business which is registered for VAT is obliged to make either a monthly or quarterly return to HMRC. On these returns, the business will enter all VAT charged on its supplies (output tax) and at the same time declare the level of VAT incurred on expenses (input tax). The difference between these figures will be the amount payable.

There are certain items of expenditure on which VAT cannot be recovered, including the purchase of motor cars, business entertainment costs and non-business items such as personal expenditure.

VAT on expenditure can be recovered only if it is attributable to a taxable supply. It therefore follows that a business which makes entirely exempt supplies cannot recover any VAT because all expenditure will be attributable to those supplies. Similarly any business which makes both taxable and exempt supplies will suffer an appropriate restriction in the recovery of VAT.

TREATMENT OF INTELLECTUAL PROPERTY

11–012 Intellectual property transactions are supplies of services by virtue of VATA 1994 s.5(2)(b):

> "anything which is not a supply of goods but is done for a consideration (including, if so done, the granting, assignment or surrender of any right) is a supply of services."

If, therefore, a UK-registered business grants a patent licence to another UK business in return for a royalty or lump sum, VAT at the standard rate is payable on the gross, pre-VAT amount even though the payer may deduct income tax at the basic rate on making the payment. This applies whether or not a royalty is described as a gross royalty from which tax is to be deducted by the payer, or as a free of tax or net royalty which has to be grossed up to arrive at the gross equivalent.

Example

Anxious Antony Ltd is in business and pays UK patent royalties and is due to pay £10,000 (gross) on September 17, 2013. The amount due he pays is as follows:

	£
Gross royalty	10,000
VAT @ 20%	2,000
	12,000
Less: income tax deducted at 20% x £10,000	2,000
Cheque to licensor	10,000
Being: net royalty	8,000
Being: VAT on gross royalty	2,000
	10,000

TREATMENT OF INTELLECTUAL PROPERTY

The £2,000 deducted will be held in charge to tax for 2013/14 or accounted for under ITA 2007 s.946 (Ch.15).

If the royalty paid by one UK business to another registered UK business is in connection with a foreign patent, VAT is still payable even though there may be no requirement to deduct income tax.

Payments of interest, royalties and certain other annual payments made between companies may be paid gross where the recipient is a company and is within the charge to tax thereon under ITA 2007 s.933 (see paras 16–006 and 16–047). Cross-border royalties to a 25 per cent associated company in an EU country where the company is beneficially entitled to the income is not liable to withholding and not liable to tax in the UK. Additionally, in respect of the payment of royalties within ITA 2007 ss.449, 901, which a UK company makes and which it reasonably believes falls within a Double Taxation Treaty, the UK company payer may withhold at the (reduced) treaty rate without HMRC consent. However, if it transpires that the recipient was not entitled under the treaty, the UK company payer must account for tax as if this rule had never applied ITA 2007 s.911.

The VAT on copyright royalties is considered further in para.18–078.

CHAPTER 12

Valuation

INTELLECTUAL PROPERTY

It is apparent that intellectual property is not, as such, of any intrinsic value although the article or work that it protects may well be. As a right to prohibit other people from exploiting or copying without permission an invention, a written work, photograph, painting, computer program, trade mark, logo, know-how or secret process, the protection given to intellectual property is a negative one. This protection shows its value in the additional profits earned by the manufacturer or publisher as a result of the monopoly given to them over the exploitation of the property. However, as intellectual property is normally assignable or licensable, the proprietor of the intellectual property can turn it to account by way of a fee or royalty for the licence to use the property or a lump sum paid on the assignment of the property in whole or part. **12–001**

There may be a number of reasons why it is necessary for commercial purposes to value intellectual property, for example, on an assignment of the interest, on entering into a licensing or franchising agreement, on a take-over or merger or purchase or sale of a company owning intellectual property, for the purposes of revaluation to justify borrowings, or to resist a take-over, or in connection with divorce proceedings, or on death, or for accounting purposes under IFRS3 and FRS7.

It may also be necessary to value intellectual property for fiscal purposes either as part of the process of valuing shares or on an assignment of the intellectual property rights in circumstances giving rise to a charge to income tax, capital gains tax, or inheritance tax.

The first stage in any fiscal valuation is to determine precisely what rights are being valued (*Borland's Trustee v Steel Brothers & Co Ltd* [1901] 1 Ch.279; *Short v Treasury Commissioners* [1948] 1 K.B. 116). In the first instance this means that it must be assumed that the rights are capable of assignment in that it has to be assumed that the assignee acquires a valid title to the intellectual property and thereafter holds that property subject to any rights or restrictions attached thereto (*Re Crossman* (1936) 15 A.T.C. 94). Intellectual property and goodwill valuations for fiscal purposes are dealt with by HMRC's Shares and Assets Valuation division.

VALUATION

MARKET VALUE

12–002 For fiscal purposes the valuation is usually at the market value, i.e. the price which the property might reasonably be expected to fetch if sold in the open market at that time (IHTA 1984 s.160; TCGA 1992 s.272; and in respect of revenue items, see *Brigg Newmann & Co v IRC* (1928) 12 T.C. 1191, and *Gold Coast Selection Trust v Humphrey* (1948) 30 T.C. 209).

The term "open market" includes a sale by auction but is not confined to that (*IRC v Clay* and *IRC v Buchanan* [1914] 3 K.B. 466, at 471):

> "A value ascertained by a reference to the amount obtainable in an open market shows an intention to include every possible purchaser. The offer is to the open market as distinguished from an offer to a limited class only, such as the members of the family. The market is not necessarily an auction sale. The (phrase) means such amount as the (property) might be expected to realise if offered under conditions enabling every person desirous of purchasing to come in and make an offer, and if the proper steps were taken to advertise the property and let all likely purchasers know that the (property) is in the market for sale." (at 475)

The phrase "open market" means the market in which the property in question would normally be dealt (*Salomon v Customs and Excise Commissioners* [1966] 3 All E.R. 871; *Glass v IRC*, 1915 S.C. 449).

12–003 The precise statutory and contractual terms setting out the rights to the intellectual property have to be considered. In the stamp duty case of *Stanyforth v IRC* [1930] A.C. 339, at 334 it was stated with regard to a sale in the open market:

> "at such a sale the property would have to be put up with all its incidents, including provisions for defeasance, either in whole or in part, powers vested in persons not controlled by the vendor to create charges taking precedence of the property sold and so forth. I really fail to understand, with all respect to those who have taken a different view, how the most drastic power of destroying the property to be sold vested in the persons over whom the purchasers could have no control could properly be disregarded."

In *Duke of Buccleuch v IRC* [1967] 1 A.C. 506, at 524 it was stated:

> "There was some argument about the meaning of "in the open market". Originally no doubt when one wanted to sell a particular item of property one took it to a market where buyers of that kind of property congregated. Then the owner received offers and accepted what he thought was the best offer he was likely to get. And for some kinds of property this is still done. But this phrase must also be applied to other kinds of property where that is impossible. In my view the phrase requires that the seller must take, or be supposed to have taken, such steps as are reasonable to attract as much competition as possible for the particular piece of property which is to be sold. Sometimes this will be by sale by auction, sometimes otherwise. I suppose that the biggest open market is the Stock Exchange where there is no auction. And there may be two kinds of market commonly used by owners wishing to sell a particular kind of property. For example, it is common knowledge that many owners of houses first publish the fact that they wish to sell and then await offers. They only put the property up for auction as a last resort. I can see no reason for holding that in proper cases the former method could not be regarded as sale in the open market."

Moreover, in *Re Lynall, Lynall v IRC* (1971) 47 T.C. 375, at 411:

> "There may be different markets or types of markets for different types of property but (in this case) the market which must be contemplated, whatever its form, must be an open market in which the property is offered for sale to the world at large so that all potential purchasers have an equal opportunity to make an offer as a result of it being openly known what it is that is being offered for sale. Mere private deals on a confidential basis are not equivalent of open market transactions."

SPECIAL PURCHASERS

It is clear, therefore, that the open market hypothesis assumes that all potential purchasers are in the market to buy the intellectual property being valued and it is necessary to consider the price that they would pay for such property. However, it could well be that in certain cases the intellectual property has a particular value to an identifiable potential purchaser, usually known as a special purchaser, because of some synergistic value that the property would give him. This could be particularly important, e.g. in the case of a patent where the master patent holder is prevented from developing the property in a particular manner because of some subsidiary patent held by another party. The master patent holder cannot develop the invention to its fullest potential without the subsidiary patent and the subsidiary patent holder cannot exploit his improvement without some agreement with the master patent holder (*Hawkings-Byass v Sassen* [1996] S.T.C. (SCD) 319). 12–004

In valuing it is therefore necessary to consider whether a special purchaser exists, and if so, whether this is likely to have an effect on the value. If the existence of a special purchaser is known, or can reasonably be inferred, this is likely to affect the price:

> "The knowledge of the special need would affect the market price and others would join in competing for the property with a view of obtaining it at a price less than that of which the opinion would be formed that it would be worth the while of the special buyer to purchase." (*IRC v Clay, IRC v Buchanan* [1914] 3 K.B. 466, at 476)

This line of reasoning is confirmed in *Glass v IRC* 1915 S.C. 449; *Raja Vyricherla, Narayana Gajapatiraju v Revenue Divisional Officer Vizagapatam* [1939] A.C. 302 and *Robinson Brothers (Brewers) Ltd v Houghton and Chester-le-Street Assessment Committee* [1938] 2 All E.R. 79. "All likely purchasers are deemed to be in the market" (*Re Lynall, Lynall v IRC* (1971) 47 T.C. 375, at 396).

REAL SALES

An actual arm's-length sale of the intellectual property in question is clearly a point that would have some bearing upon its market value for fiscal purposes (*McNamee v IRC* (1954) I.R. 214) although it would clearly be necessary to consider whether the sale in question was a true arm's length sale in the open market as many real sales do not meet the hypothetical requirements of a fiscal 12–005

VALUATION

valuation, being sales by private treaty rather than in the open market. Sales subsequent to the date of valuation should not affect the earlier fiscal valuation (*IRC v Marr's Trustees* (1906) 44 S.L.R. 647) although they may of course have some persuasive value.

It is important to remember that the fiscal valuation is on a hypothetical basis:

> "It is common ground that (property) must be valued on the basis of a hypothetical sale ... in a hypothetical open market between a hypothetical willing vendor ... and a hypothetical willing purchaser on the hypothesis that no-one is excluded from buying and that the purchaser would ... hold (the property) subject to (the legal and contractual arrangements applying to that intellectual property)." (*Re Lynall, Lynall v IRC* (1971) 47 T.C. 375, at 377; see also, *Attorney General v Jameson* [1904] 2 I.R. 644; *Re Crossman and Re Paulin* (1936) 15 A.T.C. 94; *Re Holt* (1953) 32 A.T.C. 402); *IRC v Gray (Exor of Lady Fox)* [1994] S.T.C. 360; *Walton v IRC* [1996] S.T.C. 68.

It is therefore a statutory fiction and the fact that a sale at the valuation date would be impossible (*Duke of Buccleuch v IRC* [1967] 1 A.C. 506, at 535), or illegal (*Re Aschrott, Clifton v Strauss* [1927] 1 Ch. 313, at 322), is irrelevant, see also *Marshall v Kerr* [1994] S.T.C. 638. Notional costs of disposal are not deductible (*Duke of Buccleuch v IRC* [1967] 1 A.C. 506, at 541) although actual costs of disposal would be deductible for most tax purposes (see TCGA 1992 s.38).

OPTIMUM LOTTING

12–006 When considering the intellectual property rights to be valued it is necessary to consider how these could best be packaged commercially to realise the maximum price. It may be, for example, that an invention consists of a number of elements, each of which is capable of being patented, thus widening the protection available, or there may have been material improvements to the invention capable of being patented. Similarly, when considering the copyright in a musical work, the performing rights and potential film synchronisation rights have to be considered. The law applicable to fiscal valuation allows for the optimum lotting of the various rights available:

> "The value of the property shall be estimated to be the price which it would fetch if sold in the open market. That in my opinion does not necessarily mean the price which it would fetch if sold to a single purchaser. There may be many cases where a sale to a single purchaser cannot realise 'the price which it would fetch if sold in the open market'. Take the case of an owner having property, including a colliery and a drapers shop. It is conceivable that if the colliery and the drapers shop were sold separately the best possible price might be obtained for each. On the other hand a purchaser who was anxious to buy the drapers shop might not wish to be encumbered with the colliery and vice versa and consequently if the owner insisted upon selling the whole property to one purchaser it would not obtain the market price which the act contemplates." (*Earl of Ellesmere v IRC* [1918] 2 K.B. 735)

On the other hand the principle of optimum lotting must not be carried to extremes:

> "It is sometimes said that the estate must be supposed to have been realised in such a way that the best possible prices were obtained for its parts. But that cannot be a universal rule. Suppose that the owner of a wholesale business dies possessed of a large quantity of hardware or clothing, or whatever he deals in. It would have been possible by extensive advertising to obtain offers for small lots at something near retail prices. So it would have been possible to realise the stock at much more than wholesale prices. It would not have been reasonable and it would not have been economic, but it would have been possible. Counsel for the respondent did not contend that that would be a proper method of valuation. But that necessarily amounts to an admission that there is no universal rule that the best possible price at the date of death must be taken." (*Duke of Buccleuch v IRC* [1967] 1 A.C. 506, at 526; see also, *Smyth v IRC* (1941) I.R. 643 and *Trustees of Johan Thomas Salvesen v IRC* (1930) 9 A.T.C. 43)

It may be possible to obtain the best price by selling a complete package, for example, the design of a machine could include a number of features protected by patent, copyright drawings, technical know-how and a trade mark licence, and in such cases it is reasonable to assume for valuation purposes that the most attractive package would be put together (*Attorney General of Ceylon v Mackie* [1952] 2 All E.R. 775):

> "The appellant contends that the respondent must be supposed to have taken the course which would get the largest price for the combined holding of management and preference shares and to offer for sale, together with the management shares, the whole or at least the greater part of the preference shares owned by the deceased. In their Lordships' judgment this contention is correct." (at 777)

HINDSIGHT

Fiscal valuations are usually considered by HMRC some time after the transaction has taken place, and, as a result, information is often available which would not have been at the date of valuation. It is clear that documents that were not available at the date of the valuation cannot be admissible as evidence (*Re Lynall, Lynall v IRC* (1971) 47 T.C. 375, at 383):

12–007

> "I rule out of consideration the knowledge provided by the passage of time since March 11 1948 that the company's dividend on ordinary shares has not been increased from 5 per cent and that the company has been able to avoid a public issue of ordinary shares by launching an exceedingly successful issue of new preference shares in September 1950." (*Re Holt* (1953) 32 A.T.C. 402, at 410)

On the other hand it is permissible to consider subsequent events to the extent that they may clarify or provide additional information with regard to the information available at the date of the valuation (*Trustees of Johan Thomas Salvesen v IRC* (1930) 9 A.T.C. 43, at 51; *Buckingham v Francis* [1986] 2 All E.R. 738; *Re Bradberry, National Provincial Bank Ltd v Bradberry and Re Fry, Tasker v Gulliford* [1943] Ch.35).

WILLING PARTIES

12–008 An open market assumes a sale between a hypothetical willing seller and a hypothetical willing, prudent and cautious buyer:

> "It is true that the so called willing vendor is a person who must sell, he cannot simply call off the sale if he does not like the price, but there must be on the other side a willing purchaser so that the condition of the sale must be such as to induce in him a willing frame of mind. (*Re Lynall, Lynall v IRC* (1971) 47 T.C. 375, at 392.)
> It does not mean a sale by a person willing to sell his property without reserve for any price he can obtain." (*IRC v Clay, IRC v Buchanan* [1914] 3 K.B. 466, at 476; see also, *Winter (Sutherland's Trustees) v IRC* (1961) 40 A.T.C. 361 and *Duke of Buccleuch v IRC* [1967] 1 A.C. 506)

Conversely, the purchaser must be assumed to be a man of prudence (*Trustees of Johan Thomas Salvesen v IRC* (1930) 9 A.T.C. 43 and *Re Holt, Holt v IRC* (1953) 32 A.T.C. 402), who would make diligent enquiries before buying (*Caton's Administrator v Couch* [1995] S.T.C. (SCD) 34; *Clark v Green* [1995] S.T.C. (SCD) 99; *Hinchcliffe v Crabtree* (1971) 3 All E.R. 967):

> "In estimating the price which might be fetched in the open market for the goodwill of the business it must be assumed that the transaction takes place between a willing seller and a willing purchaser and that the purchaser is a person of reasonable prudence who has informed himself with regard to all the relevant facts such as the history of the business, its present position, its future prospects and the general conditions of the industry, and also that he has access to the accounts of the business for a number of years." (*Findlay's Trustees v IRC* (1938) 22 A.T.C. 437)

The fiscal valuation therefore is based on the price at which the hypothetical sale is likely to take place, and although the effect on that price of the existence of any special purchaser has to be considered, the market value ignores the actual identity of both the vendor and purchaser (*Battle v IRC* [1980] S.T.C. 86).

The importance of producing the appropriate evidence before any appeals tribunal cannot be over-emphasised (*Denekamp v Pearce* [1998] S.T.C. 1120; *Neely v Rourke* [1988] S.T.C. 216). There is no universally accepted method of valuing intellectual property and allied rights. The Intellectual Property Office booklet "Agreeing a Price for Intellectual Property Rights" refers to "the cost method", "the market value method" and "income or economic benefit methods" such as "the relief from royalty method".

DISCOUNTED CASH FLOWS—NET PRESENT VALUE OF INCREMENTAL CASH FLOWS

12–009 Having arrived at the theoretical framework of the valuation of the intellectual property, the problem then becomes one of determining the relevant price at which the hypothetical sale would take place and this in turn is often calculated, in the real market (and equally in the hypothetical market for fiscal valuations), on the basis of the present value of the estimated future income that would be generated by the intellectual property being acquired either directly from

DISCOUNTED CASH FLOWS

royalties or any lump-sum assignments that could be possible, or indirectly from the accretion to profits which would result from the acquisition.

Although some valuations are made on the basis of the cost of replicating the research and effort which has gone into the production of the intellectual property, it is difficult in many cases to point to any real co-relation between the cost of producing the intellectual property and its value when produced.

Estimating this future income is, not surprisingly, the most difficult part of the valuation and will depend on the circumstances of each case. Experience within the industry will be of considerable assistance. For example, a drug company may, from its own experience, be able to estimate that a particular drug could be manufactured for a cost of £x per thousand pills and could be sold for £y resulting in a profit of £z per thousand. If the market is estimated at so many million pills per annum for a period of, say, five years before the drug is likely to be replaced by a rival product, the income to be generated can be calculated as a matter of arithmetic and if this income flow is then discounted back to a net present value, using an appropriate rate of discount, the current value of the income stream can be calculated. The present value of the income stream represents the amount that could be paid for the assignment of the intellectual property rights in the product, subject to the purchaser's required margin (*Re Courthope dec'd* (1928) 7 A.T.C. 538) and the cost of production.

Example

	£
x cost per thousand pills	26.00
y sale price per thousand pills	40.00
z profit per thousand pills	14.00

Estimated sales

Year 1	5 million
Year 2	10 million
Year 3	15 million
Year 4	20 million
Year 5	5 million

Estimated profit

		£
Year 1	5,000,000 x 0.014	70,000
Year 2	10,000,000 x 0.014	140,000
Year 3	15,000,000 x 0.014	210,000
Year 4	20,000,000 x 0.014	280,000
Year 5	5,000,000 x 0.014	70,000

VALUATION

Present value at 15 per cent per annum

	£
Year 1	60,869
Year 2	105,860
Year 3	138,078
Year 4	160,090
Year 5	34,802
	499,699
Less tax at, say 20 per cent	99,940
	399,759

Margin required

Say 25 per cent on cost	79,952
	319,801
Say	320,000

WEIGHTED AVERAGE COST OF CAPITAL

12–010 Any such calculation inevitably involves a number of assumptions, any one or more of which may be wrong; for example, in spite of all preparatory testing the drug may have undesirable side effects and its use be severely curtailed or banned. A rival product may appear sooner than anticipated which would reduce the potential sales of the product. Manufacturing techniques in bulk may prove more difficult than anticipated or raw materials scarcer and more expensive. On the other hand, the drug may prove highly beneficial in practice and have wider applications than were first thought, demand may greatly exceed forecast and improved manufacturing techniques might enable expensive ingredients to be synthesised, thus reducing the cost of the product. This in turn could lead to governmental interference in the price.

Factors which affect forecasts of this nature include the growth or otherwise of the market in which the business operates and anticipated changes in future years for the period of the forecast. The market share and anticipated changes which are applicable to the intellectual property being valued are also relevant, as is the anticipated level of inflation used in the forecast. Inflation levels could be forecast from the difference between the redemption yield on gilt edged securities for the period of the forecast and that on indexed linked government stocks. It is obvious that the investment in intellectual property is usually far from risk free and an element in the discount factor relates to this risk.

Various methodologies have been devised to assist in arriving at a meaningful discounting rate, such as the weighted average cost of capital (WACC) for the company owning the intellectual property.

INDUSTRY PRICE MULTIPLE—CAPITALISATION OF EARNINGS

The result of discounting cash flows at the WACC is to give an enterprise value representing the sum of the debt and equity in the business. Debt is deducted from enterprise value while surplus cash and other surplus assets are added to the enterprise value while surplus cash and other surplus assets are added to the enterprise value to reach an equity value.

12–011

- Algebraically, this is represented as WACC = k_e (E/D+E) + k_d (D/(D+E)), where:
- k_e represents the cost of equity, i.e. the return required by the shareholders;
- k_d represents the after tax cost of long-term debt, i.e. the return required by debt holders;
- E represents the value of equity; and
- D represents the value of long-term debt.

Cost of Equity, k_e

- The cost of equity is estimated using the Capital Asset Pricing Model ("CAPM"). This model hypothesises that the required rate of return on an individual security is equal to the risk-free return plus a market risk premium adjusted to reflect the volatility of the particular asset concerned.
- Algebraically, this is represented as k_e = R_f + (Beta x M) + S + F where:
  - R_f represents the risk-free rate (usually taken as the market yield on a government security at the same maturity as the investment being considered);
  - Beta represents the relative risk of the assets being valued as compared to the risk of the market portfolio – a security with a beta of 1 would be expected to change value perfectly in line with the market;
  - M represents the market risk premium, i.e. the return the market portfolio is expected to generate in excess of R_f;
  - S represents the small company premium; and
  - F represents the firm specific risk premium.

It has to be appreciated that every element in the forecast is in many ways no more than a best guess on the basis of experience within the industry.

INDUSTRY PRICE MULTIPLE—CAPITALISATION OF EARNINGS

In some industries there is an established market in the sale of intellectual property packages at a multiple of the average historical income over a period. The multiple will depend on the number of rights in the package; the broader the base, the lower the risk. It will also be affected by the volatility of the market and the specific attributes of the intellectual property involved. In such cases it is assumed that past performance may give a useful indication of the likely future income and, e.g. a publisher's back catalogue may be saleable on the basis of, say, three-and-a-half to five years' purchase of the net income generated from the

12–012

product in question for the average of the previous three years (the "net publisher's share" or NPS). However multiples of up to 15 would not be unreasonable for a catalogue of particular quality. In each case the real calculation is an estimated future income from the products in question over a period of years based on the average historical data showing the past performance of the product. Again, there are any number of uncertainties involved in that, e.g. an author included in the catalogue may become the subject of a film or television series which would increase sales enormously. Alternatively the product may turn out to be a "seven-day wonder" and pale into insignificance within a short space of time. This is particularly common in the case of a popular music catalogue although the effect of the continued success of the performing artistes could have a very considerable effect on the value of the catalogue, particularly if further successful recordings are made and extensive touring and live performances given, which could lead to a marked upturn in the anticipated level of sales.

In any commercial deal involving intellectual property, it is much easier if a number of items are involved than if a single patent or copyright work has to be valued. On the basis of experience, a publisher will take into account the fact that a number of authors included in the catalogue would be likely to become the starting point for a film or television series, although he might not be able to identify which ones will in fact so feature. Similarly, a music publishing catalogue would include a number of works which would no doubt receive a new lease of life on re-recording, or further exploitation as a result of film synchronisation rights, or the continued success of the original artistes, or others taking up the work. In such cases it would be usual to analyse the income over the various types, e.g. mechanical royalties, from the sale of recordings, performance royalties, sundry income, print royalties from the sale of sheet music and synchronisation rights. Synchronisation rights tend to be one-off and difficult to predict and may be excluded from a schedule of past income as being a distortion, the prospect of such income being taken into account in an enhanced multiple instead. Again, it is reasonable to build some expectation into a complete catalogue although it may not be possible to identify which particular works will perform better than anticipated or conversely which ones will fade into obscurity much earlier.

The growth of downloads, media on-demand viewing and music recognition applications for portable devices means that "back catalogue" and older titles frequently see a resurgence in popularity many years after their traditional "useful life" might have been expected to end. While this is not possible to predict with accuracy, the general trend is that there is now a greater potential residual value in such assets than was hitherto the case.

ROYALTY COMPARISONS—RELIEF FROM ROYALTY METHODS

12–013 In some cases the best approach may be to anticipate the royalty that would have to be paid in order to manufacture or reproduce the item under licence; that rate of royalty may be a fairly common feature of the industry in question, or derived without too much difficulty from comparable situations. This is often called the "royalty relief method". On the other hand there may not be any truly comparable licensing agreements covering the type of property under consideration and it may be necessary to consider what an arm's-length royalty might be. In order to convert a royalty rate into a present value for the whole intellectual property, it is necessary to estimate not only the royalty rate itself, but the likely production under the hypothetical royalty agreement in order to convert the royalty rate into an income stream, the present value of which can then be calculated using normal discounted cash flow techniques. In order to do this it is necessary not only to calculate the likely levels of production but the timing of that production, which will have an effect on the value.

The effect of taxation on the figures has to be considered and this will depend on whether the valuation is required for the purpose of evaluating a transfer of intellectual property itself, in which case the pre-tax value is normally required in order to calculate the potential gross value and the taxation consequences are then considered by each party. In the case of a valuation of intellectual property which forms part of a calculation of the value of shares in the company owning the property, it may be appropriate to discount the value at which it is brought into the calculation by the potential tax charge which would arise if it were to be disposed of at that figure (*Winter (Sutherland's Trustees) v IRC* (1961) 40 A.T.C. 361).

Example

Grushin Innovative Products Ltd

Valuation of Patent Rights

Instructions

We have been asked to consider the current market valuation of Grushin's rights under the patents listed on the schedule headed "Status Report on Patent Applications". The date of valuation has been taken as July 1, 2013.

Purpose of valuation

The valuation is required for the purposes of corporation tax on a chargeable gain in order to establish the value of patent rights to be acquired by a connected company within TCGA 1997 s.18(1) and ITA 2007 s.993 or CTA 2010 s.1122.

Basis of valuation

The value required is the market value, which is defined as the price which those assets might reasonably be expected to fetch on a sale in the open market.

Valuation approach

We consider it reasonable to arrive at the current value of the company's patent rights by estimating the net present value of the future royalties the company could reasonably expect to achieve if it were to license its patent rights to another manufacturer.

Valuation

VALUATION

We have been provided by the company with a forecast of its turnover in the five-year period from 2013 to 2017. At present the company achieves gross margins (after allowing for costs of sale which include manufacturing costs) in the region of 120 per cent. We therefore consider that the company could reasonably expect to receive a royalty on turnover of about one-quarter of that gross margin, say 30 per cent. In view of the uncertainty involved, however, we would reduce that rate to 20 per cent after the first three years.

As the company is forecasting a considerable increase in turnover over the next five years, arising in part from contracts which have yet to be awarded, we consider it prudent to adopt relatively high discount rates in arriving at the net present value of the assumed royalty income. We would therefore apply a discount rate of 25 per cent over the five years covered by the forecast.

The company's patents will run out by the year 2021. We have therefore added a further four years' turnover to the company's forecast, at the same level of turnover as in 2017, the last year of the company's forecast. We have, nevertheless, increased the discount rate for those final four years to 35 per cent.

On that basis the net present value is as follows:

Year	Turnover £m	Royalty level £m 30%	Royalty level £m 20%	Discount factor @ 25%	Discount factor @ 35%	Net present value of royalty £m
2013	1.9	5.7		.8		.456
2014	5.2	1.56		.64		.998
2015	8.15	2.445		.512		1.251
2016	8.325		1.665	.409		.680
2017	10.2		2.04	.327		.667
2018	10.2		2.04		.164	.334
2019	10.2		2.04		.121	.247
2020	10.2		2.04		.090	.183
2021	10.2		2.04		.066	.134
						4.950
Corporation tax at 20 per cent						0.990
After corporation tax						3.960
					Say	3.9

We therefore value the company's patent rights at £3,900,000.

HYBRID VALUATIONS—COST BASED VALUATIONS

Valuations based on the present value of future returns depend on those returns being ascertainable with reasonable certainty. When this is not possible a scenario based approach may be appropriate. Under this method a number of possible outcomes is costed and a weighting given on the basis of the probability of each outcome happening. The aggregate of the values arrived at is the current value of the intangible asset.

12–014

Example
Company A is considering an investment into a new pharmaceutical patent which has the possibility of evolving into an oral preparation which can treat a previously incurable form of alopecia.

The initial research and development will cost £1,000,000 and if this is successful human trials will be undertaken which will cost a further £500,000. If those are successful then the appropriate government licenses will be obtained and the product will be licensed on to a secure third party at an annual license fee of £1,000,000 for the first five years followed by £500,000 for the remaining lifetime of the patent.

On the assumption that the initial research and development should take a year, the trials will take a year and the costs and license fee are accounted for at the beginning of each year, then how could the valuation be approached?

Discussions with the company suggest there is a 50 per cent chance the R&D will be successful and if it is successful then there is a 75 per cent chance the human trials will also be successful. If the trials fail then we know that there would be a residual value of £100,000 in the patent as the product could be used for small animals. The return required from a successful product is judged to be 10 per cent due to the nature of the licensee. The risk free rate of return available in the market is 5 per cent.

There are three contrasting scenarios:
(1) The Research and Development fails. The chances of this are 50 per cent.
(2) The Research and Development succeeds but the trials fail. The chances of this are 12.5 per cent (50 per cent times 25 per cent).
(3) Both the Research and Development and the trials succeed. The chances of this are 37.5 per cent (50 per cent times 75 per cent).

Each of the scenarios can be valued.

Scenario 1
Immediate cost of £1,000,000 and no other benefit. Value of this scenario is thus negative £1,000,000.

Scenario 2
Cost at the beginning of year one is £1,000,000, the cost at the beginning of year two is £500,000 and the benefit at the start of year three is £100,000. The costs contribute a value of negative £1,476,190 (being £100,000 plus £500,000 discounted at the risk free rate of return for one year). The license fee of

VALUATION

£100,000 contributes a value of £82,644 being the £100,000 discounted for two years at the required rate of return of 10 per cent. The value of this scenario is thus negative £1,393,545.

Scenario 3

The contribution towards value of the costs are the same as in scenario 2 at negative £1,476,190 but the value of the license fee for the remaining 18 years of the patent is:

Discount rate

10% Beginning of year	Factor	Money (£)	Value (£)
1	1	-	-
2	0.909091	-	-
3	0.826446	1,000,000	826,446
4	0.751315	1,000,000	751,315
5	0.683013	1,000,000	683,013
6	0.620921	1,000,000	620,921
7	0.564474	1,000,000	564,474
8	0.521158	500,000	256,579
9	0.466507	500,000	233,254
10	0.424098	500,000	212,049
11	0.385543	500,000	192,772
12	0.350494	500,000	175,247
13	0.318631	500,000	159,315
14	0.289664	500,000	144,832
15	0.263331	500,000	131,666
16	0.239392	500,000	119,696
17	0.217629	500,000	108,815
18	0.197845	500,000	98,922
19	0.179859	500,000	89,929
20	0.163508	500,000	**81,754**
Total Value			5,450,999

Thus the value for this scenario is £3,974,809 (£5,450,999–£1,476,190).

Combining the values

Multiplying the value of each scenario with the chance of its occurrence gives us the following:

Scenario	Chance	Value (£)	Contribution (£)
1	50.0%	(1,000,000)	(500,000)
2	12.5%	(1,393,545)	(174,193)
3	37.5%	3,974,809	1,490,553
Total value			816,360

The value of the Patent prior to the Research and Development taking place could therefore be taken as £816,360. Say £800,000.

EXCESS PROFITS—NOTIONAL MAXIMUM ROYALTIES PAYABLE

As well as valuing for fiscal purposes an entire piece of intellectual property on its absolute assignment or a partial interest on the grant of a licence for a lump sum or royalty, it may be necessary to consider the acceptability of a commercially agreed royalty rate for tax purposes. Where there is a payment from one UK company to another, HMRC will normally be prepared to treat the payment as deductible as either an expense or annual payment as appropriate, and the income would be taxable on the recipient.

12–015

If however the royalty is seen merely as a means of moving profits between companies and not justified by the commercial circumstances the deductibility could be challenged (*Finsbury Securities Ltd v Bishop* (1966) 43 T.C. 591; *Lupton v FA & AB Ltd* (1971) 47 T.C. 580; *Thomson v Gurneville Securities Ltd* (1971) 47 T.C. 633). In a case in Hong Kong in 1996 (*Chen Hsong Machinery Co Ltd v IRC*) (D52/96) before the Board of Review, a trade mark was valued on the basis of the capitalised value, using a multiple of five, of a notional royalty of 6 per cent, less 1 per cent for the maintenance of the mark, 5 per cent net, applied to the projected turnover for the forthcoming year. The transfer pricing rules (see Ch.14) have to be considered in relation to non arm's-length transfers (TIOPA 2010 Pt 4 ss.146–217).

EXTERNAL FACTORS—COMPARABLE MARKET TRANSACTIONS

No valuation can take place in a vacuum, and the general economic and political situation is relevant both to the calculation of the likely levels of future income and to the rate of discount to be applied which is affected by market rates (*Attorney General of Ceylon v Mackie* [1952] 2 All E.R. 775; *Re Holt* (1953) 32 A.T.C. 402). The state of the industry and industry sector is also important for the same reasons (*Trustees of Johan Thomas Salvesen v IRC* (1930) 9 A.T.C. 43 and *Findlay's Trustees v IRC* (1938) 22 A.T.C. 437).

12–016

Traditionally a rule of thumb based on commercial deals over the years has indicated that a patent licensee takes the majority of the commercial risks and a royalty to the licensor which gives it somewhere between 10 per cent and 25 per cent of the net profit earned by the licenced product would be reasonable in many cases. In other cases a comparison with royalty rates used in unconnected commercial agreements may be sufficiently comparable to assist in arriving at a reasonable royalty rate. Royalty rates for trade marks are more likely to be between 10 per cent and 15 per cent. However, such data is often not readily available and full details of any deal are really required to determine whether it is a reliable comparison. Royalty rate databases seldom give sufficient detail for a realistic comparison of all the features which affect a headline royalty rate. An average royalty rate based on net sales may be in the region of 5 per cent although the rates do vary widely. See "Agreeing a Price for Intellectual Property Rights" published by the Intellectual Property Office.

GOODWILL—PREMIUM SALES PRICE—GROSS PROFIT DIFFERENTIAL

12–017 One of the most important assets of an established business is its goodwill, which is usually valued on the basis of the excess of the capitalised value of a business, on the basis of its anticipated future earnings (*Findlay Trustees v IRC* (1938) 22 A.T.C. 437), over its asset value, i.e. the market value of the various assets, less liabilities, of the business, including assets which may not be recognised on the balance sheet, such as internally generated intellectual property. The valuation case law for intangible property valuation summarised above is applicable to goodwill as well as intellectual property and unquoted shares.

In the United Kingdom intellectual property is often included in goodwill and not valued separately in arms-length sales of the whole business, and the intangible fixed assets rules introduced by CTA 2009 Pt 8 ss.711–906 recognise the difficulty of differentiating goodwill from trade and service marks, brand names and the like.

In the United States human resources available to a business are something given a separate value as "workforce in place", but this would normally be regarded as part of the goodwill in the United Kingdom.

12–018 Goodwill may, in certain cases, be inherent in the site from which the business operates and is reflected in the site value of the property itself rather than the business. Similarly businesses such as hotels, pubs, theatres, etc. are difficult to sell without the business premises from which they operate and have what is called adherent free goodwill, included in the site value, as agreed with the District Valuer of the Valuation Office Agency of HMRC. However, in *Balloon Promotions Ltd v Wilson* [2006] S.T.C. (SCD) 167, it was held that in the circumstances of that case the franchisees of Pizza Express did have personal goodwill outside the goodwill attaching to the restaurant premises.

Goodwill may be personal to one or more key individuals, whom customers would follow if they were to leave rather than remain with the business, who are retained through a mixture of incentives and restrictive covenants.

In certain trades the value is related to turnover or throughput rather than profits. Such trades include newsagents, bookmakers, chemists, employment agents, estate agents, insurance brokers, travel agents, etc. The goodwill of small businesses are sometimes valued on the basis of super profits, i.e. a number of years purchase of the profit, after reasonable management remuneration and a return on capital of 4–5 per cent above bank minimum lending rate.

BRANDS

12–019 The valuation of brands, "trade marks with attitude", in that they carry the magic ingredient of consumer loyalty, is an area of major importance both commercially and in the taxation field, with Revenue Authorities requiring, under transfer pricing rules, foreign affiliates to be charged at market rate for the use of brand names. Brand names, protected as trade marks, service marks or under passing-off prohibitions at common law, have an indefinite life, unlike the 20-year life of a patent, and the valuation of the net present value of the brand income stream, real or hypothetical, usually includes an annuity element covering future years beyond which projections can realistically be made. The problem, in practice, is to arrive at a reasonable estimate of the future results of the brand, the proportion of that income which relates to the brand or other intellectual property, and the rate of discount which is appropriate, starting with the risk-free cost of long-term debt and adding in appropriate risk factors, often termed "beta factors". Similar problems attach to domain names of websites on the internet.

Interbrand, a division of Omnicom Group, is a branding consultancy which pioneered five step brand valuation using a discounted value added methodology. It is necessary to arrive at the profit attributable to the brand after operating costs and taxation, before interest but after a charge for the capital employed. The five steps are:

- *Market segmentation* in which the brand's markets are split into non-overlapping homogenous groups of consumers.
- *Financial analysis* which identifies and forecasts income attributable to the brand for each consumer segment.
- *Demand analysis* which assesses the sale of the brand in driving demand for the product, compared with earnings from other intangibles such as patents, and other intellectual property measured by a "rate of branding index". Brand earnings are the earnings from intangibles multiplied by the branding index.
- *Competitive benchmarking* determines the risk profit of the brand, the "brand strength score" which comprises the brand's market stability, leadership position, growth trend, support, international penetration and legal protectability.
- *Brand value calculation* is the net present value of the forecast brand earnings discounted at the brand discount rate calculated on the basis of all these factors.

VALUATION

REAL OPTIONS METHODS

12–020 These methods of valuation adopt the Black-Scholes, Binomial or Monte Carlo computerised simulations for option pricing for the valuation of intellectual property, in particular to patents, which have a relatively short and ascertainable lifespan.

In the Black-Scholes methodology it is necessary to calculate the value of the various relevant factors. The formula is:

Asset value		=	$S\,N(d_1) - Ke^{-rT}\,N(D_2)$
	S		Cost of asset
	K		Strike/exercise price
	R		risk free rate of return corresponding to life of asset
	T		Time to expiration
	Sd_2		standard deviation
	e^{-rT}		continuous time present value
	N		normal distribution
	D_1		$\ln(S/K) + (r - y + sd^2/2) \times T$
	D_2		$d_1 - sd\,\sqrt{T}$
	Ln		natural logarithm

BINOMIAL MODEL

12–021 Under this model the intellectual property's commercial life is broken down into a number of time periods and builds up a tree or lattice of possible movements in the values of the IP for each period under the assumption that the value can move either up or down. It is an iterative process working backwards through the binomial value total from the IP value of each final node to the first node in the value tree which is the value of the IP. This is a relatively complex process involving statistics, probability and computer modelling which is difficult to describe in a book.

MONTE CARLO SIMULATION

12–022 A Monte Carlo simulation is a computerised statistical technique which looks at a very large number of possible values and averages the results. This involves estimating the expected risk free rate of return over the commercial life of the IP, its volatility and the volatility of the values of similar intellectual property, the expected return on the IP and the correlation between movements in the comparable IP. The technique uses computer generated random number generation over a large number of possible outcomes.

LOCATION OF ASSETS

For capital gains tax purposes the location of goodwill is where the trade or profession is carried on (TCGA 1992 s.275(1)(g)). Patents, trade marks or registered designs are situated where the, or if more than one, each register is kept and rights in licences to use are situated in the United Kingdom if they, or any right derived from them, are exercisable in the United Kingdom (TCGA 1992 s.275(1)(k)). Copyright, design right and franchises and rights to use them are situated in the United Kingdom if they, or any right derived from them, are exercisable in the United Kingdom (TCGA 1992 s.275(1)G)).

12–023

INTERNATIONAL FINANCIAL REPORTING STANDARD 3 (IFRS 3)

IFRS 3 (Business Combinations) applies to the accounting treatment for business acquisitions or mergers for which the agreement date was on or after March 31, 2004. Under the Standard, an acquirer of a business is required to identify the costs attributable to all assets and liabilities acquired, including intangible assets. Previously, the difference between the purchase price and the value of the tangible assets was generally treated as "goodwill", individual elements of acquired intellectual property must now be identified separately, provided that the fair value of the asset can be measured reliably.

12–024

The definition of an intangible asset for this purpose is as set out in International Accounting Standard 38 ("IAS 38"). Paragraph 8 of IAS 38, as issued at January 1, 2012, defines an intangible asset as "an identifiable, non-monetary asset without physical substance". An asset is identifiable, in accordance with para.12, when it:

"(a) is separable, i.e. is capable of being separated or divided from the entity and sold, transferred, licensed, rented or exchanged, either individually or together with a related contract, asset or liability regardless of whether the entity intends to do so; or

(b) arises from contractual or other legal rights, regardless of whether these rights are transferable or separable from the entity or from other rights and obligations".

Paragraph 9 of IAS 38 also gives examples of categories which may be included in intangible assets. These include:

- Scientific or technical knowledge.
- Design and implementation of new processes or systems.
- Licences.
- Intellectual property.
- Market knowledge.
- Trademarks (including brand names and publishing titles).

Specific examples of these cited in IAS 38 para.9 include computer software, patents, copyrights, motion picture films, customer lists, mortgage servicing

12–025

rights, fishing licences, import quotas, franchises, customer or supplier relationships, customer loyalty, market share and marketing rights. However, this is not an exhaustive list and IAS 38 recognises that, even where these assets exist, they may not be capable of separate or reliable valuation. Employee teams or key individuals are not regarded as assets to be valued separately, as fair value could not be measured reliably.

If any assets of this type are acquired then the basis of valuation, in the absence of an active market in that asset, is that of fair value, defined by para.8 as the price that would be received to sell an asset or paid to transfer a liability in an orderly transaction between market participants at the measurement date. (See IFRS 14 Fair Value Measurement.) It is difficult to detect any meaningful difference between this definition of fair value and the market value of assets as the price at which those assets might reasonably be expected to fetch on a sale in the open market under TCGA 1992 s.272 or IHTA 1984 s.160.

Under IFRS 3, goodwill effectively becomes a "balancing figure", valued under para.51(b) of the Standard, as "the excess of cost of the business combination over the acquirer's interest in the net fair value of the identifiable assets, liabilities and contingent liabilities". Goodwill itself is defined in para.52 as "a payment made by the acquirer in anticipation of future economic benefits from assets that are not capable of being individually identified and separately recognised".

A further point of significance is that goodwill is no longer amortised through the profit and loss account, but instead is subject to an annual (or more frequent) impairment review. Any subsequent increases in the value of goodwill are not recognised on the balance sheet.

CASE LAW

12–026 One of the few cases involving the value in which of intellectual property was *RCC v Tower MCashback LLP 1* (2011) UKSC 19 the Supreme Court found for HMRC. The case concerned a claim for capital allowances for software rights acquired by two limited liability partnerships as part of a marketed tax avoidance scheme. At [25] of the judgment Lord Hope explained that:

> "the investor members of the LLPs were individuals with large incomes who themselves put up only 25% of the consideration said to have been paid for acquiring rights in software. The remaining 75% was provided by interest-free loans on non-recourse terms, made to the investor members by special purpose vehicles set up for the purpose. HMRC rely strongly on the circularity of these transactions as more fully described below. The essential issue (simply stated but not simply resolved) is whether the LLPs incurred capital expenditure, to the extent of the whole stated consideration, in acquiring software rights for the purposes of their trades."

and at [32]:

> "Apart from the three main groups of participants two banks, both based in Guernsey, were involved in the arrangements. These were R&D Investments Ltd ("R&D") and Janus Holdings Ltd ("Janus"). As explained in more detail below,

R&D held security deposits placed with it by MCashback, which R&D in turn deposited with Janus as security for a loan by Janus to a Tower Finance company (described in the scheme's explanatory material as the "Leading SPV"). The Tower Finance company made interest-free non-recourse loans to individual investor members of the LLPs."

and at [72]:

"HMRC has now abandoned the soft finance argument as such. But it has not vanished completely, as appears from para 66 of HMRC's printed case, quoted at para 25 above. Before this Court Mr Prosser argued (though this is probably an oversimplification of his more subtle arguments) that even if an investor member did spend the money which he borrowed (say £225,000) as well as his own money (say £75,000) he did not incur expenditure of £300,000 on acquiring software rights, because only £50,000 of the money reached MCashback, and £225,000 went into a loop from which MCashback received no immediate benefit at all. If in the future money were to flow back to MCashback out of the loop it would be because of its own commercial success in generating clearing fees. Whatever the £225,000 was spent on, it was not spent in acquiring software rights from MCashback, because the £225,000 never reached MCashback (I leave open for the present the expenditure, in this example, of the odd £25,000 on fees and expenses).

75. The judge was right to emphasise that the transaction was the subject of tough negotiation between MCashback and Tower (whose founder members stood to make a large gain, when the investor members' rights had been fully satisfied, if the M Rewards scheme was as successful as both sides hoped it would be). The negotiations were tough because MCashback (unlike BGE in *BMBF*) really did need up-front finance in order to roll out its software and give effect to its business plan. It saw itself as parting with potentially very valuable rights indefinitely (the investor members dropped out after ten years, but the founder members did not) for only a modest part (just over 18% before fees and expenses, or just under 17% after fees and expenses) of the total capital apparently being raised. That was because 75% of the capital raised, although not simply a sham, was being used in an attempt to quadruple the investor members' capital allowances. That is what the tough bargain which Tower struck with MCashback enabled Tower to offer to its investor members. I have already (para.47 above) quoted Lord Goff in *Ensign* [1992] 1 A.C. 655m 682. The facts of that case were different, since in that case there was not 'in any meaningful sense' a loan at all. In this case there was a loan but there was not, in any meaningful sense, an incurring of expenditure of the borrowed money in the acquisition of software rights. It went into a loop in order to enable the LLPs to indulge in a tax avoidance scheme, Despite the shortcomings in his decision, the Special Commissioners was essentially right in his conclusion in para 138. (quoted in [56], above)"

and finally concluded at [72]:

"I would direct the conclusions and amendments in the closure notices to be amended to allow 25% only of the FYAs claimed. That is in one way generous to the LLPs, since in fact about one-third of their contribution (the £25,000 in the example given above) was devoted to fees and expenses. But I think it would, in all the circumstances, be the fair outcome in a confusing case."

In this case at first instance (*Tower MCashback LLP v RCC* 2008 S.T.C. (SCD) 1) the Special Commissioner Howard Nowlon stated:

VALUATION

"99. I have no hesitation whatsoever in concluding that the market value of the software acquired by the appellants was very materially below the price ostensibly paid for it.

100. The factor that most obviously supports this conclusion is that whether the form of the various transactions stands up to scrutiny (and that yet remains to be seen), the transactions were in economic substance contingent instalment sales where MCashback would only eventually receive the full price over a ten-year period, and indeed would receive it (assuming no sale and there was no arrangement for any sale) only if the figures of clearance fees assumed in the business plan *were material exceeded*. As a consequence, at the date of sale, MCashback would only have at its disposal an amount equal to 18.2% of the gross capital contributions made to the LLPs. If the software intended to be sold to the four LLPs was in fact worth the £143m aggregate price, why did MCashback not find the willing purchaser ready to pay this price, and why did it instead choose to proceed via a complex transaction that was only expected to deliver at the outset approximately £26m? In fact of course it produced far less than £26m because the lack of appetite on the part of genuine investors for the transaction resulted in no completion of the sales occurring until January 2005, the LLP3 transaction being completed on an instalment basis at a later date still, and by far the largest transaction, that involving LLP4, never being completed at all. And the 'outside' funds contributed into LLP1 amounted to only £700,000.

101. Consistently with the fact that whatever the form of the transactions, the deal was economically a contingent instalment sale from both the perspective of the seller and the buyers, no serious attention was ever given to the valuation issue. A business plan was produced containing staggering rising figures of revenues over a ten-year period for a software concept that had at the point of the preparation of the figures been sold to no-one. I saw absolutely no evidence that ever addressed whether the figures in the business plan were carefully calculated and cautious estimates, or whether they were 'away with the fairies'. In reality it did not particularly matter whether the figures could be supported because the proposed transaction was only ever going to be put to investors on the basis that their ceiling exposure would be for 25% of the price paid, and the expected tax relief (that could even be carried back to the previous year) was expected and represented to be worth not 25% of gross price paid, but 40%. I am not suggesting that the transaction was a fraudulent one where the aim was to sell capital allowances in relation to a fictitious sale of near worthless software. But I certainly say that the reality of the transactions meant that nobody had to give that figure, or indeed any figure that should not be more than underwritten by the tax relief expected from the exchequer.

102. It was suggested in argument by counsel for the appellants that the software was worth the full price paid on the assumption of an outright purchase by a purchaser providing the entire purchase price of his own resources. And it was then contended that if the transaction had instead been an instalment sale the price would have been much higher. I am simply unable to understand how this could be advanced as an argument. I note that this argument did at least recognise the inevitable difference in price between the price commanded in an outright sale, and that in an instalment (or I would say 'a highly contingent instalment') sale. Why it is supposed however that the parties would have failed to note that notwithstanding its form, this transaction was economically identical to a contingent instalment sale I simply cannot understand. . . .

108. My conclusions on the valuation issue are that:

- I do not purport to have any clear idea what the 13% interest in the software was worth in 2004, and I heard no evidence that could enable an experienced valuer, let alone me, to make that judgement;
- I consider that the actual figures bandied around, and inserted into the business plan, were highly optimistic, untested and unreliable aspirations. Some people *might* have genuinely believed them, but their approach to valuation would inevitably have been influenced by the fact that the proposed transaction meant that no-one would have to rely on the figures or pay either anything approaching the full price on an outright basis, or indeed even as much as the projected front-end savings, in tax;
- In my view it is ridiculous to try to support a market valuation of the software by reference to the proportion that independent people gave percentages of £143m for it, when no-one gave anything other than 25% on a very contingent instalment basis; no-one expected to spend more than 62% of their projected tax savings on their total capital contribution to the project; several investors backed off; and the sum raised from outside investors in LLP1 at as late a date as January 2005 was only about £700,000;
- In short, the appellants' valuation arguments fail to establish their case by a very wide margin indeed."

FURTHER CASE LAW

In *Iliffe News and Media Ltd & Others v Revenue & customs commissioners* (2012) UKFT 696 (TC) the valuation was considered of five-year licences of "various unregistered trade marks (UTMs) being titles of local newspapers and other periodicals, referred to as 'mastheads' (which) were assigned from the respective subsidiaries... to their parent company INML and were then licensed back to the subsidiaries by INML for consideration of various sums payable as being sums totalling £51,400,000". Ernst & Young (E&Y) were the companies' valuers. At para.93 it was stated that:

12–027

> "Three methodologies of valuation were considered, all assuming a 5 year licence. These were: the royalty relief methodology ("RRM")—which we understand to be a computation of the present value of royalty payments saved through the ownership of the licence; the elimination methodology "EM")—sometimes called 'the residual value approach', which is a method based on allocating the correct proportion of the determined value of the entire intangible assets and goodwill of a business to the assets licensed, and determining the proportion of that value attributable to the licences by application of the RRM; and the market methodology ("MM")—ascertaining the proportion of enterprise value represented by mastheads in transactions in the market place (or the price paid for mastheads sold in isolation), applying such proportion to the value of the relevant Subsidiaries' businesses and determining the proportion of the resultant ascertained value attributable to the licences by application of the RRM.
>
> 94. E&Y regarded the MM as being the 'primary analysis'. The MM was the ascertainment of market value for the licences, based on a hypothetical sale of a licence to use the masthead by a willing vendor to a willing purchaser, 'each of whom is acting for self-interest and gain and both of whom are equally well informed about [the masthead] and the market place in which it

VALUATION

operates'. It can be seen that the adoption of the MM made the question of what proportion of the enterprise value was represented by the mastheads of prime importance in reaching a valuation.

95. E&Y's valuation of 5 year licences of the HENL portfolio was between £13m and £18m, their valuation of 5 year licences of the CNL portfolio was between £16m and £21m, and their valuation of 5 year licences of the SNL portfolio was between £5m and £8m. [ie a range of £34-£47 million]. As stated above, the figures adopted in the relevant licences were: HENL—£15.5 m; CNL—£18.5m; and SNL – £6.5m [total £40.5 million]. In other words, valuations mid-point in the ranges suggested by E&Y were adopted as the consideration for the grants of the licences in question.

96. Mr Burns (the appellants' independent valuation expert) stated that in his opinion the MM represented the most robust and accurate method of valuation. He concluded that substantially all of the value of the intangible assets of HENL, SNL and SNL could be attributed to their mastheads. He accepted in cross-examination that he had based everything on the premise that virtually all the value of the intangible assets of the Subsidiaries was attributable to the values of their respective mastheads. He put values on the licences involved in the 2003 transactions as follows: HENL—between £14m and £21m; CNL—between £11m and £20m; and SNL—between £5m and £8m [total £30-49 million]. He put values on the licences involved in the 2005 Transactions in the range of between £5.3m and £11m. It will be recalled that INML charged CNL £299,000 for the grant of the licence of the UTMs sought to be assigned by CNL in 2005, and INML charged LSN £10,641,000 for the grant of the licence of the UTMs sought to be assigned by LSN in 2005. These figures total just under £11m. Mr Burns said in evidence that he thought the E&Y valuation in 2003 was 'a competent piece of professional work'. The E&Y valuation of 2005 however, focussed on the RRM, and Mr Burns, concluding that although his value range for the 2005 licences came within E&Y's valuation, considered that E&Y's valuation was 'pretty near the top of it' and that, in relying on the RRM, he considered that 'intellectually, [E&Y were] flying in fairly thin air'. . . .

98. The evidence was that the EM and the MM were similar methodologies focussing on an attribution of a proportion of enterprise value to the licences, whereas the RRM was different, and focussed on the present value of royalty expenditure saved by ownership of the licences. A difficulty faced by both Mr Burns and Mr Ryan was that there was not much relevant evidence of licences or sales of mastheads having taken place in the open market, as opposed to sales and purchases of newspaper businesses as a whole or, more usually, the companies carrying on the businesses (examples being INML's acquisition of Acorn in 2004 and LSN in 2005), although we note that Mr Burn's opinion was that when a newspaper business was acquired, the acquirer regarded the masthead as the sole asset it was seeking to acquire.

99. Mr Ryan (HMRC's independent valuation expert) stated in his original report that he regarded the RRM as the most suitable method to value the licences in issue, but he cross-checked his valuation of the UTMs by considering what proportion of intangible asset value the licences represented and the replacement cost of a local newspaper masthead. He identified what he regarded as appropriate royalty rates (5%–6% for the HENL, CNL and SNL licences and 2% for the LSN licence, because LSN publishes free newspapers only). He initially (in his written evidence) valued the licences involved as follows: HENL—£2.1m to £2.5m; CNL—£3m to £3.6m; SNL—£1.4m to £1.7m; and LSN—£1m.

100. Mr Ryan made the point that the value given by the RRM would be appropriate only if one did *not* accept his view that in the market in which the licences were granted the most likely acquirer of the licences from INML

would be the existing publisher of the newspaper concerned. (He thought—having considered the position of the newspaper publishers in nearby areas which could be said to be most likely to wish to expand into the Subsidiaries' areas—that 'the incumbent would pay the maximum value because if it purchases the masthead or the licence nobody else is going to—you go back to the position that you were in'.) Mr Ryan's view was that if one accepted this point then the value of the licences would be unlikely to be significantly higher than the cost of recreating the UTMs concerned (i.e. rebranding), which would give a lower value than that achieved by application of the RRM. If, on the other hand, there was a real risk of someone else coming into the market, the value of the licence would increase to a value calculated on a licensing-in basis (i.e. computed by using the RRM). He rejected the MM as the primary valuation methodology because, as with the most intellectual property valuations, there were not enough reference points to apply a 'top-down' valuation in a rigorous way.

101. Mr Ryan produced his Second Supplementary Report dated 12 October 2011 in the light of transcripts of evidence given at the hearing on 10 and 11 October 2011. In it he referred to evidence which Mr Richard had given which in his view emphasised the dominant nature of the paid-for newspapers (the most important of the totals concerned) operated by the appellants in their local markets. This evidence suggested to Mr Ryan that the existing publisher would be the only credible acquirer of the licences in the hypothetical market being considered and that therefore a valuation based on the costs of recreating the UTMs concerned might be a more appropriate valuation methodology.

102. In Mr Ryan's Second Supplementary Report he also considered clause 3.8 of the licences (see: paragraph 70 above), which he said he had overlooked when he wrote his two earlier reports. Clause 3.8 concerns the entitlement of the licensor (INML) from time to time at its sole discretion on at least 30 days' notice to remove any UTMs from the licence on payment of a *pro rata* refund of the licence fee attributable to UTMs so removed.

103. Mr Ryan stated that clause 3.8 significantly increased the likelihood that an existing publisher would be the only credible acquirer of the licences, essentially because of the investment needed in the business which the licences would permit, and the uncertainty attendant upon possible exercise by the licensor (INML) of its entitlement under clause 3.8. He stated his opinion that the replacement value of the UTMs which were subject to the licences was £10.8 and, on the basis that the Tribunal found that the existing publishers (notionally deprived of the right to use the relevant mastheads) were the only credible acquirers of the licences, he suggested that the appropriate valuation was based on that figure, but discounted to take account of the uncertainty created by possible exercise of the power of removal under clause 3.8. He suggested a figure of up to 35% of the cost of recreating the UTMs. This methodology gave a total valuation of £3.8m for all the licences in issue, as compared with £7.5m to £8.8m if the RRM was applied. Mr Ryan added that if the Tribunal found that the existing publishers were *not* the only credible acquirers of the licences, then he would confirm his valuation adopting the RRM method....

107. Mr Jones, in cross-examining Mr Burns, explored whether the fact that no non-competition covenant had been given by the Subsidiaries in assigning the UTMs to INML and that INML had not given any non-competition covenant on granting the licences to the Subsidiaries had had any effect on the value of the licences. Mr Jones' point was that the Subsidiaries, although without the right to use the various mastheads, remained as incumbents in their respective areas and must be assumed (as was the fact) to have retained their employees, local office facilities, distribution networks and advertiser

VALUATION

relationships, and were therefore in a position immediately to recommence publishing, albeit under a different title, the Cambridge Star, say, instead of the Cambridge Evening News. . . .

109. Mr Burns regarded the RRM as of no assistance, because the transactions providing the basic data necessary to apply it were drawn from 'non-comparable transactions in a non-comparable period a long time ago in different jurisdictions'. The cross-checking he employed for the purpose of his valuation on MM was against actual sales of companies running newspaper businesses in possession of mastheads, and for this purpose he attributed the whole of the value of the intangible assets of such companies to their mastheads. Mr Jones put to him that his begged the question of whether it was correct to make that attribution. He then said (without much enthusiasm) that instead of the RRM one could look at the expected split of profits between a licensor and a licensee, and make a cross-check of the valuation on that basis.

110. Mr Burns was disposed to agree that the non-exclusive nature of the licence between INML and LSN concluded as part of the 2005 Transactions would have had an impact on the value of that licence.

111. Mr Ryan thought it was neither possible nor realistic to regard all (or virtually all) the value of the Subsidiaries other than that attributable to tangible assets to be attributable to their respective mastheads. He made the point that a masthead was essentially a brand (Mr Richard had described it as such) and a specialist brand consultancy called Interbrand had valued the Coca-Cola brand at 50% of the value of the Coca-Cola company's intangible assets—for the McDonalds brand, the figure said to be 40%, for the Apple brand, it was 10%. In the light of that he thought it very unlikely that any brand could be worth 100% of the owning company's intangible asset value. Instead he suggested a value of 20% to 30% – which he described as 'a relatively hefty amount, in my experience', regarding at least 50% of the company's intangible asset value as attributable to its incumbency—that is, the relationships it has because it is in place as the local newspaper publishing company—which Mr Ryan regarded as distinct from brand loyalty. A newspaper brand—a masthead—told the purchaser something about what to expect in terms of the editorial comment and the style of the newspaper. It was not the newspaper itself. Thus the value of a masthead had to be supported by, for instance, editorial staff, although Mr Ryan accepted that this was less important with a free newspaper, which did not rely on the reader making a conscious decision to take (and pay for) the newspaper. On the other hand, the value of the masthead of a free newspaper was connected to the value of the newspaper's relationship with its advertisers. He made the point that the relationships supporting the value of a masthead could not be 'replaced overnight' and that the value of a masthead needed to be maintained, and could dissipate rapidly 'if the editorial content is no longer there to support it'. On the other hand, he acknowledged that if one could 'replace everything overnight' then one 'would be able to capture a lot of [the] business', adding that Mr Richard's evidence had been that it would be impossible for a newcomer to a local newspaper market to do that.

112. Mr Ryan considered that it was very advantageous to check a valuation of an intellectual property asset against other valuations of the asset computed on different methodologies. Thus, he considered it appropriate to check a valuation arrived at by the MM (a 'top-down' methodology arrived at by taking an overview of the value of the business) against the RRM or a discounted cash-flow methodology which is 'a bottom-up method which really relies on getting to grips with the business and how it works'.

113. Mr Ryan, disagreeing with Mr Burns, thought that a newspaper business which had disposed of its masthead, but otherwise retained its business

intact, would 'rebrand'—that is, publish under a different name—rather than close down or 'exit' the market. He thought (based on competition surveys which had been carried out) that it was quite possible that there could be a significant take-up of a new brand.

114. Mr Ryan's view was that the royalties implied in the licence fees charged to the Subsidiaries by INML were too high to be commercial—having regard to the alternatives available to the Subsidiaries, namely to enter the market with rebranded titles. The licence fees as a percentage of the licensees' profits were, in Mr Ryan's view, too high to be commercial—and far higher than any intellectual property valuation that he had been involved in. Even on Mr Burns's estimate (of 60% to 70% of the licensees' profits) the licence fees were too high to be commercial, in Mr Ryan's view.

That level of profit split would suggest that the product being licensed was very profitable (like a 'blockbuster pharmaceutical product') and that the market risks and the functions to be performed by the licensee were minimal.

115. Mr Ryan, differing from Mr Burns, did not regard the factor of synergies (the ability for an acquirer to make more profit out of existing assets, or to save costs) or a 'bid premium' on the licensing of the UTMs as likely to increase the market value of the licences, because he regarded the parties most likely to pay the most for the licences to be the existing publishers (the Subsidiaries) and therefore 'there are clearly no synergies because all you are doing is making it whole, effectively'. And there would be no logical basis to add a 'bid premium'. If, alternatively, a third party newspaper publisher acquired the licence and could achieve synergies by 'sweating [its assets] more', Mr Ryan's view was that those synergies would be counterbalanced by the loss of revenue it would experience by competing in the market with the existing publishers' rebranded newspapers. He acknowledged that synergies might boost the value of the licences if one could assume that the existing publishers would 'exit the market', but he made the point that Competition Commission reports had stated that many local newspapers were in effect able to operate a monopoly in a particular market, and therefore it could not be assumed that there would be a competitor for paid-for titles with a distribution network and other relationships which could give rise to synergies. . . ."

In their judgment the Tribunal stated:

"192. We however have to consider an artificial (from a commercial point of view) state of facts where only the masthead (the UTM) is alienated by a newspaper operating business, and no non-competition covenant is given by the existing publisher.

193. In that context, Mr Burns sought to support his valuation of a newspaper masthead by making the assumption that the existing publisher (who has notionally alienated only the masthead) would not try to remain in the market, and so would not be a potential purchaser of a licence of the masthead. Mr Burns thought it would be more logical for the existing publishers to distribute the proceeds of sale to their shareholders than to contemplate re-entry into the market by taking licences of the titles which they had recently disposed of (see above, paragraph 104).

194. Mr Ryan, on the other hand, was of the view that the existing publisher would be the only credible acquirer of the licence in the hypothetical market being considered (see above, paragraph 101). Indeed he thought that the existing publisher, even if unsuccessful in acquiring the licence, would be likely to use its existing business apparatus to publish under a different name ('rebrand') rather than close down (paragraph 113). This course would be

VALUATION

particularly attractive in relation to free newspapers (such as those operated by LSN). The fact that the Subsidiaries had not given covenants not to compete when assigning the UTMs to INML, and the fact that the licence taken by LSN was on a non-exclusive basis supported this view.

195. On this important issue, we favour the approach of Mr Ryan and reject that of Mr Burns. In particular we cannot understand the basis on which Mr Burns makes his assumption that the existing publisher would 'exit the business' rather than acquire the licence and in this way continue to derive value, and profit, from its existing (and notionally retained) employees, local office facilities, distribution networks and advertiser relationships. It seems to us that there is no basis to assume (as Mr Burns did, and as was not the fact) that the existing publishers had disposed of the UTMs for full value, and further that there is no basis to assume that, if they had, they would not have considered re-investing a part of that value in the acquisition of the licences. On the contrary, the assumed business realities seem to us (as they did to Mr Ryan) to point to the existing publishers being the most likely acquirers of the licences, because they retained the necessary business facilities in place to derive immediate and maximum benefit from the licences, once acquired. Any other purchaser, for example a newspaper publisher in a nearby area, or one who could achieve synergies by 'sweating [its assets] more' (*cf.* above, paragraph 115), would inevitably require a period of adjustment before it could enter the market using the licensed masthead, and this would leave a time-gap which could be exploited by the existing publisher— particularly in the area of free newspapers. . . .

198. We regard Mr Burns's use of the MM to value mastheads sold in isolation to be flawed because we do not accept his underlying assumption that the masthead represents the entirety of the intangible asset value of a newspaper business. We regard the RRM as being, in principle, an appropriate valuation methodology to use, concentrating, as it does, on the present value of royalty payments rendered necessary by the ownership of the licence. However, having reached the view that in the hypothetical market in which the licences were granted the most likely purchasers would be the existing publishers of the newspapers concerned, we are persuaded by Mr Ryan's view that the value of the licences would be unlikely to be significantly higher than the cost of recreating the UTMs concerned (ie rebranding), which would give a lower value than that achieved by application of the RRM (see above, paragraph 100).

199. In the light of Mr Ryan's evidence about the values assigned by Interbrand to the Coca-Cola brand, the McDonalds brand and the Apple brand, we would not in any event have accepted a value for the UTMs in this case which exceeded 30% of the relevant Subsidiaries' intangible asset value. We accept Mr Ryan's point that the bulk of that value is attributable to the Subsidiaries' incumbency—the relationships it has, because it is in place as the local newspaper publishing company—and his point that this is distinct from brand loyalty, or masthead value (see above, paragraph 111). . . .

205. In the result, we accept Mr Ryan's evidence (at paragraphs 1.19 to 1.21 of his Second Supplemental Report) that the value of the various licences equated to 35% of the cost of recreating the relevant UTMs which gives a total value of £3.8m, allocated between the licences as follows: HENL—£1.4m; CNL—£1.1m; SNL—£900,000; and LSN £400,000. The fees paid for the relevant licences were: HENL – £15.5m; CNL—£18.759m (£18.5m in 2003 and £259,000 in 2005); SNL—£6.5m; and LSN—£10.641m; [a total of £51.4m]. Comparison of these figures gives amounts paid by the various Subsidiaries to INML in excess of the market values of the licences concerned as follows: HENL—£14,1m; CNL—£17.659m; SNL—£5.6m; and LSN—£10.241m. these are the figures we take into account when

considering the amounts which may (or may not) rank as distributions for company law purposes by the Subsidiaries concerned to INML.

206. If we had not determined that the correct valuations were linked to the cost of recreating the relevant UTMs, we would have preferred valuations calculated by the use of the RRM, as prepared by Mr Ryan. An advantage of Mr Ryan's approach using the RRM, as against Mr Burns's approach using the MM (which we have rejected), is that Mr Ryan has cross-checked his valuations against the proportions of intangible asset value which they represented and the resultant profit split between licensor and licensee. This, in our view, added to the robustness of Mr Ryan's RRM-based valuations."

Lengthy extracts from the judgement in this case have been included because the valuation of intellectual property is rarely considered in detail in taxation cases. In fact the exercise was irrelevant because of "issue a", in paragraphs 14, 15 and 161.

"14. "The appellants submit that by each assignment in issue both UTMs (Unregistered Trade Marks) and the goodwill attaching to them were assigned, so that we do not have any attempted assignment of an UTM in gross (that is, a transfer of an UTM independently of the underlying business and goodwill to which it relates). They further submit that the UTMs were assigned intra-group and that therefore there was no risk of the assignments deceiving the public. They submit that HMRC's approach is to attempt to extend the law limiting assignments of UTMs well beyond the situations for which the rule was developed to circumstances where there is no rationale in preventing assignment.

15. HMRC submit that the purported assignments of UTMs in this case are purported assignments in gross, and that a UTM (as opposed to a registered trade mark) cannot, as a matter of law, be assigned in gross. The TMAs in this case are, in HMRC's submission, ineffective. Further HMRC originally contended that a UTM is not an intangible asset within the meaning of Schedule 29 FA 2002 (which gives 'intangible asset' the meaning it has for accounting purposes and includes, in particular, any intellectual property, which for these purposes includes 'any . . . trade mark . . . or any licence or other right in respect of [any trade mark]' (paragraph 2, Schedule 29, FA 2002). However, this latter point was withdrawn by Mr Jones in the course of argument—see: paragraphs 163 to 165 below."

Issue *a*: conclusion

"161. Our conclusion in relation to issue *a* therefore is that the purported assignments of UTMs in this case by the respective Subsidiaries to INML were assignments in gross and were void for mistake as to the assignability of the subject matter of the purported assignments (see: *Halsbury's Laws*, 4th *Edition 2007 Reissue, Vol. 13, Deeds and other instruments* paragraph 71 and the cases there cited.) It follows that no UTM, has been validly transferred to INML or licensed back by INML and on this basis the Subsidiaries' appeals in relation to their claims to write down for tax purposes the acquired licences of UTMs fall to be dismissed."

VALUATION

HMRC'S CORPORATE INTANGIBLE RESEARCH AND DEVELOPMENT MANUAL DEALS WITH VALUATION ISSUES AT CIRD10240

12–028 "**Where the value of assets needs to be considered**
Within the regime there are times when the valuation of chargeable intangible assets, or the amount charged for the use of chargeable intangible assets, needs to be considered, for example:

- Attribution of fair values to assets on acquisition in accordance with GAAP, (see CIRD30520).
- Impairment reviews in accordance with GAAP, (see CIRD20515).
- When market value is imposed on transfers between related parties, (see CIRD45030).
- When an asset ceases to be a chargeable intangible asset, (see CIRD47030).
- Where apportionments are required, (for example see CIRD11175, CIRD11685, CIRD12740, CIRD13080, CIRD13245 and CIRD25015).
- Where there are transfer-pricing considerations, (see CIRD47060).
- When a degrouping adjustment arises, (see CIRD30500 onwards)."

It also states

"Examples of useful information are:

- a full description of the product line or business, together, where relevant, with details of the filing of Patents and Trademarks, and an assessment as to the contribution those and other intangibles make to the overall success of the enterprise;
- the accounts for the last three years before the date of valuation for the entity that held the asset;
- the management accounts and other financial information that provide the historic and forecast sales/profit figures relevant to the asset, and insight into other issues such as R&D, marketing, and advertising expenditure;
- copies of any internal reports concerning feasibility, funding and expenditure programmes;
- copies of all relevant sale and licensing agreements;
- a reasoned explanation as to the value returned or royalty rate adopted – ideally to follow good valuation practice more than one approach or methodology will have been used in order to benchmark the proposals made;
- copies of any transfer pricing reports."

CIRD30515 SETS OUT NOTES ON ACCOUNTING PRACTICE FOR INTANGIBLE ASSETS UNDER FRS11 AND IAS36

12–029 "FRS11 applies to all financial statements that are intended to give a true and fair view of an entity's financial position or profit/loss for a period. There is an exemption for smaller enterprises applying the FRS for Smaller Entities, see CIRD30525.
The requirements of FRS11 apply to purchased goodwill that is recognised in the balance sheet and all fixed assets, except:

SCOPE

1. fixed assets within the scope of this FRS addressing disclosures of derivatives and other financial instruments;
2. investment properties as defined in SSAP19 "Accounting for investment properties;
3. an entity's own shares held by an ESOP and shown as a fixed asset in the entity's balance sheet under UITF 13 'Accounting for ESOP Trusts'; and
4. costs capitalised pending determination (ie costs capitalised while a field is still being appraised) under the Oil Industry Accounting Committee's SORP 'Accounting for oil and gas exploration and development activities'.

Many investments are covered by the Accounting Standards Board's project on derivatives and other financial instruments and hence are excluded from this FRS. However, investments in subsidiary undertakings, associates and joint ventures are excluded from the scope of that project and are, therefore, included within the scope of this FRS.

FRS11 does not apply to purchased goodwill that was written off to reserves under SSAP22 'Accounting for Goodwill' (a precursor standard to FRS10) and which has not been recognised on the balance sheet under FRS10 'Goodwill and Intangible Assets'."

IAS36

The equivalent IAS standard is IAS36. No departures from FRS11 that are material for tax purposes have been noted.   **12–030**

CIRD30520 COVERS FRS7/IFRS3

"The objective of FRS7 is to ensure that when one business entity is acquired by another: **12–031**

- all the assets and liabilities that existed in the acquired entity at the date of acquisition are recorded at fair values, reflecting their condition at that date, and
- that all changes to the acquired assets and liabilities, and the resulting gains and losses, that arise after control of the acquired entity has passed to the acquirer are reported as part of the post-acquisition financial performance of the acquiring group."

SCOPE

FRS7 applies to all financial statements that are intended to give a true and fair view of a reporting entity's financial position and profit or loss (or income and expenditure) for a period. Although FRS7 is framed in terms of the acquisition of a subsidiary undertaking by a parent company that prepared consolidated financial statements, it also applies where an individual company or other reporting entity acquires a business other than a subsidiary undertaking.   **12–032**

VALUATION

MEANING OF FAIR VALUE

12–033 Where an intangible is recognised, its fair value should be based on its replacement cost, which is normally its estimated market value. For certain assets it is not easy to determine current replacement cost; neither is it possible to estimate the value of the future services that an asset can provide through its continued use, because of the inherent subjectivity of such a valuation. In such circumstances the historical cost of the asset updated by the use of price indices may be the most reliable means of estimating replacement cost. Where prices have not changed materially it would be acceptable to use a carrying value based on historical cost as a reasonable proxy for fair value.

IMPAIRED ASSETS—EFFECT ON FAIR VALUE

12–034 Where the replacement cost of an acquired asset is not recoverable in full (owing, for example, to lack of profitability, under-utilisation or obsolescence), the fair value is the estimated recoverable amount. The FRS requires that a valuation at recoverable amount should reflect the condition of the asset on acquisition but not any impairments resulting from subsequent events. In some cases the recoverable amount can be determined only by considering as a whole a group of assets that are used jointly, rather than by attempting to determine the recoverable amount of each identifiable asset in that group. Aggregation in such cases serves to facilitate the attribution of cash flows to the assets that help to generate them.

CIRD30525—INTANGIBLE ASSETS: NOTES ON ACCOUNTING PRACTICE: FRS FOR SMALLER ENTITIES (FRSSE)

12–035 Under UK GAAP practice smaller companies are entitled (but not required) to draw up their accounts (apart from consolidated accounts) under the provisions of the FRS for Smaller Entities rather than under the individual FRS including FRS7, FRS10 and FRS11.

The objective of the FRS for Smaller Entities is to provide an accounting framework for smaller reporting entities which provides adequate information about their financial position, performance and financial adaptability while recognising that the accounting requirements may not need to be so detailed as for larger entities.

Under the Accounting Standards Board FRSSE (June 2008) states:

12–036 **Other intangible assets and goodwill**

6.11 Positive **purchased goodwill** and purchased **intangible assets** shall be capitalised. Internally generated goodwill and intangible assets shall not be capitalised.

6.12 An **intangible asset** purchased with a business shall be **recognised** separately from the **purchased goodwill** if its value can be measured reliably.
6.13 Capitalised goodwill and **intangible assets** shall be **depreciated** on a straight-line (or more appropriate) basis over their **useful economic lives**, which shall not exceed 20 years. THE PERIOD CHOSEN FOR DEPRECIATING GOODWILL AND THE REASONS FOR CHOOSING THAT PERIOD MUST BE DISCLOSED IN A NOTE TO THE ACCOUNTS.
6.14 The **residual value** assigned to goodwill shall be zero. A higher **residual value** may be assigned to an **intangible asset** only when this value can be established reliably, for example when it has been agreed contractually.
6.15 **Useful economic lives** shall be reviewed at the end of each reporting period and revised if necessary, subject to the constraint that the revised life shall not exceed 20 years from the date of acquisition. The carrying amount at the date of revision shall be **depreciated** over the revised estimate of remaining **useful economic life.**
6.16 Goodwill and **intangible assets** shall not be revalued.
6.17 If an acquisition appears to give rise to negative goodwill, **fair values** shall be checked to ensure that those of the acquired **assets** have not been overstated. Once this has been done, remaining negative goodwill up to the **fair values** of the non-monetary **assets** acquired shall be released in the profit and loss account over the lives of those assets. Any additional negative goodwill shall be **recognised** in the profit and loss account over the period expected to benefit from it. The amount of negative goodwill on the balance sheet and the period(s) in which it is being written shall be disclosed.

CIRD30530 states that:

"Intangible assets are defined in FRS10 as 'non-financial fixed assets that do not have physical substance but are identifiable and are controlled by the entity through custody or legal rights'.
When intangible assets should be capitalised
Internally developed intangible assets may be capitalised only when they have a readily ascertainable market value. To meet this test, FRS10 requires that the asset should belong to a homogenous population of assets that are equivalent in all material respects, and that an active market, evidenced by frequent transactions, for such assets, exists. Therefore it is clear that assets such as patents, brands, publishing titles and patented drugs should not be capitalised in the hands of the developer, as they will be unique. Once sold, however, a purchaser must capitalise them.

The general rule for an intangible asset purchased separately from the purchase of a business is that it should be capitalised at its cost. If it is purchased as part of the purchase of a business than FRS7 will apply to set the value shown.

For acquired intangible assets, these should be capitalised on acquisition in accordance with the rules in FRS7 (CIRD30520).
When intangible assets should be identified separately from goodwill

VALUATION

Where an intangible asset is acquired as part of the purchase of a business it should only be capitalised separately from goodwill if its value can be measured reliably on initial recognition. Otherwise it should be included as part of the goodwill."

CIRD30535 DEALS WITH GOODWILL

12–037   Goodwill is the difference between the consideration payable for a business and the aggregate fair value of its identifiable assets less liabilities. Much time could be spent in worrying about this definition, but the essential point is that the goodwill is the residue of the surplus value of the business after identifying specific assets to which a fair value can be attributed. From CIRD30530 it will be seen that intangible assets can only be capitalised separately from goodwill when there is an initial measurable value to them that can be recognised.

FRS10 does not attempt to define goodwill in the abstract, but it states that **internally developed goodwill should not be capitalised**.

Purchased goodwill is defined as "the difference between the cost of an acquired entity and the aggregate of the fair value of the entity's identifiable assets and liabilities".

NEGATIVE GOODWILL

12–038   It should be noted that in certain circumstances goodwill could be negative. The purchase price of a business may be less than the net value of its identifiable assets. Negative goodwill is generally attributed to two possible causes. The first is where a genuine bargain has been obtained, for example as a result of a distress sale. The other is where the purchase price is reduced to take account of future costs or losses that are not yet sufficiently certain to be recognised as liabilities at the date of acquisition.

Negative goodwill up to the fair value of the non-monetary assets acquired should be recognised in the Profit and Loss account over the same period over which the value of the non-monetary assets is "recovered" by sale or by depreciation. Any negative goodwill in excess of the fair values of the non-monetary assets acquired (which is not very likely) should be recognised in the profit and loss account in the periods expected to be benefited.

The treatment of negative goodwill involves a number of difficult problems for accountants. In practice, if this seems relevant to a tax computation, it is advisable to seek the advice of a Revenue accountant.

12–039   If there is negative goodwill it should be shown separately on the balance sheet. However, purchased goodwill arising from a single transaction should not be sub-divided into positive and negative components, but instead should be shown as one.

CIRD30540 deals with amortisation of intangible assets, CIRD 30550 covers impairment and CIRD 30555, impairment reviews, CIRD30560 refers to impairment loss and CIRD 30580 to revaluations, stating:

NEGATIVE GOODWILL

"Only where an intangible asset has a 'readily ascertainable market value', may it be revalued in a company's accounts to its market value. If one such intangible asset is revalued, all other capitalised intangible assets of the same class should be revalued.

A company can choose whether or not to make an initial revaluation of these assets but once an intangible asset has been revalued, further revaluations should be performed sufficiently often to ensure that the carrying value does not differ materially from the market value at the balance sheet date.

An asset has a 'readily ascertainable value' only if:

- The asset belongs to a homogenous population of assets that are equivalent in all material respects, and
- An active market, evidenced by frequent transactions, exists for that population of assets."

CIRD30600 sets out the accounting disclosure requirements and CIRD30650 refers to:

"Brands and Publishing Titles

FRS10 does not permit brands and publishing titles internally generated by the company that holds them to be capitalised on its balance sheet. But valuation issues may nevertheless arise in connection with purchased assets of this kind.

Techniques to value such assets have been developed by concerns that are regularly involved in the purchase and sale of such assets and may be used in applying FRS7 where the assets are acquired as part of a business (see CIRD30520). The techniques may involve 'indicators of value' such as multiples of turnover, or an estimate of the present value of the royalties that would be payable to license from a third party."

CHAPTER 13

Transfer pricing

INTRODUCTION

The rate of royalty payments between connected companies should be at market value because many countries have transfer pricing provisions whereby artificial values can be disregarded and the market value substituted. For accounting periods ending on or after April 1, 2010, the UK transfer pricing legislation is found in TIOPA 2010 Pt 4 (s.146 and following). The legislation was previously contained in TA 1988 s.770A Sch.28AA. The legislation is to be construed in such manner as to secure consistency between the basic rule on transfer pricing set out in Ch.1 and the principles of the OECD Model Convention and Transfer Pricing Guidelines for Multinational Enterprises and Tax Administrations and also any double taxation agreement which incorporates any part of art.9 of the OECD Model. On July 13, 2013 the OECD published a Revised Discussion Draft on Transfer Pricing Aspects of Intangibles, which contains some controversial proposals.

13–001

Under corporation tax self assessment taxpayers now have an obligation to use arm's-length prices in their tax returns. This chapter deals with the provisions in force at October 2013.

The main provisions

The basic rule is that an adjustment is required to the tax return of the advantaged person where a provision is made between two persons ("the affected persons") that are not at arm's length and that provision confers a potential UK taxation advantage.

13–002

United Kingdom to UK transactions were excluded from the transfer pricing provisions before April 1, 2004, provided that both parties were within the charge to UK corporation tax or income tax in respect of their profits and were not entitled to any credit relief or deduction for foreign tax payable on the profits concerned. The transfer pricing rules include UK to UK transactions on or after April 1, 2004 (April 6, 2004 for those within the charge to income rather than corporation tax). In a response to concerns that the exemption for UK to UK transactions may be in contravention of EU law, in particular following the case of *Lankhorst-Hohorst GmbH v Finanzamt Steinfurt* (C-324/00), the transfer pricing rules were extended to apply to all transactions where a UK company receives a tax advantage with effect from April 1, 2004 (April 6, 2004 for those within the charge to income rather than corporation tax). For transactions taking place between two UK companies, a compensating adjustment is made to eliminate any double counting of profits (TIOPA 2010 ss.174–180). An adjustment must be made even where the combined UK tax payable by the companies concerned remains unchanged.

In order for the transfer pricing provisions to apply, one of the affected persons must have been directly or indirectly participating in the management, control or capital of the other or the same person or persons must have been directly or indirectly participating in the management control or capital of each of the affected persons.

13–003 For accounting periods commencing on or after April 1, 2004, there are exemptions from the transfer pricing rules for small and medium-sized enterprises (TIOPA 2010 ss.166–173). Dormant companies are also outside the scope of these provisions (s.165). For the purposes of the exemptions, a company is "small" if it has fewer than 50 employees and its turnover and/or assets do not exceed €10 million. A medium-sized enterprise is one which has fewer than 250 employees and either has a turnover of less than €50 million or assets of less than €43 million. These thresholds are applied to each accounting period and on a consolidated basis, taking into account worldwide members of the group and certain "linked" enterprises. Small enterprises are exempt from the transfer pricing rules, subject to the exception mentioned below for transactions with "non-qualifying" territories. Medium-sized enterprises are outside the scope of the transfer pricing legislation on a provisional basis only: HMRC are able to apply arm's-length criteria to related party transactions undertaken by a medium-sized enterprise if they consider that there is a significant loss of UK tax.

Small and medium-sized enterprises remain within the transfer pricing rules in relation to transactions with related parties resident in certain non-qualifying countries (broadly, countries with whom the United Kingdom does not have a double tax treaty containing a suitable non-discrimination clause), or other countries specified by the Treasury. A list of the territories with appropriate double tax treaties is contained in HMRC's International Manual at INTM412090.

Notwithstanding the general exemption from the transfer pricing rules, medium-sized enterprises may be required by HMRC to make adjustments under the regime in exceptional cases where the amount of tax involved is significant. There is no equivalent power for HMRC to require a small enterprise to make transfer pricing adjustments.

13–004 The transfer pricing rules apply to companies and partnerships. They do not apply between two individuals although they may apply between an individual and a company or partnership.

Whether a body corporate or partnership is "controlled" is determined principally by reference to CTA 2010 s.1124. "Control" for this purpose means voting control or control by virtue of powers conferred by the articles of association or other document regulating the powers of a company whereby the company's affairs are conducted in accordance with the wishes of the controller. In the case of a partnership it means the right to a share of more than half the assets or income of the partnership. "Control" includes indirect control through a nominee or connected person, i.e. spouse or (from December 5, 2005) civil partner, sibling, spouse's or civil partner's sibling, ancestor or lineal descendant (or their spouse or civil partner's lineal descendant), or trustee (for the detailed

INTRODUCTION

provisions see TIOPA 2010 ss.159 and 163). In considering the definition of control under CTA 2010 s.1124, HMRC argued in *Irving v Tesco Stores (Holdings) Ltd* [1982] S.T.C. 881, that control had to be at company meeting level and not merely at board meeting level. In determining control it is not sufficient to look merely at the first named trustee of a trust holding in order to determine whether control may be exercised (*IRC v Lithgows Ltd* (1960) 39 T.C. 270).

A person ("the potential participant") is considered by the legislation to be indirectly participating in the management, control or capital of another person if he would be treated as directly participating if certain rights and powers were attributed to him. Broadly these rights and powers are rights and powers which the potential participant is entitled to acquire at a future date or which he will at a future date become entitled to acquire; rights and powers that may be required to be exercised on behalf of or under the direction or for the benefit of that person; and rights and powers of any connected person.

In relation to financing arrangements, the definition of "control" is extended to include the combined rights and powers of persons "acting together". This rule applies to financing transactions on or after March 4, 2005. A person ("P") is treated as indirectly participating in the management, control or capital of another person ("A"') if there is a provision relating to the financing of A and: **13–005**

1. A is a body corporate or partnership;
2. P and one or more others have acted together in respect of the financing arrangement; and
3. P would control A if the rights and powers of those other persons were to be taken into account.

HMRC's published guidance on the meaning of "acting together" indicates that the phrase is intentionally wide-ranging, and can include any element of cooperation, collusion, coordination or acting in concert. Furthermore, it is not necessary for P to have an equity stake in A: if P acts together with those who together would be taken to control A, P's financing arrangement with A will be within the scope of the transfer pricing provisions.

An individual is deemed to be connected to their spouse or civil partner, relative (brother, sister, ancestor or lineal descendent), spouse or civil partner's relatives and their relatives' spouses or civil partners.

A person is also considered to be indirectly participating in the management, control or capital of another person if he is one of a number of major participants in that other person. **13–006**

A person is a major participant if a 40 per cent test is satisfied. This test is satisfied where two persons each have interests, rights and powers representing at least 40 per cent of the holdings, rights and powers in respect of which they are taken to control the subordinate.

Interest

Prior to April 1, 2004, TA 1988 s.209(2)(da) (now repealed) provided that interest paid to a non-resident company by a UK company within the same 75 per cent **13–007** group should be treated as a distribution to the extent that the interest paid exceeded that which would have applied on a loan between independent companies. With effect from April 1, 2004, the thin capitalisation provisions of TA 1988 s.209(2)(da) were incorporated into TA 1988 Sch.28AA, (now TIOPA 2010 ss.161 and 162) although the transfer pricing provisions could apply to non-arm's-length loans before this date (e.g. where the 75 per cent ownership test was not satisfied). TIOPA 2010 Pt 4 operates by denying a deduction for excessive interest; the excess is not re-characterised as a distribution.

In determining whether an amount of interest is excessive, specific factors such as whether the loan would have been made were it not for the connection between the two related parties; the amount of the loan which would have been made; and the rate of interest and other terms which would have applied if the parties were acting at arm's length (TIOPA 2010 s.152). HMRC typically examine the ratio of debt to equity, taking a ratio of 1:1 to be broadly acceptable in most cases (although a higher ratio may be accepted in highly-geared business sectors, such as real estate). Interest cover is also important and although there is again no official safe harbour, HMRC view cover of around 3:1 as being acceptable.

For UK to UK loans, the compensating adjustment regime described above generally means that even where interest is disallowed, there is no overall impact on the group's UK tax liability.

The compatibility of the UK's thin capitalisation regime with EU law was examined in the case of *Test Claimants in the Thin Capitalisation Group Litigation v IRC* [2007] S.T.C. 906. The case concerned a number of UK companies with parent companies resident in other EU Member States where the subsidiary had been substantially funded by way of loans rather than equity. Under thin capitalisation principles, if a company is in receipt of shareholder or other related party loans which would not have been made on similar terms if the parties were acting at arm's length, for UK tax purposes the excess interest payable by the subsidiary would not be deductible in computing taxable profits. The Advocate General concluded that the UK's thin capitalisation rules did not infringe EU law provided that the legislation contained an exemption from the rules where it can be demonstrated without undue effort that a transaction was undertaken for genuine commercial reasons rather than for tax avoidance purposes.

Documentation and penalties

13–008   Adjustments required in order to comply with the transfer pricing legislation are made in the affected company's self assessment tax return. There are no specific record-keeping requirements set out in TIOPA 2010 Pt 4, and the general requirement under self-assessment to retain sufficient records to ensure that a return is complete and correct apply equally to transactions within the transfer pricing rules. Guidance in HMRC's International Tax Manual (INTM483030) follows that laid down in the OECD Guidelines and broadly requires that "the demonstration of an 'arm's length' result should be in accordance with the same prudent business management principles that would govern the process of evaluating a business decision of a similar level of complexity and importance".

INTRODUCTION

HMRC identify four types of records which need to be considered: primary accounting records; tax adjustment records; records of transactions with associated businesses and evidence to demonstrate an arm's length result.

In particular, a business:

- should make documentation available and accessible to HM Revenue & Customs (including, where appropriate, translation from another language), but the form in which the documentation is stored should be at the discretion of the business;
- should identify the associated businesses with which the relevant transactions took place and the nature of the association;
- should describe the nature of the business in the course of which the relevant transactions took place and the property (tangible and intangible) used in that business;
- should set out the contractual or other understandings between the associated businesses and the risk assumed by each party;
- should describe the method used to establish an "arm's-length" result and explain why that method was chosen;
- need not provide evidence about associations or transactions between businesses where those associations or transactions are not within the scope of UK transfer pricing rules;
- need not provide evidence related to each relevant transaction, but may provide aggregated evidence related to a class of similar transactions;
- need not create new evidence in relation to transactions that occur after evidence has been created in relation to transactions that are similar and there have been no material changes in the circumstances for determining an "arm's-length" result;
- need not commission the production of evidence from a professional adviser if the business is able to produce appropriate evidence itself; and
- may choose to explain its general commercial and management strategy, or that of the group of businesses of which it is a member, as well as the current and forecast business and technological environment, competitive conditions, and regulatory framework.

The above documentation should exist at the latest at the time the return is made and should be preserved until the later of four years from the end of the chargeable period to which they relate or the date on which enquiries to which the documents are relevant are complete. It is not necessary for fresh documentation to be prepared for each return period, provided that the original documentation supports a complete and correct return.

Further guidance on the type of information and documentation which may be used in support of the transfer price adopted by a company is contained in the OECD's "Transfer Pricing Guidelines for Multinational Enterprises and Tax Administrations" (Ch.V s.C).

13–009

Penalties can be charged in respect of tax lost through fraud or negligent conduct of up to 100 per cent of the tax. HMRC's internal manuals offer guidance on the application of penalties. The guidance states:

"A penalty may be due:

- if an incorrect return is made and a business has been careless or negligent in establishing the arm's length basis for the return,
- if a business does not maintain the appropriate documentation necessary to demonstrate that it has made its returns on the basis that the terms of the connected party transactions were considered to be on arm's length terms." (INTM483110)

Examples of how HMRC will interpret carelessness or negligence in transfer pricing cases are given in the Compliance Manual at CH81140 onwards for carelessness, and at INTM483120. HMRC acknowledge that what is an arm's length price is a matter of judgment and there is frequently not one "right" answer:

"Each case is to be judged on its own facts and merits, with the guiding principle being that a person is not negligent if he or she has done what a 'reasonable person would do'. There is therefore an obligation on taxpayers to do what a reasonable person would to ensure that their returns are made in accordance with the arm's length principle. This would involve, but not be limited to:

- Using their commercial knowledge and judgement to make arrangements and set prices which conform to the arm's length standard (or to make computational adjustments in their returns where they do not);
- Being able to show (for example, by means of good quality documentation) that they made an honest and reasonable attempt to comply with the arm's length standard and with the legislation;
- Seeking professional help where they know they need it."

13–010 In addition to extending the scope of Sch.28AA (now TIOPA 2010 Pt 4) to transactions between UK companies, FA 2004 introduced a temporary partial relaxation of the penalty regime for failure to keep adequate records relating to transactions within the transfer pricing rules. The relaxation applied for accounting periods beginning after December 31, 2003 and ending before April 1, 2006 (or years of assessment 2004–05 and 2005–06 for those within the charge to income tax), The £3,000 penalty per return for failure to keep proper records was removed entirely for failures to keep records in support of arm's-length transfer prices, and for the purposes of calculating any tax-geared penalty a taxpayer was not to be considered to have submitted a return negligently by reason only of his failure to keep records in support of an arm's-length provision. Records relating to all transactions, not just those between UK companies, were covered by the reduced penalty regime.

With regard to record keeping requirements, a taxpayer may be exposed to penalties if it did not make available to HMRC on request its primary accounting records, tax adjustment records or records of transactions with associated businesses, or did not make available adequate evidence demonstrating an appropriate arm's-length price.

An article at pp.345–349 in the HMRC *Tax Bulletin* October 1996 provides an insight into HMRC's views on the OECD's transfer pricing guidelines as well as practical guidance on the mutual agreement procedure contained in UK double taxation conventions. The HMRC leaflet *The Transfer Pricing Guidelines for Multinational Enterprises and Tax Administrations* contains further useful information.

Transfer pricing provisions do not apply for capital gains tax or for capital allowance purposes in view of TIOPA 2010 ss.213 and 214 except to facilitate a claim made under TIOPA 2010 s.174 where there has been a transfer pricing adjustment on the other party.

13–011

Similarly the transfer pricing provisions in TIOPA 2010 Pt 4 are explained in the HMRC Manuals at INTM410000 and in Ch.15 of the *International Tax Handbook*.

CTA 2010 s.1020 may apply to treat as a distribution, the difference between the market value and the transfer price where an undervalued asset is transferred or a liability is transferred at an overvalue unless, for transfers prior to July 17, 2012, both companies are resident in the United Kingdom (CTA 2010 s.1021).

Under self-assessment, HMRC expects taxpayers to reveal where transfer pricing adjustments are necessary and quantify the extent of the adjustment.

FOREIGN LEGISLATION

Over the years many countries have introduced transfer pricing rules including for example: Australia, Belgium, Canada, Denmark, France, Germany, Greece, Italy, Netherlands, Portugal, Russia, Spain and the United States.

13–012

Unilateral transfer pricing adjustments can give rise to economic double taxation for which no relief is available. The only remedy until recently has been to invoke the competent authority procedure under a double taxation treaty and hope the Revenue authorities of the two countries will agree a common transfer price. Relief is applied by TIOPA 2010 s.124.

ARBITRATION CONVENTION

The European Union Arbitration Convention on the elimination of double taxation in connection with the adjustment of profits of associated enterprises (EE90/436) came into force on January 1, 1995 and is applied to the United Kingdom by TIOPA 2010 s.127. This gives some protection against such double taxation arising from different transfer pricing adjustments in different countries within the European Union. The EU Joint Transfer Pricing Forum has produced a Code of Conduct in respect of the implementation of the Arbitration Convention by Member States.

13–013

THEORY OF INTERNATIONAL TRANSFER PRICING

The theory of international transfer pricing is succinctly described in art.4 para.2, of the Arbitration Convention as follows:

13–014

> "Where an enterprise of a contracting state carries on business in another contracting state through a permanent establishment situated therein there shall be attributed to that permanent establishment the profits which it might be expected to make if it were a distinct and separate enterprise engaged in the same or similar activities

under the same or similar conditions and dealing wholly independently with the enterprise of which it is a permanent establishment."

This statement forms the basis of the comparable arm's-length price calculated as if the parties to the transactions were independent persons dealing with each other at arm's length; that is the assumption underlying the Associated Enterprises Article of the OECD Model Double Taxation Convention (art.9(1) of the OECD *Transfer Pricing Report* of 1979).

In the field of intellectual property, the problem is quite simply to find a comparable situation where a royalty level has been agreed between arm's length companies in a similar situation. It is very often impossible to find such a situation and it is then necessary to try to determine from first principles what would be a fair royalty in the circumstances. The problem here is that different Revenue authorities have different approaches to this problem which in turn gives rise to the need for the Arbitration Convention. *Tax Bulletin* 25, October 1996, sets out the mutual agreement procedure in the UK double tax conventions and Arbitration Convention.

13–015 In the field of international transactions, HMRC are likely to look closely at royalty levels in view of the transfer pricing provisions in TIOPA 2010 Pt 4. These provisions apply as explained above to royalties in the same way as they apply to other transactions. Where the royalty level is greater or less than the arm's-length price which might have been expected if the parties to the transaction had been independent persons dealing at arm's length, a transfer pricing adjustment is required.

In practice the transfer pricing provisions contained in TIOPA 2010 Pt 4 are normally applied to cross-border transactions with other countries, particularly where a royalty is paid to a low tax area or tax haven.

The effect of TIOPA 2010 Pt 4 is to enable HMRC to substitute what they deem to be an arm's-length price for the price actually agreed and to levy tax accordingly. Unfortunately other countries also have similar provisions and there is no reason to suppose that different Revenue authorities would agree the same arm's-length price for the royalty arrangements. It is perfectly possible, for example, that HMRC in the United Kingdom may regard a royalty of 7.5 per cent paid to the United States as excessive and tax the licensee as if he had paid a royalty of only 5 per cent. On the other hand, the Internal Revenue Service in the United States may regard a 7.5 per cent royalty as being too low and, under s.482 of the Internal Revenue Code 1986, amend the royalty received by the licensor for American tax purposes to, say, 10 per cent. This clearly involves economic double taxation for which no relief is available under the double taxation treaty.

13–015 The transfer pricing rules are not the only rules which could affect the deductibility for tax purposes of a trading expense. Management charges paid to a connected party could be disallowed in the absence of evidence to justify the expenses as being wholly incurred for the purposes of the trade (CTA 2009 s.54 and ITTOIA 2005 s.34; *Fragmap Developments Ltd v Cooper* (1967) 44 T.C. 366; *New Zealand Commissioner of Inland Revenue v Europa Oil (NZ) Ltd* (1970) 49 A.T.C. 282). In a complex case where the arrangements were held to be designed to cheat the Public Revenue, the taxpayer's professional advisers were jailed (*R. v Charlton* [1966] S.T.C. 1418).

Any annuity or other annual payment is disallowed by CTA 2009 s.1301. Patent royalties are disallowed by CTA 2009 s.59, other than that paid by a company under the corporate intangible fixed assets scheme (see Ch.21). ITA 2007 s.448 gives tax relief to an individual who pays an annual payment from which tax must be deducted as required by ITA 2007 s.900 for annual payments or ITA 2007 s.903 for patent royalties. Prior to ITTOIA 2005, an annual payment payable out of the profits of the trade was not an allowable deduction. It remains the case that a payment out of the profits, as distinct from one made in arriving at the profits, will be disallowable, however an annual payment or patent royalty paid wholly and exclusively for the purposes of a trade or property business will be deductible. Relief under ITA 2007 s.448 is only due where the payment is not otherwise deductible.

Business entertaining expenses are disallowed by CTA 2009 s.1298 and ITTOIA 2005 s.45, and illegal bribes and extortion payments are disallowed by CTA 2009 s.1304 and ITTOIA 2005 s.55.

13–016 Where transactions take place in goods forming trading stock, for example under a franchising operation, HMRC can substitute market value for the transaction price under CTA 2009 s.157 and ITTOIA 2005 s.172B on the basis of *Sharkey v Wernher* [1955] T.C. 275; *Watson Bros v Hornby* (1942) 24 T.C. 506; *Petrotim Securities Ltd v Ayres* (1963) 41 T.C. 389; *Skinner v Berry Head Lands Ltd* (1970) 46 T.C. 377; and *Ridge Securities v IRC* (1963) 44 T.C. 373. The same principle does not apply to the provision of professional services where the Revenue has no power to substitute the market value (*Mason v Innes* (1967) 44 T.C. 326).

The capital gains tax legislation contains a number of sections under which bargains not at arm's length are treated as being disposed of for a consideration equal to market value (TCGA 1992 s.17).

Transactions between connected persons, as defined by TCGA 1992 s.286, are deemed to be bargains not at arm's length and any loss arising from such a transaction is ring-fenced so that it can only be set against gains on other transactions between the same parties (TCGA 1992 s.18), but TCGA 1992 ss.19 and 20 prevent the exploitation of the valuation rules in TCGA 1992 ss.272 and 273 to prevent the reduction in chargeable gains by transferring assets in a series of transactions to reduce the aggregate value. There are also anti-avoidance rules to prevent changes in rights. for example to shares, to move value from one asset to another without a disposal under what are known as value shifting provisions in TCGA 1992 ss.29–34.

The rules relating to distributions, loan relationships and foreign exchange dealt with in Ch.10 can also have the effect of substituting different figures for tax purposes from those agreed between the parties or for treating what would otherwise be allowable expenses as distributions out of taxed profits. Thin capitalisation rules may be applied to disallow excessive interest under TIOPA 2010 s.131, notwithstanding the EU Directive on interest and royalties 2003/49/EC. Where a special relationship exists between a paying company and the recipient results in a payment being made in excess of an amount that would have been paid between independent third parties, the exemption from tax provided under the EU interest and royalties Directive applies only to the arm's-length amount.

THE OECD TRANSFER PRICING GUIDELINES FOR MULTINATIONAL ENTERPRISES AND TAX ADMINISTRATIONS (REPORT OF JULY 22, 2010)

13–017 This report is accepted by the Revenue authorities of many jurisdictions as useful guidance for the purposes of determining transfer prices. Indeed in the case of the United Kingdom, TIOPA 2010 s.164 makes it clear that OECD principles will be used to construe UK transfer pricing rules, including (from April 1, 2004) thin capitalisation provisions.

Transfer pricing methods to arrive at the arm's-length price

13–018 One of the most difficult problems in practice in any transfer pricing adjustment is agreeing an arm's-length price for a transaction which does not, and in reality would not, take place between parties at arm's length and this report attempts to set out a basis for arriving at an arm's-length value which is likely to be fair to the taxpayers in both countries and to the Revenue authorities of both countries. The report breaks down transfer pricing comparisons into transaction-based methods and transactional profit methods.

Transaction-based methods

13–019 There are three transaction-based methods:

(1) the comparable uncontrolled price method (CUP);
(2) the re-sale price method; and
(3) the cost plus method.

An uncontrolled third party transaction may be identified for the purposes of comparison with a connected party transaction if there are no differences between the transactions being compared or between the enterprises undertaking those transactions that could materially affect the price in the open market, or such differences exist but reasonably accurate adjustments can be made to eliminate their effects. The CUP method is the most favoured method.

Comparable uncontrolled price method (CUP)

13–020 The main problem with the CUP is finding the comparable transaction, as this information is usually confidential and unlikely to be available to a trader except in the most general terms of published statistics, or where it is available from price lists and published terms of trade from competitors selling similar products. In practice this happens only rarely in a transfer-pricing investigation. It may be that the Revenue authorities have information in relation to comparable prices charged by other businesses but this information will normally be held on a confidential basis and cannot be used in evidence to support a transfer pricing adjustment.

In comparing products that are at first sight thought to be comparable it is necessary not only to consider their physical features, such as the materials out of which they are made, their expected quality and reliability and function, but also the extent to which they are readily available, the time at which they are available, the terms and date of delivery, guarantees and warranties, the market at which they are aimed, the terms of payment including transport costs, the back-up support available, such as technical support and technology transfer, the conditions of use and the volume of sales quantities, discounts available and market into which they are sold. The CUP should also take account of the brand name and advertising costs of the product which may be heavily marketed on a worldwide basis, and in practice justify a significant premium over an unbranded competitor.

The trouble with the CUP is that any such comparison is likely to highlight differences rather than similarities and even where finished products are concerned the businesses are normally trying to emphasise to their customers the differences between their product and those of their rivals, rather than the similarities. Obviously there will be cases where there are no material differences or where such differences as there are can be both quantified and adjusted for.

Re-sale price method

Because of the difficulty of finding a CUP, in practice an alternative is to look at the re-sale price. In one country X may supply goods or services to Y in another country which are incorporated into a product which Y in turn sells to unconnected customers. By deducting from the resale price from Y to the third party, customer Y's reasonable gross margin, it may be possible to arrive at the arm's-length price which X ought to have charged Y. **13–021**

The margin of Y will depend on the value which Y adds to the product or service; e.g. assembling the product or tailoring it for local use, distribution, advertising, guarantees, warranties, servicing, etc.; Y's costs, which will depend on the value added by Y to the product or service obtained from X, and may include manufacturing and assembly costs, marketing distribution, advertising, financing, administration, testing, stock holding, transportation, etc.; with an allowance for the risk taken by Y and its financing costs and perhaps the costs of supporting the brand name and exclusive franchise obtained from X.

It will be immediately apparent that a number of these costs are difficult to allocate to specific products and the allowable mark-up is a subjective figure, although it in turn should, where possible, be related to comparable third-party transactions with adjustments as necessary.

The cost-plus method

In many cases controlled subsidiaries, for which transfer-pricing adjustments may be appropriate, are not dealing with the end market but are themselves producing goods or services for fellow entities within the multinational group which are incorporated into the final product sold worldwide. In such cases the resale price method will not readily produce an arm's-length price and the cost plus method may be appropriate. This seeks to add to the costs incurred by the overseas subsidiary a reasonable margin for the value added by, and profit of, the overseas companies. This on its own is of no help where a major part of the cost arises **13–022** from the goods or services brought in from controlled enterprises, but in a typical chain transaction in a multinational chain it might provide some guidance, particularly if substantial costs are incurred locally.

In chain transactions it may be possible to look at each company in turn on the basis of its costs plus a reasonable mark-up, and compare that with a resale price method carried down through the chain from the ultimate sale price to arm's-length customers. It may, however, in such circumstances be preferable to use one of the profit methods.

Transactional profit methods

13–023　Where a lack of suitable comparisons makes a transaction-based method inappropriate, a profit-based method is perhaps the only sensible alternative.

The transactional profit-split method

13–024　In a transactional profit-split method the profit arising on the entire transaction within the group of connected enterprises is calculated and apportioned on a rational basis between the various entities, in accordance with their contribution to the overall profit. Although this is a seemingly sensible approach in theory, it is often very difficult to apply in practice. The first requirement is to be able to identify the profit per product and then to apportion it among the entities involved. This basis often uses a functional analysis by reference to the functions supplied by each to the overall product. These would include items such as management, administration and finance, manufacturing, assembling and processing, tasting, research and development, packaging, labelling, warehousing, preserving, storing, distribution, branding, marketing, wholesaling, retailing, transportation, advertising, after sales servicing, warranties and guarantees, ownership of intellectual property and brand names, and capital employed by each enterprise. The analysis of risk should take account of the commercial risk to each entity, taking account of parent company guarantees and support, liabilities to third parties, product and environmental liabilities, employee liabilities, financing costs and political and currency risks. Any such functional analysis needs to be evidenced by appropriate contemporary evidence.

The functional analysis may be complicated by set-off where, for example, patent licences are granted by the parent company to the local manufacturer who, in turn, develops the production know-how in the light of manufacturing experience and customer input, which is passed back to the parent company and perhaps ultimately incorporated in further patented developments of the product.

A profit split may have to take account of market penetration strategies whereby products are heavily discounted in a new market in order to obtain a critical market share with a view to increasing profits to acceptable levels in a reasonably short time. If such a strategy is accepted it may be a loss-split method for the whole or part of the chain.

13–025　As well as functional analysis, a contribution analysis may be useful where the profits are allocated on the basis of the relative value of the functions performed by each entity in the chain. The trouble with this approach is that it is likely to be highly subjective and difficult to obtain evidence to confirm the analysis put forward. In some cases market data may be available to support an analysis on this basis.

Residual analysis requires the total profit from the entire transaction to be allocated on the basis of a theoretical margin, dependent on the services provided by each transaction in the chain and comparing this with the overall margin resulting in a residual profit or loss, which itself is allocated to those areas most responsible for the final results. The initial split on a residual analysis may take account of the cash flow projections from the transactions being considered.

Transactional net margin method

The transactional net margin method (TNMM) examines the net profit margin relative to an appropriate base (e.g. costs, sales, assets). This method operates in a similar way to the cost plus and resale price methods. Again the problem is finding comparable data that is available in the public domain and to adjust for differences between the transactions under review and the model taken as comparison. This sort of comparison is only likely to give an acceptable result if data over several years is compared both for the controlled transactions and the chosen comparison.

13–026

Global methods

Methods that allocate profit by reference to costs of turnover, labour costs, etc. may be easy to calculate but end up by producing a result that is almost entirely arbitrary.

13–027

ARM'S-LENGTH RANGE

The problem with trying to identify an arm's-length price for transfer pricing purposes is that in most cases it does not exist, because the goods or services under consideration are not available in the same quantity and quality in unconnected transactions. The various methods suggested to try and arrive at the arm's-length price necessarily contain a substantial degree of subjective judgment and the OECD report recognises the dangers of chasing a chimera by recognising that there is a range within which a price could be said to be arm's length. There is a danger in any transfer pricing exercise, in the Revenue authorities trying to substitute their own commercial judgment for that of the enterprise which they are examining, often with the benefit of hindsight which was not available to those fixing the price for the original transactions. The OECD report warns against this danger and emphasises the requirement to find the arm's-length price for the transactions that have actually taken place, not those which the Revenue authorities wish had taken place. There are occasions when the actual transaction can be recast but only where the commercial reality of the transaction is dressed up in a manner which is different from its form, such as where interest is in reality a dividend or distribution of profits.

13–028

So far as this book is concerned the main area of interest in transfer pricing is that relating to the licensing of intangibles, not the transfer price to be attached to goods or services, although these may have relevance in, for example, a franchising operation, and the techniques mentioned *above* will normally be the most appropriate, in particular the comparable uncontrolled price method, where feasible.

With regard to services, a distinction has to be drawn between managerial, technical and commercial services which are to the benefit of the paying company's trade, and central management and servicing costs, including the costs of controlling the overall enterprise, and shareholder costs related to the production of group accounts and financial controls to safeguard shareholders' interests. The extent to which such central management costs should be passed down to the overseas subsidiaries is likely to be disputed by the local fiscal authorities and excluded from their transfer pricing calculations. Some of these control costs will actually have a direct benefit reflected in the proper management of the subsidiary and should be allowable. Methods of calculating such costs and apportioning them vary from group to group, but a direct cost charge for head office functions of benefit to the subsidiary would normally be acceptable, and an allocation by reference to turnover, profit or other arbitrary basis would often be acceptable provided that it was supported by the contractual arrangements between the parties and applied consistently from year to year in accordance with generally accepted accounting principles.

INTANGIBLES

13–029   With regard to intangibles, the OECD report distinguishes between production intangibles such as patents, know-how, designs, models, etc. and marketing intangibles such as trade marks, trade names, logos, etc. A distinction may be made between the transfer of particular intangibles such as the sale or licence of intellectual property, or the sale of goods protected by intellectual property, where the value of the patent, for example, is reflected in the price charged for the goods. In such cases where the purchaser has no benefit from the underlying intellectual property, the transaction should be regarded as sale of goods and not a transfer of intellectual property.

Another area of intangible rights coming into transfer pricing calculations is where there are group research and development facilities recharged to group companies benefiting or likely to benefit from the research and development on a cost contribution basis, or directly commissioned research and development contracts where the purchasing company specifically commissions another company in the group, in a different jurisdiction, to develop a particular product or service for the benefit of the commissioning company. In such circumstances the terms of the contract may determine who owns any resultant intellectual property and who has the right to exploit it further and on what terms. Any Revenue authority is obviously likely to be suspicious of arrangements whereby group companies in tax haven jurisdictions are commissioned to develop particular products on behalf of profitable companies and then in turn sub-contract the research and development work to high technology, high cost centres, with the result that the costs of development attract substantial tax relief but the intellectual property ends up owned by the tax haven company which is then in a position to licence worldwide at a royalty rate which reflects the pioneering nature of the invention.

Again, the main problem of applying transfer pricing rules to intangibles is the difficulty of finding comparable royalty rates for what are normally unique situations. The OECD report is very firmly in favour of the concept of the arm's-length royalty which would have been paid by the licensee to the licensor, totally rejecting the American concept of the super-royalty under which the compensation receivable by the transferor should be commensurate with the actual income which can be generated from the licensed rights. In one of the few recent cases on the value of trade marks, before the Hong Kong Board of Review, it was held that in the circumstances the use of a notional 5 per cent royalty in the valuation was correct (see Ch.12).

It is important to ensure that the licensing of intellectual property is fully recorded in written agreements and the methodology used in calculating the royalty rate is retained in order to justify to an investigating Revenue authority that this is within the range of an acceptable arm's-length price. Evidence of royalty rates is difficult to come by as few are in the public domain. It is generally accepted that it is unfair for a Revenue authority to challenge royalty levels on the basis of confidential information available to it, which cannot be produced, as evidence for their dissatisfaction with the rates actually used.

13–030

The consideration of appropriate royalty rates is dealt with in more detail in Ch.12 (see para.12–013) on the valuation of intellectual property. One of the commercial realities that makes the calculation of royalty rates difficult is that the value of the invention may have little direct relevance to the research and development costs spent on it. In the real world much research and development expenditure is inevitably abortive and some of the most valuable inventions have arisen as a by-product from efforts to develop something else entirely. This makes the use of techniques such as cash flow-based net present valuation calculations somewhat suspect.

In the field of marketing related intangibles, the activities of the licensee have to be considered as well as those of the licensor. The licensee's local advertising, for example, may have a beneficial effect on the value of the worldwide trade mark so that the licensee is not merely paying for the use of the trade mark but contributing to its development. In cases where franchising is involved, it may be possible to arrive at a useful comparison by comparing the royalty levels for arm's-length franchisees in certain territories compared with the levels charged to connected licensees in others. However, even this comparison may be influenced by questions of volume, market penetration, maturity of the market, etc. and, as in all transfer pricing negotiations, a good deal of judgment is required in considering the relevance which should be attached to any raw data.

The OECD started a project in 2010 to update the chapter of the report dealing with intangible property. An updated draft report is expected later in 2013. Some key differences between the old and the proposed new guidelines are that the new proposed guidelines will have a clear link between arm's length behaviour and arm's length pricing, and will provide guidance on the entitlement to intangible related returns ("IRRs") linked to substance and activity.

US ROYALTIES

13–031 The Internal Revenue Service of the United States has gone further than any other Revenue authority in trying to determine a set procedure for arriving at the proper royalty level in a transfer pricing situation. Inter-company transfer pricing and cost-sharing regulations were published under s.482 of the US Internal Revenue Code as amended by the Tax Reform Act of 1986. The American provisions seek to ensure that the royalty level for intangible property be commensurate with the income attributable to that property. These regulations set out a matching transaction method which is the first choice in arriving at the appropriate royalty level. It will be extremely rare to have a totally matching transaction, and the second most desirable basis is the comparable adjustable transaction method where it is possible to determine and quantify the differences between an arm's-length situation and a controlled transfer price situation. Again, it is often not easy to find suitable examples and it is then necessary to consider an arm's-length consideration determined under the comparable profit method. This method requires a comparison of the operating income that results from the consideration actually charged in a controlled transfer with the operating incomes of similar taxpayers that are uncontrolled.

It may also be possible to consider a fourth method where the comparable uncontrolled price method is inapplicable, provided that the end result can be shown to produce a result which falls within the comparable profit range ("comparable profit interval" in the United States).

The American regulations are set out in very considerable detail with the steps to be followed in each case and innumerable examples are given. The whole problem of the American approach, however, when compared with the normal arm's-length approach adopted elsewhere, is the requirement that the consideration for intangible property be commensurate with the income attributable to the intangible. In real arm's-length situations it is normal to agree a royalty level probably varying with production and covering a period of years. The licensor will, when negotiating the terms of the licensing agreement, obviously take into account the likely value of the intellectual property to the licensee and therefore the royalty level that he might be able to extract. The licensee will similarly have to have consideration for the value of the licence in terms of the profits he is likely to make after payment of the royalty. Once the agreement has been entered into, however, if the licensee is particularly successful in making profits, which would no doubt be partly attributable to the value of the licence, he would not expect the royalty level to vary other than on the basis of production as agreed in the licensing contract. Conversely, if he is less successful than anticipated, and the royalty payable does not leave him with sufficient profit, he will scale down production, subject of course to the terms of the agreement.

13–032 Very often the licensor will not know the profit generated by the licensee attributable to the intellectual property licensed and the licensee would regard such information as highly confidential. The commercial reality of licensing is therefore in immediate conflict with the American approach which envisages a renegotiation of the deal each year with the benefit of hindsight into what the IRS think it would have been had that information, which did not even exist at the time, been available to the parties. As the assumptions that are required to be made are so far away from the real world it is not surprising that it often results in a "super-royalty" that would not be acceptable to the Revenue authority of the licensee, with the result that the American parent is taxed on a royalty commensurate with the income deemed to be generated from the intellectual property, while the licensee is allowed to deduct only an arm's-length royalty such as would be payable in a real commercial situation between arm's-length companies. The economic double taxation that this gives rise to can only be mitigated if the competent authority procedure under a double tax treaty can be successfully invoked and if the two Revenue authorities involved are prepared to agree a compromise transfer price acceptable to both authorities. The multinational company sitting in the middle of this argument will often feel that it does not mind particularly what royalty level is to be used as long as it is the same one for both the licensor and the licensee and is acceptable to both Revenue authorities.

This in turn means that the likelihood of there being economic double taxation is going to increase. Although a number of double taxation agreements with the United States seek to eliminate economic double taxation through the competent authority procedure, experience would suggest that this is a slow and unsatisfactory method of dealing with the problem. Although the United States, for example, will approve an advance pricing agreement between the taxpayer, the IRS and the overseas Revenue authority, this may not be practical in the payer country if there is no procedure for agreement in advance with the Revenue authority.

The IRS has put forward a functional analysis approach to fixing royalty levels by asking what was done, what economically significant factors were involved in doing it, who performed each function, and what is the measure of economic value of each function performed by each party. In practice these questions may be answered by applying a number of methods: the matching transactions method, the comparable adjustable transaction method and the comparable profit method. The matching transaction method applies where there is an exact comparable in an arm's-length situation between the American owner of the intellectual property and a licensee abroad. It will be fairly unusual in practice to find an exact comparable in this way and the comparable adjustable transaction method is more likely to be met with in practice. This allows for an inexact comparable.

Under the comparable profit method, the total profit arising from the exploitation of the intangible is allocated in accordance with the perceived economic contribution of each party. Where more than one party is involved in the development of the intangible, one is regarded as the developer and the others assisters, all of whom must be adequately remunerated for their contribution.

13–033

The IRS approach is codified in the regulations. If the agreement covers more than one year the fact that it is accepted in one year may not make it acceptable for a subsequent year and the "commensurate within income" test has to be applied each year. The comparable profit interval used for testing the arm's-length consideration for intangibles is based on a three-year period covering the audit year and the previous and subsequent years. Cost sharing arrangements may be approved under which each party contributes to the cost of developing the product in return for a commensurate share in the resulting intellectual property.

In view of the problems arising from this American super-royalty concept, it may be preferable to substitute some form of contract manufacturing agreement for a licence agreement under which the overseas subsidiary would manufacture for the American parent which would make the sales and pay a price for the goods based on cost plus a reasonable percentage profit to the overseas manufacturer, say, cost plus 10 per cent.

In practice it is usually a good idea to have as much detail for the transfer price calculation as possible, with projected sales and results of both licensor and licensee and comparable royalty levels charged by third parties, where known, in circumstances as similar as possible, in order to build up a comprehensive picture of why the royalty level is fixed at the rate agreed and to show that the intention is merely to arrive at a commercial royalty level and not to avoid taxes.

CUSTOMS VALUATIONS

13–034 Customs, duties and VAT on goods and services passing between associated companies may be computed by reference to valuations imposed by the Excise Authorities and not necessarily by reference to the prices agreed between the connected parties or those agreed for direct tax purposes.

DOUBLE TAXATION TREATIES

13–035 Whereas double taxation treaties are designed to prevent double taxation on the same income, they do have relevance to transfer pricing in a number of respects. Although each bilateral treaty has to be examined with care, as there are substantial differences between them, the majority of treaties follow the OECD Model Tax Convention on Income and Capital published by the OECD Committee on fiscal affairs in 1992 with subsequent updates. This in turn is based on 1977 and 1963 and earlier models. There are other model treaties such as the United Nations Model Double Taxation Convention between Developed and Developing Countries published in 1980 by United Nations Publications and the Nordic Convention on Income and Capital published in 1989, as well as the US Model Double Taxation Treaty which the Internal Revenue Service attempts to impose on its treaty partners.

The business profits article (art.7) in the OECD Model Treaty, under para.2, requires each state to attribute to the taxable permanent establishment the profits which it might be expected to make, in particular in its dealings with other parts of the enterprise, if it were a separate and independent enterprise engaged in the same or similar activities under the same or similar conditions, taking into account the functions performed, assets used and risks assumed by the enterprise through the permanent establishment and through other parts of the enterprise. This requires the allocation of profits to a foreign branch or subsidiary to reflect the arm's-length principle and therefore allows for, in effect, transfer pricing adjustments where that principle has not been followed.

If royalties are charged, art.12 normally allows such royalties to be taxable only in the country of the beneficial recipient. However, art.12(4) allows the royalties paid to be adjusted to the amount which would have been agreed upon by the payer and beneficial owner had the royalty level been fixed at arm's length, where there is a special relationship between the payer and the beneficial owner, or between both of them and some other person, and the royalty paid exceeds the amount which would have been agreed in the absence of such special relationship.

Similar provisions apply for interest under art.11(6) of the Model Convention. **13–036**

The associated enterprises article (art.9) allows the Revenue authority to adjust profits of an enterprise resident in their state: (1) where an enterprise of one contracting state participates directly or indirectly in the management, control or capital of an enterprise in the other contracting state, (2) the same persons participate directly or indirectly in the management, control or capital of an enterprise of the contracting state, and (3) conditions are made or imposed between the enterprises which differ from those which would be made between independent enterprises.

The article requires the competent authorities of each state to consult on such adjustments. It is not a requirement of any such adjustment that both fiscal authorities accept the adjustment, although an aggrieved party can require the competent authority to negotiate with its colleagues in the other jurisdiction under the mutual agreement procedure (art.25 of the Model Convention). They cannot, however, force agreement and within the European Union this has given rise to the Arbitration Convention.

FUTURE DEVELOPMENTS

Transfer pricing in an international context has become an increasing high profile area of tax law within recent years. Particular concern has been expressed that a number of well-known multinational organisations generate large volumes of sales in the UK but pay little or no corporation tax, perhaps partially owing to royalty and licensing agreements with offshore affiliates located in low tax jurisdictions. The UK government has expressed its commitment to working closely with other countries in an effort to counteract profit shifting, and is dedicating additional resources to HMRC's transfer pricing units in an effort to ensure the UK legislation is operating effectively. **13–037**

In February 2013 the OECD published an initial paper examining base erosion and profit shifting and a further paper setting out suggested solutions is expected later this year. Possible options may include more rigorous enforcement of the arm's length principle, particularly in the context of the transfer pricing of intangibles where it is frequently difficult to establish comparable arm's length transactions. The OECD's revised guidance on the treatment of intangibles is expected to assist in arriving at a more consistent methodology.

CHAPTER 14

Controlled foreign companies

INTRODUCTION

The purpose of the controlled foreign company (CFC) legislation is to prevent UK companies avoiding UK tax by diverting profits to offshore tax havens. Until 1979, companies had to repatriate profits under the exchange control legislation; its abolition led to a new look at the definition of company residence for tax purposes, and proposals for the taxation of tax haven profits (first introduced in the United States) and an attack on upstream loans for offshore tax haven subsidiaries to high tax areas. Consultation documents were produced in 1981 and in 1984 the controlled foreign company legislation was enacted. The company residence changes were subsequently modified but the upstream loan legislation was dropped for the time being.

14–001

The application and scope of the UK's controlled foreign company legislation has been the subject of a case before the European Court of Justice, where it was alleged the rules are in contravention of art.43 (freedom of establishment), art.49 (freedom to provide services) and art.56 (freedom of movement of capital and payments) under the EC Treaty (*Cadbury Schweppes Plc and Cadbury Schweppes Overseas Limited v Commissioners of Inland Revenue* (C-196/04)). In this case, a UK Plc had incorporated two subsidiary companies in Ireland to benefit from the International Financial Services Centre's regime for group treasury companies. The rate of tax payable in Ireland was 10 per cent. A direction was issued by HMRC that the profits of the two Irish subsidiaries should be apportioned to Plc under the controlled foreign company rules. On the case being referred to the ECJ, it was held that EC law precluded the inclusion in the tax base of a resident company established in a Member State of profits made by a controlled foreign company in another Member State, where those profits were subject to a lower level of taxation than that applicable in the first state, unless such inclusion related only to wholly artificial arrangements intended to escape the national tax normally payable. There could be no apportionment of profits where it was proved, on the basis of objective factors which were ascertainable by third parties, that despite the existence of tax motives, the controlled foreign company was actually established in the other Member State and carried on genuine economic activities there. Following the ECJ's judgment, the UK's controlled foreign company regime was substantially modified by Finance Act 2012 with a view to eliminating those aspects which were found to be discriminatory under EC law and also focussing the provisions on the artificial diversion of profits away from the UK. The revised legislation is found in TIOPA

2010 Pt 9A and applies for accounting periods commencing on or after January 1, 2013. (For details of the legislation applying for previous accounting periods, please see earlier editions of this book.)

In outline, a CFC charge will apply where a controlled foreign company has "chargeable profits" and does not meet any of the criteria for exemption. The "chargeable profits" of a CFC are its "assumed taxable profits" calculated on the assumption that the CFC's "assumed taxable total profits" are restricted to only those profits which pass through a series of five "gateways". An adjustment is made to take into account "just and reasonable" expenses relating to the profits passing through the gateway. Where there are no chargeable profits, there is no CFC charge. This is a radical difference from the approach adopted under the former CFC provisions, which operated on an "all or nothing" basis and represents the shift in policy towards a more territorial approach to taxation and the focus on capturing only those profits which have been artificially diverted from the UK. Another notable feature of the new regime is the absence of a general "motive" test: a CFC charge could apply even where there is no underlying tax avoidance purpose if one or more of the various gateway tests are met and no exclusions apply.

For offshore intellectual property holding companies, provided the intellectual property (or other intangible asset) has not been transferred from a UK connected person within the previous six years, the new regime is more generous that its predecessor, as it enables intellectual property which is created and managed abroad to be retained outside the scope of the UK tax net.

DEFINITION OF CFC

14–002 A controlled foreign company is one which is resident outside the United Kingdom, is controlled by persons resident in the United Kingdom. The minimum interest in a CFC that will trigger an apportionment is 25 per cent. The definition of "control" for this purpose includes economic as well as legal control, and also control by reference to accounting standards.

RESIDENCE

14–003 The question of whether the company is resident outside the United Kingdom for these purposes is dealt with by TIOPA 2010 ss.371TA–371TC which provide that the company is regarded as resident in the territory in which it is liable to tax by reason of its domicile, residence or place of management (TIOPA 2010 s.371TB). There are tie-breaker provisions where the company might be regarded as resident in more than one territory, with the intention of pinning down a single jurisdiction. In the absence of an election or designation of residence under s.371TC, the territory of residence is the place of the company's effective management, which is not the same as the UK residence test of central management and control. The place of effective management, in HMRC's view, is generally understood to be the place where the head office is, not the registered office, but the central directing source where the finance director, sales director and managing director are based, together with the company records and senior administrative staff. The fact that the directors' meetings were held in a different jurisdiction would not move the place of effective management (INTM 120210, reproducing guidance originally published in ITH 348). Where the place of effective management is in two or more territories, it is the territory where the greater amount of the company's assets at the end of the accounting period is situated; if this does not pinpoint one of the territories, it is the territory where it is liable to tax by reason of its domicile, residence or place of management in which it has the greater amount of its assets situated at the end of the accounting period; if this still does not identify the territory it may be specified by a direction by HMRC (TIOPA 2010 s.371TC). If the company is not liable to tax anywhere it is presumed to be resident in a tax haven. In determining where the greater amount of a company's assets is situated at the end of the accounting period, the market value not the book value of the assets has to be considered.

A UK-resident company that is, for example, UK-resident by reason of incorporation under CTA 2009 s.14, may nonetheless be treated as non-resident under CTA 2009 s.18, if it would be regarded for the purposes of any double taxation relief arrangement as resident in a territory outside the United Kingdom and not resident in the United Kingdom.

CONTROL

A company is "controlled by persons resident in the UK" if a person has the means to secure by means of the holding of shares or the possession of voting power in or in relation to the company or any other company, or by virtue of any powers conferred by the articles of association or other documents regulating the company or any other company, that the affairs of the company are conducted in accordance with his wishes. In looking at this wide definition, two or more persons acting together who satisfy the conditions may have control, and future rights are included, as well as present rights (TIOPA 2010 s.371RD(5))   **14–004**

Rights and powers of other persons to the extent that they are required or may be required to be exercised: (1) on behalf of the person; (2) under the direction of the person; or (3) for the benefit of the person are included and in the case of loans are not confined to powers conferred in relation to the property of the borrower by the terms of any security relating to the loan.

Also included in the case of a UK resident are rights and powers of any person who is resident in the United Kingdom and connected with the person (TIOPA 2010 s.371RD(3)(c), (d)).

Further rights and powers may be attributed, see TIOPA 2010 s.371RD(7).   **14–005**

Where a company is not otherwise regarded as controlled by persons resident in the United Kingdom, it will nevertheless be treated as so controlled if there are two persons who, taken together, control the company and one of those persons is UK resident and both satisfy a 40 per cent test. This test requires that each has inherent rights and powers representing at least 40 per cent of the holdings rights and powers in respect of which the pair of them fall to be taken as controlling the company. In the case of the non-UK resident such holdings must not exceed 55 per cent (TIOPA 2010 s.371RC).

Connected persons are defined by CTA 2010 s.1122, i.e. spouse or civil partner, brother, brother-in-law, sister, sister-in-law, parent, parent-in-law, grandparent, grandparent-in-law, son, son-in-law, daughter, daughter-in-law, grandson, grandson-in-law, granddaughter, granddaughter-in-law, trustee of a settlement with the settlor and a person connected with the settlor, and a company connected with the settlement and partners. "Associates" are similarly widely defined by CTA 2010 s.882(2).

A person also controls a company if the person is the company's parent undertaking, as defined under FRS 2 and at least 50 per cent of the CFC's chargeable profits would be apportioned to the parent on the assumption that the subsidiary is a CFC (TIOPA 2010 s.371RE).

THE GATEWAYS

14–006 Only profits passing through the CFC gateway are liable to the CFC charge. The gateway therefore filters out profits which are not subject to the charge. There are five gateways to consider: profits attributable to UK activities; non-trading finance profits; trading finance profits; captive insurance business and finally, solo consolidation.

The first step is to determine which of the gateways (if any) apply to the CFC for the accounting period. If none of the gateways apply, there is no CFC charge. It is then necessary to determine the extent to which the CFC's profits fall within Chs 4–8 and therefore pass through the CFC charge gateway and detailed provisions apply to determine this amount. Where profits pass through the gateway, a CFC charge arises calculated as an amount equal to the UK corporation tax on the apportioned chargeable profits of the CFC, less the amount of creditable tax relating to those profits.

PROFITS ATTRIBUTABLE TO UK ACTIVITIES

14–007 The gateway test relating to profits attributable to UK activities potentially applies to all CFCs, unless one of conditions A to D below is met.

1. Condition A requires that at no time during the accounting period the company holds assets or bears risk under an arrangement:
   (a) the main purpose of which is to reduce or eliminate the UK tax liability of any person; and
   (b) in consequence of which arrangement the CFC expects its business to be more profitable at any time than would other be the case (negligible increases are ignored).
2. Condition B is that at no time in the accounting period does the CFC have any UK managed assets or bear any UK managed risks.
3. Condition C requires that where there are UK managed assets and/or UK managed risks, the CFC's business would be commercially affected were the UK managed assets and/or UK managed risks of the business to stop being managed in the UK.

An asset or risk is "UK managed" if the acquisition, creation, development or exploitation of the asset, or the taking on or bearing of the risk, is managed and controlled to any significant extent by "relevant UK activities", i.e. activities carried on in the UK by the CFC other than through a permanent establishment or by companies connected with the CFC through non-arm's length arrangements.

4. Condition D is that the CFC's assumed total profits consist only of non-trading finance profits or property business profits.

Conditions B and C require an analysis of the extent to which there are significant people functions (SPFs) or key entrepreneurial risk-taking functions (KERTs) being performed in the UK. The concepts of SPFs and KERTs are imports into the UK tax code from the OECD's Report on the Attribution of Profits to Permanent Establishments, and are designed to identify where the active decision making in relation to the business takes place. The focus appears to be on operational control rather than control at the highest level, and HMRC's guidance indicates that analysis of SPFs may have to take into account activities across more than one accounting period. Where UK SPFs (or KERTs in the case of a financial business) give rise to more than 50 per cent of the profit relating to particular assets or risk, those profits may pass through the gateway. An SPF is a UK SPF to the extent that it is carried out in the UK by the CFC other than through a permanent establishment or a UK connected company.

Where there are profits arising from UK SPFs, a CFC charge may still be avoided if one of the "safe harbours" within the gateway applying to profits attributable to UK activities applies. There are exemptions where the non-tax value derived from holding assets or managing risks offshore are substantial, or the arrangements entered into by the CFC in relation to the UK SPF are the same as would have been entered into had the parties been acting independently. There is also a safe harbour relating to trading profits, which requires a number of conditions to be met as follows:

1. business premises condition. This requires the CFC to have premises in the country of residence throughout the accounting period from which the CFC's activities in that country are wholly or mainly conducted. The premises must have a reasonable degree of permanence (s.371DG);
2. income condition. To meet this condition to more than 20 per cent of the CFC's relevant trading income of an accounting period can be derived from UK residents or the UK permanent establishments of non-UK resident companies. "Relevant trading income" means all trading income other than income from the sale in the UK of goods produced by the CFC in its territory of residence (s.371DH);
3. management expenditure condition. The management condition is met if the "UK related management expenditure" of the CFC for an accounting period is no more than 20 per cent of the "total related management expenditure" for that period. "UK related management expenditure" is defined as that part of the total related management expenditure relating to persons carrying on their activities in the UK, and "total related management expenditure" means the CFC's expenditure on staff (including

staff of other groups) or consultants who carry on management functions, such as managing assets and risks. The 20 per cent condition is relaxed provided the four other conditions in (a)–(e) are met, subject to further detailed requirements (s.371DI);

4. IP condition. Where a CFC holds IP derived or transferred from UK resident related persons, or the UK permanent establishment of non-UK related person, the IP condition will be met unless:
   (a) there has been a significant decrease in value of the IP held by the related person; and
   (b) if only parts of the IP were transferred to the CFC, the "significance" condition is met. This requires the parts of the IP transferred or otherwise derived are a significant part of the IP and as a consequence of the transfer, the CFC's profits are significantly higher than they would otherwise have been.

   This section applies only to IP transferred or otherwise derived in the current accounting period and the previous six years (s.371DJ); and

5. export of goods condition. This condition is met where no more than 20 per cent of the CFC's trading income arises from goods exported from the UK. Goods exported from the UK to the CFC's territory of residence are excluded from the 20 per cent calculation (s.371DK).

NON-TRADING FINANCE PROFITS

14–008 Non-trading finance profits include profits from loan relationships and non-exempt distributions. Profits arising from the investment of funds held for the purposes of a trade are not included. Further, the gateway does not apply where non-trading finance profits are no more than 5 per cent of the CFC's trading or property business profits, or exempt distribution income and it is a holding company of 51 per cent subsidiaries.

Non-trading finance profits pass through the gateway if they are attributable to UK activities, or they arise from the investment of UK monetary or non-monetary assets. Funds or other assets received in exchange for goods or services are excluded. Profits arising on arrangements with a UK resident company designed to avoid the CFC making distributions are caught if the arrangement is tax-motivated, together with certain finance lease profits (TIOPA 2010 ss.371EB–371EE).

TRADING FINANCE PROFITS

14–009 Trading finance profits are defined as profits arising on loan relationships, distributions treated as trading income and certain finance lease profits on long funding leases, and will most commonly be of application to banks and insurance companies.

Trading finance profits pass through the gateway if they arise from the use or investment of excess "free capital". Broadly, excess free capital is determined by comparing the free capital which it would be reasonable to suppose the company would hold if it were not a 51 per cent subsidiary of another company and the actual amount held. To the extent there is an excess, and it derives from UK connected capital contributions, a CFC charge will arise.

CAPTIVE INSURANCE

The profits falling within the captive insurance gateway are amounts included in the CFC's total assumed profits insofar as they arise from its insurance business or derive from a contract of insurance entered into with: **14–010**

1. a UK company connected with the CFC, or a non-UK resident company connected with the CFC operating through a UK permanent establishment; or
2. a contract of insurance entered into with a UK resident person linked to the provision of goods or services (other than insurance services) to the UK resident person by a UK connected company

and, in the case of a CFC resident in an EEA state, the CFC does not have a significant non-tax reason for entering into the contract.

SOLO CONSOLIDATION

This gateway is relevant only to banking subsidiaries of UK banks which have applied for a solo consolidation waiver. Profits pass through the gateway to the extent that the CFC's profits would not be treated as exempt if the CFC were deemed to be an overseas permanent establishment.   **14–011**

FINANCE COMPANY EXEMPTION

The finance profits exemption exempts from the CFC charge certain intra-group finance profits passing through the non-trading finance profit gateway. The exemption may be claimed by a UK resident company which would otherwise suffer a CFC charge in respect of those profits. The exemption applies only where there are "qualifying loan relationship profits", which broadly means profits arising from loan relationships where the CFC is the creditor, and the ultimate debtor is connected with the CFC and controlled by the same UK resident persons who control the CFC.   **14–012**

There are two forms of claim, one which exempts 100 per cent of a company's profits from qualifying loan relationships and a second which gives a partial exemption of 75 per cent of such profits. This means that profits falling within the partial finance company exemption will suffer tax at the rate of 5 per cent from April 1, 2015, when the standard rate of corporation tax drops to 20 per cent. "Qualifying resources" means profits of the CFC's business consisting of making loans to members of the CFC group which are used solely for the purposes of the group member's business in the relevant territory, or funds or assets received by the CFC in respect of shares held by the CFC or issued by the CFC to members of the group.

The partial finance company exemption is available where the total exemption is not claimed, and exempts 75 per cent of profits arising from qualifying loan relationships.

ENTITY-LEVEL EXEMPTIONS

14–013 Even though the company may technically be within the controlled foreign company legislation as being a non-resident under the control of persons resident in the United Kingdom, it may nonetheless escape the consequences of being a controlled foreign company, that is the apportionment of its income to UK-resident shareholders, if it falls within any one of five specific entity-level exemptions. As a practical point, it will frequently be more straightforward for a company which potentially falls within the CFC regime to consider whether one of the exemptions is available rather than going through the more complex "gateway" test.

The exemptions are "all or nothing", there is no partial application if, for example, a CFC's profits marginally exceed the thresholds set down in the low profits test.

THE TEMPORARY PERIOD OF EXEMPTION

14–014 The temporary period of exemption provides a 12-month exemption from the CFC rules for a foreign company, which would otherwise be a CFC, where control of the company is acquired by UK residents.

THE EXCLUDED TERRITORIES EXEMPTION

14–015 The excluded territories exemption applies for an accounting period of the CFC if the company is resident in an excluded territory, as specified in HMRC regulations (see the Controlled Foreign Companies (Excluded Territories) Regulations (SI 2012/3024)). Unlike the similar exemption applying under the pre-2013 rules, there are a number of additional conditions which must be met in order for a CFC resident in an excluded territory to be exempt. The CFC's "relevant income" must not exceed the "threshold amount", calculated as the greater of 10 per cent of the CFC's accounting profits for the period or £50,000 (reduced proportionately for periods of less than 12 months). Relevant income consists of:

1. income which is exempt from tax in the territory of residence or which benefits from incentive arrangements such as a tax holiday,

THE TAX EXEMPTION

2. notional interest for which a deduction is available in the CFC's territory of residence, but would not be available in computing assumed taxable total profits,
3. income accruing to the trustees of which the CFC is a settlor or beneficiary, plus its share of partnership income for the accounting period in which the CFC is a partner, and
4. income from related parties which, following the application of the transfer pricing rules, result in a reduction of income in the CFC's territory of residence with no corresponding increase in any other territory. Also included is income taxed at a reduced rate under a ruling or other arrangement of the taxing authorities in the territory of residence.

The excluded territories exemption is also subject to a specific condition relating to intellectual property. No intellectual property must have been transferred to the CFC from UK-related parties within the previous six years, unless the transfer has not had a significant impact on the CFC's profits, the value of intellectual property held the by the transferor, or the total intellectual property held by the CFC.

THE LOW PROFITS EXEMPTION

The third exemption applies where the CFC has "low profits", defined as accounting or taxable profits of no more than £50,000, or £500,000 where no more than £50,000 represents non-trading income (reduced proportionately for periods of less than 12 months). The low profits exemption is not available to companies providing the services of a UK resident individual to a UK resident client of the CFC.

14–016

THE LOW PROFITS MARGIN EXEMPTION

The forth exemption applies where the CFC's accounting profits (i.e. profits before the deduction of interest) are not more than 10 per cent of its operating costs.

14–017

THE TAX EXEMPTION

The final exemption applies to a CFC if the tax payable in the territory of residence is at least 75 per cent of the corresponding UK tax.

14–018

CLEARANCES

14–019 United Kingdom companies are entitled to request clearance as to the way any area of the CFC legislation applies in respect of a particular case. Applications for clearances should be made to: CTIAA, Outward Investment Team Registry (Controlled Foreign Company Clearances), 3rd Floor, 100 Parliament Street, London, SW1A 2BQ.

APPORTIONMENT OF CFC CHARGEABLE PROFITS

14–020 Where none of the exclusions apply and there are chargeable profits which pass through the gateway, the amount to be apportioned to a UK resident person is determined by a series of steps. The UK resident company will suffer corporation tax on the apportioned profits at the rate of tax applicable for the accounting period. The CFC charge is treated as if it were an amount of corporation tax for the period (TIOPA 2010 s.371BC). It was held in the Court of Appeal decision in *Bricom Holdings Ltd v IRC* [1997] S.T.C. 1179, that a double taxation treaty did not protect against such an apportionment.

Where profits have been brought into the UK tax net through a controlled foreign company apportionment, they cannot also be brought in under the transfer of assets abroad provisions of ITA 2007 ss.714–751. Apportionment is only made to a UK company where it or its associates are entitled to at least 25 per cent of the controlled foreign company's chargeable profits (TIOPA 2010 s.371BD). This means that there is no apportionment under the controlled foreign company legislation to an individual or trust shareholder where the anti-avoidance provisions relating to transfers of assets abroad would normally apply to prevent any avoidance of UK tax under ITA 2007 ss.714–751. Nor will an apportionment be made to an independent company holding less than 25 per cent in the controlled foreign company.

CHARGEABLE PROFITS

14–021 The starting point for the computation of chargeable profits is the CFC's "assumed taxable total profits", consisting of the total taxable profits computed in accordance with the detailed assumptions in TIOPA 2010 Pt 9A Ch.19.

Under the controlled foreign company provisions, a company is assumed to be resident in the United Kingdom, but otherwise to carry on the business it actually does (TIOPA 2010 s.371SD).

The CFC is assumed not to be a close company (TIOPA 2010 s.371SE), and is assumed to have become UK-resident at the beginning of the first accounting period in respect of which an apportionment falls to be made thereafter continues to be notionally resident until the company ceases to be controlled by UK residents. It is also assumed that for each such accounting period the chargeable profits and corresponding UK tax have been calculated so that, e.g. losses can be carried forward.

CREDITABLE TAX

Claims are notionally assumed to have been made to give the maximum relief against corporation tax, unless the company elects otherwise by notice to HMRC within 20 months of the end of the relevant accounting period (TIOPA 2010 s.371SF). Claims for the foreign branch exemption, designated currency elections and elections for leases to be treated as long funding leases are exempted from the general assumption regarding claims notionally having been made. A CFC may make a designated currency election under CTA 2010 s.9A where accounts are not prepared in accordance with generally accepted accounting practice. The CFC may also elect to be treated as having been made (or withdrawn).

Group relief is not available in computing the chargeable profits or corresponding UK tax.

Intangible fixed assets created or acquired by the overseas company before the first accounting period as a CFC are brought into account at their accounting values on the first day of the accounting period. It is assumed that a claim for rollover relief under CTA 2009 s.754 has not been made in relation to the intangible assets.

14–022

Notional capital allowances are given in computing the chargeable profits and corresponding UK tax, on the basis that, in the first accounting period for which an apportionment is made, the assets at the beginning of the period are deemed to have been brought into use at market value at that date and capital allowances calculated as if CAA 2001 Pt 2 applied.

14–023

A CFC in receipt of income from a third country, which cannot be remitted either to the United Kingdom or to its country of residence, is unable to make an unremittable overseas income claim under CTA 2009 s.1275.

An accounting period of a controlled foreign company is deemed to begin when it first comes under the control of persons resident in the United Kingdom or when it commences to carry on business, or following the end of the preceding accounting period (TIOPA 2010 s.371VB). Conversely, an accounting period ends when a company ceases to be under the control of UK residents or ceases to be liable to tax in the territory by reason of its domicile, residence or place of management, or becomes or ceases to be dual resident or ceases to have any source of income. In such circumstances the normal consequences of an accounting period ceasing, in CTA 2009 s.10, are applied, with the residual power for the Revenue to specify an accounting period of up to 12 months (TIOPA 2010 s.371VB(6)).

CREDITABLE TAX

In addition to apportioning the chargeable profits of the controlled foreign company to UK residents who are direct or indirect shareholders, the creditable foreign tax is also calculated and apportioned, and may be set against the UK corporation tax liability on the amount apportioned. The creditable tax is defined by TIOPA 2010 s.371PA as the sum of double taxation relief which would have been available had the company been resident in the United Kingdom, plus any credits for income tax deducted at source that could be set against corporation tax under CTA 2010 s.967(1)–(3), plus any UK corporation tax borne by the controlled foreign company. Apportionment may be made to those UK companies

14–024

with at least a 25 per cent interest in the controlled foreign company in accordance with their respective interests. This would normally be by reference to the percentage of the issued ordinary shares held (TIOPA 2010 ss.371QC–371QF).

CELL COMPANIES

14–025 The CFC rules in place for accounting periods commencing on or after January 1, 2013 also specifically apply to cells, whether incorporated or not, as if they were non-UK resident companies. Structures previously thought to be outside the scope of the CFC regime, such as a Jersey Protected Cell Company, will be brought within the rules with effect for accounting periods commencing on or after January 1, 2013.

DOUBLE CHARGES

14–026 There is scope for a double charge to taxation where the profits of a controlled foreign company have been apportioned to a shareholder, and the shares are subsequently disposed of, realising a price which includes the profit retained in the controlled foreign company. In contrast to the "old" rules, the CFC regime applying for accounting periods commencing on or after January 1, 2013 does not provide for relief for the disposing company in respect of amounts apportioned under the CFC rules.

FOREIGN SYSTEMS

14–027 The UK-controlled foreign company provisions are extensive and complex. They are fairly unusual in applying only to create a charge on corporate shareholders with a 25 per cent or greater interest in a controlled foreign company.

The first controlled foreign company legislation was the American sub-part F regime introduced in 1962. This was followed some 10 years later by Canada and Germany and then by Japan, France, United Kingdom, New Zealand, Australia, Sweden, Norway and Denmark, followed in 1995 by Spain, Portugal and Finland, and more recently Brazil and Korea and a number of other countries. These systems normally require the routine provision of CFC information either on completion of a return or under self-assessment rules.

CFC regulation is invariably highly complex. The scope of the legislation, i.e. whether it applies to apportion foreign profits to individuals as well as corporates, and the type of income it applies to varies from jurisdiction to jurisdiction as does the control conditions and other criteria.

CHAPTER 15

Research and Development

INTRODUCTION

At the time of the 1998 Budget, the Treasury and Department of Trade and Industry published a consultation document, *Innovating for the Future: Investing in R&D* which, in Ch.4, outlined the tax treatment of research and development (R&D) expenditure and intellectual property. The analysis was a massive over-simplification of the actual tax rules and led to a detailed review of what those rules actually were, and whether they should be changed, which led to a series of technical notes and consultation documents including *Research and Development: Definition and Appeals* in January 1999: *Reform of the Taxation of Intellectual Property and Research and Development: New Tax Incentives for Small and Medium-sized Companies*, in March 1999 and *Guidelines on the Meaning of Research and Development (R&D) for Tax Purposes*, also issued in March 1999. This led to a statutory definition for research and development taking effect from April 1, 2000 for companies, and 2000–01 for income tax purposes, in FA 2000 s.68 and Sch.19, which introduced a new definition for research and development in TA 1988 s.837A and for oil and gas exploration and appraisal in TA 1988 s.837B. Following the enactment of ITA 2007 the above definitions applied only for corporation tax purposes until redefined in CTA s.1138. The equivalent definitions which apply for income tax purposes for 2007–08 and later years are in ITA 2007 ss.1006 and 1003 respectively.

15–001

The FA 2000 s.69 introduced a new regime for enhanced relief on expenditure on research and development for small and medium-sized companies in respect of the accounting periods ending on or after April 1, 2000 with the detailed provisions being set out in FA 2000 Schs 20 and 21, now in CTA 2009 Pt 13 ss.1039–1142. This was followed by the Research and Development (Prescribed Activities) Regulations (SI 2000/2081, now superseded by SI 2004/712) which further defined the activities constituting research and development for tax purposes by reference to the *Guidelines on the Meaning of Research and Development (R&D)* issued by the Department of Trade and Industry on March 5, 2004. This was supplemented by a further technical note, *Finance Act 2000 Research and Development, Guidance on: the New Definition of Research and Development*, and *R&D Tax Credits for Small and Medium-sized Companies* issued by HMRC. In July 2003, HMRC published a consultation document entitled "Defining innovation: a consultation on the definition of research and development for tax purposes" which resulted in the "simplified" guidelines issued by the Department of Trade and Industry on March 5, 2004. The FA 2000 rules governing tax relief for expenditure on R&D were developed alongside the new regime applying to intangible assets, which was first proposed in the technical note issued on June 23, 2000 by HMRC entitled the *Reform of the Taxation of Intellectual Property, Goodwill and Other Intangible Assets*. This was followed on November 8, 2000 by *Reform of the Taxation of Intellectual Property, Goodwill and Intangible Assets: the Next Stage*, and the publication of a Treasury Consultation document in March 2001 on *Increasing Innovation*, which favoured an incremental R&D tax incentive scheme for larger companies. The consultation document was accompanied by a Treasury Report, *Productivity in the UK: Progress towards a Productive Economy*, which attempted to measure the performance in the United Kingdom compared with that in the United States, France and Germany.

A technical note was published by HMRC on March 7, 2001 on the *Taxation of Intellectual Property, Goodwill and Other Intangible Assets: The New Regime*. Further discussions led to a consultative note, *Designs for Innovation*, published by the Treasury and HMRC in December 2001, which led to tax relief for expenditure on research and development by large companies in FA 2002 s.53 and Sch.12; tax reliefs for expenditure on vaccine research in FA 2002 s.54 and Schs 13 and 14, together with some amendments to the R&D tax reliefs for small and medium sized enterprises in FA 2002 s.56 and Sch.15. It also included an entirely new regime on intangible fixed assets for companies in FA 2002 s.84 and Sch.29 which is dealt with in Ch.22. This regime is not available to sole traders or partnerships. The HMRC guidance on these new rules is contained in the *Corporate Intangibles, Research and Development Manual* (CIRD 8000 et seq).

15–002 Subsequent Finance Acts have continued to make minor adjustments to the R&D regime and reliefs for vaccine research, although the broad principles of the schemes remain unchanged.

The scientific research allowances in CAA 1990 ss.136–139, which are available for all businesses including partnerships and sole traders, were re-enacted in the Capital Allowances Act 2001 ss.437–451 and re-titled "research and development allowances"; see paras 15–011–15–013.

FRASCATI

15–003 The starting point for the definition of research and development expenditure is from what is commonly known as the Frascati Manual which is actually entitled *The Measurement of Scientific and Technological Activities: Proposed Standard Practice for Surveys of Research and Experimental Development*, and was published by the OECD in 1994, ISBN 9264142029. The Frascati Manual is a technical guide used by statisticians and uses a wider definition of R&D than that adopted for tax purposes in the United Kingdom, which is confined to activities in the fields of natural or applied science, whereas Frascati includes research and development in the Humanities and Social Sciences. The definition for UK tax purposes is now in ITA 2007 s 1006 for income tax and CTA 2010 s 1138 for corporation tax, (CIRD 82000), which defines research and development as activities that fall to be treated as research and development in accordance with generally accepted accounting practice; ITA 2007 s.1006(2)), CTA 2010 s.1138(2) but it excludes oil and gas exploration and appraisal; ITA 2007 s.1006(5), CTA 2010 s.1138(5) defined by ITA 2007 s.1003 and CTA 2010 s.1134 as activities searching for petroleum and ascertaining its extent or characteristics or reserves). The accounting definition is supplemented by regulations, ITA 2007 s.1006(3) and (4)) and CTA 2010 s.1138(3) and (4), which are the Research and Development (Prescribed Activities) Regulations (SI 2004/712), which came into force on April 1, 2004 and which give statutory force to what is, in effect, tertiary legislation, the *Guidelines on the Meaning of Research and Development (R&D) for Tax Purposes* issued by the Department of Trade and Industry (Guidelines) (see App.8).

SSAP 13 AND GUIDELINES

The Guidelines refer to the definition used for accounting purposes in the *Statement of Standard Accounting Practice* (SSAP 13). Frascati defines R&D as "comprising creative work undertaken on a systematic basis in order to increase the stock of knowledge . . . and the use of this stock of knowledge to devise new applications". However, for accounting and tax purposes the definition is confined to new scientific or technical knowledge arising from pure or applied research or the use of scientific or technical knowledge in order to produce new or substantially improved material, devices or services (SSAP 13, para.21; Guidelines, paras 3–6). Innovation within the fields of science and technology is a distinguishing feature of R&D activity, although the revised Guidelines issued on March 5, 2004 replace references to "innovation" with the concept of achieving an advance in science and technology, and these terms are further defined. (SSAP 13, para.5; Guidelines, paras 6, 15–18, 23).

15–004

R&D will normally include:

- Experimental, theoretical or other work aimed at the discovery of new knowledge or the advancement of existing knowledge.
- Searching for applications of that knowledge.
- Formulation and design of possible applications for such work.
- Testing in search for, or evaluation of, products, service or process alternatives.
- Design, construction and testing of pre-production prototypes and models and development batches.
- Design of products, services, processes, or systems involving new technology or substantially improving those already produced or installed.
- Construction and operation of prototypes and pilot plants.

The essence of R&D is the attempt to achieve an advance in science or technology through the resolution of scientific or technological uncertainty. Once the uncertainty has been resolved further development is no longer R&D (SSAP 13, para.6; Guidelines, para.33). In order for expenditure to qualify for R&D tax relief, it is not sufficient that the claimant company believes the activities to be innovative or cutting edge; the project must represent a genuine advance in science or technology (*B E Studios Ltd v Smith & Williamson Ltd* [2005] EWHC 1506 (Ch). Intra group recharged costs do not qualify as staffing costs, (*Gripple*

Ltd v RCC (2010) S.T.C. 2283, (2010) EWHC 1609 (Ch). In *Kronospan Mielec sp z oo v Dyrektor Izby Skarbowej w Rzeszowie* (2011) S.T.C. 80 it was held that R&D commissioned by a non-resident was an export of engineering services for VAT purposes.

15–005 Excluded from the definition of R&D activities are:

- Testing analysis either of equipment or a product for the purposes of quality or quantity control.
- Periodic alterations to existing products, services or processes even though these may represent some improvement.
- Operation research not tied to specific research and development activity.
- Cost of corrective action in connection with breakdowns during commercial production.
- Legal and administrative work in connection with patent applications, records and litigation and the sale or licensing of patents.
- Activity, including design and construction engineering relating to the construction, relocation, rearrangement or start-up of facilities or equipment other than facilities or equipment whose sole use is for a particular research and development project.
- Market research (SSAP 13, para.7; Guidelines, para.28).

The rules to determine whether an activity counts as R&D are complex. The Guidelines state that R&D takes place when a project seeks to achieve an advance in science or technology. The basic requirement is therefore for there to be activities which directly contribute to achieving such an advance through the resolution of scientific or technological uncertainty. If the activities "attempt to resolve an element of the scientific or technological uncertainty associated with achieving the advance", they will constitute R&D (Guidelines, para.26). The Guidelines give the following example:

"A project which seeks to, for example:

(a) extend overall knowledge or capability in a field of science or technology; or
(b) create a process, material, device, product or service which incorporates or represents an increase in overall knowledge or capability in a field of science or technology; or
(c) make an appreciable improvement to an existing process, material, device, product or service through scientific or technological changes; or
(d) use science or technology to duplicate the effect of an existing process, material, device, product or service in a new or appreciably improved way (e.g. a product that has exactly the same performance characteristics as existing models, but is built in a fundamentally different manner),

will therefore be R&D." (Guidelines, para.9)

It will be appreciated that the definition of R&D is quite restrictive and excludes not only commercial R&D but also the costs of bringing a prototype to full production. The Guidelines note that the:

"design, construction, and testing of prototypes generally fall within the scope of R&D for tax purposes. But once any modifications necessary to reflect the test findings have been made to the prototypes, and further testing has been satisfactorily completed, the scientific or technological uncertainty has been resolved and further work will not be R&D." (Guidelines, para.39)

It has been suggested that the United Kingdom is, in fact, rather good at R&D within this narrow definition but very bad at the product development stage and marketing of the new product. There has therefore been a call for the extension of this definition but whether this will result in any changes remains to be seen.

Software may qualify either as an object of the R&D or as a means of achieving R&D but only to the extent that it involves scientific or technological advances or assists in the development of such advances.

Qualifying supporting activities which will qualify if part of a larger R&D project includes:

"• Scientific and technical information services in so far as they are conducted for the purposes of R&D support (such as the preparation of the original report of R&D findings).
• Indirect supporting activities such as maintenance, security, administration and clerical activities and finance and personnel activities in so far as undertaken for R&D.
• Certain ancillary activities essential to the undertaking of qualifying R&D (e.g. taking on and paying staff, leasing laboratories and maintaining research and development equipment including computers used for R&D purposes).
• Training required to directly support an R&D project.
• Research by students and researchers carried out at universities.
• Research (including data collection) to devise new scientific or technological testing methods, survey methods or sampling methodologies.
• Feasibility studies to inform the strategic direction of a specific R&D activity (Guidelines, para.31)."

R&D however does not include:

• Work to develop non-scientific or non-technological aspects of a new or appreciably improved process, material, device, product or service.
• The production and distribution of goods and services.
• Administration and other supporting services.
• General support services (such as transportation, storage, cleaning, repair, maintenance and security).
• Elements of a company's planning activity relating to a project but not directly contributing to the resolution of scientific or technological uncertainty, such as identifying or researching market niches in which R&D might benefit a company, or examination of a project's financial, marketing, and legal aspects (Guidelines, paras 28, 37).

General and commercial activities related to, but not part of the resolution of scientific or technological uncertainty, do not count as R&D activities (Guidelines, para.28).

RESEARCH AND DEVELOPMENT

ACCOUNTING TREATMENT OF R&D EXPENDITURE

15–007 Expenditure on pure and applied research is normally written off when incurred (SSAP 13, para.8). Expenditure on new products or services, as opposed to pure or applied research, may be deferred to be matched against future revenue, but only where there is a clearly defined project and the related expenditure is separately identifiable, and if expenditure incurred together with any further development cost to be incurred on the same project, together with related production, selling and administrative cost will be more than covered by related revenues, and adequate resources will be available to enable the project to be completed, together with any consequential increases. The whole project has to be viewed in the light of its technical feasibility and ultimate commercial viability considered in the light of factors such as likely market conditions (including competing products or services), public opinion and consumer and environmental legislation (SSAP 13, paras 9–12). FRSSE 6.3–6.10 states:

> "6.3 The cost of fixed assets acquired or constructed in order to provide facilities for **research and development** activities over a number of accounting periods shall be capitalised and written off over their useful lives through the profit and loss account.
>
> 6.4 Expenditure on **pure** and **applied research** shall be written off in the period of expenditure through the profit and loss account.
>
> 6.5 **Development** expenditure shall be written off in the period of expenditure except in the following circumstances when it may be deferred to future periods:
> (a) there is a clearly defined project; and
> (b) the related expenditure is separately identifiable; and
> (c) the outcome of such a project has been assessed with reasonable certainty as to:
> (i) its technical feasibility; and
> (ii) its ultimate commercial viability considered in the light of factors such as likely market conditions (including competing products), public opinion, consumer and environmental legislation; and
> (d) the aggregate of the deferred **development** costs, any further **development** costs, and related production, selling and administration costs is reasonably expected to be exceeded by related future sales or other revenues; and
> (e) adequate resources exist, or are reasonably expected to be available, to enable the project to be completed and to provide any consequential increases in working capital.
>
> 6.6 In the foregoing circumstances **development** expenditure may be deferred to the extent that its recovery can be reasonably regarded as assured.
>
> 6.7 If an **accounting policy** of deferral of **development** expenditure is adopted, it shall be applied to all **development** projects that meet the criteria in paragraph 6.5.
>
> 6.8 If **development** costs are deferred to future periods, they shall be amortised. The amortisation shall commence with the commercial production or application of the product, service, process or system and shall be allocated on a systematic basis to each accounting period, by reference to either the sale or use of the product, service, process or system or the period over which these are expected to be sold or used.

ACCOUNTING TREATMENT OF R&D EXPENDITURE

6.9 Deferred **development** expenditure for each product shall be reviewed at the end of each accounting period and where the circumstances that justified the deferral of expenditure no longer apply, or are considered doubtful, the expenditure to the extent to which it is considered to be irrecoverable, shall be written off immediately project by project.

6.10 The amount of deferred **development** expenditure carried forward at the beginning and end of the period shall be disclosed under **intangible assets** in the balance sheet or in the notes to the balance sheet. THE REASON FOR CAPITALISING THESE COSTS AND THE PERIOD OVER WHICH THEY ARE BEING DEPRECIATED MUST BE DISCLOSED IN A NOTE TO THE ACCOUNTS. IF DEVELOPMENT COSTS ARE NOT TREATED AS A REALISED LOSS, THIS MUST BE STATED TOGETHER WITH AN EXPLANATION OF THE CIRCUMSTANCES RELIED UPON BY THE DIRECTORS TO JUSTIFY THEIR DECISION."

Only where all these requirements are met in connection with a major project may the R&D expenditure be carried forward and amortised over the period of expected benefit, i.e. the date when the revenue is likely to arise, with any amortised balance being reviewed at each accounting date and written off unless the requirements continue to be met (SSAP 13, paras 13–15). In the large majority of cases, therefore, revenue expenditure on R&D is written off in the accounting period in which it is incurred under SSAP 13.

Sub-contracted work in progress under a firm contract, which is incomplete at the balance sheet date, will normally be dealt with as contract work in progress under SSAP 9, and expenditure on locating and exploiting oil, gas and mineral deposits is specifically excluded from the definition of R&D (SSAP 13, paras 17 and 18). The accounting policies used must be disclosed (SSAP 13, paras 19 and 20).

Fixed assets acquired or constructed to provide facilities for R&D activities should be capitalised and written off over their useful life in the normal way. Such depreciation will be included in expenditure on R&D for disclosure purposes (SSAP 13, para.16).

15–008

In November 2012 the Financial Reporting Council issued FRS 100 Application of Financial Reporting Requirements and FRS 101 Reduced Disclosure Framework. FRS 102 The Financial Reporting Standard applicable in the UK and Republic of Ireland was also published, in March 2013. These new standards will apply from January 1, 2015, but may be adopted early, and are applicable to all companies and entities in the UK and Republic of Ireland, other than listed entities. They do not require any entities to apply international accounting standards that are not already required to do so. FRS 100 sets out the overall financial reporting requirements giving many entities a choice of detailed accounting requirements depending on factors such as size and whether or not they are part of a listed group. FRS 101 applies to the individual financial statements of subsidiaries and ultimate parents, allowing them to apply the same accounting as their listed group accounts, but with fewer disclosures.

Under FRS 102 Section 18.4 an entity shall recognise an intangible asset if, and only if:

(a) it is probable that the expected future economic benefits that are attributable to the asset will flow to the entity; and

(b) the cost of the asset can be measured reliably, for example, if it is separately acquired (para.18.7) or using reasonable and supportable assumptions that represent management's best estimate of the economic conditions that exist over the useful life of the asset (para.18.5). Internally generated intangible assets are classified into a research phase and a development phase, if distinguishable (paras 18.8A and 18.8B).

15–009 Internally generated goodwill, brands, logos, publishing titles, customer lists, etc. and start up costs, etc. are expenses to be written off, as is research prior to development (paras 18.8C–18.8G). The development phase is defined in paras 18.8H–18.8K.

Intangible assets are initially accounted for at cost (paras 18.9–18.13). After initial recognition all intangible assets in a class can be re-valued for accounting purposes only if the fair value can be determined by reference to an active market (paras 18.18B–18.18H).

Intangible assets should be amortised over their finite useful life, which should not exceed five years unless it is possible to make a reliable estimate of its useful life (paras 18.19–18.26). Appropriate disclosures have to be made (paras 18.27–18.29A).

TAXATION TREATMENT

15–010 As CTA 2009 s.46, for corporation tax, and ITTOIA 2005 s.25, for income tax now provide that profits of a trade, profession or vocation must be computed in accordance with generally accepted accounting practice (GAAP, as defined by ITA 2009 s.997 and CTA 2010 s.1127 subject to any adjustment required or authorised by law in computing profits for those purposes, the accounting treatment required by SSAP 13 or FRS 102 would also apply for tax purposes. Mary Arden (now the Rt Honourable Lady Justice Arden DBE, QC), in her opinion on the legal status of accounting standards reproduced as an Appendix to the forward to *Accounting Standards* in para.10, states that the immediate effect of the issue of an accounting standard is to create a likelihood that the court will hold that compliance with that standard is necessary to meet the true and fair requirements. That likelihood is strengthened by the degree to which a standard is subsequently accepted in practice. In December 1977 SSAP 13 was issued, and then revised in January 1989, so it is extremely likely that it would be treated as an authoritative view of the accounting treatment of R&D expenditure. This view is reinforced by a number of court cases such as *Threlfall v Jones, Gallagher v Jones* [1993] S.T.C. 537; *Johnston v Britannia Airways Ltd* [1994] S.T.C. 763; *Odeon Associated Theatres Ltd v Jones* (1971) 48 T.C. 257; *Chancery Lane Safe Deposit and Offices Co Ltd v IRC* (1965) 43 T.C. 83, and *Herbert Smith v Honour* [1999] S.T.C. 173.

The treatment under SSAP 13 of expenditure on R&D is normally that it is written off as incurred, although it is occasionally treated as deferred revenue expenditure and written off over a period. In this case the accounting treatment would be followed for tax purposes as deferred revenue expenditure, in accordance with *Tax Bulletin*, Issue 39, 623–625 (February 1999) and Issue 53, 859–861 (June 2001).

Although SSAP 13 is not compulsory for smaller businesses applying the Financial Reporting Standard for Smaller Entities (FRSSE), it is unlikely that the accounting policies would differ materially from those in SSAP 13 except to make it less likely that R&D expenditure would be deferred for accounting and tax purposes as it is still necessary to show a true and fair view (see *Tax Bulletin*, Issue 40, 636–641 (April 1999)). Sole traders and partnerships will therefore obtain a deduction for R&D revenue expenditure as a trading expense, following the accounting treatment, in accordance with UK GAAP. Companies will also write off R&D expenditure for tax purposes following the accounting treatment, subject to the special rules for small or medium-sized enterprises under CTA 2009 ss.1043–1073 or for large companies claiming relief under CTA 2009 ss.1074–1084, as explained below.

CAPITAL EXPENDITURE ON R&D, R&D ALLOWANCES

Research and development allowances formerly known as scientific research allowances, are available for capital expenditure on R&D within CTA 2010 s.1138 (for corporation tax purposes) and ITA 2007 s.1006 (for income tax purposes), in accordance with the Department of Trade and Industry Guidelines, (CA 61000,), which excludes capital expenditure incurred on oil and gas exploration and appraisal (CAA 2001 s.437 (CA 60100, 60200)). The special rules applicable to the Patent Box regime are explained in Ch.23. Expenditure on research and development includes capital expenditure incurred on carrying out research and development, or providing facilities for carrying out research and development, it does not include expenditure on the acquisition of rights in research and development or rights arising out of research and development such as patent rights (CAA 2001 s.438(1) and (2) (CA 60300)). Also, it does not include expenditure on the provision of a dwelling unless the rest of the building is used for research and development and no more than 25 per cent of the capital expenditure, disregarding VAT, relates to the dwelling, in which case the whole building is treated as used for research and development. Any apportionments are made on a just and reasonable basis (CAA 2001 s.438(3)–(6)).

15–011

The allowance is 100 per cent of the expenditure incurred in the qualifying period, less any disposal value brought into account for that period (CAA 2001 s.441(1)). The relevant chargeable period is that in which expenditure is incurred, or if it is incurred before the relevant trade has started, the chargeable period in which that trade commenced (CAA 2001 s.441). The allowance may be disclaimed in whole or in part (CAA 2001 s.441(3) (CA60500)).

Qualifying expenditure means capital expenditure incurred on R&D in relation to a trade carried on by the claimant, or which is subsequently set up (CAA 2001 s.439). Expenditure may only be taken into account once. Expenditure can be apportioned in a just and reasonable manner (CAA 2001 s.439(2)–(4)). R&D is related to a trade if it relates to an existing trade which may lead to or facilitate an extension of that trade or is R&D of a medical nature in relation to the welfare of

RESEARCH AND DEVELOPMENT

workers employed in that trade (CAA 2001 s.439(5)). The CAA 2001 s.439, extends to R&D undertaken on behalf of the trader, which would therefore include capital grants to universities or scientific research associations which would carry out the actual research, (see *Gaspet Ltd v Elliss* [1987] S.T.C. 362).However, R&D allowances are confined to traders, and capital expenditure on R&D in connection with a profession or vocation is not eligible for R&D allowances, (see *Salt v Golding* [1996] S.T.C. (SCD) 269). Expenditure on the acquisition of land or rights in or over land is not qualifying expenditure, except so far as it is preferable to the acquisition of a building or structure already constructed on the land, or rights in or over such a building or structure, or on plant and machinery which forms part of the building or structure, with just and reasonable apportionment as necessary (CAA 2001 s.440 (CA 60400)).

15–012 There is a balancing charge where expenditure has been written off under CAA 2001 s.441 and there is a subsequent receipt of a disposal value brought into account in a later chargeable period (CAA 2001 s.442(1) and (2)). The balancing charge is reduced to the excess of the disposal value over any unclaimed allowances where the allowance has been disclaimed in whole or part, or not been claimed (CAA 2001 s.442(3) and (4) (CA 60500)). Disposal value arises where the asset ceases to be owned or is demolished or destroyed, unless the event gives rise to a balancing charge under the plant and machinery provisions (CAA 2001 s.443(1) and (3) (CA 60600)). Where the disposal is a sale, the disposal value is the net proceeds of sale. Where the disposal is a diminution or destruction of the asset, the disposal value is the scrap value, together with any insurance proceeds or other compensation, less the costs of demolition; any other disposal is deemed to be at market value (CAA 2001 ss.443(4) and (5) and 445(1)–(3)). Where the cost of demolition exceeds the disposal value, this is treated as additional capital R&D expenditure incurred when the demolition occurs, or immediately before the discontinuance of a trade that is permanently discontinued (CAA 2001 s.445(4) and (5) (CA 60700)). The cost of demolition is not treated as expenditure on any replacement asset (CAA 2001 s.445(6)). Where there is a disposal event, it is brought into account in the chargeable period in which the event occurs, or the period in which the trade permanently ceases, if earlier (CAA 2001 s.444(1)–(3)). If the disposal event occurs before the chargeable period in which the allowance is given, i.e. before the trade commenced, the disposal value is brought into account for that chargeable period (CAA 2001 s.444(4) (CA 60600)).

Adjustments may have to be made to the capital allowances computation in respect of an additional VAT liability or VAT rebate under the VAT capital items scheme (CAA 2001 ss.547–549). An additional VAT liability is treated as capital expenditure incurred on the R&D, as if it were part of the original expenditure (CAA 2001 ss.446 and 447(1) (CA 60750)). This does not apply where the asset has been disposed of, demolished or destroyed (CAA 2001 s.447(2)). The additional relief is given in respect of the chargeable period in which the liability arises or in which the trade is set up, if later (CAA 2001 s.447(3)). A VAT rebate increases the disposal value under CAA 2001 ss.443(6) and 448(1) and (4), in the chargeable period in which the rebate accrues or in which the relevant trade is set up, if later (CAA 2001 s.448(5)). These provisions do not apply where the asset giving rise to the VAT rebate has been disposed of, demolished or destroyed or is brought into account as plant and machinery or industrial buildings allowances

(CAA 2001 s.448(2) and (3)). An additional VAT rebate can reduce the value of an unclaimed allowance proportionately, under CAA 2001 ss.442(5) and 449.

R&D allowances are given as an expense of the trade and a balancing charge as a receipt of the trade, under CAA 2001 s.450 (CA 60800). An asset ceases to be owned at the earlier of the time of completion or the time when possession is given under CAA 2001 s.451.

R&D allowances are not due where an asset was acquired other than for use in R&D activities and subsequently so used, as expenditure has to be incurred on R&D in order to qualify, CAA 2001 s.439(1). Conversely there is no withdrawal of allowances or deemed disposal on an asset acquired for R&D purposes ceasing to be so used and retained for business use generally. Where part of the allowance is disclaimed it cannot be claimed in a later year as there are no provisions for writing down or balancing allowances in CAA 2001 s.441. R&D allowances are claimed in a self-assessment tax return in the same manner as other capital allowances. Attempts to exploit these and similar provisions in complex tax avoidance schemes largely failed to achieve the desired effect in *Tower MCashback LLP v HMRC* (2011) UKSC 19, (2011) S.T.C. 1143. In *Partners of the Vaccine Research Ltd Partnership and Another v HMRC* (2013) UK FTT 073 (TC) the Tribunal judge held that a tax avoidance scheme which purportedly raised £153,370,616, less fees, etc. of £8 million, i.e. £145,370,616 through circular financing actually spent £14 million on sub-contracted research and development into vaccines for specified diseases, out of the total reliefs claimed of £192,702,989 under TA 1988 s.438(1). It was also decided that the "one-off fee" was paid for services to be provided for at least five years and potentially for 15 years. It was also held that the partnership was, to that extent carrying on a trade under TA 1988 s.439(1)(a) and the partners were entitled to sideways loss relief under TA 1988 s.381(4). Although the partnership was a Jersey limited partnership it was held that the trade was carried on in the UK. However the fees paid were not "money wholly and exclusively laid out or expended for the purposes of the trade", under TA 1988 s.74(1)(a). The interest relief claimed by the partners under TA 1988 ss.353 and 362 was allowed only to the extent that "they were used to fund (each partner's) share of the £14 million research sub-contract".

TRADING DEDUCTION FOR R&D COSTS

Revenue expenditure incurred by a trader on R&D, as defined by CTA 2010 s.1138 and ITA 2007 s.1006, but including oil and gas exploration and appraisal, related to the trade which is directly undertaken by him, or carried out on his behalf by others, is deductible as a trading expense, under CTA 2009 s.87 (for corporation tax purposes) or ITTOIA 2005 s.87 (for income tax purposes). This does not include expenditure on the acquisition of rights such as patent rights arising out of R&D CTA 2009 s.87(2); ITTOIA 2005 s.87(2)). R&D relating to a trade includes that which may lead to or facilitate an extension of the trade or is of a medical nature and has a special relation to the welfare of workers employed in the trade CTA 2009 s.87(3); ITTOIA 2005 s.87(3)). No double claim may be made of the same expenditure CTA 2009 s.87(4); ITTOIA 2005 s.87(4)).

15–013

RESEARCH AND DEVELOPMENT

A revenue payment by a trader to a scientific research association, to undertake scientific research relating to its trade, is allowable as a trading expense under CTA 2009 s.88 (for corporation tax purposes) or ITTOIA 2005 s.88 (for income tax purposes). Scientific research in this context means any activities in the field of natural or applied science for the extension of knowledge CTA 2009 s.88(3); ITTOIA 2005 s.88(3)). The scientific research must be relevant to the trade or lead to or facilitate an extension of the trade or be of a medical nature in relation to the welfare of workers employed in such trades CTA 2009 s.88(5); ITTOIA 2005, s.88(5)). A scientific research association or university, etc. carrying out the research must be approved by the Secretary of State for Trade and Industry, who also has the final decision as to whether any activities constitute scientific research CTA 2009 s.88(6); ITTOIA 2005 s.88(6)). The same expenditure cannot be allowed in more than one trade CTA 2005 s.388(7); ITTOIA 2005 s.88(7)). Patent fees and expenses are allowable as trading expenses under CTA 2009 ss.89 and 90, which applies for corporation tax purposes or under ITTOIA 2005 ss.89 and 90 for those within the charge to income tax.

R&D RELIEF FOR SMALL AND MEDIUM-SIZED COMPANIES—"SUPER DEDUCTION"

15–014   This "super-deduction" scheme was introduced by FA 2000 s.69 and Schs 20 and 21 in respect of accounting periods ending, on or after April 1, 2000 (CIRD 80100) and is now in CTA 2009 ss.1043–1073 and 1113–1142. The scheme gives R&D relief under CTA 2009 s.1044 of 225 per cent (from April 1, 2012, FA 2012 Sch.3 para.2; 200 per cent from April 1, 2011; 175 per cent from August 1, 2008, originally 150 per cent) of the qualifying R&D expenditure in the accounting period, in respect of accounting periods ending on or after April 1, 2000 (CIRD 80100). The R&D tax credit scheme is confined to small and medium-sized companies, not sole traders or partnerships. There is no minimum expenditure requirement. Prior to April 1, 2012 it was confined to companies which invested at least £10,000 in an accounting year on R&D, by CTA 2009 s.1050. A company qualifies as a small or medium-sized enterprise (SME) if it falls within the definition of a micro, small or medium-sized enterprise in the European Commission Recommendation 2003/361 dated May 6, 2003 as applied and amended by CTA 2009 s.1119–1122. This broadly applies to any company if it has, together with any company in which it holds 25 per cent or more of the share capital or voting rights:

- fewer than 500 employees, and either or both of;
- an annual turnover not exceeding €100million (about £80m);
- and an annual balance sheet total not exceeding €86m (about £68m); and
- it has less than 25 per cent of its capital or voting rights owned by an enterprise (or jointly by several enterprises) that fall outside the definition of an SME (CIRD 83000).

QUALIFYING R&D EXPENDITURE

These are the thresholds in force from August 1, 2008. Prior to that date the respective limits were 250 employees, €50 million annual turnover and €43 million annual balance sheet total.

The company will only need to calculate its turnover or balance sheet totals in Euros if it is close to the threshold. The balance sheet total should be calculated at the accounting date. The rules do not specify any particular formula for translating turnover. Any method can be used provided that it gives a reasonable result, e.g. using the average exchange rate for the accounting period. In calculating whether 25 per cent of its capital or voting rights are owned by an enterprise that is not an SME, shares held by public investment corporations controlled by central or local government or independent agencies that provide funds for companies without direct investment, venture capital companies or institutional investors, where no control is exercised either individually or jointly, are ignored. If the company cannot determine by whom its capital is held, it may be able to presume that the 25 per cent ownership restriction will not apply. A company is an SME in the accounting period in which the limits are exceeded if it was an SME in the previous accounting period. The European Commission for State Aid definition of an SME is used instead of the lower threshold which applies for UK company law and other tax purposes, because the intention is to give the maximum relief that is within the European Union State Aid rules.

CAP ON RELIEF

A cap on the amount of aid that companies can receive for a single project under the SME R&D tax relief and vaccine research relief schemes was introduced by FA 2008 Sch.10 and is now in CTA 2009 ss.1113–1118. The cap is €7.5million but may be varied by Treasury order. The introduction of the cap is intended to ensure that the SME R&D and large company vaccine research relief continues to comply with EC state aid requirements, and applies from August 1, 2008.

15–015

QUALIFYING R&D EXPENDITURE

Qualifying R&D expenditure for this scheme is revenue expenditure attributable to relevant research and development directly undertaken by the company, or on its behalf, which is incurred on staffing costs or software or consumable items, or is sub-contracted R&D. The expenditure must not normally be incurred in carrying out sub-contracted R&D for others. In the case of SME R&D relief, it is the commissioning company that obtains the relief on sub-contracted R&D, under CTA 2009 ss.1052, 1053.

15–016

Relief is not available for R&D expenditure incurred by a company in respect of work sub-contracted to it (CIRD 80200)). However, R&D relief at the large company rate of 130 per cent (125 per cent prior to April 1, 2008) may be available under CTA 2009 ss.1063–1067. An SME is entitled to large company R&D relief for its R&D expenditure without a minimum expenditure threshold. The required R&D threshold of at least £10,000 per annum in the accounting period, in CTA 2009 ss.1050 or 1015 was repealed by FA 2012 Sch.3 paras 1, 3 and 6 for accounting periods ending on or after April 1, 2012. The R&D expenditure is the aggregate of qualifying sub-contracted R&D expenditure within CTA 2009 s.1065 and the SME's own R&D expenditure within CTA 2009 ss.1044. Qualifying sub-contracted R&D expenditure under CTA 2009 ss.1063–1067 is expenditure incurred by the SME on R&D contracted out to it where the commissioner of the R&D is a large company or a person otherwise than in the course of a trade, profession or vocation taxable under ITTOIA 2005 Pt 2, Ch.2 ss.5–23 or Ch.2 of Pt 3 of CTA 2009, and the R&D is directly undertaken by the SME or on its behalf, CTA 2009 s.1065. Expenditure is directly undertaken by an SME if it is incurred on staffing costs or on software or consumable items and is attributable to relevant R&D in relation to the SME and is not of a capital nature, CTA 2009 s.1066.

R&D is directly undertaken on an SME's behalf where the expenditure is incurred on making payments to a qualifying body, individual or partnership of individuals in respect of R&D contracted out by the SME and is directly undertaken on behalf of the SME by the sub-contractor and is attributable to relevant research and development in relation to the SME and is expenditure not of a capital nature CTA 2009 s.1067 (CIRD 80500)). The expenditure must not be subsidised, CTA 2009 ss.1052, 1053 (CIRD 80300)). Relevant R&D means that it is related to a trade carried on by the company or which it intends to carry on. The R&D qualifies where it may lead to or facilitate an extension of the trade, or is of a medical nature with a special relation to the welfare of workers employed in the trade CTA 2009 s.1042.

From August 1, 2008 payments to participants in clinical trials are qualifying R&D expenditure under CTA 2009 s.1140.

STAFFING COSTS

15–017 Staffing costs, under CTA 2009 ss.1123, 1124 are the total emoluments of employees, including the secondary Class I National Insurance contributions paid by the company, and any contributions to a pension fund, so far as it relates to relevant R&D. This means that the staffing costs must be paid to, or in respect of, directors or employees directly and actively engaged in such R&D. For those employees partly engaged in R&D, expenditure incurred is subject to a straight apportionment in all cases CTA 2009 s.1124(4). Secretarial or administrative services in support of R&D are not included CTA 2009 s.1124(2). Normally 65 per cent of qualifying expenditure is allowed for externally provided workers, to exclude the provider's margin, subject to an election to apply cost of the provider which is the default treatment when such staff are provided by a connected person CTA 2009 ss.1127–1132. Staffing costs do not include director's remuneration recharged from another group company, *Gripple Ltd v RCC* (2010) S.T.C. 2283.

SOFTWARE OR CONSUMABLE ITEMS

Expenditure on computer software or consumable or transformable items, as so treated under GAAP, is attributable to R&D if such items are employed directly in such R&D (CTA 2009 ss.1125, 1126 (CIRD 82300, 82500)). Such consumable items include disposable laboratory equipment but not major items which would be capitalised. Expenditure on water, fuel and power of any kind is included CTA 2009 s.1125(2) insofar as it is directly employed in R&D. The key aspect is that the expenditure must be on items that are used for the R&D and are no longer so useable in their original form, because they are used up or transformed (CIRD 82400. CIRD 82450). Rent, rates, interest, lease payments, etc. are not software or consumable items. Receipts from disposing of waste products do not reduce the eligible cost of software and consumable items (*Tax Bulletin Special Edition*, December 2002, p.14). 15–018

OTHER CONDITIONS

There is no longer a minimum expenditure requirement on R&D to qualify for relief. Expenditure must be qualifying R&D expenditure allowable for tax purposes in computing the profits of a trade carried on in the accounting period or would have been allowable had the trading activities commenced, CTA 2009 s.1050. Sub-contracted R&D as defined by CTA 2009 ss.1063, 1065, and subsidised R&D as defined by CTA 2009 s.1138, do not qualify for the SME scheme but may qualify for large company R&D relief (as described at para.15–026 et seq), if it is allowable in computing profits for the accounting period of a trade carried on by the SME CTA 2009 s.1050(7)), if the conditions in CTA 2009 ss.1066, 1067 or ss.1071–1072 are met. 15–019

Subsidised expenditure is that which is eligible for state aid, notified to and approved by the European Commission, such as awards which are given by the Department for Business, Innovation and Skills. Where there is notified state aid deemed to be a subsidy, no part of the expenditure attributable to that R&D state aided project is allowable within the scheme (CTA 2009 ss.1052, 1053, 1138). Where the aid is not notified state aid, the grant or subsidy is merely deducted from the eligible R&D expenditure, which reduces the amount qualifying under the scheme. This also applies to that part of the cost met by any other person (CTA 2009 s.1138). Notified state aid is that notified to and approved by the European Commission but does not include R&D tax relief and R&D tax credits under this scheme, tax relief for large companies under CTA 2009 ss.1074–1084, or vaccine research under CTA 2009 ss.1138 and 1085–1142. General subsidies or grants are allocated to the R&D on a just and reasonable basis (CTA 2009 s.1138(4)).

Sub-contracted R&D, where a payment is made to a third party in respect of relevant R&D contracted out to that third party, qualifies as R&D only to the extent of 65 per cent of the qualifying expenditure on the R&D so sub-contracted (CTA 2009 ss.1133, 1136). The 65 per cent figure is designed to eliminate the sub-contractors' assumed profits so that the tax credits are only given on the actual R&D element of the costs (CIRD 80400).

SME R&D tax relief may only be claimed by a company meeting the "going concern" condition under CTA 2009 s.1046. A company is regarded as a going concern if their most recent published accounts were prepared on a going-concern basis and there is nothing to indicate that they were so prepared only on the expectation that the company would receive relief or tax credits under CTA 2009 Pt 13 ss.1039–1084.

IRREVOCABLE ELECTION FOR CONNECTED PERSONS TREATMENT

15–020   It is possible for a company and its sub-contractor to elect jointly to be treated as if they were connected. Such election is irrevocable and must be in relation to all the sub-contractor payments under the contract and be made by notice in writing to HMRC within two years of the end of the company's accounting period in which the contract, etc. is entered into (CTA 2009 s.1135). Similar rules apply to expenditure incurred on or after April 9, 2003 to externally provided workers from connected persons (CTA 2009 s.1130).

Where the company and the sub-contractor are connected persons within the normal connected person definitions of CTA 2010 ss.1122, 1123, the company can claim R&D relief on the lower of the amount paid to the sub-contractor on the sub-contracted R&D or the sub-contractor's costs in relation to software and consumable items and R&D staff as shown in its accounts prepared under UK GAAP (CTA 2009 s.1134). Where the accounts of the company and the sub-contractor are not coterminous, the sub-contractor's costs are those for a period that ends not more than 12 months after the end of the company's period of account in which the sub-contractor payment was brought into account (CTA 2009 s.1133(5)). Any apportionment of expenditure should be on a just and reasonable basis CTA 2009 s.1133(6)). The relevant expenditure of the sub-contractor consists of the staffing costs or software and consumable items costs incurred on the R&D, which are not of a capital nature and not subsidised, applying the staffing and subsidy provisions in CTA 2009 ss.1123, 1124, 1133 and 1135. The effect is to allow the R&D scheme to apply on the same basis as if the R&D had not been sub-contracted to the connected person and the sub-contractor's costs were incurred by the company. Where the payment to the connected sub-contractor exceeds the qualifying R&D expenditure, the excess is allowed as a normal trading expense (see *Tax Treatment of R&D Expenditure*, p.13).

PRE-TRADING EXPENSES

15–021   Where the trade has not yet commenced, the company may, instead of applying the normal pre-trading expenditure rules in CTA 2009 ss.61 and 330, elect to have incurred a trading loss in the accounting period in which the expenditure is incurred of 225 per cent (or 200 per cent for periods prior to April 1, 2012 and 175 per cent from August 1, 2008) of the qualifying R&D expenditure. The election must be made in writing to HMRC within two years beginning with the end of the company's accounting period to which it relates (CTA 2009 ss.1045, 1047).

SME R&D TAX CREDITS

R&D losses may be relieved in the usual way by set-off against profits for the same accounting period under CTA 2010 s.37(3)(a), carried back against profits of an earlier accounting period under CTA 2010 s.37(3)(b), or surrendered to group or consortium members under CTA 2010 ss.99–104, 137. R&D losses not so dealt with are unrelieved losses under CTA 2009 s.1056(2). Instead of claiming R&D relief for an accounting period, a company may claim an R&D tax credit where it has a surrenderable loss (CIRD 80800). The surrenderable loss is equal to the lower of the unrelieved trading loss arising under CTA 2009 ss.1044, 1045, or 225 per cent of the related qualifying R&D expenditure (CIRD 80600) see para.15–016. In computing the surrenderable loss, no account is taken of any losses brought forward from an earlier accounting period or carried back from a later accounting period (CTA 2009 ss.1054–1057). The amount of the R&D tax credit is 11 per cent of the amount of the surrenderable loss for expenditure incurred on or after April 1, 2012. The rate of tax credit relief was reduced from 12.5 per cent to 11 per cent, for expenditure incurred on or after April 1, 2012. It was 16 per cent prior to August 1, 2008 and 14 per cent thereafter, until April 1, 2011 when it became 12.5 per cent. In most cases 11 per cent of the surrenderable loss equates to 24.75 per cent of the actual expenditure on R&D. The figure is calculated on 225 per cent of the R&D expenditure, on the basis of an average 20 per cent rate of tax paid by small or medium-sized companies. The Treasury has power to change the percentage and make consequential amendments to tax credit provisions by statutory instrument (CTA 2009 s.1058(2)).

15–022

Until April 1, 2012 the credit was restricted to the total of the company's PAYE and NIC liabilities arising in the accounting period concerned.

The R&D tax credit attracts interest as if it were tax overpaid under TA 1988 s.826. HMRC may set off the credit against any unpaid corporation tax instead of paying it over to the company (CTA 2009 s.1054 (CIRD 80850)). The R&D tax credit may also be frozen if a company's tax return for the accounting period is enquired into, until the enquiry is completed, although HMRC may make a payment on a provisional basis of such amount as they think fit (CTA 2009 s.1060(4) and (5)). No R&D tax credit will be paid until any arrears of PAYE or Class 1 National Insurance contributions have been paid (CTA 2009 s.1060(6) and (7)). Where the maximum R&D tax credit is claimed, the relief for trading losses against future trading profits carried forward under CTA 2010 s.45, is reduced by the amount of the losses surrendered, which is equal to the whole of the surrenderable loss for the period. Where less than the maximum amount has been claimed by way of credit, the losses available to carry forward are reduced by the corresponding proportion of the surrenderable loss (CTA 2010 s.1138). The amount paid by way of R&D tax credit is not income of the company for tax purposes (CTA 2009 s.1061).

15–023 There is a general anti-avoidance provision in that arrangements entered into wholly or mainly for a disqualifying purpose are disregarded in determining the amount of any R&D relief or tax credit (CTA 2009 s.1084(1)). A disqualifying purpose is one where one of the main objects is to enable a company to claim R&D relief for tax credits to which it would not otherwise be entitled (CTA 2009 s.1084(2) and (3)). Consortium relief is restricted where a member of the consortium is not a small or medium-sized enterprise. Any claim for group relief is restricted to the small or medium-sized companies in the consortium (CTA 2009 s.1049 (CIRD 81100)). Where there is a claim for R&D relief in respect of pre-trading expenditure which gives rise to a trading loss, that loss may not be carried back against the preceding period unless the company was entitled to relief for pre-trading expenditure for that earlier period also (CTA 2009 s.1048(1) and 2)). When the company starts to trade, the unrelieved loss is treated as if it were a loss brought forward to set against future trading profits under CTA 2009 s.1048(3)–(5) (CIRD 80700)).

A claim must be made in a tax return under FA 1998 Sch.18 para.10(2) which includes an amendment of a return (FA 1998 Sch.18 paras 83A and 83B). A claim for an R&D tax credit must specify the amount of the relief claimed which must be quantified at the time the claim is made (FA 1998 Sch.18 para.83C). The claim may be amended or withdrawn by amending the company tax return (FA 1998 Sch.18 para.83D). A claim for R&D tax credit may be made, amended or withdrawn at any time up to the first anniversary of the filing date for the company tax return of the claimant company for the accounting period for which the claim is made, unless HMRC allow a later date (FA 1998 Sch.18 para.83E (CIRD 80900)). A penalty of up to the amount of the excess tax credit claimed may be levied where the claim was made fraudulently or negligently or was incorrect and the error not remedied without unreasonable delay (FA 1998 Sch.18 para.83F (CIRD 81000)).

APPEALS, ETC.

15–024 Appeals will follow the same procedure as other tax disputes. If a taxpayer and inspector are unable to agree whether an activity is R&D, the taxpayer's appeal will now be heard by the First Tier Tax Tribunal (FTTT). Appeals against decisions of the FTTT will go before the Upper Tribunal or the courts in the normal way. These rules do not apply to scientific research associations where appeals will continue to be made to the Secretary of State under CTA 2009 s.88(1)(a) and CTA 2010 s.491 (see *Tax Treatment of R&D Expenditure*, p.5). Excessive R&D tax credits may be recovered as an excessive repayment under FA 1998 Sch.18 para.52(2)(ba) and (5)(ab). The interest provisions are in TA 1988 s.826(3A) and (8BA).

TAX RELIEF ON R&D EXPENDITURE FOR LARGE COMPANIES

15–025 FA 2002 s.53 introduced FA 2002 Sch.12, now CTA 2009 ss.1074–1084, with effect for accounting periods ending on or after April 1, 2002, to provide a new relief for R&D expenditure by large companies (CIRD 82100), subject to a minimum of £25,000 per annum, reduced to £10,000 per annum for expenditure on or after April 9, 2003 (which was abolished by FA 2012 Sch.3 para.6, deleting CTA 2009 s.1075). A large company, under CTA 2009 s.1122, is one which is not a small or medium-sized enterprise as defined for R&D tax relief for SME's and R&D tax credits under the scheme described above (CTA 2009 ss.1119–1121). Under the large companies scheme the R&D relief is 30 per cent, (25 per cent before April 1, 2008) of the expenditure, instead of 225 per cent for SMEs. A new "above the line" tax expenditure credit is being introduced by FA 2013 s.35 and Sch.15 inserting CTA 2009 Chapter 6A ss.1040A–1040Y from April 1, 2013, see para.15–034 et seq. The ATL system will run alongside the super-deduction system until April 1, 2016. For sub-contracted work, large companies may not claim R&D credit except where the work was sub-contracted to a qualifying body under CTA 2009 s.1142, i.e. universities and other higher education institutions, charities, scientific research organisations, health service bodies; and individuals or partnerships of individuals. A large company may claim R&D tax relief for work sub-contracted to it, except where the work is sub-contracted by an SME claiming the SME R&D tax credits of 225 per cent. Conversely, where a large company sub-contracts R&D work to an SME, it cannot claim any SME R&D relief or credit; but the SME may be able to claim the large company R&D relief of 130 per cent (or 125 per cent for expenditure prior to August 1, 2008). The detailed rules are explained below (CIRD 82I75).

QUALIFYING R&D EXPENDITURE

15–026 Large companies, i.e. those that are not SMEs, CTA 2009 s.1122, throughout the accounting period, may claim relief under CTA 2009 s.1074 for qualifying R&D expenditure as defined by CTA 2009 s.1076 (CIRD 82200) as follows:

- expenditure incurred on in-house direct research and development, i.e. staffing costs, software or consumable stores, externally provided workers or relevant payments to subjects of a clinical trial CTA 2009 s.1077;
- qualifying expenditure on contracted out research and development, CTA 2009 s.1078;
- contributions to independent research and development, CTA 2009 s.1079;
- the expenditure must not be of a capital nature; and
- if the expenditure is incurred on activities sub-contracted to a large company then they must be contracted out by a large company or by any person otherwise than in the course of a trade, profession or vocation chargeable to income tax under ITTOIA 2005 Pt 2 Ch.2 (for income tax purposes with effect for 2005/06 and later years) (CTA 2009 s.1077 (CIRD 82205)).

Qualifying expenditure on sub-contracted research and development by a large company under CTA 2009 s.1078 arises where the following conditions are satisfied:

(a) the expenditure is incurred on making payments to a qualifying body, an individual or a partnership of individuals in respect of R&D sub-contracted to them;
(b) the sub-contracted R&D is directly undertaken on behalf of the company by the sub-contractor;
(c) expenditure is attributable to relevant R&D of the large company; and
(d) if the R&D was contracted out to the large company (before then being contracted out to another body), the original contracting out was by another large company, or a person otherwise than in the course of the trade, profession or vocation the profits of which are chargeable to corporation tax under CTA 2009 ss.35–45 or income tax under ITTOIA 2005 Pt 2 Ch.2 (CTA 2009 s.1078 (CIRD 82210)).

Payments to participants in clinical trials by a large company represents qualifying expenditure on R&D under CTA 2009 s.1077 in respect of expenditure incurred on or after April 1, 2006.

Contribution to independent research or development projects also qualify for relief where the following conditions are satisfied:

(a) the contributions are made to a qualifying body, individual or partnership of individuals for the purpose of funding R&D carried on by the recipient;
(b) it is expenditure on relevant R&D in relation to the company;
(c) the R&D is not contracted out to the recipient by another person;
(d) if the recipient is an individual that individual is not connected with the company; and
(e) if the recipient is a partnership, the company is not connected with any members of the partnership at the time the payment is made under CTA 2009 s.1079 (CIRD 82215)). Any connection is by reference to voting control in ITA 2008 s.993, CTA 2009 s.1316, or CTA 2010 s.1122.

THE RELIEF

15–027 The relief is 130 per cent of a company's qualifying expenditure on R&D in the qualifying period where the appropriate claim has been made (CTA 2009 s.1074 (CIRD 82250)). There are special provisions for giving relief to insurance companies in CTA 2009 ss.1080, 1081, which are outside the scope of this book (CIRD 82300). Intra-group R&D expenditure which is contracted out by Company A to Company B is treated as R&D directly undertaken by B, and where B makes a payment to a third party C for such activities it is treated as R&D contracted out by B to C (CTA 2009 s.1082 (CIRD 82350)). The group relief definition of group, in CTA 2010 s.152, is used for these provisions (CTA 2009 s.1082(2)(3)). Qualifying expenditure on sub-contracted R&D for contributions to independent R&D which is subsequently refunded is subject to recovery of the appropriate amount, being 30 per cent of the amount refunded, to claw back the relief originally granted (CTA 2009 s.1083 (CIRD 82400)). Artificially inflated claims for deduction are disregarded where one of the main objects is to enable large company R&D relief to be obtained which would not otherwise be available (CTA 2009 s.1084 (CIRD 82450)).

DEFINITIONS

15–028 The meaning of relevant research and development, staffing costs and software or consumable items for SME R&D relief in CTA 2009 ss.1042, 1123–1126, are imported directly into large company R&D relief by CTA 2009 s.1127, 1128 (CIRD 84000, 84050). A qualifying body for the purposes of contributions to independent R&D include a charity, an institution of higher education, a scientific research organisation, a health service body or other body proscribed by statutory instrument (CTA 2009 s.1142). The relief is only available in respect of expenditure actually incurred on or after April 1, 2002 (CTA 2009 Sch.2 paras 113, 114 (CIRD 82150)).

VACCINE RESEARCH RELIEF

15–029 Vaccine research relief (VRR) is only available to large companies (CTA 2009 s.1172). From April 1, 2013, it is limited to expenditure on research and development of vaccines and medicines for the prevention and treatment of tuberculosis (TB), malaria, human immune-deficiency virus (HIV) and acquired immune-deficiency syndrome (AIDS) (CIRD 86100, 86200, 86300). The expenditure allowed for tax purposes is 40 per cent of the qualifying expenditure and is given in addition to large company R&D relief under CTA 2009 ss.1074–1084 available on the same expenditure. The relief required the approval of the European Commission as state aid and applied from April 22, 2003 (CTA 2009 Sch.2 para.115 and SI 2003/1472 (CIRD 85100)).

The additional relief is 40 per cent of the expenditure qualifying for relief, CTA 2009 s.1091(3) if it is deductible in calculating the profits of the company's trade. In all other cases, relief is given at the rate of 140 per cent CTA 2009 s.1091(4). The relief is available in addition to the R&D relief for a large company (CTA 2008 ss.1087, 1091 (CIRD 85700)).

CAP ON RELIEF

15–030 A cap on the amount of aid companies can receive for a single project vaccine research relief scheme was introduced by FA 2008 Sch.10. The cap is €7.5million but may be varied by Treasury order. The introduction of the cap is intended to ensure that the SME R&D and vaccine research relief continues to comply with EC state aid requirements, and applies from August 1, 2008, CTA 2009 ss.1113–1118.

RESEARCH AND DEVELOPMENT

QUALIFYING EXPENDITURE

15–031 Qualifying vaccine research expenditure ("qualifying Chapter 7 expenditure") may be on direct R&D, sub-contracted R&D or independent R&D, CTA 2009 ss.1101, 1102. Qualifying expenditure on contributions to independent R&D for an accounting period is expenditure incurred on contributions paid in that period (CTA 2009 ss.1098–1102 (CIRD 85200)). Qualifying expenditure on direct R&D must be unsubsidised and of a revenue nature, and must be on qualifying relevant R&D directly undertaken by the company. In addition, the expenditure must be incurred on staffing costs or software or consumable items, and the R&D activities must not have been contracted out by another person to that company (CTA 2009 s.1101 (CIRD 85300)). The Treasury may make provisions by statutory instrument for further defining qualifying R&D for vaccine research relief (CTA 2009 s.1086 (CIRD 86000)). "Qualifying staffing costs", "software or consumable items", etc. are all defined by reference to CTA 2007 s.1101, in CTA 2009 ss.1086, 1123–1127, 1132, 1138, 1140.

R&D EXPENDITURE CREDITS UNDER THE LARGE COMPANY SCHEME

15–032 The R&D above the line (ATL) credit has been introduced and applies to qualifying R&D expenditure incurred from April 1, 2013. It is aimed at large companies, but will also be relevant to SMEs where, for example, R&D work has been sub-contracted out to them by a large company. The reason for its introduction is that it will be visible in the statutory accounts of companies electing to use it, unlike the current super-deduction, which lowers the effective tax rate in the accounts, but is not obvious and requires users of the accounts to read the tax note to the accounts in full.

Also, the credit in the accounts is directly linked to the qualifying R&D work carried out, whereas the super-deduction is calculated either by a company's finance function or external advisors, so the decision makers in a business who are evaluating the performance of departments would not necessarily associate the cashflow benefit of the super-deduction to the R&D department.

The ATL credit will run alongside the existing 130 per cent super-deduction scheme for large companies such that companies will have a choice as to which scheme to use. However, once a company has elected into the ATL credit it cannot elect back out again. The ATL credit system will fully replace the super-deduction from April 1, 2016.

15–033 The legislation is by way of Chapter 6A inserted into CTA 2009. CTA 2009 s.104A allows a trading company to claim an R&D expenditure credit, initially equal to 10 per cent of qualifying expenditure (49 per cent for oil and gas ring-fenced trades). The credit will be treated as a taxable receipt in calculating the profits of the trade.

The definition of qualifying expenditure for large companies claiming under the ATL scheme is the same as for the super-deduction scheme as set out at para.15–027, above.

Crucially, the ATL credit is available to both profit making and loss making companies which is by contrast to the SME tax credit scheme which can only be used by loss making companies.

SMEs may also wish to use the ATL scheme where they have incurred R&D expenditure which does not qualify under the more generous SME scheme. There are three main situations where this might be relevant:

- expenditure on sub-contracted R&D;
- expenditure on subsidised R&D; and
- capped R&D expenditure.

SME's expenditure on sub-contracted R&D—ss.104C–104E

This is relevant where the SME is carrying on R&D work that was sub-contracted to it by a large company or any person otherwise than in the course of carrying on a chargeable trade. The SME can claim for qualifying expenditure either on work it has done in-house or on work done by other parties. If the latter, then payments must have been made by the SME to a qualifying body, individual or a firm consisting solely of individual members to which the R&D work has been contracted out. 15–034

SME's expenditure on subsidised qualifying expenditure—ss.104F–104H

This is relevant where the SME's expenditure has been subsidised, as explained at para.15–020, above. 15–035

Capped R&D expenditure—s.104I

This is relevant where a company has spent more than €7.5m on the project concerned (such that the excess over this amount is not eligible for the SME scheme). 15–036

AMOUNT AND PAYMENT OF CREDIT

CTA 2009 s.104M specifies that the R&D expenditure credit is 10 per cent except in the case of companies in the oil and gas industry carrying on a ring-fenced trade when it is 49 per cent, The Treasury may change the percentage together with other consequential amendments by Statutory Instrument. 15–037

The R&D expenditure credit is relieved against various liabilities in a set order under CTA 2009 s.140N. Only once all these possibilities have been exhausted can the credit be paid in cash to the company.

There is a restriction with reference to the PAYE and NIC liabilities of the company in respect of staff engaged in R&D activities. CTA 2009 s.104P defines the total amount of a company's PAYE and NIC as that which the company is required to pay under the PAYE regulations for the accounting period, disregarding child tax credit or working tax credit, and also for National

Insurance contributions, statutory sick pay and statutory maternity pay. Apportionment is applied where appropriate. Any surrender of credit to other group companies is computed in accordance with CTA 2009 s.104Q.

15–038 CTA 2009 s.104R allows the surrender of R&D expenditure credit to any relevant group member as an alternative to discharging a corporation tax liability for any subsequent accounting period. Surrender is not taken into account when computing the profits or losses for corporation tax of either company and is not treated as a distribution.

The going concern requirement in CTA 2009 s.104S is defined by s.104T and ceases to apply if the company becomes a going concern on or before the last day for amendment of the company's tax return under FA 1998 Sch.18 para.15. Payment for R&D credit may be withheld while enquiries into the company's tax return take place or if there are outstanding PAYE or NIC liabilities. The definition of "going concern" is based on the latest published accounts where there is nothing to indicate that this was only on the basis of an expectation that R&D expenditure credits were receivable. A company is not a going concern if it is in administration or liquidation.

INSURANCE COMPANIES AND GROUPS

15–039 Insurance companies are treated as large companies under CTA 2009 s.104U. The entitlement to R&D expenditure credits under the I minus E basis is explained in CTA 2009 s.104V. Group companies which contract out R&D expenditure to other group companies are treated as if the R&D was carried out by the contractee but such expenditure contracted out to a non-group company is treated as R&D expenditure of the contractor under CTA 2009 s.104W.

ANTI-AVOIDANCE AND INTERPRETATION

15–040 Arrangements wholly or mainly made for a disqualifying purpose are disregarded in computing relief for R&D expenditure credits under CTA 2009 s.104X. A disqualifying purpose is an arrangement where a main object is to obtain or increase an R&D expenditure credit to which it would not otherwise be entitled.

CTA 2009 s.104Y sets out the interpretation of the R&D expenditure credits, by reference to the existing R&D expenditure rules in CTA 2009 Pt 13, ss.1039–1142. Various terms are defined.

FA 2013 Sch.14 Pt 2 lists the various consequential amendments required by the introduction of R&D expenditure credits which take effect from April 1, 2013. The provisions relating to the abolition of the existing super-deduction reliefs for R&D sub-contracted to SMEs in CTA 2009 Pt 13 Chapter 2, subsidised and capped R&D expenditure in Pt 13 Chapter 4 and R&D relief for large companies in Pt 13 Chapter 5. Other amendments and repeals, apply from April 1, 2016, under para.28, subject to applying earlier, i.e. from the first day of the accounting period in respect of which R&D expenditure credits are claimed, under CTA 2009 s.104A (Pt 2 para.29).

TAX RELIEF FOR TELEVISION PRODUCTION AND VIDEO GAMES DEVELOPMENTS

FA 2013 Schs 16 and 17 introduce tax relief for television production and video games development both of which allow a surrenderable loss to be converted into a tax credit, not unlike the R&D expenditure credit, but are outside the scope of this book.   **15–041**

PART 3

INTELLECTUAL PROPERTY TAXATION

CHAPTER 16

Patents

INTRODUCTION

The rules set out in this chapter apply, except as regards royalties, to "existing assets" of companies, i.e. those acquired, or created or originally acquired or created by another group company, before April 1, 2002, CTA 2009 Pt 8 Ch.16 ss.880–900. They do not apply to intangible fixed assets of a company either created by the company, or acquired from non-related parties, on or after April 1, 2002. In the case of assets acquired from related parties these fall into the corporate intangible fixed assets regime if they had been created or acquired from unrelated parties by the vendor on or after April 1, 2002, all of which are dealt with under CTA 2009 Pt 8 Chs 1–16 and 18 ss.711–879 and 901–906 and Pt 9 ss.907–931 explained in Ch.21 of this book. They continue to apply to unincorporated businesses and to limited liability partnerships which are not affected by CTA 2009 Pts 8 and 9. The Patent Box rules are set out in Ch.22. Goodwill acquired in September 2003 from a group company was a pre-April 6, 2002 asset in *Greenbank Holidays Ltd v RCC* (2010) SFTD 1101 as was that acquired from a partnership in exchange for shares in *HSP Financial Planning v RCC* (2011) SFTD 436.

16–001

There is a considerable body of statute law relating to the taxation of income from patents, introducing profit averaging which replaced forward and backward spreading of the licensor's receipts, the taxation of capital receipts as income and capital allowances for the licensee. There are also provisions relating to the treatment of UK patents as annual payments under ITA 2007 s.848, except for individuals and other persons under ITA 2007 ss.448 and 499 and FA 2013 s.15, from December 5, 2012. This effectively amounts to a withholding tax for companies at the basic rate of tax on payments made to non-resident licensors, subject to double taxation relief. Patent rights are defined by CTA 2009 s.912(3) as the right to do or authorise the doing of anything which would, but for that right, be an infringement of a patent.

ANNUAL PAYMENTS—POST-APRIL 5, 2007—PRE-DECEMBER 5, 2011—INDIVIDUALS

16–002 Patents are frequently exploited by means of a royalty payment from the licensee to the licensor. Prior to April 6, 2007, UK patent royalties, unlike most copyright royalties, were either made out of profits or gains brought into charge to income tax under TA 1988 s.348(2)(a) or not out of profits or gains brought into charge to income tax under TA 1988 s.349(1)(b).

With effect from April 6, 2007, ITA 2007 abolished the distinction between patents made or not made out of profits or out of gains brought into charge to income tax.

Whether or not the payment is made wholly out of taxable income is irrelevant and the payer in all cases must deduct tax at the basic rate from qualifying annual payments and patent royalties or other sums paid prior to December 5, 2012, in respect of the use of patents under ITA 2007 s.898(1). A qualifying annual payment is defined at ITA 2007 s.899 and includes at s.899(3)(a)(ii), royalties from intellectual property within ITTOIA 2005 s.579. If the recipient is a company the payment must be a payment charged to income tax under ITA 2007 s.899(4)(a).

16–003 Instead of holding the tax deducted in charge on accounting for it to HMRC as was done under TA 1988 s.348 or s.349, the payer has to deduct tax at the basic rate and account for the tax so deducted through his self-assessment return (ITA 2007 s.900 (2) and (3)). He then obtains relief by deducting the gross amount of the payment at step 2 of his income tax self-assessment computation under ITA 2007 Pt 8 Ch.4 ss.447–452.

The duty to deduct tax from qualifying annual payments by individuals in ITA 2007 s.900(1), arises where the payment is made for genuine commercial reasons in connection with the individual's trade, profession or vocation. It applies to partners as sole traders. Relief for the gross amount of the payment is given under ITA 2007 s.448(2), where the payment is not otherwise deductible in calculating the individual's income from any source. The relief is limited to the individual's modified net income by ITA 2007 ss.448(4) and 1025. The modified net income is the person's net income under ITA 2007 s.23, calculated in accordance with steps 1 and 2 of that section, but ignoring certain items, e.g. non-qualifying income within ITA 2007 s.1026 such as distributions from UK companies, losses brought back from a subsequent year, reliefs for qualifying annual payments and the carry back of post-cessation receipts.

ITA 2007 s.449 gives corresponding relief for other persons such as companies or trusts required to deduct tax under ITA 2007 s.901 or in the case of patent royalties that are not within the definition of a qualifying annual payment in accordance with ITA 2007 s.903 if the payment is not deductible in calculating the person's income from any source.

16–004 Section 450 of ITA 2007 denies relief for annual payments and patent royalties that can only lawfully be paid out of capital or out of income that is exempt from income tax, although this is unlikely to apply to patent royalties. The gross amount of a qualifying annual payment or patent royalty is defined at ITA 2007 s.452 as the amount of the payment before deducting income tax as required by ITA 2007 ss.898–905.

Section 902 of ITA 2007 specifies that the applicable rate for deduction of tax at source is the basic rate for the tax year in which the payment is made, in the case of qualifying annual payments and patent royalties. Annex I of the Explanatory Notes on the Bill that became ITA 2007 explains the changes in the law. Change 81 sets out in some detail the fundamental change in approach which is designed to align the approach to patent royalties with that for annual payments.

PATENT ROYALTIES—POST-DECEMBER 5, 2012

FA 2013 s.15 repeals tax relief for individuals and other persons for patent royalties paid, with effect from December 5, 2012, other than those deductible as trading expenses, because their treatment as annual payments was being exploited for tax avoidance purposes, and ITA 2007 ss.2 and 24 are amended accordingly. 16–005

Patent royalty payments made by companies must be paid under deduction of tax whether paid for commercial reasons or not except in the case of personal representatives. Section 727 of ITTOIA 2005 exempts non-commercial annual payments made by individuals from deduction of tax.

The provisions relating to the deduction of tax from patent royalties in ITA 2007 s.903, exclude those which are qualifying annual payments or annual payments for dividends or non taxable consideration within ITA 2007 s.904.

A single payment for the use of a patent would not be an annual payment and therefore would not be a qualifying annual payment within ITA 2007 s.899 and the requirement to deduct tax at source arises under ITA 2007 s.903 if the payment arises in the United Kingdom. Tax is similarly collected in the case of an individual through his self assessment return (ITA 2007 s.903(5)). Where the payment is made by another person who is liable for income tax, such as a trustee, or personal representative, or non-resident company the tax is collected though the payer's self-assessment return provided that there is some modified net income within ITA 2007 s.1025, under ITA 2007 s.903(6). In other cases the deduction of tax is accounted for to HMRC under the CT61 procedure. If the payment is by a UK resident company to a non-UK resident person deduction of tax may be made at the relevant treaty rate or in accordance with the Interest and Royalties Directive, under ITA 2007 Pt 15 Ch.8 ss.911–917. 16–006

Section 905 of ITA 2007 confirms that an individual includes a Scottish partnership if at least one partner is an individual, notwithstanding the fact that under Scottish law a partnership is a separate legal entity.

The deduction of income tax at source also applies to the proceeds of a sale of patent rights by a non-resident if that person is chargeable to income tax under ITTOIA 2005 s.587 or corporation tax under CTA 2009 s.912 in respect of the sale.

Form R185

In order to keep track of the tax deductions on annual payments, ITA 2007 s.975 provides that the licensor can request, and indeed compel, the licensee to provide a statement in writing showing the gross amount of the payment, the amount of 16–007 tax deducted and the net amount paid. Such statements are usually given on Form R185 available on *http://www.hmrc.gov.uk/menus/otherforms.htm* [Accessed August 30, 2013].

Excess charges

16–008 In the case of a company making royalty payments on patents recognised for accounting purposes before April 1, 2002, in excess of its total income for the purposes of corporation tax, relief would not be available as a charge on income. To the extent that such payments are made wholly and exclusively for the purpose of a trade carried on by the company, such excess is treated as if it were a trading expense and carried forward against future income from the same trade under CTA 2010 s.45. Royalties recognised for accounting purposes on or after April 1, 2002 are allowed on an accruals basis as a trading expense under CTA 2009 s.896, and are therefore included in the calculation of the taxable profit or loss for the accounting period.

COMPANIES—DEDUCTION OF TAX AT TREATY RATE

16–009 ITA 2007 s.911 applies to a company paying a royalty from which it is normally required to deduct tax at the basic rate under ITA 2007 ss.898–910, under the corporate CT61 procedure governed by ITA 2007 ss.945–962, or by direct payment to HMRC of the tax deducted at source under ITA 2007 s.963. If the company reasonably believes that at the time the payment is made the payee is entitled to relief in respect of the payment under a double taxation agreement the company may deduct tax at the treaty rate, including a zero rate under ITA 2007 s.911(1)(c) and (2). If however it turns out that the payee was not entitled to treaty relief, as assumed by the payer, the requirement to account for tax at the basic rate remains the liability of the payer.

Under ITA 2007 s.912 HMRC may direct the payer to deduct tax at source. For these purposes "royalty" is defined by ITA 2007 s.913, and includes payments received as consideration for the use of, or the right to use, a copyright, patent, trademark, design, process or information and the proceeds of the sale of the whole or part of any patent rights. "Payee" is defined as the person beneficially entitled to the income in respect of which the payment is made, by ITA 2007 s.913(2).

COMPANIES PAYING GROSS UNDER DIRECTIVE

16–010 Under ITA 2007 s.914, where a company making a royalty payment which it reasonably believes is exempt from income tax under the EU Interest and Royalties Directive (2003/49) under ITTOIA 2005 s.758 but there is a duty to deduct tax under ITA 2007 ss.903 or 906, a company may make the payment without deducting tax; but if it turns out that the payee was not entitled to the protection of the Directive the payer has to pay over the income tax that should have been deducted under ITA 2007 s.914(2) and (3). Section 915 of ITA 2007 gives HMRC the power to make a direction to pay royalties under deduction of tax if it is not satisfied that ITTOIA 2005 s.758 applies, although this direction may be varied or revoked. If the payee is aware that it is not exempt under the EU Directive and it becomes aware that it is not entitled to the protection of the EU Directive, it must inform HMRC and the payer. HMRC may have difficulty in enforcing this particular provision in practice, where the payer is resident within any other territory of the European Union and may be unaware of this requirement.

Where the transfer pricing provisions apply under ITTOIA 2005 s.763 which limits the exemption available under the Interest and Royalties Directive to the arm's-length amount, the exemption from the requirement to deduct tax at the basic rate at source only applies to the arms-length amount in view of ITA 2007 s.917.

ITTOIA 2005 ss.757–767 enact the withholding tax exemption for interest and royalty payments under the EU Interest and Royalties Directive.

Section 757 of ITTOIA 2005 is the introductory section and ITTOIA 2005 s.758 sets out the conditions for making payments gross. The payer must be a UK company not a branch in another territory or a UK permanent establishment of an EU company. The payee must be an EU company but not its UK permanent establishment. The two companies have to be 25 per cent associates.

The payment is treated as made by a permanent establishment (PE) if it is tax deductible in the territory in which the PE is situated, ITTOIA 2005 s.759. The permanent establishment of an EU company is to be treated as the person beneficially entitled to the royalty if it has the right or use of information which is effectively connected with the permanent establishment and it represents taxable income of the PE, ITTOIA 2005 s.760.

Section 761 of ITTOIA 2005 defines 25 per cent associates as where one company holds 25 per cent of the capital or voting rights in the other or a third company holds directly 25 per cent or more of the capital or voting rights in each of the other two companies.

16–011

The transfer pricing provisions in TIOPA 2010 ss.131, 132 apply for companies in the same way as under ITTOIA 2005 s.763 under s.764. There is a general disapplication of the relief under the anti-avoidance provisions of ITTOIA 2005 s.765 which disapplies the Directive in relation to a payment of a royalty if it was the main purpose or one of the main purposes of any person concerned with the creation or assignment of the rights in respect of which the royalty is paid to take advantage of the withholding tax exemption under ITTOIA 2005 s.758 by means of that creation or assignment.

Various terms are defined by ITTOIA 2005 s.766. The Treasury may amend these provisions by statutory instrument under ITTOIA 2005 s.767.

16–012

Foreign patents

From April 6, 2007, ITA 2007 s.899(2) specifically defines a qualifying annual payment as one which arises in the United Kingdom. An overseas patent royalty would not be an annual payment arising in the United Kingdom. This is consistent with the previous treatment where references to patent royalties in ITA 2007 ss.847–849, 898–905 referred, in the view of HMRC, to royalties in respect

16–013

of a UK patent and not in respect of an overseas patent, (BIM 45965). This interpretation was confirmed by the Financial Institutions Division of the Inland Revenue, in a letter to the authors dated July 21, 1999 (ref: 505/JAF/A26), except that UK patent for these purposes includes a UK patent granted on an overseas application under the European Patent Convention.

It often happens that the licensor provides various back-up services together with a licence to exploit the patent such as the use of a trade name, if closely connected with the user of a patent, to have any improvement of the patent made by the licensor during the currency of the agreement and to receive advice or assistance as to how best to use the patent (*Paterson Engineering Co Ltd v Duff* (1943) 25 T.C. 43). In such cases the royalties would not have been pure income profit of the licensor and tax would not have to be deducted by the licensee prior to April 6, 2007. If no services were provided by the licensor, the royalties may well have been pure income profit.

Even if the royalty were an annual payment it must be assessable on the recipient under ITTOIA 2005 s.579, or for deduction of tax to be applicable, ITA 2007 s.899. The royalty would therefore need to stem from a UK source asset. The possible sources are the patent, the trade and the licensing agreement; probably in that order. Royalties from a foreign patent are unlikely to derive from a UK source asset, unless the source is not the patent itself but is more properly the trade from which the patent has derived or the licensing agreement. If there is no UK trade and no UK agreement, it is difficult to see how a UK source could be involved, and deduction of tax would not therefore be possible. It would not arise in the UK within ITA 2007 s.899(2).

Royalties received from foreign patents by a UK resident are assessed to tax as foreign income in accordance with the normal rules (see para.9–056, above). Foreign tax deducted will usually be creditable against any UK tax liability (see para.26–015, below).

Non-residents

16–014 A non-resident is liable to UK tax in respect of UK patent royalties as investment income arising in the United Kingdom, limited to the UK tax deducted at source under ITA 2007 ss.811(4)(a), 813(1)(b), 826(a), unless he was carrying on a trade, in which case he would be liable to UK tax on the whole of the profits unless relieved under a double taxation treaty. The payer would have to deduct tax at the basic rate unless the recipient applies to HMRC for the deduction of tax at a nil or reduced rate under a double taxation treaty (see paras 16–017 and 24–015, below). HMRC would then instruct the payer to pay royalties gross or to deduct tax only at a reduced rate, under the Double Taxation Relief (Taxes on Income) (General) Regulations (SI 1970/488).

It is interesting to note that UK patent royalties, paid by a non-resident, to a UK resident licensor would still be paid under deduction of tax at the basic rate and the non-resident should account for the tax so deducted to HMRC under ITA 2007 s.963. If the non-resident does not account for the tax so deducted to HMRC (and in practice he may not do so) HMRC must nonetheless give credit for the tax notionally deducted when assessing the UK resident licensor (*Stokes v Bennett* (1953) 34 T.C. 337; IM 3961), but only where it is evident from the documentation that the sum actually transmitted was the net sum and not the gross sum (*Hume v Asquith* (1968) 45 T.C. 251). In the absence of an appropriate treaty, courts are unlikely to enforce a foreign tax claim, cf. *Government of India v Taylor* [1955] A.C. 491. However, the United Kingdom signed the Council of Europe/OECD Convention on mutual assistance in tax matters on May 27, 2007 and introduced TA 2006 s.175, and the Recovery of Foreign Taxes Regulations 2007 (SI 2007/3507) and the EU Council Directive 2006/112 was given statutory force in the United Kingdom by SI 2007/3508. The Mutual Assistance Recovery Directive 2001/44 was introduced into UK law by FA 2002 s.134 and Sch.39 and amended by SI 2005/1499. Corresponding overseas legislation could enforce a UK tax claim under these treaties, or under information exchange agreements or other bilateral or multilateral agreements.

PATENT INCOME

See Ch.22 for details of the Patent Box Rules.   16–015

According to the former Inland Revenue, in its booklet *Patents and Income Tax*, No.490 (1964) (not since revised for the advent of corporation tax or capital gains tax), expenditure and receipts in respect of patents may be of either an income or a capital nature:

> "Royalties or other sums paid in respect of the user of a patent, a term that is regarded as covering broadly payments in respect of past user [i.e. continued use or enjoyment] or future limited user, restricted as to amount or quantity, where there is no acquisition of a defined portion of the property in the patent are treated as income. There are provisions enabling certain reliefs to be claimed by inventors and others in respect of patent income. Other payments in respect of patents (e.g., for outright acquisition; for exclusive user during the whole of the unexpired life; or for the future unlimited user within a defined area or for a term of years) are, in general, treated as capital. With certain exceptions, such payments qualify for Income Tax allowances in the hands of the payer and are taxed as income of the recipient."

This definition has not been replaced by the Revenue *Manuals* so far published but is supplemented by CA 75010 and 75020 and was restated at IM 3922 (also now obsolete) as:

> "the expression 'any royalty or other sum in respect of the user of a patent' in ICTA 1988 s.349(1) applies to income payments as distinct from capital payments (see *IRC v British Salmson Aero Engines Ltd* (1938) 22 T.C. 39 at pp.39 and 42). Whether a payment is of an income nature or a capital nature depends upon the particular facts of each case, including the contractual relationship between the parties. A lump sum payment in respect of the past user of a patent, or for the future user to a limited extent (that is, restricted to the amount or quantity), where there is no acquisition of a defined portion of the property in the patent but merely a personal right of user, should be regarded as an income payment."

Lump sum payments which are in respect of the acquisition of: 16–016

(a) a patent outright by assignment,
(b) the exclusive user of a patent for the whole of its unexpired life, and

(c) the future unlimited user of a patent for a term of years, should be regarded as capital payments.

The expression "exclusive user" should be taken as applicable to the sole right to use a patent for a particular country or countries. The expression "unlimited user" should be taken as applicable to the right to use a patent, without quantitative restriction, "for a particular country or countries."

CAA 2001 s.483 defines "income from patents" as:

(1) royalties or other sums paid in respect of the use of a patent;
(2) balancing charges under CAA 2001 Pt 8 ss.464–483; and
(3) receipts from sale of patent rights under ITTOIA 2005 ss.587, 593 or 594, or CTA 2009 ss.912 or 918.

Attempts to argue that the wording of the Letters Patent gave exemption to tax, not surprisingly, failed in *Kirke v IRC* (1944) 26 T.C. 208 and *Kirke v Good* (1955) 36 T.C. 309.

Trading income

16–017 In a number of cases it has been held that patent royalties received by a trading company constituted trading income rather than investment income. Such cases include: *IRC v Anglo American Asphalt Co Ltd* (1941) 29 T.C. 7; *IRC v Rolls-Royce Ltd (No.2)* (1944) 29 T.C. 137; *IRC v Desoutter Bros Ltd* (1945) 29 T.C. 155; and *IRC v Tootal Broadhurst Lee Co Ltd* (1949) 29 T.C. 352.

It has also been held that royalties receivable in respect of manufacturing in the United Kingdom under UK patents were income arising in the United Kingdom and therefore liable to UK tax (in the absence of any double tax treaty provisions to the contrary) (*International Combustion Ltd v IRC* (1932) 16 T.C. 532). The practical effect of this is that the income would be subject to UK income tax at the basic rate under ITA 2007 ss.899–905 unless the appropriate rate of withholding tax is reduced under the double taxation treaty between the United Kingdom and the country of residence of the licensor, or the EU Interest and Royalties Directive, 2003/49.

As income from annual payments is taxable on the recipient as investment income, the tax deducted at source, if any, exhausts the UK income tax liability of a non-resident or it is excluded income under ITA 2007 ss.811, 813, 826. This does not apply where the recipient is a non-resident trust with a UK resident beneficiary, current or prospective under ITA 2007 s.812 in which case it would be liable to the rate applicable to trusts under TA 1988 s.686 (45 per cent for 2013/14, *IRC v Regent Trust Co Ltd* [1980] S.T.C. 140), unless the UK beneficiary is a life tenant, who would be liable at the higher rates, if applicable (*Williams v Singer* (1920) 7 T.C. 387; *Archer-Shee v Baker* (1927) 11 T.C. 749), or a discretionary beneficiary to whom the income has been distributed who could also have a higher rate liability with a credit for the rate applicable to trusts if different under ITA 2007 ss.493, 899. Nor does the exclusion from tax in excess of the basic rate deducted at source apply to income from a trade carried on in the United Kingdom TIOPA 2010 Sch.6. In the case of a non-resident corporate licensor there would be no corporation tax liability in view of CTA 2009 ss.5 and 19 in the absence of a permanent establishment in the United Kingdom.

Investment income

Patent income could be received by a person not carrying on a trade and would be assessed as miscellaneous income for income tax purposes under ITTOIA 2005 ss.578 and following, and under CTA 2009 s.201(2) for corporation tax purposes.

16–018

The income tax provisions of ITTOIA 2005 ss.587–599 apply to a sale by an unincorporated UK resident or a non-UK resident seller of a UK patent, unless a non-UK resident company charged to corporation tax on profits of a permanent establishment in the United Kingdom, in which case the charge would be to corporation tax under CTA 2009 ss.912–915, as explained above. The profit from the sale of patent rights is the capital sum comprised in the proceeds of sale less deductible costs, i.e. the capital cost, if any, of the rights sold and any incidental expenses in connection with the sale as reduced by any amounts allowed in connection with an earlier sale, ITTOIA 2005 s.588. The person liable to tax is the seller under ITTOIA 2005 s.589.

The income tax spreading rules are contained in ITTOIA 2005 s.590 and as for corporation tax under CTA 2009 ss.914–918 one-sixth of the amount received is chargeable in the year in which the proceeds on the sale of the patent are received and a like amount in each of the next five years. The taxpayer may elect to pay tax on the entire proceeds of sale under ITTOIA 2005 s.590(3). If the proceeds of sale are received in instalments one-sixth of each instalment is taxed in the year of receipt and the balance over the next five years under s.590(4), again subject to an election to tax the whole of the instalment when received under s.590(5). Elections under this section must be made before the first anniversary of the normal self-assessment filing date for the tax year under s.590(6), (CA 75200, 75210).

Non-residents may elect for spreading under ITTOIA 2005 s.591, which covers proceeds of sale received in one sum, and ITTOIA 2005 s.592, which covers spreading by instalments for non-residents. The same spreading provisions apply as for residents except that the taxpayer has to elect into spreading instead of electing out of spreading. The election must be made before the first anniversary of the filing date for the year of assessment in which the proceeds or the instalments are received, and any repayments and assessments as necessary to give effect to the elections may be made (ITTOIA 2005 ss.591(3) and (4) and 592(3) and (4)). Where tax has been deducted at source, any tax overpaid is repaid under ITTOIA 2005 s.596 in view of ss.591(5) and 592(5) (CA 75230).

16–019

In the case of a death, where spreading applies under ITTOIA 2005 ss.590–592, the outstanding instalments are taxed in the year in which the seller dies under ITTOIA 2005 s.593(1). This is subject to an election to be made by the personal representatives on or before the first anniversary of the normal self-assessment filing date for the tax year in which the death occurs to re-spread the instalments over the lifetime tax years, i.e. the year in which the proceeds of sale were received and each of the tax years up to and including that in which the seller died. (ITTOIA 2005 s.593(2)(4)) (CA 75220).

PATENTS

Lump sum receipts treated as capital

16–020 As with know-how payments, dealt with in Ch.19, there have been a number of cases which considered whether lump sums paid to a licensor were correctly taxed as trading receipts or were capital.

In *IRC v British Salmson Aero Engines Ltd* (1938) 22 T.C. 29, a licence was obtained by a UK company to enable it to construct, use and sell Salmson aero engines. Article 2 of the agreement provided:

> "As consideration for the Licence thus granted to them the Licensees shall pay to the Constructors the sum of £25,000 payable as follows:-
> £15,000 on the signing of this agreement. £5,000 six months after the signing of this agreement. £5,000 twelve months after the signing of this agreement.
> There shall be paid in addition to the foregoing payments and as royalty £2,500 twelve months after the signing of this agreement, and a like sum each twelve months during the following nine years."

The taxpayer argued that the entire amount was a capital sum, whereas the Revenue argued that the entire amount was taxable as income, being a sum paid in respect of the user of a patent under what is now ITA 2007 s.903. In his judgment Sir Wilfrid Greene M.R. stated:

> "The first thing to notice about it is that it is not merely an agreement under which the English Company receives the right to use a patent: under this agreement the English Company is entitled to restrain the patentees themselves from exercising the patent in the territory, and it is entitled to call upon the patentees to take steps to prevent others exercising the invention within the territory. Now those rights are, to my mind, in essence different from the mere right of user. A licensee under a patent is a person who is put into such a position that the patentee disentitles himself to complain of what would otherwise have been an infringement. That is all a patent licence is. On the other hand where the patentee himself undertakes not to exercise the invention, that is something quite different: he is restraining himself by a covenant or contract from exercising his monopoly rights, and, further, if he undertakes to prevent others from infringing his monopoly rights, he is giving an undertaking which also in its nature is quite different from what is given by a patent licence, which, in effect, is an undertaking not to complain of what would otherwise have been an infringement."

16–021 The Court of Appeal supported the Special Commissioners' decision that the sums of £15,000, £5,000 and £5,000 represented instalments of a capital sum of £25,000, whereas (at 32):

> "As regards the ten further payments of £2,500, we hold that these payments are royalties or other sums paid in respect of the user of a patent."

A case where a lump sum paid for the future use of a patent was regarded as capital is that of *Desoutter Bros Ltd v JR Hanger & Co Ltd and Artificial Limb Makers Ltd* (1936) 15 A.T.C. 49, in which it was held that the payer was not entitled to deduct tax from an instalment of what was a capital sum as though it were a royalty for the user of a patent.

Similarly, in the case of *William John Jones v IRC* (1919) 7 T.C. 310, at 312 it is stated:

> "By Clause 2 of the Indenture the purchase money of £750 was to be paid as to £300 thereof as follows: £100 on the signing of the Agreement, £100 at the expiration of one year and £100 at the expiration of two years from the date thereof and as to the balance of £450 by a royalty of 5 per cent upon the invoiced price of all machines sold by the Purchasers until such royalty should have amounted to £450. In addition the Purchasers were to pay a further royalty to the Vendors of 10 per cent upon all sales of machines and parts thereof constructed under the said inventions for a period of ten years from the date of the Indenture computed on the invoice price."

The court held that the lump sum of £750 payable by instalments was capital, but that the further royalties of 10 per cent were patent royalties taxable as income.

In the Australian case of *Hallstroms Pty Ltd v Federal Commissioner of Taxation* [1946] H.C.A. 34; 72 Clr. 634, legal costs of resisting the extension by Electrolux Pty Ltd of its refrigeration patent was held to be an income expense but the dissenting judgment of Dixon J. which was that: **16–022**

> "what is an outgoing of capital and what is an outgoing on account of revenue depends on what the expenditure is calculated to effect from a practical and business point of view rather than upon the juristic classification of the legal rights, if any, secured, employed or exhausted in the process"

was approved by Lord Wilberforce in *Strick v Regent Oil Co Ltd* (1965) 43 T.C. 1, and would be likely to be regarded as capital in the view of HMRC (BIM 35045).

Keep out covenants

In *Murray v Imperial Chemical Industries Ltd* (1967) 44 T.C. 175, ICI Ltd granted exclusive licences or sub-licences to foreign companies in various countries for the manufacture of Terylene fibre. In each licence they covenanted that they would not themselves enter the market for that country. They covenanted to keep out of that country. In return for these keep out covenants they received considerable sums of money from the overseas company. At 211 Lord Denning M.R. stated: **16–023**

> "In these circumstances I do not think it would be correct to consider a 'keepout' covenant as a thing by itself. The essence of the transaction in each case is that ICI granted to the foreign company an exclusive licence to use the patents in the country concerned for the term of the patent, and in return received remuneration in the shape of:
>
> (1) a royalty on the net invoice value of products sold or utilised (this was for use of the master patents of CPA);
> (2) a royalty of a fixed sum payable each year (this was for use of the ancillary patents of ICI);
> (3) a lump sum payable by instalments over six years (this was said to be for the 'keep-out' covenant)."

Lord Denning made repeated reference to the fact that it was an exclusive licence and continued at 212:

> "Applying these criteria in the present case, it is quite clear that the royalties for the master CPA patents and the royalties for the ancillary ICI patents were revenue receipts. That is admitted. So far as the lump sum is concerned, I regard it as a capital receipt, even though it is payable by instalments. I am influenced by the facts:
>
> (1) that it is part payment for an exclusive licence, which is a capital asset;
> (2) that it is payable in any event irrespective of whether there is any user under the licence even if the licensees were not to use the patents at all, this sum would still be payable;
> (3) that it is agreed to be a capital sum payable by instalments, and not as an annuity or series of annual payments.
>
> In these circumstances I am quite satisfied that the lump sum was a capital receipt and ICI are not taxable upon it."

This was the decision of the Court of Appeal. Such keep out covenants might now be taxable as know-how under CTA 2009 ss.176–179 (see para.20–012).

16–024 In *Kirby v Thorn EMI Plc* [1987] S.T.C. 621, it was held by the Court of Appeal that a non-competition covenant by a parent company on the sale of shares in subsidiaries was not a disposal of an asset, except to the extent that it was a capital sum derived from the exploitation of goodwill within TCGA 1992 s.22. Purchas L.J. at 633 stated:

> "The right to trade in the marketplace is a right common to all, as has already been described by Nicholls, LJ. To suggest that it is an incorporeal right within TCGA 1992, s.21 is wholly unjustifiable within the basic concept of an acquisition of an asset with its accretion in value owing to changes in economic circumstances etc, over a period of inflation followed by disposal with a realisation of a chargeable gain. With respect to those who proposed it, I think that this was a fanciful submission and was rightly rejected both by the commissioners and by Knox, J."

In *Margerison v Tyresoles Ltd* (1942) 25 T.C. 59, the taxpayer agreed not to introduce another tyresoling plant or to canvass for orders within the licensee's prescribed territory. Although the company retained the right of tyresoling tyres sent direct to its own works by persons within the said territory for their own use, the lump sum payment by the company was regarded as being effectively a capital sum for an exclusive licence or covenant not to compete.

Lump sum receipts treated as income

16–025 The mere fact that patent royalties are payable in a lump sum does not mean that they are of necessity capital.

In *Constantinesco v R.* (1927) 11 T.C. 730, an inventor was awarded a lump sum after the First World War in respect of an interrupter gear for aircraft machine guns used during the war. It was held that the payment was taxable as income. In the words of Viscount Cave L.C., at 746:

> "The payment was made in respect of the use of the invention over a period of time. The claim put in was a claim as for royalty in respect of the successive uses of the invention. In the case of patented inventions it was the practice of the Commission,

as appears from their Report which has been cited on behalf of the Appellant, to take as a basis of their award a fair royalty as between a willing licensor and a willing licensee, and I have little doubt that that basis was accepted in the present case, subject, no doubt, to certain deductions. Lastly, the patent itself, that is the corpus of the patent, was not taken away from the Appellant and his partner but still remains in them. In view of all the facts I am satisfied that the sum awarded is to be treated as profits or gains, and annual profits or gains, within the meaning of the Income Tax Act."

A similar conclusion was arrived at in the case of *Mills v Jones* (1929) 14 T.C. 769, in respect of a lump sum awarded after the First World War to the inventor of the Mills Bomb. This was held to be a royalty taxed as income for the past use of the patented bombs, in spite of an attempt to differentiate it from the *Constantinesco* case, on the ground that the amount involved some future use of the Mills Bombs. It was argued that further manufacture was unlikely in view of the considerable stocks still left of the 75,132,000 lbs of such bombs produced during the First World War. This contention was doomed to failure when the Commissioners held that the amount of future use included in the payment was negligible.

In *IRC v Rustproof Metal Window Co Ltd* (1947) 29 T.C. 243, a non-exclusive licence was granted for the manufacture of not more than 75,000 ammunition boxes for a so-called capital sum of £3,000 and a royalty of 3d per box. Both the royalty per box and the £3,000 were held to be income. As Lord Greene M.R. stated at 271:

16–026

> "The fact that parties call the £3,000 a capital sum cannot make it a capital sum if it is not. The word 'capital' is a mere label attached to the £3,000 with an eye, no doubt, to tax considerations. The fact that the agreement separates the £3,000 from the royalties is nothing more than a drafting necessity having regard to the fact that the latter are based on the actual number of boxes treated with the process while the former is paid for the right to apply the process to any number of boxes up to 75,000.
>
> If a patentee negotiating with an intended licensee who wishes to obtain the right to manufacture up to a stated number of articles in accordance with the patent states his terms to be a lump sum down and a royalty of so much per article, I can see no reason why the mere division of the price into those two separate elements should by itself necessarily produce the result that the sum down must be regarded for tax purposes as a capital receipt. Such, however, is the argument, but I cannot accept it."

A complicated case involving lump sum payments was that of *Harry Ferguson (Motors) Ltd v IRC* (1951) 33 T.C. 15, in which it was argued that lump sums received by the company were for the sale of patents relating to a plough. This argument failed because, in the words of Lord MacDermott C.J. (at 44):

> "We think that on their true construction the agreements provided for the future exploitation of the plough as a commercial profit-earning enterprise and for a division of the profits of this enterprise between the parties until the Company's share of those profits had reached an agreed total."

As there was no outright sale it was not feasible to argue that the receipts were of capital.

16-027 In *Rees Roturbo Development Syndicate v Ducker* (1928) 13 T.C. 366, it was argued that the outright sale of patents for a lump sum gave rise to a capital receipt. On the facts of the case, however, the Commissioners found that the company's sole business was the exploitation of patents as part of its trade and that the profits on the sale of patents arose in the course of the company's business and were therefore taxable as income. This finding of the Commissioners was supported by the House of Lords.

Where the royalty was paid under a guarantee it was argued, unsuccessfully, in the case of *Wild v Ionides* (1925) 9 T.C. 392, that the payments amounting to £1,000 a month should be regarded as payments on account of a capital sum. As no evidence was produced which, in the view of Rowlatt J., supported this contention, it was doomed to failure and the receipt taxed as income.

Brandwood v Banker (1928) 14 T.C. 44, was a lovely little case where a manufacturer added to the sale consideration a sum which he referred to as "shop rights" which enabled the purchaser of his equipment to use it. He then claimed that these "shop rights" were an exclusive licence and as such a capital sum.

Ingenious though this argument may have been, it fell on deaf ears and the court held that the payments for "shop rights" had to be included with the payments for the machinery in the taxable receipts of the manufacturer's business.

TAXATION OF CAPITAL RECEIPTS AS INCOME

16-028 Although it is still necessary to decide whether a lump sum royalty is capital or income, for example, to see whether or not tax has to be deducted at source, the distinction is not in practice of paramount importance to the recipient, in view of CTA 2009 s.925(4), which defines for corporation tax purposes income from patents as:

(a) any royalty or other sum paid in respect of the user of a patent,
(b) any amount subject to tax as a sale of patent rights under CTA 2009 s.912, on winding up a company under CTA 2009 s.918, or on cessation of trade under CTA 2009 s.1272, or
(c) any amount on which tax is payable for any chargeable period by virtue of CAA 2001 s.472(5), or Sch.3 para.100 as balancing charges (see CA 75010, 75020, 75120 and 75200–75230).

The corresponding income tax provisions are in ITA 2007 s.910; ITTOIA 2005 s.587; and ITA 2007 s.910. CTA 2009 s.921 provides that the grant of a licence in respect of a patent is treated as a sale of part of the patent rights and that a licence granted by a person entitled to any patent rights for the whole of the remainder of the term of the patent is treated as a sale of the whole of the patent rights. The use of a patent by the Crown or similar use by a foreign government is treated as use under a licence, CTA 2009 s.923; CAA 2001 s.482 (CA 75030). The grant of a right to acquire all the future patent rights in an invention is treated as a sale of patent rights by CTA 2009 s.922 whether or not the patent is actually granted. A payment for limited user is treated as a royalty (CA 75410).

TAXATION OF CAPITAL RECEIPTS AS INCOME

ITA 2009 s.910 and CTA 2009 ss.926–931 apply the provisions of the CAA 2001 to patents and therefore an exchange of patent rights, for example for shares, is treated as a sale by CAA 2001 s.572(1)–(3), but the arm's-length price for connected person transactions in CAA 2001 ss.567–570 are excluded by CAA 2001 s.567(1) except for a disposal to which CAA 2001 s.481 (2) applies (see para.16–039, et seq.). CTA 2009 ss.912–915, provide that where a company resident in the United Kingdom sells worldwide patent rights for a capital sum, it is to be charged to tax on one-sixth of the amount received, less any allowable costs of acquisition (the disposal value, see para.16–039 et seq.), for the chargeable period in which it is received and a similar amount in each of the next five years. The net capital sum is therefore spread over the period of six years beginning with its receipt.

If a chargeable period in the period of spread is for less than 12 months the amount chargeable in that period is reduced proportionately. **16–029**

If the capital sum is payable in instalments, the first instalment is spread over the six-year period and any subsequent instalments over the remainder of the initial six-year period CTA 2009 s.915 (CA 75200–75210), subject to an election within two years of the period of receipt to be taxed on the amount of each instalment.

The recipient, under CTA 2009 s.914 and ITA 2007 s.910 may elect within two years of the end of the chargeable period in which the capital sum was received, for the whole of it to be subject to tax for the chargeable period in which it is actually received. This it might elect to do if, for example, it had allowable losses or if it anticipated that its income would be taxed at higher rates in future periods.

In the case of *Green v Brace* (1960) 39 T.C. 281, the vendor received a capital sum of £1,000 which he subsequently had to refund, with costs and damages on failure to deliver a satisfactory prototype. He was nonetheless held taxable on the original £1,000 received that was spread over six years under the provisions of what is now ITA 2007 s.910.

Non-residents: capital sums

If a non-resident sells UK patent rights for a capital sum it is taxed under ITA 2007 s.910 to income tax under ITTOIA 2005 s.587 or corporation tax under CTA 2009 s.912 (CA 75210) and the payer must, in the absence of a relevant double taxation agreement, deduct UK income tax at the basic rate on the whole of the proceeds (CA 75230). Where a treaty applies, a claim for deduction at the treaty rate may be made, or anticipated under ITA 2008 ss.911–913. The recipient of the capital sum will be taxed as to one-sixth in the year of receipt and a further one-sixth in each of the following years under ITTOIA 2005 s.590, CTA 2009 s.914 unless the taxpayer elects for the whole of the profit to be taxed in the accounting period of receipt, under ITTOIA 2005 s.509(3) or CTA 2009 s.914(4). This does not affect the payer's liability to deduct tax at the basic rate under ITA 2007 s.910. If one-sixth of the tax deducted results in an over-deduction of tax, compared with the recipient's eventual tax liability for each year on one-sixth of the income, the excess will be repaid on finalisation of the liability for the year. A **16–030**

UK patent is defined by CTA 2009 s.912(2), as a patent granted under the laws of the United Kingdom, and in HMRC's view includes a UK patent granted abroad under the European Patent Convention.

If the vendor, although a non-resident company, is within the charge to corporation tax, for example, through having a branch or agency in the United Kingdom, it may elect under CTA 2009 ss.916, 917, by written notice to HMRC not later than two years after the end of the accounting period in which the capital sum is received, for the sum to be treated as arising rateably in the accounting periods ending not later than six years from the beginning of that in which the amount is received, provided that it remains within the charge to corporation tax.

Where the seller is a non-UK resident liable to income tax on profits from the sale of the whole or part of any patent rights under ITTOIA 2005 s.587, income tax has to be deducted by the purchaser on the sale proceeds, ignoring the seller's cost which may be deductible under ITTOIA 2005 s.588. Income tax is deductible by the purchaser on the whole of the proceeds at the basic rate under ITA 2007 s.910.

16–031 Under ITTOIA 2005 s.597, the acquisition of a license in respect of a patent is treated as the purchase of patent rights and the grant of a license is a sale of patent rights. The grant of an exclusive license for the period remaining until the rights come to an end is regarded as a sale of the whole of those rights.

The sum paid to acquire future patent rights is treated as a purchase of the rights by the payer and a sale of the rights by the recipient. If the patent is granted the amount so paid is treated as expenditure on the purchase of the rights under ITTOIA 2005 s.598. Sections 599 of ITTOIA 2005 and CTA 2009 s.919 confirm that a payment by the Crown under PA 1977 ss.55–59, or by the Government of another country under corresponding provisions, is treated as paid under a license. If the receipt is from a UK Government department, tax will normally have been deducted at the basic rate (CA 75410).

The income tax deducted from patent royalties or capital sums is treated as income tax paid by the recipient under ITTOIA 2005 s.602. Section 603 of ITTOIA 2005 provides that where a person has incurred expenditure funded directly or indirectly by a public body or another person, he is not regarded as having incurred expenditure; unless the other person is not a public body, and is not able to claim relief either as a contribution for capital allowances purposes under CAA 2001 ss.537–543, or otherwise claim a deduction in calculating the profits of a trade or profession, the expenditure may be claimed as deductible by the contributee under ITTOIA 2005 s.604. A sale of patent rights includes the exchange of property under ITTOIA 2005 s.605. Any necessary apportionments, where property is sold together with other property, are to be made on a just and reasonable apportionment irrespective of any values put on the separate items of property by the parties (ITTOIA 2005 s.606). If two or more taxpayers are affected by the apportionment, the capital allowances provisions in CAA 2001 s.563(6) specifies what question is to be determined by the Tribunal. Section 608 of ITTOIA 2005 provides that capital expenditure, and capital sums, exclude any expenditure that may be deducted in calculating the profits or gains of a trade, profession or vocation or property business or from employment earnings.

TAXATION OF CAPITAL RECEIPTS AS INCOME

Costs of acquisition

Where a company in receipt of a capital sum from the sale of patent rights originally acquired those rights for a capital sum, it is liable to tax, only on the net proceeds, under CTA 2009 s.913. If it disposes of a further proportion of the rights purchased, any unrelieved balance of the original cost may be deducted but this does not affect the purchaser's duty to deduct basic rate income tax on the whole amount unless a double taxation treaty applies CTA 2009 s.919 (CA 75200, 75210).   **16–032**

Effect of winding up

Where a company which is in receipt of a capital sum from the sale of a patent which is being taxed in instalments under the provisions of CTA 2009 ss.912–917, 919, 920, is wound up, this crystallises the charge on the remaining instalments, which are deemed to be received in the chargeable period in which the winding up occurs CTA 2009 ss.918, 1271.   **16–033**

This also applies to a non-resident company within the charge to income tax under ITTOIA 2005 s.594.

Under CTA 2009 s.1271, if the recipient of the capital sum is a partnership it is treated as if it were a company being wound up, except that the additional assessment on the balance of the instalments is apportioned to the partners in their profit-sharing ratio immediately prior to the discontinuance, and if any part is apportioned to a deceased individual partner his personal representatives have the same rights to reallocation as if he were the sole recipient, as explained below.

Lump sum for previous use

ITA 2007 s.910 and CTA 2009 ss.912–920, deal with the spreading of a lump sum capital receipt for the future use of a patented invention. TA 1988 s.527(1), applies where a lump sum royalty or other payment is received for the prior use of a patented invention where the period covered by the use is a period of six complete years or more. In such cases the royalty would normally have been taxed as income and subject to the deduction at source rules under ITA 2007 s.975 (see para.16–007). The recipient may elect, apparently within the usual six years, to spread the income received and treat it as a royalty receivable in six equal instalments made at yearly intervals, the last of which was paid on the date on which the lump sum payment was in fact made (CA 75400, RE 2010).   **16–034**

ITA 2007 s.461 provides for a similar election to spread where the period of user is two complete years or more, but less than six complete years, and the period of spread is by reference to so many equal instalments as there are complete years comprised in the period of user.

The reallocation provisions do not extend to the non-resident recipient of a capital sum which is subject to deduction of tax at the basic rate at source by reason of ITA 2007 s.910 or CTA 2009 ss.912–920, as described above. It is interesting to consider whether such provisions could be defeated by the non-discrimination article in a double taxation treaty.

Conclusion

16–035   It will be seen from the foregoing that the whole of the proceeds from the exploitation of a patent will be taxable on the recipient as income whether the sale is for a capital sum or not, although the precise manner in which the calculation proceeds will depend on whether it is an income payment of a royalty or a capital payment apportioned over six years.

EXPENSES

16–036   Under ITTOIA 2005 ss.600, 601, for income tax purposes, a non-trader's expenses for patent fees may be claimed as expenses in the year in which they are incurred against patent income, any excess being carried forward, if they would have been allowable had he been carrying on a trade. An inventor may also claim the costs of devising his invention, if not otherwise allowable, under these provisions where a patent is actually granted (CA 75310).

ITTOIA 2005 s.89 for income tax purposes, allows as a trading expense the costs of patent applications in connection with a trade, whether successful or not, including expenses in connection with the grant or maintenance of a payment or the extension of the terms of a patent; these could otherwise be disallowed as giving rise to a capital asset (CA 75300). It seems that a non-domiciled inventor can claim the costs of worldwide patenting even though he may be assessed only on remittances of royalties from non-UK patents.

Expenses relating to claims before the Royal Commission on Awards to inventors for Crown user of a patent are allowable either under ITTOIA 2005 ss.600, 601, or as a trading expense under ITTOIA 2005 s.89, as appropriate (CA 75310). Expenses on improving or extending the scope of a patent are only allowable to the extent that they are normal expenses of a trade (RE 2001–2003).

Corresponding relief for corporation tax in relation to expenses incurred in respect of patent income is given by CTA 2009 ss.910, 924, 925 and for certain contributions incurred other than by public bodies not otherwise available for relief, CTA 2009 s.927.

CAPITAL ALLOWANCES

Licensee's capital payment

16–037   A licensee paying a royalty for the use of a patent will normally claim a deduction as an expense, but this relief is not available in respect of capital expenditure on the purchase of patent rights (CAA 2001 s.466 (CA 75030)).

Post-March 31, 1986 expenditure

16–038   The system for giving capital allowances for capital sums spent on the acquisition of patent rights was totally changed in respect of qualifying expenditure incurred on or after April 1, 1986 with the introduction of what is now CAA 2001 ss.464–477. The rate of writing-down allowance is 25 per cent a year under CAA 2001 s.472(1) on the excess of the qualifying expenditure on patent rights over the disposal value on any sales, reduced proportionately for an accounting period of less than 12 months or in the year of commencement or cessation of a non-incorporated business (CAA 2001 s.472(1)–(3)). No allowance is available unless a trade is being carried on (CAA 2001 ss.467–468) or the income from the exploitation of the rights is otherwise taxable (CAA 2001 ss.467, 469) (CA 75100). Expenditure incurred prior to the commencement of trading is deemed to be incurred on the first day of trading (CAA 2001 s.468(3)) unless it had been on-sold prior to commencement. There are separate pools for each trade and for qualifying non-trade expenditure (CAA 2001 s.470).

There is a balancing charge if the disposal value of a patent exceeds the qualifying expenditure (CAA 2001 s.472(5) (CA 75110)). The qualifying expenditure for a chargeable period is the capital expenditure incurred on the purchase of patent rights during the period plus the written-down value brought forward in respect of an excess of qualifying expenditure over disposal value in earlier periods. In the words of CAA 2001, the available qualifying expenditure (AQE) (CAA 2001 ss.471, 473) allocated to the pool under CAA 2001 s.474, has to be reduced by the total of any disposal receipts (TDR) and unrelieved qualifying expenditure is the excess of AQE over TDR, less the writing down allowances, if any, claimed for the period (CAA 2001 s.475). The full writing down allowance may be reduced to a specified amount (CAA 2001 s.472 (4)), by making a reduced claim. A balancing charge is the TDR less AQE (CAA 2001 ss.471(3) and 472(5)) (CA75110, 75120, 75130).

Where the whole or any part of patent rights so acquired are sold, the disposal value is equal to the net sale proceeds, up to a maximum of the capital expenditure originally incurred (CAA 2001 ss.476, 477(1)). Any excess would be taxed as a capital receipt under the provisions of CTA 2009 ss.912–915 (see para.16–028, above). Where the patent rights have been transferred between connected persons within CTA 2009 s.839 (ITA 2007 ss.993, 994 for income tax) the capital expenditure referred to is that on the original acquisition of the rights if greater (CAA 2001 s.477(2), (3)). There is an overriding anti-avoidance provision in CAA 2001 s.481, where the purchaser and seller are connected within (ITA 2007 ss.993, 994 or CTA 2010 s.1122 onwards (CAA 2001 s.481(1)(2)) or it appears that the sole or main benefit from the transaction was to obtain a capital allowance (CAA 2001 s.481(1)(3)). Expenditure over and above the seller's disposal value is ignored in such circumstances. The disposal value is normally the net sale proceeds (CAA 2001 s.481(4)) or if the seller has no disposal value but receives a capital sum taxable under CTA 2009 ss.912–915 or ITTOIA 2005 s.587, that sum (CAA 2001 s.481(5)) or if neither of these applies, the smallest of the open market value, the capital expenditure on acquiring the rights or a connected party's acquisition costs (CAA 2001 s.481(6)).

A balancing allowance is given on any unallowed expenditure on the permanent discontinuance of the trade (CAA 2001 ss.472(6), 471(4) and (5)) or when the relevant patent rights come to an end without being revived (CAA 2001 s.471(6)), i.e. those rights acquired for a capital sum but not relieved as qualifying expenditure (CA 75210). Capital allowances are given either against the profits of the trade under CAA 2001 s.478, or against patent income under

CTA 2009 s.924 (CA 75130), for income tax under CAA 2001 s.479, and corporation tax under CAA 2001 s.480, with any excess expenditure carried forward against profits of the following period. Balancing charges are taxed as income of the individual or company respectively (CAA 2001 ss.479(4), 480(4)).

EMPLOYEE AWARDS

16–039   It is interesting to consider the tax liability of an employee in receipt of an award under PA 1977 ss.40–42.

In normal circumstances an inventor who is employed by a company to invent would be rewarded by a salary, possibly with bonuses, commissions, fringe benefits and other perquisites, all dealt with under the rules relating to employment income.

However, it is possible to apply to the court under PA 1977 s.40 (App.2), which provides for an additional payment to be made by the employer to the employee where his work has given rise to a patent of outstanding benefit to the employer. The court may award some further payment to the employee if it considers that the patent is "of outstanding benefit to the employer and that by reason of those facts it is just that the employee should be awarded compensation to be paid by the employer, the court or the comptroller may award him such compensation of an amount determined under section 41 below".

16–040   It is likely that such an award would take the form of a lump sum payment and it is quite likely that employers might make such a further lump sum, over and above the remuneration already paid, by way of out of court settlement.

It is fundamental to such a claim that the patent must be of outstanding benefit to the employer. It is not the work of the inventor that needs to be of outstanding benefit, but the patent resulting therefrom, which may or may not be directly related. On the assumption that the employee is employed to invent and has been properly remunerated, it could presumably be argued that the additional payment, arising as it does from the patent itself, which is the company's property, is not directly related to the employment, the duties of which have already been remunerated. Under Patent Act 1977 s.40(2)(d) "it is just that the employee should be awarded compensation to be paid by the employer in addition to the benefit derived from the relevant contract".

It is therefore not taxable as employment income and it is not taxable as patent income as it does not arise from the patent itself.

16–041   A claimant received a compensation payment under s.40(1) of the Patents Act 1977 following litigation reported as *JD Kelly v GE Healthcare Ltd* (2009) EWHC 181(Pat).

In this case Duncan Kelly and Ray Chiu made inventions for which patents were filed in 1987/88. The patents belonged to their employer, Amersham Plc (which was later acquired by GE Healthcare). The inventions gave rise to a blockbuster product (Myoview) that was developed and sold by Amersham/GE. The employer had no scheme that provided any award for employee inventions. DK and RC (plus another) first wrote to their employer claiming compensation for outstanding benefit from the patents under s.40(1) of the 1977 Patents Act. The employer denied outstanding benefit, so DK and RC began legal action. The third employee inventor declined to join the action. The employees did not claim at any point any inadequacy in their remuneration. The employer continued to deny outstanding benefit throughout. It made two offers to settle, the better of those barely covering the applicants' costs.

In a High court judgement of February 11, 2009, DK and RC won their claim. They were awarded £1m and £500k respectively. The entire amount was paid out by the employer, without any deductions. The court ruled that neither offer by the employer was "relevant". In other words, the applicants could not have secured an amount that was fair compensation except by court action. The award was in the form of a single lump sum, as a "once and for all" payment. The Act provides for the possibility or for "periodic payments". The award was not linked to salaries, but was determined as a notional (3 per cent) share of the patent.

In the judgment, Mr Justice Floyd stated:

Paragraph 19:

"... the rationale for the use of the word outstanding (in PA 1977 s.40) was that the employee had already been compensated for the invention through remuneration for his employment.

It must be something out of the ordinary and not such as one would normally expect to arise from the results of duties that employee is paid for..."

Paragraph 23:

"it is the benefit of the patent which must be outstanding, rather than the benefit of the invention or the benefit of sales of products made in accordance with the invention...

the notion of outstanding benefit has nothing to do with how inventive the employee was..."

Paragraph 53:

"It would be a little surprising therefore if establishing inadequate remuneration, or efforts beyond the call of duty were threshold requirements of obtaining any award under section 40."

Paragraph 179:

"There is no suggestion that either employee was paid above or below industry rates for doing the sort of work which he did."

Paragraph 202:

"... the employee's share of the value of a patent might in principle lie somewhere in the broad range from nil to as much as 33% or beyond. In the present case I think the employee's share lies towards the bottom of the scale, having regard to the factors which I have considered at length above. I have taken a very conservative figure for the valuation of the benefit. Taking the same approach to the share of the benefit, I consider that 3% of the value of the benefit represents a just and fair award to the employee claimants"...

Paragraph 203:

16–042

"Dr Kelly should receive 2% and Dr Chiu 1% of the £50 million figure I have taken as the value of the patents."

Paragraph 204:

"These combined figures represent about 0.1% of turnover. I am confident that none of the comparators show this figure to be unreasonable. Whilst it is far from perfect, the closest comparable is the Goldman licence. The lowest figure in the Goldman licence was 0.25% of turnover. Standing back, and looking at these sums in the light of all evidence I have heard, I consider them to be just and fair. It represents about three days' of the profits from Myoview at current rates."

Paragraph 205:

"Whilst I have had in mind the fact that the context of the award is employment, I have not thought it right to limit the award by reference to one year's salary, The benefit to Amersham has extended well beyond a single year."

Paragraph 206:

"Although the Act contemplates that the employee can make more than one application, I was invited to make a once and for all award, which is what I have done."

In these circumstances it appears that the compensation awarded falls within TCGA 1992 s.51(2) which states that:

"It is hereby declared that sums obtained by way of compensation or damages for any wrong or injury suffered by an individual in his person or in his profession or vocation are not chargeable gains."

Such awards are therefore not subject to tax.

In the vast majority of cases it is likely that the employee who produces a patent of outstanding benefit to the employer is an employee of considerable talent and the employer in most cases will see that the employee is properly remunerated, in view of his worth to the company, and such remuneration would be dealt with under the normal provisions relating to employment income. It is therefore likely to be only the exceptional cases that have to be considered for an award under the provisions of the PA 1977 ss.40–42.

ENTERPRISE INVESTMENT SCHEME: ROLL-OVER RELIEF ON REINVESTMENT AND VENTURE CAPITAL TRUSTS

16–043 A research and development trade is not excluded from the Enterprise Investment Scheme merely because its income arises from royalties (ITA 2007 s.195) where the company created the intellectual property and has the right to exploit it. A similar exemption from exclusion applies for roll-over relief on reinvestment under TCGA 1992 ss.150A, 150C, Sch.5B; and for venture capital trusts under ITA 2007 s.306.

CAPITAL GAINS TAX

Intellectual property such as patent rights, represent property which can be transferred and can in certain circumstances result in a chargeable capital gain or an allowable capital loss. This would be subject to the normal capital gains tax provisions, summarised in Ch.9 (see paras 9–055–9–066).

16–044

Intellectual property outside the corporate intangible fixed asset regime in CTA 2009 ss.711–931, Ch.22, does not qualify for rollover relief as it is not a relevant asset under TCGA 1992 s.155, except for know-how treated as goodwill (see para.19–010).

Such property could also qualify for holdover relief under TCGA 1992 s.165, on a gift or sale at undervalue of business assets by an individual. This relief is extended by TCGA 1992 s.260, subject to anti-avoidance rules, to gifts between UK resident individuals and into or out of UK settlements provided inheritance tax is chargeable on the transfer, albeit at the nil rate. Under these provisions the transferor and transferee can jointly elect for the transferee to take over the transferor's or transferee's base value. Where the transferee is a trustee, only the transferor need elect for the trustee transferee to take over his base value.

INHERITANCE TAX

A transfer other than by arm's-length sale under IHTA 1984 s.10, or in the course of business under IHTA 1984 s.12, could be a chargeable transfer for inheritance tax purposes equal to the reduction in the transferor's estate as a result of the transfer (IHTA 1984 s.3). It could be a potentially exempt transfer under IHTA 1984 s.3A, if inter vivos. Intellectual property could be part of a business disposed of for the purposes of business relief under IHTA 1984 ss.103–114, or could be part of the assets of a company where the disposal of shares qualifies for such relief.

16–045

There are no specific provisions relating to intellectual property as such, which means that the normal market value rules in IHTA 1984 s.160, apply to the valuation of patent rights, i.e. the price which they might reasonably be expected to fetch if sold in the open market. The value of patent right is normally calculated on the basis of the capitalised present value of its income-earning ability (see Ch.12).

STAMP DUTY

Stamp duty was abolished on instruments relating to intellectual property, executed on or after March 28, 2000 by TA 2000 s.129. Previously an exclusive non-revocable licence or assignment for consideration was subject to ad valorem duty as a conveyance on sale under the Stamp Act 1891 ss.59 and 62, but a revocable assignment or non-exclusive licence was not subject to duty (Sergeant and Sims, *Stamp Duties and Capital Duty and Capital Reserve Tax*).

16–046

VAT

Treatment of patents

16–047 Patent transactions are supplies of services for VAT purposes, as explained in Ch.11, by virtue of VATA 1994 s.5(2)(b):

> "anything which is not a supply of goods but is done for a consideration (including, if so done, the granting, assignment or surrender of any right) is a supply of services."

If, therefore, a UK-registered business grants a patent licence to another UK business in return for a royalty or lump sum, VAT at the standard rate is payable on the gross, pre-VAT amount even though the payer may deduct income tax at the basic rate on making the payment. This applies whether or not a royalty is described as a gross royalty from which tax is to be deducted by the payer, or as a free of tax or net royalty which has to be grossed up to arrive at the gross equivalent.

HMRC have been advised that tax due on an annual payment within ITA 2007 s.903 should be computed by reference to the full amount of the payment inclusive of VAT. However, no objection will be raised if the payer and recipient agree to make and accept a deduction of income tax calculated by reference to the net payment exclusive of VAT, subject to retaining the right to review the situation in the light of actual experience in the operation of VAT (IM 3900).

16–048 If the royalty paid by one UK business to another registered UK business is in connection with a foreign patent, VAT is still payable even though there may be no requirement to deduct income tax. VAT may not be payable if the licence was granted by a foreign branch as a result of the place of supply rules in VATA 1994 s.9 and this would apply to both UK and foreign patents.

For further information see Ch.11 (para.11–012).

CHAPTER 17

Trade and Service Marks and Designs

INTRODUCTION

The rules set out in this chapter apply, except as regards royalties, to "existing assets" of companies, i.e. those acquired, created or originally acquired or created by another group company, before April 1, 2002 (CTA 2009 ss.880–900). They do not apply to intangible fixed assets of a company either created by the company, or acquired from non-related parties, on or after April 1, 2002. In the case of assets acquired from related parties, these fall into the intangible fixed assets regime in CTA 2009 Pt 8 ss.711–906 if they have been created or acquired from unrelated parties by the vendor on or after April 1, 2002, all of which are dealt with in Ch.21. They continue to apply to unincorporated businesses and to limited liability partnerships which are not affected by CTA 2009 Pt 8.

17–001

Unlike patents and copyright there is practically no mention of trade marks, service marks and designs in the Taxes Acts. There are, therefore, except where CTA 2009 Pt 8 applies, no problems of capital being taxed as income, although conversely there are no capital allowances. Prior to April 6, 2007 there was normally no withholding tax in the United Kingdom on trade mark, service mark or design royalties, unless they were annual payments, or design royalties paid to a non-resident under ITA 2007 ss.906, 907, 909, see below. From April 6, 2007, if they are qualifying annual payments under ITA 2007, s.899, income tax has to be deducted from such royalties at the basic rate at the time of payment by the payer under ITA 2007 s.898. This applies if made by an individual, alone or in partnership for genuine commercial reasons in connection with the individual's trade, profession or vocation, under ITA 2007 s.900. Tax is collected through the payer's self-assessment (ITA 2007 s.900(3)). Where the payer is not an individual, tax is collected under ITA 200, ss.901, 902. In the case of a trustee payer, the tax is collected through self-assessment under ITA 2007 ss.963 and 964. If the payer is a company, the tax is collected through the CT61 procedure under ITA 2007 ss.945–962.

It may be commercially advantageous to attach a high value to trade marks and service marks as their life is indefinite. However, it should be noted that unregistered, as opposed to registered trade marks, cannot be assigned "in gross" independently from the underlying business and goodwill to which it relates, see para.12–027.

INCOME

17-002 Prior to April 6, 2005 there was no specific tax legislation dealing with income from trade marks, service marks and designs. From April 6, 2005, ITTOIA 2005 s.579 includes trademarks, service marks and designs as intellectual property. Where royalties are received by a business from exploiting a product which is protected by trade marks, service marks, registered designs or design rights, the income would be a trading receipt in the normal course of business included in the profits taxable under ITTOIA 2005 s.57, see *Orchard Wine & Spirit Co v Loynes* (1952) 33 T.C. 97.

Averaging

17-003 Amounts actually receivable after April 5, 2001 are subject to averaging under ITTOIA 2005 ss.221–225 for 2000/01 and subsequent years of assessment). The averaging scheme is based on that applicable to farmers ITTOIA 2005 ss.221–225. It enables an individual to make a claim for averaging if his profits from a qualifying trade, profession or vocation fluctuate from one year to the next (ITTOIA 2005 s.221(1)). The profits must be assessable as trading or professional income under ITTOIA 2005 ss.5–8, and arise from creative works, i.e. literary, dramatic, musical or artistic works on designs created by the taxpayer, or in a partnership by one or more of the partners, personally (ITTOIA 2005 ss.221(2) and (3)).

A claim may be made where for two consecutive years the relevant profits of one year, before loss relief, are less than 75 per cent of the profits of the other, or either year shows a nil profit, which includes a loss (ITTOIA 2005 ss.221(1) and (4) and 224(3)).

Where the profits of one year amount to less than 70 per cent of the profits of the other, the profits of the two years are averaged, i.e. the aggregate for each year is half the combined profits for the two years (ITTOIA 2005 ss.223(1)).

17-004 If the profits of one year are between 70 per cent and 75 per cent of the profits of the other a marginal relief applies. An adjustment is calculated by applying the formula:

(D x 3) – (P x 0.75)

Where D is the difference between the profits for the two years and P is the profits of the higher year. This adjustment is added to the profits of the lower year and deducted from the profits of the higher year (ITTOIA 2005 ss.223(4), 224(1).

Example

A designer has taxable profits for 2011/12 and 2012/13 of £10,000 and £7,200 respectively.

The adjustment is:

(£10,000 – £7,200) £2,800 x 3 — (£10,000 x 0.75)

i.e. £8,400 – £7,500 = £900

the profits of 2011/12 become:

£10,000 − £900 = £9,100

and for 2012/13

£7,200 + £900 = £8,300

The claim must be made by January 31, following the anniversary of the end of the later year, i.e. for a 2011/12 and 2012/13 claim by January 31, 2015 (ITTOIA 2005 ss.222 (5) and (6)).

Claims must be made sequentially, with earlier years claimed before later years because it is the adjusted averaged profit for each year that is averaged with the next year if a further claim is made (ITTOIA 2005 s.222. A claim cannot be made for the year of commencement or cessation (ITTOIA 2005 s.222(4))).

The claim is given effect to the later of the two years, to avoid re-opening the self-assessment for the earlier year, and so is calculated in terms of tax as if the earlier year had been amended and credited as if it were an increased payment on account for the later year, under TMA 1970 s.59B(1)(b) and Sch.1B as amended by ITTOIA 2005 Sch.1 para.381. 17–005

A claim may enable other claims to be made for the earlier year which are income dependant, such as marginal age relief (ITTOIA 2005 s.224(4)(5)).

A subsequent adjustment to the profits, for example, following an enquiry, cancels the averaging adjustment but may enable a revised adjustment to be made (ITTOIA 2005 s.225(4)). Various terms are defined in ITTOIA 2005 s.224(5) and Sch.1 para.381, amending TMA 1970 Sch.1B.

INVESTMENT INCOME

Trade marks, service marks, registered designs and design rights could be held as an investment other than by a business. In such cases the income is likely to be assessable as receipts from intellectual property under ITTOIA 2005 s.579. 17–006

EXPENSES

It is specifically provided under ITTOIA 2005 s.90 that the fees or expenses incurred in the registration of a design or a trade mark (which, under the Trade Marks Act 1994 as amended, would include a service mark, or in an extension of the period of copyright in a design or a renewal of the registration of a trade mark) may be treated as a trading expense, in spite of the fact that it may give rise to a capital asset which could otherwise be disallowed under ITTOIA 2005 s.33. 17–007

ROYALTIES

Prior to April 6, 2007, a licence agreement for the use of a design, service mark or trade mark would normally be for a fee or for a recurring royalty which would be taxable as a trading receipt of a business. If on the other hand a royalty is paid for the use of a trade mark, service mark or design where no services are performed 17–008 by the licensor it could (if from a UK source) be assessed on the recipient as pure income profit and therefore regarded as an annual payment of the payer and be subject to deduction of tax under the provisions of ITTOIA 2005 s.579 in the same way as patent royalties (as discussed under foreign patents at para.16–013, above). These provisions apply in respect of a United Kingdom or foreign trade mark or design whether the licensor is resident or non-resident. From April 6, 2007, ITA 2007 ss.898–902, make qualifying annual payments, which include such royalties, subject to deduction of basic rate tax at source.

In the particular instance of design rights and registered designs, royalties paid to an owner whose usual place of abode is outside the United Kingdom, must be subjected to deduction of basic rate tax at source as if they were annual payments, under ITA 2007 ss.906–909. The owner of the rights includes a recipient who whilst entitled to royalties has assigned the design or registered design right (ITA 2007 s.908(2)).

An agent making the payment is entitled to reduce the amount of royalty liable to deduction of tax by any commission to which he is entitled for services rendered (ITA 2007 s.908(1). If the commission is unknown, deduction of tax applies to the full royalty, but the agent may later claim a repayment of tax deducted (to be passed on to the royalty recipient) on proof of any commission charged (ITA 2007 s.908(2)).

The time of making the payment was, prior to April 6, 2007, defined as being the time when the royalty payment originates, and not when an agent makes the payment to the overseas recipient. Change 138 Annex I to ITA 2007 incorporated into ITA 2007 ss.900–903 makes the tax rate that in force at the time of payment. These provisions are analogous to ITA 2007 s.906 applicable to copyright royalties and are treated similarly under ITA 2007 ss.906–909. Further commentary may be found at paras 18–019 to 18–022.

LUMP SUMS

17–009 If the business consists solely of the exploitation of a trade mark or design which is sold for a lump sum, this amount would be capital as being for the total loss of the sub-stratum of the business: see Slesser L.J. in *Handley Page v Butterworth* (1935) 19 T.C. 328, at 359. It also seems from the same case that an outright sale of one of several designs, service marks or trade marks would be a capital receipt if the capital asset thereupon ceased to be owned (per Romer L.J. at 360). If it were a lump sum for a mere licence it would normally be taxed as income but could conceivably be a partial disposal of a capital asset. A disposal or part-disposal taxed as a capital receipt would be subject to assessment as a chargeable gain under TCGA 1992 s.21. A mere disposal of a trade mark or design for a single product among many is unlikely to be a capital receipt (*Orchard Wine & Spirit Co v Loynes* (1952) 33 T.C. 97).

Similar provisions would apply to an unregistered design, as in the case of *Handley Page v Butterworth* which related to the designs of the O-100, O-400 and V-1500 aircraft which were incapable of being registered as designs.

RELIEF TO PURCHASER

The purchaser of a trade mark, service mark or design, who is not himself the originator, may pay a lump sum for the use of the asset, or a royalty. A lump sum could be regarded as a capital expense rather than as a trading expense and as such would be disallowed under ITTOIA 2005 s.33. There are no provisions apart from under TA 2002 Schs 29 and 30 (see Ch.21) for giving tax relief for capital payments on the purchase of a trade mark, service mark or design and the cost could be taken account of only in a capital gains computation on a subsequent disposal. HMRC will, however, sometimes allow the acquisition costs of a trade mark, service mark or design with a limited commercial life, to be written off over a period as deferred revenue expenditure (see para.28–025). The distinction between deferred revenue expenditure and capital expenditure is vital, because if the expenditure is capital, i.e. being made not only once and for all, but with a view to bringing into existence an asset or advantage for the enduring benefit of the trade, no allowances are available (*Atherton v British Insulated and Helsby Cables Ltd* (1926) 10 T.C. 155). Vinelott J. in *RTZ Oil and Gas Ltd v Elliss* [1987] S.T.C. 512, at 541 stated:

17–010

> "It is elementary that although it may be necessary in order to give a true and fair view of the profits earned by a trade in a given year to make an allowance for the depreciation of a wasting asset on which capital has been expended no such allowance can be made in ascertaining the taxable profits for that year. The disallowance has always been founded in cases within Case 1 of Sch D on that part of rule 3 of the Rules applicable to that Case which is now reproduced (though modified so far as concerns the deduction of interest on capital) in ITTOIA 2005, s.33; (*see*, in particular, *Alianza Co Ltd v Bell* (1906) 5 T.C. 172)."

And at 546 Vinelott J. stated:

> "The legislature has not left the allowance of depreciation to be determined in accordance with accountancy principles and practice. Instead, it has imposed a general prohibition and has, since 1886, dealt with the question whether a depreciation allowance should be made in a particular case by a separate, detailed and frequently amended code. The question whether that code should not be further amended to permit the deduction claimed in the instant case is one which must be determined by the legislature and not by the court."

ROYALTIES PAID

If a royalty were paid for the use of the trade mark, service mark or design, it would normally be treated as a trading expense wholly and exclusively incurred for the purposes of the trade and therefore allowable under ITTOIA 2005 ss.25. If the royalty were paid under deduction of tax as an annual payment or under ITA 2007 ss.906–909, taxable on the licensor as income from intellectual property, it would be treated as a qualifying annual payment under ITA 2007 ss.898, 899, and deductible under ITA 2007 s.906, unless paid by a company in which case it

17–011

would be allowed on the accruals basis under the intangible fixed assets regime in CTA 2009 Pt 8 ss.711–906 for royalties recognised for accounting purposes on or after April 1, 2002, CTA 2009 s.896.

ITA 2007 in Annex 1 change 81 explains that TA 1988 s.387, is not rewritten because it is unnecessary in that *Gresham Life Assurance Society v Styles* (1892) 3 T.C. 185, shows that annual payments can give rise to a trading loss which can be dealt with in the same way as any other trading loss.

There have been no cases on the treatment of trade mark, service mark and design royalties as annual payments but the basic provisions seem analogous to royalties for secret processes and in *Delage v Nugget Polish Co Ltd* (1905) 21 T.L.R. 454, it was held that such royalties were annual payments subject to deduction of tax at source when taxable on the recipient. It is arguable that this case incorrectly attributed the royalties as arising from a UK source. Under the relevant law if the source were not UK, Sch.D, Case III would not have been in point, and deduction of tax at source would not be possible. Section 899 of ITA 2007 confirms that a qualifying annual payment has to arise in the United Kingdom for deduction at source to apply under ITA 2007 ss.900–902.

Royalties paid to 25 per cent associates within the EU may be paid gross under the EU Interest and Royalties Directives, ITTOIA 2005 ss.757–767. They may also be paid gross or at a reduced rate of withholding tax under double taxation agreements under ITA 2007 ss.911–917.

Design right royalties but not trade or service mark royalties paid to overseas settlors are subject to deduction of tax at source under ITA 2007 ss.906–909.

DEALING AND INVESTMENT

17–012 If the trade mark, service mark or design were purchased other than for the use in the buyer's trade, it could be acquired in the course of a trade of exploiting trade marks, service marks and designs. In this case, the sale proceeds less the cost would be taxed as a trading profit. No averaging under ITTOIA 2005 ss.221–225 would be available as the seller would not be the designer. Alternatively, the property may be held as an investment to exploit in return for royalties or licence fees which would be taxable income from intellectual property under ITTOIA 2005 ss.578–581, with expenses incurred in generating the income allowed under ITTOIA 2005 s.582.

In the latter case the complete assignment of the trade mark or design for a capital sum would give rise to a chargeable gain in the normal way.

STAMP DUTY

17–013 A trade mark or design is intellectual property in the same way as a patent and is, since March 28, 2000, exempt from Stamp Duty under TA 2000 s.129 (see Ch.25, below).

VAT

The VAT rules for the assignment or licence of trade marks and designs are exactly the same as for patents: see para.11–012, above. **17–014**

CHAPTER 18

Copyright

INTRODUCTION

The rules set out in this chapter apply, except as regards royalties, to "existing assets" of companies, i.e. those acquired, or created or originally acquired or created by another group company, before April 1, 2002, CTA 2009 ss.880–900. They do not apply to intangible fixed assets of a company either created by the company, or acquired from non-related parties, on or after April 1, 2002. In the case of assets acquired from related parties these fall into the corporate intangible fixed assets regime if they have been created or acquired from unrelated parties by the vendor on or after April 1, 2002, all of which are dealt with under CTA 2009 Pt 8 ss.711–906, see Ch.21. This chapter continues to apply to unincorporated businesses and to limited liability partnerships which are not affected by CTA 2009 Pt 8.

Over the years there has been a great deal of litigation on the taxation of copyright income and there are special provisions in the Taxes Acts relating to the spreading of income in certain cases. Copyright royalties, like UK patent royalties, are not automatically within the deduction of tax legislation (under ITA 2007 ss.898 and 903), but there is a limited withholding tax for copyright owners other than the author, whose usual place of abode is abroad and for qualifying annual payments made for commercial purposes, under ITA 2007 ss.906–910, 899–902 and ITTOIA 2005 ss.578–608.

The taxation of income deriving from copyright material depends to a large extent on the taxation position of the person entitled to the royalties. Although design right under CDPA 1988 Pt III is in many ways analogous to copyright, it is not within the definition of copyright for tax purposes and the taxation treatment is dealt with in Ch.17.

18–001

PROFESSIONAL INCOME

Income from the activities of a professional author, dramatist, composer, etc. are normally taxable as professional income in the same way as trading profits under ITTOIA 2005 ss.5–8 BIM. The manner in which copyright income becomes payable to the originator of the copyright material was considered in the leading cases of *Purchase v Stainer's Executors* (1951) 32 T.C. 367 and *Carson v Cheyney's Executor* (1958) 38 T.C. 240. In the *Cheyney* case, at 257, Viscount Simonds commented with regard to Peter Cheyney:

18–002

> "He was accordingly assessed during his lifetime under Case II of Sch.D in respect of the royalties so received by him after deducting therefrom all proper and allowable expenses of carrying on his profession. There is no doubt that he was rightly so assessed, and the learned Attorney-General very properly admitted that he could not lawfully have been assessed under any other Case or any other Schedule. It must be recorded also that he was consistently assessed upon a form of receipts basis, being credited with royalties upon the day when they fell due for payment, and no account being taken of the present value of royalties due at a future date".

This is the manner in which royalties are in practice normally assessed to tax on authors, composers and other producers of copyright material.

The point at issue in both *Purchase v Stainer's Executors* and *Carson v Cheyney's Executor* was that copyright continued after the death of the author, which gave rise to royalties which would nowadays be caught under the post-cessation receipts provisions of ITTOIA 2005 ss.241–259. Prior to the introduction of these provisions such income was tax free unless HMRC could show that the income arose from property, i.e. from the copyright itself and was therefore taxable under ITTOIA 2005, ss.578–582. This argument was decisively rejected in the House of Lords both with regard to the activities of Leslie Howard Stainer as an actor and film producer and for Peter Cheyney as an author. In *Carson v Cheyney's Executor*, at 260, Viscount Simonds said:

> "I doubt not that in a proper context royalties may be described as income of an investment, as in *IRC v Sangster* (1919) 12 T.C. 208, nor that, as in *Jarvis v Curtis Brown Ltd* (1929) 14 T.C. 744 copyright royalties may be merged in the receipts of a trade."

18–003 Lord Morton of Henryton stated (at 261) that so far as the author was concerned:

> "As Jenkins LJ, put it in delivering the judgment of the Court of Appeal [at p 254]: 'It',that is the copyright, 'was brought in to existence by his (Peter Cheyney's) professional activity in the writing of books and by nothing else, and it was just as much part of his profession to turn his literary labours to account by licensing the copyright he had created to publishers as it was to write the books in which the copyright subsisted.'
> If the sums in question had the quality of professional earnings during the author's lifetime, I cannot see that his death in any way changed their quality."

Lord Reid (at 264), commented:

> "I shall consider the present case on the footing ... that the sums assessed were instalments of fees payable under contracts obtained by Mr Cheyney in exploiting his copyright in books written by him by licensing publishers to publish or translate them. But I must add that even so there is an essential difference between that case and the case of a person who buys a copyright from the author and then proceeds to exploit it by granting licences to publishers. Where the author exploits his own copyright by granting licences to publishers, the fees which he receives are admittedly part of his professional earnings and are not taxable as annual payments under Case III, at least during his lifetime. But where the author sells his copyright, the price which he receives is part of his professional earnings and the fees which the purchaser gets from granting licences to publishers are from the beginning

taxable as annual payments to him irrespective of whether the author is still practising his profession. They are no part of the author's professional earnings."

Also, at 266, Lord Reid commented:

"To my mind, if a person receives as part of his remuneration an asset which yields income, that income is not the fruit of his professional activity any more than it would be if that person had received his remuneration in money and had then used that money to buy that asset. From the moment when the asset comes into his hands the source of any income which it yields is that asset and not his professional activities. There would be no question of the income falling under Case II during his life and then being taxable under some other Case after his death. The receipt by a professional man of income yielded by an asset which has been transferred to him is not a method of gaining professional income, whether or not the asset came to him as professional remuneration. But for an author exploitation of his copyright is a method of gaining professional income."

So far as the professional author is concerned, therefore, copyright royalties are taxed under ITTOIA 2005 ss.5–8 as income of the profession (BIM50705). In computing the taxable income the allowable deductions may include the reasonable expenses of producing the literary, etc. works and the expenses, including agents' commission, incurred in putting them on the market (BIM50720).

ACQUIRED COPYRIGHT ROYALTIES

18–004 The case of *Hume v Asquith* (1968) 45 T.C. 251 illustrates the difference between royalties which would have been treated as part of the author's professional income and royalties arising to third parties as a result of their ownership of copyrights. The case concerned the works of the late Sir James Barrie. The first set of royalties considered were royalties under agreements which had been entered into by Sir James Barrie during his own lifetime, which then passed by will to Lady Cynthia Asquith and by assignment to her son, Mr Asquith, the taxpayer in the case. Pennycuick J. confirmed the Commissioners' finding that these royalties were not taxable as they were post-cessation receipts of the profession, see para.18–005.

The second set of royalties were royalties under an agreement whereby Lady Cynthia Asquith assigned to Samuel French Ltd the sole and exclusive right of representation by amateur performers, as mentioned in the contract. As a result, these royalties were annual payments taxable on the recipient under ITTOIA 2005 ss.578–582 and should have been paid under deduction of tax under the provisions of what are now ITA 2007 ss.898–902.

Also considered in this case were contracts under which amounts were paid from an American company and it was held that these also arose from an agreement entered into by Lady Asquith as copyright owner and as a result the income was assessable under ITTOIA 2005 ss.578–582. Although the point was not decided in the case, as the agreement was with a foreign company apparently under a foreign contract, presumably the then Case V was the correct head of charge (BIM50725). A deduction is usually given for any agent's commission payable or other reasonable expenses incurred (BIM50720). Such income is not earned income of the acquirer.

POST-CESSATION RECEIPTS

18–005 It seems that an author who merely ceases to write is still assessed on professional income under ITTOIA 2005 ss.5–8 on royalties received, except in exceptional cases where there is a long gap between the physical cessation of writing and the republication of a work. In such cases the income could be taxed as a post-cessation receipt (BIM50740 and 80500 onwards). Similarly, income received after death by the author's executors would also be taxed as a post-cessation receipt. The author would usually have been assessed on a cash basis on royalties actually received and would therefore be assessed under ITTOIA 2005 ss.246(1) and 247(1) on post-cessation receipts. Such income would be treated as earned income, if received by the original author, in view of ITTOIA 2005 s.256(1)(b). Although the assessment is on post-cessation receipts, expenses are allowable as if the profession had continued, under ITTOIA s.254, BIM50740.

There are two important exemptions from the post-cessation receipt charge. Under ITTOIA 2005 s.243(4) sums received by a non-resident in respect of income arising directly or indirectly from outside the UK, e.g. on non-UK sales, are not taxed as post-cessation receipts. Under ITTOIA 2005 s.253(1) a lump sum paid to the personal representatives of an author, on assignment in whole or part of the copyright, is not taxed as a post-cessation receipt. There could be a capital gains tax charge on any excess of the sale proceeds over the probate value.

It is possible to elect under ITTOIA 2005 s.257 to carry back post-cessation receipts and tax them as if received on the last day of the accounting period ending with cessation. It is interesting to consider whether, if an author was non-resident at that time but subsequently returned to the United Kingdom, this could result in all future royalties being tax free, either as being deemed to arise when the author was not liable to UK tax, under ITTOIA 2005 s.257, or because in the year of discontinuance there was no profession charged to tax under ITTOIA 2005 ss.5–8 and therefore the provisions of ITTOIA 2005 ss.241–259 have no application.

There was an exemption under TA 1988 s.109, for part of the post-cessation receipts for an author born before April 6, 1917, engaged in his profession on March 18, 1968, which has been repealed as unnecessary by ITTOIA 2005 s.882.

POST-CESSATION EXPENSES

18–006 If post-cessation expenses, paid on or after November 29, 1994, and within seven years of discontinuance cannot be set against post-cessation receipts under ITTOIA 2005 ss.254–255 (TA 1988 s.105), relief may possibly be claimed under ITTOIA 2005 s.250, for damages for defective work and legal costs, insurance against such liabilities and debt collection, reduced by any unpaid expenses for which relief has been claimed on the renewals basis. Relief may be claimed against total income and then capital gains of the fiscal year of payment made within one year and 10 months from the end of that year. It is unclear whether damages for libel could fall within these provisions.

ASSIGNMENT OF COPYRIGHT

One result of assessing an author to tax as professional income under ITTOIA 2005 ss.5–8 is that the copyright in his works, although capable of assignment, does not have to be brought into the author's accounts at the market value at the time of assignment. This arises from the decision in *Mason v Innes* (1967) 44 T.C. 326.

18–007

The Revenue argued that following the decision of *Sharkey v Wernher* (1956) 36 T.C. 275, the copyright in a book which had been written by the taxpayer and given to his father was taxable at the market value. It was held that the author's copyright was not stock in trade and, therefore, that the decision in *Sharkey v Wernher* had no application. The principles were very clearly laid down in the judgment of Lord Denning M.R., at 339:

> "I start with the elementary principle of income tax law that a man cannot be taxed on profits that he might have, but has not, made: *Sharkey v Wernher* (1956) 36 TC 275. At first sight that elementary principle seems to cover this case. Mr Hammond Innes did not receive anything from 'The Doomed Oasis'. But in the case of a trader there is an exception to that principle. I take for simplicity the trade of a grocer. He makes out his accounts on an 'earnings basis'. He brings in the value of his stock-in-trade at the beginning and end of the year; he brings in his purchases and sales; the debts owned by him and to him; and so arrives at his profit or loss. If such a trader appropriates to himself part of his stock-in-trade, such as tins of beans, and uses them for his own purposes, he must bring them into his accounts at their market value. A trader who supplies himself is accountable for the market value. That is established by *Sharkey v Wernher* itself. Now, suppose that such a trader does not supply himself with tins of beans, but gives them away to a friend or relative. Again he has to bring them in at their market value. That was established by *Petrotim Securities Ltd v Ayres* (1964) 41 T.C. 389. Mr Monroe, on behalf of the Crown, contends that that exception is not confined to traders. It extends, he says, to professional men, such as authors, artists, barristers and many others. These professional men do not keep accounts on an 'earnings basis'. They keep them on a 'cash basis', by which I mean that on one side of the account they enter the actual money they expend and on the other side the actual money they receive. They have no stock-in-trade to bring into the accounts. They do not bring in debts owing by or to them, nor work in progress. They enter only expenses on the one side and receipts on the other. Mr Monroe contended that liability to tax does not and should not depend on the way in which a man keeps his accounts. There is no difference in principle, he says, between a trader and a professional man. And he stated his proposition quite generally in this way: the appropriation of an asset, which has been produced in the ordinary course of a trade or profession, to the trader's or professional man's own purposes amounts to a realisation of that asset or the receipt of its value, and he must bring it into account."

I cannot accept Mr Monroe's proposition. Suppose an artist paints a picture of his mother and gives it to her. He does not receive a penny for it. Is he to pay tax on the value of it? It is unthinkable. Suppose he paints a picture which he does not like when he has finished it and destroys it. Is he liable to pay tax on the value of it? Clearly not. These instances and they could be extended endlessly show that the proposition in *Sharkey v Wernher* does not apply to professional men."

It appears that HMRC does not normally argue that, as the value of the copyright assigned has not been charged to income tax as income within TCGA 1992 s.37, there should be a deemed disposal at market value under TCGA 1992 s.17, for capital gains tax purposes, but it is likely to raise the argument where the recipient sells the copyright for a lump sum or legal avoidance is suspected (BIM50705; 50745; 35735). Where such an argument is raised, the assignor and assignee, if individuals, might claim for the assignee to take over the nil base value of a business asset of the assignor under TCGA 1992 s.165.

Future copyright

18–008 The CDPA 1988 s.91 (see App.1) enables the copyright in works not yet created to be assigned so that when written the copyright vests in the assignee ab initio. The value of copyright in a work yet to be written cannot be great and if assigned to, say, a child's discretionary settlement, the capital gains tax and inheritance tax should be negligible and there would be no income tax liability, following *Mason v Innes*, above. This can be a useful means of transferring wealth free of tax if the work subsequently written turns out to have considerable value (see para.23–020) although this could produce a 10-yearly charge for inheritance tax purposes. It is likely that HMRC would disallow any expenses specifically relating to a work in which the copyright had been assigned, such as research expenses, unless it can be shown that these related to the profession as a whole. Whether this is likely to be a serious problem depends on the circumstances of the case.

Income of assignee

18–009 The case of *Mason v Innes* does not deal with the taxation liability of the assignee and it is to be presumed that an assessment under (Sch.D, Case III) was accepted, now as receipts from intellectual property under ITTOIA 2005 ss.578–582. It will be appreciated that the post-cessation receipts provisions would not apply to the income arising from the book where the copyright had been given away, and there is a very interesting paragraph in the case of *Hume v Asquith*, where Pennycuick J. states, at 266:

> "An aspect of this matter which was much pressed by Counsel for the Crown has given me considerable perplexity. That is the position which arises where a professional man, having entered into a royalty contract, and while still carrying on his profession, proceeds to assign the benefit of that royalty contract. In such a case it seems clear at first sight, to say no more that the royalties could not be treated as part of the professional income of the person who has made the disposition, because they are no longer his income. On the other hand, it appears that, representing as they do uncollected income owing to the person carrying on the profession, they could equally not be taxed in the hands of the assignee. That is a very strange and anomalous position. On the other hand, a comparable position appears to arise in the simple case where, whilst still carrying on his profession, a person who is charged to tax on the basis of receipts assigns uncollected fees of a non-recurrent nature due

to him. I do not know what the practice is in such a case, but the anomaly is not specific to the case of royalties or other income of a recurring nature, and I do not think that the existence of this anomaly, common to recurrent and non-recurrent payments, is a justification for attributing to the recurrent payments a character which they would not otherwise have possessed."

It should be pointed out, however, that under ITTOIA 2005 s.581, the person liable for any tax charged on income from intellectual property is the person receiving or entitled to the income. On this basis the income which would escape tax under ITTOIA 2005 ss.5–8 as not having been received by the author could nonetheless be assessed on the recipient under these provisions.

If the amount received is not assessed on the assignee as income it would be a capital amount received by him, as defined by ITA 2007 s.777(7), and as such could be assessed on the assignor under ITA 2007 ss.778(2), (3) and 779(3) as earned income if one of the main objects was the avoidance of tax. BIM50725 instructs Inspectors of Taxes to refer such cases to Business Tax (Technical).

Capital receipts

Authors have on a number of occasions tried to argue that a lump sum received from granting various rights in connection with their work is not part of their professional income assessable under ITTOIA 2005 ss.5–8 (Sch.D, Case II), but is a capital receipt. This argument has met with little success in the courts (BIM50705).

18–010

Exceptionally, the taxpayer was successful in the case of *Beare v Carter* (1940) 23 T.C. 353. In the course of his judgment MacNaghten J. stated, at 356:

> "That copyright is property and that a price paid for an out-and-out purchase of copyright is capital are propositions which are not disputed by the Crown. On the other hand royalties are income, and that is not disputed by the Respondent.
>
> The line to be drawn between the payments which are capital and those which are income is by no means clear and distinct; and even if it were clear and distinct there would still be border-line cases. The question in every case is a question of fact depending upon the circumstances of the particular case under consideration."

The Commissioners had found that the lump sum of £150 to publish a further edition of a book was a capital receipt. As a point of principle this clearly caused HMRC considerable concern, but although the taxpayer won it was made clear by MacNaghten J., at 358, that:

> "For the reasons I am about to give, I apprehend there is no question of principle in this case at all, and that it is only a question whether on the particular facts of this case there was no evidence which could support the decision of the Commissioners. There is this justification, I think, for the view that there was a question of principle, because, if the facts were that this was merely a lump sum payment for permission to publish so many copies of the work, then I apprehend that on the authority of the cases that were cited to me there is no doubt the decision of the Commissioners would be wrong."

The judge confirmed the Commissioners' decision that the licence for the sixth edition of the book was in the nature of a capital transaction inasmuch as the long-retired author sold a part of the rights he had in the book.

Film rights and outright sales

18–011 The judge's comments in *Beare v Carter* that it was not a question of principle is supported by further cases on authors attempting to argue that a lump sum received was capital. In the case of *Billam v Griffith* (1941) 23 T.C. 757, the sale of film rights of a play was held to be part of the professional receipts of the author. In this case Lawrence J. stated, at 762:

> "When such a vocation is carried on, and it is an ordinary incident of the disposition of plays either to realise them by means of royalties or by outright sale, it seems to me that it is really the realisation of what may be regarded as the circulating capital of the dramatist, his brain being his fixed capital, and his circulating capital being the plays which, no doubt, may for certain purposes be regarded as property but, at the same time, may be realised in the course of the business which he carries on."

It is not easy to reconcile this judgment with that in *Nethersole v Withers* (1948) 28 T.C. 501, in which income from the sale of film rights was held to be capital. The main distinction seems to be that in *Billam v Griffiths* the author was held still to be carrying on his profession, even though he had only ever written one successful play, whereas in the case of *Nethersole v Withers*, Miss Nethersole had given up her profession many years previously and the alternative was between a casual income charge or a receipt of capital. This view seems to be accepted by HMRC. The court drew a distinction between the partial assignment of copyright and a licence to use copyright material. As Viscount Simon stated, at 517:

> "It is not disputed that the present case is a case of assignment; the Respondent, under the relevant agreement, made a partial assignment of her copyright and ceased to be the owner of the portion assigned, receiving a sum of money in exchange. This amounts to a sale of property by a person who is not engaged in the trade or profession of dealing in such property, and the proceeds of such a sale is, for Income Tax purposes, a sum in the nature of untaxable capital and not in the nature of taxable revenue."

In *Glasson v Rougier* (1944) 26 T.C. 86, Georgette Heyer (Mrs Rougier) sold her copyright in various works for a lump sum and it was held by MacNaghten J., at 90 that:

> "Whatever Mrs Rougier receives, whether by way of royalty or by payment for the sale of her copyright, each and all are profits earned by her in her vocation which must, in accordance with the Income Tax Acts, be included in the assessment."

18–012 Again the case was distinguished from *Beare v Carter*, where the author had only ever written one book and was not at the time of the lump sum receipt carrying on the profession of an author.

ASSIGNMENT OF COPYRIGHT

Similarly in *Mackenzie v Arnold* (1952) 33 T.C. 363 the court held that the sale of copyright by Sir Compton Mackenzie for a lump sum was nonetheless a receipt of his profession as an author even though he had been resident outside the UK when the book in question had been written. A similar decision was arrived at in the case of *Household v Grimshaw* (1953) 34 T.C. 366 in respect of a lump sum received by an author on cancellation of an agreement to write a film script.

In *Howson v Monsell* (1950) 31 T.C. 529, concerning the film rights of books written by Margaret Irwin (Mrs Monsell), it was held that the amounts received for the sale of film rights should be assessed as professional income. In the words of Danckwerts J., at 534:

> "It is plain that Mrs Monsell received these sums by reason of the fact that she was carrying on the vocation of writer or authoress of historical books and that the receipt by her was plainly in the course of carrying on that vocation."

When a professional author sold his working papers to a university the receipts were taxable under Sch.D, Case II, as part of the exploitation by an author of anything produced in the course of his profession (*Professor Wain's Executors v Cameron* (1995) S.T.C. 555) (BIM35735). 18–013

The principle which clearly emerges is that the sale of copyright for a lump sum by somebody not currently carrying on the profession of author may be capital, whereas a similar sale by an author currently carrying on his profession is part of his professional income. This is because the author's brain is their fixed capital. Copyright is the product of the author's brain. It is the circulating capital and exploiting it gives rise to income (BIM50705).

Normally the income received by an author will be assessed as professional income even if, as in *Billam v Griffiths*, there is only one successful work.

Publishing and casual receipts

However, on occasions the activities of the author are inconsistent with the exercise of his profession. 18–014

In *IRC v Maxse* (1919) 21 T.C. 41, it was held that an author and publisher could divide his remuneration into two sources of income, that of publishing assessed as a trade and that of author assessed as income from a profession. In the case of *Hobbs v Hussey* (1942) 24 T.C. 153, a series of newspaper articles which were the sole literary activity of the taxpayer gave rise to profits assessed under ITTOIA 2005 s.687, as income not otherwise charged to tax because, in the words of Lawrence J., at 156:

> "Does then the fact that the present transaction involved the sale of the copyright in the Appellant's series of articles, constitute the profits therefrom capital; or is such a sale merely subsidiary to what was in its essence a performance of services by the Appellant? In my opinion, the true nature of the transaction was the performance of services."

In the case of *Housden v Marshall* (1958) 38 T.C. 233, the taxpayer did not himself write articles but provided information for articles ghosted by a newspaper journalist. The payment was held assessable as a casual receipt under what is now ITTOIA 2005 s.687 (BIM50705).

18–015 In *Alloway v Phillip* (1980) S.T.C. 490, the wife of one of the "Great Train Robbers" supplied information to a UK newspaper for use in articles published in the newspaper. As in *Hobbs v Hussey*, the profit was assessed as a casual receipt under what is now ITTOIA 2005 s.687. The case was complicated by the fact that the taxpayer was resident in Canada at the relevant time, but it was held that the income was UK source income arising from a UK contract and therefore was included within the definition of any property in the UK under what is now ITTOIA 2005 s.577(2) and is therefore still taxable.

Another case where material was provided for the use of an author was that of *Earl Haig Trustees v IRC* (1939) 22 T.C. 725. In this case the trustees of the late Earl Haig arranged for a biography of him to be written, using material from his diaries. The profits were shared between the author and the trustees. The trustees clearly could not have been assessed on professional income, as their sole activity was making the diaries available to the biographer. HMRC attempted to assess the trustees on casual profits, but the court held that by making the diaries available to the biographer they had in fact made a partial realisation of one of the assets of the estate, as the diaries could not in future be again made available in the same manner. As a result the amount received by the trustees was a capital sum, even though received in instalments. At that time such an amount was tax free, although it would now be subject to capital gains tax as a disposal of rights. In *Bradbury v Arnold* (1957) 37 T.C. 665 an introductory payment for a chance to invest in an ice show was held to be a capital receipt.

In the case of *Lawrence v IRC* (1940) 23 T.C. 333, certain royalties accrued to a charitable trust from the publication of Colonel T.E. Lawrence's writings and the charity was held to be assessed to tax on the copyright royalties as casual receipts under ITTOIA 2005 ss.578–582. Such amounts were nonetheless annual payments and so would be exempt from income tax to a charity if the income were allocated for charitable purposes only.

In *C Huhtala v HMRC* (2010) UKFTT 429 (TC) a freelance journalist and author claimed expenses of £10,000 for moving and mooring his boat in Southern France while he wrote "A Year on a Pontoon". As he was living on the boat he failed on duality of purpose.

CASUAL AUTHORS

18–016 In practice HMRC taxes an occasional author, such as a politician writing his memoirs, under ITTOIA 2005 ss.578–582 as casual receipts on royalties when received. Such income will normally be earned income if received by the originator of the work The advantage of such treatment is that a lump sum received on an absolute assignment of the copyright, as opposed to a lump sum advance or grant of a licence, would give rise to a capital gains tax liability rather than, as in the case of a professional author, be included as part of professional income (*Leeming v Jones* (1930) 15 T.C. 333 (BIM50705)).

The disadvantage is that it may be difficult to obtain relief for travel and research costs other than in the year the royalties are received on the grounds that such expenses were capital. It might be desirable to obtain an advance on royalties in such circumstances, although, in general, HMRC will allow reasonable expenses to be claimed under ITTOIA 2005 s.582 (BIM50720).

It would appear that if an author claimed to carry on a profession as author, and made a profit, HMRC would find it difficult to refuse treatment as professional income under ITTOIA 2005 ss.5–8. If the author consistently made losses then HMRC could refuse relief under ITTOIA 2005 s.66(1) and (7) unless it was shown that the profession was being carried on on a commercial basis with a view to the realisation of profits.

AVERAGING PROVISIONS

The tax spreading provisions have been replaced for 2000–01 onwards by averaging provisions under ITTOIA 2005 ss.221–225 as explained in Ch.17 in relation to designs, which also apply to copyright and artists' receipts (BIM73051, 73055, 73060).

18–017

DEDUCTION OF TAX AT SOURCE

United Kingdom patent royalties are subject to deduction of tax at source under the provisions of ITA 2007 s.898(1)(b). Copyright royalties, however, are subject to deduction of tax at source under the general provisions of ITA 2007 s.898(1)(a) only if it is a qualifying annual payment made by an individual for genuine commercial reasons in connection with the individual's trade, profession or vocation (ITA 2007 ss.899–900; ITTOIA 2005 s.579).

18–018

Non-residents

If the copyright owner's usual place of abode is outside the United Kingdom then copyright royalties may come under the provisions of ITA 2007 ss.906, 909.

18–019

Under these provisions income tax at the basic rate has to be deducted under ITA 2007 ss.906(5) and 909(2) on any copyright royalties paid to the owner of a copyright whose usual place of abode is not within the United Kingdom.

The payer's incidental expenses in connection with payment of royalties were allowed in *Curtis v Jarvis* (1929) 14 T.C. 744.

The owner of a copyright, in this connection, means the person entitled to some or all of the royalties, except that it is not extended to cinematograph films or video recordings, including the soundtrack not separately exploited. The HMRC view is that this exemption applies to the owner of the copyright in the film or video and not to the copyright in the screenplay or music held by the author or composer (ITA 2007 s.901(2)).

18–020

There is also an exception under ITA 2007 s.906(4) for copyright royalties paid in respect of copies which have been exported from the United Kingdom for distribution outside the UK which are therefore not subject to deduction of tax at source.

Where the publisher merely acts as the author's agent in arranging publication and sales, at the author's expense, any payments to the author are not copyright royalties at all, but the publisher may be taxable as agent of the author carrying on a trade in the United Kingdom under TIOPA 2010 Sch.6, inserting ITA 2007 ss.835C and 835T–835X and TCGA 1992 ss.271F–835J, and be their UK representative for self-assessment purposes.

18–021 The agent's commission may be deducted before calculating the amount on which tax is to be withheld, ITA 2007 s.908. This can be done only where the payer has proof of the commission payable to a UK agent.

These withholding tax provisions only apply to royalties and advances on account of royalties, not to lump sums payable on assignment of copyright (*IRC v Longmans Green & Co Ltd* (1932) 17 T.C. 272). They may also be affected by double taxation treaties providing for a reduced rate or zero rate of withholding tax, in which case HMRC's CAR Residency, on receipt of a competent claim for relief from the recipient, will usually authorise the payer to pay the reduced rate or not to deduct tax at all. Computer software licences authorising the user to copy programs for his own use are usually outwith these withholding arrangements.

It is not possible to enter into an agreement to avoid the deduction of tax under these provisions (ITA 2007 s.909(2)). The time of payment, under ITA 2007 s.909(1) is deemed to be when the publisher originates the payment, not the date of payment by the agent to the copyright holder.

18–022 It appears that ITA 2007 s.906 deduction of tax for certain royalties where the usual place or abode of the owner is abroad, would apply only where a UK source was involved and support for this exists in ITA 2007 s.906(4), the exception being for royalties for foreign copies as well as the *Hansard* statement (below). Thus the mere payment of copyright royalties to the owner whose place of abode is outside the UK is insufficient to require deduction of tax: location of the source in the UK is a requisite for deduction of tax at source. ITA 2007 s.906 is not a withholding tax section, i.e. it relates to sales of books or music or performances of plays, etc. within the UK only. ITA 2007 applies to copyright royalties under ITA 2007 s.907(1)(a), excluding films, s.907(2). For royalties paid to a non-UK resident author, see para.18–023.

Note that the tax deduction procedures apply under ITA 2007 s.906(2) to copyright owners whose usual place of abode is outside the United Kingdom, rather than to those who are not resident or not ordinarily resident in the UK for tax purposes. It would not be difficult to imagine the case of a person whose usual place of abode was outside the UK, but who was regarded as resident in the UK because, for example, he spends on average four months a year in the UK, or under the statutory residence rules in FA 2013 s.218, 219 and Schs 45 and 46. Tax is withheld by the payer whether the payment is made direct to the overseas recipient or to his bank or agent.

The tax deducted is accounted for to HMRC under ITA 2007 s.946(5) under the CT61 procedure in ITA 2007 ss.945–962 if paid for by a company or ITA 2007 s.963, if paid by an "other person", which means that the amount deducted is immediately paid over and is not collected through self-assessment under ITA 2007 s.964.

Non-resident authors

It is interesting to note under ITA 2007 s.906 that, in spite of appearances, the provisions do not apply to authors exercising their profession whose normal place of abode is outside the United Kingdom. The argument appears to be that so far as an author is concerned the source of his income is his brain, which is outside the UK, rather than the UK copyright as an independent asset. This interpretation was confirmed in a Parliamentary written answer on November 10, 1969 (*Hansard*, Vol.791, col.31):

18–023

> "*Overseas British National (publication fees)* Mr Ashton asked the Chancellor of the Exchequer what steps be taken to recover tax on fees paid to British nationals living abroad by publishers in this country.
> Mr Roy Jenkins: Section 391, Taxes Act 1970 (ITA 2007 s906) requires any person making such payments to deduct income tax at the (basic) rate and to pay it over to the Inland Revenue. I am advised that this does not apply to payments made to those who are authors by profession, nor does it apply if the recipient is living in a country with which we have a Double Taxation Agreement requiring us to exempt such payments."

This arrangement is referred to in the INTM 342590 which states that:

> "Payments that are made to an author by profession who usually lives overseas are therefore not subject to deduction of UK income tax at source. This follows the decisions in *Carson v Cheyney's Executor* (1958) 38 T.C. 240 and *Hume v Asquith* (1969) 45 T.C. 251."

It is interesting to note that the original rules relating to the deduction of tax from royalties paid to a copyright owner whose usual place of abode was abroad were considered in the case of *Rye and Eyre v IRC* (1935) 19 T.C. 164. Under the provisions of FA 1927 s.26, it was provided that where such a payment was made by or through any person, "that person shall forthwith deliver to the Commissioners of Inland Revenue for the use of the Special Commissioners an account of the payment", and it was held that the agents of the author were liable to deduct tax on payment to him. INTM 342590 confirms that this was incorrect.

In *IRC v Longmans Green & Co Ltd* (1932) 17 T.C. 272, the UK publishers paid a lump sum non-returnable advance to a French author and were held accountable to tax at the basic rate on the whole amount. The court rejected an argument that the advance was in fact a capital payment for the partial assignment of copyright and not a payment on account of royalties within the meaning of what is now ITA 2007 s.906.

18–024

On the facts of the case, Finlay J. held, at 280:

> "I have come to the conclusion, though not without hesitation, for I think the case near the line on this point, that this was a licence and not a complete assignment of the copyright. I think it is obvious that between a partial assignment of copyright and a licence the line may run extremely fine, and I think this does run rather fine; but, construing the agreement in the light of the authorities, and each agreement has to be construed in the light of its own facts, I think that the correct view here is that this was not an assignment of the copyright but rather a licence to do certain

specific things not, of course, to translate into every language, but to translate into one particular language, namely, English."

He contrasted this, at 283, with the situation which could have arisen:

"It may well be, indeed I think for myself that it would be, that, if for 500,000 francs or any other sum, the right of translation what I may call the unlimited right of translation, that is, the right of translating and the right of publishing any number of the expensive edition and any cheap editions that the publishers might be minded to publish if, so to speak, the whole thing, the whole English rights of translation and publication had been transferred and transferred for a lump sum, I think that it probably would be right to say that that sum would not be assessable as a royalty."

18–025 As has been seen, such a lump sum would, for a UK-resident author, be part of his normal professional income, but for someone whose usual place of abode was outside the United Kingdom a lump sum for the assignment of part of the copyright would not be within the deduction of tax at source provisions.

It is difficult to reconcile the case of *IRC v Longmans Green & Co Ltd* with HMRC's practice confirmed by the *Hansard* statement quoted above (see para.18–024), other than by recognising that the source of the income being the author himself was not argued, and INTM 342590 confirms that it was, in fact, wrongly decided in the light of later cases. This case is also interesting because it is one of the instances where the case itself was taken as a point of principle and HMRC picked up the bill for the costs of both sides in spite of being the victorious party. In the words of E.J. Macgillivray, for the Crown, at 284:

"The Commissioners do not ask for the costs of this appeal. It is an unusual case, because here the Respondents are being assessed in a representative capacity and, although they have made provision for the payment of tax, they are not in a position to recover the costs of this appeal as against the French author. In these unusual circumstances the Commissioners have agreed that they shall pay the publisher their costs of this appeal in any event."

REALISATION OF INVESTMENTS

18–026 Most of the cases so far considered concern payments in respect of copyright to authors or those who have contributed directly to the work in question. One case in which the copyright was treated as a pure investment was the case of *Shiner v Lindblom* (1960) 39 T.C. 367. In this case Ronald Shiner acquired an option for the film rights of Noel Streatfield's book *Aunt Clare* which was converted into a film in which Mr Shiner starred. The Commissioners held as a question of fact that it was Mr Shiner's intention upon acquiring the option for the copyright of the book *Aunt Clare* to use it as an investment. They then held, somewhat surprisingly, that the profit from the sale of the film rights was part of Mr Shiner's professional income as an actor, which was clearly insupportable and dismissed by Danckwerts J. HMRC also contended that the purchase and resale of the film rights constituted an adventure in the nature of trade. This was also dismissed by the learned judge at 373:

"As regards the other point, whether it was a transaction in the nature of trade, it seems to be that a conclusion can be reached on the facts which have been found by the Commissioners. It is quite plain that he had no other transactions of this nature and they have found that he acquired it as an investment and had no intention of realising it; he was not, in other words, trading in copyright or anything of that sort. It was something which he had acquired. He received an offer which was favourable and he decided to realise the investment."

The result was, at the time, a tax free capital profit which would now be subject to capital gains tax.

PRIZES AND GRANTS

A prize or gift won by or given to the originator of intellectual property is unlikely to be taxable (*Simpson v John Reynolds & Co (Insurances) Ltd* [1975] S.T.C. 271; *Moore v Griffiths* (1972) 48 T.C. 338; *Reed v Seymour* (1927) 11 T.C. 625). This would normally apply in whatever way the income is taxed, although if in excess of £30,000 and to an employee, he could be taxable under the golden handshake provisions of ITEPA 2003 ss.401–416 (*Ellis v Lucas* (1966) 43 T.C. 276; *Walker v Carnaby Harrower, Barham & Pykett* (1969) 46 T.C. 561). It would normally be argued that a prize was not a reward for services (*Ball v Johnson* (1971) 47 T.C. 155), unless part of normal remuneration (*Moorhouse v Dooland* (1954) 36 T.C. 1; *Davis v Harrison* (1927) 11 T.C. 707; *Corbett v Duff* (1941) 23 T.C. 763; *Cooper v Blakiston* (1908) 5 T.C. 347). See below for Arts Council awards and bursaries.

18–027

A gift for work well done was not taxable in *IRC v Morris* (1967) 44 T.C. 685, but may now be taxable as a gratuity under ITEPA 2003 s.62(2)(b).

A grant or subsidy directly relating to the business, however, is likely to be taxable (*IRC v Falkirk Ice Rink Ltd* [1975] S.T.C. 434; *Smart v Lincolnshire Sugar Co Ltd* (1937) 20 T.C. 643; *Temperley v Smith* (1956) 37 T.C. 18; *Duff v Williamson* [1973] S.T.C. 434; *McGowan v Brown and Cousins* [1977] S.T.C. 342). If, therefore, an author wrote a piece specifically for a competition, the prize money, if he won, would be taxable but other awards, grants, bursaries and prizes may also be taxable in the view of HMRC (BIM50710).

It is understood that the author Andrew Boyle, who won the Whitbread Award, successfully resisted HMRC's attempt to tax it as income, before the Special Commissioners. However, HMRC may challenge other cases, although it seems to accept the Booker Prize as tax free, as an unsolicited mark of honour for outstanding achievement. BIM50710 states:

18–028

"A literary etc prize which is unsolicited, and which is awarded as a mark of honour, distinction or public esteem in recognition of outstanding achievement in a particular field, including the field in which the recipient operates professionally, is not chargeable to tax."

In 1979 the Special Commissioners found for the taxpayer in a case involving a literary award. The case attracted some press publicity as a reporter was admitted to the proceedings. The book was entered for the competition by the publisher without the author's consent. The decision turned very much upon its own facts and, in particular, a finding that the award was unsolicited and did not represent the proceeds of exploitation of the book by the author personally or by his publishers as agents on his behalf. Awards may also, depending on the circumstances, possibly be taxable as emoluments, as casual profits under ITTOIA 2005 s.687 or exceptionally as annual payments under ITTOIA 2005 s.687. Awards to students may be exempt from tax as scholarship income under ITTOIA 2005 s.776 (BIM50710). Betting winnings by a golfer on matches in which he played were not taxable in *Down v Compton* (1937) 21 T.C. 60.

Arts Council awards and bursaries

18–029   BIM50715 states that:

> "The Arts Councils provide financial support through a variety of awards, bursaries and grants, to writers, artists, actors and other creative artists. The tax treatment will depend upon the nature of the payment and the circumstances of the recipient. The principles to apply are explained at BIM50710."

They could also be employment income, EIM50200. The Arts Council, on September 10, 1979, published a press release setting out the taxation treatment of awards and grant BIM:

> "The Arts Council and the Inland Revenue have now agreed this note on the tax treatment of awards and bursaries which the Council makes to artists, writers, photographers, musicians and the performing artists. Such awards and bursaries form a small but important part of the Arts Council's budget.
>
> Since the Arts Council has been introducing new types of awards there have been some difficulties in the application of the understanding reached between the Arts Council and the Inland Revenue in 1978. These notes are intended to clarify the treatment of the awards, etc. for tax purposes. They do not impinge on the rights of appeal against an assessment to tax on any individual recipient of an award or bursary.
>
> Awards and bursaries made by the Arts Council fall to be treated for tax purposes in the following categories:"

18–030   **Category A awards and bursaries which are chargeable to tax**

1. Direct or indirect musical, design or choreographic commissions and direct or indirect commissions of sculpture and paintings for public sites.
2. The Royalty Supplement Guarantee Scheme.
3. The Contract Writers' Scheme.
4. Jazz bursaries.
5. Translators' grants.
6. Photographic awards and bursaries.
7. Film and video awards and bursaries.
8. Performance Art awards.
9. Arts Publishing grants.

PRIZES AND GRANTS

10. Grants to assist with a specific project or projects (such as the writing of a book) or to meet specific professional expenses such as a contribution towards copying expenses made to a composer, or to an artist's studio expenses.

Category B awards and bursaries which are not chargeable to tax 18–031

1. Bursaries to trainee directors.
2. In-service bursaries for theatre directors.
3. Bursaries for associate directors.
4. Bursaries to people attending full-time courses in arts administration (the practical training course).
5. In-service bursaries to theatre designers and bursaries to trainees on the theatre designers' scheme.
6. In-service bursaries for administrators.
7. Bursaries for actors and actresses.
8. Bursaries for technicians and stage managers.
9. Bursaries made to students attending the City University arts administration courses.
10. Awards, known as the Buying Time Awards, made, not to assist with a specific project or professional expenses, but to maintain the recipient to enable him to take time off to develop his personal talents. These at present include the following awards and bursaries known as the Theatre Writing Bursaries, Awards and Bursaries to composers. Awards and Bursaries to painters, sculptors and print makers, Literature Awards and Bursaries.

> "It will be open to the Arts Council to make both a grant in Category A10 and an award in Category B10 to an individual and accordingly, in such a case, part only of the sum received by the individual concerned will be treated as taxable. However, it is agreed in relation to these cases that if the expenditure incurred by the individual in connection with the matters covered by the A10 grant and the B10 award exceeds the amount of the A10 grant the excess up to and including the amount of the B10 award will be regarded as covered by the B10 award, and to this extent will not be allowable as a deduction in arriving at his or her taxable profits. The remainder of any of the expenditure will be subject to the normal Sch.D expenses rules. The arrangements noted herein will be followed by the Inland Revenue, whilst the law remains as it is, in cases involving awards both for future assessments and in settlement of appeals now open. The Arts Council will, in making future awards, inform the recipient of the category applicable for tax purposes."

Public lending right

For income and corporation tax purposes, public lending right payments are treated under ITA 2007 s.907(1)(c) as copyright payments for the purposes of the return of payments under TMA 1970 s.16 and for averaging under ITTOIA 2005 ss.221–225. They are also treated as copyright royalties for the purposes of ITA 2007 s.906 for the deduction of tax on payments to copyright holders whose usual place of abode is abroad, and for post-cessation receipts purposes where ITTOIA 2005 s.254(1)(a) excludes a lump sum paid to the personal representatives of the author of a literary, dramatic, musical or artistic work as consideration for the

18–032

assignment, or partial assignment, of the copyright. They are also included in the definition of copyright for the purposes of TA 1988 s.821, where tax has been under-deducted from payments to non-UK copyright holders under TA 1988 s.821(3)(a).

Public lending right receipts will normally be included as part of the author's professional income for Sch.D purposes.

LEASING

18–033 In certain cases, in particular relating to computer software, the user may have unrestricted right to use the copyright material for his own use on payment of a fee. In other words he effectively leases the software and in many cases the contract is set out in the form of a lease agreement. As the payment is not related to the user but to time it is not a royalty (per Jenkins L.J. in *Carson v Cheyney's Executor* (1958) 38 T.C. 240), and the withholding tax provisions of ITA 2007 s.906 and other provisions relating to copyright royalties would have no effect.

EXPENSES

18–034 Reasonable expenses of producing a copyright work and of marketing it, including agents commission, should be allowable under the normal rules for trading profits computed in accordance with generally accepted accounting practice (UK GAAP) in ITTOIA 2005 s.525 subject to ss.32–94, and 582 or 687. *Salt v Buckley* [2001] S.T.C. (S.C.D.) 262; *Salt v Golding* [1996] S.T.C. (S.C.D.) 269.

PURCHASE OF COPYRIGHT

Capital allowances

18–035 There are no specific provisions giving capital allowances on the purchase of copyright except for computer software (see below) and it is doubtful whether much copyright work is within the definition of plant as originally defined in *Yarmouth v France* (1887) 19 Q.B.D. 647. In many cases this is not a problem because the acquirer is carrying on a trade of publishing or otherwise exploiting copyright and the cost of copyright purchases is written off as a trading expense or carried forward at the lower end of cost or market value as part of the publisher's stock in trade.

In the case of an investor acquiring copyright material as a capital acquisition, there is a possibility that an original manuscript may be plant. This could follow from *Munby v Furlong* [1977] S.T.C. 232, which held that books could be plant, and would be consistent with the treatment of cinematograph films and record master tapes as plant (see Inland Revenue statement of practice SP9/79, August 10, 1979, prior to CAA 1990 s.68). See below for the current rules for films and audio products.

PURCHASE OF COPYRIGHT

Wallpaper designs however, which are clearly copyright, were held not to be plant in the case of *McVeigh v Arthur Sanderson & Sons Ltd* (1968) 45 T.C. 273, but the cost of the printing blocks must include something for the cost of the designs. It should be emphasised in this case that Cross J. regarded himself bound by the decision in *Daphne v Shaw* (1926) 11 T.C. 256, although this has largely been overruled by *Munby v Furlong*, above.

Deferred revenue expenditure

Where copyright material is not stock in trade it may, nevertheless, be deferred revenue expenditure if it is not capital expenditure for tax purposes. It is capital expenditure if it is made not only once and for all but with a view to bringing into existence an asset or an advantage for the enduring benefit of the trade (*Atherton v British Insulated and Helsby Cables Ltd* (1925) 10 T.C. 155). The correct accounting treatment is to write off the expenditure over its life, under FRS 10, in accordance with generally accepted accounting practice (UK GAAP; ITTOIA 2005 s.25; ITA 2007 s.997; CTA 2009 s.180; CTA 2010 s.1127; FA 2012 s.54).

18–036

BIM42215—Deductions: timing: deferred revenue expenditure: overview provides:

> "In a number of circumstances UK GAAP either permits or requires expenditure to be 'spread' or 'deferred' in accounts; in other words, the expenditure is charged to the profit and loss account of more than one year. For example SSAP13 'Research and development' permits development expenditure, under certain conditions, to be deferred to future periods. Similarly FRS 10 'Goodwill and intangible assets' requires expenditure on the purchase of intangible assets to be spread over the expected useful economic life of the asset. Finally, recent and forthcoming changes in GAAP may make it more common for expenditure on major overhauls of plant and machinery to be spread over a number of years after the overhaul has been carried out. The changes in GAAP are FRS 12 'Provisions, contingent liabilities and contingent assets' and FRS15 Tangible Fixed Assets."

The accountancy treatment is not relevant for expenditure which is "capital" in tax terms. However, a separate issue is whether revenue expenditure which is "capitalised" by accountants is also disallowable for tax. Generally, the answer is "no".

Accountants often refer to "capitalising" expenditure without implying anything about its treatment as revenue or capital expenditure for tax. They simply mean that expenditure is taken to the balance sheet because it relates to a later year. An alternative description for capitalised revenue expenditure is "deferred revenue expenditure".

18–037

The question of whether expenditure is capital or revenue **for tax purposes** is one of tax law. It follows that expenditure which is revenue for tax purposes does not, and cannot, loose that character whether or not it is charged wholly in one year's accounts, or spread over the accounts of more than one year. In other words expenditure does not become capital expenditure by being "capitalised"; "capitalised" revenue expenditure is still revenue. Equally, capital expenditure does not become revenue expenditure when, say, depreciation is charged to the profit and loss account.

Accounting standards will be relevant for tax when it comes to deciding in which periods revenue receipts and expenses, fall, unless there is a specific tax rule which provides to the contrary. Examples of specific rules are the FA 1989 s.43 rules about late paid employment income.

18–038 Leaving aside these specific tax provisions, there is no rule of tax law that the "right" time to deduct revenue expenditure for tax purposes is the year in which it is incurred, or the year in which there is a legal liability to pay it. (*Threlfall v Jones* (1993) 66 T.C. 77, (1992) S.T.C. 77) (*Herbert Smith v Honour* (1999) 72 T.C. 130, (1999) S.T.C. 173 (1999) 72 T.C. 130). It follows that where revenue expenditure is spread over the accounts of more than one year, and this treatment accords with GAAP, there is no rule of tax law which entitles a taxpayer to deduct it all "up-front". Equally, the fact that the accounts describe some deferred revenue expenditure as having been "capitalised" does not mean that it cannot be allowed for tax as a business expense at some time.

The tax treatment of revenue expenditure should not differ from the accounts treatment where revenue expenditure is separated from capital depreciation, so no computational adjustments for deferred revenue expenditure will be necessary on a continuing basis. An adjustment is necessary if the tax treatment has differed from the accountancy treatment in prior accounting periods, see BIM42220, below.

BIM4220 DEDUCTIONS: TIMING: DEFERRED REVENUE EXPENDITURE: REACHING CONSISTENCY OF TREATMENT.

Background

18–039 In February 1999 the Revenue published an article in TB39 explaining the view that the timing of the tax treatment of deferred revenue expenditure should follow the accountancy treatment. We became aware that despite this publication, deferred revenue expenditure was being dealt with in different ways. The lack of consistency may have been partly due to ambiguous guidance caused by some unamended advice that did not reflect our publicised change of view. For example, some guidance referred to ICTA88/S74(1)(d) providing a timing rule for allowing a deduction for repairs expenditure, etc. regardless of accountancy treatment. Following the Special Commissioners' decision in *Jenners Princes St Edinburgh v Inland Revenue Commissioners* (1998) S.T.C. (SCD) 196, we accept that there is no such authority. Other guidance reflected the correct view. Previous guidance has also suggested a pragmatic approach in dealing with expenditure posted to fixed assets and this too had not been amended.

Where deferred revenue expenditure was posted to current assets on the balance sheet, following *Threlfall v Jones* (1993) 66 T.C. 77, (1993) S.T.C. 537, our guidance was consistent in explaining that no deduction for such expenditure is due when it is incurred or paid, see BIM42210.

We know that there was not a consistent approach to dealing with deferred revenue expenditure. For example, some taxpayers:

- Volunteered to follow the new approach.
- Submitted returns on the old "incurred" basis and the issue was never raised by either side.
- Submitted returns on the old "incurred" basis and accepted the Inspector's challenge to the computational adjustment.
- Submitted returns on the old "incurred" basis and the point was still open under enquiry.
- Negotiated "agreements" with their Inspector on this point.

We had to remove inconsistency to get everyone on the correct basis, but it would have been unfair to allow some taxpayers to delay computing their tax profits in accordance with the law, whilst others were at a disadvantage having complied with the law. We therefore introduced a cut-off date to enable any past inconsistencies to be removed as far as practically possible.

The cut off

June 30, 1999 is the cut off date from which the correct view of the law should be applied. By this date we think that it is reasonable to assume that details of the new approach would have become known. Any income tax or tax return, to the extent that it includes profits or losses shown in accounts for periods starting after June 30, 1999 should be settled in accordance with the law, and not to reflect computational adjustments to give relief for deferred revenue expenditure before it is deducted in the profit and loss account. 18–040

Detail

The term "accounts period" refers to a period for which accounts are drawn up. 18–041

A return and an accounts period "relate to" each other, if the return includes business profits or losses of the accounts period (disregarding losses and other amounts which for tax purposes can be carried forward or back between one period and another).

A return is "open" in the following circumstances:

(a) for periods preceding SA:
  - the accounts have not yet been agreed,
  - an appeal has not yet been determined, or
  - a return has not yet been made.
(b) For periods where SA applies:
  - the period for starting enquiries, or window for taxpayer amendment, has not yet expired,
  - an enquiry has been opened, whether or not the specific issue of deferred revenue expenditure is under consideration, or

- a return has not yet been made.

Otherwise a return is "closed".

Cases where the return is closed

18–042 If the return is closed, the treatment of deferred revenue expenditure can only be raised if the person dealing with the accounts makes a discovery.

CLAIMS FROM TAXPAYERS THAT THE CUT OFF DATE IS RETROSPECTIVE

18–043 Our view of the correct position in law for the treatment of deferred revenue expenditure was published in February 1999 in TB39. It changed from our former view as a result of evolving case law, including the decisions in *Threlfall v Jones* (1993) 66 T.C. 77 and *Herbert Smith v Honour* (1999) 72 T.C. 130. The Revenue also issues a Press Release PR138/99 in July 1999 following the *Herbert Smith* case that confirmed our revised view. We therefore consider that tax practitioners would have been aware of our view before the cut off date.

PARTICULAR SITUATIONS

18–044 In some circumstances Inspectors have entered into explicit informal understandings, that are binding on HMRC, and which perpetuate the "paid or incurred basis". They preclude the parties from applying the correct treatment for their duration. Inspectors should revisit and unwind these as soon as possible, and no such informal understanding should be renewed. In any case of difficulty, contact CT&VAT (Technical).

A payment of tax, including a quarterly instalment payment of CT, may have fallen due for an accounting period before the taxpayer was aware that the informal understanding had been withdrawn. In these circumstances, you should be prepared to accept that the correct treatment of deferred revenue expenditure should apply to relevant expenses only in relation to subsequent accounting periods. However, if the tax computations reflect the correct treatment, or if the taxpayer agrees to the correct treatment, you should follow that treatment.

CASES WHERE A NON-DEPRECIATION POLICY HAS BEEN ADOPTED

18–045 Some companies, for example, property investment companies, adopt a non-depreciation accounting policy in which revenue expenditure is capitalised without being charged to the profit and loss accounting until a much later date. If you are in any doubt about whether such treatment is in line with UK GAAP in a particular case, you should obtain advice from your local HMRC accountant.

APPEALS

There is no rule of law that enables a business to obtain relief for revenue expenditure at a time when it is not written off to the profit and loss account and you should resist any claim that relief should be given in tax computations when it is not shown as a deduction in the accounts. Under generally accepted accountancy principles, capitalised revenue expenditure will be charged to the profit and loss account either on the sale of the asset or when there is a reduction in the value of the asset which is expected to be permanent such that the value falls below the asset's original cost. Relief will only be available for tax purposes when the expenditure is charged to profit and loss account, even though this may be some time after the expenditure was incurred.

If part of an asset is sold or re-valued below cost, you can accept a reasonable allocation of agreed revenue expenditure to the profit and loss account as the amount of deduction for tax purposes.

In every case where a non-depreciation policy is adopted in the accounts but the taxpayer wishes to pursue an appeal to the Commissioners, you should submit the case to CT&VAT (Technical) before listing for a hearing.

DOUBLE DEDUCTIONS

18–046 A taxpayer may have claimed expenditure when incurred in the past and may argue that if the same expenditure is subsequently debited in the profit and loss account as deferred revenue expenditure, HMRC is now constrained to accept that treatment for tax. The effect of this would be to allow a deduction twice for the same expenditure. We do not accept that a double deduction is possible. You should submit any case where a double deduction is claimed to CT&VAT (Technical) for further advice before engaging in detailed correspondence.

COMBINED CAPITAL AND DEFERRED REVENUE EXPENDITURE DEPRECIATED

18–047 The depreciation charge in the profit and loss account may include both capital depreciation and the write off of revenue expenditure. Any capital depreciation, together with any revenue expenditure that has already been allowed on the incurred/paid basis, should be added back. Revenue expenditure will otherwise be deductible. Accept any reasonable method of identifying the revenue element provided it is consistently applied. Taxpayers and Inspectors will need to keep track of the revenue expenditure that is deferred so that it can be identified when it is written off.

APPEALS

18–048 Where attempts to settle a case by way of agreement fail, please submit the case to CT&VAT (Technical) to review before listing. Note that there is a mandatory submission instruction at IM5098e and AP3422 when any contentious case involves accountancy issues. This request for a submission will satisfy the ADM6.109 requirement about when further advice should be sought.

FILM AND AUDIO PRODUCTS

18–049 Sections 18–040 to 18–058 are obsolete but have been retained because many film financing schemes last for many years and many are still under challenge by HMRC.

Expenditure treated as revenue expense the F(No2) A 1992 rules

18–050 Expenditure on the production or acquisition of a film or record master and the intellectual property rights therein (F(No.2)A 1992 s.40A(5)) (the product) is intrinsically capital in nature giving rise to a fixed asset. It is, however, deemed to be revenue expenditure deductible under Sch.D, Case I, under F(No.2)A 1992 s.40A(1) and (4)(a) in the absence of an election under F(No.2)A 1992 s.40D, in which case the expenditure would normally qualify as plant and machinery eligible for capital allowances (see below). Although F(No.2)A 1992 s.40A, refers only to the master version of a film, this was an oversight as CAA 1990 s.68, applied to films, tapes and discs. ESC B54 reinstates the revenue treatment for expenditure on the master version of audio products (BIM56110).

Sums received from the exploitation of the product are treated as revenue receipts, whether from disposal of the master or an interest or right therein, and including insurance or compensation receipts (F(No.2)A 1992 s.40A (2), (3) and (4)(b).

The provisions of F(No.2)A 1992 ss.40A–40B, do not apply to expenditure on production or acquisition of a film that commences principal photography on or after April 1, 2006 or to acquisition expenditure on a film that commences principal photography on or after April 1, 2006 which was incurred on or after April 1, 2007 whenever the film was made (TA 2006 s.46).

Allocation of expenditure income matching method

18–051 The expenditure on the product has to be allocated to the relevant accounting period in the absence of an election for capital treatment (F(No.2)A 1992 s.40B(1)–(3)) unless the product is held as trading stock (F(No.2)A 1992 s.40C(2)). Where product is held as trading stock, the normal stock valuation rules at the lower of cost or market value apply (BIM56115). The allocation must be on a just and reasonable basis having regard to:

(1) the balance of unallocated expenditure at the beginning of the period;
(2) the proportion of the expenditure equal to:
 (a) the estimated value of the film realised in the period,
 (b) that value and the estimated remaining value at the end of the period, and

(3) (3) the requirement to allocate the expenditure over the time during which the value of the film, etc. is *expected* to be realised (F(No.2)A) 1992 s.40B(4) (BIM56075, 56080)).

Example

Expenditure	Period 1	Period 2	Period 3	Period 4
	1,200,000	–	–	–
Receipts	–	4,000,000	11,000,000	1,000,000
Allocation of expenditure factors:				
balance of expenditure at beginning of period		1,200,000	900,000	75,000
(b) allowable proportion of expenditure		4,000,000	11,000,000	1,000,000
(c) receipts plus estimated future gross income		16,000,000 0	12,000,000	1,000,000
Allocation of expenditure		300,000	825,000	75,000

(E = A (B/B+C)
Where E = allowable expenditure for period
A = total expenditure on product less already allowed
B = gross income in period
C = estimated future gross income)
(£300,000 = £1,200,000 x (((frac;£4,000,000;$4,000,000 + £12,000,000)))

Where the unrelieved expenditure exceeds the expected future income, a further allowance of the difference is given (F(No.2)A 1992 s.40B(4)(c)).

Batching, i.e. allocation on the basis of post experience in relation to other product, may be acceptable where this is exploited on a regular basis.

Allocation of expenditure cost recovery method

After the income matching calculation has been done, a claim may be made under F(No.2)A 1992 s.40B(5)–(7) for an additional amount equal to the excess of the income brought into account over the expenditure allocated to that period, up to the amount of the unallowed expenditure on a claim being submitted within one year and 10 months of the end of the fiscal year or two years of the end of a company's accounting period. This is known as the "cost recovery method" and the calculation may be short-circuited in practice to writing off the expenditure incurred against the income to date.

18–052

Miscellaneous provisions

The cost recovery method rather than the income matching method may be used by a finance lessor (BIM56230). Television films generating advertising revenue may be written off by reference to the income generation likely, effectively as deferred revenue expenditure (BIM56105). These provisions are further explained in HMRC's statement of practice SP 1/98.

18–053

Qualifying films

18–054 From March 10, 1992 pre-production costs of developing prospective qualifying films were allowed as incurred under F(No 2)A 1992 ss.41–43 and expenditure on a film could be written off at a flat rate of 33.3 per cent per annum from completion of the film, on making a claim under CAA 1990 s.68(9). The Inland Revenue press release of July 2, 1997 stated that:

> "(1) At present the costs of producing or acquiring a British qualifying film can be written off either as the film generates income or at a flat rate of 33.3 per cent per year starting when the film is completed.
> (2) The government has decided to improve the flat-rate relief for British qualifying films costing £15 million or less to make. In these cases, the new rules will allow 100 per cent write-off for production or most acquisition costs when the film is completed.
> (3) The new rules will apply to production costs incurred after Budget Day or acquisition expenditure on films completed and acquired after Budget Day, including films begun before that date. The relief will be time limited to costs incurred during the three years from Budget Day, July 2, 1997."

100 per cent write off the F(No2)A 1997 rules

18–055 The 100 per cent write off for production expenditure was duly enacted in F(No.2)A 1997 s.48(1), from July 2, 1997 and is expired on July 1, 2005 (F(No.2)A 1997 s.48(2)(a). The total production expenditure on the film must not exceed £15 million (F(No.2)A 1997 s.48(2)(b)). Where the completed film is acquired, the 100 per cent write off is limited to the total production expenditure by F(No.2)A 1997 s.48(3). A deferment, i.e. an agreed fixed sum payable at a future date contingent on the film earning income or a participation in future profits do not qualify as production expenditure unless paid at the time the film is completed or subject to an unconditional obligation to pay within four months after the date of completion (F(No.2)A 1997 s.48(6A) and (8) inserted by FA 2002 s.100 (BIM56240)). Films completed up to April 16, 2002, measured production expenditure incurred under the capital allowances rules of CAA 2001 s.5 (CA 11800) (F(No.2)A 1997 s.48(4), (6) and (9)). These rules cease to apply to production or acquisition expenditure for low budget films under F(No.2)A 1992 s.42 and F(No.2)A 1997 s.48.

Expenditure incurred with a connected person is limited to the arm's length amount (F(No.2)A 1997 s.48(7) and (10). Only expenditure incurred by the producer or on first acquisition directly from the producer qualifies for the 100 per cent write off, to prevent successive claims on recycling the film (TA 2002 s.101).

Exceptionally films and audio product may be dealt in on a one off basis, not as part of a trade, and any profit would be taxed under Sch.D, Case VI, or as part of an overseas trade under Sch.D, Case V. In both cases the special rules in F(No.2)A 1992 ss.40A–43; F(No.2)A 1997 s.48; and FA 2002 ss.99 and 101 apply as they would for a trade under Sch.D, Case 1 (BIM56260).

18–056 A qualifying film is one so certified by the Secretary of State for the Department of Culture, Media and Sport (DCMS) under the Films Act 1985 Sch.1 (F(No.2)A 1992 s.43(1)) and includes any intellectual property rights acquired with it (F(No.2)A 1992 s.43(2)). It is completed when ready for copies to be made for presentation to the general public (F(No.2)A 1992 s.43(3)). A qualifying film has to incur an agreed minimum amount of production expenditure in the UK and at least 70 per cent of the labour costs must be payable to UK, EU or Commonwealth citizens. Co-productions may also qualify without meeting these requirements.

The certificate of qualification issued by DCMS is valid for tax purposes, but the amount of production expenditure so certified is not binding on HMRC.

For tax purposes a qualifying film certified on or after April 17, 2002, unless completed between January 1 and April 16, 2002, or submitted to CDMS for certification before April 17, 2002, or a pre-production application made for a co-production before that date, must be genuinely intended for theatrical release in cinemas, under FA 2002 s.99(1)–(3) and (6). This requirement is designed to exclude television films, but there is a transitional relief for certain TV dramas commissioned before April 17, 2002, where the first day of principal photography was on or before June 30, 2002 (FA 2002 s.99(4),(6)).

Three-year spread

There is no limit on the amount of the production expenditure to enable a film to qualify, but if this is more than £15 million, or is an acquisition to the extent that it exceeds the total cost of production, the 100 per cent write off under F(No.2)A 1997 s.48, is not available. However, the expenditure may be written off over three years, one-third in the year of acquisition or completion and one-third in each of the next two years (F(No.2)A 1992 s.42(2),(5)), on making an appropriate claim by January 31 in the year of assessment following that in which the accounting period ends, for income tax on two years after the end of the accounting period for corporation tax (F(No.2)A 1992. s.42(1) and (6)). Such a claim cannot be made where the film is held as trading stock (F(No.2)A 1992 s.42(8)) or where capital allowances have been claimed under F(No.2)A 1992 s.42D, as has already been relieved under F(No.2)A 1992 s.40B (F(No.2)A 1992 s.42(1)(b) and (7)).

18–057

Preliminary expenses

Preliminary expenditure to enable a decision to be taken as to whether or not to make a qualifying film, of up to 20 per cent of the budgeted total expenditure can be treated as a deductible trading expense on a claim being made under F(No.2)A 1992 s.41. The FA 2006 s.46 withdraws relief for preliminary expenditure under F(No.2)A 1992 s.41 in respect of expenditure incurred after October 1, 2007.

18–058

Capital allowances

An irrevocable election may be made to treat all the capital expenditure on a completed qualifying film with an anticipated life of at least two years as plant and machinery qualifying for capital allowances where a claim has not been made for preliminary expenditure relief on three year spreading under F(No.2)A 1992 ss.41 or 42; F(No.2)A 1992 s.40D.

18–059

Film production is not excluded from Enterprise Investment Scheme relief merely because it generates royalties (TA 1988 ss.297(4) and 298(5), IM 7000) nor from roll-over relief on re-investment (TCGA 1992 ss.1641(5) and 164N(1)) or venture capital trust relief under TA 1988 Sch.28B paras 4(5) and 5(1).

Video tapes for rental

18–060   The Revenue, in Issue 19 of the *Tax Bulletin* (October 1995), confirmed that video tapes loaned out to users could, if their economic life exceeded two years, be treated as short-life assets for capital allowances, or accounted for on the renewals basis. Where the life of the video tapes is two years or less, it can be written off as deferred revenue expenditure by valuing the tapes at the accounting date on the basis of writing off the cost, less realisable value over their economic life on a straight line basis or by reference to anticipated income stream. Presumably the same rules apply for CDs and DVDs.

FILM RELATED TRADING LOSSES

The FA 2004 rules

Trade profits: Films and sound recordings

Film related trading losses the FA 2004 rules

18–061   With effect from December 10, 2003 FA 2004 ss.118–123 introduced anti-avoidance provisions to prevent the individuals participating in a film financing partnership from exploiting what was meant to be a deferral of tax into a tax shelter by bringing into charge to tax any otherwise non-taxable consideration or a disposal of the rights to income.

FA 2004 s.119, applied where an individual had claimed income tax relief for a film related loss defined by FA 2004 s.123 as computed under the special film relief provisions in F(No.2)A 1992 ss.40A–40C and 41–43 and F(No.2)A 1997 s.48, in order to claim sideways loss relief under TA 1988 s.380, against general income, or under TA 1988 s.381 for losses in the early years of a trade. Where an individual receives non-taxable consideration on or after December 10, 2003 or the losses claimed are greater than the individual's capital contribution, an exit event occurred. This becomes chargeable where sideways loss relief has been claimed to the extent that the consideration received would otherwise be non-taxable or the losses claimed exceed the capital contribution to the trade. The FA 2004 s.120 defines the disposal of a right of the individual to profits arising from the trade to include a disposal of a right to income, a default on the payment of income, a change in the individual's entitlement to profits or losses, and a disposal of an interest in a partnership or its distribution. The losses claimed and the individual's capital contribution to the trade are defined as sideways loss relief or relief claimed against capital gains under FA 1991 s.72, by FA 2004 s.121. The chargeable amount treated as consideration for a relevant disposal under FA 2004 s.119, is not also treated as a reduction in the capital contribution under FA 2004

FILM RELATED TRADING LOSSES

s.121, as a result of the relieving provisions of FA 2004 s.122. FA 2004 s.123 defines non-taxable consideration simply as consideration not chargeable to income tax as well as defining film-related losses.

Film related trading losses, the ITA 2007 rules

The ITA 2007 ss.796–803 re-write the provisions of FA 2004 ss.118–123 with a minor change in the law in relating to contributions to the partnership instead of to the trade. The ITA 2007 s.796, charges the amount computed under s.797 as income received in the tax year. The ITA 2007 s.797, identifies an individual making a film-related loss as defined by ITA 2007 s.800, or who disposes of the rights to profits by means of a relevant disposal as defined by ITA 2007 s.799. A taxable event occurs whenever non-taxable consideration, as defined by ITA 2007 ss.798, is received or where film-related losses exceed the individual's capital contribution as defined by ITA 2007 s.801. There may be more than one chargeable event. The income is treated as non-trading income arising when a chargeable event occurs. The amount of income received is the value of the non-taxable consideration received or the amount by which the film-related losses exceed the individual's capital contribution. Double counting is avoided under ITA 2007 s.803, power is taken by ITA 2007 s.802 re-writing FA 2004 s.122A to make regulations, which may be retrospective.

18–062

The ITTOIA 2005 rules

The ITTOIA 2005 Ch.9, re-wrote the existing rules in F(No.2)A 1992 ss.40A–43; F(No.2)A 1997 s.48; and FA 2002 ss.99–101. The FA 2005 s.59 and Sch.3 ss.60–65 amended these rules to prevent tax avoidance using film financing partnerships. Previous anti-avoidance measures in FA 2004 ss.118–123, had proved inadequate. The ITTOIA 2005 s.130, defined various terms in particular production and acquisition expenditure and preliminary expenditure in relation to a film.

18–063

The ITTOIA 2005 s.131, defined film for the purposes of the relief and s.132 defined original master version and certified master version. Film includes any record of visual images as a moving picture (including any sound track). Each part of a series is a separate film unless the Secretary of the State for the Department of Culture, Media and Sport directs otherwise under the Films Act 1985 Sch.1. The original master version is the original master negative, tape and sound track or disc and for a sound recording the original master audio tape or disc. The certified master version is the original master negative certified as such under the Films Act 1985 Sch.1, where an appropriate percentage of the total expenditure on production costs has been incurred in the UK.

The ITTOIA 2005 s.133, defines the relative period as the accounting period or basis period when no accounts have been drawn up. The ITTOIA 2005 s.134, confirms that expenditure on a film or record master is deemed to be revenue expenditure in the absence of an election for capital treatment under ITTOIA 2005 s.143. Production or acquisition expenditure is defined by ITTOIA 2005 s.135. Such expenditure has to be allocated to the relevant accounting period either under the income matching method or on a just and reasonable basis as under F(No.)A 1992 ss.40B and 40C; ITTOIA 2005 ss.136–138A re-wrote the provisions in F(No.2)A 1992 s.41 and FA 2002 s.99, in relation to preliminary expenditure and F(No.2)A 1992 s.42, in relation to production expenditure. The ITTOIA 2005 s.138A, was inserted by FA 2005 Sch.3 para.3(1) and allowed expenditure on acquiring a qualifying film for commercial release in cinemas which had not already been allocated to be written off over three years with a proportionate reduction where the accounting period is not a full year. The write off is subject to any restriction on the deduction of expenditure or where it has otherwise been relieved. The FA 2006 s.47 withdraws relief for expenditure on production or acquisition of a film within ITTOIA 2005 ss.134 and 135, where principal photography commences on or after April 1, 2006 and for preliminary expenditure under ITTOIA 2005 s.137, for expenditure incurred after January 1, 2007. The withdrawal of reliefs extends to British films under ITTOIA 2005 ss.139–144.

Production expenditure on limited budget films re-writes the provisions of F(No.2)A 1992 s.42, and F(No2)A 1997 s.48, in ITTOIA 2005 s.139, which allows a full deduction for production expenditure incurred before July 2, 2005 (extended to October 1, 2007 by FA 2005 s.58) on a qualifying film intended for commercial release in cinemas where the total production expenditure is £15m or less. The ITTOIA 2005 Sch.2 paras 31–38 re-wrote various provisions relating to expenditure incurred before June 30, 2002 or earlier. Production expenditure excludes any amount that at the time the film was completed has not been paid and which is not subject to an unconditional obligation to pay within four months after the date of completion. Disallowable expenditure or that which has otherwise been allowed is ignored. The corresponding relief for acquisition expenditure on limited budget films costing £15m or less which is incurred before July 2, 2005 is given by ITTOIA 2005 s.140, re-writing the provisions of F(No.2)A 1992 s.42; F (No.2)A 1997 s.48, and FA 2002 ss.99 and 101. The FA 2005 Sch.3 para.6(1), inserted s.140A into ITTOIA 2005 which provided that a qualifying deduction for production expenditure could not also be claimed as acquisition expenditure in the same trade or another trade to prevent a double allowance. As an anti-avoidance provision this is retrospective and applies even where the original expenditure was made before December 2, 2004. HMRC can choose which claim to allow where simultaneous deductions are claimed. The definition of total production expenditure in respect of the original master version is defined by ITTOIA 2005 s.141, re-writing the provisions of F(No.2)A 1997 s.48, and the date expenditure is incurred is defined by ITTOIA 2005 s.142, re-writing F(No.2)A 1997 s.48(9) and CAA 2001 s.5.

Anti-avoidance measures—The FA 2005 rules

18–064 On December 2, 2004, HMRC published a note on "Tax avoidance using film and partnership reliefs" which was followed by FA 2005 s.65(1), which inserted ITTOIA 2005 ss.142A–142E. These anti-avoidance provisions apply where an individual or partnership carrying on a trade or business makes a claim on or after December 2, 2004, for film acquisition relief under ITTOIA 2005 ss.138, or 138A where the claimant is or has been party to a deferred income agreement entered into on or after December 2, 2004. Any excess relief is treated as income of the relevant trade thus negating the claim. Excess relief is the proportion of the expenditure if it falls after the end of a 15-year deferral period by means of a formula D x (1 − T1/T2) where D is the deduction allowed, T1 is the number of days in the 15-year period and T2 is the number of days from the beginning of the 15-year period to the final deferral date. A deferred income agreement is defined by ITTOIA 2005 s.142B, as an agreement which guarantees any person an amount of income from exploitation of the film more than 15 years from the date of practical completion or purchase. A deferred income agreement entered into after a deduction has already been claimed for production or acquisition expenditure is regarded for corporation tax purposes as giving rise to an amount of income equal to the excess relief.

Net excess relief is defined by ITTOIA 2005 s.142D as the proportion of the expenditure which falls after the end of the 15-year period calculated by applying the same formula as under ITTOIA 2005 s.145A. These provisions had effect from April 6, 2005 unless an unconditional agreement has been entered into before December 2, 2004. The anti-avoidance provisions are aimed at artificial manipulation of the film or partnership reliefs described in Pt 2 of the technical note published by HMRC on December 2, 2004. The effect of the provisions is to limit the deferral of income through film partnerships, HMRC's note states:

> "film tax relief is commonly accessed by film makers through licensing, leasing or similar arrangements with companies or with individuals and partnerships. Typically the company or partnership (the investor) will pay to produce or acquire a film and then license or lease this film back to a producer or distributor for a specified period., Usually the investor will be guaranteed a minimum amount of license fees or lease rental payments spread over the period of the license or lease.
>
> The investor obtains accelerated relief, the cost of the film under F(No.2)A 1992 s42 or F(No.2)A 1997 s48. They then pay tax in later years on the fees or rental income. This works as a tax deferral for the investor-in effect pushing back the time that tax is paid in return for an investment in a film.
>
> The longer the period that tax is deferred the more valuable this is to the investor. The Inland Revenue has recently accepted deferral for up to fifteen years but a number of schemes have recently emerged which seek longer periods."

The effect of the provisions is to limit the period of deferral to 15 years.

On a typical film financing sale and lease back arrangement the film financing partnership will claim tax relief on the initial expenditure but will be liable for income tax on the rental income in future years; i.e. it is a tax deferral not a tax saving mechanism. The idea of replacing the existing lease with one which qualifies as a long funding finance lease of plant or machinery under ITTOIA 2005 ss.148A–148FC would normally give allowances to the lessee and the lessor's rental stream would be largely untaxed. Therefore the provisions which give this effect to a long funding finance lease are disapplied in the case of films, by ITTOIA 2005 s.148FD which applies to long funding leases entered into on or after November 13, 2008.

18–065

Where the long funding finance lease of a film was started prior to November 13, 2008, but not terminated before that date, the provisions relieving the rental income from taxation, for corporation tax under CTA 2010 s.360 and for income tax under ITTOIA 2005 s.148A are disapplied for a period of account before the relevant date. In other cases the disallowance of the exemption applies to so much of the rentals as become due on or after November 13, 2008, to the extent that it is not already regarded as reflected in the rental earnings for the period of account. These anti-avoidance provisions also permit relief for exceptional items or termination payments.

Partnership sideways loss relief was restricted by FA 2004 ss.124 and by 125 inserting TA 1988 ss.118ZE–118ZM and was further restricted by FA 2005 ss.72–79, inserting TA 1988 s.118ZN–118ZO, which were re-written as ITA 2007 ss.102–116. Sideways loss relief for individuals is restricted by FA 2008 s.60 and ITA 2007 s.27A which limits Step 2 deduction for sideways loss reliefs to £50,000 or 25 per cent of adjusted total income.

The election for expenditure on films to be treated as capital instead of income is contained in ITTOIA 2005 s.143, re-writing F(No.2)A 1992 s.40D and FA 2002 s.100. The meaning of "genuinely intended for theatrical release" under FA 2002 s.99, is re-written as ITTOIA 2005 s.144.

SETTLEMENT OPPORTUNITY

18–066 On December 20, 2012 HMRC issued a Notice introducing a settlement opportunity for participants in tax avoidance schemes, which included the following statement:

> "Outline of the settlement opportunity
> The schemes included in the settlement opportunity generally seek to create tax relief much greater than the real economic cost borne by the participants. HMRC has a high success rate in litigating these types of scheme.
> The settlement opportunity will be offered to participants in the following schemes—
>
> - Schemes which seek to use Generally Accepted Accounting Practice (GAAP) to write off expenditure or the value of assets to create losses either for sole traders, or individuals or companies in partnership
> - Schemes seeking to access the film relief legislation for production expenditure
> - Schemes seeking to create losses in partnerships through reliefs such as first year allowance, payments made for restrictive covenants, specific capital allowances
>
> There are some schemes with these features which are specifically excluded from the settlement opportunity (see FAQs). More detail will be given for individual schemes which are included but, broadly speaking, we will restrict relief so that expenditure which is not part of the real economic cost borne by the participants will be excluded when calculating losses or capital allowances. Broadly this means that, subject to the particular facts of the scheme, only amounts equivalent to the actual cash contribution funded by the participant and expended in the claimed trade will be allowed when computing losses or capital allowances. No relief will be allowed for interest on any loan used to fund contributions to the partnership in excess of the initial cash contribution. Where fees are paid for the provision of the wider funding arrangements, tax advice or litigation protection, it is likely that they will not be allowable. ...
> HMRC list the recent cases in which they have been successful including:

Commissioners for Her Majesty's Revenue and Customs v Tower MCashback LLP 1 (2011) S.T.C. 1143; *Eclipse Film Partners No 35 LLP v Revenue & Customs* 2012 SFTD 823; *Icebreaker 1 LLP v Revenue and Customs* (2011) S.T.C. 1078; *Samarkand Film Partnership No 3 v Revenue and Customs* (2012) SFTD 1; and *Alchemist (Devil's Gate) Film Partnership v HMRC* TC/2012/0618. (Other successes include *RCC v Micro Fusion 2004–1 LLP* (2010) S.T.C. 1541; *RCC v Halycon Films LLP* (2010) S.T.C. 1125; and *Patrick Degorce v RCC* (2013) UKFTT 178 (TC). An early HMRC success was *Ensign Tanks (Leasing) Ltd v Stokes* (1992) S.T.C. 226. See also, Ch.23–001–005).

Under this settlement opportunity the treatment of income that is received by the partnership, individual or company will depend on the particular arrangements. In general where there is a contingent right of future income from the asset purchased, it is expected that that income will be taxable in full. Where the income arises directly from the repayment of the circular loan finance, amounts received over and above the initial finance will be taxed as investment income on an amortised basis over the period of the unwind. The return of the initial finance will be treated as a capital receipt and not taxed.

We reserve the right to reply on all arguments available, including those that may deny any relief completely in litigation.

The settlement opportunity is open to partnerships, individual partners, company partners and sole traders who have used certain schemes. The settlement opportunity extended to partners is restricted to the specific circumstances of the schemes covered by this settlement opportunity. It is not open to partners in any other partnerships."

This was followed by a further Notice on January 9, 2013:

HMRC SETTLEMENT OPPORTUNITY—UK GAAP PARTNERSHIPS AND SIDEWAYS LOSS RELIEF

HMRC has published the terms of its "settlement opportunity" in respect of partnerships using UK GAAP schemes designed to generate sideways loss relief. In December, the government outlined plans to seek settlement of disputes involving certain tax avoidance schemes by agreement, before resorting to litigation with increased vigour. This is the first of the schemes for which detailed settlement terms have been published. **18–067**

UK GAAP PARTNERSHIPS

As part of the phased roll out of the settlement opportunity HMRC has written to individuals who have taken part in UK GAAP Partnership schemes. If you have received a letter this page sets out the broad terms under which HMRC is proposing to allow settlement. **18–068**

GAAP partnerships are those which have sought to create a loss through the write-off of expenditure or the value of rights or assets through Generally Accepted Accounting Practice.

18–069 TERMS OF SETTLEMENT

- Loss relief against other income will be allowed in an amount equivalent to your contribution to the partnership personally contributed by you as the cash contribution, less any element expended on unallowable fees.
- Unallowable fees are those spent on tax advice or circular funding arrangements. We will tell you if we believe a disallowance for fees is needed.
- The balance of the loss claim will not be allowable.
- Loan interest will only be allowable to the extent that it represents the allowable expenditure paid out of the initial cash contribution.
- Any share of income attributable to the cash element of expenditure will be taxable in full.
- Any share of income attributable to the loan financed element will only be taxable insofar as it represents investment income over and above the return of the initial capital.

Example
- Partner A invests £1m into a partnership—
   o £200,000 is cash from his own resources.
   o £800,000 is by way of loan finance as part of the scheme.
   o The objective is to claim loss relief of £1m.
- At a tax rate of 40 per cent this equates to £400,000 cash tax.
- Relief allowed under the opportunity is limited to £200,000 (less any disallowance for fees).
   - At a tax rate of 40 per cent this equates to £80,000 cash tax.

WHAT TO DO NOW

18–070 Whilst not of general applicability to partnerships, within the specific terms of this settlement opportunity HMRC is prepared to settle with individual partners, irrespective of whether or not the partnership itself continues to disagree with HMRC's view.

This new handling strategy will not apply to cases already adopted for criminal investigation. Any cases which are, during the course of an enquiry, identified as falling within HMRC's criminal investigation policy, or civil investigation of fraud procedures, will no longer be dealt with under this handling strategy.

If you wish to take advantage of this opportunity, and discuss how the precise terms of any settlement may affect your liability please call 03000 530435. HMRC's criminal investigation policy (*www.hmrc.gov.uk/prosecutions/crum-iv-policy.htm*).

An overview of the settlement opportunity, including detailed questions and answers (*www.hmrc.gpv.uk/press/settle-opp-tax-avoid.htm*).

FILM AND SOUND RECORDINGS

The FA 2006 schemes

18–071
In a dramatic change of policy the Treasury decided to abandon giving special tax reliefs to the financiers of films often organised through film partnerships. These tax reliefs were getting more and more convoluted and difficult to police, and borrowed from schemes such as the vaccine research relief to give a credit direct to the film producer as a tax relief which could be converted into immediate cash, effectively to subsidise the production costs rather than the financing arrangements. This scheme applies to qualifying expenditure on film-making activities which commenced principal photography on or after April 1, 2006. These rules were proceeded by consultation document "The Reform of Film Tax Incentives: Promoting the Sustainable Production of Culturally British Films" which was published on July 29, 2005.

The meaning of a film is defined by CTA 2009 s.1181, as any means of showing a sequence of visual images as a moving picture. In most cases each part of a series of films is treated as a separate film unless the series constitutes a self-contained work or is a series of documentaries with a common theme (see Films Act 1985 Sch.1). A film includes the soundtrack and is completed when it is in a form which can be copied and distributed for presentation to the general public.

The relief is aimed at a film production company, defined by CTA 2009 s.1182. This is a company which, otherwise than in partnership, is responsible for pre-production or principal photography, post-production and delivery of the completed film and is actively engaged in production planning and decision making and directly negotiates contracts and pays for rents, goods and services in relation to the film. There can only be one film production company in relation to a film. However, there are provisions relating to a co-production and a company is a co-producer if it makes an effective, creative, technical and artistic contribution to the film, i.e. it is more than the mere financing entity. If more than one company falls within the definition that most directly engaged is the film production company, and if no company meets all the requirements there is no film production company in relation to that film and therefore no special relief. The new scheme counts as state aid and required the approval of the European Union. A film production company can elect out of the scheme as the film tax relief is only available in respect of UK expenditure on a British film intended for theatrical releases (CTA 2009 s.1195). This is defined as release by way of exhibition to the paying public at the commercial cinema in a manner intended to obtain a significant proportion of the earnings from the film. This intention is determined at the beginning of the development, under CTA 2009 s.1196, and if genuinely so determined continues to apply irrespective of what may happen to the film, for example, the world-wide TV rights may in total exceed the cinema earnings. The film must be certified by the Secretary of State for the Department of Culture, Media and Sport under Films Act 1985 Sch.1 as amended by Films (Modification of the Definition of "British Film") Order 2000 (SI 2000/756) and the Films (Definition of "British Film") Order 2006 (SI 2006/643), under CTA 2009 s.1197. CTA 2009 s.1198 requires that at least 25 per cent of the core expenditure must be UK expenditure, within CTA 2009 s.1185. As film tax relief is not available for films made for TV, a production company may prefer to withdraw from the relief and calculate its taxable profit in accordance with UK GAAP.

A number of other terms are defined including film-making activities by CTA 2009 s.1183, the meaning of production expenditure by CTA 2009 s.1184, qualifying co-production and co-producer by CTA 2009 s.1186.

Entitlement to film tax reliefs

18–072   CTA 2009 ss.1195–1216 provide film tax relief where the appropriate conditions are satisfied, and allows the film production company to claim for an additional deduction in calculating the profit or loss of its trade in respect of qualifying expenditure on a film at least partly made in the UK, for theatrical release as a British film, CTA 2009 ss.1195–1198). Qualifying expenditure is that calculated under CTA 2009 ss.1199 and 1200 and the additional deduction is allowed in the first period of account and is the lower of the UK qualifying expenditure or 80 per cent of the total qualifying expenditure, if less, multiplied by the appropriate rate of enhancement CTA 2009 s.1200. In subsequent periods the additional deduction is re-calculated on the cumulative total less any additional deductions in earlier periods. The rate of enhancement is 100 per cent of the additional deduction for a limited budget film where the core expenditure is £20m or less, and for more expensive films, 80 per cent of the additional deduction. The 80 per cent rule is the state aid limit. A film production company may also claim a film tax credit for an accounting period of which it has a surrenderable loss which is the lower of the trading loss for the period and the available qualifying expenditure, i.e. the cumulative qualifying expenditure, less that allowed in earlier periods, i.e. it does not include the enhanced deduction CTA 2009 s.1199. The whole or any part of the surrenderable loss may be converted into a film tax credit CTA 2009 ss.1201, 1202. The payable credit for a limited budget film is 25 per cent of the loss surrendered and for any other film 20 per cent of the loss surrendered. The effective initial subsidy is therefore 80 per cent of 25 per cent, i.e. 20 per cent of the qualifying expenditure for a limited budget film and 80 per cent x 20 per cent, i.e. 16 per cent, of such expenditure for a higher budget film under CTA 2009 s.1202. HMRC, when paying the film tax credit, may deduct any outstanding liability to pay corporation tax or PAYE or tax under the foreign entertainers provisions of ITA 2007 s.966 or national insurance contributions that may be outstanding. The film tax credit is not itself taxable CTA 2009 s.1203. The trading loss is reduced by the amount surrendered for the payable tax credit under CTA 2009 s.1202.

Costs incurred on a film at the end of a period of account, under CTA 2009 s.1202, can only be included if paid within four months of the end of the period of account which is more restrictive than the normal rules for the taxation of activities of a film production company. Arrangements which have as one of their main objects the increase in the amount of film tax relief available are disregarded under CTA 2009 s.1205. The rules relating to the payment of film tax credit are set out in CTA 2009 Sch.2 para.128.

FILM AND SOUND RECORDINGS

The certification procedure for a British film is set out in amendments to the Film Act 1985 in FA 2006 Sch.5 paras 15–23, and consequential amendments in CTA 2009 ss.1206, 1207and provisional entitlement to relief is available which provides for relief to be claimed on an interim certificate of qualification as a British film and on the basis of anticipated UK expenditure and total budget. If these are over-estimated or the budget overruns and exceeds the £20m limit, the claims have to be amended in accordance with CTA 2009 ss.1212–1216.

The taxation of the activities for a film production company are set out in CTA 2009 s.1188 et seq. These provisions set out the date of commencement of the principal photography as on or after April 1, 2006. The activities of a film production company are treated as a separate trade for each film made from January 1, 2007 under CTA 2009 Sch.2 para.128. The deemed trade commences when pre-production of the film begins or income from the film is received, if earlier (CTA 2009 s.1191), pre-trading expenditure is that incurred on the development of a film, if not previously claimed (CTA 2009 s.1193). The costs of the film include expenditure in connection with exploiting the film unless specifically disallowed, such as entertaining expenditure. All expenditure on films is treated as being of a revenue nature (CTA 2009 s.1191). Income from the film includes any receipts in connection with the making or exploitation of the film including the sale of film rights or royalties, merchandising and any other income, all of which is treated as being of a revenue nature (CTA 2009 s.1190).

18–073

The calculation of the profit or loss under CTA 2009 s.1189 is arrived at by debiting the costs incurred to date and crediting the estimated total income for the film relating to the period of account. In subsequent periods of account the debit is for any additional expenditure incurred and the credit for additional estimated income earnt to date. Debits can only be included if represented in work in progress so that payments in advance are ignored until the work has been carried out and deferment payments are recognised to the extent that the work is represented in the state of completion. Unpaid amounts can only be taken into account if there is an unconditional obligation to pay which excludes conditional deferments (CTA 2009 s.1192). The formula for estimating the total income at the end of any period of account is $C/T \times I$ where C is the total of the costs to date reflected in the work done, T is the estimated total of costs of the film and I is the estimated total income from the film (CTA 2009 s.1189). CTA 2009 s.1194 requires the estimates to be made at the balance sheet date on a fair and reasonable basis taking into consideration all relevant circumstances, such as pre-sales of distribution rights. Expenditure which has already been relieved under previous film reliefs are excluded by CTA 2009 Sch.2 para.132.

Film losses are restricted while the film is in production and can only be carried forward against profits of the same deemed trade under CTA 2009 ss.1208, 1209, and this would prevent, for example, group relief being claimed. Once the film is completed or abandoned, any unrelieved trading loss brought forward becomes de-restricted under CTA 2009 s.1209 and can be set off against other profits of the company for the same or an earlier period under CTA 2010 s.37, or surrendered as group relief under CTA 2010 Pt 5, and CTA 2009 s.1210. Such losses exclude the additional deduction under CTA 2009 ss.1199, 1200 and are subject to film terminal loss relief under CTA 2009 s.1211.

18–074 Film terminal losses arising from the deemed trade of one film can be carried forward and set against the profits of a second film, which is a deemed separate trade under CTA 2009 s.1188. These provisions in CTA 2009 s.1211 are supplemented by the Corporation Tax (Surrender of Terminal Losses on Films and Claims for Relief) Regulations 2007 (SI 2007/678).

Films dealt with under the film tax relief scheme are excluded from being intangible fixed assets under CTA 2009 s.886. Transitional provisions for films that commenced principal photography before April 1, 2006 but are not completed before January 1, 2007 are covered by CTA 2009 Sch.2 para.130, and the Corporation Tax (Taxation of Films) Transitional Provisions Regulations 2007 (SI 2007/1050). The commencement date is January 1, 2007, under the Finance Act 2006 s.53(1)(Films and Sound Recordings)(Appointed Day) Order 2006 (SI 2006/3399).

Corporation tax treatment of sound recordings

18–075 CTA 2009 s.150, applies to a trading company incurring expenditure on the production or acquisition of the original master version of a sound recording which is treated as being a revenue expense. Similarly the disposal proceeds of an original master version is treated as a receipt of a revenue nature. This extends to any sums received from the disposal of any interest or right in or over the original master version or insurance proceeds or compensation. Expenditure is allocated under CTA 2009 s.151, on a just and reasonable basis taking into account the proportion of the estimated value of the original master version realised in the period and the need to bring the whole of the expenditure into account over the period during which the value of the original master version is expected to be realised. However, CTA 2009 s.151(4) allows the company also to allocate to a relevant period a further amount so long as the total amount allocated does not exceed the value of the original master version realised in the period, whether by way of income or otherwise. Various terms are defined by CTA 2009 s.152.

CAPITAL TAXES

18–076 Copyright, as intellectual property, is subject to capital gains tax and inheritance tax in the same way as patents (see Ch.17). On February 25, 1983, Mr Nicholas Ridley confirmed that "the value of a copyright for capital transfer tax (inheritance tax) is the price the property might reasonably be expected to fetch if sold in the open market at the time of the transfer" (*Hansard*, Vol.37, col.570). In practice copyright is rarely sold in isolation but any such sale would be on the basis of the discounted present value of a conservative estimate of the likely future royalties (Ch.12). Copyright would usually only become a wasting asset under TCGA 1992 s.44, more than 20 years after the author's death when the remaining life was less than 50 years.

Books, manuscripts, pictures, photographs, documents and sculptures protected by copyright are also tangible moveable property for capital gains tax purposes. This means that disposal proceeds of up to £6,000 would be exempt under TCGA 1992 s.262, and any loss on a sale for less than £6,000 would be restricted on the basis of a deemed sale price of £6,000. In the case of a gain, marginal relief is given by deducting from the gain the excess of the gain over five-thirds of the excess of the consideration over £6,000.

Example

	£	
Sale proceeds		7,200
Cost	400	
Gain		6,800
Marginal relief Sale proceeds		7,200
Less:		
Deemed cost	6,000	
Excess		1,200
5/3 excess		2,000
Gain as calculated		6,800
Relief £6,800–£2,000	4,800	
Revised gain		2,000

In other words the gain is the lower of the normal gain or five-thirds of the excess of the sale proceeds over £6,000.

Such tangible property could, in the view of the Treasury, be of national, scientific or artistic importance and thus qualify for capital gains tax exemption under TCGA 1992 s.258, if the transfer was or could have been exempt from inheritance tax as a conditionally exempt transfer under IHTA 1984 s.30 on an undertaking given under IHTA 1984 s.31 or TCGA 1992 s.258(3). The undertaking requires the property to be made available to the public and kept in the UK. On a subsequent sale or breach of undertaking where the exemption is not available there could be both a capital gains tax and an inheritance tax charge under TCGA 1992 s.258(5) and IHTA 1984 ss.32 and 33.

STAMP DUTY

18–077 Copyright is intellectual property in the same way as a patent and exempt from stamp duty for instruments executed on or after March 28, 2000, under FA 2000 s.129.

VAT

18–078 The VAT provisions relating to patents apply similarly to copyright (see Ch.11). For VAT purposes public lending right payments are different from royalty payments and cannot be treated in the same way. Public lending right is outside the scope for VAT and should not be declared on the VAT return form. Public lending right payment is not a royalty but derives from the author receiving a share of a subsidy or grant.

The public lending right registrar is not registered for VAT and no VAT is chargeable on public lending right payments. Monies distributed by the registrar under the Public Lending Right Act 1979 do not constitute considerations of a supply to the registrar and therefore no VAT is chargeable on the monies solely distributed. In case of difficulty, authors' local VAT officers should be asked to refer to VAT Administration Directorate (VAH2) quoting reference TL 1158/82 which confirms that no VAT is chargeable on public lending right monies.

Copyright royalties are often paid to authors and others whose taxable outputs are below the registration limit and who do not have to register for VAT. In such cases the royalties would be paid without any addition for VAT. Most publishers also operate a self-billing system whereby an invoice is not raised by the author but the royalties are accounted for by the publisher who produces a statement which acts as if it were an invoice from the author. This means that if the author is registered for VAT the publisher adds VAT at the standard rate to the royalties due and if the author is not so registered the publisher merely pays over the basic royalty. For a self-billed invoice to count as a tax invoice, the self-billing arrangement must have been cleared by HMRC under Value Added Tax Regulations 1995 (SI 1995/2518).

CHAPTER 19

Know-how and Show-how

INTRODUCTION

The rules set out in this chapter apply, except as regards royalties, to "pre-FA 2002 assets" of companies, i.e. those acquired, or created or originally acquired or created by another group company, before April 1, 2002, CTA 2009 Pt 8 Ch.16 s.881. They do not apply to intangible fixed assets of a company either created by the company, or acquired from non-related parties, on or after April 1, 2002. In the case of assets acquired from related parties these fall into the Corporate Intangible fixed Assets regime (see Ch.21) if they have been created or acquired from unrelated parties by the vendor on or after April 1, 2002, all of which are dealt with under CTA 2009 Pt 8 ss.711–879 and 901–906. They continue to apply to unincorporated businesses and to limited liability partnerships which are not affected by CTA 2009 Pt 8.

Although the sale of know-how has for many years normally been assessed as a trading receipt, special provisions are included in the Taxes Acts to tax as income those few receipts which would otherwise be capital. Show-how is the provision of services rather than a transfer of intellectual property and there are no special taxation provisions to consider.

19–001

Definitions

"Know-how" is defined for corporation tax purposes by CTA 2009 s.908(4) and s.176(1) as:

19–002

> "any industrial information or techniques likely to assist in (a) manufacturing or processing goods or materials , (b) in working a source of mineral deposits (including the searching for, discovery, or testing mineral deposits or the obtaining access to them), or (c) in carrying out any agricultural, forestry or fishing operations."

This is a wide definition and would include many payments normally referred to as know-how fees and could also include designs for manufactured products and secret processes. It does not, however, include commercial know-how which is becoming of greater commercial significance. A similar definition is adopted in ITTOIA 2005 Pt 2 Ch.14 s.192(1), which applies for income tax purposes with effect from April 6, 2005. In this chapter "know-how" refers to all know-how, and "industrial know-how" within CTA 2009 s.908(4) or ITTOIA 2005 s.192(1) (CA 70010). "Show-how" is the term often applied to agreements for the provision of technical assistance and training, but this term does not appear in the tax legislation. HMRC's Capital Allowances Manual of CA 70010 expands on the definition of know-how in ITTOIA 2005 s.192 and CAA 2001 s.452 as follows:

> "Know-how is a type of intellectual property. It is industrial information or techniques likely to assist in:
>
> - the manufacture or processing of goods or materials, or
> - the working of a source of mineral deposits, or
> - the carrying out of any agricultural, forestry or fishing operations.
>
> Mineral deposits include any natural deposits, including geothermal energy, capable of being lifted or extracted from the earth. A source of mineral deposits includes a mine, oil well or source of geothermal energy. Searching for, discovering or testing mineral deposits or obtaining access to them are working a source of mineral deposits.
>
> The expression "industrial information or techniques" is coloured by the words that follow—"likely to assist in the manufacture or processing of goods and materials". This means that only information relevant to industrial or technical processes is within the definition of know-how."

INCOME

19–003 Know-how is often licensed in return for royalties and as these are not patent royalties they would be taxed in the same way as royalties for trade marks and designs (see para.17–010).

Show-how fees are rather different in that show-how is, strictly, the provision of services rather than an assignment or licence of intellectual property. This means that the show-how fees would normally be taxed as trading income of the recipient and allowed as a trading expense of the payer. This would apply whether there is a single payment or lump sum fee or whether the payment is spread over a period, even if it is calculated on a royalty basis.

A know-how royalty for the use of a secret process for 40 years was, exceptionally, treated as an annual payment taxable on the licensor and as a charge on income of the licensee in the case of *Delage v Nugget Polish Co Ltd* (1905) 21 T.L.R. 454 (see above, para.17–011). Normally the services to be provided by the licensor prevent the receipt from being "pure income profit" and therefore know-how royalties are not normally annual payments.

LUMP SUMS

Case law

19–004 Know-how may be sold for a lump sum and it is then necessary to determine whether this is taxable as a trading receipt or not (CA 72000–72600). The leading case on the topic is that of *Jeffrey v Rolls-Royce Ltd* (1962) 40 T.C. 443 (CA 72000). In this case it was held that the disposal of rights to manufacture certain aircraft engines for a lump sum payment, including the provision of all technical assistance, gave rise to a trading receipt on the ground that it was merely a way of turning the company's expertise into income. As Lord Radcliffe said, at 492:

> "I cannot accept the contention that by each of these agreements the Company sold a part of that capital asset and received a price for it. There is nothing in the Case to indicate that that capital asset was in any way diminished by carrying out these agreements. The whole of its knowledge and experience remained available to the Company for manufacturing and further research and development, and there is nothing to show that its value in any way diminished."

The case was distinguished from that of *Evans Medical Supplies Ltd v Moriarty* (1957) 37 T.C. 540, under which the sale of know-how was held to be a capital receipt. The distinction was, in the words of Lord Radcliffe in the *Rolls-Royce* case, at 492:

> "In that case [*Evans Medical Supplies*] it was held that the company parted with a capital asset and received for it a capital sum. For one thing, it lost its Burmese market. And, further, it was said to be obvious that the capital value of the secret processes must have been greatly diminished by their disclosure to the Burmese Government. Every case of this kind must be decided on its own facts." (CA 72200)

The *Rolls-Royce* decision was followed in the case of *Musker v English Electric Co Ltd* (1964) 41 T.C. 556. Attempts by the company to distinguish the sale of its know-how from that in the *Rolls-Royce* case were rejected by the House of Lords.

19–005 The basic distinction is that where the know-how remains with the vendor for further exploitation, it is a trading receipt. If on the other hand the disposal is of part of the company's assets so that the information once imparted cannot again be utilised commercially, the receipt would be one of capital following *Evans Medical Supplies Ltd v Moriarty*.

The principle in the *Rolls-Royce* case was also followed in *Coalite & Chemical Products Ltd v Treeby* (1971) 48 T.C. 171.

The case of *John & E Sturge Ltd v Hessel* [1975] S.T.C. 573, not only confirmed that the sale of know-how was, in the circumstances, a trading receipt, but also that the receipt was taxable when it was earned, that is when, under the agreement, the services to be rendered were rendered.

19–006 In an early case on the topic of know-how, *British Dyestuffs Corporation (Blackley) Ltd v IRC* (1924) 12 T.C. 586, it was argued that a payment for know-how was a capital receipt in spite of the fact that it was payable by 10 annual instalments, each of £25,000.

In the words of Banks L.J., at 596, it was stated:

> "I do not myself think that the method of payment adopted in carrying through a transaction between a company, such as this, and a licensee is very much guide to the true nature of the transaction. The real question is, looking at this matter, is the transaction in substance a parting by the Company with part of its property for a purchase price, or is it a method of trading by which it acquires this particular sum of money as part of the profits and gains of that trade?"

The amount was held to be a trading receipt in that case.

19–007 Apart from the case of *Evans Medical Supplies Ltd v Moriarty*, already referred to above, the only other case where a sale of know-how was held to be capital was that of *Wolf Electric Tools Ltd v Wilson* (1968) 45 T.C. 326. In that case the company was forced either to abandon its exports to India or to set up local manufacture through a company in which it held a minority interest. It chose the latter course. It was held that the transfer of know-how to the new company in exchange for the minority interest was not a disposal of know-how for the value of the shares in the new company, but was an alteration in the company's structure. In the words of Pennycuick J., at 340:

> "In a case such as the present, the effect of the whole arrangement—and I must look at the whole arrangement—is that the trader receives a new capital asset, namely, the shares in the foreign company, in exchange for that which he previously had, namely, his connection or goodwill in the foreign country. That is a transaction of a wholly capital nature."

In *Thomsons (Carron) Ltd v IRC* [1976] S.T.C. 317, the sale of know-how in exchange for shares in the acquirer was still a revenue receipt of the vendor.

Statutory provisions

19–008 Attempts to argue that the sale of industrial know-how is a capital receipt in respect of amounts received after March 19, 1968, would be largely abortive in view of the provisions of what is now CTA 2009 s.177(1) and (2) and ITTOIA 2005 s.193(1) and (2) which state:

(1) This section applies if—
    (a) a company/person carrying on a trade receives consideration for the disposal of know-how which has been used in the trade.
    (b) the company/person continues to carry on the trade after the disposal, and
    (c) neither s.194 (disposal of know-how as part of disposal of all or part of a trade) nor s.195 (seller controlled by buyer, etc.) applies.
(2) The amount or value of the consideration is treated for corporation tax/all purposes as a trading receipt, except so far as it is brought into account under s.462 of CAA 2001 (disposal values).

There are no provisions for spreading the receipt over a period (CA 72400).

Common control

19–009 One of the exceptions to these provisions is that under CTA 2009 s.178 or ITTOIA 2005 s.193, the treatment as an automatic trading receipt does not apply where the buyer is a body of persons over whom the seller has control, or the seller is a body of persons over whom the buyer has control, or both the seller and the buyer are bodies of persons and some other person has control over both of them, and for this purpose "body of persons" includes partnerships. In such cases the sale of industrial know-how, together with the trade or part of the trade, is deemed to be a sale of goodwill giving rise to a capital gains tax charge (ITTOIA

2005 s.195). The sale of know-how by itself would normally be a trading receipt (CA 72400). No election for alternative treatment is possible.

Disposal of know-how and goodwill

If, however, the industrial know-how is sold, together with the trade or part of a trade at arm's-length, any consideration received is again, normally, treated under CTA 2009 s.178(1)–(3) and ITTOIA 2005 s.194(2) as a payment for goodwill and therefore a capital sum taxed as a chargeable gain under TCGA 1992 s.21 (CA 72300) and no disposal value is brought into account in the seller's capital allowances computation. Conversely it is treated as the purchase of goodwill by the buyer and know-how capital allowances are not available. In such arms-length transactions it is possible under CTA 2009 s.921(3), (4) or ITTOIA 2005 s.194(5) that the sale of industrial know-how will be treated as a trading receipt, even if on the disposal of a trade, where a joint election is made by the transferee and the transferor and given to the Inspector of Taxes within two years of the disposal. Nor is it to be treated as a capital transaction, in spite of being linked with the disposal of a trade, where the transferor was previously carrying on a business wholly outside the UK CTA 2009 s.178(4)–(6), ITTOIA 2005 s.194(4)). It could be advantageous, for example, where there are unused trading losses brought forward, to treat know-how proceeds as a revenue receipt rather than a capital receipt.

19–010

Non-trading know-how

Where the industrial know-how disposed of has not been used for the purpose of a trade, the receipt of a capital sum would be subject to corporation tax under CTA 2009 ss.908(1), 909(2)–(4) or income tax under ITTOIA 2005 s.583, with a deduction for the cost of the know-how if not otherwise relieved CTA 2009 s.910(1); ITTOIA 2005 s.585(2)). If such a sum is received by the devisor of the industrial know-how the income will be treated as earned income (CA 72500), and would be taxed under ITTOIA 2005 s.687, as income not otherwise charged if not employment income or from carrying on a trade or profession.

19–011

Restrictive covenants

It is not possible to avoid the statutory provisions in relation to industrial know-how receipts by entering into restrictive covenants rather than some form of licence agreement or assignment, as any receipts from such a covenant would be taxable under CTA 2009 ss.176(3), (4) and 908(1) or ITTOIA 2005 s.192(3) as a know-how receipt (CA 72600).

19–012

PLANNING ASPECTS

It might be possible in suitable circumstances to sell the pre-April 1, 2002, know-how to a subsidiary company for a capital sum in which case the provisions of CTA 2009 ss.179(1), (2), 909(5), (6) and 1316(2), would apply. If this were a

19–013

disposal of know-how there would be a capital gain, but as this would be an intra-group transaction within TCGA 1992 s.171, there would be no immediate corporation tax liability on the chargeable gain.

If the shares in the subsidiary company were then sold to an intended purchaser of the know-how there would be a chargeable gain if the shares were sold at a profit (assuming exemption is not available under the substantial shareholding provisions of TCGA 1992 Sch.7AC). If, however, the shares had been issued at par for the full value of the know-how, there would be no gain on the disposal of the shares. There would, however, be a deemed disposal of the know-how, which would crystallise on the company leaving the group under TCGA 1992 ss.178 and 179, if the transfer to the subsidiary had taken place within the previous six years. This would nonetheless be a capital gain rather than a trading receipt and could therefore be preferable.

ALLOWANCE TO PURCHASER

19-014 The net expenditure on industrial know-how (CAA 2001 s.452) incurred after March 31, 1986, if not allowable as a trading expense (CA 73000), qualifies for a "writing-down" allowance of 25 per cent a year. The available writing down allowance is proportionately reduced if the trade has been carried on for only part of a tax year or if the chargeable period is for less than one year (CAA 2001 s.458(1)–(4)). In the period to cessation a balancing allowance is made for the whole of the unallowed balance of expenditure (CAA 2001 s.458 (6)). If the disposal value exceeds the qualifying expenditure, there is a balancing charge on the excess (CAA 2001 s.458(5)).

Net qualifying expenditure is the capital expenditure during the period on the acquisition of industrial know-how (CAA 2001 s.452), not otherwise relieved (CAA 2001 s.455(1)) for the purpose of a trade carried on or to be carried on (CAA 2001 s.454) and not acquired from persons under common control (CAA 2001 s.455(2) and (3) (CA 71000)). Such expenditure on intangible property (CAA 2001 s.452) has to be pooled with a separate pool for each trade carried on (CAA 2001 ss.456 and 460) and (CA 71000) includes any previous qualifying expenditure remaining unrelieved (CAA 2001 s.461) which effectively gives a writing-down allowance of 25 per cent a year on a reducing balance basis. The net qualifying expenditure (AQE less TDV) is the available qualifying expenditure (AQE), i.e. the pool value brought forward plus the qualifying expenditure in the period (CAA 2001 ss.454, 459) less the total of any disposal values (TDV), i.e. capital sale proceeds not treated as goodwill under CTA 2009 s.178(1)–(3) or ITTOIA 2005 s.194 (CAA 2001 ss.457, 462, (CA 71200)). Know-how allowances and charges are treated as expenses and receipts of the trade (CAA 2001 s.463) (CA 71400). The capital allowances rules applicable to plant and machinery, including the pool basis and balancing allowances and charges are largely applied by CAA 2001 ss.452–463, except for the control sales rules in CAA 2001 ss.567–570, which are replaced by CTA 2009 ss.179(1)–(3), 909(5), (6), 1316(2) and ITTOIA 2005 s.195 above. Pre-trading expenditure is deemed to be incurred on commencement of the trade (CAA 2001 s.454(3)).

When industrial know-how is disposed of and is not treated as goodwill under CTA 2009 s.178(1)–(3) or ITTOIA 2005 s.194, the whole of the net proceeds will be brought into account: there is no limit by reference to the original cost of the know-how (CAA 2001 s.462(2); (CA 70020, 71300)). For the purposes of capital allowances on industrial know-how expenditure, deemed know-how, such as expenditure in relation to restrictive covenants, does not qualify for writing-down allowances, although it would normally be capital expenditure (*Associated Portland Cement Manufacturers Ltd v IRC* (1945) 27 T.C. 103; CA 6030). Industrial know-how acquired by a holding company for use by its operating subsidiaries should qualify for relief against management charges received (70040).

COMMERCIAL KNOW-HOW

19–015 Commercial know-how, outwith the definitions in CTA 2009 s.908(4) or ITTOIA 2005 s.192(1), does not qualify for capital allowances and, if capital expenditure, could only be relieved in a computation for chargeable gains on outright sale, which is unlikely to be of much assistance. Revenue expenditure can be written off immediately or over a short period as deferred revenue expenditure (see para.18–036). HMRC accept that both lump sum and recurring payments to acquire know-how for the purposes of a trade are normally revenue payments (CA 70030).

Divers

19–016 Divers and diving supervisors employed in the United Kingdom are deemed by ITTOIA 2005 s.15(2), to be carrying on a trade. Certain training courses qualify for relief as acquisition of industrial know-how (CA 74000).

STAMP DUTY

19–017 Neither know-how nor show-how are regarded as property for stamp duty purposes, although know-how is regarded as property for other tax purposes under CAA 2001 s.453 (CA 70050) and therefore no ad valorem duty is payable in respect of any agreement, assignment or licence. If an agreement covers both know-how and the sale of goodwill these elements no longer have to be clearly separated, as the goodwill transfer would be exempt from stamp duty for instruments executed on or after April 23, 2002 by FA 2002 s.116.

VAT

19–018 The provision of know-how is regarded as a service in the same way as any other assignment or transfer of intellectual property and the VAT position is the same as for patents (see para.11–012).

DOUBLE TAXATION

19–019 Occasionally, show-how fees may be treated as royalties under double tax treaties and subject to withholding tax in the overseas country.

Article 11 of the 1973 agreement with Jamaica (SI 1973/1329), for example, states:

> "*Management fees*
>
> (1) Management fees arising in one of the territories and paid to a resident of the other territory may be taxed in that other territory.
>
> (2) Management fees may also be taxed in the territory in which they arise and according to the law of that territory; but where the management fees are paid to a resident of the other territory who is subject to tax there in respect thereof the tax so charged in the territory in which those management fees arise shall not exceed 12 per cent of the gross amount thereof.
>
> (3) The term 'management fees' as used in this Article means payments of any kind to any person other than to an employee of the person making the payments, for or in respect of, the provision of industrial or commercial advice, or management or technical services, or similar services or facilities, or hire of plant or equipment but it does not include payments for independent personal services mentioned in Article 19.
>
> (4) The provisions of paragraphs (1) and (2) of this Article shall not apply if the recipient of the management fees, being a resident of one of the territories, has in the other territory in which the management fees arise a permanent establishment with which the management fees are effectively connected. In such a case the provisions of Article 5 shall apply.
>
> (5) If a resident of one of the territories who receives management fees which arise in the other territory and who is subject to tax in respect thereof in the first mentioned territory so elects for any year of assessment, or financial year, the tax chargeable in respect of those management fees in the territory in which they arise shall be calculated as if he had a permanent establishment in that territory and as if those management fees were taxable in accordance with Article 5 as industrial or commercial profits attributable to that permanent establishment.
>
> (6) Management fees shall be deemed to arise in one of the territories when the payer is the Government of that territory or a political sub-division thereof, a local authority or a resident of that territory. Where, however, the person paying the management fees, whether he is a resident of one of the territories or not, has in one of the territories a permanent establishment in connection with which the obligation to pay the management fees was incurred and the management fees are borne by the permanent establishment, then the management fees shall be deemed to arise in that territory.
>
> (7) Where, owing to a special relationship between the payer and the recipient or between both of them and some other person, the amount of the management fees paid, having regard to the advice, services or use of which they are paid, exceed the amount which would have been agreed upon by the payer and the recipient in the absence of such relationship, the provisions of this Article shall apply only to the last-mentioned amount. In that case the excess part of the payments shall remain taxable according to the law of each territory, due regard being had to the other provisions of this Agreement."

CHAPTER 20

Merchandising and endorsement

INTRODUCTION

The intellectual property aspects of character merchandising are often a mixture of design or trade mark and copyright aided by the common law rights against passing off and there are no special taxation provisions relating to this subject. Similarly, endorsement by a famous person of a product or service may be protected by the individual's copyright in his own commissioned photographs and tangible likenesses and signature, but will often involve services to be rendered, such as publicity photographs or public appearances, as well as a licence for copyright material. It may be possible to protect a "name and likeness" by registering a photograph or a trade mark or invoking the protection of the passing-off or defamation laws. Again, there are no special taxation provisions relating to endorsement.

20–001

MERCHANDISING

Character merchandising, i.e. the portrayal of fictional characters created by an author or artist on toys and other manufactured articles, has in recent times become a common means of commercially exploiting such characters. The portrayal of a character such as Peppa Pig or Paddington Bear on a child's toy without permission of the author or copyright holder could be in breach of copyright, design or trademark or passing off. It is therefore common practice to license the producers of such articles to enable them to portray the character on such goods, or to make model representations of the character. Similar issues arise in the depiction of the name and likeness of real characters such as singers, rock groups, footballers, etc.

20–002

INCOME

The income received would normally be trading income of the recipient taxed under ITTOIA 2005 Pt 2 Ch.2, and an allowable expense of the payer under ITTOIA 2005 s.34. The licence fee is not a patent royalty and not normally an annual payment and would not therefore be subject to deduction of tax at source under ITA 2007 ss.898–902.

20–003

However, ITTOIA 2005 s.579 provides that income tax is charged on royalties and other income from intellectual property. For this purpose, intellectual property means any patent, trademark, registered design, copyright, design right, performers right or plant breeders right and any rights under the law of any part of the United Kingdom which are similar to rights within para.(2)(a) or any rights under the law of any territory outside the United Kingdom which correspond or are similar to rights within paras (a) and (d) any idea, information or technique not protected by a right within paras (a), (b) or (c). In some jurisdictions, such as the United States, name and likeness can be protected and registered and certainly, for tax purposes, it would seem that the definition in ITTOIA 2005 s.579 is sufficiently wide to include merchandising and endorsement royalties. Income is therefore taxable under the provisions of ITTOIA 2005 ss.578–582.

The deduction of tax at source rules would therefore apply from April 6, 2007 under ITA 2007 ss.898–902, in the same way as a copyright royalty if it is a qualifying annual payment within ITA 2007 s.899. If the payment arises in the United Kingdom and is a royalty from intellectual property, as defined under ITTOIA 2005 s.579, and is paid by a person or company carrying on a trade or profession, then if it is a commercial payment by an individual, tax is deducted at source under ITA 2007 ss.900 and 902 again in the same way as copyright royalties. However, the question is whether the payment is an annual payment (see paras 9–056 to 9–060 et seq.).

20–004 Annual payments not otherwise charged to tax are charged under ITTOIA 2005 ss.683–686. Section 683(1) refers to annual payments that are not charged to income tax under any other provisions of ITTOIA 2005, and s.683(3) provides that the frequency with which payments are made is ignored in determining whether they are annual payments under these provisions. However there are exemptions for annual payments which include royalties under ITTOIA 2005 ss.757–767. There is no statutory definition of what constitutes an annual payment. The HMRC Savings and Investments Manual at SAIM8020 defines the characteristics of an annual payment as follows:

> "**Characteristics of an annual Payment**
> The phrase 'annual payment' is not defined in the legislation. Its meaning comes from an extensive body of case law. This has established that to be an annual payment, a sum must possess four characteristics.
>
> - It must be payable under a legal obligation. For example, a university student might receive a regular termly contribution from his or her parents towards living expenses. This is not an annual payment, because there is no legal obligation to make the contribution.
> - The obligation to make payments must extend for more than a year—the payments must be capable of recurring. But the obligation may be contingent. In the case of *Cunard's Trustees v IRC* (1945) (27 T.C. 122), sums were to be paid from the capital of a will trust in any year in which trust income was insufficient to meet the beneficiary's needs. These sums were held to be annual payments, despite the fact they were payable in some years but not in others. ITTOIA 2005 s.683(3) specifically provides that the frequency with which the payments are made does not matter.
> - It must be income, not capital, in the hands of the recipient. A capital sum may be paid in instalments—these are not annual payments.

- It must represent pure income profit to the recipient. A sum is 'pure income profit' if—like interest—it comes to the recipient without be or she having to do anything in return. It is 'pure profit' because, under ITTOIA 2005 s.684(1), it is charged on the recipient without any deduction being permitted. SAIM8030 looks at this in more detail, and SAIM8050 gives examples."

It is this final characteristic of an annual payment as pure income profit that would normally prevent endorsement fees from being annual payments and in many cases the same would apply to merchandising. If the recipient has to do anything material in connection with the payment, it is not an annual payment and therefore not subject to deduction of tax at source.

Exceptionally, the copyright owner may be holding it as an investment so that the licence income would be taxed under ITTOIA 2005 s.683 or miscellaneous income under CTA 2009 s.977 and treated as a charge on income of the payer, who would have to deduct tax at source under the provisions of ITA 2007 ss.898–902. Deduction at source could apply to a licensor who has his normal place of abode outside the United Kingdom under the provisions of ITA 2007 ss.906–909 or, as explained in Ch.18, above.

The leading case on the subject of character merchandising is *Noddy Subsidiary Rights Company Ltd v IRC* (1966) 43 T.C. 458. In this case it was held that the company carrying on the merchandising activities, i.e. granting licences to manufacturers, was carrying on a trade.   20–005

The comments of Pennycuick J. at 475 are of particular interest:

"It seems to me that, where a person owns an item of property and grants licences under it, those activities may or may not, according to the particular circumstances, amount to a trade. A number of examples were suggested in argument. I think it is better not to refer to those particular examples in case they arise in any actual case. It seems to me that where you have this position, that a person owns an asset of any kind, whether physical or not, and grants licences under it the activities which he carries on in connection with the grant of those licences may amount to a trade and then Case I of Schedule D applies. On the other hand, at the other end of the scale, the activities may amount to the mere holding of an investment, so that the receipt of income is in the nature of pure income profit and then Case III of Schedule D applies. There may be intermediate cases in which Case VI of Schedule D might apply."

Later in the same judgment (at 476) Pennycuick J. stated:

"The activities admittedly go beyond investment in the ordinary sense, and it is plain that this Company did not carry on the business of an investment company in the ordinary sense, in contradistinction to the statutory sense under the section which I have read. I can myself see no reason for denying to its activities the title of a trade and placing them in the residuary category of Case VI of Schedule D."

In the majority of cases it is likely that the activities of the copyright holder, in obtaining merchandising agreements and monitoring them, would amount to trading and the income would therefore be assessable under Sch.D, Case I.   20–006

Merchandising income is within the income caught by the foreign entertainers rules if related to performance in the United Kingdom by non-resident performers, often referred to as venue merchandising (see para.27–054) (Income Tax (Entertainers and Sportsmen) Regulations 1987 (SI 1987/530) reg.3(2); FEU 50 para.A2), as confirmed in *Agassi v Robinson* [2006] S.T.C. 1056.

ENDORSEMENT FEES

20–007 Closely allied to character merchandising is the practice of endorsement of various articles or services by well-known "personalities" who either claim to use such goods or services and find them satisfactory or merely recommend their purchase, without making it clear whether they have personally taken advantage of the goods or services in question. In either event they are likely to receive for the endorsement a fee or royalty, possibly related to the amount of goods or services sold as a result of the endorsement, or, in the case of a sportsman, his performance during a period or for particular appearances, which would, it is submitted, constitute a receipt of the person's trade or profession, taxable under ITTOIA 2005 ss.5–8. If, as frequently happens, the services of the person have been sub-contracted to a company in return for a salary, the endorsement fees would be the income of the company and the salary paid would normally be an allowable expense of the company and taxable on the person as employment income.

So far as the payer of the endorsement fee is concerned, this would be an ordinary trading expense allowable under CTA 2009 s.54, as a payment of a similar nature to advertising.

It is conceivable that HMRC could argue that endorsement fees should be taxed under ITTOIA 2005 s.687 or, for a company under CTA 2009 s.977, but it is suggested that the correct treatment would normally be trading or professional income.

20–008 A relatively common practice is for the advertiser to supply the celebrity with goods and to take publicity photographs after which the goods are handed over to the celebrity. It may be argued that these are gifts to the celebrity and not endorsement fees and in the circumstances could be tax free. There have been several cases where, for example, a room has been refurnished and redecorated in a celebrity's house at the expense of the advertiser, and HMRC has accepted that no taxation liability results.

On the other hand, the mere payment for endorsement services in kind would not escape taxation and the endorser would be taxable on the realisable value, if any, of such goods or services received (*Temperley v Smith* (1956) 37 T.C. 18).

Endorsement fees are within the foreign entertainers rules for non-UK residents if related to activities in the United Kingdom (see para.27–047) (Income Tax (Entertainers and Sportsmen) Regulations 1987 (SI 1987/530) reg.3(2); FEU 50 para.A5).

STAMP DUTY

Merchandising agreements are in reality an assignment or licence of copyright and exempt from stamp duty as intellectual property under FA 2000 s.129 in respect of instruments executed on or after March 28, 2000, in the same way as other copyright agreements. Endorsement fees would not amount to a conveyance of property and should not be liable to stamp duty. **20–009**

VAT

Merchandising agreements would be subject to VAT in the same way as patent agreements. Endorsement fees would be subject to VAT if paid to a registered or registrable business, in the same way as show-how fees (see Ch.11). **20–010**

CHAPTER 21

Corporate Intangible fixed assets

INTRODUCTION

Section 84 of the FA 2002 introduced Schs 29 and 30 (now CTA 2009 Pt 8) which set out the scheme for tax relief on capital expenditure incurred on or after April 1, 2002 in respect of corporate intangible fixed assets, including intellectual property and goodwill, but excluding financial assets. The previous law, i.e. the law as it was prior to the introduction of the FA 2002 provisions, continues to apply to expenditure incurred up to and including March 31, 2002, (FA 2002, CTA 2009 Pt.8, s.117). All references in this chapter are to CTA 2009 Pt 8, unless otherwise stated. HMRC has produced a Corporate Intangibles, Research and Development Manual (CIRD 10000; 10005; 10010) to explain their interpretation of the law under these rules, and the research and development provisions and vaccine relief, described in Ch.15. Nothing in this chapter affects the taxation of individuals, whether sole traders or partners or members of a limited liability partnership; the pre-April 1, 2002, law continues to apply to these persons.

21–001

Part 8 is divided into 17 chapters as follows:

1. Introduction.
2. Credits in respect of intangible fixed assets.
3. Debits in respect of intangible fixed assets.
4. Realisation of intangible fixed assets.
5. Calculation of tax written down value.
6. How credits and debits are given effect.
7. Rollover relief in case of realisation and reinvestment.
8. Groups of companies.
9. Application of provisions to groups of companies.
10. Excluded assets.
11. Transfer of business or trade.
12. Related parties.
13. Transactions between related parties.
14. Miscellaneous provisions.
15. Adjustments on change of accounting policy.
16. Pre-FA 2002 assets, etc.
17. Insurance companies.

SCOPE

21–002 Initially it was intended to simplify and rationalise the law relating to the taxation of intellectual property but the dividing line between, for example, trademarks, brand names and goodwill, is difficult to ascertain precisely in practice and it was decided to include as a starting point those items regarded as being included within Financial Reporting Standard (FRS) 10 "Goodwill and Intangible Assets" which applies for the preparation of accounts in accordance with generally accepted accounting practice (UK GAAP; CIRD 30010; 30055; 30060). The tax rules do not follow FRS 10 slavishly, for example, films remain outwith the corporate intangible fixed assets regime, and come within the special regime in CTA 2009 Pt 15 (see Ch.18, para.18–049 above) (CIRD 25000).

The retention of the old rules for pre-April 1, 2002, expenditure was decided upon in order to avoid the problem of having to revalue innumerable tranches of intellectual property rights and goodwill (CIRD 10140). A similar decision was made to retain the old rules for unincorporated businesses, even though they are now required to produce accounts in accordance with UK GAAP for tax purposes, because of the additional complexity and the desire to keep the capital gains tax regime available to unincorporated businesses, particularly in relation to disposals of goodwill.

BASIS

21–003 The fundamental principle of the corporate intangible fixed asset regime is to treat all costs (debits), on the acquisition or development of such assets, as depreciable for tax purposes on the same basis as for accounting purposes and to treat all royalties and disposal proceeds (credits) as income receipts. This obviously gives rise to a problem where existing intangible fixed assets are disposed of and are replaced, and there is therefore a form of rollover relief based on the replacement of business assets rollover relief provisions for chargeable gains in TCGA 1992 ss.152–159. There are also provisions for dealing with intra-group transfers without crystallising tax charges, based on the company chargeable gains provisions in TCGA 1992 ss.171–191, and the inevitable anti-avoidance provisions dealing with connected company transfers, companies leaving a group, etc. Although the rate of amortisation for each class of intangible fixed assets will normally follow the accounting treatment, the actual figures are likely to differ in most cases because of connected party or intra-group transfers and pre-April 1, 2002 expenditure (CIRD 10115, 10116).

The result of treating amortisation as an allowable expense for tax purposes is that a separate capital allowances regime is no longer required for assets acquired on or after April 1, 2002 and profits on disposal will be computed in accordance with UK GAAP which means that indexation allowances will not be available. Exceptionally, for example, where intangible fixed assets are not amortised for accounting purposes, a straight line allowance at 4 per cent per annum on such expenditure is allowed for tax purposes, on making an election under s.730.

Although the corporate intangible fixed assets regime applies mainly to capital expenditure, it is extended to include most royalties which previously have been

APPLICATION

dealt with as revenue receipts and expenses in any event (CIRD 10150). However, there may be timing changes in connection with royalties received and paid, where these have been previously taxed on a receipts basis or allowed on a payments basis as charges on income. There are anti-avoidance provisions for royalties payable to related parties not paid within 12 months after the end of the accounting period under which relief is deferred until the royalties are actually paid (CIRD 10160).

Existing assets, i.e. those held at April 1, 2002, will continue to be taxed or relieved under the pre-existing rules, explained in Chs 16–20, and remain within these rules until disposed of to an unrelated third party, who will then deal with them in accordance with the company intangible fixed assets regime (CIRD 11505; 11510). Transfers of existing assets to related parties remain within the old regime, and such transactions have normally been deemed to take place at market value. Although existing assets remain subject to the chargeable gains regime on disposal, a chargeable gain cannot normally be rolled over into the acquisition of assets within the revised chargeable gains rollover relief provisions, but instead qualifies for the reinvestment relief available for post-April 1, 2002 expenditure on company intangible fixed assets (s.898) (CIRD 10120; 10145; 20240). **21–004**

One of the effects of treating gains and losses on corporate intangible fixed assets as revenue, not capital, is to bring them within the controlled foreign company regime. They are also outwith the tax neutral treatment applicable to UK groups in respect of inter-company transfers. Normally such transfers will be treated as taking place at the arm's-length price, and the normal transfer pricing rules apply, and indeed take precedence, so far as the computation of the arms-length price is concerned. The corporate intangible fixed assets regime applies to finance lessors of intangible assets.

As well as specific anti-avoidance provisions in the corporate intangible fixed assets regime there is a general anti-avoidance provision in s.864 (CIRD 10230).

APPLICATION

A company's profits and losses on intangible fixed assets on or after April 1, 2002 are dealt with in accordance with Pt 8 of CTA 2009 (s.906(1)(2)) (CIRD 10125). **21–005**

"Intangible asset" has the same meaning as it has for accounting purposes, which means for the purposes of accounts drawn up in accordance with generally accepted accounting practice (ITA 2007 s.989, which in turn is defined in relation to a company that prepares accounts in accordance with international accounting standards as generally accepted accounting practice with respect to such accounts. For companies which do not draw up accounts in accordance with international accounting standards, "generally accepted accounting practice" means UK GAAP (ITA 2007 s.997(1)(3)). Profits are required to be computed in accordance with generally accepted accounting practice by s.46. Rules for changes of accounting basis for corporation tax purposes are contained in ss.180–182. Intangible assets include, in particular, any intellectual property, which means:

(1) Any patent, trademark, registered design, copyright or design right, plant breeders' rights or rights under s.7 of the Plant Varieties Act 1997.
(2) Any right under the law of a country or territory outside the United Kingdom corresponding to, or similar to, a right within s.(1).
(3) Any information or technique not protected by a right within s.(1) or (2) but having industrial, commercial or other economic value.
(4) Any license or other right in respect of anything within s.(1), (2) or (3) (s.2(2) (CIRD 11100, 11120)).

EXCLUDED ASSETS

21-006 Excluded assets are outwith the corporate intangible fixed assets regime (s.712(4)), either entirely (s.800(2)(a); except as regards royalties (s.800(2)(b)); or to the extent specified under s.814–815 (s.800(2)(c)) (CIRD 11100; 11120; 25010). Where an asset is excluded to an extent, it is treated as a separate asset representing so much of the asset as is excluded, with apportionment being made, as necessary on a just and reasonable basis (s.802) (CIRD 25015). Options or other rights to acquire or dispose of excluded assets are included within the definition (s.801).

Assets entirely excluded include rights enjoyed by virtue of an estate. interest or right in or over land or in relation to tangible moveable property (s.805 (CIRD 25030)), assets in respect of which capital allowances have previously been claimed (s.804(1)), oil licenses or interests in an oil license (s.809 (CIRD 25040)), and financial assets as defined for UK GAAP including loan relationships, derivative contracts, contracts for policies of insurance or capital redemption policies and rights under a collective investment scheme (s.806 (CIRD 25025, 25050)).

A financial asset is defined by FRS 13 s.2 as any asset that is:

(1) cash;
(2) a contractual right to receive cash or another financial asset from another entity;
(3) a contractual right to exchange financial instruments with another entity under conditions that are potentially favourable; or
(4) an equity instrument of another entity.

Assets entirely excluded also include shares or other rights in relation to the profits, governance or winding-up of a company, rights under a trust or an interest of a partner in a partnership unless in the latter two cases these rights would be intangible fixed assets under UK GAAP (s.807 (CIRD 25060)). There is also a general exclusion for intangible fixed assets held for a purpose that is not a

DEFINITION

business or other commercial purpose of the company, or for the purpose of activities in respect of which the company is not within the charge to corporation tax (s.726 (CIRD 25070, 25090)).

Assets excluded, except as regards royalties, include those s. held by a company for the purposes of any mutual trade or business (s.810 (CIRD 25120)). 21–007

Any fixed asset which represents expenditure by a company on the production of a film or sound recording which falls to be treated as a trade under the film tax relief provisions are specifically excluded from the intangible assets rules because a special regime applies to such assets under CTA 2009 Pt 15. Expenditure by a company on the production or acquisition of a master version of a film or sound recording under the pre-FA 2006 film tax relief rules is also excluded from the intangible assets regime (ss.811–812 (CIRD 25130)). Income (including royalties) received from films qualifying for tax relief under the CTA 2009 Pt 15 provisions is similarly outside the scope of the intangible assets regime.

The intangible asset provisions apply to acquisition expenditure incurred on the master version of a film or sound recordings.

A similar exclusion applies to computer software treated as part of the cost of related hardware, except as regards royalties (ss.813 (CIRD 25140)). Expenditure on computer software is eligible for the Annual Investment Allowance of £250,000 and writing down allowances at 18 per cent of the reducing balance which is likely to give the relief more quickly than accounts based amortisation. Computer software is treated as plant under CAA 2001 ss.71–73. See also *Tax Bulletin* Issue 9, November 1993, RI 56. 21–008

Also excluded from the company intangible fixed asset regime is expenditure which qualifies as research and development under ITA 2007 s.1006, including oil and gas exploration and appraisal (ss.814 (CIRD 25155; 25160; 25170; 25190)). The R&D tax credits regime explained in Ch.15 allows enhanced relief for such expenditure. A company can exclude capital expenditure on computer software, as can a life assurance company in respect of expenditure not referable to its basic life assurance and general annuity business, from parts of the corporate intangible fixed assets regime and instead claim capital allowances under CAA 2001, by making an irrevocable election in writing to HMRC within two years of the end of the accounting period in which the expenditure was incurred, specifying the expenditure to which it relates (ss.815 (CIRD 25180)). The election is available because tax relief may be given more quickly under the capital allowance rules. The CTA 2009 Pt.8 rules apply to disposals and reversals of previous accounting gains to the extent that the consideration has not been brought into the capital allowance computation under CAA 2001 s.72.

DEFINITION

Intangible fixed assets are defined by ss.713 as intangible assets acquired or created by the company for use on a continuing basis in the course of the company's activities (ss.713(1) (CIRD 10130; 11135; 11170)). References to intangible fixed assets include options or other rights to acquire or to dispose of such assets (ss.713(2)). Options over intangible fixed assets within ss.713(2) are 21–009 specifically excluded from the definition of options in the derivative contracts legislation by ss.589(2) and 710 (CIRD 11173). Where an option is partly to acquire or dispose of intangible fixed assets and partly other assets, apportionment is necessary under ss.800–802 and the derivative contract provisions in Pt.7 Chs 7 and 8. Other derivative contracts, such as contracts for differences based on intangible fixed assets, are nonetheless financial assets dealt with under Pt.7 Chs 7 and 8, not CTA 2009 Pt.8. Intangible fixed assets are dealt with under the corporate intangible fixed asset regime, whether or not capitalised in the company's accounts, subject to the finance leasing rules, (s.713(3) and (4)). The definition effectively replicates the standard definition of capital expenditure in *Atherton v British Insulated and Helshy Cables Limited* (1925) 10 T.C. 155. The reference in ss.713(3) to intangible fixed assets not capitalised in the company's accounts refers, for example, to internally generated intangible fixed assets which would not normally be recognised under FRS 10 s.14. This would also apply to a license to exploit an intangible fixed asset such as a patent or copyright material where the consideration consists wholly of royalties. Such assets are nonetheless within the corporate intangible fixed asset regime and disposals would be dealt with under CTA 2009 Pt.8.

ACCOUNTING ISSUES—UK GAAP

21–010 Intangible assets are defined in FRS 10 as non-financial fixed assets that do not have physical substance but are identifiable and controlled by the entity through custody or legal rights (FRS 10 s.2 (CIRD 11030; 11035; 11050; 30505; 30510)). Purchased goodwill is the difference between the cost of an acquired entity and the aggregate of the fair values of that entity as identifiable assets and liabilities. Positive goodwill arises when the acquisition cost exceeds the aggregate fair values of the identifiable assets and liabilities. Negative goodwill arises where the aggregate fair values of the identifiable assets and liabilities of the entity exceeds the acquisition cost (FRS 10 s.2 (CIRD 11070)). Positive purchased goodwill should be capitalised and classified as an asset on the balance sheet (FRS 10 s.7), internally generated goodwill should not be capitalised (FRS 10 s.8 (CIRD 30535)). An intangible asset purchased separately from a business should be capitalised at its cost (FRS 10 s.9 (CIRD 30530)). An intangible asset acquired as part of the acquisition of the business should be capitalised separately from goodwill if its value can be measured reliably on initial recognition. It should initially be recorded at its fair value, subject to the constraint that, unless the asset has a readily ascertainable market value, the fair value should be limited to an amount that does not create or increase any negative goodwill arising on the acquisition (FRS 10 s.10). If its value cannot be measured reliably, an intangible asset purchased as part of the acquisition of a business should be subsumed within the amount of the purchase price attributable to goodwill (FRS 10 s.13). An internally developed intangible asset may be capitalised only if it has a readily ascertainable market value (FRS 10 s.14 (CIRD 30580)).

Readily ascertainable market value is defined as the value of an intangible asset that is established by reference to a market where: (1) the asset belongs to a homogenous population of assets that are equivalent in all material respects, and

ACCOUNTING ISSUES—UK GAAP

(2) an active market evidenced by frequent transactions that exists for that population of assets. Intangible assets that meet these conditions might include certain operating licenses, franchises and quotas. Other intangible assets are by their nature unique: although there may be similar assets they are not equivalent in all material respects and do not have a readily ascertainable market value. Examples of such assets include brands, publishing titles, patented drugs and engineering patents (FRS 10 s.2).

Where goodwill and intangible assets are regarded as having useful economic lives, they should be amortised on a systematic basis over those lives (FRS 10 s.15 (CIRD 30540)). Where goodwill and intangible assets are regarded as having indefinite useful economic lives they should not be amortised (FRS 10 s.17).

There is a rebuttable presumption that the useful economic lives of purchased goodwill and intangible assets are limited to periods of 20 years or less. This presumption may be rebutted, and a useful economic life regarded as a longer period or indefinitely, only if: 21–011

(1) the durability of the acquired business or intangible asset can be demonstrated and justifies estimating the useful economic life to exceed 20 years; and
(2) the goodwill or intangible asset is capable of continued measurement (so that annual impairment reviews will be feasible) (FRS.10 s.19).

Where access to the economic benefits associated with an intangible asset is achieved by legal rights that have been granted for a finite period, the economic life of the asset may extend beyond that period only if, and to the extent that, the legal rights are renewable and renewal is assured. The amount of the asset that is treated as having a longer useful economic life should exclude those costs which will recur each time the legal right is renewed (FRS.10 s.24). In amortising an intangible asset a residual value may be assigned to that asset only if such residual value can be measured reliably. No residual value may be assigned to goodwill (FRS 10 s.28). The method of amortisation should be chosen to reflect the expected pattern of depletion of the goodwill or intangible asset. A straight line method should be chosen unless another method can be demonstrated to be more appropriate, (FRS 10 s.30). The useful economic lives of goodwill and intangible assets should be reviewed at the end of each reporting period and revised if necessary. If a useful economic life is revised, the carrying value of the goodwill or intangible asset at the date of revision should be amortised over the revised remaining useful economic life. If the effect of the revision is to increase the useful economic life to more than 20 years, from the date of acquisition, the additional requirements of (FRS 10) that apply to goodwill and intangible assets that are amortised over periods of more than 20 years, or are not amortised, become applicable (FRS 10 s.33).

Goodwill and intangible assets that are amortised over a finite period not exceeding 20 years from the date of acquisition should be reviewed for impairment:

(a) at the end of the first full financial year following the acquisition (the first year review); and

(b) in other periods if events or changes in circumstances indicate that the carrying values may not be recoverable (FRS 10 s.34).

Goodwill and intangible assets that are amortised over a period exceeding 20 years from the date of acquisition, or are not amortised, should be reviewed for impairment at the end of each accounting period (FRS 10 s.37). Impairment reviews should normally be performed in accordance with the requirements of FRS 11 Impairment of fixed Assets and Goodwill (FRS 10 s.39). Where an intangible asset has a readily ascertainable market value the asset may be revalued to its market value. If one intangible asset is revalued all other capitalised intangible assets of the same class should be revalued. Once an intangible asset has been revalued, further revaluations should be performed sufficiently often to ensure that the carrying value does not differ materially from the market value at the balance sheet date (FRS 10 s.43). A class of intangible assets is defined as a category of intangible assets having a similar feature, function or use in the business of the entity. Licenses, quotas, patents, copyrights, franchises and trademarks are examples of categories that may be treated as separate classes of intangible asset. Further sub-division may be appropriate, for example, where different types of license have different functions within the business. Intangible assets that are used within different business segments may be treated as separate classes of intangible assets (FRS 10 s.2). Negative goodwill up to the fair values of the non-monetary assets acquired should be recognised in the profit and loss account in the periods in which the nonmonetary assets are recovered whether through depreciation or sale (FRS 10 s.49). The accounting disclosure requirements are set out in FRS 10 ss.52–64.

The corporate intangible fixed assets regime applies to goodwill, as defined for UK GAAP via FRS 10 s.2, as explained above. If a company does not draw up its accounts in accordance with UK GAAP, the company intangible fixed asset regime is applied as if it had produced correct accounts in accordance with UK GAAP s.5 (CIRD 30065; 30070; 30090; 30105; 30110; 30120; 30130; 30140). In determining whether a company's accounts are correct, reference may be made to a view on the useful life of an asset or the economic value of an asset used for the purposes of consolidated group accounts for any group of companies of which the company is a member (s.6(1)(CIRD 30080)). Where the consolidated group accounts are prepared using a different accounting framework from that used in the company's accounts (such as accounts drawn up in accordance with international financial reporting standards) but the UK company's accounts are prepared under UK GAAP, the consolidated group accounts are ignored (s.6(2A)). Similarly, where the consolidated group accounts are prepared in accordance with foreign laws which substantially diverge from UK GAAP, the consolidated group accounts are ignored (s.6(3)). The consolidated group account treatment is not necessarily applied for the individual companies' accounts, but it means that a company may have to explain why the accounting treatment is different and in practice this is likely to be confined to cases where a company's accounting treatment is more conservative than the group treatment as a result of which the amortisation debits claimed for tax purposes are greater.

SMALLER ENTITIES

It should be noted that the generally accepted accounting practice for smaller entities is based on the Financial Reporting Standard for Smaller Entities (FRSSE) which applies to companies within CA 2006 ss.381–384 (CIRD 30525). This basically means where a company or group does not exceed two or more of the following criteria:

21–012

Turnover	£6,500,000
Balance sheet total	£3,260,000
Average number of employees	50

FRSSE (January 2007) modifies the rules in FRS 10 for such smaller enterprises (ss.6.11–6.17). The main changes are that there is no exception allowing the recognition of internally generated intangible assets with readily ascertainable market values, useful economic lives are limited to 20 years, the revaluation of intangible assets with readily ascertainable market values is prohibited.

It should be noted that intangible assets include intellectual property but are not confined to it, and, for example, agricultural quota, various types of statutory licenses and some franchise rights would normally be accounted for under FRS 10 and therefore fall within the definition of intangible assets via the reference to accounting purposes, and therefore UK GAAP, in s.2. As goodwill is treated as an intangible fixed asset under s.4 the distinction between intangible fixed assets and goodwill is in practice irrelevant. Goodwill may, in part, consist of individual assets such as customer lists or various forms of know-how both of which would be intangible assets but FRS 10, s.2, specifically excludes from the definition of intangible assets items where there is no control through custody, such as secret information, or legal rights such as patents or copyright. Such exceptions include a portfolio of clients or a team of skilled staff. However, where such assets are purchased these assets effectively fall within the mop-up definition of purchased goodwill.

IMPAIRMENT REVIEW

UK GAAP under FRS 11 recognises that it would be unnecessarily onerous for all fixed assets and goodwill to be tested for impairment every year (CIRD 30515, 30550). In general, fixed assets and goodwill need to be reviewed for impairment only at the end of the first accounting period following acquisition or if there is some indication that impairment has occurred (CIRD 30556). However, FRS 11 does not apply to derivatives and other financial instruments or to investment properties. Impairment is measured by comparing the carrying value of the fixed asset or income generating unit with its recoverable amount. The recoverable amount is the higher of the net realisable value, the amounts that can be obtained from selling the fixed asset or income generating unit and its value in use (CIRD 30557). Impairment is measured by comparing the carrying value of the fixed asset or income generating unit with its recoverable amount (CIRD

21–013

30565). The net realisable value is the amount for which the asset could be sold less direct selling costs and the value in use is the discounted present value of future cash flows arising from the asset using the rate of return that the market would expect from an equally risky investment. Detailed calculations are not required where it is obvious that the value in use is higher than the carrying value or lower than the net realisable value, in which case impairment is measured by reference to the net realisable value.

Where purchased goodwill is merged with internally generated goodwill it is necessary to calculate the value of the internally generated goodwill in order to determine whether or not impairment to the purchased goodwill has occurred. Impairment may not be permanent and events may cause it to be reversed at a future date, but increases in the recoverable amount of goodwill and intangible assets are recognised only when an external event caused the recognition of the impairment loss in previous periods and subsequent events clearly and demonstrably reverse the effect of that event in a way which was not foreseen in the original impairment calculations (CIRD 30567). Impairment losses are recognised in the profit and loss account unless they arise on a previously revalued fixed asset in which case impairment losses may be recognised in the statement of total recognised gains and losses in appropriate cases.

Impairment is defined in FRS 11 s.2, as a reduction in the recoverable amount of a fixed asset or goodwill below its carrying amount, FRS 11 does not apply to reporting entities applying the FRSSE unless preparing consolidated financial statements (FRS 11 s.4). An impairment review should be carried out if events or changes in circumstances indicate that the carrying amount of the fixed asset or goodwill may not be recoverable (FRS 11 s.10). Some examples of events and changes in circumstances that indicate an impairment may have occurred include:

- a current period operating loss in the business in which the fixed asset is involved or net cash outflow from the operating activities of that business combined with either past operating losses or net cash outflows from such operating activities or an expectation of continuing operating losses or net cash outflows from such operating activities;
- a significant decline in a fixed asset's market value during the period;
- evidence of obsolescence or physical damage to the fixed asset;
- a significant adverse change in:
  - either the business or the market in which the fixed asset or goodwill is involved, such as the entrance of a major competitor;
  - the statutory or other regulatory environment in which the business operates or any indicator of value (for example turnover) used to measure the fair value of a fixed asset on acquisition;
- a commitment by management to undertake a significant reorganisation;
- a major loss of key employees; and
- a significant increase in market interest rates or other market rates of return that are likely to affect materially the fixed asset's recoverable amount.

Where an impairment loss on a fixed asset or goodwill is recognised, the remaining useful economic life and residual value should be reviewed and revised if necessary. The revised carrying amount should be depreciated over the revised estimate of the remaining useful economic life (FRS 11 s.21). Any impairment to an income generating unit is allocated first to goodwill, then to capitalised intangible assets and lastly to any tangible assets included in the unit. An impairment review which reduces the value of an asset within the corporate intangible fixed assets provisions would usually result in an additional debit for tax purposes but whether this would follow precisely the accounting writedown would depend on the circumstances and the respective calculations for accounting and tax purposes.

COMMENCEMENT AND TRANSITIONAL PROVISIONS

The corporate intangible fixed asset regime commenced on April 1, 2002, and "after commencement" means on or after that date, and "before commencement" means before that date (CIRD 11010). Expenditure incurred before commencement is dealt with under the existing law as it was immediately before commencement and as it continues to be after commencement for unincorporated businesses. This means that the taxability of income and deductibility of expenses, subject to the transitional provisions explained below, continues under the old rules with separate regimes for patents, trademarks, designs, copyright, etc. as explained in Chs 16–20 above, and with the treatment of goodwill as a capital asset within the chargeable gains regime (s.882(1)). The rules only apply therefore to intangible fixed assets of a company that are created by the company after commencement, acquired by the company after commencement from an unrelated party, or acquired by the company after commencement from a related party which meets certain specific requirements (s.882 (1) (CIRD 11520; 11600; 11610)).

21–014

Related party acquisitions are within the company fixed assets regime where the asset acquired from the related party was a chargeable intangible asset before the acquisition, i.e. it had been acquired by the transferor after commencement, or where it is acquired from a related intermediary who acquired it after commencement from an unrelated third party, or where it was created after commencement (s.882(3)(4)(5) (CIRD 11625; 11630; 11640; 11650)). Intangible fixed assets not within the corporate intangible fixed asset regime are referred to as existing assets (ss.881). There are special rules for fungible assets, assets acquired on a transfer of business and to certain existing assets, in ss.850–891. Fungible assets are assets which do not have any separate identity such as agricultural quotas (CIRD 10220). However, they are treated as different kinds of assets if they are existing assets or acquired or created after commencement (ss.858 and 890(2) (CIRD 11760)). A disposal of fungible assets is treated as diminishing the pre-commencement existing assets in priority to diminishing the post-commencement intangible fixed asset (s.891(1)(2) (CIRD 11770)). There is an anti-bed-and-breakfast provision under which assets are identified with existing assets and not post-commencement assets if the existing assets were realised within a period beginning 30 days before and ending 30 days after the date of acquisition with assets being realised and acquired on a firstin, first-out basis, s.891(5)(6) (CIRD 11780). If it were not for this provision the company could, for example, dispose of its entire milk quota and immediately re-acquire a similar amount of quota without suffering any commercial consequences but the new quota would be tax depreciable whereas the old quota would be a non-depreciable capital asset.

Example 1

Fungible assets, say milk quota.

Cost of	100,000 units	held at	1.04.12	£200,000
Purchase	20,000 units	on	1.05.12	£41,000
Sale	50,000 units	on	5.06.12	£105,000
Purchase	60,000 units	on	30.06.12	£123,000
Sale	25,000 units	on	30.09.12	£60,000

Tax position	Existing asset			
	Units	£	Units	£
1.4.12 cost	100,000	200,000		
1.5.12 cost			20,000	41,000
5.6.12 proceeds	(50,000)	(105,000)		
	50,000	95,000		
Profit		5,000		
	50,000	100,000		
30.6.12 purchase within 30 days, cost	50,000	102,500	10,000	20,500

Tax position	Existing asset			
	Units	£	Units	£
	100,000	202,500	30,000	61,500
30.09.12 sale	(25,000)	(60,000)		
	75,000	142,500		
Profit (£60,000–£50,625)		9,375		
£25,000 x £202,500 = (£50,625) £100,000				
Balance at 31.3.13	75,000	151,875	30,000	61,500

Amortisation over 10 years
New assets only, £61,500 x 10%   £6,150

COMMENCEMENT AND TRANSITIONAL PROVISIONS

Where an asset is treated as having been sold and immediately reacquired on a no-gain, no-loss basis on a company reconstruction or amalgamation involving a transfer of business under TCGA 1992 s.139, on the transfer of a UK trade to a company resident in another EU state under TCGA 1992 s.140A, or on a transfer on formation of a Societas Europaea under TCGA 1992 s.140E, and the asset was an existing asset of the transferor company, it remains an existing asset of the transferee company (s.892). This potential mismatch was only identified in discussions between HMRC and the professional bodies after publication of the Finance Bill and therefore only applies to transfers incurred on or after June 28, 2002 (s.89 (4) (CIRD 11660)).

TCGA 1992 ss.139 and 140A, do not apply where the asset transferred was a post-commencement intangible fixed asset of the transferor though it would be a tax neutral transfer within ss.818–820. In the absence of the anti-mis-match rule the asset, in the hands of an unconnected transferee, would be treated as a post-commencement asset at its fair value as ascertained under FRS 7 s.10, based on its replacement cost, normally its estimated market value (CIRD 30520). FRS 7, fair values in acquisition accounting are designed to ensure that when a business entity is acquired all the assets and liabilities of the acquired entity at the date of acquisition are recorded at their fair values reflecting their condition at that date and any subsequent changes to the acquired assets and liabilities and any resulting gains or losses are reported as part of the post acquisition financial performance of the acquirer (CIRD 30650).

Existing telecommunication rights are fully within the corporate intangible fixed assets regime irrespective of the date of acquisition or creation (ss.897 (CIRD 11730; 11740)). Similarly, Lloyd's syndicate capacity for corporate members of Lloyd's is brought into the company intangible fixed assets regime irrespective of the date of acquisition or creation (s.905 (CIRD 11750, 12775, 20040)).

21–015 Where an existing intangible fixed asset is disposed of after commencement, which would normally be eligible for roll-over relief under TCGA 1992 ss.152 and 155, it cannot be rolled into a new asset acquired after commencement; instead the chargeable gain may be rolled over into the acquisition of further intangible fixed assets under Ch.7. Chargeable gains arising on assets eligible for rollover relief under TCGA 1992 s.155, other than corporate intangible fixed assets may not be rolled into post commencement chargeable intangible fixed assets. This means that assets eligible for chargeable gains rollover relief do not include goodwill, milk quotas, potato quotas, ewe and suckler cow premium quotas, fish quotas or, from March 22, 2005, payments under the farmers' single payment scheme (see Tolley's *Practical Tax*, July 29, 2005, Vol.26, No.16 and EC Regulation 1782/2003).

Reinvestment relief is available under Ch.7 (CIRD 10170; 10175; 10180). This is achieved by providing that disposals for chargeable gains purposes have the same meanings as for reinvestment relief and effectively extends the eligible assets for reinvestment to include intellectual property which would not have been within the list of eligible assets for rollover relief under TCGA 1992 s.155, s.130(1)(5). The exclusion of reinvestment relief for part-realisations involving a related party, under s.850, does not apply for the roll-over of an existing asset. The amount available for reinvestment relief, calculated under s.758, reduces both the consideration for disposal in calculating the chargeable gain and the acquisition cost of the new asset reintroduced by the available relief (CTA2009 Sch.1 ss.371 and 758(1)). Where a company leaves a group and there is a degrouping charge under TCGA 1992 s.179(2) or (6), and the gain on the existing intangible fixed asset is treated as arising after commencement when the company leaves the group under TCGA 1992 s.179(4) or (8), reinvestment relief is available under Ch.7 by virtue of ss.899–900. The restriction for part realisations involving a related party under s.850 does not apply (ss.899(7), 131 (4)). The deemed disposal consideration for chargeable gains purposes under TCGA 1992 s.179 is reduced by the reinvestment relief, as is the acquisition cost of the new asset (CTA 2009 Sch.1 ss.371 and 758(1)).

Definitions are scattered throughout Pt.8, including: expenditure on an asset (s.727), amounts recognised in profit and loss account (s.716), accounting value (s.719), adjustments required for tax purposes (s.721), chargeable intangible assets and a chargeable realisation gain (ss.741), royalty (s.714), and tax neutral transfer (s.776).

ROYALTIES

21–016 Royalties under the corporate intangible fixed asset regime are brought into account for both accounts and tax purposes on the normal accruals basis with the tax treatment following the accounting treatment. A royalty is defined as a royalty in respect of the enjoyment or exercise of rights that constitute an intangible fixed asset, by s.714, and would not include a quasi-royalty such as a fee related to sales (CIRD 11710).

Royalties are normally accounted for by the licensee on the basis of production or sales or usage and these figures are often subject to independent audit at the licensor's option, and audit adjustments are by no means uncommon. In complex licensing agreements such as those involving films and recorded music, there are very often chains of sub-licensees and a sale of product on sale or return terms, which can result in royalties being accounted for many months or even years after the third party sale, which theoretically gives rise to the royalty, takes place. As a result the accounting treatment tends to follow the semi-accruals basis under which the licensee accounts for royalties known to be payable in respect of its own sales and on the basis of returns received from sub-licensees, often covering different periods. The licensor brings income into his accounts on the basis of royalties for the main licensees accounting period ending in the licensor's accounting period, whether actually paid or not, and a pro rata proportion, normally calculated on a time basis, of any pipeline royalties included in the licensees next accounting under the royalty agreement, which relates to the period covered by the licensor's accounts. This accounting treatment is as close to a full accruals basis as it is practical to get and still produce accounts within a reasonable period.

Accounts prepared on this basis are in accordance with UK GAAP and should be acceptable to HMRC under s.896(1)(2). The deduction for tax purposes is the same as that for accounting purposes subject to any adjustment required for tax purposes (s.728(2)(3)). Adjustments required for tax purposes include transfer pricing adjustments under TIOPA 2010 Pt.4 (CIRD 47060).

Several assets excluded from the corporate intangible fixed assets regime are still within the scheme for the taxation of royalties, including assets held for mutual trade business, films and sound recordings and computer software, under ss.810–813.

DATE OF ACQUISITION

In determining whether an asset is a chargeable intangible fixed asset acquired on or after April 1, 2002, or an existing asset acquired before commencement (s.118), the date of acquisition has to be determined, under Ch.16 (CIRD 11690)). The general rule is that an intangible asset is regarded as created or acquired after commencement to the extent that expenditure on its creation or acquisition is incurred after April 1, 2002 (s.883(3) (CIRD 11670)). Where part of the expenditure was incurred before and part after commencement the asset is treated as if it were two separate assets, with apportionment being made on a just and reasonable basis (s.883(5)(7)). Internally generated goodwill is regarded as created before and not after commencement if the business in question was carried on at any time before April 1, 2002 by the company or a related party (s.884 (CIRD 11675, 11680)). Where expenditure is incurred on internally generated assets, which is not qualifying expenditure for capital allowances under CAA 2001, and the assets were held at any time before commencement by the company or a related party, they are deemed to have been created entirely before and not after commencement (s.885(1)(7) (CIRD 11675; 11678)). If any part of the expenditure of the asset is non-qualifying expenditure and the rest qualifies for capital allowances, only the non-qualifying part is so treated, as if it were a separate asset with any apportionment being made on a just and reasonable basis (s.883 (CIRD 11685)).

21–017

Expenditure is normally treated as incurred when it is recognised for accounting purposes (s.887(1)). However, a capital asset that does not qualify for any form of tax relief against income under the existing law is treated as incurred before commencement if it would have been so treated for chargeable gains purposes, where the contract date would normally apply under TCGA 1992 s.28 (ss.887(2) and 888ss. (CIRD 11690)). Where, however, the asset qualifies for capital allowances under CAA 2001, the expenditure is treated as incurred for the corporate intangible fixed assets regime when an unconditional obligation to pay comes into being (ss.887(2) and 889; CAA 2001 s.5).

ALLOWABLE COSTS (DEBITS)

21-018 Chapter 3 provides for the deduction for tax purposes of expenditure on intangible fixed assets written off for accounting purposes when incurred, and for the writing down of the capitalised costs of an intangible asset on an accounting basis, or on a fixed rate basis, and the reversal of previous accounting gains on intangible fixed assets (CIRD 12010; 12210; 12510). It does not apply in connection with the disposal or realisation of intangible fixed assets dealt with in Ch.4. Where expenditure is recognised in a company's profit and loss account in a period in respect of which it makes up accounts, i.e. a period of account (ITA2007 s.989) a similar deduction (debit) is allowed for tax purposes (s.728(1) (CIRD 12020, 12220)). The deduction for tax purposes is the same as that for accounting purposes subject to any adjustment required for tax purposes (s.728(2)(3) (CIRD 12530)). Adjustments required for tax purposes are defined by s.728(3) to include transfer pricing adjustments under TIOPA 2010 Pt.4, or which are required under any provision in Pt.8 of CTA 2009 (CIRD 12030; 47060; 12570). Expenditure on an asset is that for the purpose of acquiring creating or establishing title to an asset or by way of royalty in respect of the use of the asset or for the purpose of maintaining, preserving, enhancing or defending title to the asset, including abortive expenditure (s.727(1)). It does not include capital expenditure on tangible assets (s.727(2)(3)) and any necessary apportionment's are to be made on a just and reasonable basis (s.727(4) (CIRD 12240; 12250; 12260)). Recognition in a company's profit and loss account for a period include references to a statement of total recognised gains and losses or other statement of items brought into account in computing the company's profit and losses for that period, or would have been had the accounts been drawn up in accordance with UK GAAP (s.716(1)) (CIRD 12230)). Amounts recognised to correct a fundamental error in the accounts are not included. (s.716(2)(3)). A loss that represents previously capitalised expenditure is not written off as it is incurred, but allowed under the writing down rules in s.729 or on realisation under Pt 4. Although abortive expenditure on acquisition is allowed under s.133, abortive expenditure on a failed disposal is allowed under s.740 (CIRD 12270; 12550).

Certain expenditure charged to the profit and loss account is specifically disallowed for tax purposes, i.e. expenditure on business, entertainment or gifts under CTA 2009 s.1298, crime related expenditure under CTA 2009 s.1304, s.577A, expenditure on a hired car proportionate to the excess of the car's cost over £12,000 (CTA 2009 s.56), or expenditure on providing non-approved, non-taxable retirement benefits under FA 2004 s.246(2), s.865 (CIRD 12600; 12610; 12620; 12630). Employees' remuneration paid more than nine months after the period of account are deferred until paid, under s.867; cf. CTA 2009 s.1289 (RPSM05400020; CIRD 12650). Pension payments are only allowed when paid (CTA 2009 s.868 (CIRD 12640)). A debit in respect of a bad debt may only be brought into account by way of impairment loss or to the extent that the debt is released under a statutory insolvency arrangement (s.869 (CIRD 12580; 12670)).

Royalties which would normally be deductible under s.728 may have the deduction deferred until the royalty is paid, if it is payable to a related party and not paid within 12 months after the end of the period of account and the recipient does not bring the royalty into account under s.851 CTA 2009 Pt.8 (CIRD 12660). This is to prevent a deduction being claimed on an accruals basis where the recipient is possibly taxable only on a receipts basis. It is similar to the loan relationship provisions for interest in ss.372–379. Related party is defined in s.835 by reference to a related party A in relation to the company B (CIRD 45010; 45105; 45120). Under Case 1, A is a related party if it is a company and has control of and holds a major interest in B, or B has control of or holds a major interest in A. Under Case 2, A is a company and both it and B are under the control of the same persons, unless the person controlling both A and B is the Crown or similar national or international organisation (s.835(4)). Case 3 applies where B is a close company and A is, or is an associate of, a participator in B or a participator in a company that has control of, or holds a major interest in B (CIRD 45300). Case 4 applies where A is a company and B is another company in the same group Control for these purposes is voting control (s.836(1), cf. CTA 2009 s.1124) and a major interest is where at least 40 per cent of the voting control is held and a further 40 per cent is held by one other person (s.837(1)(2) (CIRD 45150; 45160; 48270)). In determining control, rights to acquire control, for example, under options or through connected persons are included (s.97), as are rights and powers held jointly (s.839). The rights and powers of a partner are not included unless he has control of a major interest in the partnership, which is determined as if the partnership were a company under ss.836–840 (CIRD 45180; 45230; 45240)). A company or partnership does not cease to be a related party by reason of insolvency or equivalent arrangements, notwithstanding that "control" over a company's affairs may pass to a liquidator or administration on the commencement of insolvency proceedings (s.835).

The normal close company definitions of a participator and associate in CA 2010 ss.448–454 are applied except that a loan creditor is not treated as a participator (s.841). The definition of connected persons in ss.842–843 includes spouses and civil partners, relatives, trustees and companies connected with the settlement, cf. CTA 2010 ss.1121–1123, and where they are related parties within s.835, Cases 1 or 2 above (s.834(4) (CIRD 45190)). Where an accounting loss reverses in whole or part, and a gain was recognised in a previous period of account in respect of which the credit was brought into account (under Ch.2 ss.720–725) the loss may be recognised for tax purposes. The amount of the loss, however, is limited to the accounting loss multiplied by the previous credit, divided by the accounting gain, formula:

21–019

A1 x PC/AG

The accounting loss (AL) is that recognised for accounting purposes, the accounting gain is the amount of gain (AG) that is reversed in whole or part, and the previous credit (PC) is the amount of credit brought into account for tax purposes in respect of the gain (s.732 (CIRD 12560)). Normally on a revaluation, s.723 only taxes amounts previously written off that have been written back on revaluation and does not tax an unrealised revaluation surplus, in the limited circumstances in which such a surplus is permitted to be brought into the accounts under FRS 10 (CIRD 12790). Therefore the formula under s.732

CORPORATE INTANGIBLE FIXED ASSETS

restricts the loss proportionately to the taxable element of the revaluation surplus. Section.732 does not relate to amortisation of the revalued asset which is dealt with under s.729.

AMORTISATION

21–020   Where an intangible fixed asset is capitalised in a company's accounts the cost is written off over the anticipated life of the asset in accordance with FRS 10, by way of amortisation or as a result of an impairment review under FRS 11. Such accounting losses are recognised for tax purposes (s.729(1) (CIRD 12710, 12755)). An impairment review does not include the initial valuation to determine the amount to be capitalised (s.729(2)). The accounting loss as a result of amortisation or impairment may need to be restricted where there is a difference between the tax cost and the accounting cost, as a result, for example, of reinvestment relief. In such cases the accounting loss (AL) has to be reduced proportionately by multiplying it by the tax cost (TLC) and dividing by the accounting cost (AC) (s.729(3) (CIRD 12760)):

AL x TC/AC

The tax cost of an asset is the accounting cost subject to any adjustment required for tax purposes under s.72, e.g. transfer pricing adjustments under TIOPA 2010 Pt.4, or a specific disallowance or deferral of the expenditure under ss.865–869 dealt with above (s.729(4) (CIRD 12720)).

In subsequent periods of account the accounting loss (AL) may again have to be proportionately reduced by multiplying by the tax (TV) value and dividing by the accounting value (AV):

AL x TV/AV

The amount of loss is the amount of loss recognised for accounting purposes, the tax value is the tax written down value immediately before the amortisation charge or impairment loss and the accounting value is the value recognised for accounting purposes immediately before the amortisation charge or impairment write-down, i.e. the tax value represents the tax cost less previous tax write-downs and the accounting value represents the amount capitalised for accounting purposes less amounts previously written off (s.729(5) (CIRD 12770)).

As Pt.8 of CTA 2009 only applies to intangible fixed assets created or acquired after April 1, 2002 (s.882(1)), any amortisation of existing assets held at April 1, 2002, will not come into the computation and will remain eligible for capital allowances in appropriate cases, or will be a tax nothing, except where there is a disposal which would be within the chargeable gains regime. See Chs 16–20 for the taxation of existing assets.

Where transactions take place between related parties, as defined by ss.835–843, explained above, the transfer of intangible assets is treated as taking place at market value (s.845), except where a transfer is at an arms-length value or adjusted to an arms-length value under the transfer pricing provisions in TIOPA 2010 Pt 4 s.848(1). The market value is also not substituted where the transfer is tax neutral under CTA 2009 Pt 8 (as defined by s.776) such as a transfer within a group under s.775 (s.848(1)). A further two exceptions apply.

First, the market value rule does not apply where there is a transfer from a company at less than market value, or to a company at more than market value and the related party is not within the corporate intangible asset regime (e.g. because it is not a company, or the asset is not a chargeable intangible asset) and the transfer is chargeable to tax as a distribution under CTA 2010 Pt.23, or as employment income within ITEPA 2003 Pt 3 (para.92 (4A) and (4B)). Where this exception applies, the market value rule does not apply to the amount taken into account in computing the profits charged to tax under those provisions. Secondly, the market value rule is disapplied where an asset is transferred to a company and the transferee makes a claim for rollover relief under TCGA 1992 s.165. In this case, the transfer is treated as taking place at the market value of the asset less the amount held over under TCGA 1992 s.165 (CIRD 45033; 45035).

Where a transaction is deemed to be at market value but the accounting value in the hands of the transferee is nil, for example, on the acquisition of internally generated goodwill, the cost or accounting value is that which would have been recognised for accounting purposes if the asset had been actually acquired at market value and the amortisation loss for tax and accounting purposes calculated accordingly (s.857 (CIRD 12780)). 21–021

The tax written-down value of an intangible fixed asset written-down on the accounting basis under s.729 is the tax cost recognised for tax purposes, less taxable debits by way of amortisation or impairment, and plus any credits brought into tax under s.723 on revaluation, subject to any adjustments on part-realisation or change in accounting policy (s.742).

FIXED RATE ALLOWANCE

As an alternative to writing-down on an accounting basis, it is possible to elect for a fixed rate writing-down allowance for tax purposes whether or not the asset is amortised for accounting purposes. An irrevocable election must be made in writing to HMRC within two years of the end of the accounting period in which the asset is created or acquired by the company making the election, and has effect in relation to the whole of the amount capitalised for accounting purposes in respect of the asset covered by the election (s.730 (CIRD 12905)). The writing-down allowance is 4 per cent of the cost of the asset, or the balance of the tax written-down value if lower, which is brought into account for tax purposes in each accounting period beginning with that in which the relevant expenditure is incurred (s.731(1) (CIRD 12910)). The write-down is reduced proportionately if the accounting period is less than 12 months (s.731(2)). The cost of the asset means that recognised for tax purposes, which will be the amount capitalised for accounting purposes subject to any adjustments required by s.731(3)(4)). If there is a partial realisation of the asset the writing-down allowance is calculated on the remainder of the capitalised cost adjusted for tax purposes if necessary (s.731(6)(7) (CIRD 12920)). 21–022

CORPORATE INTANGIBLE FIXED ASSETS

Example 2

	Tax Figures	Accounting figures
	£	£
Cost of trademark not amortised	200,000	200,000
Amortisation year 1 at 4% p.a.	(8,000)	—
Written down value	192,000	200,000
Amortisation year 2	(8,000)	—
Written down value	184,000	200,000
Part disposal a(a)	(82,800)	(130,000)
		70,000

$$\frac{\text{Tax written down value} \times \text{Reduction in Accounting Value}}{\text{Previous Accounting Value}}$$

$$£184,000 \times \frac{£90,000 \text{ (B)}}{£200,000} = £82,800 \text{ (s.737))}$$

Accounting profit		40,000
Value of remainder	101,200	110,000

$$\text{Previous tax value} \times \frac{\text{New Accounting Value}}{\text{Previous Accounting Value}}$$

$$£184,000 \times \frac{£100,000 \text{ (B)}}{£200,000} = £101,200 \text{ (s.744))}$$

AMORTISATION FOLLOWING PART REALISATION

	Tax Figures £	Accounting Figures £
Amortisation over remainder of deemed life of 25 years 1/23 p.a. (s.731(6))	(4,400)	—
Written down value	96,800	110,000

(a) difference between sale proceeds and value of remainder, taxable credit £130,000–£82,800 = £47,200
(b) book value (cost) £200,000 less value of remainder £110,000 = £90,000

The tax written-down value of an asset amortised at the fixed rate is the tax cost less previous debits for amounts written off at the fixed rate. The tax cost is the same as the accounting cost subject to any adjustment required for tax purposes under s.731, and subject to any part realisation adjustments or adjustments on change of accounting policy under ss.871–879 (s.743).

AMORTISATION FOLLOWING PART REALISATION

The tax written down value of an intangible asset following a part realisation is proportionately reduced by multiplying the previous tax value (PTV) by the new accounting value (NAV) and dividing by the previous accounting value (PTV): 21–023
PTV x NAV/PTV
The previous tax value is the tax written down value immediately prior to the part realisation, the previous accounting value is the accounting value immediately before the part realisation and the new accounting value is, not surprisingly, the accounting value of the asset immediately after the part realisation. The tax written-down value after the part realisation can then be increased by subsequent expenditure on the asset and reduced or increased by subsequent tax debits and credits (s.744 (CIRD 12798; 12920)).

Example 3

	Tax Figures £	Accounting Figures £
Cost of asset after reinvestment relief	8,000	10,000
Amortisation at say 10% p.a.	(800)	(1,000)

$$\text{(Accounting Loss} \times \frac{\text{Tax Cost (s.9(3))}}{\text{Accounting Cost}}$$

CORPORATE INTANGIBLE FIXED ASSETS

$$£1{,}000 \times \frac{£8{,}000}{£800} = £800)$$

	Tax Figures	Accounting Figures
	£	£
Written down value	7,200	9,000
Part disposal	(3,200)(a)	(7,000)
		2,000
Accounting profit		3,000
Value of remainder	4,000	5,000

$$\text{(Previous tax value} \times \frac{\text{New Accounting Value}}{\text{Previous Accounting Value}}$$

$$£7{,}200 \times \frac{£5{,}000}{£9{,}000} = £4{,}000)$$

Amortisation at say 10% p.a.	(400)	(500)

$$£500 \times \frac{£4{,}000}{£5{,}000} = £400)$$

Written down value	3,600	4,500

$$\text{(a) Tax written down value} \times \frac{\text{Reduction in Accounting Value}}{\text{Previous Accounting Value}}$$

TAXABLE RECEIPTS (CREDITS)

$$£7{,}200 \times \frac{£4{,}000}{£9{,}000} = £3{,}200 \ (\text{s.737})$$

Difference between sale proceeds and value of remainder, taxable credit

£7,000 –   £3,200 =   £3,800

The reduction in the tax written down value following the part disposal is equivalent to the amount set against the net proceeds of the part realisation, under s.737.

TAXABLE RECEIPTS (CREDITS)

Part 8 Ch.3, deals with the taxation of taxable assets arising from receipts from intangible fixed assets recognised in the profit and loss account as they accrue such as royalties, the revaluation of intangible fixed assets, credits arising in respect of negative goodwill and the reversal of previous debits (s.720(1) (CIRD 13010)). Pt.8 Ch.3 does not deal with the realisation of intangible assets, which are dealt within Pt.8 Ch.4, ss.733–740 (s.720(2) (CIRD 12280)). A receipt in respect of an intangible fixed asset will normally be of a revenue nature such as a royalty and is brought into account for tax purposes on an accruals basis (s.721(1) (CIRD 13020)). The amount brought into account for tax purposes is normally the same as that for that used for accounts purposes, except where the amount is increased following a transfer pricing adjustment under TIOPA 2010 Pt.4, under s.721(3). Receipts would normally include grants (s.852 (CIRD 13030)) except for specific tax exempt grants. Any gain recognised in a company's profit and loss account in respect of an exempt grant is disregarded for tax purposes and is added back for the purpose of computing any debits recognised in the company's profit and loss account or expenditure capitalised for accounting purposes (s.853 (CIRD 12725; 13030)).

21–024

Example 4

Purchase of asset 1.6.02	100,000
Less Exempt Grant	(10,000)
Cost per accounts	90,000
Amortisation over 10 years, per accounts	9,000 p.a.
Tax cost—not reduced by grant	100,000
Tax debit for amortisation over 10 years	10,000 p.a.

REVALUATIONS

21-025 Where an intangible fixed asset's carrying value is increased following a revaluation, a chargeable tax credit arises proportionate to the increase in value of the asset for accounting purposes, but subject to an overriding limit of the tax debits previously brought into account in respect of the asset, so that a revaluation above original cost is not taxable on the revaluation surplus, until the asset is actually disposed of. Such a revaluation is only permitted under UK GAAP where the assets have a readily ascertainable market value, where the asset is of a homogenous type dealt with on an active market or where an impairment loss is reversed on a change in circumstances under FRS 10 and FRS 11. For accounts prepared in accordance with International Financial Reporting Standards, IAS 38 permits a revaluation in similar circumstances.

The net aggregate amount of relevant tax debits previously brought into account are debits under the writing-down allowance provisions in s.729, less any previous credits, e.g. on earlier revaluations (s.723(4)). A revaluation includes the valuation of an asset shown in the company's balance sheet which has not previously been the subject of a valuation, and the restoration of past losses (s.723 (5)). Where an election has been made to write down an intangible fixed asset at the fixed four per cent rate under ss.730,731, no part of any revaluation surplus is taxable or in any way affects the fixed rate write-down (s.723(5)). The pro rata revaluation adjustment corresponding to the increase in value is the accounting adjustment (AA) being the amount of the increase in the accounting value (AV) of the asset, multiplied by the tax value (TV), i.e. the written down value of the asset immediately before the revaluation and divided by the accounting value, which is the book value of the asset prior to the revaluation (s.723(5) (CIRD 13050; 13060)).

AA x TV/AV

Example 5

	Tax Figures £	Accounting Figures £
Cost of asset	10,000	10,000
Amortisation at say 10% p.a., years 1–3	(3,000)	(3,000)
Written down value	7,000	7,000
Revaluation (a) (limited to original tax cost s.723(2)(b), £10,000–£7,000)	3,000	6,000

$$\text{Para.15(2)(a) Accounting Adjustment} \times \frac{\text{Tax Value}}{\text{Accounting Value}}$$

$£6,000 \times \dfrac{£7,000}{£7,000} = £6,000$

Adjusted values	10,000	13,000
Amortised at, say, 10% p.a., year 4(a)	(1,000)	(1,300)

$$\text{Accounting Loss} \times \dfrac{\text{Tax Value}}{\text{Accounting Value}}$$

$£1,300 \times \dfrac{£10,000}{£13,000} = £1,000$

Written down value	9,000	11,700
Amortisation year 5	(1,000)	(1,300)

$£1,300 \times \dfrac{£9,000}{£11,700} = £1,000$

Written down value	8,000	10,400

(a) Net taxable credit, year 4 £3,000–£1,000 = £2,000

NEGATIVE GOODWILL

21–026 FRS 10 paras 48–51, provides that negative goodwill (that is the amount by which the fair values of the acquired assets, after testing for an impairment, less the fair values of the acquired liabilities, is greater than the purchase price), should be recognised in the profit and loss account in the periods expected to be benefited. On a just and reasonable apportionment, the amount attributable to fixed assets taken to the credit of the company's profit and loss account in respect of negative goodwill arising on an acquisition of a business should give rise to a corresponding tax credit (s.724 (CIRD 13080)).

REVERSAL OF PREVIOUS ACCOUNTING LOSS

21-027 Just as the reversal of a previous accounting gain is treated as a tax deductible debit, by s.732, so the reversal of a previous accounting loss gives rise to a taxable credit, under s.725 (CIRD 13090). The credit is the accounting gain (AG) recognised for accounting purposes, times the tax debit (TD) brought into account in respect of the prior amortisation of the asset, divided by the accounting loss (AL) that is being reversed in whole or part (s.725(3)).

AG xTD/AL

This does not apply to revaluation gains dealt with under s.723 (s.25(4)).

CHANGE OF ACCOUNTING POLICY

21-028 Where the carrying value of an intangible asset at the end of one accounting period differs to its carrying value at the beginning of the next period as a consequence of a change in accounting policy, for example where a company moves from preparing its accounts under UK GAAP to international financial reporting standards or vice versa, the difference in value is brought into account for tax purposes in the accounting period in which the change in accounting policy takes effect under ss.871–873 (CIRD 12300). The amount of the credit or debit to be brought into account is calculated as the difference in accounting value (AD) of the asset apportioned across the tax value (TV) divided by the accounting value (AV):

AD x TV/AV

Where the accounting value and the tax written down value of the intangible asset differ, the difference between the old and new accounting values is reduced or increased accordingly (ss.872–873). If this results in a credit, the amount brought into account for tax purposes is capped at the aggregate value of previous debits brought into account in respect of that asset (s.874).

Similar rules apply where an intangible asset is disaggregated into one or more separate intangible assets following a change in accounting policy, and there is a difference in the accounting value of the old asset at the end of one period and the accounting values of the new, disaggregated assets at the beginning of the next (ss.874(1)–(3); CIRD 12310). The debit or credit to be brought into account on the change of accounting policy is calculated as the accounting difference (AD) apportioned across the old tax value (OTV) divided by the old accounting value (OAV) of the disaggregated assets (s.874(4)):

AD x OTV/OAV

Where the accounting and tax written down value of the old asset are not the same, the difference is reduced or increased accordingly. Any resulting credit which falls to be brought into account is capped at the aggregate value of previous debits brought into account in respect of the old asset (ss.872–874). The tax value of each of the disaggregated assets is determined by apportioning the tax written down value of the old asset across the new accounting values of the assets (s.875(2)).

Where an election under s.730 has been made for allowances to be made on the fixed-rate basis and there is a disaggregation of assets on a change of accounting policy, the s.730 election continues to apply to each of the disaggregated assets as it applied to the old asset. The provisions in ss.872–875 do not apply in this case, and the tax written down value of the old asset is apportioned between the disaggregated assets by reference to their new accounting values (s.876; (CIRD 12320)). If no election has been made under s.10 in respect of the old asset, an election may be made in respect of one or more of the disaggregated assets, however, the time limit for making the election is not affected by the disaggregation on change of accounting policy, and an election must be made within two years from the end of the accounting period in which the old asset was acquired or created.

In order to prevent double-counting, s.878 provides that no credit is brought into account on a change of accounting policy to the extent that a credit already falls to be brought into account under the provisions dealing with revaluation of an asset (s.723), or the reversal of an accounting gain/loss (ss.725, 732).

REALISATION OF INTANGIBLE FIXED ASSETS

21–029 Chapter 4 ss.733–740 provides for tax debits and credits to be brought into account on the realisation by a company of an intangible fixed asset (s.733 (CIRD 13210)). A realisation means where, in accordance with generally accepted accounting practice, an asset ceases to be recognised in the company's balance sheet, for example, because it has been sold, or there is a reduction in the accounting value of the asset as the result of a transaction.

A transaction includes any event giving rise to a gain recognised for accounting purposes, such as an insurance claim, but not a loss arising by way of amortisation or as a result of an impairment review, neither of which is either a transaction or an event (s.734). The disposal of an intangible fixed asset which had no book value is treated as a realisation as if it did have a balance sheet value. A reduction in the accounting value as a result of a transaction is referred to as a part realisation (s.734 (CIRD 13230)).

Where the intangible fixed asset has been amortised for tax purposes, either on the accounting basis under s.729, or the fixed rate writing down allowance under ss.730–731, the excess of the proceeds over the tax written down value not limited to the original cost, are brought into account so the whole of the profit for tax purposes, is brought into charge. If the proceeds are less than the tax written down value a debit equal to the shortfall is brought into account for tax purposes and if there are no proceeds of realisation a debit equal to the entire tax written down value is allowed for tax purposes (s.735 (CIRD 13250)). No part of the proceeds is taxable as a chargeable gain.

21–030 In the case of existing assets acquired or created prior to April 1, 2002, where the sale proceeds exceed the original cost the difference between the original cost and the tax written down value would be recovered by way of a balancing charge and any excess would be taxable as a chargeable gain. Where the sale proceeds are less than the original cost, any shortfall of the proceeds below the written-down value would qualify for a balancing allowance. Where the intangible fixed asset does not qualify for capital allowances the excess of the net proceeds over the indexed base cost would normally be taxable as a capital gain subject to reinvestment relief under Ch.7 ss.754–758. Any shortfall of the net proceeds of realisation compared with the base cost would give rise to a capital loss.

The proceeds of realisation of an asset means the amount recognised for accounting purposes less the incidental costs of realisation (s.739(1) (CIRD 13240)). Any adjustment required for tax purposes, such as under the transfer pricing rules referred to in s.728(3) has also to be included (s.739(2)). Abortive expenditure on an intended realisation which does not take place is allowed as a debit under s.740.

Where a number of assets are acquired together, the acquisition costs are allocated to particular assets in accordance with GAAP or apportioned on a just and reasonable basis (s.856(3) (CIRD 12730; 12735; 12740)). Where assets are realised together, the proceeds are apportioned to each asset on a just and reasonable basis (s.856(5) (CIRD 13245)). Where both the disposal and the acquisition are on a just and reasonable basis it is likely that the same figures would be applied to each asset for the purchaser and seller. However, where the acquisition is dealt with under UK GAAP on the basis of fair value accounting under FRS 7, there is no requirement that the allocation adopted by the purchaser would be the same as the just and reasonable allocation adopted by the seller as each is correctly applying a different method of allocation. Merely because the parties agree separate prices for each asset or even have separate contracts for each asset at a stated price does not mean that the allocation is binding (s.856(2)). Where an asset is shown as an intangible fixed asset in a company's balance sheet but has not been written down for tax purposes, for example, because it has only recently been acquired, there is a taxable credit if the proceeds of realisation exceed the costs of the asset and an allowable debit if the proceeds of realisation are less than the cost of the asset and if the asset is scrapped, so that there are no proceeds the debit is equal to the cost of the asset recognised for tax purposes (s.736(1)–(5) (CIRD 13250)). The cost of the asset for tax purposes is the accounting cost less any adjustment required for tax purposes under s.136 (s.736(6)). Where there has been a part realisation the cost element of the asset retained is that recognised for tax purposes in respect of the value of the asset immediately after the part realisation plus any further tax cost of any subsequent expenditure (s.736(8)(9)).

21–031 In the case of part realisations the tax written down value or cost (TC) of the asset shall be reduced by the reduction in the accounting value (RAV) as a result of the realisation divided by the previous accounting value (PAV) immediately before the realisation (s.737 (CIRD 13260)).

TC x RAV/PAV

Where an intangible fixed asset is not shown in the balance sheet at all, because it has been entirely written off or is an internally generated asset not recognisable under FRS 10, the taxable credit is equal to the net proceeds of realisation (s.738 (CIRD 13250)). Taxable credits in respect of intangible fixed assets under Ch.3 ss.720–725 discussed above, do not qualify for reinvestment relief whereas a realisation of intangible fixed assets under Ch.4 ss.733–739, may qualify for reinvestment relief under Ch.7 ss.754–763 (s.733(3)).

As well as actual realisations there may be deemed realisations where a company ceases to be resident in the United Kingdom, or where a non-UK resident company ceases to use the asset for the purpose of the trade carried on by its UK permanent establishment, or where an asset not previously so held begins to be held for the purposes of a mutual trade or business (s.859 (CIRD 13270, 47030)). In such cases the asset is deemed to be sold at its market value, at the time of the chargeable event and immediately re-acquired at that value which is likely to crystallise a charge under Pt 4, although the tax liability may be postponed in certain cases, under s.862 (CIRD 47040; 47050).

Where, however, an asset becomes a chargeable intangible asset on a company becoming resident in the United Kingdom, or a non-UK company beginning to hold the asset for the purpose of a trade carried on by its UK permanent establishment or on the asset ceasing to be held for the purpose of a mutual trade or business in accordance with s.863(1) (CIRD 12745, 47010, 47020). The asset is deemed to have been acquired immediately after it became a chargeable intangible asset in relation to the company for its accounting value at that time, i.e. at its net book value recognised for accounting purposes under s.719, and not its market value (s.863(2)).

Paragraph 861 postpones the tax liability on the deemed disposal on the company ceasing to be resident in the United Kingdom, under s.859(1)(a), where the asset continues to be held for the purposes of a trade carried on through a foreign permanent establishment, and where the deemed realisation proceeds exceed the original tax cost of the asset and where another UK company is a parent of the company leaving the United Kingdom, and the company leaving the United Kingdom is its 75 per cent subsidiary. The two companies may elect, within two years of a change of residence, to postpone the tax charge on the gain until either the 75 per cent subsidiary test ceases to be satisfied or the intangible fixed asset is realised (s.860(1)(2)). The postponed gain comes into charge or partially into charge, on a partial realisation, if the intangible fixed asset is realised within six years after the date on which the company ceased to be resident in the United Kingdom (s.861(1)–(3)). The appropriate proportion of the postponed gain (PG) on a partial realisation is the old market value (OV) of the asset immediately before the part realisation less the new market value (NV) of the asset retained immediately after the part realisation, divided by the old value:

PG x OV–NV/OV

There are provisions to prevent a double charge (s.861(4)), and the company becoming non-resident ceasing to be a 75 per cent subsidiary at any time crystallises a credit equal to the postponed gain, except to the extent it has already been charged (s.862(1)–(3)). There can also be a charge on the parent ceasing to be resident in the United Kingdom, which crystallises a deemed disposal immediately before it ceases to be so resident (s.109(5)). Any postponed gain becoming chargeable is treated as a non-trading credit under ss.34, 861(5), 862(5). Paragraphs 860–862 is broadly equivalent to TCGA 1992 s.187 which applies to postponement of company chargeable gains in similar circumstances.

ANTI-AVOIDANCE

21–032 Where there are tax avoidance arrangements which have as their main object, or one of their objects the obtaining or enhancing of a debit which would not otherwise have been available or to avoid having to bring in a credit that would otherwise be chargeable for tax purposes, such arrangements are disregarded (s.864 (CIRD 48010; 48020; 48030; 48105; 48110; 48120; 48130; 48140; 48150)).

It seems that local Inspectors will be expected to discuss with the technical specialists in Business Tax (Technical) before raising this general anti-avoidance provision to counter perceived tax avoidance. It should be noted that the paragraph requires tax avoidance to be a main object, i.e. purpose, of the arrangements not merely that the effect is to reduce the tax charge compared with what it otherwise might have been. In *IRC v Brebner* (1967) 43 T.C. 705, at 718, Lord Pearce in respect of the transactions in securities legislation, now ITA 2007 s.731 et seq., stated:

> "when the question of carrying out a genuine commercial transaction, as this was, is considered, the fact that there are two ways of carrying it out, one by paying the maximum amount of tax, the other by paying no, or much less, tax it would be quite wrong as a necessary consequence to draw the inference that in adopting the latter course one of the main objects is, for the purposes of the section, avoidance of tax".

The most likely target for this particular anti-avoidance provision is where transactions are entered into to depress the value of purchased goodwill in order to claim the tax write-down as a result of an impairment review under FRS 11.

It would also be aimed at attempts to inflate the acquisition cost of assets prior to acquisition or multiple transfers of assets involving non-related parties in order to turn existing assets into chargeable intangible fixed assets eligible for amortisation relief. The general nature of the anti-avoidance provision is likely to make it a potentially useful addition to the transfer pricing rules to counter offshore and cross-border arrangements.

HOW CREDITS AND DEBITS ARE GIVEN EFFECT

21–033 Credits and debits in respect of assets held for the purposes of a trade, a property business or a mine, transport undertaking etc are taxed and relieved under ss.747–749 and non-trading credits and debits are given effect to in accordance with ss.751–753 and insurance companies are dealt with under s.901 (CIRD 13520; 13530; 13540). Any apportionment necessary where an asset is used for more than one purpose is to be made on a just and reasonable basis (s.745 (CIRD 13510)).

Credits and debits in the accounting period relating to an intangible fixed asset held by the company for the purposes of a trade are given effect by treating credits as receipts of the trade and debits as expenses of the trade in calculating the profits of the trade for tax purposes (s.747). Similarly where the assets are used for a property business taxable under Sch.A or furnished holiday lettings or

HOW CREDITS AND DEBITS ARE GIVEN EFFECT

on overseas property business, the credits and debits are treated as receipts or expenses of the business (s.748). Furnished holiday lettings are those within CTA 2010, 265–268.

Where intangible fixed assets are held by a company for the purposes of a mine transport undertaking, etc. within s.39(4), credits are treated as receipts of the concern and debits as expenses in calculating its profits under Case I of Sch.D s.749.

Where there are intangible fixed assets held for commercial purposes but not within ss.747–749 the company's aggregate non-trading gain or loss on intangible fixed assets must be calculated under s.751(1). Assets not used for commercial purposes are entirely excluded by s.803. There is a non-trading gain on intangible fixed assets if there are only non-trading credits or the non-trading credits exceed the non-trading debits (s.751(2)–(5)). **21–034**

Conversely, there is a non-trading loss where there are only non-trading debits or the non-trading debits exceed the non-trading credits (s.751(6)(7)). A non-trading gain on intangible fixed-assets is charged to tax (s.752). A non-trading loss on intangible fixed assets for an accounting period may be claimed in whole or part against the company's total profits for that period (s.753(1)(3)). A claim must be made within two years of the accounting period to which it relates, or such further period as HMRC may allow (s.753(2)). If the loss is not set against total profits or surrendered by way of group relief under CTA 2010 ss.99,103,105, it may be carried forward and treated as a non-trading debit of the next succeeding accounting period (s.753(2)(5)).

A non-trading loss on intangible fixed assets may be surrendered for group relief under CTA 2010 s.99 (FA 2002 Sch.30 s.3(1)). The relief is given in a similar way to management expenses under CTA 2010 ss.99, 103–104 but does not include amounts carried forward from earlier periods CTA 2010 ss.99, 102–104 (CIRD 13550)). Non-trading gains of charities are eligible for the charitable exemption in CTA 2010 Pt.11 Ch.2.

The transfer of an intangible fixed asset to an investment company, intra-group on tax neutral terms, in order to absorb an excess of unused non-trading debits, is prevented by ss.692–702. **21–035**

Where there is a change in ownership of an investment company with an unused non-trading loss on intangible fixed assets, relief is restricted where, after the change in ownership, there is a significant increase in the amount of the company's capital or, within the period of six years beginning three years before the change, there is a major change in the nature or conduct of the business carried on by the company, or the change in the ownership occurs at a time after the scale of the activities in the business carried on by the company has become small or negligible and before any considerable revival of the business (ss.691, 677–678). The accounting period in which the change in ownership occurs is divided into two periods and the profits or losses apportioned on a time basis, or as appears just and reasonable (s.678). Relief for non-trading debits in respect of intangible fixed assets is only available for each period separately and losses cannot be carried forward through the change in ownership (s.681). The detailed rules regarding significant increases in the capital of an investment company in ss.688–691 are imported into the rules relating to non-trading debits arising from intangible fixed assets.

The profits of life insurance companies dealt with on the I-E basis are inclusive of debits and credits arising from intangible fixed assets which are dealt with under s.901 to the extent that they are not excluded from applying under s.902, i.e. royalties and computer software which remain within the company intangible fixed assets regime for insurance companies.

Corporate partners

21–036   A corporate partner under CTA 2009 Pt.17 recognises its share of partnership profits directly, and they are subjected to corporation tax and computed under corporation tax rules so far as the corporate partner is concerned. This means that the provisions of CTA 2009 Pt.8 will apply to the corporate partner's share of interests in intangible fixed assets, which could lead to some complex calculations for mixed partnerships of individual and corporate partners as the existing law treating goodwill as a capital asset within the capital gains regime and the application of the existing law for intellectual property, as explained in Chs 16–20, will mean that the income tax and corporation tax computations will be substantially different for the individual and corporate partners' shares. Nothing in s.807, which excludes interests of a partner in a partnership from being intangible fixed assets within CTA 2009 Pt.8, prevents a corporate partner's share of profits being computed under corporation tax rules under CA 2009 Pt.17.

ROLLOVER RELIEF ON REINVESTMENT

21–037   Chapter 7 of CTA 2009 Pt.8 provides for rollover relief under the corporate intangible fixed assets regime, where intangible fixed assets are realised and the proceeds re-invested (CIRD 20010). The rules are covered in ss.754–763. Rollover relief is only available if the appropriate conditions are met in relation to the old and new assets and if a claim is made, s.754 (CIRD 20020, 20025).

Rollover relief allows the whole or part of a taxable credit arising on realisation of a corporate intangible fixed asset, including goodwill, to be deferred where the various requirements are met (CIRD 20105). The amount deferred is treated as a deduction from the realisation proceeds and from the allowable expenditure on the intangible assets acquired, which both defers part of the tax charge arising on realisation and reduces the allowable debits in future both by way of amortisation or impairment and on disposal. The taxable credit may not be rolled over to the extent it prevents the recovery of previously allowed debits and is further restricted where less than the whole of the proceeds are reinvested as the non-reinvested profit over cost also remains taxable. The rollover relief is based on the capital gains rollover relief for classes of business assets under TCGA 1992 s.155. The capital gains tax relief ceases to be available for goodwill and agricultural and fishing quotas against the acquisition of new assets acquired on or after April 1, 2002, and may therefore only be rolled forward into company intangible fixed assets within s.756. The chargeable gains rollover relief continues for the remaining types of asset within TCGA 1992 s.155, for companies and the rules remain unchanged for unincorporated businesses. Rollover relief for intangible fixed assets is extended to groups.

ROLLOVER RELIEF ON REINVESTMENT

The rollover relief for intangible fixed assets differs from the capital gains tax relief in that it applies to goodwill and all intangible fixed assets not just goodwill and certain agricultural quotas. However, rollover is more restrictive in that a profit on disposal of intangible assets cannot be set against reinvestment in tangible assets. There is no requirement that the assets be used for the purposes of a trade, unlike for chargeable gains purposes. The claw-back of previously allowed debits is not eligible for rollover relief and future debits are restricted by the deemed reduction in the cost of the asset acquired on reinvestment. A part realisation to a related party cannot be rolled over. However, a major departure from the chargeable gains rules allows, in limited circumstances, reinvestment into the shares of another company owning intangible fixed assets.

21–038 The conditions which must be met in relation to the old asset and its realisation are that it must have been a chargeable intangible asset throughout the period during which it was held by the company, which means that it must be acquired or created after commencement, i.e. April 1, 2002, ss.881–905. Rollover relief for existing assets acquired pre-April 1, 2002 and sold afterwards may qualify for capital gains rollover relief under ss.898–900 (CIRD 20050). For rollover relief to apply, the proceeds of realisation must exceed the cost of the asset, or, in the case of a partial realisation, the appropriate proportion of the cost of the asset adjusted in either case for any previous realisations (s.637(1) (CIRD 20035; 20060)). If the asset was a chargeable intangible asset of the company at the time of its realisation and for a substantial part of, but not throughout, the period it was held by the company it is treated as if it were two separate assets with any apportionment necessary being made on a just and reasonable basis (s.637(2)(4)). What represents a substantial part of the period of ownership is not defined. In other cases where substantial is used in the Taxes Act it is normally accepted as amounting to 20 per cent or more. Although, exceptionally, for a substantial shareholding for reinvestment relief on the disposal of shares in subsidiaries. TCGA 1992 Sch.7AC para.8(1)(a) defines "substantial" as being not less than 10 per cent of the company's ordinary share capital, this is without prejudice to what is meant by substantial where the word appears in other contexts where the 20 per cent rule applies, see *Tax Bulletin*, Issue 62, December 2002, 985, and commentary in the *Capital Gains Manual* at p.17953. There is an exception in the case of telecommunication assets and Lloyds syndicate capacity brought within CTA 2009 Pt.8 by ss.897, 882, 905. These are treated as chargeable, intangible assets from acquisition, under ss.897(3), 905(6)(7) as such assets are brought within CTA 2009 Pt.8 even for existing assets (CIRD 20040).

The requirement for the net proceeds of realisation to exceed the costs are to prevent reinvestment relief applying to recoveries of previously tax allowed debits, which are effectively withdrawn as a result of the disposal. It is only the reinvested profit element over original cost that qualifies for reinvestment relief. In the case of capital gains tax disposals rolled over under ss.898–900, the net proceeds of realisation are the consideration less the incidental costs of making the disposal which are deductible for capital gains purposes (s.898(2)(c)), and the cost recognised for tax purposes is the indexed base cost for capital gains purposes, which is obviously the net proceeds of disposal less the chargeable gain (s.898(2)(d)). Rollover relief does not apply on a deemed realisation of an asset except in certain cases on degrouping under ss.791, 794 below, and no account is taken of any deemed reacquisition (s.763 (CIRD 20070)).

Example 6

	£
Disposal of asset A y/e 31/03/13	30,000
Cost y/e 31/03/12	(20,000)
Gain	10,000
Estimated life of asset A, five years cost	20,000
Amortisation for accounts and taxes	
20% p.a. straight line basis	4,000
Book value	
Accounting profit:	16,000
Proceeds	30,000
Less book value	(16,000)
Profit	14,000
Less recovery of amortisation	(4,000)
Gain available for roll over relief	10,000
Cost of new asset B	35,000
Less gain rolled over	(10,000)
Tax cost	25,000
Estimated life of asset B, 10 years	
Tax amortisation, year one.	2,500 p.a
Accounts amortisation	3,500 p.a.
Calculation of tax amortisation	

$$\text{Accounting loss} \times \frac{\text{Tax Cost}}{\text{Accounting Cost}}$$

$$£3,500 \times \frac{£25{,}000}{£25{,}000} = £2{,}500$$

ROLLOVER RELIEF ON REINVESTMENT

Example 7

	Tax Figures £	Accounting Figures £
Facts as in previous example		
Cost of new asset B	35,000	35,000
Less gain rolled over	(10,000)	
Cost	25,000	35,000

	Tax Figures £	Accounting Figures £

$$\text{Accounting Loss} \times \frac{\text{Tax Value}}{\text{Accounting Value}}$$

$$£3,500 \times \frac{£22,500}{£35,000} = £2,500$$

	Tax Figures	Accounting Figures
	(2,500)	(3,500)
Written down value	22,500	31,500
Tax amortisation year two	(2,500)	(3,500)

$$£3,500 \times \frac{£22,500}{£31,500} = £2,500$$

	Tax Figures	Accounting Figures
Written down value	20,000	28,000
Enhancement expenditure	10,000	10,000
Written down value	30,000	38,000
Amortisation over eight years, year three	(3,750)	(4,750)

$$£4,750 \times \frac{£30,000}{£38,000} = £3,750$$

	Tax Figures	Accounting Figures
Written down value	26,250	33,250
Amortisation year four	(3,750)	(4,750)

$$£4,750 \times \frac{£26,250}{£33,250} = £3,750$$

	Tax Figures	Accounting Figures
Written down value	22,500	28,500

CORPORATE INTANGIBLE FIXED ASSETS

Example 8

	Tax Figures £	Accounting Figures £
Cost of existing intangible fixed asset pre 1.4.02	10,000	10,000
Indexation for chargeable gains to disposal	2,500	—
	12,500	10,000
Net sale proceeds on disposal	15,500	15,500
Gain	3,000	5,500
Cost of new intangible fixed asset	12,500	12,500
Rollover relief limited to excess of cost of new asset over deemed tax cost of old asset £12,500—£11,500	(1,000)	—
Deemed cost of new asset	11,500	12,500

ROLLOVER RELIEF ON REINVESTMENT

	Tax Figures £	Accounting Figures £
Amortisation, say 10% p.a.		
£1,250 x £11,500 / £12,500 = 1,150		
	(1,150)	(1,250)
Written down value	10,350	11,250
Chargeable gain	3,000	
Less rollover relief	(1,000)	
	2,000	

Rollover relief is not available on a part-realisation where the interest in the asset realised is acquired by a related party (s.850(1)(2)), although this does not apply to chargeable gains rolled over under ss.898–900 in view of s.898(4), nor to the capital gains tax degrouping charge rolled over under ss.899–900, in view of s.899(7) (CIRD 20080; 20480).

The expenditure on the assets acquired must meet a number of conditions. It must be incurred in the period beginning 12 months before the date of realisation of the old asset or such earlier time as HMRC may by notice allow, and ending three years after the date of realisation of the old asset or such later time as HMRC may by notice allow. These time limits will only be extended in exceptional circumstances (CG60640, s.756(1) (CIRD 20110)). The expenditure must be capitalised by the company for accounting purposes (s.756(2) (CIRD 20120)). The asset on which the expenditure is incurred must be a chargeable intangible asset of the company immediately after the expenditure is incurred (s.756(3) (CIRD 20130)). A chargeable intangible asset is one where any gain on disposal would be a chargeable realisation gain (s.741(1)), and a chargeable realisation gain is one which would be taxable under Ch.4, excluding any relief for rollover on reinvestment or treatment as a tax neutral transfer (s.741(4)). The reacquisition of an asset previously realised qualifies (s.762), but not a deemed reacquisition (s.763(2) (CIRD 20140)). Expenditure is incurred for rollover relief when it is recognised for accounting purposes (s.756(4)). It is not necessarily the same as the contract date for chargeable gains purposes under TCGA 1992 s.28.

As CTA 2009 Pt.8 only applies to intangible fixed assets which are created by the company after commencement on April 1, 2002 or acquired from an unrelated company after that date (s.882(1)), an acquisition of intangible fixed assets from a related party, as defined by Ch.12, after commencement does not qualify for rollover relief unless the related party had acquired or created the asset after commencement (s.882).

The claim for rollover relief must specify the old asset to which the claim relates and the expenditure on the asset acquired on reinvestment and the amount of the relief claimed (s.757 (CIRD 20150)). There are no other requirements for

21–039

the claim which therefore falls within the general provisions as to claims and elections in FA 1998 Sch.18 Pt VII paras 54–65. Under FA 1998 Sch.18 s.55, the claim must be made within six years of the end of the accounting period to which it relates.

Where possible a claim must be made in a company tax return or amended return but if this cannot be done a stand-alone claim under TMA 1970 Sch.1A, is allowed (FA 1998 Sch.18 s.57). As the reinvestment period under s.756(1)(b) extends to three years after the date of realisation of the old asset a provisional entitlement to relief may be claimed under s.761, as for company chargeable gains rollover relief under TCGA 1992 s.153A (CIRD 20310). A declaration is required in the company's tax return for the accounting period in which the realisation takes place that the company has realised an intangible fixed asset and proposes to meet the conditions for rollover relief and is provisionally entitled to relief of a specified amount (s.761(3)). A declaration has the same effect as if the reinvestment had actually taken place (s.761(2)), until it is withdrawn or superseded by an actual claim when the reinvestment is made (s.761(4)). In any event the declaration ceases to have effect four years after the end of the accounting period in which the realisation took place (s.761(5)). On ceasing to have effect the necessary adjustments would be made to the tax computations by assessment or otherwise (s.761(6)(7)).

The computation requires the relief to be given by reducing the proceeds of realisation of the old assets and the cost recognised for tax purposes of the replacement assets by a similar amount (s.758(1) (CIRD 20205)). Where the qualifying expenditure on other assets qualifying for rollover relief is equal to, or greater than, the proceeds of realisation of the old asset, the amount available for relief is the amount by which the proceeds of realisation exceed the tax cost of the old asset (s.758(2) (CIRD 20210)). Where the qualifying expenditure on other assets is less than the proceeds of realisation, the amount of the relief is the amount if any by which the expenditure on other assets exceeds the tax cost of the old asset (s.758(3) (CIRD 20220)). The tax cost of the old asset on a partial realisation is the appropriate proportion of the tax cost or the adjusted tax cost if there has been a previous part realisation (s.758(5)(a) (CIRD 20230)). Qualifying expenditure on other assets is that which meets the requirements of ss.756,758(4), and the cost of the old asset means the total of the capitalised expenditure on the asset recognised for tax purposes (s.758(5)). A claim for rollover relief for reinvestment only affects the claimant and not any other party involved in the realisation of the old asset or the expenditure on the other assets (s.758(6)).

21–040 The limitation of the rollover relief by reference to the tax cost of the old asset ensures that the difference between the tax written down value and the tax cost on disposal is recovered under s.735 or s.736, as adjusted in the case of partial realisation by s.737.

The appropriate proportion of the cost of the old asset (COA) on a partial realisation is arrived at by multiplying the tax cost of the old asset by the reduction in the accounting value (RAV) immediately before the part realisation compared with that immediately after the part realisation and dividing by the previous accounting value (PAV), i.e. the written-down value or carrying value in the accounts immediately before the part realisation (ss.759(1) and 719 (CIRD 20230, 20235)).

ROLLOVER RELIEF ON REINVESTMENT

COA x RAV/PAV

Where there has been a previous part realisation the tax cost is the adjusted cost taking into account that realisation (s.7592(2)(3)).

Example 9

	Tax Figures £	Accounting Figures £
Cost of asset	10,000	10,000
Amortisation, say seven years at 10% p.a.	(7,000)	(7,000)
Written down value	3,000	3,000
Proceeds	14,000	14,000
Realisation credit	11,000	11,000
Cost of a new asset	16,000	16,000
Rollover relief, s.758(2)		
Proceeds less cost £14,000—£10,000	(4,000)	—
	12,000	16,000
Amortisation, say 10% p.a.	(1,200)	(1,600)
Written down value	10,800	14,400
Proceeds	15,000	15,000
Realisation credit	4,200	600
Cost of new asset	13,000	13,000
Rollover relief, s.758(3)		
Proceeds less tax cost £15,000 – £12,000 = £3,000		
Limited to excess of expenditure over cost £13,000 – £12,000	(1,000)	—
	12,000	13,000
Amortisation, say, 10% p.a.	1,200	1,300
Written down value	10,800	11,700

Where there has been a change in accounting policy resulting in the disaggregation of an asset into two or more assets under ss.871–879, the tax cost of each of the new assets is allocated across the new assets by reference to the proportion each asset's new accounting value bears to the aggregate new accounting values (s.760).

Rollover relief on reinvestment: groups

21-041 CTA 2009 Pt.8 Ch.8 ss.764–773, defines groups of companies for the corporate intangible fixed assets regime and Ch.9 ss.774–799, deals with the consequences of intra-group transactions, rollover relief on reinvestment and the charge on companies leaving a group (CIRD 20405).

As for chargeable gains within a group, rollover relief may be claimed by a company disposing of an existing asset consisting of goodwill or an intangible fixed asset into expenditure on a qualifying chargeable intangible fixed asset post-commencement where the expenditure on new assets is by another company in the same group. The normal exclusion of deemed realisations does not apply to realisations under the degrouping provisions, see below, including where the degrouping charge is reallocated to another group member. Relief is also available where the reinvestment consists of the acquisition of shares constituting a controlling interest in a company owning post-commencement chargeable intangible assets.

Rollover relief on reinvestment is available where the old asset is realised by a company which, at the time of realisation, is a member of a group and the expenditure on other assets made by another company which at the time of incurring the expenditure is a member of the same group as the disponor company, and is not a dual resident investing company (ss.109, 777(3) (CIRD 20410)). The other assets into which the reinvestment is made must be chargeable intangible fixed assets in relation to the company incurring the expenditure, and a claim must be made by both companies as if they were the same person (s.56(2)(c) and (d)). The expenditure on other assets does not include the acquisition of assets acquired from another group member on a tax neutral transfer (s.56(3)). There is no requirement that both companies are members of the same group at the same time. These provisions broadly follow the capital gains tax rules in TCGA 1992 s.175.

Rollover relief on acquisition of shares

21-042 Where company A acquires a controlling interest in company B, rollover relief is available if intangible fixed assets (underlying assets) are held by company B, which was not previously part of company A's group but becomes so on the acquisition of the controlling interest in company B (s.778(1)(2) (CIRD 20420)). The expenditure by company A on the acquisition of a controlling interest in company B is treated as expenditure on acquiring the underlying assets (s.779(1) (CIRD 20430, 20440)). This is limited to the tax written down value of the underlying assets in company B immediately before the acquisition, or, if less, the amount of the consideration for the acquisition by company A of the controlling interest in company B (s.779(2)). As a result company A is deemed to have incurred expenditure on chargeable intangible fixed assets if they are held as chargeable intangible assets by the company owning them immediately after the acquisition by company A of a controlling interest in company B. This usually means by company B or its subsidiary acquired with it (s.779(3)(4)). The relief given against the gain on the old assets need not be claimed by company A but may be claimed by another member of the group to which company A belongs.

The relief given on the realisation of the old assets is deducted from the tax written down value of the underlying assets held by company B, or the company owning the assets which joined the group as a result of company B's acquisition, and if there is more than one underlying asset the reduction in value may be allocated as the company or companies so decide or agree between them (s.779(5)(7)).

A claim for relief, in accordance with (s.757), must be made by company A jointly with the companies holding the underlying assets (s.778(4)). Company A acquires a controlling interest in company B if they were not previously part of the same group and on the acquisition, by company A of shares in company B the companies become members of the same group immediately after the acquisition (s.778(3)). Rollover relief is available on the disposal of intangible fixed assets by a group company or on a disposal of the existing goodwill or intangible assets not within CTA 2009 Pt.8 in order to defer tax due on a chargeable gain. There is no restriction where company A acquires less than 100 per cent of company B although the amount paid for the shares will be less than the entire value of the company to reflect the minority interest not acquired. This is not unusual as the whole of the gain rolled over reduces the tax written down value of the underlying assets so there is symmetry from a taxation point of view, although arguably the minority share holders are disadvantaged by such a claim in that the tax charge in company B is increased as a result of the reduction in the tax written down value which would normally be reflected in a reduced amortisation charge, and therefore an increased tax charge in company B.

The Revenue illustrated the deemed cost of new assets in the following example in their Finance Bill 2002 Notes on Clauses.

Example 10

Tax value old asset prior to realisation	Original cost of old asset	Proceeds of old asset	Cost of shares	Tax value underlying assets	Realisation proceeds rolled over
80	100	150	200	90	None (a)
80	100	150	200	180	50 (b)
80	100	150	200	140	40 (c)
80	100	150	140	200	40 (d)
80	100	150	130	140	30 (c)

Notes
(a) Tax value of underlying assets less than original cost of old asset; no relief available—ss.779(2),758(3).
(b) Tax value of underlying assets and cost of shares exceed realisation proceeds; all profit over original cost rolled over—ss.779(2), 758(2).
(c) Tax value of underlying assets less than realisation proceeds of old asset; not all proceeds reinvested; profit to be rolled over restricted to the excess of that tax value over the cost of the old asset—ss.779(2), 758(2).

(d) Cost of shares less than realisation proceeds and tax value of underlying assets (which exceeds the proceeds); relief restricted as if the cost of the shares is equal to the tax value of the underlying assets—ss.779(2), 758(2).

(e) As (d) but tax value of underlying assets does not exceed the realisation proceeds; relief again restricted as if the cost of shares is the tax value of the underlying assets.

DEGROUPING

21–043 Where the degrouping rules in ss.780–799, see below, apply, there is a deemed re-acquisition of assets which does qualify for rollover relief (CIRD 40505; 40510). The transferee company holding intangible fixed assets as the result of an intra-group transfer which then leaves the group is deemed to have sold and immediately reacquired the assets received on the intra-group transfer at market value, thus crystallising a tax charge on deemed realisation (s.780 (CIRD 40520)). In order to claim rollover relief the assets must have been chargeable intangible assets not of the transferee company leaving the group but of the transferor company in the group from which it acquired the assets. The time limits for re-investment run from the date of the triggering event of the degrouping charge not the date of the transfer of the old asset, and the proceeds of realisation are the market values of the assets included in the deemed realisation (s.791(1)–(4)(CIRD 20460)). The effect of the relief is to allow another company in the group to take over the liability deferred by the intra-group transfer in place of the company leaving the group. Therefore, the reduction in the deemed realisation proceeds does not affect the deemed reacquisition value of the transferee company (s.791(5)). The intra-group transfer would not have affected the transferee company's writing down allowances as it is a tax neutral transfer within s.775(1) and the deemed reacquisition is not expenditure on an intangible fixed asset eligible for amortisation or impairment relief, Ch.2 ss.726–732.

Where a degrouping charge arises to the transferee company under ss.780 or 785 on ceasing to be a member of a group or ceasing to satisfy the relevant conditions for membership of the new group that company (X) may elect jointly with another company (Y) that the transferor group should take over all or part of the taxable credit arising on the deemed realisation of X's intangible fixed assets (s.792(1)–(4)). An election can only be made where company Y was resident in the United Kingdom or carried on the trade in the United Kingdom through a branch or agency when company X ceases to be a member of the group or satisfies the qualifying condition, and company Y must not be a dual resident investing company within, s.793(1)–(4). An election must be made by notice in writing to HMRC not later than two years after the end of the accounting period of company X in which it leaves the group or ceases to satisfy the qualifying conditions (s.793(5)). The effect of the election is that company Y is treated as making a non-trading credit, or where it is non-resident as if it had disposed of an asset held for the purposes of a branch or agency in the United Kingdom, which effectively passes the degrouping problem from company X to company Y.

DEGROUPING

The deemed realisation is now deemed to have been made by company Y which is still part of the group and the conditions for rollover relief in s.755 are deemed to have been met, and the proceeds of realisation and tax cost of the old asset are what they would have been if there had been no election and company X had made the rollover relief claim (s.794(1) (CIRD 20470)). Company Y is now in a position to make a rollover relief claim under Ch.7 ss.754–763, on the acquisition by it of further chargeable intangible fixed assets or by another company in the group (s.792(2)–(4)).

These provisions allowing the reallocation of a degrouping charge for intangible fixed assets mirror the rollover of the chargeable gains degrouping charge in TCGA 1992 Sch.7AB. **21–044**

Where only part of the deemed gain arising on degrouping is transferred to company Y the appropriate apportionments are made and company X remains liable for the proportion of the gain not so transferred (s.794(5)(6)).

HMRC is concerned to ensure that the transferee company remains responsible for the degrouping charge where the tax has not been paid within six months of it falling due. HMRC may serve a notice under s.795 requiring another group company, which was either the principal company of the group or another company, which in the period of 12 months ending with the triggering event of the degrouping charge was a member of the same group and owned the relevant asset, or any part of it, which was subject to the degrouping charge (s.795(3)(b) (CIRD 40720, 40730)). Alternatively if the taxpayer company is not resident in the United Kingdom but carries on a trade in the United Kingdom through a permanent establishment the tax may be recovered from a controlling director of the taxpayer company or of a company which had control of that company (s.795(4)). Various terms are defined by s.796. Similar rules apply for the chargeable gains degrouping charge under TCGA 1992 ss.190, 795(1). The third party collection provisions also extend to a taxable credit on a deemed realisation, which is reallocated within the transferor group under ss.792–796.

The procedure for recovering a degrouping charge is set out in ss.795–897, which requires HMRC to serve a notice requiring the recipient, within 30 days, to pay the outstanding tax referable to the degrouping charge, or any of it which remains unpaid, and must specify the amount payable (s.795(2) (CIRD 40740)). The notice has the effect of being a notice of assessment for the requirement to pay the tax and for the purpose of interest and appeals. Changes are made to the relevant legislation to this effect (s.797(3)). A person who has paid an amount of tax in pursuance of such a notice may recover the amount from the taxpayer company, under s.797(4), although this may be difficult to enforce if the company no longer has assets or is outside the jurisdiction. A payment of tax under these provisions is not allowed as a deduction for tax purposes as it is deemed to be a payment of tax on behalf of the transferee company (s.797(5)). **21–045**

Any notice requiring payment by a controlling director must be served within three years of the final determination of the tax liability of the transferee company, or in consequence of a determination under FA 1998 Sch.18 ss.36 or 37 (s.798(1) (CIRD 40740)). Where the unpaid tax is charged under self-assessment the relevant date is when the self-assessment became final (s.798(4)(6)). In the case of a discovery assessment, the three year period starts with the date of the assessment or the determination of an appeal against it (s.798(5)(6)). Where existing goodwill and intangible assets are subject to a degrouping charge, in respect of a triggering event taking place, a chargeable gain arises which may be rolled over into chargeable intangible assets, as it cannot be rolled-over into other capital assets within TCGA 1992 s.155. The date of realisation of the old asset is taken to be the time the capital gain arises under TCGA 1992 s.179. The proceeds of realisation are the market value of the asset when it is deemed to be disposed of and re-acquired, ss.899–900. The exclusion of rollover relief in s.850(1)(2) in the case of a partial realisation involving a related party in these circumstances, is disapplied by s.899(7).

Group definition

21–046 The definition of company for group purposes is a company within the meaning of the Companies Act 2006 s.I or the Companies (Northern Ireland) Order 1986 (SI 1986/1032), a company other than a limited liability partnership constituted under any other act, including the law of a country or territory outside the United Kingdom, or a registered Industrial and Provident Society within s.499, or a friendly society within the Friendly Societies Act 1992 or a building society. Group and subsidiary are construed where appropriate in accordance with overseas laws with any necessary modifications (s.764).

A group consists of a principal company of the group and all its 75 per cent subsidiaries together with their 75 per cent subsidiaries (s.765). There is however a requirement that the group is restricted to effective 51 per cent subsidiaries of the principal company (s.766(1)). The definition is the same as that for company chargeable gains in TCGA 1992 s.170.

A 75 per cent subsidiary is defined by CA 2010 s.1154(3), as a subsidiary of another body corporate if and so long as not less than 75 per cent of its ordinary share capital is owned directly or indirectly by that other body corporate. A 51 per cent subsidiary is defined by s.52 as a subsidiary of another body corporate if and so long as more than 50 per cent of its ordinary share capital is owned directly or indirectly by that other body corporate (CTA 2010 s.1154(2)), and the parent company is beneficially entitled to more than 50 per cent of its profits and surplus assets on a winding up (CIRD 40010; 40020; 40030; 40032; 40036).

21–047 The principal company of a group cannot itself be a 75 per cent subsidiary of another company unless it and its 75 per cent subsidiary companies are excluded from the group by reason of not being effective 51 per cent subsidiaries, in which case they may constitute a separate subsidiary group, s.767 (CIRD 40038). A company cannot be a member of more than one group and there are anti-avoidance provisions to prevent the creation of artificial groups. United Kingdom subsidiaries of a foreign parent company would form a group as there is no requirement that non-resident companies be excluded from the various tests. Section 768 provides a tie-breaker test where a company would otherwise be a member of two or more groups (CIRD 40040). A group remains the same group of companies so long as the principal company remains the same and if the principal company joins another group its existing subsidiaries are regarded as part of the enlarged group which does not therefore crystallise a degrouping charge (s.769(1)(2) (CIRD 40100)). A resolution to wind up a group member is not regarded as causing that company to cease to be a member of the group (s.769(3)). There are also rules to prevent companies being treated as leaving a group where the principal company of the group becomes, or is acquired by, a Societas Europaea (s.770(1)(2)).

The definition of 75 per cent subsidiary in CA 2010 s.1154(3) is amended to include the share capital of registered Industrial and Provident Societies as ordinary share capital and imports the provisions relating to certain statutory bodies in TCGA 1992 s.170(12)–(14), s.773. The definitions in s.772 of equity holder and determination of profits available for distribution for these purposes is given by CTA 2010 Pt.5 Ch.6 .

Chapter 8 defines a group for the purpose of the corporate intangible fixed assets regime and Ch.9 ss.775–802, deals with intra-group transfers and other events. It refers to transfers of intangible fixed assets which are created or acquired from an unrelated party after commencement on April 1, 2002 (ss.881–889). Where an intangible fixed asset is transferred from one company to another, where both companies are members of the same group and the asset is a chargeable intangible asset, as defined by s.741, of the transferor company immediately before the transfer and of the transferee company immediately after the transfer, the transfer is tax neutral (s.775(1) (CIRD 40220; 40250; 40350)). This provision does not apply where the transferor or transferee is a dual resident investing company (s.775(4) (CIRD 10190)). Any adjustments which would otherwise fall to be made in accordance with the transfer pricing rules in CTA 2009 Pt.8, are ignored (para.775(3)).

Tax neutrality only applies to transfers of assets, so that, for example, the grant of a licence to exploit intellectual property for a lump sum is not a transfer. There is therefore no reason to make any adjustments for the purposes of the corporate intangible fixed asset rules, as the grant of a license will not be a transfer of an intangible asset to a related party requiring the market value rule to be applied under s.846. The calculation of the market value of intangible assets would normally be referred to the HMRC Charities, Assets and Residence, Shares and Assets Valuation, see Ch.12. In cases where the transfer pricing provisions of TIOPA 2010 Pt.4, are relevant, the arm's length price for transfer pricing is used instead of the market value if there is any difference between them (s.846(1) (CIRD 45010; 45020; 45030; 45040)).

21–048

Existing assets acquired by the transferor prior to April 1, 2002 are not chargeable intangible assets and therefore cannot be tax neutral transfers. However, they may be transferable intra group on a no gains no loss basis for company chargeable gains purposes under TCGA 1992 s.171 or s.171A. A tax neutral transfer is regarded as not involving any realisation of the asset by the transferor, or any acquisition of that asset by the transferee, and the transferee is treated as having held the asset at all times when it was held by the transferor and having done all things in relation to the asset as were done by the transferor effectively acquiring the transferor's tax history as regards the asset (ss.776(1)–(3)). In particular, the original cost of the asset in the hands of the transferor is treated as the original cost recognised for tax purposes in the hands of the transferee and all debits and credits in relation to the asset that have been brought into account for tax purposes by the transferor are treated as if they had been brought into account by the transferee (s.776(4)(5)). Rollover relief on reinvestment is available on a group-wide basis (ss.777–779), as explained above.

Degrouping charge

21-049 If it were not for the degrouping charge, a company would be able to avoid a tax charge on disposing of an intangible fixed asset by transferring it on a tax neutral intra-group basis to a shell group company and then sell the shares in the company. A similar problem arises for company chargeable gains which is solved by TCGA 1992 ss.179–181. The corporate intangible fixed asset rules are not quite so all-embracing in that where a company leaves a group for chargeable gains purposes the anti-avoidance provisions cover not only assets transferred intra-group but assets into which such assets have been rolled by the transferee company. The intangible fixed assets rules only apply to assets transferred to the transferee company which are held by it when it leaves the group.

The degrouping provisions counter the enveloping of assets within a group company by causing the disposal of the shares by which the company leaves the group to crystallise the gain deferred on the tax neutral transfer which may have taken place up to six years previously. Although the disposal triggers the charge by reference to the earlier tax neutral transfer the taxable debit or credit is chargeable on the transferee company immediately prior to its' leaving the group.

The requirements for a degrouping charge are that a transferor company, which is a member of a group, transfers a post-commencement intangible fixed asset, "the relevant asset", to a transferee company (s.780(1)(a) (CIRD 40520)). The relevant asset must be a chargeable intangible asset of the transferor immediately before the transfer and of the transferee immediately afterwards (s.780(1)(b)). A chargeable intangible asset is defined by s.741 as one which, if it were disposed of, would give rise to a chargeable realisation gain taxable under Ch.4 and it is this charge that has been avoided by a company leaving the group rather than disposing of the asset itself.

The transferee must have been a member of the group at the time of the transfer, or have subsequently become a member of the group, and ceased to be a member after the transfer within six years of the date of the transfer (s.780(1)(c) (CIRD 40600)). If the relevant asset is held by the transferee, or by an associated company also leaving the group, the transferee is treated as having realised the asset immediately after the transfer for its market value and immediately reacquired the asset at that value (s.780(2)). Note that this provision identifies what would have been the gain on a transfer between related parties at market value under ss.845–846, were it not for the tax neutral treatment given to intra-group transfers by s.775. The net debit or credit so calculated at the time of the intra-group transfer is allowed to, or taxed on, the transferee as if it had arisen immediately before the transferee ceased to be a member of the group (s.780(3) (CIRD 40610)). If the intangible fixed asset were held by the transferee, immediately after the transfer, for the purpose of a trade, business or undertaking, the charge is on a deemed trading receipt, or equivalent, under ss.747–749. If the

DEGROUPING

transferee ceased to carry on the trade or business before it ceased to be a member of the group, it would be treated as a non-trading debit or credit under ss.751–753 (s.781(5)).

Example 11

	Tax Figures £	Accounting Figures £
Group Company A		
Cost of asset	100,000	100,000
Amortisation of say 10% p.a. for four years	(40,000)	(40,000)
Written down value	60,000	60,000
Asset transferred to Group company B, at market value of £75,000 (tax neutral, s.775)	60,000	75,000
Amortisation, year five, at 10% p.a. (on deemed cost taken over)	(10,000)	(7,500)
	50,000	67,500

	Tax Figures £	Accounting Figures £
Company B leaves group in year six so deemed disposal at market value on transfer from A		
Proceeds, less tax written down value £75,000–£60,000	15,000	
Amortisation, year five		
$£10,000 \times \dfrac{£75,000}{£60,000} = £12,500$		
Less allowed £10,000	(2,500)	
Degrouping charge, year six	12,500	
Amortisation year six	(2,500)	
Net credit	10,000	

As there is no requirement, before a degrouping charge can arise that the transferor and transferee companies are members of the same group at the time of the transfer, it is possible that the transfer was not in fact done on a tax neutral basis. However, it may have been made under the company reconstruction provisions in Ch.11 ss.817–833, as a tax neutral transfer or been between parties then unrelated, which would presumably have been at market value, so no degrouping adjustment would be required or it could have been between parties that were related but not in the same group, in which case the transfer would have been at deemed market value under ss.846–849 and again no degrouping charge would actually arise.

The fiction that the transferee company had sold and immediately reacquired the asset after the transfer as a result of the degrouping charge has to take account of the fact that had this actually happened the amortisation deductions would also be affected so that the final adjustment is the net of the increase in the market value less the additional amortisation for the period between the transfer and the degrouping triggering event (ss.780(3), 785(4)). (The revised market value computed for the transferee company is used for future amortisation in that company.)

Relieving provisions

21–050   There are a number of potential let-outs where associated companies leave the group and at the same time the principal company becomes a member of another group, the company ceases to be a member of a group by reason of an exempt distribution or a merger is carried out for bona fide commercial reasons (s.780(5)). Where two or more associated companies cease to be members of a group at the same time there is no degrouping charge in relation to transfers from one to another of those companies (s.783(1) (CIRD 40530)). However, where a transferee company A, had ceased to be a member of a group of companies and had acquired an asset from a transferor company B that was also a member of the X group, and companies A and B both left the group at the same time to join the Y group and then company A ceased to be a member of the Y group, there is a degrouping charge if there is a relevant connection between the X and Y groups (s.783(2)(3) (CIRD 40540)). There is a relevant connection between the X and Y groups where, when transferee company A ceases to be a member of the Y group, the principal company of the Y group is under the control of the principal company of the X group, or which was the principal company of that group or any person who controls the principal company of the X group, or had control of the principal company of the X group; looking through a series of companies where necessary, and adopting the close company definition of control under CTA 2009s.449–451, apart from excluding a banking business holding loan capital in the ordinary course of business (s.784 (CIRD 40545)).

DEGROUPING

Where the principal company becomes a member of another group there is not normally a degrouping charge (s.785(1) (CIRD 40550)). However, if the transferee company ceases to be a 75 per cent subsidiary and an effective 51 per cent subsidiary of one or more members of the second group known as the qualifying condition, there is a degrouping charge if the transferee ceases to satisfy that condition, and the asset is still held by the transferee company or another company in the second group which the original principal company joined (s.785(2)(3) (CIRD 40560)). The transferee company is treated as through it had immediately disposed of and reacquired the asset transferred to it at its market value at that time, but the resultant debit or credit is crystallised immediately prior to the qualifying condition being no longer met (s.785) (CIRD 40610)). If the asset is used for the purpose of a trade business or concern within ss.747–749, it is treated as a trading debit or credit or its equivalent unless the trade or business has ceased prior to the breach of the qualifying condition, in which case it becomes a non-trading debit or credit (s.786). There is exemption for a bona fide commercial merger (s.785(6)).

Demergers

There is no degrouping charge where a company ceases to be a member of a group as a result of an exempt distribution on a demerger, under CTA 2010 ss.1075–1077, so long as there is no chargeable payment within CTA 2010 s.1088, within five years (s.787 (CIRD 40590)). 21–051

Bona fide commercial merger

There is no degrouping charge where a company leaves a group as a result of a merger carried out for bona fide commercial reasons and not for the avoidance of tax (s.789(1) (CIRD 40580)). A merger is defined as an arrangement or series of arrangements under which one or more companies, "the acquiring company", none of which is a member of the group, acquires, otherwise than with a view to their disposal, one or more interests in the whole or part of the business which was carried on by the transferee company leaving the group, and one or more members of the transferee company's group acquires, otherwise than with the view to their disposal, one or more interests in the whole or part of the business of each of the acquiring company's businesses, and the acquisition is by a company which was at least 90 per cent owned by the acquiring company or companies. It is also necessary that at least 25 per cent by value of each of the interests acquired by the acquiring company or companies in the transferee company's business consists of the holding of ordinary share capital. The remainder of the consideration must be a holding of share capital of any description or debentures or both. The values of the interests acquired in each case must be substantially the same and the consideration for the interests acquired by the acquiring companies must consist of, or be applied in the acquisition of those interests by businesses carried on by the acquiring companies or their 90 per cent subsidiaries (ss.789–790). 21–052

A degrouping charge does not arise on a company ceasing to be a member of a group in consequence of another member of the group ceasing to exist (s.788(1)).

For the purposes of the degrouping charge two or more companies are associated if they would, by themselves, form a group of companies and an asset acquired by a company is treated as the same asset owned at a later time by the transferee company, or an associated company, if the value of the second asset is derived in whole or part from the first asset (s.788(20(3)).

Where payments are made by one company to another in a group in respect of group roll-over relief on the reinvestment of intangible fixed assets or for the reallocation of a degrouping charge, as defined, they shall not be taken into account in computing profits or losses of either company for corporation tax purposes, nor shall they be regarded as distributions or charges on income, provided that the payment does not exceed the amount of the relief. The amount of the relief is the reduction in the charge on the realisation of an intangible fixed asset as a result of a claim for roll-over relief under ss.777–779, or the amount of the degrouping charge reallocated under s.792(1) (CIRD 40705). Any payment for the reallocation of allowances in this way should be under an agreement between the companies (CIRD 40710). As for group relief, it is the amount of the claim that may be paid for, not merely an amount equivalent to the tax consequences of the claim (s.799 (CIRD 40900)).

The election to reallocate the taxable credit on degrouping only affects that charge. Any adjustments to the amortisation figures in the transferee company remain with that company.

TRANSFER OF BUSINESS OR TRADE

21–053 Chapter 11 ss.817–833, deals with company reconstructions and transfers of trade to provide relief in respect of company intangible fixed assets similar to those which apply for chargeable gains purposes under TCGA 1992 ss.139–140B (CIRD 42010).

A company reconstruction involving a transfer of business requires a scheme of reconstruction which involves the transfer of the whole or part of the business of one company, the transferor, to another company, the transferee, under which the transferor does not receive any part in consideration for the transfer apart from the transferee company taking over the liabilities of the business. Scheme of reconstruction is defined as for chargeable gains purposes under TCGA 1992 ss.136, 818(1)–(6) (CIRD 42020; 42025).

Under TCGA 1992 s.136, a scheme of reconstruction arises where, there is an arrangement, between company A and its shareholders or debenture holders where, under the arrangement, another company, B, issues shares or debentures to those persons in proportion to their shareholdings in company A whose shares or debentures in company A are either retained by them or cancelled or otherwise extinguished (TCGA 1992 s.136(1)). Scheme of reconstruction is further defined in TCGA 1992 Sch.5AA. Where the assets transferred under such a scheme of reconstruction include chargeable intangible assets (s.741) of the transferor and transferee, the transfer is treated as tax neutral with the transferee taking over the transferor's tax history of the asset (ss.818(2), 776). Where a transfer is also an intra-group transfer the tax neutral transfer provisions under s.775 apply instead of these reconstruction rules (s.818(3)). The paragraph only applies if the reconstruction is effected for bona fide commercial reasons and does not form part of a scheme or arrangement one of the main purposes of which is the avoidance of taxation (s.818(5)), dual resident investing companies under CA 2010 s.109 (s.818(4)).

A clearance application may be made under s.832 to confirm that HMRC accept that the reconstruction is for bona fide commercial reasons and not designed to avoid tax (s.851, cf. TCGA 1992 s.138).

TRANSFER OF TRADE BETWEEN EU COMPANIES

Where a company incorporated in the European Union transfers the whole or part of a trade carried on in the United Kingdom to an EU company resident in another state, in exchange for shares issued by the transferee to the transferor, a claim may be made jointly by the transferee and transferor that any chargeable intangible assets (s.741) transferred from the transferee to the transferor may be treated as tax neutral transfers with the transferee taking over the transferor's tax history under s.776 s.819 (CIRD 42030; 42035). This provision mirrors the capital gains tax provisions in TCGA 1992 ss.140A and 140B, enacting the European Union Mergers Directive 90/434, dealing with cross-border reorganisations. The transferor must end up with not less than one quarter of the ordinary share capital of the transferee company.

21–054

A company is resident in an EU state if it is within the charge to tax of that state (s.819(3)(4)). The transfer has to be for bona fide commercial reasons and not part of a tax avoidance arrangement (ss.820(2), 831), and confirmation of this can be obtained from HMRC under s.831 (s.832).

FORMATION OF A SOCIETAS EUROPAEA BY MERGER

The transfer of an intangible asset as part of the formation of a Societas Europaea by merger (see EC Regulation 2157/2001) on or after April 1, 2005 is tax neutral for the purposes of the corporate intangible asset rules provided certain conditions are met (ss.820–832; CIRD 42080). To qualify for tax neutral treatment, there must be a merger of two or more companies who between them are resident in more than one EU Member State, and the asset transferred as part of the merger must be a chargeable intangible asset (s.741) in the hands of both the transferee and transferor (ss.821–822). The relief applies only where the merger takes place for bona fide commercial reasons and does not from part of a scheme or arrangement of which the main purpose or one of the main purposes is the avoidance of tax (ss.820(2), 831). There is a clearance procedure (s.832).

21–055

Relief under ss.820–832 does not apply where the merger falls within the scope of the company reconstruction provisions in s.818.

INCORPORATION OF AN OVERSEAS PERMANENT ESTABLISHMENT

21–056 Where a company resident in the United Kingdom, carrying on a trade outside the United Kingdom through a permanent establishment, transfers the whole or part of that trade, together with the assets used for the trade (apart from cash), to a company not resident in the United Kingdom, in exchange for shares or securities, the transfer of any chargeable intangible assets (s.741) included in the transfer may qualify for postponement of the tax charge on realisation which would otherwise apply under Ch.4 ss.733–741(s.827 (CIRD 42040; 42045; 42050)). The transferor may claim for the excess of the proceeds of realisation over the tax cost of the assets to be reduced to the extent that the consideration for the transfer consists of securities (s.828).

The gain so postponed is brought into charge to tax if the transferor realises the whole or part of the securities received in consideration for the transfer of the branch (s.829(1)(4)) if the transferee company realises any of the relevant assets the transferor must bring into charge a credit equal to the appropriate proportion of the aggregate deferred gain (s.829(3)(5)). These provisions follow the chargeable gains relief under TCGA 1992 s.140. Intragroup transfers within TCGA 1992 s.171 or Ch.8 ss.764–773, are ignored (s.830 and (7) (CIRD 42055)). The transfer has to be for bona fide commercial reasons and not part of a scheme for tax avoidance, for which clearance is available under s.832 (s.831).

CLEARANCE

21–057 Application for clearance may be made under s.832, which is similar to the clearance for chargeable gains under TCGA 1992 s.138 (CIRD 42100, 42110). Clearance is available for company reconstructions involving a transfer of business, incorporation of a non-UK branch, transfer of a non-UK trade and transfers involving the formation of a Societas Europaea by merger. It must be in writing containing particulars of the operations that are to be effected (ss.832(1)(2)). HMRC have 30 days in which to require further particulars or to give a decision on the clearance application (ss.832(3)(5), 833). If HMRC do not respond within 30 days, the application may be taken to the Tribunalfor them to decide. Non-disclosure vitiates any clearance given (ss.833(2)–(4)).

LIFE ASSURANCE BUSINESSES AND BUILDING SOCIETIES

21–058 On a transfer of life assurance businesses under the supervision of the United Kingdom or European Union courts between two companies, any transfer of chargeable intangible assets (s.741) can be treated as tax neutral (s.904 (CIRD 13560; 42120)).

Where a building society is demutualised into a company, chargeable intangible assets included in the transfer (s.741(3)(4)) may be treated as tax neutral, with the transferee company taking over the transferor society's tax history (s.776). If the society is part of the group the transfer to the transferee company does not give rise to a degrouping charge under ss.780, 785, under reliefs which correspond to the chargeable gains reliefs in TCGA 1992 s.216 (s.852(2)–(4) (CIRD 42130)). A similar relief is available for the amalgamation or transfer of engagements involving building societies, equivalent to the chargeable gains reliefs in TCGA 1992 s.215. Where the transfer includes chargeable intangible fixed assets (s.741) the transferee can take over the transferor's tax history in relation to the asset on a tax neutral transfer (ss.721, 826 (CIRD 40300, 42140)).

FINANCE LEASING

21–059 Finance leases of intangible fixed assets are treated as loans by the lessor rather than the hiring of an asset for accounting purposes, under UK GAAP, SSAP 21, as a result of which finance leasing arrangements are financial assets outside FRS 10 (CIRD 10210; 27010; 27020; 27030; 27035). Section 854 allows the Treasury to make provision by way of statutory instrument for finance leases to be brought within CTA 2009 Pt.8 as corporate intangible fixed assets, even though the asset is accounted for by the finance lessor as a financial asset. These regulations are the Corporation Tax (Finance Leasing of Intangible Assets) Regulations 2002 (SI 2002/1967) (ss.854–855 (CIRD 27050; 27090)). The asset recognised in the finance lessor's balance sheet is treated as though it were capitalised expenditure on an intangible fixed asset, except that the election for the fixed rate basis of amortisation under s.10 is not available, nor is the roll-over relief on reinvestment available as the amount so capitalised is not treated as capitalised expenditure for the purposes of s.756 (ss.854(1) (CIRD 27060)). Where an intangible fixed asset of a lessor becomes subject to a finance lease, thereby becoming a financial asset, the value of the financial asset so created is treated as the proceeds of realisation of an intangible fixed asset which is within Ch.4, ss.733-741 (ss.854–855). Assets excluded except for royalties under ss.808–813, such as computer software, films and sound recordings are entirely excluded if they are accounted for by the lessor as financial assets (s.855). Also excluded are assets leased to finance lessees chargeable to income tax, or where the asset counts as an existing asset of the finance lessee or a related party (s.855(6)). The accounting definitions are used for finance leases which includes hire purchase, conditional sale and similar arrangements (s.855(7)).

CONTROLLED FOREIGN COMPANIES

21–060 One of the consequences of bringing capital profits on the disposal of goodwill and other intangible fixed assets into an income regime such as that applicable to corporate intangible fixed assets, is that the profits then fall within the controlled foreign company regime in TIOPA 2010 Pt 9A (CIRD 10200), see Ch.14.

Consequential amendments

21–061 The introduction of the corporate intangible fixed assets regime requires a number of consequential changes to the existing tax legislation, including the surrender of non-trading losses by way of group relief, the extension of the charitable exemption to non-trading gains and the restriction of non-trading losses on a change in ownership of a company, which have been referred to above (FA 2002 Sch.30 ss.2, 3 and 4 (CIRD 48050)). The opportunity has been taken to rewrite TA 1988 ss.337, 337A and 338 in the style developed by the Tax Law Rewrite project with TA 1988 s.338, being replaced by a new s.338 and TA 1988 ss.338A and 338B (FA 2002 Sch.30 s.1).

The TA 1988 s.337 specifies when a company begins or ceases to carry on a trade including a Sch.A business or overseas property business, which includes when it comes within or ceases to be within the charge to corporation tax. A company's profits are to be computed without any deduction in respect of dividends or other distributions and without any deductions in respect of charges on income. However, no deduction is allowed in respect of interest other than under the loan relationship provisions in FA 1996 Ch.2 Pt 4, and no deduction is allowed in respect of losses from intangible fixed assets within FA 2002, CTA 2009 Pt.8, except in accordance with that Schedule (TA 1988 s.337A). Charges on income are allowed as a deduction from a company's total profits, as reduced by any other relief other than group relief, but only to the extent that the company's total profits are reduced to nil. Charges on income are only deducted if actually paid in the accounting period concerned, subject to any other express provisions in the Corporation Tax Acts (TA 1988 s.338).

Before March 16, 2005, charges on income consisted of annuities or other annual payments, within TA 1988 s.338B, qualifying donations to charity under the gift aid provisions in TA 1988 s.339, and gifts of shares to charities under TA 1988 s.587B(2)(a)(ii). Following the repeal of TA 1988 s.338B by F(No 2)A 2005, from March 16, 2005, charges on income consist only of qualifying donations to charity and gifts of shares. Any payment that is deductible from profits is not treated as a charge on income. This means that royalties in respect of intellectual property and other intangible fixed assets, which are specifically written off as incurred under s.8, are not charges on income. Royalties in respect of existing intangible assets are normally deductible on an accruals basis under s.119, if they are recognised for accounting purposes after April 1, 2002, as explained previously.

For payments made on or before March 15, 2005, an annuity or other annual payment was allowable as a charge on income if it was not specifically excluded and was made under a liability incurred for a valuable and sufficient consideration, was not charged to capital, was ultimately borne by the company and, in the case of a non-resident company, was incurred wholly and exclusively for the purposes of a trade carried on by it in the United Kingdom through a permanent establishment (TA 1988 s.338B(1) and (2)). An annual payment paid to a non-resident was only a charge on income if tax is deducted from the payment under TA 1988 s.339 and accounted for to HMRC under TA 1988 Sch.16, or it was made to the UK branch of a non-UK resident company or it was paid out of income chargeable under Sch.D, Case V, i.e. foreign income (TA 1988 s.338B(3) and (4)). An annuity or other annual payment was also not a charge on income if it was payable in respect of a company's loan relationship or is a royalty to which CTA 2009 Pt.8 applies, i.e. the corporate intangible fixed asset regime, which, under s.8, specifically allowed deductions for royalties as they accrued except where paid to a related party more than 12 months after the end of the accounting period and not brought into account by the recipient on the accruals basis, in which case the royalty was only deductible when paid, under s.94 (FA 1988 s.338B(5)). Annuities or annual payments that are gift aid donations continue to be allowable after March 16, 2005 under TA 1988 s.339.

DOUBLE TAXATION RELIEF

Because double taxation relief in the United Kingdom is given on a source-by-source basis, credits in relation to foreign tax suffered could be lost as a result of aggregating trading and non-trading debits under the corporate intangible fixed assets regime. The FA 2002 Sch.30 s.5, amends the rules to prevent this happening; TA 1988 s.795(4) is amended to ensure that where, exceptionally, the sum recognised for accounting purposes, and therefore under CTA 2009 Pt.8, is the net amount after deduction of foreign tax. The amendment ensures that such income is nonetheless grossed up and a credit allowed for the foreign tax (FA 2002 Sch.30 s.5(2)). TA 1988 s.797B is inserted by FA 2002 Sch.30 s.5(4), which applies similar rules to corporate intangible fixed assets as are applied to loan relationships by TA 1988 s.797A. A company is allowed to assume, purely for double taxation relief purposes, that corporation tax is payable on its non-trading credits without having to deduct the non-trading debits, which can be allocated in the way which preserves the maximum double taxation relief (FA 1988 s.797B (1)–(3)).

21–062

Example 12
Company A has, for the year ended March 31, 2013, the following results:

		£
Trading profits		4,000
Intangible fixed assets		
Debits	5,000	
Less credits	2,000	
(election FA 2002 Sch 29 s.30(5), foreign tax £200)		(3,000)
Income liable to corporation tax		1,000
Corporation tax at 23%		230

	£
Foreign tax credit on source basis—none—no intangible fixed asset net credits. However, for tax credit purposes only, the computation becomes:	
Trading profits	4,000
Less intangible fixed asset debits	(5,000)
	(1,000)
Intangible fixed asset credits (foreign tax £200)	2,000
Income liable to corporation tax	1,000
Corporation tax at 23%	230
Less foreign tax credit (limit £1,000 x 23%)	(200)
Net UK tax payable	30

Where non-trading excess debits on intangible fixed assets are carried forward as a loss, rather than set off against profits for a period, they can be ignored for foreign tax credit purposes as only the losses actually used in the year have to be taken into account (TA 1988 s.797B(4)). Where foreign tax is claimed by way of a deduction under TA 1988 s.811, for tax purposes, but the gross amount has been included in the accounts and would therefore normally be the measure of taxable credits under the corporate intangible fixed assets regime, TA 1988 s.797B(5), enables the net amount to be included for tax purposes.

VALUE SHIFTING

21–063 TCGA 1992 s.33A retains the efficacy of the value shifting provisions where an intangible fixed asset is transferred intra-group under the tax neutral transfer provisions in s.775, or the degrouping provisions of ss.780–785. This preserves the value shifting provisions which already counter the use of intra-group transfers under TCGA 1992 s.171, or degrouping charges under TCGA 1992 s.179.

CHAPTER 22

The Patent Box

INTRODUCTION AND BACKGROUND

Intellectual property and other intangible assets are inherently mobile, and a multinational group will be faced with a range of possible alternative strategies for holding such assets in a tax efficient manner. There were concerns that special regimes for patent income in other countries were making the UK uncompetitive and drawing business away from the UK. In particular, Luxembourg, Ireland, the Netherlands and Belgium all offer attractive incentives for intellectual property producing companies. The effective tax rate established by the Netherlands' "Innovation Box" is 5 per cent, in Luxembourg it is 5.76 per cent and in Belgium the effective rate is 6.8 per cent. The effective rate in Ireland is slightly higher at 12.5 per cent. In order to compete with these well-known intellectual property holding jurisdictions, the government announced at Budget 2009 that it would consult upon the introduction of a tax-advantaged regime for income from patents (the "Patent Box"). This move also needs to be seen as part of a much wider strategy aimed at making the UK's corporate tax system the most competitive within the G20 ("the Corporate Tax Road Map"), with comprehensive changes also being made to the UK controlled foreign company rules (see Ch.14), research and development tax credit regime (see Ch.21) and staged reductions in the standard rate of corporation tax to 20 per cent from April 1, 2015. An initial consultation document was issued in November 2010, followed by a further more detailed consultation exercise in June 2011. Draft legislation was published in December 2011, with final provisions incorporating minor amendments to the draft legislation being included within Finance Act 2012. The legislation is contained within CTA 2010 Pt 8A. Companies may elect into the Patent Box regime from April 1, 2013.

22–001

The introduction of the Patent Box is therefore a significant step towards making the UK the location of choice for holding certain intangible assets. However, the regime introduced from April 1, 2013 is more narrowly drawn than that applying in other countries, in that it applies only to patents and certain other limited intellectual property rights such as plant varieties. The Patent Box does not apply to intellectual property such as trademarks or copyright, presumably as these have a weaker or more variable link to high-tech activity and have no process of independent examination which would allow the government to be confident that the resulting product is technologically innovative. A patent, by contrast, is individually examined by an independent patent authority before being granted, to verify that the patent represents a genuinely innovative and beneficial invention. Furthermore, only UK and EU patents fall within the regime, in contrast to for example the "innovation box" applying in the Netherlands. The benefit of the Patent Box is therefore likely to be largely limited to patent-intensive industries such as pharmaceuticals, who arguably already receive relatively generous assistance through the tax system in the form of research and development reliefs. The UK's Patent Box provisions also suffers from a phased entry, such that the full benefit of the relief will not be available to companies electing into the regime until April 1, 2017. Nonetheless, the introduction of the Patent Box provides an additional incentive for companies in the UK to exploit existing patents and develop new, innovative patented products, and it should encourage companies to locate the development, manufacture and exploitation of patents in the UK, especially given the relatively wide range of income associated with a patent which potentially benefits under the regime.

OUTLINE

22–002 The Patent Box is an elective regime which allows certain income of a company's trade relating to qualifying income from patents and certain other rights to be taxed at a preferential effective rate of corporation tax of 10 per cent, although the phasing provisions means that this rate will only be available from April 1, 2017.

The Patent Box is only available to reduce the tax liabilities of companies and so although partnerships and individuals cannot use it, corporate members of a partnership can still claim the relief. This is achieved by allowing the partners to elect to be taxed as if the partnership itself had elected into the regime. The election is made on a company-by-company basis, so some partners may elect in and some may not.

To be eligible for the Patent Box, the company (or another company in the same group) must meet various ownership requirements. These require the company to be actively involved in the development of the eligible patent or the ongoing decision making connected with its exploitation. The company cannot simply hold the patent as an investment.

22–003 All businesses within the scope of UK corporation tax will potentially be eligible to elect for the Patent Box regime to apply to their trading profits.

The Patent Box specifically applies only to income from the exploitation of a patent, and detailed rules are provided to strip out any profits derived from routine manufacturing or development functions, and profits derived from exploitation of brand and marketing intangible assets, are excluded. A simplified, formulaic approach to identifying these costs is available to most claimants, although a company will be able to opt for a more precise method by reference to detailed computational rules if it so wishes.

The patent box applies to profits arising to a qualifying company on or after April 1, 2013. Where an accounting period straddles April 1, companies will be able to allocate appropriate profits to each period so that they can benefit immediately from the additional proportion of Patent Box benefits available.

ELECTIONS

22–004 A company wishing to elect into the regime must give notice to HMRC in writing specifying the first accounting period for which the election is to apply. There is no special form of words for the election but it must be made on or before the last day on which the company would be entitled to amend its tax return, under para.15 of Sch.18 of FA 1998, for the first accounting period to which it is intended to apply. In practice this means within 12 months of the fixed filing date of the return (CTA 2010 s.357G).

Once made, the election has effect from the start of the specified accounting period until such time as it is revoked. Note that it is not necessary for a company to be a "qualifying company" for Patent Box purposes in order to make an election, although naturally a company which is not a qualifying company will not be capable of obtaining the benefit of the reduced rate of corporation tax otherwise available under the regime.

A Patent Box election can be revoked by the company giving written notice to HMRC, stating the first period for which revocation is to have effect. The same time limit as above applies, so that in practice a company will be able to give notice within 12 months of the end of the fixed filing date for the return. Once an election has been revoked, a further election back into the regime cannot be made within five years of the end of the accounting period specified in the revocation notice (CTA 2010 s.357GB).

COMPANIES QUALIFYING FOR THE PATENT BOX

22–005 A company is a qualifying company for an accounting period if it is the legal owner of qualifying intellectual property rights, or an exclusive licence in respect of such rights and meets conditions relating to the "active" ownership and development of that intellectual property (CTA 2010 s.357B). It is possible for a company to make a claim in respect of income derived from intellectual property which is no longer owned, provided that the company met those conditions in a previous accounting period. Companies can also use the Patent Box where they are entitled to receive patent income or exploit a patent that has been developed under a partnership, joint venture or cost-sharing arrangement, provided that the parties to that joint arrangement own the patent or hold an exclusive licence.

Income will also fall within the Patent Box in relation to qualifying intellectual property no longer owned by the company. This could be the case, for example, in relation to income received in a period after the disposal of the patent, or where income is received as a result of infringement of a patent but not until after the patent has expired.

QUALIFYING INTELLECTUAL PROPERTY

22–006 The UK Patent Box regime is aimed at giving preferential tax treatment to profits arising from inventions which have been independently validated as innovative and useful by a patent authority. Around the world, some patent regimes do not

THE PATENT BOX

perform a full examination of patents before granting a patent application. In some jurisdictions, patents may be granted on inventions which would not be recognised as being sufficiently novel or innovative to receive patent protection if a full process of examination were undertaken. There are also significant differences in the types of invention which can be patented worldwide, with some regimes allowing patenting of things such as business models and forms of medical treatment which are not considered patentable in the UK.

However, the types of invention which can be patented in certain EU Member States are similar to those permitted in the UK, and some other Member States do require a full examination process prior to granting a patent. For these reasons, the intellectual property which qualifies is patents granted by the UK Intellectual Property Office under the Patents Act 1977 and patents granted under the European Patent Convention. It is also available in respect of national patents in Austria, Bulgaria, Czech Republic, Denmark, Estonia, Finland, Germany, Hungary, Poland, Portugal, Romania, Slovakia and Sweden (CTA 2010 s.357BB). Patents granted by non-EEA countries, most notably the US, will not qualify under the Patent Box regime. However, the Patent Box includes worldwide income earned by UK businesses from inventions covered by a qualifying patent, not just income that falls within the territorial limitations of the particular patent. For example it is possible for a UK firm to include income from licencing an invention in the US, providing it has a UK or European patent.

There are some other limited forms of intellectual property which are comparable to patents both in terms of their strong link to R&D and high-tech activity, and are included within the Patent Box regime because they are subject to examination by an independent authority prior to being granted. These rights are:

1. supplementary protection certificates relating to medicinal and plant protection products;
2. plant breeders and Community plant variety rights;
3. medicinal and veterinary products with marketing authorisations and marketing or data protection; and
4. plant protection products with data protection benefits.

22–007 As with the conditions for the patents, if the company does not own the qualifying intellectual property right then it must be an exclusive licence holder to use the Patent Box.

An exclusive licence is a licence which confers one or more rights to the licence-holder to the exclusion of all other persons (including the proprietor) in one or more countries or territories, and the right to bring infringement proceedings or to receive the whole or greater part of any damages awarded in such proceedings. The exclusive licence does not have to cover all rights in respect of the patented information provided it extends throughout a national territory (CTA 2010 s.357BB). Where the licence holder and proprietor are members of the same group, more informal arrangements are allowed in determining whether an exclusive licence has been granted. This would enable, for example, a group company which owns a patent to grant a licence to another group company, whilst retaining some management rights in relation to that patent. Under this scenario, the company with the licence would be able to elect into the Patent Box regime as if it owned all the rights relating to an exclusive licence.

THE DEVELOPMENT CONDITION

The company claiming a Patent Box tax deduction, or another company within the same group, must remain actively involved in the ongoing decision making connected with the exploitation of the patent.

The company, or group member, must have:

- created or significantly contributed to the creation of the patented invention; or
- undertaken significant activity to develop the patented item or product incorporating the patented item. This includes developing ways in which the patented invention may be used/applied (CTA 2010 s.357BD).

Development of the patent may be undertaken by a separate member of the group to the owner of the patented rights. If this is the case, HMRC guidance ("The Patent Box: Technical Note and Guide to the Draft Legislation" published December 6, 2011) states that the owner company must "actively manage" its portfolio of rights, which requires involvement in a significant number of (but not necessarily all) decisions relating to the patent.

There are four ways in which a company or group can meet the development condition. First, where a single company has carried out the qualifying development activity itself, if that company is a member of a group, the company must continue to be a member of the same group since undertaking the development activity.

Secondly, if there has been a change of ownership of the company carrying on the development activity, the company will continue to meet the development requirement provided it continues to perform development activity of the same description for at least 12 months from the date of change of ownership. Note that it is not necessary for the development activity to be carried on in relation to the same invention.

Where one member of a group meets the ownership requirements in relation to a patent or other qualifying right, and the development activity is carried on by another member of the group, the development condition will be regarded as met.

Finally, where a company which carried out the qualifying development activity is acquired by another group, the company is able to transfer the qualifying intellectual property to another company in the group. Activity done in the acquired company before acquisition can satisfy the development condition if the acquired company or another group company to which the qualifying intellectual property is transferred, perform activities of the same description for at least 12 months from when the acquired company joins the group.

The significant development activity need not necessarily occur before the patent is granted or result in further patents but it must extend beyond activities related to the management of a financial investment or the legal protection of the patent. In addition, if a company acquires a patent, or patent rights, the acquiring company must carry out the necessary development activities.

A company may meet the development condition in relation to some of its qualifying intellectual property rights but not others. In this case, the company will be able to benefit from the Patent Box in relation to those rights in relation to which the development condition is met (CTA 2010 s.357B(4)).

In the case of a corporate partner, the company will be regarded as meeting the development condition if either the partnership itself undertakes qualifying development in relation to the intellectual property rights, or a corporate partner with at least a 40 per cent interest in the partnership has carried out qualifying development (CTA 2012 s.357GB(7), (8)).

THE ACTIVE OWNERSHIP CONDITION

22–011 The Patent Box legislation is aimed at companies actively engaged in the development of intellectual property, and which are not passive intellectual property holding companies. To achieve this, the "active ownership" test conditions must be met. The test only applies where the company is a member of a group as singleton companies will have to meet the development condition and will therefore by their very nature be active rather than passive. Only qualifying intellectual property rights are considered (i.e. rights including exclusive licences for which the company meets the development condition). The company can meet the condition if either the company performs a significant amount of management activity in relation to the rights, such as making plans and decisions around the development or exploitation of the rights, or by meeting the development condition itself. "Significant" development is not defined, however, the HMRC Manuals at CIRD210210 indicate that this is determined by reference to:

> "all relevant circumstances given:
>
> - the resources the company employs;
> - the breadth of its responsibilities for the intellectual property; and
> - the significance and impact of the decisions and plans it, as opposed to other group companies, makes in relation to that intellectual property.
>
> Normally it will be reasonably clear in practice whether the company's activity is significant.
>
> The company does not necessarily have to take all decisions relating to the IP's management, particularly if normal group governance requires reference to the parent Board. But it must be actively involved in whatever activity is necessary in terms of making plans and decisions and have clear substantive responsibilities. Neither does there have to be activity in each accounting period in relation to each right, if this is commercially unnecessary for the group's holding of that right. A minimal amount of activity could then be significant in relation to the right."

It is suggested that active management would include deciding on whether to maintain protection in particular jurisdictions, granting licences, researching alternative applications for the innovation or licensing others to do so count as

CALCULATION OF IP PROFITS OF A TRADE

management activity. Where a company holds a patent for which no active market has yet been found, it should be sufficient for the company to just renew the patent annually to meet the active management condition.

A corporate partner of a partnership must itself meet the active ownership condition, even where the company is part of a group (CTA 2010 s.357GB(6)).

ELECTION

As the Patent Box is an optional regime, a company can only benefit from it if, for an accounting period, it elects into the Patent Box regime. The election must be made in writing within two years of the end of the accounting period to which the election is intended to apply.

22–012

Once a company has made a Patent Box election, the Patent Box regime will continue to apply to the company until the election is revoked. If a company revokes a Patent Box election, it will not be able to re-enter the Patent Box regime for five years.

This restriction will also apply where any other associated company acquires the trade or assets of the company which has previously opted out of the Patent Box.

CALCULATION OF RELEVANT INTELLECTUAL PROPERTY PROFITS OF A TRADE

The Patent Box rate applies to net profits, rather than gross income, and hence the need to compute the net profit attributable to patent profits. In some cases this will be a straightforward process, however, the inclusion of sale proceeds of patented products as qualifying intellectual property income means that detailed rules are required for the calculation of a qualifying company's trading profits which are eligible for the Patent Box rate (CTA 2010 s.357C).

22–013

There are six steps which fall neatly into three stages. Additionally, a seventh step may apply if profits were made previously from inventions awaiting grant of a patent if the patent is awarded in the accounting period (CTA 2010 s.357CQ).

Stage 1:
- Step 1: calculate the total gross income ("TI") of the trade.
- Step 2: calculate the proportion of "relevant intellectual property income" ("RIPI") that is included in TI, expressed as a percentage of TI.
- Step 3: attribute the same percentage to the profits or losses of the trade (adjusted by excluding finance returns and costs, and R&D additional deductions).

Stage 2:
- Step 4: remove a routine return on certain costs described at Step 4 from the attributed profits at Step 3, to arrive at "Qualifying Residual Profit" ("QRP"). If the amount of the QRP is less than nil, the third stage is ignored.

Stage 3:
- Step 5: remove the marketing assets return from QRP under the simplified "small claims" method (25 per cent of QRP).
- Step 6: deduct from QRP the actual marketing assets return.
- Step 7: where a company so elects, add profits arising before the grant of a right to the Step 5 or 6 amount (or, if the amount of QRP was not greater than nil, the Step 4 amount).

The remainder is then the relevant intellectual property profits (RIPP), which are subject to the reduced corporation tax rate or relevant intellectual property losses.

Note that as an alternative, the company can allocate profits to RIPI using the "streaming" rules set out in Ch.4. In some circumstances the company has to use this approach.

TOTAL GROSS INCOME OF TRADE (TI)

22–014 The starting point in calculating the total gross income of the trade is the revenue line (including discontinued operations) as recognised in accounts prepared under generally accepted accounting practice (CTA 2010 s.357CA). To this, certain items must be added, to the extent they are not already included in revenue—compensation proceeds of a trading nature, change of accounting basis receipts, credits on realisation of intangible assets and profits from the sale of pre-2002 patent rights under s.912 of the CTA 2009. From this must be deducted anything that is not brought into account as a credit in computing trading profits. Specifically excluded is finance income in the form of trading loan relationship credits, amounts treated as arising from a financial asset under generally accepted accounting practice such as dividends, returns that are economically equivalent to interest under CTA 2009 s.486B and credits in respect of derivative contracts (CTA 2010 s.357CB).

Where GAAP accounts are not prepared for an accounting period, then a company is required to include any amounts that would have had to be recognised as revenue were their accounts compiled in accordance with GAAP principles.

RELEVANT INTELLECTUAL PROPERTY INCOME (RIPI)

22–015 There are five heads of relevant intellectual property income arising from different ways of exploiting intellectual property rights. It should be stressed that the Patent Box includes worldwide income earned by UK businesses from inventions covered by a qualifying patent, which will avoid the need for companies to track sales made in each jurisdiction separately.

For the purposes of computing RIP, a qualifying intellectual property right (QIPR) includes a right in which the company holds an exclusive licence. Licences which include some exclusive rights along with other rights which are not exclusive are treated as two separate licences. Income from the "non-exclusive licences" is not RIPI (CTA 2010 s.357CC).

RELEVANT INTELLECTUAL PROPERTY INCOME (RIPI)

The first head includes income from the sale of items protected by a QIPR, "qualifying items". This includes not only income from items protected by a QIPR, but also profit streams derived from items which contained a (say) patented product, or items designed to be components of a patented product. Thus the profits within RIPI can include profits from the sale of items that incorporate the patented invention and any spare parts. In HMRC's view, to be incorporated, the item must be physically part of the larger item and intended to be so for its operating life. HMRC give the following examples:

"
- A patented printer cartridge is designed to be inserted in a printer and once installed not to be removed until empty, at which point it will be replaced. The printer cartridge will be incorporated in the printer. Income from the sale of a printer including the printer cartridge (whether the cartridge is installed or included separately in the box with the printer as part of a single package) can therefore qualify as RIPI, even if there were no patent over the printer itself.
- Conversely, if the printer includes a patented invention and the printer cartridge does not, then sales of the cartridges on their own will qualify as items wholly or mainly designed to be incorporated into the printer.
- In contrast a patented DVD may be designed to work with a wide variety of DVD players and after each use is intended to be removed. So it is not incorporated in the DVD player, or designed to be incorporated.
- So unless the DVD player is patented or includes a patented invention, including a patented DVD with it in a sale will not qualify the income from the player as RIPI. And similarly, if the DVD player is patented and DVDs are not, sales of the DVDs will not produce RIPI."

Special provisions are included for packaging. Largely the cost of packaging is ignored, but in some cases packaging itself may form part of a patented product if it performs a function that is essential to allow its contents to be used in the particular way they are intended to be used. HMRC give the example of a medical inhaler, where the active ingredient, gas canister and sleeve are sold together in a single product, even if each separate element were not patented, provided that one of the components is patented, profits from the sale of the entire inhaler would be regarded as derived from the patented product.

22–016

In the scenario where the packaging itself is patented but the product is not, such as a drinks carton, if the packaging materially contributes to the value of the contents a "reasonable" proportion of the sales income will be RIPI. Similarly, were items are sold together as part of a single unit at a single price, only part of which relates to a patented product, or where a single licensing agreement is entered covering patented and non-patented rights, income is apportioned between qualifying and non-qualifying elements on a just and reasonable basis, ignoring trivial amounts. HMRC guidance at CIRD 220290 indicates that figures below 5 per cent will in most circumstances be trivial (CTA 2010 s.357CF).

The second head of income comprises profits from any licence fee or royalty arising from a QIPR or any other right in respect of a qualifying item or qualifying process. This includes all royalties or licence fees received for use of an invention covered by a qualifying patent, regardless of whether the invention is used by the licensee in an industrial process or incorporated into patented products sold by them.

22–017 The third head relates to income arising from the disposal of a QIPR. This enables perhaps smaller companies which develop new patents and which do not have the scale of operations required to fully commercialise a new product in-house to benefit from the Patent Box. The amount to be included will be (for post-2002 intellectual property), the taxable credit equal to the excess of proceeds of realisation over the accounts carrying value of the QIPR (CTA ss.735, 736), or for disposals of pre-2002 patents, the profit realised on disposal. Where the company chooses to spread the profit on a disposal for tax over a six-year period, RIPI will be the part brought into charge to tax in the relevant year.

The fourth head of income relates to amounts received from infringement proceedings. Provided that the company was elected into the Patent Box regime at the time the infringement occurred, the income received will be RIPI even if it is received after expiry or sale of the patent right. An apportionment is made on a just and reasonable basis if the income relates partly to a period where the Patent Box applied and partly to a period when it did not (including periods before April 1, 2013).

The fifth and final head of income is amounts received from damages, proceeds of insurance or other compensation. This is in recognition of the fact that patents are regularly contested and that damages paid by third parties for infringing a qualifying patent largely represent compensation for lost income which would otherwise have qualified for the Patent Box.

Relevant intellectual property income excludes any income or profits which fall within the North Sea ring fence regime. However, any other income related to patented technology in the extractive industries will qualify in the same way as any other patented product or process income from exploiting non-exclusive licences.

PARTICULAR CASES: SOFTWARE

22–018 The UK and European patent offices do not generally regard computer programs as patentable. An invention which provides a technical solution may however be patentable if it is suitably novel or innovative, and the fact that the invention is incorporated in a computer program does not alter this.

Identifying the item giving rise to relevant intellectual property income is key. If a company holds a QIPR for an invention including a computer program for implementing the invention, income derived from any set of computer-readable instructions that could be considered "a computer program" and provided that the functionality defined in the patent claim will fall within Head 1 of CTA 2010 s.357CC (CIRD220170).

Where the computer program is configured to execute a piece of hardware or other system, then that piece of hardware or system would fall within Head 2 of CTA 2010 s.357CC as an item incorporating a qualifying item. This is contrasted to the position where a patent includes a claim to the hardware or system itself, either in addition to, or instead of, a claim to the computer program. In that case, the hardware or system would be considered a qualifying item in its own right and therefore fall within Head 1 of CTA s.357CC.

PARTICULAR CASES: SOFTWARE

The means through which software is exploited also requires careful analysis to distinguish between income derived from the sale of the product falling within Head 1, or licence fee income within Head 2. 22–019

HMRC's Manuals provide the following examples at CIRD220320:

Example 1: Item incorporating a patented computer program
A device uses software in respect of which a patent has been granted. The Patent Box company sells the device upon which the software is installed but the device itself is not patented. If the device and software are sold for a single price, the income from the sale is relevant IP income under Head 1 since the software is incorporated into the device.

Example 2A: Sale of boxed or downloaded software
Company X develops and sells patented software, either in the form of a CD in a box (which is then installed on the end-user's computer) or via the internet (and downloaded directly onto the end user's computer). It sometimes sells the software directly to the end user and sometimes sells the software via an intermediary third party (which simply buys and on-sells the software). In either case the income receivable from the sale of the patented software by Company X is relevant IP income under Head 1.

Example 2B: Maintenance and updates relating to the sale of boxed or downloaded software
Extending example 2A, Company X sells the software with a 12-month maintenance contract under which the end user is entitled to receive non patented software updates and telephone support. The income that derives from the sale of updates is relevant IP income under Head 1 because it is income from the sale of items that are wholly or mainly designed to be incorporated into the patented software (S357CC(2)(c)). However, the income from the sale of the telephone support is not relevant IP income. Under the mixed sources of income rules (S357CF, CIRD220290) it would be necessary to make a just and reasonable apportionment of the total sales price between the qualifying software updates and the non-qualifying telephone support (unless that element is a trivial proportion of the total income).

Example 2C: Maintenance and updates sold separate to the boxed or downloaded software
Extending example 2B, after the initial 12 month period of maintenance, the end user extends the maintenance contract with Company X. Again the income that derives from the sale of the non patented software updates is relevant IP income under Head 1. It does not matter if the end user bought the underlying software program from an intermediary third party (see example 2A) provided that the income from the software updates accrues to Company X (that is, the company holding the patent). Again the income that derives from the provision of the telephone support is not relevant IP income unless it is trivial.

There is a distinction between the "triviality test" in Examples 2B and 2C. Under Example 2B, the issue of whether telephone support is trivial should be considered in the context of the sales income from the software itself plus the updates. However, what is considered trivial in Example 2C is based on the telephone support in the context of the sale proceeds from the sale of the maintenance contract only. So the income from the telephone support could be trivial in one context but not in another.

PARTICULAR CASES: MEDICAL TREATMENTS

22–020   Methods of medical treatment are not generally patentable. However, it may be possible for a patent to be lodged in respect of a new specific medical use of certain substances or compounds. This is reflected in the 2007 European Patent Convention, which allows patenting of a substance for a specific new medical use, such as the application of a compound to treat a specific disease or condition which had not previously been treated with that compound. HMRC therefore accept that where there is a patent protecting a pharmaceutical product having an approved medical use, that will be an item falling under CTA 2010 s.357CC(2)) regardless of whether it is a "Swiss Type" claim or a new 2MU claim (CIRD 220300).

NOTIONAL ROYALTY

22–021   It will frequently be the case that a company receives income from patents which are QIPRs but the income is not itself RIPI, for example, where a manufacturing company has designed a patented process or tool, but the items produced are not themselves patented. Part of the income generated from the sale of such items is treated as a "notional" royalty under CTA 2010 s.357D, if the company so elects for it to be treated as RIPI. This is an amount equal to the royalty that would be paid to an independent owner of the QIPRs for the company's exclusive use of those rights to generate intellectual property derived income. This notional royalty must be calculated in accordance with art.9 of the July 2010 OECD Model Tax Convention and the OECD's Transfer pricing Guidelines.

The royalty is assumed to at a level which would be entered into between persons acting at arm's length and for a period matching that for which the company actually holds rights over (say) the patented process, capped at the actual income from which the notional royalty is derived. This is designed to ensure that the royalty reflects the actual value of the patent rights rather than the value being inflated by reference to a longer period. The licence giving rise to the notional royalty is assumed to be entered into on the later of the first day of the accounting period and the day the company obtained the IP right, although HMRC anticipate that in practice it should not normally be necessary to determine a new royalty rate for each new accounting period if none of the relevant facts and circumstances have changed from a previous accounting period. The notional royalty must take the form of a fixed-rate periodic royalty in order to match payments under the licence to the accounting periods in which the IP-derived income is generated as closely as possible. The royalty must be calculated as a percentage of the IP-derived income from the patent rights for their remaining life. This precludes any lump-sum upfront or milestone payments, and tiered or front-loaded or back-loaded royalties which could distort the Patent Box calculation in particular years.

The notional royalty can never be greater than the IP-derived income from which it is calculated.

CALCULATING PROFITS OF TRADE

CTA 2010 s.357CG

The trading profits used in the Patent Box calculation are, in the usual case, apportioned by using the ratio of RIPI over taxable income under CTA 2010 s.357CA, with the portion corresponding to the RIPI going into the next stage of the calculation.

Certain adjustments must be made to the taxable profits of the trade for the purposes of computing relevant intellectual property profits, prior to applying the above ratio.

Items to be added back are:

- the amount of any additional deduction provided by way of R&D tax credit relief. This will mean that companies retain the full benefit of R&D tax credit enhancement, relievable at the main rate of tax. For example if a company incurred £100 of R&D expenditure eligible for 30 per cent enhancement under the large company R&D tax credit scheme, it would have total tax deductions of £130 relating to its R&D spend. Of these, the base cost of £100 would remain within the Patent Box, but the enhancement of £30 is added back to increase the relevant profit for the Patent Box calculation;
- debits in respect of trading loan relationships and derivative contracts. Items to be deducted:
- credits in respect of finance income (see section 357CB) taken into account in calculating the profits of the trade; and
- if applicable, an adjustment for shortfall in R&D expenditure in an accounting period commencing four years following the election of the company into the Patent Box regime. A shortfall in R&D expenditure arises if the actual R&D expenditure as determined by GAAP (plus any additional amount) for an accounting period is less than 75 per cent of the average in the four years prior to electing into the Patent Box. In this case the amount of the shortfall must be added to the actual R&D expenditure as an adjustment in calculating Patent Box profits (CTA 2010 s.357CH). For an accounting period less than 12 months the average amount of R&D expenditure is proportionately reduced. If the company has traded for less than four years before electing into the Patent Box, the average amount of R&D expenditure is calculated over the period between trade commencing and the first day of the accounting period for which the company comes into the regime.

The apportionment of all remaining profit and expenses should be done on a simple pro-rata basis according to the proportion of total trading income which is qualifying income. This is where the company apportions its total profits of the trade for corporation tax purposes according to the ratio of "relevant intellectual property income" to total gross income.

In certain circumstances apportioning the profits of a trade by using the overall ratio of relevant intellectual property income to total gross income may give rise to a distorted result. This may occur where the relative proportions of income from the exploitation of intellectual property rights differs markedly from the relative proportions of profits derived from other income.

In such circumstances the streaming method can be applied. This method involves dividing income into qualifying and non-qualifying streams and arriving at profits by allocating expenses to qualifying streams on a just and reasonable basis.

22–024 The company must make a "streaming election" to use this method. No formal election procedure is set down, and a company may simply include the streaming election by way of a note to the computations in its corporation tax return for the period.

Streaming will be mandatory where a substantial proportion of gross income relates to income from non-qualifying intellectual property. 'Substantial' in this context means the lower of 20 per cent of gross income and £2 million although there is a let out from the mandatory streaming rules if the 20 per cent test produces a figure below £50,000.

ROUTINE RETURN

22–025 Valuable patents and other forms of intellectual property will produce higher profits than can be made by companies without the intellectual property. The amount of this extra profit, known as "residual profit" is a measure of the profit created by the intellectual property rather than through routine business activities. A company's residual profit is derived by deducting a simple fixed percentage return on routine expenses from the corporation tax profit attributed to qualifying income. This deduction is 10 per cent and is applied to expenses such as director and employee related expenses, premises expenses, plant and machinery expenses including capital allowances and utilities, transport, communication and consultancy fees (CTA 2010 ss.357CI, 357CJ). Routine deductions incurred by another group company on behalf of the Patent Box company are included as if they had been incurred directly by the Patent Box company.

HMRC expect it to be generally clear as to whether an amount is, or is not, a routine deduction. Where there is doubt as to whether an expense is a routine one, regard is given to the materiality of the sum in terms of its overall effect on the Patent Box claim in deciding the best way of allocating the amount (CIRD220440). A useful example of common expense items is provided at CIRD 220460.

Certain expenses are excluded from being "routine". These include debits in respect of trading loan relationships and derivative contracts, R&D expenses upon which R&D tax credits are given plus any additional deduction given by the R&D tax credit regime, research and development allowances and patent allowances under Pts 6 and 8 of CAA 2001 and deductions relating to relief given for employee share acquisitions under CTA 2009 Pt 12 to the extent they relate to staff costs of employees who are engaged in relevant R&D activities.

The remaining profit after deducting the routine return is called the "Qualifying Residual Profit" (QRP).

MARKETING ASSETS RETURN FIGURE

The qualifying residual profit will incorporate income which relates not only to the intellectual property right falling within the Patent Box, but also income attributable to other forms of intellectual property such as valuable brands and other marketing assets. These must therefore be stripped out to achieve the aim of giving preferential treatment only to qualifying intellectual property rights.

22–026

There are two possible methods for determining how much of the QRP of a company for an accounting period represents profit from intellectual property rights qualifying for the Patent Box and how much relates to brand and marketing assets. The much simpler "small claims treatment" option takes a formulaic approach, and makes a deduction of 25 per cent of QRP. Small claims treatment is available if either the company's QRP is below £1m for the accounting period (reduced proportionately for periods of account of less than 12 months), or the total amounts of QRP of each trade of the company do not exceed £3m. The £3m threshold is split between associated companies (CTA 2010 ss.25–30) which have made a Patent Box election.

For a company with QRP falling between £1m and £3m, an election for small claims treatment may be made if the company's QRP has never exceed £3m and has always adopted small claims in computing the marketing asset return, or, if QRP has exceeded £3m at some time in the past, the marketing asset return deducted is either nil or less than 10 per cent of QRP.

Where small claims treatment is not being applied, the marketing assets return figure must be deducted from the residual profits (CTA 2010 s.357CN).

22–027

Companies must use a transfer pricing calculation to deduct a notional marketing royalty (NMR) based on the price that a third party would pay to exploit the brand. If an actual marketing royalty is paid this reduces the notional royalty that is to be deducted. If the difference between the notional royalty and the actual royalty is less than 10 per cent of the residual profit for the accounting period there is no need to make any adjustment to the residual profit.

The NMR is an amount derived as a percentage of RIPI (excluding notional royalty income under CTA s.2010 s.357CD), that the company would pay for the right to exploit the relevant marketing assets of the company in the accounting period, if it could not exploit them without that payment (CTA 2010 s.357CO).

A marketing asset is a "relevant marketing asset" if the RIPI includes any income arising from things done by the company to exploit that marketing asset. In the absence of things done by the company to exploit a particular asset then there is no obligation to calculate an NMR in respect of it. Relevant marketing assets include:

22–028

1. assets where passing off (or equivalent action outside the UK) could be brought), including a registered trade mark;

2. signs or indications of geographical origin of goods and services; and
3. information about actual or potential customers.

A passing off action generally requires goodwill to attach to the business's goods or services. It is therefore necessary to include consideration of the value of goodwill in determining the level of notional royalty payable for the marketing assets. For an international business, goodwill will need to be examined in each of the territory in which the business trades or carries on activities, and it is the worldwide amount which is required to be brought into account in calculating the marketing asset return. HMRC also suggest that "jingles, celebrity endorsements and marketing campaigns are not assets in their own right, but may contribute to this goodwill and therefore act to increase the value of the marketing assets with which they are associated" (CIRD 220500).

Passing off action also requires the misrepresentation by another to be sufficiently sophisticated such as is likely to lead to the public to believe the other's goods and services are goods and services of the genuine trader. The misrepresentation may include use of a mark, trade name, designs, letters, numerals or packaging which are likely to be associated in the mind of the public with the real trader's goods or services and which are distinctive of them.

22–029 In determining the appropriate percentage NMR, the company must act in accordance with art.9 of the OECD Model Tax Convention and the OECD transfer pricing guidelines. It is to be assumed that the company and the notional owner of the intellectual property right are dealing at arm's length, and that the company has the right to exploit the marketing assets on an exclusive basis. Note that the rules require the royalty to be set according to information available at the beginning of each accounting period based on the assumption that it will continue for each succeeding accounting period for which the company will have the rights to exploit the relevant marketing assets. Although NMR must be revisited at the beginning of each accounting period, a high level consideration of any significant changes should suffice.

Actual marketing royalties paid are deducted from the NMR to give the net amount deducted from qualifying residual profits. Actual marketing royalties are the aggregate of amounts brought into account as debits in the corporation tax computation for the accounting period, and therefore includes actual royalties paid and also an amortisation charge in respect of a marketing asset.

Actual marketing royalties are split in the ratio of RIPI and non-RIPI on the same pro-rata basis as applied to other expenses (CTA 2010 s.357CP).

PROFITS ARISING BEFORE GRANT OF RIGHT

22–030 In the accounting period in which a company is granted a patent, or exclusive rights in respect of a patent) the company may elect for Patent Box treatment to apply on profits arising from exploitation of a patent during the period for which the patent was pending. Election is on a patent by patent basis. An additional amount is added to the company's RIPI in any accounting period in which a patent is granted. The election can still be made if the company received income while the patent was pending but disposed of its rights before the patent is granted (CTA 2010 s.357CQ).

The additional amount is the difference between:

- the aggregate of the RIPP of the trade for each accounting period for which the patent application was pending and which ended no more than six years prior to the grant; and
- what the aggregate of the RIPP of the trade would have been, for those accounting periods, if the patent had been granted at the date of application (or six years before the date of grant if later).

Any RIPP that are not taken into account in the Patent Box because they are off-set by a relevant intellectual property loss are disregarded.

Profits may only be included for accounting periods where the company was a qualifying company elected into the Patent Box regime. For the purposes of this section, a company is a qualifying company despite the patent not being granted or if it disposed of the patent or exclusive licence over the patent, before the date of grant. Only profit arising after April 1, 2013 may be included.

STREAMING

22–031 A company may elect to make a streaming election to allocate expenses and profits to particular income streams on a just and reasonable basis, rather than on the basis of a straightforward pro rata of RIPI to total gross income (CTA 2010 s.357D). A streaming election may be beneficial if, for example, a company's profits from patented products are significantly higher than from non-patented product sales as a simple pro rata allocation of expenses across both product lines would distort relevant IP profits (RIPP).

If a company carries on more than one trade, it can make a streaming election for one, more than one, or all of its trades. Once made, a streaming election automatically continues (subject to an exception provided for in s.357DB).

Streaming is mandatory if:

1. There are substantial credits brought into the computation of taxable profits which are not recognised as revenue under generally accepted accounting practice, such as transfer pricing adjustments.
2. The company has substantial licensing income which is not included within RIPI (such as royalties from non-UK patents). Licencing income means generally any licence fee, royalty or other payment received in respect of intellectual property of the company, as defined in s.712(3) CTA 2009, which is not a qualifying intellectual property right.

22–032 Streaming is also mandatory under certain "conduit" arrangements where a company receives non-RIPI income and receives a substantial amount of RIPI from licences it has granted, where the licensing income relates to rights that the company itself holds through exclusive licences. This is aimed at arrangements

THE PATENT BOX

whereby a company enters into onward licensing agreements which generate little, if any, profit but give rise to substantial income which would otherwise be RIPI. Without mandatory streaming, non-qualifying income of the company would benefit from the Patent Box regime.

"Substantial" in the context of the streaming provisions means the lower of 20 per cent of gross income and £2 million although there is a let out from the mandatory streaming rules if the 20 per cent test produces a figure below £50,000 (CTA 2010 s.357DC(2)).

Where streaming applies, Steps 1–4 of s.357C are replaced under CTA 2010 s.257DC with three alternative steps. The end result is that a "streamed" company's calculation is as follows:

- Streaming Step 1: All amounts included as taxable credits of the trade (including transfer pricing adjustments) net of financing income, are divided into two "streams" of income by identifying how much is relevant intellectual property income (including any notional royalty allowed by s.357CD) and how much is not relevant intellectual property income.
- Streaming Step 2: Debits deducted in arriving at taxable trading profit (excluding debits arising on loan relationships or derivative contracts, and any additional R&D tax deduction but including any amount brought in respect of a shortfall in R&D expenditure) are then allocated to the appropriate stream on a "just and reasonable" basis.
- Streaming Step 3: Deduct allocated debits from RIPI to give a figure to carry forward to Step 4.
- Streaming Step 4: Apply the 10 per cent routine return percentage to any routine deductions within the allocated debits and deduct from the figure given in Step 3 to arrive at QRP. This includes any routine deductions incurred on the company's behalf by a group member.
- Streaming Steps 5, 6 and 7: These follow the same approach as for the normal calculation described above. The only difference is in the treatment of any actual marketing royalty in Step 6. The aggregate of all actual marketing royalty amounts allocated to the RIPI stream is deducted from the notional royalty in calculating what should be deducted from QRP.

To be considered "just and reasonable", the same method of allocation must be used consistently for each accounting period, unless there is a change in circumstances which render the allocation inappropriate. In that event, unless mandatory streaming applies, the company has the option of reverting to the normal pro rata basis of apportionment. A new streaming election may be submitted in later periods if the company so wishes (CTA 2010 s.357DB).

MECHANICS OF RELIEF

22–033 Once the profits qualifying for the patent box have been established, either through streaming or the more conventional pro rata apportionment basis, the tax relief available to the company can be calculated. Relief is given in the form of a deduction from profits chargeable to corporation tax and is calculated as:

RP x MR – 10%

Where: RP = Patent Box profits (as calculated)

   MR = Applicable corporation tax rate

The introduction of Patent Box benefits is phased between April 2013 and 2017, such that the 10 per cent effective rate will not be achieved until 2017. The effective rates in the run up to 2017 are shown in the table.

Financial Year	Phasing in Percentage	Corporation tax rate	Effective rate
2013	60	23	15.2
2014	70	21	13.3
2015	80	20	12
2016	90	20	11
2017	100	20	10

LOSSES

22–034 Some thought should be given to the timing of a company's entry into the Patent Box. If a company is profitable, there are good arguments to enter the Patent Box at the earliest opportunity. However, if a company is loss-making, it may be better to wait until the losses are have been exhausted in order to avoid relief being wasted, as losses can only be relieved at the same rate at which they would have been charged to tax had they been profits.

Losses from IP assets will firstly be set against any other relevant intellectual property profits of a different trade in the year, either in the company incurring the loss or another member of the group which has elected into the Patent Box regime, thus reducing the amount that is eligible for the reduced rate of corporation tax. Where there is more than one company in the group with relevant IP profits against which the loss could be offset, the group can choose the order in which the loss is set off. Otherwise, the loss is offset against the group company with the highest level of relevant IP profits, and then the next highest and so on until the loss is exhausted or there are no further relevant IP profits in the group (CTA 2010 ss.357EA, 357EB).

Any remaining IP loss will be carried forward to reduce the amount of the total profits that qualifies for Patent Box treatment in later periods (CTA 2010 s.357EC). In contrast to the position with losses generally, brought forward IP loss set off amounts are offset against relevant IP profits of the company, plus other group members.

22–035 To take account of the phasing in of the lower tax rate on profits within the Patent Box regime between April 2013 and 2016, the loss carry forward set-off amounts are similarly reduced according to the formula 10 per cent/P, where P is the percentage given as the percentage of relevant profits applicable to the following financial year. The reduction reflects the increase in the patent box benefits of 10 per cent each year from April 2013, until 100 per cent of benefits become available in 2017.

Where there are also IP losses arising in the subsequent accounting period, and those losses cannot be offset against IP profits of a group member, the IP loss brought forward is increased by the current period loss.

If a company ceases to carry on trade, ceases to be within the charge to corporation tax in respect of the trade or the Patent Box election ceases to have effect, then any remaining set-off amounts are transferred as follows:

1. set off against the RIPP of any other trade carried on by the company;
2. against RIPP of any other group member that is a qualifying company at the time, as decided by the group members, or to the company with the largest RIPP;
3. if there are no companies with RIPP, to the company with the largest set-off amount of its own; and
4. if the company is not carrying on any other trade and is not a member of a group with members elected into the Patent Box or which are qualifying companies, then the set-off amount is reduced to nil.

22–036 Where there is a transfer of trade between group members, any IP loss set off amount is transferred to the transferee company which begins to carry on the trade (CTA 2010 s.357EE).

Note that the definition of a group in CTA 2010 s.357GD is wide and may lead to companies being grouped together unexpectedly and having to offset the Patent Box losses of other companies against their own Patent Box profits. It is therefore important that the group structure has been clearly identified before entering the Patent Box.

A payment for the set-off of IP losses in another group company does not create a tax deduction or charge, and will not be treated as a distribution, provided the payment does not exceed the amount of the relevant IP losses surrendered (CTA 2010 s.357EB).

ANTI-AVOIDANCE

22–037 The Patent Box legislation contains comprehensive and specific anti-avoidance rules. HMRC's manuals state that: "These rules are not intended to colour the approach to the vast majority of genuine claims but to provide defences against artificial attempts to exploit the rules" (CIRD 250100).

There are three areas targeted by anti-avoidance rules. The first relates to licences conferring exclusive rights, where the licence will be ignored if it is granted with a view to securing tax relief rather than for any commercial effect (CTA 2010 s.357F). The provision will not apply where an existing non-exclusive licence is renegotiated as an exclusive licence with a view to obtaining benefits under the Patent Box regime, provided that the new licence genuinely confers exclusivity and is a true reflection of the way in which the parties intend the licence to operate (CIRD 210130).

22–038 The second anti-avoidance rule targets the incorporation of patented items into a product where the main aim of the incorporation is to enable income from the sale of the item to be treated as relevant IP income (CTA 2010 s.357FA). Where there is no significant commercial rationale for incorporation of the patented item into the product, sales income will not be RIPI. Again, this provision is not intended to apply to any "reasonable" commercial transaction (CIRD 250120).

The third and final anti-avoidance provision is aimed at schemes one of the main purposes of which is to obtain a relevant tax advantage (CTA 2010 s.357FB). A "relevant tax advantage" arises where RIPI is increased as a result of the scheme and the scheme is:

- designed to avoid the application of an anti-avoidance provision;
- designed to artificially inflate the amount of RIPI brought into account in calculating the profits of the trade; or
- designed to create a mismatch between RIPI and the expenses of acquiring or developing a qualifying intellectual property right (or an exclusive licence over a qualifying intellectual property right). Such a mismatch would occur if the expense is incurred whilst the company (or a company with which it is grouped) is outside the regime, whilst the income arises once the company has elected into the regime.

As a general point, undertaking practical and commercially appropriate transactions will not be taken to be tax advantage schemes even if they have the effect of creating or enhancing Patent Box benefits. HMRC cite the following instances where the anti-avoidance rule above would not be applied:

"… the following transactions will not be tax advantage schemes:

- making an election under 357A (CIRD201020);
- delaying an election under 357A until such time as the company begins to make relevant IP profits rather than relevant IP losses;
- electing out of the regime once relevant IP profits become relevant IP losses (though of course no further S357A election will be possible within 5 years (CIRD260110));
- creating IP holding companies to crystallise income from qualifying IP in the form of royalties;
- separating trades with profitable qualifying IP income streams and those with non profitable income streams into different companies to allow decisions about whether or not to elect in to the regime to be made more easily;
- inbound businesses creating separate IP development companies for overseas tax reasons and transferring the successfully developed IP within the UK group in order to manage their overseas CFC position; or
- bringing qualifying IP into the UK.

(CIRD250130)"

COST-SHARING ARRANGEMENTS

Special rules apply where a company is a participant in a cost-sharing arrangement, which is broadly a normal commercial arrangement allowing businesses to share the costs and risks of developing, producing or obtaining assets, services or rights. If one of the parties to the arrangement holds a qualifying intellectual property right or exclusive licence and each of the parties

22–039

is required to contribute to the development of the item to which the right relates or product incorporating it, provided that each party to the arrangement is entitled to a proportionate share of the income from exploiting the right, or has one or more rights in respect of the invention as a result of which it receives income proportionate to its participation, then it is treated as if it held the relevant right itself. This means that all the participants in a cost-sharing arrangement are regarded as enjoying an exclusive licence over the QIPR, provided that they are not entitled to a financial return which is economically equivalent to interest (CTA 2010 s.357GC).

Worked Example 1 (Without streaming)

Gadget Limited has the following profit and loss account for the year ended March 31, 2015.

	£	£
Revenues		1,000,000
Damages (assumed to be excluded from Revenues under GAAP)		100,000
Profit before tax		250,000
Tax adjusted trading profits		200,000

Stage 1
Step 1: Calculate gross income of the trade

	£	£
Revenues	1,000,000	
Damages	100,000	
Gross income of the trade		1,100,000

Step 2: Calculate RIPI
(Assume that revenues from patented sales are 75 per cent of revenues)

	£	£
Head 1	750,000	
Head 5	100,000	
Total RIPI		850,000

Step 3: Calculate proportion of trade profits attaching to RIPI

	£
Tax adjusted trading profits	200,000
R&D deduction added back	50,000
Step 3 profits	250,000
Profits relating to RIPI (75 per cent, as above)	187,500

Stage 2: Deduct routine return
Step 4: Aggregate routine expenses

COST-SHARING ARRANGEMENTS

	£	£
Employment costs	300,000	
Premises costs	120,000	
Administrative expenses	30,000	
Travel	10,000	
Legal and professional fees	25,000	
Total routine expenses		505,000
Profits relating to RIPI		187,500
Routine return:		
(£505,000 x 75 per cent x 10 per cent)		(37,875)
		£
Qualifying residual profit		149,625

Stage 3: Deduct marketing assets return
Step 5: QRP is below £3 million; small claims treatment applies

Qualifying residual profit	149,625
Marketing assets return	(37,406)
(£149,625 x 25 per cent)	
Relevant profits for Patent Box	112,219

Step 6: Ignored as small claims treatment applies

Step 7: Add profits arising before the grant of patent right
Assumed to be nil

Patent Box Deduction

The deduction is calculated as: $\quad$ RP x (MR-10 per cent) / MR

However, only 70 per cent of RP can benefit from the Patent Box in the year to 31 March 2015. RP is therefore reduced by 70 per cent.

(£112,219 x 70 per cent) x $\qquad$ £41,147
(21 per cent-10 per cent) =
21 per cent

THE PATENT BOX

Worked Example 2 (Without streaming)

Widget Limited has the following profit and loss account for the year ended March 31, 2018. The company generates revenues from the sale of patented products and also receives royalties from the licensing of patents it has developed.

	£	£
Revenues		35,000,000
Profit before tax		7,300,000
Tax adjusted profit		6,200,000

Stage 1

Step 1: Calculate gross income of the trade

Assumed to be equal to revenues under GAAP.

Gross income of the trade		35,000,00

Step 2: Calculate RIPI

(Assume that revenues from patented sales are 58 per cent of revenues and royalties are 10 per cent of revenues)

Head 1		20,300,000
Head 2		3,500,000
Total RIPI		23,800,000

Step 3: Calculate proportion of trade profits attaching to RIPI

Tax adjusted trading profits		6,200,000
R&D deduction added back		2,000,000
Step 3 profits		8,200,000
Profits relating to RIPI (68 per cent, as above)		5,576,000

Stage 2: Deduct routine return

Step 4: Aggregate routine expenses

Employment costs	1,500,000	
Premises costs	450,000	
Other administrative expenses	1,830,000	
Total routine expenses		3,780,000
Profits relating to RIPI		5,576,000

COST-SHARING ARRANGEMENTS

	£
Routine return:	(257,040)
(£3,780,000 x 68 per cent	
x 10 per cent)	
Qualifying residual profit	5,318,960

Stage 3: Deduct marketing assets return
Step 5: Does not apply as QRP exceeds £3 million

Step 6: Deduction of marketing assets return
(Assumed to be £1.2 million, applying transfer pricing principles)

Qualifying residual profit	5,318,960
Marketing assets return	(1,200,000)
Relevant profits for Patent Box	4,118,960

Step 7: Add profits arising before the grant of patent right
Assumed to be nil.

Patent Box Deduction
The deduction is calculated as: RP x (MR-10 per cent) MR

£4,118,960 x (20 per cent – 10 per cent) 10 per cent = 411,896

CHAPTER 23

General Principles and Non-corporates

INTRODUCTION

As with other sources of income, the tax planning of intellectual property should concentrate on maximising the after-tax profits rather than the saving of tax as an end in itself.   **23–001**

The actual manner in which income from intellectual property can be taxed and the statutory provisions enabling it to be spread have already been considered in some detail: the purpose of this chapter is to show how these rules may be used to the best advantage of the taxpayer.

With an increasing focus on tax avoidance, it is essential in modern tax planning to ensure that any arrangements entered into can be justified commercially and are not merely inserted for a tax saving that it is hoped will result. The UK tax legislation contains a number of Targeted Anti-Avoidance Rules (TAARs) which apply where a transaction is carried out other than for bona fide commercial reasons the main purpose or one of the main purposes of which was not tax avoidance. After a lengthy period of consultation on the feasibility of a general anti-avoidance rule, Finance Bill 2013 introduces a General Anti-Abuse Rule (GAAR). The GAAR seeks to focus on the most artificial of arrangements rather than "normal" tax planning and applies to income tax, national insurance contributions, capital gains tax, corporation tax, inheritance tax, petroleum revenue tax, stamp duty land tax and the annual tax on enveloped dwellings.

Arrangements may be challenged under the GAAR if they seek to achieve an "abusive" result. Tax arrangements are "abusive" if they achieve an outcome of arrangements which cannot "reasonably be regarded as a reasonable course of action". This is known as the "double reasonableness" test, and is intended to be the principal means through which legitimate, non-abusive tax planning arrangements are excluded from the GAAR. In determining whether the arrangements may be regarded as a reasonable course of action, reference is made to all circumstances, including: **23–002**

1. whether the arrangements give a result consistent with the principles on which the particular provisions are based (whether express or implied) and the policy objectives of those provisions,
2. whether the means of achieving those results involves one or more contrived or abnormal steps, and
3. whether the arrangements are intended to exploit any shortcomings in those provisions.

The legislation specifies that tax arrangements may be abusive where:

1. the arrangements result in an amount of income, profits or gains for tax purposes that is significantly less than the amount for economic purposes,
2. the arrangements result in deductions or losses of an amount for tax purposes that is significantly greater than the amount for economic purposes, and
3. the arrangements result in a claim for the repayment or crediting of tax (including foreign tax) that has not been, and is unlikely to be, paid.

This list is not intended to be exhaustive.

Arrangements are "tax arrangements" if they have as their main purpose, or one of their main purposes, the achieving of a tax advantage. A "tax advantage" is defined as:

A "tax advantage" includes—

1. relief or increased relief from tax,
2. repayment or increased repayment of tax,
3. avoidance or reduction of a charge to tax or an assessment to tax,
4. avoidance of a possible assessment to tax,
5. deferral of a payment of tax or advancement of a repayment of tax, and
6. avoidance of an obligation to deduct or account for tax.

23–003 An independent advisory panel will review and approve HMRC's guidance on the operation of the GAAR, and also provide comment on particular cases where HMRC consider that the GAAR may apply.

HMRC's published guidance on the GAAR, including a number of helpful examples, can be found at: *http://www.hmrc.gov.uk/avoidance/gaar.htm* [Accessed September 16, 2013]. The GAAR will have effect in relation to arrangements entered into on or after July 17, 2013, the date Finance Act 2013 received Royal Assent.

The GAAR is not expected to replace existing anti-avoidance legislation or TAARS, however, it is possible that the addition of the GAAR to HMRC's arsenal of weapons against tax avoidance may lead to less reliance upon established anti-avoidance case law, and in particular the *Ramsay* principle, applicable to a series of pre-ordained transactions carried out with a view to obtaining a tax advantage (*Ramsay (WT) Ltd v IRC* [1981] S.T.C. 174). This principle follows a series of judgments including in particular the dissenting judgment of Eveleigh L.J. in *Floor v Davis* [1978] S.T.C. 436 and the House of Lords judgments in *Eilbeck v Rawling* [1981] S.T.C. 174; *IRC v Burmah Oil Co Ltd* [1982] S.T.C. 30; *Furniss v Dawson* [1984] S.T.C. 153; *Craven v White* [1988] S.T.C. 476; *Bayliss v Gregory* [1988] S.T.C. 476; *News International Plc v Shepherd* [1989] S.T.C. 617; *Ingram v IRC* [1985] S.T.C. 835; *Cairns v MacDiarmid* [1983] S.T.C. 178; *Young v Phillips* [1984] S.T.C. 520; *Magnovax Electronics Co Ltd (In liquidation) v Hall* [1986] S.T.C. 561; and *IRC v McGuckian* [1997] S.T.C. 908. The *Ramsay* principle was interpreted in the case of *Westmoreland Investments Ltd v MacNiven* [2001] S.T.C. 237, as applying only to purely legal concepts (e.g. "conveyance or transfer on sale") which have

INTRODUCTION

no broader commercial meaning. However, in *Mawson v Barclays Mercantile Business Finance Ltd* [2005] S.T.C. 1, it was confirmed that this statement was not intended to preclude a close analysis of what the statue means. It is not possible to classify all concepts as either commercial or legal. See also, *Ensign Tankers (Leasing) Ltd v Stokes* [1992] S.T.C. 226; *Tower MCashback LLP v RCC* [2007] S.P.C. 619; *IRC v Scottish Provident Institution* [2005] S.T.C. 15; *West v Trennery* (2005) S.T.C. 214; *Cadbury Schweppes Plc v Williams* [2007] S.T.C. 106; *Hitch v Stone* [2001] S.T.C. 214; and *Griffin v Citibank Investments Ltd* [2000] S.T.C. 1010.

Their Lordships held in *Westmoreland* that the *Ramsay* approach is only relevant where the statutory words under consideration refer to commercial concepts such as "loss", "gain" and "disposal". 23–004

In *Westmoreland* Lord Nicholls commented on the Ramsay "principle" as follows:

> "As I am sure Lord Brightman would be the first to acknowledge. The *Ramsay* approach is no more than a useful aid. This is not an area for absolutes. The paramount question always is one of interpretation of the particular statutory provision and its application to the facts of the case. Further *Ramsay* did not introduce a new legal principle. It would be wrong, therefore, to set bounds to the circumstances in which the *Ramsay* approach may be appropriate and helpful. The need to consider a document or transaction in its proper context and the need to adopt a purposive approach when construing tax legislation are principles of general application."

The following comments on the evolution of the *Ramsay* principle therefore are applicable only where terms having commercial meaning are being construed.

Even prior to *Westmoreland*, the mere fact that tax avoidance was a motive in the transaction does not enable it to be disregarded for tax purposes if it otherwise serves a commercial purpose (*Ensign Tankers (Leasing) Ltd v Stokes* [1992] S.T.C. 226; *New Zealand Commissioner of Inland Revenue v Challenge Corporation Ltd* [1986] S.T.C. 548, a case noted for an attempt by Lord Templeman to draw a distinction between tax avoidance, where a taxpayer seeks to avoid a liability to tax by entering into an arrangement without actually incurring the expenditure or loss, and tax mitigation, where a taxpayer obtains a tax advantage by reducing his income or by incurring expenditure in circumstances in which the taxing statutes afford a reduction in tax liability). In *Furniss v Dawson*, Lord Fraser stated (at 155): 23–005

> "The true principle of the decision in *Ramsay* was that the fiscal consequences of a pre-ordained series of transactions intended to operate as such are generally to be ascertained by considering the result of the series as a whole and not by dissecting the scheme and considering each individual transaction separately."

Lord Scarman commented (at 156):

> "I add a few observations only because I am aware and the legal profession (and others) must understand that the law in this area is at an early stage of development. Speeches in your Lordships' House and judgments in the appellate Courts of the United Kingdom are concerned more to chart a way forward between principles accepted and not to be rejected than to attempt anything so ambitious as to

determine finally the limit beyond which the safe channel of acceptable tax avoidance shelves into the dangerous shallows of unacceptable tax evasion. The law will develop from case to case. Lord Wilberforce in *Ramsay* referred to 'the emerging principle' of the law. What has been established with certainty by the House in *Ramsay* is that the determination of what does and what does not constitute unacceptable tax evasion is a subject suited to development by judicial process. The best chart that we have for the way forward appears to me, with great respect to all engaged in the map-making process, to be the words of my noble and learned friend Lord Diplock in *IRC v Burmah Oil Co Ltd* [1982] S.T.C. 30 which my noble and learned friend Lord Brightman quotes in his speech. These words leave space in the law for the principle annunciated by Lord Tomlin in *IRC v Duke of Westminster* (1936) 19 TC 490 at 520 that every man is entitled if he can to order his affairs so as to diminish the burden of tax. The limits within which this principle is to operate remain to be probed and determined judicially. Difficult though the task may be for judges, it is one which is beyond the power of the blunt instrument of legislation. Whatever a statute may provide, it has to be interpreted and applied by the Courts: and ultimately it will prove to be in this area of judge made law that our elusive journey's end will be found."

Lord Bridge commented (at 158):

"Of course, the judiciary must never lose sight of the basic premise expressed in the celebrated dictum of Lord Tomlin in *IRC v Duke of Westminster* (1936) 19 T.C. 490 at 520 that: 'Every man is entitled if he can to order his affairs so that the tax attaching under the appropriate Acts is less than it otherwise would be.' Just a year earlier Learned Hand J. giving the judgment of the United States Circuit Court (2nd Circuit) in *Helvering v Gregory* (1931) 69 F 2d 809, had said the same thing in different words: 'anyone may so arrange his affairs that his tax shall be as low as possible; he is not bound to choose that pattern that will best pay the Treasury'. Yet, whilst starting from this common principle the Federal Courts of the United States and the English Courts have developed, quite independently of any statutory differences, very different techniques for the scrutiny of tax avoidance schemes to test their validity.

The extent to which the speeches of the majority in the *Westminster* case still tend to dominate the thinking in this field of the English judiciary is well shown by the judgments in the Courts below in the instant case. In particular the *Westminster* case seems still to be accepted as establishing that the only ground on which it can be legitimate to draw a distinction between the substance and the form of transactions in considering their tax consequences is that the transactions are shams in the sense that they are not what, on their face, they purport to be. The strong dislike expressed by the majority of the *Westminster* case for what Lord Tomlin described as 'The doctrine that the Court may ignore the legal position and regard what is called the substance of the matter is not the least surprising when one remembers that the only transaction in question was the Duke's covenant in favour of his gardener and the bona fides of that transaction was never for a moment impugned'.

When one moves, however, from a single transaction to a series of inter-dependent transactions designed to produce a given result, it is, in my opinion, perfectly legitimate to draw a distinction between the substance and the form of the composite transaction without in any way suggesting that any of the single transactions which make up the whole are other than genuine. This has been the approach of the United States Federal Courts enabling them to develop a doctrine whereby the tax consequences of the composite transaction are dependent on its substance, not its form. I shall not attempt to review the American authorities, nor do I propose a wholesale importation of the American doctrine in all its ramifications into English law. But I do suggest that the distinction between form

INTRODUCTION

and substance is one which can usefully be drawn in determining the tax consequences of composite transactions and one which will help to free the Courts from the shackles which have so long been thought to be imposed on them by the *Westminster* case."

Lord Brightman in *Furniss v Dawson* (at 164) quoted Lord Diplock in the *Burmah* case as follows:

23–006

> "It would be disingenuous to suggest and dangerous on the part of those who advise on elaborate tax avoidance schemes to assume that *Ramsay*'s case did not mark a significant change in the approach adopted by this House in its judicial role to a preordained series of transactions (whether or not they include the achievement of a legitimate commercial end) into which there are inserted steps that have no commercial purpose apart from the avoidance of a liability to tax which in the absence of those particular steps would have been payable."

He continued (at 166):

> "In a pre-planned tax saving scheme, no distinction is to be drawn for fiscal purposes, because none exists in reality, between (i) a series of steps which are followed through by virtue of an arrangement which falls short of a binding contract, and (ii) a like series of steps which are followed through because the participants are contractually bound to take each step seriatim. In a contractual case the fiscal consequences will naturally fall to be assessed in the light of the contractually agreed results. For example, equitable interests may pass when the contract for sale is signed. In many cases equity will regard that as done which is contracted to be done. *Ramsay* says that the fiscal result is to be no different if the several steps are pre-ordained rather than pre-contracted …
>
> The formulation by Lord Diplock in *Burmah* expresses the limitations of the *Ramsay* principle. First, there must be a pre-ordained series of transactions; or, if one likes, one single composite transaction. This composite transaction may or may not include the achievement of a legitimate commercial (i.e. business) end … Secondly there must be steps inserted which have no commercial (business) purpose apart from the avoidance of a liability to tax—not 'no business effect'. If those two ingredients exist, the inserted steps are to be disregarded for fiscal purposes. The Court must then look at the end result. Precisely how the end result will be taxed will depend on the terms of the taxing statute sought to be applied."

The judgment in *Furniss v Dawson* did not, however, put an end to strategic tax planning, as the House of Lords confirmed in *Craven v White*, IRC *v Bowater Property Developments Ltd* (1986) 130 S.J. 15 and *Baylis v Gregory* [1988] S.T.C. 476, in which Lord Oliver said (at 507):

> "As the law currently stands, the essentials emerging from Dawson appear to me to be four in number:(1) that the series of transactions was, at the time when the intermediate transaction was entered into it, pre-ordained in order to produce a given result; (2) that that transaction had no other purpose than tax mitigation; (3) that there was at that time no practical likelihood that the pre-planned events would not take place in the order ordained, so that the intermediate transaction was not even contemplated practically as having an independent life, and (4) that the pre-ordained events did in fact take place. In these circumstances the court can be justified in linking the beginning with the end so as to make a single composite whole to which the fiscal results of the single composite whole are to be applied …

There is a real and not merely a metaphysical distinction between something that is done as a preparatory step towards a possible but uncertain contemplated future action and something which is done as an integral and interdependent part of a transaction already agreed and, effectively, pre-destined to take place. In the latter case, to link the end to the beginning involves no more than recognising the reality of what is effectively a single operation *ab initio*. In the former it involves quite a different process, viz that of imputing to the parties, ex post facto, an obligation (either contractual or quasi contractual) which did not exist at the material time but which is to be attributed from the occurrence or juxtaposition of events which subsequently took place. That cannot be extracted from Dawson as it stands nor can it be justified by any rational extension of the *Ramsay* approach. It involves the invocation of a different principle altogether, that is to say, the reconstruction of events into something that they were not, either in fact or in intention, not because they in fact constituted a single composite whole but because, and only because, one or more of them was motivated by a desire to avoid or minimise tax."

23–007 Lord Gaffat (at 511) said:

"Before the Court of Appeal, the Crown appears to have submitted that at least some kinds of 'strategic tax planning' might be caught by the principle—a submission which was, in my opinion, rightly rejected by that court."

And Lord Jauncey (at 521) tried to be helpful:

"If it were appropriate to prepare a formula defining 'composite transaction' in the light of the passages in the speeches in *Ramsay*, *Burmah* and *Dawson* to which I have referred I should be tempted to suggest the following:
A step in a linear transaction which has no business purpose apart from the avoidance or deferment of tax liability will be treated as forming part of a preordained series of transactions or of a composite transaction if it was taken at a time when negotiations or arrangements for carrying through as a continuous process of a subsequent transaction which actually takes place had reached a stage when there was no real likelihood that such subsequent transaction would not take place and if thereafter such negotiations or arrangements were carried through to completion without genuine interruption.
However, I am conscious that this may well constitute too rigid an approach to the problems and I therefore put it forward as a tentative guide rather than as a definitive exercise."

TRADING AND PROFESSIONAL INCOME

23–008 The exploitation of intellectual property can give rise to assessment as a trade, in the case of a company, under CTA 2009 Ch.2. If the trade is carried on in the United Kingdom or controlled from the United Kingdom, the assessment is in the United Kingdom (*Ogilvie v Kitton* (1908) 5 T.C. 338) and the assessment is on the worldwide income (*London Bank of Mexico v Apthorpe* (1891) 3 T.C. 143).

If the income is received by a company, the company will be liable to corporation tax on the income arising, less the expenses wholly and exclusively incurred for the purposes of the trade. As the income is assessed on a current year basis, it is only necessary to ensure that the expenses are not incurred before the trade is commenced, although expenditure incurred no more than seven years before the commencement of trade is deemed to have been incurred on the first day of trading under CTA 2009 s.61 (for corporation tax);. In the case of an individual or partnership, the pre-trading expenses provision yields a potentially relievable loss in the first period rather than an expense (CTA 2009 s.57(2)).

Although it is possible for an individual or partnership to be assessed as a trade it is more likely that the assessment would be income from a profession or vocation. From a practical viewpoint there is usually no distinction between a trade or vocation but see ITA 2007 ss.773–789 and also the loss relief restriction rules in ITA 2007 s.107.

The assessment for a business controlled from the United Kingdom would be on the worldwide income (*Davies v Braithwaite* (1933) 18 T.C. 198).

Current year basis

As explained in Ch.9, individuals and partnerships are assessed under the current year basis. However it is usually still advantageous in terms of deferral of tax to make up accounts to a date ending early in the fiscal year, say April 30, rather than late in the year, say March 31 or April 5. It also allows, at the cost of some complexity, the maximum period in which to prepare accounts and still meet the filing date requirements. 23–009

Investment income

If the assessment is, for example, on royalties from intellectual property held as an investment, the assessment under ITTOIA 2005 s.580 is normally made on the basis of the income received in the fiscal year. Each source of income is computed separately in order to arrive at the total assessment for the year (*Grainger v Mrs Maxwell's Executors* (1925) 10 T.C. 139). 23–010

If tax has been deducted from the income, it is treated as if it were a payment on account of the recipient's own liability ITA 2007 s.848.

A non-UK domiciled individual is taxed in the same manner as one domiciled in the United Kingdom. Income received by a UK company taxed under the loan relationship rules of CTA 2009 Pt 9 is taxed on an accruals basis in the same way as income assessed under CTA 2009 Pt 2.

Where income such as patent royalties has been received under deduction of tax the assessment is on a fiscal year basis. If for any reason tax has not been deducted by the payer this does not prevent it being collected from the recipient (*Grosvenor Place Estates Ltd v Roberts* (1960) 39 T.C. 433). Alternatively HMRC could collect from the payer, who in turn could recover from the recipient, if he could show that the money had been paid in full owing to a mistake of fact, for example, as to whether the payment constituted a patent royalty (*Turvey v Dentons* (1923) Ltd [1953] 1 Q.B. 218), or of law (*Kleinwort Benson Ltd v Lincoln CC* [1998] 4 All E.R. 513). 23–011

It is widely accepted that the remittance basis is a limitation of the arising basis and if this is so the cumulative assessments on a particular source during a period of residence in the United Kingdom cannot exceed the cumulative assessment on a (theoretical) arising basis.

LOSSES

23–012 One of the cardinal principles of tax planning is to make the best possible use of tax losses which may arise. The scope for planning in respect of certain losses is restricted for 2013/14 and later years by the capping of reliefs at 25 per cent of income or £50,000 if greater.

Trading losses

23–013 Under income tax self-assessment, losses of an accounting year ending in a fiscal year may be set against the total income of the preceding fiscal year effectively preserving the one year carry-back under the pre-self-assessment rules (ITA 2007 ss.213, 214). The loss is computed in the same way as a profit by reference to the accounting year ending in the fiscal year, not by reference to apportionment of the loss over the fiscal year (ITA 2007 ss.61(2), 62(2)). It is not possible to claim relief for the same loss twice nor make a partial claim for loss relief, except to the extent that the loss exceeds available income against which it can be offset. The claim must be made within one year of the filing date, i.e. one year and 10 months after the end of the fiscal year in which the loss arises.

Alternatively, relief for the loss may be claimed against total income for the fiscal year in which the loss arises with any balance in excess of available income carried back for one year (ITA 2007 ss.65, 129). Where the loss arises in the first four fiscal years of trading it may be carried back and set off against total income for the three preceding fiscal years utilising the earliest available income first (ITA 2007 s.72). Both "sideways" relief under ITA 2007 s.65 and relief for the first four years of trading under ITA 2007 s.72 are capped at 25 per cent of income or £50,000 for 2013/14 and later years.

Losses arising in the first couple of years of a trade or in a period where there is a change of accounting date can be quite complex to compute.

23–014 To the extent that trading losses are not set off against total income they may be carried forward and set off against profits of the same trade under ITA 2007 ss.23–25, 61–63, 83–85. Capital allowances are treated as expenses and will automatically be included in the computation of any loss. The relief cap does not apply to losses carried forward and offset against future profits.

Losses arising from a subscription of shares in an unquoted company may qualify for relief under ITA 2007 ss.23–25, 131–135 and be set against total income for the year in which the loss arises, subject to the relief cap from 2013/14.

A terminal loss arising in the last 12 months of trading may be carried back and set against the total income for the year of termination and the three preceding fiscal years under ITA 2007 ss.23–25, 62, 63, 89–93. The set off is against the most recent year first. The relief cap does not apply to losses arising under these provisions.

When planning loss relief claims it is important to bear in mind the time value of money, the potential loss of personal allowances and the rates of tax at which the losses will be relieved. It is often necessary to compute the available permutations for relief available, in terms of tax, in order to make the most appropriate claim.

Non-trading losses

Where income is assessable as casual but a loss arises, it may be set against any casual income in the year of loss or carried forward against future casual income (ITA 2007 ss.23–24, 152–155).

23–015

Excess charges on income incurred for trading purposes, other than capital sums paid in respect of patent rights or copyright royalties paid to a person whose normal place of abode is outside the United Kingdom, may be carried forward against future income of the trade following *Greasham Life Assurance Society v Styles* (1892) 3 T.C. 185 (ITA 2007 EN Annex 1, Change 81). Excess trading interest may be added to a loss carried forward or to a terminal loss under ITA 2007 s.88 and losses in respect of a trade carried on abroad where profits would be assessable in the United Kingdom are relieved under ITA 2007 s.95 in the same way as UK trading losses.

The above loss reliefs are not subject to the relief cap introduced for 2013/14 and later years.

POST-CESSATION RECEIPTS

In most cases of intellectual property the income is brought into account when received or when ascertained and can continue to arise for many years after the trade or profession has itself ceased. Such profits were at one time tax-free, as for example in *Purchase v Stainer's Executors* (1951) 32 T.C. 367 (see para.18–002). However, such income arising after the cessation of the trade or profession would now be taxable as post-cessation receipts under the provisions of ITTOIA 2005 ss.241–257 (see para.18–006).

23–016

If the profits had been assessed on the earnings basis, including accrued expenses and income earned but not actually received, there would be an assessment on any amounts not included in the earnings basis calculation. There are exceptions for sums received from outside the United Kingdom by a non-resident or his agent under ITTOIA 2005 s.243(3). There is also an exception for a lump sum paid to the personal representatives of an author of a literary, dramatic, musical or artistic work as consideration for the assignment by them wholly or partially of the copyright in the work, under ITTOIA 2005 s.253 and for transfers of trading stock or work in progress on cessation where it has been included in the accounts of a normal valuation (ITTOIA 2005 s.252).

It will be seen, therefore, that most sums arising after the cessation (such as royalties receivable) will be taxable under these provisions. The exception for a lump sum receipt on the assignment of copyright by personal representatives would be a disposal for capital gains tax purposes, with the probate value being the base cost under TCGA 1992 s.62.

The ITTOIA 2005 s.246 will charge to tax as post cessation receipts so far as not otherwise charged to income tax (ITTOIA 2005 s.243).

23–017

The ITTOIA 2005 ss.254–255 allows as a deduction such expenses as would have been allowed had the business continued and ITTOIA 2005 s.246(3), (4) confirms that on, for example, a change of partners the notional cessation rules also apply. However, ITTOIA 2005 s.251 states that if there is a sale of the business and post-cessation receipts are receivable by the purchaser the sale proceeds are taxable and the subsequent income is included in the purchaser's normal receipts. Similarly, on a notional discontinuance following a change in partnership there is no post-cessation receipt charge if the post-cessation income is credited to the continuing partners. The only post-cessation receipts charge would be on any amounts credited to the outgoing partners not otherwise brought into taxable income.

Where copyrights are transferred for a nominal consideration from an individual or partnership being assessed under the post-cessation receipt provisions to a connected company, the market value of the copyright should be taxed as a post-cessation receipt under ITTOIA 2005 s.251 unless the transferee carries on the trade and the company would be taxable on the subsequent royalties received.

The ITTOIA 2005 s.256 makes it clear that it is taxable as earned income. The ITTOIA 2005 s.257, gives the taxpayer the right to elect within one year from the normal self-assessment filing date to carry back the amount chargeable and have it assessed as if it were received on the last day of trading. This right is restricted to post-cessation income of six years following the discontinuance. If this election is made no claim may be made under ITTOIA 2005 s.255, setting expenses against the income carried back.

INCOME NOT OTHERWISE CHARGED TO TAX

23–018 A self-assessment under ITTOIA 2005 s.687, tax as casual income, falls to be made on the actual income arising in the fiscal year under ITTOIA 2005 s.688. In the absence of legislation to the contrary (for example, post-cessation receipts under ITTOIA 2005 s.256) the assessment would be as unearned income. The assessment extends to income of a non-resident arising in the United Kingdom, as in *Alloway v Phillips* [1980] S.T.C. 490.

It will normally be preferable to claim to be trading or carrying on a profession in the United Kingdom if the income is otherwise likely to be taxed as casual income except for a casual author who may sell his copyright for a capital sum which would be taxed as a capital gain.

CAPITAL GAINS

23–019 If a capital sum received from intellectual property is taxable as a capital gain, which, as has been seen, would be the exception rather than the rule, the assessment would be calculated in the normal way, that is, on the net sale proceeds less the cost of the asset, if any, or if the asset was held at March 31, 1982 value, its value at that date (TCGA 1992 s.35) other than for corporation tax, and any enhancement expenditure allowable under TCGA 1992 s.38. For corporation tax on chargeable gains, the value at March 31, 1982 is used if higher than the asset's original cost, or if the company had made an irrevocable election under TCGA 1992 s.35(5) to re-base the asset to its March 1982 value. Indexation relief since March 31, 1982, under TCGA 1992 s.53 applies for corporation tax purposes only to further reduce the gain arising, although indexation cannot create or augment a capital loss. Entrepreneurs' relief may apply to gains made by individuals and certain trustees (see para.9–073). If there is a part disposal, only the appropriate part of the cost can be deducted, applying the A/A x B formula under TCGA 1992 s.42. In this fraction A is the consideration received and B is the market value of the property retained.

For corporation tax purposes only, if the asset was held at April 6, 1965 the gain would be apportioned under TCGA 1992 Sch.2 para.16, by applying to the gain the fraction:

T/P x T

In this formula, T is the period from April 6, 1965 to the time of disposal and P is the period of ownership prior to April 6, 1965. Alternatively, it is possible within two years of the end of the year of assessment or accounting period in which the disposal took place to elect to substitute for the base value the market value at April 6, 1965 under TCGA 1992 Sch.2 para.17.

The case of *Mason v Innes* (1967) 44 T.C. 326, where an author gave away the copyright in one of his works, has been discussed (see paras 18–009–18–011). Although such a disposal is free of income tax under the decision, there could be a capital gains tax disposal, in view of the wide definition of assets for capital gains tax purposes under TCGA 1992 s.21. Normally an assignment of copyright by an author for cash would not be subject to capital gains tax, as there would be an income tax liability and the exemption of TCGA 1992 s.37(1) would therefore apply. However, this does not seem to be a point that HMRC normally takes, and it has accepted that TCGA 1992 s.165, roll-over relief for gifts of business assets, may apply to the gift. It would seem that any capital gains tax problem can be overcome by an author assigning the copyright in a work yet to be written which can be done under the provisions of CDPA 1988 s.91. It would be argued that at the time of the transfer no substantial asset existed for capital gains tax purposes and that there was no material reduction in the estate for inheritance tax.

ITEPA 2003

Income from an office or employment is to be assessed to tax under the ITEPA 2003. The ITEPA 2003 ss.10(2), 15(1), 21(1), 22(1), applies to a person who is resident and (before 2013/14) ordinarily resident in the United Kingdom in respect of his worldwide remuneration, except for foreign emoluments which are within ITEPA 2003 ss.10(2), 22(1),(2), 26(1). The ITEPA 2003 ss.10(2), 25(1), 27(1), applies to a person who is non-resident and is limited to the remuneration arising from an office or employment the duties of which are carried out in the United Kingdom. For years up to 2012/13, these provisions also applied to an individual resident but not ordinarily resident in the UK. Under ITEPA 2003 ss.10(2), 22(1)(2), 26(1), a non-UK domiciled individual who is resident in the United Kingdom and is in receipt of remuneration from a non-resident employer in respect of work done entirely outside the United Kingdom is assessed to tax on remittances to the United Kingdom.

23–020

Arising basis

23–021 From April 6, 1989, remuneration is assessed to tax in the year in which it is received rather than the year in which it was earned whether or not the source still exists, which overrules *Bray v Best* [1989] S.T.C. 159 and prevents avoidance of tax on the remittance basis where remitted after the end of the fiscal year in which the source ceased. Under ITEPA 2003 ss.18, 19, 31, 32, 686, earnings are treated as received at the earliest of actual payment, entitlement to payment, crediting to a director's current account, or on determination or at the end of the current period of account if determined during that period.

Remuneration under ITEPA 2003 is based on the emoluments from the employment, which includes all salaries, fees, wages, perquisites and profits whatsoever (ITEPA 2003 ss.10(2), 62(2), 327). It has been held in cases such as *Tennant v Smith* (1892) 3 T.C. 158; *Wilkins v Rogerson* (1960) 39 T.C. 344; and *Heaton v Bell* (1969) 46 T.C. 211, that a perquisite is, in the absence of specific provisions to the contrary, taxable only if it is convertible into money or money's worth. Such specific provisions are to be found in ITEPA 2003 Ch.4 of Pt 2 in relation to vouchers including season tickets and purchases by company credit card and for cash vouchers, and ITEPA 2003 ss.105 and 106 in respect of living accommodation.

Remuneration under ITEPA 2003 is normally subject to deduction of tax at source under the PAYE regulations introduced by ITEPA 2003 s.684. In respect of directors and higher paid employees, commonly called P11D employees, ITEPA 2003 Pt 3, introduced special provisions for the taxation of fringe benefits and expenses (subject to a claim for those expenses wholly, exclusively and necessarily incurred for the purpose of the employment under ITEPA 2003 Pt 5). It is not intended here to deal with the taxation of fringe benefits, which is a subject in itself, referred to briefly in Ch.9.

Two other areas of the ITEPA 2003 legislation require special consideration for tax planning purposes: "golden handshakes" and top-slicing relief.

"Golden handshakes"

23–022 If an employment ceases it may be worthwhile giving the employee a compensation for loss of office or ex gratia payment on retirement. Such payments are basically taxable under ITEPA 2003 in accordance with ITEPA 2003 s.401. The ITEPA 2003 s.403, however, exempts such payments up to £30,000.

Inducement payments

23–023 The case of *Pritchard v Arundale* (1971) 47 T.C. 680 is a useful case in which a capital payment in the form of shares was made to a self-employed individual to induce him to give up his self-employed status and become an employee. Such an inducement payment was held to be tax-free. HMRC's attempt to tax such a payment, this time to higher rates under ITEPA 2003 ss.7, 225, 226, was defeated in *Vaughan-Neil v IRC* [1979] S.T.C. 644, although they were successful in assessing under what is now ITEPA 2003, a payment to induce a change of employment in *Glantre Engineering Ltd v Goodhand* [1983] S.T.C. 1 and *Shilton v Wilmshurst* [1991] S.T.C. 88.

PENSION SCHEMES

Pension schemes are likely to feature very commonly in tax planning arrangements because, in essence, the premium paid is usually a deduction from current taxable income, is accumulated within a tax free fund, and in due course up to 25 per cent of the accumulated fund can be withdrawn tax free and the balance taken out as a taxable pension over the remaining life of the pensioner. In 2002 the Treasury and HMRC published "Simplifying the Taxation of Pensions: Increasing Choice and Flexibility for All". This identified the various schemes that had been approved, i.e. the old code schemes pre-1970, the 1970–1987 schemes, the 1987–1989 schemes and the 1989–2006 schemes. There were also approved pension schemes relating to the self-employed for those outwith occupational pension schemes which were either retirement annuity contracts or personal pension schemes. In addition there were funded unapproved retirement benefit schemes and unfunded unapproved retirement benefit schemes.

23–024

This all changed from April 6, 2006, with the introduction of registered pension funds. The relevant legislation is to be found in FA 2004 ss.149–284 and Schs 28–36; FA 2005 s.101 and Sch.10; FA 2006 ss.158–161 and Schs 21–23; FA 2007 ss.68–70 and Schs 18–20 and FA 2008 ss.90–92 and Schs 28 and 29. This primary legislation is supplemented by a considerable number of statutory instruments.

As will be appreciated with this volume of legislation and regulation it is not possible in a book of this nature to cover the subject in detail.

Under the registered pension scheme legislation existing approved schemes automatically became registered schemes with the option of opting out and suffering a 40 per cent tax charge on assets held at April 6, 2004; so almost all schemes became registered with effect from April 6, 2006. Registered schemes are exempt from tax on income and gains but the contributions are subject to a lifetime limit. The lifetime limit was set at £1.5m at April 6, 2006 and rose to £1.8m in 2011/12, before being reduced back down to the 2006 level of £1.5m from April 6, 2012. The lifetime limit will reduce further to £1.25m from April 6, 2014 (FA 2013 s.48). There are transitional provisions for schemes that exceed the lifetime limits at April 6, 2006. Subsequent reductions in the limit that broadly enable such schemes to avoid tax charges on the value of benefits accruing before the various threshold changes, although the precise details of the protection available varies. The annual allowance is applied to defined benefit schemes by assuming a capitalisation factor of 20x the members benefit. Benefits in payment prior to April 6, 2006 are capitalised using a factor of 25x the benefit to reflect the fact that commutation would normally have been taken, whether or not in fact it had been.

23–025

Instead of capping the contributions by reference to the annual earnings there is an annual allowance for the total premium paid to the scheme which was £215,000 for 2006/07 and increased by £10,000 per annum to £255,000 in

2010/11. From 2011/12 to 2013/14, the limit is £50,000 per annum, and will reduce further to £40,000 per annum from April 6, 2014. There is a further limit on members' contributions which is 100 per cent of the relevant UK earnings subject to a minimum contribution of £3,600. The relevant earnings are income from employment or self employment in the United Kingdom subject to the overall annual allowance limit. There is no limit to the employer's contributions as such apart from the annual allowance which applies to the combined contributions of the members and their employer. Employers' contributions are allowed as the tax deduction for the year in which they are paid, not on the normal accruals basis.

Members obtain tax relief on contributions by making the payment to the pension fund less tax at the basic rate, which means that a member paying tax at the higher rate has to claim the additional allowance separately. The employer may operate a net pay scheme, under which it will deduct tax on the income paid to the employee after deducting the pension contributions and therefore full tax relief is given at source for the contributions, and national insurance contributions reduced.

23–026 As well as a limit to the contributions, when benefits are taken they have to be checked against the lifetime allowance and if this had been exceeded the fund is subject to a 25 per cent tax charge and if the excess is withdrawn by the member it is subject to tax in his hands at 40 per cent giving rise to an effective 55 per cent tax charge, which is intended to recover the tax relief within the pension fund and that the excess payments are taxable as income. The minimum retirement age of 50 was increased to 55 from April 6, 2010 although there are early retirement provisions for those in special occupations such as sportsmen who can qualify for a reduced retirement age with a corresponding reduction of 2.5 per cent per annum below the normal retirement age in the lifetime allowance. On reaching retirement age a pension may be taken in the form of a scheme pension or by way of a lifetime annuity provided by an insurance company or a withdrawal from a fund subject to a limit to the notional drawdown which is allowed. From the age of 75 an alternative secured pension could be used instead of the annuity which was previously compulsory and this allowed a maximum withdrawal of 90 per cent of the relevant annuity. From April 6, 2011, it is no longer a requirement that a person reaching the age of 75 uses his pension fund to buy an annuity. Pending abolition, the age by which a person had to buy an annuity was increased to 77, provided the age of 75 had not been reached at June 22, 2010 (F(No2)A 2010 Sch.3). The rules regarding alternatively secured pensions were also repealed from April 6, 2011, and it is now possible for an individual to leave their pension fund invested in a drawdown arrangement and for income to be withdrawn up to a capped limit each year of retirement. The cap is 120 per cent of the annuity which could have been purchased with the pension fund (100 per cent prior to March 26, 2013). The cap is determined periodically, depending upon the individual's age.

On reaching retirement age, 25 per cent of the value of the pension fund (or the lifetime allowance, if lower) can generally be withdrawn as a tax free lump sum, although this amount varies where the individual chooses income drawdown or a lifetime annuity rather than a scheme pension.

Death in service benefits may be a lump sum up to the annual allowance with any excess being subject to tax at 55 per cent and a dependants' pension. After benefits have vested the residual fund on death may be used to provide a lump sum subject to tax at 55 per cent (35 per cent before April 6, 2011) and dependants' pension benefits. Any remaining fund on the death of a dependant would be subject to tax at 55 per cent. Where the member was taking an alternative secured pension any residual fund would revert to the scheme and must be used to provide a dependants' pension and where there are no dependants a surplus may be transferred to the fund of a scheme member which has been nominated by the deceased or to charity. A refund of contributions up to a limit provisionally of £20,000 (£10,800 before 2010/11), will be taxed at 20 per cent with any balance taxed at 50 per cent (40 per cent before 2010/11). Provision is made for pension sharing on divorce with the amount credited to the spouse being set against his or her lifetime allowance, which allows the divorced member to recharge his or her pension fund up to the amount of the lifetime allowance.

There are restrictions on the investments which registered schemes are allowed to hold, limited borrowing, and holding shares or granting loans to the sponsoring employer.

Unfunded pensions

The types of pensions that have been considered so far are those which are funded for in advance with an insurance company or other pension scheme. There is no reason why pensions should not be paid by a company or partnership to a former employee or partner out of the continuing profits of the business (an "employer-financed retirement benefit scheme"). In the case of a pension to a former employee, this would be a deductible expense of the company and taxed under ITEPA 2003 as earned income of the pensioner. If a company enters into an agreement to pay a pension out of continuing profits it is important that this is not included in the employee's service contract, except with the approval of HMRC as otherwise there could be a charge under ITEPA 2003 on the notional premiums that would have been required to fund the pension through an insurance company arrangement ITEPA 2003 ss.7, 10, 386 and 388.

23–027

If at a later date the company decides that it wishes to pay a lump sum to an insurance company so that future pension liabilities will be paid by the insurance company, the cost of relieving itself of the obligation to pay the pension is a trading expense, following *Hancock v General Reversionary and Investment Co Ltd* (1918) 7 T.C. 358. In practice, a Hancock scheme is often agreed with HMRC and some degree of spread of the lump sum payment is involved.

A pension may be paid to the wife or dependants of a former employee in the same way as to the employee himself.

KEYMAN INSURANCE

Employers sometimes insure the life of key employees against accidental death during the course of the employment. If the employee is unrelated to the proprietors of the business and is in an arm's-length employment, the company is

23–028

allowed to pay to the employee's dependants free of inheritance tax any amount up to the amount recovered under such keyman insurance policy. In a keyman policy the proceeds are payable to the company in the first instance. The premiums may normally be claimed as a deduction for tax purposes, in which case if the employee is killed the proceeds of the insurance would be a taxable receipt. On the other hand, HMRC will normally disallow the premiums in computing the company's corporation tax liability if the life insured has a proprietorial interest in the business and in that case would not assess to tax the amounts received from the insurance company if the employee is killed (*Greycon Ltd v Klaentschi* [2003] S.T.C. (SCD) 370).

TRUSTS

23–029 The use of trusts in the tax planning of intellectual property is no different from their use for holding other assets such as shares or loan stock and any detailed consideration of this highly complex subject would justify a book of considerable length.

So far as intellectual property is concerned it is usually advisable to make any intended transfer to a trust at the earliest possible moment. In the case of patents the trustees themselves may apply for the patent and in the case of copyright it is possible to assign future copyright before a work is written.

Income tax on trusts

23–030 Trusts are liable to income tax at the trust rate on accumulated income under ITA 2007 ss.8 and 479, which makes the effective rate of tax on such trust income 45 per cent for 2013/14. The dividend trust rate is 42.5 per cent. Trusts where a life tenant has an interest in possession are liable to tax at the basic rate and the life tenant is liable for any higher rate tax charge on the income to which he is entitled (*Archer-Shee v Baker* (1927) 11 T.C. 749; *Williams v Singer* (1921) 7 T.C. 387).

The income of a trust for the settlor's minor children is taxed on the settlor under ITTOIA 2005 ss.629–632, unless accumulated.

If a trust is revocable within six years or the settlor retains an interest the income remains that of the settlor for tax purposes under ITIOIA 2005 ss.623–627.

When income is distributed to a beneficiary he is entitled to a credit for basic rate tax paid by the trust and for the additional rate, if paid by the trust on income previously accumulated (ITA 12007 s.497).

Capital taxes on trusts

23–031 There would usually be a disposal for capital gains tax, which in the case of certain business assets may be held over on a valid election, and a chargeable transfer for inheritance tax on the creation of a trust and on subsequent distributions to beneficiaries. There may also be deemed disposals on appointment or the termination of an interest in possession, or at 10-year intervals in a discretionary trust.

PART 4

TAX PLANNING

CHAPTER 24

International tax planning

INTRODUCTION

The international dimension of tax planning runs the whole gamut from non-residence and the law of domicile through the complexities of controlled foreign companies (Ch.14) and other anti-avoidance legislation to profit engineering and the bête noire of transfer pricing, particularly American transfer pricing (Ch.13). These subjects necessarily do not form a cohesive whole and each is sufficiently complex to merit more detailed discussion than can be encompassed in a book of this nature. The overview given in this chapter is a distillation of the salient features of many different matters, and no apologies are made for the inherently piecemeal approach adopted.

24–001

Non-residents

Non-residents in receipt of income from intellectual property arising in the United Kingdom (i.e. a UK patent, defined by ITTOIA 2005 Pt 5 Ch.2 s.587, and CTA 2009 s.912, as a patent granted under the laws of the United Kingdom, royalties in respect of UK copyright under the CDPA 1988, or other rights over UK intellectual property) would be income from property in the United Kingdom and would therefore be taxable under the provisions of CTA 2009 Pt 9 Ch.3 (for corporation tax purposes) or ITTOIA 2005 Pt 5 Ch.2 (for income tax purposes) on the income arising, unless exempt or taxable at a reduced rate under a double taxation agreement (see para.24–015). The deduction of tax at source provisions apply, in effect, a withholding tax at the basic rate of 20 per cent (22 per cent up to April 5, 2008) to patent royalties paid to a non-resident, and under ITA 2007 s.906, in respect of copyright royalties paid to a person, other than the author, whose usual place of abode is outside the United Kingdom. For the rates of withholding tax under the various double taxation agreements between the United Kingdom and other countries, see App.5. Within the European Union royalties paid between associated companies will not usually be subject to withholding taxes under the Interest and Royalties Directive 2003/49/EC.

24–002

OVERSEAS RIGHTS

24–003 A UK resident in receipt of income from overseas intellectual property, such as foreign patent and copyright royalties under foreign agreements, is in receipt of income which would be assessed to income tax (from 2005/06) under ITTOIA 2005 s.579, or corporation tax under CTA 2009 s.912, as income arising from possessions out of the United Kingdom, unless included in the worldwide income of a trade or profession and subject to income tax ITTOIA 2005 Pt 2 Ch.2 or corporation tax under CTA 2009 Pt 9. The amount assessed is the income arising in the year of assessment, except where the recipient is a UK resident individual domiciled outside the United Kingdom, where the remittance basis may apply.

UK patent income is assessed under CTA 2009 s.912(2), in the case of a non-UK resident company if the trade is carried on abroad with no control from the United Kingdom (*Trustees of Ferguson, deceased v Donovan* [1929] I.R. 489). If the intellectual property income is received by a wholly owned foreign subsidiary, dividends therefrom would be assessed on a UK resident recipient under ITA 2007 s.19 and ITTOIA 2005 Pt 4 Ch.4, and in certain cases by a company under CTA 2009 ss.931A–Q (*Stanley v The Gramophone and Typewriter Ltd* (1908) 5 T.C. 358).

Income from overseas intellectual property received by a UK resident but non-UK domiciled individual, or partner in a partnership managed and controlled from overseas, is relevant foreign income within ITTOIA 2005 s.857(3), and may be taxed on the remittance basis. A UK domiciled individual is taxable on the income arising whether remitted to the United Kingdom or not.

FOREIGN PARTNERSHIPS

24–004 A UK partnership is not a separate legal entity (apart from a Scottish partnership under Partnership Act 1890 s.4(2)), but its income is computed as if it were a separate entity, and a partnership self-assessment return has to be completed on this basis. However, the profit is then allocated on the partnership statement to individual partners who are responsible for their own taxation on their share of the profits, as explained in Ch.9. Similar rules apply to limited partnerships under the Limited Partnerships Act 1907 and limited liability partnerships under the Limited Liability Partnerships Act 2000.

The ITTOIA 2005 s.6 provides that tax shall be charged in respect of any person residing in the United Kingdom from any trade, profession or vocation, whether carried on in the United Kingdom or elsewhere. The ITTOIA 2005 s.6(2) provides that tax shall be charged under the provisions of Pt 2 Ch.2, on any person, not resident in the United Kingdom, from any trade, profession or vocation exercised in the United Kingdom.

A non-domiciled individual is taxed in the same way as a UK domiciled individual under ITTOIA 2005 Pt 2 Ch.2.

24–005 Court decisions such as *Colquhoun v Brooks* (1889) 2 T.C. 490, show that it is possible for a UK resident to carry on a trade abroad as a partner and not exercise control and management of the business, and therefore avoid a tax liability under ITTOIA 2005 Pt 2 Ch.2, it being income of a foreign possession. However,

FOREIGN PARTNERSHIPS

Ogilvy v Kitton (1908) 5 T.C. 338 and *Spiers v Mackinnon* (1929) 14 T.C. 386, establish that where the head and brains of the business reside in the UK, the profits are assessed as trading or professional income, previously under Sch.D, Cases I or II. The decision in *Davies v Braithwaite* (1933) 18 T.C. 198, confirms that the whole of the worldwide profits of a profession carried on by a United Kingdom resident is liable to UK tax. Similarly, a trade carried on partly in the United Kingdom and partly abroad by a UK resident is wholly liable to UK tax following the decision in *London Bank of Mexico v Apthorpe* (1891) 3 T.C. 143.

The effect of these decisions is that UK resident partners in a partnership carrying on a business partly in the United Kingdom and partly overseas are liable to UK tax on their share of the United Kingdom and overseas income. If the overseas income arises from a permanent establishment in the foreign country it is probable that there will be a foreign tax liability on the overseas profits, which will be credited against the UK tax liability either under the terms of the double taxation treaty with the overseas country or unilaterally in the United Kingdom under TIOPA 2010 s.63 and following where the shareholding is at least 10 per cent.

When considering the foreign activities of a UK resident it is important to bear in mind that the double taxation treaties which, following *Ostime v Australian Mutual Provident Society* (1959) 38 T.C. 492, would normally overrule the UK legislation, may provide that a dual resident is deemed not to be resident in the United Kingdom. For example, a Spanish national with a home in both the United Kingdom and Spain and business interests in both countries would probably be deemed, under art.4(2)(c) of the UK/Spain double taxation agreement, to be resident in Spain and not in the United Kingdom. Similar provisions are to be found in other agreements, for example, those with the Irish Republic and with the United States. Where dual residence exists the treaty deeming provision of single residence *only* applies for treaty provision purposes and does not affect the underlying dual residence position, although in practice HMRC usually regard the treaty residence as applicable for all tax purposes.

24–006 A non-resident or deemed non-resident trading in the United Kingdom would be taxed under ITTOIA 2005 Pt 2 Ch.2 only on profits arising in the United Kingdom, following such cases as *Erichsen v Last* (1881) 1 T.C. 351, at 537; 4 T.C. 422; *Pommery & Greno v Apthorpe* (1886) 2 T.C. 182 and *Werle & Co Colquhoun* (1888) 2 T.C. 402, or the appropriate provisions of the treaty.

It will be appreciated that a UK resident may be a partner in a partnership which is managed and controlled outside the United Kingdom. ITTOIA 2005 s.857 provides:

"(1) This section applies if—
    (a) a firm carries on a trade wholly or partly outside the United Kingdom;
    (b) the control and management of the trade is outside the United Kingdom; and
    (c) a partner who is a UK resident individual–
        (i) meets condition A or B in section 831 (conditions to be met for income to be charged on the remittance basis), and
        (ii) makes a claim to that effect for a tax year.
(2) The partner's share of the profits of the trade arising in the United Kingdom is determined in accordance with sections 849 to 856.

(3) The partner's share of the profits of the trade arising outside the United Kingdom is treated as relevant foreign income for the purposes of this Act (see Part 8)."

The effect of ITTOIA 2005 s.857, and the computational rules in ITTOIA 2005 ss.849–856, limits the amount assessed on the non-UK resident partners to their share of any profits of the foreign partnership arising from activities in the United Kingdom which would be assessable in the same way as any other non-resident trading in the United Kingdom through a UK permanent establishment. The remaining income due to a UK resident and domiciled partner would be taxed under ITTOIA 2005 Pt 2 Ch.2, on his share of the worldwide income in spite of any double taxation treaty provisions overruling *Padmore v IRC (No.1)* [1989] S.T.C. 493 as confirmed in *Padmore v IRC (No.2)* [2001] S.T.C. 280. A non-UK domiciled UK resident partner would be taxed on his share of the UK income under ITTOIA 2005 Pt 2 Ch.2, and on remittances to the United Kingdom if he has claimed the remittance basis under ITA 2007 s.809B.

Control and management

24–007 To ensure that the control and management of a foreign partnership is outside the United Kingdom it is desirable to have a majority of non-UK resident partners and provisions in the partnership agreement that partnership meetings must be held outside the United Kingdom. It is not essential to have a majority in number of non-resident partners, provided that the voting control is such that they control the partnership. See, in this respect, the case of *Newstead v Frost* [1980] S.T.C. 123, in which the UK resident partner had 95 per cent of the profits of the partnership but was still assessed to income tax under ITTOIA 2005 Pt 2 Ch.2), as the control and management of the partnership were outside the United Kingdom. Whether or not both the control and management are outside this country are questions of fact, to be decided by the Tax Tribunals if necessary. Consequently, all communications from the United Kingdom to the foreign partnership must be requests and advice and not instructions.

Assessment of Foreign Income

24–008 A non-UK domiciliary is subject to income tax on income from a foreign partnership on the amount remitted to the United Kingdom (ITTOIA 2005 s.832). The remittance basis must be claimed, and for 2008/09 and later years, the annual remittance basis charge of £30,000 or £50,000 may be payable; see Ch.9.

If goods or services are transferred between a foreign partnership and an associated UK firm under common control the transfer pricing provisions in TIOPA 2010 Pt 4 ss.146–217 ensure that arms-length prices must be charged for such goods or services. Similar transfer pricing provisions are contained in most double taxation agreements and in art.9 of the OECD model double tax treaty, as explained in Ch.13, para.13–014.

The post-cessation receipts provisions of ITTOIA 2005 Pt 2 Ch.18 do not apply to relevant foreign income from a foreign partnership (ITTOIA 2005 s.243(5)). For 2007/08 and earlier years, it could apparently be argued that such post-cessation receipts are tax-free on the basis that the source has ceased and remittances from a non-employment ceased source in a tax year after that in which the source ceased are not taxable (*Joffe v Thain* (1955) 36 T.C. 199). The "source-ceasing" exemption no longer applies from April 6, 2008.

REMITTANCE BASIS

A UK resident individual is taxable on the worldwide profits of a trade or profession, *Davies v Braithwaite* (1933) 18 T.C. 198, ITTOIA 2005 s.6(1) and (3). If a sizeable proportion of the work is done overseas it may well be desirable for a non-UK domiciliary to enter into a foreign partnership within ITTOIA 2005 Pt 9, under which the income is taxable as relevant foreign income or to enter into a contract of employment with a non-resident company, in which case the remuneration would be taxed under ITEPA 2003. This would be particularly appropriate in the case of a non-UK domiciled individual because in respect of income taxed under ITTOIA 2005 Pt 2 Ch.2, a non-UK domiciled individual has no advantage under UK tax law compared with a person domiciled in the United Kingdom, whereas remuneration from a non-resident company or partnership for services performed wholly abroad would be taxed only on remittances to the United Kingdom and not on the income arising (ITEPA 2003 s.22–24, ITTOIA 2005 s.857).

24–009

Remittances from a ceased employment source are treated as emoluments for the year in which the employment ceased under ITEPA 2003 ss.17(1) and (3), 30(1) and (3).

Prior to April 6, 2008, assessments on a remittance basis included not only direct remittances to the United Kingdom but also constructive remittances, such as the satisfaction of a debt incurred in the United Kingdom under ITTOIA 2005 s.833. A cheque drawn on an American bank account was held to be a constructive remittance when sold to a UK bank (*Thomson v Moyse* (1960) 39 T.C. 291), as was a loan enjoyed in the United Kingdom (*Harmel v Wright* (1973) 49 T.C. 149). Remittances of the proceeds of foreign securities could be a remittance of capital if the securities were acquired before the taxpayer became resident in the United Kingdom (*Kneen v Martin* (1934) 19 T.C. 33), but not if purchased out of foreign income while the taxpayer was resident in the United Kingdom (*Walsh v Randall* (1940) 23 T.C. 55). Prior to April 6, 2008, a remittance of a physical asset was not a remittance of income. For 2008–09 and later years, there are specific provisions which treat a taxpayer as having made a remittance if money, property (such as artwork, antiques or cars) or services acquired using unremitted foreign income is brought into or otherwise used or received in the United Kingdom by or for the individual or another relevant person (ITA 2007 ss.809A–809Z10). A "relevant person" comprises the taxpayer, his spouse or civil partner, their minor children or grandchildren, a close company (including a company which would be close if it were UK resident) of which the taxpayer or another relevant person is a participator, the trustees of a settlement of which the taxpayer or another relevant person is a settlor or beneficiary, and anybody connected with such a settlement. For the purposes of this test, the terms "spouse" and "civil partner" include those living together as if they were married or in a civil partnership (ITA 2007 s.809L).

24–010 There are exemptions for assets brought into the United Kingdom for a temporary purpose, repair or for public display. Assets costing less than £1,000 and items for personal use (such as clothing, watches and jewellery) are also exempt from the remittance rules (ITA 2007 ss.809X–809Z(6)). The benefit of any exemption is lost if the asset is sold in the United Kingdom and a taxable remittance will arise at the time of sale. It should be noted that the above exemptions only apply to assets acquired out of unremitted foreign income: it does not extend to assets acquired out of unremitted foreign gains.

Transitional rules provide that assets acquired using untaxed foreign income and owned by the taxpayer or a relevant person at March 11, 2008 will not give rise to a remittance if brought into the United Kingdom at a later date, even if the asset was kept outside the United Kingdom on that date. Assets acquired using untaxed foreign income located in the United Kingdom at April 5, 2008 will also not give rise to a charge under the remittance basis for so long as the present owner retains the asset.

Specific rules are introduced from 2008/09 dealing with remittances from funds comprising a mix of income or gains and capital (ITA 2007 ss.809P–809R). It had been HMRC's practice to treat income as being remitted in priority to capital, on the basis that a person would exhaust their sources of income before utilising capital, however, from April 6, 2008, the legislation provides a detailed process for identifying taxable remittances using broadly a "just and reasonable" apportionment.

24–011 It should also be noted that non-UK domiciled individuals who have been resident in the United Kingdom for seven out of the previous nine tax years and who wish to continue being taxed on the remittance basis may be subject to the remittance basis charge of £30,000 per annum with effect from 2008/09; see para.9–031. This charge is increased to £50,000 p.a. if UK resident for 12 out of 14 years; ITA 2007 s.809C.

If a non-UK domiciled individual is assessable on a remittance basis, it is important to ensure that, so far as possible, remittances to the United Kingdom are out of capital. This means that he may require several bank accounts. The account containing his capital prior to becoming resident in the United Kingdom may be freely remitted. An account containing the proceeds of disposals of overseas investments could be remitted, but any chargeable gains element would be taxable on the remittance basis under TCGA 1992 s.12(1). However, the effective rate of tax applicable to capital gains is frequently less than that applicable to income. This is particularly the case from April 6, 2008, when the rate of capital gains tax is 18 per cent or 28 per cent on chargeable gains. Therefore, a remittance from an account containing the disposal proceeds from foreign chargeable assets should be made in preference to a remittance of relevant foreign income within ITTOIA 2005 s.830.

If it is likely to prove necessary to remit part of the overseas income it might be desirable to have two overseas bank accounts for such income, one relating to earned income from a foreign partnership and one relating to investment income. Such bank accounts might well be held in the Channel Islands or the Isle of Man.

Gifts overseas

24–012 Prior to 2008/09, it was relatively straightforward for a non-domiciled individual taxable on the remittance basis to make tax-free gifts overseas of funds from his foreign bank accounts to his wife, family and friends. An overseas bank account into which the gift can pass thereby avoided falling into the constructive remittance problems previously mentioned (*Carter v Sharon* (1936) 20 T.C. 229 and *Grimm v Newman* (2002) S.T.C. 84). If, for example, the wife bought a fur coat or otherwise spent the money so that her husband received no benefit, or if the children paid for their own school fees, it is considered that these would not have been constructive remittances.

The position is more complex following measures introduced to tighten the rules regarding remittances, now in ITA 2007 s.809A–Z10, however, gifts to adult children of a non-UK domiciled individual from which the donor derives no benefit may still be made without giving rise to a taxable remittance. Numerous exemptions also apply, as detailed above, however, it should be emphasised that the exemptions apply only to assets purchased out of relevant foreign income, not foreign gains and that careful record-keeping will be required in order to avoid inadvertent remittances of untaxed foreign income or gains.

For inheritance tax purposes a person who is not domiciled in the United Kingdom can be treated as so domiciled, for inheritance tax purposes, under the deemed domicile provisions of IHTA 1984 s.267. The most likely case is that of an individual who has been tax resident in the United Kingdom in at least 17 out of the previous 20 years. FA 2013 s.215 and Sch.43 introduced a detailed and complex statutory residence test with effect from April 6, 2013. The concept of ordinary residence was abolished from April 6, 2013 by FA 2013 s.216 and Sch.44, with effect from April 6, 2013.

24–013 Where the individual is not UK domiciled for both income tax and inheritance tax purposes the gifts mentioned can be made free of inheritance tax. However, if the person is deemed domiciled in the UK for inheritance tax purposes he would need to take advantage of the potentially exempt transfer provisions or other inheritance tax exemptions.

If a non-domiciled partner makes a genuine gift from his (Jersey) bank account to his UK partners by transferring funds to their own (Jersey) bank accounts, such a gift would be excluded property for inheritance tax purposes. However, it would be necessary to ensure that the UK partners had not made a transfer of assets to the foreign partnership, otherwise ITA 2007 ss.714–751, could cause the gifts to be assessable as income.

WITHHOLDING TAXES

24–014 In order to see whether the intended benefits of any overseas tax planning are in fact obtainable it is first of all necessary to consider the question of withholding taxes deducted by the countries from which the income is likely to emanate. It could be preferable for a UK resident to have the use of income which could be remitted to the United Kingdom with the result that, after credit for foreign taxes paid, the additional UK tax liability on the income would be small or at an acceptable level. On the other hand, it may be possible to set up a more sophisticated arrangement whereby the patent or copyright is owned by an offshore company.

DOUBLE TAXATION RELIEF

24–015 Many countries apply a withholding tax on royalty payments to a non-resident of that country, as does the United Kingdom, in connection with United Kingdom patent royalties and certain copyright royalties. If the recipient of the foreign royalties is resident in the United Kingdom, the rate of withholding tax is often reduced or eliminated under the appropriate double taxation treaty between the UK and the country where the royalty arises. It is important to look carefully at the definition of royalty under the particular treaty and to look at the treaty currently in force, as double taxation treaties tend to be undergoing continual revision. It is also necessary to consider the practice of the overseas country.

For example, under the old UK/US Double Tax Treaty the American Internal Revenue Service has been known to argue that record royalties are not royalties exempt within the UK/US Double Tax Treaty but are connected with income from performances in the United States and should be taxed as such. It might be necessary to resist such contentions under the law and practice of the overseas countries. The current treaty SI 2002/2848 art.12 specifically includes works reproduced or any means of sound reproduction.

It should be borne in mind that a double taxation agreement in the United Kingdom normally overrules the provisions of the Taxes Acts (*Ostime v Australian Mutual Provident Society* (1959) 38 T.C. 492 and TIOPA 2010 ss.2–7.

24–016 Under TIOPA 2010 ss.8–17, if overseas income suffers foreign tax which is not relieved under a double tax treaty, unilateral relief may be given whereby the foreign tax is treated as a credit, that is, as if it were a payment on account of the UK tax liability arising on the same income. The relief primarily applies to income tax and corporation tax but is extended to capital gains tax by TIOPA 2010 s.9, and further provisions are in TIOPA 2010 ss.18–35.

TIOPA 2010 ss.36–39, provide that the double taxation relief cannot exceed the UK income tax payable on the overseas income concerned, treating the latter as the top slice of income and ignoring the foreign tax credit (see *Yates v GCA International Ltd* [1991] S.T.C. 157 and SP7/91). Where there is a number of overseas income sources the UK tax credit appropriate to each is calculated separately by successively treating each source as the top slice of income subject to UK tax, but thereafter excluding that source in the total income computations. Thus, to maximise relief overseas sources should be dealt with in descending order of overseas tax rates with the higher tax rate source being dealt with first. The limit of foreign tax credit for capital gains tax is in TIOPA 2010 s.40 and the limit on total credit against income tax and capital gains tax is in TIOPA 2010 s.41. For corporation tax purposes TIOPA 2010 ss.42–56, provides that the double taxation relief credit cannot exceed UK corporation tax on the foreign income. If the foreign income consists of trading profits, an attribution of expenses to this income will be required to arrive at the amount of doubly taxed income.

Foreign tax unrelieved under any double taxation treaty or under the unilateral relief provisions of TIOPA 2010 ss.8–56, can, under TIOPA 2010 ss.112–115, be treated as an expense in computing the profits liable to UK tax (*Harrods (Buenos Aires) Ltd v Taylor-Gooby* (1964) 41 T.C. 450; *IRC v Dowdall O'Mahoney & Co Ltd* (1952) 33 T.C. 259). It is obviously preferable to claim foreign tax as a credit against the UK tax payable, rather than as a mere expense in computing the UK tax liability.

Royalties paid by an overseas licensee for the use of UK intellectual property in the overseas country are treated as income from overseas of the UK licensor even though, technically, the source of income is the United Kingdom, under Extra-Statutory Concession B8. Double taxation treaties also fix the source of royalties in the territory of residence of the payer in many cases. Royalties arising in more than one foreign jurisdiction in a tax year are treated as a single item of income and the foreign tax is aggregated under TIOPA 2010 ss.38 and 47 for income tax and corporation tax. 24–017

Current rates of withholding tax for royalties received by a UK resident recipient from various overseas countries are listed in App.4.

ROYALTY STRUCTURES

It may be worth considering a patent or registered trade mark owned by a company resident in a zero tax jurisdiction such as the British Virgin Islands (BVI). A patented invention, for example, could be licensed to a company in the Netherlands and in turn sub-licensed to the user in say Russia. Under the Russian/Dutch double tax treaty the rate of withholding tax on paying a patent licence fee to the Dutch company would be nil. The amount received in Holland would be subject to Dutch tax on the amount of the royalty received less the royalty paid. 24–018

The Netherlands introduced transfer pricing rules on January 1, 2002. The effect of these rules is that the "spread" must be calculated on an arm's-length basis. It is thought that in normal circumstances a spread of 7 per cent satisfies the arm's-length requirement, although this would depend on the nature of the royalties.

The agreed percentage of the royalty would be subject to Dutch tax at say 25 per cent and the balance would be paid to the BVI. There is no royalty withholding tax in the Netherlands. The tax burden suffered will be 1.75 per cent against an initial third party royalty payment of 100. It should be noted that dividends are subject to withholding tax in the Netherlands and planning is necessary if this tax is to be mitigated. Where significant profits are likely to accumulate in the Dutch BV the insertion of a Luxembourg Soparfi under the BVI but above the Dutch BV may be considered.

Structures exploiting intellectual property rights, although legitimate from a tax planning point of view, have come in for a good deal of criticism from politicians, much of it ill informed. However, international co-operation and exchange of information among tax authorities, and public criticism of companies apparently avoiding paying their "fair share" of tax, means that such structures should have a sound commercial rationale. It is generally accepted that 24–019 the current international transfer pricing rules, which date back to the 1920s, are not suited to the current digital age. The OECD is currently reviewing this.

Although the use of the Netherlands intermediate licensing company is well known it might be worthwhile exploring other potential tax havens. For example, HMRC are becoming increasingly conscious of the anti-avoidance provisions in art.12 para.5 of the UK/Dutch double taxation agreement (SI 2009/227) and it may be preferable to route royalties through the Austrian subsidiary of a non-resident Cyprus company relying on art.12 of the UK/Austrian double taxation treaty (SI 1970/1947) which has a limitation only if the UK company is more than 50 per cent controlled by the Austrian recipient. Anti-avoidance measures against cascading royalties of this nature are beginning to be applied, for example, by the IRS in the United States with wide-ranging anti-avoidance measures in the American/Dutch anti-avoidance treaty. Indeed the US/UK treaty contains such provisions. Further, since Cyprus joined the European Union on May 1, 2004, royalties may be passed directly from the United Kingdom to a Cyprus company owing to the application of the EU Directive on Interest and Royalties 2003/49/EC, provided that shareholding requirements are satisfied.

However, it may be worth considering using an independently owned Cyprus resident company which does have treaty protection. Although the profits would be liable to tax in Cyprus only the net profit after paying any outgoing royalties would be subject to tax in Cyprus. There is no Cyprus withholding tax on outgoing royalty payments (unless the asset for which the royalties are paid is used in Cyprus, in which case withholding tax applies) and the only anti-avoidance restriction in the UK/Cyprus double tax treaty is that the rate of royalties must be commercially justifiable. Therefore a structure might consist of a Jersey trust owning a British Virgin Islands company which owns the intellectual property rights and licenses these to the independently owned Cyprus resident company. This is a contractual arrangement which ensures receipt of the royalties from the Cyprus company at an appropriate level say 96 per cent of the royalties received by the Cyprus company from the licensee. This would be on a contractual basis, and therefore not dependent on the ownership of the Cyprus company. Apparently the Cyprus tax authorities will not provide pre-approvals on royalty spreads, and *Indofood International Finance Ltd v JP Morgan Chase Bank NA London Branch* [2006] S.T.C. 1195, has cast doubt on such structure, although they seem to continue to work in practice, and were upheld in *Prevost Car Inc v The Queen* [2008] T.C.C. 231, a Canadian case.

24–020 The United Kingdom itself may be used in this fashion and if it is an independently owned company which is contractually in receipt of royalties from, say, Russia and is contractually paying out royalties to some other country, say, the Bahamas both of which are independently owned, the UK company should only be subject to UK tax on the royalty spread. The United Kingdom would not charge withholding taxes on intellectual property that did not have a UK source; in other words non-UK patents and royalties from the exploitation outside the United Kingdom of material which is subject to copyright outside the United Kingdom. It is normally preferable in such circumstances to have the royalties paid into an overseas bank account and paid to the head licensor in the tax haven to emphasise the non-UK source of the income. Provided that the company is still managed and controlled from the United Kingdom, it should be eligible for the UK treaty network protection. There may be anti-avoidance provisions where the royalties emanate from, say, Germany under their legislation and it is obviously important in any form of international tax planning to take account of the liabilities and withholding tax requirement of each jurisdiction involved even though they may, like US secondary withholding tax, be difficult to enforce against a foreign company. Obviously the proper law of the licensing agreement in such circumstances should not be that of the United Kingdom.

The Republic of Ireland is also a popular venue for intermediary licensing companies as many of the Irish double tax treaties do not have limitation of benefit clauses. A combination of routing from the final licensee through an Irish company, then on to a Cyprus offshore company and finally through to the tax haven based head licensor can be worth looking at. All companies resident in Cyprus (both onshore and offshore) are subject to Cypriot corporate income tax at the rate of 12.5 per cent. Hungary has also been a popular venue for an intermediary licensing company as it is normally only necessary to leave a small spread of royalties of, say, 5 per cent which in turn are only subject to a 19 per cent rate of tax. It is important to look carefully at the treaties; for example, the Hungarian/Japanese treaty reduces the standard rate of Japanese withholding tax from 20 per cent to 10 per cent except for cultural royalties which are exempt, and include literary, artistic or scientific works, including films or tapes for cinema, television or radio.

The licensing agreement may be for a period that is much shorter than the commercial life of the intellectual property and it may be useful, for example, for the tax haven licensor to sell to the Dutch intermediary company the right to exploit the intellectual property for a period of, say, five years for a capital sum. The independently owned Dutch company will have taken into account in fixing the price to be paid the fact that the royalty income will be subject to Dutch tax but that Dutch fiscal law allows for the acquisition costs to be depreciated over the life of the licence. If this were, for example, a five-year licence, 20 per cent per annum of the original cost would be allowed as a depreciation allowance against the royalties receivable by the Dutch company. This would reduce the Dutch tax to negligible proportions. The lump sum would have been paid without any withholding tax as the Netherlands does not levy a withholding tax on intellectual property payments. This can be a useful mechanism where the royalty stream can be estimated with a reasonable degree of accuracy under the contract and it should prevent many of the anti-avoidance provisions being applied because the Dutch company is the true beneficial owner of the royalty stream by virtue of its licence and does not pay out any further royalties, merely the lump sum for the acquisition of the royalties in the first instance which may, in appropriate cases, be payable by instalments.

The Netherlands also has an "Innovation Box" regime with a 5 per cent tax rate to stimulate research and development in the country, which may be attractive in some cases.

Any treaty shopping has to take account of anti-avoidance provisions such as those relating to controlled foreign companies (Ch.14), transfer pricing (Ch.13) and offshore trust rules referred to below.

Switzerland, under a decree of the Federal Council in 1962, as amended in 1999 and 2001, may limit the rights to Swiss double tax treaty protection where Switzerland is used merely as a conduit. It only charges federal tax on intellectual property held by a domiciliary company after notional expenses at a rate of 8.5 per cent (as this tax is deductible the effective burden is 7.8 per cent) on say 50 per cent of the income is normally acceptable. However, the Swiss also require passive profits of this nature to be distributed by way of dividend of at least 25 per cent of the income received which is then subject to a hefty 35 per cent Swiss withholding tax. A solution may be a Swiss resident branch of a Luxembourg company which will qualify for the Luxembourg double tax treaty protection and would not be subject to tax in Luxembourg as it was subject to tax in Switzerland at an effective rate of less than 5 per cent and would accrue to the Swiss company as of a right as income of the branch, not by way of dividend.

FILM DISTRIBUTION AGREEMENTS

24–022 Although the United Kingdom does not levy a withholding tax on film distribution royalties many other countries do. Films can be extremely expensive to make and co-productions are common. It is possible to have a straightforward co-production between companies in two different countries where each is entitled to a proportion of the receipts throughout the world and each party has to consider the withholding taxes likely to be levied on their own share of the income. A more tax efficient structure is very often a split rights deal in which, for example, overseas distributors acquire the foreign rights of a US film and contribute to the original cost in return for a share of the eventual profit. In these deals each distributor will recover his own costs in the first instance out of the royalties receivable which would reimburse, the original investment, and as each distributor goes into profit he will start paying royalties to the other co-distributors which may be subject to withholding taxes. In such circumstances a jointly owned distribution company in a suitable intermediary licensing country such as the United Kingdom, Ireland, Netherlands or Hungary could be used to reduce the withholding taxes to a minimum. In large co-productions there may be several such intermediary distribution companies covering different territories and taking advantage of their double taxation treaty network. There may also be a general sales company covering those countries where distributors do not participate in the equity of the film.

These joint distribution agreements often require the use of an independent collection account manager to collect the receipts and make the appropriate payments under the agreements. The Netherlands is often used as the jurisdiction of the collection account manager.

AUTHORS

24–023 One of the advantages of copyright is that, at least under UK law, it can be transferred before the work to which it relates has been written, and therefore before it has acquired any significant value. One of the major problems of exploiting intellectual property is ensuring that it ends up legitimately in a suitable low-tax jurisdiction without incurring an enormous tax charge in transferring it to the offshore licensor. In the case of an author it may be appropriate to contract with a company in say Malta owned by a tax haven company, in turn owned by an offshore trust, to write a book in return for a salary to be paid by the Maltese company which would be entitled to the royalties on the eventual sale of the book. As long as the salary was reasonable the author should not become a deemed additional settlor of the trust as in *Crossland v Hawkins* (1961) 39 T.C. 493 or *Mills v IRC* (1974) S.T.C. 130. The rate of tax on profits left in the Maltese company would be 35 per cent but as it is an imputation system five-sevenths of this tax is recoverable on payment of a dividend to the trust leaving an effective rate of 10 per cent.

A variation on this theme is the use of two companies where, for example, the employment agreement is with an offshore Cyprus company which in turn licenses through a suitable treaty country such as the Republic of Ireland to the UK. The UK/Ireland treaty has no limitation of benefits clause and the Irish company would contractually pay say 98 per cent of the royalties received to the Cyprus company and the Cyprus company would be taxable on 12.5 per cent of its profits after deduction of the salary paid to the author.

There are a number of other suitable combinations such as UK/Austria, Cyprus/Norway, Cyprus/UK, Denmark/Cyprus.

DIVIDEND ROUTING

Instead of extracting royalties by way of sub-royalties through to a tax haven parent, it may be possible to take advantage of the European Community Parent/Subsidiary Directive 90/435/EC, to extract profits by way of dividend eventually routed to a tax haven parent. It seems that Gibraltar, although in the European Community, may be covered by the Directive but not all EU states accept this view. Madeira, being part of Portugal, is covered by the Directive provided that the parent based there has a Portuguese tax liability, for example from a branch in Lisbon. In such cases it may be possible to have the Madeira company owning a Dutch subsidiary holding company through which royalties are licensed and to pay the royalty up to Madeira and then extract it by way of a dividend through to a tax haven parent company as Madeira companies are not subject to a dividend withholding tax. Rather than paying royalties from the Dutch company to the Madeira company, relying on the lack of Dutch withholding tax on royalties, it may be better to pay by way of dividend in respect of which there should be no withholding tax under the directive, provided that the minimum shareholding is at least 25 per cent of the capital of the company paying the dividend.

24–024

LOAN ROUTING

24–025 A further alternative to royalties routing would be to extract profits from a royalty receiving company by financing it with loans from a tax haven-based finance company funded by means of equity participation. The loan interest, at a proper commercial rate, should be allowed as a deduction from the royalties received. The extent to which this method may be employed may be circumscribed by thin capitalisation or debt/equity rules in the interest paying country. The impact of withholding tax on interest must also be considered. The finance company must serve a proper commercial purpose (*Overseas Containers (Finance) Ltd v Stoker* [1989] S.T.C. 364).

TAX HAVENS

24–026 The choice of the appropriate tax haven will be dependent upon the countries of residence of the licensor and licensee. A route which reduces the rate of withholding taxes to an acceptable level may involve the use of an intermediate licensing company in, e.g. the Netherlands.

It is necessary also to ensure that the tax haven allows the tax-free, or low-tax accumulation of income, and taxes royalties at a low rate if at all. The country must be politically and economically stable and impose no exchange control restrictions on the movement of funds. It must have efficient banking, legal and accounting systems and have good communications. It will be necessary to show that the company is genuinely managed and controlled in the tax haven and is not a mere post box.

There may be tax charges on the existing holder of intellectual property transferring the property to the tax haven and there could be exchange control difficulties. It may be necessary to ensure that the transfer is at full market value. It will be necessary to ensure that the proposed route does not result in the royalties paid ceasing to be deductible by the licensee.

The intermediate licensing company requires a tax treaty which can be used (Switzerland, for example, by the decree of Federal Council in 1962, severely restricts the use of a Swiss company in such a manner). The treaty or national laws should also avoid the imposition of withholding taxes on royalties and dividends to be paid to the tax haven and should not require too high a proportion of royalties received to be retained in the intermediate company.

Switzerland

24–027 Switzerland may be considered as a suitable venue for a domiciliary company to hold intellectual property as it would enjoy a privileged tax treatment at cantonal level or may even be exempt from cantonal and municipal income taxes and the rate of federal income tax is a flat 8.5 per cent (as this tax is deductible the effective burden is 7.8 per cent). There are also small cantonal net worth taxes, which are all deductible for federal income tax purposes.

Switzerland has a fairly wide range of treaties but France, Belgium and Italy do not reduce their withholding taxes for a Swiss domiciliary company. The 1962 decree of the Federal Council requires the Swiss company to distribute to shareholders as a dividend at least 25 per cent of passive income received, subject to treaty relief, which then becomes subject to a Swiss anticipatory tax of 35 per cent and provides that the Swiss company must not pay more than 50 per cent of such income to its parent company as interest or royalties. Interest-bearing loans may not exceed six times the Swiss company's capital and reserves (as per the treaties, for the rest, the domestic thin capitalisation rules apply).

As a result of these restrictions Switzerland is not usually a suitable place for an intermediate licensing company but may be a very useful centre for the receipt of know-how and show-how fees for services performed outside Switzerland. A Swiss branch of a Dutch company can sometimes be useful for non-financial companies and a Swiss investment and service company may be worth considering in certain cases. Switzerland is also a suitable place for a company holding portfolio investments in quoted companies.

Liechtenstein

Holding and domiciliary companies and establishments (*anstalts*) are exempt from corporate income tax if they are not commercially active and limit their activities to the passive collection of income from holding and managing investments, and are subject to a an alternative Minimum Tax of SF 1,200 p.a. from January 1, 2011. There is no charge to tax on a capital gain on the disposal of intellectual property. There is a dividend and interest withholding tax of 4 per cent which does not apply to *anstalts*. There are no exchange control problems. As Liechtenstein has double tax treaties with only a handful of territories (Austria, Germany, Hong Kong, Luxembourg, San Marino, UK and Uruguay) it is of no use for intermediate licensing companies but could be used as an ultimate holder of intellectual property. An *anstalt* which is permitted to undertake business activities is characterised as a company for UK tax purposes under Appendix A of the second joint declaration of Liechtenstein and HMRC of September 2010. Under the Tax Act 2010 the rate of corporation tax for domestic companies was fixed as 12.5 per cent subject to a minimum corporate income tax of CHF 1,200 (which does not apply to small commercial entities).

24–028

Luxembourg

Luxembourg has double taxation treaties with more than 60 countries, several of which have a zero rate of tax on royalties, including France, Ireland, Netherlands, Norway, Russia, South Africa, and with anti-treaty shopping provisions, USA. The rate of tax to the UK and Germany is 5 per cent. The country would therefore be a contender for the intermediate holder of intellectual property. A *société de participation financère* (commonly referred to as a SOPARFI) qualifies for treaty relief and a participation privilege on dividends like a Dutch holding company. There are no exchange control difficulties, or controlled foreign company rules but there are anti-abuse and OECD style transfer pricing rules.

A SOPARFI is an ordinary Luxembourg company, SA or SARL, or limited partnership, SCA. It is subject to the standard tax regime at a combined rate of 29.22 per cent subject to a minimum tax of €3,210, including the 7 per cent

24–029

solidarity surcharge. It is however exempt from tax on dividends received where at least 10 per cent of the shares are held, and valued at at least €1.2 million. Where the participation exemption does not apply, a 50 per cent of dividends may be exempt from EU subsidiaries or treaty countries. The withholding tax on dividends paid is 15 per cent, subject to treaty relief. There is no withholding tax on interest or most royalty payments and there are no thin capitalisation rules. A SOPARFI is subject to a 0.5 per cent annual net worth tax. Capital gains on the sale of shares in a SOPARFI or on liquidation are normally tax exempt for non-resident shareholders.

Isle of Man and Channel Islands

24–030 The absence of suitable double tax treaties means that companies situated here are best used as ultimate holders of intellectual property. The standard rate of tax in the islands is 0 per cent, except for, "financial institutions" where the rate is 10 per cent. There are minor exceptions and differences among the islands' tax systems.

Republic of Ireland

24–031 Residents in the Republic of Ireland are, from November 24, 2010, no longer exempt from Irish tax on patent royalties for patents devised therein, under the Taxes Consolidation Act 1997. Individuals solely resident in the Republic are exempt from Irish tax, in respect of the first €40,000 of earnings from works of cultural or artistic merit such as books, plays, music, paintings and sculpture. International Financial Service Centres in Dublin were subject to tax at only 10 per cent until 2005 but cannot hold most forms of intellectual property except for certain computer software. From January 1, 2003 the Irish corporate tax rate on trading income was reduced to just 12.5 per cent, although a 25 per cent rate applies to passive income such as holding intellectual property. It is likely that in certain circumstances the Republic of Ireland may be usefully considered in international intellectual property licensing scenarios, in view of a 25 per cent research and development tax credit in addition to a basic 12.5 per cent rate deduction which can be converted into a payable credit of 33 per cent.

Other havens

24–032 There are many other areas of the world which could be used in appropriate circumstances. In some cases Denmark may be used instead of the Netherlands for an intermediate licensing company. The United Kingdom was for a time used for this purpose with the licence holder in Cyprus but the double tax treaty was modified to prevent Cyprus being used as a tax haven with the benefit of treaty relief with the United Kingdom although now that Cyprus no longer has a special rate for offshore companies this should no longer be a problem. The Maltese tax system has been approved by the European Union. There are no withholding taxes on dividends, interest or royalties and the corporation tax payable on profits is recoverable by the shareholders when distributed to non Maltese residents, in whole or part depending on the nature of the income, resulting in an effective 10 per cent rate on intellectual property royalties.

TRANSFERS OF ASSETS ABROAD

A further hurdle to be overcome for a UK taxpayer other than a quoted public company, are the provisions of ITA 2007 ss.714–751. These provisions contain widely drawn anti-avoidance rules to prevent ordinarily resident individuals avoiding income tax by transferring assets to non-residents. The provisions apply where there has been a relevant transfer of assets (as defined in ITA 2007 s.716) anywhere in the world at any time and as a result income is received, directly or indirectly, by a non-resident or non-domiciled individual, company or trust for the direct or indirect benefit now or in the future of an individual ordinarily resident in the United Kingdom. The transfer may or may not be in conjunction with associated operations as defined in ITA 2007 s.719. A transfer of assets by a company not controlled by the taxpayers was not within this section in *IRC v Pratt* [1982] S.T.C. 756. The transfer may have been made before the individual became resident, ITA 2007 ss.721(5) and 728(3), overturning *IRC v Willoughby* [1995] S.T.C. 143.

24–033

HMRC are empowered to apportion income of the overseas person to the UK resident transferor (or spouse, or from December 5, 2005, civil partner) if he is able to enjoy income as defined in ITA 2007 s.722, and tax is assessed under ITTOIA 2005 Pt 5 Ch.8.

The section does not apply directly to companies, but it is possible to trace a benefit through a company or a trust, although in practice HMRC would not attempt to apportion income to the shareholders of quoted companies. It is also important to ensure that a beneficiary of the trust is not an additional settlor under the decision in *Mills v IRC* [1974] S.T.C. 130 and *Crossland v Hawkins* (1961) 39 T.C. 493, and that the trust is not liable to challenge as a sham. The section does not apply to the extent that income is apportioned under the "controlled foreign companies provisions" (see ITA 2007 s.725).

A UK resident does not have to receive income; a capital sum, which includes a loan or repayment of a loan (other than one wholly repaid before the beginning of the year in which it would be charged) is also caught. A capital sum also includes an amount received by a third person (including jointly with another) by direction or assignment and which would otherwise not constitute a capital sum. There was an escape route under ITA 2007 ss.735–742, which prior to December 5, 2005, disapplied the transfer of assets abroad provisions in the case of bona fide commercial transactions not designed for the purpose of avoiding taxation or where the avoiding of taxation was not one of the purposes of the transaction. This motive defence was substantially altered with effect from December 5, 2005, and where both the relevant transfer and all associated operations (together referred to as "relevant transactions" (ITA 2007 s.715) take place after that date, the two alternative escape clauses require the taxpayer to demonstrate either that it would not be reasonable to conclude from all the circumstances of the case, that the relevant transactions were effected for the purposes of avoiding liability to taxation, or that all the relevant transactions were genuine commercial

24–034

transactions and it would not be reasonable to conclude that any one or more of those transactions was more than incidentally designed to avoid liability to taxation. The meaning of "commercial transaction" in this context is set out in ITA 2007 s.738, and excludes the making or managing of investments except to the extent that the parties concerned are not connected and are acting at arm's length. Where there are both pre and post-December 5, 2005 transactions, such as where the original transfer took place prior to that date but there is one or more associated operations after December 5, 2005, the relevant motive defence applicable to each transfer or associated operation must be satisfied in order for the exemption to operate.

Cases under these provisions include: *Aykroyd v IRC* (1942) 24 T.C. 515; *Beatty v IRC* (1940) 23 T.C. 574; *Beatty's (Admiral Lord) Executors v IRC* (1940) 23 T.C. 574; *Cottingham's Executors v IRC* (1938) 22 T.C. 344; *Lee v IRC* (1941) 24 T.C. 207; *Latilla v IRC* (1943) 25 T.C. 107; *Howard de Walden (Lord) v IRC* (1941) 25 T.C. 121; *Ramsden v IRC* 37 T.C. 619; *Corbett's Executrices v IRC* (1943) 25 T.C. 305; *Sassoon v IRC* (1943) 25 T.C. 154; *Philippi v IRC* (1971) 47 T.C. 75; and *Lord Chetwode v IRC* [1977] S.T.C. 64.

Leading cases relating to the wide ambit of this section are: *Vestey's Exors v IRC, and v Colquhoun* (1949) 31 T.C. 1; *Fynn v IRC* (1957) 37 T.C. 629; *Vestey v IRC (Nos 1 and 2)* [1980] S.T.C. 10, which overruled *Bambridge v IRC* (1955) 36 T.C. 313; and *Congreve v IRC* (1948) 30 T.C. 163. *IRC v Schroder* [1983] S.T.C. 480 confirmed that the ability to appoint trustees may not mean control over the income.

24-035   In *Rahman v Chase Bank (CI) Ltd* (Royal Court of Jersey, February 12, 1990) a widow brought a case attacking her deceased husband's trust on a number of grounds. One of these was that the powers retained by the settlor were so substantial that they breached the Jersey maxim of *"Donner et Retenir ne Vaut"*, freely translated being "to give and to retain is worth nothing". Interestingly, although the judge held that the trust was in fact in breach of this particular maxim, he also held that the trust was a sham in that:

1. The trustee did not seek remittance of the entire initial trust fund.
2. Under the trust deed, responsibility for investment policy lay with the trustees. However, the trustee never exercised that responsibility; rather the trustee left such matters wholly to the settlor who dealt exclusively with a named investment adviser.
3. The settlor unilaterally changed the investment adviser and negotiated the investment adviser's fees on behalf of the trustee.
4. On several occasions funds which had been assigned by the settlor to the trust were diverted by the settlor and used for his own purposes.
5. All payments out of the trust were made upon the settlor's instructions.
6. The trustee acted upon the instructions of the settlor without considering its fiduciary responsibilities.
7. The settlor retained the power to sign on trust accounts opened by the trustees with Geneva banks.

This is obviously an extreme case but it does serve to emphasise that the position of trustees is an onerous one and has to be taken seriously. Settlors are sometimes very domineering individuals and like to have their own way, but the trustee who allows that situation to develop is likely to face an expensive claim at the end of the day. The *Rahman* case merely emphasises the earlier decision of *Bartlett v Barclays Bank Trust Co Ltd* [1980] 1 All E.R. 139, in which Barclays were held responsible for a loss made by an underlying company owned by the trust, and the court held that they should have exercised their powers to control the situation and prevent losses being made by the underlying company. Trustees have to take a positive control over the trust for which they are responsible and a policy of merely honest inactivity is not good enough.

Liability of non-transferors

The provisions of ITA 2007 ss.731–735, are a consequence of the House of Lords' decision in *Vestey v IRC (Nos 1 and 2)* [1980] S.T.C. 10. Under that decision it was confirmed that the rules under TA 1988 s.739 (now ITA 2007 s.720) charged to tax those who took part in transfers of assets abroad together with their spouses but did not apply to others who received benefits as a result of those transactions. This section applies in respect of benefits received and relevant income arising after March 9, 1981, but irrespective of when the transfer or any associated operations took place. **24–036**

The provisions of ITA 2007 ss.731–735, complement ITA 2007 s.720, to catch the recipients of such arrangements and has effect where, as a result of a relevant transfer either alone or in conjunction with associated operations, income becomes payable to a person who is not resident or domiciled in the UK and an individual who is ordinarily resident in the United Kingdom and who is not caught by ITA 2007 s.720 itself (i.e. is not the transferor or his spouse or civil partner) receives a benefit (not otherwise taxable) from those assets which are available for the purpose. The benefit which falls within the "available relevant income" of the tax years up to and including that in which the benefit is received is treated as the income of the individual for the year of the receipt, or, to the extent to which the benefit has exceeded that relevant income, it will be treated as the recipient's income to the extent that it is within the amount of relevant income for the next following tax year, and so on. This provision prevents a benefit being arranged in anticipation of future income arising as a consequence of the transfer of assets abroad, and a further consequence is that payments cannot be made out of accumulated income of a trust whilst relevant income arises to the trust.

The steps for computing "available relevant income" are set out in ITA 2007 s.733(1). Broadly, this comprises any income arising in the year to someone who is resident or domiciled outside the United Kingdom and which in consequence of the transfer or the associated operations (as defined in ITA 2007 s.719) can be directly or indirectly used for providing a benefit to an individual or for enabling a benefit to be provided to him, and which has not been treated as arising to the individual in a previous tax year.

Income taxable under these provisions will be charged under ITTOIA 2005 Pt 5 Ch.8, and thereby will be treated as unearned income. **24–037**

These provisions do not apply to a non-UK domiciled individual, electing for the remittance basis, whether resident in this country or not, in respect of benefits received which are not brought into the United Kingdom. In the case of a non-UK domiciled individual who is ordinarily resident in this country the application of any benefit arising to him in the form of income from possessions outside the United Kingdom towards paying off a debt for money lent in or effectively received in the United Kingdom, will be subject to tax under ITTOIA 2005 Pt 5 Ch.8, on the deemed remittance (ITTOIA 2005 ss.832–832B) and will not be exempt from income tax under the foregoing provisions.

The provisions of ITA 2007 ss.731–735 will not apply where the conditions for exemption under the motive test are met in relation to the relevant transactions.

24–038 If any benefit has already been charged as a capital payment under TCGA 1992 s.87, the amount so charged reduces the income chargeable under ITA 2007 ss.731–735 as a result of ITA 2007 s.734, to prevent a double charge.

Exemption from a charge under ITA 2007 ss.714–735, is available if the individual can demonstrate to HMRC (in writing or otherwise) that, in the case of relevant transactions taking place prior to December 5, 2005 the transfer of assets and associated operations were for purposes other than tax avoidance, or were bona fide commercial transactions not designed to avoid tax, or in the case of relevant transactions taking place after that date, it would not be reasonable to conclude from all the circumstances of the case, that the relevant transactions were effected for the purposes of avoiding liability to taxation, or alternatively that all the relevant transactions were genuine commercial transactions and it would not be reasonable to conclude that any one or more of those transactions was more than incidentally designed to avoid liability to taxation. Commercial motives were established in *Clark v IRC* [1978] S.T.C. 614 and *IRC v Kleinwort, Benson Ltd* (1969) 45 T.C. 369 (TA 1988 s.741).

"Associated operation" for the purposes of the transfer of assets abroad provisions and "power to enjoy income" (for the purposes of the charge on the transferor under ITA 2007 s.720 only) are defined by ITA 2007 ss.719 and 722–723 respectively. "Assets" are defined in ITA 2007. The term "benefit" covers a payment of any kind, and encompasses not only benefits paid directly out of the income of the person abroad, but also out of the proceeds of dealing with that income, if that dealing amounts to an associated operation. References to an individual includes a spouse or, after December 5, 2005, a civil partner (ITA 2007 s.714(4)). The provisions of the sections are extended to the amount that would have been caught in the hands of a non-resident or non-domiciled person by the accrued income provisions of ITA 2007 s.747, as though it were "income payable" to such person.

24–039 Bodies incorporated outside the United Kingdom, or resident outside the United Kingdom under a double taxation agreement, have been treated as non-resident even if otherwise resident (ITA 2007 s.718) but this is being repealed through amendments in Schedule 10 FA 2013 from April 6, 2012 such that no companies treated as resident in the UK for corporation tax purposes will be treated as a "person abroad" for these purposes.

If income assessed under ITA 2007 ss.714–735, has already borne UK tax at the basic rate, for example as an annual payment made to a non-resident, the charge will be limited to the higher rates. Tax is charged under the provisions of ITA 2007 s.3, and the recipient will qualify for the same reliefs as would have

CHANGES IN THE TRANSFER OF ASSETS ABROAD RULES—FA 2013

been available if the income had actually been received by him. If the income is subsequently received it is ignored for income tax purposes so there is no double charge to UK tax (ITA 2007 s.745).

The recipient of a benefit giving rise to a charge under ITA 2007 s.724, is taxed in the year in which the benefit is received.

A non-UK domiciled individual is not chargeable to tax under ITA 2007 s.720, where, if the income had in fact been his income, he would not have been taxed on it by virtue his non-domiciled status (ITA 2007 s.726). This effectively preserves the remittance basis where the remittance basic charge, if applicable, is paid, by non-domiciled individuals assessed under ITA 2007 s.720. Similar provision is made where a non-UK domiciled individual receives a capital sum (defined in ITA 2007 s.729) which would otherwise give rise to an income tax charge under ITA 2007 s.727 (ITA 2007 s.730). 24–040

No amount of income is to be taken into account more than once in charging tax under the provisions of ITA 2007 ss.715–735. An officer of HMRC may choose who is chargeable where the choice exists and apportion income in a just and reasonable way. Such a decision may be reviewable by the First Tier Tribunal on an appeal against an assessment (ITA 2007 ss.743, 751).

Power to obtain information

HMRC has power under ITA 2007 s.748, to serve a notice in writing on any person to furnish them with such particulars as they think necessary for the purposes of deciding whether there is a charge under ITA 2007 ss.714–735, whether or not in the opinion of the person receiving the notice any liability arises. A solicitor is compelled to give only the name and address of his client and of the transferees, transferors, non-trading companies incorporated or resident outside the United Kingdom, or resident outside the United Kingdom under a double taxation agreement, which would be close companies if in the United Kingdom, or settlors in the transactions covered by the notice (ITA 2007 s.749). 24–041

Banks do not have to furnish particulars of ordinary banking transactions unless acting for the same customer in the formation of non-resident companies (with a similar exclusion for trading and non-close companies) or trusts, etc. (ITA 2007 s.750).

Nevertheless the provisions of this section are extremely wide and attempts to resist such notices were defeated in *Royal Bank of Canada v IRC* (1971) 47 T.C. 565; *Clinch v IRC* (1973) 49 T.C. 52; and *Mankowitz v Special Commissioners* (1971) 46 T.C. 707 (ITA 2007 ss.748–750).

CHANGES IN THE TRANSFER OF ASSETS ABROAD RULES—FA 2013

A package of measures was introduced through FA 2013 Sch.10 to modernise the transfer of assets abroad rules. The changes are mainly in response to an infraction noticed issued by the European Commission on February 16, 2011 arguing that the legislation breaches the EU treaty freedom of establishment and 24–042 movement of capital. The Government is also taking the opportunity to make further changes to improve the clarity of the rules.

The main change is the introduction of a new exemption which focuses on whether the nature of the transaction concerned is a genuine one (having regard to the circumstances under which it was effected and any other relevant circumstances) which, if it were to give rise to a transfer of assets charge, would be an unjustified and disproportionate restriction on an EU treaty freedom. A transaction is not to be considered to be a genuine one if it is made other than on arm's length terms. Where the assets being transferred are to be used for the purposes of, or received in the course of, activities carried out in a territory outside the UK, by a person with a business establishment in that territory, those activities must consist of the provision of goods and services to others on a commercial basis. Those activities must also involve the following:

- the use of sufficient staff with the appropriate level of competence and authority to carry them out;
- the use of premises and equipment commensurate with the size and nature of the activities; and
- the person who has the business establishment adding a commensurate level of economic value to the customers to whom the goods and services are provided.

This new exemption applies to transactions which meet all the above conditions and which take place on or after April 6, 2012. There is also a provision which allows for the bifurcation of a relevant transaction into a part which is genuine and a part which is artificial, so that the transfer of assets tax charge only falls on income from the artificial part of the transaction.

Other changes include amendments to the rules where assets are transferred to UK resident but foreign incorporated companies (referred to at para.24–040, above) and clarification that if the individual subject to the charge has already paid income tax on the deemed income then he or she will not suffer a further charge under these rules. It is questionable whether these changes are sufficient to make these rules EU compliant.

GAINS OF NON-RESIDENT SETTLEMENTS

24–043 Gains of non-resident trustees are allocated to beneficiaries in accordance with TCGA 1992 s.87.

It is first necessary to calculate the capital gains made by the trustees as if they were resident in the United Kingdom. The gains are calculated on a cumulative basis from April 6, 1981 and the total, less any amount already treated as a gain of the beneficiaries either under this section or TCGA 1992 s.89 (migrant settlements), is regarded as the trust gain for the year and is apportioned to beneficiaries in proportion to any capital sums they have received from the trust since March 10, 1981, except to the extent that it has been taken into account in allocating previous capital gains among beneficiaries. Gains chargeable on the settlor under TCGA 1992 s.86 and Sch.5 are excluded.

GAINS OF NON-RESIDENT SETTLEMENTS

The gain apportioned to a beneficiary cannot exceed the capital distribution to him. Gains apportioned to a non-UK domiciled beneficiary were not taxed for 2007/08 and earlier years, however, for 2008/09 and later years the exemption from charge for non-UK domiciliaries is removed. A non-UK domiciled but resident or ordinarily resident beneficiary of an offshore trust will be taxed on gains apportioned to him under TCGA 1992 s.87, although the remittance basis will apply if the individual has made a claim to be taxed on that basis under ITA 2007 s.809B, or the remittance basis applies automatically (ITA 2007 ss.809C, 809D). This is the case even if the asset giving rise to the capital gain is situated in the United Kingdom. Trustees may make a re-basing election for all capital assets to be treated as sold and reacquired at their open market values on April 5, 2008 for the purposes of computing the chargeable gains to be matched with capital payments after that date (TCGA 1992 s.91). The effect of the election, which is irrevocable, is to ensure that where an asset is sold after April 6, 2008, only the post-April 6, 2008 element of the gain is apportioned to non-UK domiciled beneficiaries in receipt of capital payments in 2008/09 and later years.

The trustees of a dual resident settlement who are treated as resident both in the United Kingdom and in some other territory giving rise to relief under a double tax treaty are within the non-resident settlement provisions of TCGA 1992 s.87, as if the settlement were non-resident, by virtue of TCGA 1992 s.88. **24–044**

If a UK resident settlement becomes non-resident or dual resident for a year or more any capital payments to beneficiaries in the resident period are disregarded unless made in anticipation of a disposal by the trustees in the non-resident or treaty-protected period under TCGA 1992 s.89.

If a trust is thereafter repatriated to the United Kingdom any trust gains in the non-resident or treaty-protected period which have not been apportioned to beneficiaries will be chargeable to them in proportion to capital payments subsequently received by them subject to the limitation of the gain not exceeding the amount of the capital payment.

There is an anti-avoidance provision to prevent the non-resident trust provisions in TCGA 1992 ss.87 and 89, being circumvented by transferring assets between trusts. The provisions do not apply so far as the transfer is made for consideration in money or money's worth under TCGA 1992 s.90.

Supplementary charge

The provisions of TCGA 1992 s.91 include a supplementary charge for beneficiaries of non-resident settlements who receive capital payments made on or after April 6, 1991 from the trustees or who are beneficiaries of dual resident trusts, unless the beneficiary is non-resident. **24–045**

Where a capital payment is matched with a chargeable gain which arose before the immediately preceding year of assessment, the tax payable is increased at the rate of 10 per cent a year as if it were interest. Notional interest is therefore calculated on the period from December 1 in the tax year following that in which the gain arises to November 30 in the tax year following that in which the capital payment is made, subject to a maximum of six years. The minimum period is two years, so the minimum charge is 20 per cent of the capital gains tax. As gains arising in 1990/91 or earlier are all allocated to 1990/91 the notional interest charge arises if such gains were not distributed to beneficiaries by April 5, 1992.

The tax and notional interest cannot exceed the amount of the capital payment and the rate of interest may be varied by Treasury order. The maximum charge is 28.8 per cent following the introduction of the 18 per cent capital gains tax rate for 2008/09 and up to 44.8 per cent when the maximum rate of capital gains tax was increased to 28 per cent from June 23, 2010. For 2007/08 and earlier years where the rate of capital gains tax was up to 40 per cent, the effective maximum charge was 64 per cent.

Payments by and to companies

24–046 Capital payments received from a qualifying company controlled by the trustees are taxed as if received from the trustees as are payments received by non-resident qualifying companies. A receipt by a non-resident company controlled by a UK resident is treated as capital payment received by him. If the company is controlled by two or more persons, taking each one separately, the capital payment is apportioned equally to as many UK residents as control the company under TCGA 1992 s.96.

If the company is controlled by two or more persons together, the capital payment is apportioned among the participators on a just and reasonable basis, but a participator receiving less than one twentieth of the payment actually received by the company is ignored. A qualifying company is a close company or would be if it were resident in the United Kingdom, and is controlled by the trustees if it is controlled by them under CTA 2010 ss.450 and 451 (close company control by reference to capital, income or assets). For this purpose it is possible to include with the trustees the settlor or a person connected with him. These provisions apply to capital payments received on or after March 19, 1991.

Capital payment is defined as any payment made otherwise than as income and includes a transfer to bare trustees and indirect payments. Although a loan is a capital payment it is regarded as such only to the extent that benefit is conferred thereby. A loan on normal commercial terms would not give rise to a capital gains tax charge as arm's length transactions are specifically excluded from the definition of capital payments. HMRC regard the rent-free occupation of property owned by the settlement by a beneficiary as a capital payment within TCGA 1992 s.97(1).

24–047 Capital payments received from trustees include those received indirectly under TCGA 1992 s.96, unless they are already treated as being received by a beneficiary, i.e. the recipient becomes a deemed beneficiary but not so as to treat the trustees themselves as beneficiaries on appointments or advances. The very wide information gathering provisions of ITA 2007 ss.748–750 are extended to non-resident and repatriated trusts by virtue of TCGA 1992 s.98.

Gains accruing to a non-resident company may be apportioned under TCGA 1992 s.13, to UK resident shareholders, who are thereby treated as having a proportion of the gain accruing to them under TCGA 1992 s.13(10) if they hold more than 25 per cent of the shares, from April 6, 2012, previously 10 per cent, under TCGA 1992 s.13(4), FA 2013 s.61, or are relieved from charge under s.13(5) and s.13A. From April 6, 2008, non-UK domiciled shareholders are brought within the scope of TCGA 1992 s.13, having previously been excepted from a charge under this section. Gains on foreign assets apportioned to non-domiciled UK resident shareholders will be taxed only on amounts remitted to the United Kingdom where the remittance basis applies.

A disposal of an interest in settled property is not exempt under TCGA 1992 s.76, if the trustees are non-resident unless the disponor thereby becomes absolutely entitled as against the trustees, in which case there would already be a capital gains tax charge by the combination of TCGA 1992 ss.71(1) and 87.

Trustees ceasing to be resident in United Kingdom

If trustees become neither resident nor ordinarily resident in the UK on or after March 19, 1991, and as a result cease to be within the capital gains tax charge, they are deemed to have disposed of the trust assets and immediately reacquired them at their market value at that time (TCGA 1992 s.80). See *Re Weston's Settlement* (1968) 47 A.T.C. 324 on the emigration of a trust. This exit charge may be challenged following the CJEC judgment in *De Lasteyrie du Saillant v Ministere de l'Economie, des Finances et de l'Industrie* (2004) SWTI 890.

24–048

This exit charge excludes assets used in a trade carried on in the United Kingdom through a branch or agency, which are already subject to capital gains tax under TCGA 1992 s.10. It similarly excludes assets specified in a double taxation agreement which would not have been liable to UK capital gains tax if the assets had been sold before the trustees ceased to be resident in the United Kingdom. Roll-over relief under TCGA 1992 s.152, is not available on the deemed disposal and reacquisition, unless the new assets are UK assets used for a trade carried on in the United Kingdom through a permanent establishment.

Where the emigration of the trust is caused by the death of a trustee and within six months of the trustees again becoming resident and ordinarily resident in the United Kingdom, the exit charge on the emigration of the trust is restricted to any assets which are either disposed of during the period of non-residence, or are protected by a double taxation agreement after the repatriation of the trust (TCGA 1992 s.81).

Conversely, where the trustees become resident and ordinarily resident in the United Kingdom, as a result of a trustee's death, any exit charge on re-exportation of the trust is restricted to assets acquired during the period of UK residence under the hold-over provisions relating to gifts of business assets (TCGA 1992 s.165) or gifts subject to inheritance tax (TCGA 1992 s.260).

24–049

Where the exit charge arises on the emigration of the trust and the capital gains tax is not paid within six months of the due date, HMRC may, within a period of three years beginning when the tax is finally determined, serve on the past trustees a notice (TCGA 1992 s.82).

If the trustees remain resident in the United Kingdom but become eligible to exemption from capital gains tax under a double tax treaty, because, for example, they are also resident abroad (dual resident), there is a deemed disposal and reacquisition of the treaty-protected trust assets at market value on becoming eligible for the treaty protection if this is on or after March 19, 1991 (TCGA 1992 s.83).

24–050 Where trustees are within the charge to capital gains tax for a tax year but are non-UK resident at the time an asset is disposed of, either under the terms of a double tax treaty or by reason of the trustees' non-residence and non-ordinary residence, the trustees are not able to claim treaty relief in respect of the chargeable gain arising, and the gain may be taxed on the trustees, the settlor or a beneficiary of the settlement. This provision applies in respect of gains realised on or after March 15, 2005.

Roll-over relief under TCGA 1992 s.152, is not available where on or after March 19, 1991 the new assets are acquired by dual resident trustees entitled to treaty protection in respect of those assets (TCGA 1992 s.84).

Hold-over relief under TCGA 1992 s.165 is not available on or after December 10, 2006, for gifts to trusts in which the settlor retains an interest, or where there are arrangements in place under which such an interest will or may be acquired, irrespective of whether the gift is made by the settlor or another person (TCGA 1992 s.169B). Furthermore, holdover relief will be clawed back if within six years of the end of the tax year in which the gift was made, the trust becomes settlor-interested (TCGA 1992 s.169C).

24–051 A person is chargeable to capital gains tax on the disposal of an interest in a non-resident trust under TCGA 1992 s.85. Where this has previously been the subject of an exit charge on emigration under TCGA 1992 s.80, during his period as a beneficiary, he is deemed to have disposed of and immediately reacquired his interest in the trust at the time of the emigration to avoid what would otherwise be a double charge. The effect of TCGA 1992 s.85, is that the gain in the trust up to the point of emigration is subject to the exit charge and from that date the gain on the disposal of an interest in the settlement is charged on the beneficiary disposing of it under TCGA 1992 s.85.

Alternatively, if before the trustees became non-resident they become dual resident and subject to treaty protection within TCGA 1992 s.83, the beneficiary shall be treated as having disposed of and immediately reacquired his interest in the settlement at the time the trustees became eligible for treaty protection. Thus the gain up to that date would be caught under s.83, and the subsequent gain caught on the beneficiary on the disposal of the interest in the settled property under TCGA 1992 s.85.

Where TCGA 1992 s.87, applies, which charges gains of non-resident settlements on beneficiaries, the gain is reduced by the amount already charged on the settlor under TCGA 1992 s.86 and Sch.5.

The right to recovery by the settlor who has an interest in a UK resident trust in TCGA 1992 s.78, if he pays the tax, is amended to ensure that the gains so charged and recovered are deemed to be the highest part but one of his gains, the highest part being those gains attributed to him from a non-resident trust under TCGA 1992 Sch.5.

CAPITAL GAINS TAX CHARGE ON SETTLOR

24–052 TCGA 1992 s.86 and Sch.5 apply to charge certain settlors to tax on gains of a non-resident trust as if the gains were made by the settlor. It applies where the settlement is a qualifying settlement and the trustees are not resident or ordinarily resident in the United Kingdom during any part of the year or, while resident, are regarded as resident other than in the United Kingdom under a double tax treaty.

The settlor must be domiciled in the United Kingdom at some time in the year, and resident in the United Kingdom for any part of the year or, before April 6, 2013, ordinarily resident during the year. The settlor must have an interest in the settlement as defined in TCGA 1992 Sch.5.

If the disposal of property originating from the settlor would have given rise to a chargeable gain had the trust been resident, there would be a charge to tax provided that the exceptions to the charge do not apply.

24–053 For 2007/08 and earlier years, the gains of a UK resident trust could be attributed to a settlor under TCGA 1992 s.77, if he or his spouse were beneficiaries. Following the introduction of the flat rate of 18 per cent on capital gains, the attribution provisions of TCGA 1992 s.77, in relation to UK resident trusts have been repealed. The charge on settlors of non-UK resident trusts under TCGA 1992 s.86, continue to have effect.

The gain that would have accrued to the trust had it been resident, or the treaty inapplicable, is treated as the settlor's gain and is subject to the maximum amount of capital gains tax as if it had been his own highest gain.

The settlor has an interest in a settlement if property comprised in the settlement could be applied to the benefit of a defined person under any circumstances, or income could be paid to such a beneficiary or he could benefit directly or indirectly from the property comprised in the settlement. Relevant property or income is that originating from the settlor.

24–054 A defined person is the settlor, his spouse or (from December 5, 2005) civil partner, any child of the settlor or his spouse or civil partner and any spouse or grandchild of the child, or any company controlled by such persons or associated with such a company. Control for this purpose is defined by TA 1988 s.416 (the close company definition), and a child includes a stepchild. A settlor does not have an interest in a settlement if that interest arises only on the bankruptcy of the beneficiary or his making an assignment or charge of the property, or the death of the parties to a marriage including the children under a marriage settlement or the death of a beneficiary under the age of 25 who would become entitled to the property on attaining that age. Former spouses may be ignored for these provisions.

Where the settlor is charged to capital gains tax under these provisions he has a right to recover the tax from the trustees and for this purpose may require the inspector to give him a certificate specifying the amount of the gains concerned and the amount of tax paid. It is questionable whether a UK Finance Act can give a settlor a right to recover money from overseas trustees in respect of a settlement of which he is not a beneficiary, and it could well be that such a payment could be in breach of trust.

Property originates from a settlor if it is provided by him or can be traced back to such property. Income originating from a person includes income from property originating from the person or income provided by him. Reciprocal arrangements are included.

24–055 A settlement created on or after March 19, 1991, is a qualifying settlement for the year in which it is created and subsequent years.

A settlement created before March 19, 1991, is a qualifying settlement in 1999/2000 and subsequent years of assessment unless it is a protected settlement (TCGA 1992 Sch.5 para.9(1A)). A protected settlement is where the beneficiaries are confined to children of the settlor or the spouse of the settlor who are under the age of 18 at the time of the disposal, or who were under that age at the end of the immediately preceding year of assessment, unborn children of the settlor or spouse or of a future spouse, and future spouses of any such children. A future spouse of the settlor and other persons are outside the defined categories if there is no settlor by reference to whom they can be defined (TCGA 1992 Sch.5 paras 10A and 10B). The beneficiary of a settlement and various other terms are defined in TCGA 1992 Sch.5 para.9(10C–11)).

In essence a trust created prior to March 17, 1998 for the benefit of grandchildren which remains untainted is not subject to deeming within TCGA 1992 s.86, during the minority of the beneficiaries.

HMRC may serve a notice requiring information from any person who either is or has been a trustee, beneficiary or settlor, requiring him to provide information in connection with the settlement provided that at least 28 days' notice is given, TCGA 1992 ss.98, 98A and Sch.5A.

LIMBO TRUSTS

24–056   It would seem that some of the anti-avoidance provisions can sometimes be overcome by carrying out overseas activities through what is usually known as a "limbo trust"; where a non-resident or non-UK domiciliary settles funds for the benefit of a non-resident beneficiary with power to add additional beneficiaries, although care has to be taken not to end up with a sham trust which is not a trust at all, *Rahman v Chase Bank (CI) Ltd* [1991] J.L.R. 103.

GENERAL ANTI-AVOIDANCE PROVISIONS

24–057   A number of countries have general anti-avoidance sections in their tax legislation which are intended to prevent legal avoidance of taxation. The United Kingdom until recently only had targeted anti-avoidance provisions, such as TCGA 1992 s.184G, and the disclosure of the avoidance scheme rules in FA 2004 ss.306–319 as well as numerous specific anti-avoidance measures. However, the UK has introduced a General Anti-Abuse Rule, GAAR, in FA 2013 ss.206–215 and Sch.43 with effect from Royal Assent on July 17, 2013.

FA 2013 provides that the General Anti-Abuse Rule applies to income tax, corporation tax, capital gains tax, petroleum revenue tax, inheritance tax, stamp duty land tax and the annual tax on enveloped dwellings. It does not apply to value added tax which is a European Union tax subject to the abuse of law concept to outlaw abusive VAT avoidance following *Halifax Plc and others v Customs & Excise Commissioners* (2006) S.T.C. 919.

FA 2013 s.207 defines tax arrangements as those where it would be reasonable to conclude that the obtaining of the tax advantage was a main purpose of the arrangements. Arrangements are abusive under what has become known as the "double reasonableness" test if they are arrangements which cannot reasonably be regarded as a reasonable course of action in relation to the relevant tax provisions having regard to all the circumstances. Those circumstances include:

- whether the results of the arrangements are consistent with the policy objectives of the tax law; and
- whether the result involves one or more contrived or abnormal steps intended to exploit shortcomings in the tax legislation looking at the arrangements as a whole.

Indications that arrangements are abusive are that the income profits or gains for tax purposes are significantly less than the amount for economic purposes or deductions or losses are significantly greater than the economic costs or include a claim for repayment of tax that has not been, and is unlikely to be, paid. Where the arrangements are in accordance with established practice, as previously accepted by HMRC, this might be an indication that the arrangements are not abusive.

Tax advantage is defined by FA 2013 s.208 to include an increase in relief from tax, repayment of tax, or the avoidance or reduction of a charge to tax, and includes timing differences for the avoidance of a requirement to deduct tax.

Where the GAAR applies, FA 2013 s.208 counteracts the tax advantages that are abusive by making just and reasonable adjustments to the tax charge and s.210 allows consequential relieving adjustments. The procedural requirements for counteracting a tax advantage are set out in FA 2013 Sch.43 which defines the GAAR Advisory Panel. A designated HMRC officer, as defined, must send a notice to the taxpayer of the proposed counteraction of a tax advantage which gives 45 days to the taxpayer to make representations. The GAAR Advisory Panel then considers the case and refers it to a sub-panel which gives a copy of its opinion to HMRC and the taxpayer, stating whether or not, in its view, the proposed tax arrangements are a reasonable course of action in relation to the relevant tax provisions. HMRC needs to consider the opinion of the GAAR Advisory Panel but is not bound by it, and may proceed with issuing a counteraction notice.

If the case goes to appeal, FA 2013 s.211 requires HMRC to show that the arrangements are abusive and that the counteraction adjustments are just and reasonable. The tribunal must take into account HMRC's guidance which has been subject to approval by the GAAR Advisory Panel. It must also take into account the panel's opinion about the arrangements, taking into account guidance statements or other material in the public domain and evidence of established practice at the time. FA 2013 s.212 provides that the GAAR trumps any priority rule, for example, TIOPA 2010 s.6(1) which provides that a double taxation arrangement applies despite anything in the other enactment. FA 2013 ss.213 and 214 provide consequential amendments and interpretation and s.215 provides that the GAAR has effect in relation to any arrangements entered into on or after Royal Assent, ignoring any other arrangements, unless, if these were taken into account, the arrangements would not be abusive.

CHAPTER 25

Stamp duty

INTRODUCTION

Stamp duty is chargeable in respect of specific heads of charge on instruments. It is a tax on documents: oral undocumented transactions are therefore not subject to stamp duty. Stamp duty was abolished for intellectual property in respect of instruments executed on or after March 28, 2000 by FA 2000 s.129, and for goodwill in respect of instruments executed on or after April 23, 2002, by FA 2002 s.116.

"Instrument" is an undefined term but includes every written document (Stamp Act 1891 s.122(1)).

Even if falling within one of the heads of charge, a substantial list of exempt duties removed transactions from the scope of stamp duty. The main basis for stamp duty was the conveyance or sale, chargeable ad valorem at the appropriate rate. It should be noted that the duty was expressed to be £x per £100 or part thereof, rather than a straight percentage.

25–001

INTELLECTUAL PROPERTY

An exclusive non-revocable licence or assignment for consideration was subject to ad valorem duty as a conveyance or sale under SA 1891 ss.59 and 62 but a revocable assignment or non-exclusive licence was not subject to duty.

Agreement for the sale of goodwill was property stampable under SA 1891 s.59 (*Eastern National Omnibus Co v IRC* [1939] 1 K.B. 161).

The definition of property for stamp duty purposes included patents, copyrights and trade marks (*Leather Cloth Co v American Leather Cloth Co* (1865) 11 H.L. Cas. 523), but not know-how (*Handley Page v Butterworth* (1935) 19 T.C. 328).

A non-exclusive licence was not a conveyance on transfer (*Taylor v Caldwell* (1863) 3 B.&S. 826; *Jones v IRC* [1895] 1 Q.B. 484; *Winter Garden Theatre (London) Ltd v Millennium Productions Ltd* [1948] A.C. 173; and *Street v Mountford* [1985] A.C. 809).

Where both stamp duty and VAT were chargeable, stamp duty was charged on the VAT inclusive price (*Glenrothes DC v IRC* [1994] S.T.C. 74, SP 11/91) as is the case with the more modern Stamp Duty Land Tax applicable to land transactions.

25–002

25–003

CHAPTER 26

Package deals

INTRODUCTION

The most important point to bear in mind when entering into a licensing agreement is to achieve the desired commercial result, which in turn means taking into account the taxation situations of both the licensor and licensee to ensure that each is treated in the most favourable way possible. It may well be that the taxation aspirations of both parties are incompatible, in which case a compromise is usually possible.

26–001

MANUFACTURING AGREEMENTS

In practice, if a business enters into an agreement with another business for the licensed production of a complex piece of equipment it would often be necessary to provide not only the basic permission to enter into production, but also to supply drawings and technical expertise. It may be necessary to provide moulds, tools or jigs, to supervise the installation and commissioning of machinery and to train the licensee's staff to use it. There may also be permission to use a trade mark or registered design.

26–002

It will be appreciated that such a situation would involve patent licences, agreements for the provision of copyright drawings, know-how and show-how agreements and licensed use of trade marks and registered designs, as well as the provision of tangible supplies (which is outside the scope of this book).

In respect of deals between unconnected parties, a lot of hard commercial bargaining would be necessary to arrive at the amounts payable, but there is probably a degree of flexibility in the manner in which the total payment would be apportioned amongst the various headings.

In deciding the allocation of the various payments it is necessary to consider both the commercial and the taxation positions of both the licensor and the licensee to arrive at the optimum solution. As to some extent the optimum solutions for the licensor and licensee are contradictory, some degree of compromise is essential.

Licensor's position

26–003 As far as the licensor is concerned, if he is resident in the United Kingdom, he would like commercially to receive as much as possible in advance, or "up front", as it is normally phrased, and would not want the income to be reduced by tax deductions withheld by the licensee. On the other hand, the licensor is unlikely to wish to sell outright any of the intellectual property and it is therefore unlikely that any of the proceeds would be treated as a capital receipt even in respect of pre-April 1, 2002 expenditure (Ch.19, para.19–013).

The licensor would therefore usually like to receive a lump sum payment for know-how, with a royalty for the use of a trade mark, design right and industrial copyright and drawings. These amounts would all be taxable when receivable and not subject to deduction of tax at source. The licensor would clearly like to reduce the license payment in respect of the patent to the minimum and would no doubt accept a modest royalty spread over the life of the licensed production under this head.

Stamp duty on intellectual property was abolished for instruments executed on or after March 28, 2000 by FA 2002. s.129 and Sch.34. Prior to that date, so long as there was no exclusive licence there was no stamp duty problem but if, exceptionally, the licence was to be exclusive it was possible to reduce the stamp duty by having the maximum amount under the heading of "know-how and show-how" with the minimum related to the intellectual property aspects. As far as VAT is concerned, the royalties and fees are likely to be subject to tax at the standard rate.

26–004 The licensor would also like to apply a fairly high proportion of the royalties payable to trade marks, as these do not have a limited life, and then to patents, which have a limited life of 20 years under PA 1977 rather than design right which has a limited life of 10 or 15 years from the date of first manufacture of the designed article. Although industrial copyright still exists, preventing copying of the drawing as a drawing, there is no longer protection under copyright in the manufacture of the designed article. In the United States in particular, there is some doubt as to whether the anti-trust laws would permit the artificial extension of the life of a patent by subsequent licensing of trade mark and industrial copyright, but this sort of arrangement is more likely to be effective if the agreement ab initio extends for a period beyond the life of the patent and if a large proportion of the fees are related to other forms of intellectual property.

It must always be borne in mind that HMRC may challenge the allocation of payments under licensing agreements, as, for example, in *Paterson Engineering Co Ltd v Duff* (1943) 25 T.C. 43. It is unlikely to make such a challenge, however, if the agreements entered into between arm's-length parties specifically allocate the headings under which payments are made, provided that they are not obviously totally artificial.

It is worth noting the comments in the *Paterson Engineering* case of MacNaghten J. (at 50):

> "In these circumstances, it is plain that as far as the first agreement is concerned, the case must go back to the General Commissioners to determine whether any part of that so-called 'royalty' is paid in respect of something other than 'the user of a patent'. That is a question of fact for them to determine. If they are satisfied that the

whole of the 'royalty' payable under the first agreement was paid in respect of the user of a patent, then so far as that agreement is concerned, the assessment for the year 1939–40 will stand. If, on the other hand, they think that part of the £2,000 was a sum paid in respect of something other than the user of a patent, then they will allow that sum as a deduction from the assessment.

Mr Donovan, for the Appellants, urged very strongly that, although he was entitled to have the case sent back to the Commissioners for them to ascertain what part, if any, of the royalty payable under the first agreement was paid in respect of something other than the user of a patent, the Court was bound by the provisions which the parties had inserted in their second agreement of 1st January, 1938, to hold that £100 and no more was paid under that agreement in respect of the user of a patent. I cannot accept that view.

Mr Donovan was good enough to tabulate under ten heads the various benefits which, in his view, the Appellants obtained under these agreements with the American company, the first of which is: The exclusive right to manufacture and sell in allotted territory the patented equipment, systems and processes for water treatment, ie, the right to use patents in respect of which the American company gives the licence to the Appellants to make use of. That undoubtedly is a payment in respect of the user of a patent. There is no dispute about that. Amongst the ten benefits tabulated by Mr Donovan is the right to use in the allotted territory all existing or future trade marks, trade names or designs. The exercise of that right, on the face of it, has nothing to do with the user of a patent, yet it may be that the use of a trade name is so closely connected with the use of a particular patent that a Court charged with the duty of ascertaining the facts might come to the conclusion that the sum paid for the right to use the trade name was merely incidental to the right to use the patent. It all depends upon the facts. I was asked to give some assistance to the General Commissioners as to how they should proceed to determine this question. On consideration, I do not think it is possible to give them any further assistance than this: If it is established before them that a part of the payments made by the Appellants is in fact paid in respect of something other than the user of a patent, then they should allow such part to be deducted from the assessment. The words 'a sum paid in respect of the user of a patent' are rather vague; but, as it seems to me, if construed in a narrow sense they would cover not only the right to use the patent but also such rights as might only be considered as incidental thereto, such as the right to have any improvement of the patent made by the grantors during the currency of the agreement and the right to advice or assistance as to how best to avail themselves of the patent.

Now that it is decided (so far as this Court is concerned) that these payments are not payments that come within Rule 3(1), it may be that the Inspector of Taxes and the Appellants will be able to arrive at a decision satisfactory to both; but unless they are able to, then it will be for the General Commissioners to do their best to determine this question of fact."

A licensor could well wish to assign part of his patent for a lump sum which would be spread over the following six years for tax purposes, which would mean that he has the use of the money for a considerable period before the tax on it becomes payable. However, this is difficult to achieve in most cases in practice as the licensee is likely to resist strongly the payment of a capital sum on the assignment of a patent on which he would only be able to claim capital allowances at 20 per cent per annum on the reducing balance, unless within CTA 2009 Pt 8.

Licensee's position

26–005   As far as the licensee is concerned, he would like from a commercial point of view to have royalties paid over the period of production without a large payment "up front". Royalties are usually payable gross and accounted for on an accruals basis under CTA 2009 Pt 8.

The licensee would not normally mind technical assistance fees, which would also be paid gross and provided for in the accounts on an accruals basis. The licensee would, however, like to have payments for technical assistance spread over a period of the contract so that he can claim these as a revenue expense, following *British Sugar Manufacturers Ltd v Harris* (1937) 21 T.C. 528.

Know-how charges paid as a lump sum would be an allowable expense of the licensee over the period of the agreement or on accruals basis. In respect of pre-April 1, 2002 expenditure the licensee would rather pay such fees as a royalty related to production even if he has to pay a non-returnable but recoupable advance of royalties, which would be a revenue expense rather than a lump sum of like amount dealt with under ITTOIA 2005 ss.583–586 or TA 1988 s.531.

A non-resident licensee would not normally wish to pay VAT and therefore any amount of the licence production consideration allocated to the provision of show-how or technical assistance in the United Kingdom, which would be liable to VAT, should be kept down to an absolute minimum.

Common control

26–006   If the licensor and the licensee are under common control it may still be necessary to arrive at the market value of the goods and services provided, as the licensee would be able to claim deductions only if the payments were no more than the market value (following the case of *Petrotim Securities Ltd v Ayres* (1963) 41 T.C. 389). If the licensor and licensee were in different countries it would be necessary to consider the transfer pricing provisions contained in most double taxation treaties and in the domestic legislation of many countries. In the United Kingdom the legislation is contained in TIOPA 2010 Pt 4.

PUBLISHING DEALS

26–007   If a book is produced there may be a number of agreements dealing with various rights for the publication of hardback editions, book club editions, paperback editions, film and dramatisation rights, etc. and it is necessary to consider from both the licensor's and the licensee's point of view how these may be structured. These matters are dealt with in rather more detail in Case Study 1 (at para.CS1–001, et seq.) and App.1, and it is sufficient to point out that as far as the publisher is concerned he will claim as a trading expense all payments made to authors, whether for the assignment of copyright or for the grant of a licence.

As far as the author is concerned, he may like a lump sum receipt not only from a cash flow point of view but also in order to take advantage of the averaging provisions described in para.18–021, et seq. Copyright deals are usually simpler to structure from a tax planning point of view than licensing agreements within the manufacturing industry.

ETHICAL DRUGS

26–008 The main problem with ethical drugs is the very considerable amount of research and development expenditure needed to produce an effective drug, and the substantial cost and period of time required to test the drug both in the laboratory and in clinical trials before it can actually be marketed. On the assumption that the drug company is carrying on an existing trade, it will be ploughing back a large proportion of profits into research and development for future drugs. A lot of this expenditure will consist of ordinary trading expenses allowed under ITTOIA 2005 s.34. To the extent that expenditure might be disallowed as being too remote for the existing trade or represent capital expenditure, it may qualify for research and development allowances, as explained in Ch.15 (see para.15–011). In some cases the effective exploitation of the drug will require the acquisition of patent licences which may require capital expenditure or the payment of royalties, the tax treatment of which is also explained in Ch.15. To the extent that know-how is acquired, as opposed to developed, relief for expenditure should be allowable as the acquisition of industrial know-how, see para.19–014.

Marketing costs of ethical drugs tend to be very substantial and the promotion of the trade mark of a new drug is likely to be expensive. Any expenditure will, however, normally be trading expenditure, although HMRC have been known to argue that the initial cost of advertising a new product gives rise to capital expenditure, for which no relief is available. In most cases it should be possible to resist this argument.

Where other manufacturers are licensed to produce the drug there may be lump sums received to cover know-how and licensing the patent, as well as a trade mark licence to use the proprietary name. It has to be considered whether such lump sums have to be treated as capital receipts or, as would usually be the case, income of the vendor. Capital expenditure on the acquisition of a trade mark licence should be an expense of the purchaser on which allowances are available under CTA 2009 Pt 8 (Ch.17, para.17–010). Where royalties are concerned, it has to be considered whether tax is required to be deducted at source and whether any steps can be taken to mitigate withholding taxes on cross-border licensing, as explained in Ch.24.

26–009 Where licensing and research and development are carried on within a multinational group it may be necessary to consider the controlled foreign company and transfer pricing provisions explained in Chs 14 and 13 respectively.

Costs of research and development are often so high that joint ventures seem to become more common, which from a tax planning point of view can be both a complication and an opportunity, as explained in Case Study 6 (see para.CS6–001, et seq.).

BROADCASTING

26–010 The taxation of performers and behind-the-microphone workers is dealt with in Ch.27.

Obviously, the broadcasting company is usually carrying on a trade, and the profits of that trade would be computed on the basis of usual accounting principles, and taxed accordingly. The particular areas of interest so far as this book is concerned are where the broadcasting company plays recordings on its programmes and the mechanism for paying the owners of the various rights for that broadcast. This is usually done by the broadcasting company paying a fee for the musical and lyrical composition copyright to the Performing Rights Society Ltd (PRS) in the United Kingdom which allocates the amount received, normally on a quarterly basis, and distributes it equally to the publisher and composer of each record each time it is played on the air. Phonographic Performance Ltd (PPL) also collects a fee for the sound recording copyright which is usually split three ways between the company producing the recording, the featured artistes and the session musicians, if any, who are usually paid through the Musicians' Union. Video Performance Ltd (VPL) also collects similar royalties in connection with videos shown on television; it is an associated company of Phonographic Performance Ltd. Publishing income on the sale of a recording is collected through the Mechanical Copyright Protection Society Ltd (MCPS) which works closely with the PRS in the MCPS–PRS Alliance.

These societies have their overseas equivalents in most of the important countries in the world so that wherever a recording is played on air the income should be accounted for to the performers and copyright holders.

It is obviously very difficult to ensure that the correct recipient is actually credited with the appropriate income collected by the collection societies, and in some cases they are unable to identify the correct recipients. In such cases the societies tend to accumulate the excess income for a period and then distribute it to the main payees in proportion to their allocated income. These additional monies are usually known in the trade as "black box receipts".

RECORDING AGREEMENTS

26–011 When a record company enters into an agreement with an artiste, or group of artistes, the terms of the agreement vary considerably but there is usually a royalty due to the composer, which may be split with a lyricist, and a publishing agreement under which the record company usually becomes the publisher, although a number of successful artistes do take control of their own publishing. The artistes' royalty on the production of the recording is often allocated among one or more artistes in accordance with the agreement, and in some cases this could include the producer.

As the record company will usually sell records on a worldwide basis through licensed manufacture with its overseas affiliates, there may be difficulties with withholding taxes. Royalty agreements typically have some vague provisions enabling the record company to deduct withholding taxes from royalties payable to the recipients. In practice, what often happens is that the record company suffers a withholding tax on royalties received from its overseas affiliates and licensees, and deducts an equivalent percentage from the royalties accountable to the performers or composers. In such circumstances the record company itself ought to be in a position to obtain credit for the tax deducted from its overseas affiliates and licensees in respect of any withholding taxes that remain irreducible under the appropriate double taxation treaties. Only if a withholding tax cannot otherwise be credited should it be deducted from the amount due to the recipients. The recipient will be unable to obtain credit for withholding taxes in respect of royalties due from overseas territories through the record company's sub-licensing, as they will have no direct contract with the payer of the royalties, and can only claim the cost as an expense. In certain cases the performer may have a direct contract with the overseas record company, in which case the withholding tax would be properly deducted, subject to any reduction under a double taxation treaty, and credit should then be available to the artistes.

PART 5

SPECIFIC TAXATION APPLICATIONS

CHAPTER 27

Entertainers and sportsmen

INTRODUCTION

A further class of individual who may be in receipt of royalties is the public performer, musician, actor or artiste. Such royalties from the sale of records, CDs, DVDs, tapes or films are not copyright royalties but recording or performing royalties, often known as artistes' royalties. Performances giving rise to such royalties are protected under CDPA 1988 Pt II. Although this income is not strictly from intellectual property, the taxation of such performers is so intimately connected with copyright that it warrants inclusion in this book. Sportsmen are often taxed under the same provisions as entertainers and the distinction, in practice, is becoming blurred, largely through the influence of television, and "image rights" and therefore, sportsmen are also included within the term "performer" except where the context dictates otherwise. Specific provisions relating to sportsmen are also referred to. **27–001**

Normally a person in receipt of such royalties will be exercising a profession and any royalties received from anywhere in the world would be part of the his or her professional income formerly taxed under Sch.D, Case II, as for example the singer Miss Lillian Braithwaite in *Davies v Braithwaite* (1933) 18 T.C. 198.

However, the performer may be paid a salary assessable as employment income as was the dancer in the case of *Fall v Hitchen* [1973] S.T.C. 66, or may even be carrying on a trade of, for example, running a dance band, as was Joe Loss in *Loss v IRC* [1945] 2 All E.R. 683.

It is therefore necessary to consider whether any amounts received by a performer are part of his taxable income, be it assessed as employment income or from carrying on a trade or profession.

EMPLOYED OR SELF-EMPLOYED

It is important to distinguish between a contract of *service*, as in: *Fall v Hitchen* (above); *Bhadra v Ellam* [1988] S.T.C. 239; *Sidey v Phillips* [1987] S.T.C. 87; *Walls v Sinnett* [1987] S.T.C. 236; *Cooke v Blacklaws* (1985) S.T.C. 1; *Fuge v McClelland* (1956) 36 T.C. s.571; *Andrews v King* [1991] S.T.C. 481; *Mitchell & Edon v Ross* (1961) 40 T.C. 11; *Horner v Hasted* [1995] S.T.C. 766; *Alternative Book Co Ltd* (2008) STC (SCD) 830; *Dragonfly Consultancy Ltd v RCC* (2008) S.T.C. 3030 (deemed employment under IR35, ITEPA 2003 ss.48–61); and *MKM Computing Ltd v RCC* (2008) S.T.C. (SCD) 403 (deemed employment NIC) which is an employment, or deemed employment, and a contract for services, **27–002** which is dealt with as part of the trade or profession (*Edwards v Clinch* [1980] S.T.C. 438; *Davies v Braithwaite* (1933) 18 T.C. 198; *Barnett v Brabyn* [1996] S.T.C. 716; *O'Kelly v Trusthouse Forte plc* [1983] All E.R. 456; *McManus v Griffiths* [1997] S.T.C. 1089; *Hall v Lorrimer* [1992] S.T.C. 599); *Spearmint Rhino Ventures Ltd v HMRC* (2007) EWHC 613 (Ch); *Stringfellow Restaurant Ltd v Nadine Quashie* (2012) EWCA Civ 1735; *Sherburn Aero Club Ltd v RCC* (2009) S.T.C. (SCD); *Littlewood v RCC* (2009) S.T.C. 243; *Castle Construction Chesterfield) Ltd v RCC* (2009) S.T.C. (SCD) 97; and *First World Software Ltd v RCC* (2008) S.T.C. (SCD) 389. The distinction is also important for National Insurance purposes. In *Market Investigations Ltd v Minister of Social Security* [1968] 3 All E.R. 732, Cooke J. said (at 737):

> "The observations of Lord Wright, of Denning, LJ, and of the judges of the Supreme Court in the USA suggest that the fundamental test to be applied is this: 'Is the person who has engaged himself to perform these services performing them as a person in business on his own account'. If the answer to that question is 'yes', then the contract is a contract for services. If the answer is 'no', then the contract is a contract of service. No exhaustive list has been compiled and perhaps no exhaustive list can be compiled of considerations which are relevant in determining that question, nor can strict rules be laid down as to the relative weight which the various considerations should carry in particular cases. The most that can be said is that control will no doubt always have to be considered, although it can no longer be regarded as the sole determining factor; and that factors, which may be of importance, are such matters as whether the man performing the services provides his own equipment, whether he hires his own helpers, what degree of financial risk he takes, what degree of responsibility for investment and management he has, and whether and how far he has an opportunity of profiting from sound management in the performance of his task."

This judgment was quoted with approval in *Fall v Hitchen* and in *Global Plant Ltd v Secretary of State for Social Services* [1972] 1 Q.B. 139.

Cases concerning playing in orchestras have held that in the particular circumstances the players were self-employed (*Midland Sinfonia Concert Society Ltd v Secretary of State for Social Services* [1981] I.C.R. 454; *Addison v London Philharmonic Orchestra Ltd* [1981] I.C.R. 261). However, a comedian was an employee, on the facts, in *Stagecraft Ltd v Minister of National Insurance* (1952) S.C. 288, but a part-time drama teacher was self-employed in *Argent v Minister of Social Security* (1968) 3 All E.R. 208. In *St John's College School, Cambridge v Secretary of State for Social Security*, unreported (June 12, 2000) visiting instrumental teachers are self-employed but treated as employees for National Insurance purposes by the Social Security (Categorisation of Earners) Regulations 1978 (SI 1978/1689) and the amendments Regulations 2003 (SI 2003/736).

27–003

In the case of *Ferguson v John Dawson & Partners (Contractors) Ltd* [1976] 1 W.L.R. 1213, Mr Ferguson was taken on as a self-employed member of the lump on a building site. He sustained injuries in the course of his occupation and it was necessary to determine whether he was self-employed, in which case it was his own fault, or whether he was an employee, in which case the employer had a responsibility for his safety which it had failed to observe. It was held that because the company was responsible for directing Mr Ferguson's activities and for providing him with tools and equipment, as required, that he was in reality an employee and not the supplier of independent services. He was therefore employed in reality under a contract of service and not a contract for services. A similar discussion was reached in *Lane v The Shire Roofing Company (Oxford) Ltd* [1995] T.L.R. 104.

Unusually, in *Barnett v Brabyn* [1996] S.T.C. 716, the taxpayer argued unsuccessfully that he was an employee, not self-employed, and that therefore he was not liable for tax as his "employer" should have deducted it under PAYE. Lightman J. in his judgment stated:

> "The badges of a contract of employment relied on by Mr. Way are that: (1) Mr. Barnett worked only for LTV and no one else; (2) Mr. Barnett was paid originally weekly and later monthly and took only one week's holiday during the twenty five months he worked for LTV; (3) Mr. Barnett was paid for his one week's holiday; (4) when he wanted a haircut during working hours, he sought and obtained permission; (5) Mr. Barnett never submitted invoices to LTV; and (6) LTV gave Mr. Barnett the equivalent of three months' income by three equal post dated monthly cheques on his leaving as compensation for any outstanding loss or claim.
>
> I think that these factors might in an ordinary case carry some weight indicative of his status as an employee. But the weight is very much reduced as regards (1) and (2) by the fact that Mr. Barnett insisted on the contractual right to work as much or as little as he liked: and his later decision during the period of his engagement to work full time cannot affect the character of the contract which (in the absence of any suggestion of an agreed variation) must be determined once and for all when the contract was made. As regards (3), (4), (5) and (6), their significance must be very much affected by the family relationship between Mr. Barnett and LTV and the absence of evidence from Mr. Barnett as to whether any (if so what) discussions or agreement there were pursuant to which the payments referred to in (3) and (6) were made.
>
> Mr. Way further relies as badges of a contract of employment on the existence or non existence of factors found relevant in other cases. Thus e.g. he says that Mr. Barnett (1) had no skill or experience in the work he had to perform, did not engage his own helper, invest capital or provide his own machinery or tools or price his own job all found to be badges of a contract of employment of a mason working on a building site *in Lee Ting Sang v. Chung Chi-Keung* [1990] 2 AC 374; (2) took no financial risk and had no opportunity of profiting from sound management factors found to be relevant in case of a part time interviewer held to be an employee in *Market Investigations Ltd v. Minister of Social Security* [1969] 2 QB 173; and (3) had no office or business bank account or prospect by efficiency of achieving a profit factors found to be badges of a consultant in *Hall v. Lorimer* supra. I do not find this approach helpful. Factors relevant in one situation may be irrelevant or of no weight in another. I do not find any of these factors of any substantial weight in this case.
>
> Three factors in this case in favour of Mr. Barnett being an independent contractor far outweigh any relied upon by Mr. Way. The first is (in the language of the Commissioners) that Mr. Barnett 'did have the right to control his input to LTV time wise', to enable him to exploit other interests. The second is the clear agreement that Mr. Barnett should be an independent contractor. Such an agreement cannot contradict the effect of a contract as a whole and must be disregarded if inconsistent with the substantive terms or general effect of the contract as a whole: see *Narich Pty v. Commissioner of Pay-roll Tax (Privy Council)* (1984) I.C.R. 286, quoted (1983) STI 545. But when the terms and general effect of the contract as a whole are consistent with either relationship, the parties' label may be decisive: see *Massey v. Crown Life Insurance Co.* supra. The third is the cogent factor of the previous determinations all made on this basis."

It would appear from these cases that there are five main elements in a contract of employment, taking account of written documents, oral exchanges and conduct all of which may be evidence of the agreement entered into (*Carmichael v National Power Plc* [1999] 1 W.L.R. 2042 (ESM 7005-7230); *Airfix Footwear Ltd v Cape* [1978] I.C.R. 1210; *Secretary of State for Employment v McMeechan* [1997] I.R.L.R. 353).

27–004 **First**, the employer must have control over the manner in which the employee carries out his services and as such the employer is responsible for the actions of the employee. There must be a mutuality of obligation under which the employer provides work for a reward and the employee provides his services (*Clark v Oxfordshire Health Authority* [1998] I.R.L.R. 125). The control factor, however, may be limited by the nature of the employment where the employee has specialist skills (*Marren v Swinton and Pendlebury BC* [1965] 1 W.L.R. 576).

Secondly, the employer is entitled to exploit the products or services produced by the employee by supplying them to third parties. In the literary and entertainment field it is not unusual to find that an employee is given a power of veto over the manner in which or by whom his activities may be exploited, and although it is not necessarily fatal to an employment contract to have such a veto it is nonetheless an indication of a self-employed rather than employee status. Similarly, any provision that the employee indemnifies the employer would be an indication of a self-employed status and if the employment is through a company, which ostensibly has the rights to provide the services of the employee, it is not uncommon to find that the third party consumer of such services requires an inducement letter from the employee direct. This type of letter is one in which the employee confirms that the appropriate company has the rights to his services and should it cease to have these rights he would ensure that any subsequent employer who had the rights to his services would provide them to the third party. Any such letter requires careful drafting as it could negate the employment and put the so-called employee in direct contractual relationship with the third party and therefore in a self-employed rather than employee status. It is important to ensure therefore that the inducement letter is confirmatory of intention and that the third party's rights are primarily against the employer company.

It is also common, and often desirable, for the originator of copyright work to ensure that the ownership of the copyright remains with him and does not pass automatically to the employer. This is again an indication that the contract is for services and not a service contract as under common law the products of the employee would belong to the employer. This problem can usually be solved in practice by the employee granting the employer an exclusive licence to the copyright work during the period of the employment, or as one of the terms of the contract of employment having a right to acquire copyrights at the termination of the employment for a nominal sum. It is important to have the right to acquire the copyright material under the contract of service as otherwise any transfer of the copyrights to the employee on termination would be taxable as remuneration on the market value of copyrights.

27–005 **Thirdly**, the employment contract would normally require the exclusive services of the employee (see *Express and Echo Publications Ltd v Tanton* [1999] I.R.L.R. 367, and *MacFarlane and Skivington v Glasgow CC* EAT/1277/99 (ESM 7220)), although again it is not unusual to have dual contracts with separate employers where the services are split on a territorial basis so that activities in the United Kingdom are for one employer and those outside the United Kingdom or in specified territories are for another employer. It is possible to have different employments for different services although a multiplicity of so-called employments would give rise to a potential argument that the so-called employee was in reality freelance and providing his services via different companies. It is also possible to have both an employment and a self-employed activity, although this could increase the difficulty of ensuring the bona fides of the employment (see *Mitchell & Edon v Ross* (1961) 40 T.C. 11).

Fourthly, an employment contract will provide for remuneration and reimbursement of expenses to be paid to the employee who should be in a position where he is entitled to the remuneration whatever the success his employer may have in marketing the product of his labours. Normally such remuneration would be a fixed sum paid on a monthly basis. The provision of a bonus, perhaps related to the employer's receipts as a result of the employee's activities, could also be paid, although such a provision is regarded in the United States as an indication of a contract for services rather than an employment.

Fifthly, the employment would normally be for a fixed period of time although it would not be unusual for it to continue indefinitely thereafter. A common period for a service contract would be three or five years. A service agreement should normally contain clear provisions as to how it may be terminated, for example, by giving six months' notice, or for a fundamental breach by either the employer or employee.

A leading case, involving a freelance television vision mixer, went to the Court of Appeal as *Hall (Inspector of Taxes) v Lorimer* [1994] S.T.C. 23. It concerned the case of Mr Ian Lorimer and whether his activities were as an employee carrying on a series of employments taxable as employment income or in business on his own account and properly assessed under Sch.D, Case I, as was held to be the case.

The facts were relatively simple, with Mr Lorimer joining Molinare Ltd as an electrician on February 2, 1981 and in 1983 changing his job within the company to that of vision mixer which required a nine-month period of training from Molinare's one and only vision mixer. On January 31, 1985, Mr Lorimer decided to go freelance and left Molinare's employment. A vision mixer is a type of editor who is required to have a sense of timing, a feeling for mood, anticipation and music, and dexterity in operating equipment. In a live show he has only one chance to get it right. He may have four cameras operated by four individual cameramen providing shots of an event from different positions. These shots come up on screen in front of the vision mixer. It is his function to select the one which at any moment he thinks is the most interesting for the viewer. The vision mixer works closely with the director responsible for the production. Obviously, with pre-recorded shows there is less opportunity for the vision mixer to show his skill, but it is still a very important function. A vision mixer does not use his own equipment, which is very expensive. The cost of a fully equipped outside broadcast vehicle can be £3 million.

Mr Lorimer set about getting work from his office at home where his wife assisted with the paperwork. He prepared his CV and proceeded by writing, telephoning or visiting potential customers and in this he was successful. He built up a client list of 22 companies using his services in the first 14 months and subsequently maintained his list of contacts at about this level, although the identity of the clients varied, with 14 new clients acquired in 1986/87, nine in the following year and eight in 1988/89, which was the last year under appeal. He obtained work for well over 800 days in the four years and two months from February 2, 1985 to April 5, 1989. Mr Lorimer was registered for VAT and was accepted as being in business on his own account by Customs and Excise who made the usual control visits. He paid retirement annuity policy premiums and had sickness insurance in case he was unable to work through illness. For a time Mr Lorimer used an agent but gave this up as he found he was merely being introduced to his own contacts. In a small number of cases, six in fact, he was double booked and persuaded his customers to accept a substitute for whom he paid and in respect of which he made a small profit on the differential between what he charged the customer and what he paid the substitute.

27–007   The contracts entered into by Mr Lorimer with the television companies tended to be fairly informal but normally they were written confirmation of telephone bookings followed by invoices from Mr Lorimer in varying degrees of detail. On occasions clients refused to pay the fee plus VAT and instead paid a net amount after deducting tax and national insurance for fear that the Revenue would not approve Mr Lorimer as being in business on his own account.

Mr Lorimer was for much of the time a member of the Association of Cinematograph Television and Allied Technicians but he charged more than the normal union rates of pay and worked the period of time necessary to complete the job in hand.

The Commissioner's decision in this case is very important because Mummery J. merely had to decide whether, following *Edwards (Inspector of Taxes) v Bairstow* (1956) 36 T.C. 207, the Commissioner's decision was within the band of possible reasonable decisions and not whether on the evidence he would have reached the same conclusion as the Special Commissioner.

27–008   The Special Commissioner considered Cooke J.'s admirable summary of the fine distinction between a number of casual employments and a series of contracts for services in *Market Investigations Ltd v Minister of Social Security* [1969] 3 All E.R. 732, and agreed that the fundamental test to be applied was whether or not the person who engaged himself to perform the services was performing them as a person in business on his own account. It is very interesting to note that the courts have been prepared to look to other jurisdictions such as the United States for guidance on matters of difficulty where the legal system is basically the same (*USA v Silk* (1946) 331 U.S. 704).

In the *Market Investigations* case the interviewer was held to be carrying on part-time employment in view of the high degree of control exercised over her activities. The Special Commissioner looked at *Davies (Inspector of Taxes) v Braithwaite* (1931) 18 T.C. 198 in which it was held that an actress was exercising her profession and not engaged in a series of part-time employments, contrasted with the case of *Fall (Inspector of Taxes) v Hitchen* [1973] S.T.C. 66, which concerned a professional ballet dancer engaged by Sadler's Wells under a contract which amounted to an employment agreement. The Special Commissioner also considered *O'Kelly v Trust House Forte Plc* [1984] Q.B. 90 where casual catering staff were held not to be employees and finally held that the activities of Mr Lorimer bore the hallmarks of a man who was in business on his own account. The facts outweighed substantially such details as may have been thought to militate against that conclusion.

Mummery J. in his judgment pointed out that it would be possible to have a mixture of Sch.E employments and Sch.D contracts for services as in the case of the barrister whose lecturing activities were held to be employment income (*Sidey v Phillips* [1987] S.T.C. 87). Also in *Mitchell & Edon v Ross* (1961) 40 T.C. 11, it was agreed by both sides that there was no material difference between the various contracts and they were all either Sch.E or Sch.D.

27–009

Mummery J. also referred to *Ready Mixed Concrete (South East) Ltd v Minister of Pensions and National Insurance* [1968] 2 Q.B. 497, which had also been referred to by the Commissioner, and *Lee Ting Sang v Chung Chi-Keung* [1990] 2 A.C. 374, having further judicial approval to Cooke J.'s dictum in the Market Investigations case, i.e. did Mr Lorimer perform his services as a person in business on his own account? The Crown presented a formidable argument that Mr Lorimer was not in business on his own account because he did not provide or pay for any of the equipment he used. He did not, except on the few occasions when the production company consented to the use of a substitute, engage any staff to help him in his vision mixing work. The production company controlled his time, the place and duration of each engagement and the premises where the vision mixing was to be done. The taxpayer had no say or latitude in those matters. The production company had control over the detailed planning of the programme and the taxpayer was subject to what the director wished to achieve and to the scripted directions. The taxpayer ran no financial business risk. He had not invested any capital in the productions. He had no stake in their success or failure. He had no responsibility for investment in the programme making or work or in the management of it. He had no opportunity for profit in the performance of the work, apart from the few occasions on which he hired a substitute, and his reward was not a profit from the running of the business established on his own account, but payment for the provision of his own personal skills to the production company. The risk he ran in not working for one production company under a long-term contract was that of any employee who chooses to work on a casual basis. He ran the risk of being unable to find employment or being unemployed and unpaid. Mr Lorimer's business was clearly not that of vision mixing as he did not have the premises, equipment or means to carry on such a business, so the business could only be of providing to others for reward his services as a vision mixer. However, on the authority of *Humberstone v Northern Timber Mills* (1949) 79 C.L.R. 389:

> "The essence of a contract of service is a supply of the work and skill of a man."

Mummery J. was not persuaded by this analytical approach and quoted with approval Vinelott J. in *Walls v Sinnett (Inspector of Taxes)* [1987] S.T.C. 236:

> "The facts as a whole must be looked at and a factor which may be compelling in one case, in the light of the facts of that case, may not be compelling in the context of another case."

27–010   Nor could Mummery J. be persuaded that the Special Commissioner had erred in law; he had asked himself the right question and considered in conscientious detail the essential elements of the relationship control, duration of engagements, number of engagements, provision of equipment, capital, hiring of staff, risk of profit and loss and so on. He applied the right test and came to a decision which was not open to the judge to upset. The Court of Appeal agreed with the learned judge.

This case is useful not only as a summary of the factors relevant to determining whether there is a contract of employment or a contract for services, but also to emphasise the importance of the Special Commissioners and now the First Tier Tax Tribunal as the final arbiter on questions of fact.

In *Ferguson v John Dawson & Partners (Contractors) Ltd* [1976] 1 W.L.R. 1213, at 1221 Megaw L.J. stated:

> "Mr Murray accepted that he was responsible for 'hiring and firing'. In other words, as between the defendants and the workmen, including the plaintiff, he could dismiss them. There would be no question of his being able to determine a contract between the defendants and a sub-contractor. He could move men from site to site, if he was so minded, and in support of the existence of that contractual right on behalf of the defendants he gave instances of having done so. If tools were required for the work, it was for the defendants to provide them. Again, as confirmation of that contractual obligation Mr Murray gave evidence of instances where the plaintiff had required tools for the work which he had been required to do, and the defendants had provided them. It was for Mr Murray to tell the workmen, including the plaintiff, what particular work they were to do: 'I tell him what to take and what to do.' The centurion in St Matthew's Gospel says to the man under him:' "Do this,'' and he doeth it.' The man under him is a servant, not an independent contractor. All these things are in relation to the contractual relationships existing. 'I tell him what to do,' and he does it on Mr Murray's instructions because, when legal analysis has to be applied, it is a term of the contract that the plaintiff shall carry out the defendant's instructions what to do when they tell him to do it. The men, including the plaintiff, were employed on an hourly basis. The money paid to them would be correctly described as 'a wage'.
>
> In my judgement, on the tests laid down in the authorities, all of this indicates beyond doubt that the reality of the relationship was of employer and employee a contract of service. I do not propose to lengthen this judgment by examining afresh the criteria, so fully discussed in so many cases. The judge, as I have already said, based himself on the judgment of MacKenna J. in *Ready Mixed Concrete (South East) Ltd v Minister of Pensions and National Insurance* [1968] 2 Q.B. 497. Another judgment which I have found very helpful is that of Cooke J. in *Market Investigations Ltd v Minister of Social Security* [1969] 2 Q.B. 173."

and at 1225:

> "As a matter of law I can see no reason why a general labourer should not offer his labour on some such terms as these: 'I do not mind what you ask me to do or where and when you ask me to do it but you must understand that I am not going to call you master and I will not be your servant.' Many men offer their labour on some such terms as these; the jobbing gardener is familiar to us all, as are self-employed farm workers to East Anglian farmers. When working they allow themselves to be controlled by those with whom they made a bargain. In most cases when the bargain is made nothing is said about control, but it is accepted by both parties as an implied

term that the hirer will exercise control. This does not mean either in fact or, in my opinion, in law that the hired man becomes a servant."

A recent case reviewing the classification of workers was *Wright v RCC* (2009) SFTD 84, which was referred to the First Tier Tax Tribunal as General Commissioners had erroneously attached importance to the lack of a written contract. On balance the workers, in the case were employees, distinguishing the *Castle Construction* case 2009 (S.T.C.) SC97.

In a written answer of January 21, 1982, Mr Nicholas Ridley stated:

> "I have taken steps so that, in due course and in all districts, club musicians will be brought within PAYE where appropriate." (*Hansard*, Vol.16, col.228)

It should be noted that an employer is required to deduct tax under the Pay As You Earn system (ITEPA 2003 s.684 and Income Tax (Pay As You Earn) Regulations 2003 (SI 2003/2682)). This applies if the employer has a trading presence in the United Kingdom (*Clark v Oceanic Contractors Inc* [1983] S.T.C. 35).

The HMRC website: *http://www.hmrc.gov.uk/working/intro/empstatus.htm* sets out the indicia of employment and self-employment as follows:

> "Work out if you're employed or self-employed
> Whether you're employed or self-employed depends on the terms and conditions of your work. It's important to know your employment status because it affects employment and benefit rights. and how you pay tax and National Insurance.
> Basic checks to help you decide
> You are probably self-employed if you:
>
> - Run your own business and take responsibility for its success or failure.
> - Have several customers at the same time.
> - Can decide how, when and where you do your work.
> - Are free to hire other people to do the work for you or help you at your own expense.
> - Provide the main items of equipment to do your work.
>
> You are probably employed if you:
>
> - Have to do the work yourself.
> - Work for one person at a time, who is in charge of what you do and takes on the risks of the business.
> - Can be told how, when and where you do your work.
> - Have to work a set amount of hours.
> - Are paid a regular amount according to the hours you work, and get paid for working overtime even if you do casual or part-time work, you can still be employed.
>
> You can also be employed and self-employed at the same time, perhaps by working for an employer during the day and running your own business in the evenings. Think about each contract separately you may find that you are self-employed for one but employed for another.
> There is no legal definition of employment or self-employment, so if there is doubt about someone's employment status the decision is made by referring to previous judgements—known as 'case law'. Whether you are employed or

self-employed depends upon the facts of your working arrangements, what your contract says, or a combination of both. Read our leaflet ES/FS1 'Employed or self employed for tax and National Insurance Contributions. If after reading the guidance above you are still unsure about your employment status you can use HM Revenue & Customs' online employment status indicator to help you decide following the links to *www.hmrc.gov.uk/calcs/esi.htm*."

HMRC guidance

27–013 HMRC published guidance on whether a worker was employed or self-employed in *Tax Bulletin*, Issue 28, 406, in the context of the construction industry. This guidance is more detailed than current guidance on the web, apart from the Employment Status Manual at ESM7000, et seq. The rules, however, have general application and the relevant extracts are set out below:

"**Employment status**

There is no statutory definition of 'employment'. However, the question of employment status has come before the Courts on many occasions over the years. The approach taken by the Courts has been to identify the factors which help to determine if a particular contract amounts to employment or self-employment. It is important to note, though, that the contract does not necessarily have to be in writing. It can be written, or oral, or it may be implied by the way in which the parties deal with each other. It may even be a combination of all three.

The relevant factors are:

Control—It is a feature of employment that the engager has the right to tell the worker what to do, or where or when to do it, or how it is to be done. The extent of control may vary from one case to another a contractor will probably exercise more control over an unskilled labourer than over a skilled craftsman. However, a working relationship which involves no control at all is unlikely to be an employment (*Ready Mixed Concrete (South East) Ltd v Minister of Pensions and National Insurance* (1968) 2 Q.B. 497).

The right to get a substitute or helper to do the job—Personal service is an essential element of a contract of employment. A person who has the freedom to choose whether to do the job himself or hire somebody else to do it for him, or who can hire someone else to provide substantial help, is probably self-employed (*Australian Mutual Provident Society v Chaplin* (1978) 18 A.L.R. 385).

Provision of equipment—A self-employed contractor generally provides whatever equipment is needed to do the job (though in many trades, such as carpentry, it is common for employees, as well as self-employed workers, to provide their own hand tools). Provision by the engager of the major items of equipment and/or the materials necessary to do the job will point towards employment (*Ready Mixed Concrete (South East) Ltd v Minister of Pensions and National Insurance*).

Financial risk—An individual who risks his own money by, for example, buying assets and bearing their running costs and paying for overheads and large quantities of materials, is almost certainly self-employed. Financial risk could also take the form of quoting a fixed price for a job, with the consequent risk of bearing the additional costs if the job overruns. However, this will not necessarily mean that the worker is self-employed unless there is a real risk of financial loss (*Market Investigations Ltd v The Minister of Social Security* (1968) 2 Q.B. 173).

Basis of payment—Employees tend to be paid a fixed wage or salary by the week or month and often qualify for additional payments such as overtime, long service bonus or profit share. Independent contractors, on the other hand, tend to be paid a fixed sum for a particular job. Payment 'by the piece' (where the worker is paid according to the amount of work actually done) can be a feature of both employment and self-employment (see Example 2 below).

Opportunity to profit from sound management—A person whose profit or loss depends on his capacity to reduce overheads and organise his work effectively may well be self-employed (*Market Investigations Ltd v The Minister of Social Security*). People who are paid by the job will often be in this position.

Right of dismissal—A right to terminate an engagement by giving notice of a specified length is a common feature of employment. It is less common in a contract for services, which usually ends only on completion of the task, or if the terms of the contract are breached.

Employee benefits—Employees are often entitled to sick pay, holiday pay, pensions, expenses and so on. However, the *absence* of those features does not necessarily mean that the worker is self-employed-especially in the case of short term engagements (see Example 1).

Length of engagement—Long periods working for one contractor may be typical of an employment but are not conclusive. It is still necessary to consider all the terms and conditions of each engagement. Regular working for the same contractor may indicate that there is a single and continuing contract of employment (*Nethermere (St Neots) Ltd v Gardiner* (1984) I.C.R. 612). See also Question 5 below.

Personal factors—In deciding a person's employment status it may sometimes be necessary to take into account factors which are personal to the worker and which have little to do with the terms of the particular engagement being considered. For example, if a skilled craftsman works for a number of contractors throughout the year and has a business-like approach to obtaining his engagements (perhaps involving expenditure on office accommodation, office equipment, etc) this will point towards self-employment (*Hall v Lorimer* 66 T.C. 349). Personal factors will usually carry less weight in the case of an unskilled worker, where other factors such as the high level of control exercised by the contractor are likely to be conclusive of employment.

Intention—It is the reality of the relationship that matters. It is not enough to call a person 'self-employed' if all the terms and conditions of the engagement point towards employment. However, if other factors are neutral the intention of the parties will then be the decisive factor in deciding employment status (*Massey v Crown Life Insurance Co* (1978) I.C.R. 590).

Approach to be adopted

Given the list of factors mentioned above it is tempting to try to determine a person's employment status by adding up the number of factors pointing towards employment and comparing that result with the number pointing towards self-employment. **The Courts have specifically rejected that approach**. In *Hall v Lorimer* 66 T.C. 349 Mummery J. made the following comment which was quoted with approval by Nolan L.J. in the Court of Appeal:

> 'In order to decide whether a person carries on business on his own account it is necessary to consider many different aspects of that person's work activity. This is not a mechanical exercise of running through a check list to see whether they are present in, or absent from, a given situation. . . . It is a matter of evaluation of the overall effect, which is not necessarily the same as the sum total of all the individual details. Not all details are of equal weight or importance in any given situation. The details may also vary in importance from one situation to another.'

When the detailed facts have been established the right approach is to stand back and look at the picture as a whole, to see if the overall effect is that of a person in business on his own account or a person working as an employee in somebody else's business. If the evidence is evenly balanced the intention of the parties may then decide the issue (*Massey v Crown Life Insurance Co*)."

This was followed in *Tax Bulletin*, Issue 48, 775:

"Employment status of set construction workers in the Film & TV industries
Background
In 1983 the Inland Revenue reviewed the arrangements between companies in the Film and TV industries and their casual and freelance staff. It was accepted by the industries and the Revenue that the relationships were generally that of employer and employee and as such earnings would be properly taxable under Schedule E from 6 April 1984. The only exceptions to this were the grades included on the Schedule D grading lists issued jointly by the Inland Revenue's Film and Television Industry Units. Services provided by set construction workers such as carpentry, rigging and painting do not appear on the Schedule D lists and, therefore, subject to any reviews of individual workers' employment status, income from such services is normally taxable under Schedule E. This is because typical contracts in the industry include such clauses that are typical of a contract of service and indeed the Special Commissioners. in an unreported decision, decided that the appellant set construction worker was an employee.

Under the principles of the common approach, the Contributions Agency generally adopted this line for National Insurance purposes from 1992. However, in two Secretary of State's decisions in respect of cases for *Hamilton Heritage* (1997) and *Southbrooke Studios Ltd* (1997) it was held that the set construction workers concerned were self-employed rather than employees. Secretary of State decisions are not lawful precedent and relate to the named contributors only. Following publicity surrounding these decisions it has become apparent that some Set Construction companies were incorrectly advised by local Inland Revenue (National Insurance) Offices that their workers were now self-employed and many companies also wrongly assumed that the two Secretary of State decisions applied across the industry generally.
Consequences
This has caused confusion within the industry because set construction workers can find themselves engaged on a self-employed basis with one studio and as an employee with another, whilst working under comparable terms and conditions for both. Consequently the Revenue has received representations from a number of employers in the industry requesting that it standardise the handling of these cases.
Revenue position
The Revenue still regards set construction workers as generally being employed earners because of the contractual arrangements mentioned and the Special Commissioner's case which found that the worker concerned was taxable under Schedule E. However, employment status can only be determined after establishing the individual facts and considering their relative importance. As the decisions in both of the Secretary of State cases mentioned above were found on their own facts it is reasonable to conclude they only relate to the named contributors.
Revenue Guidance to Staff
Guidance has been issued to all Revenue offices confirming the position on Set Construction workers. Any cases of doubt will be referred for advice to the Film Industry Unit at Gateshead or the TV Broadcasting Group at Manchester to review the employment status as appropriate. Whatever the final outcome on individual reviews. the agreed status will apply for both tax and NICs. This will help to ensure a more consistent treatment for tax and NICs for set construction workers in the future.'
Actors

HMRC usually accept that actors are self-employed for tax purposes (ESM 4121–4126 following Special Commissioner decisions involving Mr McCowan and Mr West in 1993, before such proceedings were formally reported).

This is so even though the standard Musicians' Union and British Actors' Equity Association standard contracts are currently accepted as employment contracts for national insurance purposes, subject to Class 1 contributions and entitling the performer to benefits when unemployed, (ESM 4145). Key talent artistes are usually self employed for NIC purposes (ESM4147) Social Security (Categorisation of Earners) (Amendment) Regulations 2003 (SE 2003 No 736). HMRC have published "Guidelines on the Special NIC Rules for Entertainers (April 2005 revised) (appendix 6).

HMRC tried to make most actors into employees from April 6, 1990, subject to those with already established self-employed status who were given 'Reserved Sch.D' status under ESC A75, but HMRC's view changed following the Special Commissioner's decisions in *McCowan* and *West* referred to above (ESM 4121, 4122)."

There are, of course, many exceptions and the engagements may be sufficiently lengthy to amount to employments as in *Fall v Hitchen* [1973] S.T.C. 66, where the taxpayer was employed as a dancer in the chorus at Sadler's Wells. Where an actor is employed, he may still have to pay agents' fees and fees of up to 17.5 per cent are deductible as wholly, exclusively and necessarily incurred in the performance of the employment (ITEPA 2003 s.352, ESM 4123). 27–014

The NIC position of TV actors has been considered recently in the case of *ITV Services Ltd v HMRC FTT* [2010] UKFTT 586 (TC), TC00836. The company has been treating several actors as employed earners and accounting for Class 1 National Insurance contributions on the amounts it paid them. From December 2006, however, it ceased to account for Class 1 NICs, treating the actors as self-employed. HMRC issued determinations charging NICs on the payments, and the company appealed. The First-Tier Tribunal reviewed the evidence in detail and allowed the appeal in part, issuing a decision in principle that the company was required to account for NICs in respect of most of the types of contracts, but not where the actors were "engaged to perform a specific role in a specific programme, engaged for a specific period of engagement, and received a single total inclusive fee". The company appealed against the decision and the case was heard by the Upper Tribunal at the end of November 2011 (FTC/12/2011 [2012] UKUT 47 (TCC)). The original decision was upheld and it was also ruled that payments under All Rights Contracts and certain Bespoke Agreements were salary and Class 1 NIC was due. The decision was confirmed on July 23, 2013 by the Court of Appeal (2013) EWCA Civ 867, except as regards all Rights Contracts where the performers were not employed earners.

Theatrical non-performing workers

People such as stage managers, designers, directors and choreographers may be either self-employed or employees depending on the terms and circumstances of their engagements. Other workers are likely to be employees but there is no hard and fast rule (ESM 4121; 4124; 4125; 4126). 27–015

Musicians

27–016   The rules for actors generally apply to musicians. The status as employee or as self-employed will depend on the contractual arrangements. Those on first call or guaranteed contracts and those with mutually owned orchestras such as the London Philharmonic are self-employed (ESM 4140).

Film and television workers

27–017   HMRC have set up special units for such workers at North East Metropolitan (Film Industry Unit) (ESM 4101) and Chapel Wharf Area Office (EMS 4110) or Trinity Bridge House in Salford (ECH 6130) (Television and Radio Unit). Front-of-camera or microphone performers are dealt with as actors, as above. Behind camera, etc. workers are either employed or self-employed depending on their grades and activities. HMRC have published Film Industry Television and Production Guidance Notes (revised April 2011) in respect of freelancers in these activities, effective from 2001 (Appendix 7), (ESM 4101–4106; 4110–4114).

On May 15, 2013 HMRC published a consultation document "National Insurance and Self-employed Entertainers" with a view to simplifying the rules and bringing entertainers within the normal Class 2 and 4 NICs, in view of the forthcoming Universal Credit. The current rules are set out in App.6.

Agency workers

27–018   Workers supplied through agencies may be taxed as employees of the agency (TITEPA 2003 ss.44–47). These rules do not apply to actors, singers, musicians or other entertainers or to artist's models ITEPA 2003 s.47(2)(a), unless working outside their profession, for example, as demonstrators.

Sportsmen

27–019   Team players, such as footballers and cricketers, are usually employees of a club and taxed as such. They may also be in receipt of endorsements or merchandising income or even record royalties which are earned outwith their employment duties and therefore taxable as receipts of a separate trade under ITTOIA 2005, ss.5–8 or as income not otherwise charged to tax under ITTOIA 2005 s.687, if received under an enforceable contract for work done, services rendered or facilities provided (*Scott v Ricketts* (1967) 44 T.C. 303).

Benefit years

27–020   In some sports, notably cricket, it is common for exceptional players to have a benefit year in which a benefit committee, independent of the cricketer or the club which employs him, raises money to give to him at the end of the year. Provided that there is no entitlement to this income under his contract of employment (*Moorhouse v Dooland* (1955) 36 T.C. 1, SE 1181; *Cooper v Blakiston* (1908) 5 T.C. 347; *Davis v Harrison* (1927) 11 T.C. 707; and *Corbett v*

Duff (1941) 23 T.C. 763) the gift should be tax-free (*Reed v Seymour* (1927) 11 T.C. 625). It is important that the benefit committee itself does not carry on a trade which would be taxable.

An unsolicited gift to a footballer for winning the World Cup was also held to be tax-free in *Moore v Griffiths* (1972) 48 T.C. 338. This has to be distinguished from a share of a transfer fee as an inducement from a past or future employer which was held to be taxable in *Shilton v Wilmshurst* [1991] S.T.C. 88. Promotional and Consultancy services provided by international footballers through personal service companies (pre-IR35) were genuine commercial agreements not part of their players' employment income (*Sports Club v HMIT* [2000] S.T.C. (S.C.D) 443).

Athletes

Merely because an athlete obtains income, including subventions, grants, sponsorship, endorsement fees, and appearance, participation or performance fees, does not necessarily mean that he is carrying on a trade on a commercial basis. He may merely be receiving a contribution to the expenses of his hobby, or a receipt taxable as income not otherwise charged to tax under ITTOIA 2005 s.687. However, an athlete may be carrying on a trade, even though retaining amateur status (BIM 50600–50690). Athlete Personal Awards from the National Lottery Sports Fund are unlikely to indicate that a trade is being carried on (BIM 50610) (*Scott v Rickets* (1967) 44 T.C. 303). However, loss of earnings support may be taxable (BIM 50660).

27–021

The usual trading expenses rules apply (IITTOIA 2005 s.34) and duality of purpose may disallow expenses on clothes (*Mallalieu v Drummond* [1983] S.T.C. 665), dietary supplements (*Ansell v Brown* [2001] S.T.C. 1166), and medical expenses (*Norman v Golder* (1944) 26 T.C. 293; *Prince v Mapp* (1969) 46 T.C. 169).

Receipts paid in kind are taxable at their encashable value (*Gold Coast Selection Trust Ltd v Humphrey* (1948) 30 T.C. 209; *Temperley v Smith* (1956) 37 T.C. 18).

An athlete may be an employee of a service company and taxable as employment income, if the company is contractually entitled to the income from the third party provider. The IR35 personal service company rules may be in point.

NATIONAL INSURANCE

An employee in employed earners' employment is liable to pay primary Class 1 earnings-related contributions and the employer is liable to pay Class 1 secondary contributions. A non-resident employer does not usually have to pay secondary contributions although primary contributions are payable by a UK employee. On taking up employment overseas the employee is liable for primary contributions for the first 52 weeks overseas if the employer has a place of business in the

27–022

United Kingdom. He may retain liability to contribute only to the DWP and not to his country of employment if there are reciprocal arrangements with the country of residence.

A self-employed individual pays Class 2 flat-rate contributions and Class 4 earnings-related contributions unless he is non-resident for at least 26 out of 52 weeks.

There is an annual maximum for contributions so far as the employee or self-employed individual is concerned and where it is anticipated that total contributions for the year will exceed these maxima, deferment of contributions under Classes 2 and 4 (and Class 1 if several employments are held) may be applied for on Form CF 351. Any excess contributions paid for a year may be reclaimed from the DWP.

Some taxpayers dealt with as self-employed such as actors and musicians, are treated as employed for national insurance purposes and pay Class 1 contributions and have to claim exemption from Classes 2 and 4 under the Social Security (Categorisation of Earners) Regulations 1978 (SI 1978/1689) as amended. They may claim income support benefit if unemployed which is brought in as income in the tax computation, or alternatively as employment income if the professional income assessment is final (*PAYE Procedures Manual*, 9662; ESM 4145; 4146; *Re Shine Ex p. Shine* [1892] 1 Q.B. 522; *Greater London Council v Minister of Social Securities* [1971] 2 All E.R. 285).

PERSONAL SERVICE COMPANIES (IR35)

27–023   FA 2000 s.60 and Sch.12 introduced a new regime for individuals providing their services through a limited company or partnership, often referred to by reference to the number of the Budget Press Release which heralded the provisions, as IR35, which is now enacted in ITEPA 2003 ss.41 and ITTOIA 2005 ss.163 and 164. This is an anti-avoidance provision designed to prevent people who would otherwise be employees of the client providing their services through an intermediary and, commonly, drawing profits through dividends to avoid national insurance contributions. It applies where the worker personally performs services for the client under a contract involving a third party intermediary, under circumstances that, if the services were provided under a contract directly between the client and the worker, the worker would be regarded for income tax purposes as an employee of the client (ITEPA 2003 s.49(I)(c)). As far as entertainers and sportsmen are concerned, although personal service companies are frequently used to provide the services of the entertainer or sportsman, the circumstances would normally be that the worker would otherwise be a self-employed individual providing his services in the exercise of his profession so that in the absence of the intermediary, the income would be taxable on the individual as his professional income, in which case the IR35 rules have no application, (see also, *Jones v Garnett* [2007] S.T.C. 1536).

Where however they do apply, the intermediary is treated as making a payment to the worker in the tax year as a deemed employment payment, which is treated as made at the end of the tax year as employment income (ITEPA 2003

PERSONAL SERVICE COMPANIES (IR35)

s.50). The provisions apply where the intermediary is a company, a partnership or an individual, with the appropriate connection to the performer, under ITEPA 2003 ss.51, 52 or 53.

The deemed employment income is calculated in accordance with a series of steps set out in ITEPA 2003 s.54:

> "• Step one aggregates all the payments and benefits received by the intermediary which are within these provisions, less a general deduction of five per cent.
> • Step two adds to this figure any payments or benefits received by the worker in respect of the engagements not otherwise taxed as employment income.
> • Step three deducts any expenses which would have been allowed had the worker been employed by the client and
> • Step four allows capital allowances that would have been available bad the worker been a direct employee of the client.
> • Step five allows deductions for pension payments and
> • Step six, allows any employers national insurance contributions paid by the intermediary.
> • Step seven allows a deduction from any payments and benefits received by the worker from the intermediary, chargeable to tax as employment income and not previously deducted."

27–024
This gives the pre-national insurance income from which is deducted, at step eight. What would have been the employers' national insurance contributions on that income and the balance is the deemed employment payment.

The meaning of earnings from employment is defined in ITEPA 2003 s.55, and tax on the deemed employment income is payable under PAYE. There is an exemption for a deemed emolument payment which relates to services performed outside the United Kingdom for a non-UK resident client where the worker would not be taxable had he been employed by the client by reason of being not UK resident, ordinarily resident or domiciled (ITEPA 2003 s.56).

The deemed employment payment may be deemed to be made prior to April 5, in the year in which the company ceases to trade, or the worker ceases to be employed by, or connected with, the company or partnership (ITEPA 2003 s.57). Where the income of the intermediary has been distributed by way of dividend there is limited relief for the double charge to tax that would otherwise arise, which is given by ITEPA 2003 s.58. The ITEPA 2003 ss.59–61, provide special provisions for multiple intermediaries and various definitions. The Revenue have issued a booklet IR175 on the personal service company rules, which is not available online.

27–025
FA 2007 s.25 inserted FA 2007 Sch.3, and introduced managed service companies (MSC) into ITEPA 2003 Pt II as a new Ch.9. It applies in addition to the agency workers provisions in ITEPA 2003 Pt II Ch.7 ss.44–47, or foreign entertainers under ITA 2007 s.966, et seq. From April 6, 2007 all payments received by individuals providing their services through managed service companies will be subject to PAYE. Costs of travel from home to place of work will be disallowed and from April 6, 2007, national insurance contributions will also be due on all payments received by individuals working through managed service companies. Where debts cannot be recovered from the managed service

company itself they may be transferred to the company's director or the managed service company provider from January 6, 2008.

The ITEPA 2003 ss.61A–61J and 688A are inserted. These rules will apply in addition to the IR35 rules in ITEPA 2003 Pt II Ch.8 ss.48–61. A managed service company is defined by s.61B as one, the business of which consists wholly or mainly of providing directly or indirectly the services of an individual to other persons and the company makes payments net of tax and National Insurance which exceed that which would have been received net of tax and National Insurance if it were employment income of the individual. It must also have an MSC provider who is a person who carries on a business promoting or facilitating the use of companies to provide the services of individuals. Section 61C allows the Treasury to exclude such persons from these provisions by statutory instrument. It also defines various other terms. Section 61D provides that the worker is treated as receiving earnings from an employment and the deemed employment payment is calculated under s.61E and F. The PAYE provisions are applied by s.61I. To prevent double counting s.61H relieves distributions made by a managed service company. Associate is determined for these purposes under s.6ll and various other terms are defined in s.61J.

The ITEPA 2003 s.688A provides for the recovery of the PAYE due from a director or office holder or an associate of the MSC, an MSC provider person who directly or indirectly has encouraged or been actively involved in the provision by the MSC of the services of the individual and a director or other office holder of an associate of an MSC provider or encourager. There is an exemption for a person providing legal or accountancy advice in a professional capacity or an agent placing the individual worker with an end-user.

RESTRICTIVE COVENANTS

27–026 In the case of *Higgs v Olivier* (1952) 33 T.C. 136, Sir Laurence Olivier was paid a lump sum under a restrictive covenant for undertaking not to act in, produce or direct any film for any other person for a period of 18 months. Sir Laurence had previously acted in a film entitled *Henry V* for which he had been fully remunerated and the restrictive covenant was with the makers of the same film. The Commissioners (at 139):

> "found it impossible to say that the sum of £15,000 under the deed came to the Respondent as part of the income from his vocation. On the contrary, it came to him for refraining from carrying on his vocation, and in our opinion was a capital receipt."

The High Court and the Court of Appeal supported the Commissioners in this.

It should be noted that had Sir Laurence been assessed as an employee, the receipt under the restrictive covenant would have been caught by the provisions of what is now ITEPA 2003 s.225, which treats payments made in respect of the giving of a restrictive undertaking, or total or partial fulfilment of the undertaking, in connection with an individual's current future or past employment earnings for the tax year in which the payment is made.

DATE ROYALTIES TAXABLE

Traditionally, royalties have normally been brought into the accounts of the recipient when received from the publisher or other paying agent. This method of accounting is normally adopted because the author or artiste is entitled to royalties on the basis of sales, less returns to the publisher. This information is available only to the publisher, although the author or artiste may have rights of auditing the publisher's records to confirm that the correct royalties have been accounted for. **27–027**

However, in the case of a self-employed author or artiste or an incorporated recipient of royalties arising from the exploitation of the services of an author or artiste, HMRC may insist that the royalties should be included on an accruals basis rather than on a receipts basis, on the basis of ITTOIA 2005 s.25. This provides that profits of a trade, profession or vocation should be computed in accordance with generally accepted accounting practice (UK GAAP) subject to any adjustment required by tax law which in practice may mean all sums reported as payable to the recipient by the publisher covering the period up to the end of the accounting date, even if not reported until after the end of the accounting period, and even if not payable until a later date. The technical justification for this treatment is that the royalties will have been earned in that the sales, less returns, will have taken place even though the information would not at the accounting date be available to the recipient. A case cited in support of this contention is *IRC v Gardner Mountain & D'Ambrumenil Ltd* (1947) 29 T.C. 69. This case concerned Lloyd's underwriting commissions. Further support of the principle is drawn from the case of *JP Hall & Co Ltd v IRC* (1921) 12 T.C. 382, and FRS 12 and FRS 18.

One of the problems of such a treatment of royalties is that the publisher itself may well be sub-contracting sales in various parts of the world to sub-publishers and agents and royalty collection societies so that the publisher at any particular accounting date of the recipient would be unaware of all royalties in respect of sales less returns that have taken place anywhere in the world and which, should theoretically be included in the accounts. It is possible to get over this problem by the practical application of the true and fair view in FRS 18(1) and the effect of measurement uncertainty and prudence in the Statement of Principles for Financial Reporting (SPFR), 5.16–5.19 and accept that the recipient has only to deal with the amounts reported by the publisher immediately after the accounting date and payable normally three or six months thereafter, applied on a consistent basis.

These problems would be avoided (and replaced by others) if the taxpayer was eligible for and elected for the cash basis under FA 2013 ss.17 and 18. **27–028**

There are transitional provisions on changing from a receipts basis to an accruals basis of royalty reporting for corporation tax in CTA 2009 ss.180–184 and for income tax in ITTOIA 2005 ss.226–240, which are designed to prevent profits falling out of assessment or being included twice.

A further problem arises in the case of blocked royalties where the amount has been reported by the publisher to the recipient but has not been paid because the publisher himself has not been paid, owing perhaps to exchange control restrictions in the country of origin of the royalty. In these circumstances HMRC

27–029 would accept that the royalty is not taxable until received or until the author or artiste enjoys the benefit of the royalty; for example, by spending the proceeds made available to him in the country where the royalty arises.

HMRC's view that royalties payable to a company should be accounted for on an accruals basis is by no means universally accepted; the argument being that provided that the accounts are prepared in accordance with proper accounting principles they should form the starting point in the determination of the profits for tax purposes (See, e.g. *Whimster & Co v IRC* (1925) 12 T.C. 813; *Duple Motor Bodies Ltd v Ostime* (1961) 39 T.C. 537; *Odeon Associated Theatres Ltd v Jones* (1971) 48 T.C. 257; and *BS. C. Footwear Ltd v Ridgway* (1971) 47 T.C. 495). Only exceptionally, as in *Willingale v International Commercial Bank Ltd* [1978] S.T.C. 75, is the accounting profit departed from for tax purposes.

In order for HMRC to succeed in adjusting accounts prepared on a royalties received basis to an accruals basis it would have to show that cash accounting of royalties received was not in accordance with UK GAAP, or that an adjustment was required by statutory or judicial authority.

It is a fundamental principle of accounting that all assets, liabilities, gains, losses and other elements would be recognised immediately they arise, but uncertainty may make it necessary to delay the recognition process (SPFR, 5.8) until such time as the uncertainty has been reduced to an acceptable level (SPFR, 5.11). It may be arguable that if, after the end of the accounting period when the accounts are being prepared the recipient of royalties cannot ascertain the amount due from the payer because the latter has not yet accounted to the recipient. The accounts of the recipient should not include amounts ultimately received even though they may relate back to a period covered by the accounts. It could be argued that the accountability by the payer is not equivalent to ascertainment of the amount receivable by the payee and the payee should not be required to hold his accounts open until the amount due from the payer at the next payment date is ascertained. There appears to be no statutory or judicial authority which covers the point. However, it may be possible to estimate the likely amount accrued but not received with sufficient accuracy to include it in the accounts, in appropriate circumstances.

27–030 The judicial authority relied upon by HMRC of *IRC v Gardner Mountain & D'Ambrumenil Ltd* (1947) 29 T.C. 69, related to insurance commission for services rendered and depended on the construction of the contract under which the commission was payable and whether or not the services had been rendered in the year. As it was held that the services had been rendered, the commission was due and therefore treated as earned in the year for tax purposes. A licence agreement under which a publisher pays a royalty for what would otherwise be an infringement of copyright is rather different from a contract under which specific services have to be performed. *JP Hall & Co Ltd v IRC* (1921) 12 T.C. 382, related to the profit on a contract, the payment of which was due on delivery, and it was held that for tax purposes the profit should be included in the period in which the delivery was made, and not that in which the contract was entered into. However, it is CTA 2009 s.46 which gives statutory authority to accounts prepared under UK GAAP.

Where royalties are paid for services rendered rather than for copyright, for example, the artiste's royalties paid to the performers of a recording, the services would have been performed during the recording and mixing and therefore all royalties relating to sales of the recording, less returns, in the accounting period should be included in the recipient's accounts for that period. However, the practical problem is that the recipient has no means of knowing what these royalties are to be and there seems no logical justification for holding the accounts open just to include the amount receivable from the immediate payer without including the amounts ultimately payable from all the various sub-publishers throughout the world. This would clearly require keeping the accounts open for a two or three-year period and is impractical (SPFR, 5.9).

Therefore, coming back to the normal basis of accounting it is suggested that accounts produced by the recipient of royalties on the basis of royalties ascertained as due to be paid and not blocked, at the accounting year end, are accounts prepared in accordance with UK GAAP and should form the starting point for the taxation computations.

SIMPLER ACCOUNTS FOR SMALL BUSINESSES

On November 7, 1989, HMRC produced a press release as follows: 27–031

> "Detailed accounts will no longer be needed from up to one million smaller businesses. Announcing this today in a written reply to a parliamentary question [HC Written Answer, 7 November 1989, Vol. 159 col. 525] the Financial Secretary to the Treasury, Mr Peter Lilley, MP said—
>
>> 'As from next April detailed tax accounts will no longer be needed from many small businesses. Taxpayers will still need to keep accurate business records, but three line accounts will be accepted with tax returns. This relaxation could simplify dealing with tax for up to a million smaller businesses.'
>
> At present, all businesses are expected to send in accounts consisting of a profit and loss account and sometimes a balance sheet. Traders have to itemise their income and expenditure for the year, for example rent, purchases of trading stock, travelling expenses, fuel, telephone, etc.
>
> From next year small businesses need only state their total turnover, total business purchases and expenses, and the resultant net profit. These simplified accounts will be accepted from individuals and partnerships who are trading with a total annual turnover of under £30,000 (from 6 April 2008) and also from people with rent from property where the gross income is less than £30,000.
>
> Taxpayers can send in the new simpler accounts with tax returns they will get next year asking them to report income for the year ended 5 April 1990. Taxpayers will still need to keep accurate business records so that they can submit correct three line accounts. The Revenue will continue to investigate business accounts and records for all sizes of business where it has reason to believe that profits may have been understated.
>
> The Revenue will be publishing more information about the new rules, to help taxpayers, including a range of leaflets, next April. Staff in local tax offices will also be able to help taxpayers with specific enquiries then."

ADVANCE ROYALTIES

27–032   In *Taylor v Dawson* (1938) 22 T.C. 189 a singer was paid an advance of royalties of £1,500 which, somewhat surprisingly, the Commissioners held to be a loan in spite of the wording of the agreement that (at 193) it:

> "shall be treated and taken in account as payments by the company on account and in advance of the royalties due under the provisions of this agreement."

The Commissioners were, however, duly overruled by MacNaghten J., who had no hesitation in holding that the construction of the agreement was a question of law. As an advance of royalties the payment was part of the recipient's Sch.D, Case II profits. Advances are not usually returnable and are therefore taxed when received, even if recoupable out of future sales. However, it is understood that the Revenue will, exceptionally, sometimes tax advance recoupable royalties when earned by sales and not when the advance is actually received. A returnable advance may be merely a loan, depending on the terms of the agreement. An advance which requires services to be performed, for example, the production of a recording, may, subject to the agreement become a recoupable non-returnable advance only when the recording is delivered and would be returnable prior to that date, if, for example, the recording was never completed, and would be taxed on delivery of the recording, not when the advance was received. *Smart v Lincolnshire Sugar Co Ltd* (1937) 20 T.C. 643, however, suggests that such advances would be income of the year of receipt and the possibility of their being repayable would not justify their exclusion from income unless that became a real likelihood.

INVESTMENT INCOME

27–033   In the case of *Mitchell v Rosay* (1954) 35 T.C. 496, Madame Rosay acquired the rights to exploit a film, which she did for a percentage of the gross receipts. Although she had herself taken part in the film, the profit she made was not part of her professional activities and therefore was not included in any professional income. Nor was she trading in the exploitation of films, so that the profit could not be treated as trading income. The film was exploited by licensing a film distributor for a share of the gross receipts and it was held that these were income assessable as annual payments. Sir Raymond Evershed M.R. quoted with approval (at 504) the following extract from the judgment of Jenkins L.J. in *Purchase v Stainer's Executors* (1951) 32 T.C. 367, at 401:

> "It is I think reasonably plain that periodical payments in respect of a contractual right to a share in the receipts or profits of the distribution of a film acquired

otherwise than in the course of a trade, profession or vocation falling within Cases I or II of Schedule D would be taxable under Case III as falling within the words 'Any... annual payment ... payable either as a charge on any property of the person paying the same ... or as a personal debt or obligation by virtue of any contract...' See *Asher v London Film Productions Ltd* [1944] 1 K.B. 133."

ANGELS

Acting as the backer for a film or stage production (usually known as an "Angel") can be done as a trading activity. In the absence of a trade, however, it is charged to tax as income not otherwise charged, under ITTOIA 2005 s.687. Assessments were made under Sch.D, Case III until 1972 on the basis of Jenkins L.J.'s comments in *Purchase v Stainer's Executors* (1951) 32 T.C. 367, at 401 (quoted above) and *Mitchell v Rosay* (1954) 35 T.C. 496. This means that tax at the basic rate must be deducted on payments of income in excess of the original investment, to non-residents by companies under ITA 2007 s.964, and in appropriate cases by unincorporated payers where the period of investment exceeds 12 months, as annual payments under ITA 2007 s.899. The true taxing provision would appear to be ITTOIA 2005 s.683 as an annual payment not otherwise charged. Losses were treated as capital losses for capital gains tax, although Mr Nicholas Ridley on March 1, 1983 (*Hansard*, Vol.38, col.101) confirmed that relief would now normally be given by set-off or carry-forward against income not otherwise charged to tax under ITTOIA 2005 s.687 under ITA 200, ss.152, 153. He did, however, point out that "whether relief is due will depend on the particular facts of a case". No one appears to have objected to the change in HMRC treatment from ITTOIA 2005 s.683 (ITTOIA 2005 s.687).

27–034

The unsuccessful backer of a film in *Lunt v Wellesley* (1945) 27 T.C. 78, was in business as an artistic film producer and the expenses he incurred, including certain guarantee payments for the film, were deductible from his professional income.

COMPENSATION

The case of *John Mills Productions Ltd (in liquidation) v Mathias* (1967) 44 T.C. 441 concerned a company which was in being to exploit the services of the actor John Mills. The company received £50,000 compensation for the cancellation of a contract from J. Arthur Rank Productions Ltd and promptly went into liquidation. A new company was formed to exploit Mr Mills' services. It was argued unsuccessfully that the compensation received of £50,000 was capital compensation for the loss of the company's substratum, its main income having previously come from Rank. This contention was rejected and the amount judged liable to tax in the company's hands as trading income.

27–035

In *John v James* [1986] S.T.C. 352, it was held that damages for breach of duty under a fiduciary relationship between a manager and Elton John, songwriter and performer, should be paid gross without deduction of tax, either

United Kingdom or foreign, following *Bartlett v Barclays Bank Trust Co Ltd* [1980] Ch.515, and distinguishing *British Transport Commission v Gourley* [1956] A.C. 185.

INDUCEMENT PAYMENTS

27–036 In some cases it may be possible to make a lump-sum payment, tax free, to induce someone to give up their current status. Examples that have been through the courts include a fee to a rugby player to give up amateur status (*Jarrold v Boustead* (1964) 41 T.C. 701), shares allotted to a chartered accountant for giving up his practice (*Pritchard v Arundale* (1971) 47 T.C. 680), and a fee paid to a barrister on giving up his profession (*Vaughan-Neil v IRC* [1979] S.T.C. 644). An inducement fee to persuade someone to join a club or business, is not, however, tax-free (*Riley v Coglan* (1967) 44 T.C. 481), nor is a payment to persuade someone to give up an existing employment and take on another (*Glantre Engineering Ltd v Goodhand* [1983] S.T.C. 1) even when paid by a person other than the prospective employer (*Shilton v Wilmshurst* [1991] S.T.C. 88).

CAPITAL RECEIPTS

27–037 An entertainer, unlike an author, has a reasonable chance of having a capital receipt, for example, on the sale of film rights acquired as an investment, taxed as a capital gain instead of as part of his professional earnings (*Shiner v Lindblom* (1960) 39 T.C. 367).

EXPENSES

27–038 Self-employed entertainers, like other people carrying on a trade or profession, are entitled to deduct those expenses incurred wholly and exclusively for the purpose of their business under ITTOIA 2005 s.34. Duality of purpose will result in a disallowance (*Prince v Mapp* (1969) 46 T.C. 169; *Murgatroyd v Evans-Jackson* (1966) 43 T.C. 581; *Norman v Golder* (1944) 26 T.C. 293; *Caillebotte v Quinn* [1975] S.T.C. 265; and *Bowden v Russell & Russell* (1965) 42 T.C. 301), unless the reason for incurring the expense was the business and any private benefit is incidental to the business purpose (*Bentleys, Stokes & Lowless v Beeson* (1952) 33 T.C. 491 and *Edwards v Warmsley, Henshall & Co* (1967) 44 T.C. 431). In practice, HMRC will often allow apportionment of expenses where there is a genuine business reason.

Entertaining expenses are specifically disallowed in most cases under ITTOIA 2005 ss.45 and 46.

A list of allowable expenses for an entertainer could include:

- accompanist, session musicians and supporting artistes' fees;
- accountancy;
- agent's fees and commission;

- fees;
- bank interest and charges;
- capital allowances on cost of equipment, car, instruments, etc.;
- chiropody and physiotherapy (for dancers);
- cleaning and repair or replacement of professional clothes and props;
- cosmetic surgery/dentistry (part);
- cosmetics;
- direct costs;
- gratuities;
- hairdressing;
- hire of rehearsal halls, studio and facilities;
- hire of television, video, hi-fi, etc.;
- insurance of clothes, instruments, public liability, etc.;
- laundry and cleaning;
- legal fees for contracts, protecting copyright, etc.;
- postage and stationery;
- professional coaching;
- professional journals;
- publicity and photographs;
- records and books, scores, etc.;
- repairs and tuning instruments;
- research assistance and materials, typing and editorial costs;
- royalty audit costs;
- secretarial assistance;
- subscriptions;
- subsistence;
- tax compliance fees;
- telephone and fax;
- theatre, concert or cinema tickets for agent, manager, etc.;
- touring expenses;
- travel and car expenses, including taxis and chauffeured cars;
- union dues;
- use of rooms as office at home (proportion of light, heat, insurance, cleaning, power, decorating, etc.);
- VAT irrecoverable on business expenses; and
- visits to theatre or cinema.

RETURNS

It should be noted that payments to entertainers have to be notified to the Revenue under TMA 1970 s.16, if a notice is required by an Inspector of Taxes. The usual notice is the return Form 46R1 and includes all payments in respect of copyright. **27–039**

EMPLOYMENT COMPANIES

27–040 It is by no means unusual for a performer, or for that matter an actor, composer or artiste, to enter into an agreement with a company whereby he is an employee of the company and draws a salary assessed to tax as employment income. The company then carries on a trade of exploiting the services of its employee and the fees, royalties or other lump sums received by the company are part of its trading income. This sort of arrangement, if properly set up and run, is perfectly effective in the United Kingdom. The arrangements may fall within the specific anti-avoidance provisions of ITA 2007 ss.773–785 but they can also have other implications, as illustrated in the case of *Crossland v Hawkins* (1961) 39 T.C. 493. In this case, Jack Hawkins was employed by a company the shares of which were owned by trustees of his father-in-law's trust in favour of his (Mr Hawkins') children. When dividends were paid by the company to the trustees and then to the children, it was held that the income so distributed was taxable on Mr Hawkins as an additional settlor of the trust. In the words of Pearce L.J., at 507:

> "The proposals were clearly proposals for achieving the result that has been achieved, namely, a family settlement financed by dividends produced by Mr Hawkins' contract to sell his services to the company at an inadequate and uncommercial rate. Had the proposals been of any other nature, the Case must inevitably have so stated. The foundation of those proposals was his earning power, and they needed not merely his assent but his active participation. He personally entered into the contract to serve for an inadequate remuneration. He was himself a director of the company when the shares were allotted to the trustees, when the large profit was made by the company's use of the contract and when the dividend was declared. And above all he himself created the source of the company's profit by acting in the film 'Fortune is a Woman'. The mere fact that he did not concern himself with some of the steps in the legal machinery involved does not make it any the less his arrangement within the Section."

The definition of "settlement" referred to is in ITTOIA 2005 s.620, and includes any disposition, trust, covenant, agreement, arrangement or transfer of assets. As a result of his being a settlor, the income of the child remained that of the parent under ITTOIA 2005 s.629. This case was followed in that of *IRC v Mills* [1974] S.T.C. 130, which was very similar to *Crossland v Hawkins*, except that the employee of the company, Miss Hayley Mills, was then aged 14 and the settlor of a trust for her absolute benefit on attaining the age of 25 was her father, John Mills. The House of Lords resisted the contention that a minor was not capable of being a settlor and entering into an arrangement such as would constitute a settlement as defined by the now repealed TA 1988 s.681(4) (which definition was the same as in ITTOIA 2005 s.620, with the omission of the reference to transfer of assets).

An extremely complex case involving the taxation of income of a performer was that involving Miss Julie Christie, *Black Nominees Ltd v Nicol* [1975] S.T.C. 372. This involved a series of transactions whereby Black Nominees Ltd, as trustees for a discretionary trust of which Miss Christie was a beneficiary, obtained large sums ostensibly as repayment of a "loan" of £475,000.

27–041 Templeman J. was unimpressed by the complexity of the scheme. At 278:

"Once Cymbeline agreed to purchase the interest of Black Nominees [the taxpayer company] under the first settlement, each participant at the meeting required to receive and pay £475,000, each participant received £475,000 and each participant paid away £475,000. No one began the meeting with £475,000 and no one left the meeting with £475,000 or with any asset remotely near that value. I assume that Knowsley were in a position to lend £475,000 when they arrived, but they departed without leaving any such sum on loan to anyone. In effect, £475,000 passed by Knowsley drafts from Knowsley to Univats to Cymbeline to Black Nominees to Swanlack to Woods to Downer to Univats and back to Knowsley, pursuant to documents which divided the profits from the Christie rights between the financiers and Black Nominees in the proportions of roughly 32 and 1/2 per cent and 67 and 1/2 per cent."

At 284:

"Tax is charged under Case VI in respect of annual profits or gains not falling under any other Case or under any other Schedule. In my judgment, the moneys received by Black Nominees in consequence of the transactions entered into in December 1965 fit within this description. If it were not the trick with the £475,000, no one would suggest that the moneys received by Black Nominees were capital. Once the trick is exposed the moneys are seen to be what they are: namely, annual profits or gains. They escape any other Case or Schedule and fall into Case VI."

It should be noted that this case was not taken beyond the High Court.

COMPANY PARTNERSHIPS

One final case has to be considered relating to income received by a performer. This is the case of *Newstead v Frost* [1980] S.T.C. 123. In this case David Frost entered into a partnership agreement with a Bahamian company, Leander Productions Ltd. The partnership was known as Leander Enterprises. The business of the partnership was to act as television and film consultants and advisers, and amongst other things to use and exploit the services of producers or directors, writers and artistes. David Frost was to participate as to 95 per cent in the profits of the partnership and 99 per cent in the capital assets of the partnership. However, the partnership was to be carried on outside the United Kingdom. It was not a sham and actually carried on business from the Bahamas. As a result, the partnership was a non-resident partnership within ITTOIA 2005 s.857, and therefore David Frost's share was assessable to tax, under the law at that time, only on the basis of remittances to the United Kingdom.

27–042

ALTERNATIVE ASSESSMENTS

It will be seen from the foregoing analysis of the case law that a performing artiste may, in the same way as an author, be taxed under various heads on income arising. The normal assessment would be as arising from the exercise of a profession or vocation. If these activities arise overseas through a non-resident partnership the assessment is under ITTOIA 2005 s.857. If the artiste is an employee of a company which exploits his services the company would be

27–043

assessed on its trading profit, and the employee on employment income. Exceptionally, the income arising may be assessed under ITTOIA 2005 ss.683 or 579 if related to the exploitation of copyright held as an investment, or under ITTOIA 2005 s.687, if the income cannot be brought within any other head of charge. It is, of course, possible that a capital profit could be made, for example, by someone purchasing film rights for a capital sum to hold as an investment and subsequently selling the entire rights at a profit. Such a profit would be subject to capital gains tax under TCGA 1992 s.21.

ANTI-CONSTELLATION PROVISIONS

27–044 An important provision that has to be considered in connection with the taxation of income from intellectual property is ITA 2007 ss.773–789, which is headed "Sale of occupation income".

The section applies where an individual (or, presumably, a number of individuals in partnership) makes arrangements to exploit his earning capacity with a view to mitigating his tax liability and as a result a capital amount is received by the taxpayer or any other person. A capital amount is extremely widely defined by ITA 2007 ss.776–779, as an amount in money's or money's worth which does not fall to be included in calculations of income for income tax purposes apart from this chapter (ITA 2007 Pt 13 Ch.4 ss.773–789).

The classic situation that the section was aimed at is that of Constellation Investments Ltd, which was a company formed to exploit the services of performers, writers and other individuals of talent. Such people would sell a right to their future income for a capital sum. As a result of ITA 2007 ss.776–779, any such capital sum would be assessed to tax as income arising to the taxpayers. These sections are sufficiently widely drawn to cover any form of capital sum received by any party, not necessarily the individual, except for the sale of a business or partnership or shares in a company so far as it is attributable to the business as a going concern, i.e. goodwill ITA 2007 s.784. The section will therefore catch the traditional situation of, for example, an author who contracts to write for a company in which he owns the shares. If in due course the income not drawn out in the form of remuneration is accumulated in the company and the shares subsequently sold, or the company put into liquidation, the capital amount received could be assessed under these provisions. There are provisions to charge capital sums indirectly derived from the individual's activities, for example, in the form of shares, and the section applies to all persons whether resident in the United Kingdom or not, to the extent that the occupation of the individual is carried on in the United Kingdom (ITA 2007 s.1015(3)). Tax must be deducted from a capital sum paid to a non-resident and accounted for to HMRC if they make a direction under ITA 2007 s.944.

27–045 There are three requirements which have to be met before the section applies to a person carrying on such personal activities.

(1) There must be transactions or arrangements to exploit the earning capacity of an individual in any occupation by putting some other person in a position to enjoy the rewards derived from the individual's activities (ITA

2007 ss.773(2)(a), 785). "Individual" almost certainly includes individuals acting together, e.g. a rock group. "Occupation" includes profession or vocation but not a trade, (ITA 2007 s.774(a)). It also includes an office or employment (ITA 2007 s.774(b)). "Income" specifically includes any receipts from copyright or any other right deriving its value from the activities, including past activities of the individual, e.g. patents obtained by an (inventor ITA 2007 s.777).

(2) A capital amount must be obtained for the individual or any other person ITA 2007 ss.778,779 "Capital amount" means any amount which does not fall to be included in a calculation of income (ITA 2007 s.777(7)).
It is possible to trace a capital amount from the individual's activities through any number of intermediaries. (ITA 2007 s.781). Income from a foreign partnership or employment assessed on a non-domiciled individual on a remittance basis may fall within the definition of a capital amount.

(3) Finally, one of the main objects of the transactions or arrangements must be the avoidance or reduction of liability to income tax (ITA 2007 s.773(2)(b)). This question of motive is hard to prove but if it can be demonstrated that there are good commercial reasons for the arrangements the section should not bite.

Although there have as yet been no cases on these provisions, a similar motive test in TA 1988 s.703(1), has been considered in: *IRC v Kleinwort, Benson Ltd* (1968) 45 T.C. 369; *IRC v Brebner* (1967) 43 T.C. 705; *IRC v Goodwin* [1976] S.T.C. 28; and *Clark v IRC* [1978] S.T.C. 614. The taxpayers argued that the transactions were in the ordinary course of business, to resist a take-over, to prevent loss of control and to buy a farm, respectively, and all were successful. In *Hasloch v IRC* (1971) 47 T.C. 50, the court upheld the Special Commissioners' finding of fact that the avoidance of taxation was a main object of the transaction.

Exemptions

The sale of goodwill of a business or of shares in a company which will carry on as a going concern is not caught by the section in view of ITA 2007 ss.784 and 785, but the going concern value must not be attributable to the prospective income from the individual's activities for which he will not receive adequate reward in an income form. This would mean that a recording artiste selling a company for a value based on prospective future record royalty income from past records would not be within the exemption, but it might be possible for an employing company to cease the employment, set up a new trade of, say, share or property dealing, with the accumulated income and sell the shares which would reflect the value of the new business as a going concern.

27–046

A capital sum received in the form of shares is not taxed until the shares are sold ITA 2007 s.785, so it could be possible to transfer a profession to a company and use the company assets to pay remuneration and pension contributions so that value is extracted before the shares are sold.

There are provisions in ITA 2007 s.786, enabling HMRC to recover tax from whoever received the capital sum if the individual assessed is unable to exercise his right of recovery within six months of the payable date. HMRC may make a direction requiring the vendor who has become entitled to the proceeds of sale to withdraw tax on payment to a non-resident purchaser of the rights, but may not make a protective assessment in advance of that entitlement, (ITA 2007 s.944, and *Energy Property Development Corporation v Pardoe* [2000] S.T.C. 286). Such sums are not charged to capital gains tax as they are liable to income tax (ITA 2007 Sch.1 paras 299, 300).

HMRC has power to obtain information under ITA 2007 s.788 which is exercised by HMRC through the Anti-Avoidance Group, which deals with cases under these provisions (BIM 35980; 35990)

NON-RESIDENT ENTERTAINERS AND SPORTSMEN

27–047 An entertainer or sportsman carrying on a relevant activity in the United Kingdom, who is not resident in the United Kingdom in the tax year in which the activity is performed, is within the provisions of ITTOIA 2005 ss.13, 14, and the detailed regulations contained in the Income Tax (Entertainers and Sportsmen) Regulations 1987 (SI 1987/530).

Such a visiting sportsman or entertainer is liable to have tax at the basic rate deducted from payments made to him including loans or transfers.

An entertainer is defined as an individual who performs, whether alone or with others (SI 1987/530 reg.2), and includes both live and recorded performances. HMRC's Guidance Notes, FEU 50, mentions, as examples of entertainers and sportsmen, athletes, golfers, cricketers, footballers, tennis players, boxers, snooker players, darts players, motor racing drivers, jockeys, ice skaters, contestants in chess tournaments, singers, musicians, conductors, models, dancers, actors, TV and radio personalities, and variety entertainers. The person may appear alone or with others in a team, choir, band, orchestra, opera company, ballet company, troupe or circus. Models are now included in the list except for photographic assignments featuring the clothes where the model is acting "as a clotheshorse", but in the age of the "supermodel" earning large fees for catwalk appearances, HMRC now argue that they are entertainers in their own right, not merely showing off clothes. Payments for ancillary services on an arm's-length basis or in respect of recording royalties are excluded (SI 1987/530 reg.3) but the provisions extend to any other activities "in his character as entertainer" including appearance fees, whether live or recorded and endorsement fees (see *Deuce and Ball v Robinson* [2003] S.T.C. (SCD) 382). They also extend, in the view of HMRC, to income from merchandising, although it would seem doubtful as to whether this can properly be described as income received as an entertainer (SI 1987/530 reg.6). There is a de minimis provision in that payments of no more than £1,000 may be made without deduction of tax although obviously connected payments have to be aggregated for this purpose (SI 1987/530 reg.4).

27–048 The entertainer is treated as carrying on a trade in the United Kingdom separate from any other activities, assessed on a current year basis with provision for losses and expenses (ITTOIA 2005 s.13(2–4)).

Payments to connected parties such as overseas companies employing the entertainer are treated as if they were made direct to the entertainer (SI 1987/530 reg.7); *Agasi v Robinson* (2006) S.T.C. 1056 and credit is given to the entertainer for the tax deducted at source (SI 1987/530 reg.12).

The person making payments has to make quarterly returns to HMRC and pay over the tax deducted within 14 days of the end of the quarter (SI 1987/530 regs 4 and 10).

Reduced withholding agreements

27–049 Where a payment is to be made subject to deduction of tax it is possible for the entertainer or the payer or recipient to apply to HMRC for a reduced withholding agreement (SI 1987/530 reg.5). The purpose of the reduced withholding agreement is to enable account to be taken of expenses which have to be met out of the fees. In order to obtain an agreement it is necessary to supply HMRC with a detailed budget, preferably before the tour commences, and agree a level of deduction from the gross payments which would equate to the entertainers' correct UK tax liability on the net income after all allowable expenses.

The problem with such a reduced withholding agreement is that it is entirely at the discretion of HMRC and they are likely to insist that marginal income such as that from merchandising is included, and will look closely at the expenses. It is unlikely in practice to be helpful to argue that the tour is unlikely to make a profit at all, even if that is the case. This suggests that the prime purpose of the tour is to promote the group's recordings, rather than to make money out of the tour itself; as a result HMRC would disallow the expenses of the tour as not wholly and exclusively related to the tour but related to promotional activity for the group's recordings, and therefore disallowable on the duality of purpose reasoning. In practice a good deal of haggling over the tour budget is common; experience suggests that the final result is likely to be reasonable.

Double taxation agreements

27–050 Most double taxation agreements have an "artistes and athletes", "artistes and sportsmen" or "entertainers and sportsmen" article which enables the visiting entertainer to be taxed in the territory in which the person is to perform. HMRC argue that these provisions enable payments made indirectly to the entertainer, for example, to a company employing him, to be treated as made to the entertainer (ITTOIA 2005 s.13(5)) and therefore there is no need to rely on what is normally para.2 of a typical "artistes and athletes" article along the lines of the OECD Model Convention. This means that even if there is not a para.2 equivalent extending to indirect payments, HMRC argue that the UK provisions treat indirect payments as paid direct to the entertainer and therefore have to be treated for double taxation agreement purposes as if they were paid direct.

Whether this line of argument is correct or whether it is possible to argue that a double taxation agreement with a simple artistes and athletes' article, which does not extend to indirect payments, could overrule the UK legislation has yet to be tested.

Within the European Union non-discrimination rules may apply (*Gerritse v Finanzamt Neukolln-Nord* (E.C.J.) (C-234/01)).

Benefits and apportionment

27–051 Payments in kind have to be valued at the cost to the provider and are then treated as a net amount which is grossed up to arrive at the tax to be deducted at source (SI 1987/530 reg.17).

Where a tour covers more than one country it is necessary to apportion expenses which relate to the entire tour to the deemed separate trade in the United Kingdom on some basis that is just and reasonable (SI 1987/530 reg.16), for example, on the number of days performed in the United Kingdom compared with the total number of days performed.

The withholding tax may be set against the finally agreed UK tax liability and repaid where appropriate in accordance with the regulations. The obligation to deduct tax may be affected by the provision of any relevant double taxation agreement.

27–052 The relevant activities are treated as part of a trade, profession or vocation exercised within the United Kingdom except where it is performed in the course of an office or employment (ITTOIA 2005 s.13(4)(b)). A payment made to a third party is treated as made to the entertainer or sportsman if a connection of the prescribed kind exists. Regulations enable credit to be obtained for expenses incurred by the third party and to prevent the third party also being taxed on the same income. The assessment is to be made on a current year basis and regulations provide for losses and expenses. The activities in the United Kingdom are treated as a separate trade carried on in the United Kingdom (ITTOIA 2005 s.13(7)). Payment is regarded as the gross amount before deducting the withholding tax. Detailed valuation rules are made in regulations for payments in kind (ITTOIA 2005 s.14). Secrecy obligations will not prevent HMRC disclosing information to payers to enable them to operate the withholding tax correctly.

The Foreign Entertainers Unit, S0708 which is part of HMRC Personal Tax International, St John's House, Merton Road, Bootle, Merseyside, L69 9AP (tel.) 0300 547 395, (fax) 0151 472 6483 administers the scheme.

IMAGE RIGHTS

27–053 Fees paid by advertisers to an entertainer or sportsman for the right to use their appearance in a photograph, film or video or in person to endorse a product are usually referred to as for "image rights" and their payment as "endorsement fees". A celebrity's likeness is, in the UK, effectively protected at common law by libel, defamation, passing off or in some cases breach of copyright or trade mark. However, in Guernsey The Image Rights (Bailiwick of Guernsey) Ordinance 2012 providing that a personage, a natural person, a legal person, two or more such persons as a joint personality or group or a fictional character may be registered as a registered personality, and protected as a form of intellectual property. The extent to which other countries will take account of registration in Guernsey remains a matter of conjecture, but it is an indication of the commercial value of a person's "name and likeness" in endorsement of goods and services.

Under the non-resident entertainers and sportsmen provisions HMRC currently regard a visiting sportsperson's endorsement income, as well as fees for appearances, as subject to tax in the UK on a proportion of the worldwide income from endorsement, calculated by reference to the person's relevant performance and training days in the UK as a proportion to their relevant performance and training days worldwide. In *Agasi v Robinson* (2006) S.T.C. 1056 the House of Lords held that payments for endorsement contracts through non-UK companies not remitted to the UK were nonetheless taxable under these provisions even though they would not have been taxed on Agasi had he been tax resident in the UK, unless remitted to the UK in view of his non-UK domicile. This peculiar state of affairs means that a non-resident sportsman or entertainer can pay more tax in the UK than his earnings from appearing in the UK. It also explains why special legislation has been introduced for major international sporting events in the UK to make the earnings including endorsement income tax free, or the competitors would not compete, see FA 2006 ss.65–68 (Olympic and Paralympic Games), FA 2010 s.63 (Champions League Final 2011), FA 2012 s.13 (Champions League Final 2013), FA 2013 s.8 (London Anniversary Games 2013), and FA 2013 s.9 (Glasgow Commonwealth Games 2014).

There is obviously pressure from other sporting events for similar tax exemption, which, it is argued, should not be confined to football and athletics.

VAT

Where a supply of services consists of cultural, artistic, sporting, scientific, educational or entertainment services, services relating to exhibitions, conferences or meetings and services ancillary to, including those organising any supply related thereto, it is treated as made where the services are physically carried out, i.e. the country in which the performance takes place (SI 1992/3121 art.15(a)). This means that if an entertainer or sportsman or a company employing him is likely to be in receipt of a sum in excess of the VAT threshold (£79,000 from April 1, 2013) (VATA 1994 Sch.1 para.1(1)) he will be liable to register for VAT as providing services in the United Kingdom. The VAT threshold in the United Kingdom is substantially higher than in other European countries and VAT rates in Europe on performance services vary widely within the European Union.

27–054

Once registered for VAT in the United Kingdom the entertainer or his employer should charge VAT at the standard rate of 20 per cent and will be able to claim input tax for VAT charged on goods and services received, such as legal and accounting fees.

Example

Skip Skyways, a Dutch resident singer, agrees to appear in the United Kingdom for five nights for a fee of £80,000. Skip has to register and submits an invoice for £80,000 plus VAT at 20 per cent, i.e. £96,000.

The fact that the entertainer is obliged to charge VAT on his services should cause no real problems in that the recipient of the services of the entertainer (i.e. the promoter) will almost certainly be VAT registered and be able to recover any VAT charged.

It is possible, however, for the entertainer to shift the obligation to account for VAT to the recipient of his services provided that the recipient is VAT registered

27–055

(VATA 1994 Sch.5 para.9). In this way VAT registration of the entertainer can be avoided although, by using this method, recovery of VAT on expenses incurred within the United Kingdom becomes more difficult. Recovery can still be made but it is necessary to make a separate application to the United Kingdom authorities and a repayment is not normally made for at least a period of six months (VATA 1994 s.39; SI 1995/2518 regs 173–197). The tax shift alternative is also available in most other EU countries.

If an entertainer decides to register for VAT in the country where he performs, it is normally necessary to appoint a fiscal representative. This can be anyone established in the country of the performance, but that representative will be jointly and severally liable for any VAT debts of the entertainer.

In the United Kingdom only, it is possible to register as an "overseas business" and in this way it is not always necessary to appoint a fiscal representative (VATA 1994 s.48(1)). It is still usually necessary, however, to authorise someone within the United Kingdom to complete and sign the VAT return forms on behalf of the entertainer.

27–056   Apart from the performer's services, ancillary services provided by the road crew, sound and lighting engineers, etc. are usually regarded as part of the performance services and take place where the performance is held (SI 1992/3121 art.15(c)). Services of intermediaries (booking agents/management) are not subject to UK VAT provided that the recipient of the service (e.g. the performer) is not registered within the United Kingdom, but is registered elsewhere in the European Union or has no business establishment anywhere within the European Union (SI 1992/3121 art.13).

If the performer does have a registration within the United Kingdom, any services provided by intermediaries will be subject to UK VAT at the standard rate.

Where a supply consists of a transfer or assignment of copyrights, licences, trade marks and similar rights, the requirement to account for VAT normally falls upon the transferee unless the performer and the transferee are VAT registered in the same country (VATA 1994 Sch.5 para.1). Where no VAT is charged, the transferee is obliged to account for VAT in his own country but can recover that VAT at the same time, subject to normal rules (VATA 1994 s.8(1)).

CHAPTER 28

Franchising

ADVANTAGE TO FRANCHISOR

Franchising is an arrangement under which a product or service has been established and the proprietors determine that they are unable to exploit it to its maximum potential on their own. Commonly, they lack the capital and expertise to develop the product or service to its maximum potential or there are local considerations such as language, infrastructure or legal requirements that require the involvement of local participation to run the business effectively. The advantage to the franchisor in such an arrangement is that he will maximise the return on the initial development by taking a profit for exploitation in areas where it is not practical to exploit the product or service on his own, and therefore take a profit that would otherwise be unobtainable. It also enables the development to be exploited in a wider area than it would otherwise be possible, and spread marketing and advertising costs over a wide market. 28–001

Very often the product or service is a way of manufacturing or distributing a product or providing a service that will often involve the exploitation by the franchisee of the franchisor's name and logo, which is likely to qualify for trade mark protection, and the provision of know-how, in its widest sense of knowledge of how the product or service may best be exploited, without necessarily falling within the limited definition of knowhow for tax purposes under ITTOIA 2005 ss.192(1), 583(4) and (5), as explained in Ch.19. This knowledge may be protected as a secret process and under the laws relating to passing off, as well as under the trade mark provisions, and there may well be written instruction manuals for the guidance of the franchisee that would be protected by copyright. It is quite common for franchising arrangements to include the providing of computer programs for assisting and monitoring the development of the franchisees' businesses.

Where a product is involved it may be protected by patents or registered design or design rights but this is not commonly an important element in a franchising operation.

ADVANTAGE TO FRANCHISEE

The advantage to the franchisee is that the franchising arrangement enables him to cut down the learning curve in running a successful business in that he can move immediately into the provision of a product or service that has an established market in the franchisor's territory, which is likely to be of similar 28–002 relevance to the franchisee's territory. The franchisee also acquires access to a branded product with an established reputation, which can be marketed further for the mutual benefit of both the franchisee and the franchisor.

DISADVANTAGE TO FRANCHISOR

28–003 The disadvantage of franchising for the franchisor is that the ability to expand the business is necessarily curtailed by having to avoid competition with the franchisees, while continuing to exploit and develop the product or service. A further disadvantage is the resources that have to be put into monitoring the franchisees' performance to make sure that the product or service supplied meets the franchisor's standards. Clearly as each franchisee is, for a fee, riding on the back of the franchisor, the reputation of both is interdependent and a rogue franchisee could quickly have an adverse impact on the reputation of the franchisor's product or service. It is easy to underestimate the resources required to ensure the proper performance of the franchisee.

It is also possible to have a franchisee who may meet the quality requirements of the franchisor but who still fails to develop the product or service to its full potential in his territory, thus inhibiting the worldwide growth and profit potential for the franchisor.

DISADVANTAGE TO FRANCHISEE

28–004 The main disadvantage as far as the franchisee is concerned is that his time, energy and resources are being put into the development of a product or service in his territory, which is building up the franchisor's reputation and profit potential rather than that of the franchisee. It is not unknown for franchisees to be a lot more successful in their territory than the original franchisor, and feel resentment to the extent that they believe they are now carrying the franchisor, whatever the original arrangement may have been.

AGREEMENTS

28–005 A well-drafted franchising agreement will often overcome many of the potential disadvantages of franchising and give the franchisor powers to ensure that the franchisee meets the appropriate quality requirements and achieves pre-agreed performance targets, and sets out with clarity the rights and duties of the franchisee and franchisor, which may include a compulsory dispute resolution procedure such as arbitration in the event of disagreement. In the United Kingdom, the Chartered Institute of Arbitrators and the British Franchise Association have established rules for a specific arbitration scheme that provides an inexpensive and informal method of resolving disputes between franchisors and franchisees, which the parties cannot resolve amicably themselves.

CODE OF CONDUCT

The British Franchise Association (*http://www.thebfa.org* [Accessed September 16, 2013]) also publishes a code of ethical conduct based on the European code of ethics for franchising produced by the European Franchise Federation.

28–006

These provide a definition of franchising including the wide definition of know-how as a body of known practical information resulting from experience and testing by the franchisor, which is secret, substantial and identified in the franchise agreement. It is also made clear that franchising takes place between independent organisations and it sets out the rights and duties of both parties, including the franchisor's commitment to continuing commercial and technical assistance.

The guiding principles require the franchisor to have himself operated the business concept, with success, for a reasonable period; to grant rights to use the name and trade mark, and to provide the franchisee with initial training and ongoing commercial and technical assistance throughout the franchise period. The duties of the franchisee are to use his best endeavours to ensure the growth of the franchise business and the maintenance of a common identity and reputation throughout the franchise network, to protect the confidentiality of information supplied by the franchisor and to provide performance and financial information relating to the franchisee's operations. The necessity in a franchise arrangement for fair play between the parties is emphasised.

In recruiting potential franchisees, the franchisor should disclose all material facts and ensure that his advertising is not misleading, subject to a requirement on the potential franchisee to keep secret all confidential information. Franchisees should be chosen who appear to have the financial and management skills necessary for the successful implementation of the franchise.

28–007

The franchise agreement should certainly comply with the national laws and international law but also with the code of ethics and the mutual requirement of the franchisee and franchisor to protect and develop the commercial reputation of the franchise network. In the case of cross-border franchising the agreement should be officially translated into the franchisee's own language and copies of the signed agreement should be given to both parties. The agreement should also set out clearly the rights and obligations of the franchisor and the franchisee in respect of the goods and services specified in the franchise agreement. The financial obligations of the franchisee should be set out as should the minimum period of the agreement, which should be sufficient to enable the franchisee to recoup his initial investment. The renewal terms of the agreement, if any, should be identified and the ability of the franchisee to sell or assign the franchise business should be explained together with any pre-emption rights for the franchisor. The franchisor's ownership of the intellectual property and the franchisee's rights to use this during the period of the franchise agreement, and the giving up of those rights on the termination of the agreement, should be clearly laid out in the agreement.

For further information on legal and commercial aspects of franchising, see M. Mendelsohn, *Guide to Franchising* (London: Thomson Learning, 2001).

FRANCHISING

THE FRANCHISOR'S TAX POSITION

Analysis of agreement

28–008 A franchise agreement may relate to the sale of goods or the provision of services and, in intellectual property terms, may combine the use of a trade mark, trade name and logo, an established market presentation and co-ordinated advertising campaign and business systems procedures which effectively amount to a combination of know-how and show-how. The products themselves may be patented or protected under the registered design or design right provisions and literature will be copyright. As has been explained earlier in this book it might be necessary to analyse payments by the franchisee to the franchisor into their constituent components by reference to the market value of the goods and services provided, in order to apply the appropriate tax rules to the particular elements, as in *Paterson Engineering Co Limited v Duff* (1943) 25 T.C. 43. In practice the franchise agreement is usually a single, all be it comprehensive, document giving the franchisee a bundle of rights within the franchise territory in which he has the exclusive right to exploit the business (without contravening the Restrictive Trade Practices Act 1976 (as amended by SI 1996/346), arts 81 and 82 of the Treaty of the European Community or other non-competition legislation). In many cases the payment to the franchisor is incorporated in the agreement for the exclusive supply of products or raw materials and it would be unusual for the Revenue to dissect such a payment to extract the intellectual property element, if any. The franchisor will be carrying on a trade and the receipts will be inflated by the enhanced sales as a result of the franchise agreement. Expenses recharged to the franchisee will also enhance the taxable trading profit of the franchisor. Under the normal accruals basis of accounting, receipts due from the franchisee will be brought into account by the franchisor over the period during which they were earned; any potential under-recovery as a result of the franchisee's inability to pay would be covered by a bad debt provision in the normal way.

Initial lump sums

28–009 It is not unusual for a franchise agreement to require the franchisee to make an initial lump sum payment to the franchisor and it has to be considered whether any part of this lump sum is a capital receipt for the sale of goodwill. In most circumstances the case law relating to the sale of know-how for a lump sum will be in point. As explained in Ch.19, cases such as: *Jeffrey v Rolls Royce Ltd* (1962) 4 T.C. 443; *Musker v English Electric Co Limited* (1964) 41 T.C. 556; *Coalite and Chemical Products v Treeby* (1971) 48 T.C. 171; *Thomsons (Carron) Ltd v IRC* [1976] S.T.C. 317; and *John & E. Sturge Ltd v Hessel* [1975] S.T.C. 573, suggest that in a majority of cases there is no diminution in the franchisor's goodwill as a result of the franchise agreement, and that any lump sum allocated to the acquisition of the franchisor's goodwill by the franchisee will nonetheless be a trading receipt of the franchisor. The fact that the lump sum is payable by instalments is irrelevant (*British Dyestuffs Corporation (Blackley) Ltd v IRC* (1924) 12 T.C. 586). Circumstances in which a lump sum payment by the franchisee for goodwill would give rise to a capital receipt, and a chargeable capital gain by the franchisor, taxable under TCGA 1992 s.21, will be limited to those cases where part of the franchisor's existing goodwill is given up in return for the receipt from the franchisee. This could arise if, for example, the franchisee takes over the franchisor's operation in an established territory, as in *Wolf Electric Tools Ltd v Wilson* (1968) 45 T.C. 326 and *Evans Medical Suppliers Limited v Moriarty* (1957) 37 T.C. 540 (CA72200). Initial sums are normally taxable when receivable (BIM 57610) if this is in accordance with the accounting treatment under UK GAAP.

It is questionable whether a trade mark or brand name disposed of without the underlying business is a disposal of a separate asset, for which roll-over relief is not available under TCGA 1992 s.155, or is a partial disposal of goodwill. CG68210 merely suggests that such cases should be referred to HMRC Capital Gains Technical Group. Disposals by companies on or after April 1, 2002 may fall within the Corporate Intangible Fixed Asset regime (Ch.21).

Amortisation

Where the franchisor has acquired goodwill by purchase, the cost is normally a capital asset in respect of which no capital allowances are available although for purchases on or after April 1, 2002 the Corporate Intangible Fixed Asset regime may allow amortisation to be claimed by a company (Ch.21). It may be that on closer inspection the acquisition relates not so much to goodwill but to the acquisition of intellectual property rights and if so, the ability of the franchisor to amortise the cost for tax purposes will depend on the rights acquired, and is considered under the various chapters related to those rights.

28–010

Restrictive covenants

Where, as is common, the franchisee acquires the rights to exploit the product or service within a particular territory this is often accompanied by a covenant from the franchisor not to compete within that territory. If any lump sum is attached to this covenant on a proper analysis of the franchise agreement, it has to be considered whether the amount received for such a keep-out covenant is capital or income. In many cases a covenant of this nature will be a capital receipt following a number of cases discussed in Ch.16 relating to lump sum receipts from patents, such as: *IRC v British Salmson Aero-engines Ltd* (1938) 22 T.C. 29; *Murray v Imperial Chemical Industries Ltd* (1967) 44 T.C. 175; *Kirby v Thorn EMI Plc* [1987] S.T.C. 621 and *Margerison v Tyresoles Ltd* (1942) 25 T.C. 59; and *Higgs v Olivier* (1952) 33 T.C. 136.

28–011

The HMRC view on restrictive covenants is that if it leads to the complete cessation of the trade, money received is likely to be capital in character. Where the trade is merely interfered with, for instance where only part of a trade ceases, then the receipt is more likely to be revenue (CG68060) although it may depend on the facts of a particular case.

A restrictive covenant given in connection with a disposal of know-how as defined for tax purposes by CTA 2009 s.908(4), is treated as a trading receipt under CTA 2009 s.176 (see para.19–012).

A keep-out covenant in these circumstances is effectively a capital receipt as a part disposal of goodwill, as was made plain in *Kirby v Thorn EMI Plc* [1987] S.T.C. 621, and, as such, taxable as a capital gain either as a part disposal of goodwill under TCGA 1992 s.21, or as a capital sum derived from goodwill under TCGA 1992 s.22 (CG68050–CG68060), unless within the Corporate Intangible Fixed asset regime.

Know-how

28–012 As explained in Ch.19, know-how outside the Corporate Intangible Fixed Asset regime is defined for corporation tax purposes by CTA 2009 s.908(4) and ITTOIA 2005 ss.192(1), 583(4) and (5) for income tax, as being limited to any industrial information and techniques likely to assist in the manufacture or processing of goods or materials, etc. which is a much narrower definition than that usually thought of in terms of franchising agreements. Where know-how is within this definition, a sale by the franchisor is treated by CTA 2009 s.177(1), (2) or ITTOIA 2005 s.193(1), as a trading receipt except to the extent that it is the sale of know-how previously purchased and treated as a disposal under CAA 2001 s.462, or is sold together with the goodwill of the trade, or part of the trade and taxed as a capital sum under CTA 2009 s.178 or ITTOIA 2005 s.194, in which case it would be taxable as a chargeable gain on the franchisor under TCGA 1992 s.21. A restrictive covenant relating to such know-how would normally be taxed as income under CTA 2009 s.176(3), (4) or ITTOIA 2005 ss.192(3), (4) and 583(1), (2), as explained above. Also as explained above, and in Ch.19, the sale of know-how, not statutorily treated as a capital receipt under CTA 2009 s.177–178 or ITTOIA 2005 ss.192–195 and 583–586 is nonetheless a trading receipt on the grounds that the transfer of the know-how to the franchisee does not, of itself, reduce the capital base of the franchisor.

Show-how

28–013 Show-how is the term often applied in the franchising context to fees received for training the franchisee's staff in the operation of the franchise, and the provision of on-going training and updating of the franchisee's staff. As such this will normally be a trading receipt of the franchisor. It is difficult to envisage a receipt of show-how fees that would be a capital receipt for the franchisor.

Advertising pools

28–014 Some franchise agreements provide for a levy on turnover from franchisees to be spent on advertising the product or services covered by the agreement, for the benefit of the franchisor and all the franchisees. The receipt of advertising fees of this nature will normally be a trading receipt of the franchisor and the expenditure an allowable trading expense of the franchisor. The accruals matching concepts of UK GAAP will normally ensure that the fees received from the franchisees will be matched with the advertising expenditure incurred by the franchisor, even when there is a timing difference between the receipt of the income and the incurring of the expenditure, for example where there are periodic advertising campaigns. See, e.g. *Threlfall v Jones, Gallagher v Jones* [1993] S.T.C. 537; *Odeon Associated Theatres Ltd v Jones* (1971) 48 T.C. 257; Inland Revenue, *Tax Bulletin*, February 1995, pp.189–93; *Johnston v Britannia Airways Ltd* [1994] S.T.C. 763; *Owen v Southern Railway of Peru Ltd (1956)* 36 T.C. 602; *IRC v Titaghur Jute Factory Ltd* [1978] S.T.C. 166; and *Commissioner of Inland Revenue v Lo & Lo* [1984] S.T.C. 366.

A mere provision for future advertising expenses that might be incurred would be insufficient to allow the franchisor an immediate deduction (*Clayton v Newcastle-under-Lyme Corporation* (1888) 2 T.C. 416; *Edward Collins & Sons Ltd v IRC* (1924) 12 T.C. 773; *Peter Merchant Ltd v Stedeford* (1948) 30 T.C. 496), and would be unlikely to come within FRS12 for UK GAAP purposes.

Royalties

The amounts which a franchisee has to pay a franchisor under the franchise agreement are normally calculated by reference to a percentage of the franchisee's sales either in monetary terms or on the basis of a levy per unit sold. In some cases the agreement requires the franchisee to purchase raw materials from the franchisor. In some cases the franchise agreement requires the franchisee to make payments for specific services, such as staff training and advertising, or contribute to the cost of the franchisor's policing of the franchise operation.

28–015

In all cases, ongoing receipts of this nature are likely to be trading profits of the franchisor in return for goods or services supplied. It may, however, be the case that the franchisor includes in the agreement intellectual property rights, the fees of which amount to pure income profit, with the result that the franchisee is making an annual payment as explained in Chs 9 and 10.

In such cases the franchisee should withhold tax at the basic rate from the amount paid to the franchisor, who will treat the income as having suffered tax at source. It will normally still be trading income of the franchisor except in the very rare cases where the franchisor does not himself carry on a trade.

Where the franchise agreement includes a licence to the franchisee allowing him to utilise the franchisor's intellectual property, protected by a UK patent, ITA 2007 ss.898–905 (Ch.16) provide that the patent royalty is, except in the case of a company, paying the royalty under the Corporate Intangible Fixed Asset regime an annual payment from which the franchisee has to deduct tax. As this will normally only be a small element of the franchise fee, the franchise agreement may itself specify a reasonable element of the total fee which relates to the patent licence, which will be treated as an annual payment, with the balance being related to the other services provided by the franchisor and paid in full without deduction of tax.

28–016

A franchisee has to deduct tax from royalties under the franchise agreement where they relate to copyright and the franchisor's usual place of abode is outside the United Kingdom, under ITA 2007 s.906, as explained in Ch.18 (see para.18–023 onwards), although a company may, at its own risk, reasonably assume that the recipient will be entitled to relief under an appropriate double taxation agreement and withhold tax at the treat rate, if any, under ITA 2007 ss.911, 912. Where the franchise agreement provides for trade mark or know-how royalties, there is no withholding tax requirement on such income.

This book is only concerned with the taxation of a UK resident franchisor, as the rules applicable to a non-resident franchisor will depend on those of the country of residence. Where, however, a UK franchisor licenses a non-UK resident franchisee, the local law may require the franchisee to deduct withholding tax from fees paid to the UK resident franchisor if not exempt under a double taxation treaty, in respect of which he will normally be able to claim double taxation relief against the UK tax due on the franchise income, either under an appropriate double taxation treaty entered into under TIOPA 2010 s.2, or by way of unilateral relief under TIOPA 2010 ss.8–17.

28–017 There can be a problem arising from the UK treatment of double taxation relief on a source by source basis, where foreign rates of withholding tax are relatively high and there are substantial expenses incurred in the United Kingdom in relation to the franchise income, so that the UK tax on the profit is less than the foreign tax suffered. In *Yates v GCA International* [1991] S.T.C. 157, as explained by SP7/91, means that the foreign tax paid in excess of UK tax due on the franchisor's franchise income cannot be relieved, and can therefore only be claimed as an expense under TIOPA 2010 s.112.

Whether the franchise fees are treated as royalties subject to withholding tax, when paid by the franchisee, will depend on the local rules in the franchisee's country and may be substantially different from the UK rules requiring deduction of tax at source. In particular, in certain countries, the definition of royalty subject to withholding tax includes service charges, which would normally be regarded as a fee for services rendered and outside the scope of any definition of royalties. Where the franchisee is non-resident it is very important to ensure that the franchise agreement recognises the franchisee's liability to withhold tax at source on some or all of the franchise fee payments. This has to be taken into account both in the agreement itself, in requiring the franchisee to obtain confirmation of tax withheld to substantiate a claim for the tax so deducted to be relieved as a credit or expense by the franchisor in the United Kingdom, and commercially to ensure that the franchise agreement leaves the franchisor with sufficient profit, after taking into account both UK and foreign tax, to make the operation worthwhile.

Most of the expenses incurred by the franchisor in connection with the franchising operations will be incurred wholly and exclusively for the purpose of the franchising trade and deductible for tax purposes under CTA 2009 s.54, or ITTOIA 2005 s.34, unless the expenditure relates to a capital asset such as goodwill, on which no relief is available, or plant and machinery, industrial buildings, agricultural buildings, hotels or buildings in an enterprise zone for which capital allowances may be available, as explained in Chs 9 and 10. Where the franchisor's expenditure is on the acquisition of intellectual property rights, relief for the acquisition may be available (as explained in Pt 3).

Turn-key operations

In some cases the franchisor, either alone or in conjunction with the franchisee, will identify suitable premises for the franchisee's operations and fit these out with the appropriate decoration, trade marks, signs, equipment and whatever else is necessary for the franchisee to commence business, in return for a fee. This fee would normally be part of the franchisor's trading income and the expenses incurred allowable expenses of the franchisor's trade. It is unlikely that the franchisor would be regarded as carrying on a separate trade of fitting out premises for franchisees and it will be all part of the franchisor's normal trade. In some cases, however, the franchisor will retain ownership of the premises and/or some or all of the equipment, and recharge these to the franchisee by way of a rent, which may be an inclusive rent or a rent for premises, and operating or finance leases on the equipment. In these cases the premises will remain an asset of the franchisor, and the rent from the premises will be property income, while the rent for the use of equipment will be trading income. The franchisor will claim any capital allowances available on the premises or equipment and these will no doubt be reflected in the rental charge to the franchisee. Whether the rental of the equipment will constitute a separate leasing trade carried on by the franchisor or will be subsumed within the franchisor's general trade, will depend on the circumstances. The taxation of this income and the allowances available are explained generally in Chs 9 and 10.

28–018

THE FRANCHISEE'S TAX POSITION

In many cases the franchisee's taxation treatment will mirror that of the franchisor, but this is not necessarily the case. Normally the purchase of goods and services from the franchisor will be wholly and exclusively for the purpose of the franchisee's trade and allowable under CTA 2009 s.54 or ITTOIA 2005 s.34. However, merely because the payment is treated as a trading receipt of the franchisor does not automatically mean that it is a revenue expense of the franchisee.

28–019

Initial payment

It is common in franchise arrangements for the franchisee to be charged an initial sum. In the case of a company, the payment will normally be deductible as written off for accounting purposes under the Corporate Intangible Fixed Asset regime. In other cases, to determine whether an initial payment is capital or revenue, so far as the franchisee is concerned, it is necessary to consider whether it is in connection with the fixed capital of the business, in which case it is not an allowable revenue deduction (*Beauchamp v FW Woolworth Plc* [1989] S.T.C. 510) or whether it relates to circulating capital and is therefore prima facie a revenue expense (*Pattison v Marine Midland Ltd* [1984] S.T.C. 10). Although it may be fairly obvious that, for example the acquisition of premises or plant and machinery from the franchisor is fixed rather than circulating capital, it is not necessarily clear whether the payment for the initial training of the franchisee and

28–020

its staff, or the right to become a franchisee and use the franchisor's expertise and trade marks for which further fees will be paid, is a payment on capital or revenue account. One of the leading judgments is that of Viscount Cave in *Atherton v British Insulated and Helsby Cables Ltd* (1925) 10 T.C. 155, in which he decided that expenditure is normally capital if "made not only once for all but with a view to bringing into existence an asset or advantage for the enduring benefit of the trade". This is, however, rather more than acquiring the ability to commence or remain in business (*Lawson v Johnson Matthey plc* [1992] S.T.C. 466). The expenditure has to be wholly and exclusively for the purpose of the franchisee's trade, which can give rise to problems where the trade will be carried on through a group of associated companies (*Garforth v Tankard Carpets Ltd* [1980] S.T.C. 251), although it might be possible to argue that the company incurring the expenditure is doing so wholly and exclusively for its own trade and any benefit to a fellow subsidiary or associated company is incidental (*Vodaphone Cellular Ltd and others v Shaw* [1997] S.T.C. 734).

Strick v Regent Oil Co Ltd (1965) 43 T.C. 1, provides a useful review of the distinction between a revenue and capital expense. In this case the observation of Lord Dunedin in *Vallambrosa Rubber Co Ltd v Farmer* (1910) 5 T.C. 529, was quoted with the approval:

> "It is not a bad criterion of what is capital expenditure and what is income expenditure to say that capital expenditure is a thing that is going to be spent once and for all and income expenditure is a thing that it is going to recur every year".

Also considered were Dixon J.'s comments in *Sun Newspapers Ltd v Federal Commissioner of Taxation* (1938) 61 C.L.R. 337, at 359 (Australia):

> "the distinction between expenditure and out-goings on revenue account and capital account corresponds with the distinction between the business entity, structure or organisation set up or established for the earning of profit and the process by which such an organisation operates to obtain regular returns by means of regular outlay. The difference between the outlay and returns representing profit or loss".

28–021 Lord Read stated (at 31):

> "when one comes to intangible assets there is much more difficulty. To help the conduct of his business a trader obtains a right to do something on someone else's property or an obligation by someone to do, or refrain from doing, something or makes a contract which affects the way in which he conducts his business, or the right or obligation or the effect of the contract may endure for a short or a long period of years. The question then arises whether the sum which he has paid for that advantage is a capital or revenue expense. As long ago as 1914 it was settled in *Usher's Wiltshire Brewery Ltd v Bruce* (1915) 6 T.C. 399 that in determining profit, a deduction is to be made or not to be made according, as it is or is not, on the facts of the case a proper debit item to be charged against in-comings of the trade when computing the balance of profits of it . . . One reason at least for refusing to allow a lump sum payment as a debit against incomings and therefore treating it as a capital outlay is that to allow it as a debit would distort the profit and loss account. Counsel agreed that a taxpayer is always permitted to bring the whole of any item of revenue expenditure into the profit and loss account of the year in which the money was spent. The Counsel for the Crown suggested that the taxpayer might be permitted to spread it over more than one year but certainly the Revenue cannot insist on that. So

THE FRANCHISEE'S TAX POSITION

if the whole of a payment made to cover several years is brought into one year's account the profit for that year will be unduly diminished."

Lord Morris of Borth-y-Gest stated (at 45):

"I consider that a tie of the kind now being examined is a capital asset. If a lump sum is paid for such a tie for five years (or for a lesser number of years) it would give a false and unreal picture if the whole sum were debited to the profit and loss account for the first year or for the year in which the payment was made. If it is said to be hard that no part of the lump sum can be a debit in the profit and loss account that is merely to voice a regret that there is no statutory provision which enables periodic allowances to be made. That, however, is not a matter for the Courts.

If regard is had to the language of metaphor which is found in some of the cases, a tie would seem to appertain to the structure of the selling organisation or income earning machine of the appellant. If it is argued that a tie for a shorter period than a year may seem to possess the same nature as a tie for a longer period, I think that it can be said that a tie for a period of less than a year (being a right which, so to speak, evaporates within the year) is so closely linked with the selling operations during the year that it becomes different in nature and does not qualify to attain 'the dignity of a capital asset'. See *Henriksen v Grafton Hotel Ltd* (1942) 24 T.C. 453. In that case it was held that payments in respect of the monopoly value payable upon the grant of a licence for a period of three years were of a capital nature. Du Parq LJ said that 'the right to trade for three years as a Licensed Victualler must be regarded as attaining the dignity of a capital asset'."

It may be worth noting that Lord Upjohn (at 51) stated: **28–022**

"I only desire to say that I regard the decision in *Henriksen v Grafton Hotel Limited* (1942) 24 T.C. 453 as a very special case, a decision which, if it can be supported at all, can be justified solely upon its own particular facts within the realm of licensing laws".

Lord Morris also stated (at 42):

"in the *Nchanga* Case (*Commissioner of Taxes v Nchanga Consolidated Copper Mines Ltd* [1964] A.C. 948) Lord Radcliffe, at 960 said that 'Courts have stressed the importance of observing a demarcation between the cost of creating, acquiring or enlarging the permanent (which does not mean perpetual) structure of which the income is to be the produce or fruit, and the cost of earning that income or performing the income earning operations."

In *Robert Addie & Sons Collieries Ltd v CIR* (1924) 8 T.C. 671, at 676, Lord President Clyde posed the question:

"are the sums in question part of the trader's working expenses, are they expenditure laid out as part of the process of profit earning, or, on the other hand, [are they] capital outlays, [are they] expenditure necessary for the acquisition of property or of rights or a permanent character, the possession of which is a condition of carrying on the trade at all?"

Lord Morris also quoted with approval Lord President Clyde in *IRC v Coia* **28–023** (1959) 38 T.C. 334, at 339, in a case involving a garage proprietor receiving a money payment for a tie with a petrol company, in which he stated that it was capital "as a consideration for giving up his freedom of trading and changing the structure of this part of his business". He also quoted Lord Patrick, at 339:

> "he parted with what I regard as a valuable asset of a capital nature, the right to obtain the supplies of fuel oils which were his stock-in-trade from such sources as he might consider most suited to the varying nature of the demands made by his customers."

Lord Macintosh (at 340) said that the tie plainly:

> "affected the overall structure of Mr Coia's garage business. He became hence-forth for a ten-year period tied to the Esso Petroleum Co for all his supplies instead of being at liberty from 1953 onwards to buy and sell all the particular brands of motor fuel which were then on the market".

In *Tucker (HMIT) v Granada Motorway Services Limited* [1977] S.T.C. 353, the House of Lords held as capital, expenditure incurred by Granada for a variation of its lease which, though non-assignable.and hence having no balance sheet value, was valuable to its trade, and hence a capital asset. The expenditure was designed to make the lease more advantageous and was therefore undoubtedly a payment of a capital nature.

28–024 As will be apparent from these comments, under many franchise agreements it is possible for HMRC to argue that an initial payment which brings the franchise into being is capital expenditure by the franchisee and not deductible for tax and not falling within any of the classes of assets for which capital allowances are available (BIM 57620).

CG68270 argues that although a franchise is an asset for capital gains tax purposes, being property within the meaning of TCGA 1992 s.21(1), it is not regarded as goodwill and therefore not within any of the classes qualifying for roll-over relief under TCGA 1992 s.155, outside the Corporate Intangible Fixed Asset regime.

HMRC's established view was that in the case of a franchise the only form of goodwill that can be increased by the franchisee's efforts is his personal goodwill which is not capable of sale as any improvement to the goodwill of the franchise accrues to the benefit of the franchisor. Therefore any disposal of the franchise is a disposal of the franchise itself not a disposal of goodwill and therefore roll-over relief is not available. However, *Balloon Promotions Ltd v Wilson* [2006] S.T.C. (SCD) 167, held otherwise, but see *Tax Bulletin* 83, 1291–1292. HMRC's position following the *Balloon Promotions Case* is to review each case on its merits depending upon the strength of the franchisor's brand. A dealership however may, unlike a franchise, develop free goodwill which is capable of sale as such (CG68270). CG68109 (now removed) quoted *IRC v Earl Fitzwilliam* [1913] 2 K.B. 593, as "authority for the concept that it is the franchise and not the goodwill that has value".

Deferred revenue expenditure

28–025 It may be possible to argue on the correct analysis of the agreement that expenditure is actually incurred for the purposes of the trade and if the proper accounting treatment is to write off the expenditure either immediately or over a period of years as deferred revenue expenditure, there seems no reason to deny relief for the expenditure as a trading expense of the franchisee merely because it is paid in a lump sum up front although HMRC may argue otherwise (BIM 57620), even if the lump sum is paid by instalments on the basis of *S Ltd v O'Sullivan* ((1972) TL(I) 108). The matter will probably be put beyond doubt by the franchise agreement providing that any initial payment is for specified revenue services such as training or a non-returnable recoupable advance of franchise fees that will become payable under the agreement once the business commences. This can of course be reflected commercially in the franchise fees agreed.

The question of deferred revenue expenditure is a difficult one. As quoted above, *Strick v Regent Oil Co Ltd* (1965) 43 T.C. 1, itself refers with approval to the concept of writing off expenditure to profit and loss account over a period of years and if this is consistent with proper accounting principles the tax treatment should follow, on the basis of cases such as *Johnston v Britannia Airways Ltd* [1994] S.T.C. 763. The accounting treatment is not, however, conclusive (*EEC Quarries Ltd v Watkis* [1975] S.T.C. 175). The fact that HMRC accept the concept of deferred revenue expenditure is confirmed by the now obsolete Statement of Practice on expenditure on producing films and similar assets, SP9/79, and applies to video tapes for rental in certain cases under *Tax Bulletin*, Issue 19, October 1995, 249, and more generally in Issue 39, February 1999, 623 and Issue 53, June 2001, 859.

If it has to be accepted that part of the initial expenditure relates to capital assets, it is worth considering whether any of the expenditure could qualify as plant (as discussed under the purchase of copyright, Ch.18, para.18–036) to the extent that the initial sum includes a licence for a patent or know-how as restrictively defined for tax purposes by CTA 1988 s.908(4) or ITTOIA 2005 ss.192(1) and 583(4), (5). Relief for capital expenditure may be available as explained in Ch.16 on Patents and Ch.19 on Know-how. There is, however, no corresponding deduction for capital expenditure on the right to use trade marks on copyright material outside the Corporate Intangible Fixed Asset regime.

28–026 CG68270 suggests that the initial payment by the franchisee is normally a capital expense, even though it would normally be a revenue receipt in the hands of the franchisor.

In setting out the contention that the initial fee payable by the franchisee is generally a capital sum the HMRC *Manual* at BIM 57620 refers to *Atherton v British Insulated Helsby Cables Ltd* (1925) 10 T.C. 155 and *S Ltd v O'Sullivan* (1972) T.L. (I) 108. However, BIM 57620 recognises that an apportionment of the initial fee may be appropriate dependent on the facts; for example, the agreement may show that the franchisor charged a specific part of the initial fee for a revenue service such as the training of staff (other than the franchisee) and if the charge is justifiable in relation to the actual services provided then apportionment may be appropriate. If, however, the agreement terms are such that no part of the initial lump sum fee is specifically attributed to revenue items, then inspectors should critically examine claims for apportionment. In practice apportionments for which franchisees contend may be made without reference to the franchisor and may be difficult to justify in relation to the services provided. For instance, some franchisors are unwilling to negotiate special terms with individual franchisees and the same lump sum is payable irrespective of the actual services required from the franchisor; for example, the number of staff needing training may be irrelevant. The facts may also show that no part of the initial lump sum fees can be attributed to services of a revenue nature provided by the franchisor because such services are separately charged for in the annual fees.

Where the initial fee is accepted as capital, the trader may seek capital allowances under CAA 2001 ss.452 and 453, such claims are not generally acceptable. Agreements vary but typically the franchise fee will be for items which do not satisfy the statutory definition of know-how in CTA 2009 s.908(4) or ITTOIA 2005 ss.192(1), 583(4)(5) although, if the franchisee can demonstrate that a reasonable part of the total payment was for the acquisition of industrial know-how, then a just and reasonable part apportionment should be negotiated (see also, *Tax Bulletin*, Issue 17, June 1995). In most cases the franchisee will be trading through a company and amortisation of the initial fee would be claimed under the Corporate Intangible Fixed Asset regime.

Advertising contributions

28–027 Where the franchise agreement requires the franchisee to contribute specifically to advertising expenditure incurred, or to be incurred, by the franchisor this should be allowable as a trading expense for the franchisee, being wholly and exclusively incurred for the purpose of the franchisee's trade.

Occasionally the advertising pool will be set up in the form of a trust for the benefit of the franchisees but this could lead to complications and is to be avoided if possible. The accounting treatment will probably be to write off payments to the trust fund when made or accrued over a period when the advertising campaign takes place and is therefore properly regarded as expenditure wholly and exclusively for the purpose of trade. However, it is arguable that the payment is a settlement on the trustees and arguably not expenditure on advertising itself, and therefore not expenditure for the purposes of the trade. The position is best avoided by having the advertising pool under the control of the franchisor with a provision for a refund to the franchisees, if the advertising pool is not expended within an agreed period. In this case any payment to the pool should be an allowable expense when payable and any recovery from the pool a trading receipt of the franchisee when received.

Pre-trading expenditure

28–028 In many cases the franchisee will incur the initial expenditure in setting up the franchise and making the arrangements to trade before the trading actually commences, which would be when the services are first provided, or sales take place (*Birmingham and District Cattle By-Products Co Ltd v IRC* (1919) 12 T.C. 92). In practice this is not a problem because relief for pre-trading expenditure given by TA 1988 s.401 or ITTOIA 2005 s.57, provides that expenditure incurred within the seven years prior to commencement of trade is treated as incurred on the day the trade actually commences.

VAT

There is no direct reference to franchising in the Value Added Tax Acts and the normal VAT rules apply, as explained in Ch.11. The only cases that appear to have arisen in connection with franchising involve the supply of instruction manuals by the franchisor to the franchisee and whether these can be zero-rated as books rather than standard rated. In the *Franchise Development Services Ltd* case (LON/95/2530A July 1996 (14295)) it was held that the franchisor was providing a composite service with a single charge and the instruction manuals and other printed materials did not qualify for zero rating. This was contrasted with the case of *Force One Training Ltd* (LON/95/1594A October 1995 (13619)) where it was held that a company providing instruction was making a separate supply of the course material, which qualified for zero rating.

Franchise fees will normally follow the general rule that what is not a supply of goods is a supply of services.

28–029

INTERNATIONAL CONSIDERATIONS

Where the franchisor is not based in the United Kingdom, it is necessary to decide whether the franchisor's activities take place entirely outside the United Kingdom, in which case there will be no exposure to UK tax, or whether activities which do take place in the United Kingdom are limited to visits by the franchisor's personnel to the UK-resident franchisees, where the franchisor would not normally be liable to UK tax unless there was a permanent establishment in the United Kingdom, provided that the franchisor was resident in a country where there is a double taxation treaty with the United Kingdom. This is considered in more detail in Ch.24 (international tax planning). If the franchisor does have a branch or subsidiary company in the United Kingdom this would be subject to UK tax on its profits and this may involve transfer pricing considerations when considering how much of the franchisor's overall profit arises in the United Kingdom (see Ch.13).

Similarly a UK franchisor with overseas franchisees may operate through a branch or subsidiary in overseas jurisdictions to supervise the franchisees, and thereby become liable to overseas taxation, and will have to consider the international tax planning points mentioned in Ch.24 as well as transfer pricing (Ch.13) and the controlled foreign companies' legislation (Ch.14). The other main problem arising from cross-border franchising, which has already been mentioned in this chapter and is further discussed in Ch.24, is the question of withholding taxes and how these may be relieved.

28–030

CHAPTER 29

Computer software, the internet and the Cloud

INTRODUCTION

The widespread and rapid development of computer technology, and in particular the globalisation of business facilitated by the internet, has not in general been matched by international tax legislation designed to deal with the taxation of payments generated by the exploitation of computing technology and software, or online transactions where the creation of value may be remote from the location of any physical activity. The OECD Model Treaty does not currently address the specific issues which arise from e-commerce and, along with the majority (if not all) double tax treaties, are framed around conventional business models which envisage a correlation between the physical place of supply of goods or services and liability to tax. In a digital context, the geographical boundaries are much less distinct and determining the taxable base becomes correspondingly more complex **29–001**

In addition to the difficulties in identifying the taxable base in e-commerce transactions, separate issues arise in connection with the acquisition and exploitation of computer software.

SOFTWARE

In the United Kingdom, the Capital Allowances Act 2001 contains provisions for capital allowances relating to capital expenditure on computer software (see para.29–006, below), but there is no precise definition of the term "computer software" which generally has two related but separate meanings. It can refer simply to the programs that allow computers to operate in the desired way ("operating systems") but it can also refer to the program and the accompanying instruction manuals and other materials necessary to make full use of the program. The program itself will be provided to the user in an "object code" which the computer recognises but it will have been written in a "source code" which will usually be retained by the owner of the software. The user of the software will thus have to revert to the owner to sort out any problems or develop the program further, as it is usually impossible to deduce the source code from the object code in any useful way. The licensing agreement could well in any event prohibit interference by the user. **29–002**

There is also some blurring of the distinction between the terms "software" and "hardware". "Hardware" generally includes the physical parts of the computer system such as the display screen, the computer itself, keyboard, mouse, or laptop, netbook, tablet or smartphone. In each case, some software is permanently stored in the computer's hard disk (or equivalent). An acquisition of software may be bundled with hardware, such as where an operating system is pre-loaded onto a PC or laptop. For tax purposes, the accounting treatment is generally followed such that the acquisition is treated as if the software were part of the hardware and capital allowances will be available on the composite cost if acquired for use in a qualifying business activity (see para.29–006 below).

As the user does not usually "buy" the software but simply obtains a licence to use it, it is important to separate ownership of the download or disk, etc. on which the program is recorded from the rights in the program itself.

New media

29–003 "New media" is a catch-all term encompassing content distributed or exhibited digitally, for example by a computer or smartphone and includes apps, electronic books, computer games, CD-ROMs and DVDs as well as downloadable or on-demand content. From a taxation point of view such products are often based on a series of licences and can be broken down into their constituent parts in order to consider their treatment as capital or revenue expenditure, royalties or business expenses.

THE INTERNET

29–004 Where the internet is used merely as a means of ordering or paying for physical goods, then the position is relatively unproblematic and is akin to more conventional transactions such as mail order. The supplier is likely to have a tax liability at the base from which such goods or services are supplied.

New media is increasingly downloaded directly over the internet, and fiscal authorities face a severe problem in the tracking of online payments made by credit or debit card or through online payment transfer websites. Although the purchaser might not have great security for his purchase, he can sample software and other media packages such as music files or apps and then pay for the full version by credit card. The purchaser may not even be aware of the origin of the software to which he is acquiring a licence, or indeed that he is acquiring a licence at all. Whilst consumer-based taxes such as VAT sit comfortably with online transactions, the application of tax principles underlying the allocation of profits to a taxable base is more complex. It has been suggested that the international corporate tax system requires fundamental overhaul in order to accommodate the increase in trading over the internet and the transfer of digital goods and services. The two main areas of concern relate to transfer pricing principles and the application of the concept of a permanent establishment to e-commerce. It has been suggested that fiscal authorities will eventually be forced to concede defeat and recognise that tax cannot be recovered where the vendor has no permanent establishment. In the case of the downloading of music, apps or books, the sales transaction takes place through a website, and it is generally held that a website has its location where the host server is located. The United Kingdom has taken the view that a website of itself is not a permanent establishment and that a server is insufficient of itself to constitute a permanent establishment of a business that is conducting e-commerce through a website on that server, see INTM 266100. This is the case irrespective of whether the server is owned, rented or otherwise at the disposal of the business through which the e-commerce activity is being conducted. The analogy appears to be that the storage of physical goods in a warehouse in the UK, rented or otherwise, would not of itself give rise to a permanent establishment, and therefore the storage of data on a server in the UK should be treated in a similar way. There are difficulties with this proposition and some other countries take a different view (see various OECD commentaries on e-commerce available on *http://www.oecd.org*, in particular the "Clarification on the Application of the Permanent Establishment Definition in E-commerce", December 2000 and commentary to art.5 of the OECD Model Convention at paras 42.1–42.10). In particular, Spain and Portugal do not accept that a physical presence is required in order for a permanent establishment to exist in the context of e-commerce. The difficulties in applying the permanent establishment concept to internet based transactions and their ever greater use in business has led to a re-examination of the report entitled "Are the Current Treaty rules for Taxing Business Profits Appropriate for E-Commerce?" (November 2003). Whilst recognising the challenges faced in this area, the report does not recommend any changes to the current treaty rules and therefore the concept of a permanent establishment remains fundamental in determining the taxation of e-commerce.

THE CLOUD

Cloud computing is a relatively recent development and refers to a type of internet-based computing where servers, storage and applications are shared over the internet rather than through local servers. Services are typically provided through a Cloud service provider (CSP), enabling on-demand access to software applications and hardware without the traditional requirement to purchase or licence them. **29–005**

Cloud computing adds further strain to tax rules, already stretched by the difficulties posed by the internet and e-commerce generally. For the user of Cloud services, the tax treatment of the payment to the CSP will be dictated by the nature of the services being provided. The provisions of the service agreement or contract are therefore key. In many cases, the user will be acquiring a mix of services, such as access to software, storage capacity or infrastructure. Where the Cloud user does not acquire any property from the CSP, and the agreement does not amount to a license to use applications beyond the life of the contract, it is likely that the user's payment will be in the nature of a subscription or service fee and deductible in accordance with the normal rules in ITTOIA 2005 s.34 (for income tax) or CTA 2009 s.54 (for corporation tax). Where the agreement provides for property or IP rights to be transferred from the CSP to the user, the payment will be in the nature of a royalty and withholding taxes may apply.

HMRC's Manuals give an example at CIRD220325 of a company licensing patented software via the Cloud, where it is clearly envisaged that the income so derived will be royalties (and potentially therefore within the Patent Box—see Ch.23).

The Cloud is a virtual concept which does not have a fixed address, and a CSP is able to provide Cloud services in any geographical location in which users have the necessary technology to access it. Cloud technology gives rise to similar issues in terms of whether or not a permanent establishment as for more traditional internet-based businesses. Further, servers used in processing a single service or transaction may be located in more than one jurisdiction, making identification of where a transaction takes place particularly difficult, and potentially risking double or multiple taxation. Given that the concept of a permanent establishment also entails the identification of a "source" of profits (in that profits of a non-resident entity are only taxed in the jurisdiction of the permanent establishment if they are sourced there), the nature of the Cloud as relying upon shared resources presents practical difficulties as to determining where income has its source.

ACQUISITION FOR DISTRIBUTION

29–006 A person acquiring software to sell on as a distributor or retailer will usually obtain a licence to do so from the software owner, who might be the original developer or someone to whom the developer has sold the intellectual property rights over the software. The retailer will make payments, usually described as royalties or licence payments, to the owner. There could be an initial lump sum which might or might not be set off against future payments. The Inland Revenue's *Tax Bulletin* of November 1993 (TB9F) sets out their approach to the treatment of expenditure on computer software in general and in particular whether payments are capital or revenue (see BIM 35810). The payment of regular amounts by a distributor for the licence to distribute will undoubtedly be classified as revenue. Where a significant initial lump sum is payable by a distributor to the owner, the cost should be written off on a prudent basis over the likely period of its recovery. The payment cannot be treated as a capital asset but as deferred revenue expenditure (see para.29–007 below). See *Tax Treaty Characterisation Issues Arising from E-commerce*, OECD, February 1, 2001.

EXPLOITATION FOR OWN USE

29–007 The user of software might make an initial payment for his own use of the software in the first year and further annual payments to include maintenance and support in subsequent years, or in the case of packaged software he might make a single payment to a retailer for the licence and a maintenance contract. HMRC's guidance of BIM 35810 stresses that payments akin to rental are categorised as revenue. Correct accounting practice in accordance with UK GAAP or International Accounting Standards will determine the time of the deduction.

If a lump sum has been paid, it is necessary to look how the software is used in the trade of the licensee. Generally speaking, HMRC will accept revenue treatment where software is expected to have a useful life of less than two years. Correct accounting procedure will again determine the timing of the deduction. A company may claim under the Corporate Intangible Fixed Assets regime, Ch.21.

HMRC could argue that, where the software will be a tool of the taxpayer's trade for several years, the initial payment, if significant, should be treated as capital. A software product, however, generally requires regular updating in order not to become obsolete. That being so, it is reasonable to argue that it is more prudent to meet the initial payment as revenue, again taking the deduction on the basis of the accounting treatment. If the purchase of the software is a major expense, however, HMRC might insist on its being treated as capital, unless the user "trades up to new versions at intervals which are short enough to give a particular version only a transitory value to that business" (BIM 35815).

CAPITAL ALLOWANCES

29–008 If capital treatment is appropriate for expenditure on computer software, the position in the United Kingdom regarding capital allowances is dealt with by CAA 2001 s.71, which has effect from March 10, 1992. Before that date there was doubt as to whether or not capital allowances were available to software licensees. Under s.71, the licensee's software expenditure is now treated as plant or machinery belonging to him.

A short-life asset election under CAA 2001 ss.83–88 can accelerate allowances where the software is scrapped or destroyed before the eighth anniversary of the end of the chargeable period in which it was acquired. This also applies in the unlikely circumstances of a sale of the rights to the software within eight years. For acquisitions of software before April 1, 2011 (April 6, 2011 for income tax), the eight year period was four years.

REVENUE EXPENDITURE

29–009 Where expenditure is treated as revenue, the accounting treatment under UK GAAP or International Accounting Standards is central to the timing of relief. Where payments are made overseas from the United Kingdom this is of particular importance to determine whether or not tax should be deducted at source but it is also important for the manner and timing of the deduction against taxable profits. Payments for computer software will in almost all circumstances be treated as usual expenses of the trade rather than as "annual payments". "Annual payments" are, generally speaking, amounts due under legally enforceable agreements representing "pure income profit" in the hands of the recipient. "Pure income profit" is profit which is not in return for any other consideration from the recipient.

ROYALTIES

29–010 The conclusions of the 1992 OECD report on the *Tax Treaty Characterisation Issues Arising from E-commerce*, February 2001, appear to have been accepted for all practical purposes by HMRC with regard to payments for software made in the United Kingdom. The report favours limitation of the term "royalty" to circumstances where there is a limited grant of rights (not amounting to a change in ownership) for the commercial development or exploitation of software. In particular, payments for software for personal or business use and payments for the alienation of all rights attached to software do *not* represent royalties. If, however, an original owner receives payment quantified by the user where a third party has developed the software, that payment will usually be given royalty treatment. Where royalty treatment is applicable, UK withholding tax may have to be deducted as copyright royalties to an owner whose usual place of abode is abroad, under ITA 2007 s.906, subject to any double taxation treaty relief (see para.18–023 onwards).

WITHHOLDING TAX

29–011 Income payable from overseas to the United Kingdom for the use of software is often subject to a significant level of withholding tax which may well exceed the UK tax against which it can be credited. There are various strategies for minimising levels of withholding tax.

If the creation of a permanent establishment defined in the United Kingdom by CTA 2010 ss.1141–1143, in the country producing the income can be avoided and there is a bilateral tax treaty in place, business profits will not be taxed in that country. Article 5 of the OECD Model Treaty sets out in detail the factors which determine whether or not there is a permanent establishment. If there is no treaty in place, local law will have to be considered.

If a permanent establishment, defined in the United Kingdom by CTA 2010 ss.1141–1143, cannot be avoided, items that are tax-deductible can be maximised within the limitation imposed by the OECD Model Treaty that the permanent establishment's profits must be calculated on an arm's length basis.

If the licence fee is paid direct by an overseas user to an owner in the United Kingdom, the local jurisdiction could impose withholding tax. In these circumstances the precise nature of the payment and any treaty protection available have to be studied. Under the OECD Model Treaty, licence fees for software will usually be treated as commercial income (not royalties—see above) and will not usually be subject to withholding tax, but not all countries follow the OECD model. If a particular country does treat licence fees as a royalty and thus subject to withholding tax, consideration can be given to allocation of part of the overall payment to maintenance and support, which would escape withholding tax.

"TREATY SHOPPING"

Many jurisdictions, the United States especially, are taking measures to ensure that bilateral treaties established with other states are not used as stepping stones to create treaty protection where there is no direct treaty between the jurisdiction of the user and that of the owner. "Treaty shopping" and the use of conduit companies is thus becoming more difficult and may be less likely to provide the answer to the problem than previously, although there is still considerable scope for careful routing in many cases (see para.24–018 onwards). 29–012

DEVELOPMENT EXPENDITURE

SSAP 13, *Accounting for Research and Development*, sets out the criteria which are used to decide whether expenditure on research and development should be capitalised as deferred development expenditure which will be written off against anticipated revenues, or should be written off to the profit and loss account when incurred. Pure research expenditure is written off in the year incurred whereas development expenditure can be deferred to later periods if there is a clearly defined project with separately identifiable costs and sufficient funding, which is technically and commercially viable, with costs to be covered by future revenues. Unless, however, development expenditure is recoverable from a customer, most software developers write off development expenditure as it is incurred, see Ch.15, para.15–010 onwards. 29–013

Capitalising development expenditure may prevent its deduction as a revenue deduction for tax purposes, unless it can be classified as deferred revenue expenditure (see above) or brought within the R&D or Corporate Intangible Fixed Asset regimes (Chs 15 and 21 respectively). Expenditure written off as incurred, however, will usually be deductible on the same basis as that used for accounts purposes. If software has been developed for use in a company's own business, HMRC can argue that expenditure should be treated as capital expenditure even if written off as incurred for accounts purposes. HMRC's approach is summarised in BIM 35810, which sets out the November 1993 Inland Revenue *Tax Bulletin* TBF9. If the expenditure has a sufficiently enduring nature, which is determined by reference to the function of the software in the trade in question, HMRC will seek to categorise it as capital and capital allowances should be available (see above). If the software is expected to have a useful life of less than two years, revenue treatment will be accepted.

TRANSFER PRICING

United Kingdom legislation allows the income from transactions between related parties to be taxed on the basis of the income that would have arisen if the transaction had been carried out at arm's length (TIOPA 2010 Pt 4) The UK transfer pricing legislation was extended to apply to UK transactions from April 1, 2004 to try and make them EU compatible. 29–014

The OECD Transfer Pricing Guidelines for Multinational Enterprises and Tax Administrations, most recently updated in 2010, identifies five methods for determining an arm's length price, dividing these into traditional transactional methods and transactional profit methods, although it is acknowledged that other methods not described in the Guidelines may be used provided an arm's length result is derived. The traditional transaction methods are: comparison with prices in similar arm's length transactions; deduction of an appropriate mark-up from retail prices; and the addition of an appropriate mark-up to a supplier's costs. The transactional profit methods are: profit split and the transactional net margin method. Unlike the previous (1995) version of the Guidelines, there is no absolute hierarchy of preferred methods in the 2010 Guidelines, although a "natural hierarchy" is anticipated which would favour a comparable uncontrolled price or comparable uncontrolled transaction method. The allocation of profit by reference to some non-profit-related factor such as turnover or size of workforce is not recommended (see Ch.13).

If a UK company licensing software to a subsidiary outside the United Kingdom also licenses software to third parties on a similar basis there is clearly a comparable price which it would be difficult to gainsay. If there are no similar third-party arrangements, usual pricing structures within the industry as a whole would have to be considered. There is always a difficulty, however, where there are no directly comparable products.

The taxation of global business, particularly web-based multinationals, has been a subject of much debate by international fiscal authorities and the effectiveness of existing transfer pricing rules is under review. HMRC issued a paper entitled "Taxing Multinationals: transfer pricing rules" on May 2, 2013, and the OECD is currently consulting on Transfer Pricing Aspects of Intangibles, as part of its review of Base Erosion and Profit Shifting (BEPS) (*http://www.oecd.org/ctp/transfer-pricing/revised-discussion-draft-intangibles.pdf* [Accessed September 16, 2013]).

VAT

29–015 The correct VAT treatment of the supply of software depends on:

1. whether the software is a standard "*off-the-shelf*" package or a *bespoke* package;
2. the VAT status of the customer; and
3. whether the customer belongs inside or outside the European Union.

The sale of an "*off-the-shelf*" package on a tangible carrier medium (e.g. CD) to a customer registered for VAT in the European Union is treated as a supply of goods and can be zero-rated from the UK, as the customer will be able to account for the VAT due on acquisition of the goods in its own EU country. If the sale of an "*off-the-shelf*" package is to a non-VAT registered customer in the European Union, UK VAT must be added, except that if the seller arranges delivery and the distance selling threshold is exceeded in any particular country, the seller must register for VAT in that EU country and add VAT at the local rate.

Supplies of software to non-EU customers are zero-rated provided that sufficient evidence is retained of their export and the usual export conditions are satisfied.

Sales of *bespoke* software and electronically supplied "off the shelf" software in the EU are supplies of services and subject to the complicated "place of supply" rules. **29–016**

If a UK seller supplies such software, the supply will normally be outside the scope of UK VAT if the customer is in business in another European Union state and receives the software for **business** use. The "reverse charge" provisions will apply in that case. However, under EU VAT law, this position can in certain cases, be overridden by the place where effective use and enjoyment of the services takes place. These use and enjoyment rules have not been implemented in all EU Member States, therefore it is always necessary to check the position in each EU country concerned with the supplies being made.

If the customer is in another EU state and receives the software for **non-business** purposes, UK VAT must normally be added by the seller. This is because currently, supplies of e-services made by a business located in one EU Member State to a private consumer located in a different EU Member State ("intra EU B2C supplies") are taxed in the country where the business is established.

Since July 1, 2003, services supplied electronically by non-EU businesses to private individuals and non-business organisations in the European Union are subject to VAT where the customer belongs. **29–017**

To avoid such businesses having to register in every EU Member State where they make supplies, an optional simplified Special Scheme was introduced with effect from July 1, 2003 by VATA 1994 Sch.3B (FA 2003 s.23 and Sch.2).

The Special Scheme allows such businesses to register in a single Member State of their choice and electronically declare the EU tax due on a single VAT return where registered. That particular EU state will then distribute the VAT due to the appropriate EU Member States (VATA 1994 Sch.3B). Further significant changes to the place of supply rules for telecoms, broadcasting and electronically supplied services will be introduced from January 1, 2015.

In particular, from January 1, 2015, the current rules for non-EU businesses will be extended to apply to **all** supplies of electronically supplied services to private/non-business customers (whether by EU persons or non-EU persons) and the rules will then also apply to telecoms and broadcasting services, to ensure that the services are taxed in the EU Member State of consumption. **29–018**

This means that the place of supply of all such services will, after January 1, 2015, always be the country of the customer, regardless of where the supplier is located.

Also, from January 1, 2015, a Mini One Stop Shop (MOSS) system will also be introduced to allow businesses that make intra EU B2C supplies of telecoms, broadcasting and e-services, the option of VAT registering in a single Member State, from where they can account for VAT due in all EU Member States by submitting a single VAT return.

PART 6
CASE STUDIES

Case Study 1: Peter Roberts, author

INTRODUCTION

The purpose of this case study is to consider the taxation planning opportunities of an author resident and domiciled in the United Kingdom and the way in which the commercial and taxation considerations are intertwined. The study has been kept as realistic as possible in order to illustrate the planning decisions as they arise and is not to be regarded as an optimum solution, as it is usually only possible with hindsight to decide what the best tax planning would have been had all the subsequent developments been known from the beginning. **CS1–001**

The study illustrates, in particular, the use of the copyright averaging provisions, personal service companies, trusts and overseas companies.

THE PRODUCT

Peter Roberts, an author of children's books, wrote a book called *Strompy and the Flying Alligator*. He sent the manuscript to his literary agents who in turn took it to a well-known publisher of children's books. The publisher liked the manuscript and agreed to publish the book. It was decided that the book should be illustrated and the publishers and Peter Roberts agreed to approach Ann Pyke to prepare the illustrations. **CS1–002**

An agreement was entered into between Peter Roberts and the publisher whereby he agreed to grant a licence to the publisher to publish a hardback edition of the book in return for a royalty of 12 per cent for the first 5,000 copies and thereafter 15 per cent calculated on the retail selling price of the book in the United Kingdom. The publisher originally asked for a complete assignment of the copyright but Peter Roberts had in mind to write a series of "Strompy" books, since he thought that the character might prove popular, and he was therefore unwilling to part with more than a licence to publish.

The publisher was sufficiently enthusiastic about the book to agree to a non-returnable recoupable advance of royalties on the basis of an anticipated sale of 4,000 copies. The book was expected to retail for £14.95 in the hardback edition.

CASE STUDY 1: PETER ROBERTS, AUTHOR

INITIAL INCOME

CS1–003 Peter Roberts had spent 18 months writing the first *Strompy* book.

Ann Pyke also entered into an agreement with the publishers whereby she became entitled to a 2.5 per cent royalty based on the published price, for her illustrations, with a similar advance payment on the basis of 4,000 copies as a non-returnable recoupable advance.

The royalty income for both Peter Roberts and Ann Pyke were taxed as part of their professional earnings. Both Peter and Ann may elect to average profits under ITTOIA 2005 ss.221–225, if their respective profits for the current year are not more than 70 per cent of the profit of the next year or vice versa. There is restricted relief available where the difference is between 70–75 per cent.

CS1–004 *Strompy and the Flying Alligator* met with a good reception and a reprint was arranged on the basis of a royalty of 15 per cent on all copies for Peter Roberts and 2.5 per cent for Ann Pyke. Peter Roberts' agents also started negotiations with a publisher of children's paperbacks for the paperback rights of *Strompy and the Flying Alligator*. The paperback royalties were agreed at 17.5 per cent of the published price of £4.95 per copy. The non-returnable recoupable advance, this time, was based on 8,000 copies. Ann Pyke's illustrations were again used, this time for a lump sum on partial assignment of the copyright for the purposes of the paperback print for a fee of £7,500, which was again brought into her professional earnings when received.

In the meantime Peter Roberts had written *Strompy Goes Hunting* and *Strompy and the Lost Brontosaurus*. Peter Roberts' original publishers agreed to publish the two new books at six-monthly intervals on the basis of a 20 per cent royalty on the published price of £18.49 on condition that there would be no paperback edition within 12 months of the hardback publication and with a recoupable advance of royalties on the basis of expected sales of 7,500.

A royalty agreement was entered into between the publishers and Ann Pyke for her to produce the illustrations for the two new books on the basis of a fee of £10,000 in addition to a 2.5 per cent royalty.

For both Mr Roberts and Miss Pyke the periodic royalties were brought into their accounts when received.

THE COMPANIES

CS1–005 By this time Peter Roberts was convinced that Strompy would prove successful and he formed a series of companies (see diagram at para.CS1–017). As he was genuinely self-employed previously the personal service company (IR35) rules did not apply.

He formed Strompy Creations Ltd and entered into a service contract with the company under which he agreed to be employed by the company for a period of five years at a salary of £35,000 per annum, and during that period he would write five books incorporating the character of Strompy and would grant the company an exclusive 10-year licence for the UK editions of such books, both hardback and paperback. The shares in Strompy Creations Ltd were owned as to

THE DISCRETIONARY TRUST

50 percent by Peter Roberts, 25 per cent by his wife Sandra and 25 per cent by his children, Alexander, Rona and Brian, equally.

As well as forming Strompy Creations Ltd he also formed Strompy Films Ltd, Strompy Records Ltd, Strompy Performances Ltd and Strompy Merchandising Ltd. The shareholdings in these four companies were held as to 25 per cent by Peter Roberts, 25 per cent by Sandra and 50 per cent on discretionary trusts for their three children.

Peter's shares in these four companies were entitled to any capital appreciation on winding up the company, but had no votes and were not entitled to any dividends. The trust shares were entitled to any dividends declared but had no votes and had no entitlement to any surplus on a liquidation. Sandra's shares were entitled to the votes but had no rights as to dividends or to any surplus on winding-up. The purpose of the multiple rights was to reduce the value of the shares so far as possible both at the time of issue and at any future date, while still preserving the possibility of paying a sizeable lump sum to Peter should the opportunity occur. The settlement provisions in ITTOIA 2005 ss.619 onwards were considered and thought not to apply. **CS1–006**

To these companies he granted a 10-year exclusive licence of the UK rights in respect of films (including television films), records and songs, dramatic rights and rights in manufactured goods and designs, incorporating the character of Strompy. The consideration for the licence was, in each case, £5,000, which was agreed to be a fair market value of the rights at that stage, there being no immediate possibility of commercial exploitation of the Strompy character in such formats. Peter Roberts, however, believed in planning for the future. He had considered an absolute assignment but was advised that this could make it expensive in tax terms to reacquire the rights in his own name should he desire to do so.

THE DISCRETIONARY TRUST

Peter Roberts had a friend living in the Bahamas who wished to set up a discretionary trust (see diagram at para.CS1–018). The settlor decided that the beneficiaries of the discretionary trust should be the Bahamian settlor's nephew and his wife, with the trustees having the power to appoint additional beneficiaries not ordinarily resident in the United Kingdom (which might include Peter Roberts if he ever fulfilled that criterion). Peter Roberts might therefore one day be included as a beneficiary. A protector was appointed who was resident in the Isle of Man. **CS1–007**

It was decided that the trust should be formed in Bermuda with trustees in Bermuda, Guernsey and Hong Kong. The trustees incorporated a company in the British Virgin Islands (BVI), Creative Enterprises (BVI) Ltd to whom Peter Roberts assigned the overseas film, recording and dramatic rights arising from "Strompy" for a fee of £12,500, which again was regarded as the fair market value of those rights at that time. This time it was thought desirable to dispose of the rights absolutely as Peter wished to sever his interest in the rights completely.

CASE STUDY 1: PETER ROBERTS, AUTHOR

The overseas publishing rights were licensed for a fee of £15,000 for a 10-year period to Creative Publishing (BVI) Ltd, another company in the BVI owned by the Bermudian trust.

The overseas merchandising rights for portraying the character of Strompy on manufactured goods were licensed for a 10-year term to a Jersey company, Strompy Overseas Merchandising Ltd, the shares of which were owned by Peter Roberts himself and which had two directors resident in the Channel Island of Jersey. This company was a company established for the benefit of non-Jersey residents to grant licences to overseas manufacturers. As there was no present possibility of such licences being taken up it was agreed that the fair market value of the overseas rights should be fixed at £7,500, which was the amount the Jersey-based company paid to Peter Roberts. All the fees for the assignments and licences were included in Peter Roberts' professional income as received.

STROMPY TAKES OFF

CS1–008 The scene was now set for the commercial exploitation of Strompy and Peter Roberts sat down to write *Strompy Goes Sailing, Strompy on the Moon, Strompy on Safari, Strompy Goes to School* and *Strompy in Hospital*.

Strompy Films Ltd entered into negotiations with an established film making company, Kiddikartoon Ltd, for the production of an animated cartoon film for television called *The Adventures of Strompy*, as a joint venture. The film consisted of a number of short episodes based on events in the various Strompy books and was illustrated by a professional cartoon animator using as a basis Ann Pyke's original portrayal of Strompy. Strompy Films Ltd, on behalf of the joint venture, entered into an agreement with Ann Pyke for the portrayal of Strompy and his friends in any form other than book illustrations for a fee of £25,000.

Strompy Films Ltd and Kiddikartoon Ltd granted a licence to the BBC for *The Adventures of Strompy* for one showing and two repeats for the sum of £45,000.

CS1–009 Under the joint venture agreement, Kiddikartoon Ltd paid the cartoonist's costs of £25,000 on behalf of the venture and split the balance of £20,000 between Strompy Films Ltd and itself in equal shares. Strompy Films Ltd showed in its accounts a trading receipt of £10,000 less half the cost of the acquisition of the rights from Ann Pyke of £25,000. HMRC argued, however, that the royalty paid to Miss Pyke of £25,000 although taxable on her as income, would nonetheless be regarded as a capital payment so far as the company was concerned and was therefore a capital sum amortised as a corporate intangible fixed asset on the accounts basis.

The television film was licensed to Creative Films (BVI) Ltd an international business company in the BVI, which in turn licensed the film to Creative Enterprises BV, its immediate parent incorporated in the Netherlands. Creative Enterprises BV licensed the film to China, Japan and a number of European countries, including the Netherlands. The terms agreed were that 93 per cent of the income less expenses received by the Dutch company would be paid over to Creative Films (BVI) Ltd as the fee for the sub-licence. The object of the exercise was to obtain the maximum benefit of the double taxation agreements between the Netherlands and other countries outside the United Kingdom so that the royalties and licence fees received were not subject to any more than the minimum withholding tax under the various double taxation treaties between the Netherlands and the contracting country. The sub-licence fee paid to the BVI represented an arm's length price. Creative Enterprises BV therefore made a small profit in the Netherlands subject to Dutch tax at 20 per cent and a substantial profit accrued to Creative Films (BVI) Ltd in the BVI. Creative Films (BVI) Ltd paid a dividend to Creative Enterprises BV which was exempt from tax in the Netherlands, under the participation privilege. Creative Enterprises BV in turn paid the same dividend to Creative Enterprises Soparfi, Creative Enterprises Soparfi retained the dividend. It is intended that sometime in the future that the Soparfi be liquidated and the liquidation proceeds distributed to Creative Enterprises (BVI) Ltd without deduction of withholding tax.

The liquidation proceeds received by Creative Enterprises (BVI) Ltd would not be subject to tax in the BVI.

The licence fee between Creative Films (BVI) Ltd and the producers of the film (Strompy Films Ltd and Kiddikartoon Ltd) was at a relatively modest level as Creative Films (BVI) Ltd already had the sole rights to exploit the character of Strompy in film form outside the United Kingdom. A substantial profit was therefore accruing in the BVI for the eventual benefit of the discretionary trust and, in due course, Peter Roberts or members of his family, if and when they might become not resident in the United Kingdom and be appointed beneficiaries of the trust.

CS1–010

As a result of the film a number of toys and games were devised by various manufacturers portraying Strompy in the form of soft toys, puppets, jigsaws, scrap books, posters, T-shirts, crockery and various other paraphernalia.

Strompy Merchandising Ltd granted the various licences to UK manufacturers and Strompy Overseas Merchandising Ltd granted overseas licences for the manufacture of such articles.

SELLING OUT

After five years Peter Roberts sold his shares in Strompy Overseas Merchandising Ltd for £300,000 to an arm's length purchaser on the basis of the accumulated profits and likely future profits for the remainder of the 10-year licence term.

CS1–011

HMRC argued that Peter was in receipt of a capital sum within ITA 2007 s.720. Peter argued that he merely disposed of shares in an overseas company and had obtained a capital gain. He argued that ITA 2007 s.720 did not apply as the original assignment of the merchandising rights was at a commercial price and therefore was a bona fide commercial operation within ITA 2007 ss.736–742. HMRC accepted that the original assignment was for a bona fide commercial price but argued that Peter Roberts had not shown that the sale was not designed with the avoidance of tax as a main object and therefore the escape mechanism was not available. It was agreed that the merchandising income would have been part of Peter Roberts' professional income in the absence of the assignment to Strompy Overseas Merchandising Ltd and the income of the company was therefore assessed under ITA 2007 s.720 on Peter as part of his professional income for the years in which it arose. The object of setting up the Jersey company was therefore entirely defeated by the transfer of assets abroad provisions.

Peter had rather more luck with the UK merchandising company which he sold at the same time because here ITA 2007 s.720 et seq, had no application, although HMRC argued that Peter was in receipt of a capital amount under ITA 2007 ss.773–785, and that as the licensing agreement had five years to run the protection of ITA 2007 s.784, for the sale of goodwill was not available. Peter was able, however, to show both that the original assignment was on commercial terms with the avoidance of tax not being a main reason for the transfers, as it was still within the United Kingdom, and that in view of such matters as limited liability there were good commercial reasons for operating through a company. It was therefore accepted that the shareholders received a capital gain.

CS1–012 HMRC's argument that the accumulated income of the company should be assessed on him as settlor of an arrangement following the decisions of *Crossland v Hawkins*, and *IRC v Mills* (see para.27–042) was defeated on proof that the original assignment had been on proper commercial terms. This, of course, emphasised the advantage of planning the commercial exploitation of Strompy from the earliest possible moment.

Following the success of the film, a musical was developed using the Strompy characters and royalties were paid to Strompy Performances Ltd.

A DVD of the musical was produced and royalties were paid to Strompy Records Ltd. After five years Strompy Records Ltd was sold for £250,000 to an arm's length purchaser, which gave rise to a capital gain. As the whole of the goodwill was sold with the company ITA 2007 ss.773–785 did not apply, in view of ITA 2007 s.784, and the value did not depend to a material extent on the future income from Peter Roberts' own personal activities.

THE BENEFICIARIES' INCOME

CS1–013 When Alexander reached the age of 18 he went to live in Spain for a period and Creative Enterprises Ltd paid a dividend of the equivalent of £200,000 to the Bermudian trust which in turn appointed a Channel Islands resident as an additional beneficiary of the trust and paid him £200,000. The Channel Islands resident in turn paid the sum to Alexander. HMRC attacked the arrangement under ITA 2007 s.716 onwards, on the grounds that there had been a transfer of assets, namely the assignment of the overseas films rights, and a capital sum had been received by Alexander. However, as Alexander was at the time of payment not resident in the United Kingdom there was no UK resident to charge. HMRC could not successfully argue that the payment was in reality to Peter Roberts even if he had been the settlor of the trust, which he argued he was not, in spite of the fact that he was the transferor of the film rights. A claim under ITA 2007 ss.773–785 was defeated on the grounds that the sum did not arise from the activities of the individual, Peter Roberts, but from the creation of the film, which was a corporate activity involving many people.

THE TRADING TRUST

At the end of 10 years, the UK merchandising rights reverted to Peter Roberts and he then entered into a partnership with a trading trust whereby he licensed the Strompy UK merchandising rights to the partnership for a five-year period in return for 65 per cent of the partnership profits. The remaining partnership profits were received by trustees of a discretionary settlement for Alexander's daughter, Rebecca and any further children of Alexander. HMRC threatened to assess the entire partnership profits on Peter on the ground that it was an arrangement which constituted a settlement within ITTOIA 2005 s.619, but were persuaded that it was not a settlement of income in view of the partnership liabilities shared by the trustees.

Peter Roberts decided to assign the copyright in a proposed new book *Strompy Underground* to Mrs Lirtl, his mother-in-law who had recently been widowed. It was argued that as there were no rights currently in existence there could be little or no capital gains tax or inheritance tax on the disposal and there would be no income tax charge on Peter arising from the disposal as a result of *Mason v Innes*. It was accepted that Mrs Lirtl would be liable to tax on the royalties arising. Although it could possibly be argued, following Pennycuick J.'s comments in *Hume v Ascquith* (1968) 45 T.C. 251, that the income was tax free (see para.18–009), it would not be wise to do so in view of the likely charge under ITA 2007 ss.773–785 (TA 1988 s.775), which would then be raised on Peter Roberts.

THE FUTURE

Peter Roberts is still writing about Strompy and no doubt his adventures—and his author's tax planning saga—will continue.

CASE STUDY 1: PETER ROBERTS, AUTHOR

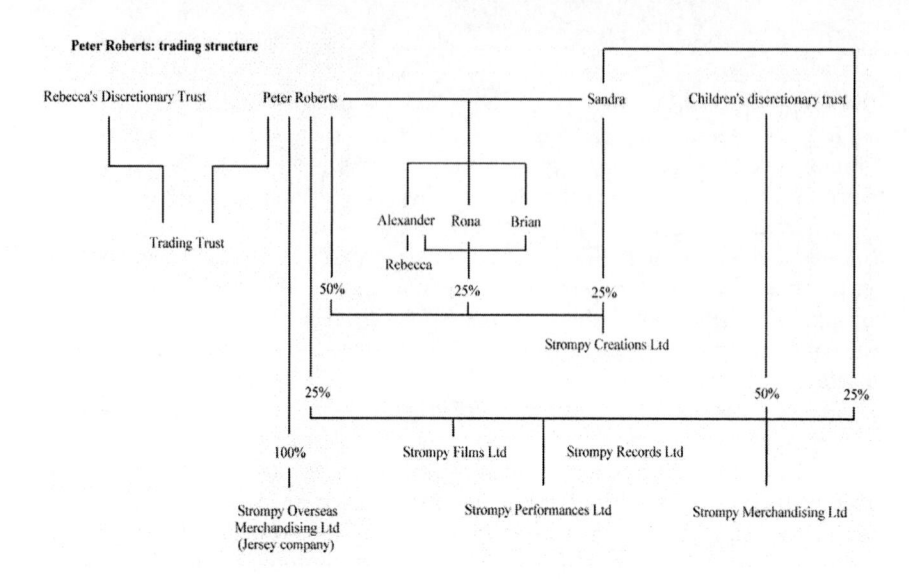

Peter Roberts: trading structure

- Rebecca's Discretionary Trust
- Peter Roberts
- Sandra
- Children's discretionary trust
- Trading Trust
- Alexander, Rona, Brian
- Rebecca

Strompy Creations Ltd — Peter Roberts 50%, Rona 25% (with Alexander/Rebecca/Brian), Sandra 25%

- Strompy Overseas Merchandising Ltd (Jersey company) — 100% (via 25% holding chain)
- Strompy Films Ltd
- Strompy Records Ltd
- Strompy Performances Ltd
- Strompy Merchandising Ltd — 50% / 25% (Children's discretionary trust)

THE FUTURE

Discretionary trust arrangement

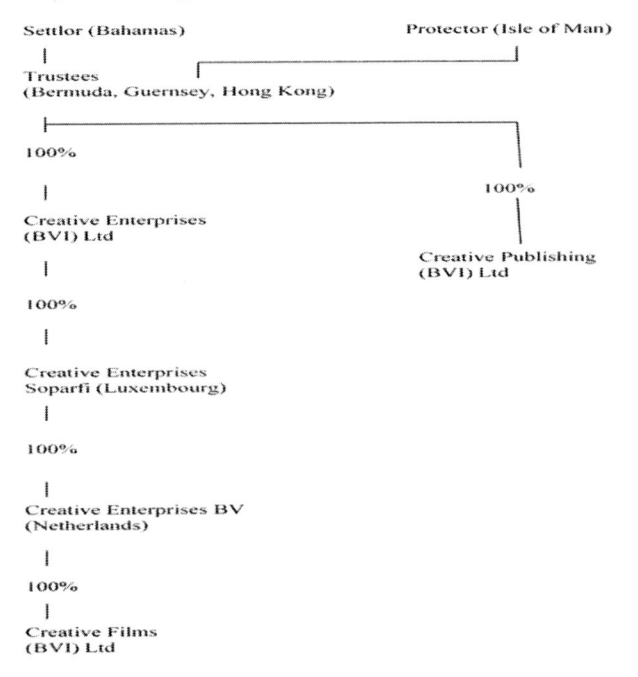

```
Settlor (Bahamas) ─────────────┬───────────── Protector (Isle of Man)
        │                      │
Trustees
(Bermuda, Guernsey, Hong Kong)
    ├──────────────────────────────────────┐
   100%                                    │
    │                                    100%
    │                                      │
Creative Enterprises                   Creative Publishing
(BVI) Ltd                              (BVI) Ltd
    │
   100%
    │
Creative Enterprises
Soparfi (Luxembourg)
    │
   100%
    │
Creative Enterprises BV
(Netherlands)
    │
   100%
    │
Creative Films
(BVI) Ltd
```

Case Study 2: Andrew Rankin, inventor

INTRODUCTION

The second case study, like the others, involves a practical commercial and tax structure development rather than an optimum solution, this time for an inventor, and illustrates scientific research allowances, intermediate licensing companies and trusts, sale of goodwill, capital gains, partnerships, patent income averaging, loss claims, inheritance tax and capital gains tax on gifts.   **CS2–001**

THE PRODUCT

Andrew Rankin was an engineer employed by a water company who became interested in the development of fuel-saving devices for motor cars. Andrew had a small workshop of his own and produced an elementary prototype of a fuel-saving device which showed encouraging results. Over the next 18 months, he devoted his spare time to the development of the idea and eventually produced a device which consistently showed a 15 per cent fuel-saving when fitted to his Plus 8 Morgan. Andrew consulted a patent agent and after some preliminary searches it was decided that the device was sufficiently different from other fuel-saving inventions to make it patentable. He therefore, through his patent agent, filed the necessary preliminary application for a UK patent. At this stage he realised that to date the device had cost him a great deal of time and a not inconsiderable amount of money; furthermore, commercial exploitation was likely to prove difficult. However, Andrew's Great-Aunt Matilda had recently died leaving him a sufficiently large sum of money to enable him to rent some premises and commence limited manufacture of the device, which he had by this time christened the "Mizermyle".   **CS2–002**

Andrew then left his job to concentrate on the development and sale of his Mizermyle. Andrew was convinced from the start that the device would make his fortune and he therefore consulted his accountant to decide how best to handle the idea.

CASE STUDY 2: ANDREW RANKIN, INVENTOR

THE COMPANY

CS2–003 His accountant suggested that before commencing to exploit the invention, the patent be assigned to a UK company, Mizermyle Ltd, in exchange for shares, as otherwise he would be taxed on his professional income as an inventor on the whole of the income arising worldwide, which did not seem a particularly good idea. By transferring the patent in exchange for shares there was no capital gains tax problem as the company merely issued shares at par for the expenses incurred by Andrew to date. The par value of the shares was treated as income, but covered by the expenses, and the company could have claimed capital allowances under the corporate intangible fixed asset rules. Instead, however, the company claimed scientific research allowance on the expenditure, successfully arguing that it was in relation to the development of a prototype, the relief being given in one year under CAA 2001 ss.437–451.

By issuing shares for the expenditure incurred before the trade commences the problem of the valuation of any goodwill attached to the embryo business under TCGA 1992 s.162 was avoided.

THE CHILDREN'S TRUST

CS2–004 As it was anticipated that the company should prove fairly profitable in the long run Andrew immediately issued further shares to a discretionary settlement which he had set up in favour of his children, Jennifer and Stephen. Thirty per cent of the shares were then held by the children's trust (see diagram at para.CS2–013).

Great-Aunt Matilda's husband, Colin, decided to spend the remainder of his days in the Algarve and promptly emigrated from the United Kingdom. Great-Uncle Colin wished to create a trust in Bermuda (No.1) with intended beneficiaries Jennifer and Stephen should they become not ordinarily resident in the United Kingdom and he transferred £10,000 to the trustees resident in Bermuda to start the settlement. A Guernsey-resident protector was also appointed.

The trustees incorporated a company in the BVI and subscribed for share capital of $12,000, the balance of the trust fund being placed on deposit.

The BVI company was managed and controlled from Bermuda. The company was called Rankin Overseas (BVI) Ltd. Rankin Overseas (BVI) Ltd bought from Andrew the right to patent his invention outside the United Kingdom for the sum of £2,000. This modest amount was agreed as the full market value, as at this stage the Mizermyle had yet to be commercially exploited in the United Kingdom and the overseas rights were largely based on hope. Nonetheless, Rankin Overseas (BVI) Ltd borrowed further funds on security of a guarantee given by Great-Uncle Colin and used the proceeds to patent the Mizermyle in the United States, Canada, France, Germany, the Netherlands, Japan and South Korea.

FIRST YEAR'S GROWTH

Mizermyle Ltd in the United Kingdom employed a sales representative and Andrew concentrated on the production and development of the device. At the end of the first year of the company's trade he had produced some 5,000 units, the vast majority of which had been sold by mail order as his sales representative was having difficulty persuading wholesalers to accept an invention, which sounded about as plausible as the philosopher's stone, from an unknown company.

Andrew, however, had continued to develop the product on behalf of the company and was now regularly achieving a 20 per cent reduction in fuel consumption. He arranged to have the device independently tested by the AA and the RAC Technical Departments which confirmed his findings. Largely as a result of these independent evaluations, Andrew's salesman was somewhat overwhelmed to receive an order for 12,000 units from one of the leading independent motor vehicle spares factors. This order was considerably in excess of the first year's entire production and Andrew did not have the financial resources to expand production to the required extent. He approached his bank for a facility of £50,000 to acquire additional premises and machinery, together with the necessary working capital, in order to expand production to 30,000 units per annum. The bank manager viewed his request with a somewhat jaundiced eye, having recently had an unfortunate experience with another customer whose brilliant invention was going to produce a fortune, and on which the bank had had to write off £20,000 as a bad debt. The invention had proved a commercial disaster (mainly on the grounds of a total failure to comply with the advertised claims). Andrew did eventually find another bank which was prepared to lend £40,000 on the basis of Andrew's personal guarantee and a second mortgage on his house. Andrew was extremely loath to involve his personal assets in his business ventures but decided to accept the gamble and duly increased production.

OVERSEAS TRADING INCOME

After a further two years Mizermyle Ltd had pushed its annual sales to 100,000 and was beginning to export the device. Export sales were made through Rankin Overseas (BVI) Ltd as that company had the rights to exploit the invention outside the United Kingdom. Although the Mizermyle was sold in the UK with a gross profit of 100 per cent, the export prices to Rankin Overseas (BVI) Ltd were at cost plus 50 per cent, thus enabling the overseas company to make a worthwhile profit. Andrew's accountant was somewhat concerned with the provisions of the transfer pricing legislation in the United Kingdom but came to the conclusion that there was no problem in view of the fact that the beneficial ownership of Mizermyle Ltd in the United Kingdom and Rankin Overseas (BVI) Ltd were such that they were not under common control and therefore the transfer pricing provisions did not apply.

The real breakthrough came when a Japanese car manufacturer wished to install the device as original equipment in one of its high-volume production cars. Rankin Overseas (BVI) Ltd therefore entered into a licence agreement through its new Netherlands subsidiary with the Japanese manufacturer who agreed to pay a royalty of $10 per unit. In order to reduce the rate of Japanese withholding tax on the patent royalties on the Mizermyle, Rankin Overseas (BVI) Ltd had formed a wholly owned Dutch subsidiary company, Rankin Netherlands BV, which had in turn sub-licensed the Mizermyle to the Japanese company. It was considered that an arm's length margin would be 7 per cent. This 7 per cent would be left in the Netherlands and the balance paid by way of licence fee to Rankin Overseas (BVI) Ltd. The 7 per cent left in the Netherlands was subject to Dutch Corporation tax at 25 per cent. This enabled the Japanese withholding tax to be reduced to 10 per cent under the Dutch/Japanese Double Tax Treaty whereas it would otherwise have been 20 per cent on a direct payment to Rankin Overseas (BVI) Ltd.

SELLING OUT

CS2–007 Andrew at this stage was beginning to realise that although his family were now very well catered for through Rankin Overseas (BVI) Ltd, his own position in the United Kingdom, although not exactly penurious, was rather less healthy than he would have wished. He realised that he was unlikely to expand significantly the UK production of the Mizermyle unless it was accepted as original equipment by one of the leading UK manufacturers. He entered into discussions with one of the UK manufacturers who showed interest for the possible outright sale of Mizermyle Ltd.

Andrew had under development a new form of anti-skid device which prevented a car's wheels locking under excessive braking in slippery conditions. This invention he had named the "Safteemyle" and he had provisionally agreed with Rankin Overseas (BVI) Ltd to exploit the overseas rights. It was, however, recommended that the new invention be dealt with by its own separate overseas company and Rankin Overseas (BVI) Ltd, out of its profits, settled cash on the trustees of another trust in Bermuda (No.2) who used the funds to form a new company, Angus Developments (BVI) Ltd, in the BVI. Rankin Overseas (BVI) Ltd had the power to settle funds in this manner, which is not uncommon. The overseas rights of the new invention were sold by Andrew for £30,000, being the estimated market value of the rights to the new invention, which although purely in the embryo stage, nonetheless had the precedent of the Mizermyle to enhance considerably its commercial appeal.

A wholly owned subsidiary was formed in the Netherlands, Angus Europe BV, to reduce withholding taxes to a minimum in the same way as with Rankin Netherlands BV.

CS2–008 Andrew agreed to sell Mizermyle Ltd to the UK motor manufacturing company for £5 million payable partly in cash and partly in quoted shares and unsecured loan stock of the UK manufacturer. His children's discretionary settlement elected to take shares and loan stock and roll over the gain. Andrew elected to take cash for his shares and decided to accept a capital gains tax charge of 28 per cent.

Andrew's accountant was concerned that the receipt of a capital sum could possibly fall within the provisions of ITA 2007 ss.773–785 and therefore become liable to income tax instead of merely being taxed as a capital gain. However, the sale of the shares of Mizermyle Ltd included the goodwill of the company and all the UK rights relating to the product, which was where the real value lay; and the personal services of Andrew, who remained with the company on a part-time basis under a five-year service contract, were not a significant part of the deal and therefore the section would not have any application, under ITA 2007 s.784.

THE SAFTEEMYLE PARTNERSHIP

When he first started to think about Safteemyle, Andrew realised that certain aspects of the device were outside his professional competence and he approached an engineering friend of his who had considerable experience in dynamics, with a view to the joint development of the idea. His colleague, John Geddes, was interested and Andrew related the success that he had had with the Mizermyle through arranging things to the best possible advantage from the start; he explained that this was why he had just sold the overseas Safteemyle rights to Angus Developments (BVI) Ltd for £30,000. Rankin Overseas (BVI) Ltd settled funds on a new discretionary trust (No.3), this time in Guernsey, for the benefit of John's children. The new trust acquired 30 per cent of the shares in Angus Developments (BVI) Ltd, the company designed to exploit the overseas rights of the Safteemyle, by way of a further issue of shares by the company.

The lump sum of £30,000 that Andrew received from Angus Developments (BVI) Ltd was a lump sum on the disposal of patent rights and therefore subject to averaging.

Andrew and John decided to develop the Safteemyle in the United Kingdom through a Limited Liability Partnership and under the profit-sharing arrangements John was to receive 40 per cent of the overall profits with a minimum profit share of £20,000 per annum, but to share in only one per cent of any losses. Andrew and his wife, Doreen, were the remaining partners in the business, which started on January 1, 2010. Doreen kept the books of the partnership and ordered the necessary materials, while Andrew and John developed the Safteemyle. It took 18 months to make the Safteemyle work satisfactorily in practice and the partnership therefore showed a loss for the first period, 99 per cent of which was available to Andrew to set against his other income but he elected to carry back the loss against previous years' total income.

The partnership accounts were made up to April 6 and in the third year the success of the Safteemyle was assured and a large contract entered into with one of the UK manufacturers for a licence to manufacture the product for a volume production car. Andrew and his partners were not willing to sell the business outright. They therefore agreed to the non-exclusive UK licence of the Safteemyle for a royalty of £1 per unit payable annually on the basis of the production in the proceeding calendar year but with a non-returnable but recoupable advance royalty of £800,000 payable in two equal instalments on April 3, 2012 and April 3, 2013. The production in the first three years amounted to 950,000 units.

On April 6, 2015, however, Doreen resigned from the partnership and a professional book-keeper was employed to take over her duties and at the same time the business was converted to a company.

HMRC at first argued that Doreen's contribution to the partnership was insufficient to justify her share of profit, but it was pointed out that the partnership profit share was for the partners themselves to decide and there was no question of having to justify the partners' shares of profit in the same way as for remuneration. Once it was shown that Doreen was actively engaged in the partnership, which she indubitably was, there was no mechanism for HMRC to avoid assessing her on her share of the income, short of showing that her share of profits was effectively a settlement created by Andrew, which they were unable to do given her contribution to the business over a period of more than five years.

SAFTEEMYLE LTD

CS2–011 On April 10, 2015 it was decided to transfer the partnership to a limited company and claim the capital gains tax roll-over relief under TCGA 1992 s.162.

A company, Safteemyle Ltd, was therefore formed and the goodwill and other trading assets of the partnership sold to the company at cost, the shares previously having been issued for cash at par. This gave rise to a transfer at an undervalue but as the assets were business assets within TCGA 1992 s.165, the capital gains tax charge could be held over. It was argued that even without business property relief there was no inheritance tax on the transfer, as the reduction in the estate resulting from the partial gift of goodwill was balanced by the increase in the estate resulting from the transfer of the goodwill to the company, the shares of which constituted part of the transferor's estate.

It was decided that some of the shares should be transferred to a discretionary settlement for Andrew's children, Jennifer and Stephen, but as this would involve a transfer for inheritance tax purposes it was decided to issue deferred shares in the company to the trust. These shares were of a class that carried no rights to participate in dividends or a surplus on liquidation and carried no votes, for a period of 15 years. At the end of the 15-year period, however, the shares would rank pari passu with the existing ordinary shares. The issue of the deferred shares was made at market value to avoid allowing value to pass out of the existing shares which would have given rise to an inheritance tax charge under IHTA 1984 s.98, and a capital gains tax charge on the deemed disposal at market value of the existing shares under TCGA 1992 s.29. In view of the lack of rights attaching to the shares for a very considerable period the value for inheritance tax purposes was ultimately agreed with Shares and Assets Valuation of HMRC at £1.50 per share, the price at which they were issued.

Andrew and John started considering further products for Safteemyle Ltd.

ANDREW RANKIN: TRADING STRUCTURE

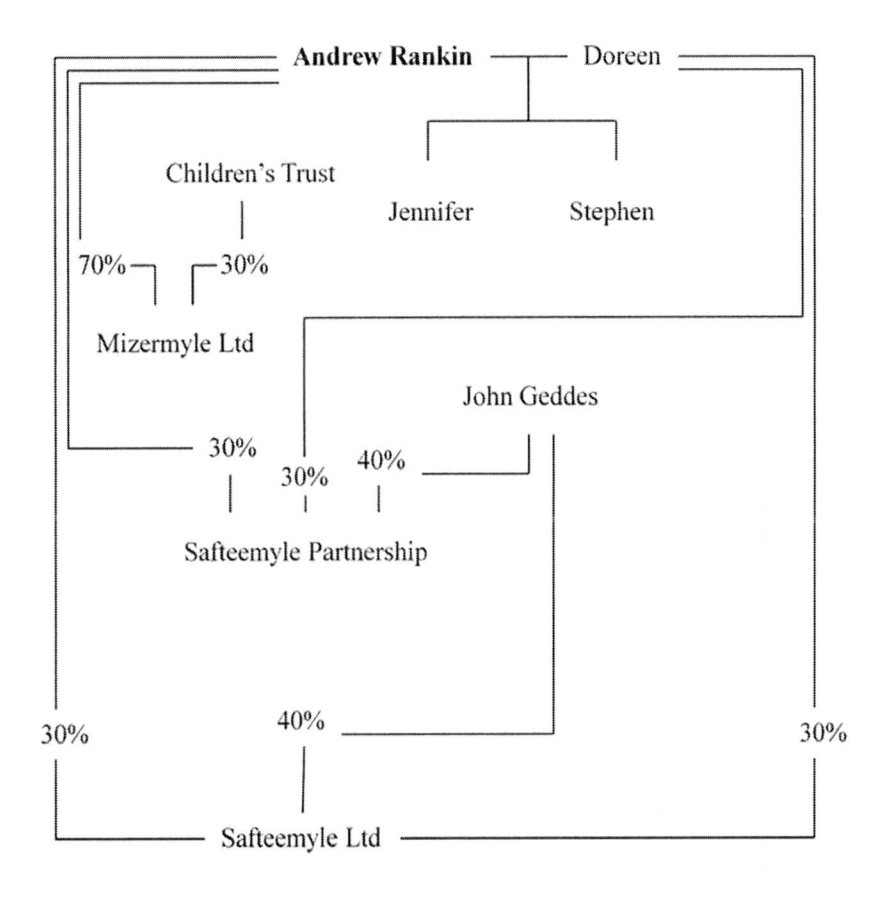

```
          ┌─────────── Andrew Rankin ──┬── Doreen ───────────┐
          │                            │                     │
          │              ┌─────────────┴─────────────┐       │
          │    Children's Trust                      │       │
          │              │                Jennifer   Stephen │
          │              │                                   │
      70%─┤          ┌─30%                                   │
          │          │                                       │
        Mizermyle Ltd                                        │
                                                             │
                                   John Geddes               │
          ┌────── 30%         40% ──────┐                    │
          │             30%    │                             │
          │              │     │                             │
              Safteemyle Partnership                         │
          │                                                  │
          │                                                  │
          │              40% ──────────┐                     │
    30%   │               │            │               30%   │
          └──────── Safteemyle Ltd ────┴─────────────────────┘
```

CASE STUDY 2: ANDREW RANKIN, INVENTOR

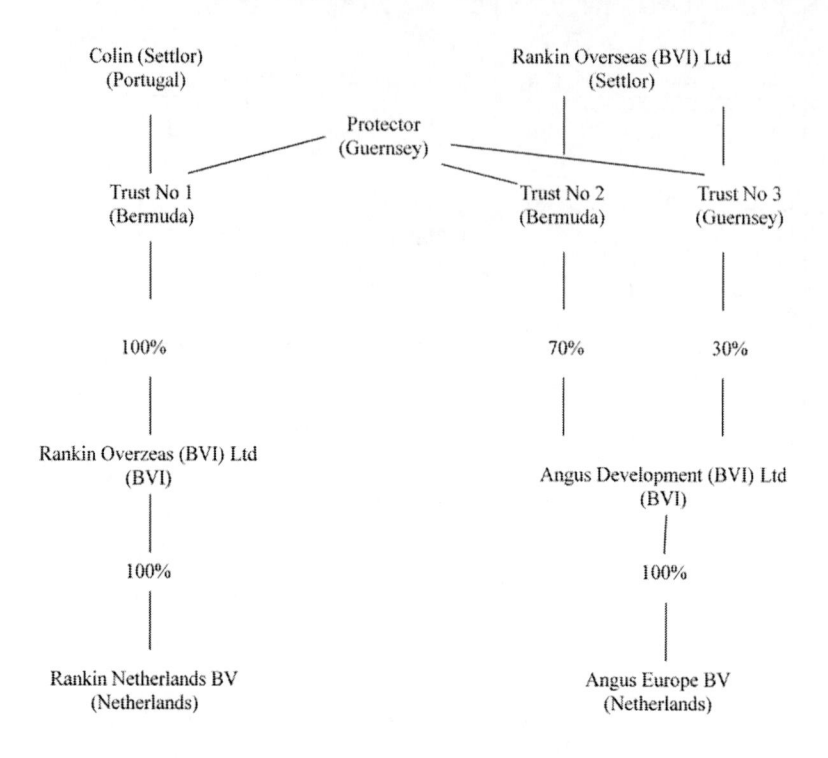

```
Colin (Settlor)                              Rankin Overseas (BVI) Ltd
(Portugal)                                          (Settlor)
    |                                                   |
    |           Protector                               |
    |----------(Guernsey)----------------               |
    |                    |              \               |
Trust No 1           Trust No 2          Trust No 3
(Bermuda)            (Bermuda)           (Guernsey)
    |                    |                   |
   100%                 70%                 30%
    |                    |                   |
Rankin Overzeas (BVI) Ltd       Angus Development (BVI) Ltd
      (BVI)                              (BVI)
    |                                      |
   100%                                   100%
    |                                      |
Rankin Netherlands BV             Angus Europe BV
    (Netherlands)                   (Netherlands)
```

Case Study 3: Brighton Rock, entertainers

INTRODUCTION

This case study illustrates the possible treatment of the composing, performing and publishing income of a rock group. It deals with partnerships, employment companies and their shareholdings, pension schemes, small company rates, overseas and UK trusts, foreign earnings employment provisions, post-cessation receipts, royalty planning and gifts of future copyright. **CS3–001**

THE PRODUCT

Brighton Rock is the name of a rock group formed between Agatha Bentley, Cedric Dawson, Elizabeth Farrow and Gordon Hepplewhite (see diagram at para.CS3–019). All four were resident in the United Kingdom. Gordon retained his domicile of origin which was in Guernsey, where his family had lived for generations, but the other three members were all domiciled in England. **CS3–002**

Agatha was aged 26 and divorced with a two-year old daughter, Ingrid. Cedric, aged 28 was married to Jemima, aged 24, and they had two young children, Kathleen and Leslie. Elizabeth, aged 22, was married to the group's manager, Morris and they had two children, Naomi and Ophelia. Gordon, aged 32, was divorced from his wife, Petra, by whom he had two sons, Quentin and Richard and was now living with Sylvia by whom he had two children, Teresa and Ursula.

The group originally began playing at various gigs as a support band. The group was assessed to taxation as a partnership on the modest profits then made.

Towards the end of the next year Agatha and Gordon started to write their own songs with some assistance from Morris and from a friend of Agatha's, Vernon Wallace, who was not a member of the group. As some of their own compositions seemed to be having a good reception where they played, the band thought it would be desirable to put together an album, ideally for release during the pre-Christmas period. Vernon then talked to a friend of his, Xavier Yates, who had produced a number of records for which Vernon had written some of the songs and Xavier, having heard the group play, agreed to produce an album for them but pointed out that the suggested timescale was hopelessly unrealistic. **CS3–003**

CASE STUDY 3: BRIGHTON ROCK, ENTERTAINERS

Xavier arranged for a company with which he was connected, Zombie Productions Ltd to publish the DVD which would be manufactured and distributed by Zombie Records Ltd.

The recording was duly produced in the middle of the following year under the title "Peer West" and was a modest success, reaching nineteenth position in the UK album charts.

Brighton Rock: dramatis personae

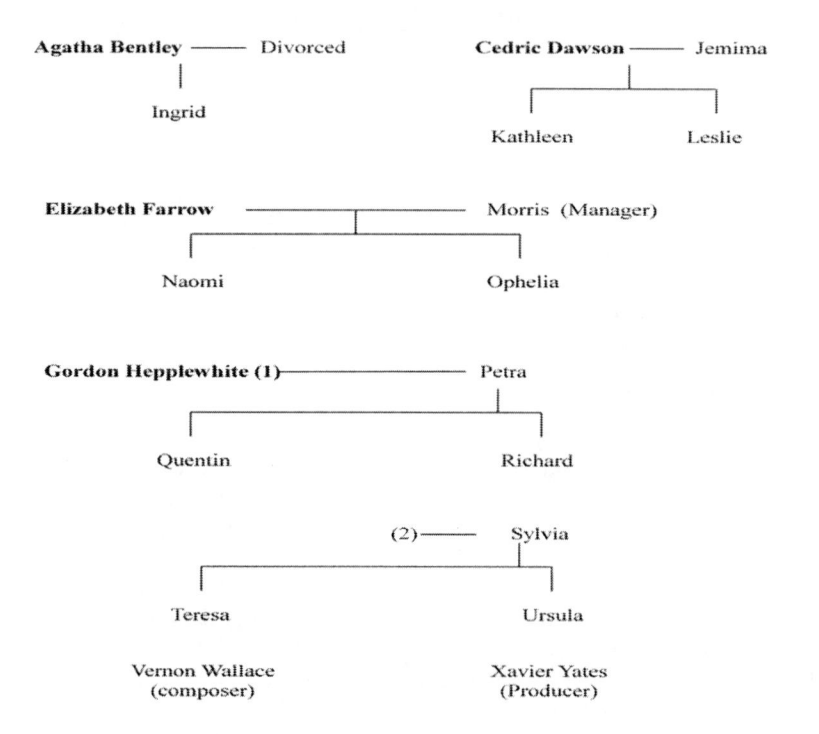

Agatha Bentley —— Divorced
  |
  Ingrid

Cedric Dawson —— Jemima
  |
  ┌───────┴───────┐
  Kathleen   Leslie

Elizabeth Farrow ———————— Morris (Manager)
  ┌───────┴───────┐
  Naomi   Ophelia

Gordon Hepplewhite (1) ———————— Petra
  ┌───────┴───────┐
  Quentin   Richard

                (2) —— Sylvia
  ┌───────┴───────┐
  Teresa   Ursula

Vernon Wallace   Xavier Yates
(composer)   (Producer)

THE PARTNERSHIP'S INCOME

CS3–005 The group was entitled to an artistes' royalty of 10 per cent of the retail price of CDs sold in the United Kingdom (see diagram at para.CS3–019). This was a partnership receipt and was included in the professional income of the partnership.

The composers of the various songs were entitled to a royalty totalling 6.25 per cent of the retail value of the recording of which the publishers, Zombie Productions Ltd, took 3 per cent. The producer, Xavier, took 1 per cent, leaving 2.25 per cent to be divided among the composers of the songs. It was agreed that the apportionment should be in accordance with the playing time of each track and Agatha and Vernon were each entitled to 0.75 per cent, Gordon 0.5 per cent and Morris 0.25 per cent.

THE COMPANIES

Each of the composers had set up a new business assessed to tax as professional income as a songwriter.

The publisher's and composers' royalties on performances were collected by the Performing Rights Society Ltd to whom the copyright was assigned for collection. Such royalties were payable whenever any track from the recording was played on the radio or television or performed in public, either by a live band or discotheque. The publishing and composing royalties were paid by the manufacturer, Zombie Records Ltd, with the artistes' royalties on the sale of DVDs.

THE COMPANIES

At this stage Morris thought, somewhat belatedly, that it would be a good idea to consider some more sophisticated financial planning for the group and consulted an accountant and a solicitor experienced in the music industry. **CS3–006**

One of the main problems of the popular music world is the relative shortness of the earnings period of many performers and the high earnings concentrated into a short period of time, which in the absence of avoiding action would nearly all be taxed at the top rate of tax, 45 per cent.

It was therefore decided to set up a series of companies for each group member and for Morris who, as the group's manager, was entitled to 10 per cent of the gross earnings and was therefore likely to receive nearly as much as a performing member of the group (see diagram at CS3–019). Vernon Wallace, the outside writer, and Xavier Yates already had their own company through which they operated.

Consideration was given to setting up Gordon's company outside the United Kingdom but it was thought that it would be preferable to have a UK company which could then pay premiums to fund a pension scheme. **CS3–007**

It was decided that the shares in the individuals' companies should be owned as to 70 per cent by the group member and as to 30 per cent by a discretionary settlement set up for each of their children, except that Agatha decided to own all the shares in her company personally, on the ground that the financial maintenance of her daughter was a responsibility of her former husband.

Each member of the group then entered into an employment contract with the company under which they undertook to compose and record for the company in return for a salary. There was a territorial limitation in that the contract applied only to work done in the United Kingdom. As they had previously been self-employed the personal service company anti-avoidance provisions (IR35) would not apply.

The partnership remained entitled to the artistes' royalties from the sale of the DVD "Peer West" and also continued to receive the income for public performances in the UK. The songwriting royalties for the tracks of "Peer West" were received by the individuals, except for Vernon and Xavier whose royalties were paid to their own companies. **CS3–008**

It was appreciated that the formation of the companies would not enable profits to be built up and the companies then sold for a lump sum subject only to capital gains tax. Such a lump sum would be likely to be caught as a capital amount (ITA 2007 ss.773–785) and the profit would then be liable to tax as income not otherwise charged to tax in one year. The purpose of the company was to make the profits subject to corporation tax after paying out a reasonable remuneration which would be taxed under ITEPA 2003 as employment income.

THE PENSION FUNDS

CS3–009 The actual saving between the top rates of personal taxation of 45 per cent and NICs and corporation tax at 22 per cent was attractive and when the National Insurance savings were considered it did justify a pension fund being set up for the benefit of each of the group members. This in turn enabled a tax deductible ordinary annual contribution, within the statutory limits to the salary drawn to be paid into the pension fund by the company. This premium would be saved up within a tax free fund for the benefit of the individual group members.

As the funds were self-administered each group member was, as a trustee of the pension fund, able to decide on the investment policy he or she preferred within the tax free structure of the fund, so long as the HMRC guidelines were adhered to. The pensioneer trustee for the funds was able to agree with HMRC that in view of the fund members' income coming from the rock music world the normal retirement age would be 40 instead of the more usual retirement age of 60. So far as Morris was concerned, however, as a manager it was not possible to agree a normal retirement age below the age of 60.

The Small Self-Administered Scheme (SSAS) enabled the money to be saved up in a tax-free environment for the future benefit of the group members when, from age 40 onwards, they would be able to draw a pension taxable as earned income. They would also be able to commute part of this pension entitlement for a tax-free lump sum equal to 25 per cent of the fund reduced by 2.5 per cent for each year below the normal retirement date, i.e. 37.5 per cent at age 40, reducing the commutation to 62.5 per cent of 25 per cent based on the number of years the employment had continued.

THE CHILDREN'S TRUSTS

CS3–010 It was intended to pay dividends from the companies to the children's discretionary settlements, thus transferring some money into the hands of the trustees where, to the extent that it was accumulated, it would suffer tax at the effective rate of 45 per cent. It was appreciated that as the parents were the settlors any income not accumulated but distributed to the children would be taxed as the parents' income during the children's minority. Consideration was given to making friends or grandparents the settlors of the trust, which would then buy the shares in the companies. However, it was thought that HMRC would argue that the true settlors of the trust funds were in any event the parents and that such an exercise would therefore be pointless.

THE SMALL COMPANIES' RATE

The existence of the partnership meant that the four companies of the group members were associated companies for the small companies' rate and it was therefore decided to look carefully to see whether the partnership could be wound up without adverse tax consequences at a fairly early stage. Any profits left in the companies would then be taxed only at the small companies' rate of 20 per cent rather than the 22 per cent which would apply if profits of more than the lower relevant limit were accumulated within the companies. This limit was £300,000 for the year beginning April, 2013. Profits in a single company (with no associated companies) of between this and the upper relevant limit of £1,500,000 would be taxed at the marginal small companies' rate. However, the payment of salaries and pension fund contributions would enable the profits to be kept within the small companies' rate for the first period. The proposed reduction of the standard rate of corporation tax to 20 per cent would soon remove any problem of rate differential.

CS3–011

ANOTHER RECORD

The songwriters in the group were meanwhile working on another DVD entitled "Palace Promises" and in view of the success of "Peer West" Morris was able to negotiate slightly better terms. The group were entitled to an artistes' royalty of 11 per cent of the retail value and publisher Zombie Productions Ltd agreed to split the publishing and composing royalties 70/30 in the writers' favour. All the income from both the latter sources went to the individuals' own companies and was largely paid out by way of remuneration and pension fund contributions.

CS3–012

THE OVERSEAS COMPANIES

Morris now planned for the group to make an overseas tour and, as this involved activities outside the United Kingdom, a further company was set up for each individual and consideration given as to whether this should be a non-UK resident company.

CS3–013

Setting up an overseas company seemed an attractive solution until the anti-avoidance provisions were looked at in more detail (ITA 2007 ss.716–750). Under these provisions it seemed that the income of the company could be regarded as the income of the individuals unless there was a good commercial reason for having an overseas company. Other anti-avoidance provisions would in any event prevent the build-up of a capital sum outside the United Kingdom through overseas companies (ITA 2007 ss.773–785), and therefore it was decided to form UK resident companies wholly owned by the group members for the overseas activities, except for Gordon, as in any event it was likely that the majority of the income would at some stage be taken out by way of remuneration or pension contribution.

In view of his non-UK domiciled status, Gordon's company was set up in Jersey as a non-resident company which was beneficially owned by a Guernsey resident and domiciled friend of Gordon's, to forestall any HMRC arguments on transfer of assets abroad (ITA 2007 s.720). Gordon, however, had a service agreement with the company whereby he was entitled to 95 per cent of the company's profits as remuneration. As emoluments from a foreign employment with a non-resident company for duties carried out wholly overseas, the remuneration would be taxed only on the full amount of any remittances to the United Kingdom.

Gordon accepted the risk that the service agreement itself might constitute a transfer of assets and therefore cause Gordon to be assessed on the profits of the company.

DOUBLE TAXATION

CS3–014 So far as the United States was concerned, however, it was decided that each individual group member would be employed by the American tour operator, which was a locally managed and controlled American company. The reason for this was that the Internal Revenue Service could tax the earnings of the group members' employing companies as if it were the income of the individual group members personally (UK/US Double Tax Treaty Agreement (SI 2002/2848) art.16). The effect of this, however, was not merely to make employing companies ineffective from an American tax point of view, but would result in the Internal Revenue Service subjecting the income of the employing company to tax in the United States as if it were the employee's income and to that extent the UK company would have a foreign tax credit. However, if the company then paid out its income in the form of remuneration to the group member, which was the object of the exercise, it would have no UK tax liability against which it could absorb the foreign tax credit. Although HMRC had been known to look through the company in the same way as the Internal Revenue Service and give relief for the American tax against the individual's own UK income from the company, this was a concessionary treatment and could not be relied upon. Attempts to resolve this problem with HMRC had so far proved unsuccessful. HMRC'S view was supported in *RCC v Anson* (2003) S.T.C. 557 which involved a Delaware LLC with a UK resident member who could not claim relief for the US tax paid. It was therefore decided that each group member's activities in the United States should be as employee of the US tour operator, which would give rise to a tax liability on employment income with double taxation relief for the US tax already suffered. Gordon claimed the remittance basis as he was not domiciled in the United Kingdom.

The tour was a modest success and helped considerably in the sale of both "Peer West" and "Palace Promises". The group's third record, "The Beach", produced following the overseas tour, was an instant success.

By now the group was well established in the United Kingdom and was becoming established overseas. Substantial sums of money were flowing into the UK companies. The partnership had outlived its original purpose and was now wound up; the continuing royalty income from "Peer West" was taxed on the individuals in accordance with their profit shares as self-employed earnings not as post-cessation receipts as they continued to be entertainers.

THE FILM

Cedric and Elizabeth had decided that there was a possibility of writing a screenplay for a film involving the group while Gordon and Agatha thought it would be desirable to release a new record before the success of "The Beach" was forgotten. Morris, however, wanted to arrange another overseas tour which would help DVD sales, particularly in Germany, Japan and the United States. It was decided to combine these activities and to produce the new DVD outside the United Kingdom so that the royalties could legitimately flow to the companies dealing with the overseas activities. For the fourth DVD, entitled "Regency Relics", Vernon Wallace was not involved and Agatha and Gordon between them composed all the tracks. The record was actually written and produced in Spain, although still released by Zombie Records Ltd in the United Kingdom and by its subsidiary, Zombie Records Inc, in the United States.

While Agatha and Gordon had been writing the songs for the DVD, Cedric and Elizabeth had been in Corfu producing a screenplay for the proposed film.

When the DVD had been produced and released the overseas tour commenced, structured in the same manner as previously. By this time the group had been outside the United Kingdom for about eight months and Agatha and Gordon returned to the United Kingdom because Agatha was homesick and did not care about money and Gordon was happy with the remittance basis in spite of having to pay the remittance basis charge. Elizabeth and Cedric, however, decided to remain outside the United Kingdom for a further four months.

CS3–015

THE FILM

So far as the film was concerned it was decided to set up a traditional royalty strip (see diagram). A friend of Agatha's resident and domiciled in Jersey settled $10,000 on a Cayman Islands trust, the beneficiaries of which were resident outside the United Kingdom but with power to add additional beneficiaries. The trustees incorporated a company in the BVI called Venah (Holdings) (BVI) Ltd which in turn formed a Netherlands subsidiary company Venah BV. Venah (Holdings) (BVI) Ltd acquired by way of assignment the screenplay from Cedric and Elizabeth for $100,000 which was thought to be a fair market value. This was taxed as professional income of the two writers.

Venah (Holdings) (BVI) Ltd also entered into a contract with each of the group members' UK employing companies for their services for a fee of $50,000 each to appear in the film. This was again thought to be a fair market rate for the work involved.

Venah (Holdings) (BVI) Ltd sub-contracted the production of the film to a UK company, which duly produced the film on its behalf. Venah (Holdings) (BVI) Ltd then licensed its Netherlands subsidiary company, Venah BV, which in turn sub-licensed the film to distributors in various countries. The royalties for the showing of the film were largely paid to Venah BV without deduction of any withholding taxes, in view of the double tax agreements between the countries where the film was shown and the Netherlands. It was considered that 7 per cent represented an arm's length royalty turn, which remained in the Netherlands. This would be taxed at an effective 25 per cent. The remaining 93 per cent of the income would be paid by way of royalty to Venah (Holdings) (BVI) Ltd in the

CS3–016

CASE STUDY 3: BRIGHTON ROCK, ENTERTAINERS

BVI without any Netherlands withholding tax. Venah (Holdings) (BVI) Ltd distributed its profits by way of dividend to the trustees of the Cayman Islands trust free of all further taxes. By this means the majority of the profits from the film were accumulated in the Cayman Islands for reinvestment. At some future date members of the group expected to become not resident in the United Kingdom. It was possible that they might then be made additional beneficiaries of the trust. It was thought that once they had become non-resident HMRC would not be able to tax any sum distributed to them under the anti-avoidance provisions ITA 2007 ss.714–751 and it was argued that the film royalties were not income arising from the activities of any individual (ITA 2007 ss.773–789), which would have made the capital sum taxable in the UK whether or not the individual was then not resident. The application of the General Anti-Abuse Rule in FA 2013 ss.206–215 and Sch.43 was thought not to apply because of the treaty relief, but this could not be guaranteed.

The royalty income of the group members' own companies was regarded as trading income and not investment income because the entitlement to the income arose from the activities of the company and not from copyrights acquired by purchase. Income arising from the reinvestment of undistributed royalties, however, would be investment income. Thus the majority of such reinvestment took place through the self-administered pension funds rather than in the company itself. This helped to ensure that the companies did not become close investment-holding companies, which are not entitled to the small companies' rate (CTA 2010 ss.19–32 and 34).

GIFT OF FUTURE COPYRIGHT TO TRUST

CS3–017 When the group came to write a fifth record "Black Rock", Agatha had decided that it would be a good idea to set up a discretionary settlement for her daughter, Ingrid, after all. As her own company was relatively valuable by this time she decided, in view of the capital gains tax and inheritance tax implications, not to transfer the shares in her company to the settlement but instead to give the trustees the copyright in the songs she was about to write for the record "Black Rock". It was argued that as she had not yet written the songs there could be no reduction in her estate for inheritance tax purposes. It was also argued that as the rights had not been created there could be no material capital gains tax charge. The songwriting activities in the United Kingdom were part of Agatha's own professional income and therefore it was not necessary to bring into her professional receipts any notional income from the copyrights transferred to the settlements. As the income would be accumulated within the trust it would be subject only to tax at the rate applicable to trusts of 45 per cent and could in due course be paid out as income to Ingrid at some stage after she reached her majority.

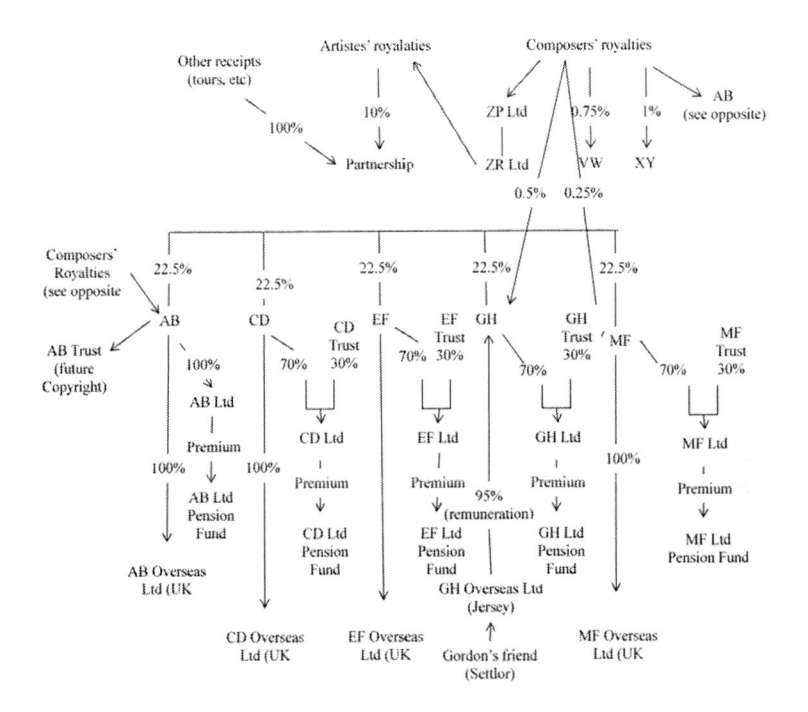

BRIGHTON ROCK: STRUCTURE

BRIGHTON ROCK: STRUCTURE

Other receipts (tours, etc) — 100% → Partnership

Artistes' royalties — 10% → Partnership

Composers' royalties:
- → ZP Ltd → ZR Ltd (0.5%)
- 0.75% → VW (0.25%)
- 1% → XY
- → AB (see opposite)

Composers' Royalties (see opposite):

- 22.5% → AB
  - AB Trust (future Copyright)
  - 100% → AB Ltd → Premium → 100% → AB Ltd Pension Fund → AB Overseas Ltd (UK)

- 22.5% → CD
  - CD Trust 70% / 30%
  - 100% → CD Ltd → Premium → 100% → CD Ltd Pension Fund → CD Overseas Ltd (UK)

- 22.5% → EF
  - EF Trust 70% / 30%
  - EF Ltd → Premium → EF Ltd Pension Fund → EF Overseas Ltd (UK)

- 22.5% → GH
  - GH Trust 70% / 30%
  - GH Ltd → Premium 95% (remuneration) → GH Ltd Pension Fund → GH Overseas Ltd (Jersey) ← Gordon's friend (Settlor)

- 22.5% → MF
  - MF Trust 70% / 30%
  - 100% → MF Ltd → Premium → MF Ltd Pension Fund → MF Overseas Ltd (UK)

CASE STUDY 3: BRIGHTON ROCK, ENTERTAINERS

BRIGHTON ROCK: FILM STRUCTURE

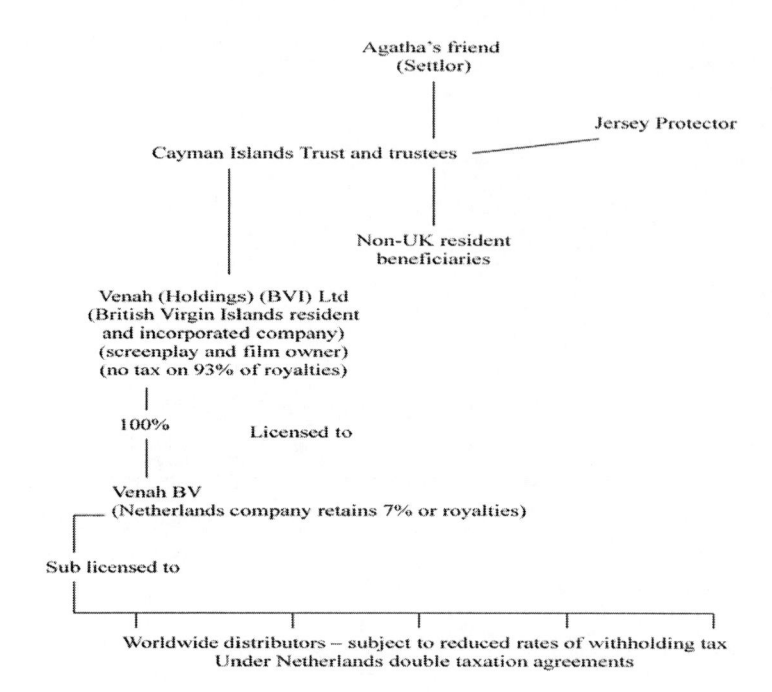

```
                        Agatha's friend
                           (Settlor)
                              |
                              |                    Jersey Protector
        Cayman Islands Trust and trustees ─────────
               |                      |
               |                      |
               |                   Non-UK resident
               |                    beneficiaries
               |
   Venah (Holdings) (BVI) Ltd
   (British Virgin Islands resident
     and incorporated company)
   (screenplay and film owner)
   (no tax on 93% of royalties)
               |
             100%          Licensed to
               |
           Venah BV
    ─── (Netherlands company retains 7% or royalties)
   |
Sub licensed to
   |
   ┌───────┬───────┬───────┬───────┐
   Worldwide distributors – subject to reduced rates of withholding tax
              Under Netherlands double taxation agreements
```

Case Study 4: Albert Potcher, bricklayer extraordinare

INTRODUCTION

This case study is designed to illustrate the interrelationship between the various types of intellectual property rights applied to industrial manufacture. CS4–001

THE PRODUCT

Albert Potcher was a bricklayer. He had originally worked for various large construction companies but after a few years found that he enjoyed life much more working as an independent contractor and advertising through the local newspaper and on the internet. He was self-employed, worked as few or as many hours each week as he wanted to, weather permitting, and generally enjoyed life. What irritated him was that sometimes, despite his best efforts, brickwork shifted. He was constantly at the mercy of people who wanted work done but who tried to economise on the materials. A particular problem in his area was garden retaining walls. He had lots of good contacts among the local landscape gardeners, and was often called on to build retaining walls for terraces. All too often, subsequent ground movement or the activities of the landscape gardeners themselves caused the walls to move, generating dissatisfaction among his customers and the occasional complaint. CS4–002

Potcher decided something had to be done and turned his mind to whether an improvement could not be achieved, by using for such retaining walls bricks that allowed a little more grip both between themselves and with the mortar than that obtained with conventional substantially flat-sided bricks. Working away with cold chisel and masonry saw he took some relatively soft bricks (since they were easier to work) and tried changing the shapes, giving them different surface configurations. To his delight he found that there were ways of shaping some of the faces of bricks that gave improved results.

PROTECTING THE IDEA

Albert was quite excited by his discovery and fortunately the first person he told about it was his accountant, with whom he had, of course, a professional confidential relationship as between client and accountant. His accountant, aware CS4–003

CASE STUDY 4: ALBERT POTCHER, BRICKLAYER EXTRAORDINARE

from several past experiences with other clients that secrecy was of the utmost importance in these matters, counselled Albert to tell no-one about the idea before he saw a patent agent. Albert, who trusted his accountant implicitly, duly did so and was received by the patent agent with interest. The agent listened to Albert's description of how the bricks were shaped to give a self-locking action when installed in a certain way and advised Albert that certainly it would seem to be the sort of subject matter for which a patent might be obtained, provided of course that no-one had previously had much the same idea.

Albert asked whether one could find that out but was horrified to learn how much it would cost to do so. The patent agent advised filing a patent application since that was really the only way of getting any protection on the basic idea, if such was available, and it was cheaper to file an application than it was to try to do a search. This seemed good advice and Albert instructed that an application be prepared. The patent agent took down the details and drafted a specification. The agent felt that there were really two slightly separate inventions, one being the shape of the bricks themselves and the other being the way in which they were fitted together, but he wrote descriptions of the article and the method into a single patent application and, having secured Albert's approval of them, filed the written documents at the Patent Office.

This took several weeks, but after that Albert knew that he was at least initially protected, to the extent that he could now go and talk to other people about his idea.

This he did, first to a specialist brickmaker to see if special shaped bricks could be produced to enable a proper test of the idea to be carried out and then to the more reliable of his landscape gardening friends who might be interested. The parties seemed enthusiastic and, although the bricks were obviously going to be more expensive, the area in which they both worked was well populated by people with more money than sense and the landscape gardener thought he could persuade some of them to pay up adequately in return for the promise of a better construction. After a lot of fuss and bother, bricks were produced and used in three or four different sites. They aroused some interest and unquestionably seemed to work. Of course, no-one could be quite sure whether the walls in question would have moved or stayed put anyway, but everybody seemed pleased.

BEGINNING COMMERCIAL EXPLOITATION

CS4–004 By this time Albert thought he might be on to something and he and the landscape gardeners decided to do a deal. The landscape gardeners would promote the system and try to get orders and in return Albert would supervise the works and have a slice of the profits derived from that particular area of the business. This sounded quite attractive to Albert but he was by no means certain that it was the right way to go. His experience of bricklaying had taught him that bricks were useful in more than building retaining walls in gardens and he wondered whether the potential might not be rather greater. He accordingly approached a civil engineering company of some standing and told them about his ideas. He showed them the patent application, then some eight months old, and they were pleased that he had taken that first step. They said they would like to evaluate the idea but that it would take time and they would let Albert know. Albert communicated this to his patent agent who said that this was all very well but if the idea really was going to take off then it would be desirable to try to secure patent protection on a somewhat broader basis geographically. Albert thought the construction company had been sufficiently enthusiastic to make that a real possibility but he was somewhat daunted by the cost. He therefore went to the contractors and offered them a deal.

He said that he would not try to sell the idea to anyone else within the next 12 months if they would put in some effort to testing the idea on a large scale and additionally put up some money to start securing foreign patent protection. The contractors were keen, particularly since they had just been asked to tender for some very substantial reservoir works where they felt the invention could be advantageously used and in respect of which the cost of patenting was insignificant compared to the potential value of the contract. They therefore advanced some money to Albert, which he used for filing, on the basis of his original British application, some applications in other countries, notably North America, Japan, some Commonwealth countries and a European application designating 15 countries. The original British application was used just as a basis for claiming priority.

During this time, Albert had reserved for himself and his landscape contractor friends the ability to go on buying bricks and using them and they were continuing to operate in that way. The brickworks themselves were beginning to be interested. The brickmakers in fact wanted to make more of these bricks since they commanded a better margin and it was naturally of assistance in promoting their business as specialist brickmakers to be associated with a new development in bricks. Indeed the brickmakers went so far as to start offering to supply the new sort of brick to third parties, which infuriated Albert when he heard about it and which in turn led to displeasure on the part of the brickmakers when they found Albert wanted to stop them. The brickmakers had never asked Albert for a penny piece in connection with making the moulds or anything like that and effectively told him to get lost. Albert wrote them a letter saying that he had all rights in the new bricks and that he would sue them, whereupon the brickworks instructed their solicitors to enquire gently what the problem was.

At this stage Albert, realising that the brickworks were not terribly happy, **CS4–005** started to consider his position more carefully. The brickworks had originally worked from a specimen handmade brick which he had produced for them and Albert's patent agent said that it was by no means certain that there was any copyright in the brick itself. Albert had not done any drawings of the brick so no copyright was to be found there. Albert had heard of registering designs and suggested that, but the patent agent pointed out that by this time the brick had already been manufactured and sold, and indeed used, so that requisite novelty for registering a design no longer existed. There being no special contract between Albert and the brickworks, his position was very weak, so he decided to be conciliatory and point out to the brickworks that, while he had no great wish to stop exploitation of the idea, he did feel that he was entitled to something on all their sales of bricks and, in any case, has had made a patent application and in due course hoped that patents would be granted which would protect him against

CASE STUDY 4: ALBERT POTCHER, BRICKLAYER EXTRAORDINARE

that sort of activity. The brickworks, unhappy to build up a business which might be liable to attack if Albert ever obtained his patent and in ignorance, of course, of what the patent said (the papers had not yet been published by the Patent Office), decided to do a deal with Albert where they would give him one per cent of the value of any order for the bricks. Albert thought that this was mean but agreed to it.

The brickworks wanted to promote the brick with a little bit of advertising in the trade and wanted a name for it. Albert suggested Frogmate which had a certain allusiveness but was probably registrable. The brickworks asked their solicitors to take the necessary action and applied to register the name in respect of bricks and other non-metallic building materials. This caused further ructions with Albert when he found out about it, since he felt the name was his, but the matter remained unresolved and the brickworks started doing some advertising.

THE COMPANY

CS4–006 Around this time Albert's accountant, realising that his client might have hit on something that could really make money, suggested that it would be a good idea to set up a little company to exploit the idea and, since there was a little change left over from the money advanced by the contractors, Albert did this. Albert, still annoyed by the actions of the brickworks, called it Frogmate Limited.

After a few months the contractors finished their testing and agreed that the system worked and worked well. Unfortunately, they had not secured the reservoir tender so their enthusiasm was waning. Albert by this time had formed a good working relationship with the people who had been doing the testing and they were enthusiastic about the idea, so when the contractors finally decided not to go ahead and to write off the expenditure, Albert was left free, or at least freer, to try to exploit the invention.

He was still tied down by the fact that he had only one supplier of the bricks in question, who would clearly never be capable of supplying the enormous quantities of bricks which, by now, Albert had decided that the world needed, so he went to see one of the major brickmaking companies. They offered to buy out Albert lock, stock and barrel at that stage but Albert, who was beginning to enjoy wheeling and dealing, rejected the offer and said he was prepared to do a deal with them provided they would help him disentangle himself from his present brickmakers. This they agreed to do and, furthermore, they agreed to promote the system and pay Frogmate Limited a royalty.

CS4–007 The major brickworks were persuaded by Albert to pay £10,000 as an advance against royalties, which he then used to try to sort out what was going on, on the following basis: first, he transferred all the patent applications that were in his name into that of Frogmate Limited. He then applied to register "Frogmate" in the name of "Frogmate Limited" at the Trade Marks Registry, feeling sure that that application would then come into conflict with the earlier application made by the brickmakers and thus that neither party would get anywhere with registering the trade mark for some time. In this respect he was right and eventually the small brickmakers, by then finding themselves being elbowed out, simply faded out of the act. Albert also caused Frogmate Limited to employ one of the contractor's people who had recently been made redundant to try to develop the system a little further. This man, Tom Smith, had been employed in testing the bricks for the contractors. He settled down with Frogmate and improved on the design of the brick and designed some alternative brick types. By virtue of his contract, the property in the new designs was Frogmate's. Albert thought these looked rather good and this time was determined not to lose out on the possibility of getting some early useful protection, so he first of all had drawings made and dated and deposited with his solicitor of each of the new brick types and then he had a set of the drawings sent to his patent agent for considering whether it might not be possible to register the new bricks as designs. The patent agent pointed out that it could be argued that the brick design was purely functional but that nevertheless it did seem to have sufficient features of shape or configuration to make it new. Applications were accordingly filed and Albert was very pleased when they all resulted in certificates of registration being issued a few months later. He advised the big brickworks and they agreed, in respect of the modified types, to mark any bricks so produced with the registered design number. Albert wondered about designs overseas and was advised that this was possible but perhaps of questionable value. Anyway, he did nothing about it.

By this time the large brickworks were beginning to sell substantial quantities and received a number of enquiries about the new bricks. Some difficulties were being experienced in the field since people did not know exactly how to manage them, so Albert and the development man settled down and produced a handy guide as to how the bricks could be used. This went out as a brochure from Frogmate Limited, the originators of the bricks, and was widely distributed in the trade. Inevitably, the trade press gave the matter some publicity and one or two unsolicited enquiries started to come into Frogmate from overseas.

TAKING THE IDEA ABROAD

At this stage Albert went to see his accountant again who advised that if the British potential looked good, the overseas potential was probably good also, and suggested to Albert that a basic decision had to be made as to whether to attempt to exploit via the British company or whether an overseas company should be set up with a view to attempting to generate, and subsequently exploit, business abroad. Albert chose the latter course and his accountant put the necessary wheels in motion. Since the business overseas was very much a hope rather than an actuality, there was little value to be ascribed to the only assets, which immediately had to be placed at the disposal of the overseas company, i.e. the overseas patents. By this time, Albert was pleased to see that, not without fairly substantial expenditure, patent offices around the world were beginning to grant patents on the basis of the applications made. Armed with these patents and wearing his overseas company's hat, Albert set off on an expenses-paid trip to try to drum up business abroad.

CS4–008

He did well in North America, finding several interested parties who were willing to enter into royalty agreements with the overseas company. His greatest surprise came in Japan where an enquirer confided to him after several days of polite negotiation that, although possible exploitation could be arranged in Japan, it was quite impossible to use the trade mark "Frogmate" in connection with the system, not only because of the difficulties of pronouncing that word in Japan but because of the fact that the mispronounced word could be taken as a pun in somewhat bad taste. However, the Japanese were friendly and letters of intent were exchanged.

ANOTHER TRADE MARK

CS4–009   On coming back to the UK, Albert decided that a new name did have to be found and after a fair amount of searching and clearance with Trade Mark Registries via his patent agent the name CYLOCK was settled on. This could be written as a logo with part of the Y intruding into part of the C, thus symbolising in a vague way some of the interlocking features of the brick types which had now been developed. Registration of the trade mark was sought in a number of countries and subsequently secured. Frogmate Limited kept its name but the overseas company changed its name to incorporate the word "Cylock" and "Cylock" became the company's main house mark. There were always two elements to the trading arrangements with overseas customers; first the patent licensing strand, and secondly a trade mark licence strand, the latter enabling the arrangements to have, potentially, a very long life.

The business was now running satisfactorily and Albert decided to try to develop other schemes of an analogous nature. He worked himself on developments and collaborated with Tom Smith and third parties, but they never came up with anything quite as good as the original Frogmate idea. In respect of that idea, the business had now acquired a momentum of its own and both Albert and Tom were enjoying the benefits of arrangements made via the overseas company and he and Tom made appropriate arrangements for their respective spouses and families. What Albert particularly enjoyed was travelling around the world either doing licensing deals or beavering away with lawyers and others in exploiting the intellectual property.

THE COMPETITORS

CS4–010   The patents proved surprisingly difficult to obtain in some countries, but early initial successes in obtaining patents in North America acted as a valuable springboard, persuading quite a lot of people outside to take licences rather than fight when they too had started to modify bricks or paving slabs or other constructional units embodying the basic idea underlying the Frogmate bricks. The United States proved a valuable ground for exploitation but not, initially, for Albert. Several small companies set up, obviously wishing to imitate the invention, not doing quite as well but severely underselling the legitimate licensee, who naturally complained. Albert, working on the assumption that he had a US patent (which he had), promptly sued and unleashed a small army of lawyers all eager to win, but not all working for the same side. Discovery proceedings dragged on with substantial depositions and even though all of the original papers (such as they were) concerning the British company were not directly in question, discovery being against the overseas company that owned the US patents, the piles of paper rapidly grew (as did the lawyers' bills). The counter-claim by the infringers not only asserted patent invalidity but fraud on the US Patent Office and there were various collateral anti-trust claims and unnerving statements in the pleadings about the defendants being entitled to substantial awards of money in their favour from Albert's company because of anti-trust violations. Before too long it became apparent that both parties were dug in for a good fight but also that there was room for everyone to make some money and on appropriate terms the American infringers took licences. Most of the American licensees simply took patent licences rather than sell "Cylock" bricks but Albert did not mind this because to his mind the Cylock brand bricks sold by his main licensee were rather better manufactured and he was jealous of his own reputation in the United States.

Parallel litigation in the United Kingdom went well and he secured damages from several parties who had used the system in major construction works without asking for permission first. In Germany, despite valiant efforts, Albert never secured his patent, which was a pity since several German steelmakers had adopted the system for brick linings for furnaces. There was a continuous problem in trying to keep everyone in order in Europe because each one of his licensees thought they were getting a worse deal than the others and kept threatening to invoke art.101 TFEU. However, the business was not so substantial as to attract the attention of the Commission on its own account and the various parties were all making satisfactory money out of the arrangements they had and so they never pushed the matter too far.

THE OUTCOME

This story ends happily: Albert retired overseas to a house architect-designed and **CS4–011** built at great expense using the Cylock brick.

Case Study 5: Tanaday, the pill or potion to help you love the sun

THE PRODUCT

Dennis Frankinsop, Professor of Dermatology at Regents College, Oxbridge, discovered that an extract from the Yucca plant caused a reaction in skin cultures which destroyed melanomas caused by skin cancer or even naturally occurring moles, but which discoloured the skin to a pleasing golden brown not unlike the Mediterranean tan of a Swedish nymph besporting herself on the Costa Del Sol. He discovered that this skin discolouration also acted as a block, which even in strong sunlight failed to allow the sun's rays to cause any further damage to the skin and therefore had the effect of preventing sunburn.

CS5–001

Sensing the commercial possibilities of this discovery, Professor Frankinsop applied for European patent registration through the UK patent office in the joint names of himself and Regents College. Loot Pharmaceuticals Plc, a substantial UK incorporated unquoted company, founded by, and still very much under the control of, Sir Sinbad Loot, became aware of this development and protracted discussions with Professor Frankinsop and the Bursar of Regents College led to an agreement under which they would attempt jointly to develop the professor's discovery into a commercial product for the benefit of mankind in general and Sir Sinbad in particular.

LOOT PHARMACEUTICALS PLC

Sir Sinbad's grandfather, Yefim Lutskii had emigrated in rather a hurry from Russia in 1917 and ended up in Paris where he worked for a small French perfumery. In the late 1930s, however, Yefim emigrated once more with his family, fearing the generally xenophobic attitudes that appeared to be developing in continental Europe and came to the United Kingdom where he changed his name to Loot and founded Loot Cosmetics Ltd. He eventually retired in the early 1960s to California where he died, happily, at the age of 92. A number of Yefim's relations had remained in Russia and a spasmodic and guarded correspondence took place between Yefim and his family members as it was always his desire to return to his native land if ever it were to become free of what he had regarded as the Communist totalitarian yoke. His son, Jacques, who had been born in France, took over the reins of Loot Cosmetics on his father's retirement and Loot Cosmetics continued to prosper and diversified by both internal growth and

CS5–002

CASE STUDY 5: TANADAY

acquisition into the ethical drugs market, changing its name in the process to Loot Pharmaceuticals. In the mid-1980s Jacques founded a charitable trust in the United Kingdom known as the Loot Foundation, which he financed by substantial gift aid payments from the company. The foundation was part of a general restructuring of Jacques Loot's business affairs, during which it was argued on his behalf that he was domiciled in Russia, his father never having acquired a domicile of choice in France where Jacques had spent his entire childhood. Jacques' emigration and business success in England had not prevented him retaining the family desire to return to Russia in the then unlikely event of there being a change in regime. With some reluctance HMRC accepted his position as retaining a Russian domicile of origin which also determined the domicile of his own children, including Sinbad the eldest son. A structure of overseas trusts and companies was therefore set up to augment and control Loot Pharmaceuticals and its associated companies. The Loot Foundation had financed some university research, which, unexpectedly, produced a most useful drug in the treatment of anorexia which was immediately snapped up by one of the rivals to Loot Pharmaceuticals, which proceeded to make substantial profits out of the drug. Sinbad's apoplexy at this event was slightly mollified by his own knighthood and the fact that he has now become chief executive of Loot Pharmaceuticals, his father having retired first of all to Spain to enjoy the sunshine and then in 1993 to his native Russia. Unfortunately, Jacques had been killed while exercising his passion for flying in light aircraft, when an over-exuberant Russian aerobatics champion attempted a manoeuvre in a Yakovlev 52 at a height that prevented even his consummate skill from achieving it successfully, which resulted in the demise of both of them. However, the non-UK trusts that controlled the Loot Pharmaceuticals empire ensured that the business continued with no perceivable effect arising from Jacques' untimely death. Sir Sinbad stoutly upheld the family tradition of claiming a Russian domicile of origin and refused to accept any suggestions from HMRC that having been born and educated in the United Kingdom and having lived his entire life to date in the United Kingdom, it was only reasonable to assume that he had acquired a UK domicile of choice. Sinbad's advisers pointed out that as long as he maintained a definite intention to return to Russia, the land of his grandfather, he would not have acquired the intention to remain in England permanently or indefinitely, which was a prerequisite of acquiring an English domicile of choice. The fact that Sir Sinbad had never been to Russia and that his only property overseas was the family villa in Spain, inherited from Jacques, did not affect the situation.

THE JOINT DEVELOPMENT AGREEMENT

CS5–003 Professor Frankinsop and Regents College were unwilling to enter into any agreement with Loot (Cayman Islands) Ltd for the further development of the Professor's discoveries, but were persuaded that it was perfectly proper for English academics to enter into a joint development agreement with Loot (Ireland) Ltd, which had substantial research and development laboratories in the countryside of West Cork, close to Ballydehob. Loot (Ireland) Ltd was commissioned by Loot (Cayman Islands) Ltd to develop the Professor's discoveries in return for the 50 per cent interest in the patent rights, which had not been retained by professor Frankinsop or Regents College (see diagram, para.CS5–006).

Loot Pharmaceuticals' marketing consultants in the United Kingdom were appointed by Loot (Cayman Islands) Ltd to devise an appropriate name and logo for the product, which resulted in the name Tanaday and the well-known trade mark of the stylised lettering, with the white marble Grecian goddess T changing colour to the light golden brown of the Y, said to resemble a beautifully tanned Swedish maiden. Under the terms of the commissioning contract, Loot (Cayman Islands) Ltd retained copyright in all the artwork and arranged for the trade mark to be registered in the European Union as a community trade mark and in a number of other countries under the Madrid Protocol or nationally.

The initial manufacturing of the product took place in a new purpose-built factory at Gurteenroe, close to the Irish research facility in order to obtain the benefit of the Irish corporate taxation rate of 12.5 per cent and some extremely persuasive European Union grants. The terms of the assignment of the patent rights from Loot (Ireland) Ltd to Loot (Cayman Islands) Ltd involved a lump sum payment of £2 million, which funded the new factory and an ongoing royalty of 8 per cent of the wholesale selling price from any Loot associated company to a third party, which mirrored the terms of the royalty payable jointly to Professor Frankinsop and Regents College. Under the terms of the UK/Ireland Double Taxation Treaty, Loot (Ireland) Ltd was able to pay the royalty without deduction of withholding tax in Ireland. The Professor was subject to UK tax on the share of royalties he received, as professional income, as exercising his profession as inventor, as well as employment income in the form of his salary from the college. The college, as a registered charity was not subject to tax on the royalties received, the funds being ploughed back into other research projects.

LICENCES AND SUB-LICENCES

The manufacturing company in Ireland was, for commercial reasons, separate from Loot (Ireland) Ltd and called Tanaday Products Ltd, both companies being wholly owned by Loot Investments Ltd, a Jersey company. Tanaday Products Ltd was able to licence other manufacturers to produce the developed product, which was available either in the form of a pill that could be taken once a day to ensure 24-hour protection from sunshine or in the form of a spoonful of liquid taken, similarly once a day, neat or mixed in with drinks. A milder formulation called Tanaday Junior was available for young children and babies to ensure protection from the sun from the earliest ages. Because the research and development had taken place in the Republic, Loot (Ireland) Ltd was able to sub-licence under the protection of the Irish double tax treaty network to manufacturers in Germany, France, Spain, Italy and the United States, the royalties received being tax-free in Ireland. Patent royalties payable by Tanaday Products Ltd, the Irish manufacturing company, to Loot (Cayman Islands) Ltd were routed through Loot Netherlands BV in order to avoid Irish withholding taxes.

CSS–004

CASE STUDY 5: TANADAY

Ninety per cent of the output of Tanaday Products Ltd was sold to Loot Retailers Ltd, the chain of retail stores in the United Kingdom within the Loot Pharmaceuticals empire and Loot Mail Order Ltd, the UK mail order branch of the group. HMRC in the United Kingdom had expressed dissatisfaction at the high price charged by Tanaday Products Ltd to its UK associated distributors and were seeking an adjustment to the submitted tax computations under TIOPA 2010 Pt 4 ss.146–217, on the grounds that the transfer pricing between the manufacturer and the distributors was not at arm's length. The remaining 10 per cent of the output of Tanaday Products was being distributed to overseas agents with a view to test-marketing the product in various countries, pending the conclusion of overseas manufacturing licences; these sales were at a very much reduced price compared with the sales to the United Kingdom. In the overseas markets Tanaday Products was responsible for marketing and spending a lot of money on television and magazine advertisements. However, in the UK Loot Retailers and Loot Mail Order undertook the marketing and advertising of the product, which was the cause of HMRC's enquiries.

FURTHER DEVELOPMENT OF THE DISCOVERY

CS5–005 Professor Frankinsop had further developed his discovery to concentrate the cancer treatment attributes of his Yucca extract and he was now able to synthesise the active ingredient. This development was taken up by one of the major international drug companies, again on a joint venture basis with the professor and Regents College, but Loot Pharmaceuticals objected to the patent for the new drug on the grounds that it was in breach of its patents for Tanaday. As neither organisation wished to get involved in a major legal dispute, which could become time-consuming and expensive, as well as severely inhibiting the ability of the medical profession to use the new drugs in the treatment of skin cancers, agreement was reached between the organisations under which the international drug manufacturer agreed to pay a royalty to the patent holder, Loot (Cayman Islands) Ltd, which resolved the dispute. The Professor and Regents College were naturally entitled to a share of this royalty under the original assignment agreement with Loot (Ireland) Ltd. Loot (Cayman Islands) Ltd also took action against the UK manufacturers of a sun cream called Tan Delight, on the grounds that the logo used reflected the change from white to golden brown in the Tanaday logo and were able to enforce an injunction against the makers of Tan Delight and an order for accounting for profit, being the proceeds of the sale of Tan Delight during the relatively short time it had been on the market prior to the injunction being obtained. This amount was payable to Tanaday (Cayman Islands) Ltd as owner of the world-wide trade marks. As the accounting represented a payment of damages, there was no UK withholding tax payable on the amount due.

The research chemists at Loot (Ireland) Ltd also developed from the product a sunburn relief cream for those foolish enough not to use Tanaday prior to their sunbathing. Although neither Professor Frankinsop nor anyone else at Regents College were involved in this development, it was accepted that it relied upon the developments of the master patent for Tanaday and a further licence was entered into between Loot (Ireland) Ltd, Professor Frankinsop and Regents College. Again, patent royalties under this new agreement were payable without deduction of withholding tax under the UK/Ireland Double Taxation Treaty and also with Loot (Cayman Islands) Ltd as holder of the other 50 per cent of the master patent. Loot (Ireland) Ltd then licensed the manufacturing rights to Tanaday Products Ltd and other manufacturers worldwide. A logo and trade mark for the new product were devised in the style of the original Tanaday logo and registered by Tanaday (Cayman Islands) Ltd, which licensed the appropriate manufacturers for the territory under their domain.

TANADAY: TRADING STRUCTURE

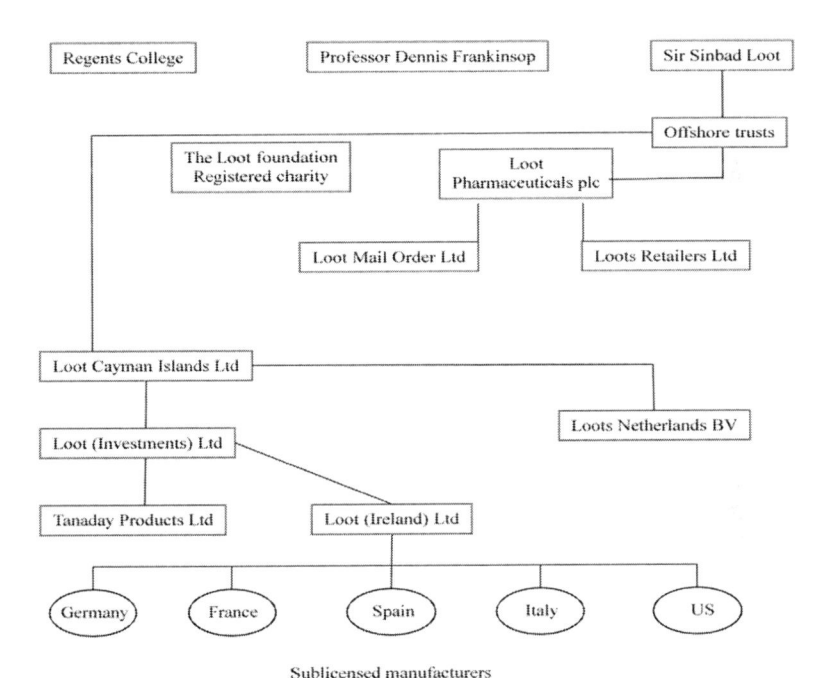

```
┌─────────────────┐   ┌─────────────────────────────┐   ┌─────────────────┐
│ Regents College │   │ Professor Dennis Frankinsop │   │ Sir Sinbad Loot │
└─────────────────┘   └─────────────────────────────┘   └─────────────────┘
                                                               │
                                                        ┌──────────────┐
                                                        │Offshore trusts│
                                                        └──────────────┘
        ┌──────────────────────┐   ┌──────────────────┐
        │ The Loot foundation  │   │      Loot        │
        │  Registered charity  │   │ Pharmaceuticals plc │
        └──────────────────────┘   └──────────────────┘
                 │                    │            │
            ┌────────────────┐   ┌─────────────────┐
            │Loot Mail Order Ltd│   │ Loots Retailers Ltd │
            └────────────────┘   └─────────────────┘

┌─────────────────────────┐
│ Loot Cayman Islands Ltd │────────────────────────┐
└─────────────────────────┘                        │
         │                                ┌──────────────────┐
┌─────────────────────┐                   │Loots Netherlands BV│
│ Loot (Investments) Ltd│                 └──────────────────┘
└─────────────────────┘
         │              │
┌─────────────────┐   ┌──────────────────┐
│Tanaday Products Ltd│   │ Loot (Ireland) Ltd │
└─────────────────┘   └──────────────────┘
                           │
   ( Germany ) ( France ) ( Spain ) ( Italy ) ( US )

              Sublicensed manufacturers
```

Case Study 6: Gribs by Night

THE PRODUCT

Eymos Films Inc has entered into a merchandising licence agreement with Valcav CS6–001
Inc, in connection with the names and static visual likenesses of the fictional
characters depicted in the live action science-fiction motion picture entitled *Gribs
by Night*, excluding the picture dialogue, storylines and plot elements from the
picture, except as specifically agreed in writing and in advance by Eymos Films
Inc. The proprietary subject matter of the licence specifically includes the
characters' names, likenesses (as portrayed by the live talent) and other elements
referred to including, if applicable, the names of actors, voice-over artists and
other elements, only to the extent of the licensor's ownership or control thereof
and only as specifically depicted in and as part of the picture and subject to the
actor's approval of the sculpting. The licensee is specifically granted the picture's
trade mark and its logo and any derivative live action movie rights, for example
books, television, videos, etc. during the three-year term commencing on January
1, 2008, and in the territory covered by the licence, namely the universe,
excluding South America, Australia and New Zealand. The licensee is also
granted the right to use footage including the actors' voices in a television
commercial subject to the actors' approval. Valcav Inc is licensed to produce
action figures of all sizes and materials with and without special features, toy
vehicles, play sets scaled to the size of the dolls of all sizes and materials and
fashions and accessories, board games, non-board games including skill under
action, playing cards, puzzles, role play and dress up sets including play sets,
helmets, weapons, communication devices, etc. with pedal or foot-powered
ride-ons, ride-on accessories, wind-up toys, activity toys, compounds, play sets,
mechanical drawing, audio-visual including projection toys, along with cartridges, software, play microphones and toy cameras, inflatables, bath toys,
pre-school toys and collectible figures. The licensee obtains the right to negotiate
with third parties for the manufacture and distribution of toys covered by the
licence.

TERMS OF THE MERCHANDISING LICENCE AGREEMENT

Valcav Inc is required to make an advance royalty payment of £150,000 on CS6–002
account of royalties of 8 per cent as a non-returnable, recoupable advance against
royalties, which are calculated on the net wholesale selling prices of the articles
by the licensee and its subsidiaries, affiliates or co-venturers, with no royalties

payable on close-out sales at a net selling price of less than 50 per cent of the licensee's usual price to its customers and made in contemplation of ceasing sales of the articles.

Detailed royalty reports are required, quarterly, including a product sales breakdown by product and style number, article description, unit sales, royalty base price, gross sales and net sales of each and every licensed article. Royalty payments are to be made within 45 days of the end of each calendar quarter. The licensee must deduct any applicable withholding taxes from the licensor's royalties. The licensee must pay and hold the licensor forever harmless from all other taxes, customs duties, levies, etc. which charges may not be deducted from the licensor's royalties.

There is a guarantee under the agreement that the minimum royalties for the three-year period will be £500,000, any shortfall in royalties being payable within 45 days of the expiration of the licence.

CS6–003 The licensee undertakes that the licensed articles are of the highest standard and quality and that the manufacture, distribution, sale promotion and advertisement of the licensed articles comply with all federal, state and local laws and regulations. The licensee also agrees to submit articles for prior approval by the licensor. The licensee acknowledges that the licensor owns and controls the copyrighted works which underlie the licence and agrees not to attack the licensor's rights therein or any trade marks based thereon and agrees to co-operate with the licensor in undertaking the registration of any copyright, trade mark, service mark or other intellectual property, registration or filing in connection with the licensed articles.

The licensee has a sell-off period of 120 days on the expiration of the licence to sell off licensed articles that are on hand or in process at the time of the expiration, with accounting 30 days after the end of the sell-off period of any royalties in connection with sales other than close-out sales, at less than 50 per cent of the licensee's usual price.

Three hours before the agreement is due to be signed, Eymos Films Inc requires a further clause in the contract, stating that if withholding taxes are based on the licensor's direct net income the licensee may deduct the required amount from royalties prior to remitting them to the licensor, with a copy of such withholding tax payment prior to deducting it from the royalties and to provide the licensor with the appropriate tax credit forms within 60 days of payment of the withholding tax and to afford all necessary co-operation and support to the licensor in order to get reimbursed or credited. If the licensee does not provide the appropriate tax credit form within 60 days of payment it has to reimburse the licensor for the amounts deducted from the royalties in respect of withholding taxes.

Both Eymos Films Inc and Valcav Inc are quoted American public companies.

EXPLOITATION OF THE LICENCE

CS6–004 Valcav Inc considers that the *Gribs by Night* is likely to be very popular and that the alien beings (i.e. the Gribs) are likely to appeal to children and that the battle scenes with the humans depicted in the film are likely to give scope for substantial sales in the toy market. Although Valcav Inc has considerable experience in the toy market, it has not previously had experience in creating multi-media games or die-cast metal models and therefore, enters into discussions with EBE Plc, a UK quoted company that has considerable experience in both these fields and also with Render Ltd, a company resident in the Irish Republic at the cutting edge of multi-media technology. Valcav Inc, EBE Plc and Render Ltd, decide to exploit the licence through Vebe Ltd, a company incorporated in the Cayman Islands and owned one-third each by the three companies (see diagram).

Vebe Ltd is neither a controlled foreign company for UK tax purposes nor a controlled foreign corporation for American tax purposes. Under the terms of the joint venture, any sales of product in the United States will be made by Valcav Sales Inc, a wholly owned subsidiary of Valcav Inc. Valcav Sales Inc will buy the licensed articles from product manufacturers and account for the royalty out of its trading profit, the royalty being payable to Valcav Inc, which would on pay it to Eymos Films Inc. Similarly EBE Plc in the United Kingdom would sell product through its wholly owned subsidiary, EBE (UK) Ltd which in turn would buy direct from product manufacturers. Render Ltd provides know how to EBE plc for which it receives a fee.

EBE (UK) Ltd will export products to Europe and Valcav Sales Inc will export products to the remainder of the licensed territory.

MANUFACTURE OF LICENSED ARTICLES

Manufacture of licensed articles and games will be undertaken by independent manufacturers in a number of European countries, Hong Kong and the Peoples' Republic of China. The distribution sub-licence between Valcav Inc and Valcav Sales Inc requires payment of a royalty of 10 per cent, which may be paid without deduction of any withholding tax as a payment within the United States. The distribution licence with EBE (UK) Ltd requires a royalty of 10 per cent of the wholesale price in respect of sales in Europe, which may be paid gross under the UK/USA Double Taxation Treaty.

CS6–005

Valcav Inc sub-licenses the manufacturing rights to Vebe Ltd for a royalty of 5 per cent. Vebe Ltd contracts with EBE (Multi-Media) Ltd for the design of a multi-media package entitled Gribs by Night in return for a fixed fee, which it is envisaged will give EBE (Multi-Media) Ltd a net profit of 10 per cent on the contract.

Vebe Ltd licenses the manufacturing of multi-media games and die-cast toys direct to independent manufacturers in Hong Kong. The contracts are supervised by EBE (HK) Ltd, a subsidiary of EBE Plc that charges a commercial fee of 2 per cent of the manufacturer's sale price for its services. The manufacturers sell to EBE (UK) Ltd and Valcav Sales Inc and to a distributor in Brazil who has the distribution licence for that country and New Zealand. Manufacturers are only allowed to sell to licensed distributors.

CASE STUDY 6: GRIBS BY NIGHT

THE TAX POSITION

CS6–006 There are no withholding taxes on royalties paid from Hong Kong to Vebe Ltd. Vebe Ltd also sub-licenses manufacturing of other licensed articles to Vebe BV in the Netherlands, which manufacturers certain items and sub-licenses to other manufacturers in Germany, France, Belgium and Switzerland. Vebe BV is owned by Vebe SA Soparfi in Luxembourg, which is wholly owned by Vebe Ltd. Withholding taxes on royalties received via Vebe BV are kept to a minimum under the Dutch treaties with the sub-licensee manufacturers' countries and there are no withholding taxes on royalties paid from the Netherlands to Vebe Ltd in the Cayman Islands. A return on sublicensing royalties of 7 per cent is retained in Vebe BV, as are the Dutch manufacturing profits until paid up by way of dividend free of withholding tax to Vebe SA prior to its liquidation. Vebe Ltd also owns Vebe (Cyprus) Ltd, which is licensed for manufacture in the United Kingdom. These manufacturing rights are in turn sub-licensed to Vebe Austria, which in turn licenses manufacturers of certain articles in the United Kingdom. Under the appropriate double taxation treaties with Austria, copyright royalties are not subject to withholding taxes and the anti-avoidance provisions against treaty shopping in the UK/Netherlands Treaty are not applicable to the Austrian Treaty. Vebe Austria suffers a small amount of tax on the spread of royalties left in that country. Trade marks are licensed direct by Vebe Ltd to the UK manufacturers as such royalties may be paid gross without withholding taxes.

Royalties accumulated in Vebe Ltd are retained and lent to EBB Plc, Valcav Inc and Render Ltd at commercial rates of interest.

It is assumed that the manufacturing royalties can be justified commercially as arm's length arrangements, in view of the contractual arrangements entered into by the various parties.

GRIBS BY NIGHT: TRADING STRUCTURE

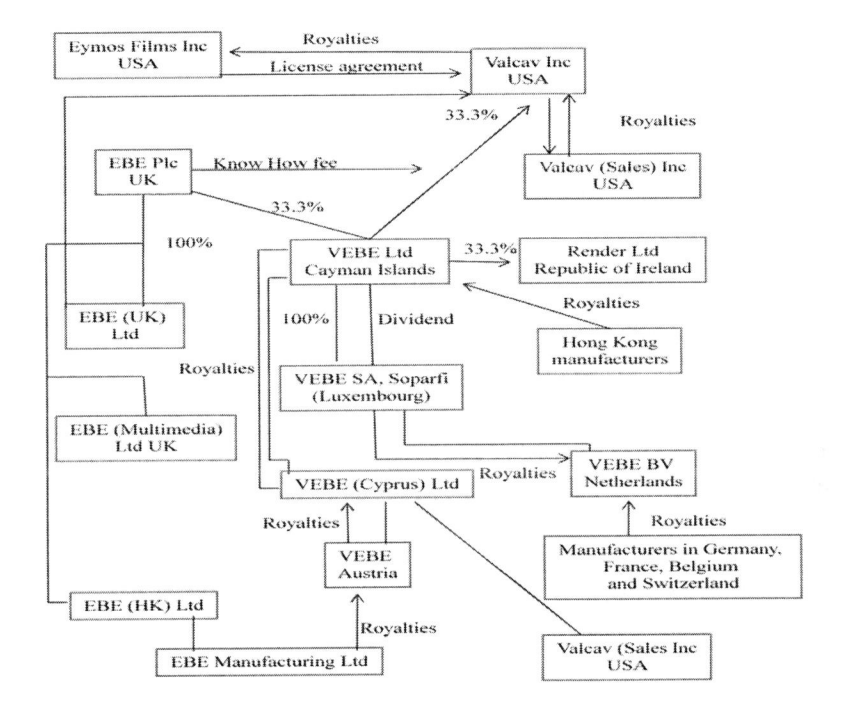

```
Eymos Films Inc  ←— Royalties ——  Valcav Inc
    USA          —— License agreement ——  USA
                                    ↑  ↕ Royalties
                           33.3%    Valcav (Sales) Inc
                                        USA
EBE Plc ——— Know How fee ———→
  UK        33.3%
   |100%                    VEBE Ltd  ——33.3%——→  Render Ltd
                          Cayman Islands           Republic of Ireland
EBE (UK)                                    ←—— Royalties ——
   Ltd              100% │ Dividend
         Royalties                          Hong Kong
                    VEBE SA, Soparfi        manufacturers
                    (Luxembourg)
EBE (Multimedia)
   Ltd UK               VEBE (Cyprus) Ltd —Royalties→ VEBE BV
                                                      Netherlands
                  Royalties                           ↑ Royalties
                  VEBE              Manufacturers in Germany,
                 Austria            France, Belgium
                    ↑                and Switzerland
EBE (HK) Ltd    Royalties
              EBE Manufacturing Ltd    Valcav (Sales Inc
                                            USA
```

Case Study 7: Nuttabun, fast food for the third millennium

THE PRODUCT

Black Hole Developments Ltd, a wholly owned subsidiary of Intergalactic Foods Plc, has recently developed a new form of bun that it thinks will revolutionise the fast food market. The fundamental property of the bun is that the dough out of which it is made contains all the protein, carbohydrate, sugar, starch, vitamins and other ingredients needed to have the same nutritional value as a three-course lunch. The ingredients, however, are based broadly on a mixture of cereals, pulses and nuts with appropriate chemical additives and flavourings. **CS7–001**

The bun made from the dough has a very pleasant moist texture and is equally palatable hot or cold. The basic bun is entirely without flavour of any description, which means that the same basic mixture can be used for every flavour of Nuttabun.

The secret of the success of Nuttabun is the development of a flavour injection microwave, which is a fully patented process under which a bun is placed in the "Flavourator" for a period of two seconds, during which the molecules of the Nuttabun are impregnated with the desired flavour.

The Flavourator is capable of impregnating the Nuttabun with any one of 87 different flavours, ranging from salmon and cucumber to beef bourguignon and including trout with almonds, sole Walewska and rack of lamb with mint sauce, amongst many others. **CS7–002**

The Nuttabun obviously has many advantages over the traditional hamburger or vegeburger, in that, whatever the flavour, it contains no meat or milk and is suitable for vegetarians and vegans as well as the carnivorous members of the populace. It does not require any filling to be cooked separately as it has no filling and this reduces the labour required to run a Nuttabun Express Emporium, the outlet through which Nuttabuns are to be sold to the public. The absence of filling means a corresponding absence of waste, the elimination of dangers of food poisoning and the absence of complaints from customers of the filling running out all over their fingers when trying to eat the delicacy.

The technical success of the Nuttabun depends upon the dough mixture, which is a highly complex recipe, the precise formulation of which is the copyright of Black Hole. However, because the formulation is so complex it can only be made in very large, computer-controlled production lines with careful pre-processing of the raw materials and precise control over every stage of the mixing phase. The Nuttabun manufacturing process produces golf ball sized extrusions of dough mixture which grow to hamburger-bun size Nuttabuns during the Flavourator process. It is considered that this is the optimum size for Nuttabuns in terms of customer acceptance, as preliminary trials had suggested that leaving the Nuttabun the original golf-ball size suggested to customers that they had not truly had the equivalent of a three course meal, while puffing up the Nuttabun to melon or even pumpkin size encouraged customers to share their Nuttabun with friends with the obvious result that everybody ended up hungry. The dough-making process required the development of machinery to extract from the raw materials what was wanted for the production of Nuttabun dough mixture and the successful recovery of any remaining raw materials for conversion into Nuttabake concentrated food for cows and sheep. The marketing department, however, has objected strongly to the use of the name Nuttabake for this material on the grounds of possible confusion, with the potentially unfortunate results of feeding Nuttabuns to the cows or Nuttabake to hungry travellers which, while it would actually cause no real harm to either party, would not improve the marketing image. A number of aspects of this extraction process from the basic raw materials involved the development of new techniques, which had been patented worldwide. The names "Nuttabun", "Nuttabake", "Flavourator", and "Nuttabun Express Emporium" have been registered under the Madrid Protocol and in other countries where trade marks under the Protocol are not yet recognised.

THE COMPANIES

CS7–003 Black Hole has run a number of trial Nuttabun Express Emporia in railway stations and airports in the United Kingdom and abroad and has confirmed public acceptance of the products and appreciation of the speed of service, lack of mess and interesting flavours available. Intergalactic Foods has therefore decided to sponsor a new company, Nuttabun Express (BVI) Ltd, to which it has transferred the intellectual property rights developed by Black Hole (see diagram, para.CS7–009). Nuttabun Express (BVI) Ltd is 75 per cent owned by Intergalactic Foods Plc and 25 per cent by Optima Greed, an investor resident in the Cayman Islands. The rights were transferred for a payment of £10 million to Black Hole, which produced a 25 per cent profit on the development expenditure in relation to Nuttabun. Nuttabun Express International BV is a wholly owned subsidiary of Nuttabun Express (BVI) Ltd and is resident in the Netherlands. It has set up a manufacturing plant for the dough mixture in the Republic of Ireland to take advantage of the 12.5 per cent tax rate applicable to trading income within the Republic. This plant is owned by a local company, Nuttabun Express (Ireland) Ltd. A similar dough manufacturing plant has been set up in California as a joint venture between a wholly owned Delaware subsidiary, Nuttabun Express (USA) Inc and a local American fast food chain, Yukki Super Fast Inc, which was so impressed by the process that it acquired 37.5 per cent of Nuttabun Express (BVI) Ltd from Intergalactic Foods Plc, reducing that company's holding to 37.5 per cent.

FRANCHISE OUTLETS

A third manufacturing plant has been set up on the outskirts of Moscow as a joint venture between the wholly owned Russian subsidiary, Joint Stock Company Nuttabun Express, and the local Joint Stock Company Cosmonautica, named after Yuri Gagarin. The existing Nuttabun Express outlets within the United Kingdom will in future be run by Nuttabun Express Emporia Ltd, a wholly owned subsidiary of Intergalactic Foods Plc, but it has been decided to limit the number of directly controlled outlets to 50. It is, in addition, intended to exploit Nuttabuns within the UK through franchise outlets, the terms of which include the franchisee paying a fee of £50,000 to cover the initial training and know-how for the sale of Nuttabuns and running a Nuttabun Express Emporium that will meet the high standards of service and cleanliness demanded by Intergalactic Foods. CS7–004

The franchisee will also pay a royalty of two pence per Nuttabun for the use of the Nuttabun, Flavourator and Nuttabun Express Emporium trade marks.

A franchisee will also have to buy Nuttabun dough from one of the Nuttabun manufacturing plants and will have to lease the Flavourator from a Dublin based company, Nuttabun Leasing (Ireland) Ltd, a wholly owned subsidiary of Nuttabun Express International BV.

Nuttabun Express (BVI) Ltd will also charge a patent royalty for the use of the patented Flavourator process through a series of intermediate licensing companies. Intergalactica SL, a Hungarian non-resident company managed and controlled outside Hungary, had been set up for this purpose as a wholly owned subsidiary of Nuttabun Express NY. Under art.12 of the UK/Hungarian Double Taxation Treaty (SI 1978/1056) patent royalties may be paid gross by the UK franchisees to Intergalactica SL which in turn is licensed by a Cyprus company. Intergalactica Cyprus Ltd, a fellow subsidiary of Nuttabun Express (BVI) Ltd, will receive a royalty without Hungarian withholding tax, which in turn it will pay without withholding tax to Nuttabun Express (BVI) Ltd. Profits on the royalty margin of 5 per cent retained in the Hungarian non-resident company originally suffered tax at 5.4 per cent but the benefits of a Hungarian non-resident company ceased from January 1, 2006 and the current corporate tax rate is 19 per cent, which compares unfavourably with Cyprus at 12.5 per cent, or Malta, under its royalty withholding tax imputation system of an effective 10 per cent and the royalty routing is being reconsidered. In Malta there is a withholding tax of 35 per cent but 25 per cent is immediately refundable. CS7–005

Trade mark royalties by UK franchisees used to be paid direct to Nuttabun Express (BVI) Ltd as there are normally no withholding taxes payable on trade mark royalties from the United Kingdom, but these are now routed through Cyprus.

The purchase of Nuttabun dough is the purchase of goods by the franchisee from an arm's-length supplier and there are no UK tax implications. The initial franchise fee, payable by franchisees, has been considered by HMRC and regarded in part as a capital payment for commercial know-how, which is a corporate intangible fixed asset, the amortisation of which is allowable for corporation tax purposes under CTA 2009 Pt 8 s.729. The balance of the franchise initial payment is accepted as an up-front staff training expense, which HMRC will allow to be amortised over three years, following the guidance in *Tax Bulletin* No.17. It has been agreed that of the fee of £50,000, £20,000 should relate to know-how and the balance of £30,000 to staff training, allocable as to £15,000 in year one and £7,500 in years two and three.

OTHER LICENSES AND AGREEMENTS

CS7–006 Nuttabun Express (BVI) Ltd has agreed to license a manufacturer of Nuttabun dough in Germany in return for a lump sum know-how payment of £1 million and a royalty on invoiced sales of 5 per cent for the first three years, increasing to 7 per cent for the next four years and 8 per cent thereafter, for a period of 20 years. The licence agreement allows the German manufacturer, Komet AG, the exclusive right to sell Nuttabun dough within Germany, Poland, France, Austria and Switzerland.

Komet AG will also pay a fee for production advice to Black Hole Developments Ltd of €500,000 in year one and €300,000 in years two and three.

Nuttabun Express (BVI) Ltd is in negotiation with potential franchisees who wish to open Nuttabun Express Emporia in a number of countries within the expanded European Union.

CS7–007 Flavourators are manufactured in Southern China to the exclusive order of Nuttabun Leasing (Ireland) Ltd and may not be sold to any third party, although the manufacturers are seeking a licence to enable them to sell Flavourators in specific areas within the Pacific region.

The production equipment for Nuttabun dough is made to the exclusive order of Nuttabun Express (BVI) Ltd and will be leased through Nuttabun Leasing (Ireland) Ltd.

Intergalactic Foods Plc is incorporated in the United Kingdom but quoted on the London, New York and Tokyo Stock Exchanges.

THE FUTURE

CS7–008 The group structure of Intergalactic Foods Plc is currently being reviewed as a result of the anticipated success of the revolutionary Nuttabun product. Currently, Nuttabun Express (BVI) Ltd is neither a controlled foreign company for UK purposes nor a controlled foreign corporation for US purposes as it is controlled in neither country.

The scientists at Black Hole Developments are currently working on the Slimabun which has half the calorie content of the normal Nuttabun but all the vitamins needed for a healthy diet, the Trencherbun which is aimed specifically at sports people and others engaged in strenuous physical activities and the special small size Kiddibun formulated for children, specially prepared to taste its best with added ketchup.

NUTTABUN: TRADING STRUCTURE

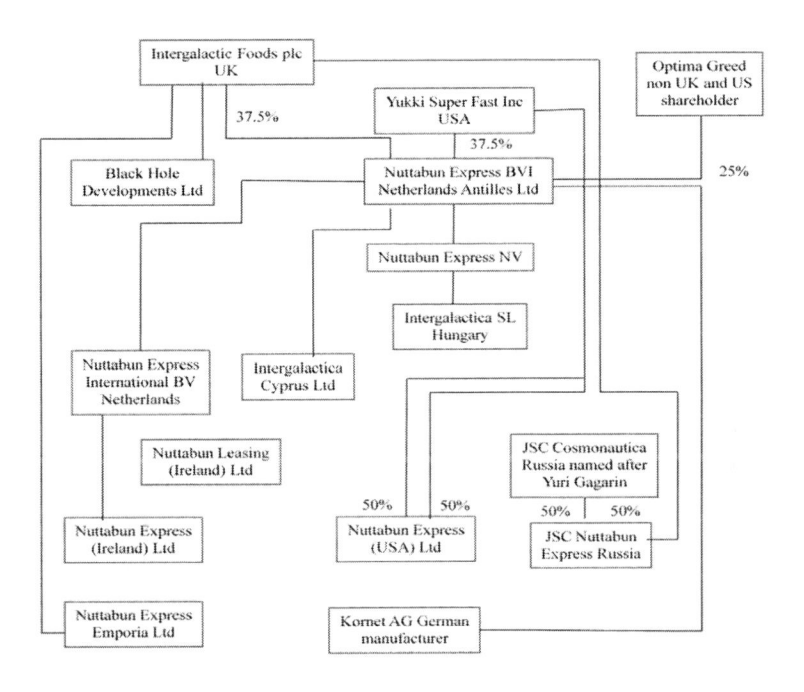

```
                    ┌─────────────────────┐                                    ┌──────────────────┐
                    │ Intergalactic Foods plc │                                │ Optima Greed     │
                    │        UK           │                                    │ non UK and US    │
                    └─────────────────────┘                                    │ shareholder      │
                         │        │        ┌─────────────────────┐             └──────────────────┘
                         │     37.5%       │ Yukki Super Fast Inc │                   │
                         │        │        │        USA          │                   │
                         │        │        └─────────────────────┘                   │
                         │        │                 │ 37.5%                          │
                    ┌──────────────┐       ┌─────────────────────────┐       25%    │
                    │ Black Hole   │       │ Nuttabun Express BVI    │──────────────┘
                    │ Developments │       │ Netherlands Antilles Ltd│
                    │ Ltd          │       └─────────────────────────┘
                    └──────────────┘                 │
                                            ┌─────────────────┐
                                            │ Nuttabun Express NV │
                                            └─────────────────┘
                                                     │
                                            ┌─────────────────┐
                                            │ Intergalactica SL│
                                            │    Hungary      │
                                            └─────────────────┘
         ┌────────────────┐        ┌────────────────┐
         │ Nuttabun Express│       │ Intergalactica │
         │ International BV│       │ Cyprus Ltd     │
         │ Netherlands     │       └────────────────┘
         └────────────────┘
                │                                              ┌──────────────────┐
         ┌──────────────────┐                                  │ JSC Cosmonautica │
         │ Nuttabun Leasing │                                  │ Russia named after│
         │ (Ireland) Ltd    │                                  │ Yuri Gagarin     │
         └──────────────────┘                                  └──────────────────┘
                                    50%       50%              50%       50%
         ┌──────────────────┐   ┌──────────────────┐   ┌──────────────────┐
         │ Nuttabun Express │   │ Nuttabun Express │   │ JSC Nuttabun     │
         │ (Ireland) Ltd    │   │ (USA) Ltd        │   │ Express Russia   │
         └──────────────────┘   └──────────────────┘   └──────────────────┘

         ┌──────────────────┐   ┌──────────────────┐
         │ Nuttabun Express │   │ Kornet AG German │
         │ Emporia Ltd      │   │ manufacturer     │
         └──────────────────┘   └──────────────────┘
```

Case Study 8: Transporterplane, economic transport for the 21st century

THE PRODUCT

Transporterplane International Developments Plc, a consortium company in which major aeronautical engineering companies in the United Kingdom, United States, Germany, France and Spain had varying interests, entered into a joint development agreement with the Chkalov Aero Hydro-Dynamic Institute, named after Andrei Alexandrov in the Russian Federation, to develop a vertical take-off and landing amphibious transport aircraft, which would be used for long-distance travel over the sea, flying at very low level in ground effect in order to conserve fuel when over water. The idea would be to develop the Chkalov Institute's expertise in the field of Ekranoplan or wing-in-ground-effect vehicle design and to ally that to the high efficiency engine technology and fly-by-wire avionics available within the Transporterplane consortium. **CS8–001**

It was important that the vehicle should be able to travel at high speed within ground effect as this would reduce the fuel consumption to one-tenth of that required to fly as an aeroplane. It was, however, necessary to be able to fly as an aeroplane as it was likely for practical purposes that part of each journey would be overland and, in order to arrive at the desired final destination, it was appropriate for the vehicle to be able to take off and land vertically. The amphibious capability enabled it to take off or land wherever there was an appropriate stretch of water and the aircraft was therefore ideally suited to be able to deliver goods and cargo at long distances economically, and without the need of major airport or docking facilities at the point of departure or destination.

APPLICATIONS FOR PATENTS

An application for a master patent on the concept was challenged on the grounds of lack of innovation. It had been pointed out that the Bartini VVA-14 of the early 1960s had all the major attributes of the Transporterplane in that it was amphibious, able to take off from water and from land, was designed for the provision of lift engines to enable it to take off and land vertically, as well as using a runway like a conventional aircraft, and was fitted with forward engines to create a wing-in-ground effect cushion to enable the aircraft to travel at high speed in ground effect, using the forward engines for initial production of the ground effect air cushion and thereafter travelling on the power of the aft **CS8–002** mounted engines only. The objectors pointed to the remains of the original VVA-14 currently residing at the Monino Aircraft Museum outside Moscow and a master patent based on the overall concept of the Transporterplane was rejected. However, the Bartini VVA-14 had proved less than 100 per cent successful with the technology available in the 1960s and the new Transporterplane incorporated a number of innovative features, which individually were capable of being patented. It also relied on a great deal of know-how from the joint venturers, and the computer-generated drawings for the construction of the vehicle were copyright. Consideration was given to registering the entire design but this was considered to be inappropriate in view of *Handley Page v Butterworth* (1935) 19 T.C. 328.

Although it proved impossible to arrange a meaningful patent on a number of the more revolutionary attributes of the Transporterplane, as they were already in the public domain (despite having previously been regarded as top secret within the old Soviet Union), it was nevertheless possible to patent sufficient of the secondary systems to prevent a competitor copying closely the design and the expertise provided by the Chkalov Institute. The membership of the consortium was sufficient to ensure a practical, competitive lead based more on know-how and competitive position in the market than any individual aspect of intellectual property.

THE CONSORTIUM COMPANY

CS8–003   In view of the very substantial development costs, the consortium members wished to take their share of such costs against the profits of their other activities in their home countries and a UK-based consortium company was formed primarily to co-ordinate the project. Detailed designs and manufacture was spread around members of the consortium as near as possible, in proportion to their share in the overall venture with design leadership for the structure and control systems being with the Chkalov Institute, the avionics being with the German consortium member and the engines with the UK consortium member.

THE OUTCOME

CS8–004   Final construction took place in one of the former Soviet military aircraft factories close to the Caspian Sea, which would allow for initial trials in relatively uncluttered waters. The major financing of the project was provided by the members of the consortium. It was decided that it was unlikely that outright sales of the Transporterplane would be possible in the near future, except via an international leasing structure. Advice was taken in connection with the leasing arrangements in order to ensure that capital allowances for tax depreciation were available, preferably in more than one territory; and the use of currency swaps and preference share funding would provide an effective fiscal subsidy to the ultimate lease charges, thereby encouraging operators to bring the Transporterplane into service at the earliest possible opportunity.

Case Study 9: Yuri Rakovsky, conductor/composer

INTRODUCTION

Yuri Rakovsky, a Russian emigrant, is 30 years old and a brilliant conductor/ **CS9–001**
composer. In the last two years he has conducted a number of leading orchestras. He has also penned (much of it in the air!) three major symphonies and several minor works, although he had not attempted to have them published due to a possessive and secretive trait in his character. He has now been persuaded (by his informal agent, Kurt Hausseman, a mysterious Swiss individual) to publish the symphonies and two publishing companies have expressed interest in his entire output. The Australian Philharmonic Orchestra (APO) is negotiating to play the latest of his symphonies in their 2014 programme.

Yuri has agreed (and has signed up) to a world tour with the Taiwan Free Philharmonic Orchestra. The tour starts in December 2015. Over 50 performances are scheduled in venues in Japan, Germany, France, Spain, the UK, Sweden, Australia, Argentina, Mexico, South Africa, Canada and the US (California). The tour will close in Taiwan in August 2016. The idea is to video major parts of the programme and Hausseman has arranged a Luxembourg company to undertake this work; it is suspected that Hausseman owns the company and Yuri expects to get some of the "action" on top of royalties due to him.

"Jacko" Records, a major American record company, has offered Yuri a 10-year recording contract, and his intention is to accept it.

Yuri left his Moscow home and place of work in March 2007. He moved **CS9–002**
briefly to New York and after a major argument over immigration rules moved to Amsterdam in September 2007, where he is now principally residing. He has expressed his intention of moving his principal residence away from Amsterdam but is undecided between Stockholm and Paris. He has personally acquired homes in London, Amsterdam, Nice, New York and Moscow. He has a Greek girlfriend (a very clever water-colourist) who is pregnant with his child. He is also often seen accompanied by the young, beautiful and charismatic new German opera star Uli Schubert and Kurt has suggested there are some very definite musical partnership possibilities here, especially in recording. He has hinted that Yuri may be writing an opera based on the novel *One Day in the Life of Ivan Denisovitch*.

CASE STUDY 9: YURI RAKOVSKY, CONDUCTOR/COMPOSER

Yuri and Kurt have asked for your assistance in planning his future arrangements to minimise his worldwide tax exposure, maintain personal life-style flexibility and safeguard the confidentiality he demands in his business affairs. What is your advice?

NATIONALITY

CS9–003 It seems that Yuri Rakovsky remains a citizen of the Russian Federation and there are no immediate plans to change this.

DOMICILE

CS9–004 Yuri clearly has a Russian domicile of origin. There is nothing to suggest that he has as yet decided to live permanently or indefinitely in any particular state and has not thereby obtained a domicile of choice. His domicile of origin will therefore remain, notwithstanding the fact that he is living outside Russia, unless or until this is displaced by a domicile of choice elsewhere.

RESIDENCE

CS9–005 Yuri would appear to have accommodation available for his use in London, Amsterdam, Nice, New York and Moscow. He is not currently living in the Russian Federation and therefore it seems unlikely that the Russian tax authorities would have any effective claim to tax him either on the basis of residence, domicile or nationality. The home available for his use in the United Kingdom does not create a UK tax problem as it is his only UK tie and he is only likely to be treated as UK tax resident if he spends more than 183 days in the United Kingdom in any one tax year.

He seems to have been spending most of his time in Amsterdam since September 2007 and is likely to be resident in the Netherlands for Dutch tax purposes.

Although he has a home in Nice it seems that he has not spent more than 183 days in France and is unlikely to be regarded as resident for French tax purposes and would therefore only have a French tax liability on French source income.

CS9–006 He has a home in New York and may have spent more than five months in the United States in 2011, which could have made him a resident alien if he had spent any material time in the United States in 2011 or 2012.

If, as planned, he moves his principal place of residence from Amsterdam he might become resident in Sweden under Swedish law. He might also move to Paris and thereby become resident in France with appropriate tax consequences. He was previously considering becoming resident in London in view of the generous UK treatment of non-domiciliaries then available who, in principal, were only taxable on income originating in the UK and income from abroad remitted to the UK, although these rules have now been changed and the complexity of the new rules has caused him to think again.

It could be worth establishing a peripatetic existence under which Yuri was not resident for tax purposes in any country. Although this is initially attractive, it would mean that the full level of withholding taxes would be levied without the benefit of any double taxation relief.

SOURCES OF INCOME

Yuri is both a conductor and a composer. As a conductor he provides services for which he is likely to obtain performance fees. To the extent that these performances might be recorded and produced as a record, film or video, he would be entitled to what are normally referred to as royalties, that is, performance fees calculated by reference to the sales of product. Radio or TV interviews or live performances would similarly attract fees, with repeat fees on subsequent broadcasts. Where recordings of his performances are played in public or on the air, he would only be entitled to any remuneration if he were the publisher or composer under the rules of most countries' performing rights royalty collection societies, although in some countries the performing rights are also paid to the performers of the recording as well as to the publisher and composer. **CS9–007**

There is no indication, nor is it likely, that Yuri is involved in publishing any of his works personally and he will therefore receive the composer's share and in some jurisdictions, also the artiste's share of the performing rights and royalties on the sale of music, and the composer's royalty in respect of performances in which he is not involved.

It appears that a lot of the composing has been outside the Netherlands, or indeed any other state in which he might become resident, which could be important for tax purposes. In some jurisdictions it is important to consider where the works were written and if he were, for example, to become resident in the United Kingdom, the fact that these works had been written outside the United Kingdom during a period when he was neither resident nor domiciled there, should mean that continuing royalties would not be subject to UK tax unless remitted to the United Kingdom. If, on the other hand, he continued to write as a UK resident, he would be taxable on the worldwide income of his profession and royalties would be regarded as part of his professional income following *Davies v Braithwaite* (1933) 18 T.C. 198. It would be sensible to employ him through a non-resident company for his composing services outside the United Kingdom: any remuneration paid from the royalties received by the employing company would be tax-free in the UK unless remitted.

Royalties and performing rights fees would usually be subject to withholding tax from the country of payment unless exempt under a double taxation treaty with the country of residence of the employing company. **CS9–008**

If Yuri becomes resident in the United Kingdom it might be appropriate to have royalties collected by a UK company to take advantage of the UK double taxation treaties, but for the UK company to contract with an overseas company for the benefit of Yuri's services outside the United Kingdom. In many cases royalties paid to the British company would be paid gross or subject to a reduced withholding tax under the appropriate double taxation treaty with the United

CASE STUDY 9: YURI RAKOVSKY, CONDUCTOR/COMPOSER

Kingdom, notwithstanding the fact that the majority of the royalties would then be paid out by way of a fee to the non-resident company before being paid through to Yuri as employment income.

The APO will no doubt be negotiating with whichever of the publishing houses is chosen to publish Yuri's works and the fee payable by the APO may well include "mechanical" and performing rights royalties if the concert of his symphonies is to be recorded. The Australian withholding tax, if any, payable will depend on the country of residence of the publishing house which, in turn, may deduct withholding taxes when accounting to Yuri or his employing company.

WORLD TOUR

CS9–009 Yuri's income from the world tour is likely to arise from a number of possible sources. There is likely to be a fee as conductor per performance, which may be a fixed fee or related to the ticket sales directly or indirectly. If the performance is videoed there would ultimately be royalties from the sale of videos. If the concert is recorded there would be artiste's royalties for the performance. To the extent that the performance is of Yuri's own works, he would be entitled to the composer's proportion of the performing rights fees and the composer's proportion of the publishing royalties for the video and record sales.

It is also quite likely that Yuri will be paid a fee from the orchestra itself for practising with the orchestra in rehearsals, not constituting public performances.

In view of the popular nature of the works there is also a possibility that merchandising material, in particular badges and T-shirts, would be produced, which could give rise to a fixed fee or more likely a royalty based on sales of merchandise.

CS9–010 From a taxation point of view, it is going to be necessary to consider whether the countries in which the tour operates are likely to charge tax in respect of the performances in their country and, if so, on what basis.

It is probable that every country visited will seek to charge tax whether as a provisional withholding tax, which can be amended to a final figure on submission of the appropriate tax return, or a withholding tax as a final tax. It is also worth considering the income to which any withholding tax is to be applied. It may be limited to the performance fees or may extend to include other income.

In relation to performances in the United Kingdom, if Yuri is not a resident of the United Kingdom, there will be entertainers' withholding tax at the basic rate of 20 per cent on payments to members of the Taiwan Free Philharmonic Orchestra and also for performance fees payable to Yuri. In addition, entertainers' withholding tax would be charged on merchandising income due to Yuri and any fees for personal appearances, endorsement, interviews, etc. Recording royalties and composer's royalties would not be subject to the entertainers' withholding tax as such but would be subject to copyright royalty withholding tax as paid to a person whose normal place of abode was outside the United Kingdom, to the extent that they are derived from sales in the United Kingdom, subject to reduction of withholding tax under a double taxation treaty with Yuri's country of residence. Fees relating to rehearsals or consultancy fees in relation to the running of the orchestra should not be subject to UK tax unless they represent employment income for work done in the United Kingdom, in which case they would be taxable as UK employment income and subject to deduction of tax at source under the PAYE scheme.

If Yuri were resident in the United Kingdom, it is probable that he should receive performance fees personally in the United Kingdom and to be employed by a non-UK company for services in the rest of the world, particularly because he is not UK domiciled. The choice of employment company to be used in such circumstances would depend on the proportion of income likely to arise from each venue compared with the time spent in each country. Consideration might be given to using a United Kingdom, American or Dutch company specifically to run the world tour. **CS9–011**

If a UK company were to be used there would be liability to UK tax but only on the profits of the company after payment of all fees and remuneration. In some jurisdictions the use of a company in a high tax area with double tax treaties may be preferable to the use of a company in an offshore tax haven and this would be particularly important where there is a double taxation treaty with only a basic entertainers' and sportsmen's clause, which would not apply to a non-resident company employing Yuri for his services in the country of the performance. In more recent treaties a tax charge on entertainers' services may apply even where payments are made to an employing company.

VAT ON THE TOUR

Consideration should be given to the possible advantages of subcontracting the tour to a special-purpose company formed in the country of the performance in order to enable VAT paid on expenses to be recovered. Alternatively, it may be possible or desirable to appoint a fiscal representative in a country where VAT is in place or to arrange for the local promoter organising ticket sales to act as fiscal representative or to comply with the VAT requirements by self-supply and recover VAT suffered by direct refund, in which case it is important to make claims on time and to have the appropriate original documentation available. VAT is an area where local advice is essential. **CS9–012**

THE VIDEO

If Kurt Haussenman's company in Luxembourg were to video the performance in the United Kingdom, it is unlikely that HMRC would regard this as a taxable event in the absence of a permanent establishment of the Luxembourg company in the United Kingdom. If Yuri receives royalties from the video, HMRC would seek to apply the foreign entertainer's rules to the income. It would probably be desirable however, to produce the video elsewhere and consider mixing and finishing and adding additional elements with specific controlled payments being made for each element to contain tax costs. **CS9–013**

CASE STUDY 9: YURI RAKOVSKY, CONDUCTOR/COMPOSER

JACKO RECORDS

CS9–014 Although Jacko Records is an American record company, it no doubt has subsidiaries worldwide and it is worth considering whether the local contract should be with Yuri personally or with a company employing his services and whether there should be a separate recording deal with the American company for American sales and with, say, a Dutch subsidiary for sales in the rest of the world. It seems that the works composed by Yuri have been written outside the United States and outside the United Kingdom, but it is probable that at least part of the writing has taken place in the Netherlands which has been his base since September 2007. It may be necessary to consider whether any of the writing took place in the United States in case the Internal Revenue Service were to argue that the composer's royalties were a reward for services performed in the United States and taxable as earnings in the United States rather than merely being subject to a withholding tax as royalties arising from the United States. It is similarly worth considering whether a recording should actually be made in the United States or whether they should be recorded in a jurisdiction in which Yuri is not resident.

If Yuri were a resident of the United Kingdom it would be desirable for the recordings to be made outside the United Kingdom and for Yuri to be employed by a non-resident company for his recording services. This would enable him to take advantage of the remittance basis for earnings of a non-UK domiciliary from a non-resident employer.

GIRLFRIEND

CS9–015 The existence of the pregnant Greek girlfriend may not, at first glance, seem to have any taxation effects but it could influence the country of residence that Yuri is likely to choose in view of a potential paternity suit if he decides not to continue to live with his girlfriend and support their child. It could also have inheritance or estate tax implications, in that the child could acquire forced heirship rights under the provisions of Greek law and be entitled to a substantial portion of Yuri's estate. If this is a real possibility it might be appropriate to consider structuring Yuri so that the rights to his activities are held by companies, in turn owned by appropriate trusts and, if so, consideration should be given to the type of trust that might be appropriate, bearing in mind his responsibilities to his child and its mother.

ULI

CS9–016 Yuri's increasing interest in Uli is suspected as being not entirely platonic and this could give rise to further problems with the Greek girlfriend and an asset protection trust in a jurisdiction with suitable legislation such as Cyprus is looking increasingly attractive, irrespective of the taxation situation. As far as the opera is concerned, whether this will be written by Yuri in his own capacity or as employee of a suitable company would seem largely dependent on where he is likely to reside for tax purposes. It would also seem that there are considerable possibilities of Yuri conducting opera recordings in which Uli will star as one of the soloists. Jacko Records is particularly interested in such recordings and wish to produce the records under the proposed recording agreement. There may be an opportunity to establish a commercial partnership between Yuri and Uli, whatever other partnership interest may be developing.

APPENDICES

Sources of Appendices

Appendix 1: Copyright, Designs and Patents Act 1988
http://www.ipo.gov.uk/cdpactl988.pdf

Appendix 2: Patents Act 1977
http://www.ipo.gov.uk/patentsactl977.pdf

Appendix 3: Treaty on the Functioning of the European Union
http://eur-lex.europa.eu/LexUriServ/LexUriServ.do?wri+0J:C:2010:083: 0047:0200:en:PRD

Appendix 4: Countries with Double Taxation Agreements with the UK – rates of withholding tax for the year ended April 5, 2012
http:/www.hmrc.gov.uk/cnr/withholding-tax.pdf

Appendix 5: HMRC FEU50, A Guide to Paying Foreign Entertainers
hrrp://www.hmrc.gov.uk/leaflets/feu50_0300.htm

Appendix 6: Guidelines on the Special NIC Rules for Entertainers

Appendix 7: Film, Television and Production Industry Guidance Notes 2003 edition

Appendix 8: Guidelines on the Meaning of R&D for Tax Purposes

Appendix 1 Copyright, Designs and Patents Act 1988

Note Only those sections of the Act which are of particular relevance to tax planning are reproduced here.

Chapter V Dealings with rights in copyright works

Copyright

90. Assignment and licences

(1) Copyright is transmissible by assignment, by testamentary disposition or by operation of law, as personal or moveable property.

(2) An assignment or other transmission of copyright may be partial, that is, limited so as to apply_
- (a) to one or more, but not all, of the things the copyright owner has the exclusive right to do;
- (b) to part, but not the whole, of the period for which the copyright is to subsist.

(3) An assignment of copyright is not effective unless it is in writing signed by or on behalf of the assignor.

(4) A licence granted by a copyright owner is binding on every successor in title to his interest in the copyright, except a purchaser in good faith for valuable consideration and without notice (actual or constructive) of the licence or a person deriving title from such a purchaser; and references in this Part to doing anything with, or without, the licence of the copyright owner shall be construed accordingly.

91. Prospective ownership of copyright

(1) Where by an agreement made in relation to future copyright, and signed by or on behalf of the prospective owner of the copyright, the prospective owner purports to assign the future copyright (wholly or partially) to another person, then if, on the copyright coming into existence, the assignee or another person claiming under him would be entitled as against all other persons to require the copyright to be vested in him, the copyright shall vest in the assignee or his successor in title by virtue of this subsection.

(2) In this Part_

"future copyright" means copyright which will or may come into existence in respect of a future work or class of works or on the occurrence of a future event;

and "prospective owner" shall be construed accordingly, and includes a person who is prospectively entitled to copyright by virtue of such an agreement as is mentioned in subsection (1).

(3) A licence granted by a prospective owner of copyright is binding on every successor in title to his interest (or prospective interest) in the right, except a purchaser in good faith for valuable consideration and without notice (actual or constructive) of the licence or a person deriving title from such a purchaser; and references in this Part to doing anything with, or without, the licence of the copyright owner shall be construed accordingly.

92. Exclusive licences

(1) In this Part an "exclusive licence" means a licence in writing signed by or on behalf of the copyright owner authorising the licensee to the exclusion of all other persons, including the person granting the licence, to exercise a right which would otherwise be exercisable exclusively by the copyright owner.

(2) The licensee under an exclusive licence has the same rights against a successor in title who is bound by the licence as he has against the person granting the licence.

93. Copyright to pass under will with unpublished work

Where under a bequest (whether specific or general) a person is entitled, beneficially or otherwise, to
 (a) an original document or other material thing recording or embodying a literary, dramatic, musical or artistic work which was not published before the death of the testator, or
 (b) an original material thing containing a sound recording or film which was not published before the death of the testator, the bequest shall, unless a contrary intention is indicated in the testator's will or a codicil to it, be construed as including the copyright in the work in so far as the testator was the owner of the copyright immediately before his death.

93A. Presumption of transfer of rental right in case of film production agreement

(1) Where an agreement concerning film production is concluded between an author and a film producer, the author shall be presumed, unless the agreement provides to the contrary, to have transferred to the film producer any rental right in relation to the film arising by virtue of the inclusion of a copy of the author's work in the film.

(2) In this section "author" means an author, or prospective author, of a literary, dramatic, musical or artistic work.

(3) Subsection (1) does not apply to any rental right in relation to the film arising by virtue of the inclusion in the film of the screenplay, the dialogue or music specifically created for and used in the film.

(4) Where this section applies, the absence of signature by or on behalf of the author does not exclude the operation of section 91(1) (effect of purported assignment of future copyright).

(5) The reference in subsection (1) to an agreement concluded between an author and a film producer includes any agreement having effect between those persons, whether made by them directly or through intermediaries.

(6) Section 93B (right to equitable remuneration on transfer of rental right) applies where there is a presumed transfer by virtue of this section as in the case of an actual transfer.

Right to equitable remuneration where rental right transferred

93B. Right to equitable remuneration where rental right transferred

(1) Where an author to whom this section applies has transferred his rental right concerning a sound recording or a film to the producer of the sound recording or film, he retains the right to equitable remuneration for the rental.
The authors to whom this section applies are_
    (a) the author of a literary, dramatic, musical or artistic work, and
    (b) the principal director of a film.

(2) The right to equitable remuneration under this section may not be assigned by the author except to a collecting society for the purpose of enabling it to enforce the right on his behalf.
The right is, however, transmissible by testamentary disposition or by operation of law as personal or moveable property; and it may be assigned or further transmitted by any person into whose hands it passes.

(3) Equitable remuneration under this section is payable by the person for the time being entitled to the rental right, that is, the person to whom the right was transferred or any successor in title of his.

(4) The amount payable by way of equitable remuneration is as agreed by or on behalf of the persons by and to whom it is payable, subject to section 93C (reference of amount to Copyright Tribunal).

(5) An agreement is of no effect in so far as it purports to exclude or restrict the right to equitable remuneration under this section.

(6) References in this section to the transfer of rental right by one person to another include any arrangement having that effect, whether made by them directly or through intermediaries.

(7) In this section a "collecting society" means a society or other organisation which has as its main object, or one of its main objects, the exercise of the right to equitable remuneration under this section on behalf of more than one author.

93C. Equitable remuneration: reference of amount to Copyright Tribunal

(1) In default of agreement as to the amount payable by way of equitable remuneration under section 93B, the person by or to whom it is payable may apply to the Copyright Tribunal to determine the amount payable.

(2) A person to or by whom equitable remuneration is payable under that section may also apply to the Copyright Tribunal_
- (a) to vary any agreement as to the amount payable, or
- (b) to vary any previous determination of the Tribunal as to that matter; but except with the special leave of the Tribunal no such application may be made within twelve months from the date of a previous determination. An order made on an application under this subsection has effect from the date on which it is made or such later date as may be specified by the Tribunal.

(3) On an application under this section the Tribunal shall consider the matter and make such order as to the method of calculating and paying equitable remuneration as it may determine to be reasonable in the circumstances, taking into account the importance of the contribution of the author to the film or sound recording.

(4) Remuneration shall not be considered inequitable merely because it was paid by way of a single payment or at the time of transfer of the rental right.

(5) An agreement is of no effect in so far as it purports to prevent a person questioning the amount of equitable remuneration or to restrict the powers of the Copyright Tribunal under this section.

Appendix 2   Patents Act 1977

Note Only those sections of the Act which are of particular relevance to tax planning are reproduced here.

Employees' inventions

Right to employees' inventions

39. (1) Notwithstanding anything in any rule of law, an invention made by an employee shall, as between him and his employer, be taken to belong to his employer for the purposes of this Act and all other purposes if_
- (a) it was made in the course of the normal duties of the employee or in the course of duties falling outside his normal duties, but specifically assigned to him, and the circumstances in either case were such that an invention might reasonably be expected to result from the carrying out of his duties; or
- (b) the invention was made in the course of the duties of the employee and, at the time of making the invention, because of the nature of his duties and the particular responsibilities arising from the nature of his duties he had a special obligation to further the interests of the employer's undertaking.

(2) Any other invention made by an employee shall, as between him and his employer, be taken for those purposes to belong to the employee.

(3) Where by virtue of this section an invention belongs, as between him and his employer, to an employee, nothing done_
- (a) by or on behalf of the employee or any person claiming under him for the purposes of pursuing an application for a patent, or
- (b) by any person for the purpose of performing or working the invention, shall be taken to infringe any copyright or design right to which, as between him and his employer, his employer is entitled in any model or document relating to the invention.

Compensation of employees for certain inventions

40. (1) Where it appears to the court or the comptroller on an application made by an employee within the prescribed period that_
- (a) the employee has made an invention belonging to the employer for which a patent has been granted,

(b) having regard among other things to the size and nature of the employer's undertaking, the invention or the patent for it (or the combination of both) is of outstanding benefit to the employer, and

(c) by reason of those facts it is just that the employee should be awarded compensation to be paid by the employer, the court or the comptroller may award him such compensation of an amount determined under section 41 below.

(2) Where it appears to the court or the comptroller on an application made by an employee within the prescribed period that_

(a) a patent has been granted for an invention made by and belonging to the employee;

(b) his rights in the invention, or in any patent or application for a patent for the invention, have since the appointed day been assigned to the employer or an exclusive licence under the patent or application has since the appointed day been granted to the employer;

(c) the benefit derived by the employee from the contract of assignment, assignation or grant or any ancillary contract ("the relevant contract") is inadequate in relation to the benefit derived by the employer from the invention or the patent for it (or both); and

(d) by reason of those facts it is just that the employee should be awarded compensation to be paid by the employer in addition to the benefit derived from the relevant contract;

the court or the comptroller may award him such compensation of an amount determined under section 41 below.

(3) Subsections (1) and (2) above shall not apply to the invention of an employee where a relevant collective agreement provides for the payment of compensation in respect of inventions of the same description as that invention to employees of the same description as that employee.

(4) Subsection (2) above shall have effect notwithstanding anything in the relevant contract or any agreement applicable to the invention (other than any such collective agreement).

(5) If it appears to the comptroller on an application under this section that the application involves matters which would more properly be determined by the court, he may decline to deal with it.

(6) In this section_

"the prescribed period", in relation to proceedings before the court, means the period prescribed by rules of court, and

"relevant collective agreement" means a collective agreement within the meaning of the Trade Union and Labour Relations (Consolidation) Act 1992, made by or on behalf of a trade union to which the employee belongs, and by the employer or an employers' association to which the employer belongs which is in force at the time of the making of the invention.

(7) References in this section to an invention belonging to an employer or employee are references to it belonging as between the employer and the employee.

Amount of compensation

41. (1) An award of compensation to an employee under section 40(1) or (2) above shall be such as will secure for the employee a fair share (having regard to all the circumstances) of the benefit which the employer has derived, or may reasonably be expected to derive, from any of the following_
- (a) the invention in question;
- (b) the patent for the invention;
- (c) the assignment, assignation or grant of_
    - (i) the property or any right in the invention, or
    - (ii) the property in, or any right in or under, an application for the patent,

to a person connected with the employer.

(2) For the purposes of subsection (1) above the amount of any benefit derived or expected to be derived by an employer from the assignment, assignation or grant of_
- (a) the property in, or any right in or under, a patent for the invention or an application for such a patent; or
- (b) the property or any right in the invention; to a person connected with him shall be taken to be the amount which could reasonably be expected to be so derived by the employer if that person had not been connected with him.

(3) Where the Crown or a Research Council in its capacity as employer assigns or grants the property in, or any right in or under, an invention, patent or application for a patent to a body having among its functions that of developing or exploiting inventions resulting from public research and does so for no consideration or only a nominal consideration, any benefit derived from the invention, patent or application by that body shall be treated for the purposes of the foregoing provisions of this section as so derived by the Crown or, as the case may be, Research Council.

In this subsection "Research Council" means a body which is a Research Council for the purposes of the Science and Technology Act 1965.

(4) In determining the fair share of the benefit to be secured for an employee in respect of an invention which has always belonged to an employer, the court or the comptroller shall, among other things, take the following matters into account, that is to say
- (a) the nature of the employee's duties, his remuneration and the other advantages he derives or has derived from his employment or has derived in relation to the invention under this Act;
- (b) the effort and skill which the employee has devoted to making the invention;
- (c) the effort and skill which any other person has devoted to making the invention jointly with the employee concerned, and the advice and other assistance contributed by any other employee who is not a joint inventor of the invention; and
- (d) the contribution made by the employer to the making, developing and working of the invention by the provision of advice, facilities and other

assistance, by the provision of opportunities and by his managerial and commercial skill and activities.

(5) In determining the fair share of the benefit to besecured for an employee in respect of an invention which originally belonged to him, the court or the comptroller shall, among other things, take the following matters into account, that is to say_
- (a) any conditions in a licence or licences granted under this Act or otherwise in respect of the invention or the patent for it;
- (b) the extent to which the invention wasmade jointly by the employee with any other person; and
- (c) the contribution made by the employer to the making, developing and working of the invention as mentioned in subsection (4)(d) above.

(6) Any order for the payment of compensation under section 40 above may be an order for the payment of a lump sum or for periodical payment, or both.

(7) Without prejudice to section 32 of the Interpretation Act 1889[1] (which provides that a statutory power may in general be exercised from time to time), the refusal of the court or the comptroller to make any such order on an application made by an employee under section 40 above shall not prevent a further application being made under that section by him or any successor in title of his.

(8) Where the court or the comptroller has made any such order, the court or he may on the application of either the employer or the employee vary or discharge it or suspend any provision of the order and revive any provision so suspended, and section 40(5) above shall apply to the application as it applies to an application under that section.

(9) In England and Wales any sums awarded by the comptroller under section 40 above shall, if a county court so orders, be recoverable by execution issued from the county court or otherwise as if they were payable under an order of that court.

(10) In Scotland an order made under section 40 above by the comptroller for the payment of any sums may be enforced in like manner as an extract registered decree arbitral bearing a warrant for execution issued by the sheriff court of any sheriffdom in Scotland.

(11) In Northern Ireland an order made under section 40 above by the comptroller for the payment of any sums may be enforced as if it were a money judgment.

(12) In the Isle of Man an order made under section 40 above by the comptroller for the payment of any sums may be enforced in like manner as an execution issued out of the court.

Enforceability of contracts relating to employees' inventions

42. (1) This section applies to any contract (whenever made) relating to inventions made by an employee, being a contract entered into by him_

---

[1] To be construed as a reference to sections 12 and 14 of the Interpretation Act 1978.

(a) with the employer (alone or with another); or
(b) with some other person at the request of the employer or in pursuance of the employee's contract of employment.

(2) Any term in a contract to which this section applies which diminishes the employee's rights in inventions of any description made by him after the appointed day and the date of the contract, or in or under patents for those inventions or applications for such patents, shall be unenforceable against him to the extent that it diminishes his rights in an invention of that description so made, or in or under a patent for such an invention or an application for any such patent.

(3) Subsection (2) above shall not be construed as derogating from any duty of confidentiality owed to his employer by an employee by virtue of any rule of law or otherwise.

(4) This section applies to any arrangements made with a Crown employee by or on behalf of the Crown as his employer as it applies to any contract made between an employee and an employer other than the Crown, and for the purposes of his section "Crown employee" means a person employed under or for the purposes of a government department or any officer or body exercising on behalf of the Crown functions conferred by any enactment or a person serving in the naval, military or air forces of the Crown.

Supplementary

43. (I) Sections 39 to 42 above shall not apply to an invention made before the appointed day.

(2) Sections 39 to 42 above shall not apply to an invention made by an employee unless at the time he made the invention one of the following conditions was satisfied in his case, that is to say_
(a) he was mainly employed in the United Kingdom; or
(b) he was not mainly employed anywhere or his place of employment could not be determined, but his employer had a place of business in the United Kingdom to which the employee was attached, whether or not he was also attached elsewhere.

(3) In sections 39 to 42 above and this section, except so far as the context otherwise requires, references to the making of an invention by an employee are references to his making it alone or jointly with any other person, but do not include references to his merely contributing advice or other assistance in the making of an invention by another employee.

(4) Any references in sections 39 to 42 above to a patent and to a patent being granted are respectively references to a patent or other protection and to its being granted whether under the law of the United Kingdom or the law in force in any other country or under any treaty or international convention.

(5) For the purposes of sections 40 and 41 above the benefit derived or expected to be derived by an employer from an invention or patent shall, where he dies before any award is made under section 40 above in respect of it, include any benefit derived or expected to be derived from it by his personal representatives or by any person in whom it was vested by their assent.

(5A) For the purposes of sections 40 and 41 above the benefit derived or expected to be derived by an employer from an invention shall not include any benefit derived or expected to be derived from the invention after the patent for it has expired or has been surrendered or revoked.

(6) Where an employee dies before an award is made under section 40 above in respect of a patented invention made by him, his personal representatives or their successors in title may exercise his right to make or proceed with an application for compensation under subsection (1) or (2) of that section.

(7) In sections 40 and 41 above and this section "benefit" means benefit in money or money's worth.

(8) Section 533 of the Income and Corporation Taxes Act 1970[2] (definition of connected persons) shall apply for determining for the purposes of section 41(2) above whether one person is connected with another as it applies for determining that question for the purposes of the Tax Acts.

---

2 To be construed as a reference to section 839 of the Income and Corporation Taxes Act 1988.

Appendix 3   Treaty on the Functioning of the European Union

Article 101 (ex Article 81 of the Treaty establishing the European Community (TEC))

The following shall be prohibited as incompatible with the common market: all agreements between undertakings, decisions by associations of undertakings and concerted practices which may affect trade between Member States and which have as their object or effect the prevention, restriction or distortion of competition within the common market, and in particular those which:

(a) directly or indirectly fix purchase or selling prices or any other trading conditions;
(b) limit or control production, markets, technical development, or investment;
(c) share markets or sources of supply;
(d) apply dissimilar conditions to equivalent transactions with other trading parties, thereby placing them at a competitive disadvantage;
(e) make the conclusion of contracts subject to acceptance by the other parties of supplementary obligations which, by their nature or according to commercial usage, have no connection with the subject of such contracts.

Any agreements or decisions prohibited pursuant to this Article shall be automatically void.

The provisions of paragraph 1 may, however, be declared inapplicable in the case of:

_ any agreement or category of agreements between undertakings;
_ any decision or category of decisions by associations of undertakings;
_ any concerted practice or category of concerted practices,

which contributes to improving the production or distribution of goods or to promoting technical or economic progress, while allowing consumers a fair share of the resulting benefit, and which does not:

(a) impose on the undertakings concerned restrictions which are not indispensable to the attainment of these objectives;
(b) afford such undertakings the possibility of eliminating competition in respect of a substantial part of the products in question.

Article 100 (ex Article 82 TEC)

Any abuse by one or more undertakings of a dominant position within the common market or in a substantial part of it shall be prohibited as incompatible with the common market insofar as it may affect trade between Member States.

Such abuse may, in particular, consist in:
- (a) directly or indirectly imposing unfair purchase or selling prices or other unfair trading conditions;
- (b) limiting production, markets or technical development to the prejudice of consumers;
- (c) applying dissimilar conditions to equivalent transactions with other trading parties, thereby placing them at a competitive disadvantage;
- (d) making the conclusion of contracts subject to acceptance by the other parties of supplementary obligations which, by their nature or according to commercial usage, have no connection with the subject of such contracts.

Only European Community legislation printed in the paper edition of the Official Journal of the European Union is deemed authentic.

Appendix 4 Countries with Double Taxation Agreements with the UK – rates of withholding tax for the year ended April 5, 2012

This table shows the maximum rates of tax those countries with a Double Taxation Agreement with the UK can charge a UK resident on payments of dividends, interest, royalties and management/technical fees. **The table only includes agreements which are currently in force.**

Abbreviations: NA = No Article.
                 S   = There is a 'subject to tax' condition.

630 *Appendices*

Territory	Dividends paid to portfolio investors	Interest	Royalties	Management/technical fees	Notes
Antigua and Barbuda	Zero (S)	NA	Zero (S)	NA	
Argentina	15%	12%	15% (Note 1)	NA	1. 3% on news. 5% on copyright royalties other than for films and television. 10% on payments for the use of industrial or scientific equipment.
Australia	15% (Note 1)	10%	5%	NA	1. Only unfranked dividends carry withholding tax.
Austria	15%	Zero	Zero	NA	
Azerbaijan	15%	10%	10% (Note 1)	NA	1. 5% on copyright royalties.
Bangladesh	15%	10%	10%	NA	
Barbados	Zero (S)	15% (S)	Zero (S) (Note 1)	NA	1. 15% on cinematograph and television royalties.
Belarus*	Zero	Zero	Zero	NA	
Belgium	10%	15%	Zero	NA	
Belize	Zero (S)	NA	Zero (S)	NA	
Bolivia	15%	15%	15%	NA	
Bosnia-Herzegovina	15%	10%	10%	NA	
Botswana	12%	10%	10%	$7\frac{1}{2}\%$.	
Brunei	Zero (S)	NA	Zero (S)	NA	
Bulgaria	10%	Zero	Zero	NA	
Burma	Zero (S)	NA	Zero (S)	NA	

Appendix 4 631

Territory	Dividends paid to portfolio investors	Interest	Royalties	Management/ technical fees	Notes
Canada	15%	10% (Note 1)	10% (Note 2)	NA	1. Zero if loan guaranteed by UK ECGD or Canadian EDC or if Canadian government or local authority bond. 2. Zero if copyright royalties (excluding films and television).
Chile	15%	15%	10%	NA	
China	10%	10% (Note 1)	10% (Note 2)	10% (Note 3)	1. Exempt in certain circumstances (see Art 11(3)). 2. Payments for the use of, or right to use, any industrial, commercial or scientific equipment 10% of 70% of the gross amount of the royalty. 3. On 70% of gross fees.
Croatia	15%	10%	10%	NA	
Cyprus	Zero	10%	Zero (Note 1)	NA	1. 5% on film and television royalties.
Czech Republic	15%	Zero	10% (Note 1)	NA	1. Zero on copyright royalties.
Denmark	15%	Zero	Zero	NA	
Egypt	20%	15% (Note 1)	15%	NA	1. Exempt if loan guaranteed by UK ECGD.
Estonia	15%	10% (Note 1)	10% (Note 2)	NA	1. Exempt in certain circumstances (see Art 11(3)). 2. 5% on royalties for the use of industrial, commercial or scientific equipment (see Art 12(2)(6)).

Territory	Dividends paid to portfolio investors	Interest	Royalties	Management/ technical fees	Notes
Falkland Islands	(Note 1)	Nil (Note 2)	Zero	15%	1. See the Double Taxation Manual at **www.hmrc.gov.uk/manuals/index.htm** 2. Exempt if loan guaranteed by UK ECGD.
Faroes	15%	Zero	Zero	N/A	1. DT treaty effective in Faroes from 1 January 2009 and in UK from 6 April 2009
Fiji	15%	10%	15% (Note 1)	15%	1. Zero if copyright royalties (excluding films and television).
Finland	Zero	Zero	Zero	NA	
France	15%	Zero	Zero	NA	
Gambia	Zero (S)	15% (S)	12.5% (S)	15% (S)	
Georgia	10%	Zero	Zero	NA	
Germany (Note 1)	15% (S) (Note 2)	Zero (S) (Note 2)	Zero (S) (Note 2)	NA	1. New DT treaty effective in Germany from 1 January 2011. Effective in UK from 1 January 2011 for taxes withheld at source. 2. 'Subject to tax' condition applies only to income paid before 1 January 2011.
Ghana	15% (S)	12.5% (S)	Zero (S)	NA	
Greece	NA	Zero (S)	Zero (S)	NA	
Grenada	Zero (S)	NA	Zero (S)	NA	
Guernsey	NA	NA	NA	NA	
Guyana	15%	15% (S) (Note 1)	10%	10% (Note 2)	1. Exempt if loan guaranteed by UK ECGD. 2. A smaller percentage where Guyana Minister of Finance applies Section 39(10) of the Income Tax Act, Chapter 81:01.

Territory	Dividends paid to portfolio investors	Interest	Royalties	Management/ technical fees	Notes
Hungary (Note 1)	10% (Note 2)	Zero	Zero	NA	1. New DT treaty, effective in Hungary from 1 January 2012. Effective in UK from from 1 January 2012 for taxes withheld at source. 2. The prior treaty rate of 15% applies to dividends paid before 1 January 2012.
Iceland	15%	Zero	Zero	NA	
India	15%	15%	20% (Note 1)	NA (Note 1)	1. Article includes fees for technical services. For first five years of Convention, 15% where payer is Government. 15% for all royalties, etc. after the five years. Some forms of royalty, 10% throughout.
Indonesia	15%	10% (S)	15% (Note 1)	NA	1. 10% on payments for the use of industrial, commercial or scientific equipment (see Art 12(2)(6)).
Ireland	15% (Note 1)	Zero	Zero	NA	1. Exempt where paid to a charity, superannuation fund or insurance companies in respect of pension fund business.
Isle of Man	NA	NA	NA	NA	
Israel	15% (S)	15% (S)	Zero (S) (Note 1)	NA	1. See treaty for cinematograph or television royalties.
Italy	15% (S)	10%	8%	NA	
Ivory Coast	15% (Note 1)	15%	10%	10%	1. 18% where paid by an Ivory Coast company exempt from tax or paying at less than normal rates on profits.

Territory	Dividends paid to portfolio investors	Interest	Royalties	Management/ technical fees	Notes
Jamaica	15%	12.5% (Note 1)	10%	12.5%	1. Exempt if loan guaranteed by UK ECGD.
Japan	10%	10%	Zero	NA	
Jersey	NA	NA	NA	NA	
Jordan	10%	10%	10%	NA	
Kazakhstan	15%	10% (Note 1)	10% (Note 2)	NA	1. Exempt if loan guaranteed by UK ECGD. 2. Unless election is made for net profit basis.
Kenya	15% (S)	15% (S)	15% (S)	12.5%	
Kiribati	Zero (S)	NA	Zero (S)	NA	
Korea	15%	10% (Note 1)	10% (Note 2)	NA	1. Exempt where loan is guaranteed by UK ECGD. 2. 2% on equipment leasing payments.
Kuwait	15%	Zero	10%	NA	
Latvia	15%	10% (Note 1)	10%	NA	1. Exempt if loan guaranteed by UK ECGD or Bank of England.
Lesotho	Zero (S)	NA	Zero (S)	NA	
Libya (Note 1)	Zero	Zero	Zero	NA	1. New DT treaty effective in Libya from 1 January 2011. Effective in UK from 6 April 2010.
Lithuania	15%	10% (Note 1)	10% (Note 2)	NA	1. Exempt in certain circumstances (see Art 12(2)(6)). 2. 5% on royalties for the use of industrial, commercial or scientific equipment (see Art 12(2)(6)).

Appendix 4   635

Territory	Dividends paid to portfolio investors	Interest	Royalties	Management/ technical fees	Notes
Luxembourg	15%	Zero	5%	NA	
Macedonia	15%	10%	Zero	NA	
Malawi	Zero (S)	Zero (S)	Zero (S)	NA	
Malaysia	10%	10% (S) (Note 1)	8%	8%	1. Exempt if an approved loan (see Art 11).
Malta	(Note 1)	10% (S)	10% (S)	NA	1. Tax not to exceed that chargeable on the profits out of which the dividends are paid.
Mauritius	15%	No limitation (Note 1)	15% (S)	NA	1. Exempt when paid to UK banks.
Mexico	Zero	15% (Note 1)	10%	NA	1. A lower rate or exemption will apply in certain circumstances (see Art 11(2)).
Moldova	10%	5% (Note 1)	5%	NA	1. Exempt in certain circumstances (see Art 11(3))
Mongolia	15%	10%	5%	NA	
Montenegro	15%	10%	10%	NA	
Montserrat	Zero (S)	NA	Zero (S)	NA	
Morocco	25%	10%	10%	NA	
Namibia	15%	20%	Exempt (S) (Note 1)	NA	1. Copyright royalties only. Other royalties: the lesser of 5% and one half of tax that would otherwise be charged.
Netherlands	15%	Zero	Zero	NA	
New Zealand	15%	10%	10%	NA	
Nigeria	15% (S)	12.5% (S)	12.5% (S)	NA	
Norway	15%	Zero	Zero	NA	

Territory	Dividends paid to portfolio investors	Interest	Royalties	Management/ technical fees	Notes
Oman (Note 1)	10%	Zero	8% (Note 2)	NA	1. DT treaty amended by Protocol, effective in both Oman and UK for taxes withheld at source from 1 January 2012. 2. The prior treaty rate of Zero(S) applies to royalties paid before 1 January 2012.
Pakistan	20% (Note 1)	15%	12.5%	12.5%	1. See the Double Taxation Manual, DT14956 and Art 10, at **www.hmrc.gov.uk/manuals/index.htm**
Papua New Guinea	17%	10%	10%	10%	
Philippines	25%	15% (Note 1)	25% (Note 2)	NA	1. 10% where paid by a public issue bond etc. Exempt where loan is guaranteed by a UK government agency. 2. 15% on royalties for films, television or radio.
Poland	10%	5%	5%	NA	
Portugal	15%	10% (S)	5% (S)	NA	
Qatar	Zero	Zero	5%		1. New DT treaty effective in Qatar from 1 January 2011. Effective in UK from 1 January 2011 for taxes withheld at source.
Romania	15%	10%	15% (Note 1)	12.5% (Note 2)	1. 10% on copyright royalties. 2. Rate applies to commissions. See the Double Taxation Manual, DT16054 at **www.hmrc.gov.uk/manuals/index.htm**

Appendix 4 637

Territory	Dividends paid to portfolio investors	Interest	Royalties	Management/ technical fees	Notes
Russian Federation	10% (S)	Zero	Zero	NA	
St Christopher-Nevis (St Kitts)	Zero (S)	NA	Zero (S)	NA	
Saudi Arabia	5%	Zero (Note 2)	5% or 8% (Note 3)	NA	1. DT treaty effective in Saudi Arabia from 1 January 2010 and in UK from 6 April 2010 2. Income from debt-claims 3. 5% for royalties paid for use of, or the right to use, industrial, commercial, or scientific equipment, 8% in all other cases
Serbia	15%	10%	10%	NA	
Sierra Leone	Zero (S)	NA	Zero (S)	NA	
Singapore	0% (Note 1)	10%	10%	NA	1. Treaty allows for 15% but there are currently no withholding taxes on dividends.
Slovak Republic	15%	Zero	10% (Note 1)	NA	1. Zero on copyright royalties (see Art 12(3)(6)).
Slovenia	15%	5%	5%	NA	
Solomon Islands	Zero (S)	NA	Zero (S)	NA	
South Africa	15%	Zero (S)	Zero (S)	NA	
Spain	15%	12%	10%	NA	
Sri Lanka	No limitation	10% (Note 1)	10% (Note 2)	NA	1. Only reduced to this rate where paid on loan, etc. made after 21 June 1989. 2. Only reduced to this rate where rights are granted after 21 June 1989.

Territory	Dividends paid to portfolio investors	Interest	Royalties	Management/ technical fees	Notes
Sudan	15% (Note 1)	15% (S)	10% (S)	NA	1. Exempt if the dividends are exempt under Sudan law when paid to non-residents.
Swaziland	15%	NA	Exempt	NA	
Sweden	5%	Zero	Zero	NA	
Switzerland	15%	Zero	Zero	NA	
Taiwan	10% (S)	10% (S)	10% (S)	NA	
Tajikstan*	Zero	Zero	Zero	NA	
Thailand	20% (Note 1)	25% (Note 2)	5% (Note 3)	NA	1. Rate only applies to a dividend from a company carrying on an industrial undertaking. 2. 10% if paid to a financial institution. 3. 15% on patent royalties.
Trinidad and Tobago	20%	10%	10% (Note 1)	10%	1. Copyright royalties are exempt.
Tunisia	20%	12%	15%	NA	
Turkey	20%	15%	10%	NA	
Turkmenistan*	Zero	Zero	Zero	NA	
Tuvalu	Zero (S)	NA	Zero (S)	NA	
Uganda	15%	15%	Zero (S)	NA	
Ukraine	10% (S)	Zero (S)	Zero	NA	
United States of America	15%	Zero	Zero	NA	
Uzbekistan	10%	5%	5%	NA	
Venezuela	10%	5% (Note 1)	7%	NA	1. Exempt if paid on a loan guaranteed by UK ECGD.
Vietnam	15%	10% (S)	10% (S)	NA	
Zambia	15% (S)	10% (S)	10% (S)	NA	
Zimbabwe	20% (S)	10% (S) (Note 1)	10% (S)	10% (S)	1. Exempt if paid on a loan guaranteed by UK ECGD.

* *UK/Soviet Union agreement applies*

Appendix 5   HMRC FEU50, A Guide to Paying Foreign Entertainers

1 A Guide to paying Foreign Entertainers

As the withholding tax system relies on Payers knowing how to carry out their role we have designed a guide specifically for them. However, much of the information it contains is also useful for payees, entertainers and sportspeople. The Guide contains the following sections:

2 Contents

- How the Scheme works
- What can be classed as payments?
- Does it matter who gets the payments?
- What type of appearance is covered?
- What is the link between the payment and the UK appearance?
- Which entertainers and sportsmen are involved?
- How do I know if they are non-UK-resident?
- Which payments are excepted from Withholding Tax?
- What the payer must do
- Is Withholding Tax due on payments made to Groups, Theatre Companies, Productions, etc, which include both UK resident and non-resident entertainers?
- How to work out the Withholding Tax
- VAT Implications
- How do you deal with payment chains?
- Middleman applications
- How and when do you pay the tax that you have deducted and/or accounted for?
- Completing form FEU 1
- What record does the payee get of the payment?
- Application to HMRC to limit the amount of tax withheld
- How to make a reduced tax payment application
- How do you know that a reduced tax payment has been authorised?
- How are payments dealt with in your Self Assessment or Corporation Tax accounts?
- Assessments
- Appeals
- Interest

- Information and inspection
- List of forms
- Where can I get help and information?

To avoid repetition the term 'entertainer' is used in this Guide to cover both non-resident entertainers and sportsmen and women. **Examples in the Guide assume a basic rate of tax of 20 per cent**. The basic rate in force in any particular year can be obtained from the 'Rates and Allowances' section of the HM Revenue & Customs (HMRC) website.

3 How the Scheme Works

Any payer who makes a payment to or on behalf of any person, which in any way arises directly or indirectly from a UK appearance by a non-resident entertainer must deduct or account for tax at the basic rate.

There are certain exceptions from the scheme. You will find details in the section Which payments are excepted from withholding tax?

4 What can be classed as Payments?

Payments include cash, cheques, bank transfers, online transfers and also a loan of money. The list below gives some examples of payments:
- appearance fees
- achievement bonus
- exhibition income
- box office percentages
- TV rights
- broadcasting/media fees
- tour income
- tournament winnings
- prize money
- advertising income
- merchandising income
- endorsement fees
- film fees

The scheme also applies to transfers of assets, for example, a motor car for a 'hole in one' during a golf competition. Where assets are transferred Withholding Tax does not apply to the payment for the acquisition of the asset but tax should be accounted for on the transfer to the entertainer. The scheme also applies to expenses paid on behalf of the entertainer. See How to work out the withholding tax.

5 Does it matter who gets the payments?

The short answer is no!

Any payment made in respect of a non-resident entertainer, to any other individual or organisation, whether they are resident in the UK or overseas, falls within the scheme and is subject to Withholding Tax.

6 What type of appearance is covered?

Any appearance by the entertainer in the UK for which a payment is made, will be within the scheme.

A simple case would be the entertainer appearing in his or her recognised profession. This might be an actor performing in the theatre or a golfer competing in the Open Championship.

However the scheme is much wider than this. It also covers promotional activities, advertising and endorsement of goods or services. This may include a photocall, TV/radio interview or other appearances.

The appearance does not have to be in front of an immediate audience. It may include film work, video, radio or live/recorded television.

7 What is the link between the payment and the UK appearance?

Any payment which arises directly or indirectly from a UK appearance will be within the scheme. In most cases it will be easy to find the link. For example, a tennis player competes at Wimbledon and receives prize money or a singer is paid for performing at a concert at Wembley.

The payment does not have to have a direct connection with the UK appearance. Endorsement fees paid to a tennis player using sports equipment in a UK tournament would be linked.

8 Which entertainers and sportsmen are involved?

The following list is not exhaustive. athletes, golfers, cricketers, footballers, tennis players, boxers, snooker players, darts players, motor racing drivers, jockeys, ice skaters, contestants in chess tournaments, singers, musicians, conductors, models, dancers, actors, TV and radio personalities, variety entertainers. The person may appear alone or with others in a team, choir, band, group, orchestra, opera company, ballet company, troupe or circus.

9 How do I know if they are non-UK-resident?

In most cases it will be obvious.

You may know from the agent or management company, perhaps from the need to obtain a work permit or visa.

A UK national who is non-resident also comes within the scheme. They should not be treated any differently from a non UK national for Witholding Tax purposes.

If you are uncertain about the residence position of an entertainer then you must obtain clarification from the entertainer, their manager or representative.

If there is still any doubt as to the residence position of an entertainer then Withholding Tax must be deducted.

10 Which payments are excepted from Withholding Tax?

If you engage a non-resident entertainer as an employee and operate Pay as You Earn on payments to that entertainer, you do not need to deduct additional Withholding Tax on those payments.

Withholding Tax does not apply to payments made in respect of copyright, royalties or advances on royalties. For the treatment of such payments please see Section 906 Income Tax Act 2007 (Opens new window).

You do not need to deduct and account for tax on payments made direct to an entity for ancillary services such as:
- hall hire
- security
- damages/carpentry
- stage hands
- PA equipment
- lighting etc
- equipment hire
- advertising
- ticket printing
- hire of chairs, barriers or marquees etc.

You do not have to deduct and account for tax on payments made to an entertainer for record sales (including vinyl, cassette, CD and Audio only USB sticks) where the payment relates to one of the following:
- is based on the proceeds of sales
- a non-returnable advance on account of future sales
- sales at a live performance

Do not withhold tax if the total payments made to an individual or group, including any connected payments by an associate, will be equal to or less than the UK Personal Allowance for the tax year. The tax year runs from 6 April in one year to 5 April in the following year. The Personal Allowance normally changes each year, the current years Personal Allowance can be obtained from the 'Income Tax rates and allowances' section of the HMRC website.

The total payment for this purpose includes not only cash, but also expenses paid on behalf of the entertainer such as airfares or the cost of an asset transferred to the entertainer.

If you are making the first payment and it is less than the current Personal Allowance but you know in advance (for example, from the contract) that the total payments for the tax year will be more than the current Personal Allowance, then you should deduct tax even from the first payment.

11 Example

The payer knows in advance that he will be making total payments of £12,000, made in three installments.

1st payment = 4,000
Less tax withheld at 20% = 800
Net payment to entertainer = **3,200**
2nd payment = 4,000
Less tax withheld at 20% = 800
Net payment to entertainer = **3,200**
3rd payment to entertainer = 4,000
Less tax withheld at 20% = 800
Net payment to entertainer = **3,200**
Total payments = 12,000
Tax withheld = 2,400
Net payments = 9,600

Payments made direct to any payee included on the following lists may be made gross (without the deduction of tax):
- Simplified tax system for classical music
- List of Approved Promoters, Agents and Merchandisers (Rock and POP)

If you are in any doubt at all about which payments are excluded from the scheme please contact the Foreign Entertainers Unit for advice.

12 What the payer must do

Each time you make a payment you must deduct tax at the basic rate, **unless** an arrangement has been made with the Foreign Entertainers Unit and they have issued an authorisation to deduct an amount of tax other than the basic rate tax. (see Application to HMRC to limit the Amount of tax withheld) or the payments are excepted from withholding tax (see Which payments are excepted from Withholding Tax?).

You may be liable for the payment of Witholding Tax if you do not deduct the tax when it is due.

13 Is Withholding Tax due on payments made to Groups, Theatre Companies, Productions, etc, which include both UK resident and non-resident entertainers?

For example, a music group or a theatre company which includes both UK resident and non-resident performers.
- Yes, Withholding Tax is due
- Unless advised otherwise by the Foreign Entertainers Unit the payer must account for Withholding Tax on the total payment, including expenses, made to or in respect of the group or theatre company.
- If the payee/group/theatre company want the payer to calculate and deduct tax only on the non UK resident performers, the payee/group/theatre company must apply to the Foreign Entertainers Unit for agreement.to do this.

14 How to work out the Withholding Tax

Where you are paying or transferring **money** it is very straightforward to work out the tax.

Assuming the basic rate percentage for the year of payment is 20 per cent then you should deduct this percentage from each payment made.

15 Example

Gross Payment = £10,000
Tax (10,000 × 20%) = £2,000
Net amount paid to entertainer = **£8,000**

The same applies to a loan of money. You should deduct tax from the amount of the loan.

All payments of Withholding Tax made to HMRC must be made in sterling. If you make a payment directly or indirectly to an entertainer in a foreign currency you should calculate the Withholding Tax due using the rate of exchange at the time when the payment is made or at the rate used at the time the foreign currency was purchased. The rate of exchange used should be shown on your return form FEU 1.

If the transfer of an **asset** is involved (for example, a motor car for a 'hole in one' during a golf competition) you must account for the tax as if the asset's cost to you or in connection with providing it was the net amount of the payment.

Withholding Tax is also due on expenses provided for an entertainer.

For example, hotel accommodation, airfares, UK transport etc.

In the absence of an agreement with the Foreign Entertainers Unit, Withholding Tax must be accounted for and paid by the payer, from its own funds, on payments made in respect of expenses provided for an entertainer.

The Withholding Tax due must be calculated as follows:
1. The cost of the expenses, to the payer, must be grossed up, at the basic rate of tax, to give the true cost of the benefit to the artiste.
2. Withholding Tax due must be calculated at the basic rate on the grossed up value of the expenses.
3. The withholding tax calculated must be paid by the payer from its own funds: it must not be deducted from the overall payment made to the artiste.

16 Example

The airline ticket costs you £1,000. You need to work out the gross amount of the payment and pay tax on that amount. To work out the gross amount you do the following sum.

Net amount of payment £1000 × 20 (basic rate of tax) divided by 80 (100% – 20 basic rate of tax) = £250

Add the tax amount £250 to the net payment £1000 to get the gross payment £1250

Add the result to the net payment to get the gross payment.

£250 + £1,000 = £1,250

Tax (£1,250 × 20%) = £250

17 VAT Implications

VAT is not chargeable on Withholding Tax and you should therefore exclude the VAT when calculating Withholding Tax due.

1. When calculating the amount of tax due on a payment to be made either to, or in respect of an entertainer you must not include VAT (if any) charged to you.
2. If you are a venue paying the gross ticket sales to a promoter or entertainer, the VAT element of each individual ticket price must be taken out.

18 How do you deal with payment chains?

Some activities may give rise to a chain of payments. Every payer in the chain must deduct tax as required by law unless the payment is exempt. (Which payments are excepted from Withholding Tax?)

19 Example

A concert is arranged at a venue. The venue owners control the box office and pay over the ticket proceeds to the promoter less their costs and Withholding Tax. The promoter is then required to deduct Withholding Tax from the fee payable to the entertainer. The promoter should deal with this as follows:

- He must deduct Withholding Tax (where it is due) from the payment made to the entertainer and pay over the net amount.
- He must issue a tax deduction certificate form FEU 2, to the entertainer confirming the pay and tax details.
- He declares the payment made and the tax deducted on the form FEU 1 (boxes 5 & 6) and shows the tax already withheld from the payment made to him in box 8.

20 Example

A Promoter engages a non-resident entertainer to appear at a UK venue.

The Entertainer is the only non-resident entertainer the promoter engages in the quarter. The sequence of payments is as follows:

The Venue pays £100,000 less £20,000 tax to the Promoter
The Promoter pays £60,000 less £12,000 tax to the Entertainer

The Promoter is liable to account to HMRC for £12,000 but as the payment he has received has had £20,000 Withholding Tax deducted from it he can treat the £12,000 as paid.

21 Entries on the Promoter's return form FEU 1

The amount and income tax columns of the Promoter's return for the relevant period should be completed as follows:

Payment	Amount	Tax
	60,000	12,000
Less tax already paid by Venue		12,000
Tax payable now		Nil

Evidence of the tax already paid must be provided with the FEU1 return by including part 3 of the FEU2 tax deduction certificate which is supplied by the Venue.

You will find details of how the payment is treated in the Promoter's company accounts and of the repayment of tax in certain circumstances at How are payments dealt with in your Self Assessment or Corporation Tax Accounts?

22 Middleman Applications

Payers can ask for an arrangement which moves the withholding point further down the chain so that payments between specified payers can be made without deduction of tax. This can only be done with the Foreign Entertainers Unit's approval.

If the concert promoter makes a 'Middleman' application, the Unit may agree to the promoter being the witholding point, therefore the venue will not have to withold tax. The promoter will then have to deduct tax at basic rate on his or her payment or a reduced amount if an entertainer's application for a reduced tax payment has been made and agreed.

The Unit will ask for certain information in support of any 'Middleman' application you make, for example, a copy of any contract, dates of appearances, and probably a copy of the budget. If you are submitting a 'Middleman' application for the first time the Unit will be happy to advise you on the procedure and level of information required.

23 How and when do you pay the tax that you have deducted and/or accounted for?

You must pay the tax within 14 days after the end of the return period during which the payment was made. The return periods for each tax year are:
- 30 June
- 30 September
- 31 December
- 5 April

24 Completing form FEU 1

HMRC will send you a form FEU 1 before the end of each Return period. If you want to use your own form FEU 1 you must submit it to the Foreign Entertainers Unit for approval before you do so.

It is your responsibility to make a return of payments. HMRC will not notify you when a return is due. If you have not received form FEU 1 by the end of the return period, please telephone The Foreign Entertainers Unit.

Any new payers must contact the Foreign Entertainers Unit who will issue a Starter Pack which will contain the relevant information and forms.

The form FEU 1 must be completed and returned to the Accounts Office, Shipley within 14 days of the end of the relevant period. Please note the return should include every payment made including those below the Personal Allowance and those where tax has not been deducted (Which payments are excepted from Withholding Tax?).

Where tax is due, if it is not paid within 14 days of these dates you may become liable to an interest charge.

25 What record does the payee get of the payment?

Whenever you make a payment from which you have deducted Withholding Tax, you must complete a tax deduction certificate, form FEU 2.

This form is in 3 parts
Part 1 : Send to Accounts Office Shipley together with your form FEU 1.
Part 2 : Keep this for your own records.
Part 3 : Give this to the payee as a certificate of the payment made and tax withheld.

If the payee loses the original certificate and requests a duplicate, **this must not be issued**, tell them to contact the Foreign Entertainers Unit.

You are not required to issue a form FEU 2 where, for whatever reason you have not deducted withholding tax (Which payments are excepted from Withholding Tax?).

Withholding tax deducted is regarded as a payment on account of the final UK tax liability of the entertainer.

26 Application to HMRC to limit the amount of tax withheld

An application may be made in writing by the entertainer or anyone else authorised to do so on their behalf. Where the application is agreed, it allows the payer to deduct an amount other than the basic rate of tax which corresponds as near as to the entertainer's final UK liability on that payment.

An application to HMRC to limit the amount of tax withheld may be made in writing or on form FEU 8 (PDF 105K). Any letter which advises the Unit that detailed figures are to follow is considered to constitute an advance notification of an application **but does not constitute the application itself**.

Applications to the Foreign Entertainers Unit must be made no less than 30 days before the date the payment is due.

If the application is **not** agreed tax must be accounted for at the basic rate on all related payments.

27 How to make a reduced tax payment application (RTPA)

The information required to enable an agreement to be made includes:
- dates of arrival in and departure from the UK
- whether the entertainer is likely to return to the UK again before the 5 April
- a projection of actual or estimated total income due from all sources
- a schedule confirming; the date of each performance/event, the name and address of the venue and the name and address of the promoter
- a schedule of the projected actual or estimated expenses which will be incurred
- a copy of each relevant engagement contract or agreement (these do not need to be signed copies).

The application should give sufficient information to show how figures have been arrived at (including the basis for any estimates) and how expenditure appropriate to several countries has been apportioned.

In some cases you may be authorised to deduct a reduced rate of tax, a fixed sum or no tax from the gross payment. This could apply, for example, where an entertainer has to meet substantial expenditure out of a gross fee thus reducing the expected UK tax liability.

In reaching an agreement the Foreign Entertainers Unit will make allowances for admissible expenses. What can be allowed depends on the general rules covering expenditure allowable in arriving at taxable business profits under Section 34 Income Tax (Trading and Other Income) Act 2005 (Opens new window) and the facts of each case. Normally allowances will be made for:
- general subsistence expenses
- commission, manager's and agent's fees
- UK travel
- international air fares to and from the UK where the entertainer comes to the UK to perform and returns directly to his or her home country

Other expenses may be allowable. What is allowable in each case will need to be agreed with the Foreign Entertainers Unit including the proportion of any costs appropriate to several countries.

Further information can be obtained about Reduced Tax Payment Applications including **further advice** regarding the preparation of an entertainer RTPA.

If the point you wish to check is not covered in this guidance or at the above link then contact the Foreign Entertainers Unit.

28 How do you know that a reduced tax payment has been authorised?

The Foreign Entertainers Unit will authorise you to deduct a reduced amount of tax by sending you a form FEU 4. Even where you have been a party to the agreed arrangement with HMRC you must wait until you get the form FEU 4.

If you have not received an authorisation form FEU 4 by the time the payment is due you must deduct tax at the basic rate on all related payments.

29 How are payments dealt with in your Self Assessment or Corporation Tax accounts?

If the income you receive is attributed to the entertainer under the rules set out in Regulation 7 Income Tax Regulations 1987 (Opens new window) then the tax withheld from the payment you receive will be treated as a payment on account of the entertainer's UK liability.

You will not be charged to UK tax on that income and there will be no repayment of the Withholding Tax to you.

But if:
1. you are UK resident and
2. the income you receive is not attributed to the entertainer under the above rules then the payment you receive will be a receipt of your own business

The amount of the assessable income will be the payment received plus the amount of the Withholding Tax which has been deducted. You will be able to claim the gross payment you make as a deduction in your UK Income Tax or Corporation Tax accounts.

'Gross payment' means the payment to the entertainer or intermediary plus the tax accounted for to HMRC.

If you make the payment in a series of payments as described at How to work out the tax, you may be entitled to set off tax withheld from payments you receive against your UK tax liabilities or claim a repayment of tax.

30 Example

A UK Venue pays box office income of £100,000 to a UK Promoter in respect of the performance of a non-UK resident entertainer. The Entertainer is paid a fee of £60,000 by the Promoter

31 Withholding Tax

A venue pays £80,000 to the promoter. This is £100,000 less £20,000 which is 20% tax. The £20,000 tax is paid to HMRC.

The promoter pays £48,000 to the entertainer. This is £60,000 less £12,000 which is 20% tax. The £12,000 tax is paid to HMRC.

32 Treatment in the accounts

The Venue is allowed the expense of £100,000 (that is the gross payment shown in his accounts).

The Promoter has a receipt of £100,000 as income and is allowed £60,000 as an expense in its accounts.

33 Tax set offs

The Promoter can claim to set the excess Withholding Tax of £8,000 against its Income Tax/Corporation Tax liability for that accounting period. i.e. £20,000 less the payment of £12,000.

If the Promoter had a tax liability of less than £8,000 it can claim a repayment of the amount by which £8,000 exceeds its Income Tax/Corporation Tax liability for that accounting period.

34 Assessments

If a payer does not deduct Withholding Tax from a payment, or does not pay over tax which he has deducted, then HMRC may make an assessment (Opens new window) to recover the tax due direct from the payer.

An assessment may be made on the payments made in the tax year or for a particular period (see How do you pay the tax that you have deducted and/or accounted for?). The tax charged in the assessment is regarded as being due and payable by the 14th day after the end of the relevant return period for which it was originally due.

You will see therefore that there is no advantage in delaying payment and waiting for an assessment. The tax will be treated as due at the normal time and interest calculated accordingly.

35 Appeals

Any appeal against an assessment made to recover Withholding Tax should be made in writing to the Foreign Entertainers Unit. The appeal should be made within 30 days from the date the notice of assessment was issued.

36 Interest

Interest may be charged and recovered by HMRC if Withholding Tax is paid late. (How do you pay the tax that you have deducted and/or accounted for?).

37 Information and inspection

The Foreign Entertainers Unit will be able to call for information from payers, providing due notice is given. The information which the Inspector can request is fully set out in Regulation 9 of the Income Tax (Entertainers and Sportsmen) Regulations 1987 (Opens new window).

38 List of forms

The forms shown below are those that the **payer** may require/receive:

FEU 1 Return of payments made to non-resident entertainers
FEU 1(CS) Payer's Return continuation sheet
FEU 2 Foreign Entertainers Unit tax deduction certificate
FEU 4 Payer's notification that basic rate Withholding Tax is not appropriate

The forms shown below are those that the **payee** may require/receive:

FEU 2 Foreign Entertainers Unit tax deduction certificate
FEU 8 (PDF 105K) Application for Reduced Tax Payment (not mandatory: applications can be made by letter or fax).

39 Where can I get help and information?

If after reading this guide you have any questions or require further information, please contact the Foreign Entertainers Unit.

Appendix 6   Guidelines on the Special NIC Rules for Entertainers

Introduction

1. The NIC treatment of entertainers is different to that which applies for tax. Following the Special Commissioners' case for *McCowen and West* the Inland Revenue accepted that most performers/artistes in the entertainment sector, engaged under Equity contracts, were engaged under contracts for services and would generally be assessable to tax under Schedule D. However, it was recognised that to follow this line for NIC purposes would mean that the majority of entertainers who had previously paid Class 1 NICs would only be liable for Class 2 and Class 4 NICs which would not provide them with universal title to contributory benefits.

2. DSS Ministers, therefore, decided that they would introduce regulations which would treat the majority of entertainers as employed earners for NIC purposes. This would enable entertainers to build up entitlement to contribution based Jobseeker's Allowance and ensure that, in a precarious industry, new talent could be encouraged to weather long periods without work whilst they established themselves.

3. Prior to 1998, the main category of performers in the entertainment industry not paying Class 1 contributions were certain 'Key Talent' stars who were generally regarded as having been engaged on productions because of their celebrity status. To try and ensure this practice continued The Social Security (Categorisation of Earners) (Amendment) Regulations 1998 were introduced from 17 July 1998 which created a liability for Class 1 NICs for entertainers whose earnings consisted 'wholly or mainly of salary'. Those for whom a fee was negotiated or received rights and additional use payments, higher than the salary element were not liable to pay Class 1 NICs but were regarded as self-employed as such payments did not come within the definition of 'salary', derived from case law.[1]

---

[1] There is no statutory definition of the word 'salary'. Remuneration does, however, have to have all of the following characteristics to be regarded as 'salary':
- It is paid for services rendered or to be rendered
- It is paid under some contract or appointment
- It is computed by reference to time worked
- It is payable at a specified time or at specified intervals
- It is paid for regular work

4. Most entertainers in the theatre industry are mainly remunerated by salary and would be subject to the 1998 Regulations. However, it has become the usual practice for the majority of entertainers in the Film industry and some in the TV industry to receive as part of their remuneration package pre-purchase payments as compensation for the loss of future repeat fees and rights and royalties worth many times the salary element. In addition Equity agreements in the TV industry typically provide for repeat fees to be paid as and when those repeats are transmitted. Over time the value of these in many cases exceeds the level of salary. Few actors were, therefore, paid 'wholly or mainly' by salary and it was realised that the regulations did not achieve the desired object of bringing most entertainers into Class 1.
5. The Revenue, therefore, accepted that the 1998 regulations were not sustainable and new regulations were introduced from 6 April 2003. These were the Social Security (Categorisation of Earners) (Amendment) Regulations 2003[SI 2003 No. 736]. Equivalent regulations SI 2003 No 733 apply for Northern Ireland.
6. These guidance notes explain:
    - the criteria from 6 April 2003 to determine whether an entertainer is to be treated as an employed earner;
    - how the regulations affect all parts of the entertainment industry;
    - how engagers and entertainers can claim refunds of wrongly paid Class 1 contributions as a consequence of the 1998 regulations;
    - how further help and information about the tax/NIC treatment of entertainers can be obtained.
7. The notes are divided into two sections to provide details about the NIC position of entertainers as a consequence of these changes:
    - Section A explains the 2003 regulations in detail.
    - Section B gives information on the arrangements for enabling engagers and entertainers to claim refunds of Class 1 NICs paid in error as a consequence of the superseded regulation.

SECTION A

THE SOCIAL SECURITY(CATEGORISATION OF EARNERS) (AMENDMENT) REGULATIONS 2003

1. The regulations from 6 April 2003 reflect the fact that instead of a 'wholly or mainly' salary test, those entertainers[2] whose remuneration includes any element of salary, as defined below, will be treated as

---

The above statements are based on the cases of Re Shine, ex parte Shine [1892, 1QB522] and Greater London Council v Minister of Social Security [1971, 2 All ER285]

[2] Entertainer is defined in the Social Security (Categorisation of Earners) Regulations 1978 as a "person employed as an actor, singer or musician or in any similar performing capacity." This includes such professions as dancers, voice-overs and walk–on parts. TV Presenters and news reporters are not regarded as entertainers for the purposes of the legislation.

employed earners. Once subject to the regulations there will be liability for Class 1 NICs on all earnings from the engagement (including rights payments.)

2. The regulations are aimed at reflecting the NICs position of entertainers prior to July 1998, when there was a distinction between entertainers regarded as self-employed and those regarded as employees, based on the terms and conditions of their engagements. The vast majority of entertainers are engaged on the basis of payments of salary, but a small proportion are only paid a fee for an engagement which is not dependent upon the time worked.

3. Where the payment is a fee for the production, not a salary – and this would have to be made clear in the contract – the entertainer will remain self – employed for NICs purposes and liable to Class 2 and Class 4 NICs.

4. For the avoidance of doubt the position with regard to liability for Class 1 NICs on rights payments from contracts entered into where services are provided after April 2003 is:
    - If the initial payment under the terms of the contract (including pre-purchased rights payments) is not subject to NICs because no salary element is included in the remuneration then any subsequent rights payments made will not be subject to Class 1 NICs;
    - If there is a liability for Class 1 NICs on the initial payment because any part of that payment satisfies the definition of salary then any subsequent rights payments will also be subject to Class 1 NICs. This applies even if the contract period has ended and the repeat programme is not broadcast by the original production company as in the case of the BBC/PACT agreement (from January 2004) whereby the BBC take out a licence to use the programme and pay the production company for any repeat fees due. In this event the original production company will continue to be the liable secondary contributor in respect of the entertainer as defined by regulation 4 of the 2003 regulations [see paragraph 7 below]. The broadcaster must, therefore, inform the production company that it will have ongoing liability for Class 1 NICs. Those broadcasting companies not subject to the PACT agreement will need to inform the relevant production company when the repeat broadcast takes place and the amounts paid.

5. 'Salary' is now defined in the 2003 regulations which requires that the following four tests need to be satisfied:
    - made for services rendered;
    - paid under a contract for services;
    - where there is more than one payment, payable at a specified period or interval; and
    - computed by reference to the amount of time for which work has been performed.

6. The third bullet point ensures that those entertainers engaged on a single day or two-day engagement are covered by the legislation. This means that the policy intention of ensuring that the regulations apply to film extras and walk-on parts is achieved. The last bullet point, should apply to all entertainers, apart from a very small minority, who are contracted to appear in productions for which their remuneration is not directly calculated according to the period of weeks or months they are assigned to the production. Revenue solicitors have confirmed that the words "by reference to" in this context should be interpreted widely to the extent that, should there be any link between the amount of the fee paid and the number of days worked or the period of the engagement, (whether or not there is a contractual requirement for work to be performed on each and every day,) then this bullet will be satisfied.

7. The legislation also includes provisions which amend paragraph 10 of Schedule 3 to the Social Security (Categorisation of Earners) Regulations 1978 to ensure that in all cases where the entertainer is treated as an employed earner by the regulations, the secondary contributor is treated as the producer of the entertainment in respect of which the payments of salary are made. Since the first edition of this guidance was published it has become apparent that some confusion has arisen throughout the industry over the wording of this provision.

8. Because *the person* to whom the payments of salary are made is not described in column A of para 5A of Schedule 1 it was necessary for the draftsman to refer to the column B description "any person in employment described in para 5A in column (A) . . ." Although these words appear under the heading 'Person excepted from the operation of column (A)' this does not negate the effect of the regulation nor does it override the effect of the Intermediaries legislation (IR35) which provides that where an entertainer provides his services to a client through a personal service company it is the latter which is the secondary contributor.

9. As part of the function of Government, Inland Revenue Officers are required to carry out periodic compliance checks. Where there is evidence that entertainers are paid a salary but the contract has been framed in such a way so as to treat the payment as a fee in order to avoid Class 1 NICs the Inland Revenue will investigate such arrangements and seek to collect any unpaid Class 1 NICs due as a result of these investigations.

Special Cases

10. Session Musicians:
Session musicians is a term which describes the elite group of musicians who did not pay Class 1 NICs prior to July 1998. In accordance with the Revenue's policy intention Session Musicians and their deputies will not fall under the 2003 regulations.

11. Disc Jockeys:
    Disc jockeys, although engaged under Equity contracts would not fall to be included in the definition of 'entertainer' and, therefore, are not covered by the 2003 regulations. However, disc jockeys who provide additional services which satisfies the definition of entertainer may be covered depending on the nature of the contract.
12. Regular Members of Orchestra or Chorus:
    With the exception of the major London orchestras, musicians and singers who are permanent members of major orchestras and choruses are generally engaged under contracts of service and chargeable to tax under the employment income rules with Class 1 NICs liability.
13. Entertainers from Overseas:
    Where an entertainer comes from a member state of the European Economic Area or a country which has a reciprocal agreement with the UK and provides a form E101 or equivalent certificate of continuing liability under their own domestic legislation, the special rules for entertainers will not apply. This will be the case even if the individual is engaged in the UK and remuneration includes a salary element. Instead the entertainer will remain in the category of earner determined by it's own country's domestic legislation.

Further Information

14. If theatre engagers or their representatives have any questions about the status of entertainers in the light of this legislation or any individual wishes to query their status they should contact their local Inland Revenue office. Engagers and workers in the TV Industry should ring the TV Industry Unit on 0161 2613255.
    Film Production companies and their advisors may contact the Film Industry Unit on 0191 490 3662.

SECTION B
ARRANGEMENTS FOR CLAIMING REFUNDS OF CLASS 1 NICs PAID IN ERROR

Who can claim refunds

1. The 1998 Regulations have led to some entertainers being wrongly categorised as employed earners because their remuneration did not consist 'wholly or mainly of salary' and therefore any primary or secondary Class 1 contributions which have been paid in relation to entertainers on the footing that they were employed earners may have been incorrectly paid. There is provision under National Insurance legislation for the return of contributions which have been paid in error and refund claims will be invited for appropriate periods between 17 July 1998 and 5 April 2003 (and in some cases beyond).

2. As previously notified the Inland Revenue waived the legislation restricting refund claims to 2 years provided for in section 19A of the Social Security Contributions and Benefits Act 1992 for the purposes of this exercise but this concession ended on **5 April 2005**, so any claims for refunds under this guidance made after this date will be subject to the normal rules.
3. However, entertainers can choose not to have their primary contributions refunded, but to let them count instead towards their Additional Pension (AP) entitlement, as if they had been correctly paid. This does not prevent the engager from seeking a refund of the wrongly paid secondary contributions or the entertainer notifying the Revenue before they reach pension age that they now wish to claim a refund. Any such claim in these circumstances would be subject to the normal time limits for the claiming of refunds of erroneously paid contributions.
4. Primary Class1 NICs refunded to entertainers will be reduced by the amount of any Class 2 and 4 contributions which were due from them as self-employed earners, and of any contribution based Jobseekers Allowance paid on the basis of the incorrect Class 1 contributions.

How do I know if I am entitled to claim a refund?

5. If Class 1 NICs have been paid between 17 July 1998 and 5 April 2003 in respect of entertainers whose remuneration in respect of services performed between those dates did not satisfy the 'wholly or mainly by salary' criteria in the 1998 regulations then the engager is entitled to apply for an immediate refund of those contributions. For example, remuneration made up of 60% Rights Payments and 40 % Salary would not be 'wholly or mainly by salary' and there would have been no liability for Class 1 NICs. However, Class 1 NICs were properly payable in cases where, at the time of the engagement, it was known that the salary element of the remuneration exceeded any residuals.
6. We have obtained legal advice in cases where the salary exceeded the fee element at the time of the engagement but subsequent rights payments made as and when they arose resulted in the rights payments ultimately exceeding the salary. Solicitors have advised there are two further scenarios to consider:
    (i) If Class 1 NICs have been paid up to or beyond 5 April 2003 in respect of entertainers whose remuneration in respect of services provided between 17 July 1998 and 5 April 2003 has subsequently been exceeded by the amount of rights payments, then a refund claim can be made immediately on the basis that remuneration is no longer 'wholly or mainly by salary'.
    (ii) Where Class 1 NICs have been paid up to or beyond 5 April 2003 for those entertainers in respect of whom rights payments may not at present exceed salary but would, however, on the balance of probabilities exceed the salary level either before 5 April 2005 or beyond that date then, subject to satisfactory evidence, a refund may be claimed on that basis.

7. The following table should help you decide whether or not the various elements of remuneration under any of the standard BBC/Equity, ITVA/Equity or PACT/Equity contracts satisfy the case law definition of salary (see page 1):

TYPE OF PAYMENT	SALARY/ RIGHTS PAYMENT
Engagement Fee	Salary or Rights payment depending upon contract type
Attendance days	Salary
Standby days	Salary
Holiday pay	Salary
Overtime	Salary
Additional Use fee	Rights payment for pre-purchase
Retainer	Salary – to ensure services available when needed
Royalty	Rights payment – at each sale of programme
Residual	Rights payment – either pre-purchase or at each sale.
Option fee	Rights payment – to ensure an engager has priority use of an entertainers services.

How to make a claim

8. An engager or entertainer who considers that Class 1 NI contributions may have been incorrectly paid after 17 July 1998 in the circumstances described in these guidance notes may apply for a refund. Claims for all tax years should be submitted together. Anyone who wishes to do so in the belief that workers previously treated as employed earners should have been regarded as self-employed should write to:

National Insurance Contributions Office,
Refunds Group,(Erroneous 4)
Room BP1001
Benton Park View,
Newcastle upon Tyne
NE98 1ZZ

Alternatively they should telephone Refunds Group on 084591 –54042 to request a claim form [calls will be charged at BT local rates.]

9. As an alternative to the written application form applicants may find it more convenient to submit claims for refunds by CD-Rom or floppy disk. Engagers should indicate which method they prefer.

What we need to know from you

10. Please give as much information as possible when making a claim i.e. Full name of individual / Stage Name (where appropriate)/ NI NO/ Date of Birth/ Correct address. You will also be required to declare:
    (i) All Basic and Rights Payments made in each tax year for which a claim is made.
    (ii) Total earnings on which NICs were deducted and total amount of NICs paid.
    (iii) Amounts of employers and employees contributions.
    (iv) The type of contract under which the individual has been engaged; If it is either of the standard BBC/EQUITY, ITVA/EQUITY or PACT/EQUITY contracts then, subject to IR audit requirements, no other documentary evidence of payment will be required. Contracts and/or invoices will be required in all other cases.

Additional Evidence

11. For claims under scenario (1) in para 6 above an additional statement that for the individuals concerned rights payments of a 'X' amount had now exceeded salary of 'Y' amount, showing evidence of the date this occurred would suffice.
12. For claims under scenario (2), i.e. where rights payments have not at the time of the claim yet exceeded salary but are expected to in the future, the Revenue would need to be satisfied that a sufficiently high percentage of entertainers had already received rights payments in excess of salary. This evidence should be in the form of industry statistics which would satisfy us as to prevalence and anticipated future trends in repeats. In other words evidence that would support the contention that because the entertainer has so far received salary of 'Y' amount and rights payments of 'X' amount, on the basis of anticipated future repeats the salary amount will be exceeded. This would need to be accompanied by a covering statement from an authorised representative of the engager that "for all of the refund claims submitted it is expected that the repeat fees and royalties will exceed the salary payments for the particular programme."

If information is incomplete or incorrect

13. We will be unable to proceed with your claim and you will be asked to provide the additional information.

What happens when we receive your claim

14. On receipt the claim will be registered and if sufficient information is supplied, all secondary Class 1NICs confirmed as erroneously paid will be refunded. All claims will be dealt with in the order they are received and will be processed as soon as possible. Employees named on the claim form whom, as a result of previous refund action have already notified the Inland Revenue that they did not wish to claim a refund of primary NICs, will not be contacted but applications will be accepted from those individuals who choose not to allow their wrongly paid contributions to remain on their NI record. Immediate applications for refund of primary NICs will also be accepted from individuals who can provide evidence that their engager has already received a refund of their secondary NICs on the basis of probability that future repeat fees and royalty payments will eventually exceed salary (see para 12 above.)
15. If you are in any doubt about the categorisation of entertainers you have engaged or you are an entertainer yourself and wish to query your own position then contact your nearest Inland Revenue office and ask to speak to a member of the Status team. Enquiries about entertainers engaged by TV Broadcasting Companies should be made to the TV Industry Unit on 0161 2613255

Appendix 7 Film, Television and Production Industry Guidance Notes 2003 edition

THESE NOTES PROVIDE FURTHER ADVICE WITH REGARD TO THE APPLICATION OF PAYE AND NATIONAL INSURANCE CONTRIBUTIONS TO NON-PERMANENT, CASUAL AND FREELANCE WORKERS IN FILM AND TELEVISION PRODUCTION, UK AND FOREIGN TELEVISION BROADCASTING INDUSTRY.
THEY ARE INTENDED FOR GUIDANCE ONLY.
PLEASE BE AWARE THAT THE GUIDANCE AND RATES IN THE HYPERLINKED GUIDANCE MAY CHANGE AND YOU SHOULD ALWAYS CHECK THE LINK TO ENSURE YOU USE THE LATEST UP TO DATE INFORMATION.

CONTENTS

1. OPERATION OF PAYE
2. EXCLUSIONS FROM PAYE
3. ISSUE OF FORM P45
4. PAYMENTS TO SERVICE COMPANIES
5. CONSTRUCTION INDUSTRY CERTIFICATES
6. OVERSEAS PRODUCTIONS
7. WORKERS FROM ABROAD
8. PAYMENTS TO OVERSEAS PERSONALITIES
9. COMPANY DIRECTORS
10. TAX TREATMENT OF EXPENSES PAYMENTS
11. RETURNS OF PAYMENTS MADE
12. SPECIAL NIC RULES FOR ENTERTAINERS
13. VALUE ADDED TAX
14. DIRECTORY

APPENDIX 1

1. OPERATION OF PAYE

- refer to guidance on hmrc website HM Revenue & Customs: PAYE for employers

2. EXCLUSIONS FROM PAYE

2.1 STAFF WORKING IN SPECIFIED SELF EMPLOYED GRADES

It is your responsibility to correctly determine the employment status of your workers.

You need not apply PAYE to payments made to non-permanent, casual or freelance staff working in the grades shown in Appendix 1 to these Guidance Notes, provided that they fulfil any specific requirements shown in the list. HMRC has reviewed the contractual and working arrangements applicable to these grades in detail and it is accepted that the terms of engagement do not normally constitute a contract of employment.

When deciding whether PAYE is to be applied you should consider only the grade in which the worker is currently engaged. Qualification for or previous engagements in a higher grade should be ignored.

Appendix 1 does not list every grade in the industry; it shows only those grades for which PAYE need not be operated. This list is always under review by HMRC and representatives of the Film & Production and TV Broadcast industry. All parties are agreed that some new grades may fall to be self-employed whereas there will be others that will be appropriate to employee status

If you have a grade that is not recognisable in Appendix 1 you can use the guidance in the hyperlink below and any additional assistance you require can be obtained from the Film & Production and TV Broadcast helplines – see the Directory on page 12 for contact numbers.

HM Revenue & Customs: Employment status: employed or self-employed?

2.2 LETTERS OF AUTHORITY

In certain circumstances where a worker has a business structure that includes a number of separate, short engagements, a worker may be regarded as self employed, even though each of his engagements, viewed in isolation, would suggest that he was an employee. Engagers are not expected to make any additional enquiries; these cases are identified by the Film & Production Industry Unit, Washington or the Television Broadcasting Unit Manchester and special letters of authority are issued to workers for production to engagers before payment is made.

> **Employers should only accept without question letters that contain a valid expiry date.**
>
> **ONLY letters issued by Film & Production Unit, TV Broadcasting Unit or Foreign Broadcasting should be accepted.**
>
> **Letters from any other HMRC Office or from Accountants must be ignored; as should Self-Assessment or any other Tax Reference Numbers provided by the worker.**

There are two kinds of Letters of Authority:-

SPECIAL LETTERS OF AUTHORITY have been issued to all workers who, although not usually working in a grade listed in Appendix 1, have satisfactorily demonstrated that their overall pattern of activity amounts to self employment. In these cases, the letter authorises you to make gross payment in respect of payments for **short** engagements. In this context, 'short' means ten days or less. You should however telephone the contact number shown in the letter:-

- if the engagement is expected to last for more than ten days, or
- If there is an arrangement for the worker to be engaged regularly for short periods.

When telephoning, you should provide the worker's full name and National Insurance number and the unique serial number shown on the Special Letter of Authority, together with brief details of the engagement. We will either authorise the use of gross payment or will give additional advice on the operation of PAYE. Workers who dispute the operation of PAYE should be referred to the Film & Production Unit or the TV Broadcasting Unit.

Special Letters of Authority are not of course required where the worker is engaged in one of the self employed grades listed at Appendix 1 and fulfils the necessary criteria.

2.3 SPECIFIC OPINION LETTERS

Specific letters are occasionally issued to a small number of individuals working in a grade not normally recognised as self employed in accordance with the published list of self employed grades at Appendix 1. In those cases a worker successfully demonstrated to HMRC that self employed status may be granted for this particular engagement only.

> **Please remember to disregard letters from other HMRC Offices or from Accountants.**

2.3 THE "SEVEN DAY" RULE

Because many employed workers in the Film, Production & TV Broadcasting industry have short engagements with a succession of different employers, the normal operation of PAYE is impractical and would in many cases result in excessive deductions of tax. The Seven-Day Rule is intended to alleviate the hardship, which might arise from such excessive deductions.

You need not apply PAYE to payments made to workers engaged for less than one week – that is, for six consecutive days or less.

The period of six consecutive days includes rest days and weekends if these fall between the first and last days of engagement. For example, if a worker is engaged for Wednesday, Thursday and Friday and for the following Monday and Tuesday, the intervening weekend must be counted and the limit of six days will be exceeded.

> **The Seven-Day Rule applies only to Income Tax; it does not apply to National Insurance Contributions, which must be accounted for in the normal way. Operation of the Seven-Day Rule does not change the nature of the contract and the worker remains an employee.**

Except in the circumstances set out below the Seven-Day Rule applies to each engagement separately. Successive engagements should not be aggregated, nor should PAYE be applied retrospectively.

The Seven-Day Rule does NOT apply:-
- **If it is known at the time of payment that the worker is to be re-engaged and the total period of engagement (inclusive of rest days and weekends) is more than six days.**
- **If there are arrangements for the worker to be engaged frequently or at regular intervals.**

In either of the above situations PAYE should be operated in the normal way.

3. ISSUE OF FORM P45

3.1 IF TAX HAS NOT BEEN DEDUCTED UNDER PAYE

If you have not operated PAYE because:-
- the worker was engaged in a grade listed in Appendix 1, and all necessary conditions were met (see Paragraph 2.1), or
- the worker produced a valid letter of authority and you were authorised to make gross payment (see Paragraph 2.2).

You do not need to prepare a form P45, because the worker was not regarded as an employee.

> **If you did not operate PAYE because the engagement was covered by the Seven-Day Rule (see Paragraph 2.3) or you engaged an Actor/ Entertainer, you should complete form P45, give Part 1A only to the worker, and destroy parts 1, 2 and 3.**

4. PAYMENTS TO SERVICE COMPANIES (LOAN OUTS)

Some individuals have set up service companies or partnerships to provide the services of a single worker to production companies in circumstances where – if the worker had been engaged directly by the Film, Production or TV Broadcasting Company – a contract of employment would otherwise have existed. In the following advice, reference to a service company should be regarded as applying equally to a partnership. The use of service companies in the manner described above allows the Film, Production or TV Broadcasting Company to make payments to the service company instead of to the worker, so avoiding the deduction of PAYE or NI Contributions.

The Intermediaries legislation, more commonly referred to as IR35, seeks to ensure that what is properly employment income is taxed as such and tackles tax and National Insurance avoidance through the use of intermediaries, such as service companies.

The statutory provisions to counter such avoidance impose obligations directly upon the service company and do not affect the entitlement of the Film, Production or TV Broadcasting Company to make such payments gross.

It is not however sufficient that a service company exists; it is the duty of the Film, Production or TV Broadcasting company to satisfy itself that there is in fact a *bona fide* contract **with the service company** for the provision of the worker's services. If you have any doubt about the existence of a valid contract, payment should be made directly to the worker and the PAYE and NIC provisions should be applied in the normal way. If you fail to exercise reasonable care in this regard, you may be held liable for the deductions that ought to have been made.

If the worker's services are provided in circumstances such that if the worker had been employed directly you would have been able to make payment gross by virtue of Paragraphs 2.1 or 2.2 above, you may make gross payments to the service company without further enquiry.

In any case of dispute or difficulty, engagers or workers may obtain further advice from Film & Production Industry Unit or TV Broadcasting Unit.

Workers who seek further information about the application of the statutory provisions mentioned above in relation to their service company should be referred to:-

IR35 Customer Service Unit
HMRC
Ground Floor North
Princess House
Cliftonville Road
Northampton
NN1 5AE

Telephone: 0845 303 3535 (8.30 – 16.30 Monday – Friday)
Fax: 0845 302 3535
Email IR35@hmrc.gov.uk

The telephone and fax numbers are available for IR35 queries only. Further information about IR35 issues can be found on the HMRC website at www.hmrc.gov.uk/ir35

A copy of the disputed contract will be required, and an initial contact by telephone is recommended so that callers can be advised of any further information which may need to be provided in particular cases.

5. CONSTRUCTION INDUSTRY SCHEME

- refer to guidance on hmrc website – HM Revenue & Customs: Construction Industry Scheme

6. OVERSEAS PRODUCTIONS

- refer to guidance on hmrc website – HM Revenue & Customs: Employee going to work abroad

7. WORKERS FROM ABROAD

- refer to guidance on hmrc website – HM Revenue & Customs: Employees coming to the UK from abroad

Workers from overseas engaged in the grades listed in Appendix 1, fulfilling the criteria, may however be regarded as self-employed and should be treated in the same way as United Kingdom workers engaged in those grades.

8. PAYMENTS TO OVERSEAS PERSONALITIES

- for tax refer to guidance on hmrc website – HM Revenue & Customs: Foreign Entertainers Unit
- for National Insurance refer to guidance on hmrc website –
- NIM33000 – Special Cases: People Going to or Coming from Abroad – Contents
- NIM33014 – Special Cases: Class 1: Workers Going to and Coming from Abroad – Reciprocal Agreement Countries – contents
- NIM33019 – Special Cases: Class 1: Workers Going to and Coming from Abroad – Rest of the World (ROW) – contents

9. COMPANY DIRECTORS

Advice should be sought from Film & Production Industry Unit or TV Broadcasting Unit before making any gross payment to a director of your company in respect of 'other work' performed for the company.

10. TAX TREATMENT OF EXPENSES PAYMENTS

– refer to guidance on hmrc website:-

HM Revenue & Customs: 480 (2011) – Expenses and benefits
HM Revenue & Customs: Expenses and benefits A to Z
HM Revenue & Customs: Expenses payments
P11D – Expenses Payments and Benefits

* The existing Subsistence rates shown at paragraphs 10.2.1 and 10.2.2 in the April 2011 publication can continue to be used until March 2013, these are:-

Meal Allowances
Breakfast	£6.00
Mid-day Meal	£7.00
Evening Meal	£12.00

Accommodation Allowances

London	Per night, exclusive of meals	£75.00
	Per night, inclusive of all meals	£100.00
Elsewhere	Per night, exclusive of meals	£60.00
	Per night, inclusive of all meals	£85.00

You should begin to use HMRC's Benchmark Scale Rates, links are above, with effect from April 2013.

11. RETURNS OF PAYMENTS MADE

In addition to the issue of forms P45 in the circumstances set out in Paragraph 3 above, you may be required to make returns of payments made to your workers as instructed below.

11.1 SELF-EMPLOYED WORKERS

Workers engaged in grades listed in Appendix 1 who fulfil any specific requirements shown in the list (see Paragraph 2.1 above) and workers who have produced a valid letter of authority (see Paragraph 2.2 above) are regarded as self-employed. If requested to do so you should complete a Section 16 Return for each such worker to whom you have made payments exceeding £1,000, **inclusive of any payments of expenses,** during the relevant return period. The necessary forms and instructions for their completion may be obtained from:-

HMRC
Centre for National Intelligence (CNI)
Ty Glas
Llanishen
CARDIFF
CF14 5TS
Telephone: (029) 2032 7456

11.2 EMPLOYED WORKERS COVERED BY THE SEVEN DAY RULE

Where the engagement was covered by the Seven-Day Rule, a form P14 is still required for NIC purposes, even though no tax will have been deducted. Each form P14 should show the dates of commencement and cessation, the total pay for that engagement and the appropriate NIC deductions. If you comply with the above requirements you need not complete a form P38A in respect of payments made without deduction of tax.

Please also remember to issue form P45 Part 1A on completion of each engagement covered by the Seven-Day Rule (Paragraph 3.2 above).

11.3 ACTORS/ ENTERTAINERS

A form P14 is still required for NIC purposes, even though no tax will have been deducted. Each form P14 should show the dates of commencement and cessation, the total pay for that engagement and the appropriate NIC deductions – if the actor/ entertainer is continuing after 5 April you should for administrative purposes enter '5 April' in the cessation date box.

If gross payment is in excess of £1,000 you should provide full details on the annual Section 16 Return.

12. SPECIAL NIC RULES FOR ENTERTAINERS

– refer to guidance on hmrc website – http://www.hmrc.gov.uk/guidance/nicrules-ents.pdf

13. VALUE ADDED TAX

Within the Film & Production &TV Broadcasting industry, HMRC accept that any VAT registration requirement will follow from the status decision made in accordance with these Guidance Notes. This means that individuals will be liable to register and account for VAT if their income exceeds the prescribed limit (or if they elect to register voluntarily) provided that

- They are engaged in grades regarded as self-employed by virtue of Paragraph 2.1 above,

or

- They hold a Special Letter of Authority as described in Paragraph 2.2 above.

The view of HMRC is that regular working for short periods is indicative of self-employment and therefore of a potential liability to register for VAT. Workers whose earnings from short period contracts exceed the registration threshold and who request a status review with a view to obtaining a Special Letter of Authority (see Paragraph 2.2) should at the same time consider that they may be liable to register for VAT. The outcome of the review will be accepted as determining status both for Income Tax and for Value Added Tax.

Further information can be found on the HMRC website and in the HMRC Notice 700/1 '*Should I be registered for VAT?*'

This guidance does not limit the worker's right to make an application for VAT registration, nor to appeal to a Tribunal if that application is refused. Any queries about VAT can be dealt with by the VAT Excise and Customs Duties Helpline on 0845 010 9000 or 0845 000 0200 for those with hearing difficulties or 0845 010 0300 for those who wish to speak to someone in Welsh.

14. DIRECTORY

General PAYE & Self Assessment enquiries in the Film, Production & TV Broadcast Industry should in the first instance be made to –

HMRC Contact Centre telephone number 0845 300 0627

All other enquiries, including, actors, 7 Day Rule, employer expenses, employment status of grades, special letters or dispensations in the Film & Production Industry should be made to –

Film & Production Unit
Floor 2
Weardale House
Washington
Tyne & Wear NE37 1LW

Telephone: 0191 419 8800
Fax: 0191 419 8782
Email a.filmproductionunitmailbox@hmrc.gsi.gov.uk

Employment status queries about workers engaged by Television Broadcasting Companies should be addressed to –

TV Broadcasting Unit
4th Floor
Trinity Bridge House
2 Dearmans Place
SALFORD
M3 5BH

Telephone: (0161) 261 3254/3255/3691
Fax: (0161) 261 3197

Enquiries about workers engaged by Foreign Broadcasting Companies should be addressed to –

Specialist Employer Compliance
Grayfield House
5 Bankhead Avenue
Edinburgh

EH4 7DL
Telephone 0131 453 8780
Fax 0131 453 8806

APPENDIX 1

LIST OF ACCEPTED SELF EMPLOYED GRADES

IMPORTANT NOTES

1. SCOPE

This list applies to all sectors of the Film & Production Industry and to Television Broadcasting.

2. MAXIMUM DURATION OF ENGAGEMENT

In certain circumstances the status of a worker may be influenced by the duration of an engagement. Workers in grades marked with an asterisk* in the following list may be regarded as self-employed provided that they are engaged:-

- for a one-off production such as a feature film or a single drama or documentary, **or**
  (if the worker is to be engaged on a separate production following the completion of the one off production then where this is known at the outset of the second production PAYE should be considered from the commencement of the second production. If this happens after a break, where it can be shown that the worker was seeking or worked elsewhere then the worker can be treated as self employed. Note – a break is a natural break rather than a contrived one such as Christmas holiday, annual vacation.)
- for less than 9 months on a series or a specific strand of a programme.
  (if the worker is engaged for 9 months on a series and a second series is commissioned then as the series are linked the worker can continue to be treated as self employed on the second series.)

In exceptional circumstances the period of 9 months may be extended if specific authority is sought from Film & Production or TV Broadcasting Unit.

Workers in grades not marked with an asterisk may be regarded as self-employed regardless of the length of the engagement, **provided that they fulfil the necessary criteria.**

3. ASSISTANTS

Assistant grades are **NOT** included unless specifically identified in the list.

4. OTHER GRADES

Payments to workers in grades not shown in the following list should be taxed under PAYE (except where the Seven Day Rule applies) and should be subjected to Class 1 National Insurance Contributions.

> **Remember that the Seven Day Rule does not apply to National Insurance Contributions!**

5. DEFINITIONS

5.1 PREMISES PROVIDED BY THE ENGAGER

These embrace studios, locations or any other facilities provided by or at the direct expense of the engager, whether or not the engager is occupier of those premises.

5.2 SUBSTANTIAL PROVISION OF MATERIALS/EQUIPMENT

This means the provision of major items which play an important and fundamental role in the work of the grade in question and which are of significant value, such provision being an integral requirement of the contract of engagement. It does **not** include tools of the trade (see below). The significance of the provision of equipment in determining tax status is the financial risk which such provision entails. It follows that in general equipment must be owned by, or at the permanent disposal of the worker. Provision of hired equipment, whether or not hired in the worker's name, is relevant only if obtained entirely independently of the engager. Such provision should be disregarded if the financial risk is effectively underwritten by the engager. If a worker is treated as self-employed by virtue of the substantial provision of equipment, the engager must retain full details of the equipment provided for production to HMRC on request.

5.3 TOOLS OF THE TRADE

It is customary for most craftsmen to provide their own tools, whether engaged as employees or as self-employed contractors. Such tools should be disregarded in considering the value of equipment provided, even though the contents of a joiner's or electrician's toolbox may have substantial intrinsic value.

5.4 PROVISION OF FACILITIES BY WORKER

This means that the work is performed mainly away from the engagers premises and/or that the worker provides office equipment, other relevant equipment and the necessary space to facilitate the relevant work activities.

5.5 WORK OF LOCATION MANAGER

Completes preliminary planning, arranging accommodation, setting the stage, restoring the site to original condition and within this role should provide a complete office service and may hire staff and equipment.

ADVANCE RIGGER	Where the contract requires substantial provision of equipment (See Note 5.2).
* ANIMAL HANDLER	
* ANIMATION DIRECTOR	
* ANIMATION PRODUCTION CO-ORDINATOR	
ANIMATOR	Where the work is performed other than on premises provided by the engager and the contract requires substantial provision of equipment (See Note 5.1 & 5.2)
* ANIMATRONIC MODEL DESIGNER	
ARCHIVE RESEARCHER	Where work is performed other than on premises provided by the engager (See Note 5.1)
* ART DIRECTOR	
ASSISTANT ART DIRECTOR	Where the work is performed other than on premises provided by the engager (See Note 5.1)
ASSISTANT COSTUME DESIGNER	Where the work is performed other than on premises provided by the engager or the contract requires substantial provision of materials (See Note 5.1 & 5.2)
* ASSOCIATE PRODUCER	Except where engaged primarily for general research
* AUDITIONER	
BACKGROUND ARTIST	Where the work is performed other than on premises provided by the engager (See Note 5.1)
CAMERA OPERATOR	Where the contract requires substantial provision of equipment (See Note 5.2)
* CASTING DIRECTOR	

* CHAPERONE/TUTOR	
* CHOREOGRAPHER	
* COMPOSER	
CONSTRUCTION MANAGER	Where the contract requires substantial provision of equipment (See Note 5.2)
CONTINUITY	Where script breakdown is an integral part of the contract
CONTRIBUTOR	Where payment is made on a per contribution basis.
* CO PRODUCER	
COSTUME DESIGNER	Where the work is performed other than on premises provided by the engager or the contract requires substantial provision of materials (See Note 5.1 & 5.2)
COSTUME SUPERVISOR	
* CRICKET SCORER	
DIGITAL SET DESIGNER	Where work performed other than on premises provided by the engager (See Note 5.1)
* DIRECTOR	
* DIRECTOR OF PHOTOGRAPHY	
DRESSMAKER	Where the work is performed other than on the premises provided by the engager (See Note 5.1)
DRIVER	Where the contract requires the driver to provide his own vehicle
* EDITOR	
* EXECUTIVE PRODUCER	
* FIGHT ARRANGER	
* FILM STYLIST	
* FIRST ASSISTANT DIRECTOR	
FOLEY ARTIST	Where the contract requires substantial provision of equipment (See Note 5.2)
GAFFER	Where the contract requires substantial provision of equipment (See Note 5.2)

GRAPHIC ARTIST	Where the work is performed other than on the premises provided by the engager (See Note 5.1)
GRAPHIC DESIGNER	Where the work is performed other than on the premises provided by the engager (See Note 5.1)
GRIP (Including KEY GRIP)	Where the contract requires substantial provision of equipment (See Note 5.2)
HAIRDRESSER	Where the contract requires substantial provision of equipment (including wigs), or 50% or more of the work is performed other than on premises provided by the engager (See Note 5.2 & 5.1)
***HEAD OF ART DEPARTMENT**	
HEAD OF DEPARTMENT RIGGER	Where the contract requires substantial provision of equipment (See Note 5.2)
LANGUGAGE ASSESSOR	Where used on an occasional basis to check style and delivery of foreign language broadcasts
LETTERING ARTIST	Where the work is performed other than on premises provided by the engager (See Note 5.1)
LETTERING DESIGNER	Where the work is performed other than on the premises provided by the engager (See Note 5.1)
LIGHTING CAMERAPERSON	Where responsible for designing lighting or photography
LIGHTING DIRECTOR	Where responsible for designing lighting or photography
***LINE PRODUCER**	
LOCATION MANAGER	See Note 5.5
MAKE-UP ARTIST	Where the contract requires provision of a standard make-up kit by the worker, or 50% or more is performed other than on premises provided by the engager (See Note 5.1)
***MATRON**	

MODEL CAMERA	Where the contract requires substantial provision of equipment (See Note 5.2)
MODEL DESIGNER	Where the engagement requires the provision of facilities and equipment/materials by the individual (See Note 5)
MODEL MAKER	Where the engagement requires the provision of facilities and equipment/materials by the individual (See Note 5.2 & 5.4)
* MODELLER	
MUSICAL ARRANGER	Where the work is performed other than on premises provided by the engager (See Note 5.1)
* MUSICAL ASSOCIATE	
MUSICAL COPYIST	Where the work is performed other than on premises provided by the engager (See Note 5.1)
* MUSICAL DIRECTOR	
* MUSICAL SCORE READER	
* NURSE	
* PHOTOGRAPHIC STYLIST	
* POST PRODUCTION SUPERVISOR	
* PRODUCER	
PRODUCTION ACCOUNTANT	Where the contract requires provision of relevant facilities by the worker (See Note 5.4)
PRODUCTION ASSISTANT	Where script breakdown is an integral part of the contract
* PRODUCTION BUYER	
* PRODUCTION DESIGNER	
* PRODUCTION MANAGER	
* PRODUCTION SUPERVISOR	
PROPERTY MASTER	Where the contract requires substantial provision of equipment (including props) (See Note 5.2)

PROPERTY HAND	Where the contract requires substantial provision of equipment (including props) (See Note 5.2)
PROVIDER OF OCCASIONAL INFORMATION (including LEGMEN)	Embraces tip-offs, racing tips, news, sports news and similar information
*** PUBLICIST**	
SCENIC ARTIST	Where 50% or more of the work is performed other than on the premises provided by the engager (See Note 5.1)
SCENIC DESIGNER	Where 50% or more of the work is performed other than on premises provided by the engager (See Note 5.1)
SCRIPT READER	Where the work is performed other than on premises provided by the engager (See Note 5.1)
SCRIPT SUPERVISOR	Where script breakdown is an integral part of the contract
*** SCRIPTWRITER**	Excluding reporting scripts
*** SCULPTOR**	
*** SENIOR FLOOR MANAGER**	
*** SENIOR SPECIAL EFFECTS TECHNICIAN**	
SET DECORATOR	Where the contract requires set design performed other than on premises provided by the engager (See Note 5.1)
SET DRESSER	Where the contract requires set design performed other than on premises provided by the engager (See Note 5.1).
SOUND MAINTENANCE ENGINEER	Where the contract requires substantial provision of equipment (See Note 5.2)
SOUND MIXER	Where the contract requires substantial provision of equipment (See Note 5)

Appendix 7   679

SOUND RECORDIST	Where the contract requires substantial provision of equipment (See Note 5.2)
SPECIAL EFFECTS SUPERVISOR	Where the contract requires provision of necessary equipment by the worker (See Note 5.2)
SPECIAL EFFECTS WIREPERSON	Where the contract requires provision of substantial equipment by the worker (See Note 5.2)
SPECIALIST RESEARCHER	Where the worker has either an existing profession outside of the Film Industry (Academic, Legal Adviser, Doctor, etc) or specialist knowledge of the programme content to be researched and the worker is engaged for a specific project and is not a regular contributor
***SPORT STATISTICIAN**	
STAGE MANAGER	Where the contract requires provision of equipment (including props) (See Note 5.2)
STILLS PHOTOGRAPHER	Where the contract requires provision of all cameras by the worker
***STORYWRITER**	Excluding news reporting
STORYBOARD ARTIST	Where the work is performed other than on premises provided by the engager (See Note 5.1)
***STYLISTS**	Film or photographic styling
TRANSCRIPT TYPIST	Where the work is performed other than on premises provided by the engager (See Note 5.1)
TRANSLATOR	Where the work is performed other than on premises provided by the engager (See Note 5.1)
TRANSPORT MANAGER	Where the worker provides vehicles
***TUTOR**	
UNIT MANAGER	Where the contract requires provision of facilities by the worker (See Note 5.4)

VIDEO TECHNICIAN	Where the contract requires substantial provision of equipment (See Note 5)
WARDROBE (INCLUDES WARDROBE SUPERVISOR AND STYLIST)	Where the work is performed other than on the premises provided by the engager or the contract requires substantial provision of materials (See Note 5.1 & 5.2)
* WARM UP	
WIGMAKER	Where the work is performed other than on premises provided by the engager (See Note 5.1)
WIREPERSON	Where the contract requires provision of necessary equipment by the worker
WRITER	Excluding reporter

Appendix 8   Guidelines on the Meaning of R&D for Tax Purposes

1 CIRD81900 – R&D tax relief: conditions to be satisfied: BIS Guidelines (formerly DTI Guidelines) (2004) – text

These Guidelines are issued by the Secretary of State for the Department of Trade and Industry for the purposes of **Section 837A Income and Corporation Taxes Act 1988**. They replace the previous version issued on 28 July 2000

1. Research and Development ('R&D') is defined for tax purposes in **ICTA88/S837A**.[1] This says the definition of R&D for tax purposes follows GAAP. SSAP13 Accounting for research and development is the SSAP which defines R&D. The accountancy definition is then modified for tax purposes by these guidelines, which are given legal force by Parliamentary Regulations. These guidelines explain what is meant by R&D for a variety of tax purposes, but the rules of particular tax schemes may restrict the qualifying expenditure.[2]
2. In these guidelines a number of terms are used which are intended to have a special meaning for the purpose of the guidelines. Such terms are **highlighted** on first appearance and defined later.

[1] For the purposes of research and development allowances (Part 6 CAA01) this definition is extended to include oil and gas exploration and appraisal as defined in **ICTA88/S837B**. These guidelines apply to this extended definition as well.

[2] The original footnotes 2 and 3 to the 2004 Guidelines (which were not themselves part of the Guidelines) have been removed. This is because those footnotes stated that the qualifying indirect activities (QIAs) listed in para 31 are R&D tax relief depends on a number of factors, but there is no blanket exclusion. For further explanation see, for example, HMRC guidance at CIRD83000. These revised footnotes are not part of the Guidelines. Revised footnote prepared by Department for Business, Innovation and Skills in consultation with HMRC December 2010.

2 The definition of R&D

3. R&D for tax purposes takes place when a **project** seeks to achieve an advance in science or technology.
4. The activities that **directly contribute** to achieving this advance in science or technology through the resolution of scientific or technological uncertainty are R&D.

5. Certain **qualifying indirect activities** related to the project are also R&D. Activities other than qualifying indirect activities which do not directly contribute to the resolution of the project's scientific or technological uncertainty are not R&D.

3 Advance in Science or Technology

6. An advance in science or technology means an advance in a **overall knowledge or capability** in a field of **science** or **technology** (not a company's own state of knowledge or capability alone). This includes the adaptation of knowledge or capability from another field of science or technology in order to make such an advance where this adaptation was not readily deducible.
7. An advance in science or technology may have tangible consequences (such as a new or more efficient cleaning product, or a process which generates less waste) or more intangible outcomes (new knowledge or cost improvements, for example).
8. A process, material, device, product, service or source of knowledge does not become an advance in science or technology simply because science or technology is used in its creation. Work which uses science or technology but which does not advance scientific or technological capability as a whole is not an advance in science or technology.
9. A project which seeks to, for example:
    1. extend overall knowledge or capability in a field of science or technology; or
    2. create a process, material, device, product or service which incorporates or represents an increase in overall knowledge or capability in a field of science or technology; or
    3. make an **appreciable improvement** to an existing process, material, device, product or service through scientific or technological changes; or
    4. use science or technology to duplicate the effect of an existing process, material, device, product or service in a new or appreciably improved way (e.g. a product that has exactly the same performance characteristics as existing models, but is built in a fundamentally different manner), will therefore be R&D.
10. Even if the advance in science or technology sought by a project is not achieved or not fully realised, R&D still takes place.
11. If a particular advance in science or technology has already been made or attempted but details are not readily available (for example, if it is a trade secret), work to achieve such an advance can still be an advance in science or technology.
12. However, the routine analysis, copying or adaptation of an existing product, process, service or material, will not be an advance in science or technology.

4 Scientific or technological uncertainty

13. Scientific or technological uncertainty exists when knowledge of whether something is scientifically possible or technologically feasible, or how to achieve it in practice, is not readily available or deducible by a competent professional working in the field. This includes **system uncertainty**. Scientific or technological uncertainty will often arise from turning something that has already been established as scientifically feasible into a cost-effective, reliable and reproducible process, material, device, product or service.
14. Uncertainties that can readily be resolved by a competent professional working in the field are not scientific or technological uncertainties. Similarly, improvements, optimisations and fine-tuning which do not materially affect the underlying science or technology do not constitute work to resolve scientific or technological uncertainty.

5 Other definitions

6 Science

15. Science is the systematic study of the nature and behaviour of the physical and material universe. Work in the arts, humanities and social sciences, including economics, is not science for the purpose of these guidelines. Mathematical techniques are frequently used in science, but mathematical advances in and of themselves are not science unless they are advances in representing the nature and behaviour of the physical and material universe.
16. These guidelines apply equally to work in any branch or field of science.

7 Technology

17. Technology is the practical application of scientific principles and knowledge, where 'scientific' is based on the definition of science above.
18. These guidelines apply equally to work in any branch or field of technology.

8 Project

19. A project consists of a number of activities conducted to a method or plans in order to achieve an advance in science or technology. It is important to get the boundaries of the project correct. It should encompass all the activities that collectively serve to resolve the scientific or technological uncertainty associated with achieving the advance, so it could include a number of different sub-projects. A project may itself be part of a larger commercial project, but that does not make the parts of

the commercial project that do not address scientific or technological uncertainty into R&D.

9 Overall knowledge or capability

20. Overall knowledge or capability in a field of science or technology means the knowledge or capability in the field that is publicly available or is readily deducible from the publicly available knowledge or capability by a competent professional working in the field. Work that seeks an advance relative to this overall knowledge or capability is R&D.
21. Overall knowledge or capability in a field of science or technology can still be advanced (and hence R&D can still be done) in situations where:
    -
        - several companies are working at the cutting edge in the same field, and are doing similar work independently; or
        - work has already been done but this is not known in general because it is a trade secret, and another company repeats the work; or
        - it is known that a particular advance in science or technology has been achieved, but the details of how are not readily available.
22. However, the routine analysis, copying or adaptation of an existing process, material, device, product or service will not advance overall knowledge or capability, even though it may be completely new to the company or the company's trade.

10 Appreciable improvement

23. Appreciable improvement means to change or adapt the scientific or technological characteristics of something to the point where it is 'better' than the original. The improvement should be more than a minor or routine upgrading, and should represent something that would generally be acknowledged by a competent professional working in the field as a genuine and non-trivial improvement. Improvements arising from the adaptation of knowledge or capability from another field of science or technology are appreciable improvements if they would generally be acknowledged by a competent professional working in the field as a genuine and non-trivial improvement.
24. Improvements that arise from taking existing science or technology and deploying it in a new context (e.g. a different trade) with only minor or routine changes are not appreciable improvements. A process, material, device, product or service will not be appreciably improved if it simply brings a company into line with overall knowledge or capability in science or technology, even though it may be completely new to the company or the company's trade.
25. The question of what scale of advance would constitute an appreciable improvement will differ between fields of science and technology and

will depend on what a competent professional working in the field would regard as a genuine and non-trivial improvement.

11 Directly contribute

26. To directly contribute to achieving an advance in science or technology, an activity (or several activities in combination) must attempt to resolve an element of the scientific or technological uncertainty associated with achieving the advance.
27. Activities which directly contribute to R&D include:
    1.
        1. activities to create or adapt software, materials or equipment needed to resolve the scientific or technological uncertainty, provided that the software, material or equipment is created or adapted solely for use in R&D;
        2. scientific or technological planning activities; and
        3. scientific or technological design, testing and analysis undertaken to resolve the scientific or technological uncertainty.
28. Activities which do not directly contribute to the resolution of scientific or technological uncertainty include:
    1.
        1. the range of commercial and financial steps necessary for innovation and for the successful development and marketing of a new or appreciably improved process, material, device, product or service;
        2. work to develop non-scientific or non-technological aspects of a new or appreciably improved process, material, device, product or service;
        3. the production and distribution of goods and services;
        4. administration and other supporting services;
        5. general support services (such as transportation, storage, cleaning, repair, maintenance and security); and
        6. qualifying indirect activities.

12 System uncertainty

29. System uncertainty is scientific or technological uncertainty that results from the complexity of a system rather than uncertainty about how its individual components behave. For example, in electronic devices, the characteristics of individual components or chips are fixed, but there can still be uncertainty about the best way to combine those components to achieve an overall effect. However, assembling a number of components (or software sub-programs) to an established pattern, or following routine methods for doing so, involves little or no scientific or technological uncertainty.

30. Similarly, work on combining standard technologies, devices, and/or processes can involve scientific or technological uncertainty even if the principles for their integration are well known. There will be scientific or technological uncertainty if a competent professional working in the field cannot readily deduce how the separate components or sub-systems should be combined to have the intended function.

13 Qualifying indirect activity

31. These are activities which form part of a project but do not directly contribute to the resolution of the scientific or technological uncertainty. They are:
    1.
        1. scientific and technical information services, insofar as they are conducted for the purpose of R&D support (such as the preparation of the original report of R&D findings);
        2. indirect supporting activities such as maintenance, security, administration and clerical activities, and finance and personnel activities, insofar as undertaken for R&D;
        3. ancillary activities essential to the undertaking of R&D (e.g. taking on and paying staff, leasing laboratories and maintaining research and development equipment including computers used for R&D purposes);
        4. training required to directly support an R&D project;
        5. research by students and researchers carried out at universities;
        6. research (including related data collection) to devise new scientific or technological testing, survey, or sampling methods, where this research is not R&D in its own right; and
        7. feasibility studies to inform the strategic direction of a specific R&D activity.
32. Activities not described in paragraph 31 are not qualifying indirect activities.

14 Commentary on particular questions which arise
15 Start and end of R&D

33. R&D begins when work to resolve the scientific or technological uncertainty starts, and ends when that uncertainty is resolved or work to resolve it ceases. This means that work to identify the requirements for the process, material, device, product or service, where no scientific or technological questions are at issue, is not R&D.
34. R&D ends when knowledge is codified in a form usable by a competent professional working in the field, or when a prototype or pilot plant with all the functional characteristics of the final process, material, device, product or service is produced.

35. Although the R&D for a process, material, device, product or service may have ended, new problems which involve scientific or technological uncertainty may emerge after it has been turned over to production or put into use. The resolution of these problems may require new R&D to be carried out. But there is a distinction to be drawn between such problems and routine fault fixing.

16 Planning as part of R&D

36. Scientific or technological planning activities associated with a project directly contribute to resolving the scientific or technological uncertainty associated with the project, and are therefore R&D. These include defining scientific or technological objectives, assessing scientific or technological feasibility, identifying particular scientific or technological uncertainties, estimating development time, schedule, and resources of the R&D, and high-level outlining of the scientific or technical work, as well as the detailed planning and management of the work.
37. Elements of a company's planning activity relating to a project but not directly contributing to the resolution of scientific or technological uncertainty, such as identifying or researching market niches in which R&D might benefit a company, or examination of a project's financial, marketing, and legal aspects, fall outside the category of scientific or technological planning, and are therefore not R&D.

17 Abortive projects

38. Not all projects succeed in their aims. What counts is whether there is an intention to achieve an advance in science or technology, not whether ultimately the associated scientific or technological uncertainty is completely resolved, or resolved to the degree intended. Scientific or technological planning activities associated with projects which are not taken forward (e.g. because of insurmountable technical or commercial challenges) are still R&D.

18 Prototypes, pilot plants

39. A prototype is an original model on which something new or appreciably improved is patterned, and of which all things of the same type are representations or copies. It is a basic experimental model possessing the essential characteristics of the intended process, material, device, product or service. The design, construction, and testing of prototypes generally fall within the scope of R&D for tax purposes. But once any modifications necessary to reflect the test findings have been made to the prototypes, and further testing has been satisfactorily completed, the

scientific or technological uncertainty has been resolved and further work will not be R&D.

40. Similarly the construction and operation of pilot plants while assessing their operations is R&D until the scientific or technological uncertainty associated with the intended advance in science or technology has been resolved.

19 Design

41. When achieving design objectives requires the resolution of scientific or technological uncertainty within a project, work to do this will be R&D. Design activities which do not directly contribute to the resolution of scientific or technological uncertainty within a project are not R&D.

20 Cosmetic and aesthetic effects

42. Cosmetic and aesthetic qualities are not of themselves science or technology, and so work to improve the cosmetic or aesthetic appeal of a process, material, device, product or service would not in itself be R&D. However, work to create a desired cosmetic or aesthetic effect through the application of science or technology can require a scientific or technological advance, and resolving the scientific or technological uncertainty associated with such a project would therefore be R&D.

21 Content delivered through science or technology

43. Information or other content that is delivered through a scientific or technological medium is not of itself science or technology. However, improvements in scientific or technological means to create, manipulate and transfer information or other content can be scientific or technological advances, and resolving the scientific or technological uncertainty associated with such projects would therefore be R&D.

22 Examples/Illustrations

Examples in these guidelines are illustrative, designed to cast light on the principles explained in the guidelines, and should be read in that context.

23 A. The R&D process

A1. A company conducts extensive market research to learn what technical and design characteristics a new DVD player should have in order to be an appealing product. This work is not R&D (paragraph 37). However, it does identify a potential project to create a DVD player incorporating a number of technological improvements that the company's R&D staff (who are competent professionals) regards as genuine and non-trivial. This project would be seeking to develop an appreciably improved DVD player (paragraphs 23 – 25) and would therefore be seeking to achieve an advance in science or technology (paragraph 9 (c)).

A2. The company then decides on a detailed specification for the desired new product, and devises a plan for developing it. Some elements of this plan involve planning of activities that directly contribute to resolving the project's scientific or technological uncertainties (such as the system uncertainty associated with an improved control mechanism for the laser that 'reads' the DVD). This element of planning is R&D (paragraph 36), as are the activities themselves (paragraph 4). Other elements of the plan focus on obtaining intellectual property protection or cosmetic design decisions, for example, which do not directly contribute to resolving the project's scientific or technological uncertainties and are not qualifying indirect activities (paragraph 31) and are therefore not R&D. Neither this planning (paragraph 37) nor these activities (paragraph 28) are R&D.

A3. The scientific or technological work culminates in the creation of a series of prototype DVD players, and ultimately a 'final' prototype is produced and tested which possesses the essential characteristics of the intended product (circuit board design, performance characteristics, etc.). All the activities that directly contributed to resolving the scientific or technological uncertainty of creating the DVD player up to this point (such as the testing of successive prototypes) are R&D (paragraphs 34 and 39).

A4. Several copies of this prototype are made (not R&D; paragraphs 4–5 and 26–28) and distributed to a group of consumers to test their reactions (not R&D; paragraph 28 (a)). Some of these consumers report concerns about the noise level of the DVD player in operation. Additional work is done to resolve this problem. If this involves a routine adjustment of the existing prototype (i.e. no scientific or technological uncertainty) then it will not be R&D (paragraph 14); if it involves more substantial changes (i.e. there is scientific or technological uncertainty to resolve) then it will be R&D.

24 B. Equal applicability in any branch or field of science or technology

B1. The guidelines apply equally to work in any branch or field of science or technology (paragraphs 15 – 18). This means that work in software engineering, for example, is subject to the same fundamental criteria for being R&D as work in textile science, or nanotechnology, or anything else.

B2. This equality also applies to the methods used to resolve scientific or technological uncertainty. For example, it is sometimes possible to implement functionality in a product or process by means of software or of hardware. As long as the scientific or technological uncertainty cannot readily be resolved by a competent professional working in the field, hardware and software methods are both equally R&D in these circumstances.

25 C. Abortive projects

C1. Not all projects achieve the advance in science or technology they are seeking. For example, work to insert a particular gene into a gene sequence may simply fail, while an attempt to appreciably increase the life of a battery may only yield a marginal improvement. In both cases, the project seeks to achieve an advance in science or technology and work to resolve the scientific or technological uncertainty would be R&D (paragraph 10).

26 D. Advance in science or technology

D1. Searching for the molecular structures of possible new drugs would be an advance in science or technology, because it applies existing knowledge of science (which compounds are known to cause particular physiological effects) in search of new or improved active compounds (paragraph 9(b)). This is true even if the method used to search for those molecular structures (e.g. running a computer program on a particular set of data) is itself entirely routine; the activity directly contributes to the resolution of scientific or technological uncertainty (paragraph 27(c)) and so would be R&D (paragraph 4). Work to identify new uses of existing compounds would also be creative work in science or technology, because it seeks new scientific knowledge about those molecules (paragraph 9(a)).

D2. However, the development of software intended for the analysis of market research data (which is not scientific or technological knowledge; paragraphs 15 – 18) which was not expected to result in the development of a scientific or technological advance in the field of software as a whole (such as an algorithm which extends overall knowledge or capability in the field of software) would not be R&D (paragraph 8). Work to adapt such software to analyse, say, customer-spending patterns would also not be R&D.

D3. An advance in science or technology need not imply an absolute improvement in the performance of a process, material, device, product or service. For example, the existence of high-fidelity audio equipment does not prevent a project to create lower-performance equipment from being an advance in science or technology (for instance, if it incorporated technological improvements leading to lower cost through more efficient circuit design or speaker construction) (paragraph 9(d)).

27 E. Scientific or technological uncertainty

E1. A firm's project involves finding a new active ingredient for weed-killer (an advance in overall knowledge or capability in the particular field of science or technology; paragraphs 6, 20), and developing a formula incorporating the new active ingredient for use in a commercial product (paragraph 9(b) or (c)). Both of these would constitute an advance in science or technology.

E2. In order to achieve this advance, a programme of investigation by computer to pick likely ingredients and the systematic testing of possible ingredients and products based on those 'trial' ingredients is undertaken. The work involves the adaptation of existing software to tackle the specific problem, and product formulation and testing using established methods. This investigation and testing evaluates the weed-killing performance and other relevant characteristics of the formulations (for example, toxicity to humans and wildlife, water solubility, adhesion to weeds, damage done to other plants). All of these activities would therefore be R&D (paragraphs 4, 26, 27).

E3. The company also does work to assess what characteristics a new weed-killing product should have in order to appeal to consumers. This activity does not directly contribute to the resolution of scientific or technological uncertainty (paragraph 28(a)) and is not a qualifying indirect activity (paragraph 31), and is therefore not R&D (paragraph 4).

28 F. Direct contribution to the resolution of scientific or technological uncertainty

F1. Work to compare the effectiveness of two possible designs for controlling part of a new manufacturing process would directly contribute to resolving the scientific or technological uncertainty inherent in the new process, and hence the activity would be R&D (paragraphs 4, 26). But work to raise finance for the project, while indirectly contributing to the resolution of scientific or technological uncertainty (e.g. by paying for work) does not of itself help resolve the uncertainty, and hence is not R&D (paragraph 28(a)). Human Resources work to support the R&D is a qualifying indirect activity (paragraph 31) and hence is also R&D (paragraph 5), though it does not directly contribute to the resolution of scientific or technological uncertainty (paragraph 28(e) and (f)).

29 G. Testing as part of R&D

G1. Scientific or technological testing and analysis, which directly contributes to the resolution of scientific or technological uncertainty, is R&D (paragraph 26). So for example if testing work is carried out as part of the development of a pilot plant, this would be R&D, but once the design of the 'final' pilot plant had been finalised and tested, any further testing would not be R&D (paragraph 39). However, if flaws in the design became apparent later on, then work to remedy them would be R&D if they could not readily be resolved by a competent professional working in the field (in other words, if there was scientific or technological uncertainty around how to fix the problem; paragraph 14).

30 H. Cosmetic and aesthetic effects

H1. A company is seeking to make a water-breathable fabric for use in hiking gear. A test fabric with the required physical characteristics is produced through R&D. This new fabric is then produced in small quantities (not R&D) and market tested with a number of trial users. The user tests are not R&D, because they are concerned with testing the commercial potential of the new material and assessing its appeal to users (paragraph 42).

H2. One of the results of these tests is that users do not like the feel of the new fabric against their skin, and dislike its shiny appearance. The company decides to investigate variants of its new fabric, which require significant changes to the material's weave and physical structure, to overcome these problems. Because there is scientific and technological uncertainty around whether a material with the desired physical characteristics can be made, the R&D continues.

31 J. Project, prototype and end of R&D

J1. A company develops new spark plugs for use in an existing petrol engine. The scientific or technological uncertainty associated with this work is resolved once prototype plugs have been fully tested in the engine. The activities directly contributing to this work, including the construction of prototypes and their testing in the engine, would be R&D.

J2. The same company decides to design a new engine to incorporate the new spark plugs, involving a new combustion chamber design, lighter materials and other improvements such that the overall engine is appreciably improved (it uses less petrol to achieve slightly greater power output performance, and generates less pollution than current models). The activities directly contributing to this work, including the design of the separate components (not all of which need be different from those used in previous models) and their integration into a new engine, are R&D. The uncertainty associated with this work is resolved, and R&D is complete once a functionally final prototype has been tested.

INDEX

This index has been prepared using Sweet and Maxwell's Legal Taxonomy. Main index entries conform to keywords provided by the Legal Taxonomy except where references to specific documents or non-standard terms (denoted by quotation marks) have been included. These keywords provide a means of identifying similar concepts in other Sweet and Maxwell publications and online services to which keywords from the Legal Taxonomy have been applied. Readers may find some minor differences between terms used in the text and those which appear in the index. Suggestions to *sweetandmaxwell.taxonomy@thomson.com*.

All references are to paragraph number

Accounting periods
  corporation tax, 10–011—10–012
Accounts
  adjusted accounts
    self-employment, 9–048
  amortisation, 21–011, 21–028
  change of accounting policy, 21–028
  intangible fixed assets
    amortisation, 21–011, 21–028
    fixed assets, 15–008
    generally, 15–007
    intangible assets, 15–009
    useful economic life, 21–011
    valuation, 21–010
  performers, 27–031
  research and development
    fixed assets, 15–008
    generally, 15–007
    goodwill, 15–009
    intangible assets, 15–009
  reversal of previous accounting loss, 21–027
  self-assessment, 9–015
  self-employment, 9–048
  sportsmen, 27–031
  true and fair value, 12–030—12–033
  useful economic life, 21–011
  valuation, 12–028, 21–010
Accumulation trusts
  taxation of income, 10–018
Acquired royalties *see* **Royalties**
Acquisitions
  shares
    roll-over relief, 21–042
    software for distribution, 29–006
Actors *see* **Performers**
Adjustment
  capital expenditure
    research and development, 15–012

  sportspersons, 27–032
  transfer pricing, 13–010
Advance royalties *see* **Royalties**
Advertising
  franchising
    franchisee, 28–027
    franchisor, 28–014
Agency workers
  employment status, 27–018
Allowances
  see also **Capital allowances**
  employee taxation, 9–042
  fixed rate allowances
    corporate intangible fixed assets, 21–022
  pension schemes
    annual allowances, 23–025
    lifetime allowance, 23–026
  personal allowances, 9–003
  research and development, 15–002, 15–011
Amortisation
  accounts, 21–011, 21–028
  following part realisation
    anti-avoidance, 21–032
    change of accounting policy, 21–028
    corporate partners, 21–036
    generally, 21–023
    method of giving credits and debits, 21–033—21–035
    negative goodwill, 21–026
    realisation, 21–029—21–031
    revaluations, 21–025
    reversal of previous accounting loss, 21–027
    rollover relief on acquisition of shares, 21–042
    rollover relief on reinvestment, 21–037—21–040
    taxable receipts, 21–024
  franchising, 28–010

693

generally, 21–020—21–021
"Angels"
taxation, 27–034
Animal varieties
biotechnology protection, 8–004
Annual allowances
pension schemes, 23–025
Annual payments
patents, 16–002—16–008
self-employment, 9–056—9–057
Anti-avoidance
see also **Tax avoidance**
corporate intangible fixed assets, 21–032
international tax planning, 24–059—24–060
Patent Box, 22–037—22–038
targeted anti-avoidance rule (TAAR)
corporation tax, 10–002
Applications
design protection, 3–003—3–004
trade marks
content, 4–006
distinctiveness, 4–007
geographical indications, 4–006
opposition, 4–008
publication, 4–008
search, 4–007
Apportionment
controlled foreign companies, 14–020
non-resident entertainers and sportsmen, 27–051—27–052
Arbitration
transfer pricing, 13–013
Arm's length transactions
transfer pricing, 13–018, 13–028
Assets see **Intangible fixed assets**
ordinary business, 15–012
Assignment
copyright, 18–007—18–015
design right, 5–009
patents, 2–019
trade marks, 4–013
Athletes see **Sportspersons**
Authors
case study, CS1–001—CS1–015
casual authors
copyright, 18–016
deductions, 18–023—18–025
international tax planning, 24–025
Averaging profits
copyright, 18–017
designs, 17–003—17–005
Balancing adjustments
see also **Capital allowances**
research and development, 15–012
Belgium
effective rate of taxation, 22–001
Benefits in kind
employee taxation, 9–039

Berne Convention for the Protection of Literary and Artistic Works 1886
copyright protection, 5–015
Biotechnology
application of intellectual property rights
animal varieties, 8–004
copyright, 8–005
enerally, 8–002
morality, 8–003
patents, 8–005
plant varieties, 8–004
Brand names
valuation, 12–018
Broadcasting
application of intellectual property rights, 8–010—8–011
package deals, 26–010
Building societies
intangible fixed assets, 21–058
Business activities see **Economic activities**
Capital allowances
copyright, 18–035
fixed rate allowances
intangible fixed assets, 21–022
know-how, 19–014
patents, 16–037—16–038
self-employment, 9–051—9–052
software, 29–008
Capital expenditure
research and development
adjustment, 15–012
allowances, 15–011
assets acquired for ordinary business, 15–012
balancing adjustments, 15–012
qualifying expenditure, 15–012
Capital gains
individuals, 9–072
Capital gains tax
individuals
capital gains, 9–072
capital losses, 9–072
de minimis exemption, 9–071
entrepreneurs' relief, 9–073—9–075
generally, 9–070—9–071
losses, 9–073, 9–076
other provisions, 9–080
residence, 9–020
restructuring of companies, 9–078
roll-over relief, 9–079
transfers between spouses, 9–077
patents, 16–044
settlors
international tax planning, 24–054—24–057
tax planning
generally, 23–019
trusts, 23–031
trusts, 10–020

INDEX

Capital losses
  capital gains tax
    individuals, 9–072
Capital receipts
  patents, 16–028—16–035
  performers, 27–037
  sportspersons, 27–037
Capital transfer tax *see* **Inheritance tax**
Cash flows
  discounted cash flow
    valuation, 12–009
Certification marks
  nature, 4–002
  nature of, 4–002
Channel Islands
  tax havens, 24–032
Character merchandising
  case study, CS6–001—CS6–007
  copyright, 5–013
  taxation, 20–002
Charges
  corporation tax, 10–005
Clearances
  controlled foreign companies, 14–019
  degrouping
    intangible fixed assets, 21–057
Close companies
  inheritance tax, 9–094
Cloud computing
  meaning, 29–005
  nature of concept, 29–005
  taxation, 29–005
Codes of conduct
  franchising, 28–006—28–007
Collective marks
  nature of, 4–002
Commercial activities
  copyright
    character merchandising, 5–013
    licensing, 5–012
  designs, 3–008
  introduction, 7–001
  meaning, 7–001
  policy
    development, 7–002—7–003
    implementation, 7–004
    reputation, 7–004
  taxation, 7–001
  trade marks
    assignment, 4–013
    franchising, 4–014
    generally, 4–011
    licensing, 4–012
Common law
  endorsement, 6–009
  introduction, 6–001
  know-how and show-how, 6–008
  unfair competition
    copyright, 6–005

    generally, 6–002—6–003
    lotteries, 6–006
    misleading and comparative advertising, 6–005
    passing off, 6–004—6–005
    patents, 6–003
    raising actions, 6–007
    registered designs, 6–004
    trade marks, 6–004
Community patents
  introduction, 2–031
Companies *see* **Controlled foreign companies; Corporation tax; Large companies; Small and medium-sized enterprises; Tax planning**
Comparative advertising
  unfair competition law, 6–005
Compensation
  entertainers, 27–035
  sportspersons, 27–035
Composers
  case study, CS9–001—CS9–016
Computer games
  research and development, 15–041
Computer software *see* **Software**
Computers
  application of intellectual property rights
    databases, 8–008
    digital copying, 8–005
    hardware, 8–008
    software, 8–008
    trade marks, 8–009
Connected persons
  research and development, 15–020
  transfer pricing, 13–004—13–006
Consumable goods
  research and development, 15–018
Controlled foreign companies
  apportionment, 14–020
  cell companies, 14–020
  control, 14–004—14–005
  creditable tax, 14–024
  definition, 14–002
  double charges, 14–026
  excluded territories
    generally, 14–015
    low profits, 15–017
    tax, 14–018
  exclusions
    clearances, 14–019
    excluded territories, 14–015
    finance companies, 14–012
    foreign systems, 14–027
    introduction, 14–001
    residence, 14–003
    temporary period of exemption, 14–014
  gateways
    captive insurance, 14–010

non-trading finance profits, 14–008
overview, 14–006
profits attributable to UK activities, 14–007
solo consolidation, 14–011
trading finance profits, 14–009
intangible fixed assets, 21–060—21–061
meaning, 14–002
profits, 14–021—14–023

Copyright
averaging profits, 18–017
biotechnology, 8–005
broadcasting, 8–010—8–011
bursaries, 18–029—18–031
capital allowances, 18–035
capital taxes, 18–076
casual authors, 18–016
casual receipts, 18–014—18–015
commercial activities
　character merchandising, 5–013
　licensing, 5–012
computers, 8–007—8–009
conclusion, 5–017
deductions, 18–018–18–025
deferred revenue expenditure, 18–036—18–042
duration, 5–005
expenses, 18–034
film products, 18–049—18–060
film related trading losses, 18–061—18–065
film tax relief, 18–061—18–065
films
　GAAP partnerships, 18–068—18–070
franchising, 8–013
from of protection, 5–004—5–005
grants, 18–027—18–028
international copyright
　Berne Convention, 5–015
　overview, 5–014
　Universal Copyright Convention, 5–017
introduction, 5–001, 18–001
leasing, 18–033
musical works, 5–003
obtaining protection, 5–002—5–003
ownership, 5–003
post-cessation expenses, 18–006
post-cessation receipts, 18–005
prizes, 18–027—18–028
professional income
　generally, 18–002—18–003
　public lending right, 18–032
　publishing income, 18–014—18–015
　realisation of investments, 18–026
　sound recordings, 18–061, 18–071—18–075
　stamp duty, 18–077
　VAT, 18–078
qualified person, 5–003
settlements, 8–012, 18–066—18–067
stamp duty, 18–077
taxation
　acquired royalties, 18–004

Arts Council awards, 18–029—18–031
assignment of copyright, 18–007—18–015
three-dimensional marks, 5–001
unfair competition law, 6–005

Corporate intangible fixed assets *see* **Intangible fixed assets**

Corporation tax
accounting periods, 10–011—10–012
background, 10–001
charges on income, 10–005
deductions, 10–009
disclosure of tax avoidance schemes, 10–013
dividend receipt, 10–010
groups of companies, 10–007
losses, 10–004
payments, 10–011
residence, 10–001
sound recordings, 18–075
structure, 10–002
substantial shareholding exemption, 10–008
targeted anti-avoidance rule (TAAR), 10–002
tax rates, 10–003—10–004
trading companies, 10–006

Counterfeits
use, 4–001

Customs value
transfer pricing, 13–035

Databases
protection, 8–008

De minimis
capital gains tax individuals, 9–071

Death benefits
pension schemes, 23–026

Declarations of invalidity
designs, 3–007

Deductions
Copyright
　generally, 18–018—18–025
　introduction, 18–018
　non-resident authors, 18–023—18–025
　non-residents, 18–019—18–025
corporation tax, 10–009
research and development, 15–013

Demergers
intangible fixed assets, 21–051

Design right
assignment, 5–009
development, 5–006—5–011
duration, 5–008
interaction with copyright, 5–010
introduction of, 5–002
licensing, 5–009
meaning, 5–006
scope of protection, 5–007
spare parts and accessories, 5–009

Designs
commercial activities, 3–008
conclusion, 3–012

INDEX

declarations of invalidity, 3–007
form of protection, 3–006
international systems
    European Community design system, 3–010—3–011
    fees, 3–011
    generally, 3–009
    international design deposit system, 3–010
introduction, 3–001
obtaining protection
    applications, 3–003—3–004
    database of applications, 3–005
    individual character, 3–003
    meaning, 3–002
    novelty, 3–003
taxation
    averaging profits, 17–003—17–005
    dealing, 17–012
    expenses, 17–007
    income, 17–002
    introduction, 17–001
    investment income, 17–006
    investments, 17–012
    lump sums, 17–009
    relief to purchaser, 17–010
    royalties, 17–008, 17–011
    stamp duty, 17–013

Digital technology
copyright protection, 8–006

Discounts
investment income
    individual taxation, 9–065

Discretionary trusts
taxation of income, 10–018

Distinctiveness
trade marks, 4–007

Distribution agreements
international tax planning, 24–024

Divers
know-how, 19–016

Dividends
corporation tax, 10–010

Domicile
individual taxation
    business investment relief, 9–038
    generally, 9–028—9–030
    gifts overseas, 9–037
    remittance basis, 9–031—9–036

Dormant companies
transfer pricing, 13–003

Double tax relief
intangible fixed assets, 21–062
international tax planning, 24–017—24–019

Double taxation
controlled foreign companies, 14–026
know-how, 19–019
non-resident entertainers and sportsmen, 27–050
transfer pricing, 13–036—13–037

Drugs
package deals, 26–008—26–009

Dual residence
individuals, 9–027

Duration
copyright, 5–005
design right, 5–008, 5–009

Economic activities
application of intellectual property rights
    biotechnology, 8–002—8–005
    broadcasting, 8–010—8–011
    computers, 8–007—8–009
    conclusions, 8–014
    film, 8–012
    franchising, 8–013
    introduction, 8–001

Electronic filing
self-assessment, 9–013

Emoluments
employee taxation, 9–044

Employees
employees' inventions, 16–039—16–042
individual taxation
    allowances, 9–042
    benefits in kind, 9–040
    emoluments, 9–044
    generally, 9–030
    P11Ds, 9–041
    PAYE, 9–043

Employees' inventions
patents, 16–039—16–042

Employment income
arising basis, 23–021
ex gratia payments, 23–022
generally, 23–020
inducements, 23–023

Employment status
actors, 27–014
agency workers, 27–018
benefit years, 27–020
film industry, 27–017
generally, 27–002—27–012
HMRC guidance, 27–013
musicians, 27–016
sportspersons, 27–021
taxation
    income, 20–007—20–008
    introduction, 20–001
    stamp duty, 20–009
    VAT, 20–010
team players, 27–019
television workers, 27–017
theatrical non-performing workers, 26–016, 27–015

Enterprise investment schemes
patents, 16–043

Entrepreneurs' relief
capital gains tax, 9–073—9–077

Estimates
  self-assessment, 9–011
European companies
  creation by merger
    intangible fixed assets, 21–055
European Patent Office
  generally, 2–030
  role, 2–004
European Union
  design protection, 3–010—3–011
  exports
    VAT, 11–004
Ex gratia payments
  employment income, 23–022
Exempt transfers
  conditionally exempt transfers
    inheritance tax, 9–092
Exhaustion of rights
  patents, 2–024
Expenses
  copyright, 18–034
  designs, 17–007
  franchising
    pre-trading expenses, 28–028
  patents, 16–036
  performers, 27–038
  post-cessation expenses
    copyright, 18–006
  pre-trading expenses
    franchising, 28–028
    research and development, 15–021
  research and development
    minimum expenditure, 15–019
    pre-trading expenses, 15–021
    qualifying expenditure, 15–012, 15–016, 15–026—15–027, 15–031
  software
    development expenditure, 29–013
    revenue expenditure, 29–009
  sportspersons, 27–038
  trade marks, 17–007
Exploitation
  see also **Commercial activities**
  own use
    software, 29–007
Exports
  VAT, 11–004
Fair dealing
  designs, 17–012
  trade marks, 17–012
Film industry
  employment status, 27–017
Films
  application of intellectual property rights, 8–012
  copyright
    GAAP partnerships, 18–068—18–070
    generally, 18–049—18–060
    settlements, 18–066—18–067

    tax relief, 18–049—18–060
    trading losses, 18–061—18–065
  distribution agreements copyright
    international tax planning, 24–024
Finance leasing
  corporate intangible fixed assets, 21–059
Fixed assets
  see also **Intangible fixed assets**
  research and development, 15–008
Food industry
  inventions
    case study, CS7–001—CS7–009
Foreign companies
  degrouping
    intangible fixed assets, 21–056
Foreign legislation
  transfer pricing, 13–012
Foreign partnerships *see* **Overseas partnerships**
Franchising
  advantages
    franchisee, 28–002
    franchisor, 28–001
  agreements, 28–005
  application of intellectual property rights, 8–013
  codes of conduct, 28–006—28–007
  disadvantages
    franchisee, 28–004
    franchisor, 28–003
  franchisee's position
    advertising contributions, 28–027
    deferred revenue expenditure, 28–025—28–026
    generally, 28–019
    initial payment, 28–020—28–024
    pre-trading expenditure, 28–028
  franchisor's tax
    advertising pools, 28–014
    amortisation, 28–010
    analysis of agreement, 28–008
    initial lump sums, 28–009
    know-how, 28–012
    restrictive covenants, 28–011
    royalties, 28–015—28–017
    show-how, 28–013
    turnkey operations, 28–018
  international considerations, 28–030
  trade marks, 4–014
  turnkey operations, 28–018
  VAT, 28–029
Frascati Manual
  research and development, 15–003
Generally Accepted Accounting Principles
  valuation, 12–034
Geographical indications
  trade marks, 4–006

INDEX

Gifts
  domicile
    individual taxation, 9–037
    international tax planning, 24–014—24–015
  reservation of benefits
    inheritance tax, 9–087
Goods
  place of supply
    VAT, 11–003
Goodwill
  intangible fixed assets, 21–026
  negative goodwill
    corporate intangible fixed assets, 21–026
Grants
  copyright, 18–027—18–028
Groups of companies
  corporation tax, 10–007
  intangible fixed assets
    bona fide mergers, 21–052
    building societies, 21–058
    clearance, 21–057
    conditions, 21–049
    demergers, 21–051
    European companies, 21–055
    generally, 21–043—21–045
    group definition, 21–046—21–048
    life assurance business, 21–058
    overseas permanent establishments, 21–056
    relieving provisions, 21–050
    transfer of business, 21–053
    transfer of trade between EU companies, 21–054
  research and development, 15–039
Hardware
  software distinguished, 29–002
Hindsight
  valuation, 12–007
HMRC guidance
  research and development, 15–001
  transfer pricing, 13–008, 13–009
Image rights
  entertainers, 27–053
  sportsmen, 27–053
Income
  Copyright
    generally, 18–002–18–003
    professional income, 18–002—18–003
    publishing income, 18–014—18–015
  deemed income
    individuals, 9–002
  designs
    generally, 17–002
    investment income, 17–006
  employment income
    arising basis, 23–021
    ex gratia payments, 23–022
    generally, 23–020
    inducements, 23–023
  endorsements, 20–007—20–008

know-how, 19–003
land
  from individual taxation, 9–061—9–063
  high value residential property, 9–064
merchandising, 20–003—20–006
not otherwise charged to tax, 23–018
patents, 16–015—16–027
trade marks
  generally, 17–002
  investment income, 17–006
trading income
  current year basis, 23–009
  generally, 23–008
Income tax
  residence, 9–018—9–027
  trusts
    generally, 10–015—10–016
    tax planning, 23–030
Individual character
  designs, 3–003
Individuals
  capital gains tax
    capital gains, 9–072
    capital losses, 9–072
    de minimis exemption, 9–071
    entrepreneurs' relief, 9–073—9–075
    generally, 9–071
    losses, 9–073, 9–076
    other provisions, 9–080
    restructuring of companies, 9–078
    roll-over relief, 9–079
    transfers between spouses, 9–077
  casual profits, 9–069
  deemed income, 9–002
  domicile
    business investment relief, 9–038
    generally, 9–028—9–030
    gifts overseas, 9–037
    remittance basis, 9–031—9–036
  employees
    allowances, 9–042
    benefits in kind, 9–040
    emoluments, 9–044
    generally, 9–039
    P11Ds, 9–041
    PAYE, 9–043
  foreign possessions, 9–067, 9–068
  foreign securities, 9–067, 9–068
  general principles, 9–001
  high value residential property, 9–064
  income from land, 9–061—9–063
  inheritance tax
    close companies, 9–094
    conditionally exempt transfers, 9–092
    generally, 9–090
    gifts with reservation of benefits, 9–096
    other provisions, 9–098
    pre-owned assets, 9–097
    reliefs, 9–095

taxpayer's estate, 9–091
trusts, 9–093
investment income
  discounts, 9–065
  interest, 9–065
  taxed investment income, 9–066
national insurance, 9–070
personal allowances, 9–003
rate of tax, 9–004
residence
  capital gains tax, 9–020
  dual residence, 9–027
  income tax, 9–018—9–027
  ordinary residence, 9–001, 9–026
  temporary visitors, 9–026
  UK domiciliaries, 9–002
self-assessment
  accounts
    Submission, 9–015
  amendment of returns, 9–011
  disclosure of tax avoidance schemes, 9–008
  electronic services, 9–013
  estimates, 9–011
  internet services, 9–013
  introduction, 9–005
  mistakes, 9–006
  payment of tax, 9–010
  penalties for incorrect returns, 9–012
  penalties for late payment, 9–010
  post-transaction rulings, 9–016
  repayments, 9–017
  tax enquiries, 9–009
  tax returns, 9–006
self-employment
  adjusted accounts, 9–048
  annual payments, 9–056—9–057
  capital allowances, 9–051—9–052
  cash basis, 9–049—9–050
  current year basis, 9–046—9–047
  failure to deduct tax, 9–058
  generally, 9–045
  high value residential property, 9–064
  loss relief, 9–053—9–054
  pure income profits, 9–059—9–060
Inducements
employment income, 23–023
performers, 27–036
sportspersons, 27–036
Infringement
patents, 2–015, 2–016
trade marks, 4–010
Inheritance tax
close companies, 9–094
conditionally exempt transfers, 9–092
copyright, 18–076
generally, 9–091
gifts with reservation of benefits, 9–096
other provisions, 9–098
patents, 16–045

pre-owned assets, 9–097
reliefs, 9–095
taxpayer's estate, 9–091
trusts, 9–093, 10–022—10–023
Insurance companies
research and development, 15–039
Intangible assets
see also **Intangible fixed assets**
transfer pricing, 13–029—13–030
Intangible fixed assets
accounts
  amortisation, 21–011
  useful economic life, 21–011
  valuation, 21–010
allowable costs, 21–018—21–019
amortisation
  accounting issues, 21–011
  generally, 21–020—21–021
amortisation following part realisation
  anti-avoidance, 21–032
  change of accounting policy, 21–028
  corporate partners, 21–036
  generally, 21–023
  method of giving credits and debits, 21–033—21–035
  negative goodwill, 21–026
  realisation, 21–029—21–031
  revaluations, 21–025
  reversal of previous accounting loss, 21–027
  rollover relief on acquisition of shares, 21–042
  rollover relief on reinvestment, 21–037—21–040
  taxable receipts, 21–024
commencement of regime, 21–014—21–015
controlled foreign companies, 21–060—21–061
degrouping
  bona fide mergers, 21–052
  building societies, 21–058
  clearance, 21–057
  conditions, 21–049
  demergers, 21–051
  European companies, 21–055
  generally, 21–043—21–045
  group definition, 21–046—21–048
  life assurance business, 21–058
  overseas permanent establishments, 21–056
  relieving provisions, 21–050
  transfer of business, 21–053
  transfer of trade between EU companies, 21–054
double tax relief, 21–062
excluded assets, 21–006—21–008
finance leasing, 21–059
fixed rate allowance, 21–022
impairment losses, 21–013
introduction, 21–001
meaning, 21–005, 21–009
negative goodwill, 21–026

INDEX

royalties
  allowable costs, 21–018—21–019
  date of acquisition, 21–017
  generally, 21–016—21–019
scope, 21–002
smaller entities, 21–012
tax basis, 21–003—21–004
transitional provisions, 21–014—21–015
value shifting, 21–063

Intellectual property
  characteristics, 1–001—1–004

Interest
  individual taxation, 9–065
  transfer pricing, 13–007

International law
  franchising, 28–030
  transfer pricing, 13–014—13–016

International tax planning
  anti-avoidance provisions, 24–059—24–060
  authors, 24–025
  capital gains tax charge on settlor, 24–054—24–057
  designs
    European Community design system, 3–010—3–011
    generally, 3–009
    international design deposit system, 3–010
  dividend routing, 24–026
  double tax relief, 24–017—24–019
  film distribution agreements, 24–024
  foreign partnerships
    assessment of foreign income, 24–010
    control and management, 24–009
    generally, 24–004—24–006
  gains of non-resident settlements
    generally, 24–045—24–046
    payments by and to companies, 24–048—24–049
    supplementary charge, 24–047
    trustees ceasing to be resident in UK, 24–050—24–053
  introduction, 25–001
  limbo trusts, 24–058
  loan routing, 24–027
  non-residents, 24–002
  overseas rights, 24–003
  remittance basis
    generally, 24–011—24–013
    gifts overseas, 24–014—24–015
  royalty structures, 24–020—24–023
  tax havens
    Channel Islands, 24–032
    generally, 24–028
    Isle of Man, 24–032
    Liechtenstein, 24–030
    Luxembourg, 24–030
    other tax havens, 24–034
    Republic of Ireland, 24–033
    Switzerland, 24–029

trademarks
  Berne Convention, 5–015
  Universal Copyright Convention, 5–017
transfers of assets abroad
  generally, 24–035—24–037
  liability of non-transferors, 24–038—24–042
  power to obtain information, 24–043
  withholding tax, 24–016

Internet
  cloud computing, 29–005
  globalisation, 29–001
  new media, 29–003, 29–004
  software, 29–004

Inventions
  nature of, 2–002

Inventors
  case study, CS2–001—CS2–012

Investment income
  copyright, 18–026
  designs, 17–006
  discounts, 9–065
  interest, 9–065
  performers, 27–033
  sportspersons, 27–033
  tax planning, 23–010—23–011
  taxed investment income, 9–066
  trade marks, 17–006

Investments
  designs, 17–012
  trade marks, 17–012

Ireland
  effective rate of taxation, 22–001

Isle of Man
  tax havens, 24–032

"Keyman insurance"
  pension schemes, 23–028

Know-how
  common law protection, 6–008
  franchising, 8–013, 28–012
  taxation
    capital allowances, 19–014
    commercial know-how, 19–015
    divers, 19–016
    double taxation, 19–019
    income, 19–003
    introduction, 19–001
    meaning, 19–002
    sale for lump sum, 19–004—19–012
    stamp duty, 19–017
    tax planning, 19–013
    VAT, 19–018

Large companies
  research and development
    qualifying expenditure, 15–026
    tax relief, 15–025

Leasing
  copyright, 18–033

Letters patent *see* **Patents**

Licensing
  copyright, 5–012
  design right, 5–009
  patents, 2–020—2–023
  trade marks, 4–012
Liechtenstein
  tax havens, 24–030
Life assurance companies
  degrouping
    intangible fixed assets, 21–058
Life interests
  taxation of income, 10–017
Lifetime allowances
  pension schemes, 23–026
Limited liability partnerships
  basis of taxation, 9–087—9–089
  disguised employment relationships, 9–088
  reform proposals, 9–088—9–089
Limited partnerships
  basis of taxation, 9–086
Loss relief
  self-employment, 9–053—9–054
Losses
  capital gains tax
    individuals, 9–073, 9–076
  film copyright, 18–061—18–065
  non-trading losses
    tax planning, 23–015
  tax planning
    generally, 23–012, 23–013—23–014
    non-trading losses, 23–015
    trading losses, 23–013—23–014
Lotteries
  unfair competition law, 6–006
Lump sum payments
  designs, 17–009
  know-how, 19–004—19–012
  trade marks, 17–009
Luxembourg
  effective rate of taxation, 22–001
  tax havens, 24–031
"Madrid protocol system"
  trade mark protection, 4–019
Manufacturing agreements
  case study, CS4–001—CS4–011
  common control, 26–006
  generally, 26–002
  licensee's position, 26–005
  licensor's position, 26–003—26–004
Market value
  valuation, 12–002–12–003, 12–016
Medical research
  vaccine research
    tax credits, 15–029
    tax relief, 15–001, 15–029
Medical treatment
  Patent Box, 22–020

Merchandising
  taxation
    character merchandising, 20–002
    income, 20–003—20–006
    introduction, 20–001
    stamp duty, 20–009
    VAT, 20–010
Mergers
  intangible fixed assets
    European companies, 21–055
    generally, 21–052
Misleading advertising
  unfair competition law, 6–005
Morality
  biotechnology protection, 8–003
Musical works
  copyright protection, 5–003
National insurance
  individual taxation, 9–070
  performers, 27–022
  sportspersons, 27–022
Netherlands
  effective rate of taxation, 22–001
  Innovation Box, 22–001
Non-residents
  deductions
    authors, 18–023—18–025
    generally, 18–019—18–025
  international tax planning, 24–002
  performers
    apportionment, 27–051—27–052
    double taxation agreements, 27–050
    generally, 27–047—27–048
    payments in kind, 27–051—27–052
    reduced withholding payments, 27–049
  settlement gains
    generally, 24–045—24–046
    payments by and to companies,
      24–048—24–049
    supplementary charge, 24–047
    trustees ceasing to be resident in UK,
      24–050—24–053
Novelty
  designs, 3–003
OECD guidelines
  transfer pricing
    generally, 13–009
    methods to arrive at arm's length price,
      13–018
    profit methods, 13–023—13–027
    transaction-based methods, 13–019—13–022
Office for Harmonisation in the Internal Market
  role of, 4–016—4–018
Opposition
  trade marks, 4–008
Overseas partnerships
  assessment of foreign income, 24–010
  basis of taxation, 9–084

INDEX

control and management, 24–009
generally, 24–004—24–006
P11D
   employee taxation, 9–041
"Package deals"
   broadcasting, 26–010
   drugs, 26–008—26–009
   introduction, 26–001
   manufacturing agreements
     common control, 26–006
     generally, 26–002
     licensee's position, 26–005
     licensor's position, 26–003—26–004
   publishing deals, 26–007
   recording agreements, 26–011
Paris Convention for the Protection of Industrial Property 1883
   international patent systems, 2–026—2–027
Partnerships
   corporate partnerships, 9–085
   disguised employment relationships, 9–088
   foreign partnerships
     assessment of foreign income, 24–010
     basis of taxation, 9–084
     control and management, 24–009
     generally, 24–004—24–006
   limited liability partnerships, 9–087—9–089
   limited partnerships, 9–086
   non-resident partners, 9–082
   performers, 27–042
   reform proposals, 9–088—9–089
   self-assessment, 9–014, 9–081, 9–082
   sportspersons, 27–042
Passing off
   unfair competition law, 6–004—6–005
Patent applications
   examination, 2–011
   generally, 2–009
   search, 2–010
Patent attorneys
   role, 2–012
Patent Box
   active ownership condition, 22–011
   anti-avoidance, 22–037—22–038
   availability, 22–002, 22–003
   background, 22–001
   calculation of profits of a trade, 22–013
   cost-sharing arrangements, 22–039
   development condition, 22–008—22–010
   elections, 22–001, 22–004, 22–012
   introduction, 22–001
   losses, 22–034—22–036
   marketing assets return figure, 22–026—22–029
   meaning, 22–001
   mechanics of relief, 22–033
   medical treatment, 22–020
   outline, 22–002—22–003
   profits
     calculation, 22–022—22–024

     pre-grant profits, 22–030
     qualifying residual profit, 22–025, 22–026—22–029
   qualification, 22–005
   qualifying intellectual property, 22–006—22–007
   relevant intellectual property income, 22–015—22–017
   residual profit, 22–025
   routine deductions, 22–025
   royalties, 22–021
   scope, 22–001
   software, 22–018—22–019
   special regime, 22–001
   total gross income of trade, 22–014
   transfer of income streams, 22–031—22–032
Patent Cooperation Treaty 1970
   scope, 2–028—2–029
Patentability
   inventions, 2–006—2–007
Patents
   biotechnology, 8–005
   commercial activities
     assignment, 2–019
     exhaustion, 2–024
     introduction, 2–018
     licensing, 2–020—2–023
   conclusion, 2–036
   description, 2–003
   form of protection, 2–013—2–017
   international systems
     International Convention, 2–026—2–027
     introduction, 2–025
     Patent Cooperation Treaty, 2–028—2–029
     United States, 2–032—2–033
   introduction, 2–001, 2–005
   inventions
     nature of, 2–002
     novelty, 2–008
   patent agents, 2–012
   patent applications, 2–009—2–011
   patent attorneys, 2–012
   Patent Offices, 2–004
   patentability, 2–006—2–007
   petty patents, 2–034—2–035
   protection
     form, 2–013—2–017
     introduction, 2–005
     novelty, 2–008
     patent agents, 2–012
     patent applications, 2–009—2–011
     patent attorneys, 2–012
     patentability, 2–006—2–007
   stamp duty, 16–046
   taxation
     annual payments, 16–002—16–008
     capital allowances, 16–037—16–038
     capital gains tax, 16–044

capital receipts treated as income, 16–028—16–035
employee awards, 16–039—16–042
enterprise investment schemes, 16–043
expenses, 16–036
foreign patents, 16–013
inheritance tax, 16–045
introduction, 16–001
non-residents, 16–014
patent income, 16–015—16–027
royalties, 16–002—16–012
stamp duty, 16–046
VAT, 16–047—16–048
unfair competition law, 6–003

PAYE
employee taxation, 9–043

Payments
franchising, 28–009, 28–020—28–024
payments in kind
non-resident entertainers and sportsmen, 27–051—27–052

Penalties
self-assessment
incorrect returns, 9–012
late payment, 9–010
transfer pricing, 13–009, 13–010

Pension schemes
annual allowances, 23–025
death benefits, 23–026
generally, 23–024—23–026
keyman insurance, 23–028
lifetime allowance, 23–026
registered pension funds, 23–025
unfunded unapproved schemes, 23–027

Performers
accounts, 27–031
alternative assessments, 27–043
angels, 27–034
anti-constellation provisions, 27–044—27–046
capital receipts, 27–037
case study, CS3–001—CS3–019, CS9–001—CS9–016
company partnerships, 27–042
compensation, 27–035
double taxation agreements, 27–050
employment companies, 27–040—27–041
employment status
actors, 27–014
agency workers, 27–018
film industry, 27–017
general1, 27–002—27–012
musicians, 27–016
television workers, 27–017
theatrical non-performing workers, 27–015
expenses, 27–038
image rights, 27–053
inducements, 27–036
introduction, 27–001
investment income, 27–033

musicians
employment status, 27–017
national insurance, 27–022
non-residents
apportionment, 27–051—27–052
payments in kind, 27–051—27–082
personal service companies (IR35), 27–023—27–025
reduced withholding payments, 27–049
restrictive covenants, 27–026
royalties
advance royalties, 27–032
date royalties payable, 27–027—27–030
small business accounts, 27–031
tax returns, 27–039
VAT, 27–054—27–056

Personal allowances
individual taxation, 9–003

Personal service companies (IR35)
performers, 27–023—27–025
sportspersons, 27–023—27–025

Pharmaceuticals
case study, CS5–001—CS5.006

Place of supply
VAT
goods, 11–003
services, 11–005

Plant varieties
biotechnology protection, 8–004

Post-cessation receipts
copyright, 18–005
tax planning, 23–016—23–017

Pre-owned assets
inheritance tax, 9–088

Pre-trading expenses
franchising, 28–028
research and development, 15–021

Prizes
copyright, 18–027—18–028

Profits
casual profits
individual taxation, 9–069
controlled foreign companies, 14–021—14–023
Patent Box, 22–022—22–024
transfer pricing
calculation of arm's length price, 13–024—13–025
OECD guidelines, 13–023—13–027

Public lending right
taxation, 18–032

Publication
trade marks, 4–008

Publishing
income
copyright, 18–014—18–015
package deals, 26–007

Real property
income from individual taxation, 9–061—9–063

INDEX

Realisation
  intangible fixed assets, 21–029—21–031
  investments
    copyright, 18–026
Receipts
  casual receipts
    copyright, 18–014—18–015
  intangible fixed assets, 21–024
Recovery of tax
  VAT, 11–009
Registered designs
  unfair competition law, 6–004
Registered pension schemes
  tax planning, 23–025
Registrability
  trade marks, 4–005
Registration
  trade marks, 4–002—4–003
Reinvestment relief
  operation, 21–041
Reliefs
  degrouping
    intangible fixed assets, 21–050
  designs, 17–010
  double taxation relief
    intangible fixed assets, 21–062
    international tax planning, 24–017—24–019
  film copyright, 18–049—18–060
  inheritance tax, 9–095
  rate, 15–027
  research and development
    cap, 15–015, 15–030
    computer games, 15–041
    large companies, 15–025
    loss relief, 15–022
    television production, 15–041
  roll-over relief
    acquisition of shares, 21–042
    individuals, 9–079
    reinvestment, 21–041
  small and medium-sized entities, 15–019
  trade marks, 17–010
  trusts, 10–018
  vaccine research, 15–029
Remittance basis
  domicile
    individual taxation, 9–031—9–036
  international tax planning
    generally, 24–011—24–013
    gifts overseas, 24–014—24–015
Republic of Ireland
  tax havens, 24–033
Resale price
  transfer pricing
    calculation of arm's length price, 13–021
Research and development
  accounts
    fixed assets, 15–008
    generally, 15–007
    goodwill, 15–009
    intangible assets, 15–009
  allowances, 15–002
  anti-avoidance, 15–040
  appeals, 15–024
  capital expenditure
    adjustment, 15–012
    allowances, 15–011
    assets acquired for ordinary business, 15–012
    balancing adjustments, 15–012
    qualifying expenditure, 15–012
  commercial activities, 15–006
  computer games, 15–041
  connected persons
    irrevocable election, 15–020
  consumables, 15–018
  deductions, 15–013
  definitions, 15–028
  DTI guidance, 15–001
  Frascati Manual, 15–003
  general activities, 15–006
  groups of companies, 15–039
  HMRC guidance, 15–001
  insurance companies, 15–039
  interpretation, 15–040
  introduction, 15–001
  large companies
    qualifying expenditure, 15–026
    tax relief, 15–025
  meaning, 15–001
  minimum expenditure, 15–019
  pre-trading expenses, 15–021
  qualifying expenditure
    generally, 15–016
    independent R&D, 15–026
    large companies, 15–026
    scope of, 15–031
    sub-contracted research, 15–026
  qualifying supporting activities, 15–006
  reliefs
    scheme for SMEs, 15–014
    super dediction, 15–014
  scientific research allowances, 15–002
  SME tax relief, 15–019
  software, 15–006, 15–018
  SSAP, 15–004—15–005
  SSAP 13, 15–004—15–005
  staffing costs, 15–017
  sub-contracted R&D
    generally, 15–019
    qualifying expenditure, 15–026
  tax credits
    amount of credit, 15–037—15–038
    loss relief, 15–022
    payment of credit, 15–037—15–038
    scheme for SMEs, 15–034, 15–035
    treatment, 15–022—15–023
    vaccine research, 15–029

tax relief
  cap, 15–015, 15–030
  large companies, 15–025
  rate, 15–027
  vaccine research, 15–029
tax treatment, 15–010
television, 15–041
vaccine research
  reliefs, 15–001, 15–029
  tax credits, 15–029
Research and development allowances
research and development, 15–002
Residence
companies, 10–001
controlled foreign companies, 14–003
individuals
  capital gains tax, 9–020
  dual residence, 9–027
  income tax, 9–018–9–027
  ordinary residence, 9–019—9–021, 9–026
  post-April 6, 9–022—9–025, 2013
  temporary visitors, 9–025
temporary visitors, 9–025
Restrictive covenants
franchising, 28–011
performers, 27–026
sportspersons, 27–026
Revaluation
corporate intangible fixed assets, 21–025
Revenue expenditure
copyright, 18–036—18–042
franchising, 28–025—28–026
Reverse charge
VAT, 11–006
Roll-over relief
capital gains tax
  individuals, 9–079
corporate intangible fixed assets
  reinvestment, 21–041
intangible fixed assets
  acquisition of shares, 21–042
Royalties
acquired royalties
  copyright, 18–004
advance royalties
  entertainers and sportsmen, 27–032
copyright, 18–004
designs, 17–008, 17–011
franchising, 28–015—28–017
intangible fixed assets
  allowable costs, 21–018—21–019
  date of acquisition, 21–017
  generally, 21–016—21–019
international tax planning, 24–020—24–023
Patent Box, 22–021
patents, 16–002—16–012
performers
  advance royalties, 27–032
  date royalties payable, 27–027—27–030

software, 29–010
trade marks, 17–008, 17–011
transfer pricing, 13–031—13–034
valuation, 12–013
Scientific research
qualifying expenditure, 15–026
Searches
trade mark applications, 4–007
Securities
foreign securities
  individual taxation, 9–067
Self-assessment
individuals
  accounts
    submission, 9–015
  amendment of returns, 9–011
  disclosure of tax avoidance schemes, 9–008
  electronic services, 9–013
  estimates, 9–011
  introduction, 9–005
  mistakes, 9–007
  payment of tax, 9–010
  penalties for incorrect returns, 9–012
  penalties for late payment, 9–010
  post-transaction rulings, 9–016
  repayments, 9–017
  tax enquiries, 9–009
  tax returns, 9–006
partnerships, 9–014, 9–081, 9–082
transfer pricing, 13–010
Self-employment
adjusted accounts, 9–048
annual payments, 9–056—9–057
capital allowances, 9–051—9–052
cash basis, 9–049—9–050
current year basis, 9–046—9–047
failure to deduct tax, 9–058
generally, 9–045
high value residential property, 9–064
loss relief, 9–053—9–054
pure income profits, 9–059—9–060
Service marks
see also **Trade marks**
taxation
  averaging profits, 17–003—17–005
  dealing, 17–012
  expenses, 17–007
  income, 17–002
  introduction, 17–001
  investment income, 17–006
  investments, 17–012
  lump sums, 17–009
  relief to purchaser, 17–010
  royalties, 17–008, 17–011
  stamp duty, 17–013
Shareholdings
corporation tax
  substantial shareholding exemption, 10–008

INDEX

"Show-how"
  common law protection, 6–008
  franchising, 8–013, 28–013
  taxation
    income, 19–003
    introduction, 19–001
    meaning, 19–002
Small and medium-sized enterprises
  research and development taxation
    tax reliefs, 15–019
Small businesses
  intangible fixed assets, 21–012
  performers, 27–031
  sportspersons
    accounts, 27–031
Software
  acquisition for distribution, 29–006
  capital allowances, 29–002, 29–008
  copyright protection, 8–008
  development expenditure, 29–013
  exploitation for own use, 29–007
  hardware distinguished, 29–001
  internet, 29–004
  Patent Box, 22–018—22–019
  research and development, 15–006, 15–018
  revenue expenditure, 29–009
  royalties, 29–010
  transfer pricing, 29–014
  treaty shopping, 29–012
  VAT, 29–015—29–018
  withholding tax, 29–011
Sound recordings
  copyright, 18–061, 18–075
  corporation tax, 18–075
Spare parts and accessories
  design right, 5–009
Sportspersons
  employment status
    benefit years, 27–020
    generally, 27–002—27–012, 27–021
    team players, 27–019
  image rights, 27–053
  inducements, 27–036
  introduction, 27–001
  investment income, 27–033
  national insurance, 27–022
  non-residents
    apportionment, 27–051—27–052
    double taxation agreements, 27–050
    generally, 27–047—27–048
    payments in kind, 27–051—27–052
    reduced withholding payments, 27–049
  personal service companies (IR35), 27–023—27–025
  restrictive covenants, 27–026
  VAT, 27–054—27–056
Spouses
  transfers between
    capital gains tax, 9–077

SSAP 13
  research and development, 15–004—15–005
"Staffing costs"
  research and development, 15–017
Stamp duty
  copyright, 18–077
  designs, 17–013
  endorsements, 20–009
  instruments, 25–001
  introduction, 25–001
  know-how, 19–017
  merchandising, 20–009
  patents, 16–046
  property, 25–002
  rules, 25–002—25–003
  trade marks, 17–013
Substantial shareholding exemption
  corporation tax, 10–008
Supply of goods
  place of supply, 11–003, 11–005
  supply of services distinguished, 11–002
  time of supply, 11–007
Supply of services
  place of supply, 11–003, 11–005
  supply of goods distinguished, 11–002
  time of supply, 11–005
Switzerland
  tax havens, 24–029
Tax assessments
  see also **Self-assessment**
  current year basis
    self-employment, 9–046—9–047
  performers, 27–043, 27–044
  sportspersons, 27–043, 27–044
Tax avoidance
  corporation tax, 10–013
  self-assessment, 9–008
Tax credits
  research and development
    loss relief, 15–022
    scheme for SMEs, 15–034, 15–035
    treatment, 15–022—15–023
    vaccine research, 15–029
Tax enquiries
  self-assessment, 9–009
Tax havens
  international tax planning
    Channel Islands, 24–032
    generally, 24–028, 24–058
    Isle of Man, 24–032
    Liechtenstein, 24–030
    Luxembourg, 24–031
    other tax havens, 24–034
    Republic of Ireland, 24–033
    Switzerland, 24–029
Tax planning
  capital gains, 23–019
  employment income
    arising basis, 23–021

ex gratia payments, 23–022
generally, 23–020
inducements, 23–023
income not otherwise charged to tax, 23–018
international tax planning
   anti-avoidance provisions, 25–059—25–060
   authors, 24–025
   capital gains tax charge on settlor, 24–054—24–057
   dividend routing, 24–026
   double tax relief, 24–017—24–019
   film distribution agreements, 24–024
   foreign partnerships, 24–004—24–006
   gains of non-resident settlements, 24–045—24–049
   introduction, 24–001
   limbo trusts, 24–058
   loan routing, 24–027
   non-residents, 24–002
   overseas rights, 24–003
   remittance basis, 24–011—24–013
   royalty structures, 24–020—24–023
   tax havens, 24–028
   transfers of assets abroad, 24–035—24–044
   withholding tax, 24–016
introduction, 23–001—23–007
investment income, 23–010—23–011
know-how, 19–013
losses
   generally, 23–012
   non-trading losses, 23–015
   trading losses, 23–013—23–014
package deals
   broadcasting, 26–010
   drugs, 26–008—26–009
   introduction, 26–001
   manufacturing agreements, 26–002—26–006
   publishing deals, 26–007
   recording agreements, 26–011
pension schemes
   annual allowances, 23–025
   death benefits, 23–026
   generally, 23–024—23–026
   keyman insurance, 23–028
   lifetime allowance, 23–026
   registered pension funds, 23–025
   unfunded unapproved schemes, 23–027
post-cessation receipts, 23–016—23–017
stamp duty
   introduction, 25–001
   rules, 25–002—25–003
trading income
   current year basis, 23–009
   generally, 23–008
trusts
   capital gains tax, 23–031
   generally, 23–029
   income tax, 23–030

Tax rates
   corporation tax, 10–003—10–004
   individual taxation, 9–004
   VAT, 11–008
Tax relief *see* **Reliefs**
Tax returns
   performers, 27–039
   self-assessment
      amendment, 9–011
      electronic services, 9–013
      estimates, 9–011
      generally, 9–006
      penalties for errors, 9–012
   sportspersons, 27–039
   trusts, 10–019
Three-dimensional marks
   copyright protection, 5–001
Trade marks
   applications
      content, 4–006
      distinctiveness, 4–007
      geographical indications, 4–006
      opposition, 4–008
      publication, 4–008
      search, 4–007
   certification marks, 4–002
   collective marks, 4–002
   commercial activities
      assignment, 4–013
      franchising, 4–014
      generally, 4–011
      licensing, 4–012
   computers, 8–009
   conclusions, 4–021
   counterfeits, 4–001
   form of protection
      generally, 4–009
      infringement, 4–010
   franchising, 8–013
   international systems
      basic framework, 4–015
      Community Trade Marks Office, 4–016—4–018
      Madrid Agreement, 4–019
      rest of world, 4–020
   introduction, 4–001—4–003
   meaning, 4–002
   obtaining protection, 4–004
   registrability, 4–005
   registration, 4–002—4–003
   stamp duty, 17–013
   taxation
      averaging profits, 17–003—17–005
      dealing, 17–012
      expenses, 17–007
      income, 17–002
      introduction, 17–001
      investment income, 17–006
      investments, 17–012

INDEX

lump sums, 17–009
relief to purchaser, 17–010
royalties, 17–008, 17–011
stamp duty, 17–013
VAT, 17–014
unfair competition law, 6–004
Trading
corporation tax, 10–006
Trading income
current year basis, 23–009
generally, 23–008
Transfer of business
intangible fixed assets, 21–053
Transfer of income streams
Patent Box, 22–031
Transfer pricing
acting together, 13–004, 13–005
Arbitration Convention, 13–013
arm's length range, 13–028
control
  meaning, 13–005
controlled, 13–004, 13–005
cost plus method
  calculation of arm's length price, 13–022
customs valuations, 13–035
documentation, 13–008
dormant companies, 13–003
double taxation treaties, 13–036—13–037
foreign legislation, 13–012
future developments, 13–038
HMRC guidance, 13–008
intangibles, 13–029—13–030
interest, 13–007
international transfer pricing, 13–014—13–016
introduction, 13–001
key provisions, 13–002—13–004
OECD guidelines
  generally, 13–009
  methods to arrive at arm's length price, 13–018
  profit methods, 13–023—13–027
  transaction-based methods, 13–019—13–022
participation in management, 13–006
penalties, 13–009, 13–010
self-assessment
  declaration of adjustment, 13–010
  software, 29–014
  thresholds, 13–003
US royalties, 13–031—13–034
thresholds, 13–003
Transfers of assets abroad
generally, 24–035—24–037
liability of non-transferors, 24–038—24–042
power to obtain information, 24–043
"Transport invention"
case study, CS8–001—CS8–004
Treaty shopping
software, 29–012

Trustees
residence
  gains of non-resident settlements, 24–050—24–053
Trusts
accumulation trusts, 10–018
capital gains tax, 10–020
discretionary trusts, 10–018
foreign trusts, 10–021
income tax, 10–015—10–016
inheritance tax, 9–093, 10–022, 10–023
introduction, 10–014
life interest trusts, 10–017
limbo trusts, 24–058
tax planning
  capital gains tax, 23–031
  generally, 23–029
  income tax, 23–030
tax relief, 10–018
tax returns, 10–019
Unfair competition
copyright, 6–005
generally, 6–002—6–003
lotteries, 6–006
misleading and comparative advertising, 6–005
passing off, 6–004—6–005
patents, 6–003
raising actions, 6–007
registered designs, 6–004
trade marks, 6–004
Unfunded unapproved schemes
tax planning, 23–027
Universal Copyright Convention 1952
copyright protection, 5–016
Utility models
nature, 2–034—2–035
Valuation
accounts, 12–028, 21–010
binomial model, 12–020
Black-Scholes methodology, 12–019
brand names, 12–018
capitalisation of earnings, 12–012
case law, 12–025—12–026
discounted cash flow, 12–009
excess profits, 12–015
external factors, 12–016
Generally Accepted Accounting Principles, 12–034
goodwill, 12–017, 12–035—12–037
hindsight, 12–007
HMRC guidance, 12–027—12–037
hybrid valuations, 12–014
impaired assets, 12–033
industry price multiple, 12–012
International Financial Reporting Standard 3, 12–023—12–024
location of assets, 12–022
market value, 12–002—12–003, 12–016
Monte Carlo simulation, 12–021

optimum lotting, 12–006
present value, 12–009
real sales, 12–005
reasons to value intellectual property, 12–001
royalty comparisons, 12–013
special purchasers, 12–004
true and fair value, 12–030—12–033
weighted average cost of capital, 12–010—12–011
willing parties, 12–008

Value shifting
intangible fixed assets, 21–063

VAT
collection of VAT, 11–011
copyright, 18–078
endorsements, 20–010
entertainers, 27–054—27–056
European Union
  exports out of or into, 11–004
franchising, 28–029
introduction, 11–001
know-how, 19–018
merchandising, 20–010
patents, 16–047—16–048
place of supply of goods, 11–003
place of supply of services, 11–005
rates of VAT, 11–008
recovery of VAT, 11–009
reverse charge services, 11–006
software, 29–015—29–018
sportsmen, 27–054—27–056
supply of good/services distinction, 11–002
time of supply, 11–007
trade marks, 17–014
treatment of intellectual property, 11–012
vatable persons, 11–010

Will trusts
see also **Trusts**
international tax planning, 24–058

Withholding payments
non-resident entertainers and sportsmen, 27–049

Withholding tax
international tax planning, 24–016
software, 29–011